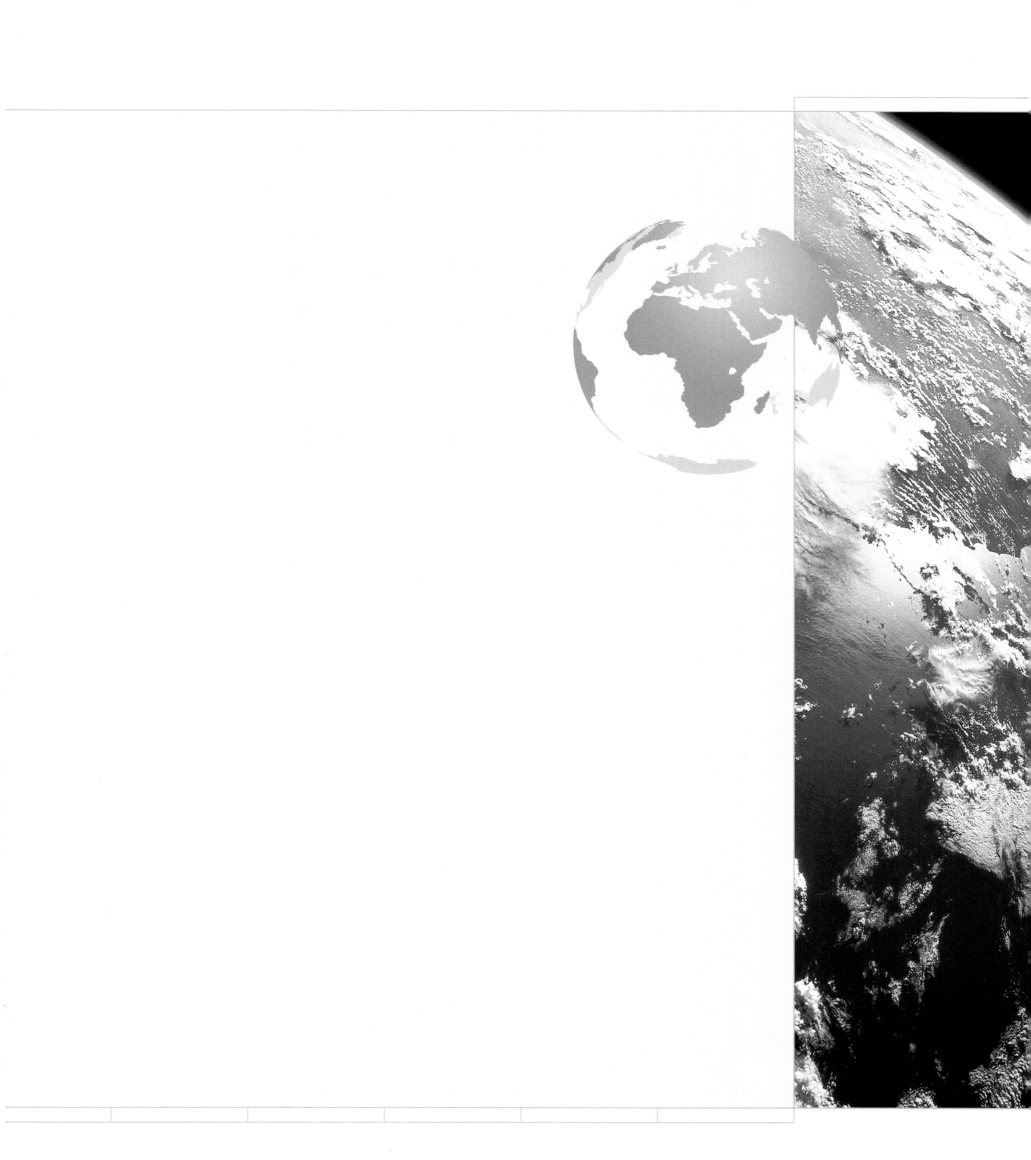

The blue planet: The Earth was created billions of years ago from cosmic dust and gas –water, vital to all life on Earth, covers more than two-thirds of the planet's surface.

The delta of the Mississippi River on the Gulf of Mexico – the mixing of water from the gulf and the river is vividly apparent in the satellite photograph below.

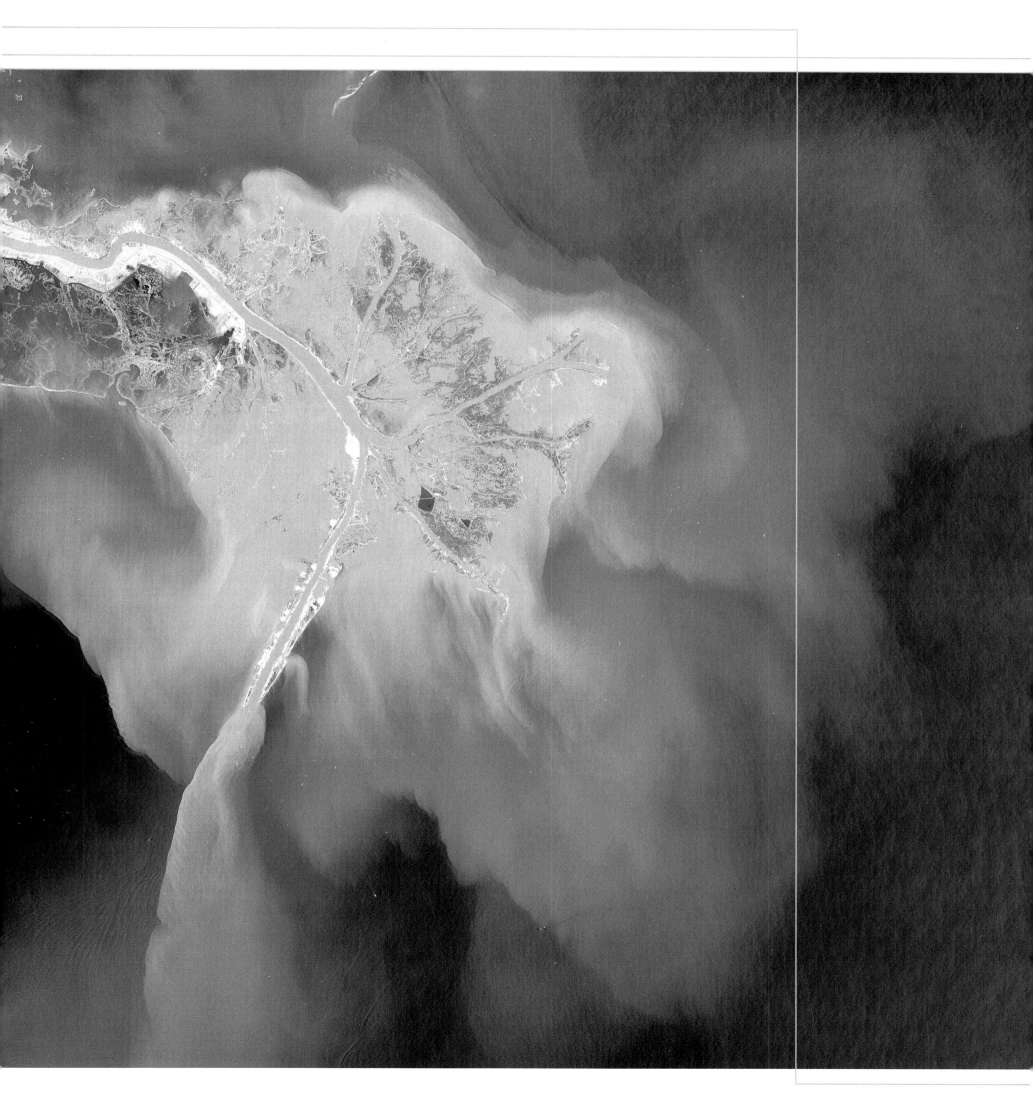

The power of wind and water erosion shaped
the beautiful landscapes of the Colorado Plateau – including the sandstone arches in
Arches National Park

WORLD TRAVEL ATLAS

Florence, the historic capital of Tuscany (Italy), with its Renaissance buildings and countless artistic masterpieces, is a jewel of European culture.

Preface

"The world is a book, and those who do not travel read only a page." – St. Augustine of Hippo (354–430 AD).

St. Augustine's quote is as true now as it was during his lifetime. The world has experienced many dramatic changes since then – empires have fallen, new nations have been born, and technology and global communications have made our world a smaller place – but travel remains as fascinating as ever.

In recent centuries, scientists and explorers have discovered every "terra incognita" and now use satellites to survey and photograph the Earth with incredible accuracy. Our planet, however, still offers countless surprises, adventures, and exotic wonders: the vastness of Asia, the isolated islands of the Pacific, the dense rainforests of Africa, Alaska's wilderness, ancient villages in Europe, and the summits of the Andes. Presenting all of these, and the many other fascinating places on our planet, is a difficult but rewarding task.

"A journey of a thousand miles begins with the very first step" – Lao-tzu (Chinese philosopher, 4th century BC).

And now we can begin our journey with the new World Travel Atlas. The groundbreaking concept of the atlas serves several functions: the first is to offer basic geographic knowledge of our planet with detailed and clear cartography. Further, it functions as a comprehensive travel guide in which more than 17,000 fascinating attractions are highlighted – including landscapes, national parks, cities, cultural attractions, monuments, holiday destinations, and travel routes. These sites are presented through a new system of pictograms, developed specifically for this book. With more than 2,000 texts covering the geographic and cultural aspects of the world's regions, the atlas also serves as a travel encyclopedia. Finally, it is a visually stimulating illustrated book with numerous beautiful photographs from around the world.

It is our hope that the World Travel Atlas will inspire in our readers the feeling that they are "citizens of the world" and serve as a "first step" on a fascinating journey of discovery to the countless wonders of the planet we call home. This atlas should deepen our understanding of our Earth and its multifaceted splendor, and awaken our curiosity, tolerance, and feelings of responsibility towards one another as inhabitants of this planet.

In the words of the famed Indian poet Rabindranath Tagore: "We live in this world as long as we love it".

The Publisher

Table of Contents

Islamic heritage in southern Spain: La Mezquita cathedral, once the Great Mosque of Córdoba, is a beautiful example of Moorish architecture with large chambers and splendid facades.

Beautiful landscapes on the Li River: The green, craggy mountains around the city of Guilin are located in one of China's most scenic regions.

Table of Contents

Marrakech (Morocco): Djemâa el-Fna square, located near the Koutoubia mosque, is a lively meeting place for vendors, street artists, traditional storytellers, and tourists.

Wet Tropics National Park in north-eastern Australia features fascinating flora and fauna as well as beautiful landscapes such as Milla Falls.

Map locator

Europe

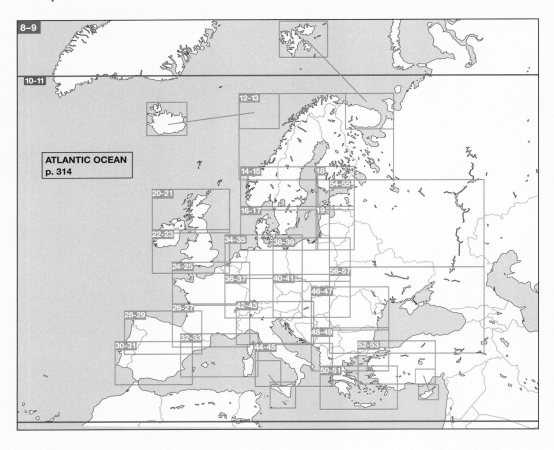

8–9
10–11
12–13

ATLANTIC OCEAN
p. 314

14–15
18–
64–55
20–21
16–17
19–
22–23
34–35
38–39
24–25
36–37
40–41
66–57
46–47
26–27
42–43
28–29
48–49
32–33
44–45
52–53
30–31
50–51

Southeastern Asia, Australia/Ocea

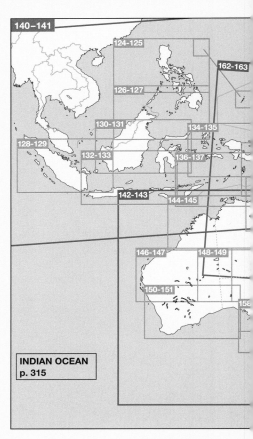

140–141
124–125
162–163
126–127
130–131
134–135
128–129
132–133
136–137
142–143
144–145
146–147
148–149
150–151
158

INDIAN OCEAN
p. 315

Near and Middle East, Northern Asia, Central Asia, Southern Asia

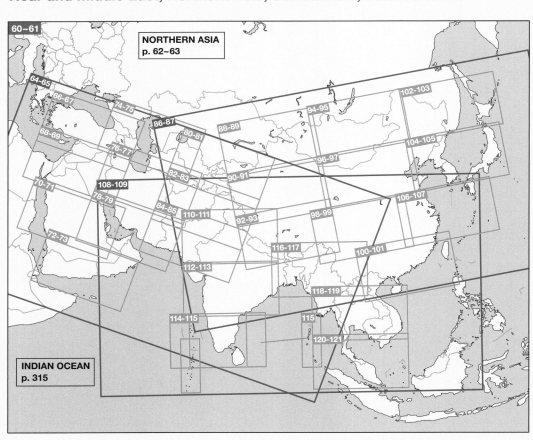

60–61

NORTHERN ASIA
p. 62–63

64–65
66–6
74–75
102–103
68–69
86–87
80–81
88–89
94–95
76–77
104–105
70–71
82–83
90–91
96–97
108–109
78–79
106–107
84–85
110–111
92–93
98–99
72–73
116–117
100–101
112–113
118–119
114–115
115
120–121

INDIAN OCEAN
p. 315

Africa

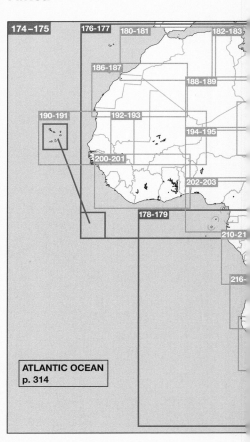

174–175
176–177
180–181
182–183
186–187
188–189
190–191
192–193
194–195
200–201
202–203
178–179
210–21
216–

ATLANTIC OCEAN
p. 314

Map locator

The impressive modern skyline of Chicago, along the shores of Lake Michigan. The city is a leading commercial and financial center.

Easter Island was once home to an advanced civilization. The more than 300 stone sculptures (moai) scattered around the island are the most important remnants of this culture.

North and Central America

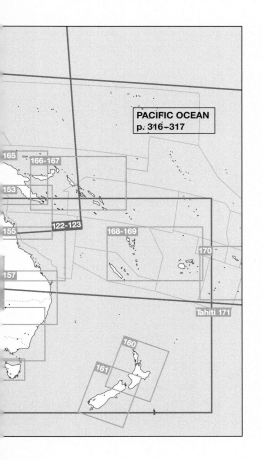

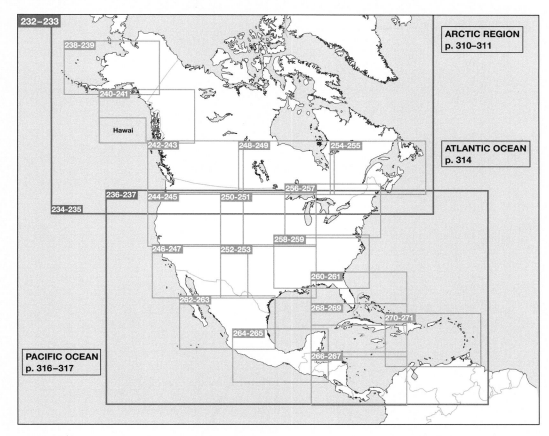

PACIFIC OCEAN p. 316–317

165
166-167
153
155
122-123
168-169
170
157
Tahiti 171
160
161

232–233
238-239
240-241
Hawai
242-243
248-249
254-255
236-237
244-245
250-251
256-257
234-235
258-259
246-247
252-253
260-261
262-263
268-269
270-271
264-265
266-267

ARCTIC REGION p. 310–311

ATLANTIC OCEAN p. 314

PACIFIC OCEAN p. 316–317

South America

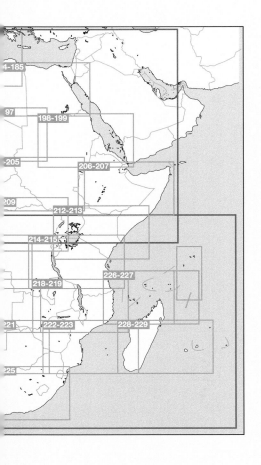

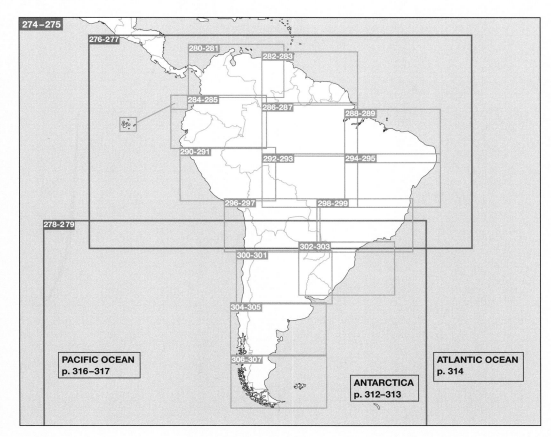

4-185
97
198-199
205
206-207
209
212-213
214-215
218-219
226-227
221
222-223
228-229
225

274–275
276-277
280-281
282-283
284-285
286-287
288-289
290-291
292-293
294-295
296-297
298-299
278-279
302-303
300-301
304-305
306-307

PACIFIC OCEAN p. 316–317

ANTARCTICA p. 312–313

ATLANTIC OCEAN p. 314

Legend · Natural geographical features

The Polynesian island of Moorea is the remnant of a massive volcano. The island, like so many in the Pacific Ocean, is surrounded by coral reefs.

The Scottish Highlands in the United Kingdom feature a variety of romantic and beautiful landscapes, including craggy mountains, pristine lakes, and rugged valleys.

Bodies of Water

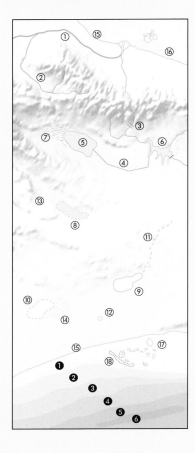

1. Stream, river
2. Tributary with headstreams
3. Waterfall, rapids
4. Canal
5. Lake
6. Reservoir with dam
7. Marsh, moor
8. Intermittent lake
9. Salt lake
10. Intermittent salt lake
11. Intermittent river (wadi)
12. Well, spring
13. Salt swamp
14. Salt pan
15. Shoreline
16. Mud flats
17. Island, archipelago
18. Coral reef

Depth tints

❶	0 – 200 meters
❷	200 – 2000 meters
❸	2000 – 4000 meters
❹	4000 – 6000 meters
❺	6000 – 8000 meters
❻	below 8000 meters

Topography

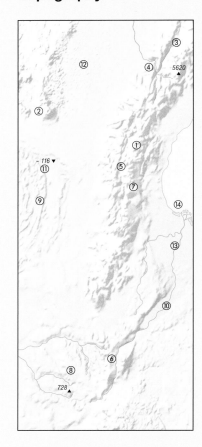

1. High mountain region
2. Volcano
3. V-shaped valley
4. Gorge
5. U-shaped valley
6. Canyon
7. Glacier
8. Highland with valleys
9. Escarpment
10. Rift Valley
11. Depression
12. High dunes in arid areas
13. Lowland
14. Delta

Color tints of climate and vegetation zones

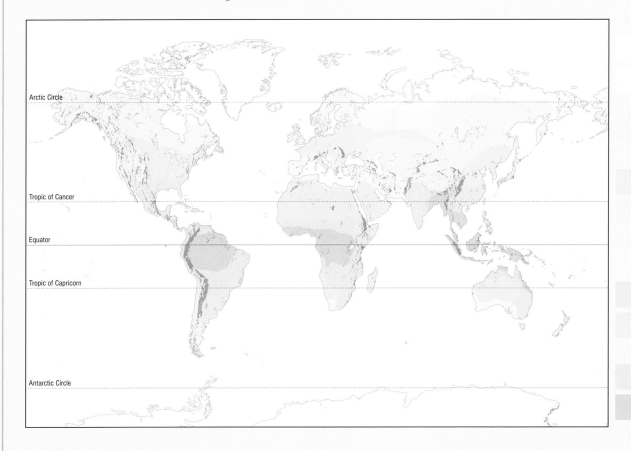

Polar and subpolar zone

Perpetual frost, all months below 0° C (32° F)

Arctic flora and Tundra (lichens, mosses, grasses, dwarf shrubs)

Boreal zone

Taiga, northern coniferous trees; pines, firs, larches, spruces

Temperate zones

Rainy climates with mild winters; deciduous broadleaf forests, mixed forests

Winter-cold desert and semidesert climates; steppe, prairie, grasslands, semideserts

Subtropics

Mediterranean climate with dry summers and moist winters; broadleaved evergreen forests

Warm, summer-humid moist climate; subtropical forests

Desert and semidesert climates; open shrub lands

Tropics

Humid and dry savannas with dry seasons; woody savannas

Tropical rainforest, rainy climate with no winter; high temperatures

Manmade geographical features · **Legend**

Beijing's historic Forbidden City was the main residence of China's monarchs and the great imperial court for many centuries.

A full moon above the skyline of San Francisco in northern California. The city's beautiful Golden Gate Bridge is one of the world's longest suspension bridges.

Settlements and transportation routes

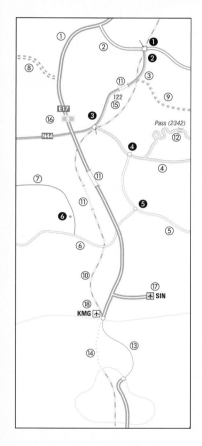

Transportation routes

① Interstate highway/motorway
② Multilane divided highway
③ Primary highway
④ Secondary highway
⑤ Main road
⑥ Secondary road
⑦ Unimproved road
⑧ Interstate highway/motorway under construction
⑨ Primary highway under construction
⑩ Railroad
⑪ Tunnel
⑫ Pass with elevation in meters
⑬ Ferry, shipping route
⑭ Railroad ferry
⑮ Distances in kilometers (in miles within USA and UK)
⑯ Road numbers
⑰ International Airport with IATA-code
⑱ Airport with IATA-code

Settlements

❶ Urban area
❷ City, over 1 million inhabitants
❸ City, 100,000 - 1 million inhabitants
❹ Town, 10,000 - 100,000 inhabitants
❺ Town, under 10,000 inhabitants
❻ Hamlet, research station

Typefaces of cities and towns

① **NEW YORK**
② **Stuttgart**
③ **Narvik**
④ Porta Westfalica
⑤ **Storuman**
⑥ White Owl
⑦ Glenayle
⑧ **BEIJING (PEKING)**
⑨ **Firenze (Florence)**
⑩ Tikal
⑪ Grand Canyon du Verdon

① City, over 1 million inhabitants
② City, 100,000 - 1 million inhabitants
③ Significant city, 10,000 - 100,000 inhabitants
④ City, 10,000 - 100,000 inhabitants
⑤ Significant town, under 10,000 inhabitants
⑥ Town, under 10,000 inhabitants
⑦ Hamlet, research station
⑧ City, over 1 million inhabitants with translation
⑨ Town 100,000 - 1 million inhabitants with translation
⑩ Point of cultural interest
⑪ Point of natural interest

Political and other boundaries

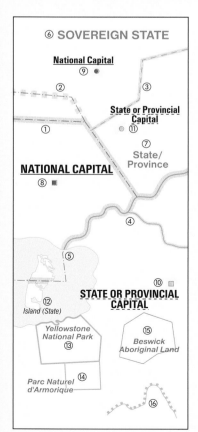

① International boundary
② Disputed international boundary
③ Administrative boundary
④ Boundary on rivers
⑤ Boundary in lake or sea
⑥ Country name
⑦ Administrative name
⑧ Capital with more than 1 million inhabitants
⑨ Capital below 1 million inhabitants
⑩ Administrative capital with more than 1 million inhabitants
⑪ Administrative capital with less than 1 million inhabitants
⑫ Dependent territory with administering country
⑬ National parks and biosphere reserves
⑭ Nature parks and other protected areas
⑮ Reservation
⑯ Walls (Great Wall of China, Hadrian's Wall)

Typefaces of topographic features

① *PACIFIC OCEAN*
② *GULF OF MEXICO*
   Gulf of Thailand
③ *Antalya Körfezi*
④ *Elbe*   *Rio Grande*   *Murray*
⑤ *White Nile*   *Suez Canal*
⑥ *HIMALAYA*
⑦ *Great Plains*
⑧ *Mt. Olympus* ▲ 2424
⑨ - 116 ▼ *Danakil Depression*
⑩ *Tahiti*
⑪ *Cape of Good Hope*
⑫ 325
⑬ 5425
⑭ *Mexican Basin*
⑮ *Mariana Trench*

① Ocean
② Gulf, bay
③ Small bay, strait
④ River, lake, canal
⑤ River, lake, canal (translated)
⑥ Mountain name
⑦ Area name, landscape name
⑧ Mountain name with elevation above sea level in meters
⑨ Depression with depth below sea level in meters
⑩ Island name
⑪ Cape name
⑫ Elevation of lake above sea level
⑬ Depth in oceans and lakes
⑭ Undersea landscapes, mountains and trenches
⑮ Deepsea trench

Explanation of symbols

The passenger train services that pass through South Africa's Garden Route offer spectacular views of the Indian Ocean and the Karoo Mountains.

The landscapes of Los Glaciares National Park, including large glaciers and mountains, are among the most spec-tacular in the region of Patagonia. Photo: Fitz Roy Massif (3,128 m).

Principal travel routes

Remarkable landscapes and natural monuments

Beautiful natural landscapes, fascinating wildlife, historic architecture, and vibrant cities – our world is rich in wonders. The modern cartography and layout of the World Travel Atlas highlight many of the world's attractions – unspoiled wilderness areas, the most famous and significant historic sites, culturally diverse urban areas, holiday resorts, and sporting venues. The system of pictograms developed speci-fically for this atlas gives the reader a clear impression of the diverse attractions in the world's regions. All of the picto-grams featured on each map are listed and labeled in a legend at the bottom of the respective page.

The following pages offer brief characterizations of the various pictograms used in the atlas. The pictograms are divided by color into two groups: green and blue pictograms represent natural attractions, while yellow pictograms represent cultural attractions and other man-made sites. The names of significant towns and cities are highlighted in yellow through-out the atlas. Blue pictograms represent sporting and recre-ational facilities. Important and well-known transportation routes, including highways and shipping routes, are also fea-tured in the atlas. These routes are not only highlighted by pic-tograms but also by distinctly-colored lines that identify each type of route.

Auto route
The maps display many of the world's most famous and historically signi-ficant roads and routes, such as the ancient Silk Road in Asia and historic Route 66 in the United States, The maps also feature im-portant modern highways, including the Pan-American Highway that stretches through the Americas from Alaska to Tierra del Fuego, the high-way stretching between Bangkok in Thailand and Singapore, and the Stuart Highway, which traverses the fascinating landscapes in Australia's sparsely populated interior.

Railroad
The age of the railroads started in 1804 when the world's first steam locomotive began operation in Wales. By the end of the 19th century it was possible to travel through most re-gions of Europe and North America and much of Asia and South America by train. The Orient Express, Eu-rope's first long-distance luxury pas-senger line, began operation in 1883 and traveled between Paris. Bucha-rest, and Istanbul. The Trans-Siberian line was constructed between 1891 and 1916 with the goal of connecting Siberia to European Russia. The Trans-Siberian still runs between Moscow and Vladivostok on the Pacific Ocean almost 100 years after construction ended.

High speed train
The Eurostar trains travel at speeds up to 300 kilometers an hour and trans-port passengers between London and Brussels or Paris in less than three hours. Japan's Shinkansen line, also known as the "bullet train", connects several of the country's major cities. In Europe, France and Germany main-tain the most extensive networks of high speed trains.

Shipping route
Millions of passengers travel on cruise ships every year and experi-ence one of the most leisurely and comfortable forms of long-distance travel. Thousands of cruise ships tra-verse the oceans, seas, and rivers of the world. The Caribbean Sea, Medi-terranean Sea, Scandinavia, and Alaska are among the most popular locations for cruises on the open seas. Modern cruise ships offer an astounding variety of attractions including casinos, entertainment, fine restaurants, and shops.

UNESCO World (Natural) Heritage
Since 1972, UNESCO, a body of the United Nations, has compiled a grow-ing list of specially designated natu-ral attractions and wonders that are deemed to be of outstanding impor-tance and "universal" significance.

Mountain landscape
Mountain ranges are among the most scenic areas in the world. Many of the world's ancient low-mountain ranges, including the Appalachians and the Central Massif, feature heavily eroded and rounded peaks. Other, younger mountain ranges feature jagged and high peaks that are often covered by snow and glaciers.

Rock landscape
Many of the world's most interesting stone formations were shaped by wind and water erosion, including the natural attractions of Monument Valley National Park in the USA.

Ravine/canyon
Canyons and gorges are narrow and often deep valleys created by river and wind erosion. The Grand Can-yon, in the American state of Arizo-na, is the most famous and one of the most spectacular canyons on the planet.

Extinct volcano
Volcanoes are formed when solid, liquid, or gas-like materials from the Earth's interior rise to the planet's surface. Magma passes through the structure of a volcano and leaves its crater as lava, often accompanied by plumes of hot ash. An extinct vol-canoe is a volcano that has not expe-rienced an eruption in the last 10,000 years.

Active volcano
Geologists consider any volcano that has erupted in the last 10,000 years to be an active volcano. Most of the world's active volcanoes are con-centrated in geologically active re-gions, such as areas near the bound-aries of the world's tectonic plates or mid-ocean ridges. The Pacific Ring of Fire is an area of relatively frequent volcanic activity.

Geyser
Active geysers are hot springs that occasionally release plumes of water into the air. Geysers are located in vol-canically active regions.

Cave
Caves are formed during the crea-tion of stone formations (mountains, underground layers of stone, etc.) or emerge later due to the eroding effects of water that seeps into stone and often carves out entire networks of large caves containing lakes and rivers.

Glacier
Glaciers are large fields or rivers of ice that often migrate through moun-tain valleys. Glaciers are formed above the snow line in mountainous areas such as the Alps or in regions with cold climates such as Alaska, northern Canada, and Greenland.

River landscape
The eroding power of flowing water formed many of the world's valleys and canyons. Many of the world's early civilizations emerged in fertile river valleys such as Mesopotamia or the Indus Valley. Many rivers in low-land areas have large branching del-tas containing delicate ecosystems.

Waterfall/rapids
Waterfalls are formed when rivers flow over an area with a sudden drop in elevation. They come in a variety of heights and lengths and are among the most stunning natural attractions on the planet.

Lake country
Most of the world's major lakes were created by glaciers during the ice ages. Several regions have a large number of lakes, often interconnec-ted and located near one another. In addition to glacial lakes, many lakes were created as a result of tectonic and geological activity.

Desert
Vast landscapes covered by sand dunes, sand fields, or stone with sparse rainfall. Deserts are the most arid regions on the earth and only a few types of plants and animals can survive in these harsh environments. Most deserts have major differences between night and daytime temper-atures. Most of the world's deserts remain sparsely populated.

Oasis
Oases are fertile islands surrounded by barren, arid deserts or steppes. They are supplied with water by riv-ers, springs or subterranean ground-water repositories.

Explanation of symbols

Thick clouds above Mount Taranaki (2,158 m) on New Zealand's North Island, one of many active volcanoes in the Pacific Ring of Fire.

Dresden, the capital of the German state of Saxony, became a major cultural center in the 18th century. The city's waterfront along the Elbe River features many historic landmarks.

Remarkable cities and cultural monuments

Depression
Depressions are small basins located on land but at significant depths below sea level. Many depressions – including the Dead Sea – were created through tectonic activity.

Fossil site
Fossils are the ancient remnants and traces of animals and plants that have inhabited our planet during its long history.

Nature park
Conservation areas have been created to protect local flora and fauna. Most designated nature parks tend to be relatively small in size.

National park (landscape)
These large conservation areas to protect areas of natural beauty and significant national or international importance. Development and industry are forbidden or heavily restricted in such area. Yellowstone National Park, in the US-State of Wyoming, is the world's oldest national park.

National park (flora)
This symbol designates national parks with interesting local flora.

National park (fauna)
This symbol designates national parks with unique local wildlife.

National park (culture)
National park with cultural attractions such as the Native American historic sites in Mesa Verde National Park.

Biosphere reserve
Undeveloped conservation areas with pristine examples of distinct climate or vegetation zones. Many biosphere reserves exhibit high levels of biodiversity.

Wildlife reserve
Conservation areas created for the protection of endangered animals. Selous Game Reserve in Tanzania is home to herds of African elephants.

Whale watching
Boat tours providing the chance to observe whales or dolphins in their natural habitats.

Turtle conservation area
Several countries in the world have specially designated coastal areas where endangered sea turtle species live or lay their eggs.

Protected area for sea lions/ seals
Some countries have coastal areas that have designated conservation sites to preserve the natural habitats of endangered seals and sea lions.

Protected area for penguins
These protected areas were created to preserve threatened penguin colonies and to observe these wonderful creatures in their habitats.

Zoo/safari park
Zoos are park-like areas that feature collections of animals, mostly from a variety of regions. Safari parks are large properties open to tourists that feature wildlife in open wilderness.

Crocodile farm
Most crocodile farms are commercial operations where the animals are bred. Many are open to the public.

Coastal landscape
Coastal areas often feature diverse landscapes including beaches, cliffs, tidal flats, and marshlands. Some coastal areas are flat with sand dunes, while others are lined by rock formations, stony beaches, and high cliffs. The beautiful fjords of Scandinavia are among the most stunning coastal areas in the world.

Beach
Beaches are major tourist attractions and often offer diverse recreational activities. Sand beaches are common in flat areas. Many of the world's beaches are now heavily developed.

Coral reef
Coral Reefs are formed by small animals called coral in warm saltwater. Many of the world's large coral reefs exhibit astonishing biodiversity and are accessible to divers. The world's largest coral reef is the Great Barrier Reef off the coast of Australia.

Island
Islands are land masses surrounded by water. Most islands are part of island groups. The islands on our planet have a combined land area of 10.5 million km². Many of the world's islands and island groups have become popular tourist destinations.

Underwater reserve
Underwater conservation areas have been created to protect local marine flora and fauna.

UNESCO World (Cultural) Heritage
Since 1972, UNESCO has compiled a list of specially designated cultural sites that are deemed to be of outstanding importance. The list now includes hundreds of cultural and historic sites around the world.

Remarkable city
Large and small cities of global importance or with an abundance of tourist attractions are highlighted in yellow on our maps.

Pre- and early history
Sites related to ancient human cultures and their ways of life during times before the emergence of written records. The most grandiose prehistoric sites include large megaliths created by different cultures, such as the circle of stone pillars at Stonehenge in the United Kingdom.

Prehistoric rockscape
Prehistoric paintings, carvings and reliefs created by nomadic peoples during ancient times. Such sites have been found on all of the world's inhabited continents and often provide scientist, with valuable information about life in the times before the first civilizations emerged on our planet.

The Ancient Orient
Sites related to the ancient cultures that developed in the region comprising modern Anatolia (Asia Minor), Syria, Iraq, Israel, Lebanon, Iran, and in some cases Egypt, during the period between 7000 BC and the time of Alexander the Great (400 BC). The Sumerians developed one of the first urban civilizations on the planet. They also developed one of the first number systems. After 2000 BC, the first large empires emerged in the region including the kingdoms of the Babylonians, Assyrians, and Hittites. The region features temples, ziggurats, and palaces from ancient times.

Ancient Egypt
One of the greatest ancient civilizations developed on the banks of the Nile River in Egypt. Around 3000 BC, Egypt was unified under the reign of one ruler for the first time. Between this time and the period of Alexander the Great's conquests, Egypt was ruled by more than 31 dynasties. The all-powerful pharaohs were considered living gods in Ancient Egypt. The ancient Egyptians developed a

writing system, a calendar, and eventually advanced building techniques. The greatest legacy of this fascinating culture is the spectacular pyramids. The arts of the ancient Egyptians were devoted primarily to religion and mythology.

Ancient Egyptian pyramids
The monumental pyramid tombs of Egyptian pharaohs were constructed during the Old Kingdom. The largest and most impressive pyramid is the 137-meter-high Great (Cheops) Pyramid at Giza.

Minoan culture
The advanced Bronze-Age culture of the Minoans flourished on the island of Crete during ancient times. Minoan civilization first emerged during the 3rd millennium BC, after which the Minoans rapidly became the dominant power in the eastern Mediterranean. Modern Crete features the remnants of Minoan villas with impressive frescoes and interior design.

Phoenician culture
During ancient times the area encompassing modern Israel, Lebanon, and Palestine was once the center of Phoenician culture. The Phoenicians were the dominant trading power in the Mediterranean for several centuries and founded many colonies.

Early African culture
Ancient African civilizations include the cultures of the Kingdom of Ghana, Axum (Ethiopia), the Great Zimbabwe culture, and Kush, a complex and advanced society that developed south of Egypt.

Etruscan culture
The Etruscans probably originated in central Italy. During the 10th century BC, they conquered large sections of the Italian Peninsula before they were conquered by the Romans. Italy has numerous archeological and historic sites related to the culture of the ancient Etruscans.

Greek antiquity
No other civilization has had a greater influence on European culture than that of Ancient Greece. The city-state of Athens was one of the first basic democracies in history. The art, philosophy and architecture of Ancient Greece continue to inspire and shape our modern world. Ancient Greece was divided into city-states, many of

Explanation of symbols

Sunset above the Pyramids of Giza: the enormous pyramids were constructed as monumental tombs during the reign of ancient Egypt's pharaohs.

Borobudur: the Buddhist complex in Indonesia features numerous sculptures and reliefs. The site was buried beneath volcanic ash for centuries until it was rediscovered in the 19th century.

Remarkable cities and cultural monuments

which founded distant colonies in Southern Europe, the Middle East, and North Africa. Ancient Greek art dealt mostly with subjects related to Greek mythology. The Greek city-states constructed many great structures including impressive temples and amphitheaters. During the Hellenistic period – after the death of Alexander the Great – Greek-speaking cities outside the mainland, including Alexandria in Egypt, replaced the city-states as the centers of Greek civilization.

Roman antiquity
Over a period of centuries the once small city of Rome emerged as the center of a powerful empire. The Roman Empire was at its largest under the reign of the Emperor Trajan (98–117 BC); during this period its borders extended from North Africa to Scotland and from Iberia to Mesopotamia. The Roman state that existed between 509 and 27 BC is referred to as the Roman Republic. The Roman state that was created after the reforms of Caesar Augustus is known as the Roman Empire. Roman art and culture was greatly influenced by Ancient Greek and other Mediterranean cultures. The Romans constructed impressive structures including amphitheaters, temples, and aqueducts.

Nabatean culture
The ancient city of Petra (in modern Jordan) was first settled by the Nabateans in the fifth century BC. By the 1st century BC, the Nabateans ruled a powerful trading empire. The monumental ruins of Petra are the greatest remnant of this ancient culture.

Vikings
Between the 9th and 11th centuries, Scandinavian Vikings conquered territories throughout Europe. During their centuries of conquest, the Vikings founded numerous settlements and trading posts in Russia, Western Europe, and in the British Isles.

Ancient India
India has a wealth of cultural and historic attractions. The Indus Valley civilization (2600–1400 BC) was one of the first urbanized civilizations to emerge on the planet. Indian culture reached one of its high points during the period between the 7th and 13th centuries. Many of India's greatest

Buddhist and Hindu architectural masterpieces, as well as artworks, were created during these centuries. During the Mogul era (16th and 17th century), many impressive works of Islamic architecture were created throughout the country, including modern India's most famous structure, the Taj Mahal.

Ancient China
The oldest remnants of early Chinese culture date from the era between 5000–2000 BC. The Shang dynasty (1600–1000 BC) was the most influential and advanced bronze-age culture in China. Daoism and Confucian philosophy were both developed in China during the 5th century BC. The first great unified Chinese Empire was forged around 220 BC by Ying Zheng, the king of Qin. After the emergence of the first Chinese Empire, China was ruled by various dynasties and experienced many periods of cultural and technological advancement. The country's most impressive historic sites include the Great Wall of China, the tomb of Emperor Qin with its army of terracotta warriors in Xi'an, and the Forbidden City in the capital city Beijing.

Ancient Japan
The Yamato period of Japanese history began around AD 400. During this period, the country was ruled by an imperial court in Nara. During the 5th century the Japanese adopted the Chinese writing system and in the 6th century Buddhism arrived in Japan. The Fujiwara clan dominated the country for more than 500 years, starting in the 7th century. During this period the country's imperial capital was moved from Nara to Kyoto. Between 1192 and 1868, Japan was ruled by a series of shoguns (military rulers). The Meiji Era (1868–1912) saw the restoration of imperial power and the emergence of modern Japan.

Mayan culture
The Maya are an Amerindian people in southern Mexico and Central America. During pre-Colombian times, the Maya developed an advanced and powerful civilization that ruled over a vast territory. Mayan Civilization reached its cultural and technological peak around AD 300 and was eventually devastated by the arrival of the Spanish in the 16th century. Central America and Mexico have many impressive Mayan ruins.

Inca culture
The Inca culture emerged around Cusco during the 12th century. By the 15th century, the Inca ruled a vast empire that encompassed parts of modern Peru, Bolivia, Ecuador, Chile, and Argentina. Although their empire was shortlived, the Inca left behind impressive stone monuments and structures throughout western South America. The Inca city of Machu Picchu in Peru is one of the most impressive sites in South America.

Aztec culture
At some point during the second millennium BC, the Aztec people migrated into Mexico where they eventually established a powerful empire. The Aztec capital, Tenochtitlan (modern Mexico City), was founded in 1325 and was once one of the world's largest cities. The Aztecs constructed many grand temples and pyramids throughout their empire and made important cultural advances, including the creation of a writing system and calendar. Central Mexico has numerous Aztec cultural sites.

Other ancient American cultures
Advanced Amerindian cultures appeared in both North America and the Andean regions of South America. Countless Amerindian historic sites, including the remnants of ancient settlements, can be found throughout the Americas.

Places of Jewish cultural interest
Judaism is the oldest of the world's major monotheist religions. The Jerusalem temple was a great achievement of early Jewish culture – now only a section of its walls remain (the Western Wall). Historic synagogues can be found throughout the world, a legacy of the Jewish Diaspora.

Places of Christian cultural interest
Christianity is the world's most practiced and widespread religion. Christianity is based on the teachings in the old and new testaments of the Bible, and emerged in western Asia during the first century AD. Christian religious sites, including churches, cathedrals, and monasteries, can be found in most regions of the world.

Places of Islamic cultural interest
Islam, one of the world's major religions, was founded by Mohammed (AD 570–632). The teachings of the

Quran (Koran) are its basis. Muslims around the world pray in the direction of Mecca in Saudi Arabia, Islam's holiest city.

Places of Buddhist cultural interest
Buddhism is based on the teachings of Siddhartha Gautama (around 560–480 BC), also known as the Buddha. Most of the world's Buddhists live in East Asia. Important Buddhist sites include temples, pagodas, stupas, and monasteries.

Places of Hindu cultural interest
Most of the at least one billion followers of Hinduism, one of the world's most practiced religions, live on the Indian subcontinent. Hinduism encompasses a variety of beliefs and practices, many of which are thousands of years old.

Places of Jainist cultural interest
Most followers of Jainism live in India. It is based on the teachings of Mahavira, who lived in the 5th century BC. India features many Jainist sites including temples and monasteries.

Places of Sikh cultural interest
The Sikh religious philosophy emerged in 16th-century northern India, as an attempt to merge the teachings of Islam and Hinduism. The "Golden Temple" in Amritsar is the most important Sikh religious center.

Places of Shinto cultural interest
Shinto, the indigenous religion of Japan, is based on the reverence of kami (nature spirits) and ancestral spirits. Historic Shinto shrines can be seen throughout Japan.

Sites of interest to other religions
Sites related to other religious and spiritual communities.

Places of cultural interest to indigenous peoples (native peoples)
Sites related to the culture or history of a the indigenous peoples in different regions around the world.

Aborigine land reserves
The almost 500,000 Aborigines form only a small portion of Australia's population. Many Aborigine communities administer large land reserves.

Places of Aboriginal cultural interest
Cultural sites of the Aborigines, including rock paintings, are among the interesting attractions in Australia.

Explanation of symbols

Spanish settlers built Nuestra Senora church in Cholula, Mexico atop a series of ancient Amerindian pyramids. The historic church lies close to the snow-capped volcano Popocatepetl.

Las Vegas, the largest city in the American state of Nevada, is a popular tourist destination with numerous casinos, theme hotels, and amusement parks.

Sport and leisure destinations

Native American reservation
Most of the Native American reservations in North America were founded during the 19th century. Despite the history of low living standards on some reservations, many Native American communities have successfully protected their traditions.

Pueblo Indian culture
The Pueblo Indians are a group of Native American communities who have lived in the southwestern United States for centuries. Their traditional settlements – known as pueblos – consist of adobe buildings.

Places of Amerindian cultural interest
The different regions of North America feature hundreds of sites related to the history and cultures of Native Americans.

Amazonian Amerindians/protected area
The rainforests of South America are home to many Amerindian communities. Land reserves have been created to protect the Amerindian cultures in the Amazon basin.

Cultural landscape
The symbol refers to areas with landscapes that have been shaped by human settlement or cultivation.

Historical cities and towns
Historic cities and towns with well-preserved architectural attractions.

Impressive skyline
Cities featuring modern skylines, such as New York City, Chicago, and Hong Kong.

Castle/fortress/fort
Europe features the greatest concentration of these structures.

Caravansary
Historic inns along the ancient caravan routes of the Middle East, Central Asia, and North Africa.

Palace
Grand castles and palaces that once housed nobility and royalty can be found in many different regions. Europe has many historic residences.

Technical/industrial monument
Man-made attractions related to the achievements of industrialization and modern times.

Dam
The largest and most important dams and retaining walls on the planet.

Remarkable lighthouse
Many coastal areas feature beautiful or historic lighthouses.

Remarkable bridge
Many of the world's ancient and modern great bridges are considered engineering marvels.

Tomb/grave
Mausoleums, monuments, burial mounds, and other grave sites.

Theater of war/battlefield
Site where important battles occurred, including Waterloo in Belgium.

Monument
Sites dedicated to historic figures and important historical events.

Memorial
Site dedicated to the victims of wars and genocides.

Space mission launch site
Landing and launch sites of manned and unmanned space missions.

Space telescope
Radio, X-ray, and gamma-ray telescopes are important tools of modern astronomy.

Market
Important markets where people gather to trade and purchase goods.

Festivals
Large celebrations of music and culture, including Rio de Janeiro's Carnaval, and Mardi Gras in New Orleans.

Museum
Important collections of man-made works (art, technology, anthropology) and natural relics.

Theater
Famous theaters presenting opera, musicals, and other productions.

World exhibition
Cities that have hosted world expositions, including London in the United Kingdom and Seville in Spain.

Olympics
Cities and towns that have hosted the modern summer or winter Olympic Games.

Arena/stadium
The largest and most famous sporting venues in the world – including stadiums for football (soccer), baseball, rugby, hockey, and other popular sports.

Race track
Auto and motorbike racing are popular sports in many of the world's regions. The atlas highlights many of the most famous auto-racing venues, including Formula 1 and NASCAR race tracks in Indianapolis, Melbourne, and numerous other cities.

Golf
Golf has become an increasingly popular sport around the world in recent years. The atlas highlights several of the most famous and beautiful golf courses as well as areas that host important golf tournaments.

Horse racing
Horse racing has a long history in many of the world's regions. Several well-known race tracks and events are highlighted in the book, including the Ascot racecourse in England, a major event for Britain's high society. The Kentucky Derby remains one of the most popular annual sporting events in the United States, while Hong Kong's Happy Valley draws thousands of visitors every week.

Skiing
The maps in the atlas point out the most important ski areas in the world, including Chamonix in the French Alps, St. Moritz in Switzerland, and Aspen in the Rocky Mountains of Colorado. Many of these areas also offer facilities for other winter sports, including snowboarding.

Sailing
Once a sport for the wealthy, sailing is now enjoyed by millions of people. The atlas highlights areas with good conditions for recreational sailing.

Diving
Beautiful, colorful coral reefs, fascinating shipwrecks, and close encounters with marine life – the atlas presents popular dive sites around the world.

Wind surfing
A mix of surfing and sailing, windsurfing is a popular aquatic sport. The atlas points out coastal areas well suited to the sport.

Surfing
Popular coastal areas with adequate waves for surfing are highlighted – including well-known beaches in Australia, California, Europe, and in Hawaii, the birthplace of surfing.

Canoeing/rafting
Travelers can enjoy both adventurous and relaxing journeys along many of the world's rivers and lakes in canoes or rafts.

Seaport
Shipping remains vital for the global economy. The largest and busiest harbors in the world are highlighted.

Deep-sea fishing
The atlas highlights several of the best and most well known locations on the world's seas and oceans for recreational fishing.

Waterskiing
Popular beaches, coastal areas, and lakes with ideal conditions for waterskiing.

Beach resort
Many of the world's beachside communities feature a laid-back atmosphere and excellent tourist facilities. The atlas highlights popular beaches and redorts.

Mineral/thermal spa
The atlas locates several historic and beautiful towns with spas that have attracted visitors for centuries.

Amusement/theme park
Modern amusement parks offer diverse attractions. The parks highlighted in the atlas include Walt Disney World in Orlando, Sea World in California, Disneyland Paris, and Tivoli in Copenhagen.

Casino
Well known casinos, including the historic casino of Monte Carlo and the resort-hotels of Las Vegas.

Hill resort
Exclusive resorts located in temperate highland areas. Mostly in Asia, hill resorts were once very popular destinations, especially for European colonial officials.

Lodge
Comfortable and luxurious camps or inns in pristine wilderness areas, mostly in Africa and North America.

A view over the crater of Mount St. Helens, an
active volcano which last erupted in 1980.
Mount St. Helens is proof of the awesome natural forces which continue to shape our planet.

The world

Fascinating Planet Earth: The blue jewel of the solar system. Created 4.6 billion years ago from a cloud of dust and gas, the Earth today has a fascinating mix of landscapes, flora, and fauna. In addition to this wealth of natural features, our planet is also home to countless manmade wonders, all created in the last few thousand years.

The world – physical map

The total surface area of the Earth covers 510 million km², 71 % of which is covered by water and 29 % by land. Most of the **world's water** is contained in the four vast oceans on our planet: Pacific, Atlantic, Indian, and the relatively small Arctic Ocean. The world's **land area** is divided between the seven continents: North America, South America, Europe, Asia, Africa, Australia, and Antarctica. While the surface of the planet's south-

ern hemisphere is dominated by the oceans, the northern hemisphere is almost equally covered by land and water. The shape of the Earth's surface and the creation of the continents are the result of tectonic plate movements, a process that began billions of years ago. Catastrophic volcanic eruptions and

Light and water are the sources of all life on Earth.

Heavy snowfall, extremely cold temperatures, permafrost, bright summers and dark winters are common in the world's **polar regions**. Antarctica and the Arctic (top photo) contain at least 90 % of the planet's ice masses. The polar regions border on large tundras. Tundras (bottom photo) are cool regions with little precipitation and sparse, rugged vegetation.

The **taiga** is the world's largest belt of continuous forests and the world's northernmost forested biome. This immense climate zone is 1,000 kilometers wide at its widest. The taiga belt stretches though Alaska and Canada in North America as well as Scandinavia in Europe and Siberia (top photo). The vast boreal forests of the taiga (bottom photo) cover around 13 % of the world's land surface.

The **temperate regions** are home to vast forests with tall and green broad-leafed trees (top photo: Mixed forests in the Rocky Mountains of North America). Another side of the temperate zones are its vast grasslands and steppes, located primarily in Central Asia (Kazak Steppe), North America (Great Plains), and South America (Pampas). These mostly treeless regions receive relatively little precipitation and were once home to large numbers of animal herds (middle photo). The temperate zones also feature many of the world's most productive farming areas.

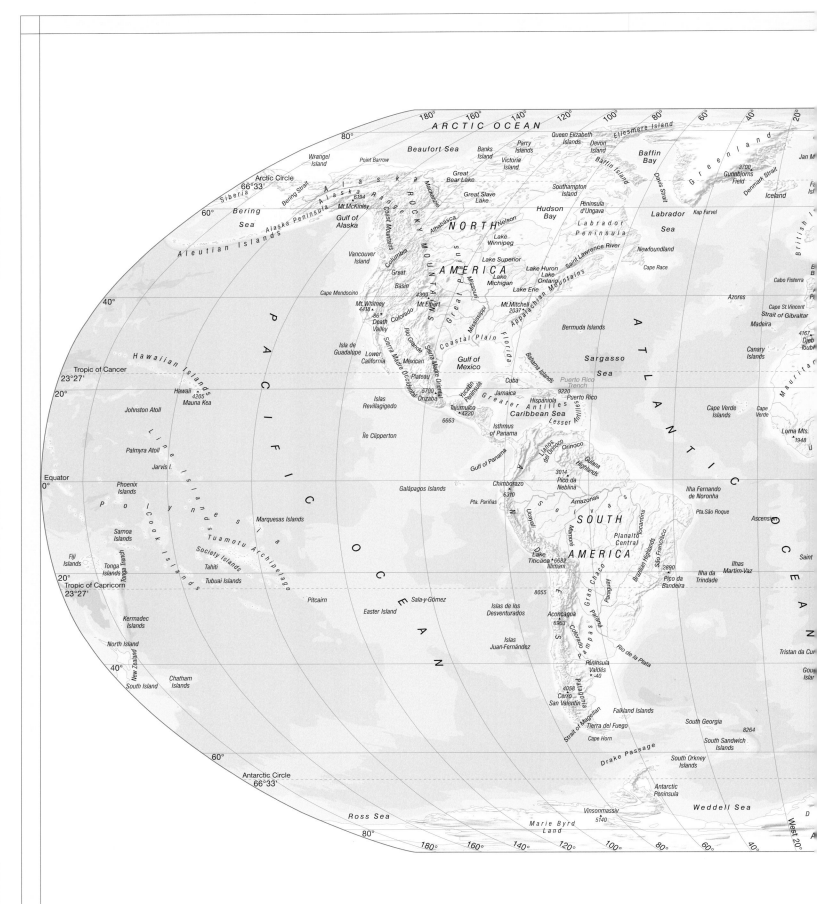

Scale 1:85,000,000

0   400   800 Kilometers

powerful earthquakes are not uncommon along the edges of the various tectonic plates.

Compared to the total diameter of the Earth (12,700 km) the height variations on our planet's surface are small. Mount Everest, the world's tallest mountain, rises 8,850 meters, while the deepest point in the ocean, the Mariana Trench in the Pacific, extends 11,034 meters beneath the planet's surface. Including

Mount Everest there are 14 mountains rising above 8,000 meters; all of them are located in Asia.

Most of the world's highest mountains are located in massive mountain chains, several of which cover large sections of the continents. The Pyrenees in Europe are the westernmost chain in an almost continuous belt of mountain systems stretching to Southeast Asia. The world's largest body of water, the Pacific Ocean,

is surrounded by the circumglobal mountain belt and East Africa has a long mountain belt. Mountain chains are the source of many rivers. The longest rivers on Earth are the Nile (6,671 km) in Africa, the Amazon (6,400 km) in South America, and the Yangtze (Chang Jiang) in East Asia (6,300 km).

The location of the world's various climate and vegetation zones is dependent on many factors, including the Earth's rota-

tion, the tilt of the Earth's axis, and ocean currents, among others. In equatorial regions constant heavy rainfall leads to the growth of thick vegetation coverage. Many tropical and subtropical regions border large arid regions; the Sahara in Africa is the world's largest desert (nine million km²). The world's temperate regions are home to green deciduous and mixed forests, and often border taiga and tundra regions.

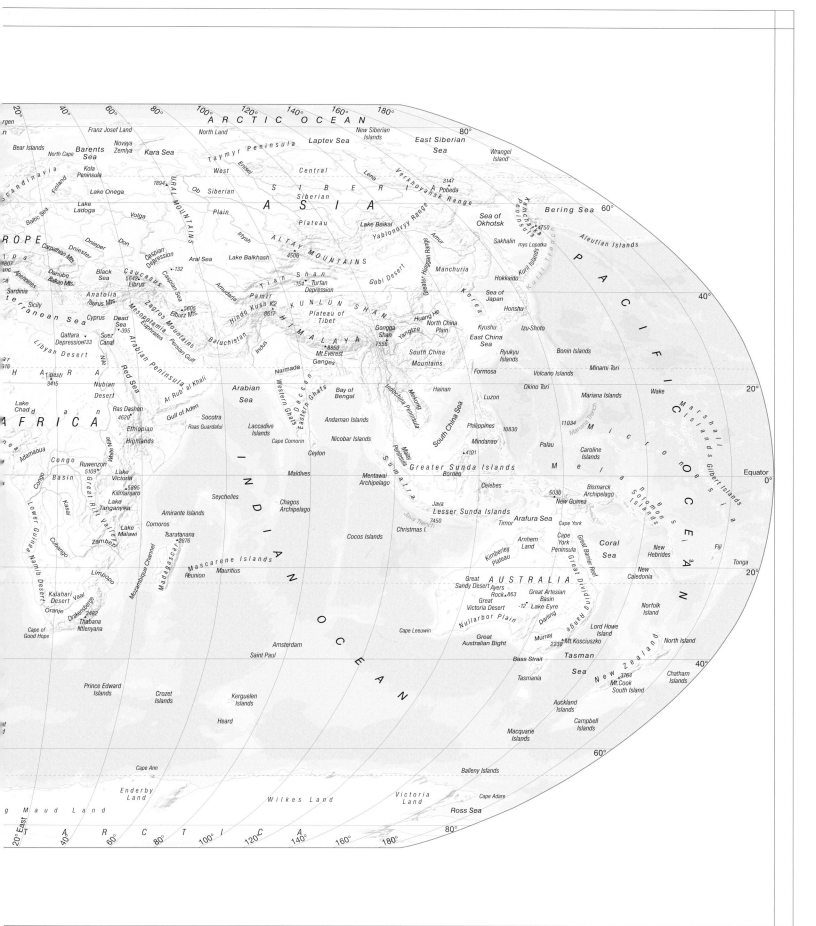

The world's **subtropical regions** are located between areas with temperate and tropical climates. Regions with Mediterranean climates (top photo) have warm summers as well as rainy winters and often border **semi-arid regions** or **deserts** (middle photo). **Humid subtropical forests** (ferns, palms, and mangroves) often grow along the edges of the tropical regions around the equator (bottom photo).

Most of the regions situated between the Tropics of Cancer and Capricorn have **tropical** or **subtropical climates**. To the north and south of most tropical rainforests are large **humid subtropical forests** or **savannahs** (top photo: Africa). The world's tropical rainforests are home to countless species of plants and animals and thick foliage (bottom photo: Brazil).

Mountain Systems (photo: Cerro Paine in Patagonia) often form distinct "climatic islands" inside larger climate zones. Many mountain ranges feature a variety of vegetation types at different elevations. The Himalayas in Asia are the world's highest mountain system.

The world – political map

At the beginning of the 21st century there were 194 sovereign nations on our planet. During the last centuries the shape of borders around the world were changed many times. Two world wars, the decline of European colonialism, and the collapse of Communism in Europe and the Soviet Union were especially important factors in the rise of many new nations and the fall of others. At the beginning of the 20th century most of Africa was

controlled by colonial powers; today the continent has 54 independent states, more than any other continent. After Africa comes Asia with 47 states, then Europe with 44, North America with 23, Australia/Oceania with 14, and South America with 13. Antarctica is the only "stateless" continent; the southernmost landmass is

United Nations headquarters along the East River in New York City.

The **United Nations (UN)** is the most famous and one of the more controversial international organizations on our planet. The United Nations was founded in 1945 and declares supporting world peace, increased international cooperation, and the development of underdeveloped nations as its main goals. New York City is the site of UN headquarters but the organization has bases and offices around the world. The UN has 191 member nations; only Taiwan, the Vatican, and West Sahara (occupied by Morocco) have not joined. The major divisions of the UN are the General Assembly, the Security Council, the Economic and Social Council, the International Court of Justice, and the Secretariat. In addition, the UN also operates several organizations and special programs, including the World Health Organization (WHO), UNICEF, and UNESCO. Photos from top to bottom: United Nations flag, the Palace of Nations in Geneva, The General Assembly, The Security Council.

One of the UN's major concerns is the fight against hunger around the world. The **UN World Food Program (WTF)** was set up in 1963 to provide assistance in areas where food is in short supply. In 2001, the WTF fed 77 million people in 81 countries, including many of the world's refugees.

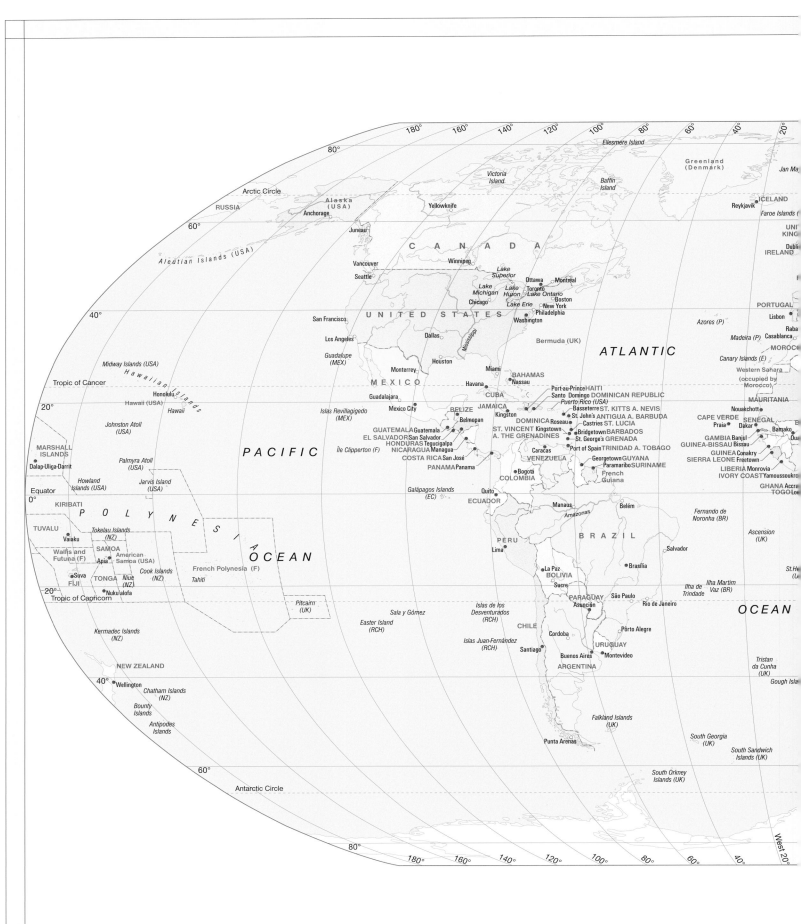

Scale 1:85,000,000

0   400   800 Kilometers

international territory according to the Antarctic Treaty of 1961.

Russia is the world's largest nation in terms of area. The country covers around 17.1 million km² on two continents and occupies one-ninth of the world's land surface. The **smallest sovereign nation** on Earth is the Vatican, the spiritual center of the Roman Catholic Church. The small city-state covers 0.44 km² and is entirely surrounded by the city of Rome.

Many of the world's political **borders** developed along natural barriers such as rivers and mountains. The straight linear borders found in some countries are the result of political developments; the border between the United States and Canada is an example of such a border.

The many different nations of the world are connected to one another in many ways. **Globalization** is a popular term used to describe the increasing integration of cultures and economic markets around the world. Globalization involves not only the **trade of natural resources** and manufactured goods, but also increasingly the exchange of information, skills, and services.

In October 1999, the **world's population** exceeded six billion for the first time in history. The population density of our planet is unevenly distributed between different regions. Western Europe and India are the world's most densely populated regions. China is the most populous country with 1.3 billion inhabitants. In the year 2000, India became the second nation with a population exceeding one billion. Since 1960 the world population has doubled in size. At least 90 % of current population growth occurs in the so-called developing nations; this imbalance contributes to the problems of mass hunger and poverty in many of the world's poorer regions.

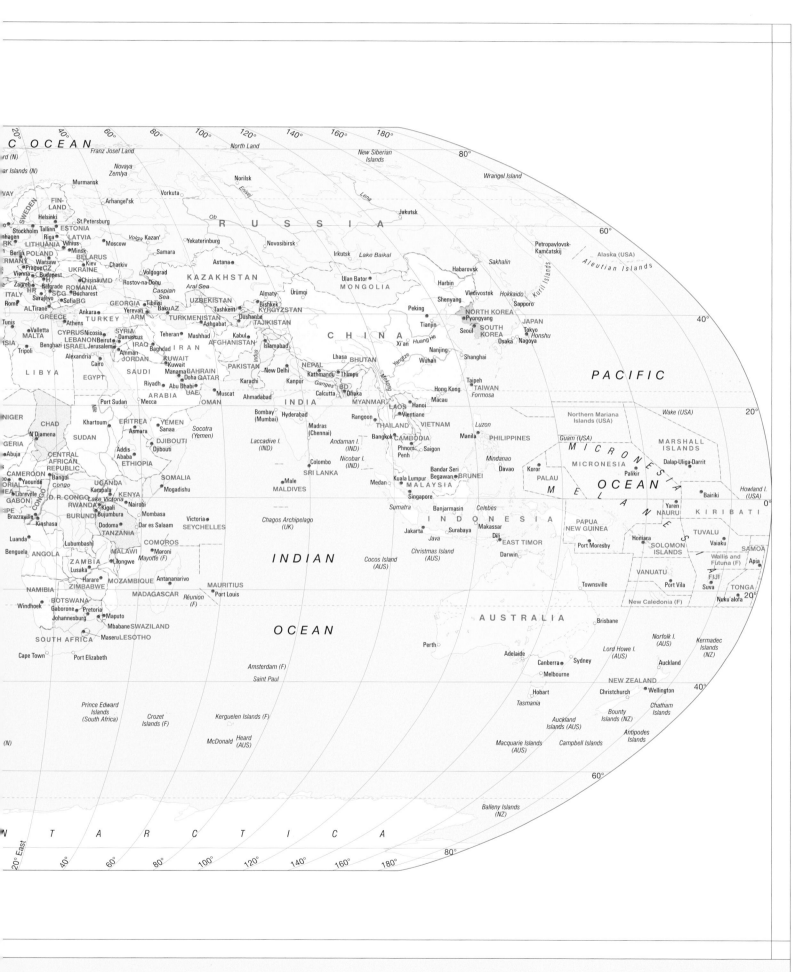

The **UN Security Council** is the only UN body authorized to make binding decisions for all of its members. The Council has 15 members, including five permanent members.

The **United States of America** is the last remaining superpower. The White House (top photo) in Washington D.C is the residence of American presidents. The United States' Senate meets in the Capitol (bottom photo).

The Kremlin has been a center of political power in **Russia** since the 13th century and is today the seat of the Russian parliament.

In 1949, Mao Zedong proclaimed the establishment of the **People's Republic of China** in fronz of Beijing's Gate of Heavenly Peace (top photo) on Tiananmen Square (bottom photo).

Paris is the cultural, economic, and political center of **France**. Photo: Place de la Concorde and the National Assembly.

Great Britain: Once the leader of a vast empire, Britain is now an important member of the European Union. Photo: The Houses of Parliament in London.

Salzburg (top): The Hohensalzburg fortress towers above the picturesque old town.
Andalusian countryside (bottom): storm clouds above a village in the Sierra Nevada.

Bilbao (left): The futuristic architecture of Bilbao's Guggenheim museum.
Stonehenge (right): An early Stone Age monument built to observe the stars.

Europe

The fjords and cliffs of the north, the vast green forests of Central Europe, the snow covered peaks of the Alps and Pyrenees, the sun drenched coasts of the Mediterranean, the legacy of ancient Greeks and Romans, medieval cathedrals, baroque castles, modern cities, and colorful traditions... All this and more is Europe.

With an area of 10.5 million km², Europe is the second smallest continent in size. Separated in the east from Asia by the Ural Mountains, Europe extends over 5,000 kilometers to the western coast of Ireland. From the North Cape to Crete in the Mediterranean, Europe stretches over 4,000 kilometers north to south. The **Atlantic Ocean** marks the western borders of Europe, the Mediterranean and Black Sea border the continent in

the south and the Arctic Ocean lies north of the continent.

The topography Southern and Central Europe's is dominated by a bow shaped series of **mountain chains**. The mountain system extends from the Sierra Nevada, to the Pyrenees, the Alps, and the Carpathian Mountains. North of this

The beatiful rolling hills of Tuscany (Italy).

mountain belt lies a series of **medium elevation ranges** – including the French Massif Central, the Harz Mountains, and the Tatras – that gives way to the plains of northern and Central Europe. One of the most striking features of Europe's geography is the large number of **peninsulas** (Scandinavia, Iberia, Greece, etc.) on the continent. The European mainland is also surrounded by many **islands**, including Great Britain and Sardinia.

Europe's diverse landscapes developed over many millions of years and were largely shaped by the last ice ages. The ice and snow-covered **mountainous tundra** of northern Scandinavia – including Lapland (top photo) – is a rugged and sparsely populated region. North of the tall Alps, a series of **medium-height ranges** stretches through much of Central Europe (middle photo: Sächsische Schweiz in Germany). There are also many rocky landscapes and high hills along Europe's Mediterranean coastlines (bottom photo).

The **Alps** stretch in a long band from west to east. The highest peaks are in the western areas of the Alps, including the highest alpine mountain Mont Blanc (4,807 m). The 4,478-meter-high Matterhorn (top photo) is the third highest mountain in the Alps. The second highest mountain chain in Europe is the Sierra Nevada in Spain, which encompasses many high peaks including Mulhacen (3,478 m).

Many of the world's most famous **rivers** are located in Europe. The longest rivers in Europe are the Volga (3,530 km), the Danube (2,850 km), and the Ural (2,428 km); all three flow into the Caspian or Black Sea (top photo: the Danube in Budapest). The Rhine (1,320 km), Loire (1,020 km), and Oder (868 km) are all among the longest rivers in Europe (bottom photo: The Rhine in Switzerland).

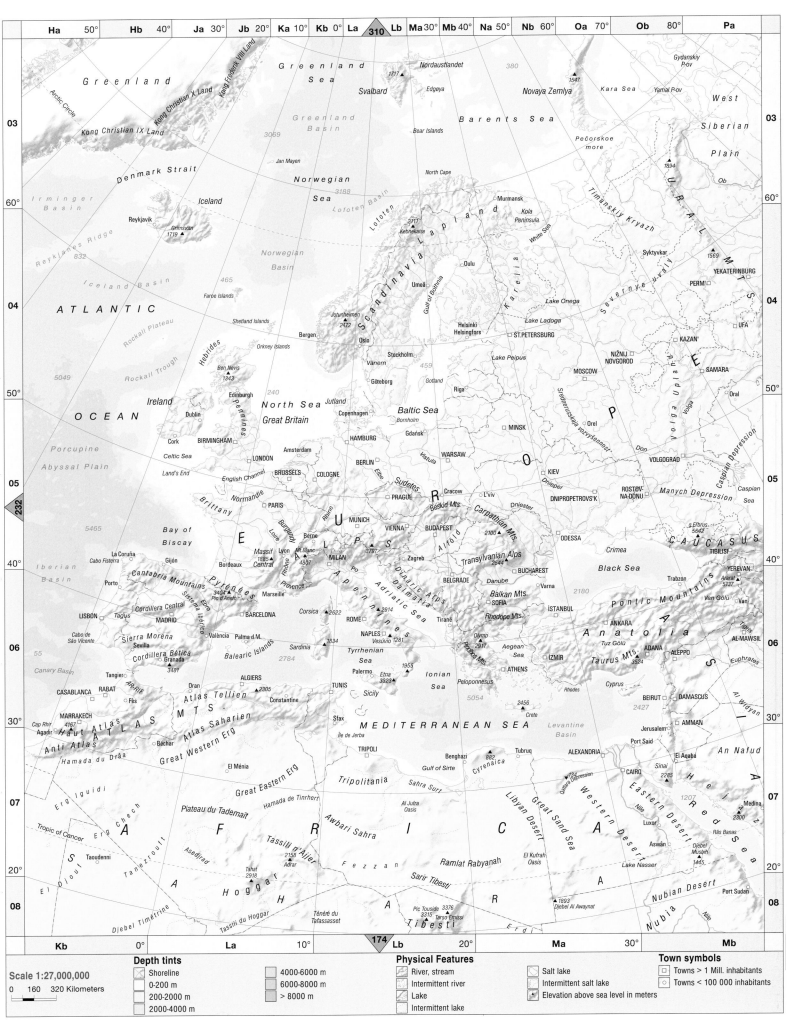

Scale 1:27,000,000

0   160   320 Kilometers

Depth tints		Physical Features		Town symbols	
Shoreline	4000-6000 m	River, stream	Salt lake	Towns > 1 Mill. inhabitants	
0-200 m	6000-8000 m	Intermittent river	Intermittent salt lake	Towns < 100 000 inhabitants	
200-2000 m	> 8000 m	Lake	Elevation above sea level in meters		
2000-4000 m		Intermittent lake			

With a **population** of 740 million, Europe is the third most populous continent. Several European states have populations exceeding 50 million – including Italy, France, the United Kingdom, Russia, and Germany. Immigrants from outside Europe have changed the faces of many once homogenous European nations since the second half of the 20th century. With the relatively recent **political development** in Eastern Europe – the collapse of the Soviet Union for example – many new states have emerged on the continent. The **migration** of people from eastern to western Europe and between southern and northern Europe continues to bring the continent's diverse cultures and nations closer together.

Left: Swedish child.
Right: A young Russian woman.

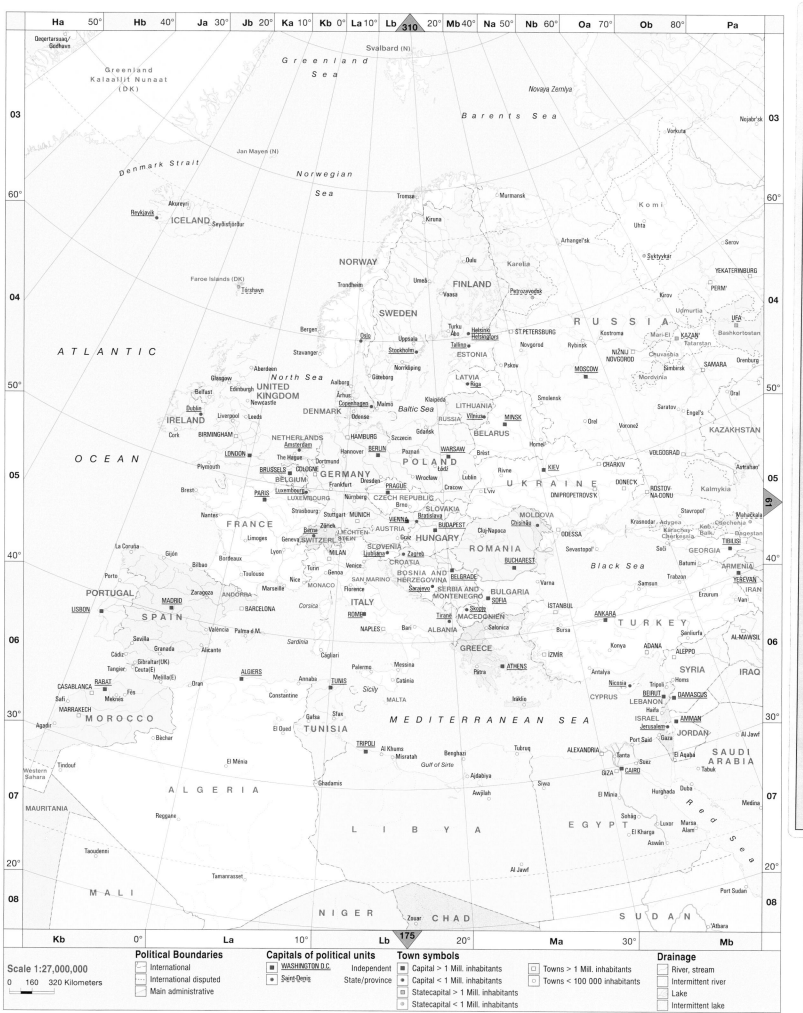

Countries and Flags

- Albania
- Andorra
- Austria
- Belarus
- Belgium
- Bosnia and Herzegovina
- Bulgaria
- Croatia
- Cyprus
- Czech Republic
- Denmark
- Estonia
- Finland
- France
- Germany
- Greece
- Hungary
- Iceland
- Ireland
- Italy
- Latvia
- Liechtenstein
- Lithuania
- Luxembourg
- Macedonia
- Malta
- Moldova
- Monaco
- Netherlands
- Norway
- Poland
- Portugal
- Romania
- Russia
- San Marino
- Serbia and Montenegro
- Slovakia
- Slovenia
- Spain
- Sweden
- Switzerland
- Ukraine
- United Kingdom
- Vatican City

A blue flag with twelve golden stars is the official emblem of the **European Union**. Founded in the 1950s, the European Union was originally a trade alliance of six nations.

Scale 1:27,000,000

0   160   320 Kilometers

Political Boundaries
- International
- International disputed
- Main administrative

Capitals of political units
- ▪ WASHINGTON D.C. — Independent
- ● Saint-Denis — State/province

Town symbols
- ▪ Capital > 1 Mill. inhabitants
- ● Capital < 1 Mill. inhabitants
- ■ Statecapital > 1 Mill. inhabitants
- ● Statecapital < 1 Mill. inhabitants
- □ Towns > 1 Mill. inhabitants
- ○ Towns < 100 000 inhabitants

Drainage
- River, stream
- Intermittent river
- Lake
- Intermittent lake

Europe

The continent of Europe is surrounded by the Atlantic Ocean, Arctic Ocean, and several marginal seas – including the Mediterranean Sea – on three sides: north, south, and west. The Ural Mountains and the Ural River are generally considered the natural boundaries that separate Europe from Asia. Geographically, Europe and Asia can be seen as two parts of a larger continent called Eurasia. Because Europe lacks a definitive border to

Asia, certain regions such as Anatolia (Asia Minor) may or may not be considered European in different situations. Iceland lies on the boundary between the Eurasian and North American continental plates but is considered a European nation. Islands and peninsulas form around 34 % of Europe's total area.

The Dolomites, a craggy section of the Alp's in South Tyrol-Alto Adige (Italy).

Despite the presence of several high mountain ranges including the Alps, Europe has an average height of just 300 meters above sea level, the lowest average elevation of any continent.

Europe is a relatively small land mass but the continent features an incredible diversity of **landscapes** and geographically distinct regions including numerous islands and peninsulas. The mountain ranges in western Scandinavia and northern

Iceland Volcanic island located just south of the Arctic Circle – 103,125 km² – highest mountain, Hvannadalshnukur (2,119 m).

The British Isles Great Britain and Ireland are the main islands in this group – smaller island groups include the Shetlands, Orkneys, and Hebrides – highest mountain, Ben Nevis (1,344 m) – photo: Dorset.

The North Sea Flat marginal sea of the Atlantic Ocean – surface covering 0,575 million km² – maximum depth, 294 meters – extreme tidal range (0,5 to 7 m).

The European Plain Series of plains encompassing lowlands in France, northern Germany (photo), and eastern Europe – stretches from the Atlantic Coast to the Urals.

Massif Central Unique mountainous region in France – consists of craggy mountains (photo) and plateaus – the Rhone Valley separates the area from the Alps.

Iberian Peninsula Encompasses Spain and Portugal – circa 585,560 km² – Atlantic and Mediterranean coasts – the Pyrenees form a natural boundary between Iberia and France.

Apennine Peninsula The "boot" of Italy – named after the 1,500 kilometer long Apennine Mountain Range – Sicily lies to the southwest – photo: Mount Etna.

Scale 1:18,000,000

0   160   320 Kilometers

Depth tints
- Shoreline
- 0-200 m
- 200-2000 m
- 2000-4000 m
- 4000-6000 m
- 6000-8000 m
- > 8000 m

Physical Features
- River, stream
- Intermittent river
- Lake
- Intermittent lake
- Salt lake
- Intermittent salt lake
- Elevation above sea level in meters

Europe

Great Britain border lowlands and rolling hills around the North Sea, the Baltic Sea, and the English Channel. Lowlands also dominate the northwestern edges of mainland Europe in France and the Benelux countries. Most of Eastern and Central Europe is covered by a series of vast plains stretching to the Ural Mountains. A long belt of mountain ranges extends from the western coast of mainland Europe to the eastern edges of the continent. This mountain belt encompasses the Pyrenees, the Alps, the Carpathian Mountains, and several smaller ranges. Most of the mountain ranges in southern and southeastern Europe – including the highlands on the Balkan Peninsula – are lateral branches of the main continental mountain belt.

Most of Europe's regions have temperate continental **climates**. Mild ocean currents (including the Gulf Stream) and winds have a significant impact on the continent's climates. During winter, Eastern Europe is often significantly colder than the western sections of the continent where the effect of ocean currents on the weather is greater. During summer, major differences in temperature between northern and southern Europe are common.

With the exception of a few areas in northern Europe with arctic and sub-arctic climates, most of Europe lies within the temperate zone. Much of the continent is covered by forests and heavily cultivated farmland. Southern Europe's coastal areas, around the Atlantic Ocean, Mediterranean, and Black Sea, have warm "Mediterranean" climates with mild winters and dry hot summers.

The many islands of the Mediterranean Sea include some of the driest and warmest areas in Europe.

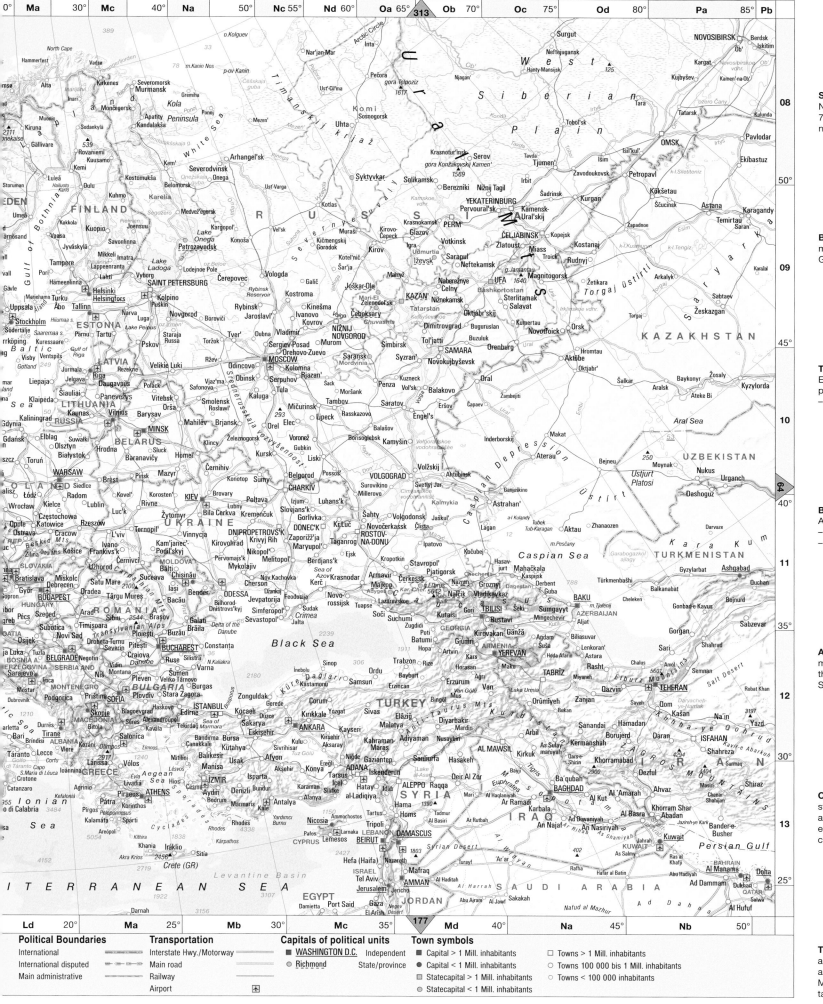

Scandinavian Peninsula Encompasses Norway, Sweden, and northern Finland – 750,000 km² – jagged western coast – numerous fjords.

Baltic Sea Sea in northern Europe – maximum depth, 459 meters – largest island, Gotland (Sweden) – photo, Rügen (Germany).

The Alps High mountain range in Central Europe – length: 1,300 kilometers – highest peak, Mont Blanc in France (4,807 m) – photo, alpine glacier in Switzerland.

Balkan Peninsula Located between the Adriatic and Black Seas – circa 476,000 km² – Balkan, Pindus, and Rhodope Mountains – photo, the Dalmatian coast.

Aegean Islands Island group belonging mostly to Greece – includes the Cyclades, the Sporades, Rhodes and Crete – photo: Santorini.

Carpathian Mountains Mountain system stretching 1,300 kilometers – between 50 and 150 kilometers wide – consists of several distinct ranges – tallest mountain, Gerlachovsky in Slovakia (2,655 m).

The Caucasus Mountain range stretching around 1,100 kilometers between the Black and Caspian Seas – heavily glaciered – Mount Elbrus (5,642 m), the highest mountain in Europe.

Political Boundaries
International
International disputed
Main administrative

Transportation
Interstate Hwy./Motorway
Main road
Railway
Airport

Capitals of political units
■ WASHINGTON D.C. Independent
● Richmond State/province

Town symbols
Capital > 1 Mill. inhabitants
Capital < 1 Mill. inhabitants
Statecapital > 1 Mill. inhabitants
Statecapital < 1 Mill. inhabitants
Towns > 1 Mill. inhabitants
Towns 100 000 bis 1 Mill. inhabitants
Towns < 100 000 inhabitants

Northern Scandinavia, Iceland, Spitsbergen

Most of Northern Scandinavia's fascinating landscapes were formed during the last three ice ages, the most recent ending 13,000 years ago. The region boasts numerous ■ treeless plateaus (**fjell**), **mountain valleys**, and ■ **fjords**. Norway's Vestfjorden is the longest fjord in the region and one of the most stunning. The Scandinavian Mountains cover most of northern Norway and stretch across the border into Sweden. Many

small islets and islands are located off the jagged northern coast of Norway. Northern Norway also features numerous pristine rivers that flow from the interior into the sea. Lapland, a fascinating region of moors and tundra, lies north of the Arctic Circle. The region is divided between Norway, Sweden, Finland, and Russia.

The Mørsvikfjorden in Northern Norway. **Lh12**

Iceland Despite its name, ice and glaciers cover only 10 % of this large volcanic island in the North Atlantic. Iceland's largest glacier ▲ Vatnajoekull is also the largest glacier in Europe. The country has more than 200 ■ volcanoes including Hekla, the most active in the country (eruption every 40 to 50 years). Photos from top to bottom: Dettifoss (**Kb13**), Hekla (**Ka14**), Jökulsárlon Glacier (**Kb14**).

North Cape/Nordkapp ■ Rocky coast on the edge of an icefield – the northernmost point in Norway. **Mc10**

Lofoten Norwegian ■ island group north of the Arctic Circle – jagged mountains and fascinating rugged landscapes. **Lg11/12**

Hurtigruta Famous ■ ferries that travel regularly along the Norwegian coast from Bergen to Kirkenes.

Trondheim Capital of Norway during the Middle Ages – ▲ Nidarosdom, Norway's royal cathedral – the Nidelv River (photo). **Le14**

Scale 1:4,500,000
0   40   80 Kilometers

Principal travel routes
- Auto route
- Rail road
- Shipping route

Remarkable landscapes and natural monuments
- UNESCO World Natural Heritage
- Mountain landscape
- Rock landscape
- Ravine/canyon
- Active volcano
- Geyser
- Cave
- Glacier
- River landscape
- Waterfall/rapids
- Nature park
- National park (landscape)
- National park (fauna)
- National park (culture)
- Whale watching
- Protected area for sea-lions/seals

Most of Finland's more than 180,000 lakes were formed during the ice ages. Russia's Lake Ladoga, near the Finnish border, is the largest lake in Europe. Another lake in the region, Lake Onega, is the second largest in Europe. The two most famous natural phenomena in this part of Europe are the **Aurora Borealis (northern lights)** and the **midnight sun**. In areas north of the Arctic Circle, the sun is visible during all 24 hours of the day around the 21st of June. In winter, this process is reversed and the region experiences long periods without sunlight. The spectacular light shows of the Aurora Borealis are created when energized particles from the sun plunge through the Earth's atmosphere. Like many of the world's large volcanic islands, Iceland was formed along what geologists refer to as a hotspot. On this hotspot a stream of magma rising from the earth's core breached the surface and cooled.

Iceland features active volcanoes, geysers, and gigantic glaciers. At least two-thirds of the island's territory is uninhabited. The majority of the country's population is concentrated in coastal cities and towns – including the capital Reykjavik. The more than 700 hot springs on the island provide a reliable source of heat for most of the country's households.

Svalbard is an isolated Norwegian island group in the Arctic Ocean. The islands lie just 1,000 kilometers away from the North Pole. More than two thirds of the islands' land area is covered by large glaciers. The highest mountain in the island group Newtontoppen rises 1,717 meters. Svalbard is home to around 2,500 people living in a few scattered settlements. Most of the islands' inhabitants work in the fishing or coal mining industries.

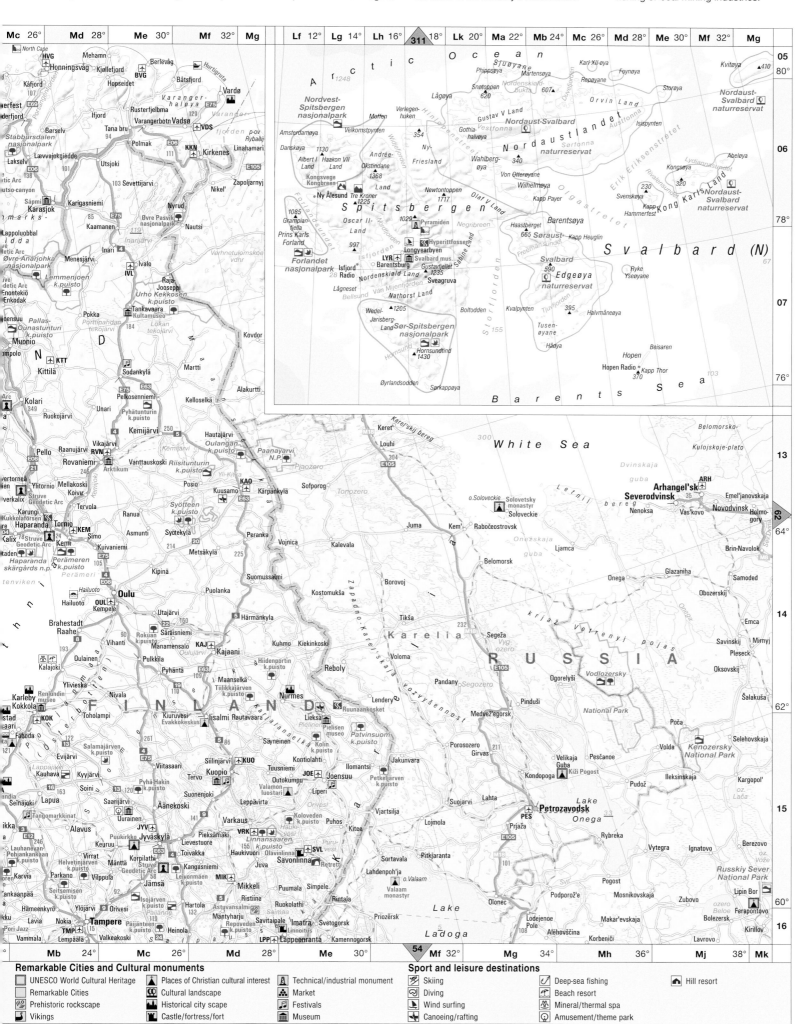

Svalbard This Norwegian island group boasts fascinating mountain landscapes and large glaciers (top photo). The national parks on the islands are home to reindeer, walruses (bottom photo), and many unique bird species.

The Sámi Once known as the Lapps, around 50,000 Sámi live in Lapland. Their nomadic ancestors lived primarily from reindeer herding in the northernmost regions of Scandinavia.

Lake Inari The second largest lake north of the Arctic Circle – 1,085 km² – maximum depth, 96 meters.   **Md-Me11**

Savonlinna Historic city surrounded by numerous lakes – Burg Olavinlinna, built in 1475.   **Me15**

Solovetsky Monastery Historic fortified Orthodox monastery on an island – UNESCO world heritage site.   **Mh13**

Kiži Pogost Two beautiful historic wooden churches – on an island in Lake Onega – UNESCO world heritage site.   **Mh14**

Remarkable Cities and Cultural monuments

- UNESCO World Cultural Heritage
- Remarkable Cities
- Prehistoric rockscape
- Vikings
- Places of Christian cultural interest
- Cultural landscape
- Historical city scape
- Castle/fortress/fort
- Technical/industrial monument
- Market
- Festivals
- Museum

Sport and leisure destinations

- Skiing
- Diving
- Wind surfing
- Canoeing/rafting
- Deep-sea fishing
- Beach resort
- Mineral/thermal spa
- Amusement/theme park
- Hill resort

Southern Norway, Central Sweden

Norway covers the western half of the Scandinavian Peninsula. The country is a land of mountains, fjords, and valleys. The 400-million-year old **Scandinavian Mountains** extend through most of Norway. The mountain range stretches over 1,500 kilometers from Southern Norway to the Arctic Ocean.

The **Jotunheimen Range**, a section of the Scandinavian Mountains, includes the two highest mountains in Scan-

dinavia: Galdhøpiggen (2,469 m) and Glittertind (2,472 m). Most of the population in southern Norway and central Sweden live near or along the coast. In Norway, 80 % of the population lives within 15 kilometers of the sea. Norway's capital city, Oslo, is also the largest city in the country – with a popu-

Ålesund, the center of Norway's fishing industry, is an attractive city. **Lf28**

Geirangerfjorden One of the most spectacular fjords in Norway – connected to the larger Storfjord. **Lg28**

Røros Former mining center – historic town center is a UNESCO world heritage site – 350-year-old wooden houses. **Lm28**

Urnes Stave Church The oldest stave church – made entirely of wood in the 12th century – UNESCO world heritage site. **Lg29**

Jostedalsbreen National Park Mountainous national park containing the largest glacier in Norway – glacier museum in Fjaerland. **Lg29**

Lustrafjorden Fjord in southwestern Norway – deep blue water surrounded by the Sognefjell plateau. **Lg29**

Bergen The second largest city in Norway and the leading port on the country's western coast – Bryggen, the medieval quarter with historic warehouses is a UNESCO world heritage site – 12th century church – interesting museums. **Le30**

Oslo Norway's capital and largest city – Akerhus fortress and the interesting modern city hall (photo) – Karl Johans Gate, major city center boulevard – Royal Palace – Bygdoy museum island – the ski jump of the 1952 Olympic winter games is a local landmark. **Ll31**

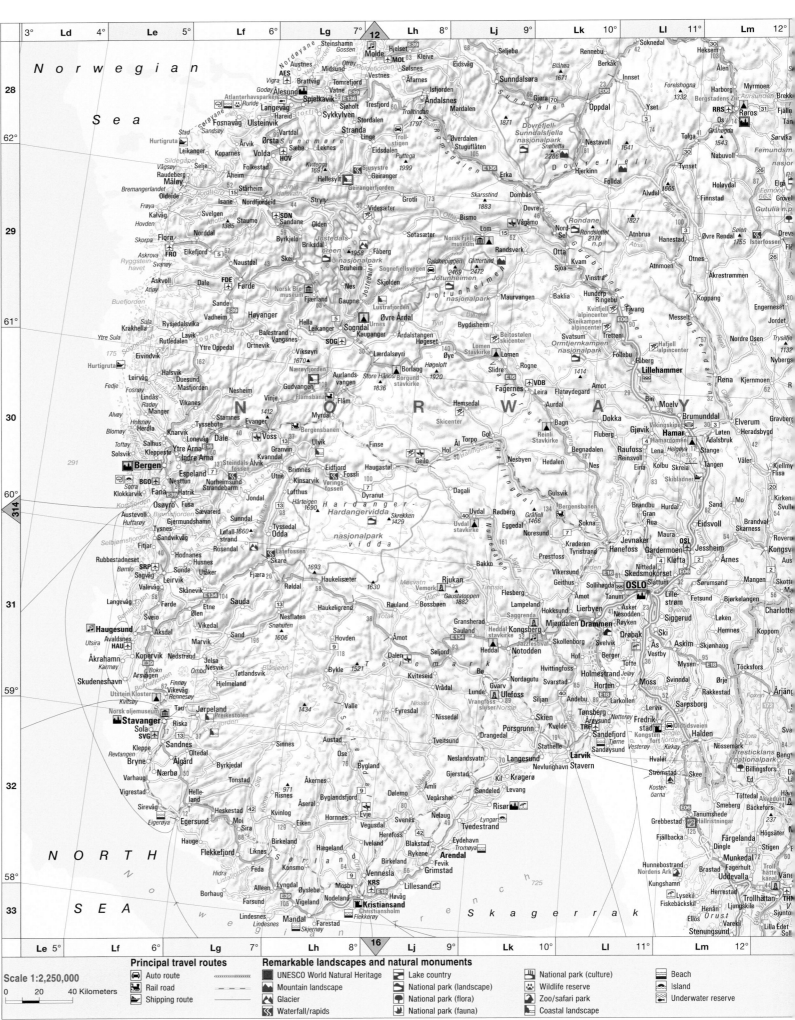

Scale 1:2,250,000

0   20   40 Kilometers

Principal travel routes
- Auto route
- Rail road
- Shipping route
- UNESCO World Natural Heritage
- Mountain landscape
- Glacier
- Waterfall/rapids

Remarkable landscapes and natural monuments
- Lake country
- National park (landscape)
- National park (flora)
- National park (fauna)
- National park (culture)
- Wildlife reserve
- Zoo/safari park
- Coastal landscape
- Beach
- Island
- Underwater reserve

lation approaching 800,000. The city is situated on the Oslofjord in southeastern Norway and is surrounded by forested hills and mountains.

The numerous ⬛ **fjords** on Norway's western coast were formed during the last ice age around 10,000 years ago. Today these deep flooded valleys are among the most popular tourist attractions in the country. The longest fjords stretch over 200 kilometers inland and

the deepest, Sognefjord, has a maximum depth of 1,244 meters. Eastern Norway contains many plateaus and barren treeless patches of rocky land. The area is popular with Norwegian hikers during summers. Dovrefjell and ⬛ **Hardangervidda**, between Oslo and Bergen, are two of the larger plateaus in the countries. Hardangervidd is one of the largest elevated plateaus in Europe with a total area of 10,000 km².

Central Sweden is an expansive region of countless rivers, large virgin forests, and fertile valleys. The thousands of ⬛ lakes in the region are ideal for swimmers and recreational sailors.

The area between Oslo and Stockholm features several of Europe's largest lakes – including Lake Vanern (5,600 km²), the continent's third largest lake. Sweden's Baltic coast is lined by countless small ⬛ islands and islets. Many of the islands

near Stockholm are popular weekend destinations for city dwellers. Stockholm, the capital of Sweden, is the largest and most cosmopolitan city on the Scandinavian Peninsula.

Despite their northern locations, both southern Norway and central Sweden have temperate climates with cold winters and warm summers. The Gulf Stream, an ocean current, has a major effect on the climates of both regions.

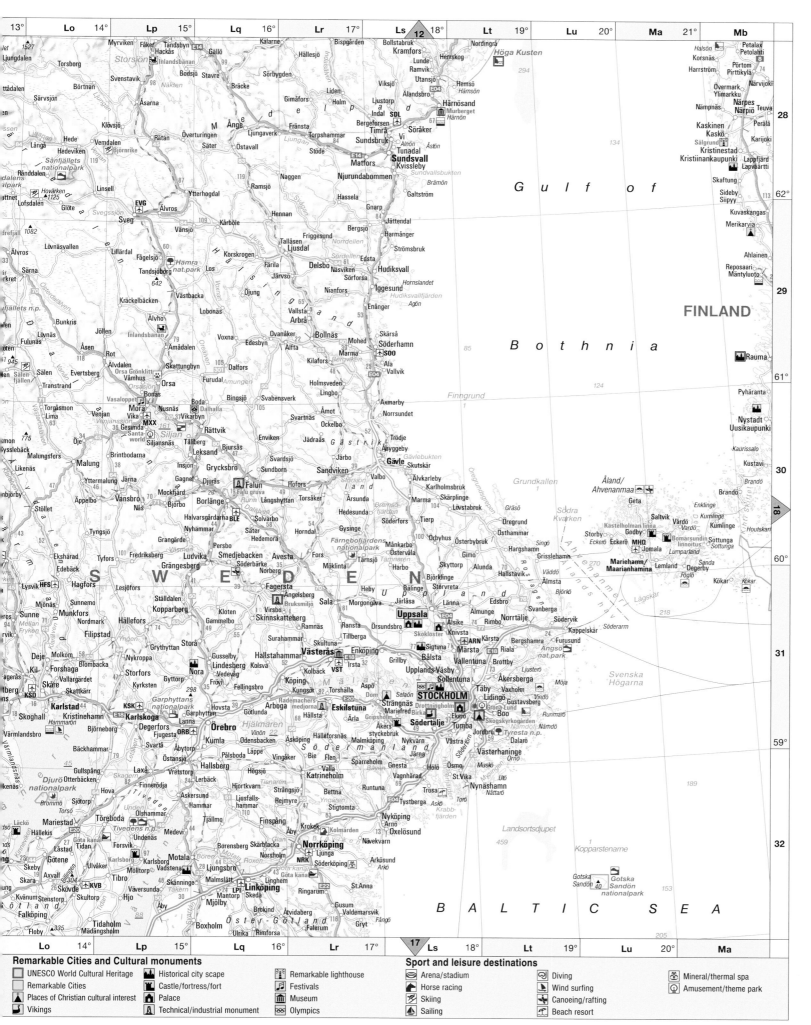

Falun The oldest ⬛ copper mine in the world – in use for over 1,000 years – UNESCO world heritage site – ⬛ museum and visitors center. **Lq30**

Darlana Province in central Sweden – beautiful Lake Siljan – expansive virgin forests cover most of the province's southeast – popular ⬛ ski areas. **Lp29/Lp30**

The Åland Islands Group of over 6,500 ⬛ islands and islets – province of Finland – most of the population are Swedish speakers – ⬛ Kastelholm, medieval castle. **Lu30**

Gripsholm Castle Historic ⬛ castle – built in the 16th century – on the shore of Lake Malaren. **Lr31**

Drottningholm Palace Baroque palace – UNESCO world heritage site – residence of the Swedish Royal Family. **Ls31**

Stockholm The capital of Sweden since 1634 (750,000 inhabitants) – built on fourteen islands between the Baltic Sea and a lake (Mälaren) – Gamla Stan, medieval old town – museum church on the island Riddarholmen – the national parliament – the ⬛ Vasa Museum, Scandinavia's most visited museum. **Ls31**

Skargard Islands near Stockholm Archipelago of more than 30,000 ⬛ islands between Stockholm and the Baltic Sea. **Lt31**

Legend

Remarkable Cities and Cultural monuments

☐ UNESCO World Cultural Heritage	⬛ Historical city scape
⬛ Remarkable Cities	⬛ Castle/fortress/fort
⬛ Places of Christian cultural interest	⬛ Palace
⬛ Vikings	⬛ Technical/industrial monument
⬛ Remarkable lighthouse	
⬛ Festivals	
⬛ Museum	
⬛ Olympics	

Sport and leisure destinations

⬛ Arena/stadium	⬛ Diving	⬛ Mineral/thermal spa
⬛ Horse racing	⬛ Wind surfing	⬛ Amusement/theme park
⬛ Skiing	⬛ Canoeing/rafting	
⬛ Sailing	⬛ Beach resort	

Denmark, Southern Sweden

Denmark is a small nation of rolling hills, forests, and fertile plains. The country has around 1,000 lakes and 7,300 kilometers of coastline – at least 5,000 kilometers of which feature sandy beaches. No area in Denmark is more than 55 kilometers distance from the sea. Of the 400 Danish islands, around 380 are located in the Baltic Sea.

Denmark's capital city, **Copenhagen**, is located on the country's largest and most

densely populated island, ▨ **Seeland**. Much of the land on Seeland is used for agriculture but the island also has large forests, dunes, and ▨ long sand beaches. Denmark's second largest island ▨, **Funen**, is surrounded by many smaller islands and islets. Funen is heavily forested but it is also one of the most important

A Viking burial site near Aalborg (Denmark). **Lk33**

fruit and vegetable farming areas in the country. **Jutland** – a peninsula between the Baltic and North Seas – is the largest Danish region and the only part of the country connected to mainland Europe. **Limfjord**, a body of water that cuts through northern Jutland, is a popular recreational destination. Most of Jutland's western coast consists of ▨ large dunes, broad sandy ▨ beaches, and scattered bluffs. Southern Jutland features large

Århus Denmark's second largest city – Modern city hall – ▨ Frue Kirke – open air museum ▨ Den Gamle By (photo). **Ll34**

Egeskov Castle ▨ Beautiful Renaissance-era castle on Funen – beautiful gardens – ▨ classic car museum. **Ll35**

Roskilde Former residence of the Danish monarchs – ▨ gothic cathedral built in the 12th century, burial site of Danish royalty and UNESCO world heritage site (photo) – ▨ hall with preserved Viking ships. **Ln35**

Kronborg Castle Shakespeare's ▨ Hamlet Castle (Elsinore) – on the Öresund strait – UNESCO world heritage site. **Ln34**

Frederiksborg Castle ▨ Renaissance era castle built in the 17th century – on a lake near Hillerod in Seeland. **Ln35**

Copenhagen Capital city of Denmark since 1417. More than a million people live in the city and its surrounding area. The city is also the country's leading ▨ port and cultural center. The city's most famous landmark is the (top photo) ▨ Little Mermaid statue. South of the ▨ Nyhavn district (bottom photo), with its bars and historic architecture, lies ▨ Slottsholmen Island and ▨ Christiansborg Castle. **Ln35**

Scale 1:2,250,000

0   20   40 Kilometers

Principal travel routes
🚗 Auto route
🚆 Rail road
⚓ Shipping route

Remarkable landscapes and natural monuments
▨ UNESCO World Natural Heritage
▨ Rock landscape
▨ Lake country
▨ Nature park
▨ National park (landscape)
▨ National park (flora)
▨ National park (fauna)
▨ Protected area for sea-lions/seals
▨ Zoo/safari park
▨ Coastal landscape
▨ Beach
▨ Island

coastal marshlands and pastures. **Rebild Bakker National Park** south of Aalborg encompasses moorlands and the largest forest in Denmark. The eastern half of Jutland is an important agricultural region. The coastal areas of eastern Jutland are narrower than those on the peninsula's western coast. Several long and narrow bays are located on the eastern coast of Jutland. **Bornholm**, the easternmost Danish island, has the

country's finest beaches and a variety of interesting landscapes. The **Öresund** strait separates Denmark from **Southern Sweden**. **Scania**, the southernmost region of Sweden, is covered by plains and scattered hills. Scania is densely populated and agriculture is an important sector in the region's economy. The coasts of Scania are lined with fine sand beaches. To the north of Scania lies **Blekinge**, a region of rolling hills, forests, and

meadows. The **Småland** region has the most diverse collection of landscapes in Southern Sweden. Småland's natural attractions include a hilly upland, vast forests, countless moors, around 5,000 lakes, and a coast lined by many small islands. The highest elevation in Småland is **Tomtabacken** (378 m), a hill southwest of Nässjö. **Vättern**, Sweden's second largest lake, is located to the northwest of Tomtabacken. **Öland** and

Gotland, off the southwestern coast of Sweden, are the country's two largest islands. Both islands have steep, rocky western coasts and smooth sandy eastern coasts. The historic landscapes of Öland's countryside comprise a designated world heritage site.
Southern Sweden is the location of five national parks. **Store Mosse National Park** encompasses the largest Swedish moorland outside of Lapland.

Gothenburg Important port and Sweden's second largest city – beautiful historic old town – important art museum. **Lm33**

Öland Island off the southwestern coast of Sweden – UNESCO world heritage site – Sta Birgitta Chapel (photo). **Lr34**

Kalmar Castle Renaissance era fortified castle – splendid interior design – beautiful fountains. **Lr34**

Gotland Because of its mild climate and sandy beaches, Sweden's largest island is a popular holiday destination. Gotland's many attractions include large unique rock formations called Raukar (top photo) and Visby (bottom photo), a historic city and UNESCO world heritage site on the island's coast. **Lt33**

Bornholm The easternmost and fourth largest Danish island has a rocky northern coast, while its southern coast has sandy beaches, idyllic fishing villages, and historic sites. The island's landmarks are its round churches, all of which were built in the 12th and 13th centuries – including the Olskirke (bottom photo). **Lp-Lq35**

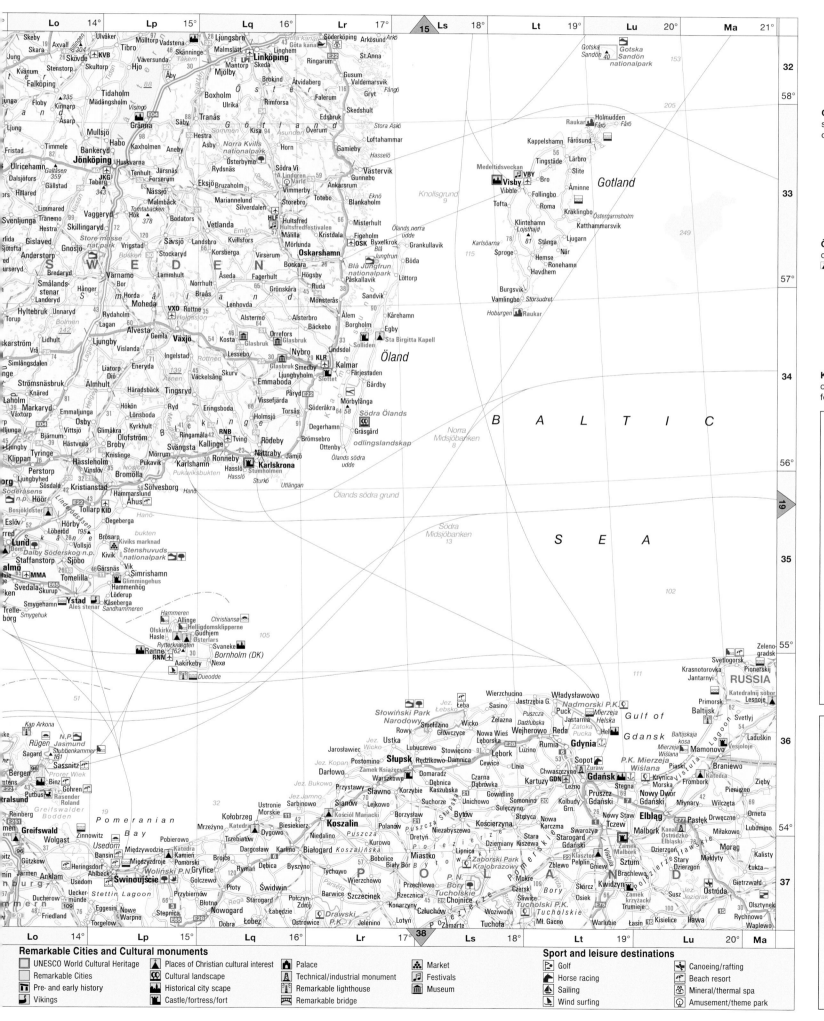

Remarkable Cities and Cultural monuments		Sport and leisure destinations	
UNESCO World Cultural Heritage	Palace	Market	Canoeing/rafting
Remarkable Cities	Technical/industrial monument	Horse racing	Beach resort
Pre- and early history	Remarkable lighthouse	Festivals	Mineral/thermal spa
Vikings	Remarkable bridge	Museum	Amusement/theme park
Places of Christian cultural interest	Golf		
Cultural landscape	Sailing		
Historical city scape	Wind surfing		
Castle/fortress/fort			

Southern Finland, Northern Baltic States

The Finns call their country **Suomi**, a name meaning marshland and one that accurately describes much of southern Finland. There are at least ⊡ **55,000 thousand lakes** in southern Finland, many of which are interconnected by streams and rivers. During the ice ages, Finland was covered by large glaciers. When these glaciers melted, they created most of the country's lakes. Finland is a heavily forested country – at least 70 % of the country

is covered by woodlands. Finland's coast is lined with thousands of ⊡ **small islands**, only 80 of which are permanently inhabited. The islands south of the Finnish city Turku Åbo are parts of the **Skargardshavet National Park**.
The **Baltic Sea** lies southeast of the **Bay of Finland**. **Saremaa** (2,710 km²) and

The Curonian Spit off the coasts of Lithuania and Kaliningrad. **Ma35**

Southern Finland's Lakes ⊡ Lake Saimaa in southeastern Finland is the largest lake in the country, with a total area of 1,460 km². The lake is just one of at least 55,000 lakes in southern Finland alone. **Md-Na28/29**

Rauma ⊡ Port city on the Baltic Sea – ⊡ Historic district with wooden houses – UNESCO world heritage site. **Mb29**

Helsinki Finland's capital city hosted the 1952 ⊡ Olympics. Senate Square is the site of an impressive ⊡ cathedral (top photo). The ⊡ Suomenlinna fort and the National Opera House (bottom photo) are attractions. **Me30**

Tallinn (Reval) The capital of Estonia has a beautiful medieval ⊡ old town (top photo). Town Hall Square (bottom photo) has stunning historic architecture. **Me31**

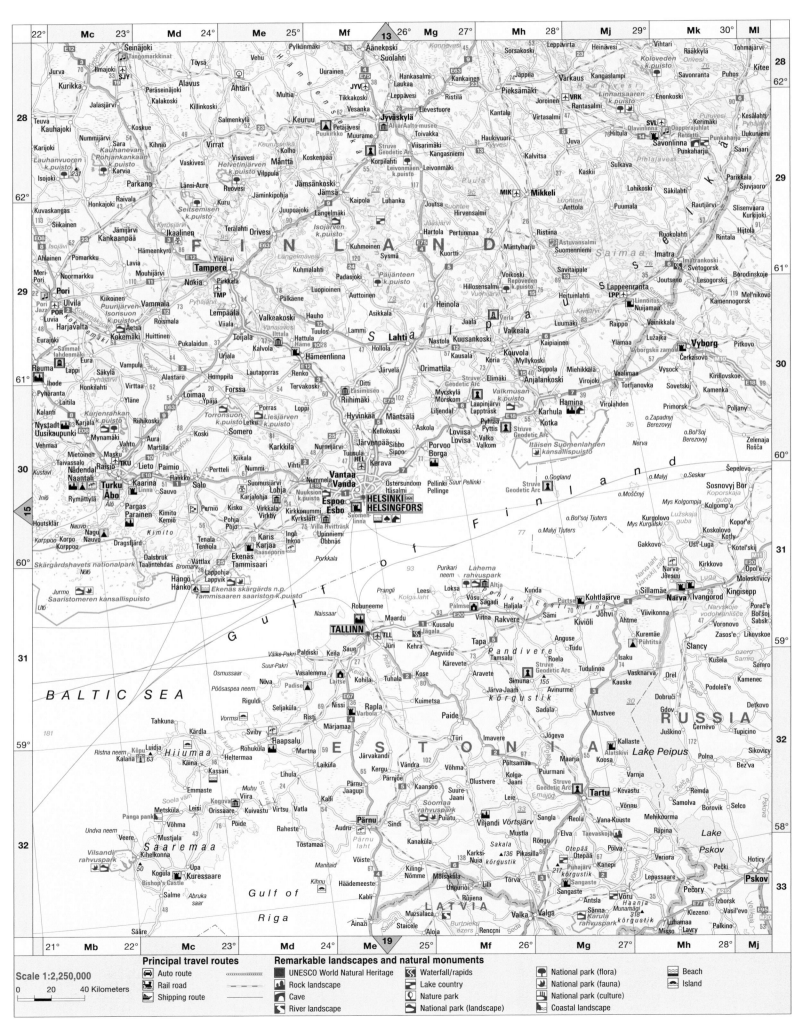

Scale 1:2,250,000
0   20   40 Kilometers

Principal travel routes
- Auto route
- Rail road
- Shipping route
- Auto route ----
- ---- ----

Remarkable landscapes and natural monuments
- UNESCO World Natural Heritage
- Rock landscape
- Cave
- River landscape
- Waterfall/rapids
- Lake country
- Nature park
- National park (landscape)
- National park (flora)
- National park (fauna)
- National park (culture)
- Coastal landscape
- Beach
- Island

Hiiumaa (960 km²) are the largest of the 1,500 islands off the coast of Estonia. Most of Estonia's land is covered by low hills and plains. Marshland and lakes cover at least a fifth of the country. The country has extensive forests and wood products are among its leading exports. Estonia is a very flat country with no major elevations. Munnamagi, a hill rising 318 meters, is the highest point in the country. **Lake Peipsi** (2,673 km²) is

the largest of Estonia's 1,400 lakes. Finland's capital city, Helsinki, is situated on the Gulf of Finland's northern edge across from Tallinn, the capital of Estonia. The two cities are separated by around 90 kilometers of water and linked by frequent ferry services.
The former Soviet republics **Estonia**, **Lithuania**, and **Latvia** are collectively referred to as the Baltic States. Large sections of Latvia are situated below sea

level. Only the eastern and western areas of the country rise significantly above sea level. Latvia's coastline consists primarily of long sandy beaches. The western coast borders the Baltic Sea and farther east the large Gulf of Riga extends deep into the country's interior. Most of eastern Latvia consists of low lying plains, while the western section of the country is covered by numerous lakes and rolling hills. Western Latvia

also features extensive, virgin forests of pine, spruce, and birch trees.
Northern and southeastern Lithuania have many high sand dunes, small lakes, and hills. The **Curonian Spit** is a narrow 98-kilometer-long strip of land between the Baltic and the Curonian Lagoon. The Neman (Nemunas) River flows from Belarus to the Baltic Sea and forms the border between Lithuania and the Russian exclave Kaliningrad.

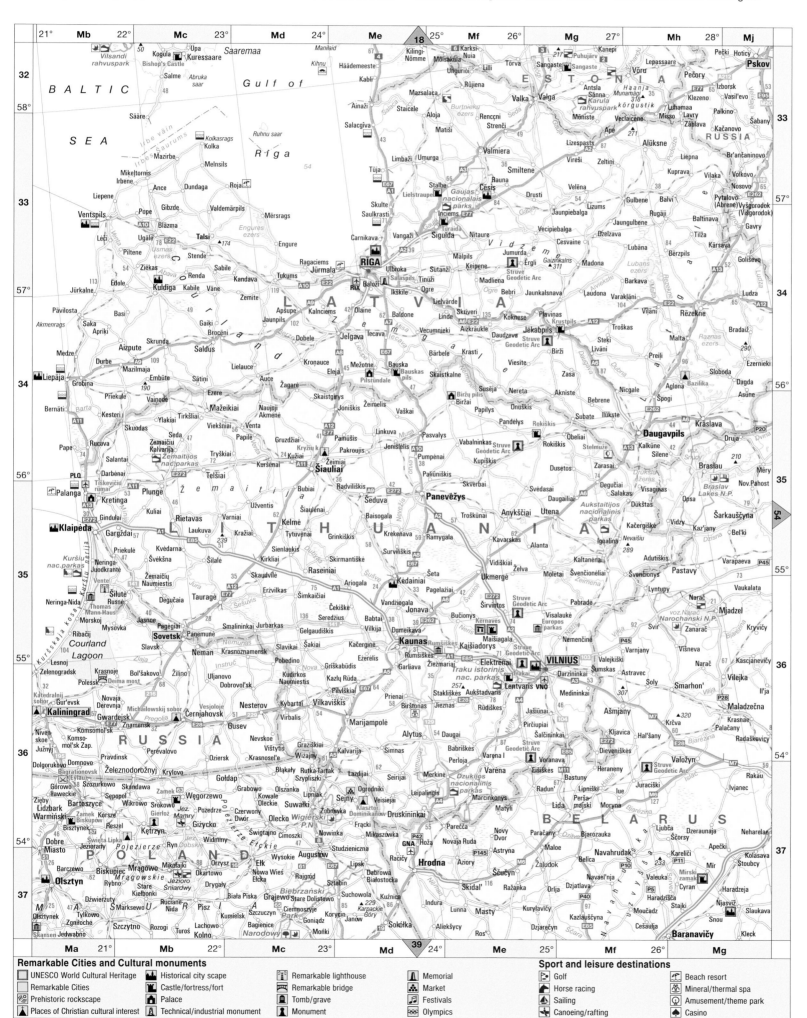

Riga St. Peter's Church (top photo) in Latvia's capital city was built in 1209. The city's historic old town (bottom photo) boasts well preserved medieval buildings and is a UNESCO world heritage site. **Me34**

Kaunas The second largest city in Lithuania – historic Jesuit church (photo) – beautiful riverside district. **Md36**

Vilnius Lithuania's capital city has a beautiful old town – UNESCO world heritage site – cathedral (photo) built in 1783. **Mf36**

Trakai Capital of the Lithuanian kingdom during the Middle Ages – island castle (photo) in an area with many lakes. **Me36**

Kaliningrad Russian exclave surrounded by Poland and Lithuania – the city was once predominantly German speaking and was called Koenigsberg – cathedral (photo) with a memorial to Immanuel Kant. **Ma36**

Remarkable Cities and Cultural monuments

- UNESCO World Cultural Heritage
- Remarkable Cities
- Prehistoric rockscape
- Places of Christian cultural interest
- Historical city scape
- Castle/fortress/fort
- Palace
- Technical/industrial monument
- Remarkable lighthouse
- Remarkable bridge
- Tomb/grave
- Monument
- Memorial
- Market
- Festivals
- Olympics

Sport and leisure destinations

- Golf
- Horse racing
- Sailing
- Canoeing/rafting
- Beach resort
- Mineral/thermal spa
- Amusement/theme park
- Casino

Northern Great Britain encompasses several regions and political divisions: Northern England, Scotland, the Shetland Islands as well as the Orkney and Hebrides Islands off the coast of Scotland. Northern Ireland is a political division of the United Kingdom and shares a border with the Republic of Ireland. **Northern England** is distinctly hilly and the **Pennines**, a low mountain range, stretches through most of the region.

Lake District National Park boasts some of the most beautiful landscapes in England. The national park also features Scafell Pike (978 m), the highest point in England. The coast of **Northumberland** has many attractive fine sandy beaches and is a popular area for bird and seal watching.

Spectacular Glen Coe in the Scottish Highlands. **Kp34**

Isle of Skye Island in the Inner Hebrides – interesting attractions; Loch Coriusk and 🏔 the Cullin Hills. **Ko33**

Giant's Causeway 🏞 Natural attraction on the coast of Northern Ireland – consists of over 40,000 black basalt columns leading to the sea – created by lava 60 million years ago – UNESCO world heritage site. **Ko35**

Dunluce Castle Picturesque ruins of a 🏰 castle atop a small stone hill – built in the 16th century. **Ko35**

Achill Island The largest island off the coast of Ireland – hills, moors, and meadows in the island's interior – beautiful views – 🏖 good beaches. **Kk37**

Connemara National Park in the Republic of Ireland with fascinating coastal landscapes (top photo). The large 🏞 national park features many pristine landscapes, includind moors and heaths. Doo Lough (bottom photo) often called the "black lake" is situated in a beautiful valley near Clew Bay. The park contains several nature trails and hiking paths. **Kk-Kl37**

Clifden Castle 🏰 Once the home of John d'Arcy, founder of the city of Clifden – now a beautiful ruin. **Kl37**

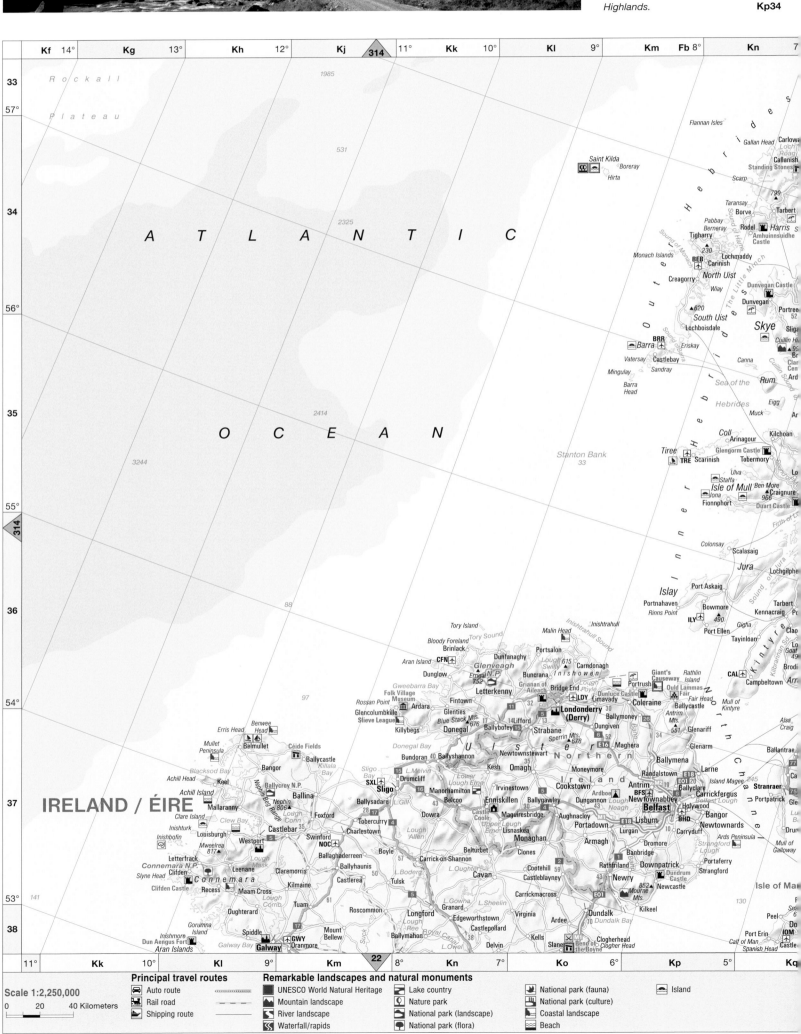

Scotland can be divided into three distinct geographic regions: the Southern Uplands are a region of low hills and undeveloped coasts, the Central Lowlands – the most densely populated and fertile region, and the mountainous Scottish Highlands with its stunning landscapes. The most sparsely populated regions in Great Britain are the beautiful northern and western Highlands of Scotland. Ben Nevis (1,344 m), the highest mountain in Great Britain, and ⊠ Loch Ness are two of the most popular tourist attractions in the Highlands. ⊠ **Loch Lomond and the Trossachs National Park** in central Scotland encompass beautiful mountains and valleys. Firth and loch are Scottish words used to designate the many ⊠ bays, inlets, and estuaries along the country's coast. The ⊠ **Orkney Islands** and the ⊠ **Hebrides** are island groups off the coast of Scotland.

Like the more distant ⊠ **Shetland Islands**, the Hebrides and Orkneys feature many ⊞ prehistoric sites and fascinating landscapes. Much of the land on the Scottish islands is cultivated. Small scale farming together with fishing dominate the local economies of the Shetlands, Orkneys, and Hebrides.
The interior of Ireland is covered by lakes and fertile plains, while the coastal areas are rocky and hilly. The north and north-west of **Ireland** feature tree covered hills, jagged coasts, and low mountains. The summit of Slieve Donard (825 m) in the ⊠ Mourne Mountains is the highest point in Northern Ireland. ⊠ Glenveagh, ⊠ Connemara, and ⊠ Ballycroy **National Parks** are three fascinating and beautiful nature reserves in the Republic of Ireland. The ⊠ Giant's Causeway is one of many beautiful stone formations on the coast of Northern Ireland.

The Orkney Islands A group of 70 islands off the northern coast of Scotland – several of the ⊞ prehistoric sites including the Ring of Brodgar (photo) are UNESCO sites. **KrKs31/32**

Scotland's castles Scotland has numerous historic castles and forts. Many of these building are well preserved and have extensive gardens. Some are also open to visitors. Photos from top to bottom: Dunnottar Castle, Stalker Castle, and Eilean Donan Castle.

Scottish Clans The Scottish clan system was first established in 13th century. The clan system was the suppressed during the 18th and 19th centuries. Many of the surviving clans still have their own unique tartans.

Edinburgh Scotland's capital and one of the most beautiful cities in the United Kingdom – ♫ annual festival – Edinburgh Castle towers above the city – medieval ⊠ old town and Georgian new town – important ⊠ museums. **Kr35**

Hadrian's Wall ⊞ The wall was built in the 2nd century. UNESCO site and Britain's most important Roman ruin. **Ks35/36**

Remarkable Cities and Cultural monuments
- ⊡ UNESCO World Cultural Heritage
- ⊡ Remarkable Cities
- ⊞ Pre- and early history
- ⊠ Roman antiquity
- ▲ Places of Christian cultural interest
- ⊡ Cultural landscape
- ⊠ Historical city scape
- ⊠ Castle/fortress/fort
- ⊠ Palace
- ⊠ Remarkable bridge
- ⊠ Tomb/grave
- ⊠ Theater of war/battlefield
- ⊠ Market
- ⊠ Festivals
- ⊠ Museum

Sport and leisure destinations
- ⊠ Golf
- ⊠ Horse racing
- ⊠ Skiing
- ⊠ Sailing
- ⊠ Diving
- ⊠ Wind surfing
- ⊠ Seaport
- ⊠ Beach resort

Southern **Great Britain** consists of Wales as well as central and southern England. This small region encompasses diverse landscapes, including some of the most beautiful areas in the British Isles. Most of southern Britain is covered by rolling low hills and fertile plains. The southwest of England is the location of Dartmoor and Exmoor National Parks, both of which contain pristine moorlands. Millions of visitors travel to England's south-

ern coast to enjoy the many sandy beaches and majestic cliffs in the region. Devon, the Isles of Scilly, and the Isle of Wight have the mildest climates in Great Britain as well as attractive coastlines. The Isle of Wight is also home to an abundance of wildlife including many unique bird species. The Jurassic

Durdle Door, an ancient natural arch on the Dorset coast. **Ks40**

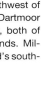

Clonmacnoise Ruins of an early Christian monastic settlement on the banks of the Shannon River – first settled by Celtic monks in the 7th century. **Kn37**

Cliffs of Moher One of the Europe's most beautiful coastal cliffs – 203 meters above the ocean. **Kl37/38**

Dublin Capital and cultural center of the Irish Republic – modern and cosmopolitan city – two historic cathedrals – Temple Bar, neighborhood with vibrant nightlife – museums – O'Connell Bridge (photo) – Trinity College. **Ko37**

Snowdonia National Park Popular national park with tall mountains and deep valleys. **Kq-Kr37/38**

Conwy Castle Impressive example of medieval fortified architecture in the historic Welsh county of Gwynedd – the imposing structure was built in the 13th century during the reign of Edward I. – UNESCO world heritage site. **Kr37**

Tintern Abbey This Cistercian abbey in the Wye Valley is one of Wales' most impressive ruins – built in Gothic style during the 13th century. **Ks39**

Land's End The westernmost point in Great Britain – located in Cornwall – high stone cliffs – popular tourist destination. **Kp40**

Scale 1:2,250,000

0   20   40 Kilometers

Principal travel routes
- Auto route
- Rail road
- Shipping route

Remarkable landscapes and natural monuments
- UNESCO World Natural Heritage
- Mountain landscape
- River landscape
- Lake country
- National park (landscape)
- National park (flora)
- National park (fauna)
- National park (culture)
- Zoo/safari park
- Coastal landscape
- Beach
- Island

Coast between East Devon and Dorset features prehistoric rock formations and many important fossil sites. Outside London and its suburbs, South East England is a largely rural character. The South East with its mild climate is one of England's most fertile regions and comprises deep valleys, idyllic pastures, and famous white chalk cliffs. **East Anglia** is a low-lying region with extensive fenlands, historic towns and small seaside resorts – located northeast of London. Much of East Anglia consists of land reclaimed from the sea through the use of canals and dikes. The **Midlands** in central England is a diverse region with both idyllic rural settings (including Cotswolds) and large industrial urban areas such as Birmingham, Britain's second largest city. North of the Midland lies the historic county of Yorkshire, which features the Yorkshire Dales and the ⌂ North York Moors. ⌂ Lake District National Park in Cumbria has fascinating landscapes and is considered by many to be the most beautiful area in England. **Wales** is largely mountainous, with the Cambrian Mountains and their foothills stretching through most of the country. ⌂ Snowdonia National Park in North Wales is the location of Mount Snowdon, the highest British mountain outside Scotland. ⌂ Pembrokeshire National Park on the Welsh coast encompasses fascinating seaside landscapes and small islands. The interior of **Ireland** has numerous rivers and lakes. Most of the Republic of Ireland's land is covered by hills, moors, and fertile pastures. Carrauntoohil (1,038 m), near the ⌂ southwestern coast, is the highest mountain in Ireland. The southwestern coast of Ireland also features the ⌂ Ring of Kerry, a fascinating region of beautiful landscapes.

Lake District ⌂ National park with spectacular landscapes and lakes – waterfalls, mountains, and gorges.   **Kr-Ks36**

Blenheim Palace Largest ⌂ private residence in Britain – impressive architecture and gardens – UNESCO world heritage site. **Kt39**

London ⌂ The capital city of the UK and a leading financial center. The cosmopolitan city has numerous attractions including; ⌂ the Tower Bridge (top photo), ⌂ Buckingham Palace, the ⌂ British Museum. Several London attractions including the ⌂ Tower of London, ⌂ the Houses of Parliament (bottom photo), and ⌂ Westminster Abbey are UNESCO sites.   **Ku39**

Stonehenge Famous ⌂ prehistoric site consisting of several large stones in a circle – built between 3000 and 1500 BC – the site's origins and early history remain largely unknown – world heritage site.   **Kt39**

Canterbury One of the oldest cities in southern England – home to a magnificent historic cathedral begun in the 12th century AD, a UNESCO world heritage site.   **Lb39**

The Chalk Cliffs of East Sussex This area boasts many beautiful high ⌂ chalk cliffs, including the Seven Sisters.   **La40**

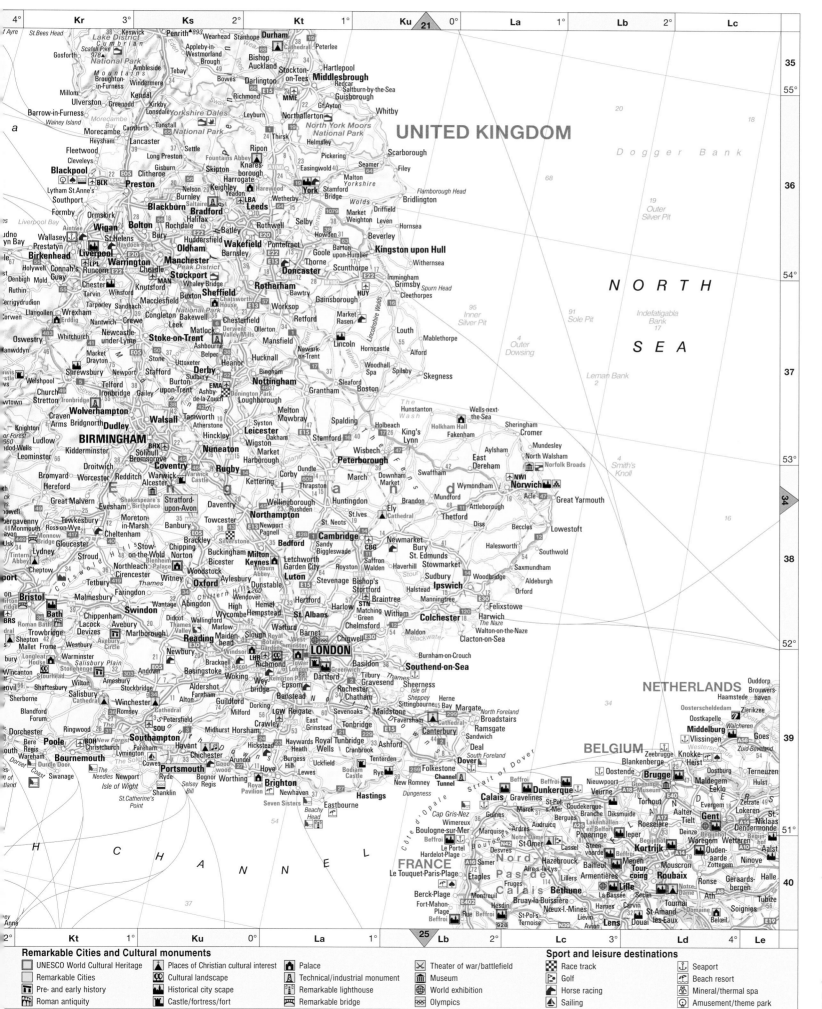

Remarkable Cities and Cultural monuments

- ☐ UNESCO World Cultural Heritage
- ☐ Remarkable Cities
- ⌂ Pre- and early history
- ⌂ Roman antiquity
- ⌂ Places of Christian interest
- ⌂ Cultural landscape
- ⌂ Historical city scape
- ⌂ Castle/fortress/fort
- ⌂ Palace
- ⌂ Technical/industrial monument
- ⌂ Remarkable lighthouse
- ⌂ Remarkable bridge

Sport and leisure destinations

- ⌂ Theater of war/battlefield
- ⌂ Museum
- ⌂ World exhibition
- ⌂ Olympics
- ⌂ Race track
- ⌂ Golf
- ⌂ Horse racing
- ⌂ Sailing
- ⌂ Seaport
- ⌂ Beach resort
- ⌂ Mineral/thermal spa
- ⌂ Amusement/theme park

Belgium, Northern France

Belgium is one of the smallest and most densely populated states in Europe. The country is divided into two distinct geographic regions seperated by the Maas/Meuse river. The south and east of Belgium is a highland region, in contrast to the country's low lying north and west. Beyond Belgium's 70 kilometers of coastline, with its dunes and ⌂ beaches, lies a flat region of fertile polders – land reclaimed from

the sea – and the hills of the Kempenland. **Central Belgium** is a region of rolling green hills, that rise to 200 meters in height. To the south and east of the Maas/Meuse lies the **Ardennes**, a densely forested region and the location of countless caves, gorges, and the Hohen Venns plateau (694 m).

The famous medieval abbey Mont Saint Michael. **Kt42**

Brittany's Coast Beautiful ⌂ cliffs – beaches – charming port cities including St. Guénolé (Photo). **Kq43**

Carnac Center of a prehistoric culture – Sites with ancient man-made stone formations and 3,000 stone monoliths. **Kr43**

La Rochelle ⌂ Port city (71,000 inhabitants) – interesting ⌂ old town center – attractive Vieux Port. **Kt44**

Loire Valley From Sully-sur-Loire to Chalonnes this fertile ⌂ river valley forms part of a UNESCO world heritage site. Highlights of the ⌂ region include the ⌂ palaces at Chambord (photo, top) Chenonceaux, Amboise, and Azay-le-Rideau. Historic Blois (photo, bottom) also has a ⌂ palace and the town of ⌂ Saumur is dominated by an impressive castle. **Lb43**

Amiens Traditional capital of Picardy, located on the Somme river – the large Gothic cathedral Notre Dame built in the 13th century – UNESCO world heritage site. **Lc41**

Versailles ⌂ Louis XIV's grandiose palace, today a national museum – symbol of absolutism – the historic hall of mirrors – beautiful surrounding parks (UNESCO world heritage site). **Lc42**

Scale 1:2,250,000
0   20   40 Kilometers

Principal travel routes
- Auto route
- Rail road
- Shipping route

Remarkable landscapes and natural monuments
- UNESCO World Natural Heritage
- Mountain landscape
- Ravine/canyon
- Cave
- River landscape
- Waterfall/rapids
- Lake country
- Nature park
- National park (landscape)
- National park (fauna)
- Biosphere reserve
- Wildlife reserve
- Zoo/safari park
- Coastal landscape
- Beach
- Island

Northern France is dominated by the plains of Normandy and Picardy and the hills of Brittany. The Atlantic and English Channel coasts of France are rich in contrasts: the white ⬛ chalk cliffs of the northern channel coast, the endless ⬛ beaches in Picardy and Normandy, the jagged coastline, bays, and ⬛ islets in Brittany. The ⬛ Channel Islands, dependencies of the United Kingdom, present some of most interesting landscapes in

the region and a wealth of unique flora and fauna. The unusual chalk formations of the ⬛ Côte de Granit Rose in Northern Brittany and the marsh landscape Marais Poitevin are among the many other interesting landscapes in the region.
The Loire River delta is situated to the south of Brittany. The Loire stretches over 1,000 kilometers through France and is the country's longest river. Between Orleans and Angers the Loire pas-

ses through a ⬛ region with an abundance of interesting cultural attractions including numerous ancient towns, palaces, and cathedrals.
The Paris basin is located in the center of northern France. Paris, the capital of France, is one of the world's most diverse cities and the largest urban area in France by far. The city's numerous cultural, historic, and architectural highlights attract millions of visitors to the region

every year. The river Seine flows 770 kilometers though the region's farmland and beyond into the region Champagne, a major center of wine production. In the eastern basin, the forests of the ⬛ French Ardennes run along the border between France and Belgium. The ⬛ Vosges mountain range extends through the area to the southeast of the Paris basin. The range has a maximum height of 1,426 meters and descends into the Rhine Valley.

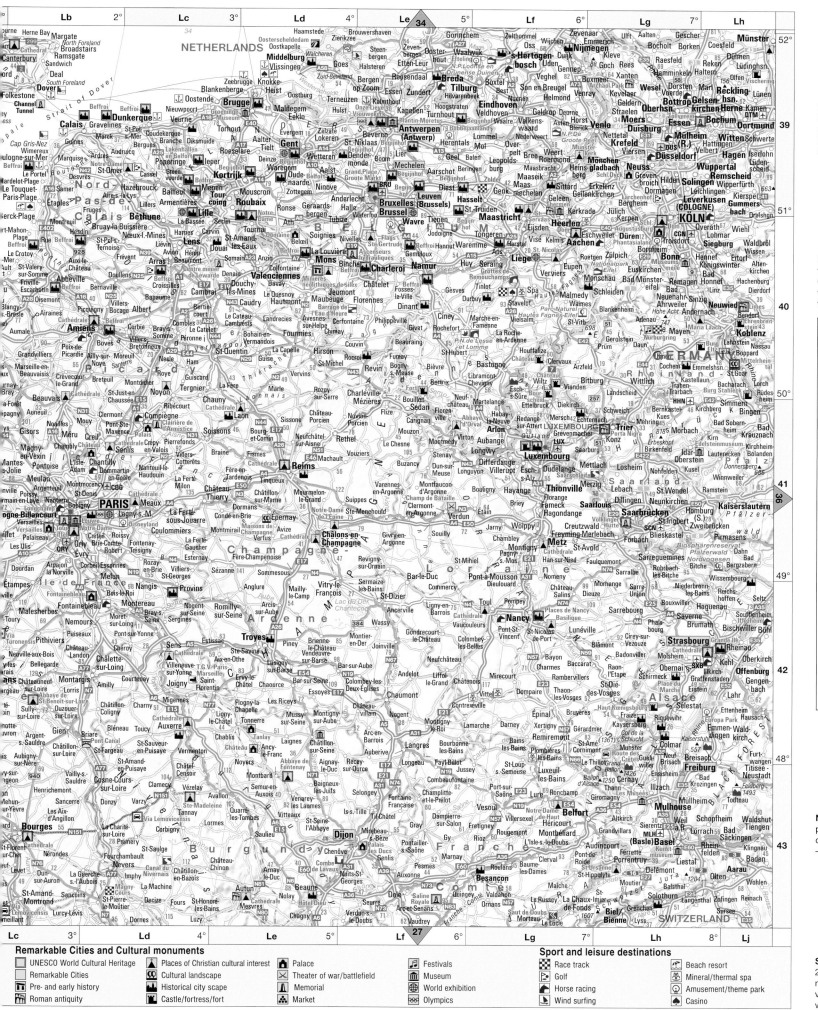

Bruges The traditional capital city of western Flanders – well-preserved ⬛ Gothic city center with historic warehouses and guild houses – world heritage site – photo: Roezenhof wharf and the Belfried tower. Ld39

Brussels Capital of Belgium and administrative center of the EU (pop. 950,000) – UNESCO world heritage site: La Grand Place (photo) with its guild houses and the city hall – important 🏛 museums – ⚛ Atomium. Le40

Paris The capital of France (metro area pop. 12 million) has countless attractions. The banks of the Seine from the ⬛ Eifel Tower to the gigantic 🏛 Louvre and including the ⬛ cathedrals Notre Dame and Saint Chappelle make up a UNESCO world heritage site. Photos from top to bottom: The Louvre, Arc de Triomphe, the Eifel Tower. Lc42

Nancy Charming city center rich in impressive 18th ⬛ century architecture – three city plazas are UNESCO world heritage sites – Art Nouveau 🏛 museum. Lg42

Strasbourgh Capital of Alsace (pop. 256,000) and home of the European Parliament and the Council of Europe – medieval ⬛ city center and cathedral (UNESCO world heritage site). Lh42

Remarkable Cities and Cultural monuments

- ⬜ UNESCO World Cultural Heritage
- ⬜ Remarkable Cities
- ⬜ Pre- and early history
- ⬜ Roman antiquity
- ⬜ Places of Christian cultural interest
- ⬜ Cultural landscape
- ⬜ Historical city scape
- ⬜ Castle/fortress/fort
- ⬜ Palace
- ⬜ Museum
- ⬜ Theater of war/battlefield
- ⬜ Memorial
- ⬜ Market
- 🎵 Festivals
- 🏛 Museum
- 🌐 World exhibition
- 🏅 Olympics

Sport and leisure destinations

- ♟ Race track
- ⛳ Golf
- 🐎 Horse racing
- 🏄 Wind surfing
- 🏖 Beach resort
- ♨ Mineral/thermal spa
- 🎢 Amusement/theme park
- ♣ Casino

Southern France

Southern France comprises several distinct geographic regions. In the southwest, the Bay of Biscay, an arm of the Atlantic Ocean, borders the Aquitaine Basin. West of the Aquitaine Basin are the highlands of the Massif Central, which are separated from the French Alps by the Rhone River Valley. The Pyrenees Mountains separate France from the Iberian Peninsula.
The Aquitaine Basin, located south of the Paris basin, is a scenic region of rolling

hills crossed by many rivers such as the **Garonne**. The flat southeastern coast between the Spanish border and the Gironde Delta consists of long sand beaches with many sand dunes. This area has several seaside freshwater lakes including Lac de Lacanau and Etang de Cazaux. The 105-meter-high and 2,700-

The village of Roussilon in Provence lies atop an ancient stone hill. **Lf47**

Lascaux Caves Cave in the Vezere Valley features ancient cave paintings – UNESCO world heritage site – tourists can visit an exact replica of the paintings. **Lb45**

Saint-Émilion Historic city built around two hills in a winemaking region – well preserved architecture – UNESCO world heritage site. **Ku46**

The Pyrenees High mountain range stretching from the Atlantic Ocean to the Mediterranean Sea – lush green valleys – unique wildlife and vegetation. **Kt-Lc47/48**

Carcassonne Historic city with a largely intact medieval old town surrounded by a city wall – UNESCO world heritage site – the wall is over three kilometers long and includes 52 towers – medieval castle. **Lc47**

Languedoc Region west of Provence – Cevenne Mountains and a sunny coastline – interesting gorges. **Ld46**

Roman relicts in France Southern France boasts many remnants from the Roman era (200 BC–400 AD) including temples (Nimes), triumphal arches, amphitheaters (Orange), aqueducts (Pont du Gard, top photo), and arenas (Arles, bottom photo). Many are UNESCO world heritage sites. **Le47**

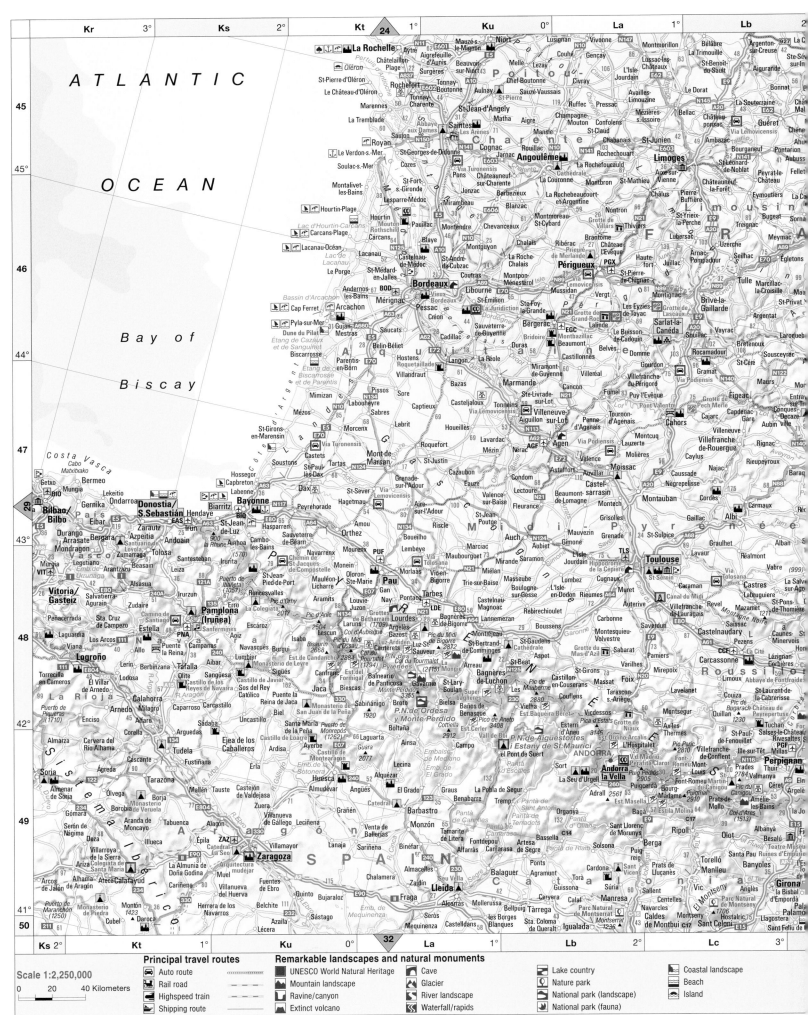

Scale 1:2,250,000

0   20   40 Kilometers

Principal travel routes
- Auto route
- Rail road
- Highspeed train
- Shipping route
- .... (travel route dashed)

Remarkable landscapes and natural monuments
- UNESCO World Natural Heritage
- Mountain landscape
- Ravine/canyon
- Extinct volcano
- Cave
- Glacier
- River landscape
- Waterfall/rapids
- Lake country
- Nature park
- National park (landscape)
- National park (fauna)
- Coastal landscape
- Beach
- Island

meter-long **Dune du Pilat** is the longest sand dune in Europe. **Côte d'Argent** near the Spanish border encompasses Europe's largest pine forest.
France's Bordeaux region is one of the most productive and famous 🍷 wine-making regions in the world. Dordogne to the west of Bordeaux is a hilly region of forests, pastures, and vineyards.
France's 🏔 **Pyrenees** are green and steep. The area around the French Pyrenees is one of the most pristine in Western Europe. Cirque du Gavarnie, a gigantic natural stone half-circle in 🏞 Pyrenees Occidentales National Park is the most famous attraction in this region. The Massif Central which covers most of Southeastern France is a large mountainous highlands region. The **Auvergne Mountains**, a range of extinct volcanoes, form the core of the Massif Central. Between the Massif Central and the French Alps

stretches the **Rhone River Valley**. The 🏞 **Camargue** in the Rhone Valley is a unique wetlands area with interesting local wildlife and nature reserves.
France's **Mediterranean coast** has a warm climate with most rainfall concentrated in the winter months. The most visited section of the coast is the French Riviera or **Côte d'Azur**, as it is known in French. This world famous coastal area has beautiful cliffs and

vibrant seaside resort towns. **Provence**, a charming region in southeastern France, contains many natural attractions including 🏞 Gorges du Verdon, Europe's deepest canyon and the 🏔 **Luberon Mountains**. The magnificent French Alps stretch from Lake Geneva to just north of the Mediterranean Coast. Mont Blanc rises 4,807 meters above sea level and is the highest mountain in Europe outside of Russia.

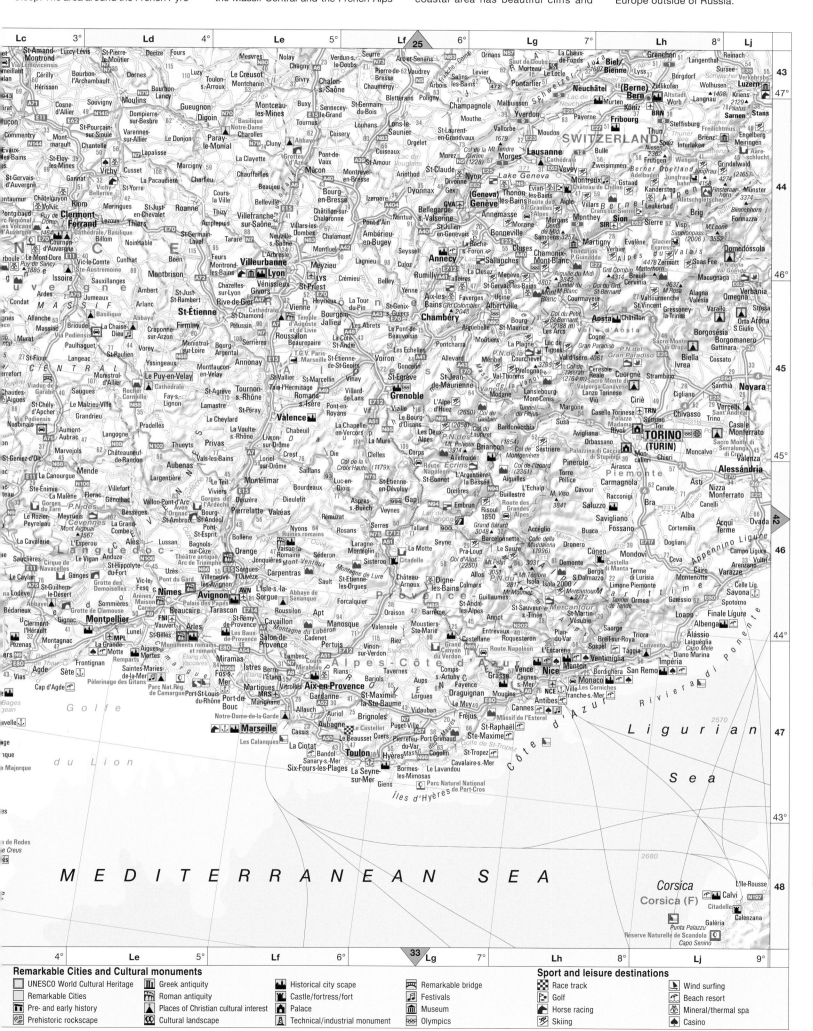

Lyon 🏛 The second largest urban area in France has a historic city center with Roman ruins, medieval buildings, and Renaissance-style patrician houses – UNESCO world heritage site. **Le45**

Mont Blanc The highest 🏔 mountain in Europe outside of Russia – rising 4,807 meters – covered by several glaciers. **Lg45**

Avignon Once a papal residence during the Middle Ages – 🏛 historic city architecture – large 🏰 Palace of the Popes – 🎭 annual theater festival. **Le47**

Abbaye de Sénanque 🏛 Cistercian abbey in Provence – simple harmonious architecture – beautiful cloister. **Lf47**

The French Riviera (Côte d'Azur) The Côte d'Azur is the section of the Mediterranean coast between Cassis and Menton. The 🏔 Massif de l'Estérel (top photo) is a series of beautiful hills directly on the coast. Famous towns on the Riviera include 🏖 Nice, 🏖 St. Tropez, and 🎵 Cannes, site of an annual 🎵 film festival. **Lg-Lh47**

Monaco Small principality on the Mediterranean coast – famous for its historic 🎰 casino in Monte Carlo – annual 🏎 Grand Prix auto race. **Lh47**

Legend

Remarkable Cities and Cultural monuments

- ▢ UNESCO World Cultural Heritage
- ▢ Remarkable Cities
- ▢ Pre- and early history
- ▢ Prehistoric rockscape
- ▲ Greek antiquity
- ▲ Roman antiquity
- ▲ Places of Christian cultural interest
- ▲ Cultural landscape
- ▦ Historical city scape
- ▦ Castle/fortress/fort
- ▦ Palace
- ▦ Technical/industrial monument
- ▦ Remarkable bridge
- ▦ Festivals
- ▦ Museum
- ▦ Olympics

Sport and leisure destinations

- ▦ Race track
- ▦ Golf
- ▦ Horse racing
- ▦ Skiing
- ▦ Wind surfing
- ▦ Beach resort
- ▦ Mineral/thermal spa
- ▦ Casino

Northern Portugal, Northern Spain

The Bay of Biscay, an arm of the Atlantic Ocean, and the Pyrenees Mountains border the Iberian Peninsula to the north. Spain covers around four-fifths of the Iberian Peninsula's area, while Portugal and the small nation of Andorra comprise the remaining area.

The ⛰ **Pyrenees** separate Iberia from France. **Monte Perdido**, the highest mountain in the Pyrenees, rises 3,350 meters above sea level. West of the

Pyrenees rises the **Cordillera Cantábrica Range**. The highest mountain in the range, ⛰ **Picos de Europa**, rises 2,600 meters. The Cordillera Cantabrica is also the source of the 928-kilometer-long **Ebro River** – Spain's second longest river. The Ebro River 🔺 delta on the Spanish Medditerranean coast is a

The historic skyline of Segovia (Spain).　**Kq50**

Camino de Santiago Also known as the Way of St. James, this route has attracted pilgrims for thousands of years. The route leads to the cathedral in Santiago de Compostela (bottom photo; **Km52**), with the tomb of Saint James. The 800-kilometer-long route passes through Astorga (top photo; **Ko52**).

Picos de Europa National Park Mountainous ⛰ nature reserve around the city of Covadonga – chamois, wolf, and bear populations – 30 kilometers from the coast – hiking trails.　**Kp-Kq53**

Porto The largest city in northern Portugal – the 🏛 old town is a UNESCO world heritage site – port wine cellars.　**Km51**

Bragança Portuguese town with a largely intact 🏰 castle built in the 12th century – the 🏛 old town is surrounded by an ancient city wall.　**Ko51**

Salamanca Historic university town (pop. 170,000) – UNESCO world heritage site – beautiful 🏛 Plaza Mayor – famous 🏛 twin cathedrals.　**Kp50**

Ávila The highest city in Spain – medieval 🏛 town center – 2,500-meter-long city wall with 86 towers – UNESCO world heritage site.　**Kq50**

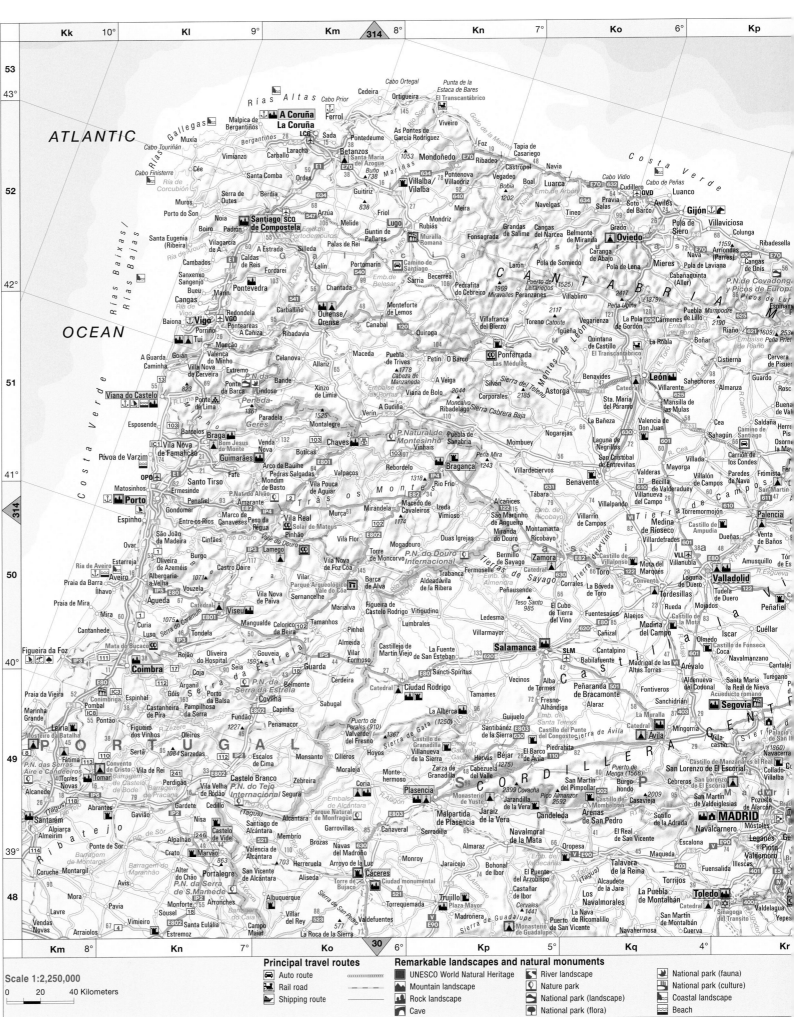

Scale 1:2,250,000

0　20　40 Kilometers

Principal travel routes
- 🚗 Auto route
- 🚆 Rail road
- 🚢 Shipping route
- ········
- ········

Remarkable landscapes and natural monuments
- 🏛 UNESCO World Natural Heritage
- ⛰ Mountain landscape
- 🪨 Rock landscape
- 🕳 Cave
- 🌊 River landscape
- 🌲 Nature park
- National park (landscape)
- National park (flora)
- National park (fauna)
- National park (culture)
- Coastal landscape
- 🏖 Beach

Northern Portugal, Northern Spain

conservation area, home to many rare and fascinating birds.

Spain's **Meseta** is a large elevated plateau covering much of the country. The northern Meseta is separated from the other sections of the plateau by the **Cordillera Central** Range. Several major rivers flow through the Cordillera Central including the Tajo (Tejo: Portuguese) River in the south and the Douro River in the north. The northwestern coast of the

Iberian Peninsula has a rainy maritime climate. Northwestern Iberia encompasses many inland valleys with mild climates – including the ⌂ **Douro Valley** in Portugal and the **Rioja** region, both major winemaking regions. The Meseta region and the Ebro River Basin get scorching temperatures in summer months, while the climate of the warm Mediterranean coast is moderated by sea breezes. During winter, strong winds can cause tem-

peratures below freezing and even snowfall in Madrid and the Meseta.

The mountains of northern Iberia receive abundant snowfall during the winter months. The Pyrenees are a popular destination for the enjoyment of ⌂ winter sports such as skiing and snowboarding. The northernmost regions of Spain are often referred to as "green Spain" because of their lush vegetation and abundant rainfall. Galicia is the wettest

region in Spain and the region's coast is indented by several bays. Spain's Basque Country is home to a people with a unique culture. The origins of the Basque people are unknown and their language is unrelated to any other. The Basque city of San Sebastian/Donostia is one of the most beautiful seaside towns in Europe. Portugal's ⌂ **Costa Verde**, a major tourist destination, features ⌂ sandy and rocky beaches.

Altamira ⌂ Cave with Stone Age paintings – world heritage site – cave painting replica in the neighboring museum. **Kq53**

San Sebastián/Donostia Elegant ⌂ seaside town on the Bay of Biscay – ⌂ La Concha beach (photo) is between Monte Urgull and Monte Igueldo. **Kt53**

Pamplona Capital of Navarre – the city has medieval ruins and a ⌂ historic center – location of the famous ⌂ Fiesta de San Fernin, where young men run through narrow alleys chased by a herd of bulls. **Kt52**

Ordesa y Monte Perdido National Park Located in the central ⌂ Pyrenees – the national park was founded in 1918 and has several high mountain hiking trails. **La52**

Zaragoza Once the residence of the kings of Aragon, today a large modern city – ⌂ Basilica del Pilar (photo). **Ku51**

San Lorenzo de El Escorial Enormous ⌂ monastic castle northwest of Madrid – built by Phillip II. in the 16th century – burial site of Spanish monarchs since Charles V. **Kq50**

Madrid Capital of Spain and the largest city on the Iberian Peninsula – ⌂ Royal Palace – ⌂ Prado art museum – Plaza de la Cibeles (photo) is the intersection of several major boulevards – historic buildings on Plaza de la Villa and Plaza Mayor. **Kr50**

Remarkable Cities and Cultural monuments

- UNESCO World Cultural Heritage
- Remarkable Cities
- Pre- and early history
- Prehistoric rockscape
- Roman antiquity
- Places of Jewish cultural interest
- Places of Christian cultural interest
- Cultural landscape
- Historical city scape
- Castle/fortress/fort
- Palace
- Remarkable bridge

Sport and leisure destinations

- Market
- Festivals
- Museum
- Golf
- Horse racing
- Skiing
- Wind surfing
- Seaport
- Beach resort
- Mineral/thermal spa
- Amusement/theme park

Southern Portugal, Southern Spain

The southern half of the Iberian Peninsula encompasses many mountain ranges, called Sierras or Cordilleras in Spanish and Serra in Portuguese. Spain's highest **mountain, Mulhacén** rises 3,481 meters above sea level and is situated 20 kilometers from the Mediterranean coast in the ◪ **Sierra Nevada Mountains**. The name Sierra Nevada means "snowy mountains" and the range gets abundant snowfall during winter.

Sintra Once the residence of Portuguese monarchs – UNESCO site – ◪ Paço Real palace – Palácio da Pena (photo). **Kl48**

Lisbon Capital city of Portugal on the delta of the Tejo River – the old town district ◪ Alfama has historic plazas and palaces – Oceanario de Lisboa aquarium – UNESCO world heritage site: Mosteiro dos Jerónimos, Torre de Belém. **Kl48**

Algarve This region in southern Portugal is a popular destination for tourists – beaches and ⛳ golf courses – sandbanks and lagoons in the eastern Algarve. **Km-Kn47**

Seville Capital of Andalucia and the largest city in southern Spain – the Gothic ◪ cathedral is a UNESCO world heritage site – Alcázar Castle. **Kp47**

Córdoba ◪ Mezquita Cathedral (photo) is a world heritage site; the cathedral is a converted mosque containing more than 850 columns. **Kq47**

Ronda Historic ◪ town in Andalucia – the two sections of the town are connected by the 98 meters high ◪ Puente Nuevo bridge – Spain's oldest bullfighting arena. **Kp46**

Gibraltar British overseas territory – located on a rocky peninsula – Europe and Africa are between 14 and 44 kilometers apart in the Strait of Gibraltar. **Kp46**

Spain's **Meseta** is a large elevated plateau that extends over much of the country. The sections of the Meseta south and southeast of Madrid produce most of the country's grain and are known as the "breadbasket of Spain." Saffron, the most expensive spice in the world, is also harvested in this region. Southern

Windmills in La Mancha, a Spanish region south of Madrid. **Ks49**

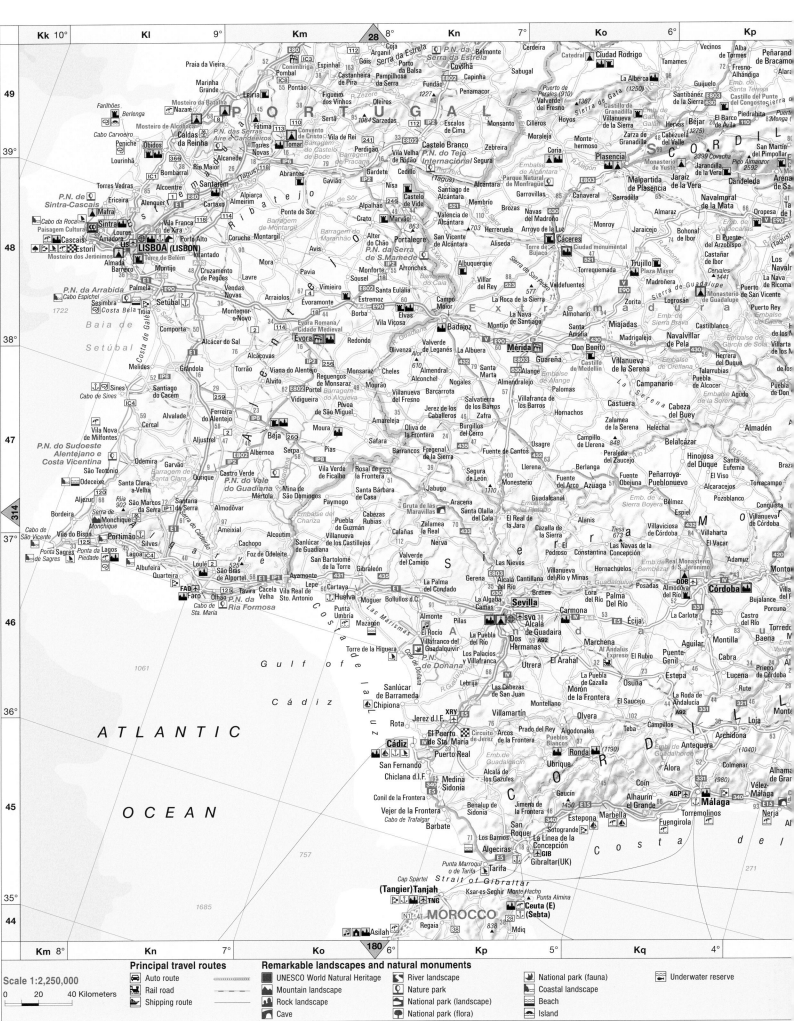

Scale 1:2,250,000

0   20   40 Kilometers

Principal travel routes
- 🚗 Auto route
- 🚂 Rail road
- Shipping route

Remarkable landscapes and natural monuments
- ■ UNESCO World Natural Heritage
- ■ Mountain landscape
- ■ Rock landscape
- ■ Cave
- ■ River landscape
- ■ Nature park
- ■ National park (landscape)
- ■ National park (flora)
- ■ National park (fauna)
- ■ Coastal landscape
- ■ Beach
- ■ Island
- ■ Underwater reserve

Southern Portugal, Southern Spain

Portugal comprises two vast plain-covered regions: the **Alentejo** and the **Ribatejo**. The Ribatejo is a major cattle ranching center, while the Alentejo produces much of Portugal's grain and most of the world's cork supply.

Most of Portugal's Atlantic coast consists of sandy strips of land but the **Algarve** region has many picturesque rocky bays. The southernmost regions of Portugal, including **Ponta de Sagres**, have Mediterranean climates with hot sunny summers and mild wet winters. Portugal's central coast (around Lisbon) is cooler and wetter than the southern coast because of strong Atlantic winds. **Gibraltar**, a British territory, comprises a five kilometer long and 1.4 kilometer wide peninsula bordering Spain's **Costa del Sol**. The Costa del Sol with its Mediterranean beaches is one of Spain's most popular tourist destinations.

The interior of the Iberian Peninsula has a continental climate with abundant sunshine and significant differences between the seasons. In addition to grain production, citrus farming is widespread in the warmer regions of Iberia. Olive trees are common in most Mediterranean regions including Spain and Portugal.

Due to deforestation that began in the Bronze Age, southern Iberia has suffered from water shortages since the Roman era. Numerous dams have been built throughout the Iberian Peninsula to provide water for irrigation and household consumption. The few remaining wetlands in the region, including the **Tablas de Daimiel** and **Río Guadalquivir** Delta, are part of **national parks** established in recent decades. During winter, these areas are home to large colonies of migrating birds. Both of these wetlands are home to endangered animals such as the Spanish lynx.

Toledo Historic city surrounded by the Rio Tajo – medieval architecture – museum in the former home of 17th century master painter El Greco. **Kq49**

Aranjuez Castle and retreat of the Spanish Royal Family – gardens surrounding the castle – world heritage site. **Kr50**

Monasterio de Guadalupe Monastery, west of Toledo – UNESCO world heritage site – major pilgrimage site because of its Black Madonna statue. **Kp49**

Granada The town features the Alhambra Palace (UNESCO site), built during the Moorish era – Renaissance-era cathedral. **Kr47**

Sierra Nevada Mountain range with a large national park – ski areas – 16 peaks rising above 3,000 meters. **Kr-Ks47**

Spanish Bullfighting Traditional Spanish bullfighting (corrida de toros) is a national passion in Spain. Bullfighting season runs from Easter until October. Picadores and banderilleros encite the bulls before a matador in an elaborate costume begins the main event.

Benidorm Resort city on the Costa Blanca. The town was a sleepy fishing village until the tourism boom of the 1960s. **Ku48**

Remarkable Cities and Cultural monuments

- UNESCO World Cultural Heritage
- Remarkable Cities
- Phoenecian culture
- Roman antiquity
- Places of Jewish cultural interest
- Places of Christian cultural interest
- Cultural landscape
- Historical city scape
- Castle/fortress/fort
- Palace
- Space telescope
- World exhibition

Sport and leisure destinations

- Race track
- Golf
- Horse racing
- Skiing
- Sailing
- Diving
- Wind surfing
- Seaport
- Beach resort
- Mineral/thermal spa
- Amusement/theme park
- Casino

Catalonia, Balearic Islands, Corsica, Sardinia

The 🏔 **Pyrenees** stretch through much of **northern Spain** and separate the Iberian Peninsula from France. In addition to mountains, northern Spain also comprises fertile plains, river valleys, and beautiful 🏖 coastal areas. The **Costa Brava** and **Costa Daurada** are both popular tourist destinations. Catalonia's capital, **Barcelona** is the second largest urban area in Spain and a major economic center.

The **Balearic Islands** consist of **Majorca (Mallorca)**, **Minorca**, **Formentera**, **Ibiza**, as well as numerous minor islands. 🏝 **Cabrera**, one of the minor islands includes the Cabrera National Park.
In northwestern **Majorca** rise the mountains of the Serra de Tramuntana range, while the southeast is covered by the

Les Calanche, beautiful granite stone formations on Corsica. **Lj48**

The Costa Brava Rocky 🏖 coast north of Barcelona – popular 🏖 beach towns including Cadaques. **Lc-Ld48/49**

Monserrat Monastery The most revered religious site in Catalonia – 🏛 basilica containing a Black Madonna statue. **Lb49**

Barcelona Catalonia's leading city is one of the most vibrant 🏖 coastal cities on the Mediterranean. In addition to its many 🏛 museums the city also has an abundance of interesting architecture including Casa Mila (top photo) and 🏛 Palau de la Música Catalana (bottom photo), both UNESCO world heritage sites. **Lc49**

The Balearic Islands The 🏝 islands are popular tourist destinations with many diverse landscapes, picturesque villages, beautiful bays, and beaches. Photos from top to bottom: Ibiza (**Lb51/52**), beach on Majorca, Palma de Mallorca (**Lc-Ld51**).

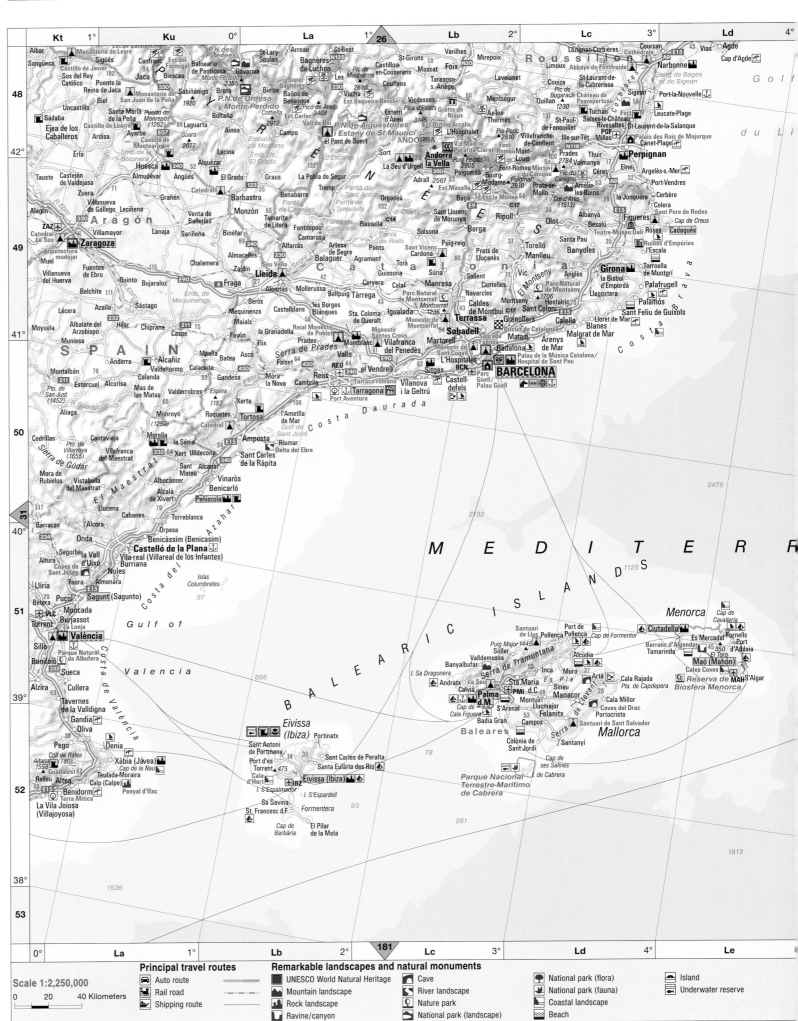

Scale 1:2,250,000

0   20   40 Kilometers

Principal travel routes
- 🚗 Auto route
- 🚃 Rail road
- ⛴ Shipping route

Remarkable landscapes and natural monuments
- ⬛ UNESCO World Natural Heritage
- Mountain landscape
- Rock landscape
- Ravine/canyon
- Cave
- River landscape
- Nature park
- National park (landscape)
- National park (flora)
- National park (fauna)
- Coastal landscape
- Beach
- Island
- Underwater reserve

Serra de Llevant. Between the two uplands lies a large fertile plain. Majorca's ⬜ coastal areas comprise beautiful beaches, cliffs, and bays.
Minorca's 200 kilometers of coastline include some of the most spectacular bays in the Mediterranean. The island's interior consists of fertile hills in the north and barren grassy areas in the south.
Hilly **Ibiza** has beautiful ⬜ coasts and is one of Spain's most popular tourist desti-

nations. Neighboring **Formentera** lies only a few kilometers south of Ibiza and has numerous undeveloped white ⬜ sand beaches. Both Ibiza and Formentera feature coastal nature reserves.
Politically, **Corsica** is a region of France but the island has a distinctive local culture and is situated closer to Italy than France. A ⛰ mountain range running from the northwest to the southeast divides Corsica into two regions. The west-

ern half of the island is a region of bays and hills, while the eastern half of the island is a region of plains with numerous ⬜ sandy beaches. The large Regional Nature Park of Corsica was created in the 1970s. It covers a third of Corsica's total area and encompasses protected areas on the island's coast and in the mountainous interior.
The Italian island, **Sardinia**, boasts many beautiful 🕳 caves and grottos. A ⛰ moun-

tainous highland covers most of Sardinia's interior. Around 14 % of the island's territory is covered by plains, including the fertile Campidano region between the cities of Cagliari and Oristano. Sardinia also features many important archeological and historical sites including remnants of the Roman and Neolithic eras. Costa del Sud in southern Sardinia is the location of the finest ⬜ beaches on the island.

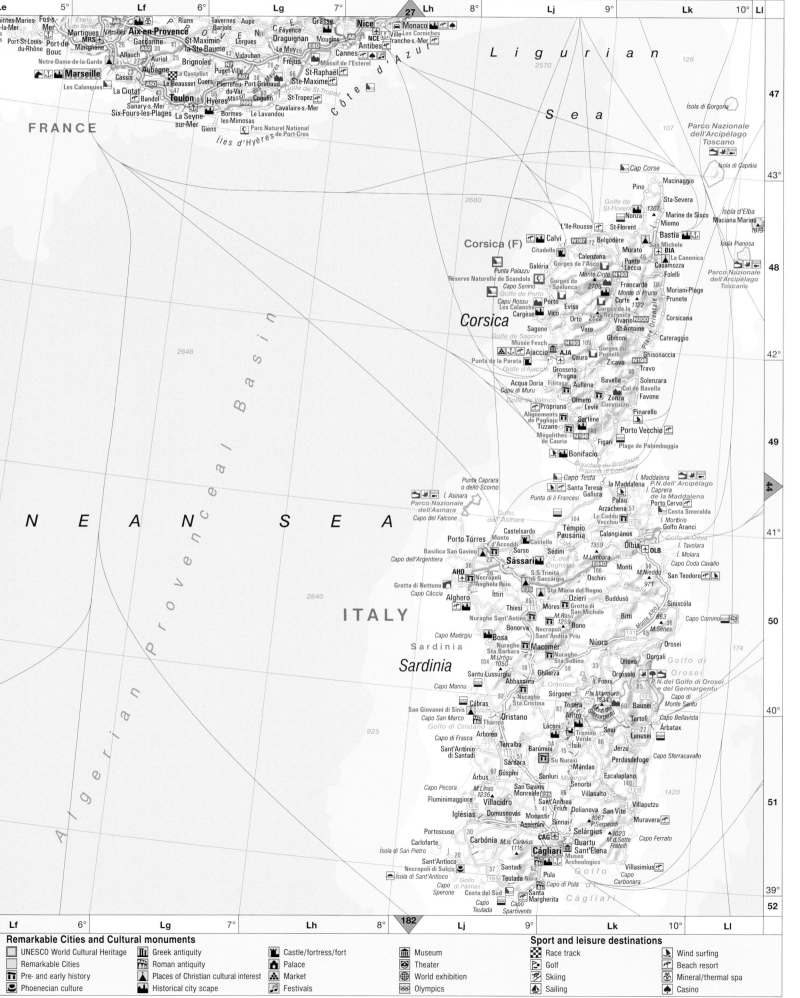

Calvi Picturesque Corsican ⬜ town with beautiful ⬜ beaches – La Marine, harbor district – ⬜ medieval citadel.　　**Lj48**

Gulf of Porto One of the most beautiful ⬜ coastal areas on Corsica – rocky Cape Porto is a designated UNESCO world natural heritage site.　　**Lj48**

Corte ⬜ Historic Corsican city with a vibrant student population – ⬜ citadel – 🏛 Musée de la Corse, Corsican culture museum.　　**Lk48**

Bonifacio Ancient ⬜ city in southernmost Corsica – lively lower town – historic sailors' cemetery.　　**Lk49**

Costa Smeralda Popular tourist destination on Sardinia – ⬜ picturesque bays – turquoise blue sea.　　**LK49**

Su Nuraxi ⬜ Large prehistoric structure built by an ancient culture around 2,500 years ago – round structures – bastion with four towers and defensive walls.　　**Lk51**

Capo Cáccia Steep cliffs on the Sardinian coast – Escala di Cabiro (656 steps) lead to the 🕳 Grotta di Nettuno.　　**Lj50**

Remarkable Cities and Cultural monuments

⬜ UNESCO World Cultural Heritage	🏛 Greek antiquity	🏰 Castle/fortress/fort
⬜ Remarkable Cities	🏛 Roman antiquity	⬜ Palace
⬜ Pre- and early history	🔺 Places of Christian cultural interest	⬜ Market
⬜ Phoenecian culture	⬜ Historical city scape	🎵 Festivals

🏛 Museum	
🏛 Theater	
🌐 World exhibition	
⬜ Olympics	

Sport and leisure destinations

♟ Race track	🏄 Wind surfing
⛳ Golf	🏖 Beach resort
⛷ Skiing	♨ Mineral/thermal spa
⛵ Sailing	⬜ Casino

Netherlands, Northern Germany

Germany is divided into several distinct geographic regions. The northern half of the country is dominated by plains and in certain areas by low mountains. The **flat, low-lying areas** in the most northern regions of Germany are relatively unfertile and are dotted with moors, small lakes, and heaths. **The North and East Frisian Islands** in the ⬛ **North Sea** encompass many fascinating landscapes, including the three ⬛ **national**

parks in the ⬛ **Wattenmeer**, a muddy tideland. The German **Baltic Sea coast** is an area of bays, sandy beaches, and hanging cliffs. The largest German islands in the Baltic Sea are Fehmarn, Rügen, Hiddensee, and Usedom. Behind the Baltic coast is the region called ⬛ Holstein's Switzerland and ⬛ Mecklenburg's lake

Kinderdijk-Elshout: historic windmills in the Dutch countryside. **Le39**

Hanseatic Towns ⬛ The Hanseatic League was founded in the 13th century as a union of trading towns with Lübeck (top photo), now a world heritage site, as its center. Other Hanseatic towns in northern Germany include Hamburg, Wismar (bottom photo), and Greifswald.

Hamburg Germany's largest port and second largest city (pop. 1,7 million) is a major cultural center encompassing several urban lakes – most important tourist attraction: the ⬛ harbor (photo). **Ll37**

Amsterdam Capital of the Netherlands (pop. 730,000) – a multicultural city with a reputation for tolerance – historic villas and guild houses – picturesque ⬛ canals – photo: Canal with houseboats. **Le38**

De Keukenhof A large ⬛ park near Lisse – flowers, trees, waterways, a sea of tulips and other colorful flowers. **Le38**

Rotterdam Second largest city of the Netherlands – busiest ⬛ harbor in the world – photo: ⬛ Erasmus bridge. **Le39**

Cologne ⬛ Important cultural and convention center (pop. 960,000) – most famous landmark: ⬛ Cologne Cathedral (photo): UNESCO site – historic churches. **Lg40**

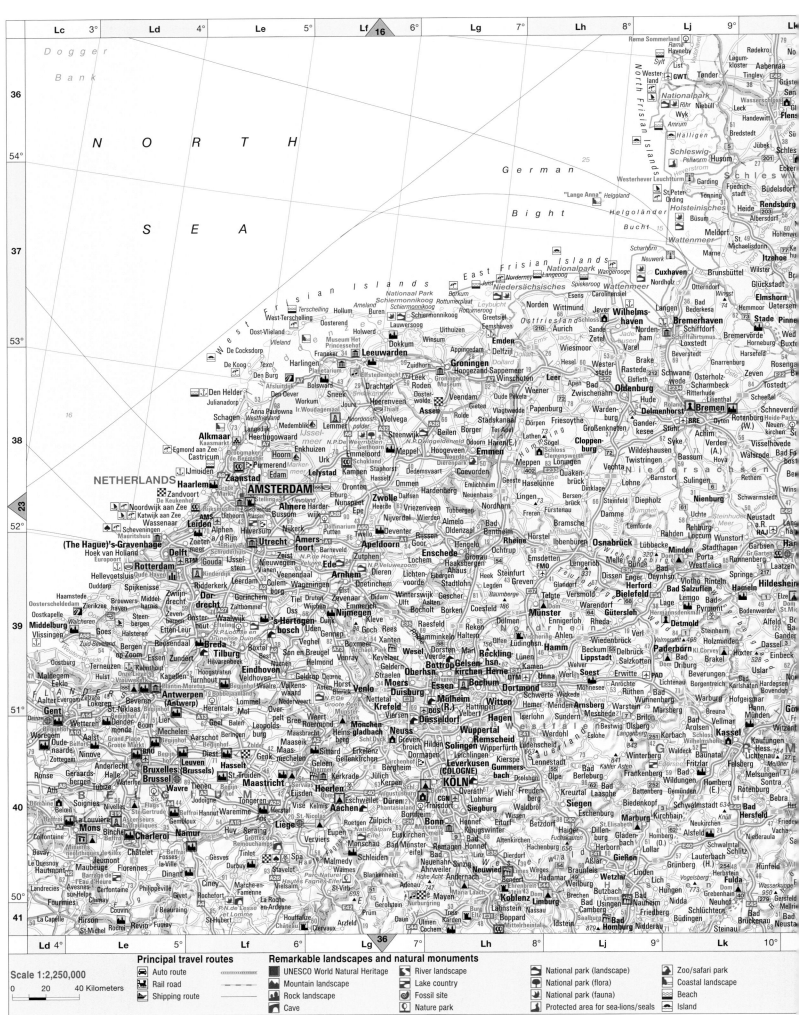

Scale 1:2,250,000
0   20   40 Kilometers

Principal travel routes
- Auto route
- Rail road
- Shipping route

Remarkable landscapes and natural monuments
- UNESCO World Natural Heritage
- Mountain landscape
- Rock landscape
- Cave
- River landscape
- Lake country
- Fossil site
- Nature park
- National park (landscape)
- National park (flora)
- National park (fauna)
- Protected area for sea-lions/seals
- Zoo/safari park
- Coastal landscape
- Beach
- Island

district. The land surrounding the coastal bays are fertile plains that give way to the foothills of central Germany's mountains. The ■ **low mountain ranges** of central Germany stretch through a heavily forested region. The region ranges between 450 and 1,200 meters in elevation. Central Germany's uplands feature scenic river valleys, unique eroded stone formations, and beautiful lakes. The highest mountains in the region are the Fichtelberg (1,214 m) in the Erz Mountains and the Brocken (1,142 m) in the ⌂ Harz Mountains.

The most important 🡒 rivers in the northern half of Germany are the **Rhine**, the **Elbe**, and the **Weser**. The largest urban area in the region is the Rhine-Ruhr area, which encompasses the major cities of Cologne and Düsseldorf as well as the industrial centers along the Ruhr River. Most of the **Netherlands** is located on the same vast plain that covers most of northern Germany. More than half of the country's land area is situated below sea level and much of the country's territory consists of land reclaimed from the sea through the use of dikes and canals. Despite having a high population density, most of the land in the country is used for agriculture. The Netherlands also has extensive forests and meadow landscapes. The country is criss-crossed by numerous canals and protected from the sea by a series of dunes and dikes. There are many good 🡒 beaches along the northern and northwestern coasts. The highest point of the Netherlands is in the country's hilly southeast (Vaalser 322 m).

The most densely populated region in the country is the Randstad, which comprises several major cities, including Amsterdam and Rotterdam.

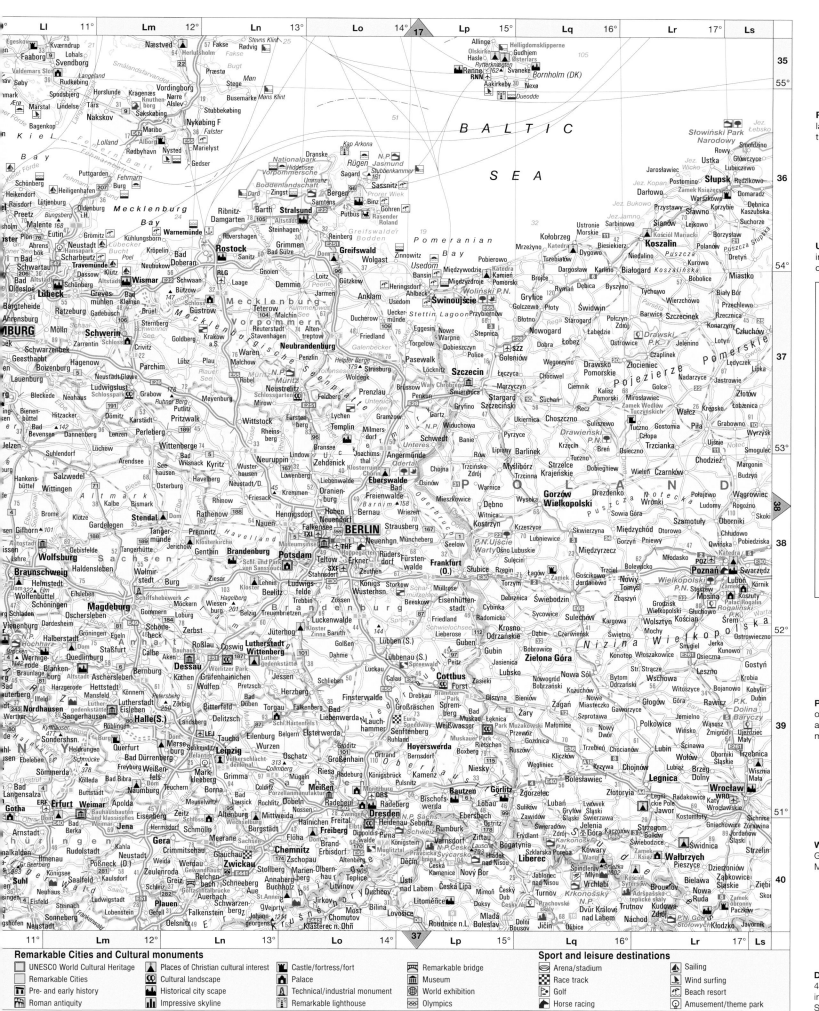

Rügen ⌂ Baltic Sea island with diverse landscapes – white chalk cliffs (photo) in the Jasmund ⌂ National Park. **Lo36**

Usedom Historic 🡒 seaside resort with interesting architecture – long white 🡒 beaches – wealth of flora and fauna. **Lp36**

Berlin The German capital (pop. 3.39 million) has been one of Europe's leading cities since its reunification. The city has numerous cultural offerings, important 🏛 museums, and the best nightlife in Germany. The city's most famous landmark is the 🏛 **Brandenburg Gate** (photo, bottom). One of the city's most impressive buildings is 🏰 **Charlottenburg palace** built in the 17th and 18th centuries (photo, top). **Lo38**

Potsdam-Sanssouci Summer residence of Frederick the Great – 🡒 park and 🏰 palace are world heritage sites – lakeside manor on Heiligen See (photo). **Lo38**

Wartburg Impressive 🏰 castle in central Germany – UNESCO world heritage site – Martin Luther's study – museum. **Ll40**

Dresden "Florence on the Elbe" (pop. 480,000) – important 🏛 art collection and impressive 🏰 historic buildings: Zwinger, Semperoper opera house, palace. **Lo39**

Remarkable Cities and Cultural monuments

- ☐ UNESCO World Cultural Heritage
- ☐ Remarkable Cities
- ☐ Pre- and early history
- ☐ Roman antiquity
- ☐ Places of Christian cultural interest
- ☐ Cultural landscape
- ☐ Historical city scape
- ☐ Impressive skyline
- ☐ Castle/fortress/fort
- ☐ Palace
- ☐ Technical/industrial monument
- ☐ Remarkable lighthouse
- ☐ Remarkable bridge
- ☐ Museum
- ☐ World exhibition
- ☐ Olympics

Sport and leisure destinations

- ☐ Arena/stadium
- ☐ Race track
- ☐ Golf
- ☐ Horse racing
- ☐ Sailing
- ☐ Wind surfing
- ☐ Beach resort
- ☐ Amusement/theme park

Southern Germany, Switzerland, Austria

The terrain of **southern Germany** is distinctly more mountainous and hilly than that of northern Germany. The region encompasses several **mountain ranges** and **highlands**. The highlands in the region include the **Upper Rhine Uplands**, an area comprising the Black Forest and the Palatinate region. The Upper Rhine Uplands are a major center for wine and fruit production because of their mild climate. The **South German**

"**Stufenland**" is a hilly area with many natural caves in the regions of Swabia and Franconia. Between the "Stufenland" and the Rhine Basin lie numerous fertile valleys with terraced vineyards.

The **Upper Palatinate** and Bavarian Forests are heavily forested areas with sparsely populated river valleys. The

The Matterhorn is one of the most beautiful peaks in the Alps.   **Lh45**

Feldberg (1,493 m) in the Black Forest and Grosser Arber in the Bavarian Forest are the highest mountains in southern Germany outside of the Alps.

The region south of the Danube River in Bavaria forms a transition zone between the hilly uplands and the Alpine foothills with their lakes and moors. In Germany, the **Alps** rise abruptly in the southernmost sections of the country. The German Alps are a 30 to 40 kilometer wide strip of

The Moselle Valley German river valley and a major 🍇 winemaking area – 🏰 Burg Eltz (photo), a beautiful historic castle.   **Lh41**

The Rhine Valley The central section of the 🏞 Rhine Valley is a UNESCO site – numerous castles and fortresses – restored 🏰 Burg Stahleck castle (photo) – Lorelei Rock.   **Lh41**

Heidelberg Historic city on the Neckar River (photo) – picturesque 🏘 old town – ruins of a 🏰 medieval castle.   **Lj41**

Lake Constance Lake divided between Germany, Austria, and Switzerland – 🏝 Reichenau Island is a UNESCO world heritage site – winemaking area – 🏰 historic castle in Meersburg (photo).   **Lj-Lk43**

Zurich Largest city (36,000 inhabitants) and economic center of Switzerland – the ⛪ Grossmuenster church (12th/13th century, photo) is a city landmark – important 🏛 museums: Rietberg Museum, Art Museum, and Swiss National Museum.   **Lj43**

Lake Thun The prettiest 🏞 lake in the Berner Oberland region – the 🏰 several historic castles including Oberhofen (photo), Thun, and Spiez castles.   **Lh44**

Berner Oberland One of Switzerland's most beautiful regions with many lakes and 🏔 mountains including Moench (photo) and Jungfrau (4,158 m).   **Lg-Lh44**

Principal travel routes

- Auto route
- Rail road
- Shipping route

Remarkable landscapes and natural monuments

- UNESCO World Natural Heritage
- Mountain landscape
- Rock landscape
- Ravine/canyon
- Cave
- Glacier
- River landscape
- Waterfall/rapids
- Lake country
- Fossil site
- Nature park
- National park (landscape)
- National park (flora)
- National park (fauna)
- National park (culture)
- Zoo/safari park

Scale 1:2,250,000

0   20   40 Kilometers

high mountains with many picturesque lakes. The **Zugspitze** (2,962 m) near the Austrian border in Bavaria is the highest mountain in Germany.

The Swiss Alps are divided into two main ranges – northern and southern – by the **Rhone** and **Rhine** rivers. More than two-thirds of **Switzerland's** territory is covered by the Alps. Switzerland's tallest mountains including the Matterhorn (4,478 m) and Monte Rosa (4,637 m) are located in the southern range. The **Jura Mountains**, a range in the Alps, covers most of northwestern Switzerland. Between the Jura Mountains and the southern range lies the densely populated central region of Switzerland which stretches from Lake Geneva in the west to Lake Constance in the northeast. In addition to its mountain peaks, Switzerland also features many rivers and lakes.

Austria is a small nation with a great variety of landscapes and an abundance of natural attractions. Like Switzerland, much of Austria is covered by the mountains of the Alps. Austria's tallest mountains – all in the Salzburg, Tyrol, and Carinthia regions – are collectively referred to as **"Hohe Tauern."** The Grossglockner in East Tyrol rises 3,798 meters and is the highest mountain in the country. Northern Austria is dominated by the foothills of the Alps. The mountains north of the Danube are covered by large forests. The **Pannonian plain**, a fertile lowland, encompasses large sections of eastern Austria. Austria's capital, Vienna, is situated in a basin between mountain ranges and the Pannonian plain.

The **Inn** and the **Danube River** are the most important waterways in the country. Floods and avalanches in mountainous regions are the only significant natural threats to the country.

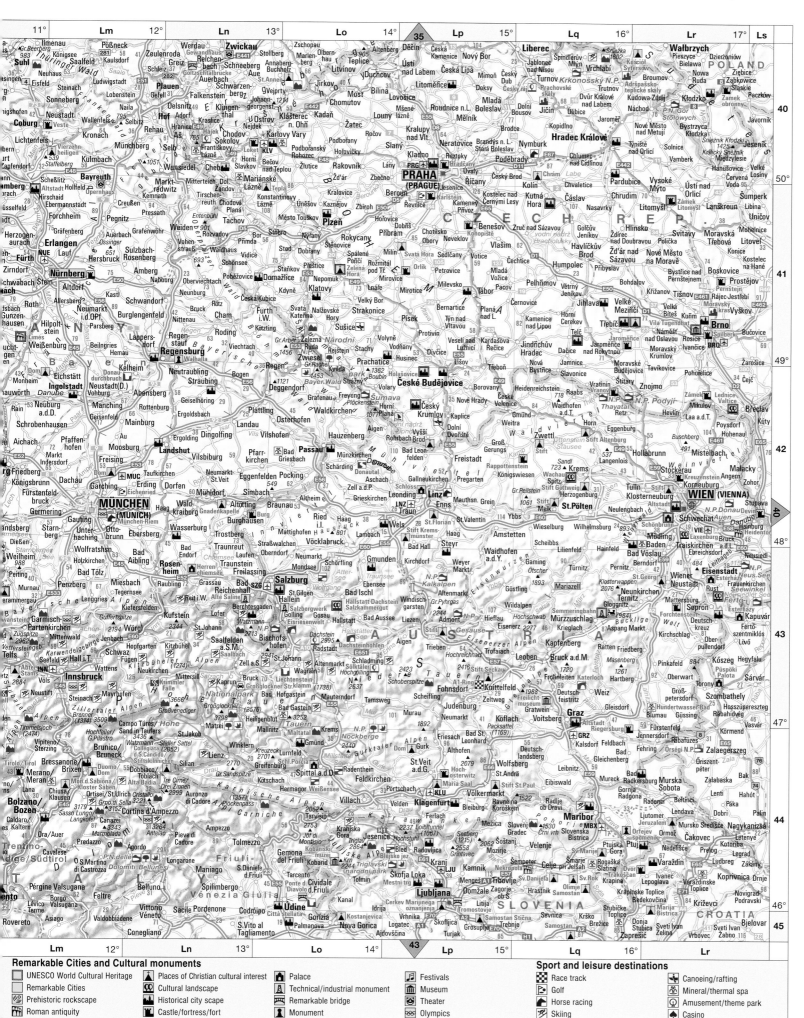

Germany's Romantic Road This popular tourist route between Würzburg and Füssen passes many popular tourist attractions. Highlights include Würzburg's royal residence (UNESCO world heritage site, top photo) and the idyllic medieval town of Rothenburg (bottom photo). **Lk41**

Bamberg City in Franconia – the historic old town is a UNESCO world heritage site – the old town hall (photo) is built atop a 15th century bridge. **Ll41**

Augsburg Bavarian city with a history stretching over 2,000 years – Renaissance-era city hall (photo). **Ll42**

Munich The beautiful capital city of Bavaria has a vibrant cultural scene and countless historic buildings – Marienplatz – The English Garden, Europe's largest city park – medieval Church of our Lady (photo). **Lm42**

Neuschwanstein Castle World famous "fairy tale" castle built by Bavaria's Ludwig II. – beautiful towers and pinnacles. **Ll43**

Salzburg City in western Austria – the birthplace of Wolfgang Amadeus Mozart – annual music festival – Baroque old town – historic palaces, churches, and squares – Hohensalzburg fortress. **Lo43**

Remarkable Cities and Cultural monuments

- UNESCO World Cultural Heritage
- Remarkable Cities
- Prehistoric rockscape
- Roman antiquity
- Places of Christian cultural interest
- Cultural landscape
- Historical city scape
- Castle/fortress/fort
- Palace
- Technical/industrial monument
- Remarkable bridge
- Monument
- Festivals
- Museum
- Theater
- Olympics

Sport and leisure destinations

- Race track
- Golf
- Horse racing
- Skiing
- Canoeing/rafting
- Mineral/thermal spa
- Amusement/theme park
- Casino

Poland

Poland can be seen as either the western-most nation in Eastern Europe or the easternmost in Central Europe. The country can be divided into three distinct geographic regions stretching parallel to one another from north to south: the plains of western Poland, hilly areas in central Poland, and the mountainous east. Poland borders the Baltic Sea to the north. The country's 500-kilometer-long **Baltic coast** consist mostly of broad

white ▭ sandy beaches. Several large bays and seaside lakes are located on the Baltic coast separated from the sea by narrow spits of land. South of the coast in **Pomerania** lies a hilly region with hundreds of lakes and moors. The **Vistula**, Poland's longest river, flows through the center of Pomerania.

Pristine birch forests are common in the Polish region of Masuria. **Ma-Mc37**

Szczecin Historic ⊞ port city on the Baltic coast – Gothic town hall in the old town – national museum. **Lp37**

Gdańsk (Danzig) Major ⊞ port city that was once a leading member of the Hanseatic League – restored historic ⊞ old town – the historic ⊠ crane built in the 15th century is the city's landmark. **Lt36**

Malbork Historic city in northern Poland (40,000 inhabitants) – famous ⊠ brick castle built in the 14th century by the Knights of the Teutonic Order – UNESCO world heritage site – the castle consists of three separate structures. **Lu36**

Frombork Town with a Gothic town hall built on a fortified hill in the 14th century – famed astronomer Copernicus lived here in the 16th century. **Lu36**

Masuria Region in northeastern Poland with many ⊠ lakes and forests – destination with many ⊠ recreational opportunities. **Ma-Mc37**

Święta Lipka Baroque ⊠ pilgrimage church – built in the 17th century – located in a heavily forested area. **Mb36**

Białowieski National Park National Park on the Belorussian border – the park encompasses sections of Europe's largest remaining ⊠ virgin forest – ⊠ bison herds inhabit the park. **Md-Me38**

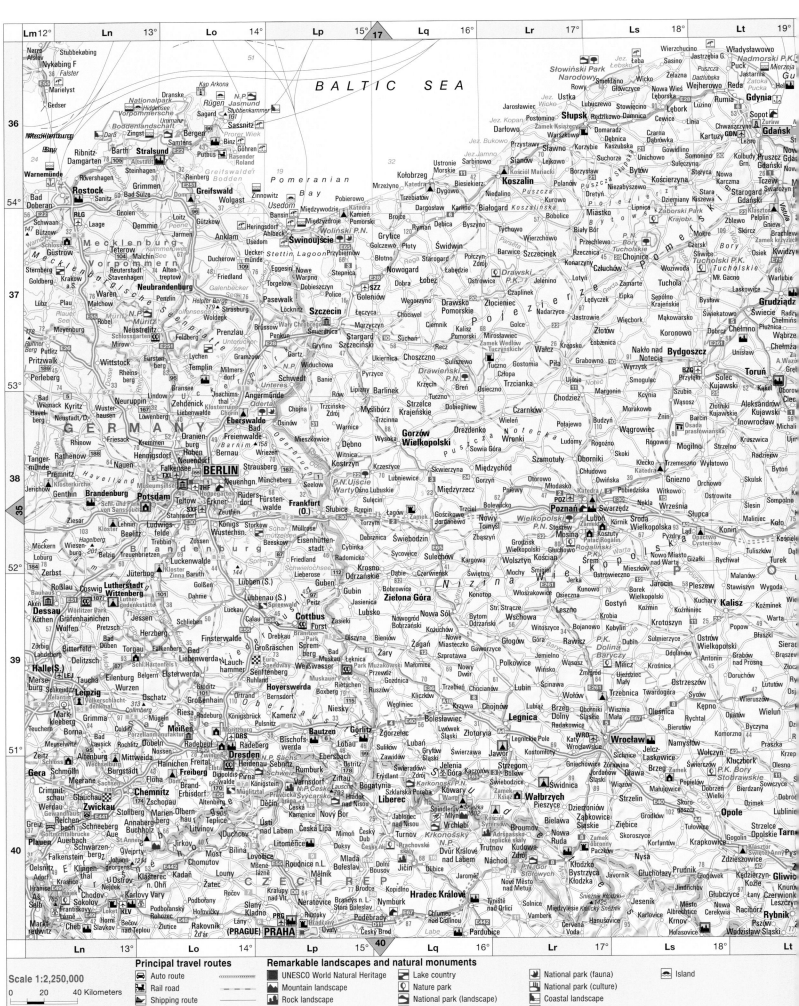

Scale 1:2,250,000

0   20   40 Kilometers

Principal travel routes

- 🚗 Auto route
- 🚂 Rail road
- ⚓ Shipping route

Remarkable landscapes and natural monuments

- UNESCO World Natural Heritage
- Mountain landscape
- Rock landscape
- River landscape
- Lake country
- Nature park
- National park (landscape)
- National park (flora)
- National park (fauna)
- National park (culture)
- Coastal landscape
- Beach
- Island

The Oder and Neisse Rivers form most of the border between Poland and Germany. German's capital city Berlin lies just 80 kilometers away from the Polish border. Most of Poland is covered by vast **plains** and much of the country's land is used for agriculture. Warsaw, Poland's capital lies on the banks of the Vistula River in a lowlands region. The Vistula is 1,066 kilometers long and its basin covers over 200,000 km².

South of central Poland's plains lie the hills and uplands of Silesia and southeastern Poland. Krakow, Poland's second largest city, is located in the country's southeast. The city contains an impressive collection of well-preserved historic architecture. The southernmost region of Poland is the most mountainous region in the country. The **Sudeten Mountains** form a natural border between Poland and the Czech Republic.

The western **Carpathian Mountains** separate the country from the Slovak Republic. Since the collapse of the Soviet Union two new nations now border Poland to the east: Ukraine with its vast plains and heavily forested Belarus. Northeast of Poland lies Lithuania, a country that, together with Poland, ruled a vast empire during the Middle Ages. The Russian enclave of Kaliningrad was part of the historic German kingdom of

Prussia until the end of the Second World War. Kaliningrad is now separated from mainland Russia by the territory of Lithuania and Belarus. Poland has a temperate continental climate with cold winters and warm summers. The climate of the country's coastal areas is significantly different from that of the interior. The Baltic coast tends to be cooler than the interior in summer and warmer than the interior in winter.

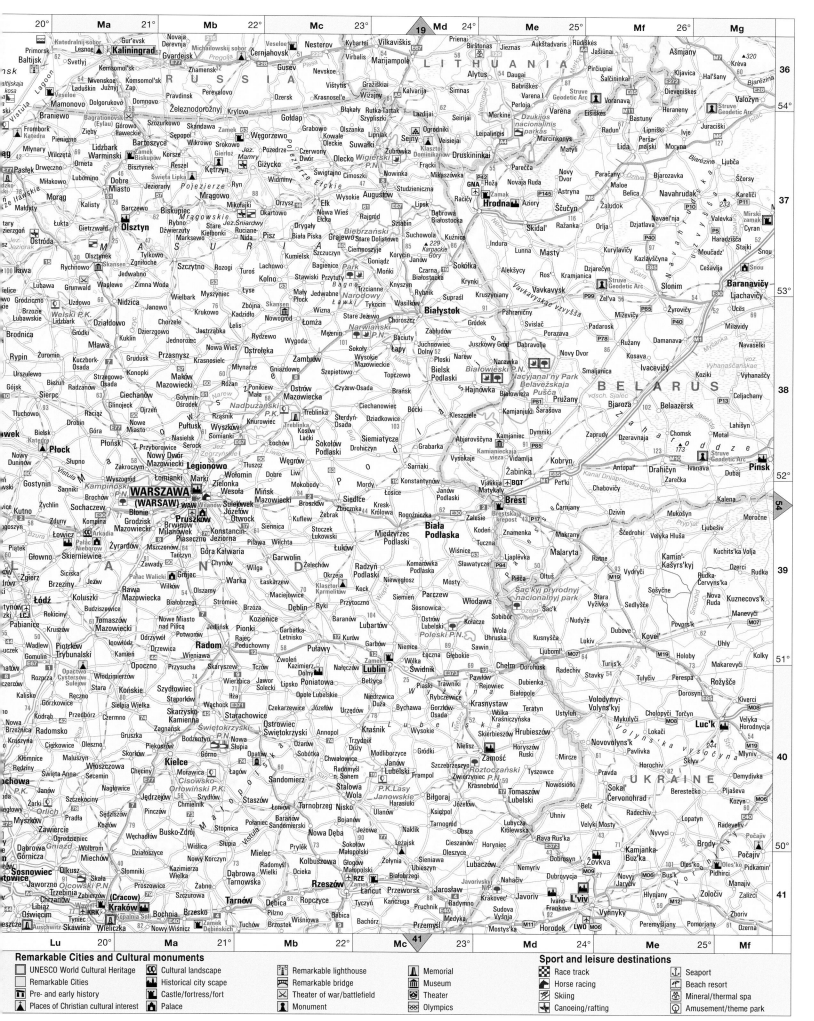

Warsaw The city's 🏛 old town (UNESCO site) was largely destroyed in the Second World War and later restored. The city features the former 🏰 Royal Palace and ⛪ St. John's Cathedral (top photo). Market Square is surrounded by historic houses (bottom photo). **Ma38**

Wrocław (Breslau) Capital of Silesia (pop. 643,000) – Gothic town hall in the 🏛 old town district of Rynek – historic church and cathedral on Tum Island. **Ls39**

Jawór The town has a 🏛 "Church of Peace" built in the 17th century (photo) – the church was designated a UNESCO world heritage site in 2001. **Lr39**

Kraków The cultural center (pop. 745,800) and former capital of Poland. The city's beautiful 🏛 old town is a UNESCO world heritage site. Major attractions include the cathedral, the former 🏰 Royal Palace (top photo), and the impressive large market square (bottom photo). **Lu40**

Zamość In 1508, the town was built in a wilderness on the orders of Poland's ruler Jan Zamoyski – the historic 🏛 old town is a UNESCO world heritage site. **Md40**

Remarkable Cities and Cultural monuments

- ☐ UNESCO World Cultural Heritage
- ☐ Remarkable Cities
- ☐ Pre- and early history
- ☐ Places of Christian cultural interest
- Cultural landscape
- Historical city scape
- Castle/fortress/fort
- Palace
- Remarkable lighthouse
- Remarkable bridge
- Theater of war/battlefield
- Monument
- Memorial
- Museum
- Theater
- Olympics

Sport and leisure destinations

- Race track
- Horse racing
- Skiing
- Canoeing/rafting
- Seaport
- Beach resort
- Mineral/thermal spa
- Amusement/theme park

Eastern Austria, Czech Republic, Slovakia, Hungary

Before the First World War the countries in this Central European region were all parts of the Austro-Hungarian Empire ruled by the Habsburg dynasty. The region has diverse landscapes and many cultural attractions. Most of the region is covered by mountains and rolling hills. **Bohemia** in the Czech Republic is surrounded by several ⛰ mountain ranges including sections of the Erz and Sudeten Mountains which form a natural

boundary between the Czech Republic and Germany, Poland, and Austria. The **Bohemian Basin** contains the Labe and Vltava, the longest rivers in the Czech Republic.
Slovakia, officially known as the Slovak Republic, is a small mountainous nation. Slovakia's highest mountains are located

Budapest, Hungary's historic and beautiful capital on the Danube River. **Lu43**

Mariánské Lázně Famous 🛁 spa town in Bohemia – grand colonnades – historic architecture including hotels. **Ln41**

Prague The capital city of the Czech Republic was founded in the 10th century. The city's extensive 🏛 old town is a UNESCO world heritage site. Prague old city hall (top photo) was constructed in the 13th century from a row of seperate houses. Historic 🌉 Charles Bridge and 🏰 Prague Castle are two of the city's most visited attractions (bottom photo). **Lp40**

Karlštejn Castle Castle 28 kilometers southwest of Prague – built by Charles IV. in the 14th century. **Lp41**

Český Krumlov The 🏛 old town features a hilltop castle – UNESCO world heritage site – historic Latran district – 🏛 Egon Schiele Art Center. **Lp42**

Bratislava Slovakia's capital and largest city – in the foothills of the Carpathian Mountains – university city – 🏛 national museum – 🏛 historic old town – 🏰 Gothic St. Martin's Cathedral. **Ls42**

Spišský hrad Largest 🏰 castle in Slovakia – founded in the 12th century – UNESCO world heritage site. **Ma42**

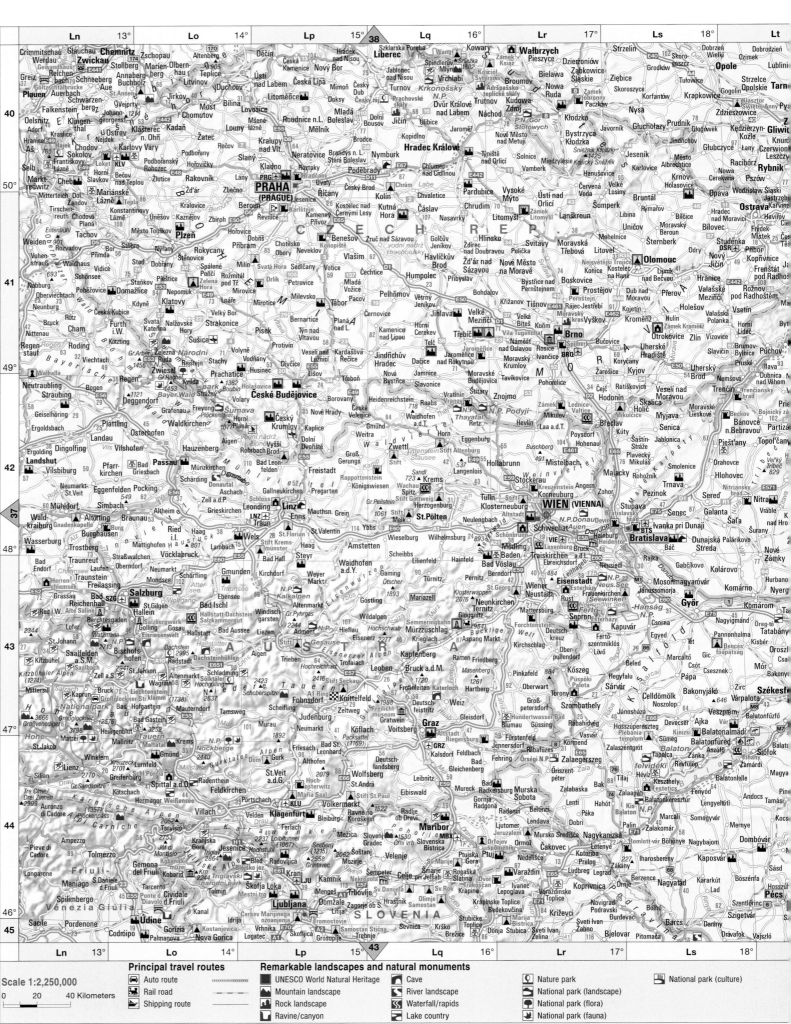

Scale 1:2,250,000

0   20   40 Kilometers

Principal travel routes
🚗 Auto route
🚃 Rail road
⚓ Shipping route

Remarkable landscapes and natural monuments
▪ UNESCO World Natural Heritage
▪ Mountain landscape
▪ Rock landscape
▪ Ravine/canyon

▾ Cave
▾ River landscape
▾ Waterfall/rapids
▾ Lake country

♦ Nature park
♦ National park (landscape)
♦ National park (flora)
♦ National park (fauna)

▥ National park (culture)

in the ⛰ **High Tatra Mountains**, along the Polish-Slovakian border. Gerlachovsky Stit, the highest Slovak mountain, rises 2,655 meters. Slovakia's capital city, Bratislava, lies in the ⬚ **Danube River Basin**. The Slovakian section of the basin stretches to the Ukrainian border and is the flattest region in the country. The **Carpathian Mountains** begin near Bratislava and stretch through Slovakia, Romania, Poland, and the Ukraine.

In contrast to neighboring Slovakia, **Hungary** is mostly flat country. The vast **Pannonian plain** is the remnant of an ancient lake and covers most of southern and eastern Hungary. A major agricultural area, the Hungarian sections of the plain are called the Great Alföld or Great Hungarian Plain. Northwestern Hungary is covered by the Little Alföld, a smaller plain separated from the Great Alföld by a low mountain range. The ⬚ **Danube**

River flows through the middle of the Great Alföld and passes through Budapest. Hungary's capital and largest city, Budapest, is built on a series of hills. ⬚ **Lake Balaton** (592 km²) in western Hungary is the largest freshwater lake in Central Europe. The shallow lake has an average depth of just 3.5 meters.
Hungary and neighboring **Austria** were once the dominant nations in the vast Astro-Hungarian Empire that once ruled

most of Central Europe. Vienna, the capital of modern Austria, was once the administrative center of the empire. The region around Vienna is a transition zone between the Pannonian plain and the **Alps**. More than two-thirds of Austria's land is covered by the Alps. The ⬚ **Hohen Tauern** in western and central Austria include some of the country's highest mountains including the Großglockner (3,798 m), Austria's highest peak.

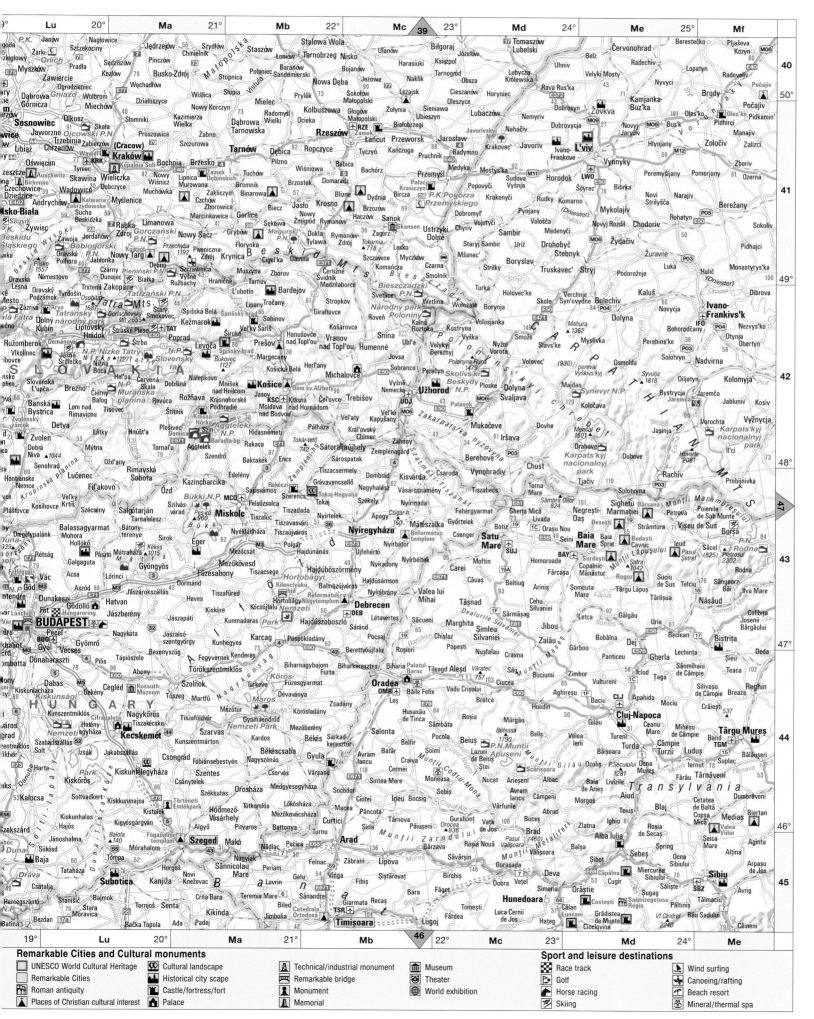

Hallstatt Picturesque village in Austrian Alps along ⬚ Lake Hallstatt – historic salt mines – UNESCO world heritage site. **Lo43**

Wachau Austrian 🍇 winemaking region along the ⬚ Danube – idyllic village – photo: Dürnstein. **Lq42**

Vienna Once the center of a vast empire, Vienna is now the capital of the Austrian Republic. The charming city on the Danube is a popular tourist destination. Vienna's ⬚ medieval center is surrounded by Baroque and 19th century buildings. The ⛪ St. Charles' and ⛪ St. Stephan's cathedrals (top photo) are Vienna's most famous landmarks. The ceremonial room (bottom photo) in Vienna's old national library is the largest Baroque library chamber in the world. **Lr42**

Budapest Hungary's capital city boasts countless art and architectural treasures. ⬚ Castle Hill is a UNESCO world heritage site. The famous chain bridge, near the Hungarian parliament building, was completed in 1849. The area around beautiful Fisherman's Bastion (photo) offers good views of the city. **Lu43**

Hortobágyi National Park Hungarian national park – grazing areas in the Puszta – photo: cattle herd. **Mb43**

Remarkable Cities and Cultural monuments

- ⬚ UNESCO World Cultural Heritage
- ⬚ Remarkable Cities
- Roman antiquity
- Places of Christian cultural interest
- Cultural landscape
- Historical city scape
- Castle/fortress/fort
- Palace
- Technical/industrial monument
- Remarkable bridge
- Monument
- Memorial
- Museum
- Theater
- World exhibition

Sport and leisure destinations

- Race track
- Golf
- Horse racing
- Skiing
- Wind surfing
- Canoeing/rafting
- Beach resort
- Mineral/thermal spa

Northern Italy, Slovenia, Croatia, Bosnia-Herzegovina

Northern **Italy** consists of the northern half of the Italian mainland on the Apennine peninsula, which takes its name from the Apennine Mountains. The northernmost regions of Italy are covered by the 🏔 **Alps**, the alpine foothills and many mountain lakes. Northeast of 🌊 **Lake Garda**, Italy's largest lake, rise the 🏔 **Dolomites**, a fascinating section of the Alps with high, craggy mountains. Mont Blanc (4,807 m), the highest mountain in

Western Europe, is situated on the border between France and northern Italy. The region to the south of the alpine foothills consists of fertile plains including the 🌊 **Po Valley**. The 🏔 **Apennine Mountains** form a natural barrier between the western and eastern sections of the Italian peninsula. The western regions of

Rolling hills cover much of Tuscany (Italy).   **Ll-Lm47**

The Dolomites 🏔 Alpine mountains east of Bolzano in northernmost Italy – famous peak: Marmolada (3,343 m) – winemaking village St. Magdalena (photo) in the Villnos Valley.   **Lm44**

Milan The economic center of Italy and a major center of the international fashion industry – population, 2.3 million – landmark: 🏛 Duomo cathedral (photo) – historic shopping center Galleria Vittorio Emanuele II. – 🏛 La Scala opera house.   **Lk45**

Lake Garda The largest lake in Italy covering 370 km² – name taken from the town Garda – 🎡 amusement parks – 🏰 Rocca Scalgera in Sirmione (photo).   **Ll45**

Cinque Terre Beautiful rocky coast, interesting coastal islands (UNESCO world heritage site) in northern Italy – 🏞 national park – picturesque villages – Vernazza (photo) has a charming harbor.   **Lk46**

Tuscany's Historic Cities and Towns
The beautiful cities and towns of Tuscany draw millions of tourists to the region. The 🏛 cities feature spectacular collections of priceless art and architectural masterpieces. Photos from top to bottom: Florence (**Lm47**), 🏛 Pisa (**Ll47**), and Siena (**Lm47**). All three cities are designated UNESCO sites.

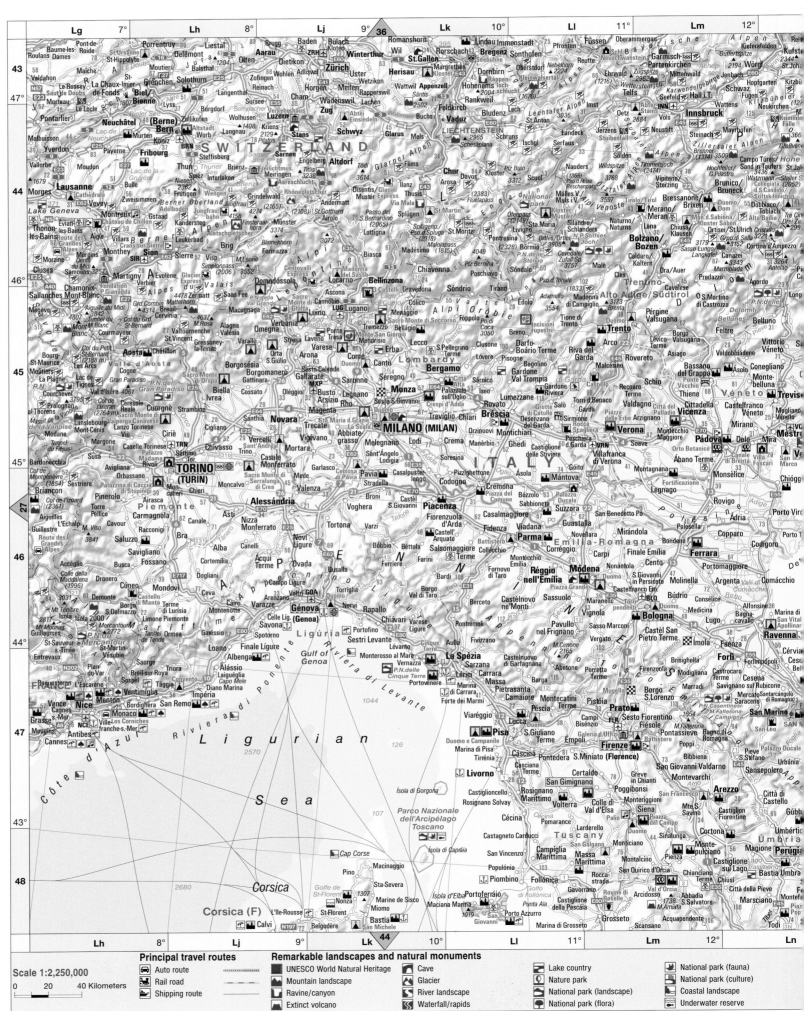

Scale 1:2,250,000

0   20   40 Kilometers

Principal travel routes
- Auto route
- Rail road
- Shipping route

Remarkable landscapes and natural monuments
- UNESCO World Natural Heritage
- Mountain landscape
- Ravine/canyon
- Extinct volcano
- Cave
- Glacier
- River landscape
- Waterfall/rapids
- Lake country
- Nature park
- National park (landscape)
- National park (flora)
- National park (fauna)
- National park (culture)
- Coastal landscape
- Underwater reserve

Northern Italy, Slovenia, Croatia, Bosnia-Herzegovina

the northern peninsula are covered by rolling hills and basins, while the eastern regions consist of mountain ridges and river valleys extending up to the narrow coastal areas. Northern Italy's ■ **coasts** comprise sandy beaches, steep cliffs, lagoons, and rocky bays.

The ■ Julian Alps stretch through most of mountainous Northwestern **Slovenia** – a region with many lakes and ■ **Triglav** (2,864 m), the country's highest mountain. Between Triglav National Park and Slovenia's coastal region lies an area with interesting natural sights including plateaus, rivers, and numerous caves. The areas south of the basin, around Ljubljana, have rolling hills covered by vineyards and fruit farms. Beyond the Mur River, in the easternmost regions of Slovenia, lie sections of the vast **Pannonian plain**.

Croatia can be divided into three distinctive geographic regions: the ■ coastal region along the **Adriatic**, the areas on the **Pannonian plain**, and the ■ **mountainous regions**. Croatia's jagged Adriatic coast, a popular tourist attraction, features sandy beaches, cliffs, and numerous coastal islands. The mountainous regions of Croatia include the mountains (up to 2,000 meters high) near the northern coast and between the Istria peninsula as well as the hills of northern Croatia. In eastern Croatia, the Pannonian plain stretches between the Drava and Sava rivers.

Bosnia-Herzegovina is a mountainous nation with fertile lowlands in the northern sections of the country. Central Bosnia is a heavily forested area encompassing several large valleys. The country's short ■ Adriatic coast is only 20 kilometers long. Devastated by an ethnic civil war in the 1990s, the country is now in the process of rebuilding.

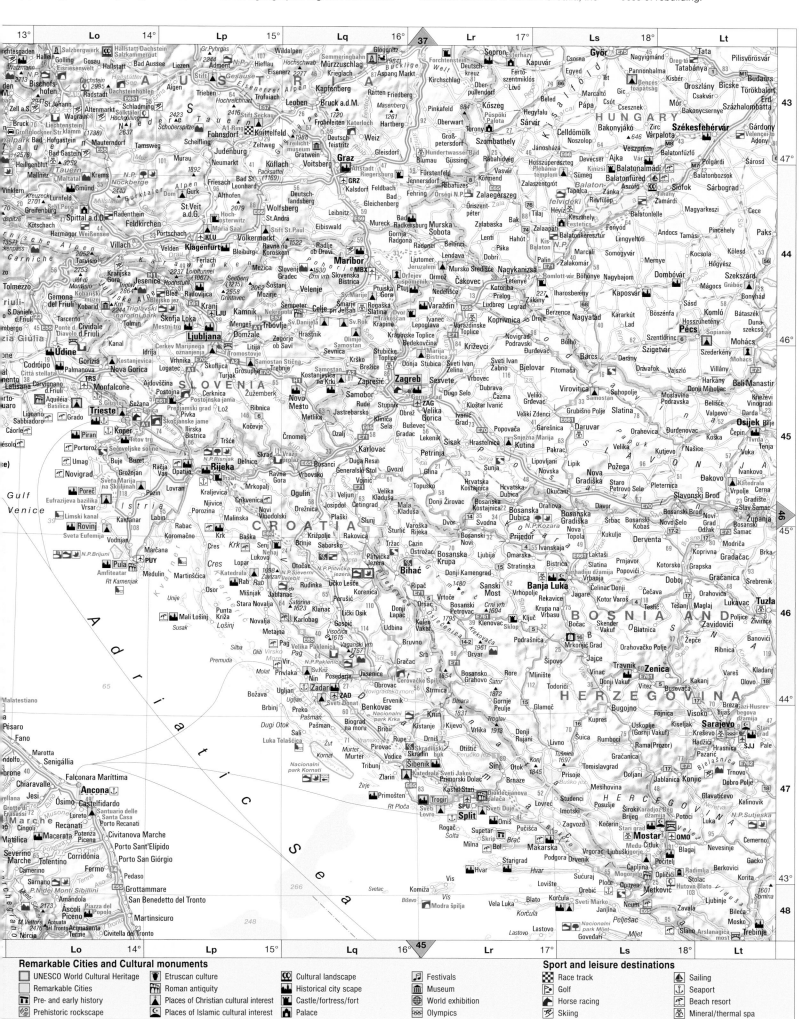

Venice ■ UNESCO world heritage site, containing San Marco Piazza, St. Mark's Basilica, and the ■ lagoon. Gondolas (top photo) are floating symbols of the city. The Rialto Bridge on the Canal Grande (bottom photo) is one of Venice's 400 bridges. **Ln45**

Ravenna City on Italy's Adriatic coast – ■ San Vitale Basilica contains interesting mosaics (photo) – grave of the poet and author Dante Alighieri. **Ln46**

Ljubljana ■ Capital and largest city in Slovenia – Baroque and art deco architecture in the city center – castles, palaces, and palatial houses. **Lp44**

Istria Peninsula in northwestern Croatia – ■ towns with historic Venetian architecture – Roman ■ amphitheater in Pula – ■ Rovinj cathedral (photo). **Lo45**

Plitvicka Jezera This Croatian ■ national park is a UNESCO world heritage site – diverse ■ fauna and flora – ■ beautiful lakes – ■ waterfalls and river rapids. **Lq46**

Trogir Historic ■ old town on a small coastal island – UNESCO world heritage site – numerous historic churches including the ■ St. Lawrence cathedral – ■ palaces from the Venetian era. **Lr47**

Remarkable Cities and Cultural monuments

- □ UNESCO World Cultural Heritage
- □ Remarkable Cities
- 🏛 Pre- and early history
- Prehistoric rockscape
- Etruscan culture
- Roman antiquity
- Places of Christian cultural interest
- Places of Islamic cultural interest
- Cultural landscape
- Historical city scape
- Castle/fortress/fort
- Palace
- Festivals
- Museum
- World exhibition
- Olympics

Sport and leisure destinations

- Race track
- Golf
- Horse racing
- Skiing
- Sailing
- Seaport
- Beach resort
- Mineral/thermal spa

Europe **43**

Southern Italy, Malta, Albania

The **Apennine Mountains** stretch through the entire boot-shaped southern half of the Italian Peninsula. The region of Abruzzo contains the highest peaks in the Apennines, including the mountains of the Gran Sasso d'Italia Range, several of which rise higher than 2,500 meters. The area north of Italy's capital city **Rome** consists of rolling hills and lakes that were formed in ancient volcanic craters. Vatican City, the spiritual center of millions of Roman Catholics, is a small sovereign state in the middle of Rome. The flat plains of Italy's southwestern coast – especially **Calabria** and the area around **Naples** – are the most volcanically active regions in Italy. In addition to the active volcanoes Mount Etna and Mount Vesuvius, the region also features dormant volcanoes and large fields of volcanic stone. Numerous rivers flow parallel to the coast through the mountainous regions of southwestern Italy. The small peninsula in southeastern Italy is covered by heavily cultivated, flat plains. The coastal areas in Italy's far south feature kilometers of long white sand beaches and beautiful cliffs. Italy's **Amalfi Coast** region is a popular tourist destination with lush vegetation and rocky coastlines.

Mount Etna on Sicily is the highest active volcano in Europe. **LpLq53**

Rome The "eternal city" has been a center of western civilization for more than 2,000 years. The city, built on seven hills, has important historic buildings including the Forum Romanum and countless art treasures. The city also boasts many historic churches. Photos from top to bottom: the Spanish Steps, Arch of Constantine, and the Pantheon. **Ln49**

Vatican City (The Holy See) Small sovereign enclave in Rome – residence of the Pope – Palace of the Vatican – The Sistine Chapel – St. Peter's Basilica. **Ln49**

Pompeii When Mount Vesuvius erupted in 79 AD, the city of Pompeii was buried under a layer of ash and lava. More than three-quarters of the city (top photo) has been excavated. One of the most impressive sights is the Villa del Misteri (bottom photo) with its frescoes. The neighboring Roman town of Herculaneum was also buried after the eruption. **Lp50**

Capri The most beautiful island in the Gulf of Naples – grand villas – beautiful gardens – historic town center – Grotta Azzura, the world famous Blue Grotto. **Lp50**

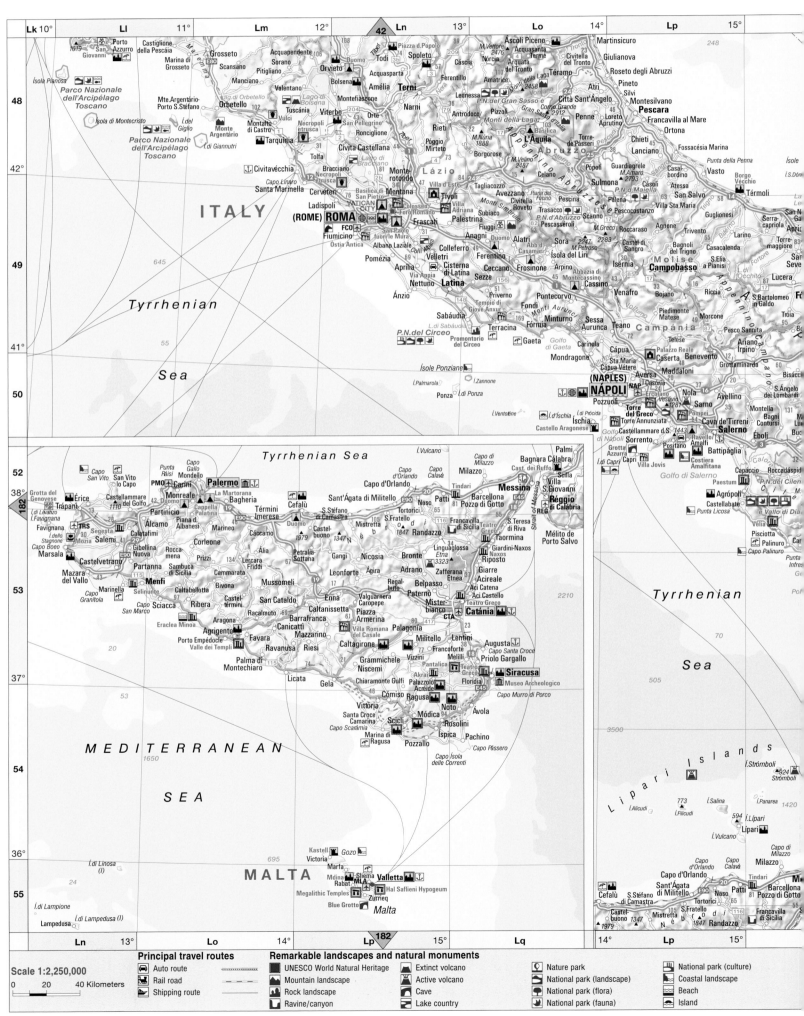

Scale 1:2,250,000
0   20   40 Kilometers

Principal travel routes
- Auto route
- Rail road
- Shipping route

Remarkable landscapes and natural monuments
- UNESCO World Natural Heritage
- Mountain landscape
- Rock landscape
- Ravine/canyon
- Extinct volcano
- Active volcano
- Cave
- Lake country
- Nature park
- National park (landscape)
- National park (flora)
- National park (fauna)
- National park (culture)
- Coastal landscape
- Beach
- Island

The 405-kilometer-long **Tiber River** is the longest river in southern Italy.

Sicily, the largest Italian island, is separated from the mainland by the **Strait of Messina**. The densely populated island is geologically active and earthquakes are not uncommon on Sicily. Northern Sicily is dominated by craggy mountains, while the island's south is a hilly yet fertile region. **Mount Etna**, Sicily's highest mountain is an active volcano which has erupted several times in recent decades. The **Aeolian Islands** off the northern coast of Sicily contain two more active volcanoes: Strómboli and Vulcano.

Malta is a nation consisting of a group of dry islands with no rivers and few sources of freshwater. The largest island in the group, also called **Malta**, is covered by hills in the southeast and valleys and fruit fields in the northwest. **Gozo**, the second largest Maltese island, is more fertile than neighboring Malta and covered by a large plateau. **Comino**, the smallest of the three inhabited islands, has many attractive beaches. The country has a pleasant Mediterranean climate and tourism is an important sector of Malta's economy.

More than three-quarters of **Albania's** territory is covered by mountains. The highest mountains are located in the northern and northeastern sections of the country. Korab, the country's highest mountain, rises 2,764 meters. Western Albania, including the coastal areas, is the least mountainous and most densely populated region in the country. Most of Albania's coast consists of marshy areas with numerous lagoons, while the south has a rocky coastline. Albania's three largest lakes are all situated along the country's borders with neighboring countries.

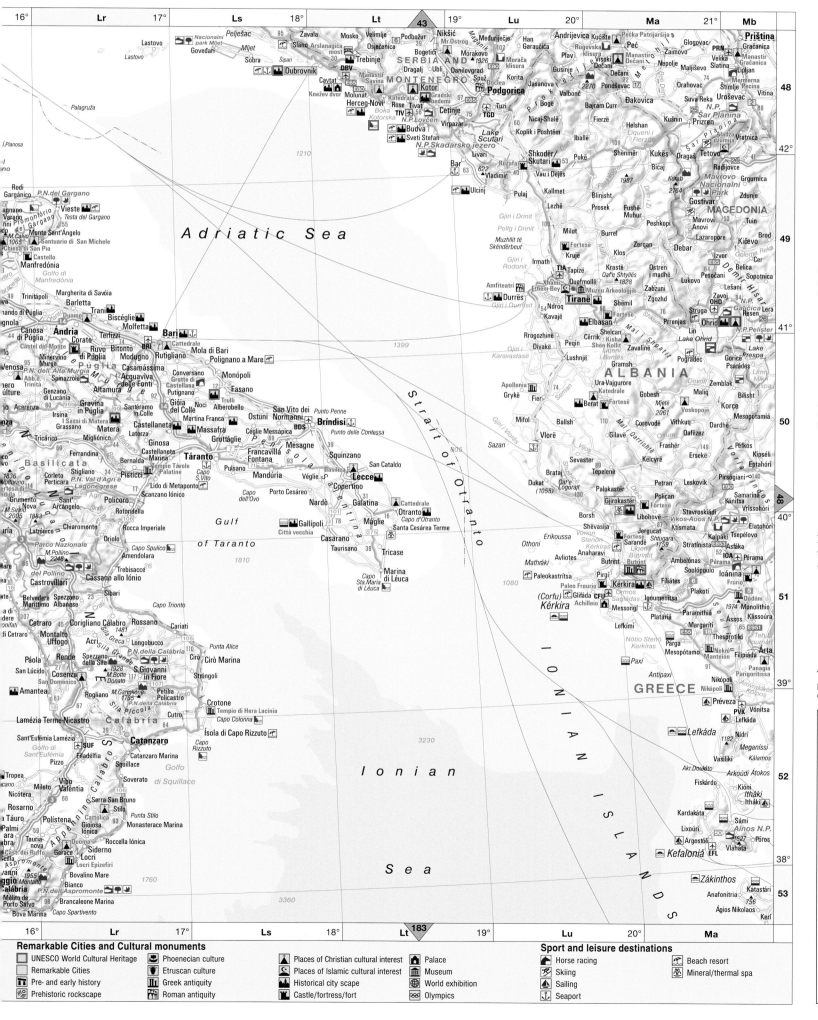

The Amalfi Coast One of Europe's most beautiful coastal areas – UNESCO world natural heritage site – Positano (one of the oldest settlements in Italy) has charming pastel colored cottages and palaces – Santa Maria Assunta church. **Lp50**

Castel del Monte Unique octagonal castle built by Frederick II in the 13th century – ornamental windows – UNESCO site. **Lr49**

Aeolian Islands Seven volcanic islands north of Sicily – Strómboli and Vulcano are active volcanoes – ancient ruins. **LpLq52**

Agrigento Founded as a Greek colony between 600-500 BC – Greek temples in the Valley of Temples – well preserved Temple of Concord (photo). **Lo53**

Temple of Segesta Impressive and well-preserved building erected by the Dorian Greeks and never completed. **Ln53**

Malta Malta's capital city Valletta (top photo) has one of the most attractive harbors in Europe and is a UNESCO world heritage site. Valletta has baroque and renaissance architecture. The Grand Master's Palace is one of the most impressive sights. Maesaxlockk (bottom photo) is a beautiful fishing village. **Lp54/55**

Remarkable Cities and Cultural monuments

- UNESCO World Cultural Heritage
- Remarkable Cities
- Pre- and early history
- Prehistoric rockscape
- Phoenecian culture
- Etruscan culture
- Greek antiquity
- Roman antiquity
- Places of Christian cultural interest
- Places of Islamic cultural interest
- Historical city scape
- Castle/fortress/fort
- Palace
- Museum
- World exhibition
- Olympics

Sport and leisure destinations

- Horse racing
- Skiing
- Sailing
- Seaport
- Beach resort
- Mineral/thermal spa

Northern Serbia, Romania, Moldova

West of Romania, the vast plains of the Carpathian Basin stretch south from the city of Budapest in Hungary to Belgrade in Serbia. North of Budapest rise the mountains of the ■ **Mátra Range**, which stretches north to the Tatra Mountains in Slovakia.

The ■ **Danube River** is the most important waterway in this region of Europe. Before it reaches its delta on the Black Sea, the Danube passes through many

large cities, including Belgrade and Budapest. Large cargo ships transport goods along the Danube and the river is one of the busiest transport routes between Western Europe and the Balkan nations. River cruises offer tourists the chance to enjoy the Danube's beauty. Since the collapse of Yugoslavia, Rom-

One of the wider sections of the Danube; near Orsova in Romania. **Mc46**

Bistriţa Monastery Orthodox monastery built in the 16th century – located in the eastern Carpathian Mountains. **Me43**

Cluj-Napoca Historic ■ university town – the city has a very long and rich history – ■ St. Michael's church (photo). **Md44**

Sighişoara Well preserved ■ medieval center – UNESCO site – birthplace of Vlad Tepes, the inspiration for Dracula myths. **Me44**

Biertan Large ■ church complex in Transylvania – fortified towers and high defensive walls. **Me44**

Alba Iulia The largest ■ fortress complex in Romania – ten-kilometer-long defensive walls – ■ orthodox cathedral. **Md44**

Timişoara Largest city in Romania's Banat region – ■ historic architecture from the era of the Habsburg Empire. **Mb45**

Beograd (Belgrade) Capital city of Serbia and Montenegro on the Danube River – population: 1.2 million – ■ Kalemegdan Fortress. **Ma46**

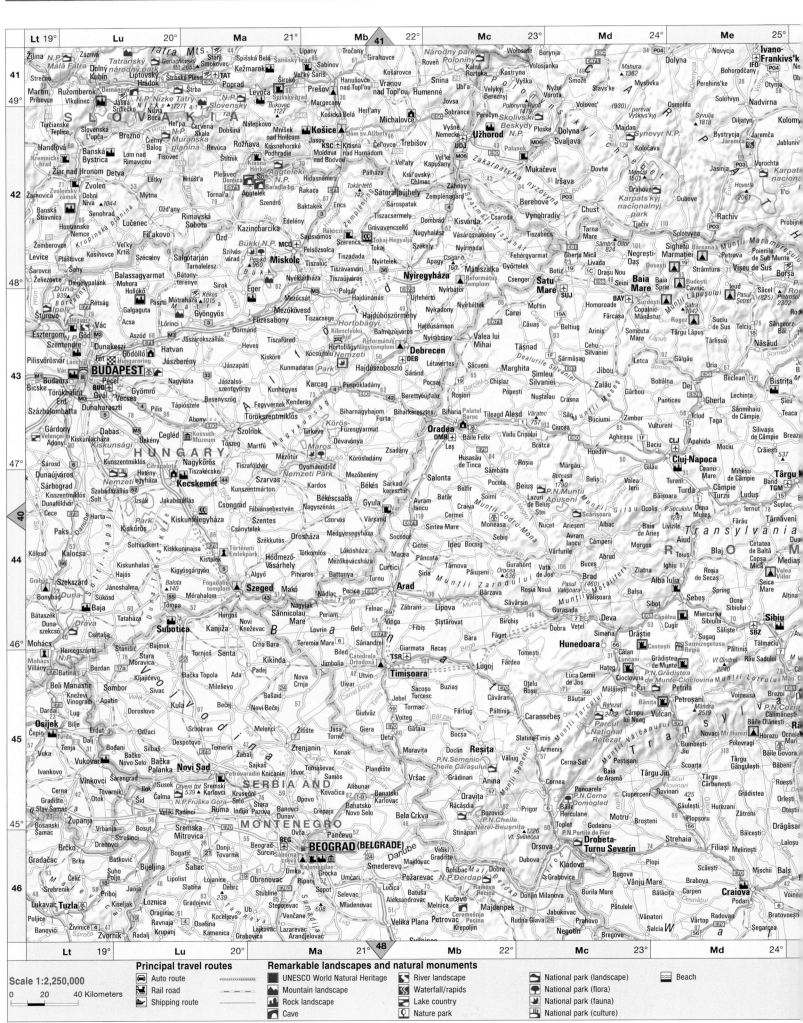

Principal travel routes

Scale 1:2,250,000

0   20   40 Kilometers

- Auto route
- Rail road
- Shipping route

Remarkable landscapes and natural monuments

- UNESCO World Natural Heritage
- Mountain landscape
- Rock landscape
- Cave
- River landscape
- Waterfall/rapids
- Lake country
- Nature park
- National park (landscape)
- National park (flora)
- National park (fauna)
- National park (culture)
- Beach

...ania is the largest nation in southeastern Europe. The country consists mostly of three historic regions separated by ◫ mountain ranges and ⬖ rivers: Wallachia, Romanian Moldavia, and Transylvania. The Banat region in southeastern Romania, was Hungarian territory from the late 18th century until the end of the First World War.

The ◫ **Carpathian Mountains** stretch through Romania from the southeast to the northern areas along the Ukrainian border. Transylvania is a hilly region surrounded by mountains – including **Moldoveanu**, the highest mountain in Romania, rising 2,544 meters. The Romanian region of Moldavia encompasses many river valleys, inactive ◫ volcanic mountains, and the largest forest in Romania. Southern Romania is a mostly flat region containing the most productive grain growing areas in the country.

The interior area around the Black Sea coast is a fertile flat plain stretching to the Bulgarian border – a border that has been the subject of dispute more than once. The many streams and tributaries in the Danube river delta form a natural boundary between Romania and Ukraine.
Moldova is a small landlocked country between the Danube and Prut ⬖ Rivers. Before its independence in 1991, Moldova was a republic in the Soviet Union.

Moldova consists mainly of rolling hills and plains as well as numerous rivers. Mount Balanesti, the highest point in the country, rises just 430 meters. The country has an abundance of fertile land, a good climate, and a large winemaking industry. Modern Moldova encompasses most of the historic Romanian-speaking region of Bessarabia and still has strong cultural and historic connections to Romania.

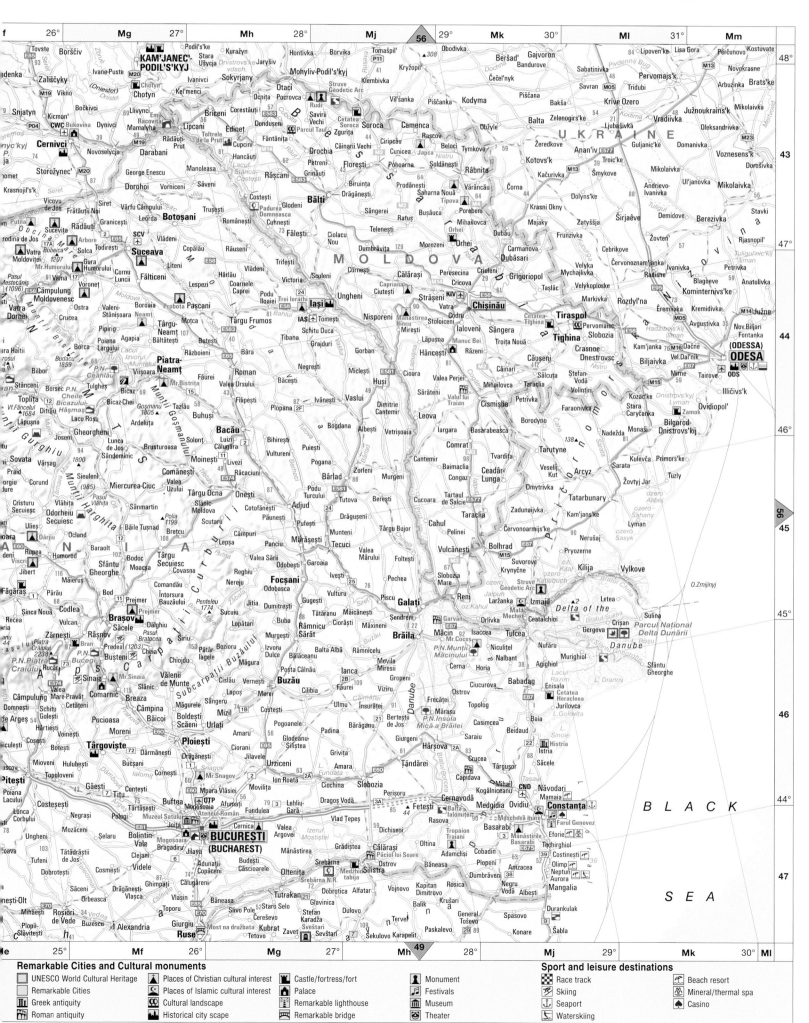

Romania's Monasteries Many of the beautifully painted ◫ churches and monasteries of northeastern Romania are UNESCO world heritage sites – including Putna (top photo), Sucevita (middle photo) with its well-preserved wall paintings, and Humor Monastery (bottom photo). **Mf-Mg43**

Chişinău Capital of Moldova – largely Stalinist era architecture – historic orthodox churches. **Mj43**

Bran Castle ◫ Also known as Dracula's castle – once a citadel against the Ottoman armies – center of "Dracula" tourism. **Mf45**

Bucureşti (Bucharest) Capital of Romania – population 2.1 million – the former palace (photo) of the dictator Ceausescu now houses Romania's parliament. **Mg46**

Danube River Delta ⬖ UNESCO world natural heritage site – around 150 fish species – habitat for migrating birds. **Mk45/46**

Remarkable Cities and Cultural monuments

- ▣ UNESCO World Cultural Heritage
- ▣ Remarkable Cities
- 🏛 Greek antiquity
- 🏛 Roman antiquity
- ✝ Places of Christian cultural interest
- ☪ Places of Islamic cultural interest
- ◫ Cultural landscape
- ▣ Historical city scape
- ⊠ Castle/fortress/fort
- ▣ Palace
- ⛴ Remarkable lighthouse
- ⟡ Remarkable bridge

Sport and leisure destinations

- ▲ Monument
- ▣ Festivals
- ▥ Museum
- ▣ Theater
- ♘ Race track
- ⛷ Skiing
- ⚓ Seaport
- ⛵ Waterskiing
- ⛱ Beach resort
- ♨ Mineral/thermal spa
- ♠ Casino

Southern Serbia and Montenegro, Bulgaria, Macedonia, Northern Greece

The borders in the southern Balkans have been changed many times throughout history, most recently, during the conflicts following the collapse of Yugoslavia in the early 1990s. Geographically, the southern Balkans are a region of ⛰ mountain ranges, pristine forests, and 🏖 coastal areas along the Adriatic, Aegean, and Black Seas. The high mountain range west of the steppe between Belgrade and Nis in Serbia has several peaks rising

over 2,500 meters. 🏞 **Durmitor National Park** is a UNESCO world heritage site with unique wildlife and the 61-kilometer-long 🏞 Tara Canyon. Brown bears, chamois, and wild cats are just a few of many interesting animals inhabiting the park. While **Kosovo** comprises two large basins surrounded by mountains, neigh-

Sveti Stefan: resort island on the Montenegro's Adriatic coast. **Lt48**

boring Albania is a mountainous country with a marshy coast. On the border between **Albania** and the Former Yugoslav Republic of **Macedonia** lies ⛰ Lake Ohrid. The large lake is surrounded by mountains and is the deepest lake in the Balkans, with a maximum depth of 295 meters. Macedonia's interior is covered by expansive mountain forests.
Bulgaria is a relatively small nation with a great variety of landscapes. South of

Bay of Kotor Historic Montenegrin port city – UNESCO world heritage site – medieval wall – 🏛 cathedral. **Lt48**

Budva 2,500-year-old 🏛 city on Montenegro's Adriatic coast – surrounded by 🏖 17 beautiful beaches, considered by many to be among the best in the region. **Lt48**

Gjirokastër Albanian 🏛 city – the birthplace of Albania's former Stalinist dictator Enver Hoxha – distinctive architecture – 🏰 Gjirokaster Castle. **Lu50**

Lake Ohrid Mountain 🏞 lake between Albania and Macedonia – UNESCO world heritage site. **Ma49/50**

Corfu One of the most visited Greek Islands – diverse landscapes and lush vegetation – historic palaces and monasteries – sandy 🏖 beaches. **Lu51**

Metéora 🏛 Spectacular monasteries in northern Greece built on large rock formations – UNESCO world heritage site. **Mb51**

Mount Athos The monastic community on Greece's 🏛 Athos Peninsula is an important religious center encompassing 20 monasteries. Around 3,000 monks live on Mount Athos. The area is accessible by ferry only. **Me50**

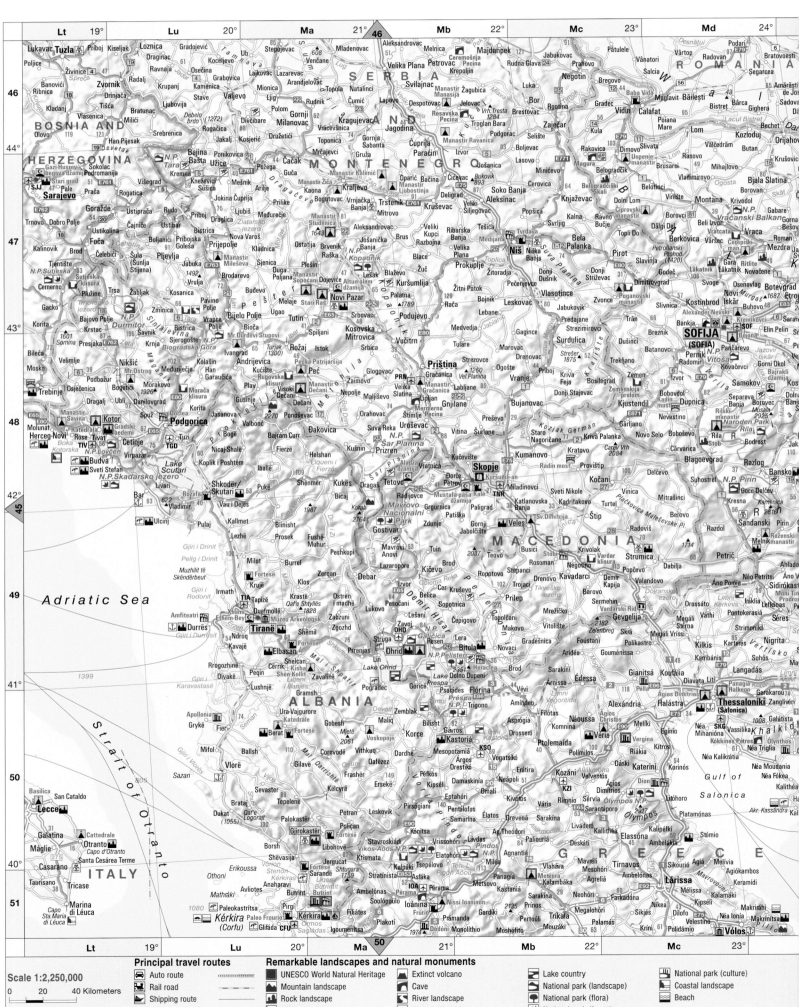

Scale 1:2,250,000

0   20   40 Kilometers

Principal travel routes	Remarkable landscapes and natural monuments		
🚗 Auto route	⬛ UNESCO World Natural Heritage	🌋 Extinct volcano	⬛ Lake country	⬛ National park (culture)
🚆 Rail road	⬛ Mountain landscape	⬛ Cave	⬛ National park (landscape)	⬛ Coastal landscape
⚓ Shipping route	⬛ Rock landscape	⬛ River landscape	⬛ National park (flora)	⬛ Beach
	⬛ Ravine/canyon	⬛ Waterfall/rapids	⬛ National park (fauna)	

Southern Serbia and Montenegro, Bulgaria, Macedonia, Northern Greece

the capital city Sofia, rise the forested mountains of the ▲ **Vitoša Range** which extend up to the ▲ **Rila Mountains**. Mustala in the Rila Mountains rises 2,925 meters and is the tallest mountain in the country. According to legend, the **Rhodope Mountains** along the Greek-Bulgarian border were the home of the mythological figure Orpheus. The Balkans region is named after the **Balkan Mountains**, a long mountain range

which stretches through central Bulgaria and eastern Serbia.

The **Danube River** forms a natural border between Bulgaria and Romania. The areas along the river's banks are the most fertile in the region. Bulgaria's 378-kilometer-long ▦ Black Sea coast is rocky in the north and covered by ▦ sandy beaches in the south. The coast is a major tourist attraction and has become increasingly popular in recent

years. A 400-kilometer-long roadway connects the Bulgarian port city of Bourgas to Istanbul, the largest city in Turkey. **Istanbul** is situated on the Bosporus, a strait between the Black Sea and the Sea of Marmora. The **Dardanelles**, another important strait, connects the Sea of Marmora with the Aegean Sea. Northern Greece, like most of the country consists largely of mountainous highlands and hills. The region has a

Mediterranean climate with mild winters and hot summers. **Chalkidiki Peninsula** on the coast of northern **Greece** features many beautiful beaches. The peninsula is also the location of Mount Athos, an important spiritual center of the Greek Orthodox religion. Thessaloniki, the largest city in northern Greece, is located just north of ▲ **Mount Olympus**, the home of the Greek gods in ancient mythology.

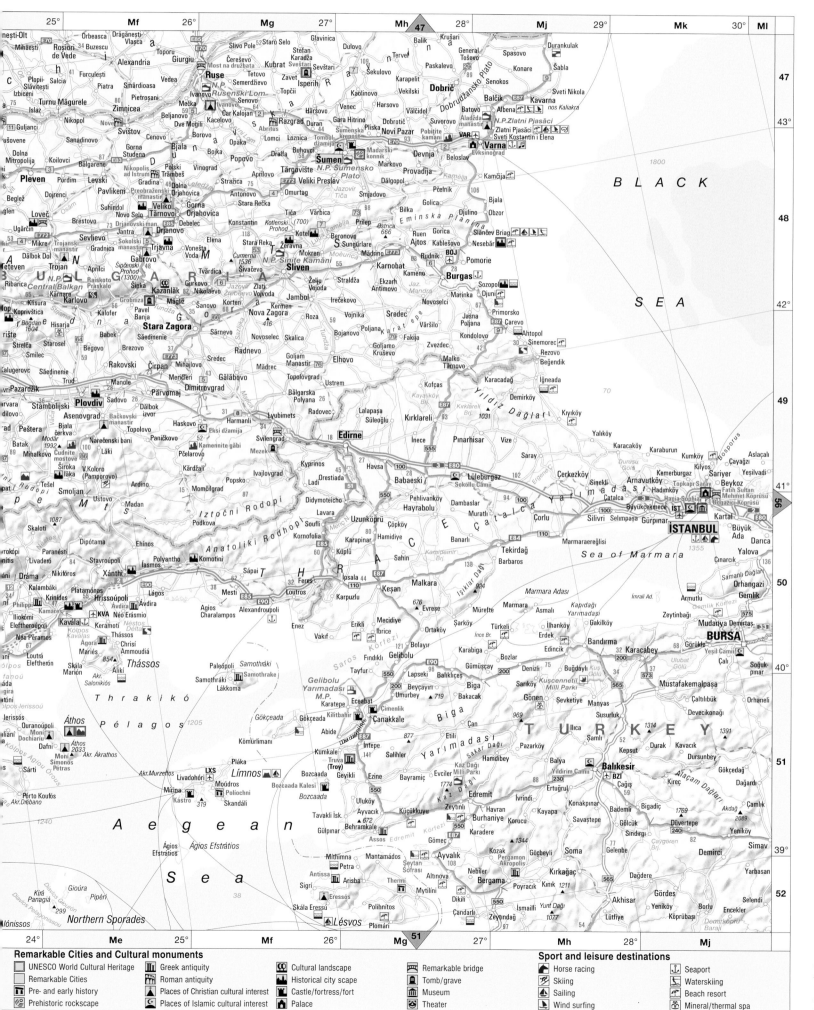

Sofia Capital city of Bulgaria – ▣ Alexander Nevsky Cathedral (photo) – ▣ St. George's Church, built in the 4th century – ▥ Archeology Museum. **Md48**

Rila Monastery Bulgarian ▣ monastery (UNESCO world heritage site) founded by Ivan Rilski in the 10th century. The unique complex has been destroyed and rebuilt several times and is an important national symbol. Photos: (top) historic church in the monastery's interior, (bottom) interior wall paintings. **Md48**

Plovdiv The second largest city in Bulgaria – ▥ Roman amphitheater – around 300 protected ▣ buildings. **Me48**

Veliko Tărnovo Former ▣ capital of Bulgaria (1185–1393) – picturesque riverside architecture – ruins of Tsaravets Citadel. **Mf47**

Pobitite Kamani Fields of interesting ▣ stone pillars – created by erosion millions of years ago. **Mh47**

Nesebăr Ancient city first settled in the 2nd century BC – historic ▣ city on a peninsula – the city is a designated UNESCO world heritage site – 19th century Black Sea region architecture (photo) including buildings made of stone and wood. **Mh48**

Remarkable Cities and Cultural monuments

▢	UNESCO World Cultural Heritage
▣	Remarkable Cities
▣	Pre- and early history
▣	Prehistoric rockscape
▥	Greek antiquity
▥	Roman antiquity
▣	Places of Christian cultural interest
▣	Places of Islamic cultural interest
▣	Cultural landscape
▣	Historical city scape
▣	Castle/fortress/fort
▣	Palace

▣	Remarkable bridge
▣	Tomb/grave
▥	Museum
▣	Theater

Sport and leisure destinations

▣	Horse racing
▣	Skiing
▣	Sailing
▣	Wind surfing
▣	Seaport
▣	Waterskiing
▣	Beach resort
▣	Mineral/thermal spa

Southern Greece, Southwestern Turkey

Southern Greece consists of the southern half of mainland Greece including the Peloponnesus peninsula and most of the Greek islands, which combined comprise around one fifth of the country's land area. The region is mostly mountainous with craggy coasts, while the western Peloponnesus has a smooth coast with many sand beaches.

The ⛰ **Pindos Mountains** run through the western section of mainland Greece

parallel to the coast. This mountain range looks distinctly alpine and snow covers much of the area between December and April.

Athens and its surrounding areas are located in the **Attica Basin**. The basin is the most densely populated region in Greece and is home to almost half of the coun-

The Colossus of Rhodes stood near Rhodes harbor in ancient times. **Mj54**

Zakynthos 🏛 Byzantine Museum – historic town Zakynthos – beaches including the 🏖 "shipwreck beach" (photo). **Ma53**

Delphí Site of the 🏛 ancient Delphic Oracle, dedicated to the Greek god Apollo – the area is a UNESCO world heritage site – Temple of Apollo – remains of an ancient arena – Tholos temple. **Mc52**

Corinth, Temple of Apollo 🏛 Ruin of an ancient Hellenic city – Temple of Apollo remnants (photo). **Mc53**

Athens Greece's capital and largest urban area is not usually considered beautiful, but it is a fascinating city with several ancient sites. The 🏛 **Acrópolis** (top photo) – with the ancient Parthenon, Erechtheum, and Propylaea – towers over the center of the city. The **Odeon** (bottom photo) is the site of an annual 🎵 theatre festival in summer. **Md53**

Aegina Interesting island – the 🏛 Temple of Aphaia (photo), built around 500 BC and one of Greece's most famous temples. **Md53**

Epídauros Birthplace of Asclepius in Greek mythology – the well preserved amphitheater is considered a masterpiece of classic Hellenistic architecture. **Md53**

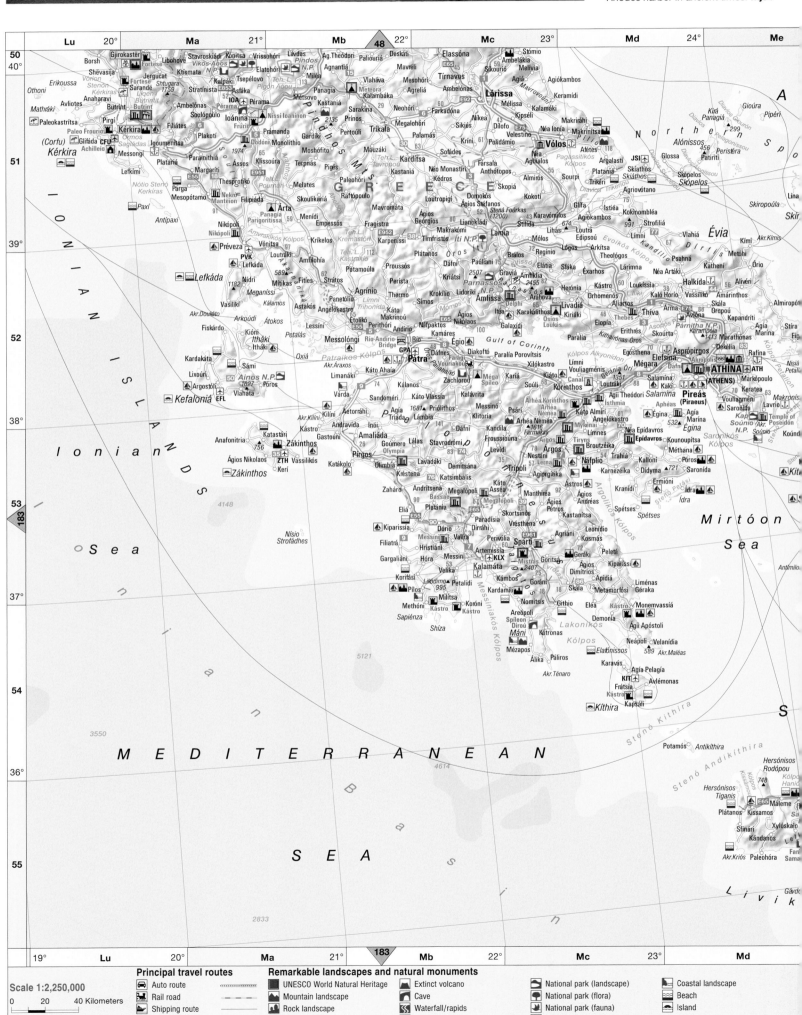

Scale 1:2,250,000

0   20   40 Kilometers

Principal travel routes
- 🚗 Auto route
- 🚂 Rail road
- 🚢 Shipping route

Remarkable landscapes and natural monuments
- UNESCO World Natural Heritage
- Mountain landscape
- Rock landscape
- Ravine/canyon
- Extinct volcano
- Cave
- Waterfall/rapids
- Lake country
- National park (landscape)
- National park (flora)
- National park (fauna)
- National park (culture)
- Coastal landscape
- Beach
- Island

try's population. The **Thessaly Plain** and the **Peloponnesus** are two of the more fertile regions in Greece. There are several large bays and gulfs between the Peloponnesus and the Isthmus of Corinth. Greece's 🏖 **Aegean Islands** are covered by rolling hills and mountains. The islands are divided into several groups: the Cyclades, including Mykonos and Delos, the Dodecanese, near the coast of Asia Minor, and the Sporades. Euboea is the

largest of the Aegean Island, with a total land area of 3,580 km². The eastern Aegean Islands including the Dodecanese are generally wetter than their western counterparts. Rhodes has an area of 1,398 km² and is the largest island in the Dodecanese. The island was once the site of the Colossus of Rhodes, one of the "seven wonders" of the ancient world. The 🏛 **Ionian Islands** are situated off the western coast of southern Greece. The

Ionians consist of seven main islands and many smaller ones with lush green vegetation. 🏖 **Crete**, the largest of the Greek islands, has a long history and beautiful landscapes including mountains and sandy beaches. Crete also features many important archeological sites, including many linked to the ancient Minoan civilization (3000–1400 BC). **Southwestern Turkey** is a region with rolling hills, lakes, ancient towns and

important archeological sites. 🏛 **Pamukkale** – a spectacular site consisting of terraced white chalk formations and thermal pools – is the most interesting natural attraction in the region. The western 🏖 **Aegean coast** features several bays. Southwest of Marmaris lies the so-called 🏖 **Turkish Riviera**. 🏖 **Ölü Deniz Bay** has fine sandy beaches and is one of the most attractive areas in the region.

Mykonos 🏖 This Aegean island is a popular tourist destination – traditional white cubic houses – windmills – beaches. **Mf53**

Páros One of the Cyclades islands – 🏛 Katapoliani church in Parikia (photo) – highest mountain, 🏔 Profitis Ilias (775 m). **Mf53**

Delos This was a sacred island for the ancient Greeks – "birthplace" of Apollo – 🏛 the largest site of ancient Greek ruins – Terrace of the Lions with large lion statues – Temple of Apollo. **Mf53**

Náxos Charming island – 🏛 historic towns with Venetian architecture – reconstructed 🏛 Temple of Demeter. **Mf53**

Santorini Fascinating 🏞 crater landscapes – typical Aegean Island architecture – 🏘 Oia is the prettiest village on the island. **Mf54**

Crete The largest of the Greek islands has many diverse landscapes. Crete was home to the Minoan culture, one of the first civilizations in Europe. Around 2000 BC the Minoans built impressive palaces on the island – including the 🏛 **Palace of Knossós** (top photo). 🏘 **Réthimno** (bottom photo) is one of the prettiest towns on Crete with a historic old town and an idyllic harbor. **Md–Mg55**

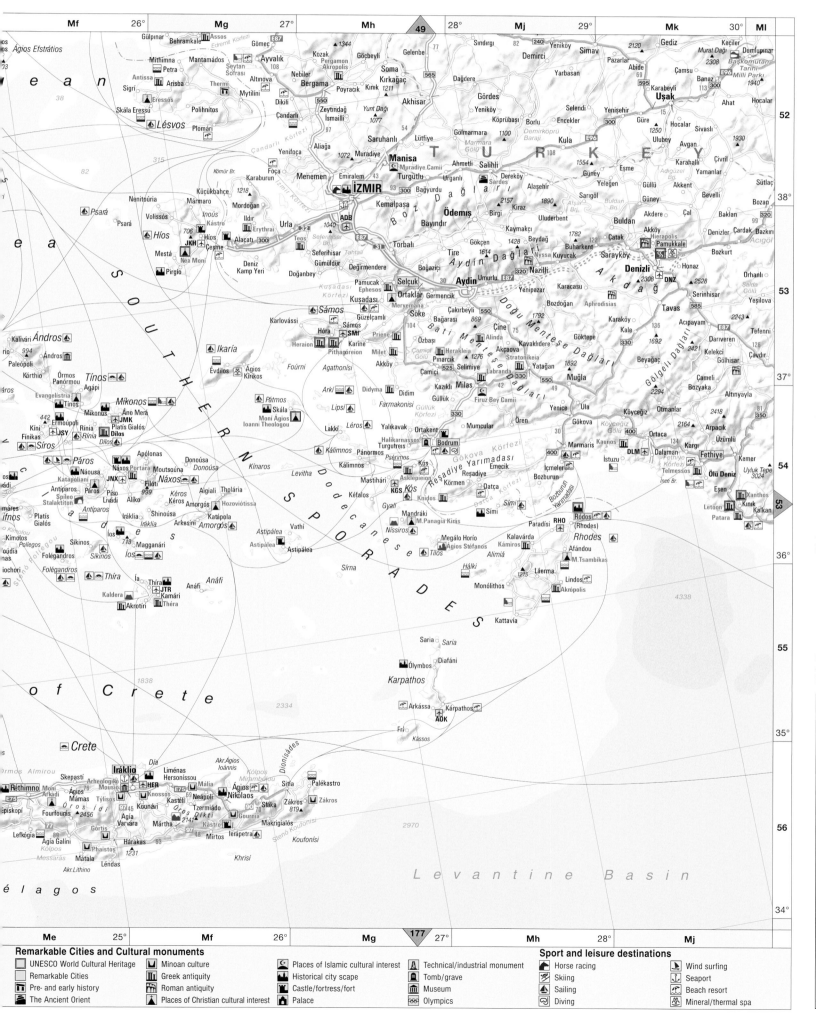

Remarkable Cities and Cultural monuments

UNESCO World Cultural Heritage	Minoan culture	Places of Islamic cultural interest
Remarkable Cities	Greek antiquity	Historical city scape
Pre- and early history	Roman antiquity	Castle/fortress/fort
The Ancient Orient	Places of Christian cultural interest	Palace

Technical/industrial monument	
Tomb/grave	
Museum	
Olympics	

Sport and leisure destinations

Horse racing	Wind surfing	
Skiing	Seaport	
Sailing	Beach resort	
Diving	Mineral/thermal spa	

Southern Turkey, Cyprus

"Like the head of a mare galloping from Asia into the Mediterranean", is how the famed Turkish poet Nazim Hikmet described the shape of his native country. Istanbul,the largest city in Turkey, was once the capital of the mighty Ottoman Empire. Most of **Istanbul** lies in the small European portion of Turkey (3 %) on the Bosporus, a strait separating Europe from Anatolia (Asia Minor). This region between two continents has been a melting pot of different cultures since ancient times.

Turkey is a country surrounded by seas on three sides. The **Black Sea** and the **Sea of Marmara** are north of mainland Turkey. To the west is the **Aegean Sea** and to the south lies the Mediterranean Sea. Many of the numerous islands off the western coast of Turkey belong to Greece. Ionia was the name of the coastal areas of western Turkey in ancient times. The ancient Ionians were ethnically Greek and the region features the **ruins** of several ancient Hellenic cities – including Pergamon, Ephesus, Bodrum (Halicarnassus), and a site believed by many to be the "legendary" city of Troy. Turkey's **southern coast** is a transition zone between mountains and the

Sunset near Lamarka on Cyprus. **MnMp55/56**

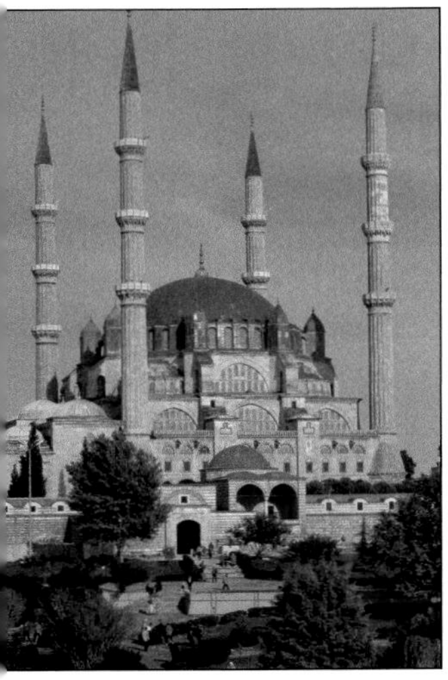

Edirne City in European Turkey – the Selimiye Mosque (photo), a masterpiece of Ottoman religious architecture – Ottoman bridges. **Mg49**

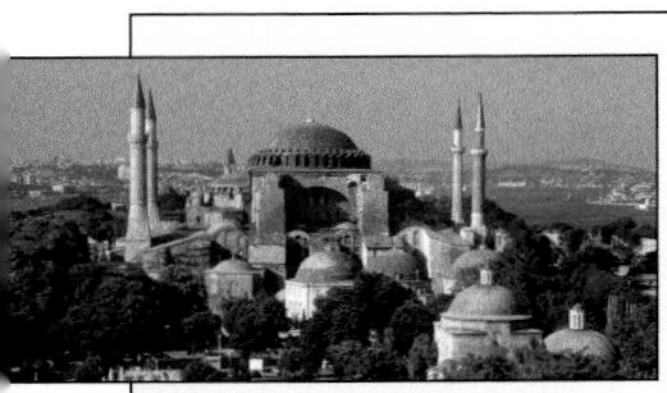

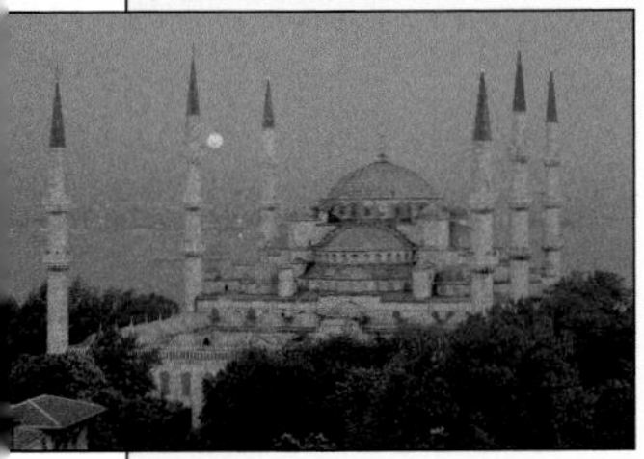

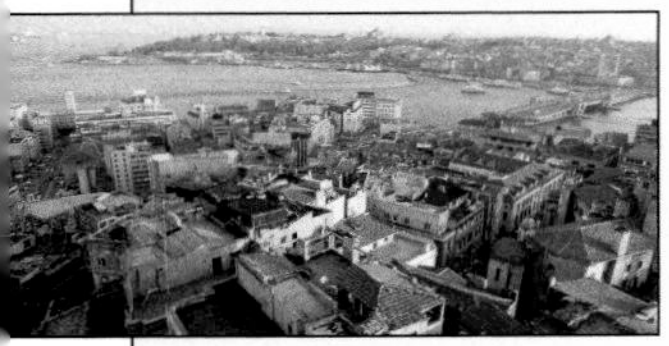

İstanbul Turkey's largest city (population, 13 million) has attractions from the Roman to the modern era – including the Hagia Sofia (top photo), the Blue Mosque (middle photo), and a historic old town (bottom photo). The city is located in both Europe and Asia. **Mj-Mk49/50**

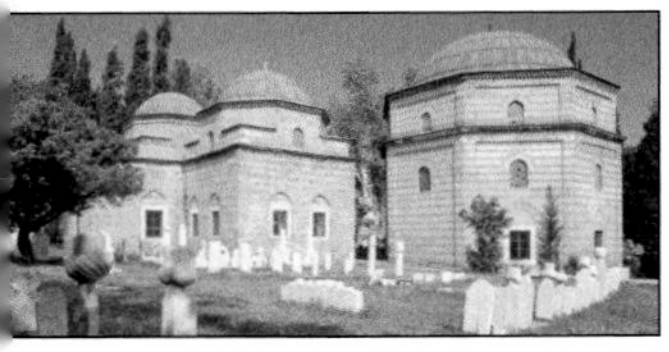

Bursa City in northwestern Turkey – once the residence of Ottoman sultans – historic old town – The Green Mosque – Islamic cemetery (photo). **Mk50**

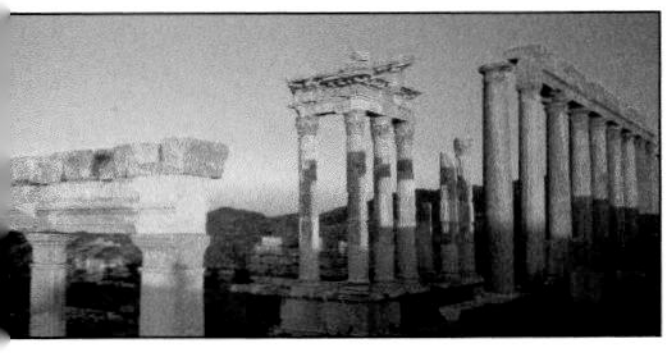

Pergamon This ancient coastal city was the center of an important Hellenic kingdom – large altar to Zeus and Athena – ruins of the Dionysus Temple. **Mh51**

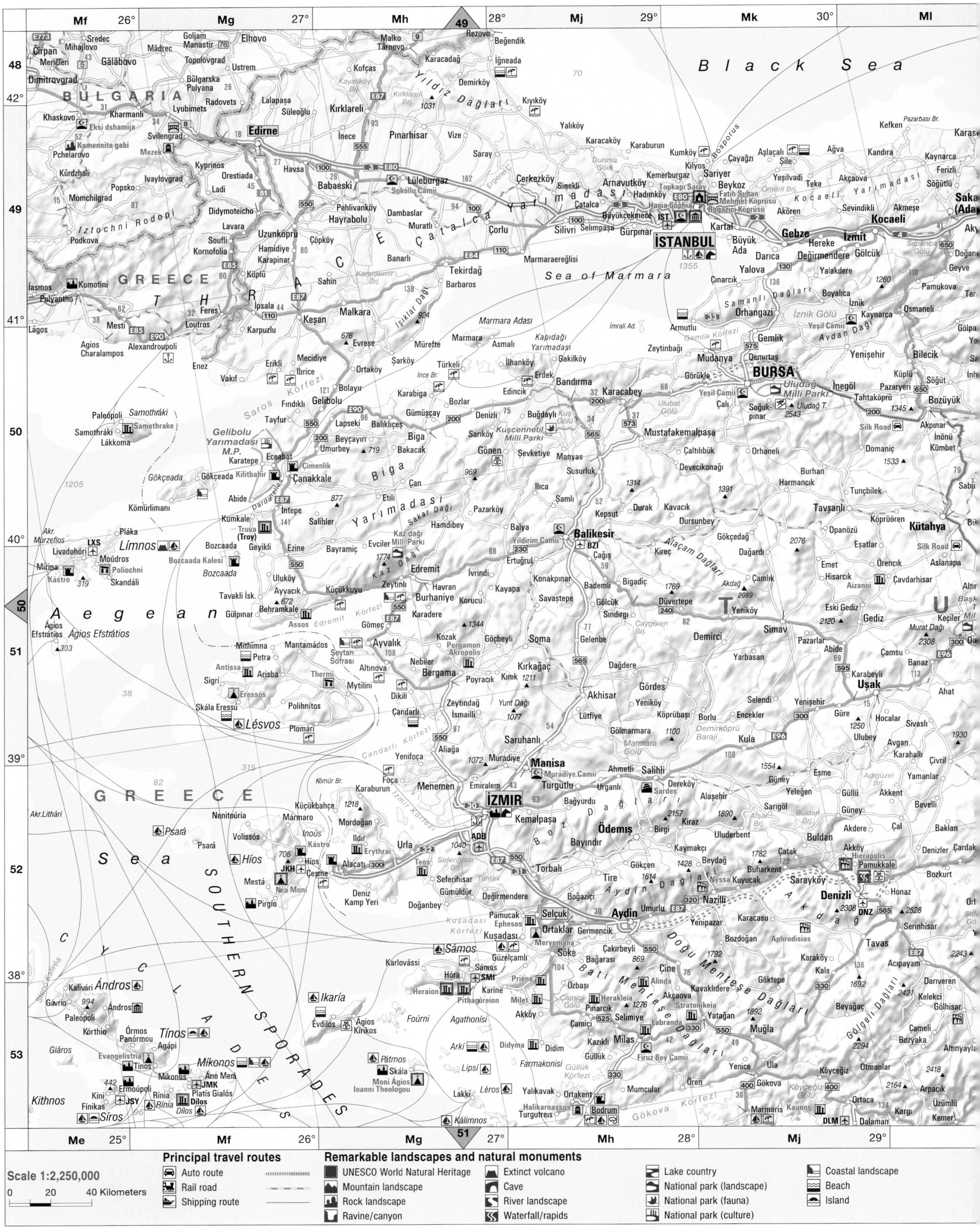

Scale 1:2,250,000

0 20 40 Kilometers

Principal travel routes

- Auto route
- Rail road
- Shipping route

Remarkable landscapes and natural monuments

- UNESCO World Natural Heritage
- Mountain landscape
- Rock landscape
- Ravine/canyon
- Extinct volcano
- Cave
- River landscape
- Waterfall/rapids
- Lake country
- National park (landscape)
- National park (fauna)
- National park (culture)
- Coastal landscape
- Beach
- Island

Mediterranean Sea. The southern coast has many beautiful bays and the **Lycian Coast** between Marmaris and Antalya is a popular tourist destination with long, white beaches.

Two large mountain ranges cover most of Western Turkey: the **Pontus Mountains** in the north and the **Taurus Mountains** in the south. Between these two mountain ranges lies a large, flat plateau around the large and shallow salt lake **Tuz Gölü**, the second largest lake in Turkey. Many of the settlements on the edges of the highlands in western Turkey have ancient histories and were founded by different ancient cultures, including the Romans, Hittites, and the Phrygians.

Central Anatolia features many historic sites connected to the different cultures that once lived in the region. The ruins of Huttusa, the ancient capital of the Hittites, and Ankara, the capital of modern Turkey since 1923, are both located on Anatolia's central plateau. The city Konya has a rich collection of early Islamic art and is the birthplace of the Whirling Dervishes sect. Near Konya, lies the prehistoric ruin of Çatal Hüyük, an ancient town first settled around 7000 BC.

The region around the city of Göreme has been known by the name **Cappadocia** for many centuries and contains many unusual "lunar" landscapes as well as several active volcanoes – including Erciyes Dağı (3,916 m) and Hasan Dağı (3,253 m). Cappadocia's most fascinating attractions are the many homes, churches, and monasteries built into caves and stone formations during ancient times.

Cyprus is an island in the eastern Mediterranean located south of Turkey. The country's population consists mostly of ethnic Greeks and Turks.

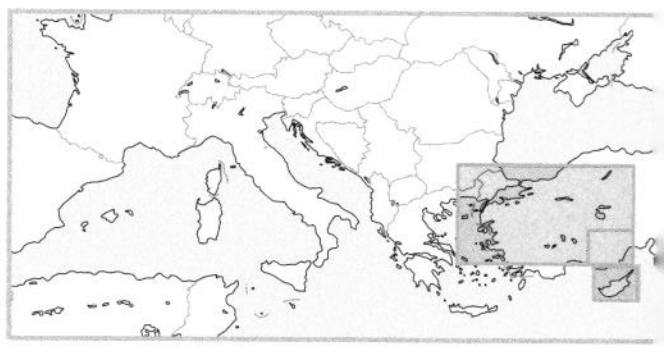

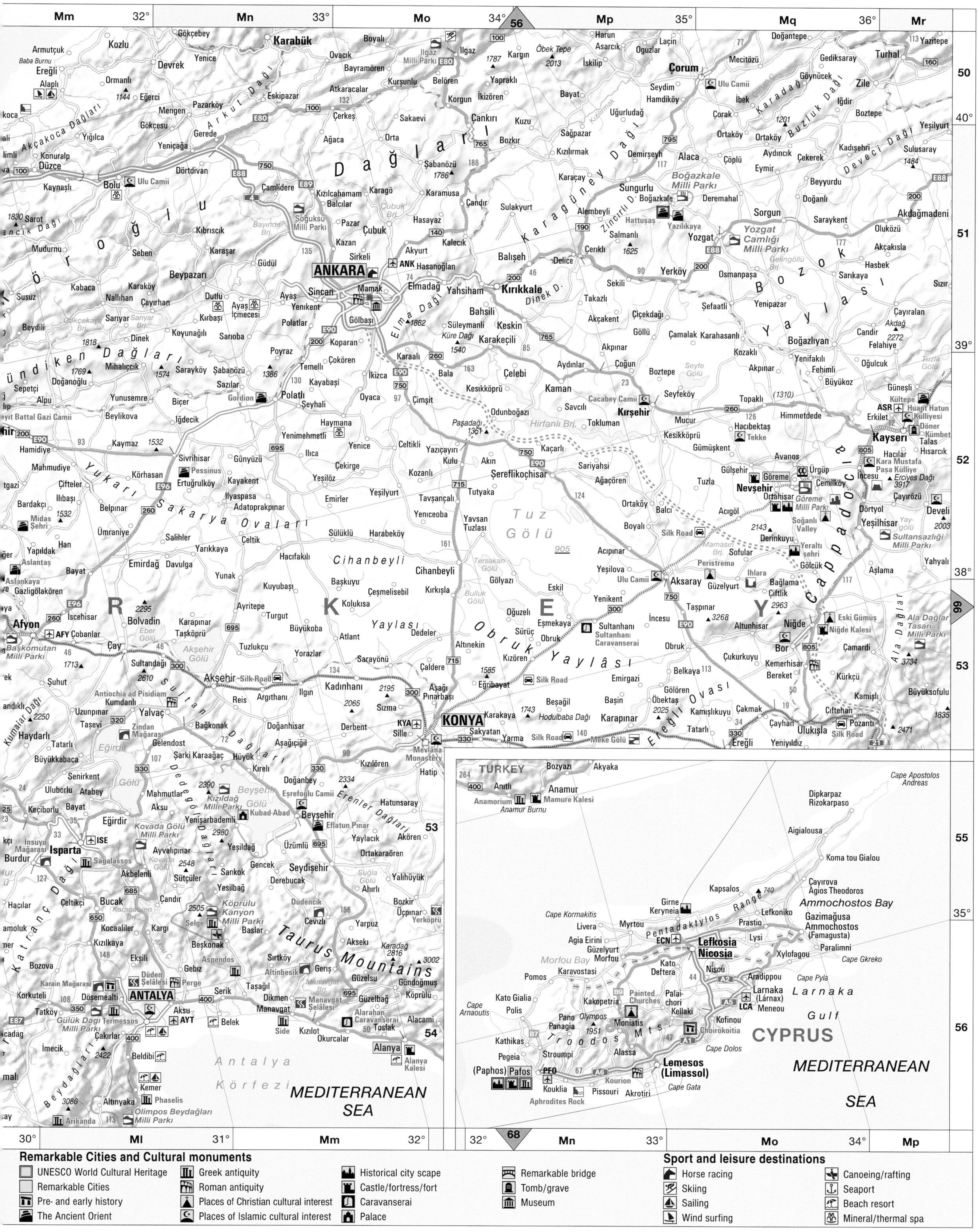

Remarkable Cities and Cultural monuments

- UNESCO World Cultural Heritage
- Remarkable Cities
- Pre- and early history
- The Ancient Orient
- Greek antiquity
- Roman antiquity
- Places of Christian cultural interest
- Places of Islamic cultural interest
- Historical city scape
- Castle/fortress/fort
- Caravanserai
- Palace
- Remarkable bridge
- Tomb/grave
- Museum

Sport and leisure destinations

- Horse racing
- Skiing
- Sailing
- Wind surfing
- Canoeing/rafting
- Seaport
- Beach resort
- Mineral/thermal spa

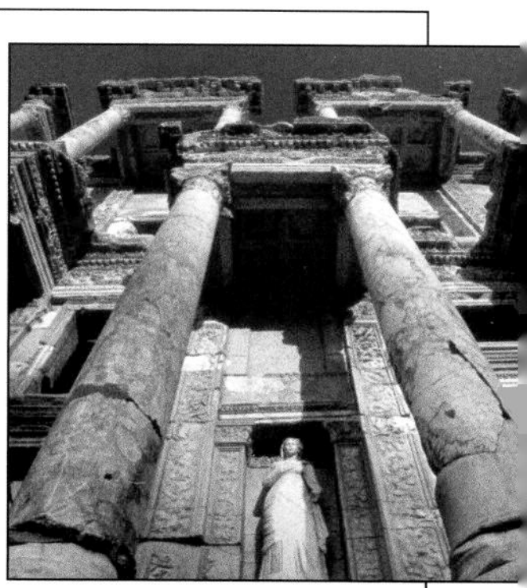

Ephesus An important city during the ancient Greek era. Ephesus contains the ruins of temples and ceremonial sites. The Celsus Library (photo) is the most intact ancient site. **Mh53**

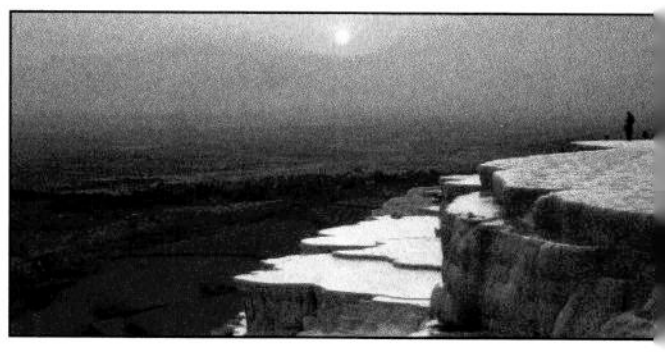

Pamukkale Fascinating natural attraction – UNESCO world heritage site – museum – ancient amphitheater. **Mk53**

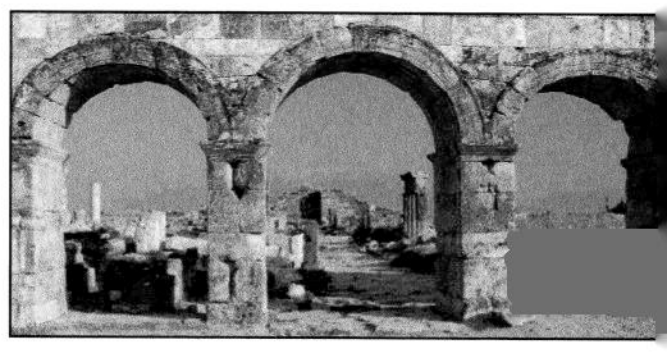

Hierapolis Ruins of a Greek/Roman settlement (photo) – UNESCO world heritage site – largest necropolis in Asia. **Mk53**

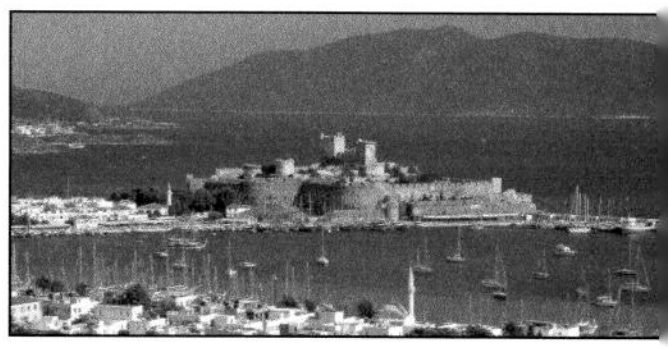

Bodrum Popular seaside resort – St. Peter's Castle (photo); the historic building contains a museum. **Mh53**

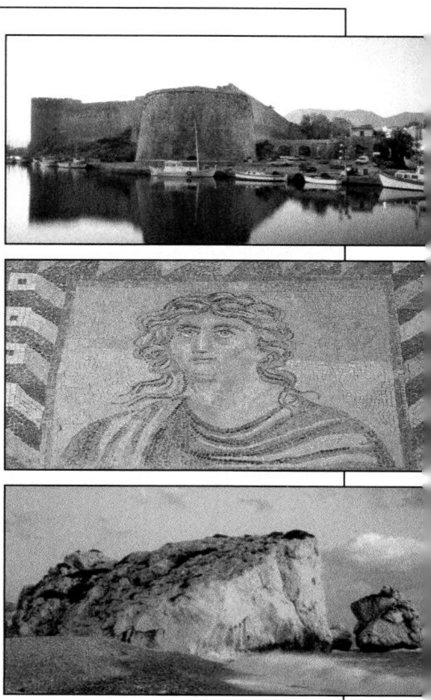

Cyprus The island is a popular tourist destination. Photos from top to bottom: the harbor of Girne, Dionysus mosaic in Paphos, Aphrodite's Rock. **Mn-Mp55/56**

Belarus, Western Russia

Russia's Valdaisky National Park contains many lakes. Mg17

Russia is the largest nation in the world in terms of area. The enormous size of the country has always had an influence on Russia's economy and culture. Russia stretches through two continents, numerous climate zones, and twelve time zones.

The country has a total land area of 17,075,400 km² and a population around 150 million. Most of European Russia comprises a series of vast **plains** stret-

ching up to the Ural Mountains. South of Russia's capital city, Moscow, lies a lowland region encompassing sections of the **Don and Oka river basins**. This lowland borders the **Central Russian Upland**, a large region of rolling hills. The **Volga Upland**, which has a maximum height of 358 meters above sea

St. Petersburg The former capital of the tsars was founded in 1703 and has an abundance of beautiful architecture – UNESCO site. Alexander Column (top photo) was erected in front of the Winter Palace. Smolny Cathedral (bottom photo) was the Soviet headquarters during the Russian Revolution. Mf16

Palaces of the Tsars St. Petersburg is home to several grand palaces from the time of the tsars including Catherine the Great's summer palace in Zarskoje Selo (top photo) and the Peterhof, the "Russian Versailles" (bottom photo). Mf16

Novgorod City in northwestern Russia – during the Middle Ages Novgorod was a leading trading center – St. Sophia's – Museum of Wooden Architecture. Mf16

Minsk Capital city of Belarus – population, 1.8 million – Belarusian National Museum – national circus – heavily damaged during the Second World War – 20th century socialist architecture. Md19

Mir Castle Complex Historic 16th century castle in Belarus – Gothic architecture – UNESCO world heritage site. Md19

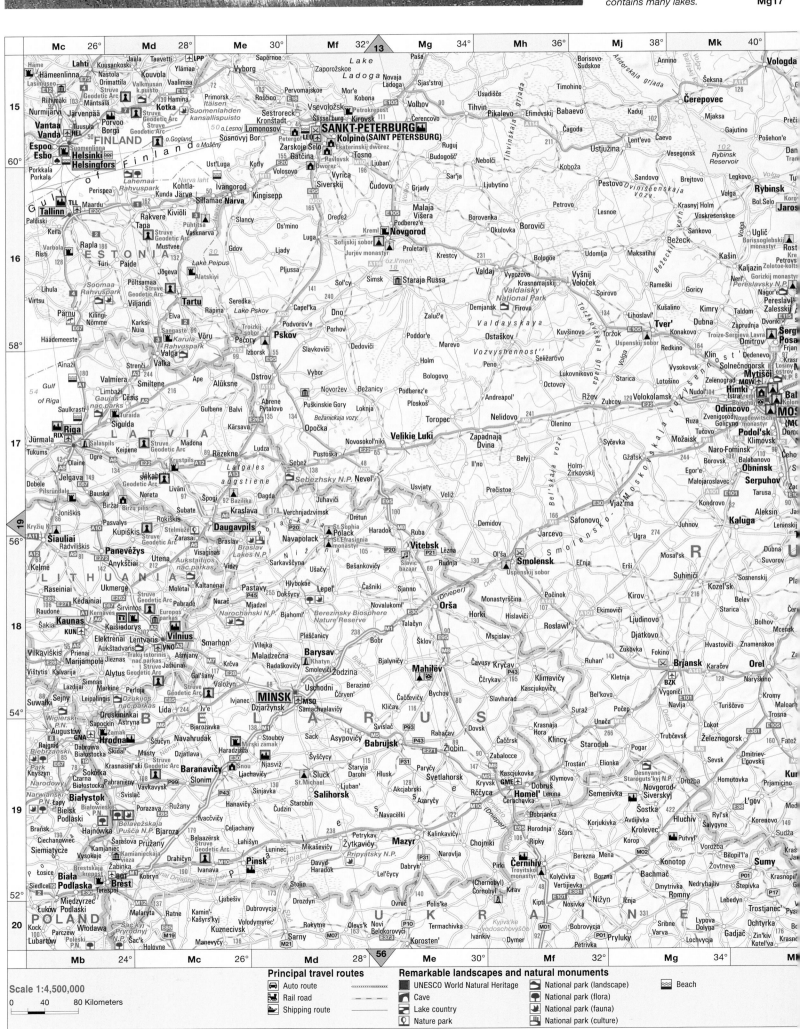

Scale 1:4,500,000

0   40   80 Kilometers

Principal travel routes
- Auto route
- Rail road
- Shipping route
- Auto route

Remarkable landscapes and natural monuments
- UNESCO World Natural Heritage
- Cave
- Lake country
- Nature park
- National park (landscape)
- National park (flora)
- National park (fauna)
- National park (culture)
- Beach

level, is located to the west of the Volga River. The European section of Russia is home to most of the Russian population and is the country's cultural heartland. European Russia is crisscrossed by many powerful ✈ rivers running from north to south – including the 1,870-kilometer-long **Don River** and the 3,350-kilometer-long **Volga River**.

When Peter the Great founded the city of **St. Petersburg** in the 18th century he wanted to give his nation a major port on the Baltic Sea and a "window to the West". The largest city in Russia is the nation's capital city **Moscow**. From 1922 to 1991 the city was also the capital of the powerful Soviet Union. Northwestern Russia features many large ✈ lakes. **Lake Ladoga**, north of St. Petersburg, is the largest lake in Europe with a total area of 18,000 km². Most of European Russia has a continental climate with long, cold winters and short, dry summers. The area between the **Baltic States** and the plains of Russia and Belarus consists of large marshlands with many lakes and forests. The area is also a transition zone between the maritime climate zone of the Baltic region and the continental climate zone in most of Eastern Europe.

Belarus is located just west of European Russia and has a total land area of 207,595 km². Most of the country's territory is covered by flat plains. Agriculture and lumbering are both important sectors of the country's economy. The hills around Belarus' capital, **Minsk**, rise no more than 346 meters in height. The basins of the Desna and the Dnieper rivers encompass large marshlands including the ✈ **Pripyat marshes** along the Ukrainian border. The country has a temperate continental climate with mild winters and cool summers.

Kostroma Historic city trade center on the banks of the Volga river – ▲ Ipatievsky Monastery – resurrection church (photo). **Na17**

Pereslavl Zalessky City on the shore of Lake Pleshcheyevo – ▲ Goritsky Monastery, 14th century structure (photo). **Mk17**

Suzdal' Largest city on the Golden Ring – ▲ impressive citadel (kremlin) – 🏛 museum of wooden architecture. **Na17**

Sergiyev Posad Near Moscow – ▲ Trinity Monastery, spectacular fortress) – 🏛 art history museum – 🏰 tsarist palace. **Mk17**

Moscow The capital city of the Russian Federation (approximately eight million inhabitants) is the nation's leading cultural and economic center. Moscow has an interesting mix of medieval Russian, tsarist, and Stalinist architecture. The historic 🏰 Kremlin (top photo) is Russia's most famous national landmark. Red Square (bottom photo) was once a market square and lies near the ▲ St. Basil's Cathedral (built in 1553). **Mj18**

Volgograd Industrial city on the lower Volga – known as Stalingrad before 1961 – reconstructed in Stalinist style after the Second World War – ⚔ war memorial (photo). **Nc21**

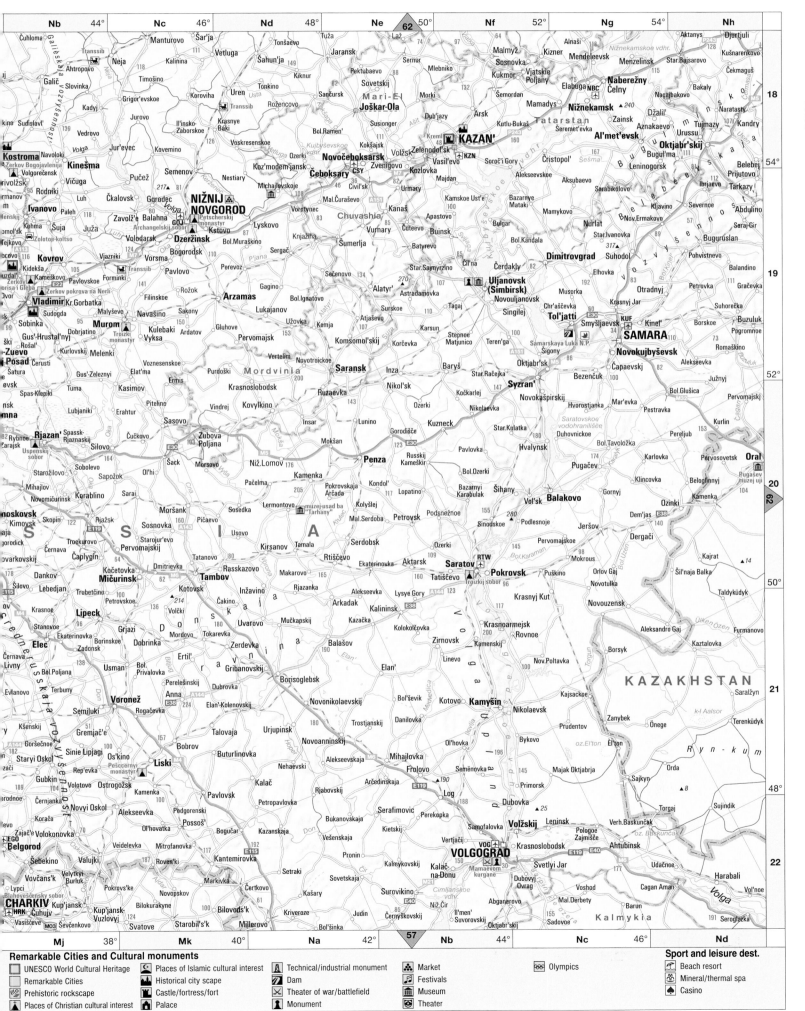

Ukraine, Southern Russia, Black Sea

Before it became an independent nation in 1991, **Ukraine** was politically aligned to neighboring Russia, first in the Russian Empire and later in the Soviet Union. The country is the second largest nation in Europe with a total area of 604,000 km². At least 100 distinct ethnic groups live in Ukraine. Ethnic Russians, who form one fifth of the country's population, are the largest minority group. The Crimean Peninsula was once home to a large distinct

Tatar community before they were expelled from the region by Stalin in 1944. Most of Ukraine is covered by vast **plains** and few areas of the country are situated more than 500 meters above sea level. The plains of Ukraine are covered by fertile, black soil and agriculture is an important sector in the nation's economy. The 🏔

Mount Elbrus in the central Caucasus. **Na24**

L'viv The former capital of the historic region Galicia. L'viv, a UNESCO world heritage site, has an abundance of 🏛 beautiful architecture. The city's opera house (top photo) was built in the Viennese neo-Renaissance style. The medieval market square (bottom photo) is well preserved. **Mc21**

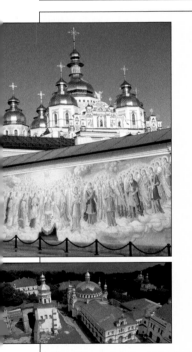

Kiev The capital city of Ukraine was founded in the 5th century. 🏛 St. Sophia's Cathedral (top photo) was completed in 1037. Lavra Monastery (bottom photo) is a pilgrimage site for Orthodox Christians. **Mf20**

Monument to the Motherland Massive Soviet-era 🗽 monument to the victory in the Second World War. **Mf20**

Odessa Ukrainian port city on the Black Sea – 🏛 beautiful baroque and neo-classical architecture. **Mf22**

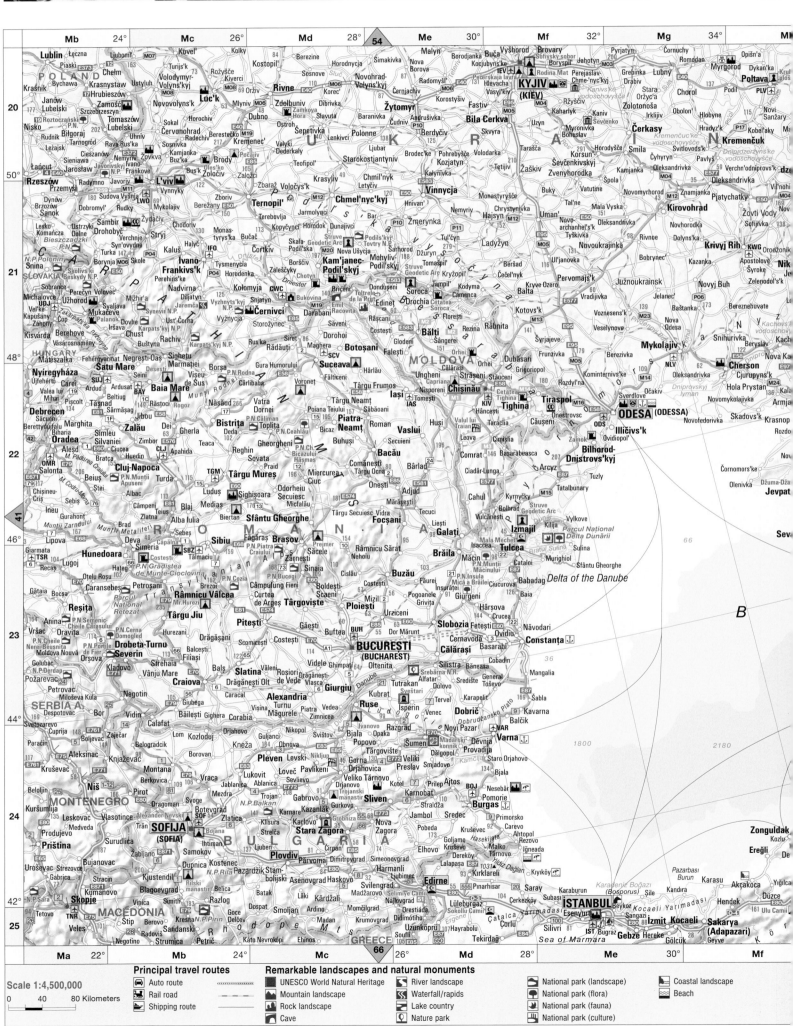

Scale 1:4,500,000

0   40   80 Kilometers

Principal travel routes
- Auto route
- Rail road
- Shipping route

Remarkable landscapes and natural monuments
- UNESCO World Natural Heritage
- Mountain landscape
- Rock landscape
- Cave
- Nature park
- River landscape
- Waterfall/rapids
- Lake country
- National park (landscape)
- National park (flora)
- National park (fauna)
- National park (culture)
- Coastal landscape
- Beach

Ukrainian Carpathians in western Ukraine are a 280-kilometer-long mountain range covered by large forests of beech and fir trees. The mountain Hora Hoverla rises 2,061 meters above sea level and is the highest mountain in Ukraine. Most of southern Ukraine is covered by steppes, while the northern and eastern sections of the country feature expansive forests.

The **Black Sea** (maximum depth, 2,243 m) is connected to the Mediterranean Sea by the Bosporus, the Dardanelles, and the Sea of Marmara. The **Sea of Azov** is a section of the Black Sea connected to the main body of water by the Kerch Strait. The **Crimea** consists mostly of mountain ranges, prairies, and coastal areas with numerous natural harbours and bays. The Black Sea coasts are divided between Ukraine, Russia, Bulgaria, Romania, Turkey, and Georgia. The coastal areas around the Black Sea have a climate similar to that of the Mediterranean with dry, warm summers and wet, mild winters. Western Ukraine has a temperate continental climate with wet, warm summers and cool winters. Most of eastern Ukraine, however, has a continental climate with long, cold winters and short summers. Three major rivers flow through Ukraine: the **Dniester**, the **Bug**, and the 2,200-kilometer-long **Dnieper River**. All three of these rivers flow from north to south into the Black Sea. Kiev, Ukraine's capital city, lies on the Dnieper River and stretches over seven hills.

The Greater Caucasus Mountains are located between the Black and the Caspian Seas. The mountain range is more than 1,000 kilometers long and up to 180 kilometers wide. It is also the site of several high, extinct volcanoes including Mount Elbrus, the highest mountain in Europe.

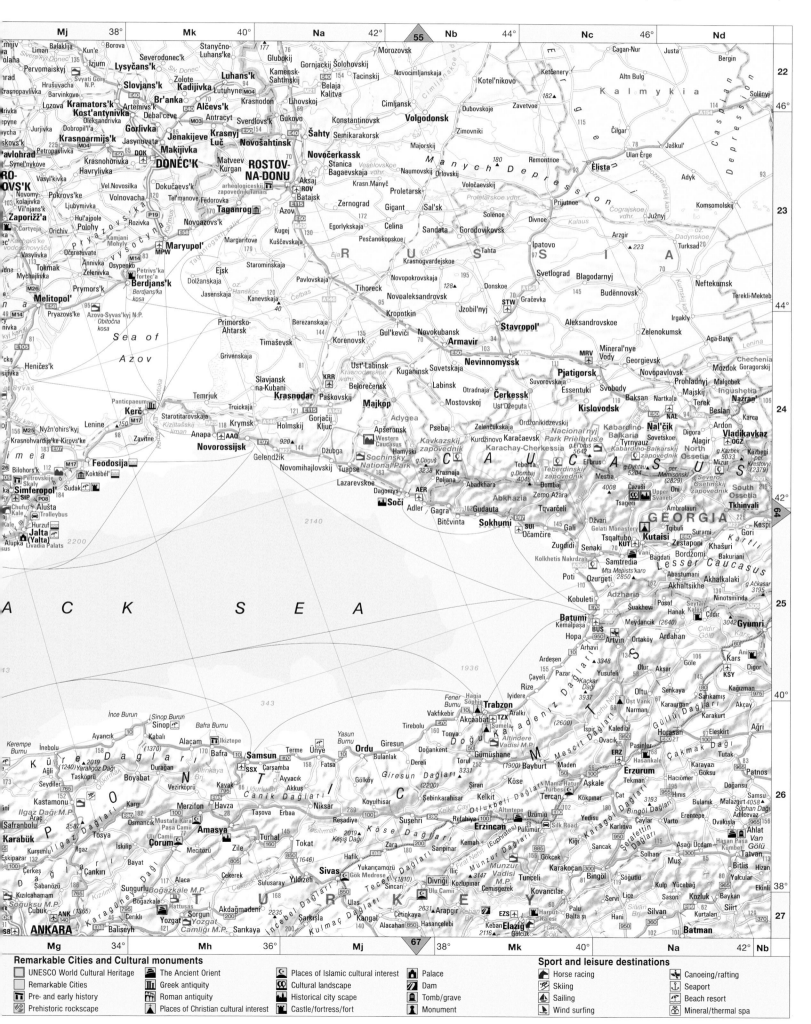

Crimea In 1783 Empress Catherine II annexed the Crimean Peninsula for the Russian Empire. Before the Russia Revolution, the Russian elite and wealthy foreign visitors built grand villas in Crimea. Photos from top to bottom: Livadia Palace, Alupka Palace, the Swallow's Nest. **Mh23**

Sudak Fortified complex on a small peak rising out of the sea – built by Genovese traders in the 14th century. **Mh23**

Mount Elbrus The highest mountain in Europe – in the western Caucasus – twin peaks, western peak rises 5,642 meters. **Nb24**

Mestia Capital of the mountainous Georgian region Svaneti – located in the Greater Caucasus – traditional art museum. **Nb24**

Kutaisi Center of the Imereti region in western Georgia – cathedral, completed in 1033 – distinct local stone architecture. **Nb24**

Remarkable Cities and Cultural monuments

- UNESCO World Cultural Heritage
- Remarkable Cities
- Pre- and early history
- Prehistoric rockscape
- The Ancient Orient
- Greek antiquity
- Roman antiquity
- Places of Christian cultural interest
- Places of Islamic cultural interest
- Cultural landscape
- Historical city scape
- Castle/fortress/fort
- Palace
- Dam
- Tomb/grave
- Monument

Sport and leisure destinations

- Horse racing
- Skiing
- Sailing
- Wind surfing
- Canoeing/rafting
- Seaport
- Beach resort
- Mineral/thermal spa

Itsukushima (top): Shinto shrine in one of Japan's most beautiful coastal regions.
Hong Kong (bottom): The glittering skyline of China's leading financial center.

Taj Mahal (left): A monument to eternal love and Islamic architecture at its finest.
Borobudur (right): The largest Buddhist temple complex in the world.

Asia

Sweeping deserts, foggy rainforests, and the tallest mountains on Earth can all be found in Asia. The ancient cultures of Mesopotamia were among the earliest civilizations. The ancient philosophies of China, Islam, Hinduism, Buddhism, as well as many other religions and cultures make Asia a continent with an incredibly rich cultural legacy.

Asia · The continent

Asia has a total area of 44.4 million km² and encompasses around one-third of the world's land. The continent has a maximum length of 11,000 kilometers from east to west and a maximum length of 8,500 kilometers from north to south. The vast majority of Asia's land area is situated above the equator in the northern hemisphere. Only a few areas in Southeast Asia and the Indian subcontinent are located south of the equator. The

Mount Everest (8,850 m), the world's tallest mountain.

continent borders the Arctic Ocean in the north, the Pacific Ocean in the east, and the Indian Ocean in the south. In the west, Asia borders Europe, the Mediterranean Sea, North Africa and the Red Sea. The Bering Sea, a section of the Pacific, separates Siberia in northern Asia from North America. The Arabian Penin-

sula, India, the Malay Peninsula, Korea, and Kamchatka are the largest and most significant of the many peninsulas on the continent. The Japanese Islands are located off the northeastern coast of mainland Asia. A large belt of mountain systems extends from the Caucasus (maximum height, 5,642 m) and the Pontic Mountains (3,937 m) in western Asia to the **Himalayas** and farther east into Southeast Asia.

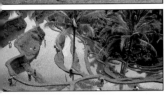

Asia stretches from the frozen tundra above the Arctic Circle to the hot and humid tropics along the equator. Northern Asia is home to vast treeless plains (top photo) and central Asia encompasses many large deserts (middle photo). The climates of South and Southeast Asia (bottom photo: the Philippines) are greatly influenced by monsoon winds.

All of the world's 14 mountains rising above 8,000 meters are located in Asia, most in the Himalayas. Mount Everest in the Himalayas is the world's tallest mountain. K2 (photo), with a height of 8,611 meters is the world's second tallest mountain.

The Chang Jiang (Yangtze) River in China is the longest river in Asia with a total length of 6,300 kilometers (top photo). The Huang He/Yellow (5,460 km), Mekong (4,500 km), Amur (4,415 km), and Ob (5,400 km) Rivers are all among the longest rivers in the world. The Aral Sea, a large inland body of water (bottom photo), has an area of around 33,640 km². In recent decades the sea has shrunk dramatically in size.

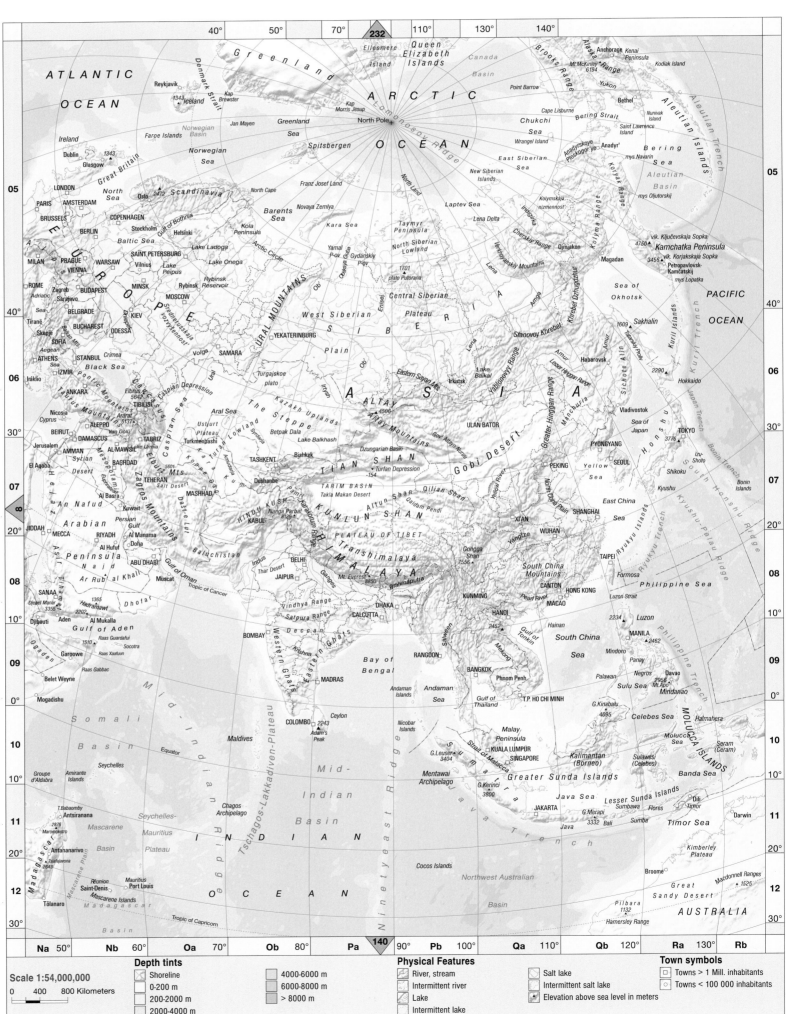

Scale 1:54,000,000

0   400   800 Kilometers

Depth tints
- Shoreline
- 0-200 m
- 200-2000 m
- 2000-4000 m
- 4000-6000 m
- 6000-8000 m
- > 8000 m

Physical Features
- River, stream
- Intermittent river
- Lake
- Intermittent lake
- Salt lake
- Intermittent salt lake
- Elevation above sea level in meters

Town symbols
- Towns > 1 Mill. inhabitants
- Towns < 100 000 inhabitants

Asia is by far the most populated of the world's seven continents. The continent's **population** of more than 3.4 billion is unequally distributed. Sparsely populated Mongolia has a population density of just two inhabitants per square kilometer. Bangladesh, one of the world's most crowded nations, has a population density in excess of 900 inhabitants per square kilometer. China and India, the world's most populous nations, are both home to more than one billion people. Most of the **world's major religions** were founded in Asia many centuries ago. Judaism, Islam and Christianity all originated in western Asia. India was the birthplace of Hinduism and Buddhism, while Taoism and Confucianism both originated in China.

Left: Veiled woman in Oman.
Right: Balinese dancer.

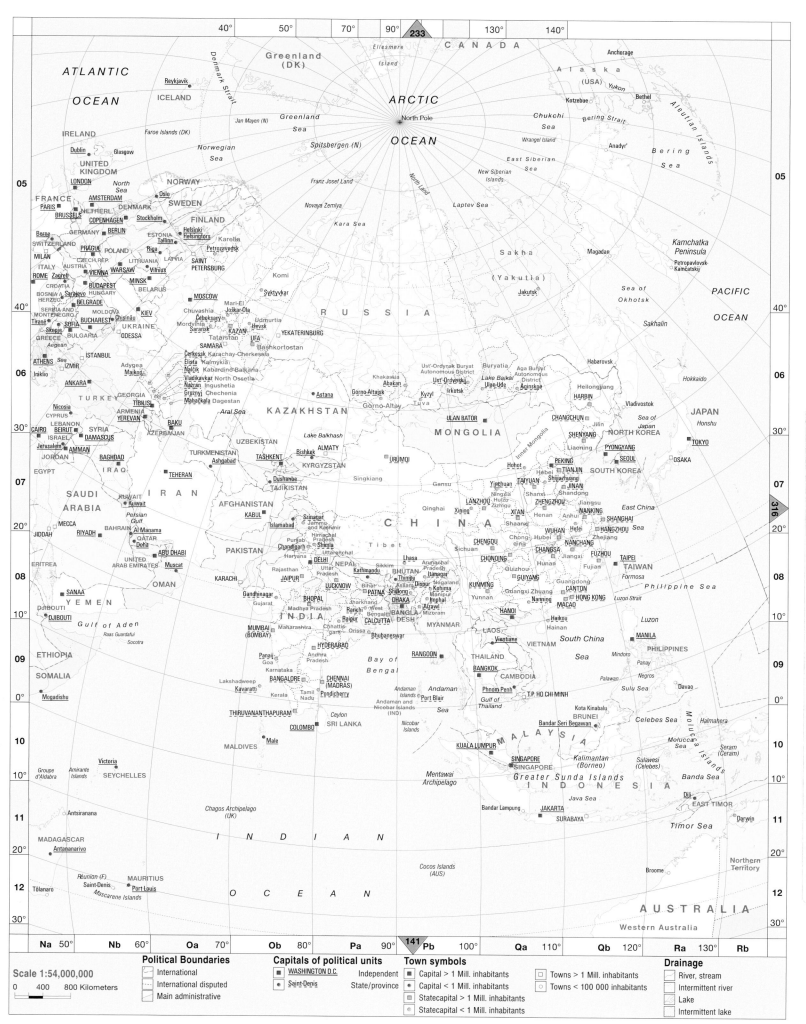

Countries and Flags

Afghanistan
Armenia
Azerbaijan
Bahrain
Bangladesh
Bhutan
Brunei
Burma
Cambodia
China
East Timor
Georgia
India
Indonesia
Iran
Iraq
Israel
Japan
Jordan
Kazakhstan
Korea, North
Korea, South
Kuwait
Kyrgyzstan
Laos
Lebanon
Malaysia
Maldives
Mongolia
Nepal
Oman
Pakistan
Philippines
Qatar
Saudi-Arabia
Singapore
Sri Lanka
Syria
Taiwan
Tajikistan
Thailand
Turkey
Turkmenistan
United Arab Emirates
Uzbekistan
Vietnam
Yeman

Scale 1:54,000,000

0   400   800 Kilometers

Political Boundaries	Capitals of political units	Town symbols		Drainage
International	■ WASHINGTON D.C. Independent	■ Capital > 1 Mill. inhabitants	□ Towns > 1 Mill. inhabitants	River, stream
International disputed	● Saint-Denis State/province	● Capital < 1 Mill. inhabitants	□ Towns < 100 000 inhabitants	Intermittent river
Main administrative		■ Statecapital > 1 Mill. inhabitants		Lake
		● Statecapital < 1 Mill. inhabitants		Intermittent lake

In 1967, ten Southeast Asian nations joined together to form ASEAN, a community founded to increase economic and cultural cooperation in the region. The ten members of ASEAN are Brunei, Indonesia, Cambodia, Laos, Malaysia, Myanmar (Burma), Singapore, Thailand, the Philippines, and Vietnam. ASEAN is now home to more than 500 million people and comprises several rapidly developing economies.

Northern Asia

The 2,000-kilometer-long **Ural Mountains** form a natural boundary between Asia and Europe. Naroda, the tallest peak in the mountain range, rises 1,894 meters above sea level. The Urals stretch from the steppes of southern Russia near the border of Kazakhstan to the Russian Arctic Ocean coast. East of the Urals lies **Siberia**, a region encompassing most of Russia's territory. Siberia stretches over 7,000 kilometers from the Urals to the

Pacific Ocean and the greatest distance from north to south in Siberia is around 3,500 kilometers. The **West Siberian Plain**, the world's largest plain, covers 2.6 million km² and is drained by the Ob River and its many tributaries. The plain is rich in valuable mineral resources including natural gas and oil.

Coastal wetlands on the Kamchatka Peninsula.

Ural Mountains The "border" between Europe and Asia – Komi virgin forests, UNESCO world heritage site.

West Siberian Plain The series of lowlands has a total area of around 2.6 million km² – large marshlands – more than 2,000 rivers – frequent flooding in summer.

Yenisei River Major river in Siberia – 4,130 kilometers long – the river's basin spans 2.6 million km².

Central Siberian Plateau Series of plateaus – Putoran Mountains, tallest peak 1,701 meters – taiga and permafrost ground.

Altai The name of a region and mountain range containing Siberia's tallest mountains. Beluha, the tallest mountain rises 4,506 meters. The region encompasses diverse landscapes including steppes, forests, sub-alpine and alpine regions. Altai is also home to several rare animal species such as snow leopards.

Sayan Mountains Mountain range between central and northern Asia – highest mountain, Munku Sardyk (3,491 m) in the Eastern Sayan Mountains.

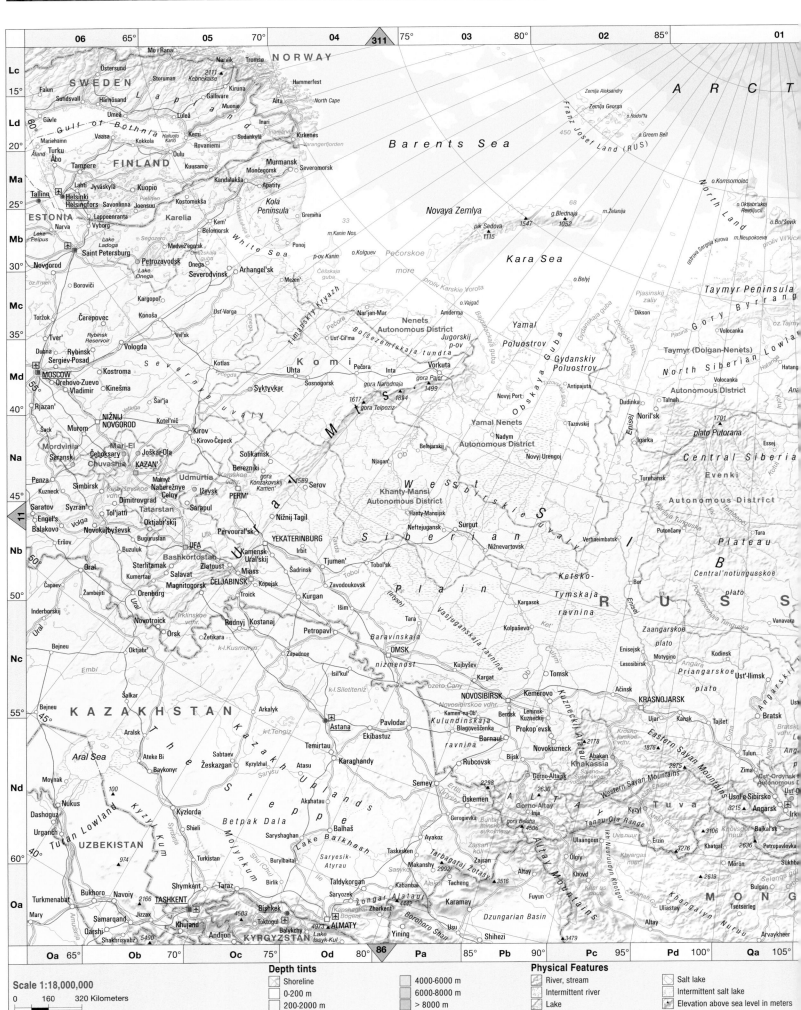

Scale 1:18,000,000

0   160   320 Kilometers

Depth tints

- ⊠ Shoreline
- ☐ 0-200 m
- ☐ 200-2000 m
- ☐ 2000-4000 m
- ☐ 4000-6000 m
- ☐ 6000-8000 m
- ☐ > 8000 m

Physical Features

- River, stream
- Intermittent river
- Lake
- Intermittent lake
- Salt lake
- Intermittent salt lake
- ▲ Elevation above sea level in meters

Directly to the east of the West Siberian Plain lies the **Central Siberian Plateau**. The plateau, located between the **Yenisey** and **Lena Rivers**, covers around 3.5 million km². The tallest peak in the plateau region lies in the Putoran Mountains and rises 1,701 meters. The **North Siberian Lowlands**, a region of vast plains, stretch between the plateau and the **Taymyr Peninsula**. The archipelago Severnaya Zemlya is situated north of

this region and off the Arctic Ocean coast of Russia. **Lake Baikal** in southern Siberia is the largest freshwater lake in Asia and the world's deepest with a maximum depth of 1,620 meters. East of Lake Baikal in southern Siberia lies a region of high mountain ranges that stretch to Russia's southeastern borders. The various ranges in this region include the Altai Mountains, the Stanovoy Range, and the Eastern and Western Sayan Range.

Northeastern Siberia is also a mountainous region with numerous mountain ranges and tall peaks. The **Verkhoyansk** and **Kolyma Mountain Ranges** stretch through much of the region. The Yana, Indigirka, and Kolyma plains consist of vast infertile moorlands. The Chukchi Peninsula is mainland Siberia's easternmost region. East of the peninsula is the Bering Strait, which connects the Bering Sea and the Arctic Ocean. **Kamchatka**,

a 1,250-kilometer-long peninsula in Siberia's far east, separates the Sea of Okhotsk from the Pacific Ocean. Around seven million square kilometers of Siberia's land is covered by permafrost, a layer of frozen rock and soil. There are three distinct climate and vegetation zones in Siberia: the barren arctic northern islands, a broad strip of tundra along the Arctic coast, and a large taiga region with sub-arctic forests.

Lake Baikal 31,500 km², 636 kilometers long, and 40 to 80 kilometers wide – deepest freshwater lake on Earth, maximum depth 1,620 meters.

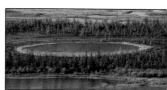

Yakutian Taiga Sub-arctic mixed forests consisting mostly of larches – permafrost ground.

Russia's Arctic Coast Long coast consisting of barren, uninhabited moorlands, river deltas, and steep rocky areas – photo: coastal area near Anadyr.

The Bering Strait Named for the Russian explorer Vitus Bering – connects the Bering Sea and the Arctic Ocean – photo: Cape Dezhnev.

Kamchatka A chain of volcanoes runs through this 1,200-kilometer-long peninsula. The peninsula covers 350,000 km². Southeastern Kamchatka is home to many geysers. Photos from top to bottom: Kliuchevskoi (4,750 m), Mutnovsky, Karymsky.

Near and Middle East

The Middle East is a term encompassing a variety of different nations. The term usually refers to the countries along the eastern coast of the Mediterranean, on the Arabian Peninsula, and along the Persian Gulf.

Anatolia (Asia Minor) contains most of Turkey's territory. Anatolia consists of a large central plateau flanked by two tall mountain ranges; the **Taurus Mountains** in the south and the **Pontus Mountains**

in the north. The two mountain ranges stretch from western Turkey to the eastern edges of the country. **Lake Van**, Turkey's largest lake, is located in eastern Anatolia near the Iranian border.

The **Arabian Peninsula** is located between the Persian Gulf and the Red Sea and is the westernmost of Asia's sub-

The Indus River has a total length of 3,200 kilometers.

Anatolia (Asia Minor) Large central plateau flanked by tall mountain ranges – salt lakes – photo: mountains in western Anatolia.

Jordan Rift Valley The Dead Sea is the lowest point on the Earth's surface (-829 m) – Sea of Galilee (photo) – Jordan River.

Negev Desert covering most of southern Israel – the southern sections are the driest – photo: hills near the Red Sea.

Sinai Peninsula Arid peninsula in Egypt – between the Gulf of Suez and the Gulf of Aqaba – photo: Mount Sinai.

Euphrates River 2,500-kilometer-long river – forms the boundaries of Mesopotamia together with the Tigris River – the two rivers merge to form the Shatt al-Arab River.

Rub al'Khali/The Empty Quarter Large sand desert covering almost a third of the Arabian Peninsula – sparsely populated region.

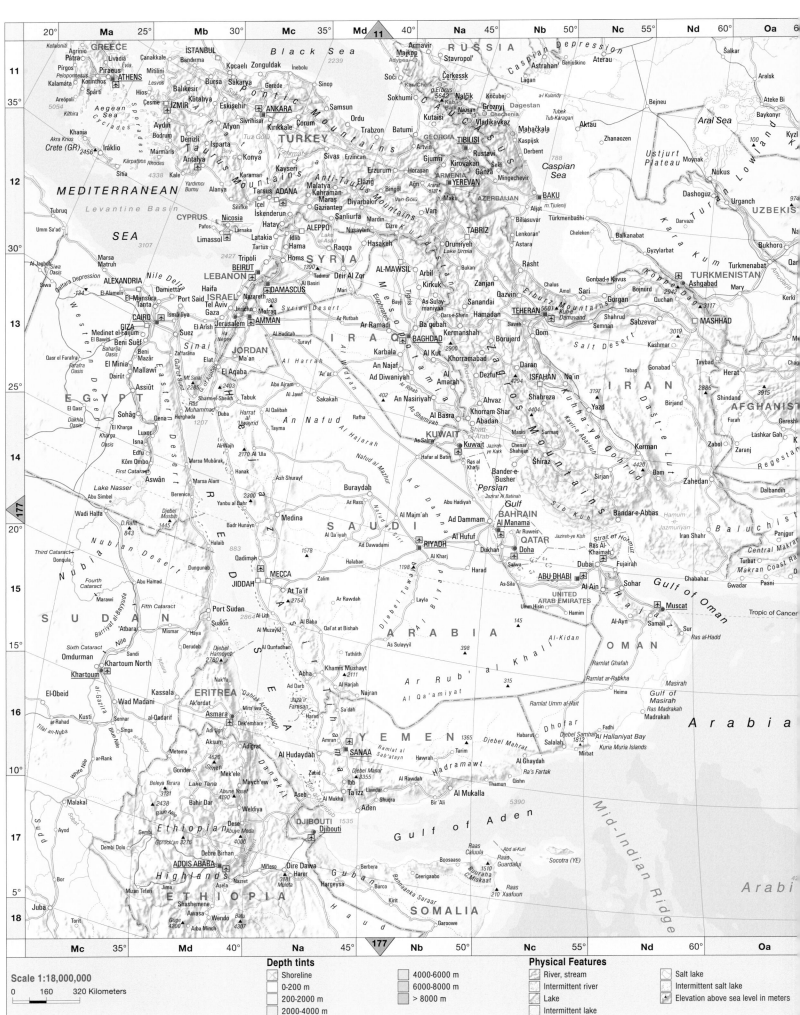

Scale 1:18,000,000

0   160   320 Kilometers

Depth tints
- Shoreline
- 0-200 m
- 200-2000 m
- 2000-4000 m
- 4000-6000 m
- 6000-8000 m
- > 8000 m

Physical Features
- River, stream
- Intermittent river
- Lake
- Intermittent lake
- Salt lake
- Intermittent salt lake
- Elevation above sea level in meters

continents. The peninsula consists overwhelmingly of vast barren deserts and the area is an extension of Africa's Sahara Desert. The coastal mountains in northwestern Arabia border a region of interior highlands. The peninsula's interior is also the location of its most barren deserts including the **Nafud Desert** with its red sands and the Rub'al Khali. The **Rub'al Khali** covers 780,000 km² and is often referred to as the Empty Quarter

because most of the area is uninhabited. Historic **Mesopotamia**, the mountainous highlands of Iran, Armenia, and the Caucasus nations are located north of the Persian Gulf. Iran is one of the most mountainous nations in the Middle East. The large **Alborz** and **Zagros Mountain ranges** cover most of western and northern Iran. Damavand (5,601 m), Iran's highest peak, is located in the Alborz Mountains. Eastern and Central Iran contain large

basins with numerous salt lakes and vast deserts. **Dasht-e-Lut**, a large sand desert in central and eastern Iran, is one of the hottest places on the Earth.
The **Caspian Sea**, the world's largest inland body of water, is around 1,200 kilometers long from north to south. The Caspian Sea basin is bounded in the west by the **Caucasus Mountains**. A region of vast semi-arid lowlands is located to the east of the Caspian Sea. This region

encompasses the almost uninhabited **Ustjurt plateau** and the **Kara Kum** desert, a section of the **Turan lowlands**. A large endhoric body of water, the **Aral Sea**, borders this arid region.
The **Hindu Kush** mountain range in Afghanistan contains several peaks rising more than 7,000 meters including Tirich Mir (7,707 m). The range is a branch of the **Pamir Mountains**, a mountain system extending to the Himalayas.

Hajar Mountains Mountain range in Oman in southeastern Arabia – tallest mountain, Jabal Shams (3,108 m).

The Steppes and Deserts of Central Asia Includes the vast arid and semi-arid region east of the Aral Sea; the Turan lowlands, Kazahk steppes, and Kara Kum deserts.

Alborz Mountains Range in northern Iran, extending to the Caspian Sea coast – photo: Damavand (5,601 m).

Hindu Kush Mountain range in northeastern Afghanistan – more than 20 mountains above 7,000 meters – Tirich Mir (7,707 m).

Toba Kakar Range Mountain range in Pakistan and Afghanistan – southeast of Kandahar – Sakir (3,092 m).

Pamir Mountains A combination of several tall mountain ranges located near the Himalayas – highest peak, Kungur (7,719 m).

Political Boundaries
International
International disputed
Main administrative

Transportation
Interstate Hwy./Motorway
Main road
Railway
Airport

Capitals of political units
■ WASHINGTON D.C.   Independent
◉ Richmond   State/province

Town symbols
● Capital > 1 Mill. inhabitants   □ Towns > 1 Mill. inhabitants
● Capital < 1 Mill. inhabitants   ○ Towns 100 000 bis 1 Mill. inhabitants
▣ Statecapital > 1 Mill. inhabitants   ○ Towns < 100 000 inhabitants
◉ Statecapital < 1 Mill. inhabitants

Turkey, Caucasus Region

With a total area of 780,576 km² and a population around 68 million the Republic of Turkey has a relatively low population density. The country's territory lies on two continents: Europe and Asia. The province of Thrace which encompasses three percent of Turkey's territory is geographically European, while the rest of Turkey lies in Asia.

The historic Turkish city of **Istanbul** is situated on the Bosporus strait, the

boundary between Europe and Asia. With more than ten million inhabitants Istanbul is the most populous city in Turkey. Turkey is divided into 80 provinces ruled from the national capital **Ankara** in the mountains of Anatolia.

Turkey is home to a variety of unique landscapes and regions. The country's

Natural stone formations near Göreme (Turkey). **Mh26**

The Turkish Riviera The coastal area contains ancient historic 🏛 sites and beautiful ⚓ bays. Antalya has the most beautiful ⚓ harbor in the region. Photos from top to bottom: ancient burial site near Daylan, the beach of Ölu Deniz, Antalya harbor. **Me-Mf27**

Ankara Turkey's capital – 🏛 Roman ruins – Museum of Anatolian Civilization – photo: Atatürk mausoleum. **Mg26**

Konya 🕌 Former capital of the Seljuk Empire – Mevlevi Convent – photo: Whirling Dervishes. **Mg27**

Göreme Rocky landscapes and the site of unique stone churches (top photo) in the heart of Anatolia. Göreme Museum Park (bottom photo) is a world heritage site. **Mh26**

Scale 1:4,500,000
0   40   80 Kilometers

Principal travel routes
- Auto route
- Rail road
- Shipping route

Remarkable landscapes and natural monuments
- UNESCO World Natural Heritage
- Mountain landscape
- Rock landscape
- Ravine/canyon
- Cave
- Waterfall/rapids
- Nature park
- National park (landscape)
- National park (flora)
- National park (fauna)
- National park (culture)
- Coastal landscape
- Beach
- Island

southern and western coasts contain numerous ancient 🏛 archeological sites including the ruins of **Pergamon**, **Troy**, and **Ephesus**.

Northern Turkey is covered by the tall mountains and foothills of the 🏔 **Pontic Mountain Range** which extend to the Turkish Black Sea coast. Like the north, southern Turkey is also a mountainous region. The 🏔 **Taurus Mountain Range** and its foothills extend through most

of southern Turkey. The highlands of eastern Turkey contain the nation's highest mountain 🏔 **Mount Ararat**, an extinct volcano which rises 5,165 meters. Anatolia's large central plateau features many of Turkey's unique natural and cultural attractions. Several large 🌊 **salt lakes** including Tuz Gölü are located in the region. **Cappadocia**, a historic region on the central plateau, is home to hundreds of unique ancient 🏛 churches

carved into rock formations. The ruins at Hattusa are ancient remnants of the Hittite civilization and 🏛 Konya is the spiritual center of the Whirling Dervishes, a religious sect famous for its unique spiritual dances.

The Firat (Euphrates) and Dicle (Tigris) Rivers are the principal rivers in eastern Turkey. Several large dams constructed on the rivers have helped to transform eastern Turkey into a fertile region with

productive agriculture. Eastern Turkey is the traditional homeland of Turkey's large Kurdish minority. The region is also home to 🌊 **Lake Van**, Turkey's largest lake. Mountainous northeastern Turkey is covered by the foothills of the Caucasus which stretch into neighboring countries. Turkey's 🏖 **Black Sea coast** is a fertile region with heavy rainfall throughout the year. The coast is the site of numerous ancient settlements and historic 🏛 ruins.

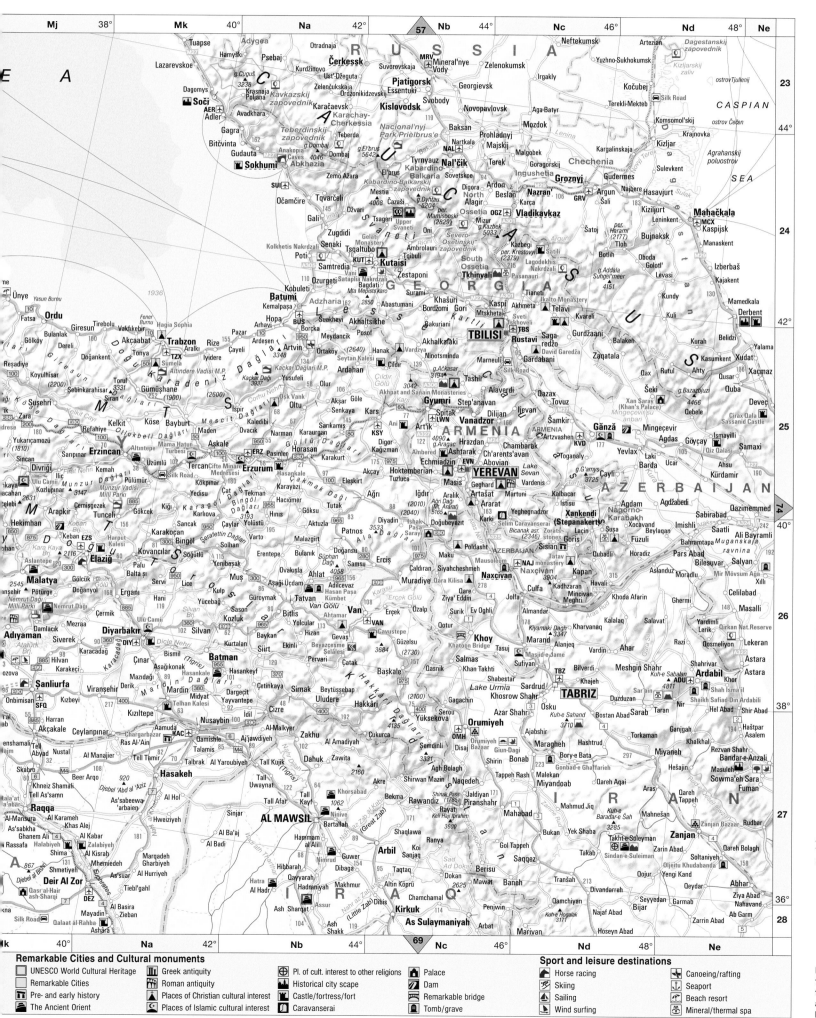

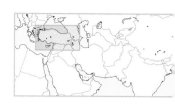

Hattuşa 🏛 Ancient ruins in the Anatolian highlands – once the center of Hittite civilization – preserved city gates (photo) – UNESCO world heritage site. **Mh26**

Nemrut Daği 🏛 Extensive burial site of Antiochus I. (69–38 BC) – large statues of kings and gods (photo). **Mk26**

Lake Van The largest lake in Turkey was first settled around 840 BC. Photos from top to bottom: the ruins of 🏛 Ahtamar church, 🏛 Hasan Paşa Kümbret, 🏰 castle ruins, 🌊 waterfalls near Muradiye. **Nb26**

Aleppo Ancient 🏛 trading and cultural center in Syria – 🏰 citadel containing a mosque and a Mamluk palace (photo). **Mj27**

Hatra 🏛 Historic remnants of an ancient fortified city in Mesopotamia (Iraq) – Parthian architecture – large temple to Greek and Parthian gods (photo) – UNESCO world heritage site. **Nb28**

Lebanon, Syria, Israel, Jordan, Iraq

North of the **Arabian Peninsula** is a large triangle shaped region covered mostly by deserts and semi-arid plains. Situated along the Mediterranean coast, the western section of the region is home to several mountain ranges and rift valleys. The **Lebanon** and **Anti-Lebanon Mountains** are the region's principal coastal mountain ranges. Both ranges merge with a series of smaller mountain ranges in Syria and Jordan. The **Gulf of Aqaba**

and the **Jordan Rift Valley** are sections of an enormous fracture zone that also encompasses the Great Rift Valley in Africa. The surface of the salty **Dead Sea** lies around 829 meters below sea level and is the lowest point on the Earth's surface. The coasts, coastal mountains, and interior mountains of Israel, Lebanon, Syria,

Camels were once vital for travel through the Syrian desert. **MjMk27**

Baalbek Spiritual center for the ☉ Phoenicians and ☉ Romans – Temple of Jupiter (photo) – UNESCO world heritage site. **Mj28**

Damascus ⬛ Capital city of Syria – the old town is a UNESCO world heritage site – ☉ Omayyad Mosque – ☉ Saladin's mausoleum – "burial site" of St. John. **Mj29**

Acre (Acco) ⬛ Port city in Israel – medieval town center – historic "crusaders" buildings – ☉ Ahmed-al-Jazzar mosque. **Mh29**

Jerusalem The capital of Israel is a holy city for three major religions; Judaism, Christianity, and Islam. The ☉ Dome of the Rock (top photo) is at the center of the Temple mount in the old city. The ☉ al-Aqsa mosque also lies in the old town. At the foot of the Temple mount is the ☉ Western Wall (bottom photo), a Jewish holy site. The Via Dolorosa stretches from the ☉ Sacred Tomb to Golgotha, where Jesus Christ was crucified. **Mh30**

The Dead Sea Saline lake – the surface, 395 meters below sea level, is the lowest point on the Earth's surface. **Mh30**

Petra Capital of the ☉ Nabataean civilization – palaces and temples carved into stone walls – UNESCO world heritage site. **Mh30**

Scale 1:4,500,000

0   40   80 Kilometers

Principal travel routes
- Auto route
- Rail road
- Shipping route

Remarkable landscapes and natural monuments
- UNESCO World Natural Heritage
- Mountain landscape
- Rock landscape
- Ravine/canyon
- Cave
- Waterfall/rapids
- Lake country
- Desert
- National park (landscape)
- National park (fauna)
- Wildlife reserve
- Coastal landscape
- Beach
- Coral reef
- Island
- Underwater reserve

and Jordan are fertile areas that have been densely populated since ancient times. In stark contrast to these areas, many places farther in the interior are covered by sparsely populated deserts with extremely hot daytime temperatures and freezing winters.

Beyond the barren ⊠ **deserts of Syria** and the ⊠ **Nafud Desert** in Saudi Arabia lie the ◹ **Euphrates** and ◹ **Tigris Rivers**. The Tigris and Euphrates both have their sources in the mountains of eastern Turkey. Together the two rivers nourish and define the historic region of Mesopotamia. ◹ **Mesopotamia** covers a large section of modern Iraq and the region is often referred to as the "cradle of civilization" because of the relatively advanced cultures that inhabited the region during ancient times.

With the use of modern technology and irrigation techniques Israel has made major agricultural advances in the extremely dry ⊠ **Negev Desert** and sections of eastern **Sinai**. The Negev is dotted by numerous dried river beds called wadis which can suddenly fill with water during winter floods. The well preserved remnants of ⌂ **Petra**, the ancient capital of the Nabataean culture, are located in a gorge near the Wadi Araba valley. The city was once a major trading center along the ancient trade route be-tween Mesopotamia and the Mediterranean coast. The grand historic architecture in Syrian cities such as Damascus and Tadmor (Palmyra) are evidence that these cities were once major centers of commerce and trade.

Israel's capital city, Jerusalem, has been a melting pot of different religions and cultures since the Roman era. The city continues to attract many pilgrims of various faiths from around the world.

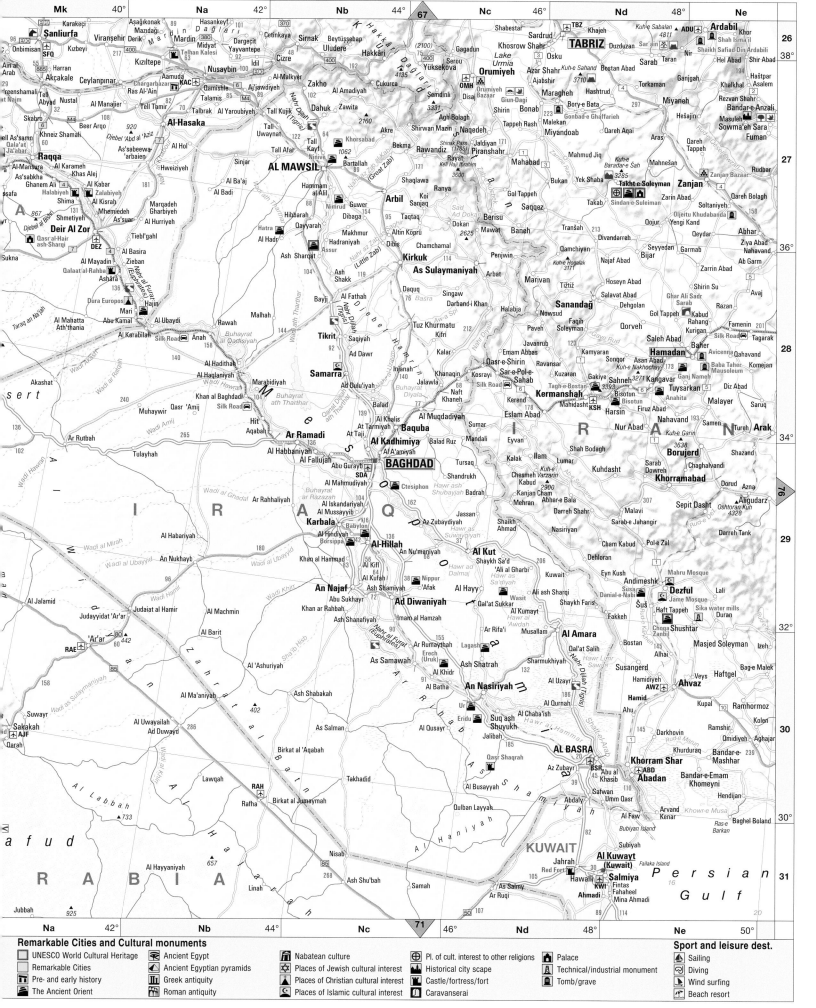

Palmyra/Tadmor ⌂ ruins of an ancient city in Syria – 4,000 years old – UNESCO world heritage site – ⌂ museum. **Mk28**

Samarra Shiite ⌂ pilgrimage site in Iraq – ruins of caliphal palaces – spiral minarets of the ⌂ Great Mosque. **Nb28**

Bagdad Capital of Iraq – population, 4.5 million – Tahrir Square (photo) – palaces from the Abbasids era – ⌂ historic Umm el-Mahare mosques. **Nc29**

Sumerian and Babylonian Culture
The Sumerians wandered into southern Mesopotamia around 4000 BC and founded the city states of Ur and Babylon. In addition to colorful mosaics, remnants of Sumerian sculpture have also been found throughout southern Mesopotamia. Arabian nomads mixed with the Sumerians around 3500 BC. The new culture founded Ur and the world's first dynasty around 2500 BC. Photos from to bottom: section of the Babylon's Ishtar Gate, temple in Uruk, ziggurat in Ur.

Euphrates The longest ◹ river in western Asia, 2,375 kilometers – source in Turkey, flows through Syria and Iraq – delta on the Persian Gulf – several large dams have been constructed along the river. **Mj-Nd27/30**

Remarkable Cities and Cultural monuments

☐ UNESCO World Cultural Heritage	☐ Ancient Egypt
☐ Remarkable Cities	☐ Ancient Egyptian pyramids
☐ Pre- and early history	☐ Greek antiquity
☐ The Ancient Orient	☐ Roman antiquity

☐ Nabatean culture	⊕ Pl. of cult. interest to other religions
☐ Places of Jewish cultural interest	☐ Historical city scape
☐ Places of Christian cultural interest	☐ Castle/fortress/fort
☐ Places of Islamic cultural interest	☐ Caravanserai

☐ Palace	
☐ Technical/industrial monument	
☐ Tomb/grave	

Sport and leisure dest.

☐ Sailing	
☐ Diving	
☐ Wind surfing	
☐ Beach resort	

The kingdom of **Saudi Arabia** comprises the vast majority of the Arabian Peninsula – including the central section of the peninsula with the Islamic holy cities of Mecca and Medina. Most of western Saudi Arabia is covered by a large plateau containing ⊠ **vast barren stone and sand deserts**. The plateau descends in "steps" in the east and in the west it merges with the Hijaz Mountains which contain peaks rising more than

3,000 meters above sea level. Along the Red Sea coast, the Hijaz Mountains drop abruptly to the sea. Saudi Arabia is home to some of the most expansive deserts in the world including the Nafud desert in the country's north and the Rub'al Khali (Empty Quarter) in the south. The interior of Saudi Arabia contains numer-

A desert highway on the Persian Gulf coast. **Ne32**

Madain Salah Spectacular Nebetaean 🏛 rock tombs with well-preserved facades – 300 kilometers north of Medina. **Mj32**

Medina Historic city in western Saudi Arabia – Masjid Al Nabawi (photo), mosque and the ⊠ burial site of the Islamic prophet Muhammad. **Mk33**

Harrat Rahat Arid volcanic lava field south of Medina – one of twelve lava field deserts in Saudi Arabia. **Na34**

Jeddah Modern port city on the Red Sea. The city has a restored 🏛 old town (top photo) with historic architecture and an old marketplace. 60-kilometer-long coastal road Corniche with beautiful ⊠ mosques (bottom photo), 🏛 palaces, and villas. **Mk35**

Mecca The most holy spiritual center of Islam – pilgrimage site visited by millions annually during the Hajj – the Prophet's ⊠ Mosque containing the Kaaba (photo), which pilgrims circle seven times – Mount Arafat is 15 kilometers from the city. **Mk35**

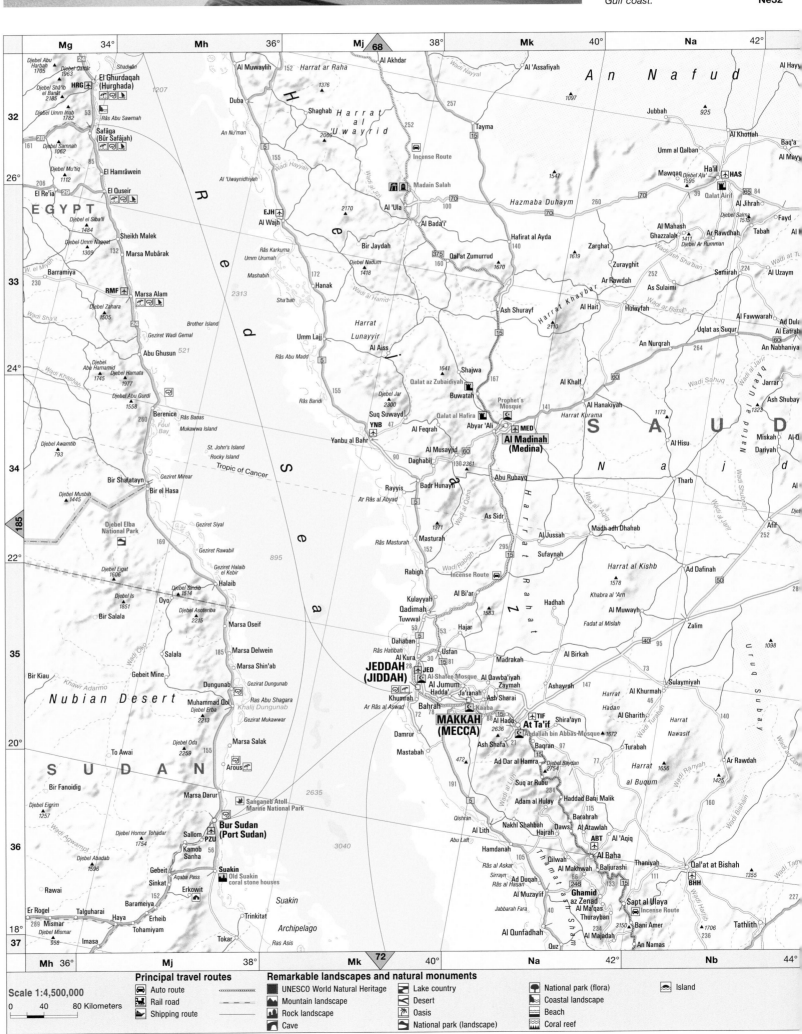

Scale 1:4,500,000

0   40   80 Kilometers

Principal travel routes

- Auto route
- Rail road
- Shipping route

Remarkable landscapes and natural monuments

- UNESCO World Natural Heritage
- Mountain landscape
- Rock landscape
- Cave
- Lake country
- Desert
- Oasis
- National park (landscape)
- National park (flora)
- Coastal landscape
- Beach
- Coral reef
- Island

ous 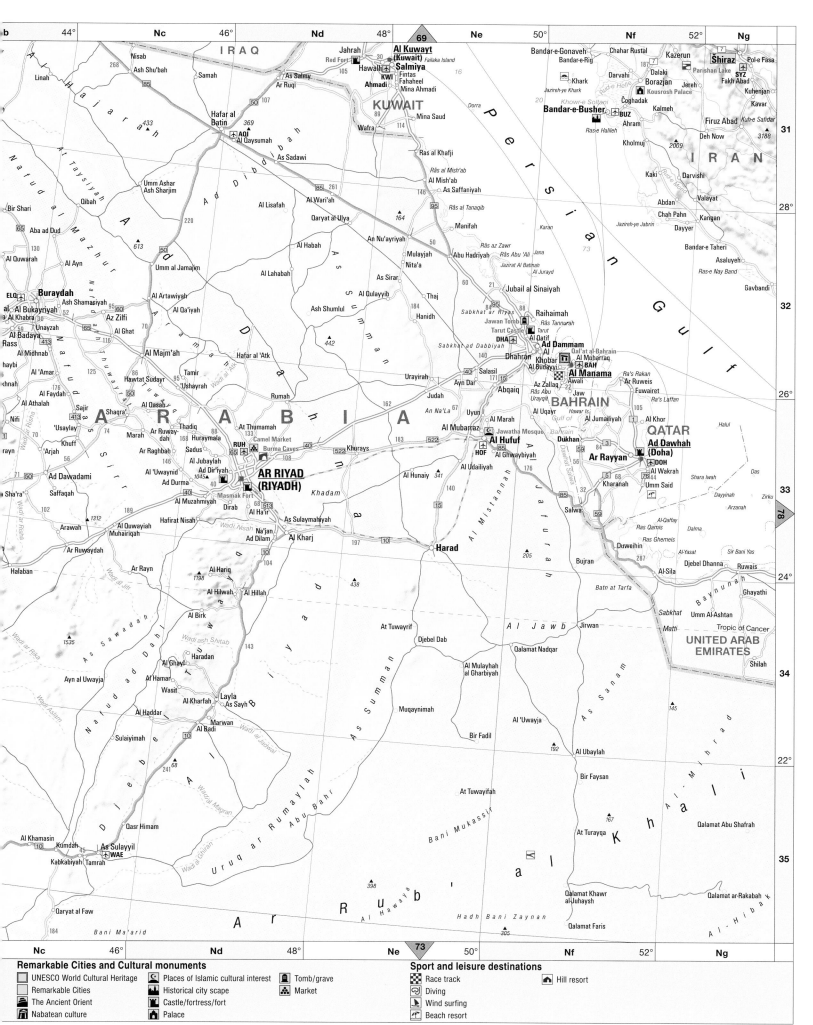 wadis, dry river beds that can flood suddenly after rainfall.

The desert state **Kuwait** is situated on the northwestern edge of the Arabian Peninsula. The country consists of a mostly flat ⊠ **desert** interior and a short coastline along the Persian Gulf. Kuwait's deserts rise in elevation towards the Iraqi border and eventually rise to a maximum height of 300 meters above sea level.

The Kingdom of **Bahrain** encompasses 33 islands in the Gulf of Bahrain. The kingdom's main island, Bahrain, consists mostly of sand dunes and marshes.

Qatar is an arid peninsula, located fifty kilometers south of Bahrain, along the western edge of the Persian Gulf. The country's interior ⊠ is mostly flat, expansive deserts and semi-arid areas.

The **United Arab Emirates** is a federation of small emirates on the eastern edge of the Arabian Peninsula. More than two-thirds of the country's territory is covered by ⊠ deserts. The deserts of the country extend to just before the Persian Gulf coast. A narrow three-kilometer-wide strip of fertile land stretches along the coast. Dates, mangos, bananas, and vegetables are widely cultivated in this area. The economies of the countries in northern Arabia are dominated by the region's large oil and natural gas deposits.

Saudi Arabia's interior contains some of the hottest areas on the planet. Many of these desert areas remain almost totally uninhabited. Most of the settlements in the Saudi interior are built near oases or near the edges of the desert. Despite the high temperatures common throughout the region, low humidity makes the climates tolerable in many places. During summer, temperatures in northern Arabia often exceed 40° C and in the some areas even 50° C.

Kuwait City Capital city of the desert nation Kuwait. The three Kuwait Towers (photo) are the city's principal landmark. Major attractions include the 🕌 old town, fishing harbor, and the 🏛 Sief palace. **Nd-Ne31**

Al Manama Bahrain's capital city – skyscrapers and 🕌 traditional architecture – ⊠ Al Fateh mosque (photo). **Nf32**

Doha Capital city of Qatar on the Persian Gulf – traditional dhows (boats) in the harbor (photo). **Nf33**

Riyadh Saudi Arabia's capital city – Dira Square with the Friday ⊠ Mosque – ⊠ markets – 🏛 National Museum – futuristic Ministry of the Interior building (photo). **Nd33**

Ad Dir'iyah The traditional home of the Al-Saud royal dynasty – 🏛 ruins of the house of Al-Saud – north of Riyadh. **Nd33**

Remarkable Cities and Cultural monuments

- ⬜ UNESCO World Cultural Heritage
- ⬛ Remarkable Cities
- ⬛ The Ancient Orient
- 🏛 Nabatean culture
- ☪ Places of Islamic cultural interest
- 🏛 Historical city scape
- 🏰 Castle/fortress/fort
- 🏛 Palace
- ✠ Tomb/grave
- ⊠ Market

Sport and leisure destinations

- 🏁 Race track
- 🤿 Diving
- 🏄 Wind surfing
- 🏖 Beach resort
- 🏠 Hill resort

Southern Arabian Peninsula

Traditional architecture in Wadi Doan (Yemen). **Ne38**

The south of the Arabian Peninsula encompasses Oman, Yemen, and the southernmost regions of Saudi Arabia. **Yemen** is situated on the southwestern edge of the Arabian Peninsula. The country has an area of 527,968 km². **Tihamah**, a narrow arid plain, stretches along the Red Sea coast in Western Yemen. The region is bounded in the west by a series of ▲ mountain ranges. The country's tallest mountain, Jabal an Nabi Shu'ayb, is located in the mountain ranges of western Yemen. Across the border in Saudi Arabia, the ▲ **Asir Mountain range** features several mountains taller than 3,000 meters. Monsoon winds from the Indian Ocean bring sporadic rainfall to the highlands of western Yemen during summer. In ancient times, most of western Yemen was ruled by the powerful **Kingdom of Saba (Sheba)**, which controlled Arabia's valuable **frankincense trade**. North of Yemen's southern coast stretches a chain of plateaus and ▲ volcanoes. The **Jol mountain plateau** covers a large area in the center of the country. Around 160 kilometers inland, the Yemeni highlands drop abruptly to the flat desert that covers much of the country's interior.

Clay Buildings Common in Saudi Arabia's Asir Mountains region, a popular summer destination with a temperate climate. **Na36**

Najran Saudi province containing a large ▣ oasis – ▣ along the ancient frankincense route – Ibn Madi palace (photo). **Nc37**

Sanaa The city's unique architecture includes traditional tower buildings (photo). The ▣ old town is a UNESCO world heritage site. The city's ▣ Great Mosque contains important old handwritten versions of the Koran. Sanaa has a vibrant marketplace (bottom photo). **Nc38**

Wadi Dahr Contains the Dar al-Hajar rock palace (photo) – ▣ summer residence of local imams. **Nc38**

Sa'dah Location of the Al Hadi mosque (photo) – ▣ center of the Zaydi Shiites – ▲ historic old town. **Nb37**

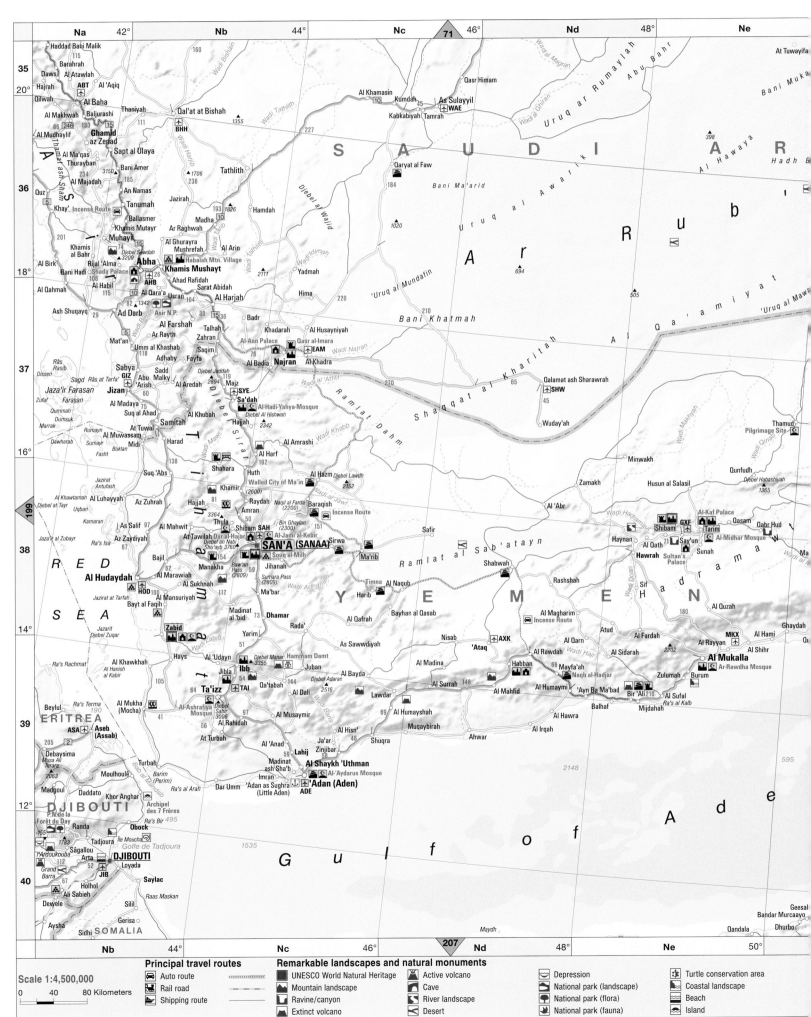

Scale 1:4,500,000

0   40   80 Kilometers

Principal travel routes
- Auto route
- Rail road
- Shipping route
- Mountain landscape
- Ravine/canyon

Remarkable landscapes and natural monuments
- UNESCO World Natural Heritage
- Active volcano
- Extinct volcano
- Cave
- River landscape
- Desert
- Depression
- National park (landscape)
- National park (flora)
- National park (fauna)
- Turtle conservation area
- Coastal landscape
- Beach
- Island

Yemen's interior is home to several large dried watercourses called wadis including the ⬜ Wadi Hadhra-mawt, the largest wadi in Arabia. ⬜ Socotra Archipelago, a Yemeni island group in the Indian Ocean is home to unique flora. Major dams and irrigation projects are vital to agriculture in arid Yemen.

Yemen coastal regions – including the Tihamah – have hot humid climates, while most of the country's highlands have temperate climates. In Yemen's vast desert regions, including the Wadi Hadhramawt and the Ramlat Al-Sab'atayn, temperatures regularly exceed 50° C during summer. Yemen has around 20 million inhabitants and is the second most populous country on the Arabian Peninsula. Yemen's capital Sanaa is located in a mountainous interior region. Most of the country's population is concentrated in the temperate mountainous regions. ⬜ Najran province in Saudi Arabia has strong cultural and historic connections to Yemen. Most of southern Saudi Arabia is covered by the vast and almost totally uninhabited ⬜ Ar Rub' al Khali desert – also widely known as the Empty Quarter. The Sultanate of Oman is situated on the southern edge of the Arabian Peninsula, to the east of Yemen. Oman varies between 200 and 700 kilometers in width from north to south. The Umm as Samim is a unique desert landscape with salt marshes and quicksand fields located in central Oman, along the edges of Saudi Arabia's Rub'al Khali desert. Oman's largest island territory, Masirah Island, is an important habitat for migratory birds and a breeding ground for sea turtles. ⬜ Jiddat al-Harasis is an expansive rocky desert in central Oman that contains sanctuaries for the Arabian oryx (antelope) population.

The villages and cities of the Yemeni highlands The ⬜ highlands of western Yemen are the wettest and most heavily populated region in the country. 1000-meter-high terraced agriculture (grain, coffee, etc.) has been practiced in the area since ancient times. Tall ⬜ tower buildings are common in the region's cities. Photos from top to bottom: terraced farms near Al Mahwit, Thula, Tiwala. **Nb38**

Habban Village between Aden and Mukalla at the foot of a large plateau – once home to a large community of Jewish silversmiths – ⬜ palaces. **Nd38**

Socotra Archipelago of volcanic islands in the Indian Ocean – ⬜ nature reserves – frankincense trees – ⬜ dragon blood trees – ⬜ sea turtles. **Nh39**

Wadi Hadhramawt Situated in a valley surrounded by high plateaus, this area is the economic center of eastern Yemen. Dates, grains, and fruits are all grown here. The towering buildings of Shibam, a UNESCO site (top photo) are surrounded by an old city wall. The city of Say'un is home to a large ⬜ sultan's palace (bottom photo). **Ne37/38**

Remarkable Cities and Cultural monuments

- ⬜ UNESCO World Cultural Heritage
- ⬜ Remarkable Cities
- ⬜ The Ancient Orient
- ⬜ Places of Islamic cultural interest
- ⬜ Cultural landscape
- ⬜ Historical city scape
- ⬜ Castle/fortress/fort
- ⬜ Palace
- ⬜ Remarkable bridge
- ⬜ Tomb/grave
- ⬜ Market

Sport and leisure destinations

- ⬜ Diving
- ⬜ Seaport
- ⬜ Beach resort
- ⬜ Mineral/thermal spa
- ⬜ Hill resort

Caspian Sea Region

The **Caspian Sea** covers 371,000 km² and is the largest inland body of water in the world. The sea has a maximum depth of 1,000 meters and its surface lies around 28 meters below sea level. Five nations have borders along the Caspian Sea; Russia, Kazakhstan, Turkmenistan, Azerbaijan, Armenia, and Georgia. The ☁ Caucasus is a mountainous region – between the Caspian and Black Seas – comprised of Armenia,

Azerbaijan, and Georgia. The Caucasus nation of **Georgia** has an area of 69,700 km². Georgia's capital city **Tbilisi** is located along the banks of the Mtkvari River in the southwest. The Mtkvari flows from Georgia to its delta near Baku, Azerbaijan on the Caspian Sea coast. Most of northern Georgia is covered by the

Mount Ararat rises 5,165 meters in northeastern Turkey. **Nc26**

snowy mountains and foothills of the ☁ **Greater Caucasus** mountain range. Georgia's Black Sea coast consists of fertile plains with a subtropical climate and abundant rainfall. The country's eastern coast along the Caspian Sea is an arid region with a cool climate. The ☁ **Lesser Caucasus** mountain range covers most of southwestern Georgia and stretches over the border into Armenia.

Caucasus Mountains 1,200-kilometer-long ☁ range – Greater and Lesser Caucasus – world heritage site. **Mk-Ne23/25**

Svaneti Region in Georgia's ☁ Greater Caucasus mountains – historic homes with defensive towers (photo) – hot springs – numerous scenic hiking trails. **Nb24**

Mtskheta First settled around 3000 BC – Capital of the Georgian Kingdom of Iberia in ancient times – ☁ Svetitskhoveli cathedral, a world heritage site (photo). **Nc25**

Tbilisi Georgia's capital and largest city – ☁ spas with sulfur springs – historic old town – Narikala fortress – ☁ Metekhi church (photo). **Nc25**

Haghpat Monastery In the Bazum Mountains of northern Armenia – fortified ☁ monastery from the 10th century – UNESCO world heritage site. **Nc25**

Geghard Monastery Located in Armenia's Azat Valley – ☁ stone monasteries built in the 4th century – the main building was completed in 1215 – UNESCO site. **Nc25**

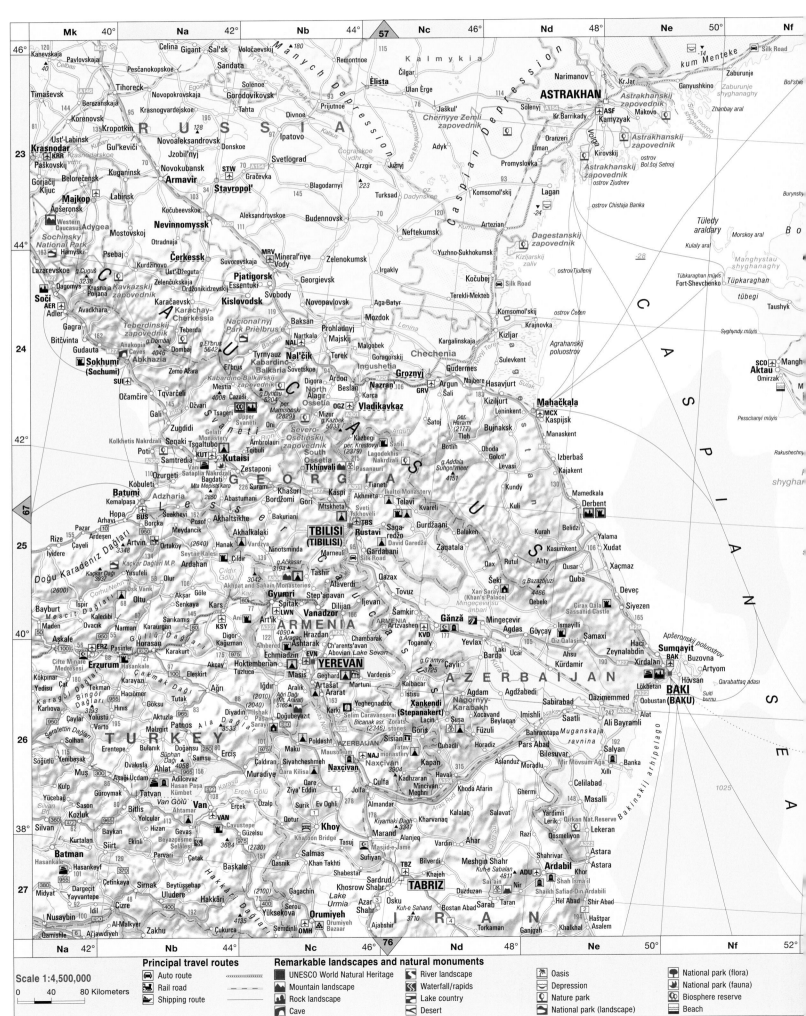

Principal travel routes

Scale 1:4,500,000

0   40   80 Kilometers

- 🚗 Auto route
- 🚂 Rail road
- ⚓ Shipping route

Remarkable landscapes and natural monuments

- ■ UNESCO World Natural Heritage
- ■ Mountain landscape
- ■ Rock landscape
- ■ Cave
- ~ River landscape
- Waterfall/rapids
- Lake country
- Desert
- Oasis
- Depression
- Nature park
- National park (landscape)
- National park (flora)
- National park (fauna)
- Biosphere reserve
- Beach

Armenia is a mountainous nation with a total area of 29,800 km² and a population around 3.8 million. Armenia is situated in a geologically active region and the country is home to several 🌋 dormant volcanoes. The country's tallest mountain is Aragats Lerrnagagat (4,090 m) near the Turkish border. Armenia's capital city **Yerevan** is surrounded by highlands with cool continental climates. **Lake Sevan** is situated in eastern Armenia at a height of

1,897 meters above sea level. In addition to Turkey and Georgia Armenia borders several other nations; in the southwest the country borders the Azeri exclave **Naxçivan**, in the far south Iran, and in the east mainland Azerbaijan.

The Azeri region of **Nagorno-Karabakh** has a mostly Armenian speaking population. The region has been at the center of a dispute between **Azerbaijan** and Armenia since the collapse of the Soviet

Union. Azerbaijan is the largest of the Caucasus nations with a total area of 86,600 km². Most of northern Azerbaijan is covered by the foothills of the Greater Caucasus range. Azerbaijan's tallest mountain, Bazarduzu Dagi, rises 4,466 meters. The 🌊 Kura River basin is a fertile area bordered by vast steppes. Azerbaijan's capital **Baku** is situated on the **Apsheron Peninsula**. The **Üstyurt plateau** in Kazakhstan lies northeast of the Caspian

Sea and west of the **Turan lowlands**. The **Aral Sea** is situated between these two regions. In recent decades, the Aral Sea has shrunk dramatically as a result of evaporation and irrigation projects. Turkmenistan's Caspian Sea coast is broken by several large bays. Garabogazkol was once the largest bay next to the Caspian Sea but the two bodies are now separated by a narrow strip of land created after a drop in the Caspian Sea's water level.

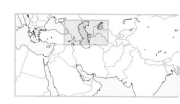

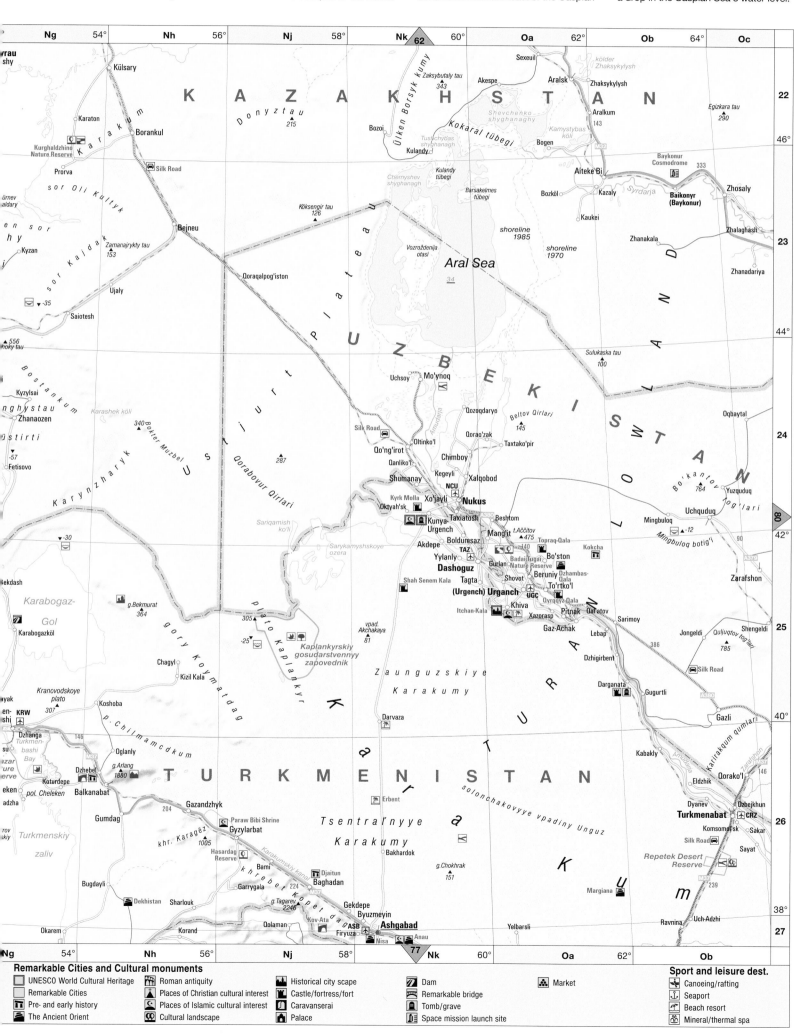

Echmiatsin A holy city for Armenian Christians. The city is the site of a historic 🏛 basilica, a UNESCO world heritage site with colorful frescoes and clock towers. **Nc25**

Baku Azerbaijan's capital city on the Caspian Sea – 🏛 old town with historic city wall (12th century) – UNESCO world heritage site – palace of Shrivan Shah – 🕌 medieval mosques and palaces. **Ne25**

Baikonur Kazahkstan – 🚀 launch site for the Russian space program – the first manned space flight started here in 1961. **Ob23**

Khiva Fascinating city in Uzbekistan – the 🏛 old town Ichan Kala is surrounded by a city wall – 🕌 mosque and palaces. **Oa25**

Remarkable Cities and Cultural monuments

☐ UNESCO World Cultural Heritage	⌂ Historical city scape	🌊 Dam
☐ Remarkable Cities	⌂ Castle/fortress/fort	🌉 Remarkable bridge
☐ Pre- and early history	⌂ Caravanserai	⚰ Tomb/grave
☐ The Ancient Orient	⌂ Palace	🚀 Space mission launch site

🏛 Roman antiquity	🛒 Market
✝ Places of Christian cultural interest	
☪ Places of Islamic cultural interest	
🏞 Cultural landscape	

Sport and leisure dest.

🛶 Canoeing/rafting
⚓ Seaport
🏖 Beach resort
♨ Mineral/thermal spa

Northern Iran

The narrow  **Alborz mountain range** covers much of northern **Iran** and contains the country's tallest mountain, Damavand, which rises 5,601 meters above sea level. **Teheran**, the capital of the Islamic Republic of Iran is situated on the southern edges of the Alborz Mountains. Teheran is also the largest Iranian city with around seven million residents. Northwestern Iran is a mountainous region along the country's borders to Tur-

key, Azerbaijan, and Armenia. This region features narrow and shallow **Lake Urmia**. Along the Caspian Sea coast in the northwest lies a strip of fertile and heavily cultivated plains. Most of northwestern Iran has cold winters with heavy snowfall and temperate dry summers with only sporadic rainfall.

Damavand (5,601 m), Iran's tallest mountain. **Ng28**

Maku Town near Mount Ararat – pilgrimage site for Armenian Christians – Qara Kilisa, ancient "black church" (photo). **Nc26**

Tabriz Near the volcano Sahand – traditional bazaar – capital of Persia in the 14th century – Blue Mosque (photo). **Nd26**

Teheran The capital of Iran is situated at the foot of the Alborz Mountains. Teheran's sites includes the Golestan Palace, the mausoleum of Ayatollah Khomeini and Shahyad's Tower (photos). **Nf28**

Kermanshah Historic city in northeastern Iran – sculptures and reliefs – tomb of the Sassanian king Ardashir (photo). **Nd28**

Shush (Susa) First settled around 4000 BC – capital of ancient Elam – tomb of the biblical prophet Daniel (photo). **Ne29**

Tchogha Zanbil Ruins of the ancient holy city of the Elamites – world heritage site – site of Iran's only terraced palace. **Ne29**

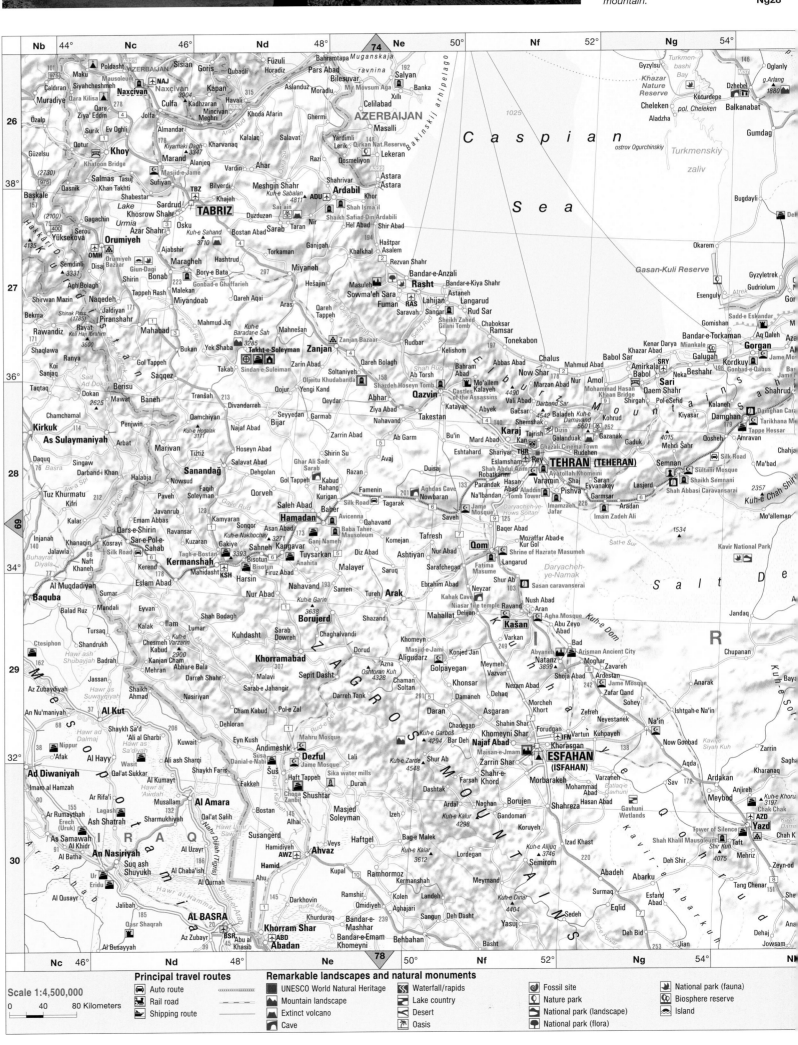

Scale 1:4,500,000
0   40   80 Kilometers

Principal travel routes
- Auto route
- Rail road
- Shipping route

Remarkable landscapes and natural monuments
- UNESCO World Natural Heritage
- Mountain landscape
- Extinct volcano
- Cave
- Waterfall/rapids
- Lake country
- Desert
- Oasis
- Fossil site
- Nature park
- National park (landscape)
- National park (flora)
- National park (fauna)
- Biosphere reserve
- Island

Earthquakes are common in northern Iran. The geologically active region is situated near the boundaries of the Arabian and Eurasian tectonic plates. The area between the cities Tabriz and Ardabil encompasses many natural hot springs and a chain of extinct volcanoes.

The 🏔 **Zagros Mountains**, a series of parallel ranges, stretch from the northwest to the southeast near the borders to Iraq and Turkey. Iran's Zagros Mountains contain the source of the **Karun River**, the country's only major navigable river. The river flows from Khorramshahr to the Shatt al-Arab river along the Iran-Iraq border. Iran's Central Plateau is situated west of the Zagros Mountains and has an average height of 1,220 meters. The plateau borders two large deserts: ⬩ **Dasht-e Kavir** and ⬩ **Dasht-e Lut**. Dasht-e Kavir covers 200,000 km² and is the largest salt desert in the world. It stretches between the cities Teheran, Mashhad, and Yadz. The Dasht-e Lut desert covers 166,000 km² and stretches to the Iran's borders with Pakistan and Afghanistan. The Iranian province of Khuzestan consists of marshlands along the Shatt al-Arab river southwest of the Zagros Mountains. Located along the border to Iraq, **Khuzestan** has major oil deposits.

Iran's southwest, southeast, and coastal areas along the Persian Gulf have humid and hot climates. Most of the country's interior regions however have hot and arid climates with little rainfall. Iran has a diverse **population** with many distinct ethnic groups. Ethnic Persians form around one half of Iran's population. Azeris, Kurds, and smaller ethnic groups comprise the remaining half of the population. The smaller ethnic groups are mostly concentrated near Iran's borders.

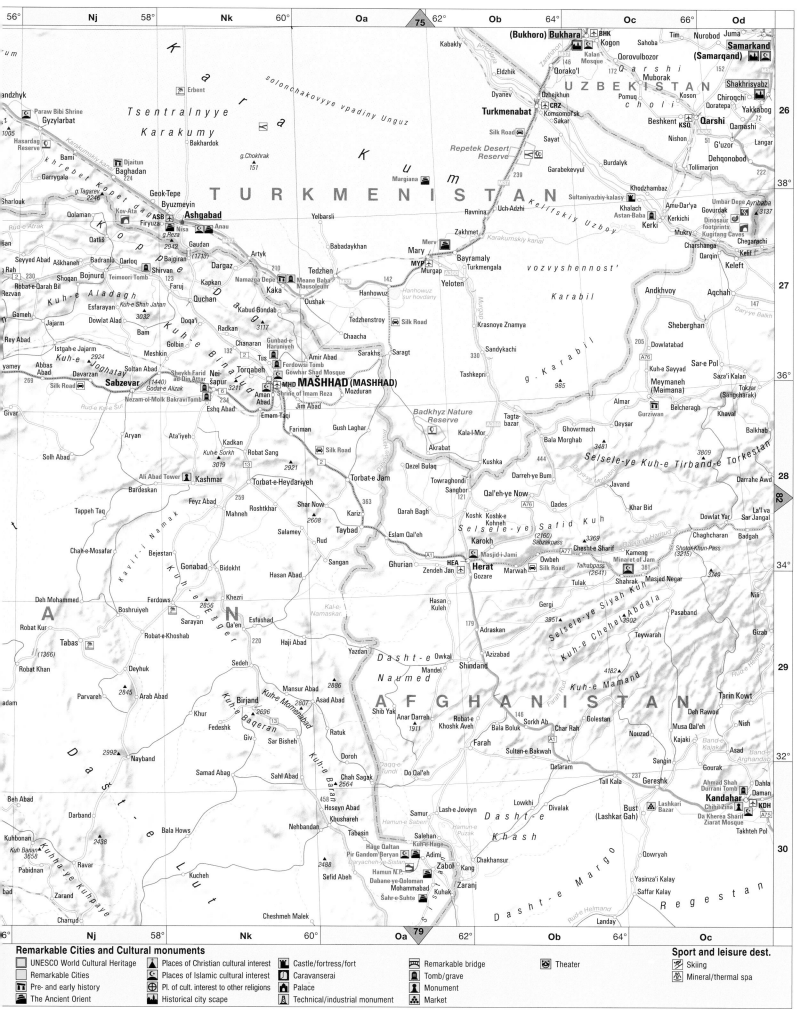

Qom Pilgrimage site and important Iranian 🕌 religious center – training schools for Shiite clerics – the 🕌 tomb of Fatima, sister of Imam Reza, (photo) is the town's principal attraction. **Nf28**

Kashan 🕌 Oasis town on the edge of a large salt desert – unique local architecture – Tabatabai House (photo). **Nf28/29**

Isfahan The 🏙 city is often considered the most beautiful urban area in Iran. Isfahan lies on the Zayandeh River between the mountain ranges. The Meidan Emam 🕌 mosque (both photos) is a UNESCO world heritage site. **Nf29**

Yazd Beautiful 🏙 old town – traditional homes topped by wind towers for cooling – center of silk production. **Nh30**

Masshad The shrine of Imam Reza (top photo) is the most revered Shiite 🕌 holy site in Iran. The shrine's golden towers were built in the 17th century. Masshad contains many historic caravansaries (bottom photo). **Nk27**

Remarkable Cities and Cultural monuments

- ▢ UNESCO World Cultural Heritage
- ▢ Remarkable Cities
- ▢ Pre- and early history
- ▢ The Ancient Orient
- ▲ Places of Christian cultural interest
- ▲ Places of Islamic cultural interest
- ⊕ Pl. of cult. interest to other religions
- ▲ Historical city scape
- ▲ Castle/fortress/fort
- ▲ Caravanserai
- ▲ Palace
- ▲ Technical/industrial monument
- ▣ Remarkable bridge
- 🏛 Tomb/grave
- 🏛 Monument
- 🏛 Market
- 🎭 Theater

Sport and leisure dest.
- ⛷ Skiing
- ♨ Mineral/thermal spa

Southern Iran, Persian Gulf

The regions along the coasts of the **Persian Gulf** contain a fascinating variety of unique landscapes. With the exception of the ▢ **Al Hajar Mountains** in Oman most of the Arabian Peninsula's Persian Gulf coast consists of flat desert regions. Because of its hot and dry climate along the Persian Gulf most of the region's large towns and cities lie directly on the coast. The Persian Gulf is the site of major oil deposits and oil exports

dominate the economies of several countries in the region including **Oman** (309,500 km²) and the **United Arab Emirates**. The United Arab Emirates (77,700 km²) is a federation consisting of seven emirates; Abu Dhabi, Ajman, Dubai, Fujairah, Ras al-Khaimah, Sharjah, and Umm al-Qaiwain. The **Al Batinah** coastal plain

Jebel Akhdar (3,018 m) in Oman's Al Hajar Mountains. **Nj34**

Naghshe-Rostam ▢ The tombs of four ancient Persian Kings including Darius the Great and Xerxes II. – built into the side of stone cliffs – large reliefs. **Ng30**

Persepolis ▢ The center of the Persian-Achaemenid Empire was founded by Darius I. and destroyed by Alexander the Great around 330 BC. The **Apadana** (top photo) or reception hall was decorated with large reliefs, some depicting battles between animals (bottom photo). **Ng31**

Kerman Provincial capital on the edge of the Dasht-e Lut desert. The city is known for its carpets, the ▢ Ganj-Ali-Khan Museum, ▢ 13th century mosque, and bazaar. Gonbad-e Jabalieh (top photo) and the Vakil tea house (bottom photo) are also popular attractions. **Nj30**

Bam, Arg-e-Bam Historic Iranian city with unique architecture – ▢ citadel (photo) – historic mosque and palaces – damaged by major earthquake in 2003. **Nk31**

Ras al-Khaimah Sheikdom in the United Arab Emirates – ▢ mountainous regions with wadis and scattered oases. **Nj33**

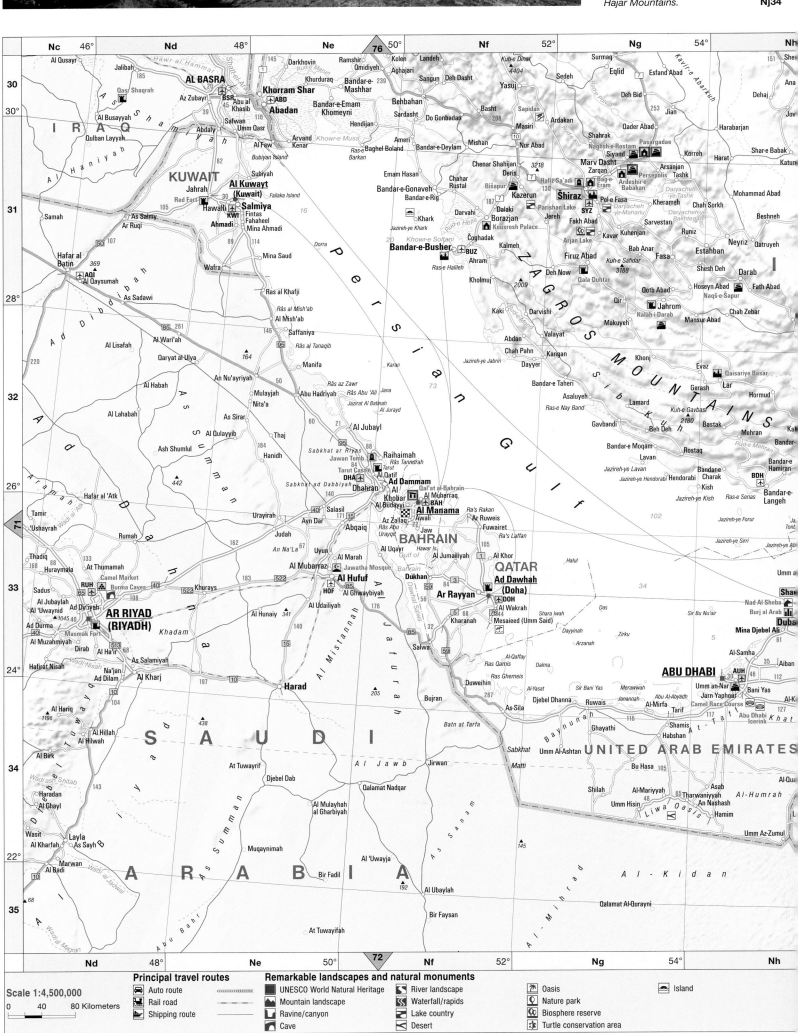

Scale 1:4,500,000

0   40   80 Kilometers

Principal travel routes
- Auto route
- Rail road
- Shipping route

Remarkable landscapes and natural monuments
- ▢ UNESCO World Natural Heritage
- ▢ Mountain landscape
- ▢ Ravine/canyon
- ▢ Cave
- ▢ River landscape
- ▢ Waterfall/rapids
- ▢ Lake country
- ▢ Desert
- ▢ Oasis
- ▢ Nature park
- ▢ Biosphere reserve
- ▢ Turtle conservation area
- ▢ Island

in Oman is a hot region with temperatures often exceeding 50° C and extreme humidity in summer. Despite the harsh climate, the majority of Oman's 2.5 million inhabitants live on the coastal plain. Oman's mountainous regions have a warm but moderate climate with abundant rainfall in winter.

The **Zagros Mountains**, a series of tall ridges, extend from northwestern Iran to the country's southeast. The Zagros Mountains rise abruptly to around 3,000 meters above sea level just beyond Iran's Persian Gulf coast.

Oman and Iran are separated by just 80 kilometers of water along the narrow **Strait of Hormuz**. The strait is situated between the Persian Gulf and the Gulf of Oman. The tall craggy mountain ranges of Southern Iran and Pakistan are far younger than the heavily eroded plateaus of Southern Arabia. Several large basins are situated between the mountains of southern Iran. These basins are covered by large ⊠ deserts, including the Dasht-e Lut, which contain numerous salt lakes. Because of high temperatures and evaporation many of these lakes have extremely salty water and are dry during most of the year. Southern Iran's scattered oasis towns including **Bam** and **Kerman** are dependant on groundwater supplies. Bam, one of the most ancient cities in Iran, was heavily damaged by a powerful earthquake in 2003. The Zagros Mountains of Iran and Balochistan in Pakistan have been inhabited for thousands of years. **Persepolis**, the center of an ancient Achaemenid Empire was founded around 600 BC. The city of **Shiraz** is situated on a large oasis and became an important settlement in the 7th century when it fell under the control of a powerful Arab dynasty.

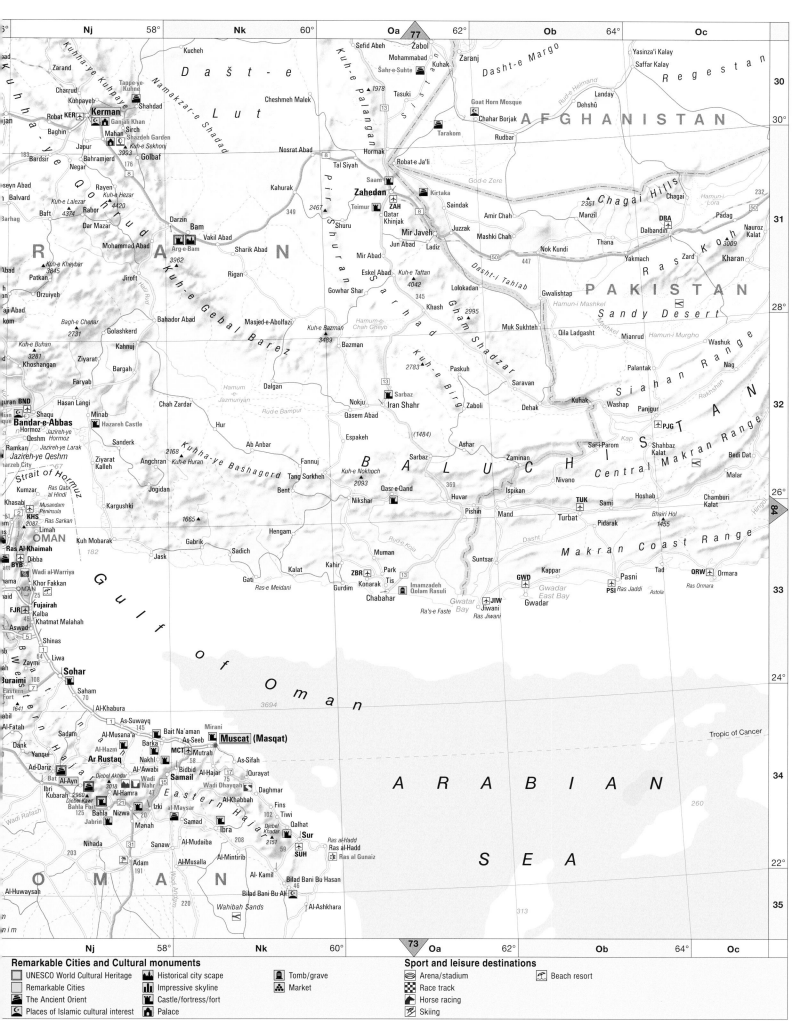

Dubai Economic center of the United Arab Emirates. The city has a modern skyline including the 🏙 World Trade Center and Burj al-Arab hotel (bottom photo). The city's traditional sites include the 🕌 Jumeirah mosque and the Deira district. **Nh33**

Abu Dhabi Capital of the United Arab Emirates – more than 20 parks – 🏰 Al-Husn, historic fort – long seaside road (photo) – the island of Umm an-Nar features ancient graves from the 3rd century BC. **Nh33**

Fort Nakhl 🏰 Historic fort located southwest of Muscat in Oman – defensive towers on the Nakhl oasis – ♨ hot springs. **Nj34**

Muscat The capital city of Oman – major port city with a natural harbor – the 🏰 forts Al Jalali (photo) and Al Mirani were built in the 16th century – 🏰 Al Alam, sultan's palace – dhow harbor. **Nk34**

Bahla Fort Clay 🏰 fort built during the pre-Islam era – UNESCO world heritage site – expanded between the 12th and 15th centuries – long ring wall. **Nj34**

Archeological sites Bat/Al Ayn/Al Khutm 🏛 Bronze Age settlements including the necropolis Al Ayn – built during the 3rd millennium BC – world heritage site. **Nj34**

Remarkable Cities and Cultural monuments

- ▫ UNESCO World Cultural Heritage
- ▫ Remarkable Cities
- ▫ The Ancient Orient
- ▫ Places of Islamic cultural interest

- 🏛 Historical city scape
- 🏙 Impressive skyline
- 🏰 Castle/fortress/fort
- 🏛 Palace

- 🪦 Tomb/grave
- 🏪 Market

Sport and leisure destinations

- 🏟 Arena/stadium
- 🏁 Race track
- 🐎 Horse racing
- ⛷ Skiing

- 🏖 Beach resort

Central Asia

The shrinking 🌊 **Aral Sea** lies on the **Turan Plain**, a vast arid lowland that rises no more than 34 meters above sea level. A long chain of mountain ranges stretches between the Aral Sea and the arid **Tarim Basin** in China. These ranges contain several of the world's highest mountains including **K2** (8,611 m), the world's second highest mountain, in the Karakoram Range and Cummunism Peak (7,494 m) in the ⛰ **Pamir Range**. The section of the

⛰ **Tian Shan Mountains** around Lake Issyk-Kul in Kyrgyzstan contains dozens of mountains taller than 4,000 meters. Kyrgyzstan has a total area of 2,717,300 km² and is the world's ninth largest nation in terms of size. Most of the country consists of large deserts and arid steppes.

The mountains of the Pamir Range cover most of Tajikistan. **OfOg26/27**

Kazakhs Kazakhs, the second largest Turkic ethnicity in Central Asia, are famous for their horse riding skills.

Kzyl-Orda Former capital of Kazakhstan (1925–1929) – vast underground water reserves – fortress ruins (photo). **Oc23**

Tashkent Capital of Uzbekistan – major transportation center – 🏛 old town with historic mosques, mausoleums, and 🏛 bazaars. **Oe25**

Buhkara Located on an oasis in the Kyzylkum Desert – 🏛 old town, a UNESCO world heritage site – 🕌 Kalan Mosque (photo) – Ark citadel. **Oc26**

Samarkand One of the world's grandest 🏛 cities during the 14th century, Samarkand is now a world heritage site. There are three historic 🏛 Islamic schools on the central square Registan (bottom photo) including the Shirdar (top photo). **Od26**

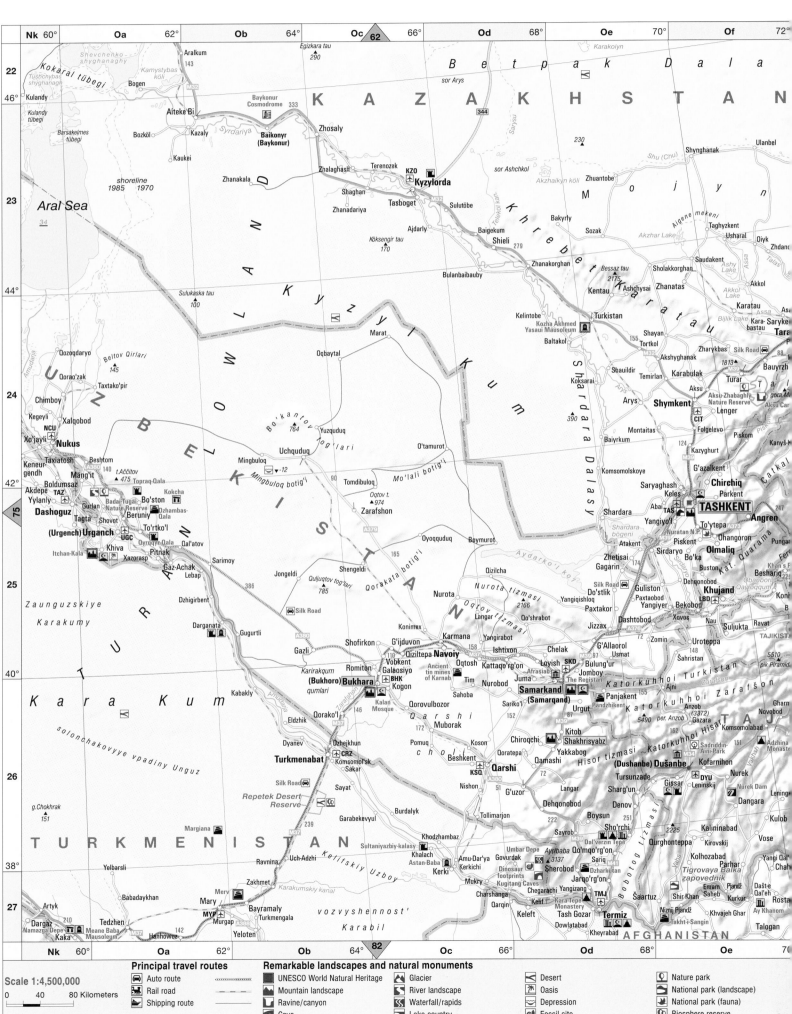

Scale 1:4,500,000

0   40   80 Kilometers

Principal travel routes
- Auto route
- Rail road
- Shipping route

Remarkable landscapes and natural monuments
- UNESCO World Natural Heritage
- Mountain landscape
- Ravine/canyon
- Cave
- Glacier
- River landscape
- Waterfall/rapids
- Lake country
- Desert
- Oasis
- Depression
- Fossil site
- Nature park
- National park (landscape)
- National park (fauna)
- Biosphere reserve

80 Asia

the Tian Shan Range forms a natural boundary between the two countries. **Kyrgyzstan** is a mountainous nation and more than half of the country's territory (198,500 km²) lies at heights above 3,000 meters. A large percentage of Kyrgyzstan's population lives from traditional sheep herding in rural areas. Most of the country's major towns are concentrated in river valleys and in the areas around Lake Issyk-Kul. Kyrgyzstan's capital **Bish-**

kek is the nation's largest city with a population of around 650,000. The most isolated mountainous regions are home to abundant wildlife including bears, wolves, eagles, and rare snow leopards. The area around Jalal Abad features large pristine forests. Around four percent of Kyrgyzstan's area consists of designated nature reserves and national parks.
Like neighboring Kyrgyzstan, **Tajikistan** is a mountainous nation and the Pamir

Range stretches over much of its territory. The majority of Tajikistan's population is concentrated in the country's fertile river valleys. The country's capital, Dushanbe, is located near the border to Uzbekistan. Livestock ranching, cotton farming, and silk production are important sectors in the country's economy. Centuries ago many of Uzbekistan's towns including **Samarkand**, **Khiva**, and the capital **Tashkent** were

important trade centers along the **Silk Road** trade route. More than three quarters of Uzbekistan is covered by arid steppes and deserts including the vast **Kara Kum** desert. The country has a mostly continental climate with hot summers and cold winters.
The mountainous areas of Uzbekistan and Tajikistan are home to large glaciers including the Inylchek Glaciers and snow capped mountains.

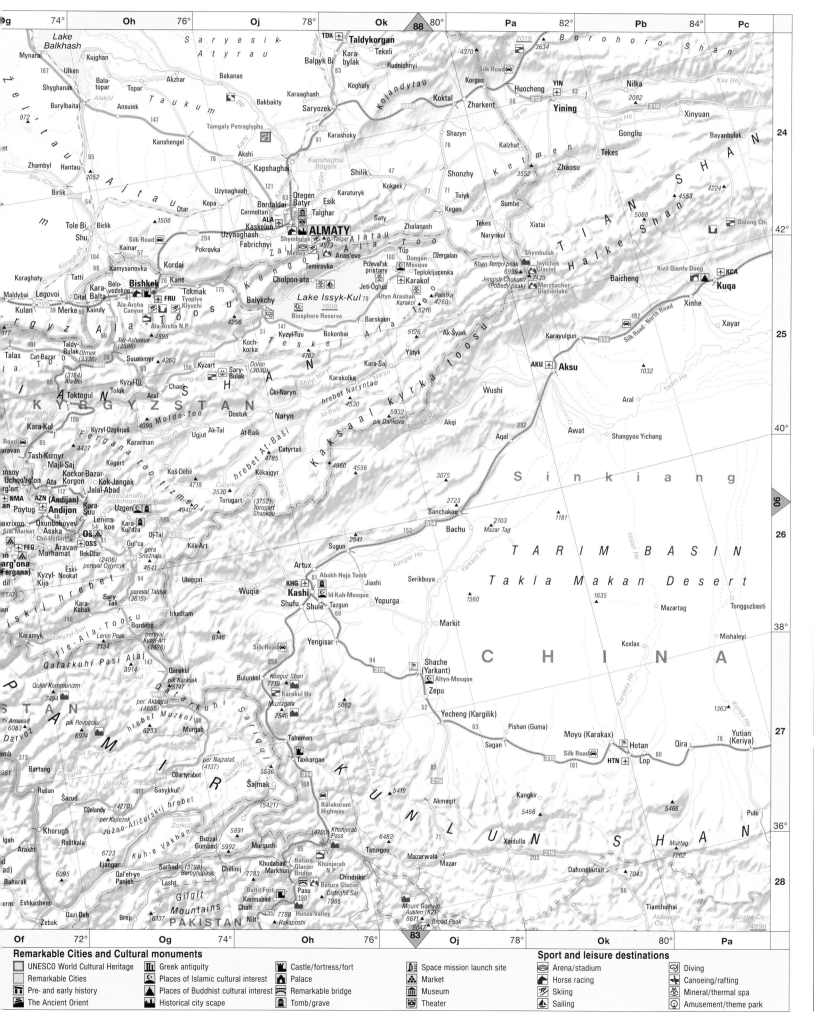

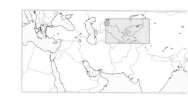

Almaty The largest city in Kazakhstan – former national capital and leading economic center – Zenkov cathedral – university – Pushkin Library – Palace of Culture – National Museum. **Oj24**

Lake Issyk-Kul Mountain lake – hot springs along the shore – national park and UNESCO biosphere reserve. **Oj24**

Tian Shan Mountains Mountain range encompassing Jengish Chokusu (7,439 m), Khan Tengri (6,995 m) – Inylchek Glacier. **Of-Pc24/25**

Kyrgyzstan The Kyrgyz are a Turkic people and form the majority of Kyrgyzstan's population. Most Kyrgyz are Sunni Muslims and many raise livestock in rural areas. Yurts (photos) made of wood and animal hide are the traditional homes of the Kyrgyz.

Pamir Mountains This mountain range (photos) stretches through much of Central Asia and has a total area of 60,000 km². Many of the mountains are covered by glaciers and several peaks rise above 7,000 meters. **Of-Og26/27**

Remarkable Cities and Cultural monuments

- UNESCO World Cultural Heritage
- Remarkable Cities
- Pre- and early history
- The Ancient Orient
- Greek antiquity
- Places of Islamic cultural interest
- Places of Buddhist cultural interest
- Historical city scape
- Castle/fortress/fort
- Palace
- Remarkable bridge
- Tomb/grave

Sport and leisure destinations

- Space mission launch site
- Market
- Museum
- Theater
- Arena/stadium
- Horse racing
- Skiing
- Sailing
- Diving
- Canoeing/rafting
- Mineral/thermal spa
- Amusement/theme park

Afghanistan, Northern and Central Pakistan

The landlocked country of **Afghanistan** has a total land area of 652,090 km². Most of Afghanistan's territory is covered by mountain ranges and valleys. Around half of the country lies at heights between 600 and 1,800 meters above sea level. The vast **Kara Kum desert** stretches over many of the regions near the border to Turkmenistan in north-western Afghanistan. The country's south and southwest consist primarily of large basins

and deserts including the Dasht e-Margo or "desert of death."

The high **Hindu Kush mountain range** begins in southwestern Afghanistan and extends through most of the country including the central highlands. In northeastern Afghanistan the peaks of the Hindu Kush rise above 7,000 meters in

Rakaposhi massif (7,788 m) in Pakistan's Hunza Valley. **Oh27**

Mazar-e Sharif City in Afghanistan – Blue Mosque is reputed to be the tomb of Ali, son in law of Islamic prophet Mohammed. **Od27**

Bamiyan Valley Region containing unique Buddhist art – several large historic Buddha statues were destroyed by the Taliban – UNESCO site. **Od28**

Panjshir Valley Difficult to access region north of Kabul with narrow canyons and valleys. **Oe28**

Kabul Afghanistan's capital and largest city (pop. 1.5 million) – Babur gardens – Timur Shah mausoleum – citadel and historic city wall. **Oe28**

Herat One of Afghanistan's most attractive cities – ancient citadel (top photo) – old town and Masjid I. Jami mosque (bottom photo). **Ob28**

Khyber Pass 53-kilometer-long path through the Hindu Kush between Pakistan and Afghanistan. **Of28**

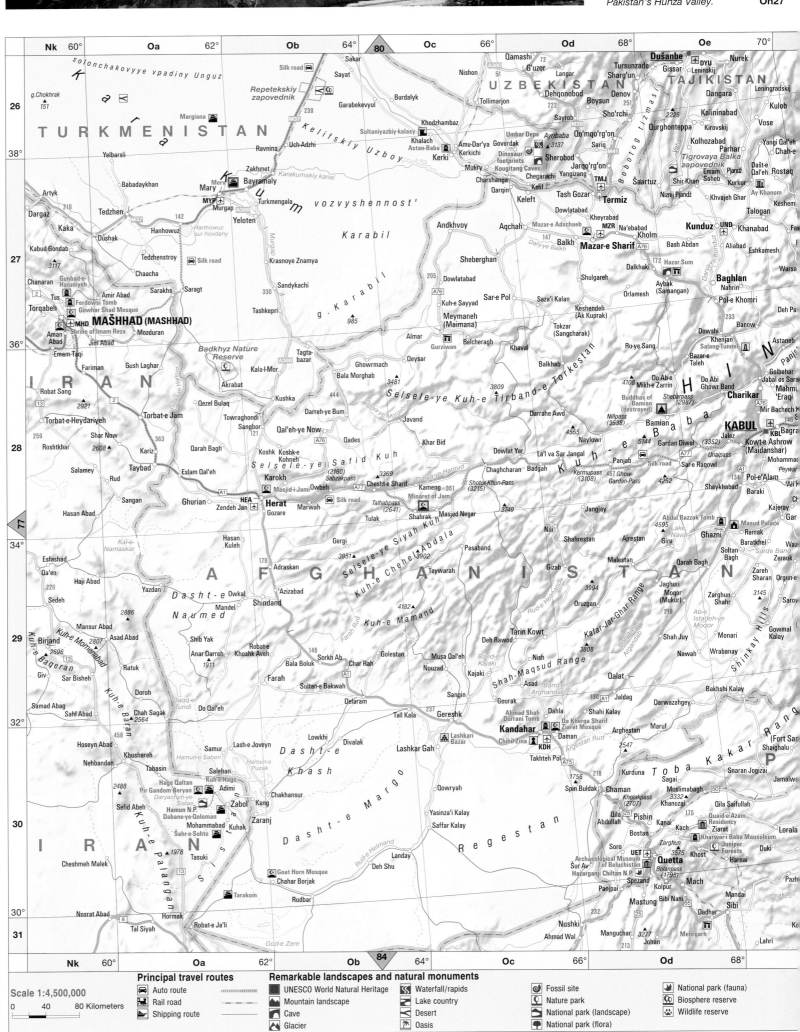

Scale 1:4,500,000

0   40   80 Kilometers

Principal travel routes
- Auto route
- Rail road
- Shipping route
- Mountain landscape
-

Remarkable landscapes and natural monuments
- UNESCO World Natural Heritage
- Mountain landscape
- Cave
- Glacier
- Waterfall/rapids
- Lake country
- Desert
- Oasis
- Fossil site
- Nature park
- National park (landscape)
- National park (flora)
- National park (fauna)
- Biosphere reserve
- Wildlife reserve

height, while the tallest peak in south-western Afghanistan barely tops 4,000 meters. **Kabul**, the capital of Afghanistan is situated in a mountainous region at a height of 1,800 meters above sea level and has a population around 1.5 million. Afghanistan's central highlands have a continental climate with hot summers and bitter cold winters. Southeastern and eastern Afghanistan have arid sub-tropical climates.

Northern **Pakistan** is covered by expansive ⛰ mountain ranges that stretch into neighboring China to the east. In this region, two of the world's tallest mountain ranges border one another: the Karakoram, a section of the Hindu Kush, and the Himalayas.
The Gilgit mountain range in Baltistan is home to numerous fertile ⛰ river valleys with green meadows and farms. Many of the mountains in the region are covered

by snow and long ❄ glaciers. The Siachen Glacier, is around 72 kilometers long. The ⛰ **Indus River** begins in Tibet and flows south through many mountain ranges in a long narrow valley. South of Peshawar, the Indus River flows through a large plain which is dissected by many of the river's tributaries including the Chenab, Ravi, Jelum, and Sutlej Rivers. The Indus River plain covers almost half of Pakistan's terri-

tory and stretches over the border into neighboring India.
Most areas in northern and central Pakistan have temperate continental climates with warm summers and cold winters. In the Punjabi city of Lahore, temperatures usually exceed 30° C in summer, while frost covers many of the region's mountains during the same time. The wet monsoon season occurs between July and October in Pakistan.

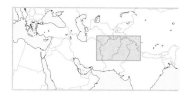

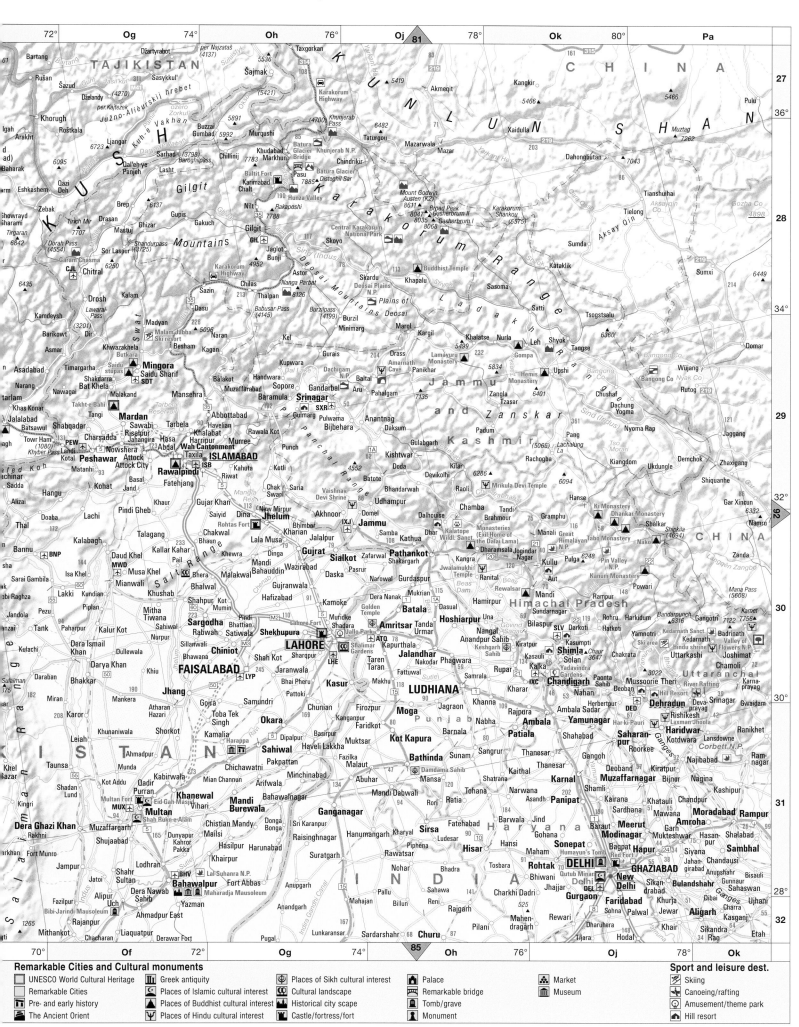

Karakoram Mountain range divided between India, China, and Pakistan: Broad Peak (8,047 m), Gasherbrum I (8,068 m, top photo), K2 (8,611 m, bottom photo). **Oh-Ok27/28**

Nanga Parbat Mountain (8,126 m) on the western edge of the ⛰ Himalayas – first climbed in 1953. **Oh28**

Baltit Fort 600-year-old ⛰ fort in the Hunza Valley (Pakistan) – Tibetan-influenced architecture. **Oh27**

Karakoram Highway Road stretching from Islamabad in Pakistan to China. Passes the ❄ Batura glacier (top photo) and suspension bridges (bottom photo) over the Gilgit River. **Oh27**

Rawalpindi City near Islamabad – southeast of Taxila archeological site – once the center of the ancient ⛰ Gandhara kingdom. **Og29**

Remarkable Cities and Cultural monuments

☐ UNESCO World Cultural Heritage	Ⅲ Greek antiquity	⚑ Places of Sikh cultural interest	⛪ Palace
☐ Remarkable Cities	▲ Places of Islamic cultural interest	◙ Cultural landscape	⌂ Remarkable bridge
☐ Pre- and early history	▲ Places of Buddhist cultural interest	◘ Historical city scape	⌂ Tomb/grave
☐ The Ancient Orient	▼ Places of Hindu cultural interest	⛫ Castle/fortress/fort	◻ Monument

	Sport and leisure dest.
⛩ Market	⛷ Skiing
⛩ Museum	⛵ Canoeing/rafting
	◉ Amusement/theme park
	⛰ Hill resort

Central and Southern Pakistan

The southern and central regions of **Pakistan** are situated east of Iran and Afghanistan, between the Arabian Sea and the Toba Kakar mountains. These regions contain a diverse group of landscapes including the deserts of Makran, the flood threatened Indus River Valley, and the arid steppes of Balochistan. The delta of the ⚓ **Indus River** is situated on the Arabian Sea, just east of Karachi. The Pakistani section of the Indus alone

is around 2,200 kilometers long. Tibet in China is the location of the Indus River's source. Many smaller rivers flow into the Indus along its path south to the Arabian Sea. The river's delta encompasses more than 60,000 km² of wetlands.
The name of the **Punjab** region means "land of five rivers." Punjab is home to

The Toba Kakar Mountains in western Pakistan. **Od-Oe30**

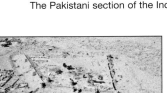

Mehrgarh Southeast of Quetta in Balochistan – ⬚ first settled around 7000 BC – excavation sites (photo) – early center of agriculture – ancient pottery. **Od31**

Mohenjo Daro ⬚ Ruins of an ancient city and trade center built in the 3rd millienium BC – UNESCO world heritage site – ⬚ citadel – ⬚ Buddhist temples. **Oe32**

Hyderabad Economic center of Sindh province – historic 18th century ⬚ fort built by Ghulam Shah Kalhora – towers of Char Minar (photo) – ⬚ Mausoleum of Sheikh Makki. **Oe33**

Karachi Because of its natural harbor (top photo), Pakistan's largest city has long been a major center of trade. Muhammed Ali Jinnah, the founder of Pakistan was born in the city. The ⬚ Qiad-e-Azam mausoleum (middle photo) was built in his honor. The city is home to several ⬚ markets including the Empress Market (bottom photo) where local goods are sold. **Od33**

Chaukundi Located 30 kilometers east of Karachi – historic burial site (16.–18. century) – ⬚ graves decorated with floral and geometric reliefs. **Od33**

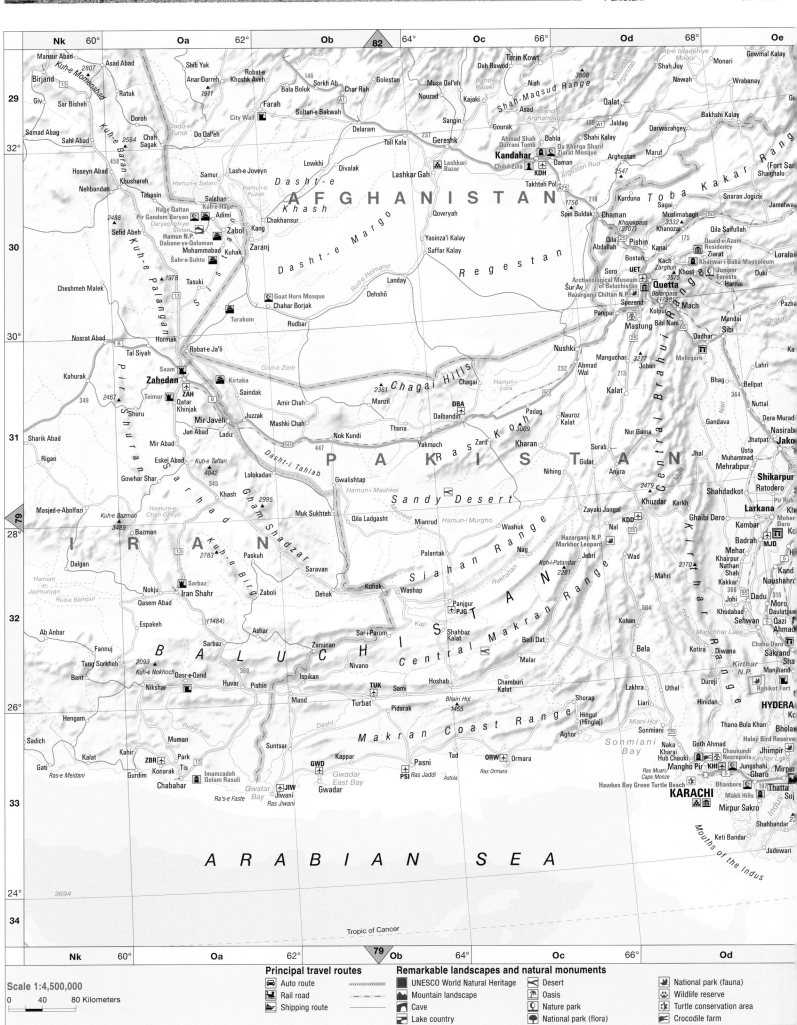

Scale 1:4,500,000
0   40   80 Kilometers

Principal travel routes
- 🚗 Auto route
- 🚆 Rail road
- 🚢 Shipping route
- ·········· Auto route
- ──── Mountain route

Remarkable landscapes and natural monuments
- ⬚ UNESCO World Natural Heritage
- ⬚ Mountain landscape
- ⬚ Cave
- ⬚ Lake country
- ⬚ Desert
- ⬚ Oasis
- ⬚ Nature park
- ⬚ National park (flora)
- ⬚ National park (fauna)
- ⬚ Wildlife reserve
- ⬚ Turtle conservation area
- ⬚ Crocodile farm

several major rivers, most of which flow into the Indus. This fertile region – which is divided between India and Pakistan – was once a center of the **Sindu-Indus River civilization**, an ancient culture founded during the 3rd millennium BC. At least one-third of Pakistan's territory is covered by the basin of the Indus and its tributaries. These regions are home to the majority of Pakistan's 145 million inhabitants. The port city of Karachi,

on Pakistan's southern coast, is the country's largest city and most important economic center. **Balochistan** is an arid region consisting of vast steppes and numerous salt pans. The region covers southwestern Pakistan and several areas across the border in Iran and Afghanistan. Balochistan is bounded by three mountain ranges: the Siahan Range, the Central Makran Range, and the Coastal Makran Range. The

Sulaiman Mountains are situated in central Pakistan, on the northeastern edges of Balochistan. Most of northern Balochistan is covered by large sand deserts. The **Thar Desert** is located east of the Indus River and encompasses a large area divided between Pakistan and India. Lahore, the second largest city in Pakistan, lies near the Indian border and has a population of around 4.5 million.

Pakistan has two significant climate types: subtropical and temperate continental climate. During the rainy season, monsoon winds bring heavy rainfall to most of the country. The Indus River Valley gets little precipitation outside of winter and Balochistan is dry during the entire year. Pakistan's southern coast is a hot and humid area, while the mountains in the far north are covered by frost and snow during most of the year.

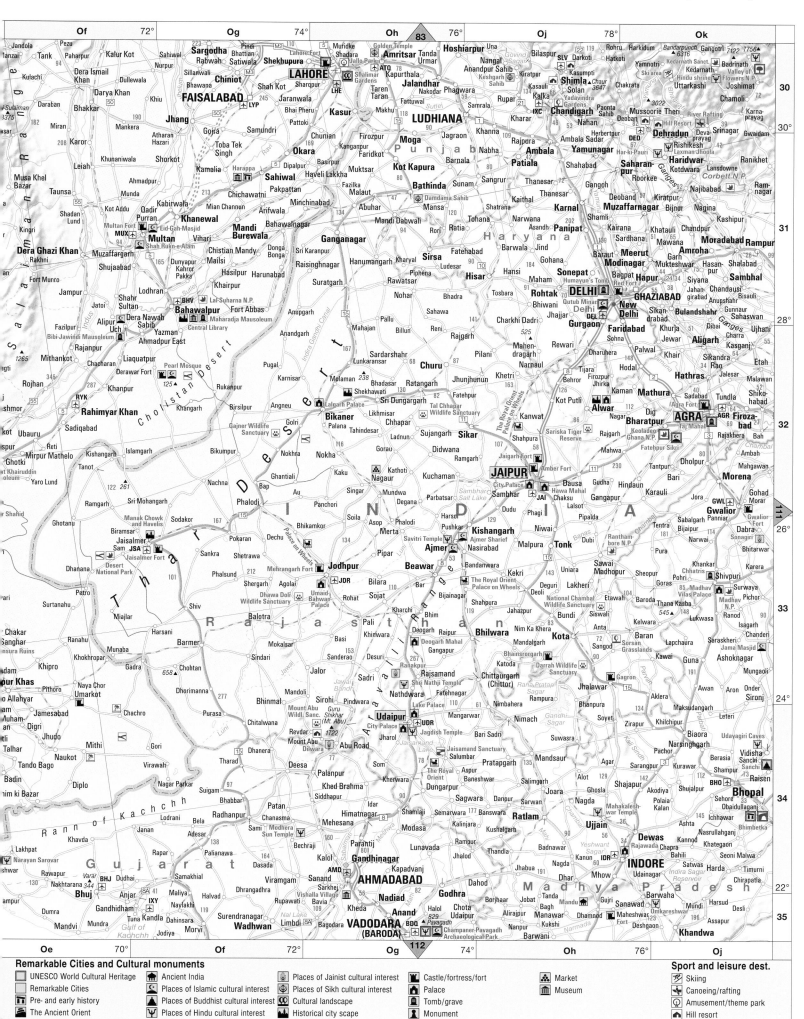

Lahore The capital of Punjab province, Lahore, flourished under the rule of the Mogul Empire during the 16th and 17th century. Lahore's fort (top photo), world heritage site, was expanded during this era. Badshahi mosque (middle photo) accommodates 60,000 worshippers. The Wazir Khan mosque (bottom photo) was built with Persian architectural influences. **Oh30**

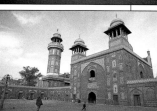

Shalimar Gardens Large gardens with terraces, canals, pavilions in Lahore – UNESCO world heritage site. **Oh30**

Multan Fortified city in the Indus Valley – mausoleum of Rukn-i-Alam (photo) – silk production. **Of30**

Uch Center for Islamic scholars in the 12th and 13th centuries – Persian architecture – the tomb of Bibi Jawindi (photo) was completed in 1494. **Of31**

Makli Hills Necropolis Large field of tombs near Thatta, a UNESCO world heritage – mausoleum of Tarkhan. **Od33**

Remarkable Cities and Cultural monuments

- UNESCO World Cultural Heritage
- Remarkable Cities
- Pre- and early history
- The Ancient Orient
- Ancient India
- Places of Islamic cultural interest
- Places of Buddhist cultural interest
- Places of Hindu cultural interest
- Places of Jainist cultural interest
- Places of Sikh cultural interest
- Cultural landscape
- Historical city scape
- Castle/fortress/fort
- Palace
- Tomb/grave
- Monument
- Market
- Museum

Sport and leisure dest.
- Skiing
- Canoeing/rafting
- Amusement/theme park
- Hill resort

East Asia

The **People's Republic of China** is the third largest nation on earth with a total area of 9.6 million km². With around 1.3 billion inhabitants, China is also the world's most populous nation. The vast **Plateau of Tibet** in western China is the world's largest continuous upland region. Much of the plateau is covered by the **Himalayan Range** which features **Mount Everest** (8,850 m), the world's tallest mountain. The Himalayas sepa-

rate the highlands of Central Asia from tropical South Asia. The **Karakoram Range**, an extension of the Hindu Kush, is situated northwest of the Himalayas. The Karakoram features many large glaciers and high mountains – including **Nanga Parbat** (8,126 m) and K2 (8,611 m), the world's second highest

The Karakoram Mountains, a section of the Himalayas.

Tian Shan Mountain range in central China, rising 5,000 meters – borders large deserts, steppes, and oases.

Takla Makan Sand desert in the Tarim basin – Northwestern China – around 400,000 km².

Karakoram Mountain range in Afghanistan and Pakistan – contains four mountains rising over 8,000 meters.

Tibet Tibet consists mostly of a two million km² large mountainous plateau. The region is widely known as the "roof of the world." Tibet's capital Lhasa was once the home of the Dalai Lama, the spiritual leader of Tibetan Buddhism. Photos from top to bottom: barren landscape in central Tibet, Yamdrok Tso lake, Brahmaputra river, Cho Oyu.

North Tibetan Mountains Peaks rising above 7,000 meters – source of the Huang He and Chang Jiang Rivers – salt lakes.

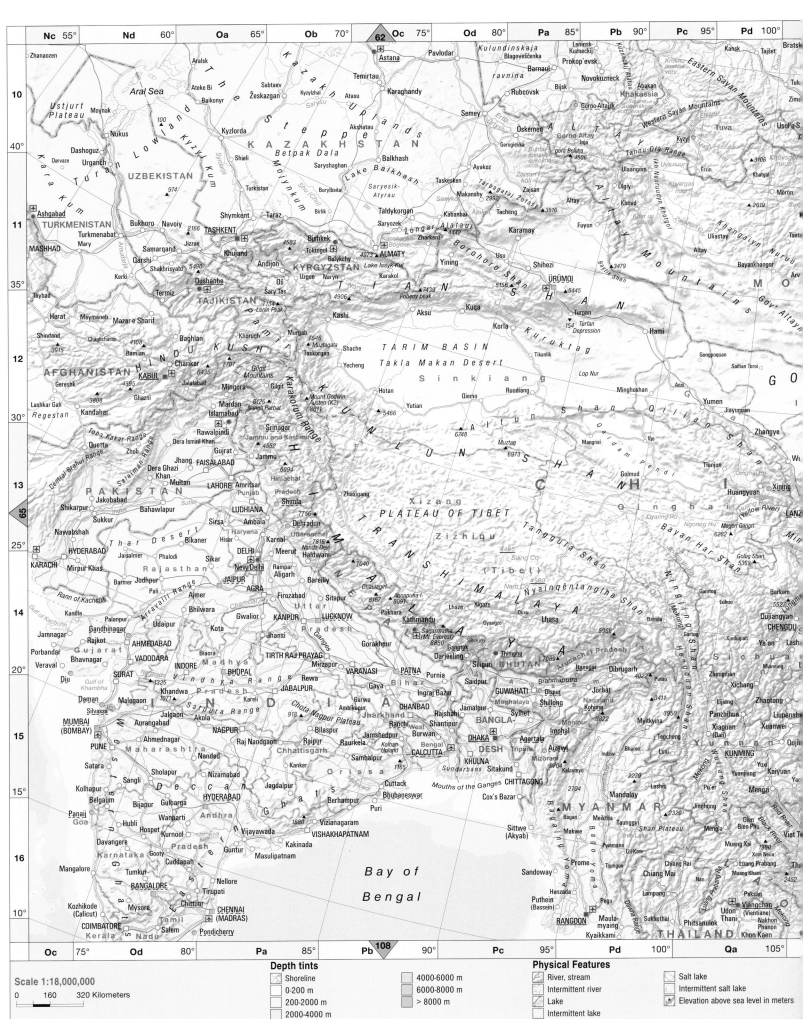

Scale 1:18,000,000

0   160   320 Kilometers

Depth tints

- Shoreline
- 0-200 m
- 200-2000 m
- 2000-4000 m
- 4000-6000 m
- 6000-8000 m
- > 8000 m

Physical Features

- River, stream
- Intermittent river
- Lake
- Intermittent lake
- Salt lake
- Intermittent salt lake
- ▲ Elevation above sea level in meters

mountain. The **Quidam Basin** in central China is an arid basin between the Altun Shan and branches of the Kunlun Range.

Two large basins, the **Tarim basin** and the **Dzungaria basin** stretch through northwestern China. Most of the arid Tarim basin is covered by the vast and sandy Takla Makan desert. The two basins are separated by the mountains of the **Tian Shan Range**. The vast **Gobi**

Desert starts to the east of the Tian Shan Range. The Gobi has an extreme climate with hot summers and bitter cold winters. It covers around 1.2 million km² in China and Mongolia. The Gobi is bordered in the northwest by the **Mongolian Altai**, a section of the large Altai mountain system.

Manchuria in northeastern China is bounded by three mountain ranges: the Greater and Lesser Khingan in the north

and the Changbai range in the east. The Greater and Lesser Khingan ranges are relatively low mountain ranges which rise no higher than 2,000 meters.

Much of the Great Manchurian Plain in southern Manchuria is crossed by the **Huang He River**. The 4,845-kilometer-long Huang He is China's second longest river. China's longest river, the **Chang Jiang (Yangtze) River**, is around 6,300 kilometers long.

Japan is an archipelago of volcanic islands situated off the eastern coast of mainland Asia. Japan consists of four main islands: Hokkaido, Honshu, Shikoku, and Kyushu; and at least 3,300 smaller islands. All of the Japanese islands are summits of an undersea mountain range. A long mountain range stretches through the middle of the main Japanese islands and most of the country's territory is mountainous.

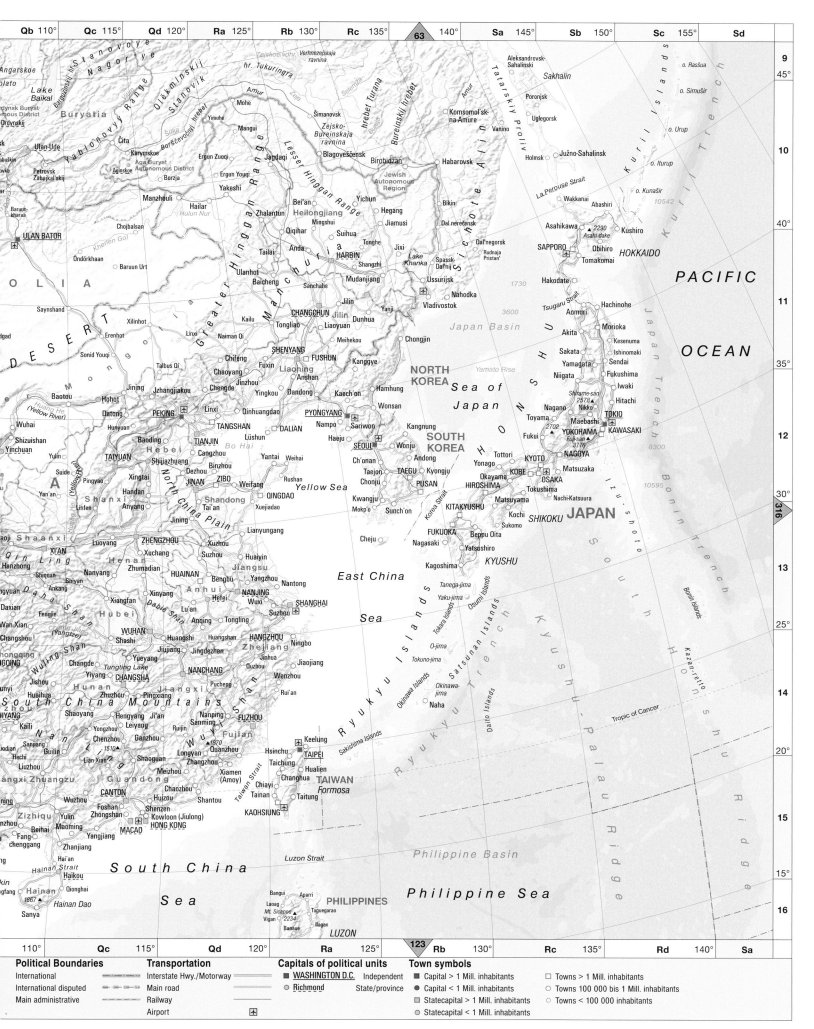

Gobi Desert East Asia's largest desert is surrounded by mountain ranges – located in northern China and southern Mongolia – dramatic climate with hot summer and bitter cold winters.

Mongolian Altai Section of the Altai mountain range, divided between Russia and Mongolia – arid eastern sections – stretches into the Gobi Desert.

Highlands of Central China Several mountain ranges stretch through the region – beautiful landscapes – tallest mountain, Magên Gangri (6,282 m).

Huangshan Picturesque mountains west of Hangzhou – popular Chinese tourist destination – UNESCO world heritage site.

Guilin Beautiful landscapes containing unique stone formations – along the Li River – numerous lake and rivers.

Japanese Islands The volcano Mount Fuji (top photo) rises 3,776 meters on Japan's largest island Honshu. The Ryukyu Islands (bottom photo) are situated between Kyushu and Taiwan.

Political Boundaries		Transportation		Capitals of political units		Town symbols	
International		Interstate Hwy./Motorway		■ WASHINGTON D.C. Independent		■ Capital > 1 Mill. inhabitants	□ Towns > 1 Mill. inhabitants
International disputed		Main road		⊙ Richmond State/province		● Capital < 1 Mill. inhabitants	○ Towns 100 000 bis 1 Mill. inhabitants
Main administrative		Railway				▣ Statecapital > 1 Mill. inhabitants	○ Towns < 100 000 inhabitants
		Airport	✈			▢ Statecapital < 1 Mill. inhabitants	

This section of Central Asia is a region of vast sparsely populated steppes and uninhabited deserts. The region encompasses sections of five nations; Kazakhstan, Tajikistan, Kyrgyzstan, and China. Many historic trade routes including the Silk Road passed through the heart of Central Asia during ancient times. Most of the larger cities in the region were, however, only founded in recent centuries. Bishek, the capital of **Kyrgyz-**

stan, is situated in the Chu River valley. The foothills of the Trans Alay Range – a section of 🏔 **Tian Shan** mountain system – are located just outside the city. The glacier-covered Tian Shan mountain range covers most of northeastern Kyrgyzstan where it rises to a maximum height of 4,000 meters. Most of north-

A lush valley in China's Xinjiang province. **Pb24**

Trans-Ili Alatau 🏔 Mountain range south of Lake Issyk-Kul – (photo) Kazakh shepherds near Almaty. **Oj-Ok24**

Dzungarian Gate 🏔 Mountain pass between China and Kazakhstan – 3,000 meters above sea level – (photo) a satellite view of the Dzungarian Gate. **Pb23**

Sayram Hu Lake in China at a height of 2,019 meters above sea level – 🗠 457 km² – maximum depth of 86 meters – colorful mountain vegetation in summer. **Pa23**

Tian Shan Mountain System 🏔 The system encompasses several ranges. The tallest peaks Khan Tengri (top photo; **Pa24**) and Pik Pobedy are in Kazakhstan. 🏔 Inylchek Glacier (photo) is around 60 kilometers long. The turquoise lake 🗠 Tian Chi is located west of Urümqi at an elevation of 2,000 meters (bottom photo; **Pe24**).

Scale 1:4,500,000

0   40   80 Kilometers

Principal travel routes
- 🚗 Auto route
- 🚆 Rail road
- 🚢 Shipping route

Remarkable landscapes and natural monuments
- ■ UNESCO World Natural Heritage
- 🏔 Mountain landscape
- Ravine/canyon
- 🏔 Glacier
- River landscape
- Waterfall/rapids
- Lake country
- Desert
- Fossil site
- Nature park
- National park (landscape)
- Biosphere reserve
- Wildlife reserve

eastern Kyrgyzstan's population is concentrated in two densely populated valleys; the Talas River valley and the valley around ⊠ **Lake Issyk-Kul**. The lake (6,000 km²) has a maximum depth of 700 meters and is one of the deepest freshwater lakes in the world. ⛰ Pik Pobedy (7,439 m) and ⛰ Khan Tengri (6,995 m), the tallest mountains in Kyrgyzstan, are both located near the border to China.

Most of southeastern **Kazakhstan** is covered by vast flat steppes and grasslands. The region is also the location of several mountainous areas including sections of the Tian Shan and Altai mountain systems. ⊠ **Lake Balkhash** is a long and narrow body of water stretching over 600 kilometers from west to east though the steppes of southern Kazakhstan. The shallow western sections of the lake contain fresh water,

while the deeper eastern sections of the lake contain salty water.

The Tian Shan Mountains separate the low lying northern sections of China's **Xinjiang Autonomous Region** from the Tarim Basin in the southern sections of the region. Most of northern Xinjiang is covered by the **Dzungarian (Junggar) Basin**. The basin itself consists of steppes and a ⊠ large desert. The basin is bounded to the north by the ⛰ **Altai**

Mountains in Mongolia. The Altai Mountain Range rises to a maximum height above 4,000 meters. Mongolia's mountains are the source of the Irtysh River, which flows through ⊠ **Lake Zaysan** in southeastern Kazakhstan. The northeastern section of the Altai stretches into the mountainous Russian republics of **Altai** and **Tuva**. The Altai is bordered to the east by a series of arid basins dotted with lakes and oases.

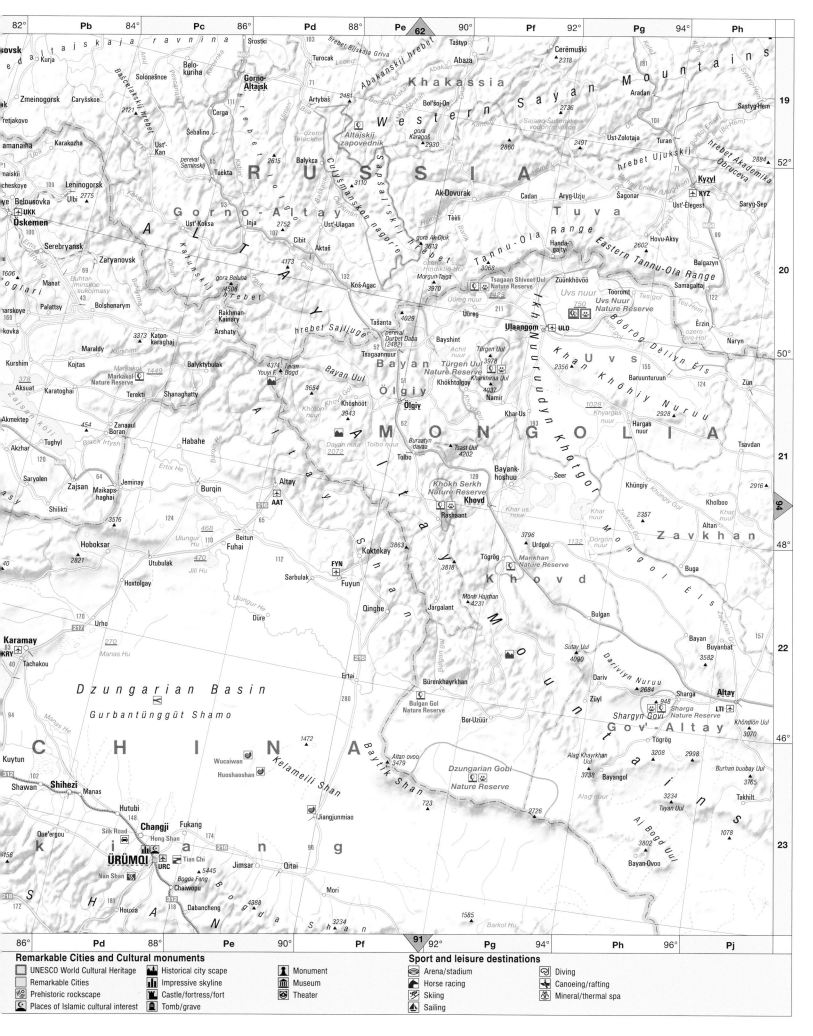

Mongolian Altai Forested ⛰ mountain range in Mongolia with a maximum height of 4,374 meters. **Pe-Pj21/23**

Dzungarian (Junggar) Basin ⊠ Basin with grasslands and deserts. Photos from top to bottom: Grazing sheep, desert, wild camels. **Pd-Pe22/23**

Ürümqi The pagoda (built in 1788, top photo) on the Red Hill is the major landmark of Ürümqi (pop. 1.25 million, bottom photo), 🏛 capital of Xinjiang Autonomous Region. **Pd24**

Remarkable Cities and Cultural monuments

- ☐ UNESCO World Cultural Heritage
- ☐ Remarkable Cities
- ☐ Prehistoric rockscape
- ☐ Places of Islamic cultural interest
- 🏙 Historical city scape
- 🏙 Impressive skyline
- 🏰 Castle/fortress/fort
- ⛩ Tomb/grave
- 🏛 Monument
- 🏛 Museum
- 🎭 Theater

Sport and leisure destinations

- ◬ Arena/stadium
- 🐎 Horse racing
- ⛷ Skiing
- ⛵ Sailing
- 🤿 Diving
- 🛶 Canoeing/rafting
- ♨ Mineral/thermal spa

Tarim Basin, Western China

Northwestern China is home to several large basins surrounded by large mountain ranges. The largest of these basins is the massive Tarim basin which covers an area of 975,000 km². The Tarim Basin is bounded in the north, west, and south by three mountain ranges. The ▲ **Tian Shan range** which rises to a maximum height of around 7,000 meters is situated north of the Tarim basin. The ▲ **Altun Mountains** and ▲ **Kunlun Mountains**

stretch to the south and west of the basin. The climates in the basin range from semi-arid to very arid and most of the basin is covered by the large ⊠ **Takla Makan** desert. Because of its extreme climate, the Takla Makan is totally uninhabited. The only settlements in the basin lie along its edges outside of the desert and

Bezeklik Valley: tall stone walls and numerous caves. **Pe24**

Takla Makan Large ⊠ sandy desert covering the Tarim basin – scattered ▣ oasis settlements along the edges of the desert. **Pa-Pb26**

Karakoram Highway 1,300-kilometer-long mountain roadway between Pakistan and China. Photos from top to bottom: ▣ Taxkorgan, ▣ Muztagata, ⊠ Lake Karakul. **Oh26/27**

The Tomb of Abahk Hoja ▣ Beautiful tomb in the city of Kashi – ▣ mosques and historic fountains on the premises. **Oj26**

Id Kah Mosque The largest ▣ mosque in China – yellow brick facade – oldest sections constructed in 1445. **Oj26**

Kuqa ▣ The Thousand Buddha caves (photo) contain important Buddhist art made between the 3rd and 8th centuries. **Pb25**

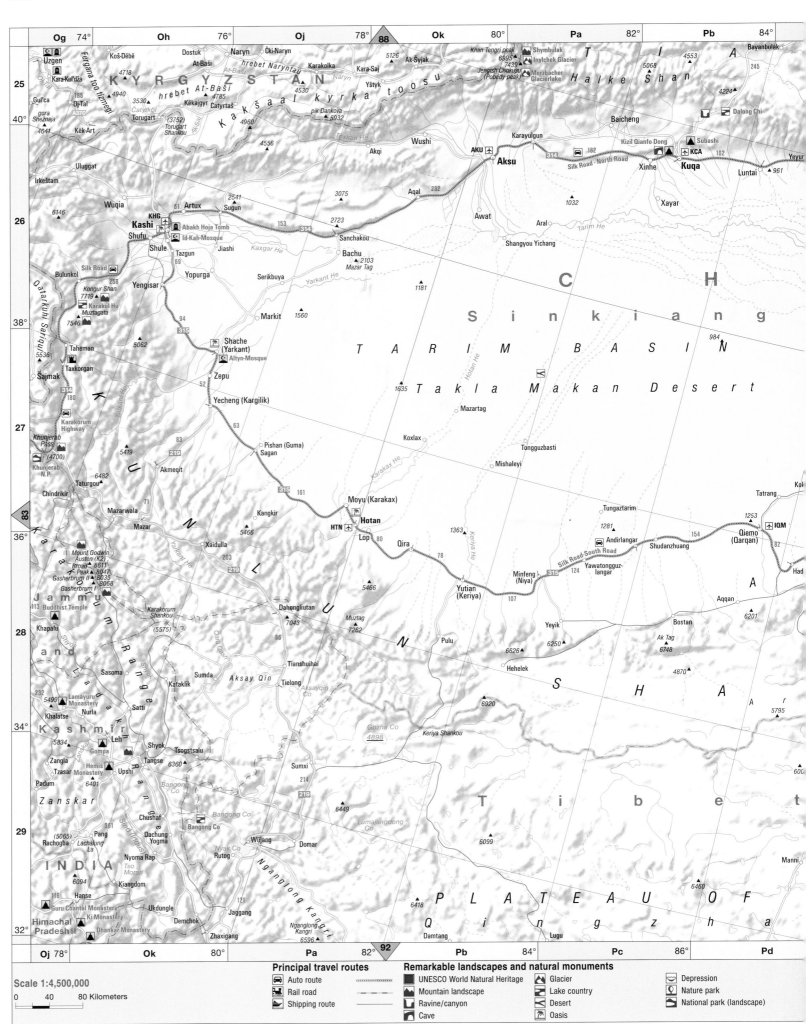

Scale 1:4,500,000

0   40   80 Kilometers

Principal travel routes
- 🚗 Auto route
- 🚂 Rail road
- ⚓ Shipping route

Remarkable landscapes and natural monuments
- ■ UNESCO World Natural Heritage
- ▲ Mountain landscape
- ▲ Ravine/canyon
- ▲ Cave
- ⊠ Glacier
- ⊠ Lake country
- ⊠ Desert
- ▣ Oasis
- ⊠ Depression
- ⊠ Nature park
- ▣ National park (landscape)

depend on water from snow-covered mountains. 🚇 **Turpan**, on the northeastern edge of the basin, is one of the largest towns in the region. It lies in the Turfan Depression, which has a maximum depth of 505 meters below sea level. The depression is the second lowest point on the Earth's surface, after the Dead Sea. Turpan and its surroundings are well known throughout China for their grape farms and Central Asian atmosphere. The town of Dunhuang is located in the western foothills of the Qilian Mountains along the historic Silk Road. The **Silk Road** was a historic trade route along which traders carried valuable Chinese silk to Europe and the Middle East.

The 🏛 **Mogoa Grottoes** contain impressive Buddhist cave paintings and historic statues made between the 4th and 7th centuries. The grottoes are the major cultural attraction in the region around Dunhuang. 🚇 **Kaski**, a city in the northwestern Tarim basin, is home to many different Central Asian ethnicities including Ka-zakhs, Uzbeks, Kyrgyz, and Uighurs. The city lies near China's borders to Kyrgyzstan, Tajikistan, and Afghanistan.

The 🔺 **Karakoram Range** – an extension of the Hindu Kush – starts to the west of Kunlun Mountains. The Karakoram forms part of the border between China and Pakistan. K2, the world's second tal-lest mountain (8,611 m) is situated on the Chinese-Pakistani border.

Most of the eastwest extension of the Kunlun Mountains lies just north of the vast **Tibetan Plateau**. The southeastern sections of the Kunlun Mountains extend into the 200,000-km²-large Qaidam basin. The arid basin consists of sand hills, salt lakes, and marshlands. There are only a few scattered settlements in this inhospitable region.

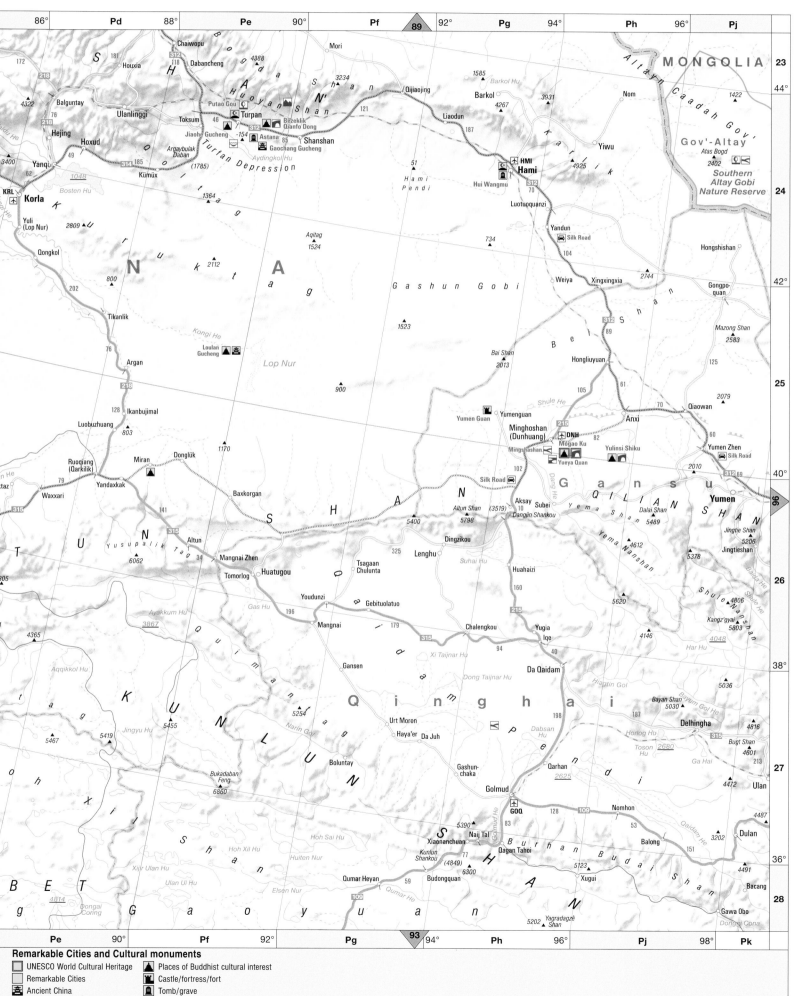

Jiaohe 🔺 Ruins of a city abandoned in the 13th century – well preserved remnants of the city gates and Buddhist monasteries. **Pe24**

Turpan Oasis in a deep depression – 🕌 Emin mosque and the Sugong Ta (photo) minaret, built in the 18th century. **Pe24**

Bezeklik The 🔺 Thousand Buddha Caves – 70 grottoes containing wall paintings made between the 5th and 9th century. **Pe24**

The Silk Road The historic route was first used by traders carrying silk from China to Persia around 200 BC. In addition to silk, weapons, horses, and art were traded along the road. Photo: near Dunhuang. **Ph25**

Mogao Grottoes 🔺 5th century temple constructed into the side of a stone cliff – Buddhist art from different centuries. **Ph25**

Crescent Moon Lake Lake surrounded by large sand dunes – beautiful views from the top of 🕌 Mingsha Shan dune. **Ph25/26**

Remarkable Cities and Cultural monuments

- ☐ UNESCO World Cultural Heritage
- ☐ Remarkable Cities
- ⛩ Ancient China
- ☪ Places of Islamic cultural interest
- ▲ Places of Buddhist cultural interest
- ⛫ Castle/fortress/fort
- ▲ Tomb/grave

Tibet, Nepal, Bhutan

Because of its high elevation, the expansive Plateau of Tibet is often referred to as the "Roof of the World." The mountainous plateau encompasses most of Tibet and sections of China's Qinghai province. With an average elevation of 4,500 meters above sea level, the Plateau of Tibet is the highest plateau in the world. It consists of a large basin that declines in elevation to the north, numerous mountain ranges, and wide valleys. Thousands of lakes and salt lakes are scattered throughout the area of the plateau. The largest lake, ⊠ **Nam Co**, covers 1,920 km² and is considered a sacred site by Tibetan Buddhists. The highlands of Tibet and especially the **Tanggula Shan mountain range** contain the sources of many important rivers

Sunset above the Tibetan Himalayas. **Pa30**

Annapurna 40-kilometer-long mountain mass in the ▲ Himalaya – Annapurna I (8,091 m). **Pb-Pc31**

Pokhara City at the foot of the mountain ▲ Machhapuchare (6,997 m) – lakes and forests in the surrounding area. **Pc31**

Royal Chitwan National Park ⊠ Situated in a pristine section of Nepal's Terai region – UNESCO world heritage site. **Pc32**

Kathmandu Valley The region of Nepal has been designated a UNESCO world heritage sites. The royal cities ⊠ Kathmandu and ⊠ Patan (middle photo) are home to several medieval palaces and other historic buildings. ⊠ Stupas (top photo) are the holiest temples for Nepal's Buddhist community. The royal city Bhaktapur is the location of the Nyatapola (bottom photo) and ⊠ Pashupatinath temples. **Pc32**

Scale 1:4,500,000

0   40   80 Kilometers

Principal travel routes
- Auto route
- Rail road
- Shipping route

Remarkable landscapes and natural monuments
- ⬛ UNESCO World Natural Heritage
- Mountain landscape
- Ravine/canyon
- Glacier
- Lake country
- National park (landscape)
- National park (flora)
- National park (fauna)
- ⊠ Wildlife reserve

that flow through East and Southeast Asia, including the Chang Jiang (Yangtze), Huang He, and Mekong Rivers. Because of the extreme climate, the highest elevated sections of the plateau are generally uninhabited. Much of the plateau's population lives in the numerous canyons and rivers valleys in the region's southeastern section. Southeastern Tibet is the location of several glacier covered mountains ranges and

at lower elevations expansive **subtropical forests** with abundant flora and fauna including rare Tibetan white pines and (white-lipped) Thorold's deer.
The most populous area of Tibet is the valley of the 🌊 **Yarlung-Zangbo (Brahmaputra) River** which flows from west to east at an elevation around 4,000 meters. According to traditional Tibetan beliefs the valley was the original "birthplace" of the Tibetan people. The valley

is bordered to the north by the 🏔 **Kailas Mountains** and to the south by the main range of the 🏔 **Himalayas**. The Himalayas are divided between Tibet and several neighboring countries: India, Nepal and Bhutan. **Mount Everest** (8,850 m), the world's highest mountain, is located in the Himalayas along the border between Nepal and Tibet. The Yarlung-Zango river valley features the majority of Tibet's cultural and religious

attractions including the ancient cities of 🏛 Lhasa and Xigaze.
Despite its small size, the **Kingdom of Nepal** has a wealth of breathtaking landscapes and cultural treasures. The country's culture has been heavily influenced by neighboring Tibet and India. Nepal is 800 kilometers long from east to west but its territory encompasses several climate zones including polar mountainous regions and subtropical marshlands.

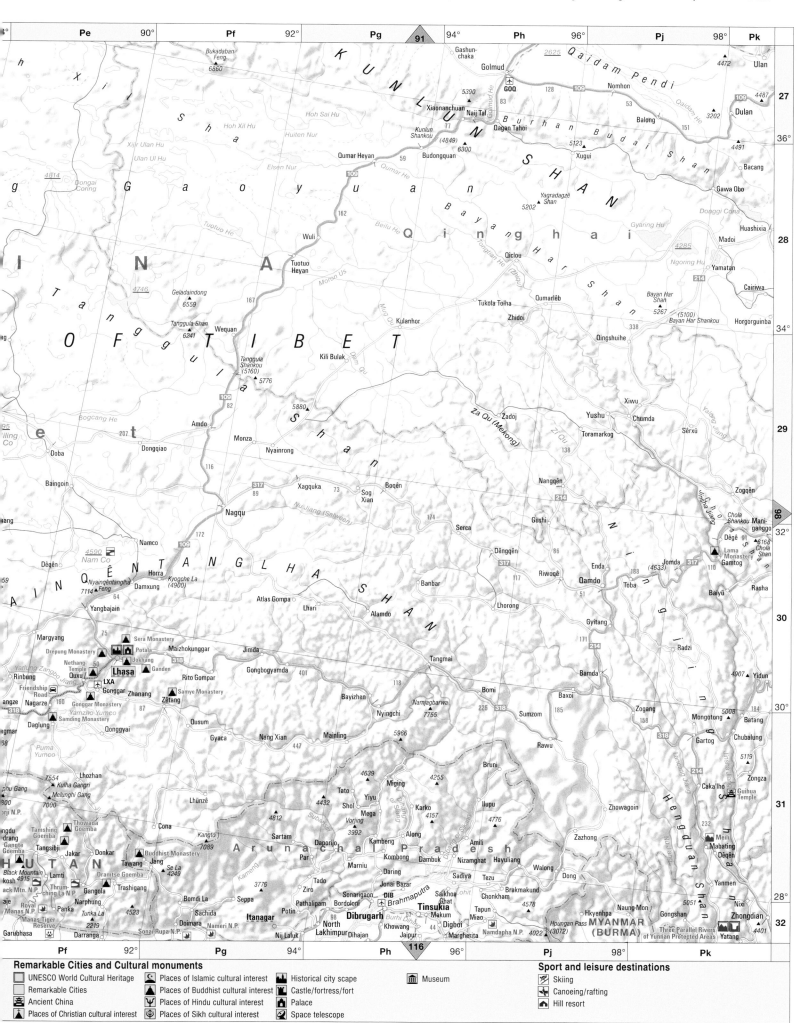

The Roof of the World The Himalayas and their foothills encompass many of the world's great mountains including 🏔 Mount Everest (Nepalese: Sagarmatha, 8,850 m, photo), which was first climbed in 1953. **Pd31/32**

Sagarmatha National Park The area contains glaciers, valleys, and 🏔 tall peaks including Mount Everest – world heritage site – 🏛 Tengpoche monastery (photo). **Pd32**

Lhasa The 🏰 Potala Palace towers above Lhasa and was once the summer residence of the Dalai Lamas. The 🏛 Johkang Temple contains the beautiful Meitreya chapel (bottom photo). **Pf31**

The Monasteries of Tibet 🏛 Tashilhungpo (top photo; **Pe31**) monastery, founded in 1447. 🏛 Samye monastery, Tibet's oldest, (bottom photo; **Pf31**) was founded around 767 AD.

Remarkable Cities and Cultural monuments

- ▢ UNESCO World Cultural Heritage
- ▢ Remarkable Cities
- ▲ Ancient China
- ▲ Places of Christian cultural interest
- ⚜ Places of Islamic cultural interest
- ☪ Places of Buddhist cultural interest
- ☸ Places of Hindu cultural interest
- ☬ Places of Sikh cultural interest
- ⛪ Historical city scape
- ⛫ Castle/fortress/fort
- ⛩ Palace
- 🔭 Space telescope
- 🏛 Museum

Sport and leisure destinations

- ⛷ Skiing
- 🚣 Canoeing/rafting
- 🏨 Hill resort

Southern Baykal Ragion, Northern Mongolia

Mongolia in eastern Central Asia is a nation of large plateaus, arid **steppes** and vast **deserts**. Around 80 % of the country's territory is covered by mountain plateaus and lies at elevations above 1,000 meters. The western and southern sections contain several tall mountain ranges including the Mongolian-Gobi Altai which rises to a maximum height of 4,000 meters. Numerous large basins are situated between the mountains of the south

and west and many of the region's mountains are covered by glaciers. In northwestern Mongolia the mountains of the Eastern and Western Sayan mountain ranges rise to maximum heights around 3,000 meters.

The **Hangayn Mountains** are a range of low and heavily eroded mountains. They

Lake Baikal in Siberia, the world's deepest freshwater lake. **Qb–Qe19/20**

Irkutsk Russian city in eastern Siberia – Kazanskaya Church, built in the 17th century (photo). **Qc19**

Lake Khovsgol National Park Located in northeastern Mongolia, Lake Khovsgol (top photo) is the second largest lake in Mongolia. Yaks (bottom photo) are the most valuable animals for the region's inhabitants. **Qa20**

Khorgo Terkhiin Tsagaan Nuur National Park The crater of Khorgo volcano was created around 8,000 years ago – 2,240 meters high – mountain scenery. **Pk21**

Mongolian/Gobi Altai This expansive mountain system is inhabited by Mongolian nomads (top photo). The region's wildlife includes snow leopards and argali sheep. Böön Tsagaan (bottom photo) is the largest salt lake in the area. **Pk-Qb23**

Orkhon Valley Contains the meandering Orkhon River – Orkhon waterfalls – archeological sites. **Qa-Qb22**

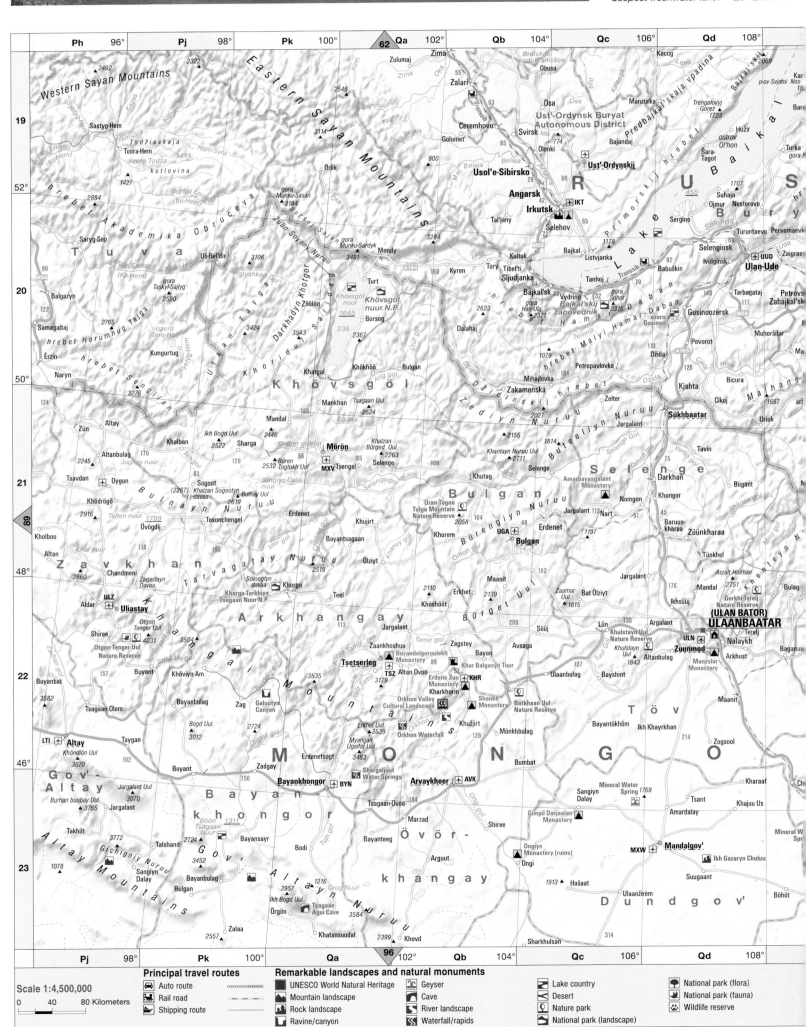

Scale 1:4,500,000

0   40   80 Kilometers

Principal travel routes
- Auto route
- Rail road
- Shipping route

Remarkable landscapes and natural monuments
- UNESCO World Natural Heritage
- Mountain landscape
- Rock landscape
- Ravine/canyon
- Geyser
- Cave
- River landscape
- Waterfall/rapids
- Lake country
- Desert
- Nature park
- National park (landscape)
- National park (flora)
- National park (fauna)
- Wildlife reserve

cover much of central Mongolia and are broken by numerous large plains. Around nine percent of Mongolia's territory is covered by forests, many of which are concentrated in the center of the country. The northern foothills of the Hangayn Mountains comprise an area of forested steppes which are mostly used for livestock grazing. In contrast to the northern foothills, the southern edges of the Hangayn Mountains are a mostly treeless area covered by large grasslands. Central Mongolia features numerous lakes and smaller bodies of water, many of which contain saline water.

The Mongolian section of the ☒ **Gobi Desert** consists primarily of arid steppes. The desert covers much of southern Mongolia and is bordered to the north by mountain ranges and dense taiga. The ☒ Gobi is around 2,000 kilometers long. Its sandy deserts, marshes, and grassy steppes where livestock is grazed. Eastern Mongolia consists of a large plateau that is situated at heights between 800 and 1,000 meters above sea level. This plateau contains large basins with numerous salt lakes and vast steppes covered by grass. Mongolia's rivers flow in three directions: south into China, north into Russia, and east to the Pacific Ocean.

Lake Baikal is the largest freshwater lake in Asia and the deepest lake on the planet with a maximum depth of approximately 1,620 meters. At least 1,000 unique species inhabit the lake but its biodiversity is threatened by manmade pollution.

Mongolia has an arid and cool continental climate. Winters are dry and cold, while summers are temperate with plentiful rainfall. In Mongolia's capital **Ulaanbaatar (Ulan Bator)** temperatures often fall below -47° C during winter.

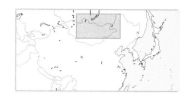

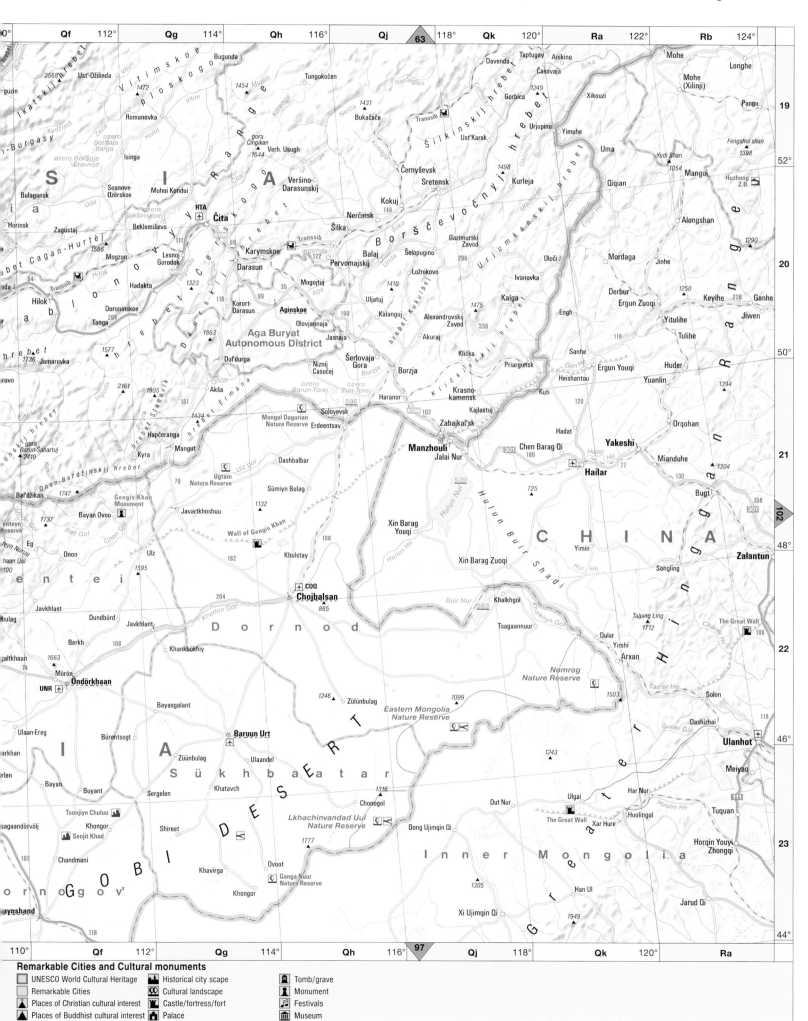

Amarbayasgalant Buddhist ▲ monastery built in the 17th century. The monastery is situated in a picturesque Mongolian valley.   **Qc21**

Ulaanbaatar (Ulan Bator) Mongolia's capital and largest city – the former ⊡ Winter Palace now contains a museum – Mongolian temples (photo).   **Qd22**

Erdene Zuu Monastery Oldest Mongolian ▲ temple, founded in 1586 – damaged in the 1930s and recently renovated.   **Qb22**

Shankh Monastery ▲ Heavily damaged during the early Communist era – now in the process of reconstruction.   **Qb22**

Ikh Gazaryn Chuluu ⊡ Stone formation near Mandalgov' – many interesting granite formationes in the suroounding area.   **Qd23**

Khan Khentii Nature Reserve The birthplace and burial site of Genghis Khan, according to traditional beliefs.   **Qe21**

Remarkable Cities and Cultural monuments

☐	UNESCO World Cultural Heritage	⊞	Historical city scape	⌂	Tomb/grave
☐	Remarkable Cities	⊠	Cultural landscape	⊞	Monument
▲	Places of Christian cultural interest	⊠	Castle/fortress/fort	⊡	Festivals
▲	Places of Buddhist cultural interest	⊡	Palace	⌨	Museum

Northern China

Northern China is a region of high plateaus, deserts, and craggy mountains. Northern China's topography resembles the shape of a stairway. The region's elevation rises from east to west like a series of steps or ridges. The **Alxa Plateau** in the far west of Northern China is the first in a chain of sparsely populated high plateaus covered by deserts and arid grasslands. The plateau stretches between the Mongolian border in the north and the 🏔

Qilian Shan Mountains in the south. The **Gansu (Hexi) Corridor** is over 1,000 kilometers long and stretches through the Gansu province. The corridor has been a major transport route to western China since ancient times. The Gansu Corridor was once part of the ancient **Silk Road** and the Great Wall of China runs parallel

The Great Wall of China is 6,700 kilometers long. **Qg25**

Bayanzag 📷 The valley contains excavation sites with dinosaur fossils – around 100 intact skeletons have been found here. **Qb23**

Dafo Si 🏛 Large Buddhist temple built in the 11th century – largest reclining Buddha statue in China; 35 meters long. **Qa26**

Wuwei The city of Wuwei is home to three major tourist attractions: the 🏛 Han tomb of Leitai, the 🏛 tomb of the princesses, and the 🏛 Haizang temple. **Qb27**

Ta'er Si Large 🏛 monastery complex built by Tibetan Buddhist lamas in the 16th century – beautiful landscapes – historic sculptures. **Qa27**

Xixia Wangling Burial site containing the tombs of 72 kings and nobles from the Xixia Kingdom (1038–1227) – often called the "Pyramids of China". **Qc26**

Jiayuguan Large historic 🏛 fortress built in the 14th century – the surrounding walls are ten meters high. **Pk26**

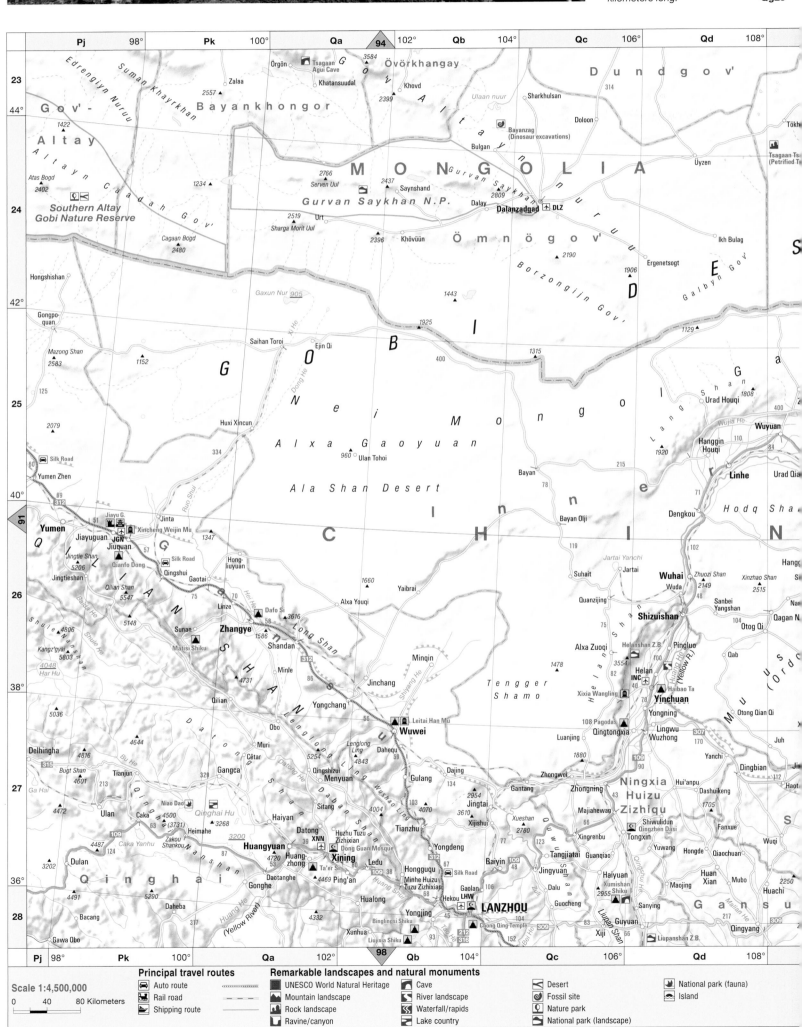

Scale 1:4,500,000

0   40   80 Kilometers

Principal travel routes
- 🚗 Auto route
- 🚂 Rail road
- ⛴ Shipping route

Remarkable landscapes and natural monuments
- ◼ UNESCO World Natural Heritage
- ◼ Mountain landscape
- ◼ Rock landscape
- ◼ Ravine/canyon
- ◻ Cave
- ◻ River landscape
- ◻ Waterfall/rapids
- ◻ Lake country
- ◻ Desert
- ◻ Fossil site
- ◻ Nature park
- ◻ National park (landscape)
- ◻ National park (fauna)
- ◻ Island

to the corridor for much of its length. The Silk Road was not only a trade route but also a meeting point for many different cultures and religions. The numerous beautiful ⌂ mosques and ▲ Buddhist temples scattered throughout northwestern China are reminders of the cultural interactions that took place in the region during ancient times.

The center of Northern China is covered by the **basin of the** ⌐ **Huang He (Yellow) River**. The basin area is often considered the craddle of Chinese civilization. The Chinese name Huang-He literally means the "Yellow River" and comes from the yellow color of the silt in the river. Every year the river transports around 1.6 billion tons of silt, much of which gets deposited along its banks. The river flows north in the shape of a bow, around the Ordos Plateau. This large plateau is covered by deserts and

extends east to the ▲ highlands of Shaanxi province. Wutaishan, the tallest mountain in Shaanxi province rises 3,058 meters above sea level.

The eastern sections of Northern China consist mostly of densely populated plains dissected by many rivers and canals. The ▤ **Great Wall of China**, a UNESCO world heritage site, begins in this region. It is, however, just one of many historic monuments and attrac-

tions in the region. ⌂ **Beijing**, the capital of China is home to many important Chinese historic sites including Tiananmen Square and the ⌂ **Forbidden City**, once the residence of China's emperors. **Qufu**, the birthplace of Confucius and the mountain ▲ **Taishan** are also located in the region and both are highly revered by the Chinese. Northern China extends east to the delta of the Huang He River on the coast of **Bo Hai**, an arm of the Pacific.

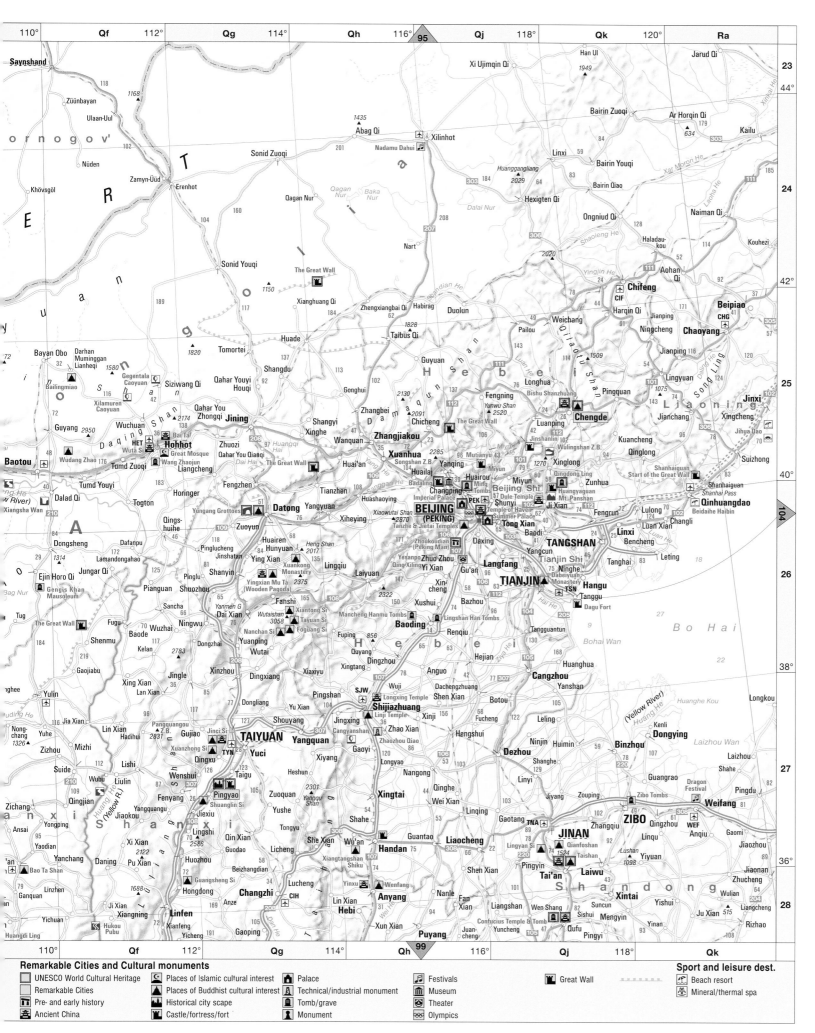

Yungang ▲ 53 grottoes with Buddhist sculptures and bas-reliefs, a UNESCO world heritage site – created in the 5th century. **Qg25**

Chengde Summer ⌂ palace of the Qing dynasty – Buddhist temple complex – UNESCO world heritage site. **Qj25**

The Great Wall The ▤ section near Badaling has been restored – built under the Ming dynasty – 🏛 museum. **Qh25**

The Imperial Ming Tombs ⌂ Burial site of the Ming dynasty (1368–1644) – UNESCO world heritage site – sculptures. **Qj25**

Beijing China's capital is both a historic and modern city. Photos from top to bottom: the ⌂ Forbidden City, the ⌂ Imperial Summer Palace, the ⌂ Temple of Heaven, a UNESCO world heritage site. **Qj26**

Remarkable Cities and Cultural monuments

			Sport and leisure dest.
▢ UNESCO World Cultural Heritage	⌂ Places of Islamic cultural interest	▤ Festivals	⛵ Beach resort
▢ Remarkable Cities	▲ Places of Buddhist cultural interest	🏛 Museum	♨ Mineral/thermal spa
⟁ Pre- and early history	⌂ Palace	▦ Theater	
⛩ Ancient China	⚙ Technical/industrial monument	⬚ Olympics	
	⌂ Historical city scape	⌂ Tomb/grave	▤ Great Wall
	⌂ Castle/fortress/fort	⌂ Monument	

Central China

Central China contains an incredible wealth of important cultural and natural attractions. The region also features a fascinating mix of distinct climate zones and topographies.

The western edges of Central China are covered by the **highlands of Qinghai** province and sections of the **Tibetan Plateau**. This area is home to major rivers flowing from to north to south and expansive mountain systems including the

Hengduan Shan along the border between China and Myanmar (Burma). Also in the region, the craggy and tall Daxue Shan range rises above 7,000 meters in Sichuan province. The source of the **Jinsha Jiang River** lies in Tibet. The river forms the western borders of Sichuan. Near Yibin, the Jinsha Jiang

Arid plains and rugged mountains near Labrang. **Qb28**

Labrang Si Monastery The largest Tibetan Buddhist (Lamaism) monastery outside of Tibet – golden stupas. **Qb28**

Jiuzhaigou National park – waterfalls, steppes, and grasslands – rare plants and animals. **Qb29**

Huanglong Mountain valley – hot thermal springs and tall stone formations – large glaciers. **Qb29**

Wolong Giant Panda Reserve Protected habitat of giant pandas and other endangered animals – research area for panda preservation. **Qb30**

Leshan Giant Buddha Large Buddha statue built into the side of a stone wall – temple and pagoda built during the Tang era. **Qb31**

Lijiang Historic town with wooden houses and cobblestone streets – UNESCO world heritage site – traditional Naxi culture. **Qa32**

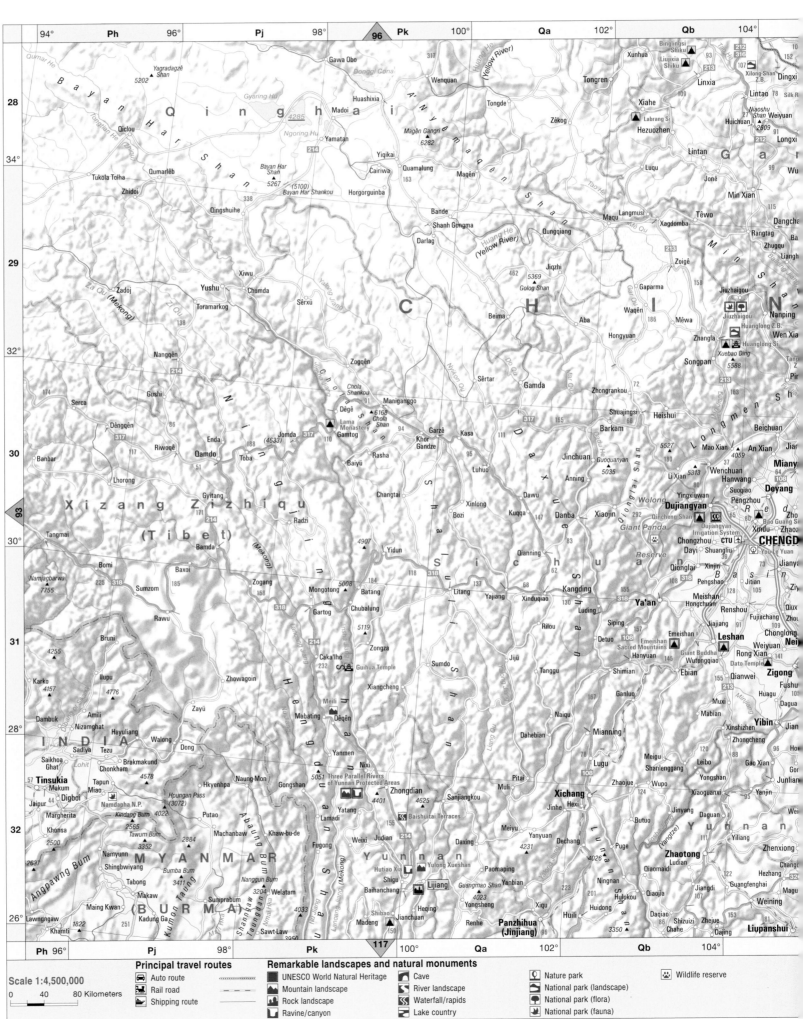

Scale 1:4,500,000

0   40   80 Kilometers

Principal travel routes
- Auto route
- Rail road
- Shipping route

Remarkable landscapes and natural monuments
- UNESCO World Natural Heritage
- Mountain landscape
- Rock landscape
- Ravine/canyon
- Cave
- River landscape
- Waterfall/rapids
- Lake country
- Nature park
- National park (landscape)
- National park (flora)
- National park (fauna)
- Wildlife reserve

becomes the Chang Jiang (Yangtze) River, Asia's longest river.

The Chang Jiang flows through the large Sichuan Basin, which covers most of eastern Sichuan. The basin is also widely known as the **Red Basin**, a reference to its rich red soil. The mountainous western edge of the basin is home to many important natural and cultural attractions. The sacred mountain **Emei**, the **Giant Panda Reserve** near

the city of Chengdu, **Huanglong National Park** and **Juizhaigou National Park** are among the more popular attractions in the region.

Near Fengjie, the river passes through the first of the famous **Three Gorges**, a group of scenic gorge landscapes. After passing Yichang, the river flows through a large plain containing many lakes and rivers. The plain comprises sections of both the Chang Jiang River

basin and the delta of the Han River. **Dongting Hu**, situated on the plain, is China's second largest freshwater lake. The **Qin Ling Mountains** are located just north of the Sichuan Basin. The mountain range separates the subtropical regions to its south from the more temperate areas to the north. Many Chinese consider the Qin Ling Mountains a boundary between Northern and Southern China. The Wei River flows along the

edges of the Qin Ling Mountains and the Wei river valley contains the city **Xi'an**. The city was once the starting point of the ancient Silk Road and is home to several important historic sites. The Wei empties into the **Huang He (Yellow) River** near the city of Tong'guan. East of the city **Luoyang**, the Huang He flows into the **North China Plain**. The large plain covers 400,000 km² and is one of China's most densely populated regions.

Xi'an Once a capital of China and site of the Wild Goose Pagoda (top photo) and the terracotta army in Qin Shi Huangdi's tomb (bottom photo). **Qe28**

Longmen Shiku Grottoes containing historic Buddhist art – over 2,000 statues and bas-reliefs. **Qg28**

Wudang Sacred mountain for Taoists – highest peak rises 1,612 meters – Ming era temple and 36 monasteries. **Qf29**

Chang Jiang (Yangtze) Some of the landscapes in the beautiful Three Gorges (top photo) will be submerged after the completion of the gigantic Three Gorges Dam (bottom photo). **Qf30**

Dazu Buddhist caves – around 50,000 colorful sculptures and bas-reliefs from the Tang and Song eras. **Qc31**

Remarkable Cities and Cultural monuments

				Sport and leisure destinations
UNESCO World Cultural Heritage	Cultural landscape	Dam	Market	Mineral/thermal spa
Remarkable Cities	Historical city scape	Remarkable bridge		Amusement/theme park
Ancient China	Castle/fortress/fort	Tomb/grave		
Places of Buddhist cultural interest	Palace	Theater of war/battlefield		

Southern China is a region of low mountains and rolling hills dissected by a network of rivers and canals. Most of the region has a subtropical climate and experiences heavy rainfall.
The ⬛ **Highlands of Southern China** are bordered on their western edges by the large Yunnan Plateau which contains the source of many rivers including the ⬛ Wu River, a major tributary of the Chang Jiang (Yellow) River. A long chain

of ⬛ mountains and hills stretch northwest of the highlands and into the provinces Guangdong, Jiangxi, and Fujian. **Heng Shan**, one of the five holy mountains in Taoism and the incredibly tall "Dragon's Backbone Terrace" near Longsheng are two of the most fascinating natural attractions in the region. The

Stunning landscapes along the Lijiang River near Yangshuo. **Qf33**

Guilin Beautiful landscapes along the ⬛ Li River. Photos from top to bottom: Hills along the Li River, Moon Hill near Yangshuo, traditional fishers. **Qf33**

Longsheng Village in northeastern Guangxi province – Dragon's Backbone Terrace – ⬛ terraced rice fields on steep hills. **Qf33**

Sanya City on the southern edge of Hainan, an island off the southeastern coast of China – ⬛ beautiful sand beaches. **Qe36**

Hoa Binh Province in northern Vietnam – ancient Vietnamese ⬛ historic sites along the ⬛ Black River – ▲ Perfume Pagoda. **Qc35**

Halong Bay ⬛ Bay of the descending Dragon – 1,600 islands – stone formations – UNESCO world heritage site. **Qd35**

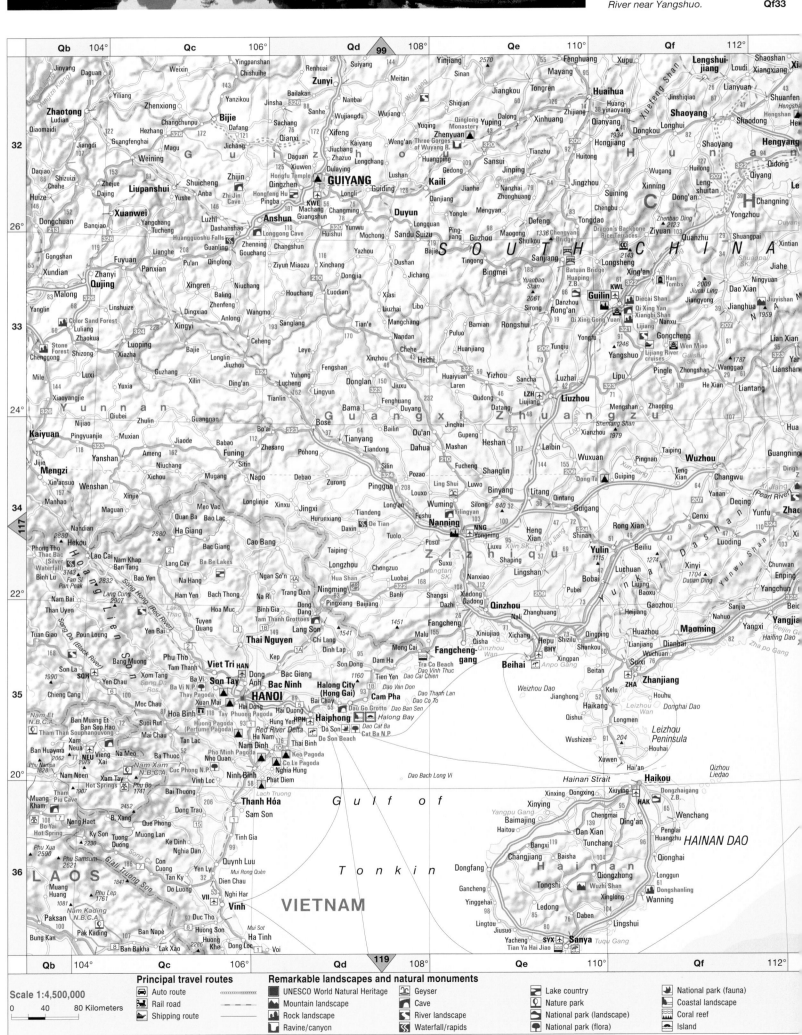

Principal travel routes

Scale 1:4,500,000
0   40   80 Kilometers

- 🚗 Auto route
- 🚆 Rail road
- Shipping route

Remarkable landscapes and natural monuments

- ⬛ UNESCO World Natural Heritage
- Mountain landscape
- Rock landscape
- Ravine/canyon
- Geyser
- Cave
- River landscape
- Waterfall/rapids
- Lake country
- Nature park
- National park (landscape)
- National park (flora)
- National park (fauna)
- Coastal landscape
- Coral reef
- Island

tall stone formations along the ◩ **Lijiang River** near Yangshuo and Guilin are known throughout China for their unique beauty. The ◩ **Lianhua Shan range** is a small mountain ridge stretching through the coastal areas of southeastern China. Much of Guangdong province's population is concentrated in or near the ◩ **delta of the Pearl River**. In addition to the Pearl River, several other rivers also flow into the large delta. The historic port

city of Guangzhou (Canton) is situated on the northern edge of the delta.
The northeastern section of Southern China consists of hills and low mountains extending to a coast which is broken by many bays and peninsulas. **Taiwan**, the largest island in the region is separated from mainland China by the Taiwan Strait, which has a maximum width of 200 kilometers. The majority of Taiwan's 21 million inhabitants live on

the plains of western Taiwan. Most of the eastern and central sections of the island are dominated by ◩ mountain ranges. Although the island has historic ties to mainland China, Taiwan has been governed seperately from the mainland since the end of the Chinese Civil War in 1949. **Macau** and ◩ **Hong Kong** are both situated on peninsulas along the southern coast of China. Hong Kong was a British colony for more than a century

and remained politically seperated from China until the city and it surroundings were integrated into the People's Republic of China in 1997. **Hainan**, a large tropical island in southernmost China, is bordered to the west by the Gulf of Tonkin. Along the western edge of the Gulf of Tonkin lies northern **Vietnam** with the country's capital Hanoi and the densely populated region in and around the ◩ **Red River delta**.

Hong Kong Modern ⌂ skyline with beautiful towers along the waterfront (top photo). Victoria Peak offers the best views of the city (bottom photo). **Qh34**

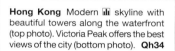

Macau ⌂ St. Paul's Cathedral (top photo) and the ◩ casino (bottom photo) draw many visitors to this former Portuguese colony. **Qg34**

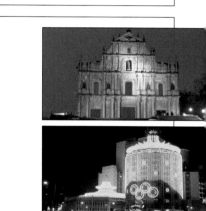

Taipei Taiwan's capital – population, three million – ◩ Chiang Kai-shek Memorial (photo) – national opera and concert halls. **Ra33**

Taroko National Park Deep ◩ gorges – waterfalls, caves, and historic temples – ⌂ hot thermal springs. **Ra33**

Kaohsiung Taiwanese city – ◩ Three Phoenix Palace – ◩ Dragon and Tiger Pagodas (photo) are connected by a bridge. **Ra34**

Remarkable Cities and Cultural monuments

UNESCO World Cultural Heritage	Places of Christian cultural interest	Historical city scape
Remarkable Cities	Places of Islamic cultural interest	Impressive skyline
Prehistoric rockscape	Places of Buddhist cultural interest	Castle/fortress/fort
Ancient China	Cultural landscape	Remarkable bridge

Tomb/grave	
Monument	
Festivals	
Museum	

Sport and leisure destinations

Horse racing	Seaport
Sailing	Beach resort
Diving	Mineral/thermal spa
Wind surfing	Hill resort

Northeastern China, Southeastern Russia, Hokkaido

Large sections of China's three north-eastern provinces are covered by expansive forests. In the past, this region of China was widely known as **Manchuria**. One of the largest forests in China stretches along the edges of the 🚂**Lesser Khingan Range**. Southwest of the range lies the densely populated Manchurian Plain, the economic center of the region. The major industrial cities **Qiqihar** and **Daqing** are both situated on the

plain. **Harbin** in Heilongjiang province is the region's cultural center. The northeastern section of China's Northeast (Manchuria) is covered by large marshlands and bogs. This area is dissected by many rivers including the numerous tributaries of the 🚢**Amur River** (Heilong Jiang) such as the Songhua Jiang and Naoli He.

The jagged coastline of the Shakotan Peninsula (Japan).   **Sa24**

With a total length of 4,416 kilometers, the Amur River is the fifth longest river in Asia. The Amur River – together with its tributary the 🚢**Ussuri River** (Wusuli Jiang) – forms a long section of the northern border between northeastern China and Russia. **Lake Khanka** (Xingkai Hui) is a shallow lake near the border with a total area of 4,380 km² and a maximum depth of ten meters. The Laoye Ling Mountains and the eastern foothills of

Trans-Siberian Railway The famous 🚆 rail link was completed in 1916 and stretches over 9,290 kilometers in both Europe and Asia. The journey between Moscow and Vladivostok takes ten days on the Trans-Siberian.

Vladivostok 🏙 Russian port city on the Pacific coast – important industrial and trade center.   **Rf24**

Lake Wudalianchi 🏞 Nature reserve – five interconnected lakes – 🕳 caves containing hot thermal springs.   **Rd21**

Harbin 🏛 Ice and Snow Festival held every January – illuminated sculptures and buildings made of ice (photo).   **Rd23**

Lake Jingpo The lake 🏞 is 45 kilometers long, surrounded by forests, and dotted with small islands. The beautiful 20-meter-tall 🏞 Diaoshuilou waterfall is located near the lake's shore.   **Re24**

Scale 1:4,500,000

0   40   80 Kilometers

Principal travel routes
- 🚗 Auto route
- 🚆 Rail road
- 🚢 Shipping route

Remarkable landscapes and natural monuments
- ■ UNESCO World Natural Heritage
- ■ Mountain landscape
- ■ Active volcano
- ■ Cave
- River landscape
- Waterfall/rapids
- Lake country
- Nature park
- National park (landscape)
- National park (fauna)
- Wildlife reserve
- Coastal landscape

the ⛰ Wanda Shan Range stretch along the eastern border of northeastern China. A wide strip of Russian territory lies between the northernmost sections of China's Northeast and the Pacific Ocean. The ⛰ Sikhote Alin mountain system stretches more than 1,200 kilometers along the Pacific coast of southeastern Russia between Vladivostok to the Amur River delta. 🏝 Sakhalin, the largest Russian island, is separated from the main-

land by the Tartar Strait. In recent years, the island has become an important center of the Russian oil industry.

Hokkaido is the northernmost of the four main Japanese islands. The sparsely populated island encompasses 20 % of Japan's total land area but is home to less than 5 % of the national population. The island is home to three significant mountain ranges: the Kitami Range in the north, the Hidaka Range in the south,

and the Ishikari Mountains in central Hokkaido. Hokkaido's tallest mountain, Asahidake, rises 2,290 meters above sea level. 🏞 **Daisetsuzan National Park** in central Japan is the largest national park in Japan and contains beautiful landscapes with many high volcanoes, lakes, and forests. 🏞 Shiretoko National Park is situated on an isolated peninsula in northernmost Hokkaido. 🏞 **Akan National Park** in eastern Hokkaido

contains the largest crater lake in Japan. 🏞 **Lake Mashu**, one of the cleanest lakes in the world, has stunningly clear water. The largest body of water on Hokkaido, 🏞 **Lake Kutcharo**, has an area of 80 km². Hokkaido's climate is significantly cooler from those of the other Japanese main islands. The average temperature in summer is around 20° C and the island experiences heavy snowfall in winter.

Shiretoko National Park 🏞 Peninsula in northern Hokkaido – rugged landscapes encompassing several volcanoes. **Sc23**

Akan National Park 🏞 Mountains, forests, and lakes – 🏞 crater lakes: Lake Mashu and Lake Kutcharo – ♨ hot springs. **Sc24**

Daisetsuzan National Park Japan's largest 🏞 national park – mountains, plains, and gorges – mountain vegetation. **Sb24**

Sapporo ⊡ The capital city of Hokkaido prefecture – tree-lined central boulevard, Odori (photo) – 🏛 Ainu Museum – 🌿 botanical gardens. **Sa24**

Shikotsu Toya National Park The park contains diverse landscapes including 🌋 volcanoes, 🏞 crater lakes, and many ♨ hot springs. Photos from top to bottom: Lake Toya, Mount Yotei, Lake Shikotsu. **Sa24**

Remarkable Cities and Cultural monuments

☐ UNESCO World Cultural Heritage	☪ Places of Islamic cultural interest	🏛 Palace
☐ Remarkable Cities	☸ Places of Buddhist cultural interest	🏛 Technical/industrial monument
☐ Ancient China	🏙 Historical city scape	🎵 Festivals
✝ Places of Christian cultural interest	🏰 Castle/fortress/fort	🎭 Theater

Sport and leisure destinations

🏇 Horse racing
⛷ Skiing
⚓ Seaport
♨ Mineral/thermal spa

◈ Olympics

Korea, Honshu (Central Japan)

Korea, the "land of the morning calm", and Japan are home to many of the wealthiest and most economically developed regions in Asia. At their closest, South Korea and the Japanese island Honshu are separated by just 160 kilometers of water. North Korea shares a long border with China and a small 17 kilometer long border with Russia. Most of the **Korean Peninsula** consists of mountainous land, with the tallest mountains concentrated

in the north. The 🏔 **T'aebaek Mountains** stretch along the peninsula's eastern coast and the highest peak in the range, Sorak, rises 1,708 meters. Korea is situated between regions with subtropical and cold continental climates but the peninsula itself has a mostly temperate climate with abundant rainfall.

Mount Fuji is Japan's most revered mountain. **Rk28**

Pyongyang Capital of North Korea – numerous monuments, including the Tower of the Juche Idea (photo). **Rc26**

Kaesong 🏛 Burial site of ancient kings – once the capital of the Koryo kingdom – one of Korea's oldest cities. **Rd27**

Changdeokgung Palace Originally built during the Joseon Kindgom, the historic 🏛 palace in Seoul has been destroyed and reconstructed several times. **Rd27**

Seoul Capital of South Korea and the largest city on the peninsula – historic Old Seoul district – 🏛 ancient royal palaces. **Rd27**

Haeinsa Temple 🏛 Buddhist holy site in South Korea's 🏞 Kayasan National Park – location of the Tripitaka Koreana, a Korean cultural treasure. **Re28**

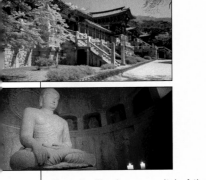

Kyongju The former capital of the ancient Silla Kingdom. The Pugulska temple (top photo) is considered a 🏛 holy site and masterpiece of Silla architecture. The 🏛 Seokguram Grotto houses a historic Buddha statue (bottom photo). **Re28**

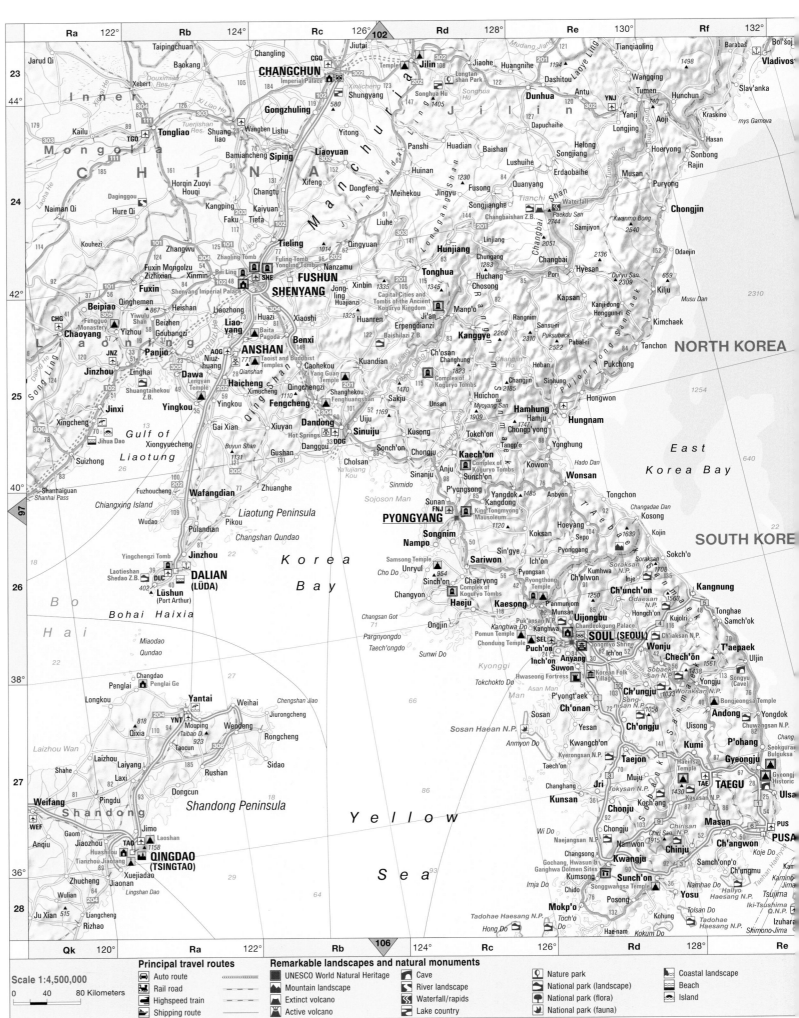

Scale 1:4,500,000

0   40   80 Kilometers

Principal travel routes
- Auto route
- Rail road
- Highspeed train
- Shipping route

Remarkable landscapes and natural monuments
- UNESCO World Natural Heritage
- Mountain landscape
- Extinct volcano
- Active volcano
- Cave
- River landscape
- Waterfall/rapids
- Lake country
- Nature park
- National park (landscape)
- National park (flora)
- National park (fauna)
- Coastal landscape
- Beach
- Island

Korea, Honshu (Central Japan)

Despite the strong cultural influence of Japan and China, the Koreans have been able to preserve their own unique culture. Since the Korean War ended through a ceasefire in 1953, the Korean Peninsula has been divided between capitalist South Korea and communist North Korea. Since the 1970s, South Korea has undergone an incredible transformation from a poor country to a major exporter with a relatively high standard of living.

In addition to its populated islands, **Japan** also consists of at least 3,000 small uninhabited islands. The country has four ⬛ main islands: Hokkaido, Shikoku, Kyushu, and Honshu. Honshu is the largest and most populous Japanese island. From north to south, the main islands extend over a distance of 4,000 kilometers. The vast majority of the mountainous nation's land is unsuitable for agriculture. All of the Japanese islands are part of a large underwater mountain system and the country is situated in a geologically active region where earthquakes occur frequently. In addition to earthquakes, Japan is also threatened by other natural hazards including cyclones, tsunamis, and volcanic eruptions. There are approximately ⬛ 265 volcanoes in Japan, around 60 of which are active. The tallest and most famous Japanese mountain is Mount Fuji which rises 3,776 meters.

There are many lakes scattered throughout the countryside and Japan's national parks. The country's largest lake, ⬛ **Lake Biwa**, covers 674 km² on the island of Honshu. There are three distinct climate zones in Japan but most of the country has a temperate humid climate with plentiful rainfall. The country's largest cities, including the capital Tokyo, are among the most modern and wealthy urban areas in the world.

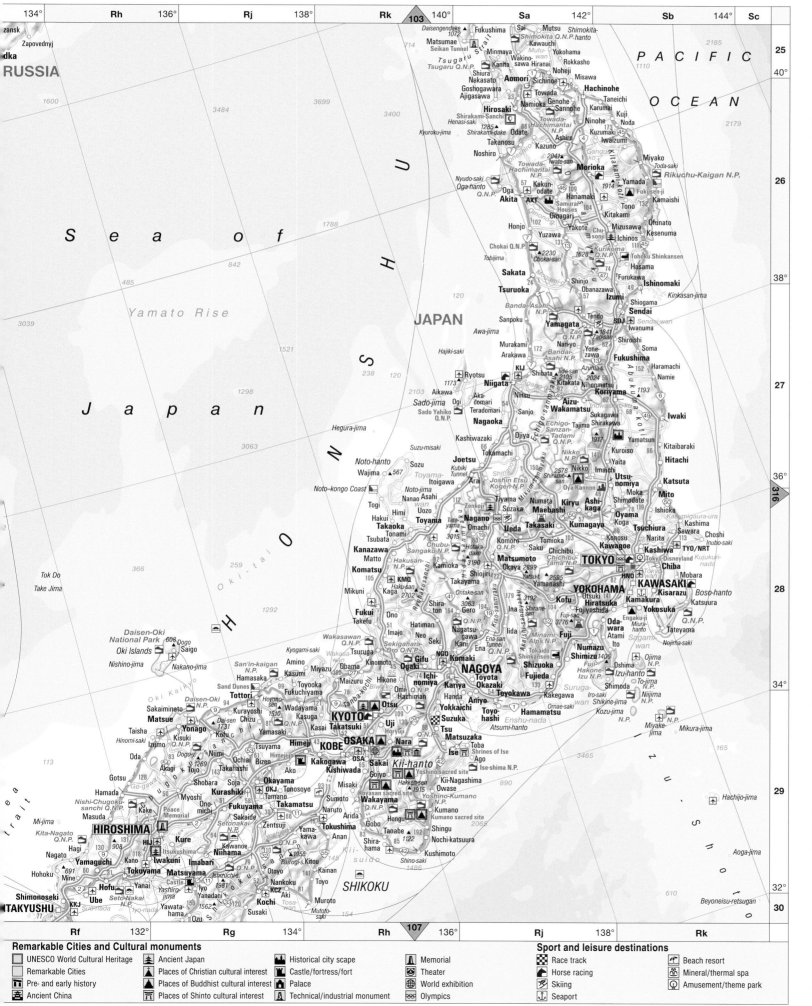

Nikko National Park ⬛ Conservation area north of Tokyo – Toshugu shrine (photo) – ⬛ Shinto and Buddhist architecture – rivers and waterfalls.　**Rk27**

Tokyo Japan's capital and largest city – ⬛ Imperial Palace – Tokyo Tower (333 m) in Shiba Park – ⬛ Ginza shopping district – ⬛ Shinto shrines – modern skyscrapers.　**Rk28**

Yokohama Japan's second largest city – leading ⬛ port city in East Asia – large Chinatown.　**Rk28**

Kyoto Japan's historic cultural center – population 1.5 million – traditional wooden architecture – Golden Pavilion (photo) – Imperial Palace – Nanzen-ji Temple – Kyoto National Museum.　**Rh28**

Nara Capital of Japan until 784 AD – ⬛ Todai-ji Temple, the world's largest wooden temple – ⬛ Yakushiji Temple – ⬛ Nara National Museum.　**Rh28**

Himeji ⬛ the "White Heron Castle" – Japan's best preserved medieval castle – 31 buildings and 21 towers – built in the 14th century and expanded in 1581.　**Rh28**

Itsukushima Shinto Shrine Important Shinto holy site on a small island near Hiroshima – built in the 13th century – world heritage site – the Red Torii gates stand on the water before the shrine (photo).　**Rg28**

Map labels

RUSSIA, Sea of Japan, Yamato Rise, JAPAN, PACIFIC OCEAN

Major cities and places: Fukushima, Aomori, Hirosaki, Hachinohe, Morioka, Akita, Sakata, Tsuruoka, Yamagata, Sendai, Niigata, Nagaoka, Aizu-Wakamatsu, Koriyama, Iwaki, Nagano, Toyama, Takaoka, Kanazawa, Fukui, Matsumoto, Takasaki, Maebashi, Utsunomiya, Mito, TOKYO, YOKOHAMA, KAWASAKI, Chiba, Nagoya, Gifu, KYOTO, OSAKA, KOBE, Nara, Tottori, Matsue, Yonago, Okayama, Kurashiki, HIROSHIMA, Kure, Yamaguchi, Shimonoseki, Takamatsu, Tokushima, Kochi, Matsuyama, Imabari, SHIKOKU

Legend

Remarkable Cities and Cultural monuments
- UNESCO World Cultural Heritage
- Remarkable Cities
- Pre- and early history
- Ancient China
- Ancient Japan
- Places of Christian cultural interest
- Places of Buddhist cultural interest
- Places of Shinto cultural interest
- Historical city scape
- Castle/fortress/fort
- Palace
- Technical/industrial monument
- Memorial
- Theater
- World exhibition
- Olympics

Sport and leisure destinations
- Race track
- Horse racing
- Skiing
- Seaport
- Beach resort
- Mineral/thermal spa
- Amusement/theme park

Eastern China is one of the world's most populous regions. The region can be divided into three distinct geographic areas. The southern sections of the region consist of rolling hills and mountains that stretch from the interior to the coast along the East China Sea. Eastern China's highlands tend to decline in height from south to north. The 🖫 **Chang Jiang (Yangtze) River** basin covers the central section of eastern

China. This area consists of densely populated and low lying plains between the cities 🖫 **Wuhan**, 🖫 **Nanjing**, and 🖫 **Shanghai**. The northern section of eastern China includes parts of the temperate North China Plain. The plains in this region are dissected by many rivers and canals. Several large lakes including

Thousand Islands Lake near Hangzhou (China). **Qk31**

Qufu Impressive 🖫 Qing-era temple at the birthplace of Confucius – UNESCO world heritage site. **Qj28**

Kaifeng 🖫 City on the Huang River – Dragon Pavilion (photo) – Xiang Guo monastery – the Iron Pagoda. **Qh28**

Nanjing 🖫 Ancient imperial city on the Yangtze River – 🖫 well preserved Ming era city walls – Ming era tombs with human and animal statues. **Qk29**

Huang Shan The 🖫 "Yellow Mountain" has inspired many poets and painters throughout Chinese history. Lotus Flower Peak rises 1,841 meters and is the tallest peak in the Huang Shan range. **Qk30**

Lushan 🖫 National Park around Lake Poyang – UNESCO world heritage site – caves, ponds, waterfalls, steep cliffs, and jagged peaks. **Qj31**

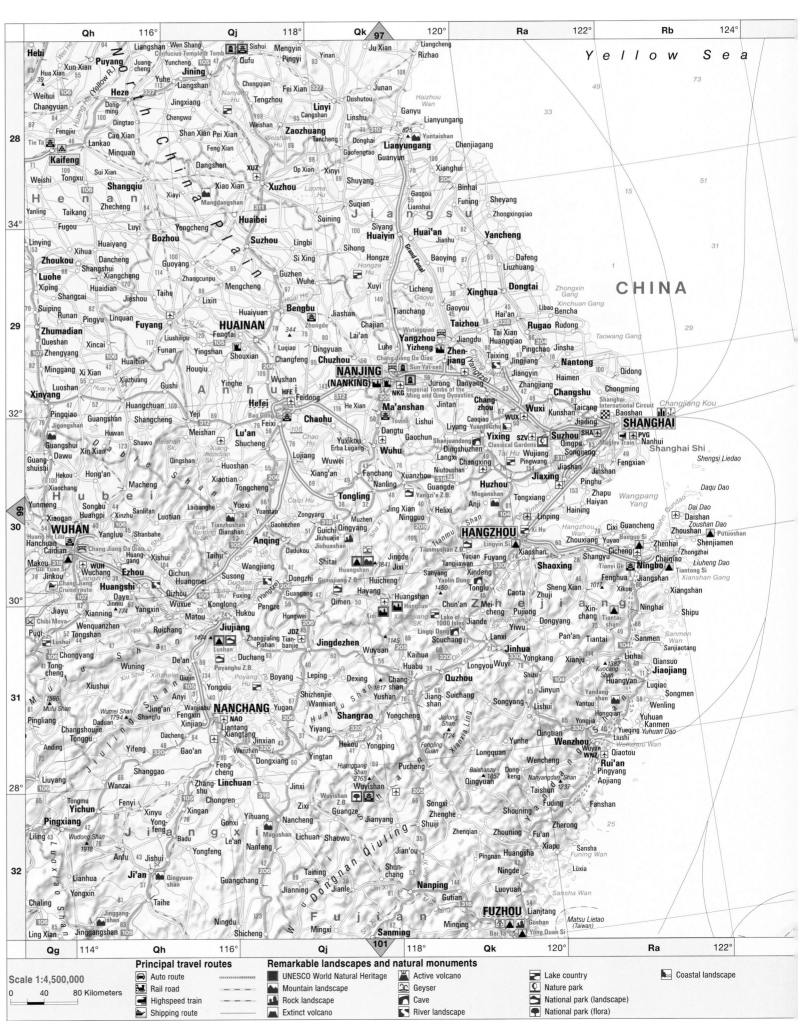

Scale 1:4,500,000

0   40   80 Kilometers

Principal travel routes
- Auto route
- Rail road
- Highspeed train
- Shipping route

Remarkable landscapes and natural monuments
- UNESCO World Natural Heritage
- Mountain landscape
- Rock landscape
- Extinct volcano
- Active volcano
- Geyser
- Cave
- River landscape
- Lake country
- Nature park
- National park (landscape)
- National park (flora)
- Coastal landscape

Eastern China, Kyushu, Ryukyu Islands (Southern Japan)

◪ **Hongze Hu** and ◪ **Nanyang Hu** are scattered throughout the region.
The vast basin of the Chang Jiang (Yangtze) River encompasses not only the river but its many tributaries and numerous lakes. The largest lake in the basin, ◪ **Po-yang Hu**, covers 3,500 km² and is also the largest freshwater lake in China.
There are many beautiful landscapes scattered throughout the highlands of eastern China including beautiful ▲

Mount Wuyi which rises 1,500 meters above sea level and the peaks of the ▲ **Huang Shan** and ▲ **Jiuhua Shan** mountain ranges. ◪ **"Thousand Island Lake"** in Zhejiang province is surrounded by lush green hills. The city ◪ **Hangzhou** is one of the starting points of the 2,000-kilometer-long **Grand Canal**, the world's longest man-made waterway.
The southern islands of **Japan** are separated from eastern China by the East

China Sea. **Kyushu** is the southernmost of Japan's four main islands. Most of Kyushu is covered by rolling hills and mountains. In addition to its many historic sites, there are also many natural attractions on Kyushu including ♨ hot springs, geysers, and active ▲ volcanoes. ◪ **Aso National Park** features pristine landscapes around the volcano Aso and is one of several national parks on Kyushu. The subtropical Ryukyu

Islands stretch over a distance of 1,200 kilometers between Kyushu and Taiwan. The islands are the southernmost Japanese island group. Despite the strong cultural influence of the Japanese main islands, the people of the **Ryukyu Islands** have maintained a distinct indigenous culture. **Okinawa**, situated halfway between Taiwan and Kyushu, is the largest and most populous island in the Ryukyu archipelago.

Shanghai China's largest city is a booming economic center. The Bund, a central boulevard, and Frenchtown contain historic western style architecture. In recent years, modern skyscrapers have been built in the ▥ Pudong district (top photo). The Oriental Pearl Tower (bottom photo) has become a city landmark. **Ra30**

Suzhou City on the shore of Lake Tai – major center of silk production – traditional ▣ Chinese gardens. **Ra30**

Hangzhou The ◪ West Lake is famous for its beautiful pavilions and bridges. ▲ Lingyin Temple contains ancient stone sculptures and the laughing Maitreya Buddha (photo). **Ra30**

Aso National Park Located on Kyushu – ▲ Aso San (1,592 m), large caldera containing five volcanic cones – hot springs. **Rf29**

Yakushima Island National Park ◪ UNESCO world heritage site – 40 peaks above 1,000 meters – Japanese cedars. **Rf30**

Ryukyu Islands Okinawa is the largest island – Gusuku, UNESCO world heritage site – historic palaces (photo). **RdRe31/32**

Remarkable Cities and Cultural monuments

- ☐ UNESCO World Cultural Heritage
- ☐ Remarkable Cities
- △ Ancient China
- △ Ancient Japan
- ▲ Places of Buddhist cultural interest
- ▲ Places of Shinto cultural interest
- ▥ Historical city scape
- ▥ Impressive skyline
- ▣ Castle/fortress/fort
- ▣ Palace
- ▣ Remarkable bridge
- ▣ Tomb/grave
- ✕ Theater of war/battlefield
- ▣ Market
- ▥ Museum

Sport and leisure destinations

- ▦ Race track
- ⚓ Seaport
- ▣ Beach resort
- ♨ Mineral/thermal spa
- ⚲ Amusement/theme park

Southern Asia

The section of Asia south of the Himalayan Mountain Range and China is generally divided into two distinct regions: South Asia and Southeast Asia. South Asia stretches south to the island Sri Lanka off the coast of India. The region encompasses almost the entire Indian subcontinent. A series of mountain ranges running from north to south through Pakistan and Afghanistan define the western boundaries of South Asia. The

mountain ranges in the far west of South Asia include sections of the **Hindu Kush**, the **Toba Kakar Range**, the **Central Brahui Range**, and the **Makran Coast Range**. The Indian and Bangladeshi borders to Myanmar (Burma) are generally considered the borders between South Asia and Southeast Asia.

The Mekong River in the highlands of Laos.

The **Thar Desert** covers a vast area between the Indus River Valley and Central India. Only a small percentage of the desert's 200,000 km² is covered by sand, the majority of desert consists of rocky arid land broken by hills.

The Indian subcontinent covers 3,287,782 km² and encompasses the majority of South Asia, with the notable exception of Sri Lanka. The northern sections of the subcontinent are cover-

Jammu and Kashmir Beautiful mountainous region – numerous lakes and lush mountain valleys.

The Ganges India's holiest river is 2,500 kilometers long and has a large delta (top photo). Important religious ceremonies occur in many places along the river.

Vindhya Range 1,000-kilometer-long mountain range – sandstone plateaus – mountain valleys – waterfalls.

Tamil Nadu Mountainous region in southern India – beautiful coastlines – Dravidian culture – Nilgiri Mountains.

Kerela Backwaters 1,500-kilometer-long network of canals and lagoons in Kerela (Southern India).

Sri Lanka Island republic off the coast of India – large coastal plains – mountainous interior – Adam's Peak (2,243 m).

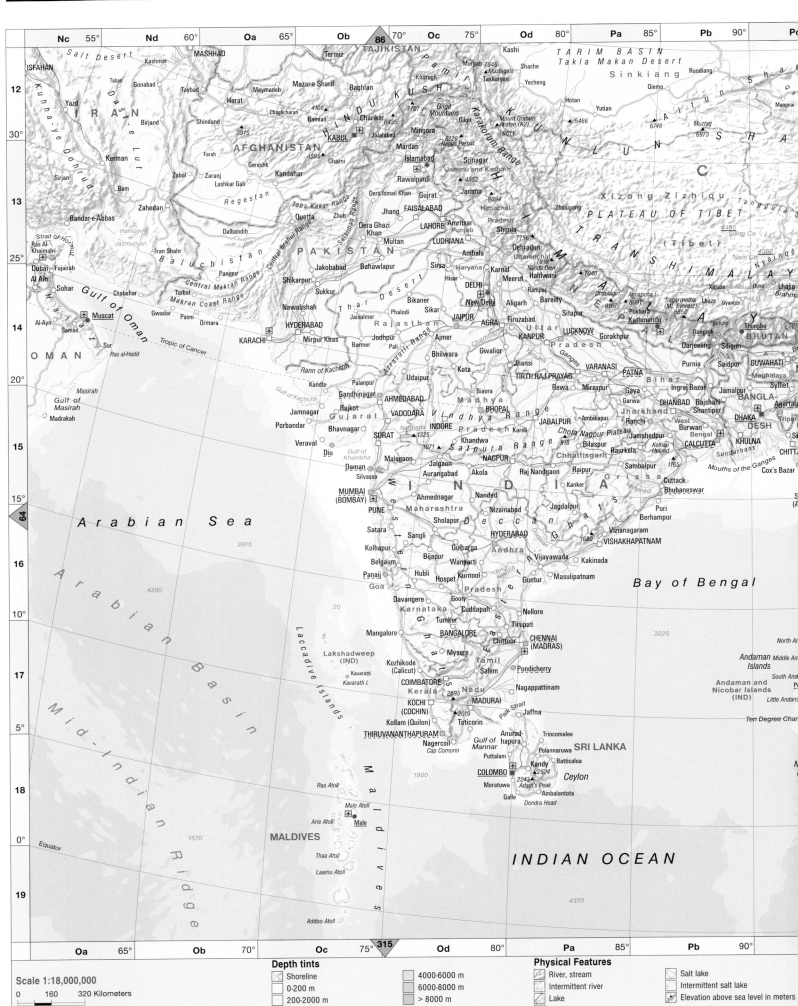

Scale 1:18,000,000

0   160   320 Kilometers

Depth tints
- Shoreline
- 0-200 m
- 200-2000 m
- 2000-4000 m
- 4000-6000 m
- 6000-8000 m
- > 8000 m

Physical Features
- River, stream
- Intermittent river
- Lake
- Intermittent lake
- Salt lake
- Intermittent salt lake
- Elevation above sea level in meters

ed by the plains stretching out from the Ganges and Brahmaputra Rivers. South of the plains lies a series of mountain ranges and hills including the Vindhya Range and the Aravalli Hills. The **Deccan Plateau** is a massive plateau covering most of Central and Southern India. The plateau is bounded by two mountain ranges on its eastern and western edges: the Eastern and Western Ghats. The island nation of **Sri Lanka** is situated off the southeastern coast of India. Sri Lanka's north is covered by savannahs which give way to the tall mountain ranges in the island's central and southern sections. The **Maldives** are a group of small coral island and atolls in the Indian Ocean. An independent country, the Maldives have a land area of 300 km². In northeast India, the **Ganges** and **Brahmaputra** Rivers flow into a vast delta which covers 44,000 km². The fertile region in and around the delta is densely populated. The outer edges of the delta are covered by large mangrove forests called **Sundarbans**. The Patkai and Arakan mountain ranges stretch along the border between India and Myanmar, the westernmost country in Southeast Asia. The Irrawaddy River is Myanmar's longest river and principal commercial waterway. The 2,000-kilometer-long river flows south to its delta on the Indian Ocean. East of the Irrawaddy River basin, mountainous highlands cover most of eastern Myanmar. Southern Thailand, Cambodia, and southern Vietnam consist primarily of vast low-lying plains. This region contains the deltas of several major rivers – including the **Mekong River delta** – Southern Asia is home to many distinct regions including tropical rain forests, grassy plains, and semi-arid savannahs.

Himalayas The world's tallest mountain range boasts 14 mountains higher than 8,000 meters. Photos from top to bottom: Annapurna, Sagarmatha National Park, Runbuk Glacier.

East Indian Highlands The Eastern Ghats, a mountain range on the edge of the Deccan Plateau – Simlipal National Park (photo).

The Mekong 4,500-kilometer-long river – source in the Tibetan mountains – several waterfalls – the Mekong Delta (70,000 km²).

Thai Highlands The highest mountains are concentrated in the far north – Doi Inthanon (2,590 m).

Halong Bay Unique coastal landscape near Hanoi – around 3,000 limestone formations dot the bay.

Political Boundaries
International
International disputed
Main administrative

Transportation
━━━ Interstate Hwy./Motorway
━━━ Main road
━━━ Railway
✈ Airport

Capitals of political units
■ WASHINGTON D.C. Independent
◉ Richmond State/province

Town symbols
■ Capital > 1 Mill. inhabitants
● Capital < 1 Mill. inhabitants
□ Statecapital > 1 Mill. inhabitants
○ Statecapital < 1 Mill. inhabitants
□ Towns > 1 Mill. inhabitants
○ Towns 100 000 bis 1 Mill. inhabitants
○ Towns < 100 000 inhabitants

Pakistan, Northern India

Few regions on the planet encompass as many contrasting landscapes as the northern section of the Indian subcontinent. The mountainous highlands of Pakistan (Central Grahui Range, Sulaiman Range, etc.) border the vast plains of the Indus River basin. The 3,200-kilometer-long ⊠ **Indus River** nourishes the fertile plains of Punjab, a region whose name means the land of five rivers. Further south, the Indus flows through a 130-

kilometer-wide river oasis in southern Pakistan, a mostly arid region. This oasis is the most important economic center in Pakistan. The ⊠ **Thar Desert** stretches over a vast area to the west of the Indus River basin and has a total area of 250,000 km². Most of the desert is situated in the Indian state of **Rajastan**. Arid

Mehrangahr Fort towers above the ancient city of Jodhpur. **Og32**

Jaisalmer Traditional home of Rajasthan's royalty – 🏰 large historic fortress – 🏛 grand villas. **Of32**

Nagaur The site of India's largest 🐂 cattle and camel market, held January and February – camel races. **Og32**

Alwar Trade center with many historic 🏛 buildings – impressive 🏰 palace complex built in 1793. **Oj32**

Jaipur The capital of Rajasthan; major attractions: 🏰 Jaipur Palace (top photo), marketplace (bottom photo). **Oh32**

Ajmer Marble pavilions – 🕌 the grave of the Sufi saint Muin-ud-din, a pilgrimage site for Muslims. **Oh32**

Udaipur City in Rajasthan on Lake Pichola with 🏰 palaces and a beautiful natural setting. **Og33**

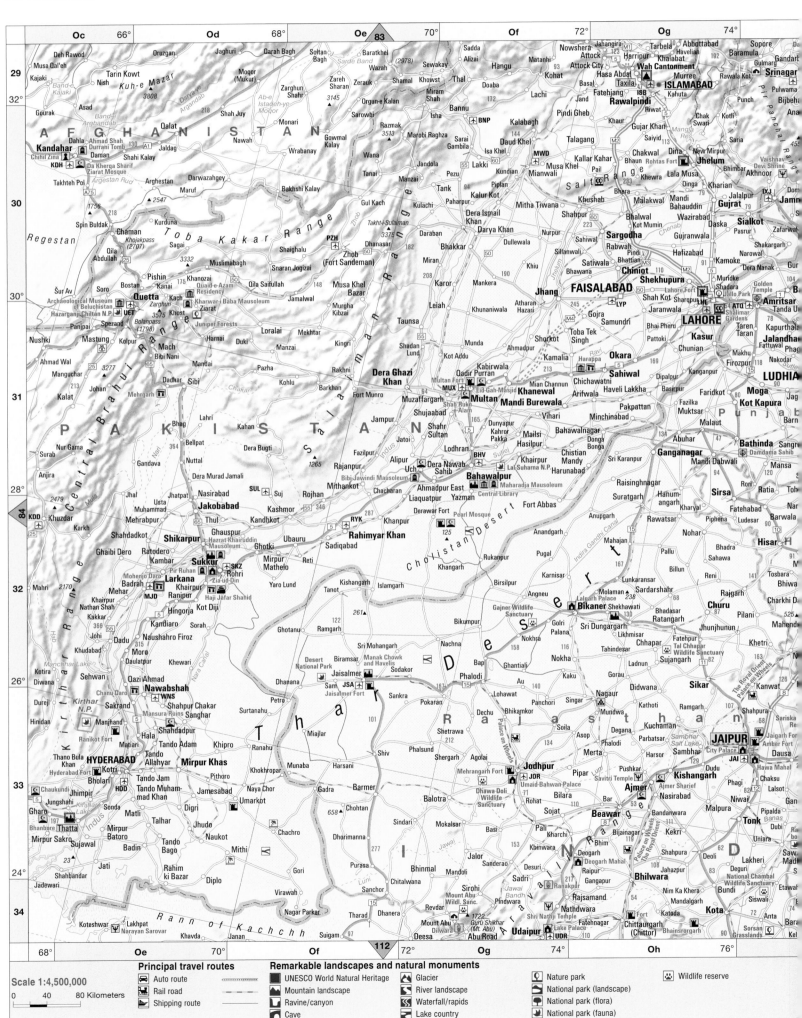

Principal travel routes

Scale 1:4,500,000
0   40   80 Kilometers

- 🚗 Auto route
- 🚆 Rail road
- 🚢 Shipping route
- ⸺⸺ (route line)

Remarkable landscapes and natural monuments

- ◼ UNESCO World Natural Heritage
- ◢ Mountain landscape
- ◣ Ravine/canyon
- ◥ Cave
- ◼ Glacier
- ◼ River landscape
- ◼ Waterfall/rapids
- ◼ Lake country
- ◼ Nature park
- ◼ National park (landscape)
- ◼ National park (flora)
- ◼ National park (fauna)
- ◼ Wildlife reserve

steppes and large sand dunes cover most of the desert. The arid desert is the driest region in India. The fertile plains of the Ganges and Brahmaputra river basins are bordered to the north by the Himalayas and to the west by the Thar Desert. The 2,700-kilometer-long ⛴ **Ganges River** and its most important tributary, the **Yamuna**, flow south from their sources in the Himalayas. The two rivers merge near the Indian city of Allahabad. A large

alluvial plain subject to frequent ⛴ floods lies at the foot of the Himalayas. The plains of northern India include some of the most fertile areas in the country. An elevated plain around **Delhi** separates the Indus basin from the plains in the Ganges basin. To the north, the plains of the Ganges basin are bounded by sections of the Himalayan Range.
The 🏔 **Himalayas** are the highest mountain range in the world. The range was

formed millions of years ago by collisions between the Indo-Australian and Eurasian tectonic plates. The Himalayas stretch in the shape of a bow through Afghanistan, Pakistan, northern India, Nepal and Tibet (China). There are several mountains in the range that exceed 8,000 meters in height. Mount Everest (8,850 m), the world's highest mountain, is situated along the border between Tibet and Nepal. The Himalayas separate

Central Asia with its cool climates from the tropical and subtropical regions of South Asia. The Indus-Yarlung suture, an ancient trench, separates the Trans-Himalayas (Tibetan Himalayas) from the main sections of the range.
The **Tibetan Plateau**, one of the world's largest plateaus, covers around two million km² and is situated mostly at elevations between 4,000 and 5,000 meters above sea level.

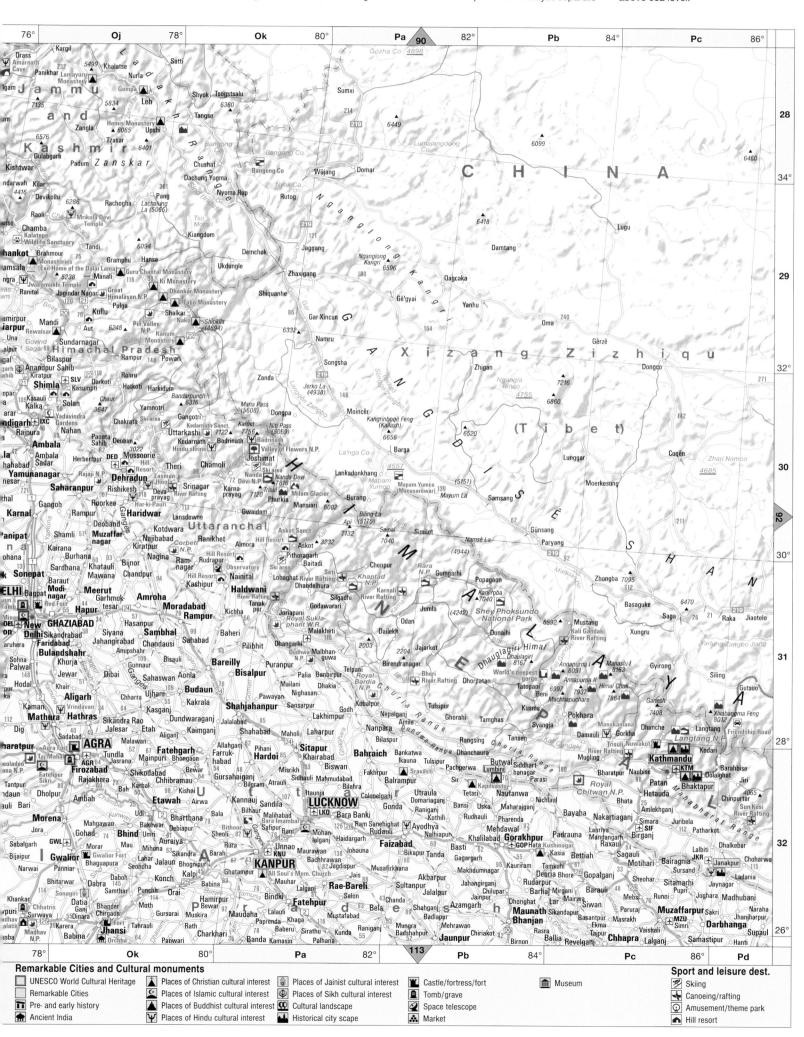

Ladakh Craggy mountainous landscapes (top photo) and the site of important Tibetan Buddhist 🏔 monasteries (bottom photo). **Oj-Ok28/29**

Amritsar The spiritual center of India's Sikh community – ☸ Golden Temple – Granth Sahib, a Sikh holy book. **Oh30**

Delhi The capital city of India – population, 7.3 million – 🏛 Humayan's Tomb (photo), a world heritage site – 🏰 The Red Fort. **Oj31**

Taj Mahal 🏛 Mausoleum built by Emperor Shah Jahan in memory of his wife Mumtaz Muhal – UNESCO world heritage site. **Oj32**

Fatehpur Sikri 🏛 Residence of Emperor Akbar – built in the 16th century – UNESCO world heritage site. **Oj32**

Remarkable Cities and Cultural monuments

▢ UNESCO World Cultural Heritage	Places of Christian cultural interest	Places of Jainist cultural interest
Remarkable Cities	Places of Islamic cultural interest	Places of Sikh cultural interest
Pre- and early history	Places of Buddhist cultural interest	Cultural landscape
Ancient India	Places of Hindu cultural interest	Historical city scape

Castle/fortress/fort	🏛 Museum
Tomb/grave	
Space telescope	
Market	

Sport and leisure dest.

Skiing	
Canoeing/rafting	
Amusement/theme park	
Hill resort	

Central India

The **Rann of Kachchh** is a vast area of salty mudflats in central India that stretches along the country's Arabian Sea coast. The Gulf of Kachchh separates this area from the **Kathiawar Peninsula**. The peninsula is mostly flat and agriculture is an important part of the local economy. The vast **Deccan Plateau** covers a large section of the Indian subcontinent. To the north, the plateau borders the fertile plains of northern India and

several upland areas including the 🏔 **Vindhya Range** and 🏔 **Saptura Range**. The Deccan Plateau is situated at heights between 800 and 1,000 meters. Together with the coastal plains on its edges, the plateau covers around half of India's territory. Several major rivers including the Godavari (1,450 km) and Krisna

Ancient Fort Golconda near Hyderabad. Ok37

Palitana Important 🛕 spiritual center of Jainism – temple district on Shetrunjaya Hill encompasses 863 buildings (photo). **Of35**

Ajanta Caves Crescent shaped caves in the side of a stone wall containing 🔺 Buddhist art. The caves are a UNESCO world heritage site. **Oh35**

Ellora Caves The caves contain 🔺 Buddhist, 🔶 Jain, and 🛕 Hindu temples and monasteries – world heritage site. **Oh35**

Mumbai (Bombay) India's largest city is home to more than ten million people – large film industry (Bollywood). **Og36**

Elephanta Island Stone temples carved into caves – 7th and 8th century sculptures – UNESCO world heritage site. **Og36**

Goa The former Portuguese colony, with its beautiful beaches, is a popular tourist attraction. Goa's historic churches are world heritage sites. **Og38**

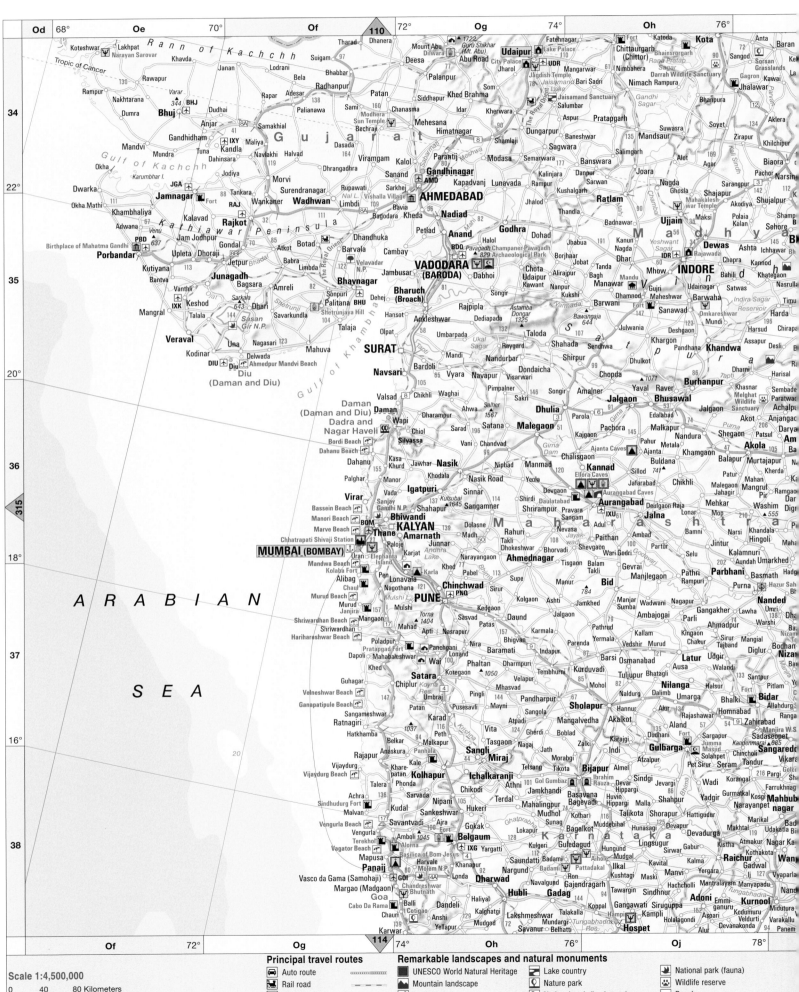

Scale 1:4,500,000

0   40   80 Kilometers

Principal travel routes
- Auto route
- Rail road
- Shipping route

Remarkable landscapes and natural monuments
- UNESCO World Natural Heritage
- Mountain landscape
- Rock landscape
- Cave
- Lake country
- Nature park
- National park (landscape)
- National park (flora)
- National park (fauna)
- Wildlife reserve
- Beach

(1,250 km) Rivers flow through the plateau. The majority of the rivers on the plateau empty into the Bay of Bengal. The water levels in these rivers are greatly affected by monsoon winds. Most of the Deccan Plateau's terrain is dominated by hills, river basins, and mountain ranges. The northern section of the Deccan Plateau is covered by rich volcanic soils and many of the fields in the area are used to grow cotton. During the monsoon season, the northern sections of the plateau get abundant rainfall. In contrast to the north, the center of the Deccan Plateau is a semi-arid region with sparse rainfall. Sorghum, grain, and peanuts are common crops in the region.

The Deccan Plateau is bounded on its western and eastern edges by two mountain ranges. The **Western Ghats** bound the plateau to the west and separate it from the 🖼 **Malabar plains**, a narrow strip of lowlands along the Arabian Sea coast. The **Eastern Ghats** bound the Deccan Plateau in the east and descend gradually to the 🖼 **Coromandel Coast**. The plains on the Coromandel Coast are significantly wider than those on India's western coast. Situated on the Coromandel Coast, the deltas of the Krishna and Mahanadi Rivers extends out into the Bay of Bengal. Devodi, the tallest mountain in the Eastern Ghats range rises 1,680 meters above sea level. Both the Eastern and Western Ghats get abundant rainfall and both ranges are major centers of agriculture. Rice, tea, coffee, and palm trees are the most important crops grown in the highlands.

Most of central India has a tropical climate. Central India's climate is greatly influenced by **monsoon** winds and the region has dry summers, a warm rainy season, and mild winters.

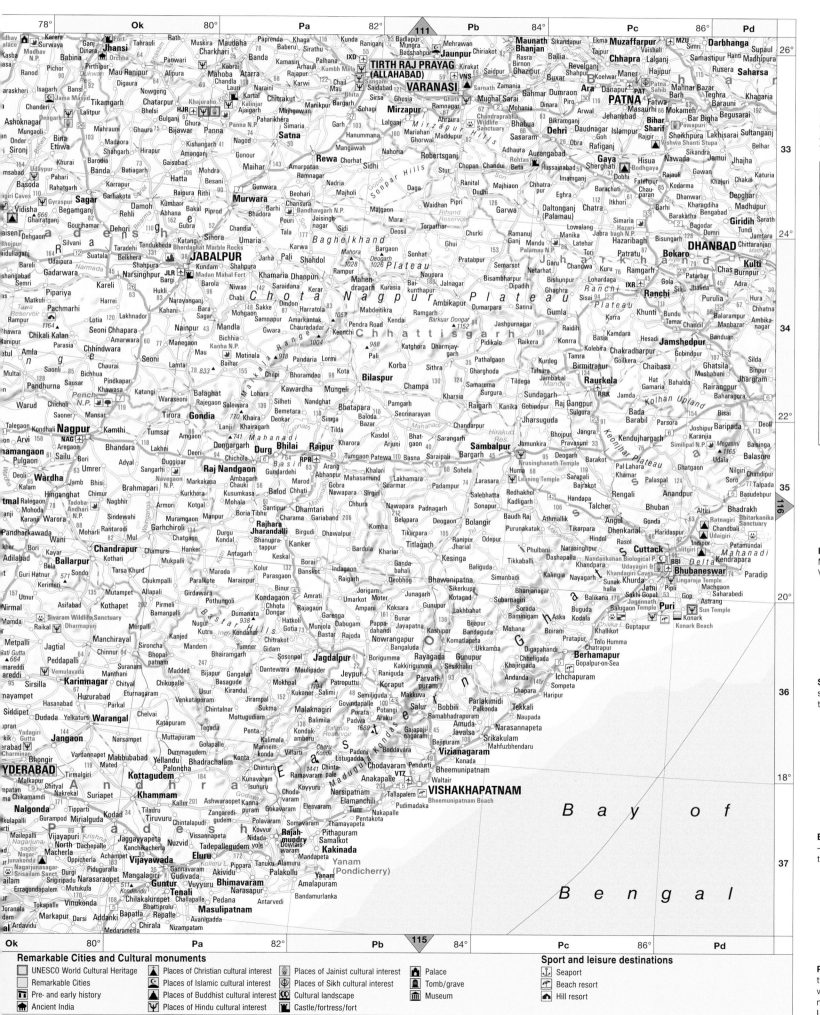

Khajuraho The 🛕 temple is a masterpiece of Hindu architecture (approximately 1000 AD) – UNESCO world heritage site – famous for its sculptures. **Ok33**

Varanasi (Benares) For around 2,500 years, Hindu pilgrims have traveled to this holy city for ceremonial baths in the Ganges River. The pilgrims descend steps (ghats) into the holy river. The most important religious building in the city is the 🛕 Vishvanatha temple dedicated to Shiva. **Pb33**

Bodhgaya Buddhist spiritual center – ▲ Mahabodi temple, built in the 2nd century – Vajrasana – museum. **Pc33**

Sanchi The oldest ▲ stupa (Buddhist shrine) in India is a UNESCO site – built over the burial site of Buddha. **Oj34**

Bhubaneswar Site of historic Indian temples – 🛕 Muktesvara temple (photo) was built in the 10th century. **Pc35**

Puri 🛕 Jagannath temple (photo), built in the 12th century, has several 65-meter-tall white pagodas – pilgrimage sites – ceremonies in honor of Jagannath (God of the Universe) – Rath Yatra Festival. **Pc36**

Remarkable Cities and Cultural monuments

- ⬜ UNESCO World Cultural Heritage
- ⬛ Remarkable Cities
- 🏛 Pre- and early history
- ▲ Ancient India
- ✝ Places of Christian cultural interest
- ☪ Places of Islamic cultural interest
- ▲ Places of Buddhist cultural interest
- 🛕 Places of Hindu cultural interest
- Places of Jainist cultural interest
- ☬ Places of Sikh cultural interest
- Cultural landscape
- Castle/fortress/fort
- Palace
- Tomb/grave
- 🏛 Museum

Sport and leisure destinations

- ⚓ Seaport
- Beach resort
- 🏠 Hill resort

Southern India, Maldives, Sri Lanka

The Maldives are a group of coral atolls located 700 kilometers off the coast of India in the Indian Ocean. The coral islands of the  **Maldives** are situated atop a long underwater ridge with a total length of around 1,000 kilometers. Because none of the islands lie more than three meters above sea level, the small nation's existence is threatened by a possible rise in sea level that could occur as a result of global war-

ming. The Huvadhoo Atoll has a diameter of 80 kilometers and is the country's largest atoll.
The **Eastern** and **Western Ghats** are situated on the edges of the **Deccan Plateau** in southern India. The two mountain ranges merge and form the Palani Hills in the far south of India. The mountains

The Maldives are home to many beautiful sandy beaches. **Og41/46**

The Maledives This small nation encompasses 19 groups of coral islands and atolls in the Indian Ocean. The islands are home to many good diving sites. **Og42-46**

Hampi Once the capital of the Vijayanagar Empire, today it consists of large ruins – UNESCO world heritage site. **Oj39**

Kochi (Cochin) The port city's attractions include a historic Jewish Quarter with India's oldest synagogue and the famous Theyyam temple dancers (photo). **Oj42**

Kollam (Quilon) Holiday resort on the Malabar Coast – access to the Backwaters region – lakes and lagoons (photo). **Oj42**

Thiruvananthapuram (Trivandrum) Capital of Kerala – museum – palm tree lined Kovalam Beach. **Oj42**

Madurai 2,000-year-old city in Tamil Nadu state – site of the large 17th century Meenakshi temple (photo) – Hall of 1,000 Pillars. **Ok42**

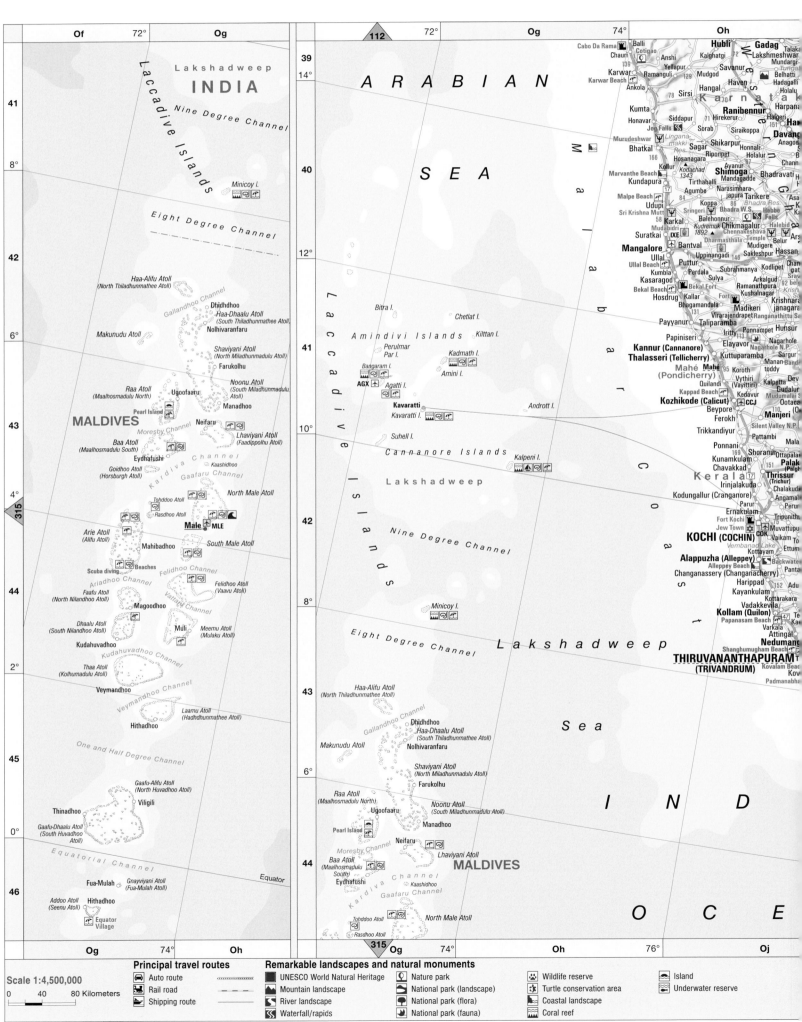

Scale 1:4,500,000
0   40   80 Kilometers

Principal travel routes
- Auto route
- Rail road
- Shipping route

Remarkable landscapes and natural monuments
- UNESCO World Natural Heritage
- Mountain landscape
- River landscape
- Waterfall/rapids
- Nature park
- National park (landscape)
- National park (flora)
- National park (fauna)
- Wildlife reserve
- Turtle conservation area
- Coastal landscape
- Coral reef
- Island
- Underwater reserve

of the Western Ghat fall abruptly to the 1,500-kilometer-long Malabar Coast. The Indian state Kerala is the location of several mountain ranges – including the ⌂ **Nilgiri Hills,** which rise to a maximum height of 2,600 meters. The ⌂ **Malabar Coast** is a narrow strip of coastal plains which increases in width from north to south. Cape Comorin is the southernmost point on the Indian subcontinent. The **Kaveri River** flows 475 kilometers from its source in the Western Ghats to its delta on the Bay of Bengal.

The Gulf of Mannar and shallow Palk Bay separate the island nation ⌂ **Sri Lanka** from the Indian subcontinent. **Adam's Bridge,** a chain of sand bars and coral islands between the Gulf of Mannar and Palk Bay are visible reminders of an ancient land bridge that once connected the island to India. Most of northern Sri Lanka is covered by lowlands and coast-al plains. Adam's Peak is the tallest mountain in the country's central highlands with a height of 2,243 meters above sea level. Adam's Peak is highly revered by all four major religious communities on the island. Two sudden drops in elevation mark the transition between the central highlands and the plains of northern Sri Lanka. The transition zone between the two regions is home to many beautiful landscapes including a large number of waterfalls. There are noticeable differences between the topography of Sri Lanka's coastal areas. The western coast is lined by several long spits, while the eastern coast consists primarily of broad sandy beaches. The **Andaman** and **Nicobar Islands** are situated in the eastern Bay of Bengal. Both island groups belong to India. Most of the 223 islands are mountainous and most of their populations live in river deltas or on coastal plains.

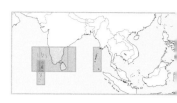

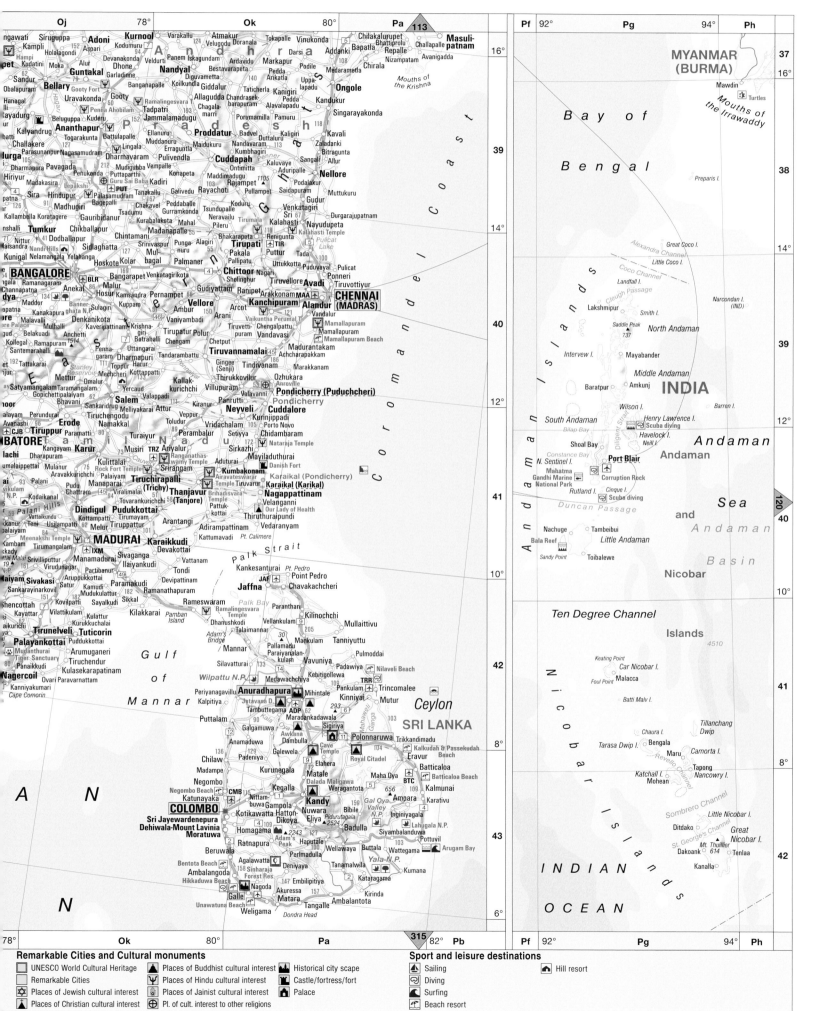

Mahabalipuram ⌂ The Shore Temple was built in the eighth century and is now a world heritage site – ⌂ large bas-reliefs.   **Pa40**

Anuradhapura The city became the first royal capital of Sri Lanka in the fourth century – ruins area covering 20 km², a world heritage site – ⌂ Buddhist shrines.   **Pa42**

Sigiriya The ruins of King Kasyapa's palace built into the "Lion Rock" – beautiful frescoes – UNESCO world heritage site.   **Pa42/43**

Dambulla Five ⌂ cave temples, a UNESCO world heritage site – 14 meter long reclining Buddha statue.   **Pa43**

Kandy Historic city in the Sri Lankan highlands – ⌂ Dalada Maligawa, the temple of the sacred tooth – Esala Perahera, Hindu pageant – UNESCO world heritage site.   **Pa43**

Andaman Islands This island group in the Bay of Bengal is surrounded by waters with beautiful ⌂ coral reefs. The islands are a popular destination for ⌂ diving.   **Pg39/40**

Remarkable Cities and Cultural monuments

- ☐ UNESCO World Cultural Heritage
- ☐ Remarkable Cities
- ✡ Places of Jewish cultural interest
- ⌂ Places of Christian cultural interest
- ▲ Places of Buddhist cultural interest
- ⌂ Places of Hindu cultural interest
- ⌂ Places of Jainist cultural interest
- ⌂ Pl. of cult. interest to other religions
- ⌂ Historical city scape
- ⌂ Castle/fortress/fort
- ⌂ Palace

Sport and leisure destinations

- ⌂ Sailing
- ⌂ Diving
- ⌂ Surfing
- ⌂ Beach resort
- ⌂ Hill resort

Eastern India, Bangladesh, Northern Myanmar

The eastern section of the Indian subcontinent encompasses several distinct landscapes. The  Himalayas are the world's tallest mountain range. The highest mountains in the range including Mount Everest (8,850 m) and Lhotse (8,516 m) are situated near the border between Nepal and Tibet (China). The lower eastern section of the Himalayas located in Bhutan, the Indian state of Arunachal Pradesh, and Yunnan (China) is

situated between 4,000 and 5,000 meters above sea level. The Kingdom of **Nepal** consists of several distinct regions with major differences in elevation. Around one fourth of the kingdom's territory lies more than 4,000 meters above sea level. The Kathmandu Basin has an average elevation of 1,300 meters. In contrast to

Shwesandaw temple in Bagan; built in the 11th century. **Ph35**

Simtokha Dzong Historic fortified  monastery in Bhutan – located on a steep hillside – founded in 1644 and rebuilt after a fire in 1907. **Pe32**

Darjeeling Indian town situated in a scenic highlands area – the historic Darjeeling Himalayan Railway (photo) is a UNESCO world heritage site. **Pe32**

Kaziranga National Park This conservation area contains the world's largest population of one-horned rhinoceros – elephant herds – world heritage site. **Pg32**

Dhaka Bangladesh's capital and largest urban area – Historic mosque (photo) in the area of Lalbagh Fort. **Pf34**

Sundarbans National Park This park, located in the Ganges delta (top photo), contains the world's largest mangrove forest. It was designated a UNESCO world heritage site in 1987. Around 250 rare Royal Bengali Tigers (bottom photo) inhabit the park. **Pe35**

Kolkata (Calcutta) India's second largest city – Victoria Memorial Hall (photo) contains an art museum. **Pe34**

Scale 1:4,500,000

0   40   80 Kilometers

Principal travel routes
- Auto route
- Rail road
- Shipping route

Remarkable landscapes and natural monuments
- UNESCO World Natural Heritage
- Mountain landscape
- Rock landscape
- Ravine/canyon
- Extinct volcano
- Cave
- River landscape
- Waterfall/rapids
- Lake country
- Fossil site
- Nature park
- National park (landscape)
- National park (flora)
- National park (fauna)
- Wildlife reserve

these regions, however, the subtropical plains of southern Nepal rise no higher than a few hundred meters above sea level. The 2,700-kilometer-long **Ganges River** flows into Bangladesh from the west, while the 3,000-kilometer-long **Brahmaputra** enters the country from the northeast. The two rivers merge near Dhaka, the capital city of Bangladesh. The shared delta of the two rivers covers an area of 56,000 km² and extends out

into the Bay of Bengal. Because of frequent tropical storms and Bangladesh's low elevation, the risk of devastating floods is the major natural threat to the country. In recent decades, several major floods have caused severe economic damage and many fatalities in densely populated Bangladesh.
The eastern edge of the Indian subcontinent and western Myanmar (Burma) are dominated by a series of mountain

ranges. The Irrawaddy River basin covers much of central Myanmar. The Shan Plateau is located to the east of the basin. The expansive plateau encompasses numerous high mountains. The powerful ⚓ **Salween River** flows from north to south through the plateau. Myanmar's far north is dominated by the **eastern Himalayas**.
The highlands of southeastern China feature many high mountains and

several major rivers. The **Mekong (Lancang Jiang) River** flows east from its source in Tibet into Southeast Asia. After it leaves China, the river forms sections of the borders separating Laos from Myanmar and Thailand. The **Chang Jiang (Yangtze) River** is the longest waterway in Asia. The upper course of the river flows through a series of beautiful gorges in the highlands of southern China.

Kunming 🏞 The stone forest of Shilin, a group of unusual stone formations formed over 200 million years ago. **Qb33**

Golden Triangle This ⚓ region at the junction of Myanmar, Laos, and Thailand is where the Ruak River flows into the powerful Mekong. The area's name comes from its history as a major center of illegal drug production and trafficking. The traditional homelands of the Shan people (bottom photo) are located along the northwest edges of the triangle. **Qa35**

Monywa 🏛 Thanboddhay temple – the temple contains 845 small stupas – constructed between 1939 and 1952. **Ph34**

Inle Lake Unique 🌾 "floating gardens" – 🏛 Phaung Daw Oo monastery with the royal barge (photo) – Nga Phe monastery. **Pj35**

Bagan 🏛 Religious center of the Bamar people – around 2,000 well preserved and beautiful historic buildings. **Ph35**

Louangphrabang (Luang Prabang) Town in Laos – 🏛 Wat Xieng Thong temple, built in 1850 – traditional architecture. **Qb36**

Remarkable Cities and Cultural monuments

- ☐ UNESCO World Cultural Heritage
- ☐ Remarkable Cities
- 🏛 Ancient China
- ☐ Places of Islamic cultural interest
- ☐ Places of Buddhist cultural interest
- ☐ Places of Hindu cultural interest
- ☐ Places of Jainist cultural interest
- ☐ Pl. of cult. interest to indig. peoples
- 🌾 Cultural landscape
- ☐ Historical city scape
- ☐ Castle/fortress/fort
- ☐ Palace
- ☐ Remarkable bridge
- ☒ Theater of war/battlefield
- 🏛 Museum

Sport and leisure destinations

- ⚓ Canoeing/rafting
- ☐ Beach resort
- ☐ Mineral/thermal spa
- 🏔 Hill resort

Northern Thailand, Laos, Cambodia, Central Vietnam

Much of mainland Southeast Asia is covered by heavily forested highlands and fertile plains in the basins of the region's many powerful rivers. The Irrawaddy, Salween, Chao Phraya, and Mekong Rivers are the most important waterways in the region.

The **Irrawaddy River** flows south from its source in the Himalayas through the center of Myanmar. Its delta in southern Myanmar covers 47,800 km² and en-

compasses one of the largest rice farming areas in the world. A narrow mountain range separates the Irrawaddy from the **Thanwin River** which flows from north to south near the border to Thailand. The Bilauktaung Range stretches south from the Dawna Mountains in eastern Myanmar into the **Malay Penin-**

Elephant riders near Siem Reap in Cambodia. Qc39

Kyaik Hti Yo Pagoda Myanmar's most important ▲ pilgrimage site – located atop the "golden rock". **Pj37**

Yangon (Rangoon) Myanmar's capital – ▲ Shwedagon Pagoda (photo), a historic holy site with a 98-meter-tall golden stupa. **Pj37**

Chiang Mai The largest city in northern Thailand – ▲ Wat Chedi Luang – ▲ Wat Phra Singh (photo) – ▲ night market. **Pk36**

Sukhothai Capital of the Thai Empire in the 13th century – historic park containing ancient ruins, a UNESCO world heritage site – remnants of ▲ Wat Mahathat (photo). **Pk37**

Bangkok The ▣ Chao Phraya River (bottom photo) flows through Thailand's capital and largest city. Bangkok is home to modern skyscrapers and historic architecture including the ▲ Wat Phra Kaeo. The Wat Phra Kaeo complex contains the Royal Pantheon (top photo). **Qa39**

Ayutthaya Thailand's capital and leading city until the 17th century – UNESCO world heritage site – ▲ Wat Yat Chai Mongkol. **Qa38**

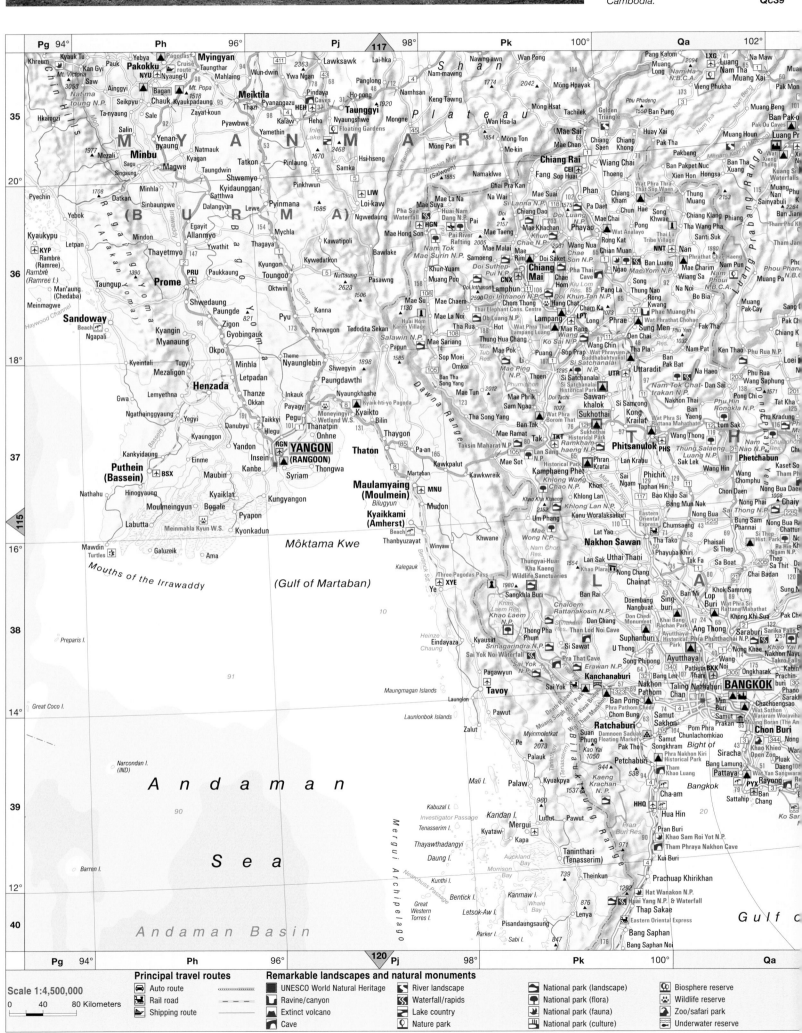

Scale 1:4,500,000
0   40   80 Kilometers

Principal travel routes
- Auto route
- Rail road
- Shipping route

Remarkable landscapes and natural monuments
- UNESCO World Natural Heritage
- Ravine/canyon
- Extinct volcano
- Cave
- River landscape
- Waterfall/rapids
- Lake country
- Nature park
- National park (landscape)
- National park (flora)
- National park (fauna)
- National park (culture)
- Biosphere reserve
- Wildlife reserve
- Zoo/safari park
- Underwater reserve

sula. Thailand's principal river, the Chao Phraya, flows though the country's central plain, one of the most productive rice and fruit farming regions in Asia. The central plain is also considered the cradle of Thai civilization. After leaving the plain, the Chao Phraya flows south to its large delta near Bangkok.

The highlands of northern and western Thailand are home to many steep narrow mountain valleys. Thailand's highest mountain, **Doi Inthanon** (2,590 m), is located in the northern highlands near Chang Mai. The **Golden Triangle** region is divided between Thailand, Laos, and Myanmar. In addition to its interesting indigenous cultures, the Golden Triangle also encompasses some of the most spectacular landscapes in Southeast Asia. Northeastern Thailand is dominated by mountain ranges and the hills of the **Khorat Plateau**.

The 4,500 meter long **Mekong River** is the fourth longest river in Asia. It flows from its source in Tibet to its delta in southern Vietnam. The river forms a long section of the border between Laos and Thailand. Further south it enters the plains of Cambodia before crossing the border into Vietnam where it reaches its 70,000-km² delta on the South China Sea. Most of eastern Laos is covered by the mountains of **Annamite Chain**, which rises to a maximum height of 2,500 meters. The mountain chains form a natural barrier between Vietnam and Laos. Vietnam is a long nation from north to south but relatively narrow from east to west. The smallest distance from the western border to the eastern coast in central Vietnam is 60 kilometers. Central Vietnam consists of mountainous highlands in the interior and a narrow strip of coastal plains.

Hue Former imperial capital of Vietnam – the city contain many historic buildings – UNESCO world heritage site. **Qd37**

My Son Ruins of an ancient Cham ▲ religious center – damaged during the Vietnam War – UNESCO world heritage site. **Qd38**

Hoi An The ▥ old town is a UNESCO world heritage site – Hoi An's central street Duong Tran Phu is a center of the Chinese community (photo) – ⌂ Japanese Bridge. **Qe38**

Angkor ▲ The city was the center of the Khmer Empire (802–1432 AD). Bayon temple complex features many towers with depictions of human faces (top photo). Wat Ta Prohm (middle photo) was completed in 1186. The temple Angkor Wat (bottom photo) is one of the the most impressive historic buildings in Asia. **Qb39**

Wat Phu Large ▲ temple complex at the foot of Phu Pasak (1,200 m) – the oldest sections were completed in the 5th and 6th centuries – beautiful bas-reliefs. **Qc38**

Remarkable Cities and Cultural monuments

▢ UNESCO World Cultural Heritage	◷ Cultural landscape
◻ Remarkable Cities	⬚ Historical city scape
▲ Places of Buddhist cultural interest	⬛ Castle/fortress/fort
▮ Pl. of cult. interest to indig. peoples	⬚ Remarkable bridge
⊠ Theater of war/battlefield	⌂ Museum
⬚ Monument	
⬚ Memorial	
⬚ Market	

Sport and leisure destinations

◇ Diving	
⬚ Canoeing/rafting	
⬚ Beach resort	
⬚ Mineral/thermal spa	

Southern Thailand, Malaysian Peninsula

The **Malay Peninsula** was created around 150 million years ago. The peninsula is around 40 kilometers wide at its narrowest. Several long mountain ranges stretch from north to south through the 1,500-kilometer-long peninsula. Until recently, the ⛰ mountains were a major obstacle to overland travel between the two coasts of the peninsula. Southern Thailand's pleasant climate and its many beautiful beaches attract

tourists from around the world to the region. Situated off the west coast of the southern Thailand, ☐ **Phuket** is the country's largest island and a major center of the Thai tourism industry. The ☐ **Similan Islands**, a small island group north of Phuket, offer some of finest diving sites in Thailand.

Phuket, Thailand's largest island, is a popular tourist destination. **Pk41/42**

Khao Luang (1,793 m) is the tallest mountain in a long mountain chain that stretches through much of southern Thailand. The mountain is surrounded by a national park with fascinating flora and fauna. The mountains in this area are home to many ancient and heavily eroded ⛰ stone formations as well as countless ☐ caves.
The alluvial plains in the western parts of the Malay Peninsula contain extensive

Koh Samui Island in the Gulf of Thailand (247 km²) – beautiful ☐ Chaweng beach – waterfalls: Na Muang and Hin Lat – large Buddha statue (photo). **Qa41**

Phuket Thailand's largest island (800 km²) – Phuket (town) contains historic Sino-Portuguese architecture – rainforests in ☐ Khao Phra Taeo National Park – long ☐ beaches on the island's western coast. **Pk41/42**

Georgetown Capital of the Malaysian state Penang – the majority of the city's population is of Chinese descent – Chinatown (photo) – ☐ Khoo Kongsi Temple. **Qa43**

Kek Lok Si Temple Located on the island Penang – ☐ Buddhist pilgrimage site – "the pagoda of 10,000 Buddhas". **Qa43**

Batu Caves Site of the ☐ Thaipusam festival, a large Hindu religious gathering in Malaysia. **Qa44**

Kuala Lumpur Malaysia's capital city was founded in the middle of the 19th century. The city is now the economic and cultural center of the country. Kuala Lumpur's ☐ Petronas Towers (452 m, photo) are among the tallest buildings in the world. **Qa44**

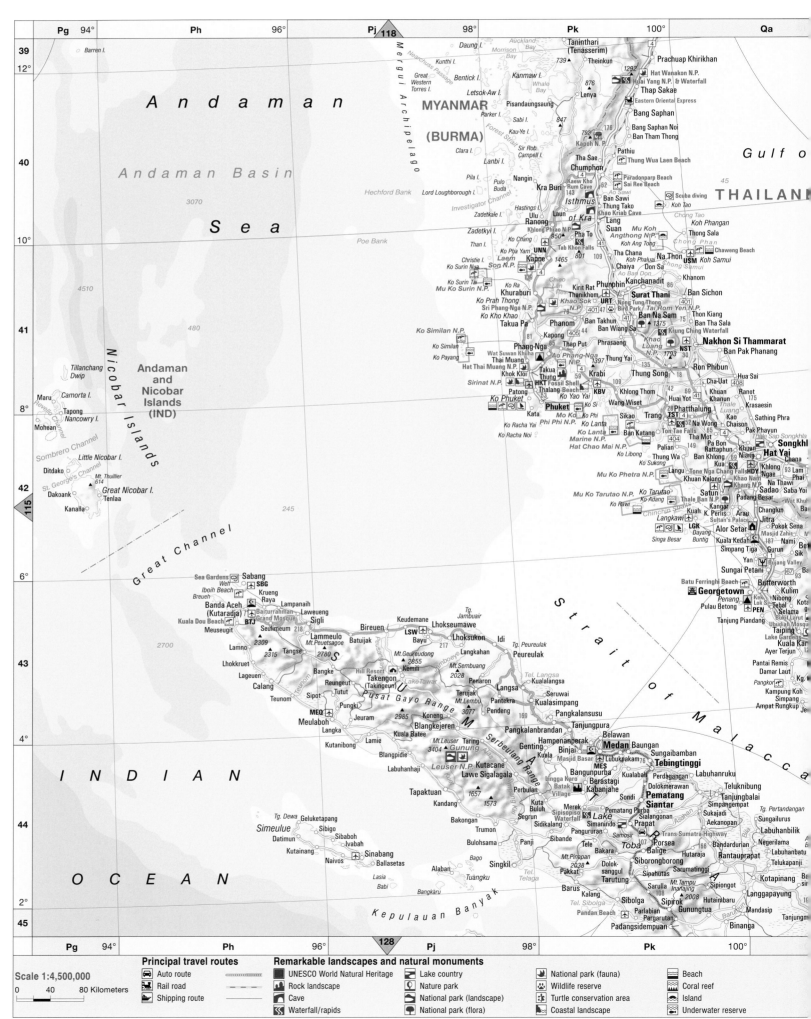

Scale 1:4,500,000

0   40   80 Kilometers

Principal travel routes
- Auto route
- Rail road
- Shipping route

Remarkable landscapes and natural monuments
- UNESCO World Natural Heritage
- Rock landscape
- Cave
- Waterfall/rapids
- Lake country
- Nature park
- National park (landscape)
- National park (flora)
- National park (fauna)
- Wildlife reserve
- Turtle conservation area
- Coastal landscape
- Beach
- Coral reef
- Island
- Underwater reserve

rice growing areas. The peninsula was once totally covered by dense tropical rainforests: today the **tropical rainforests** cover only a portion of the region but they contain an incredible level of biodiversity. Many of the larger mammals in the forests including local tigers and rhinoceroses are considered endangered. Smaller animals such as apes, insects, and butterflies continue to flourish in the forests. The forests of the Malay

Peninsula are also home to many birds, including several species of hornbills. **Taman Negara National Park** is the largest national park in Malaysia and contains large virgin rainforests. Because of logging and agriculture, only around 12 % of the Malay Peninsula is covered by tropical rainforests. Expansive palm, rubber, and coconut plantations now occupy large sections of the countryside where rainforests once were.

Southern Thailand and Peninsular Malaysia both have tropical **climates** with high humidity and heavy rainfall during much of the year.
The Indonesian island of Sumatra is separated from Malaysia and southern Thailand by the Strait of Malacca. The western section of the island is dominated by a long mountain range. These mountains border a large plain that covers much of northeastern Sumarta.

The forests in **Mount Leuser National Park** are the only remaining habitats of the endangered Sumatran orangutans. Western Sumatra's most popular attraction is **Lake Toba**, a large lake in an ancient volcanic crater.
Southern Thailand is home to most of the country's large Muslim minority. Most Malaysians are practicing Muslims but the country also has large Buddhist and Hindu communities.

Ho Chi Minh City (Saigon) Vietnam's largest city with a population of 4.5 millions – Temple of the Jade Emperor with a Taoist pantheon – Mariamman temple – Chinatown Cho Lon. **Qd40**

Mekong-Delta The 4,500-kilometer-long Mekong River is the longest river in Southeast Asia. The river's basin covers much of southern Vietnam. The delta features an extensive network of canals, rivers, and streams. **Qd40**

Cameron Highlands Mountain region – between 600 and 2,000 meters above sea level – major tea growing area. **Qa43**

Taman Negara 4,350-km²-large national park containing pristine rainforests – river rapids at Lata Berkoh. **Qb43**

Singapore The island nation is connected to Peninsular Malaysia by a one-kilometer-long causeway. The ethnically diverse city (pop. 3.7 million) is home to many notable attractions including the colonial era Raffles Hotel, markets in Orchard Road, Mariamann temple, and Jamae Mosque. Singapore is the busiest port in Southeast Asia. **Qb45**

Remarkable Cities and Cultural monuments
- UNESCO World Cultural Heritage
- Remarkable Cities
- Ancient China
- Places of Islamic cultural interest
- Places of Buddhist cultural interest
- Places of Hindu cultural interest
- Pl. of cult. interest to other religions
- Historical city scape

Sport and leisure destinations
- Race track
- Horse racing
- Sailing
- Diving
- Wind surfing
- Seaport
- Beach resort
- Mineral/thermal spa
- Hill resort

Southeast Asia

Southeast Asia is composed of six nations on mainland Asia: Vietnam, Cambodia, Laos, Thailand, and sections of Malaysia. The region also includes the countless islands that form Indonesia and the Philippines. The island of Borneo is divided between the small sultanate Brunei, Indonesia, and two Malaysian states. Myanmar (Burma), the westernmost nation in Southeast Asia features a variety of landscapes and topographies. The

eastern, northern, and western sections of Myanmar are dominated by mountains and plateaus. Myanmar is also home to numerous river valleys, rolling hills, and large lowland areas. The **Malay Peninsula** is divided between Thailand and Malaysia. A long chain of mountains stretches from north to south through the

Rainforest in the highlands of Borneo.

Malay Peninsula South of southern Thailand – Peninsular Malaysia and the capital Kuala Lumpur – Singapore off the southern coast.

Sumatra Large Indonesian island – plains in the east – the Barisan Mountains dominate the west – Lake Toba, the largest crater lake in Southeast Asia.

Borneo The world's third largest island is one of the Greater Sunda Islands. The island's craggy highlands rise to 4,100 meters at Mount Kinabalu, Borneo's tallest peak. Several national parks protect some of the island's rare flora and fauna. Photos from top to bottom: Mount Kinabalu, Gunung Mulu National Park (middle photos), Tanjung Putting National Park.

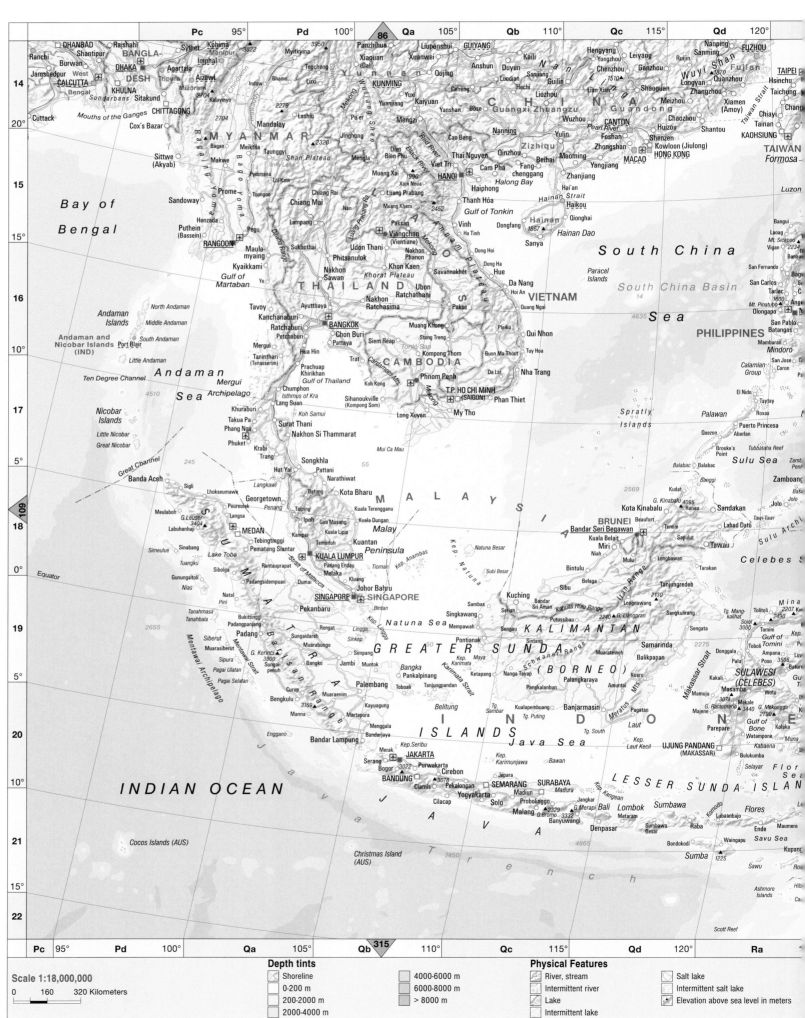

Scale 1:18,000,000
0   160   320 Kilometers

Depth tints
- Shoreline
- 0-200 m
- 200-2000 m
- 2000-4000 m
- 4000-6000 m
- 6000-8000 m
- > 8000 m

Physical Features
- River, stream
- Intermittent river
- Lake
- Intermittent lake
- Salt lake
- Intermittent salt lake
- Elevation above sea level in meters

center of the peninsula. Singapore, a small island nation, is situated off the southern coast of the peninsula. The Malay Peninsula is home to many sandstone mountain ranges with unique stone formations and extensive networks of subterranean caves.

Indonesia is a large mosaic of islands that were once part of an ancient subcontinent that connected Australia and Asia. The nation is the largest archipel-

ago in the world and encompasses more than 15,000 islands. Indonesia is located near the edges of the Eurasian, Pacific, and Indo-Australian tectonic plates. The geologically active archipelago is home to a long chain of volcanoes, several of which are still active. Borneo, Java, Sumatra, Sulawesi, and the Lesser Sunda Islands are the most important islands in Indonesia. The northern section of Borneo, the world's third largest island, is

occupied by Brunei and the Malaysian states, Sabah and Sarawak. Much of Borneo's interior is covered by dense tropical rainforest, while the island's coastal areas contain large swampy plains.

New Guinea is the world's second largest island. The western half of the island forms the Indonesian province of Papua – officially known as Irian Jaya before 2002. The eastern half of the island belongs to Papua New Guinea, an independent na-

tion since 1975. More than half of New Guinea is covered by tropical rainforest. The **Philippines** is an archipelago of more than 7,100 islands off the southeastern coast of mainland Asia. The archipelago is located inside the so-called Pacific Ring of Fire and there are several active volcanos in the area. Luzon, the Visayas, Mindanao, Mindoro, and Palawan are the most important islands and island groups of the Philippines.

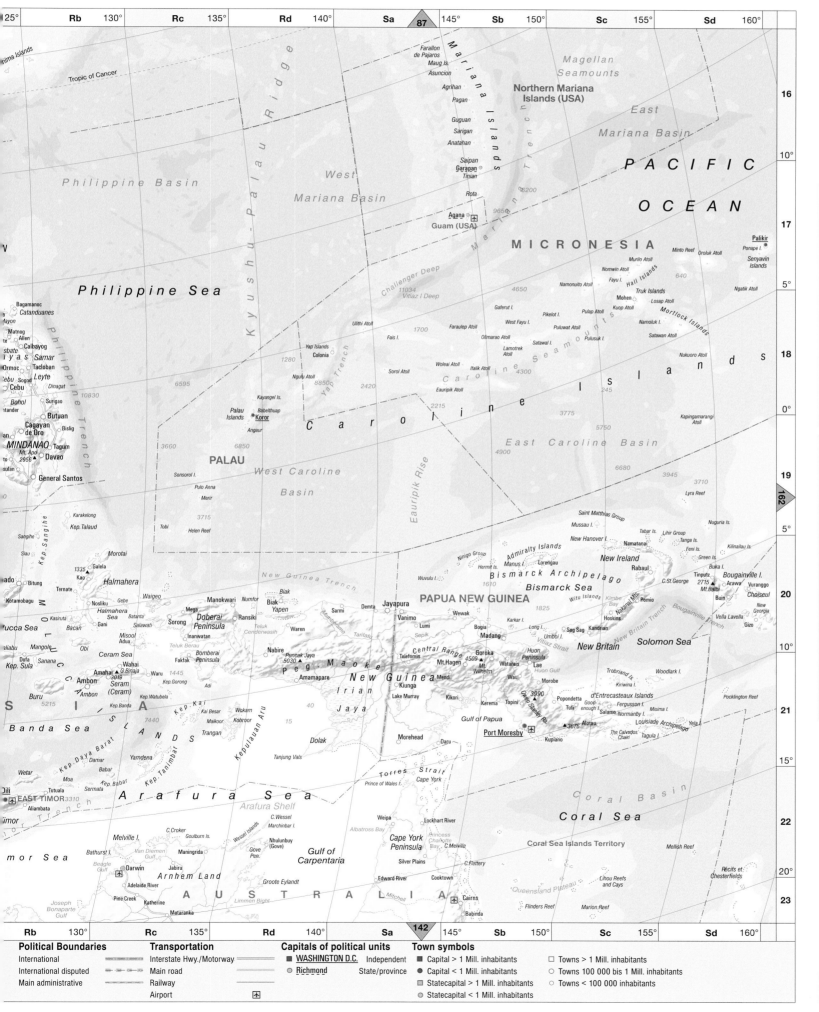

The Philippines More than 5,000 islands – active volcanoes including Mount Pinatubo (photo) – Luzon, largest island and location of the capital Manila.

Sulawesi The Indonesian island consist of several long peninsulas with tall mountains, savannahs, traditional villages and coral reefs off the coast.

Lesser Sunda Islands The island group includes Bali (photos), Lombok, Sumba, Flores, and Komodo, home of the fascinating Komodo Dragons.

New Guinea The world's second largest island (771,900 km²) – rainforests – tallest mountain, Puncak Yaya (5,030 m).

Political Boundaries
International
International disputed
Main administrative

Transportation
Interstate Hwy./Motorway
Main road
Railway
Airport

Capitals of political units
■ WASHINGTON D.C. Independent
⊙ Richmond State/province

Town symbols
■ Capital > 1 Mill. inhabitants
● Capital < 1 Mill. inhabitants
□ Statecapital > 1 Mill. inhabitants
◎ Statecapital < 1 Mill. inhabitants
□ Towns > 1 Mill. inhabitants
○ Towns 100 000 bis 1 Mill. inhabitants
○ Towns < 100 000 inhabitants

Northern Philippines, Palau

The **Philippines** is a large archipelago encompassing more than 7,100 islands off the southeastern coast of mainland Asia. The island nation has a total land area of 300,000 km². Only around 900 of the islands that form the Philippines are permanently inhabited. The Philippines have a maximum length of 1,850 kilometers from north to south and from east to west a maximum length of 1,060 kilometers. The archipelago borders the

South China Sea in the west and the Pacific Ocean in the east. To the north, the archipelago is separated from Taiwan by the **Luzon Strait**.

Like Indonesia, the vast number of islands in the Philippines means the country has one of the longest coastlines of any nation in the world. The Philip-

The islands of Palau are covered by lush tropical forests. **Rh42**

Paoay Church The historic ⛪ church was built in the Baroque style and completed in 1894. Paoay church is a designated UNESCO world heritage site. **Ra37**

Vigan Spanish colonial houses in the Kamestizoan district, a world heritage site – ⛪ cathedral – 🏛 Ayala Museum. **Ra37**

Lake Taal Beautiful 270-km²-large 🌊 crater lake – the volcano 🗻 Taal is located in the middle of the lake. **Ra38/39**

Manila The capital of the Philippines has one of the best natural harbors in Asia. The city (top photo) is home to around ten million people. Colorful jeepneys (bottom photo) are an important means of transport in Manila. **Ra38**

Puerto Galera On the island Mindoro – beautiful natural harbor – 🏖 beaches – popular tourist destination. **Ra39**

Mount Pinatubo 🗻 Volcano on the island Luzon – the eruption in 1991 created a 25-kilometer-high plume of smoke. **Ra38**

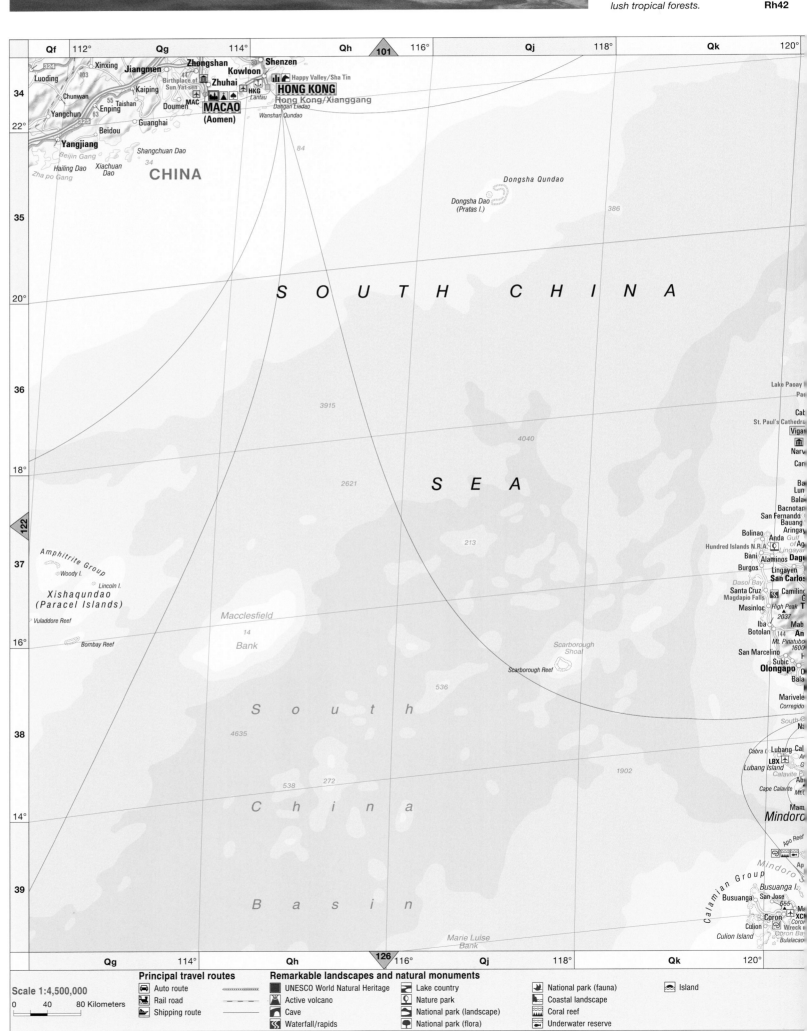

Scale 1:4,500,000

0   40   80 Kilometers

Principal travel routes
- Auto route
- Rail road
- Shipping route
- ···· (dotted)

Remarkable landscapes and natural monuments
- UNESCO World Natural Heritage
- Active volcano
- Cave
- Waterfall/rapids
- Lake country
- Nature park
- National park (landscape)
- National park (flora)
- National park (fauna)
- Coastal landscape
- Coral reef
- Underwater reserve
- Island

pines are situated along the edges of several tectonic plates. Many of the Philippine islands are mountainous and the country is home to several active volcanoes. The **Philippines Trench**, located off the archipelago's eastern coasts, has a maximum depth of 10,830 meters. Both the Pacific Trench and the Philippine islands were created through the collision of tectonic plates in the Earth's crust. Millions of years ago the largest

Philippine islands – including Luzon – were connected to mainland Asia by land bridges. After the last ice age, massive glaciers that covered much of the planet's surface began to melt, causing the oceans to rise. The land bridges disappeared beneath the sea and the Philippines became a mosaic of several thousand small scattered islands.
Of the 37 ☒ volcanoes on the Philippines, 18 are still active including ☒

Mount Pinatubo (1,600 m) on the island of Luzon. In 1991, a major eruption of Mount Pinatubo devastated the areas surrounding the volcano.
Luzon is the largest island in the Philippines and encompasses more than a third of the country's total area. The island is home to several powerful rivers that deposit large amounts of rich sediments in their deltas and river valleys. The **Cagayan River**, the longest river on

Luzon, has a total length of 354 kilometers. ☒ **Laguna de Bay**, the largest lake in the Philippines, is located south of Manila and covers an area of 932 km². **Palau** is a small island group on the western edge of Micronesia, a section of the Pacific Ocean. Most of Palau's larger islands are located near a 110-kilometer-long barrier reef. Palau has a tropical climate with warm temperatures throughout the year.

Palau The island group Palau consists of 343 ☒ islands around 1,000 kilometers east of the Philippines. Coral atolls (top photo) surrounded by reefs and the ☒ Rock Islands (bottom photo) are among Palau's attractions. **Rh42**

Rice Terraces of Ifugao The high terraces in Luzon's highlands are a UNESCO world heritage site. The highest of the narrow ☒ terraces, held up by stone and clay walls, rises approximately 1,500 meters. **Ra37**

Indigenous People Most Filipinos are ethnic Malays but around 12 % of the population consist of indigenous people whose ancestors lived on the islands before the Malays arrived. There are around 60 indigenous ethnic groups in the Philippines.

Pagsanjan ☒ River near Santa Cruz – deep gorges around ☒ Pagsanjan (Magdapio) Falls (photo). **Qk38**

Mount Mayon 2,462-meter-tall ☒ volcano with a beautiful cone shaped peak – several eruptions in recent centuries. **Rb39**

Remarkable Cities and Cultural monuments

- ☐ UNESCO World Cultural Heritage
- ☐ Remarkable Cities
- ☐ Places of Christian cultural interest
- ☐ Cultural landscape
- Historical city scape
- Impressive skyline
- Monument
- Memorial
- 🏛 Museum

Sport and leisure destinations

- Horse racing
- Sailing
- Wind surfing
- Seaport
- Deep-sea fishing
- Beach resort
- Casino

Southern Philippines, Northern Borneo

The many islands of the Philippines can be divided into four distinct large island groups. The northernmost group consist of the largest Filipino island Luzon and the islands surrounding it. The  Visayas group containing the major islands of Cebu and Bohol, is located south of Luzon.

Palawan is located to the west of the other main islands in the Philippines archipelago and is separated from Bor-

Beautiful El Nido Bay in northern Palawan. **Qk40**

neo by a narrow strait. **Mindanao** and the **islands of Sulu** Province are located in the southeastern section of the Philippines.

The **Chocolate Hills**, a major tourist attraction on Bohol, are a series of brown cone shaped hills with average heights of 30 meters. **Negros**, the fourth largest

island in the Philippines is situated between the islands Cebu and Panay. Negros is home to fertile mountainous areas with extensive forests, subterranean caves, and large sugar plantations. The coasts of the island **Panay** contain many of the finest beaches in the Philippines. Panay also has several important rice farming areas, including the plains around the city of Iliolio. **Mindanao**, the largest island in the southern Philippines is

Paglugaban Island In the Bacuit archipelago, an island group west of El Nindo – beautiful beaches. **Qk40**

Underwater Biodiversity The waters surrounding the Philipines are home to many unique plants and animals. The Tubbataha reef (top photo) **(Qk41)** contains more than 300 types of coral. Honda Bay, north of Puerto Princesa **(Qk41)** is also home to interesting marine life. Turtle Island Marine Park **(Qj42)** contains sea turtle (bottom photo) breeding sites.

Kinabalu National Park Large rainforests – the world's largest flower – Mount Kinabalu (4,101 m). **Qj42**

Brunei The small sultanate of Brunei is a wealthy nation with large oil reserves. The capital city Bandar Seri Begawan is home to the Sultan Omar Mosque (top photo) and the large Istana Nurul Imam palace (bottom photo: palace interior). **Qh43**

Gunung Mulu National Park Large underground cave systems – Sarawak Chamber is the largest cave chamber – UNESCO world heritage site. **Qh43**

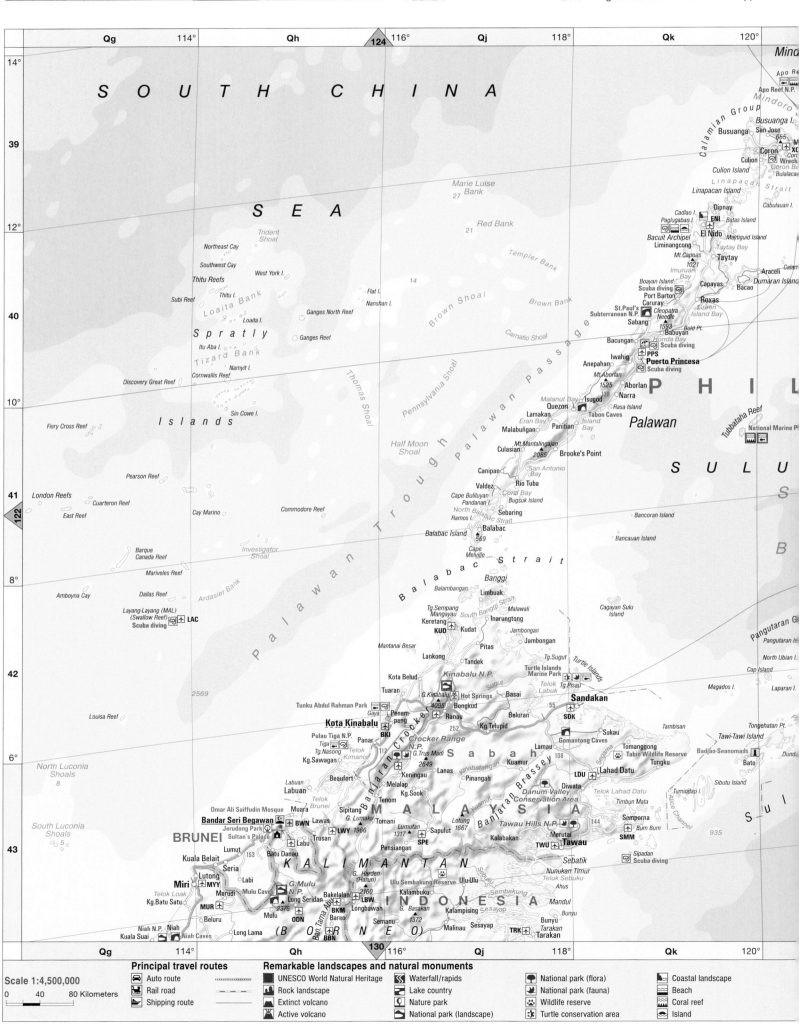

Scale 1:4,500,000
0   40   80 Kilometers

Principal travel routes
- Auto route
- Rail road
- Shipping route

Remarkable landscapes and natural monuments
- UNESCO World Natural Heritage
- Rock landscape
- Extinct volcano
- Active volcano
- Waterfall/rapids
- Lake country
- Nature park
- National park (landscape)
- National park (flora)
- National park (fauna)
- Wildlife reserve
- Turtle conservation area
- Coastal landscape
- Beach
- Coral reef
- Island

Many of Sumatra's mountainous regions are home to dense tropical rainforests that grow at elevations below 1,000 meters. Moss covered cloud forests are common in mountainous areas above 1,000 meters. The rainforests of Sumatra grow in areas with hot humid climates and contain an incredible abundance of flora and fauna.

A chain of small and medium-sized islands is located just off the western coast of Sumatra. ⊓ **Nias**, the largest island in the chain, is home to historic stone altars, traditional architecture, and a distinctive local culture.

With a population of more than two million inhabitants, **Medan** is the largest city on Sumatra and the island's main economic center. Medan's city hall and main train station were built during the colonial period when the Dutch ruled Indonesia. The section of Sumatra's eastern coast between Medan and Palembang is covered by mangrove forests. The **Trans Sumatra Highway**, completed in the 1980s, runs between Medan and the southern tip of Sumatra. Eastern Sumatra's plains are crossed by numerous rivers and small streams.

Sumatra produces many of Indonesia's most important exports – including oil, natural gas, rubber, cinnamon, coffee, tea, and tobacco.

The Strait of Malacca is a body of water with a width of just 67 kilometers at its narrowest section. It separates Sumatra from Peninsular **Malaysia** and **Singapore**, an island nation with the busiest port in Asia.

The densely populated island **Java** is located southeast of Sumatra on the opposite side of the Sundra Strait. **Borneo** is separated from Sumatra by the Karimata Strait.

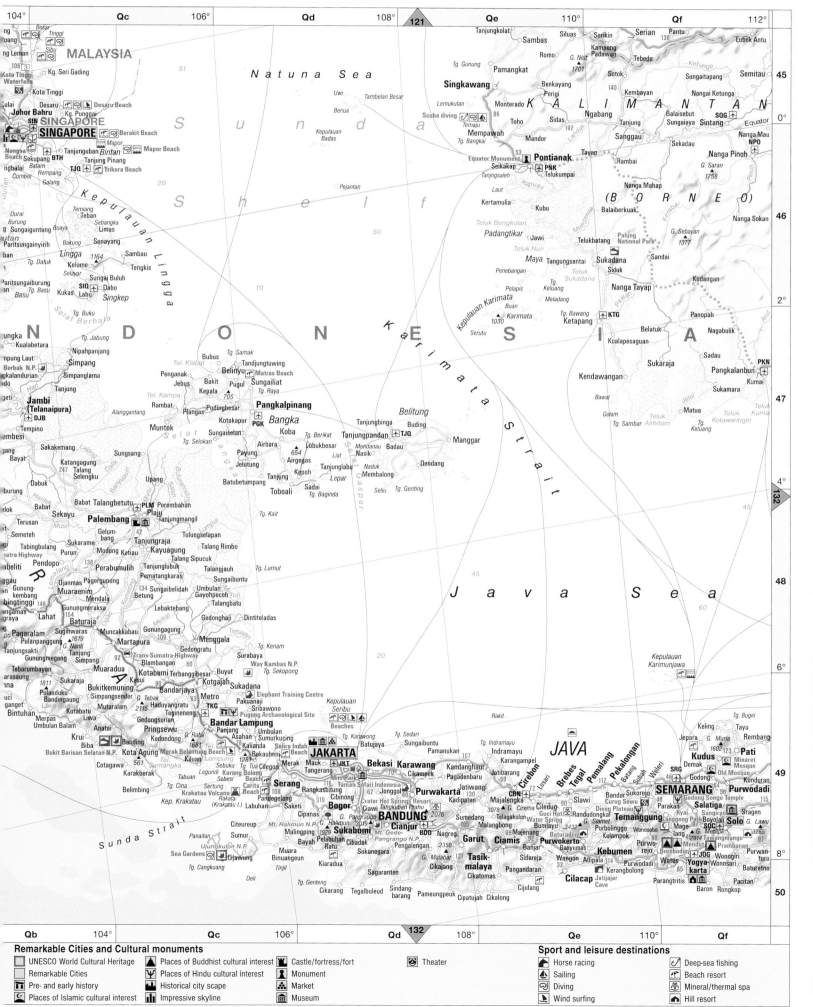

Sianok Canyon The walls of this steep canyon are 100 meters high – lush vegetation – suspension bridge. **Qa46**

Gunung Kerinci 3,800-meter-high volcano in the Barisan range – eruption in 1982 – Kerinci Seblat National Park. **Qa46**

Kerinci Seblat National Park The park features tropical plains, large mountain rainforests, and cloud forests. The park is home to many interesting animals including large numbers of macaques (top photo). Sumatran tigers (bottom photo) inhabit the coastal forests and highlands of the park. **Qa46**

Mentawai Island Siberut is the largest island in this group off the western coast of Sumatra. The islands are home to many endemic plant and animal species. The origin of the indigenous Mentawai people (photo) is unknown. Their culture, language, and appearance differ from those of the peoples on neighboring islands. **Pk-Qa46/47**

Palembang The largest city in southern Sumatra – oil refineries – traditional houseboats – 🏛 Balaputra Museum – historic Dutch colonial 🏰 fortress. **Qc47**

Remarkable Cities and Cultural monuments

- ▢ UNESCO World Cultural Heritage
- ▢ Remarkable Cities
- ▣ Pre- and early history
- ◉ Places of Islamic cultural interest
- ▲ Places of Buddhist cultural interest
- ▲ Places of Hindu cultural interest
- ▦ Historical city scape
- ▦ Impressive skyline
- ▦ Castle/fortress/fort
- ▥ Monument
- ▦ Market
- ▦ Museum
- ◙ Theater

Sport and leisure destinations

- Horse racing
- Sailing
- Diving
- Wind surfing
- Deep-sea fishing
- Beach resort
- Mineral/thermal spa
- Hill resort

Borneo, Sulawesi

Kalimantan (Borneo) and Sulawesi together with Java and Sumatra form the **Greater Sunda Islands**, an island group in the large Indonesian archipelago. Because of their locations near the equator all of these islands have hot tropical climates with high humidity and warm temperatures throughout the year.
Indonesia shares ⌂ **Borneo**, the world's third largest island, with two other nations. Most of northern Borneo is occu-

pied by two Malaysian states and the small nation Brunei. The two Malaysian states, **Sarawak** and **Sabah** are covered by tropical rain forests with lush vegetation and interesting wildlife.
Brunei was once the center of a large and powerful empire that ruled over large sections of Borneo and the Philip-

Kuching, the capital of Sarawak, is situated on the Sarawak River. **Qf45**

Bako National Park ⌂ Lush tropical vegetation – ⌂ hornbills and gibbons – ⌂ interesting stone formations (photo). **Qf45**

Uma Daro The village consists of buildings constructed on stilts along the ⌂ Rajang River, the longest river (560 km) in Sarawak – only accessible by boat. **Qf44**

National Parks of Kalimantan The tropical rainforests in ⌂ Tanjung Putting National Park **(Qg47)** are home to rare birds (top photo) and orangutans (middle photo). ⌂ Palung National Park encompasses mangrove forests, swamps, plains, mountain forests, and the habitats of colorful hornbills (bottom photo; **Qf46**).

Banjarmasin Important port city on the Barito River in southern Kalimantan – canals and streams – ⌂ floating market – large main ⌂ mosque. **Qh47**

Scale 1:4,500,000

0   40   80 Kilometers

Principal travel routes
- Auto route
- Rail road
- Shipping route
- ---- (mountain route)

Remarkable landscapes and natural monuments
- ■ UNESCO World Natural Heritage
- ■ Mountain landscape
- ■ Rock landscape
- ■ Extinct volcano
- ▲ Active volcano
- ⌂ Cave
- ⌂ Waterfall/rapids
- ⌂ Lake country
- ⌂ Nature park
- ⌂ National park (landscape)
- ⌂ National park (flora)
- ⌂ National park (fauna)
- ⌂ Coastal landscape
- ⌂ Coral reef
- ⌂ Island
- ⌂ Underwater reserve

pines. Today the country is a small sultanate with an impressive wealth of oil and natural gas reserves.

The Indonesia section of Borneo is called **Kalimantan** and covers most of the island. Borneo's interior is dominated by highlands which border large swampy plains that cover the south and coastal areas of the island. These plains are crossed by many streams and large ⌕ rivers. The large oil deposits on Bor-

neo and the logging industry dominate the economy of Kalimantan. Indonesian and foreign concerns operate oil drilling sites and oil refineries along the eastern coast of the island around the cities Tarakan, Bontang, and Balkpapan.

Kalimantan is a sparsely populated region. The majority of its 12.3 million inhabitants are concentrated in cities and towns along the coast. In the western section of Kalimantan, the population

consists mostly of Malays and ethnic Chinese. The majority of the population in Kalimantan's interior consists of **Dayaks** – a term encompassing hundreds of distinct indigenous tribes. The ancestors of the Dayaks first settled Borneo more than 2,000 years ago.

The island of ⌕ **Sulawesi** has a distinctive shape, consisting of four long arms of land extending out from the center of the island. The "arms" of the island con-

sist of mountainous areas and volcanic massifs. The coastal areas of Sulawesi are the traditional homelands of the several indigenous ethnic groups with distinct cultures, including the **Makassar people**. The **Toraja people** are well known for their elaborate funerals and burial practices. The ancestors of many indigenous coastal people on Sulawesi came to the island from the Asian mainland thousands of years ago.

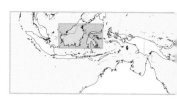

Bunaken Marine National Park Extensive ⌕ coral reefs (photo) – abundant marine life – good ⌕ diving sites.   **Rc45**

Dumoga Bone National Park Home to abundant flora and fauna including Borneo tarsiers – pristine ⌕ jungle wilderness in Minahasa.   **Rb45**

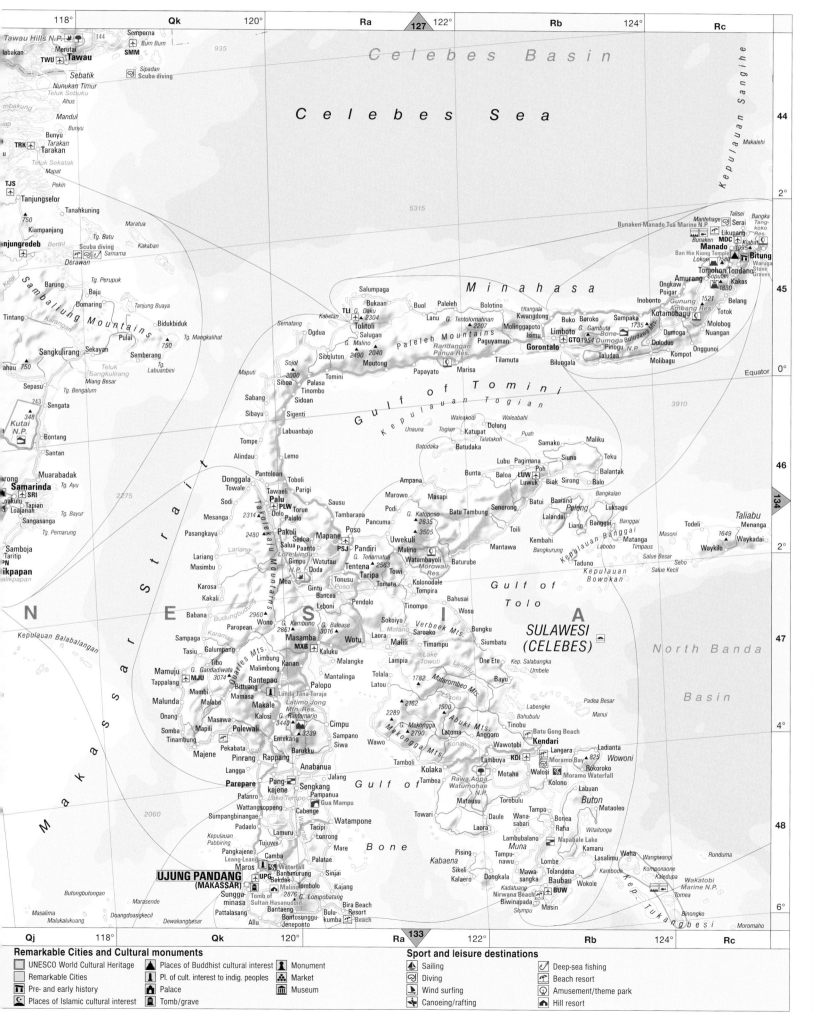

The Toraja This ethnic group lives in central Sulawesi and around the Gulf of Tomini. Death is very important in Toraja culture. The Toraja devote much of their time to organizing elaborate burial ceremonies and "death festivals." Photos from top to bottom: traditional homes, burial site with figures, sacred stones.   **Qk47**

Tukangbesi Islands Wakatobi National Park, southeast of Sulawesi, contains delicate underwater ⌕ ecosystems with large coral reefs and abundant marine life.   **Rb-Rc48**

Remarkable Cities and Cultural monuments

- ▢ UNESCO World Cultural Heritage
- ▢ Remarkable Cities
- ▢ Pre- and early history
- ▢ Places of Islamic cultural interest
- ▲ Places of Buddhist cultural interest
- ▲ Pl. of cult. interest to indig. peoples
- ▲ Palace
- ▲ Tomb/grave
- ☖ Monument
- ☖ Market
- ☖ Museum

Sport and leisure destinations

- ⛵ Sailing
- 🤿 Diving
- 🏄 Wind surfing
- 🚣 Canoeing/rafting
- 🎣 Deep-sea fishing
- 🏖 Beach resort
- 🎡 Amusement/theme park
- 🏔 Hill resort

Java, Lesser Sunda Islands

Like neighboring Sumatra, Java and the Lesser Sunda Islands are located on the southwestern edge of the Eurasian tectonic plate. The southern coasts of Java of the Lesser Sunda Islands border deep underwater trenches in the Indian Ocean while the northern coasts of these islands border the relatively shallow Java Sea. After the end of the last ice age around 10,000 years ago, the **Sunda continental shelf** was flooded

by the rising seas and Indonesia, the world's largest archipelago was formed. The archipelago encompasses more than 15,000 islands and islets.
The large number of 🌋 **volcanoes** located on the islands of **Indonesia** is evidence of the archipelago's location in the collision zone of two tectonic plates. A

Bromo Semeru mountain massif in eastern Java. **Qg49**

Jakarta Capital and largest city of Indonesia – 🏛 National Museum – 🐟 fish market – 🏚 historic Batavia district – Sunda Kelapa harbor – Ancol amusement park. **Qd49**

Mount Gede 🌋 Active volcano (2,958 m) in 🌲 Mount Gede Pangrango National Park – rare flora. **Qd49**

Prambanan The large 🛕 temple complex, built towards the end of the 9th century, is the largest Hindu holy site in Indonesia. The complex encompasses 190 buildings including eight large temples. The 47-meter-high main temple is dedicated to Shiva and the complex is a UNESCO world heritage site. **Qf49**

Borobodur One of the largest 🛕 Buddhist temples in Southeast Asia – built in the 9th century by the Sailendra dynasty – UNESCO world heritage site. **Qf49**

Yogyakarta Sultanate in Indonesia, founded in the 17th century – 🏰 Sultan's Palace with the central mosque – bird market – 🏛 Sono Budoyo Museum. **Qf49**

Krakatau Site of several major eruptions in recent centuries – new 🌋 volcanic island formed in 1928. **Qc49**

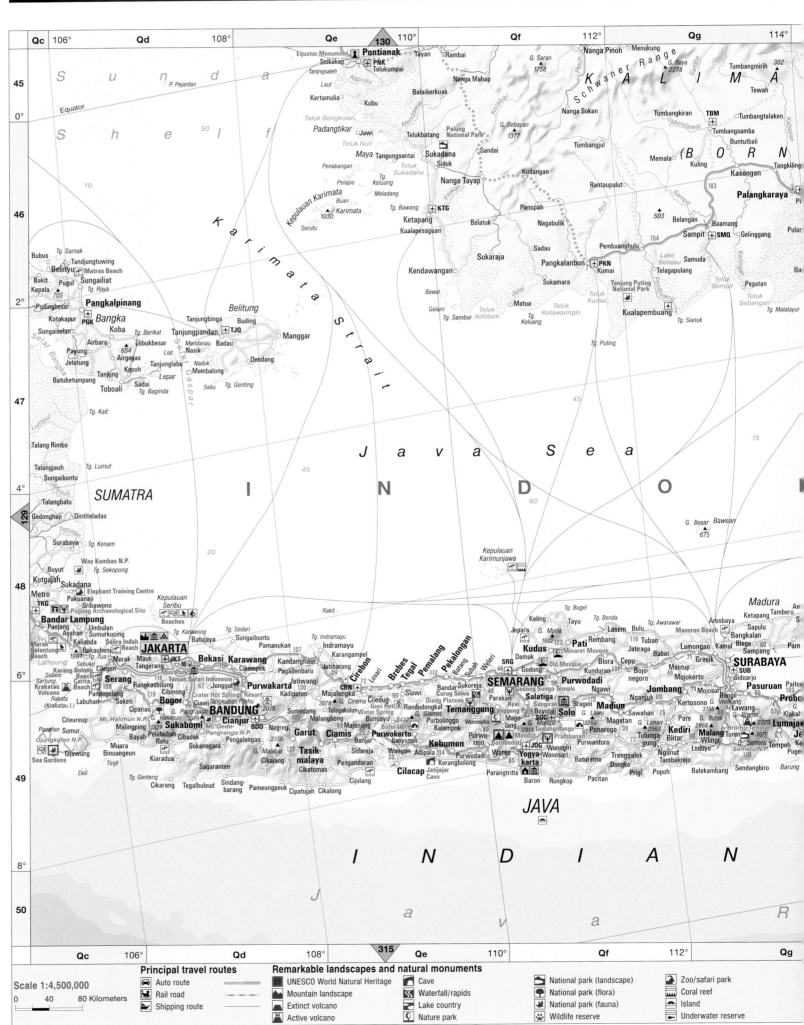

Scale 1:4,500,000
0   40   80 Kilometers

Principal travel routes
- 🚗 Auto route
- 🚂 Rail road
- 🚢 Shipping route

Remarkable landscapes and natural monuments
- UNESCO World Natural Heritage
- Mountain landscape
- Extinct volcano
- Active volcano
- Cave
- Waterfall/rapids
- Lake country
- Nature park
- National park (landscape)
- National park (flora)
- National park (fauna)
- Wildlife reserve
- Zoo/safari park
- Coral reef
- Island
- Underwater reserve

long belt of volcanoes stretches through peninsular Malaysia, Sumatra, Java and Bali. This volcanic belt also stretches east into the Lesser Sunda Islands and the island of Sulawesi. Around 76 of the volcanoes in Indonesia have been active in recent centuries and Java alone contains 35 active volcanoes including Mount Semuru (3,676 m). The volcano **Krakatau**, off the west coast of Java, was the site of a major eruption in 1883.

The fertile plains and foothills on the island of **Java** are used primarily for rice farming. Rice has been the staple food throughout most of Indonesia for many centuries and the rice trade financed the construction of several historic temples including the Buddhist ▲ **Borobudur** temple and the Hindu temple complex ⊻ **Prambanan**. Both of these temples have been designated world heritage sites by UNESCO because of

their historic architecture. Java is one of the most densely populated regions in the world. At least two-thirds of Indonesia's 200 million inhabitants live on the island. Archeological sites suggest that Java was also one of the earliest sites of human settlement in Asia.

The island of **Bali**, like neighboring Java, is dominated by ▲ volcanic mountain chains. Bali is the only majority ⊻ Hindu region in Indonesia, the world's most

populous majority Muslim nation. The island's culture, architecture, and beautiful landscapes attract many tourists from around the world. The indigenous Sassaks form the majority of the population of **Lombok's** population. Most Sassaks practice a religion indigenous to Lombok called ⊕ Wetu Tulu. Komodo, one of the smaller Lesser Sunda islands is home to the fascinating Komodo Dragons, the largest lizards in the world.

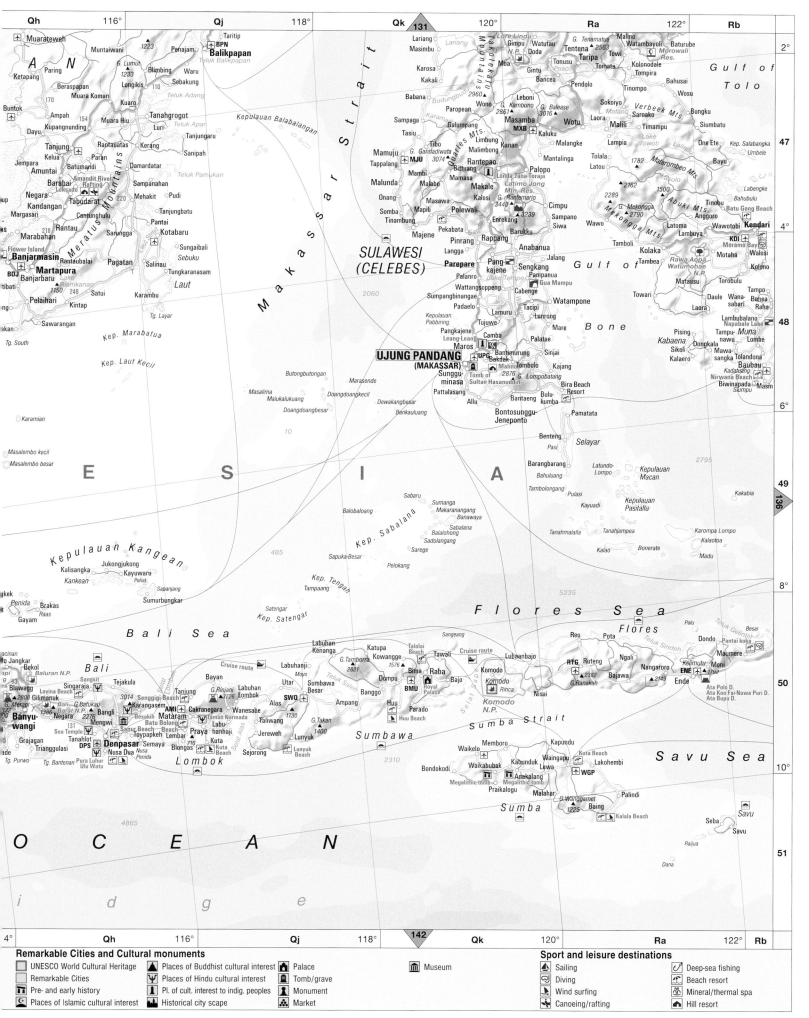

Bali The Hindu enclave in predominantly Muslim Indonesia is home to unique local cultures and religious practices. ⊻ Pura Ulun Danu (top photo), in the middle of Lake Bratan, is dedicated to the Hindu deities Shiva and Vishnu. ⊻ Pura Kehen (bottom photo) is one of the six holiest temples on Bali. The island's rural areas have many large ⊠ rice terraces (middle photo). Bali coasts encompass countless beautiful beaches. **Qh50**

Kecak Dance The "monkey dance" is one of the most fascinating traditional Balinese dances. A performance of the dance involves more than 100 actors. The actors sit around a main stage where stories of the Ramayana myth are performed. Most of the actor's portray soldiers in the monkey army of the general Hanuman.

Sumba Island (11,080 km²) in the Lesser Sunda group – traditional grass covered buildings – ancient ⊓ stone megaliths scattered around the island – burial sites with large stone animal and human figures (photo). **Qk-Ra49/50**

Komodo Lesser Sunda Islands – ⊡ national park, a UNESCO world heritage site – home of the Komodo Dragons (photo), the largest lizards in the world. **Qk49**

Remarkable Cities and Cultural monuments

- ⬜ UNESCO World Cultural Heritage
- ⬜ Remarkable Cities
- ⊓ Pre- and early history
- ◯ Places of Islamic cultural interest
- ▲ Places of Buddhist cultural interest
- ⊻ Places of Hindu cultural interest
- ⊕ Pl. of cult. interest to indig. peoples
- ⬛ Historical city scape
- ▮ Palace
- ⬛ Tomb/grave
- ⬥ Monument
- ✦ Market
- 🏛 Museum

Sport and leisure destinations

- ⛵ Sailing
- 🤿 Diving
- 🏄 Wind surfing
- 🛶 Canoeing/rafting
- 🎣 Deep-sea fishing
- 🏖 Beach resort
- ♨ Mineral/thermal spa
- ⛰ Hill resort

Molucca Islands, Irian Jaya

The Moluccas island group was once known throughout the world as the **Spice Islands**. The island group, called Maluku in Indoniesian, is situated on both sides of the equator – between Sulawesi to the northwest and Irian Jaya (Papua) to the southeast – in one of the most geologically active regions on the planet. Like the rest of Indonesia, the Moluccas were once part of a vast sub-continent that connected Australia and

Southeast Asia. Millions of years ago, rising seas submerged the low-lying areas of this subcontinent.
The **Moluccas** comprise more than 1,000 islands and form two Indonesian provinces: Maluku and Maluku Utara. The production of spices such as saffron, ginger, and coriander dominated the

Palm trees and beautiful beaches are abundant in the Moluccas. **Rd45**

Manado Important port city and capital of North Sulawesi – fascinating 🐠 coral reefs in Tua Marine National Park on the island Bunaken (photo). **Rc45**

Ternate Circle shaped island – historic Dutch 🏰 fort, built in 1511 – administrative center of Maluka Utara (Northern Moluccas) – 🏔 Gamalama (photo). **Rd45**

Biak population 70,000 – 🐾 nature re-serves – numerous white sand beaches including 🏖 Adoki Beach (photo). **Rh-Rj46**

Pandaidori Islands Small island group east of Biak – large 🐠 coral reefs – 🏖 beaches and 🤿 diving sites on the islands' coasts. **Rj46**

Yapen Island south of Biak – main settle-ment Serui – 🌳 rainforests – numerous bird species including hornbills and cockatoos – beautiful bays. **Rh-Rj46**

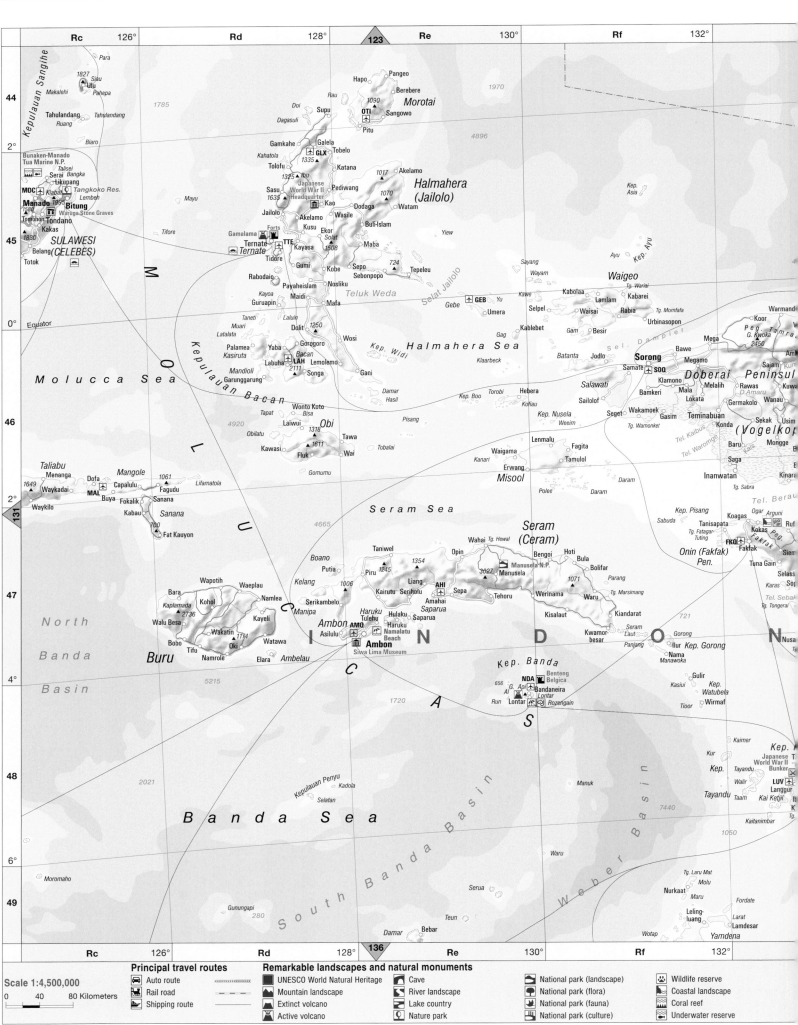

Scale 1:4,500,000
0   40   80 Kilometers

Principal travel routes
- 🚗 Auto route
- 🚂 Rail road
- ⚓ Shipping route

Remarkable landscapes and natural monuments
- ▪ UNESCO World Natural Heritage
- ▪ Mountain landscape
- ▲ Extinct volcano
- ▲ Active volcano
- Cave
- River landscape
- Lake country
- Nature park
- National park (landscape)
- National park (flora)
- National park (fauna)
- National park (culture)
- Wildlife reserve
- Coastal landscape
- Coral reef
- Underwater reserve

Molucca Islands, Irian Jaya

islands' economies for many centuries. Before the 16th century, the spice trade on the Moluccas was dominated by Arab and Indian traders. In 1511, the Portuguese built their first base in the region on the island of ▣ Ternate. Shortly afterwards, the first Portguese trade ships arrived at **Ambon** and the Banda Islands, the most important centers of spice production. Ambon City is the provincial capital of Maluka and the most important

economic center in the region. Fish, nickel, oil, and timber are now the leading exports of the Moluccas.
The Moluccas are home to countless beautiful ▣ beaches and there are extensive ▣ coral reefs near the coasts of many islands. The interiors of many islands in area are covered by dense **tropical rainforests** with an incredible abundance of unique plants. In addition to its fascinating plant life, the islands are

also home to an interesting collection of land and marine animals.
With a total area of 733,000 km², ▣ **New Guinea** is the second largest island in the world. The eastern half of the island comprises most of Papua New Guinea, an independent nation since 1975. The western half of the island (**Irian Jaya**, province: Papua) has been a part of Indonesia since 1969. More than half of Papua's land is cov-

ered by dense tropical rainforests and the mountainous central highlands are home to expansive cloud forests. The tallest mountain in the province, ▣ **Puncak Jaya**, rises 5,030 meters above sea level and its peak is covered by snow during the entire year. Many of the areas in the province's interior are difficult to access. The coastal areas of the province are dominated by vast swampy plains.

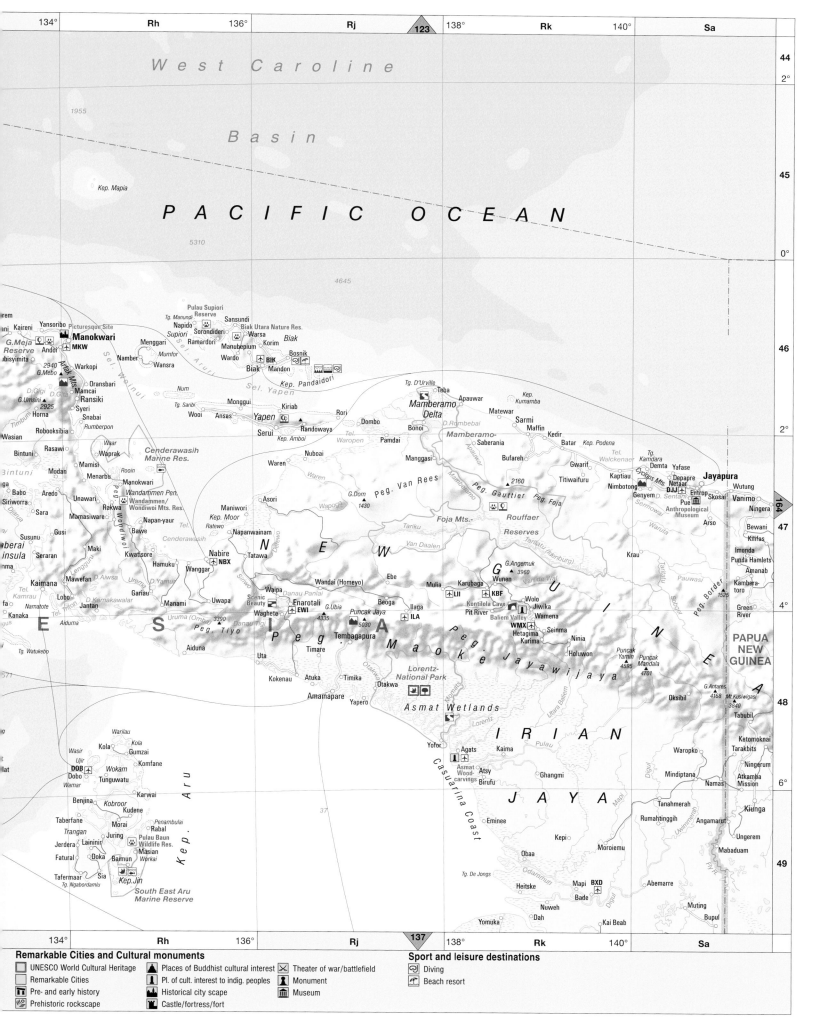

Jayapura Capital city of Papua (Irian Jaya) – located near the Cyclops Mountains, a range of ▣ rainforest-covered mountains – unique birds and orchids. **Sa47**

Baliem Valley The valley in Irian Jaya (Papua) is situated 1,700 meters above sea level. The indigenous ▣ Dani people form the majority of the area's population. Many small Dani villages consisting of grass covered huts are scattered throughout the valley. Like the other inhabitants of New Guinea's isolated highlands, the Dani have their own unique social systems and traditions. Photos from top to bottom: lush mountain vegetation, suspension bridge over the Baliem River, Dani people in traditional costumes. **Rk48**

Jayawijaya Mountains Long mountain range in central Irian Jaya (Papua). The Jayawijaya highlands contain villages inhabited by the Dani, Lani, Jali, and Eipomek peoples. **Rk48**

Remarkable Cities and Cultural monuments

- ▢ UNESCO World Cultural Heritage
- ▢ Remarkable Cities
- ▢ Pre- and early history
- ▢ Prehistoric rockscape
- ▲ Places of Buddhist cultural interest
- ▢ Pl. of cult. interest to indig. peoples
- ▢ Historical city scape
- ▢ Castle/fortress/fort
- ✕ Theater of war/battlefield
- ▢ Monument
- ▢ Museum

Sport and leisure destinations

- ▢ Diving
- ▢ Beach resort

Timor, Arafura Sea

Southeastern Indonesia is a region containing several thousand islands scattered thorough three different seas. The region is home to a unique diversity of cultures, ethnicities, and landscapes. Southeastern Indonesia consists of the southern tip of Sulawesi, Timor, the Southern Moluccas, and the southwestern coast of Papua (Irian Jaya), an Indonesian province on New Guinea. The islands of southeastern Indonesia are located near the

northernmost tip of Australia. Millions of years ago, the regions were connected by a land bridge and animals migrated in both directions between Asia and Australia. The Arafura Sea stretches over a large section of the area once occupied by the prehistoric land bridge. It is a shallow sea with a maximum depth of just 130 meters.

Isolated beach in Wakatobi Marine National Park.   **RbRc48**

Timor The western section of the politically divided island contains vast tropical rainforests. Photos from top to bottom: the harbor of Dili, Mount Ramelau in East Timor, rainforest on Mount Mutis.   **Rc50**

Seram Central Moluccas – high mountains – dense rainforests – ⬛ Manusela National Park – unique birds – photo: the harbor of Seram.   **Re-Rf47**

Banda Islands The islands are widely scattered and were once a center of nutmeg production. Photos from top to bottom: beach, historic ⬛ Fort Benteng Belgica, traditional boat. **Re-Rf48**

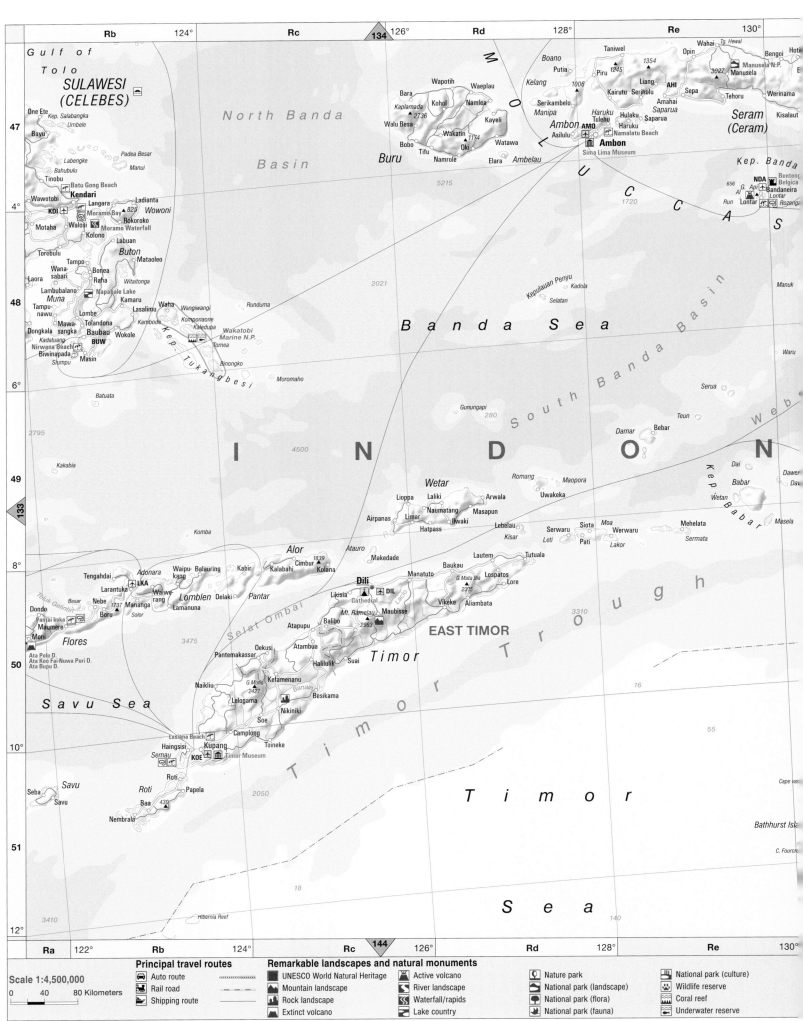

Principal travel routes
- Auto route
- Rail road
- Shipping route

Scale 1:4,500,000
0   40   80 Kilometers

Remarkable landscapes and natural monuments
- UNESCO World Natural Heritage
- Mountain landscape
- Rock landscape
- Extinct volcano
- Active volcano
- River landscape
- Waterfall/rapids
- Lake country
- Nature park
- National park (landscape)
- National park (flora)
- National park (fauna)
- National park (culture)
- Wildlife reserve
- Coral reef
- Underwater reserve

Timor is the largest island in the Lesser Sunda group and is divided between two nations. East Timor was a Portuguese territory for several centuries before it was occupied by Indonesia in 1975. After a long period of violent unrest, East Timor was granted its independence from Indonesia in 2002. The country is home to around 800,000 people and the port city Dili is the national capital. West Timor is a province of Indonesia. Like neighboring Sumba, Timor is located in the western section of the Lesser Sunda island group. Timor is separated from Australia by the Timor Sea which contains the Temor Trough, an underwater trench with a maximum depth of 3,300 meters. Central Timor is dominated by a 500-kilometer-long mountain range that is interrupted by several grassy plateaus. The tallest mountain on the island, **Mount Ramelau**, rises 2,963 meters. The remaining sections of Timor's virgin rainforests are home to many fascinating birds. With the exception of some areas dominated by swampy mangrove forest, most of the coastal areas are covered by grassy plains with scattered acacias and eucalyptus trees. The coasts are home to unique plants and animals. The flora and fauna of coastal Timor is similar to that found on other islands in the region.

The Aru Islands in the Southern Moluccas are covered by dense rainforests, home to a variety of plants and animals. The islands are located 200 kilometers off the southwestern coast of **New Guinea**. The Indonesian province Papua, formerly known as **Irian Jaya**, covers the western half of New Guinea. **Lorentz National Park** stretches from the swampy coast of Papua to the foothills of the province's central highlands.

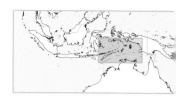

Kai Islands Three islands with approximately 100,000 inhabitants – main settlement Tual (photo) – beautiful beaches. **Rg48**

Aru Islands South East Aru Marine Reserve – Pulau Baun Wildlife Reserve – many lagoons and coral reefs – dolphins and sea cows. **Rh48/49**

Lorentz National Park The national park in Indonesia's Papua province is a UNESCO world heritage site. The park features rainforests (top photo). Many animals including birds of paradise (photo) inhabit the park. **Rj48**

Asmat The name refers to a swampy area in western New Guinea and an indigenous ethnic group that lives in the area. The Asmat are well known for their traditional wood carvings. Photos from top to bottom: Asmat men and traditional body paintings. Wood carving, Asmat community gathering. **Rk48**

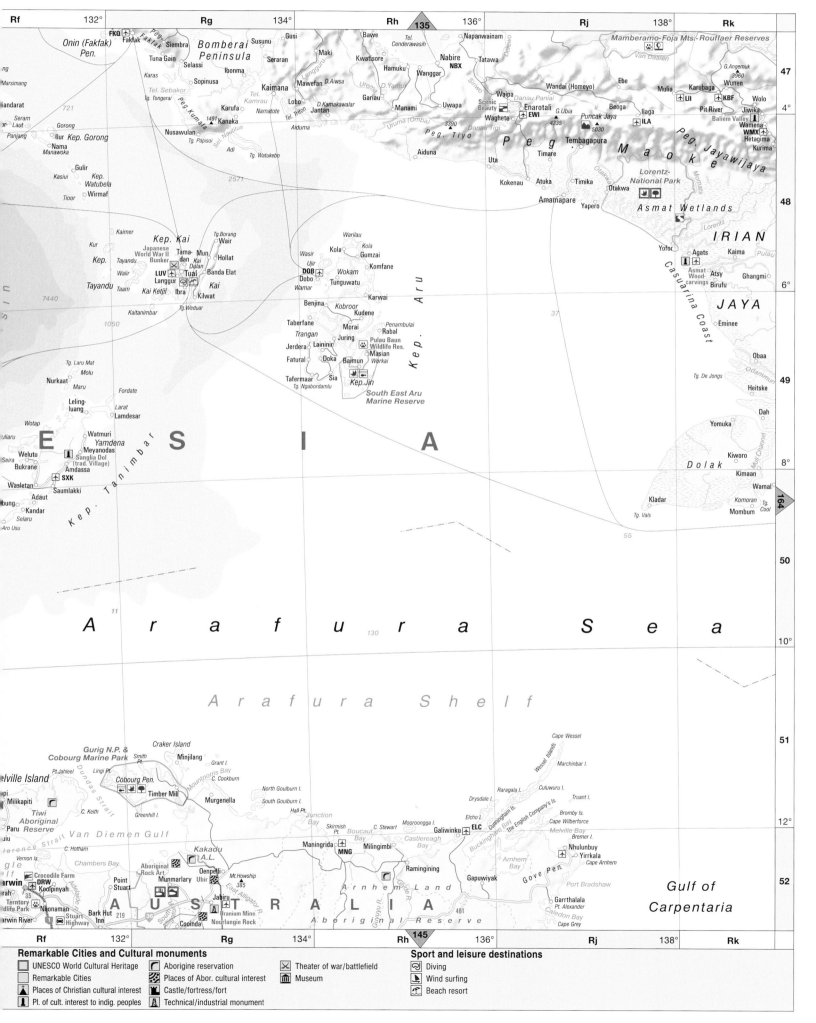

Remarkable Cities and Cultural monuments

- UNESCO World Cultural Heritage
- Remarkable Cities
- Places of Christian cultural interest
- Pl. of cult. interest to indig. peoples
- Aborigine reservation
- Places of Abor. cultural interest
- Castle/fortress/fort
- Technical/industrial monument
- Theater of war/battlefield
- Museum

Sport and leisure destinations

- Diving
- Wind surfing
- Beach resort

The Olgas (top): Spectacular rock formations in the "red heart" of Australia.
Sydney (bottom): Australia's largest city with its famous Opera House and the Harbour Bridge.

Milford Sound (left): A stunning fjord landscape on New Zealand's South Island.
Moorea (right): One of Polynesia's most beautiful islands; Moorea is covered by lush forests.

Australia/Oceania

Australia is the land of the "dreamtime." The blue waters of the Great Barrier Reef, the green rainforests in the wet tropics, the red rock formations of Central Australia, and the golden sand dunes of Nambung National Park make Australia a fascinating continent rich in color and diversity.

Australia/Oceania · The continent

This region of the world is comprised of two unequal parts: the massive landmass of **Australia** and the countless scattered islands of the South Pacific. The region's islands range from the very smallest of islets to large islands such as New Guinea and New Zealand.

Australia is a continent of vast distances. Most of Central and Western Australia consist of deserts. Australia's largest desert, The Great Sandy Desert, covers

Sunset at Ayers Rock (Uluru).

520,000 km². Ayers Rock, also known by its Aboriginal name Uluru, is located near the geographic center of Australia. Australia's highest mountains are in the Australian Alps, a section of the Great Dividing Range which stretches along the eastern coast. Mount Kosciuszko (2,228 m) is the highest mountain on the continent.

The Great Barrier Reef off the northeastern coast of Australia is the world's largest coral reef. It has a total length of more than 2,000 kilometers from north to south.

The **islands of Oceania** are usually divided into three regions: Micronesia, Melanesia, and Polynesia. The thousands of islands in Oceania, scattered over 70 million km² in the Pacific Ocean, have a total land area around 1.3 million km².

The regions of Oceania near the equator have lush and thick vegetation (top photo: rainforest in New Guinea). **Subtropical vegetation** in Australia's Northern Territory (middle photo, top). Mungo National Park in New South Wales (middle photo, bottom). **The Great Barrier Reef** off the eastern coast of Australia (bottom photo).

Snow covered Mount Cook (Aoraki) in the New Zealand Alps is the tallest mountain in **New Zealand** (3,764 m, top photo). Fjordland National Park encompasses some of the most beautiful and unspoiled landscapes on the South Island of New Zealand (bottom photo: Milford Sound).

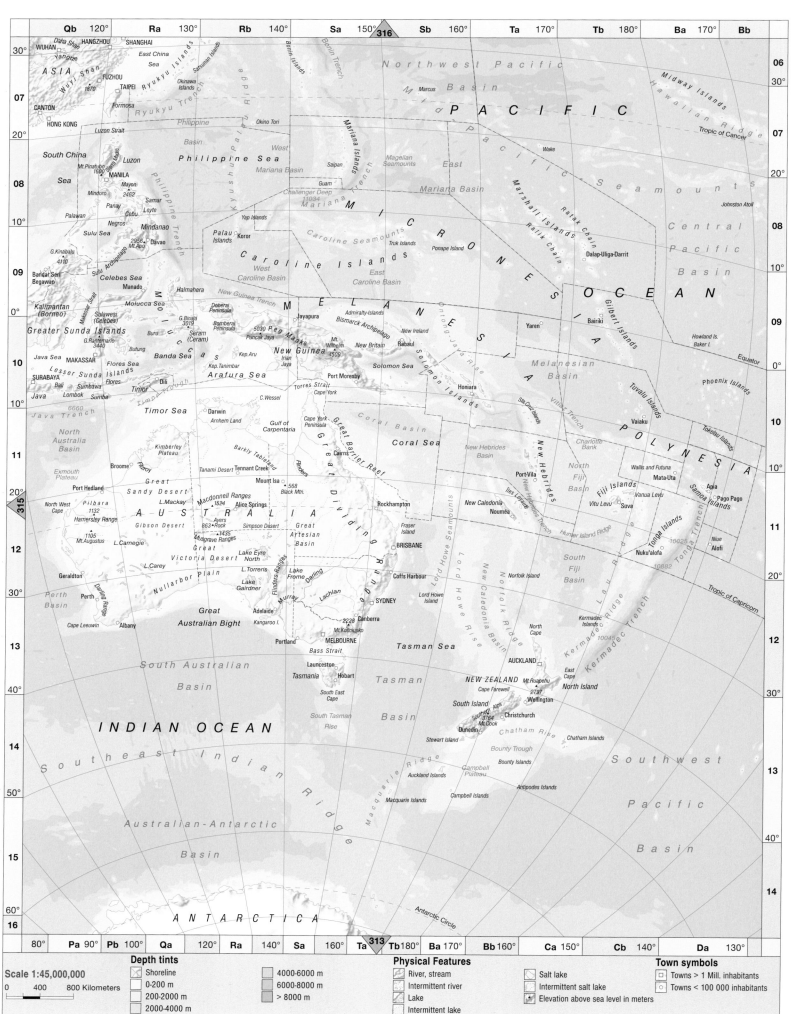

Many of the **Pacific islands** were created from coral reefs. Countless small islands scattered throughout the region remain uninhabited (photo: small island in the Palau archipelago), while other have been populated for thousands of years. Many islands are home to unique flora and fauna.

Scale 1:45,000,000

0   400   800 Kilometers

Depth tints
- Shoreline
- 0–200 m
- 200–2000 m
- 2000–4000 m
- 4000–6000 m
- 6000–8000 m
- > 8000 m

Physical Features
- River, stream
- Intermittent river
- Lake
- Intermittent lake
- Salt lake
- Intermittent salt lake
- Elevation above sea level in meters

Town symbols
- Towns > 1 Mill. inhabitants
- Towns < 100 000 inhabitants

Around 90 % of Australia's 19.7 million inhabitants occupy just 3 % of the continent's land. The continent's population is concentrated in the Southeast with the majority of people living in a few large coastal cities. **Aborigines**, the continent's indigenous people, represent just 2.2 % of the population. Most Australians are the descendants of European immigrants. After the arrival of the first Europeans at the end of the 18th century, the Aborigi-

nal population began to decline. Like the Aborigines, the **Maori** of New Zealand and the **Papua** of New Guinea were dramatically affected by the European colonization of their countries. These ethnic groups still struggle to preserve the most important aspects of their cultures including their languages and traditional arts.

Left: Aboriginal man of Australia.
Right: Warrior of Papua New Guinea.

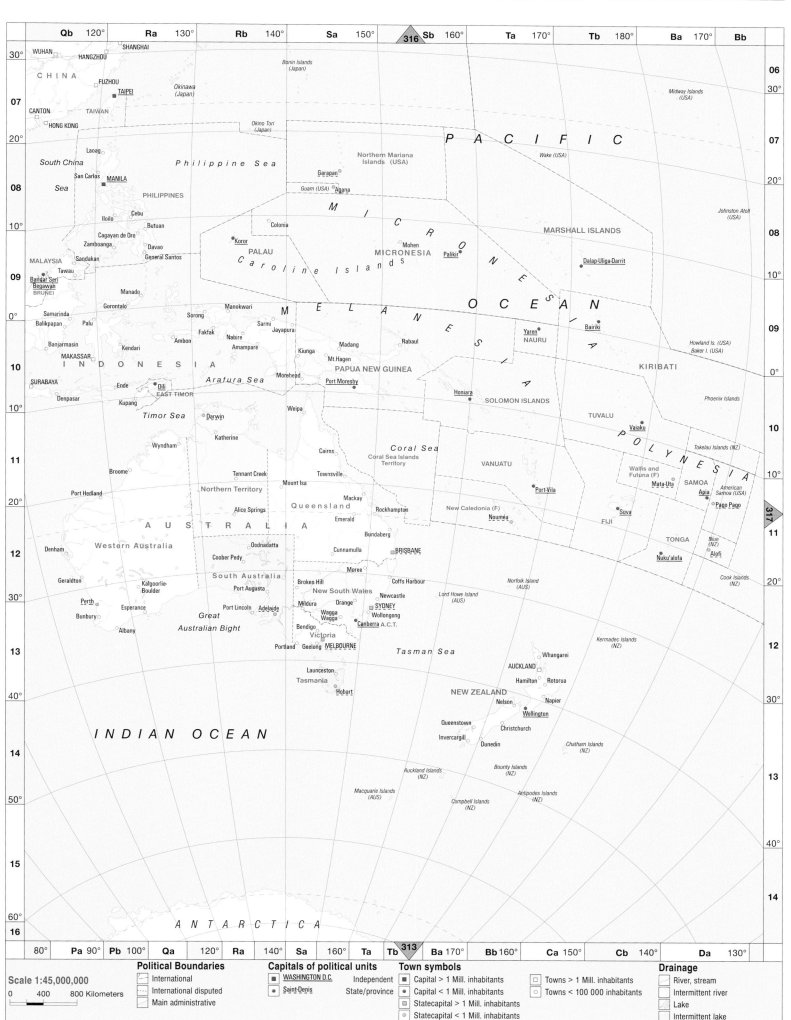

Countries and Flags

- Australia
- Fiji
- Kiribati
- Marshall Islands
- Micronesia
- Nauru
- New Zealand
- Palau
- Papua New Guinea
- Samoa
- Solomon Islands
- Tonga
- Tuvalu
- Vanuatu

Since the 19th century the islands of the Pacific have been divided into three distinct regions: **Melanesia** in the western Pacific, **Micronesia** in the northern Pacific, and **Polynesia** in the central Pacific. Melanesian ethnic groups include the Chimbu, Enga, Motu, and Foi. Among the more famous Micronesian ethnic groups are the Chamorro, Marshall Islanders, and Palauans. The Polynesians include the indigenous Hawaiians, the Maori of New Zealand, and the Samoans. In all traditional Pacific island societies, dance, song, and traditional storytelling play important roles in the preservation of culture. Photos from top to bottom: Huli man of New Guinea, Samoan, Micronesian man, Polynesian women (all in traditional headdresses).

Scale 1:45,000,000

0   400   800 Kilometers

Political Boundaries
- International
- International disputed
- Main administrative

Capitals of political units
- WASHINGTON D.C. — Independent
- Saint-Denis — State/province

Town symbols
- Capital > 1 Mill. inhabitants
- Capital < 1 Mill. inhabitants
- Statecapital > 1 Mill. inhabitants
- Statecapital < 1 Mill. inhabitants
- Towns > 1 Mill. inhabitants
- Towns < 100 000 inhabitants

Drainage
- River, stream
- Intermittent river
- Lake
- Intermittent lake

Australia, New Zealand

Australia is the smallest of the world's seven continents with a total area of 7.7 million km². The continent can be divided into three large geographic regions. The **Great Western Plateau** covers much of western and central Australia. It is situated at elevations between 200 and 800 meters above sea level. The plateau features vast deserts, including the **Great Sandy Desert**, as well as unique stone formations. The **Great Dividing Range** stretches the entire length of Australia's eastern coast. A narrow strip of low-lying coastal plains is located to the east of the range. Southeastern Australia is the most densely populated region on the continent. Australia's two largest cities – Melbourne and Sydney – are located in this region.

Pristine Lake Burbury on the Australian island of Tasmania.

Arnhem Land Aboriginal land reserve in Australia's Northern Territory – aboriginal art – Gove Peninsula – Mary River (photo).

The Kimberley Region (not easily accessed) in Western Australia – 350-million-years old stone formation, Bungle Bungle (photo); a UNESCO world heritage site.

Macdonnell Ranges Range of hills and mountains in central Australia – mountains rise above 1,500 meters – fascinating gorges – national park.

Central Australia's Stone Formations Uluru (Ayers Rock) is 348 meters high with a diameter of nine kilometers (photo) – 600 million years old – The Olgas (Kata Tjuta): a group of red sandstone formations.

Australia's Western Coasts Shark Bay World Heritage Area is home to rare animals including humpback whales and manatees – Ningaloo Reef Marine Park.

Australia's Southern Coasts Walpole-Nornalup National Park encompasses the Valley of the Giants with its tall Karri Trees – Whale watching off the coast near Albany – Limestone Coast.

South Australia The state's interior comprises large deserts and semi-arid grasslands – Stuart Highway – Eyre Highway – capital city of Adelaide – Eucla Desert (photo).

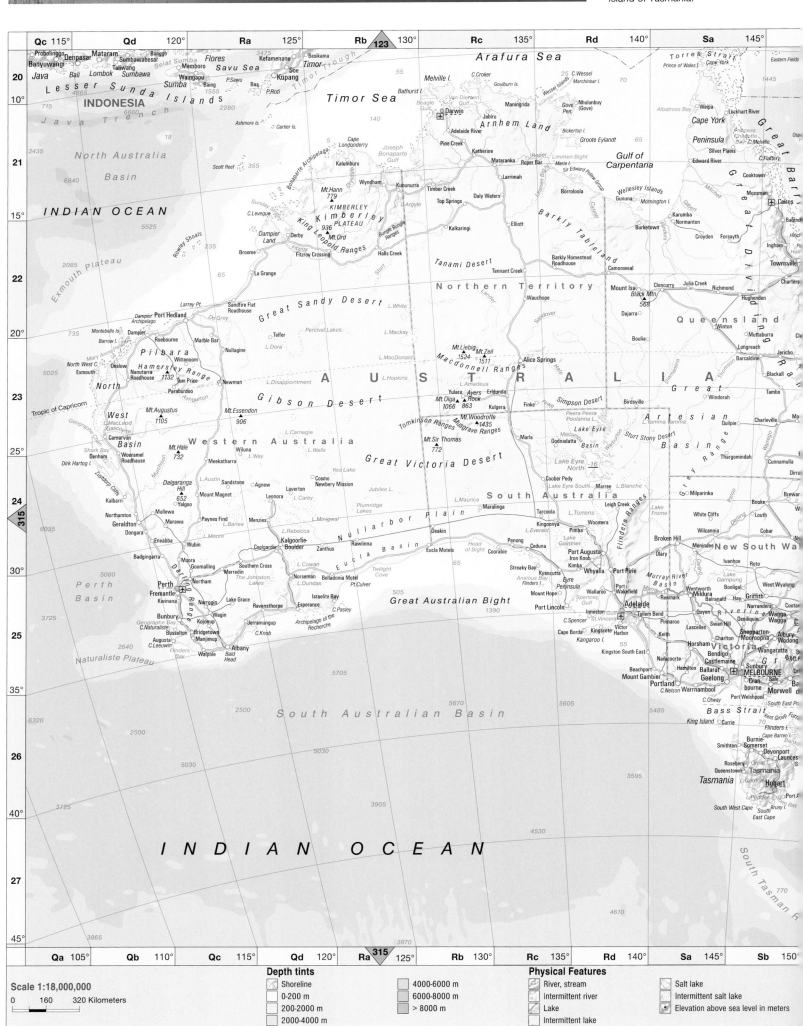

Scale 1:18,000,000

0   160   320 Kilometers

Depth tints
- Shoreline
- 0-200 m
- 200-2000 m
- 2000-4000 m
- 4000-6000 m
- 6000-8000 m
- > 8000 m

Physical Features
- River, stream
- Intermittent river
- Lake
- Intermittent lake
- Salt lake
- Intermittent salt lake
- Elevation above sea level in meters

Situated between the Western Plateau and the mountains of eastern Australia, a vast basin covers most of central Australia. This arid region is covered by large sandy deserts, such as the **Great Victoria Desert**, as well as large salt lakes. The region is extremely sparsely populated and has no large cities. There are several vast livestock ranches scattered throughout central Australia. The major tourist attractions in central Australia are the region's unique red sandstone formations including **Uluru (Ayers Rock)** and the **Olgas**.

The **Great Barrier Reef**, located off the northeastern coast of Australia, is the world's longest coral reef. The reef is more than 2,000 kilometers long and houses 400 types of coral and 1,500 fish species. **Tasmania**, Australia's largest island, features pristine forests and unique wildlife.

The ancestors of Australia's Aborigines arrived on the continent more than 50,000 years ago. There are now around 400,000 Australians of Aboriginal descent. The Aborigines have been granted Australian citizenship and control of large land reserves in recent decades.

Fiji and **Vanuatu (New Hebrides)** are island groups situated east of Australia in the Pacific Ocean. **New Zealand** consists of two main islands as well as numerous smaller ones. New Zealand's North Island (115,000 km²) has many geysers and several active volcanoes. The South Island (151,000 km²) features tall mountain ranges, fjords, and large glaciers. The country's capital, Wellington, and the largest city, Auckland, are both situated on the North Island. In recent decades, the government of New Zealand has taken steps to preserve the culture of the indigenous Maori people.

Northern Queensland Daintree National Park (photo): rain forests, bird watching, tours along the Daintree River – Cape Tribulation with coastal rainforests.

Whitsunday Islands Island group close to the Great Barrier Reef – around 70 islands – the islands are the peaks of an underwater mountain system.

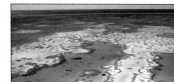

Great Barrier Reef The largest coral reef in the world – off the coast of Queensland – UNESCO world natural heritage site.

Great Dividing Range Mountain range along the eastern coast of Australia – Blue Mountain National Park (photo).

Tasmania Island (68,000 km²) around 300 kilometers south of mainland Australia – hilly terrain – temperate rain forests – 14 national parks – historic architecture in Hobart.

New Zealand The two main islands of this Pacific nation are home to a diverse group of beautiful landscapes. The North Island has active volcanoes including Mount Ngauruhoe (top photo). The South Island is home to the Southern Alps and Westland National Park (bottom photo).

Political Boundaries
International
International disputed
Main administrative

Transportation
Interstate Hwy./Motorway
Main road
Railway
Airport

Capitals of political units
■ **WASHINGTON D.C.** Independent
⊙ Richmond State/province

Town symbols
■ Capital > 1 Mill. inhabitants
● Capital < 1 Mill. inhabitants
■ Statecapital > 1 Mill. inhabitants
● Statecapital < 1 Mill. inhabitants
□ Towns > 1 Mill. inhabitants
○ Towns 100 000 bis 1 Mill. inhabitants
○ Towns < 100 000 inhabitants

Northwestern Australia

Northwestern Australia comprises areas in the state of Western Australia and the Northern Territory of the Australian continent. The climate in this part of the country is mostly tropical except for a few arid areas, including the ⬛ **Tanami Desert**, in the southern section of the region. The **Kimberley** (in the western part of the region) is a series of rugged plateaus and spectacular gorges near the ⬛ Timor Sea coast.

The region, which has been inhabited by Aborigines for centuries, was barely explored up until the last few decades. Many areas are still difficult to travel into, a fact which has helped preserve the fascinating nature of the region. Although northwestern Australia is three times the size of England it has just 25,000 inhabitants.

The Bungle Bungle: bizarre rock formations in Western Australia. **Re54**

Bonaparte Archipelago ⬛ A lone tropical island 850 kilometers north from Broome, off the jagged Kimberley coast. **Rc53**

Prince Regent Nature Reserve ⬛ nature reserve in the Kimberley region – heavy annual rainfall – the area is difficult to access – the reserve contains more than 500 unique plant species. **Rc53/54**

Lake Argyle Largest ⬛ man-made lake in Australia – 45 kilometers south of the Kununurra – the damming of the ⬛ Ord River made agriculture possible in the Kimberley. **Re54**

Argyle Diamond Mine World's most productive diamond ⬛ mine – produces one-third of the world's natural diamonds – source of rare pink diamonds. **Re54**

Wolfe Creek Crater Second largest ⬛ meteor impact crater on Earth – on the edge of the Great Sandy Desert – only visible from the air – around 300,000 years old. **Rd55**

Windjana Gorge National Park (Kimberleys) ⬛ Large gorge on the Lennard River (top photo). The sandstone walls of the gorge are as high as 90 meters. The area is renowned for old Aboriginal ⬛ rock paintings. The most impressive paintings portray the cloud gods (bottom photo). **Rc54**

Scale 1:4,500,000
0   40   80 Kilometers

Principal travel routes
- 🚗 Auto route
- 🚆 Rail road
- ⚓ Shipping route
- ·······
- Mountain landscape
- Rock landscape
- Ravine/canyon

Remarkable landscapes and natural monuments
- UNESCO World Natural Heritage
- Geyser
- Cave
- River landscape
- Waterfall/rapids
- National park (landscape)
- National park (flora)
- National park (fauna)
- National park (culture)
- Wildlife reserve
- Crocodile farm
- Coastal landscape
- Underwater reserve

One of the region's most interesting attractions is the ⌐ **Bungle Bungle (Purnululu)** – a group of colorful stone formations first discovered during the filming of a television program in 1982. Kinunurra is the gateway to the Kimberley. The town was built in the 1960s as part of a plan to dam the nearby Ord River and irrigate the surrounding area. South of the Kimberley lies the city of Broome ⌐, famous for its beaches and local pearl industry.

The northern part of the region including **Darwin**, the capital of the Northern Territory, is called the "Top End" by Australians. Darwin and its surroundings have a humid subtropical climate. The city with 100,000 inhabitants is the only large city in the region. For the Australian economy Darwin is the "gateway to Asia" and for many tourists the city is also important as the gateway to ⌐ **Litchfield** and ⌐ **Kakadu** National Parks.

In both the Top End and the Kimberley there are only two distinct seasons during the year. The Dry Season lasts from May until September, while the Wet Season lasts from November until the end of March. April and October are the transitional months between the two seasons. During the Wet Season, many areas in northwestern Australia, including Arnhem Land and Kakadu National Park, are flooded over and can only be reached by

airplane. Temperatures in the region regularly exceed 35° C, and humidity is high during the entire year. Coastal storms often move inland bringing heavy rainfall and floods to the interior. The coast it>self is regularly threatened by powerful cyclones. July and August offer the most appealing weather for tourists wanting to explore the region, despite many areas being parched because of the low rainfall during these months.

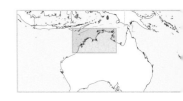

Arnhem Land ⌐ Region on the edge of northwestern Australia – floods during the wet season – towns: Nhulunbuy and Yirrkala – under Aboriginal administration. **Rh52/53**

Litchfield National Park ⌐ Spectacular national park with Florence Falls and "The Lost City": a rock formation. **Rf52**

Kakadu National Park Covering 20,000 km² the ⌐ national park is inhabited and governed by Aborigines. The national park, a UNESCO world heritage site, lies in the drainage area of the Alligator River. Kakadu is home to over 1,000 different plant, 300 bird, and 75 reptile species. Ubirr and Nourlangie Rock are sites of important aboriginal rock paintings. **Rg52**

Nitmiluk National Park ⌐ The major attraction in this national park is ⌐ Katherine Gorge, a 30-kilometer-long series of 13 gorges – cliffs with ❀ rock paintings. **Rg52/53**

Devil's Marbles According to aboriginal myths these rock formations are eggs laid by the Rainbow Serpent – large round ⌐ stones along the Stuart Highway. **Rh56**

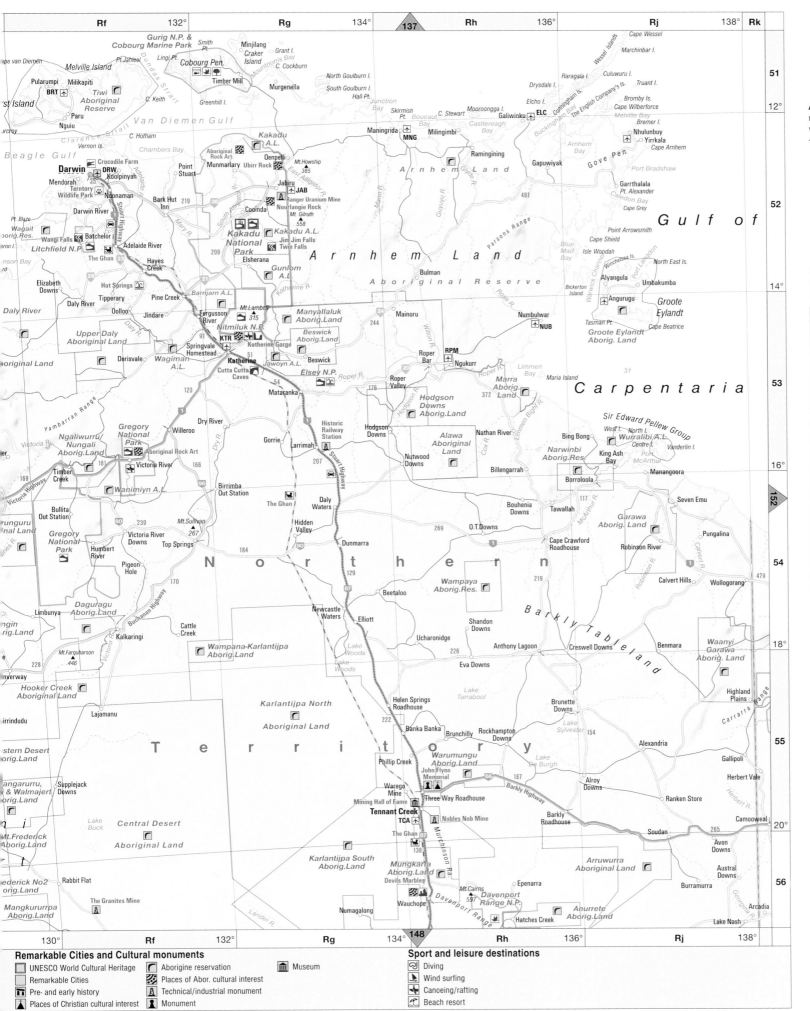

Remarkable Cities and Cultural monuments

☐ UNESCO World Cultural Heritage	☐ Aborigine reservation	🏛 Museum	
☐ Remarkable Cities	☐ Places of Abor. cultural interest		
☐ Pre- and early history	☐ Technical/industrial monument		
☐ Places of Christian cultural interest	☐ Monument		

Sport and leisure destinations

- Diving
- Wind surfing
- Canoeing/rafting
- Beach resort

Western Australia

If the Australian state of Western Australia were an independent country it would be the ninth biggest nation on Earth. The state covers the western third of the continent and has a land area of 2.5 million km². Western Australia is incredibly rich in natural resources. 🔲 **Pilbara**, a rocky region in Western Australia, has vast iron ore deposits. Most of the communities in the area, including Newman and Tom Price, depend on mining for their econo-

mic well being. The rock formations in Pilbara's **Hamersley Range** are estimated to be at least three million years old. In recent decades, significant reserves of natural gas and oil have been found off Western Australia's coast. Western Australia coasts feature many delicate and unique ecosystems. The marine and

Storm clouds above the Great Sandy Desert. **Rb56**

Dampier Archipelago 🔲 Island group near the port city of Dampier – rare plant and animal species. **Qj56**

Hamersley Range Pilbara Region – vast iron ore deposits – 🔲 Karijini National Park – gorges, rivers, and waterfalls. **Qj-Qk57**

Australia's West Coast 🔲 Cape Range National Park has many fine beaches and coral reefs; the park is part of the 🔲 Ningaloo Marine Park (UNESCO natural heritage site) **(Qg 56/57)**. The Ningaloo reef comprises at least 250 different types of coral. 🔲 Shark Bay Marine Park was named for the tiger sharks in the area **(Qg-Qh 58/59)**. Stromatolites (colonies of primitive microbes) are one of the major reasons Shark Bay was designated a world natural heritage site by UNESCO. The 🔲 underwater reserves around Shark Bay and Ningaloo Reef were created to protect the animals and plants in the area. 🔲 Francois Perron National Park in Shark Bay is home to rare bird species **(Qg58)**.

Kalbarri National Park 🔲 River basin along the Murchison River – canyons and beautiful coastline. **Qh59**

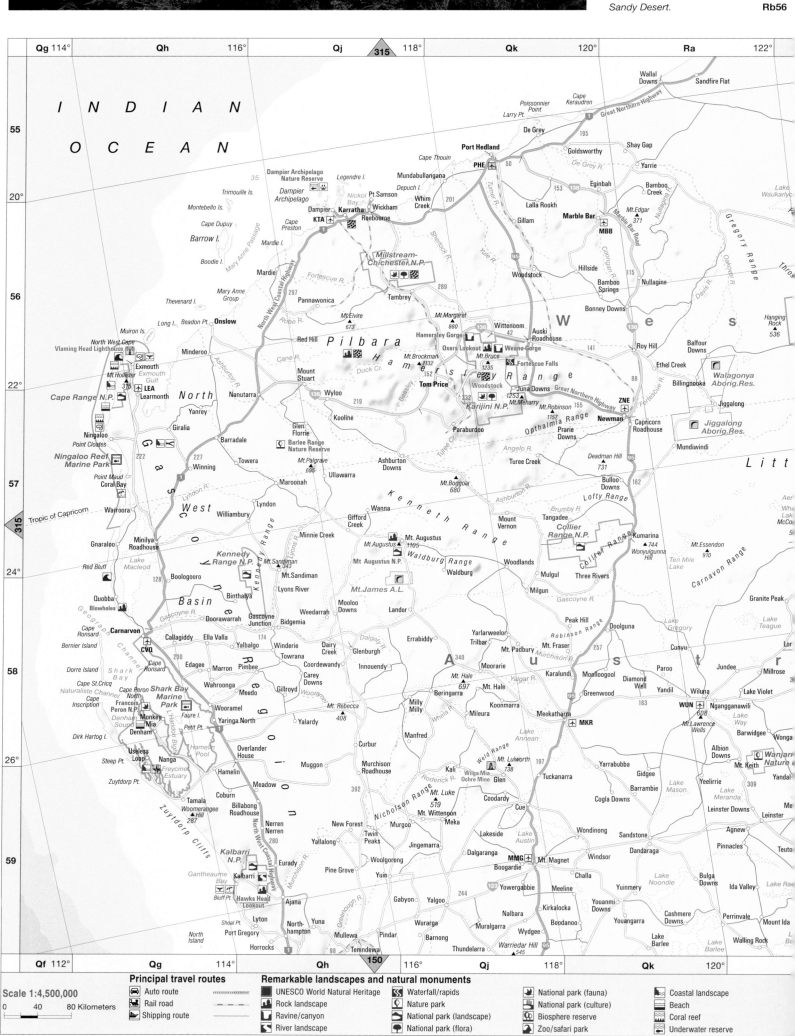

Scale 1:4,500,000

0   40   80 Kilometers

Principal travel routes	Remarkable landscapes and natural monuments		
Auto route	UNESCO World Natural Heritage	Waterfall/rapids	National park (fauna)	Coastal landscape
Rail road	Rock landscape	Nature park	National park (culture)	Beach
Shipping route	Ravine/canyon	National park (landscape)	Biosphere reserve	Coral reef
	River landscape	National park (flora)	Zoo/safari park	Underwater reserve

national parks around 🏖 **Shark Bay** and the 🏖 **Ningaloo Reef** have been designated UNESCO world natural heritage sites. Rare plants and animals are found in both areas. Whales, dolphins, and manatees are among the many animals visitors can discover in these areas. Shark Bay is also home to what may be the oldest life forms still living on earth – the stromatolites. Stromatolites are structures consisting of bacteria layers that grow in warm saline water. The oldest stromatolite fossils in Shark Bay are more than three billion years old.

The interior of Western Australia consists mostly of 🏜 deserts and semi-arid land. Visitors to the interior will encounter a land of red sand dunes, spinifex grass, beautiful rock formations, sleepy isolated towns, and the largest livestock ranches in the world. Western Australia also encompasses the hottest areas on the continent. During the 1920s temperatures exceeding 38°C were recorded for 160 consecutive days in the town of **Marble Bar**. Despite the high temperatures, heavy rainfall often leads to severe flooding in the interior of Western Australia. These floods can cause major damage to roads and buildings. The northern sections of Western Australia above the Tropic of Capricorn are situated in a hurricane risk zone. Many Australian towns in this area have been heavily damaged by these powerful storms in recent decades.

The **Aborigines** of Western Australia have gained control of large areas of 🟥 land in the region after a series of court rulings in recent years. Many Aboriginal leaders hope that land ownership and limited self-government will increase the confidence, influence and economic well-being of their communities.

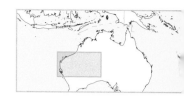

Western Australia's deserts Rudall River national park is the largest in Western Australia. Mostly 🏜 desert, the park contains a system of salt lakes (Lake Dora and Lake Blanche) **(Rb57)**. 🟥 The Gibson Desert Nature Reserve is home to large herds of wild horses and camels **(Rc58)**. Large sections of Western Australia's interior are under Aboriginal control.

Warburton Range Typical desert mountain range – in the center of a large 🟥 Aboriginal land reserve. **Rd59**

The Outback The Outback ist the name Australians give to their most sparsely populated regions. Most of the Outback is desert but some ot the largest farms and ranches in the country can be found here. Many dirt roads and paths in the Outback are only accessible with all terrain vehicles and some only with permission from local authorities. Several paved highways stretch through the Outback including the Stuart and Matilda Highways.

Remarkable Cities and Cultural monuments

- ☐ UNESCO World Cultural Heritage
- ☐ Remarkable Cities
- ☐ Aborigine reservation
- ☐ Places of Abor. cultural interest
- 🏛 Historical city scape
- 🏭 Technical/industrial monument
- 🗼 Remarkable lighthouse
- 🗿 Monument
- 🏛 Museum

Sport and leisure destinations

- 🤿 Diving
- 🏄 Wind surfing
- 🏄 Surfing
- 🎣 Deep-sea fishing
- ⛱ Beach resort

Central Australia

The sparsely populated interior of the world's smallest continent encompasses sections of Western Australia, South Australia, Queensland, and the Northern Territory. The region consists mostly of ⌧ deserts and semi-arid regions including the **Great Victoria Desert**, **Gibson Desert** and the **Simpson Desert** with its gigantic red sand dunes. The mesa landscape is dotted with several mountain chains, including the Mac-

donnell Ranges, rising between 1,000 and 1,500 meters in height. The famous stone monolith **Uluru** (⛰ **Ayers Rock**) towers over the surrounding countryside and is – after Western Australia's Mt. Augustus – the second largest monolith on the planet. The ⛰ **Olgas** (a group of red stone formations) are one of the most

The Olgas: sandstone formations in the "red heart" of Australia. **Rf58**

The **Aborigines** arrived on the Australian continent about 50,000 years ago. As hunters and gatherers they migrated throughout the continent with the help of songlines – oral maps passed on through the generations. The myths of the "dreamtime" are an important element of Aboriginal culture. In recent decades, the Aborigines have won many legal rights.

Kings Canyon In Watarrka National Park – ⬛ steep canyon walls – the Lost City: a cluster of rock formations – swimming holes – "The Garden of Eden" (photo). **Rf58**

Uluru (Ayers Rock) and **the Olgas (Kata Tjuta)** are the highlights of Central Australia's national parks. ⛰ Uluru (863 m) is 600 million years old and is considered sacred ground by many Aborigines (top/middle photo). ⛰ The Olgas (bottom photo) comprise 36 round rock formations surrounded by gorges and valleys. **Rf 58**

Scale 1:4,500,000

0   40   80 Kilometers

Principal travel routes
- 🚗 Auto route
- 🚆 Rail road
- Shipping route

Remarkable landscapes and natural monuments
- ⬛ UNESCO World Natural Heritage
- Rock landscape
- Ravine/canyon
- Geyser
- Cave
- Desert
- Nature park
- National park (landscape)
- National park (flora)
- National park (fauna)
- National park (culture)
- Biosphere reserve
- Zoo/safari park

fascinating natural attractions in the region. The red color of the Olgas and much of central Australia is caused by the high level of oxidized iron in the region's soil and rocks. The 🖼 **Lake Eyre Basin** is the world's largest salt pan, containing a lake of the same name that is both Australia's largest lake as well as the largest salt lake in the world. The basin's watershed covers one sixth of the continent and the area is usually parched

and lifeless. Only after periods of extremely strong rainfall does the area become fertile, but this happens no more than three or four times in a century. The Lake Eyre Basin is part of the **Great Artesian Basin**, the world's largest reservoir of groundwater (1.8 million km²). During summer temperatures in Central Australia often exceed 40° C. Winters in the region are more pleasant, with temperatures consistently around 20° C.

The outback town of **Alice Springs** is situated near the geographical center of the Australian continent. The countryside around Alice Springs is well known as the red heart of Australia and tourists flock to the region to enjoy its natural beauty. In 1987 the first paved highway through Central Australia was completed. The Stuart Highway runs between Darwin, in the Northern Territory, and Port Augusta, in South Australia. Large sections of Central

Australia are tribal lands under the control of Australia's indigenous people – the Aborigines. Most of these lands are only open to visitors who have been granted permission before their arrival. The famous artwork of the Aborigines can be found throughout Central Australia. The Aboriginal paintings depict myths from the "dreamtime" and are an important element in the ceremonies and spirituality of Australia's indigenous people.

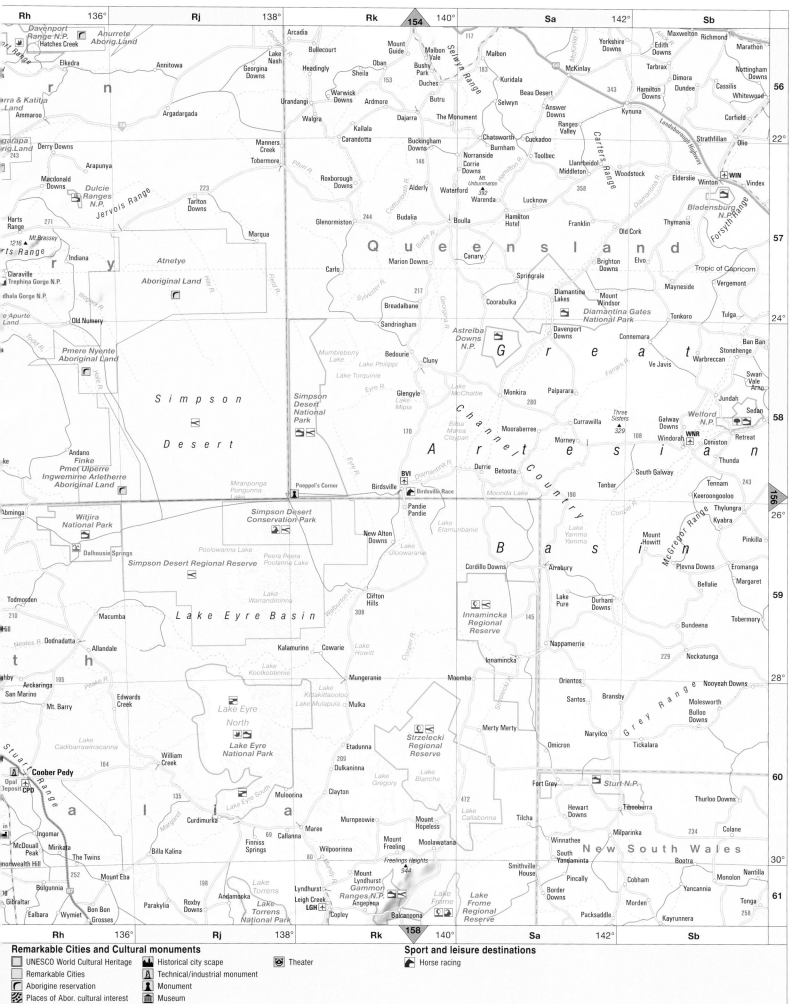

Macdonnell Ranges 🖼 Mountain chain – tallest peak: Mount Liebig (1,524 m) – numerous valleys and gorges in the area – 🖼 traditional Aboriginal rock paintings. **Rg57**

Finke Gorge National Park canyon along the Finke river – 🖼 Palm Valley with rare red cabbage palms. **Rg58**

Henbury Meteorite Craters Thirteen meteorite 🖼 craters – the largest crater is 15 meters deep and has a diameter of 180 meters – created 5,000 years ago. **Rg58**

Chambers Pillar High red 🖼 sandstone formation on the edge of the Simpson Desert – the landmark was once used by early outback explorers for orientation through the empty desert interior. **Rg58**

Trephina Gorge National Park 🖼 Conservation area with streams and lush riverside vegetation – John Hayes Rockhole: a long narrow gorge. **Rh57**

Simpson Desert National Park Large national park with beautiful 🖼 desert landscapes – large sand dunes up to 20 meters tall and 100 kilometers long. **Rk58**

Coober Pedy 🖼 Opal mining center in the Australian outback – subterranean homes – 🖼 Mine Museum. **Rh60**

Remarkable Cities and Cultural monuments

☐ UNESCO World Cultural Heritage	☐ Historical city scape	☑ Theater
☐ Remarkable Cities	☐ Technical/industrial monument	
☐ Aborigine reservation	☐ Monument	
☐ Places of Abor. cultural interest	☐ Museum	

Sport and leisure destinations

☐ Horse racing

Southwestern Australia

Southwestern Australia covers one-third of the state of Western Australia. The region's attractions include the marine life of ⊠ **Shark Bay**, giant trees in the south, beautiful beaches on the Indian Ocean in the west, and the red sand dunes of the ⊠ **Great Victoria Desert** in the east. The distance from Perth in the far west to Eucla (on the border to the neighboring state South Australia) is around 1,450 kilometers. The greater part

of southwestern Australia is sparsely populated rural outback land. The terrain consists mostly of semi-arid grasslands and parched deserts including the ⊠ **Great Sandy Desert**. The **Nullarbor Plain** is a vast flat grassland with a total area of 250,000 km². It is situated atop a series of underground rivers and caves. Much

The Pinnacles: a group of limestone formations in the desert.   **Qh61**

Rottnest Island Island with nice 🏖 beaches – automobiles are banned on the island – 🌿 diverse flora and fauna – home of Rottnest Quokka, a mammal – 🏄 Surfing area.   **Qh61**

Perth 🏙 Capital and economic center of Western Australia (population 1.3 million) – vibrant cultural scene – 🏖 beaches on the Indian Ocean.   **Qh61**

Leeuwin National Park 🌲 National park along the coast – around 250 kilometers south of Perth – large 🕳 caves – vineyards and holiday camps.   **Qh62/63**

Walpole Nornalup National Park Giant Karri trees in the 🌲 Valley of the Giants – Tree Top Walk: steel walkways with trees 40 meters above ground.   **Qj63**

Albany Oldest European settlement in Western Australia (1823) – former whaling port – 🏛 18th century buildings (photo: Two People's Bay).   **Qj63**

Wave Rock 350 kilometers east of Perth – a massive 🪨 stone formation resembling a wave – the formation is 15 meters high and 100 meters long.   **Qk62**

Fitzgerald River National Park 🌿 Nature reserve on the southern coast of West Australia– the area is home to a variety of rare plants and animals – deep gorges, tall cliffs, and secluded beaches.   **Qk62/63**

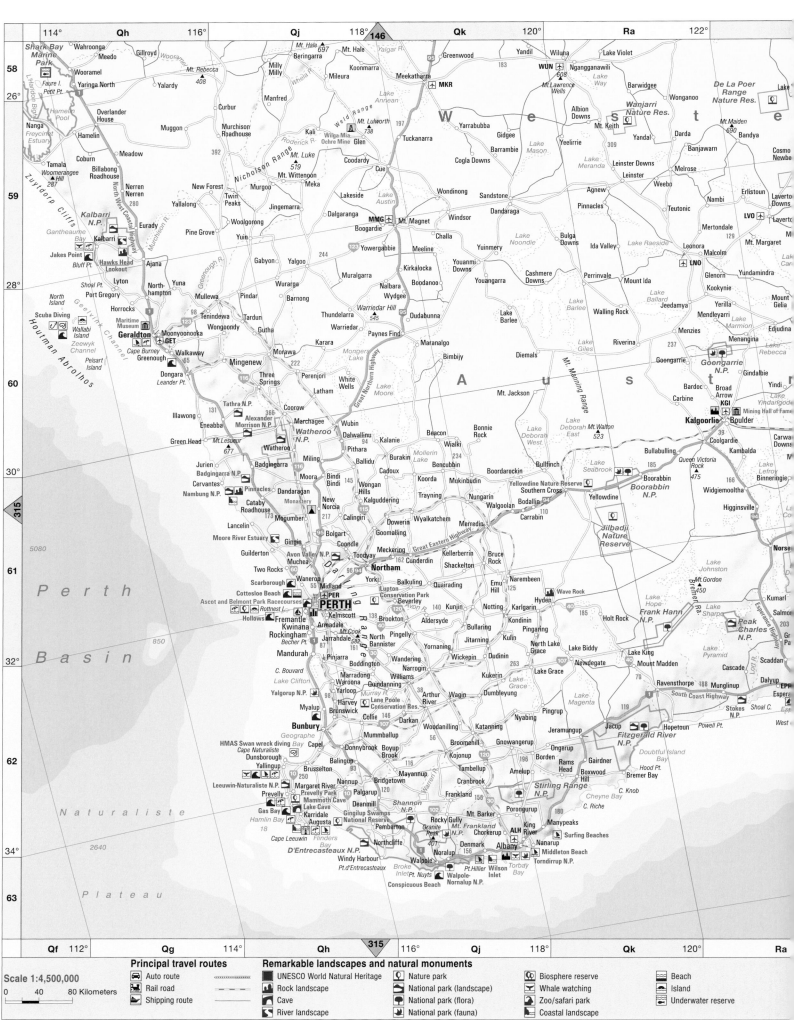

Scale 1:4,500,000

0   40   80 Kilometers

Principal travel routes
- 🚗 Auto route
- 🚆 Rail road
- Shipping route
- · · · · · (dotted route)
- — — — (dashed route)

Remarkable landscapes and natural monuments
- ⬛ UNESCO World Natural Heritage
- Rock landscape
- Cave
- River landscape
- Nature park
- National park (landscape)
- National park (flora)
- National park (fauna)
- Biosphere reserve
- Whale watching
- Zoo/safari park
- Coastal landscape
- Beach
- Island
- Underwater reserve

of the plain's surface is covered by expansive agricultural fields.

Perth is the state capital and largest city of Western Australia. The area surrounding the city is known as the "Heartland." **Perth** – the "city of lights" – is situated between the Indian Ocean and the Swan River and is considered one of the most attractive cities in Australia. The sprawling city is the political, economic, and cultural capital of Western Australia. It is

also the most isolated major city on the continent. Perth has a pleasant Mediterranean climate with mild winters and long hot summers.

Southwestern Australia has a milder climate than most of the continent and plentiful rainfall. The region's coastal areas feature numerous vineyards, olive tree groves, fruit gardens, and lush forests with tall karri trees. The coast is also the location of several attractive and

historic seaside towns including Margaret River and Yallingup.

The so-called Heartland stretches from the edge of Perth to the eastern goldfields near Kalgoorie. It is a largely rural area with an economy heavily dependent on agriculture. Most of the area is covered by vast golden fields of grain. In recent years, an increasing number of farmers near the coast have started growing olive trees instead of more traditional crops.

The coast is also the location of many of the region's most important natural attractions. The so-called Pinnacles (in **Nambung National Park**) are a series of pointy limestone formations. **Wave Rock**, another fascinating natural attraction in the region, is a 15-meters-tall rock formation that resembles the crest of a wave. It is located near the town of Hyden in a reserve that features several other unique rock formations.

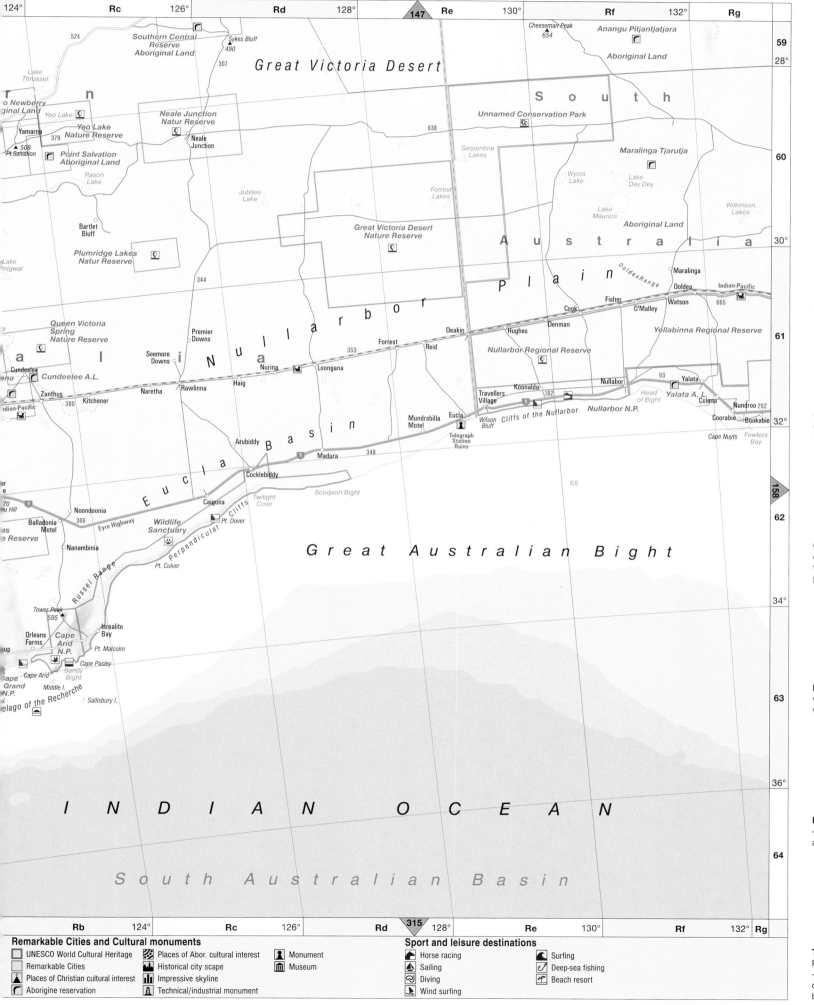

Kalgoorie-Boulder Twin gold rush towns in the outback – historic mines and architecture. **Ra61**

Esperance Bay Small port city – popular holiday destination – beaches – sailing and deep-sea fishing. **Ra62**

Cape Le Grand National Park Hilly coastline – impressive bays with long white beaches. **Rb62**

Cape Arid National Park Unique hill and coastal landscapes – beaches – important conservation area for birds – natural pools with rare plants and animals. **Rb62**

Nullarbor Plain The area is almost totally waterless – Australia's largest karst – little vegetation. **Rc-Rf60/61**

Nullarbor Cliffs In Nullarbor National Park – jagged coast – cliffs up to 80 meters above the Great Australian Bight. **Re-Rf61**

Trans-Australian Railway (Perth-Sydney) Route of the legendary Indian Pacific line – runs 4,000 kilometers in just under three days – 480 km straight through the Nullarbor Plain without curves or turns.

Legend

Remarkable Cities and Cultural monuments

- UNESCO World Cultural Heritage
- Remarkable Cities
- Places of Christian cultural interest
- Aborigine reservation
- Places of Abor. cultural interest
- Historical city scape
- Impressive skyline
- Technical/industrial monument
- Monument
- Museum

Sport and leisure destinations

- Horse racing
- Sailing
- Diving
- Wind surfing
- Surfing
- Deep-sea fishing
- Beach resort

Northern Australia

The northernmost region of Australia consists of ※ **Arnhem Land** in the Northern Territory and **Cape York Peninsula** in the state of Queensland. The entire region has a tropical climate with high temperatures throughout the year and heavy rainfall during the so-called wet season. Much of region is inaccessible by road during the wet season because of frequent flooding. A large portion of Northern Australia is under the administration

of local ⬚ aboriginal communities. Between Arnhem Land and Cape York Peninsula lies the **Gulf of Carpentaria**, a large body of water that indents Australia's generally smooth coastline.

Both parts of northern Australia are rich in **mineral resources**. Arnhem Land is major source of bauxite (aluminum ore).

Daintree National Park encompasses Australia's most ancient rainforests. **Sc54**

Aboriginal Dance A gathering of the Corroboree tribe on ⬚ Groote Eylandt off the coast of Arnhem Land – traditional legends and history are told through dance. **Rj52/53**

Mornington Island In the Wellesley Island group – under the administration of local ⬚ Aborigines – main settlement is Gununa. **Rk54**

Nicholson River Delta Typical central Australian basin landscapes – usually flooded or parched. **Rk54**

Lizard Island Coral island in the northern section of the ⬚ Great Barrier Reef National Park – fascinating marine life. **Sc53**

Rock Paintings near Laura Hundreds of ※ rock paintings – some are open to the public – Split Rock and Guguyalangi are well known and easy to reach. **Sc53**

Cooktown Captain Cook stopped here in 1770 to repair his ship Endeavour – gold rush on the Palm River in 1872 – 🏛 James Cook Museum. **Sc53**

Cedar Bay National Park 🔲 Tropical river delta on the Coral Sea – ⬚ Wujal Wujal Aboriginal village located in the park. **Sc53**

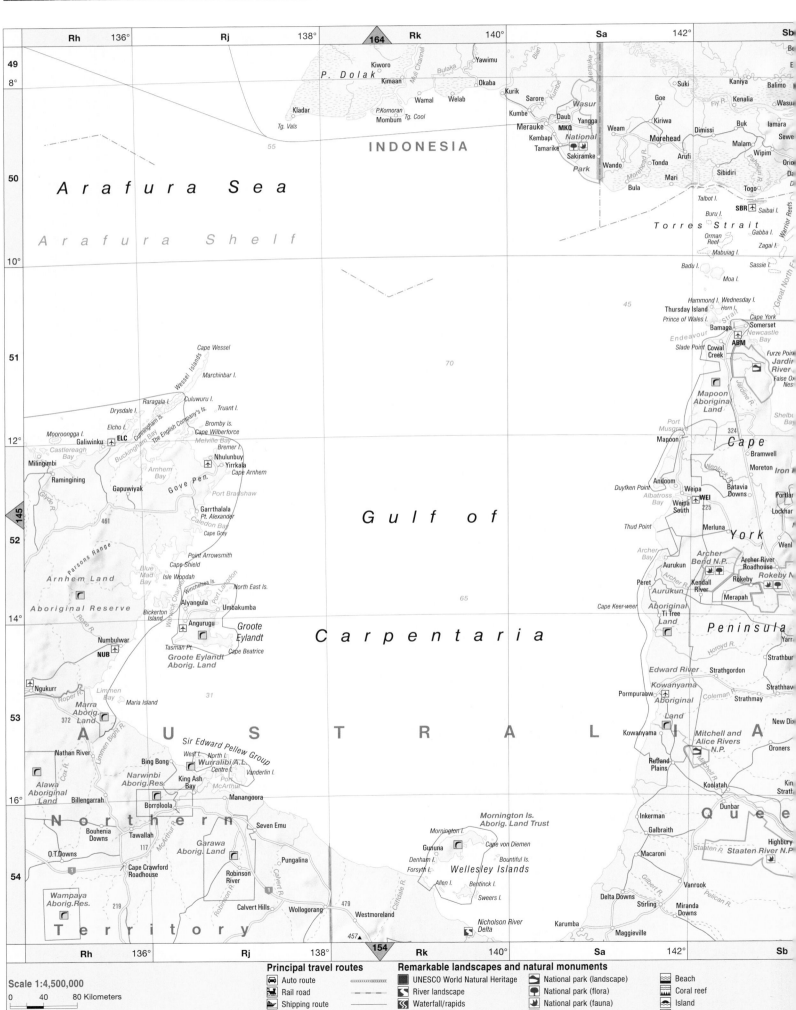

Scale 1:4,500,000

0   40   80 Kilometers

Principal travel routes
- 🚗 Auto route
- 🚃 Rail road
- Shipping route

Remarkable landscapes and natural monuments
- ⬛ UNESCO World Natural Heritage
- River landscape
- Waterfall/rapids
- Nature park
- National park (landscape)
- National park (flora)
- National park (fauna)
- Coastal landscape
- Beach
- Coral reef
- Island
- Underwater reserve

Cooktown on the Cape York Peninsula has been a gold mining center since the end of the 19th century and Weipa on the peninsula's west coast is home to the largest bauxite mine in the world.

The tip of the **Cape York Peninsula** is the northernmost area in Australia. It is a region of thick rainforests, flooded plains, crocodile infested rivers, large cattle ranches, mines. The area also features several isolated Aboriginal communities with interesting cultural attractions. North of the peninsula lie the **Torres Strait Islands**: the most northern of these islands are separated from Papua New Guinea by only a few kilometers of water. The Great Barrier Reef is located off the coast of northeastern Australia. With its coral islands and diverse marine life, the Great Barrier Reef is one of the world's natural wonders. The reef's existence and its incredible biodiversity is threatened by rising ocean temperatures that may be caused by global warming. The best starting point for any expedition to the Great Barrier Reef is the city of **Cairns**. The stretch of coastline to the north and south of Cairns is one of the most popular holiday destinations in the country for both Australians and foreign tourists. Between October and April the waters off the northeastern coast are inhabited by the highly poisonous Box Jellyfish, a potential danger to swimmers in the area.

The **Atherton Tableland**, a section of the Great Dividing Range is just 10 to 15 kilometers away from the coastal area around Cairns. The 900 meter tall plateau was created 10,000 years ago as a result of volcanic activity. The breathtaking landscapes in the tableland include several crater lakes, high waterfalls and vibrant green rainforests.

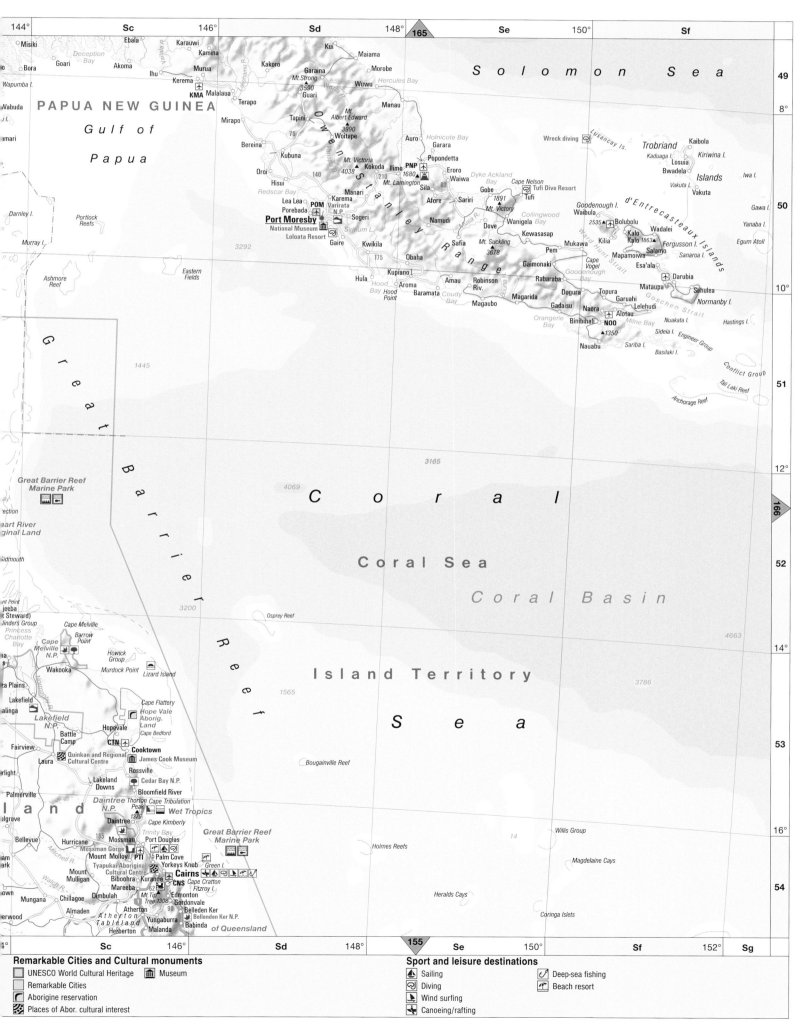

Cape Tribulation Rainforest and ocean reefs – long beaches – several ecotourism resorts. **Sc54**

Daintree National Park The Daintree tropical forest is home to many rare birds and small mammals including the Brush-tailed possum (middle and bottom photos). The region's flora includes palms, ferns (top photo), and vines. **Sc54**

Port Douglas This popular tourist destination is a good area for sailing and diving. The barrier reef is close to the coast. The Rainforest Habitat provides information on local forests. **Sc54**

Cairnes-Kuranda train route An hour and a half-long journey around curves and through tunnels – passes rainforests and waterfalls – the Skyrail: the world's longest cable car. **Sc54**

Remarkable Cities and Cultural monuments

- ☐ UNESCO World Cultural Heritage
- ☐ Remarkable Cities
- ▲ Aborigine reservation
- ▨ Places of Abor. cultural interest
- 🏛 Museum

Sport and leisure destinations

- ⚓ Sailing
- 🤿 Diving
- 🏄 Wind surfing
- 🛶 Canoeing/rafting
- 🎣 Deep-sea fishing
- 🏖 Beach resort

Northeastern Australia, Great Barrier Reef

Northeastern Australia can be roughly divided from east to west into four areas. The world's largest coral reef, the Great Barrier Reef, with its many islands, are located in the west. The reef, a UNESCO world heritage site, is over 2,300 kilometers long. It borders a narrow fertile coastal strip that extends inland up to the Great Dividing Range. The Great Dividing Range is bordered in the west by the large flat Carpentaria Basin.

The ▥ **Great Barrier Reef** is a chain of over 2,500 separate coral reefs that starts south of the Tropic of Capricorn and stretches almost to New Guinea. The entire reef was designated a world heritage site in 1981. Countless species of marine life inhabit the reef, including at least 400 colorful types of coral, 4,000

Underwater bounty: the Great Barrier Reef. **Sd-Sg53/58**

Lawn Hill National Park 🏞 Green oasis in the outback – abundant wildlife – gorges and sandstone ranges. **Rk55**

Fossil Mammal Site Part of Lawn Hill National Park – 🦴 paleontologists have found fossils of extinct mammals on the site – UNESCO world heritage site. **Rk55**

Porcupine Gorge National Park The 🏞 park is home to a canyon of the same name with 150-meter-high walls. **Sc56**

Milla Milla Falls In the Atherton Tableland – 65-meter-wide 💧 waterfalls – most impressive during the rainy season. **Sc54**

Wet Tropics National Park The last remnants of the northern Australian rainforest are in this national park (UNESCO world heritage site). Photos from top to bottom: Mossman Gorge **(Sc54)**, Wallaman Falls **(Sc55)**, tree kangaroo. **Sc-Sd54/55**

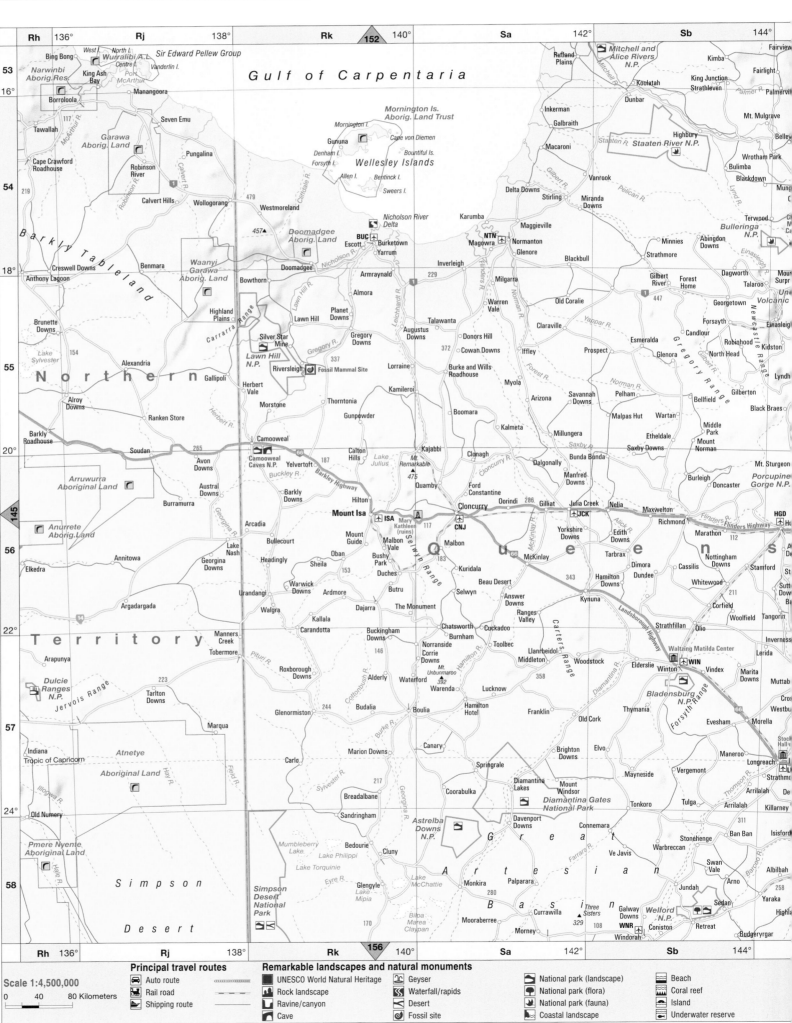

Scale 1:4,500,000

0   40   80 Kilometers

Principal travel routes
- 🚗 Auto route
- 🚂 Rail road
- ⚓ Shipping route
- ⋯⋯ (auto route)
- ⋯⋯ (rail road)
- ⋯⋯ (shipping route)

Remarkable landscapes and natural monuments
- ◼ UNESCO World Natural Heritage
- ◻ Rock landscape
- ◻ Ravine/canyon
- ◻ Cave
- ◻ Geyser
- ◻ Waterfall/rapids
- ◻ Desert
- ◻ Fossil site
- ◻ Coastal landscape
- ◻ National park (landscape)
- ◻ National park (flora)
- ◻ National park (fauna)
- ◻ Beach
- ◻ Coral reef
- ◻ Island
- ◻ Underwater reserve

species of mollusks, 2,000 fish species, as well as rare sea turtles and manatees. Global warming and coastal pollution are major threats to the health and long term survival of the reef.

Large sections of the reef are protected nature reserves, whiles others are open to tourists – most traveling from coastal towns such as MacKay or Townsville. In addition to tourism, agriculture also plays an important role in the regional econ-

omy of Northeastern Australia. Sugar cane is one of the most important crops grown in the region.

The mountains of the ⛰ **Great Dividing Range** stretch along the entire eastern coast of Australia. In northeastern Australia, the range reaches a maximum height of 1,300 meters. The **Wet Tropics World Heritage Site** encompasses several large national parks. It contains the remaining sections of a vast rain

forest that covered most of Australia 50 million years ago.

Between the Great Dividing Range and the Gulf of Carpentaria lies the Carpentaria Basin. It is a hot, dry region covering most of the state of **Queensland**. Despite the dry climate, floods are a major problem in the region during the rainy season, bushfires in the dry season. The main industries in Northeastern Australia's sparsely populated outback are

sheep and cattle ranching as well as mining. The town of Mt. Isa has an area as large as Switzerland within its city limits, with a population of less than 25,000 inhabitants. Because of the vast distances, airplanes play a vital role in the lives of many Outback residents. Many people rely on the Flying Doctor Service for medical care and many of the region's children are educated by the School of the Air.

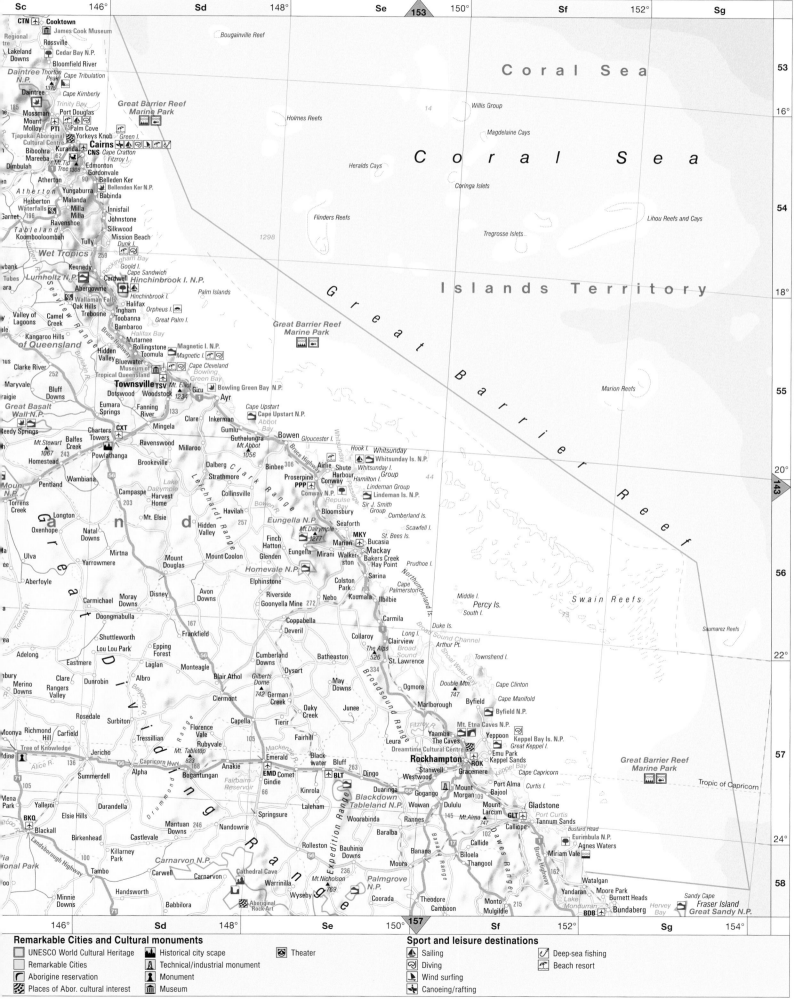

Hinchinbrook-Island National Park 🏞
Nature reserve – Mangroves and tropical forests – Mount Bowen (1,142 m).   **Sd55**

Whitsunday Island National Park 🏞
National park with azure blue water, sandy white beaches and tropical vegetation.   **Se56**

Great Barrier Reef Not all of the islands in this world heritage site are coral islands; some are the remnants of mountains chains that were submerged and surrounded by coral. 🏞 Reefs are formed when tiny animals called coral secrete small shells made of limestone. The accumulation of limestone eventually results in the formation of reefs. The Great Barrier Reef is home to over 2,000 fish species. Photos from top to bottom: Coral island, Reef shark, Coral formation, Clown Anemone Fish.   **Sd-Sg53/58**

Remarkable Cities and Cultural monuments

☐ UNESCO World Cultural Heritage	🏛 Historical city scape
☐ Remarkable Cities	⚙ Technical/industrial monument
☐ Aborigine reservation	🗿 Monument
☐ Places of Abor. cultural interest	🏛 Museum
🎭 Theater	

Sport and leisure destinations

⛵ Sailing	🎣 Deep-sea fishing
🤿 Diving	🏖 Beach resort
🏄 Wind surfing	
🛶 Canoeing/rafting	

Eastern Australia

Eastern Australia covers portions of two Australian states: (northern) New South Wales and (southern) Queensland. The region itself is divided into three distinct sections: a narrow ⌧ **coastal region**, the ⌧ **Great Dividing Range**, and the open spaces of the **Outback**. The majority of the population is concentrated near the coast. **Brisbane**, the third largest city in Australia, is the economic center of the region and the capital of Queensland.

The region's economy is supported primarily by agriculture and tourism. The region's most visited tourist destination is ⌧ Surfer's Paradise on the Gold Coast. The area around Coffs Harbour is a major center for banana farming. Pineapples and sugar cane are important crops on the Sunshine Coast.

Wilpena Pound in Flinders-Ranges-National Park. **Rk61**

Salt Lakes The largest salt lakes in the region are Lake Eyre, Lake Torren, Lake Frome and Lake Gairdner. They are all remnants of a large inland sea. All of the lakes are located in the Great Artesian Basin. **Rh-Rk60/61**

Flinders Ranges National Park One of the oldest landscapes on earth – ⌧ landscape with unusual stones – the park's major attraction is Wilpena Pound, a large natural amphitheater – ⌧ Arkaroo Rock: site of Aboriginal rock paintings. **Rk61**

Giant Red Kangaroo This type of Kangaroo grows up to two meters tall and is the largest marsupial in Australia. They can jump over ten meters and can run at speeds of 80 km/h. They can dig one meter deep to search for water in the dry outback deserts.

Mutawintji National Park ⌧ Beautiful sandstone landscape – green canyons scattered around the park – more than 300 ⌧ sites with ancient Aboriginal art – several camp sites. **Sb61**

Kinchega National Park On the west bank of the Darling River home to numerous species of aquatic birds (photo: Giant Eucalyptus Tree on Menindee Lake). **Sb62**

Principal travel routes

- Auto route
- Rail road
- Shipping route

Remarkable landscapes and natural monuments

- UNESCO World Natural Heritage
- Rock landscape
- Extinct volcano
- Geyser
- Cave
- Waterfall/rapids
- Lake country
- Desert
- National park (landscape)
- National park (flora)
- National park (fauna)
- Biosphere reserve
- Zoo/safari park
- Coastal landscape
- Beach
- Coral reef

Scale 1:4,500,000

0   40   80 Kilometers

Off the coast of eastern Australia lies a series of sand islands, including ⛴ **Fraser Island** – the largest sand island in the world and a UNESCO world heritage site. The southern portion of the ⛴ **Great Barrier Reef** begins just north of Fraser Island. The climate on the coast is entirely subtropical and becomes warmer from south to north.

The mountains and hills of the ⛰ **Great Dividing Range** are located between the Outback and the coast. The Great Dividing Range, with mountains rising above 1,600 meters, stretches along the east coast of Australia. The Great Dividing Range area has a mild climate and heavy rainfall. The area's thick rainforests include many unique ecosystems. A network of ⛴ national parks and nature reserves protect the flora and fauna of the area including the unique Antarctic Beech. Many of these national parks have the interesting feature of encompassing both subtropical rainforests and temperate rainforests at higher elevations.

The western Great Dividing Range borders the flat expanses of the Australian Outback. The thinly populated **Outback** is dotted by many small settlements. Towns in the Outback are usually no more than one paved road and a few small buildings. The region also possesses some of the world's largest farms and cattle ranches. Kangaroos, Australia's "national" animals, are common in the continent's interior. Farther inland, the region's climate becomes increasingly drier and farms and ranches are replaced by parched deserts and semiarid regions. Despite the raw climate there are a few scattered settlements deep in the interior. Most of these cities are mining towns such as Broken Hill, a center for silver mining.

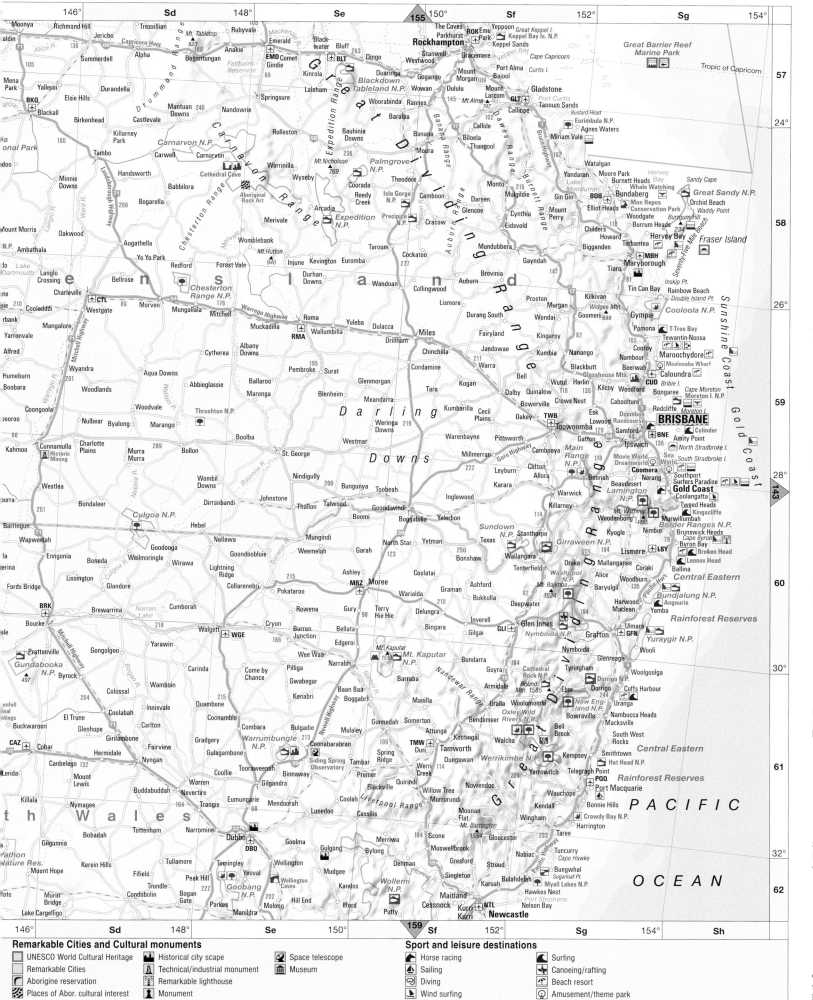

Koalas Koalas live in the eucalyptus forests of Australia and have a diet consisting exclusively of eucalyptus leaves. Koalas are an endangered species due to human intrusion into their habitats and forest fires.

Fraser Island UNESCO world heritage site – the world's largest sand island – tall sand dunes – rainforest in the interior. **Sg58**

Moreton Island National Park ⛴ Mount Tempest (world's tallest sand dune) – beautiful 🏖 beaches – 🐋 whale-watching. **Sg59**

Brisbane Population 1.5 million – botanical gardens – Southbank Parklands – Cultural Center (theater, concerts, museum). **Sg59**

Surfers Paradise 🏖 40 kilometers of beaches – 300 days of sunshine annually – large 🎡 amusement parks. **Sg59**

Subtropical Rain Forest Parks 🌳 National Parks in the interior – humid rainforests – diverse flora and fauna. **Sg60/61**

Cape Byron The easternmost point of Australia – lighthouse with an impressive view – 🏨 tourist resorts in Byron Bay. **Sg60**

Remarkable Cities and Cultural monuments

- ☐ UNESCO World Cultural Heritage
- ☐ Remarkable Cities
- ⚑ Aborigine reservation
- ⚑ Places of Abor. cultural interest
- ⚑ Historical city scape
- ⚑ Technical/industrial monument
- ⚑ Remarkable lighthouse
- ⚑ Monument
- ⚑ Space telescope
- 🏛 Museum

Sport and leisure destinations

- ⚑ Horse racing
- ⚓ Sailing
- ⚑ Diving
- ⚑ Wind surfing
- ⚑ Surfing
- ⚑ Canoeing/rafting
- ⚑ Beach resort
- ⚑ Amusement/theme park

Southern Australia, Tasmania

The climate of southern Australia fits the pattern of most of the continent. The farther inland an area is, the less rainfall it gets. The region covers portions of three states: New South Wales, Victoria, and South Australia. A large percentage of the region has a subtropical climate with plentiful rainfall. Southeastern Australia is the most densely populated region on the continent and encompasses several large cities including 🏙 **Sydney** and ❉ **Mel-**

bourne. Australia's national capital, Canberra, is also situated in the region. The 🏔 **Great Dividing Range** – a long mountain range that runs along the entire east coast of Australia – begins just north of Melbourne. Mount Kosciuszo, the highest mountain in Australia, rises 2,228 meters above sea level. The mountain is

The Twelve Apostles near Melbourne in the state of Victoria. **Sb65**

Mungo National Park ⚘ 40,000-year-old relicts of early Aboriginal culture – 🏖 "Walls of China," a line of white sand dunes (UNESCO world heritage site). **Sb62**

Adelaide Capital of the state of South Australia – population 1.2 million – vibrant cultural scene – one of the world's largest arts and culture 🎵 festivals. **Rk63**

Flinders Chase National Park Located on the western edge of Kangaroo Island – high cliffs and interesting rock formations – 🦭 seal and sea lion colonies. **Rj63**

Tasmania About the size of Ireland, this hilly island was "discovered" by Abel Tasman in 1642. The 🏝 island is Australia's southernmost state. Tasmania has some of the world's few remaining pristine temperate rain forest ecosystems as well as an abundance of rare animals, historic sites and 14 national parks. The Tasmanian Devil and the Wombat are two fascinating animals native to Tasmania. Photos from top to bottom: Cradle Mountain, Mount Field National Park, South West National Park. **Sc-Se66/67**

Scale 1:4,500,000

0   40   80 Kilometers

Principal travel routes
- 🚗 Auto route
- 🚆 Rail road
- ⚓ Shipping route
- ⋯⋯ Auto route

Remarkable landscapes and natural monuments
- ▣ UNESCO World Natural Heritage
- ▣ Rock landscape
- ▣ Extinct volcano
- ▣ Cave
- Waterfall/rapids
- Lake country
- Desert
- Fossil site
- Nature park
- National park (landscape)
- National park (flora)
- National park (fauna)
- Biosphere reserve
- Zoo/safari park
- Coastal landscape
- Beach

located in the Snowy Mountains, a section of the Great Dividing Range. In the higher elevations of the mountain range snowfall, rare in Australia, is common in winter, while in summer mountain flowers cover the sides of the peaks.

The source of the country's longest river, the ◧ **Murray River**, is located in the Great Dividing Range. The Murray River flows over 2,500 kilometers from east to west before reaching its delta

near the city of Adelaide in South Australia. Most of Southern Australia, like the rest of the continent, consists of dry and sparsely populated countryside. Only a limited percentage of the land in the region is arable but irrigation projects have opened large areas to farming in recent decades. Countless fascinating rock formations are scattered throughout the southern outback including the sand-stone mountains in the **Grampians**

and the rock formations in ◧ **Mungo National Park**, the **Mount Lofty Ranges**, and the **Flinders Range**.

The bluffs west of Melbourne with their views of the ◧ **Twelve Apostles** stone formations are one of the most visited natural attractions in the region.

Kangaroo Island off the coast of South Australia is the third largest Australian island. The island is home to interesting wildlife including, koalas, wallabies, and

kangaroos. The island also includes pristine coastal areas and unique flora.

◧ **Tasmania** (64,880 km²) is separated from the Australian mainland by the 200-kilometer-wide Bass Strait. Tasmania's terrain is mostly hilly. Mount Ossa (1,617 m) is the highest point on the island. Tasmania's national parks with their temperate rainforests and unique fauna encompass some of the world's most pristine natural settings.

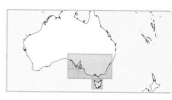

Blue Mountains Mountains rising up to 1,000 meters – named for the blue hue of the local eucalyptus trees – ◧ Three Sisters (tall rock formations). **Se-Sf62**

Sydney The economic ⬛ center of Australia has a population of four million. Sydney is an attractive city renowned for its Harbour Bridge and the Opera House (bottom photo). The well-known Bondi and Manly beaches are popular with surfers and swimmers. **Sf62**

Canberra Capital of Australia – population 310,000 – planned city – important ⬛ museums and parks. **Se63**

Sovereign Hill ◧ Historic gold mining town in the Ballarat region – famous for the Eureka Stockade, a revolt by local gold miners against license fees in 1854. **Sb64**

Melbourne Capital of Victoria – population 3.5 million – second largest city in Australia – ⬛ important museums include the National Gallery of Victoria (art) and the Melbourne Museum (local history). **Sc64**

Great Ocean Road Fascinating coastal route with cliffs, beaches, and forests – The ◧ "Twelve Apostles" – (photo: cliffs near the Great Ocean Road). **Sa-Sc67**

Remarkable Cities and Cultural monuments

- ☐ UNESCO World Cultural Heritage
- ☐ Remarkable Cities
- ☐ Aborigine reservation
- ☐ Places of Abor. cultural interest
- ⬛ Cultural landscape
- ⬛ Historical city scape
- ⬛ Impressive skyline
- ⬛ Castle/fortress/fort
- ⬛ Space telescope
- ⬛ Museum
- ⬛ Theater
- ⬛ Olympics

Sport and leisure destinations

- ⬛ Race track
- ⬛ Horse racing
- ⬛ Skiing
- ⬛ Sailing
- ☐ Diving
- ☐ Wind surfing
- ☐ Surfing
- ☐ Canoeing/rafting
- ☐ Deep-sea fishing
- ☐ Beach resort

New Zealand

The islands of New Zealand were created after the collision of two tectonic plates around 100 million years ago and are relatively young by geologic standards. New Zealand is one country but it consists of two mains islands and countless smaller ones. The South Island is a land of hills, mountains, lakes, and fjords. Most of the **South Island's** are the result of centuries of glacial activity. Snow-covered Mount Cook (Aoraki) in the South-

ern Alps is the highest mountain in New Zealand rising 3,764 meters above sea level. Volcanic eruptions, earthquakes, and the forces of erosion continue to shape the land of South Island.
The North Island is home to a chain of volcanoes stretching from ⛰ Ruapeha (2,797 m) in Tongario National Park

Milford Sound in Fiordland National Park on the South Island.　**Td68**

Cape Reinga Meeting point of the Pacific Ocean and Tasman Sea – lighthouse (photo).　**Tg63**

Maori The indigenous inhabitants of New Zealand are of Polynesian descent. Traditionally, the Maori lived in clans and had no concept of private property. Traditional face tattoos (moko) are becoming less common.

Auckland Cultural and economic center of New Zealand – largest city in the country – population 1.1 million – panoramic views of the city from 🗼 the Sky Tower.　**Th64**

White Island Volcanic island 59 kilometers from the mainland – last eruption in 1966 – steaming ⛰ crater.　**Tj64**

Tongariro National Park 🏞 A UNESCO world heritage site – ⛰ Mount Ruapehu (2,797 m, last eruption in 1996).　**Th65**

Taranaki National Park 🏔 In the vicinity of the volcano Mount Taranaki (2,518 m) – open to mountain climbers.　**Th65**

Wellington National capital – population 350,000 – Lambton Quay shopping area – Botanic Gardens – 🏛 Katherine Mansfield's childhood home – waterfront – 🏛 National Museum Te Papa.　**Th66**

Principal travel routes

Scale 1:4,500,000

0　40　80 Kilometers

- 🚗 Auto route
- 🚂 Rail road
- ⚓ Shipping route

Remarkable landscapes and natural monuments

- 🏛 UNESCO World Natural Heritage
- 🏔 Mountain landscape
- ⛰ Rock landscape
- 🌋 Active volcano
- ♨ Geyser
- 🕳 Cave
- ❄ Glacier
- 🏞 River landscape
- 🌊 Lake country
- 🌳 Nature park
- 🏞 National park (landscape)
- 🌲 National park (flora)
- 🐾 National park (fauna)
- 🏖 Coastal landscape
- 🏖 Beach

down to **White Island** in the Bay of Plenty. At the center of the North Island lies a volcanic plateau containing a large number of geysers, hot springs, boiling mud pools, and steam vents.
The flora and fauna of New Zealand were able to develop isolated and undisturbed for over 80 million years until the first humans arrived on the islands. The first people to settle New Zealand were Polynesians – the ancestors of the Maori

who took their name from large (now extinct) birds called moa. The early European colonists introduced new animals , including deer and possums that thrived in the New Zealand countryside. The most famous bird species in the country are the keas (mountain parrots) as well as the bizarre **kiwis**, the national symbol of New Zealand. The tuatara is a small reptile indigenous to New Zealand. It is often called a living fossil because it is the

last surviving member of an ancient class of animals that appeared on earth even before the dinosaurs. Depending on the season, coastal New Zealand is an excellent location for watching whales, dolphins, or penguins.
Ferns are common in all of New Zealand's warmer regions. There are around 180 fern species in the country. Kauris are giant spruce trees that grow up to 50 meters in height. Most of the kauri forests

were chopped down in the 19th century, but in recent decades ◨ nature reserves and national parks have been created to save the remaining trees. The two main islands have several climates zones. The North Island with a subtropical climate is warmer than the South Island. The South Island has the more interesting landscapes of the two islands. The weather on both islands is greatly affected by ocean currents and winds.

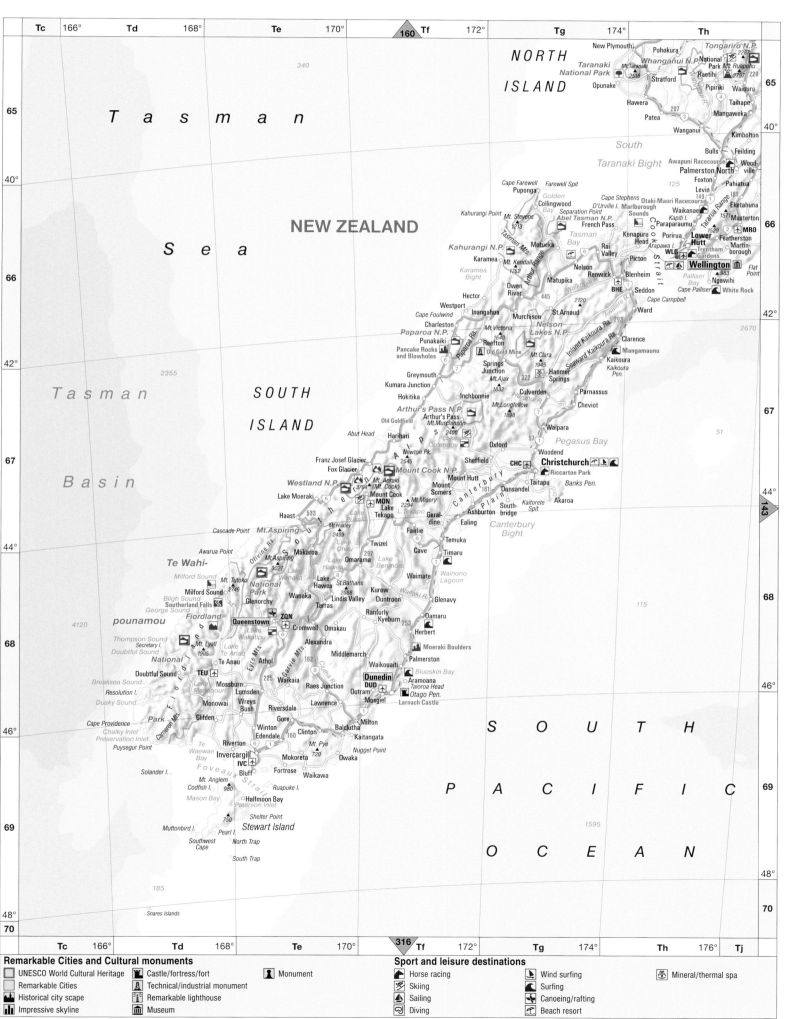

Pancake Rocks Pancake shaped ⛰ limestone formations – 🏞 Paparoa National Park – natural fountains. **Tf67**

Lake Coleridge ⬡ Mountain lake at the foot of Craigieburn Range – an hour from Christchurch – nearby 🗻 Washpen Falls – Rakaia Gorge. **Tf67**

Queenstown Popular tourist destination on ⊞ Lake Wakatipu (Hayes) at the foot of the Remarkables mountain range. **Te68**

Mount Aspiring National Park Unspoiled wilderness area in the majestic Southern Alps – mountain climbing and ski areas – beautiful 🏞 mountainous landscape in the park's river valleys. **Te68**

Westland National Park UNESCO world heritage site on the South Island – 60 glaciers including the ⛄ Franz Josef Glacier and Fox Glacier – 🏞 Lake Matheson (photo) with reflections of Mount Cook (Aoraki) and Mount Tasmen. **Te67**

Mount Cook National Park 🏞 National park and world heritage site encompassing New Zealand's highest mountain – Mount Cook is also known by its Maori name Aoraki. **Tf67**

Fiordland National Park New Zealand's largest 🏞 national park (12,095 km²) – UNESCO world heritage site – Milford Track – 🗻 Sutherland Falls (580 m high). **Td68**

Remarkable Cities and Cultural monuments

☐ UNESCO World Cultural Heritage
☐ Remarkable Cities
▦ Historical city scape
📊 Impressive skyline
🏰 Castle/fortress/fort
⚒ Technical/industrial monument
🗼 Remarkable lighthouse
🏛 Museum
🗿 Monument

Sport and leisure destinations

🐎 Horse racing
⛷ Skiing
⛵ Sailing
🤿 Diving
🏄 Wind surfing
🏄 Surfing
🚣 Canoeing/rafting
🏖 Beach resort
♨ Mineral/thermal spa

Islands of the South Pacific

The South Pacific is home to thousands of islands, most of them small and uninhabitable. The Pacific Ocean has an average depth of 4,188 meters below sea level, with the western Pacific containing the deepest ocean trenches on Earth. The **Tonga Trench** drops 10,025 meters below the surface of the ocean. The **Mariana Trench** is the world's deepest ocean trench with a maximum depth of 11,034 meters. The largest trenches in the

South Pacific and the "bow" shaped series of island groups stretching from New Guinea to the New Hebrides are all situated along the edges of the Indian-Australian tectonic plate.

Collisions between the Indian-Australian and Pacific plates resulted in the formation of the western Pacific's volcanic islands and certain mountain chains

Sunset on Fiji.

Guam Territory of the United States – large military base – War of the Pacific National Historic Park – ancient stone pillars and in Latte Stone Park.

Palau The republic consists of 343 islands, only nine of which are inhabited. The surrounding large coral reef has the richest collection of plants and animals of any island nation in the region.

Eastern Caroline Islands The volcanic island Truk encompasses the world's largest lagoon (top photo). The island Kosrae (bottom photo) has an interior covered mostly by lush tropical rainforests.

New Guinea The world's second largest island – western portion is Papua – eastern portion is Papua New Guinea.

Bismarck Archipelago Many colorful and often rare fish inhabit the archipelago's coral reefs – (photo) a swarm of snappers.

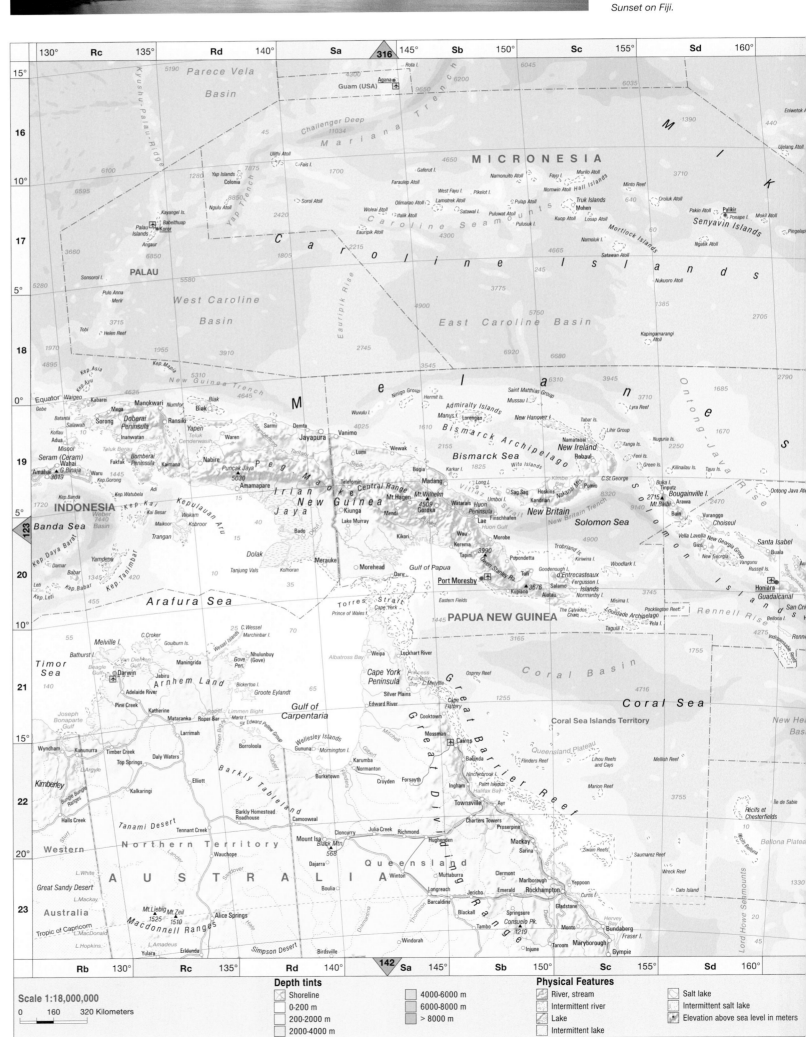

Scale 1:18,000,000

0   160   320 Kilometers

Depth tints
- Shoreline
- 0-200 m
- 200-2000 m
- 2000-4000 m
- 4000-6000 m
- 6000-8000 m
- > 8000 m

Physical Features
- River, stream
- Intermittent river
- Lake
- Intermittent lake
- Salt lake
- Intermittent salt lake
- Elevation above sea level in meters

Islands of the South Pacific

including the central highlands of New Guinea. New Guinea's highest mountain Puncak Jaya rises 5,030 meters above sea level. The many volcanic islands in the region including Fiji, Bougainville Island, and Tonga are the peaks of massive underwater mountain chains. Extreme variations in the elevation of islands and their surrounding waters are not uncommon in the region. The Bougainville Trench has a maximum depth

of over 9,000 meters, while the highest peak on Bougainville Island rises 2,175 meters above sea level.
The **Pacific "Ring of Fire"** runs along the entire edge of the Pacific Ocean. The Ring of Fire encompasses 80 % of the active volcanoes on the Earth's surface. Volcanic eruptions and earthquakes are common occurences in the geologically active region. Underwater earthquakes often result in the creation of destructive

waves called tsunamis that can reach 300 kilometers in length and 35 meters in height. The numbers of islands dotting the Pacific tends to decreases from west to east. Micronesia which means "small islands" consists entirely of coral islands and atolls. The islands of Micronesia are located parallel to the Melanesian islands. The large islands of Melanesia, including New Guinea and New Caledonia, are all of volcanic orgin.

The flora and fauna of the small Pacific Islands are relatively unimpressive compared to the abundance of species found on New Guinea and Australia. Animals and plants introduced by humans in recent centuries (pigs, dogs, chickens, etc.) have caused significant damage to indigenous ecosystems. Even the coconut palm, the most cliché symbol of the South Pacific, was introduced to the region by human settlers.

Marshall Islands Island nation consisting of two chains of atolls with over 1,200 coral islands – (photo) Reef sharks in Bikini Atoll.

Tarawa Atoll One of the 17 Gilbert Islands – part of the Republic of Kiribati – the main settlement is Bairiki.

Nendo Island Part of the Santa Cruz Group in the Solomon Islands – good diving areas – traditional villages.

Tanna Island The island belongs to the Republic of Vanuatu. There are five active volcanoes in the archipelago encompassing Tanna. Tanna's attractions include mountain climbing on Jasur (bottom photo) and Hot Springs Lake (top photo).

Fiji Island group in Melanesia – the largest islands are Vanua Levu and Viti Levu – sunset in Naidi on Vanua Levu (photo).

Tonga Polynesian kingdom – located on the international dateline – the capital is Nuku'alofa on Tongatapu – beautiful harbor on Vava'u (photo).

Political Boundaries
International
International disputed
Main administrative

Transportation
Interstate Hwy./Motorway
Main road
Railway
Airport

Capitals of political units
WASHINGTON D.C. Independent
Richmond State/province

Town symbols
Capital > 1 Mill. inhabitants
Capital < 1 Mill. inhabitants
Statecapital > 1 Mill. inhabitants
Statecapital < 1 Mill. inhabitants
Towns > 1 Mill. inhabitants
Towns 100 000 bis 1 Mill. inhabitants
Towns < 100 000 inhabitants

Papua New Guinea

New Guinea, the world's second largest island, is located in the southwestern Pacific Ocean. The island is separated from Australia to the south by the narrow Torres Strait.

New Guinea owes its existence to its location near the meeting points of the Indian-Australian and Pacific tectonic plates. The collision of these plates led to the formation of the island and the mountain chain that runs through its cen-

ter. The island can be divided into three distinct geographic regions. In the center of New Guinea extends a 2,500 kilometer long chain of ▲ mountain ranges (Maoke Mountains and Central Range). The central highlands are covered by thick tropical rainforests. The highest peaks in the region are more than 4,000

New Guinea's Central Highlands are covered by dense vegetation. **Sb49**

Sepik River The ▨ region along New Guinea's longest river is ▯ home to many different tribes including the Yamis and the Yawangs. Traditional masks (middle photo) are an important element of local culture. **Sa-Sc47/48**

Lake Kutubu National Park ▨ Fascinating body of water with 14 unique species of fish – rare birds and butterflies. **Sb49**

Mount Bosavi The mountain (2505 m) is the source of several major ▨ rivers – mountain rainforests. **Sb49**

Kikori River Region Pristine rainforests – stretching from the dense mountain forests of the Central Range to the coastal areas along the Gulf of Papua. **Sb-Sc49**

Scale 1:4,500,000

0   40   80 Kilometers

Principal travel routes
- Auto route
- Rail road
- Shipping route

Remarkable landscapes and natural monuments
- UNESCO World Natural Heritage
- Mountain landscape
- Active volcano
- Cave
- River landscape
- Waterfall/rapids
- Lake country
- Nature park
- National park (landscape)
- National park (flora)
- National park (fauna)
- Wildlife reserve
- Beach
- Underwater reserve

meters high. The highest mountain on the island, **Puncak Jaya** (5,030 m), lies in Papua (Irian Jaya), the western half of New Guinea and a province of Indonesia. The central portions of the highlands are home to several active ⛰ **volcanoes** and earthquakes are common in the area. The isolated and difficult-to-access mountain valleys in the highlands are inhabited by tribes of subsistence farmers. The swampy plains south of the highlands form another distinct region of New Guinea. This region is criss-crossed by numerous rivers that flow from the mountains into the **Arafuru Sea** and **Gulf of Papua**. Because of heavy rainfall and erosion in the mountains the rivers contain large amounts much of silt, which gets deposited on the southern plains. The **Fly River,** on the southwest coast, nourishes one of the world's largest wetland areas. These wetlands were once one of the most inaccessible regions in Papua New Guinea. But mining opera-tions have expanded in recent years, threatening the delicate ecosystem in the area. To the north of the central highlands lies a region of hills and plains. The **Sepik** and **Tariku** rivers are two of the most important rivers in the north. The waters off the northern coast contain large coral reefs. Around 60 % of New Guinea is covered by dense rainforests.

New Guinea's climate is tropical but frost is not uncommon at higher elevations in the highlands. The entire island gets heavy rainfall throughout the year, especially during the rainy season from December to March.

Most of the islands to the east and northeast of New Guinea are of volcanic origins including the Bismarck Archipelago and the Trobriand Islands. This area features numerous large coral reefs.

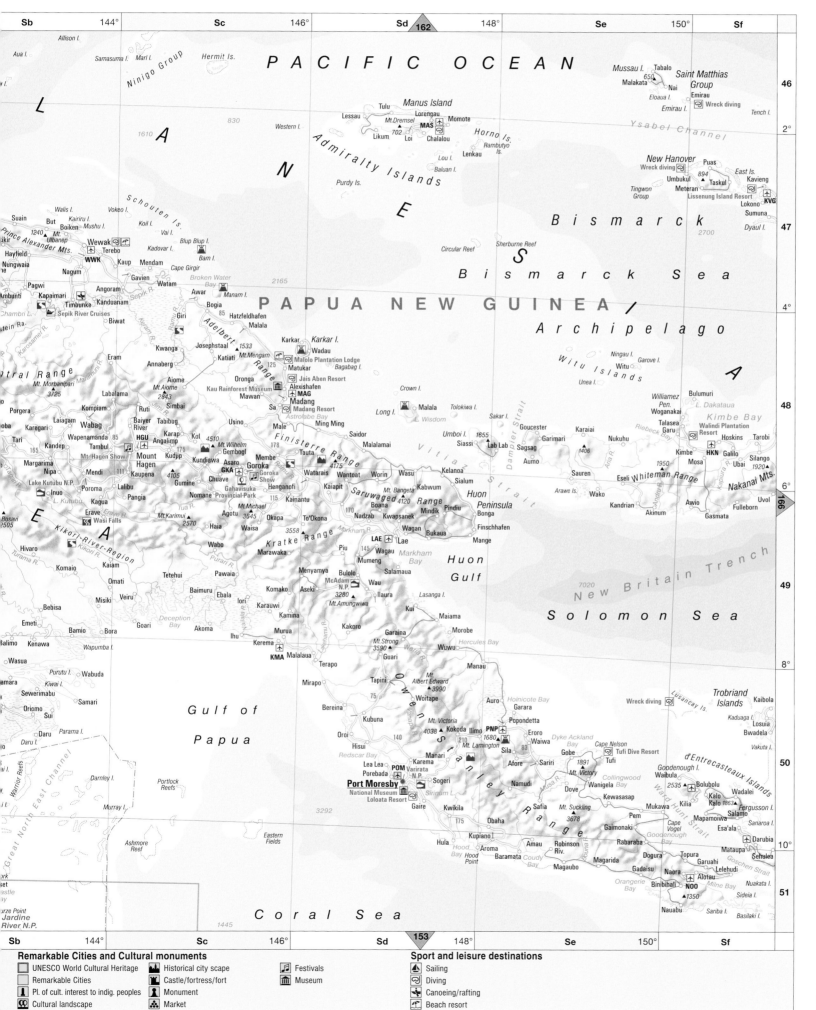

Finisterre Range Peaks over 4,000 meters – home to some of the most isolated communities in New Guinea. Sc48

Ramu River ⛴ Flows parallel to the coast – forms a single flood plain with the Sepik River during the rainy season. Sc-Sd48/49

Mount Hagen Show ♫ A gathering of clans and an impressive display of indigenous cultures. The clans compete in a "sing sing" contest with fascinating performances. Sc48

Owen Stanley Range ⛰ Mountain range north of Port Moresby – waterfalls – home to isolated mountain tribes. Sd-Se50

Remarkable Cities and Cultural monuments

- ▢ UNESCO World Cultural Heritage
- ▢ Remarkable Cities
- ▣ Pl. of cult. interest to indig. peoples
- ▣ Cultural landscape
- ▢ Historical city scape
- ▢ Castle/fortress/fort
- ▢ Monument
- ▢ Market
- ♫ Festivals
- ▣ Museum

Sport and leisure destinations

- ⛵ Sailing
- ▣ Diving
- ▢ Canoeing/rafting
- ▢ Beach resort

Bismarck Archipelago, Solomon Islands

The Bismarck Archipelago has two main islands: New Britain and New Ireland. Both the Bismarck Archipelago and the nearby Solomon Islands lie in the collision zone of two tectonic plates: the Indian-Australian and Pacific plates. The New Britain Trench is situated in the Solomon Sea between New Britain and the Solomon Islands. The trench reaches a depth of 9,140 meters at its deepest point. In the area around the trench, tec-

tonic forces continue to suck pieces of the ocean's floor into the Earth's mantle, causing the trench to expand.

The Solomon Islands and the **Bismarck Archipelago** are located inside the Pacific "Ring of Fire," which extends along the edges of the Pacific Ocean. Volcanic islands and active volcanoes

Coral islands in the New Georgia archipelago. **Sj49/50**

New Britain The island has several ▲ active volcanoes (top photo). The fire dances of the Bainings tribe are fascinating (bottom photo). **Se-Sg48/49**

Trobriand Islands These flat coral islands are home to a proud people with rich traditions. Photos from top to bottom: Aerial view of Kiriwina Islands, Kula dancers, spear fisher, harvest festival in a Yam village. **Sf50**

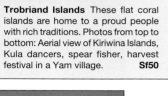

New Georgia The people of New Georgia were once known as headhunters – today their traditional culture attracts visitors. **Sj50**

Scale 1:4,500,000

0   40   80 Kilometers

Principal travel routes
- Auto route
- Rail road
- Shipping route
- Shipping route

Remarkable landscapes and natural monuments
- UNESCO World Natural Heritage
- Extinct volcano
- Active volcano
- Waterfall/rapids
- Coastal landscape
- Beach
- Coral reef
- Island
- Underwater reserve

are common in this region. Earthquakes and volcanic eruptions are constant threats to the islands. The Bismarck Archipelago belongs to Papua New Guinea and consist of more than 200 islands – most covered by dense rainforests. There are several ▲ active volcanoes in the archipelago including Vulcan and Tavurvur. New Britain and New Ireland are the two largest islands in the archipelago.

The territory of the Solomon Islands is divided between two parallel island groups. The Solomons are located southeast of **Bougainville Island**, an island territory of Papua New Guinea. With more than 1,000 islands and a total land area of 28,000 km², the Solomon Islands form one of the largest archipelagoes in the Pacific Ocean. The island nation lies around 1,860 kilometers from Australia and stretches over a distance of approximetely 1,400

kilometers from north to south. The main islands in the archipelago (Choiseul, New Georgia, Santa Isabel, Makira, and Guadalcanal) are all of volcanic origin and are covered by thick forests. The economy of the Solomon Islands is heavily dependent on the export of crops and timber, but the abundant mineral wealth of the islands is being increasingly exploited.

Coral reefs are common along the coastline of many islands in this region of the

Pacific, some extending above the water. The Louisiade Archipelago is an island group off the southeastern coast of New Guinea. The archipelago includes several large islands of volcanic origin as well as many small coral islands. Both the Bismarck Archipelago and the Solomon Islands get abundant rainfall, especially during the rainy season. This is also the time when the risk of cyclones is greatest in the region.

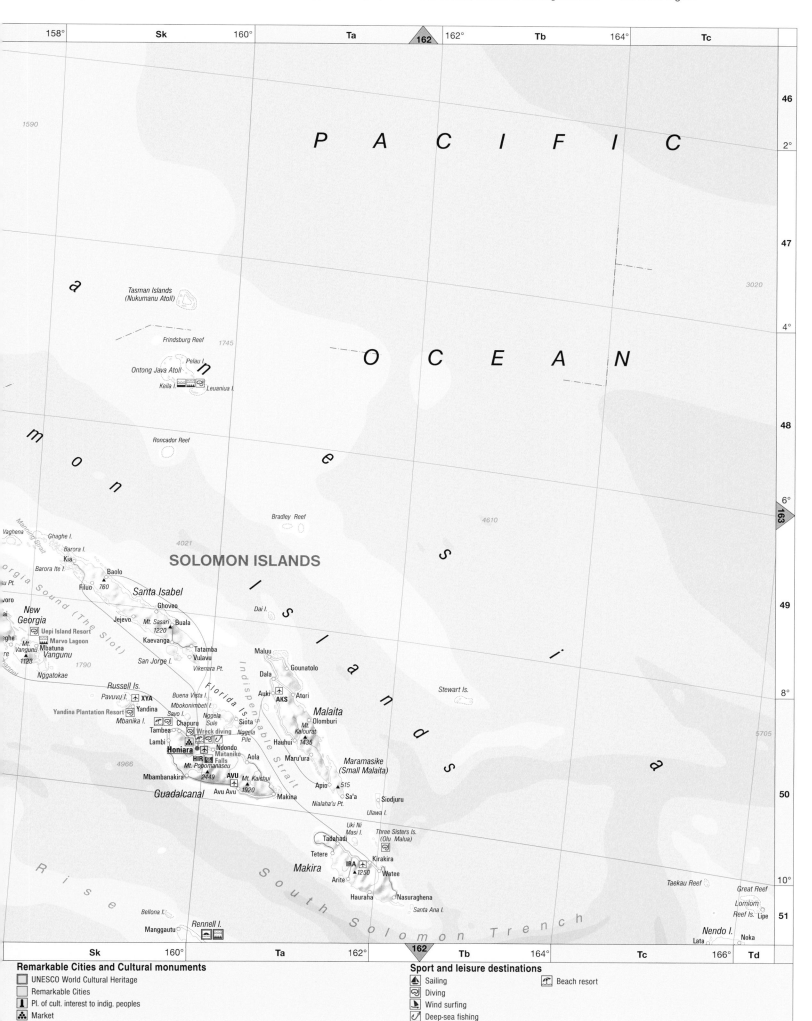

The Coral Reefs of the Solomon Islands The beautiful coral reefs off the coast of the Solomon Islands among the country's most popular attractions. The country's reefs are home to a diverse collection of marine plants and animals. Coral reefs are formed over many years, in warm (minimum temperature, 20° C) saltwater, by colonies of coral – tiny marine animals. Photos from top to bottom: Coral reefs off the coast of the Solomon Islands, Moray eel, Clown fish, Toadstool coral, Boxfish.

Solomon Islands Melanesian ◪ island group – independent nation since 1978 (photo: A wedding).   **Sh-Tb48/51**

Rennell Island Located south of Guadalcanal – total area of 650 km² – traditonal dance troupes (photo) – the ◪ coral island is a UNESCO world heritage site – national park.   **Sk-Ta51**

Map

Remarkable Cities and Cultural monuments
- ☐ UNESCO World Cultural Heritage
- ☐ Remarkable Cities
- ☐ Pl. of cult. interest to indig. peoples
- ⚒ Market

Sport and leisure destinations
- ⛵ Sailing
- 🤿 Diving
- 🏄 Wind surfing
- 🎣 Deep-sea fishing
- 🏖 Beach resort

New Caledonia, Vanuatu, Fiji Islands

New Caledonia, Vanuatu and Fiji are all located in the South Pacific to the east of Australia. Many of the islands in this region are part of an expansive ancient underwater ⛰ mountain chain. 🏝 New Caledonia is 400 kilometers long and has a maximum width of 50 kilometers. The island has an extraordinary wealth of mineral resources including deposits of nickel, gold, copper, iron and silver. Just north of New Caledonia's main island lie

two large parallel coral reefs, the 🪸 **Grand Récif de Cook** and the **Récif de Français**. With the exception of the main island, most of New Caledonia's islands are flat coral islands. The tallest mountain in the archipelago is the ⛰ **Massif de Humboldt** (1,635 m).

The culture of New Caledonia has been greatly influenced by the cultures of

Dusk on a Fijian island. Tj-Ua54/55

Espíritu Santo Largest island in Vanuatu – inaccessible interior – sunken warships at 🖼 Million Dollar Point. **Td53**

Ambrim Two active 🌋 volcanoes in the island's interior – striking statues – (photos) traditional dances. **Te54**

Tana The volcano 🌋 Mount Yasur is the island's major attraction – manatees near Port Resolution. **Te55**

New Caledonia 🪸 Reefs and coral islands surround the main island (top photo). The ⛰ highlands contain beautiful waterfalls including 🖼 Chute de la Madeleine (bottom photo). **Tc-Td56/57**

Lifou The largest and most populated of the Loyalty Islands – major town 🖼 We – the local language is Drehu. **Td56**

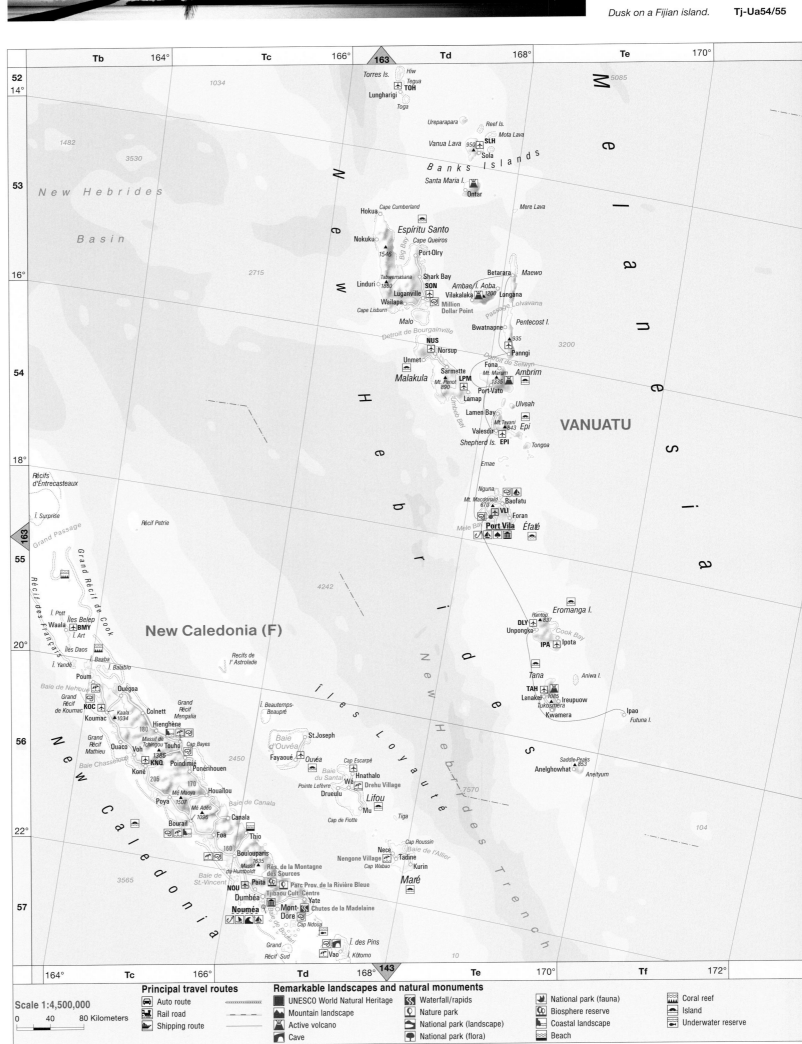

Scale 1:4,500,000

0   40   80 Kilometers

Principal travel routes
- Auto route
- Rail road
- Shipping route

Remarkable landscapes and natural monuments
- UNESCO World Natural Heritage
- Mountain landscape
- Active volcano
- Cave
- Waterfall/rapids
- Nature park
- National park (landscape)
- National park (flora)
- National park (fauna)
- Biosphere reserve
- Coastal landscape
- Beach
- Coral reef
- Island
- Underwater reserve

France and the surrounding Melanesian islands. The island has been politically linked to France since the middle of the 19th century, and French is the dominant language on New Caledonia and the smaller islands around it. The indigenous people of New Caledonian – the Melanesian Kanaks – now make up less than half of the current population.

Melanesia, along with Polynesia and Micronesia, is one of the three regions into which the islands of the South Pacific are divided. Melanesia was given its name by 19th century Europeans because of the dark skin tones of its indigenous people. Vanuatu, also known as the 📷 **New Hebrides**, consists of over 70 islands located in the southern part of Melanesia. Most of the Melanesian islands are surrounded by large 📷 coral reefs with diverse and unique marine life. 📷 **Éfaté**, the most populated island in Vanuatu, is the location of the country's capital city, Port Vila. The islands north of Efaté have a distinct climate with high temperatures and humidity. The large northern island Espiritu Santo has several good diving areas where divers can view several shipwrecks from the Second World War.

Vanua Levu (5,534 km²) and 📷 **Viti Levu** (10,388 km²) are by far the largest of the 330 **Fiji Islands**. Most of the smaller Fiji islands are separated from the two larger islands by the Nanuku Passage. There are many large reefs off the coast of the Fiji islands including the 📷 **Great Sea Reef** near Vanua Levu. The population of Fiji is almost equally divided between the indigenous (Melanesian) Fijians and Fijians of Indian descent. In recent years, ethnic tension between the two communities has led to government instability and violent clashes.

Yasawa Islands Part of the Fiji Islands – beautiful beaches – good 📷 diving areas – local 🚢 cruise ship lines. **Tj54**

Viti Levu Largest of the Fiji Islands – tropical 🏔 highlands – 📷 Sigatoka Sand Dunes National Parks. **Tj-Tk54/55**

Coral Reefs The 100-kilometer-long 📷 Great Astrolabe Reef near Kadavu one of the world's most fascinating reefs. The Great White Wall, a white coral reef, lies in the 📷 diving areas off the coast of Taveuni. **Tk55**

Vanua Levu Second largest island in Fiji – major cities: Labasa and Savusavu – 🚢 cruise lines and 📷 diving areas. **Tk54**

Taveuni Volcanic "garden island" – 📷 Buma National Park with the crater lake, Lake Tagimaucia. **Tk-Ua54**

Map labels

PACIFIC OCEAN

Micronesia

Polynesia

North Fiji Basin

Fiji Islands

TUVALU

Charlotte Bank

Rotuma

Wallis and Futuna (F)

Niulakita

Cikobia

Great Sea Reef

Yasawa Group

Vanua Levu

Koro Sea

Ringgold Isles

Udu Point

Lagalaga

Nabavatu

Labasa

Bua

Savusavu

Buca

Somosomo

Taveuni

Bouma N.P.

Naitaba

Yacata

Kanacea

Vanua Balavu

Lomaloma

Mago

Northern Lau Group

Southern Lau Group

Lakeba Passage

Cicia

Tuvuca

Nayau

Lakeba

Tubou

Bukatatonoa Reefs

Reid Reef

Moala

Totoya

Matuku

Vuaqava

Namuka-Hau

Kabara

Moce

Yagasa Cluster

Fulaga

Ogea Levu

FIJI

Viwa

Naviti

Waya

Mamanuca Group

Malolo

Tavarua

Lautoka

Viseisei

Nadi

Ba

Tavua

Rakiraki

Nabouwalu

Bligh Water

Koroyanitu N.P.

Tomaniivi

Keiyasi

Lawaki

Korovou

Ovalau

Levuka

Sigatoka

Colo-i-Suva Forest Res.

Korolevu

Lami

Navua

Nausori

Suva

Sawaleke

Nairai

Gau

Sigatoka Sand Dunes N.P.

Coral Coast

Frigates Passage

Orchid Island

Beqa

Vatulele

Garden of the Sleeping Giant

Great Astrolab Reef

Tavuki

Vunisea

Ono

Kadavu

Kadavu Passage

Viti Levu

Bua Bay

Naravuka

Nasorolevu

Natewa Bay

Savusavu Bay

Great Sea Reef

Vatu-i-Ra Channel

Legend

Remarkable Cities and Cultural monuments

- ☐ UNESCO World Cultural Heritage
- ☐ Remarkable Cities
- ☑ Places of Hindu cultural interest
- ☑ Pl. of cult. interest to indig. peoples
- ☐ Historical city scape
- ☐ Monument
- ☐ Museum

Sport and leisure destinations

- ⛵ Sailing
- 📷 Diving
- 🏄 Wind surfing
- 🏄 Surfing
- 🎣 Deep-sea fishing
- 🏖 Beach resort
- ♠ Casino

Tonga, Samoa, French Polynesia

The island kingdom of Tonga and its northern neighbor Samoa are both **Polynesian islands**. These island nations are located in the South Pacific to the northeast of New Zealand. The island groups in this section of the Pacific Ocean are separated from one another by relatively large distances. The Kingdom of **Tonga** consist of 169 islands in two parallel island chains. Tonga encompasses both coral islands and islands of volca-

nic origin. The island kingdom is home to several active volcanoes. The frequent volcanism in Tonga is the result of the country's location near the collision zone of the Pacific and Indian-Australian tectonic plates.

The **Tonga Trench** has a maximum depth of 10,882 meters. Most of Tonga's

Sunset above Rangiroa atoll in French Polynesia.   Cg53

Savai'i Largest Samoan island – several volcanoes and lava fields – mountainous interior – beaches and waterfalls.   **Bd52**

'Upolu The second largest Samoan island – beautiful beaches in the southeast – waterfalls.   **Be52**

Manua Islands Three islands; Olosega, Ofu, and Ta'u – sandy beaches – mountains reaching 1,000 meters in height.   **Bf53**

The Samoans Family and community play an important role in the lives of Samoa's 200,000 inhabitants.

Vava'u The most beautiful of Tonga's island groups – boat expeditions through the islands – accessible caves.   **Bc-Bd55**

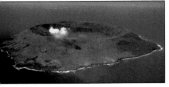

Tofua Islands Home to Tonga's most active volcanoes – the site of the famous mutiny on the ship Bounty in 1789.   **Bc55**

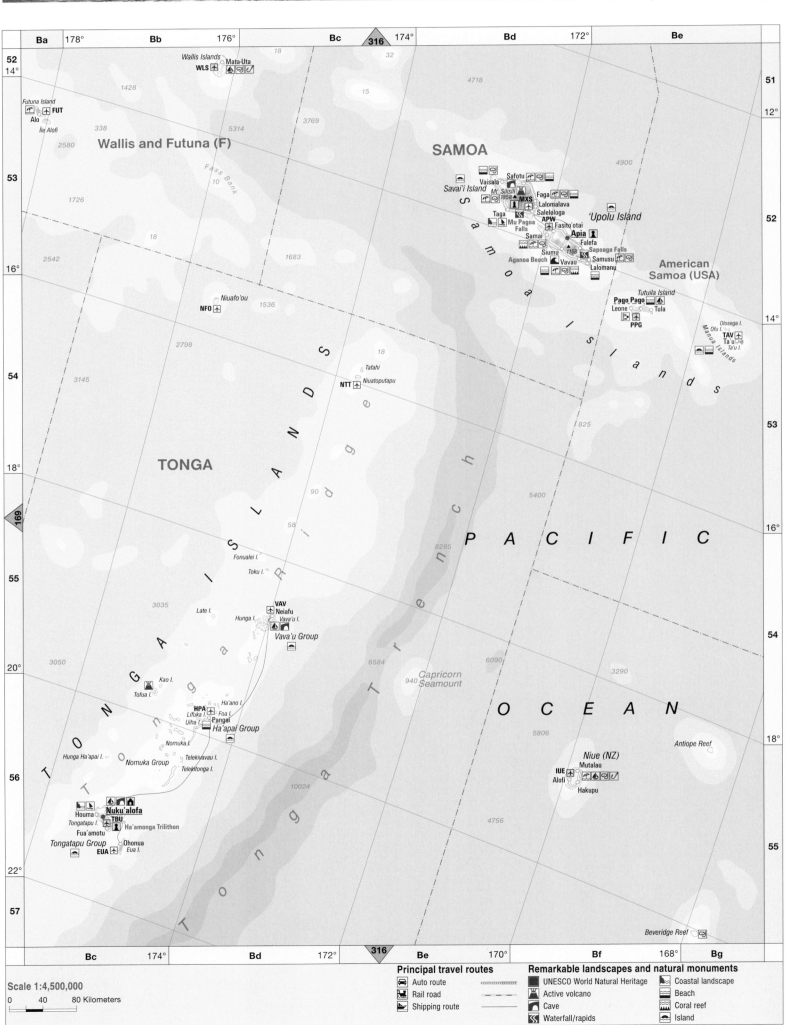

Scale 1:4,500,000

0   40   80 Kilometers

Principal travel routes
- Auto route
- Rail road
- Shipping route

Remarkable landscapes and natural monuments
- UNESCO World Natural Heritage
- Active volcano
- Cave
- Waterfall/rapids
- Coastal landscape
- Beach
- Coral reef
- Island

eastern islands – including the largest island Tongatapu – are coral islands, while most of the western islands are of volcanic origin.

The largest islands in **Samoa** are the peaks of large underwater volcanic mountain chains. ▲ **Mount Matavanu** is located at the center of Savai'i, the largest Samoan island. The volcano's last major eruption in 1905 forced much of the local population to permanently leave the island. Because of the lovely beaches, waterfalls, and fascinating culture the Samoan Islands are considered one of most attractive destinations in the South Pacific. Despite the influence of American and European culture, the Samoans have preserved many aspects of their traditional culture.

French Polynesia consists of five archipelagos comprising more than 120 islands. The French territory is scattered over 4.5 million km² near the eastern edges of Polynesia. The volcanic **Marquesas Islands** are one of the largest island groups in French Polynesia. Poitanui (1,232 m) is the highest volcano in the Marquesas. Over 1,000 kilometers southwest of the Marquesas Islands lie the **Tuamotu Islands** – an island group consisting entirely of atolls. The ◩ **Society Islands** are the most famous island group in French Polynesia. **Tahiti**, the economic and cultural center of French Polynesia, lies at the geographic center of the territory. The capital and largest city in French Polynesia is Papeete on Tahiti. The Society Islands are divided into two groups: the Leeward and Windward Islands. All of the Society Islands are volcanic islands with rich tropical vegetation. Mount Orohena on Tahiti is the highest mountain in the territory, rising 2,241 meters above sea level.

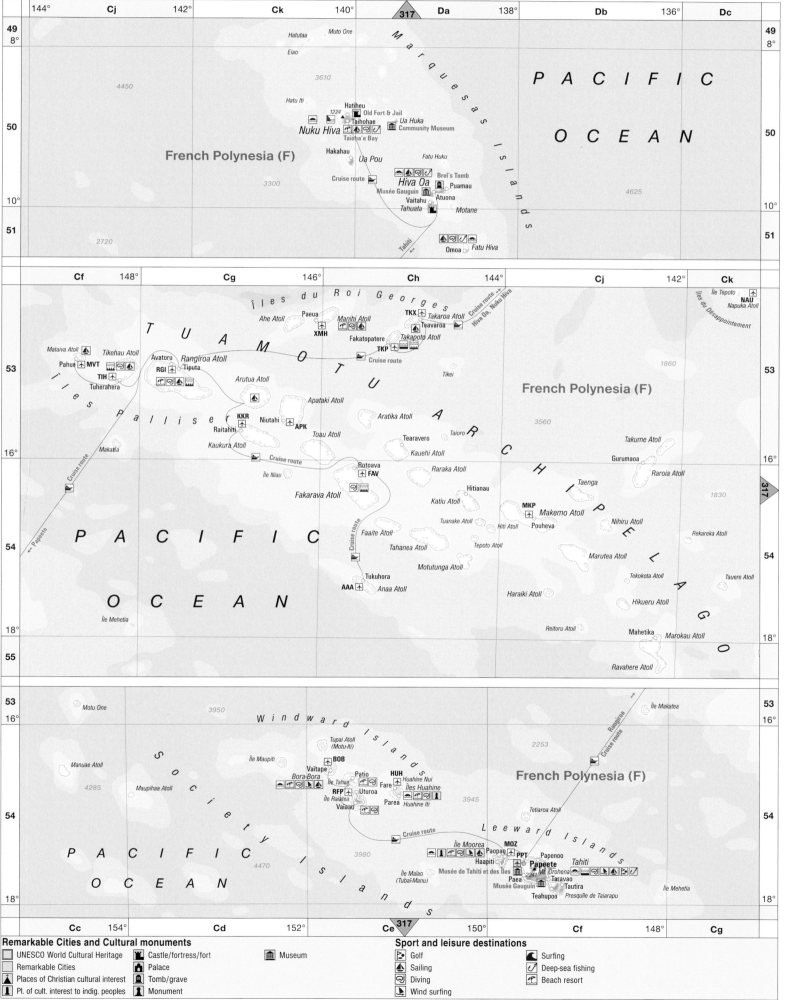

Nuku Hiva Largest of the Marquesas Islands – several deep bays – fascinating stone formations – historic ⌖ fort. **Ck50**

Fatu Hiva Considered the most beautiful of the Marquesas Islands – formed from two volcanic craters – ⛵ sailing areas. **Da51**

Bora Bora Often called the "pearl of the Pacific", the island in French Polynesia has an area of 38 km². Bora Bora boasts several beautiful blue lagoons surrounded by long sandy white beaches. Regular ferries link the island to nearby Tahiti. **Ce54**

Moorea Island with peaks and lush vegetation – panoramic views from Belvedere lookout – ruins of ancient ⌖ temples. **Cf54**

Tahiti 🏛 Gauguin Museum – 🏛 Musée de Tahiti et des Îles (local history and culture) – tall cliffs and peaks – capital: Papeete. **Cf54**

Remarkable Cities and Cultural monuments

- ◻ UNESCO World Cultural Heritage
- ▪ Remarkable Cities
- ▪ Places of Christian cultural interest
- ▪ Pl. of cult. interest to indig. peoples
- ▦ Castle/fortress/fort
- ▦ Palace
- ▦ Tomb/grave
- ▦ Monument
- 🏛 Museum

Sport and leisure destinations

- Golf
- Sailing
- Diving
- Wind surfing
- Surfing
- Deep-sea fishing
- Beach resort

Namaland (top): Quiver trees, a type of Aloe, are common in the deserts of southern Namibia.
Abu Simbel (bottom): Colossal statues of Ramses II before the temple at Abu Simbel.

Kruger National Park (left): A leopard relaxes in South Africa's most famous national park.
The Seychelles (right): A tourist paradise in the Indian Ocean.

Africa

Africa was and is the continent of explorers and adventurers. The continent's wonders include vast wildernesses, the world's largest desert, the Virunga Volcanoes, steamy rainforests, the Victoria Falls, the majesty of Kilimanjaro, Egypt's pyramids, Morocco's palaces, the ruins of Great Zimbabwe, as well as its fascinating indigenous cultures.

Africa · The continent

Africa has an area of approximately 30.4 million km². The world's second largest continent encompasses around 20 % of the Earth's total land area. From north to south, Africa stretches over 8,000 kilometers. Africa is separated from Europe by the Mediterranean Sea, but at the **Strait of Gibraltar** the two continents are less than 14 kilometers apart. The Red Sea is situated between northeastern Africa and the Arabian Peninsula. In the west, Africa

is bordered by the Atlantic Ocean, while the Indian Ocean borders the continent to the east and southeast. The coasts of Africa are remarkably smooth with few peninsulas and large natural harbours. **Madagascar** is situated near a series of smaller island groups including the Comoros and the Seychelles. Several small island

Beautiful Mount Kilimanjaro is comprised of three volcanoes.

groups – including the Cape Verde Islands – are located near Africa's western coast. The terrain of Africa is dominated by a series of basins, including the immense Sahara basin, the Niger-Chad-White Nile basin, and the Congo basin. The **Great Rift Valley**, an ancient fracture on the Earth's surface, stretches through East Africa. Many of Africa's tallest mountains – including Kilimanjaro and Mt. Kenya – are located in or near the Great Rift Valley.

With the exception of a few areas near the Mediterranean and southeastern coast on the Indian Ocean, most of Africa has three types of climate/vegetation zones. The north and southwest of the continent have **arid** and **semi-arid climates** (top photo: Dunes in the Libyan Desert). Central Africa and West Africa have humid **tropical climates** (middle photo: Rain forest in the Congo basin). The landscape in East Africa and most of Southern Africa is primarily **savannah** (bottom photo: Serengeti National Park in Tanzania).

The highest mountains in Africa (in descending order) are Kilimanjaro (5,895 m), **Mt. Kenya** (photo: 5,199 m), Mt. Ruwenzori (5,109 m), and Ras Dashen Terara (4,620 m). The **Atlas Mountains** is the highest range in North Africa. In southern Africa, the **Drakensberg Mountains** rise to a maximum height of 3,482 meters. Lake Assal (-155 m) in Djibouti is the lowest point on the continent's surface.

The longest river in Africa is the 6,671-kilometer-long **Nile River** (top photo). Other major rivers include the **Congo** (4,374 km), the **Niger** (4,184 km), and the **Zambezi** (2,376 km). The **Victoria Falls** (middle photo) on the Zambezi River are the continent's largest waterfalls. The largest lakes in Africa are **Lake Victoria** (68,000 km²), **Lake Tanganyika** (34,000 km²), and Lake Malawi (30,800 km²: bottom photo).

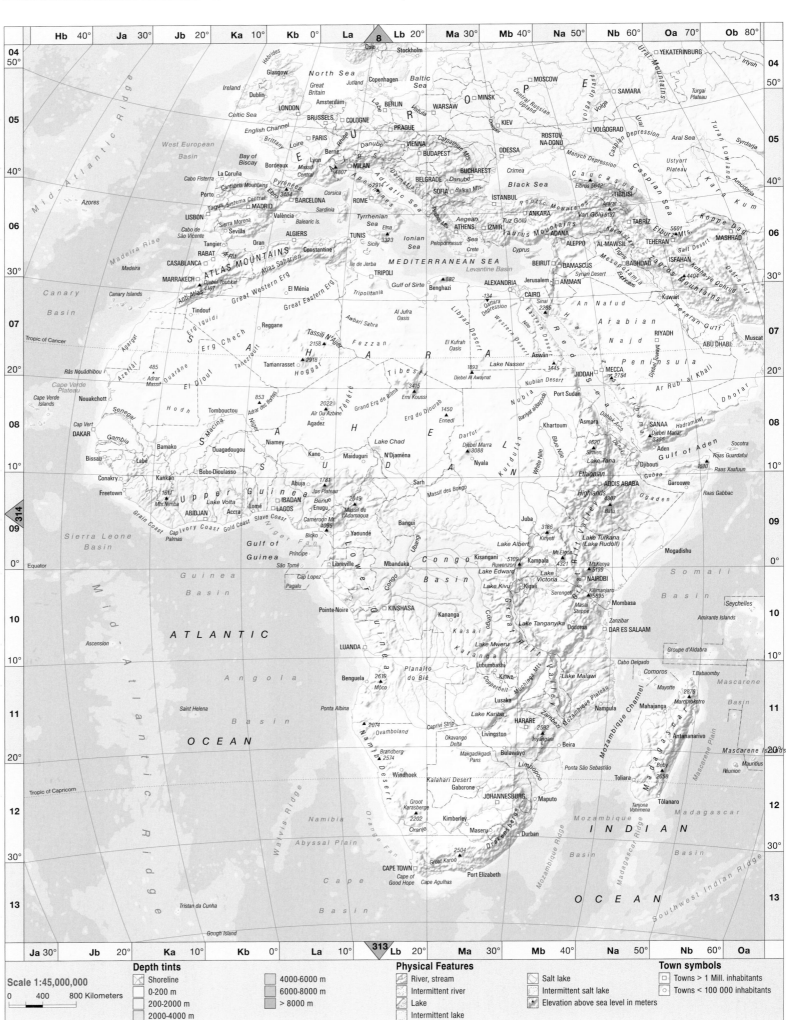

Scale 1:45,000,000

0   400   800 Kilometers

Depth tints

- Shoreline
- 0-200 m
- 200-2000 m
- 2000-4000 m
- 4000-6000 m
- 6000-8000 m
- > 8000 m

Physical Features

- River, stream
- Intermittent river
- Lake
- Intermittent lake
- Salt lake
- Intermittent salt lake
- Elevation above sea level in meters

Town symbols

- Towns > 1 Mill. inhabitants
- Towns < 100 000 inhabitants

Africa is home to more than 700 million people. North Africa is inhabited by a variety of ethnicities, including **Arabs**, **Berbers**, and the **Tuareg**. The areas south of the Sahara are populated mostly by dark-skinned black African ethnicities. Most black Africans are categorized into one of two distinct groups: **Bantu speaking** and **Sudanic** ethnicities. Other major ethnic groups in Africa include the **Somalis**, **Ethiopians**, and the **San**.

Africa has the highest birthrates of any continent. The rapid population growth is seen by many as a major obstacle to the continent's economic and social development. Despite widespread social problems, several African states have experienced positive economic and political developments in recent years.

Left: A Tuareg man.
Right: Maasai girl in Kenya.

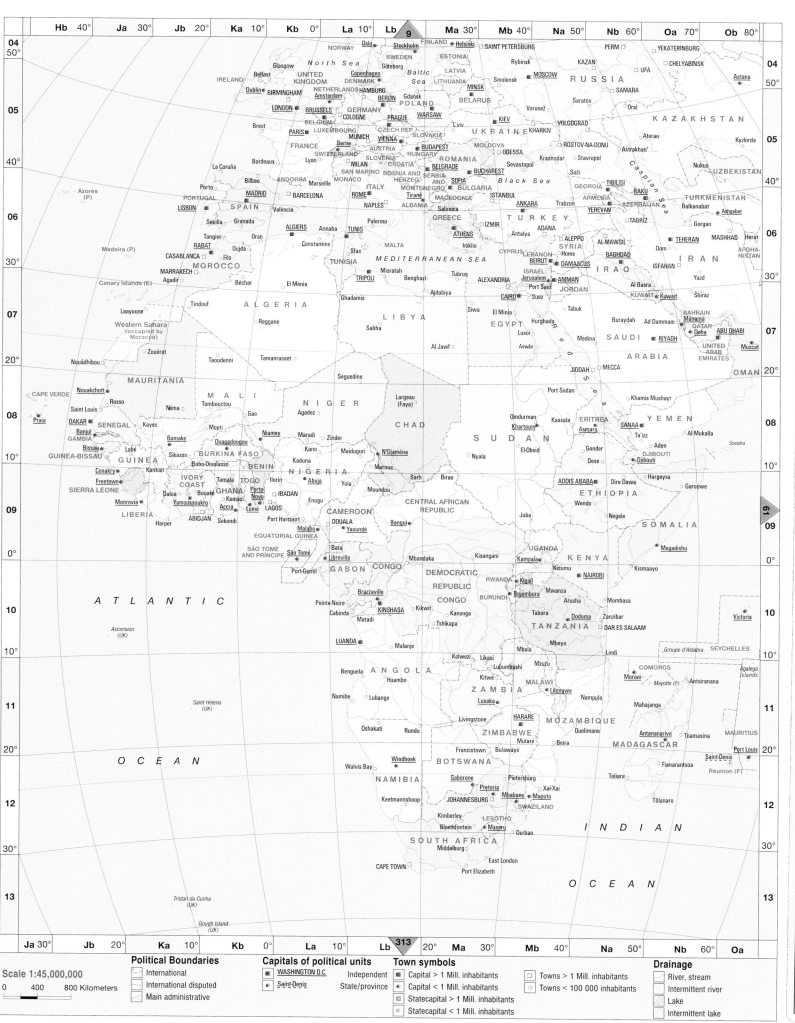

Countries and Flags

Algeria
Angola
Benin
Botswana
Burkina Faso
Burundi
Cape Verde
Cameroon
Central African Republic
Chad
Comoros
Congo, Democratic Republic
Congo, Republic
Côte d'Ivoire
Djibouti
Egypt
Equatorial Guinea
Eritrea
Ethiopia
Gabon
Gambia
Ghana
Guinea
Guinea-Bissau
Kenya
Lesotho
Liberia
Libya
Madagascar
Malawi
Mali
Mauritania
Mauritius
Morocco
Mozambique
Namibia
Niger
Nigeria
Rwanda
Sao Tome e Principe
Senegal
Seychelles
Sierra Leone
Somalia
South Africa
Sudan
Swaziland
Tanzania
Togo
Tunisia
Uganda
Western Sahara
Zambia
Zimbabwe

Scale 1:45,000,000
0   400   800 Kilometers

Political Boundaries
International
International disputed
Main administrative

Capitals of political units
■ WASHINGTON D.C.   Independent
▪ Saint-Denis   State/province

Town symbols
■ Capital > 1 Mill. inhabitants
□ Capital < 1 Mill. inhabitants
■ Statecapital > 1 Mill. inhabitants
□ Statecapital < 1 Mill. inhabitants
□ Towns > 1 Mill. inhabitants
□ Towns < 100 000 inhabitants

Drainage
River, stream
Intermittent river
Lake
Intermittent lake

Northern Africa

The northern half of Africa features many contrasting climate and vegetation zones. The Sahara Desert stretches between Africa's Mediterranean coast and the tropical regions of central and western Africa. The **Sahara**, the world's largest desert, covers more than nine million km². Between the Atlas Mountain range on the northwestern edge of the Sahara and the Mediterranean lies a coastal area with a hospitable subtropical climate. The

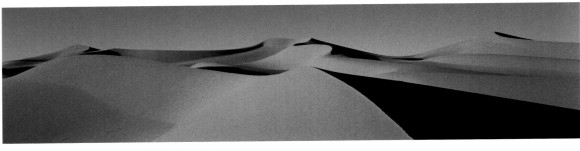

The vast Sahara Desert covers most of North Africa.

Sahel along the southern edges of the Sahara is a transition zone between the desert and the tropical regions of Africa. This region consists mostly of semi-arid savannahs and stretches from Senegal in West Africa to Kenya in East Africa. Centuries ago, Arab traders and geographers gave the Sahel its name, an Arabic word

Canary Islands Spanish island group off the western coast of Africa – the highest point on the Canary Islands is Pico del Teide (photo) with a height of 3,717 meters.

Atlas Mountains The Atlas mountain chain stretches through Morocco, Algeria, and Tunisia. The High Atlas (top photo, Morocco), the highest section of the chain, rises above 4,000 meters. The Sahara Atlas range (bottom photo) borders the Sahara Desert.

The **Sahara Desert** encompasses a variety of contrasting landscapes including high sand dunes, heavily eroded highlands with unusual stone formations, and flat monotonous fields of sand. Numerous fertile oases are scattered throughout the desert. Photos from top to bottom: Erg Chebbi in Morocco, The Hoggar Mountains in Algeria, Saharan village.

Niger River 4,184 kilometers long – the river flows from the highlands of Guinea through the Sahel into the deserts of Mali and Niger – rainforests around the Niger's delta (photo).

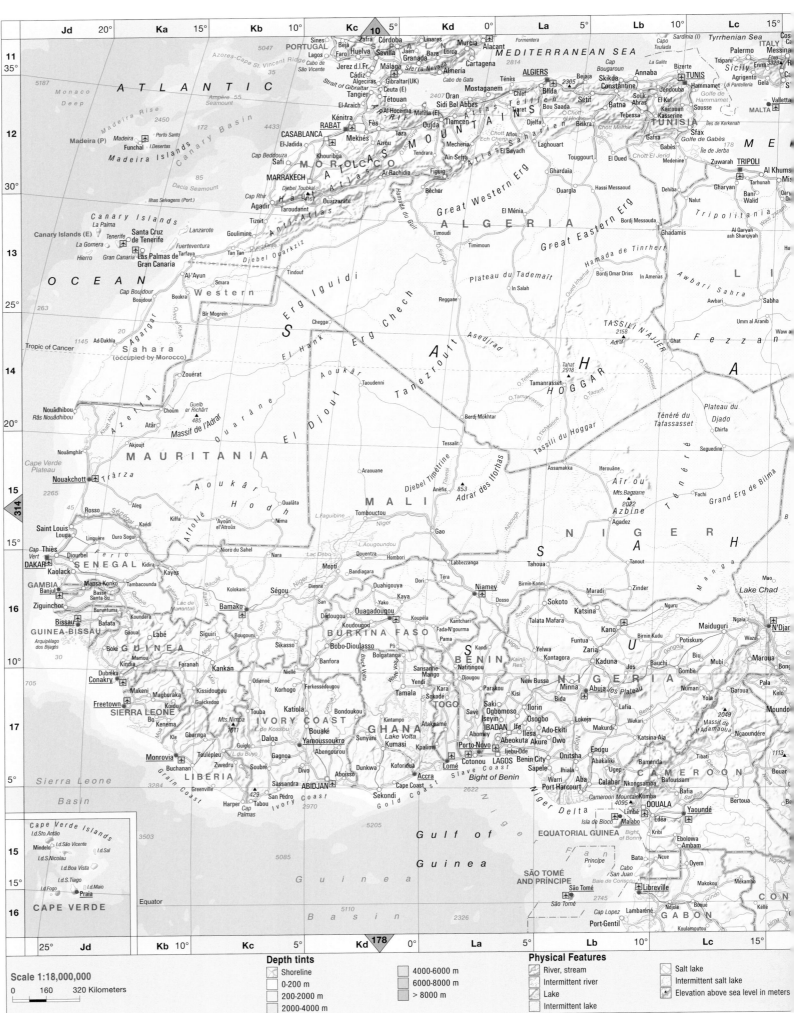

Scale 1:18,000,000

0   160   320 Kilometers

Depth tints
- Shoreline
- 0–200 m
- 200–2000 m
- 2000–4000 m
- 4000–6000 m
- 6000–8000 m
- > 8000 m

Physical Features
- River, stream
- Intermittent river
- Lake
- Intermittent lake
- Salt lake
- Intermittent salt lake
- Elevation above sea level in meters

meaning shore or border. Because of natural desertification and human land use, the Sahel is gradually expanding south. The majority of the Sahel's inhabitants are subsistence farmers or nomads. South of the Sahel lies a belt of **forested savannahs** and **tropical rainforests** stretching from the Atlantic coast to the Great Rift Valley in East Africa. The region is home to many ecosystems with unique flora and fauna. Rapid population growth in the region is a significant threat to this biodiversity.

The **Congo basin** encompasses the world's second largest area of tropical rainforests. Many of these forests have been designated conservation areas in recent years but illegal logging remains a problem in the region. The Congo basin is also home to many valuable mineral resources including diamonds, oil, gold, and iron ore. Unfortunately this mineral wealth has also contributed to environmental damage and the outbreak of armed conflicts in the region.

Centuries ago, European traders established bases and forts in West Africa and on islands near the region's coast. Many settlements on the West African coast would eventually become centers of the international slave trade. For many centuries, Arabian traders had a major presence on the continent's eastern coast.

Many traders and armies once traversed the deserts of North Africa in large caravans. Northern Africa's rivers – including the Nile and Niger – have been an important means of transport through the continent's interior for many centuries. The **Niger** is the longest river in West Africa with a length of 4,184 kilometers. Africa's longest river, the **Nile**, flows north from its source in Uganda to the continent's Mediterranean coast.

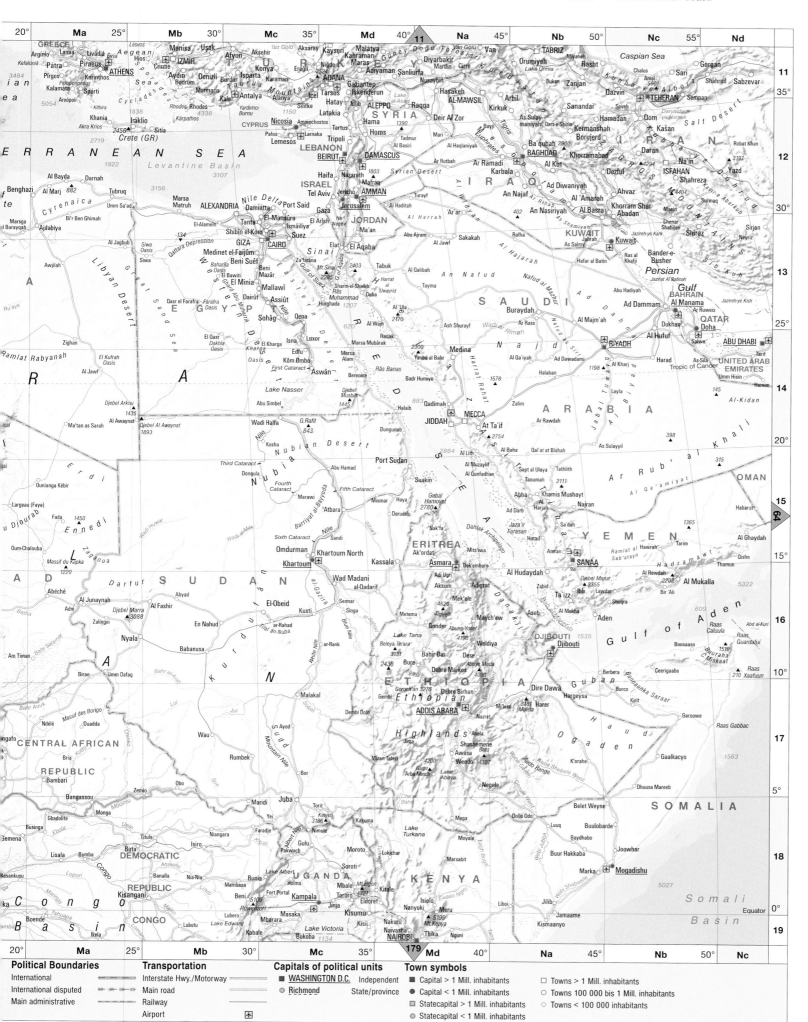

The Nile The Blue Nile and the White Nile Rivers begin in Ethiopia and Uganda and merge near Khartoum in Sudan. The Nile, Africa's longest river, flows north to its delta on the Mediterranean coast. Photos from top to bottom: Cairo, near Aswan, Blue Nile Falls in Ethiopia, the source of the White Nile in Uganda.

Eritrea Mountainous arid nation – capital city Asmara – fertile coastal strip along the Red Sea.

The Highlands of Ethiopia Mountainous areas cover much of Ethiopia. The country's highlands contain several massifs taller than 4,000 meters.

Somalia Desert country on the Horn of Africa – home to many desert nomads – dry river beds (photo).

Political Boundaries

International	───────
International disputed	─ ─ ─ ─
Main administrative	───────

Transportation

Interstate Hwy./Motorway	───────
Main road	───────
Railway	───────
Airport	✈

Capitals of political units

■ WASHINGTON D.C.	Independent
⊙ Richmond	State/province

Town symbols

■ Capital > 1 Mill. inhabitants	□ Towns > 1 Mill. inhabitants
■ Capital < 1 Mill. inhabitants	□ Towns 100 000 bis 1 Mill. inhabitants
▣ Statecapital > 1 Mill. inhabitants	○ Towns < 100 000 inhabitants
⊙ Statecapital < 1 Mill. inhabitants	

Southern Africa

The section of Africa between the equator and the continent's southern tip offers a variety of distinct climate zones, including areas with tropical and Mediterranean climates. The terrain of southern Africa is dominated by a series of large basins including the **Kalahari Basin** with its arid deserts. The **Okavango Basin** encompasses the world's largest wetland – a conservation area with abundant wildlife. The Afro-Arabian Rift Valley, an

ancient geographic feature, stretches from southern Africa to western Asia. In East Africa, the Rift Valley diverges into two branches: the **Western** and **Eastern (Great) Rift Valleys**. Lake Victoria, Africa's largest lake, is located in a basin between the two branches of the Rift Valley. The Great Rift Valley contains many fas-

The Blyde River flows through the Drakensberg Mountains of South Africa.

Congo Basin The basin of the Congo River contains vast tropical rainforests, home to countless plants and animals.

Great Escarpment The transition zone between southern Africa's highlands and coasts has beautiful, craggy landscapes.

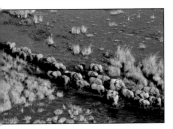

Okavango Delta Inland river delta in Botswana (15,000 km²) – numerous small streams – home to large animal herds.

Namib and **Kalahari Deserts** Large arid areas in Botswana and Namibia. The Namib Desert (top photo) located near the Atlantic Ocean gets almost no rainfall. The arid and semi-arid steppes of the Kalahari Desert contain several seasonal rivers.

The region around the **Cape of Good Hope** (bottom photo) in South Africa has some of the country's most beautiful landscapes, unique flora, attractive beaches, and a pleasant Mediterranean climate.

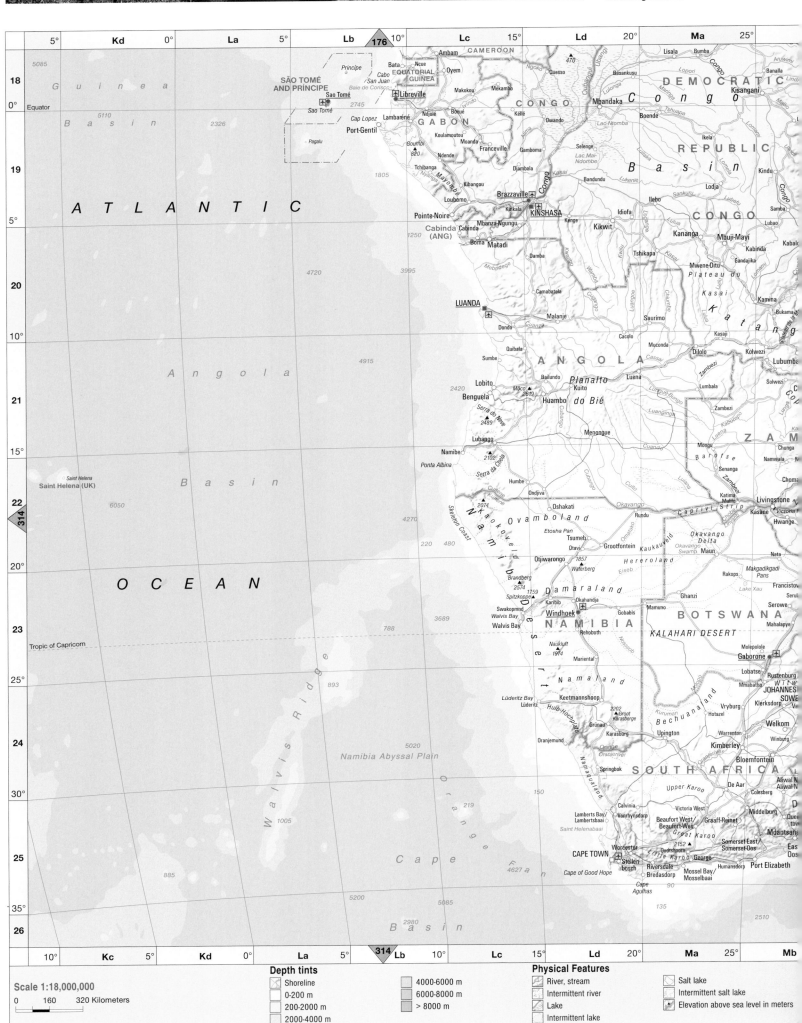

Scale 1:18,000,000

0   160   320 Kilometers

Depth tints
- Shoreline
- 0-200 m
- 200-2000 m
- 2000-4000 m
- 4000-6000 m
- 6000-8000 m
- > 8000 m

Physical Features
- River, stream
- Intermittent river
- Lake
- Intermittent lake
- Salt lake
- Intermittent salt lake
- Elevation above sea level in meters

cinating landscapes including numerous high volcanoes and large lakes. **Mount Kilimanjaro** (5,895 m), Africa's highest mountain, lies in the Great Rift Valley near the border between Tanzania and Kenya. East Africa features several large national parks and conservation areas with fascinating wildlife – including **Ruwenzori Mountains National Park** (Uganda), **Serengeti National Park** (Tanzania), and the **Masai Mara Reserve** in Kenya.

Southern Africa features a long series of highlands. These highlands rise gradually to the south of the enormous Congo River basin and extend to the southern edges of the continent in South Africa. The highlands of Zimbabwe, known as the **High Veld**, consist of heavily cultivated areas where tobacco and grains are farmed. Namibia's arid and semi-arid highlands are inhabited mostly by ranchers and cattle herders. The **Okavango** and **Zam-**

bezi Rivers are the two most significant rivers in Southern Africa. During the wetter months of the year, the Okavango Delta is transformed into a fertile wetland. The Zambezi flows east from its source in northeastern Zambia and forms the spectacular **Victoria Falls** when it crashes over a narrow gorge in Zimbabwe. Two large man-made lakes have been created along the course of the Zambezi in recent decades: Lake Kariba

and Cabora Bassa Reservoir. The dams constructed on the Zambezi are vital sources of electricity for Mozambique and Zimbabwe. **Madagascar** is the largest island off the African coast and the world's fourth largest island. The island's interior is dominated by humid tropical highlands. Because of its geographic isolation, Madagascar has a unique collection of endemic flora and fauna.

Mount Kilimanjaro Africa's highest mountain rises 5,895 meters – located in northern Tanzania – UNESCO world heritage site.

Vast **steppes** and **savannahs** cover much of East Africa, especially Kenya and Tanzania. This region features some of the continent's most famous national parks – including Serengeti National Park and the Masai Mara National Game Reserve.

The **Great Rift Valley** and **Western Rift Valley** are ancient fault systems in Africa. Both encompass numerous volcanoes and a series of large lakes. Photos: the volcano Ol Doinyo Lengai, Lake Malawi.

Drakensberg Mountains UNESCO world heritage site – mountain range in South Africa and Lesotho – thousands of ancient rock paintings created by the San people.

The Highlands of Madagascar Highlands cover much of the island's interior – humid tropical and subtropical climates – national parks with diverse flora and fauna.

Political Boundaries
International
International disputed
Main administrative

Transportation
Interstate Hwy./Motorway
Main road
Railway
Airport

Capitals of political units
■ WASHINGTON D.C.   Independent
◉ Richmond   State/province

Town symbols
■ Capital > 1 Mill. inhabitants
■ Capital < 1 Mill. inhabitants
▣ Statecapital > 1 Mill. inhabitants
◉ Statecapital < 1 Mill. inhabitants
□ Towns > 1 Mill. inhabitants
□ Towns 100 000 bis 1 Mill. inhabitants
□ Towns < 100 000 inhabitants

Morocco, Northwestern Algeria

Morocco and Algeria occupy the north-western edges of Africa. There are however major geographic and political differences between the two neighboring nations. Morocco's territory is dominated by the four sections of the 🏔 Atlas mountain system. The **Anti-Atlas range** in southern Morocco borders the Sahara Desert. The **High Atlas range**, the tallest section of the Atlas system, contains several mountains taller than 4,000 me-

ters. The central range of the Atlas Mountains borders a large fertile plateau called the Meseta. Northeastern Morocco is dominated by the **Rif Mountains**, the northernmost section of the Atlas Mountains in the country. Morocco contains only a small section of the Sahara but the Moroccan territory Western Sahara

The high mountains of the Atlas Range in Morocco. **Kg30**

Casablanca Morocco's largest city – important industrial and commercial center – major 🚢 port city – the 🕌 Grand Mosque Hassan II. (photo) can accommodate up to 100,000 worshippers. **Kg29**

Volubilis Capital of the 🏛 Roman province Mauritania Tingitania (42–285 AD) – historic ruins and mosaics – UNESCO site. **Kh28**

Fès (Fez) Royal city – 🕌 Fès al Bali (photo), a UNESCO world heritage site, with historic 🕌 mosques, Islamic schools – the tomb of the city's founder Moulay Idriss II. is a pilgrimage site. **Kh29**

Meknès 🕌 Royal City – UNESCO world heritage site – city gate Bab el-Mansour (photo) – royal palaces. **Kh29**

Marrakech 🕌 Royal city – historic 🏰 city wall, souks (Arab markets), and the 🕌 Koutoubia Mosque – Djemaâ el-Fna square (photo) with vendors and street performers – UNESCO world heritage site. **Kf30**

Tizi-n-Tichka Pass Mountain pass situated 2,260 meters above sea level in the 🏔 Atlas Mountains. **Kg30**

Aït Ben Haddou UNESCO world heritage site in Morocco – features ancient, ornamental adobe 🏰 casbahs built by the Ben Haddou Berbers on the edge of the 🏔 High Atlas mountain range. **Kg30**

Scale 1:4,500,000

0   40   80 Kilometers

Principal travel routes
- 🚗 Auto route
- 🚆 Rail road
- 🚢 Shipping route
- ⋯⋯ (dotted route)

Remarkable landscapes and natural monuments
- UNESCO World Natural Heritage
- Mountain landscape
- Rock landscape
- Ravine/canyon
- Cave
- Waterfall/rapids
- Desert
- Oasis
- National park (landscape)
- National park (flora)
- National park (fauna)
- National park (culture)
- Biosphere reserve
- Coastal landscape
- Beach

Morocco, Northwestern Algeria

(250,000 km²) consists almost entirely of desert. Western ⌖ **Sahara**, a former Spanish colony, was annexed by Morocco in the 1970s. The region has a population of around 250,000 and is believed to have valuable mineral resources. Morocco is a popular tourist destination and the country's attractions include the four so-called **royal cities**, historic North African architecture, and long sand ⌖ beaches on the Mediterranean coast.

The Moroccans have preserved many aspects of their traditional culture despite centuries of foreign influence. The Alaouite Dynasty has been the ruling family of Morocco continuously since the 17th century.
In contrast to Morocco's history of political stability, **Algeria** has experienced political unrest and armed conflicts since its independence from France in 1962. Northern Algeria is the most fertile and

densely populated region in the country. The majority of Algeria's more than 30 million inhabitants live in this region. Algeria's capital and largest city, **Algiers**, is situated on the country's Mediterranean coast. The **Tell mountain range** separates the fertile area on Algeria's Mediterranean coast from the country's interior. Further south, the **Sahara Atlas mountain range** rises to a maximum height of 2,328 meters above sea level.

Most of Algeria's territory (2,381,741 km²) is occupied by sections of the ⌖ Sahara Desert. The sand dunes of the **Grand Erg Occidental** – near Timimoun – are among the most fascinating natural attractions in the interior. The ⌖ **oasis towns of the M'zab region** contain distinct local architecture. This region is inhabited by the M'zabites, a Berber ethnic group with a unique culture developed during centuries of isolation.

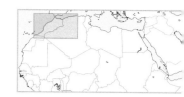

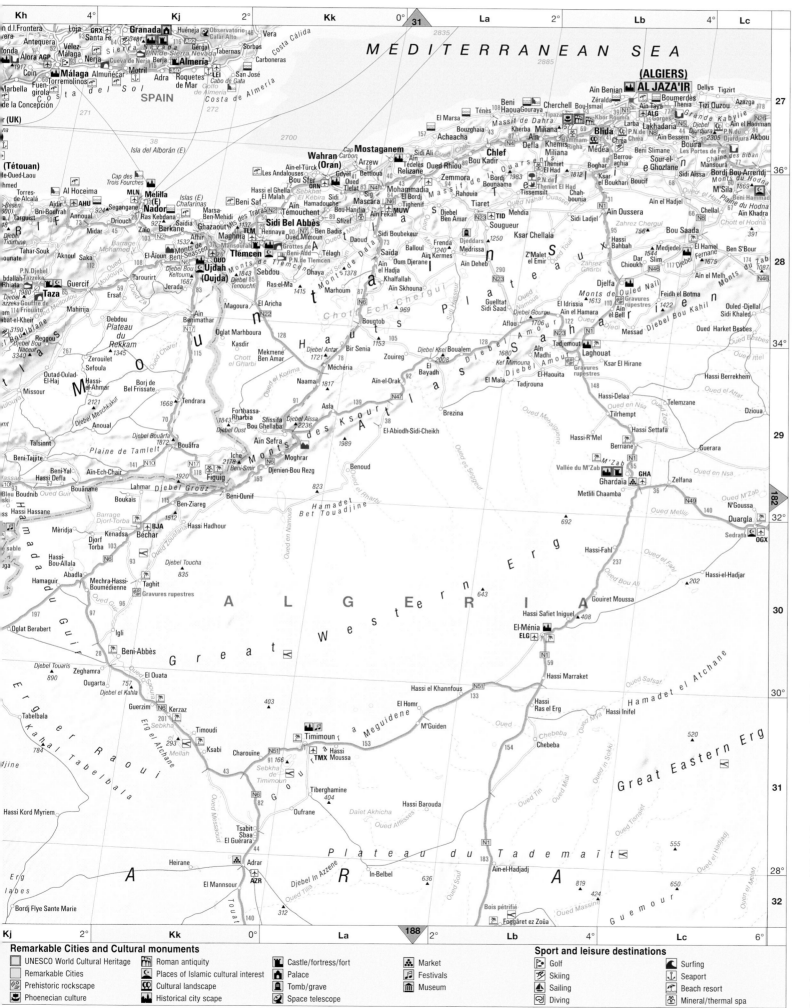

Drâa Valley Fertile ⌖ oasis on the Drâa River – numerous small farms, palm groves, traditional gardens, adobe villages, and historic kasbahs. **Kg-Kh30**

Todra Gorge Beautiful ⌖ gorge near the southern edge of the High Atlas mountain range – near Tinerhir. **Kh30**

Merzouga Large erg (stretch of ⌖ sand dunes) in southeastern Morocco near Tafilalt Oasis. **Kh30**

Tipaza Algerian town – former ⌖ Roman port founded by the Phoenicians – Kbor er Roumia tomb (photo) – UNESCO world heritage site. **Lb27**

Great Kabylie ⌖ Mountainous region in eastern Algeria – large Berber population – principal city, Tizi Ouzou – cedar forests – Djebel Djurdjura National Park. **Lb-Lc27**

Ghardaïa ⌖ Largest town in the M'zab Valley – UNESCO world heritage site – distinct culture of the M'zabite Berbers – the town's unique Saharan architecture inspired prominent modernist architects. **Lb29**

Taghit ⌖ Oasis village surrounding by large sand dunes – located in the Grand Erg Occidental – ⌖ historic rock carvings. **Kj30**

Remarkable Cities and Cultural monuments

- UNESCO World Cultural Heritage
- Remarkable Cities
- Prehistoric rockscape
- Phoenecian culture
- Roman antiquity
- Places of Islamic cultural interest
- Cultural landscape
- Historical city scape
- Castle/fortress/fort
- Palace
- Tomb/grave
- Space telescope
- Market
- Festivals
- Museum

Sport and leisure destinations

- Golf
- Skiing
- Sailing
- Diving
- Surfing
- Seaport
- Beach resort
- Mineral/thermal spa

Northeastern Algeria, Tunisia, Northern Libya

The Mediterranean coasts of Libya, Algeria, and Tunisia are home to more remnants of ancient 🏛 Roman civilization than any other region in Africa. Numerous temples, amphitheaters, villas, and aqueducts from the Roman era are scattered throughout this part of the continent. Like the other countries of North Africa, the culture of Libya, Tunisia, and Algeria was shaped mostly by **Arabs** who migrated to the region

from the Middle East during the 7th and 8th centuries. After their arrival in North Africa, the Arabs rapidly replaced the indigenous **Berbers** as the dominant ethnic group in the region. The Berber populations of Libya and Tunisia have largely adapted Arab culture and there are few significant differences between

A herd of camels near the Douz oasis in Tunisia. **Le29**

The Phoenicians In the 9th century BC, the Phoenicians founded the city of Carthage where Tunis now stands. The city became Rome's greatest challenger for control of the Mediterranean. The two powers fought three wars before Carthage was conquered.

The Romans in North Africa Around 44 BC, the Romans under the leadership of Caesar Augustus gained control over much of North Africa. The province of Africa Proconsularis encompassed most of modern Tunisia. Photos from top to bottom: Djemilla (**Lc27**), Sufetula (**Le28**), Djem (**Lf28**).

Tunis Tunisia's capital and principal city – historic 🕌 medina, a world heritage site with historic markets and mosques – 🏛 Bardo Museum – Roman and Phoenician ruins in 🏛 Carthage. **Lf27**

Kairouan 🕌 Religious center founded in 670 AD – historic medina: a world heritage site – 🕌 Sidi Oqba mosque (photo). **Lf28**

Sousse Port city with a vibrant 🕌 medina (photo), a UNESCO world heritage site – 🕌 Ribat, fortified complex and mosque built in the 9th century – kasbah. **Lf28**

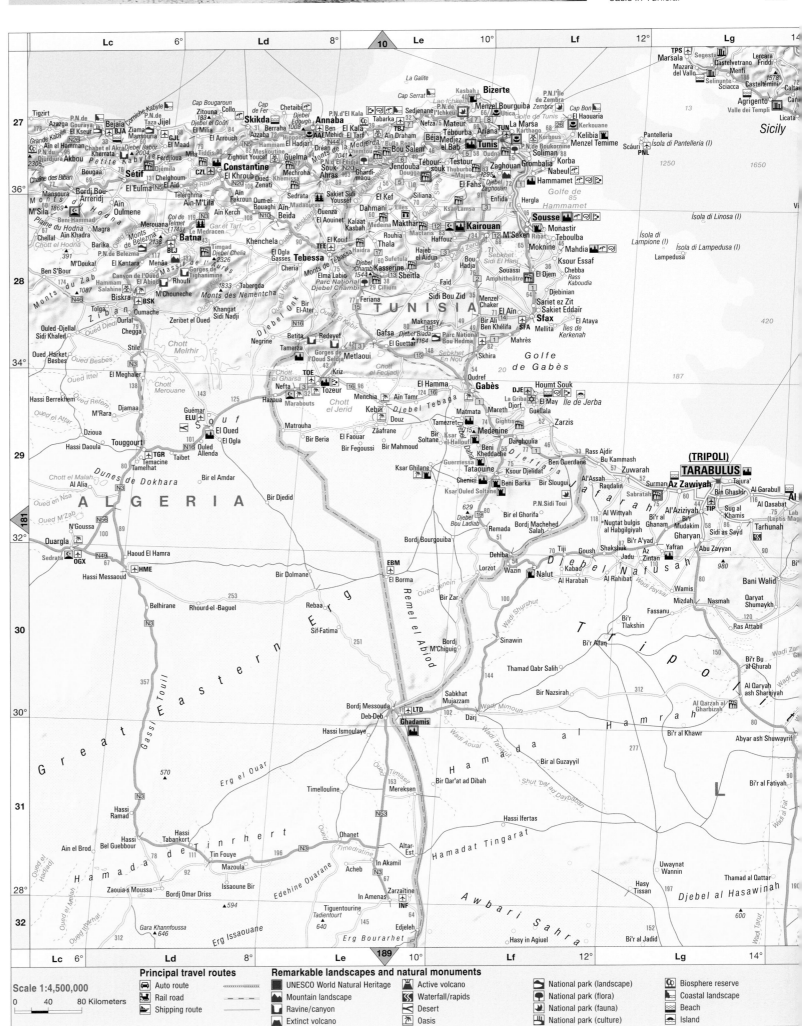

Scale 1:4,500,000
0   40   80 Kilometers

Principal travel routes
- 🚗 Auto route
- 🚂 Rail road
- Shipping route
- Mountain landscape
- Ravine/canyon

Remarkable landscapes and natural monuments
- ◼ UNESCO World Natural Heritage
- ▲ Active volcano
- Waterfall/rapids
- Desert
- Oasis
- Extinct volcano
- National park (landscape)
- National park (flora)
- National park (fauna)
- National park (culture)
- Biosphere reserve
- Coastal landscape
- Beach
- Island

the two ethnicities in Libya and Tunisia. In Algeria, a large segment of the Berber population retreated to the highlands of the Atlas Mountains after the Arabs arrived in the region. Because of their isolation, the Algerian Berbers were better able to preserve their languages and traditions.

Northeastern Algeria and most of Tunisia are dominated by the foothills and mountains of the **Atlas mountain system**. In contrast to these regions, **Libya** is dominated by the vast Sahara Desert. The desert extends through the country's interior and along the Mediterranean coast. Most of Libya's **desert** consists of flat monotonous fields of sand, unlike the deserts of Tunisia and Algeria, which contain many fascinating landscapes – including the sand dunes of the **Grand Erg Oriental** and numerous shining salt flats.

Tunisia, the smallest nation in North Africa, borders the Mediterranean Sea to the north and east. The country is one of the most popular tourist destinations in Northern Africa. Tunisia's attractions include its long Mediterranean **beaches**, the beautiful **mountain villages** of the Berbers, **desert oases**, and traditional markets. The coastline between the cities Djerba and Nabeul contains many modern hotels built with local North African architectural influences. **Libya's** main tourist attractions include its ancient **archeological sites** and desert interior. Islam is the dominant religion in all of the North African countries. In Algeria, tensions between Islamic fundamentalists and the country's government have led to political instability. In Tunisia, a moderate interpretation of Islam dominates society. Polygamy is forbidden and women have the same legal rights as men in the country.

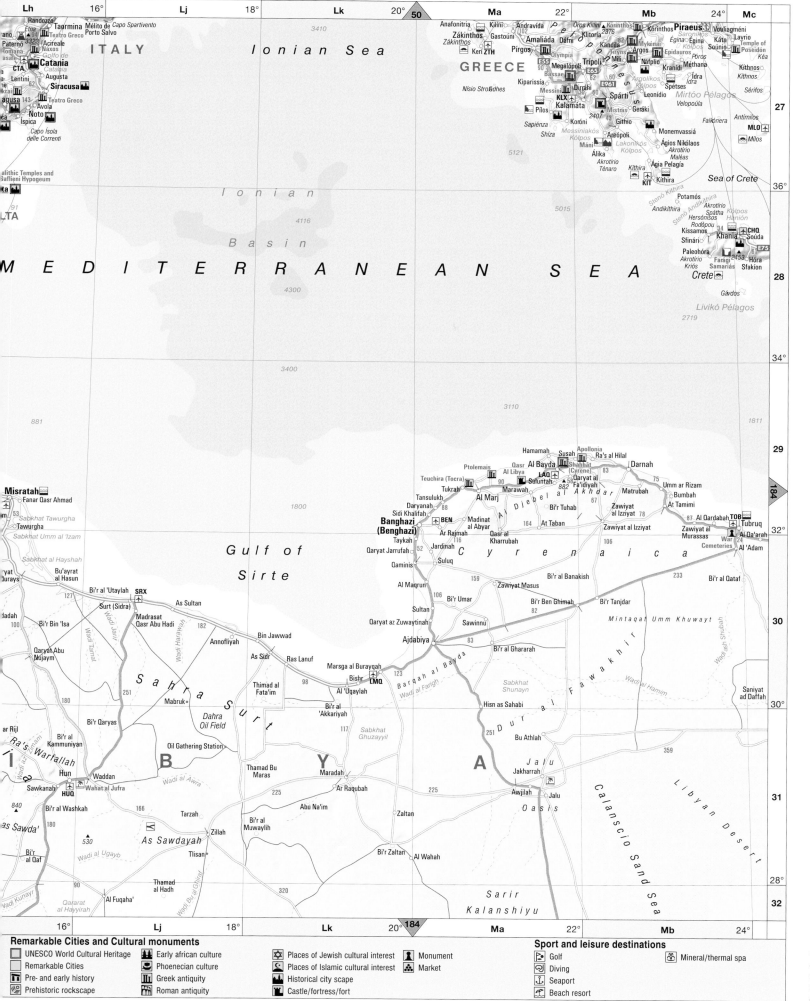

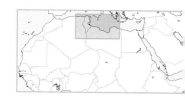

Djerba Island in the Gulf of Gàbes – Houmt Souk, a historic marketplace – La Ghirba synagogue – Jewish community since the 1st century AD – Berber architecture – sandy beaches. **Lf29**

Cave Dwellings in Matmata Unusual village in the highlands of southeastern Tunisia – underground dwellings – several scenes from the Star Wars films were filmed in the town. **Le29**

Tataouine Southernmost major town in Tunisia – historic mosque in Guermessa (photo), 20 kilometers from Tataouine. **Lf29**

Chenini Picturesque Berber village built on a hillside – cave dwellings – Mosque of the Seven Sleepers. **Lf29**

Sabratah Well preserved remnants of a Roman town on the Mediterranean coast – amphitheater, temple of Isis, and main plaza (forum) – world heritage site. **Lg29**

Leptis Magna Ancient city in Libya – birthplace of the "African" emperor Septimus Severus – site of the most beautiful ruins in North Africa – world heritage site. **Lh29**

Ghadamis UNESCO world heritage site – once a major trade center along a caravan route – walled old town – traditional Saharan architecture; white washed buildings and arched alleyways. **Le30**

Remarkable Cities and Cultural monuments

- UNESCO World Cultural Heritage
- Remarkable Cities
- Pre- and early history
- Prehistoric rockscape
- Early african culture
- Phoenecian culture
- Greek antiquity
- Roman antiquity
- Places of Jewish cultural interest
- Places of Islamic cultural interest
- Historical city scape
- Castle/fortress/fort
- Monument
- Market

Sport and leisure destinations

- Golf
- Diving
- Seaport
- Beach resort
- Mineral/thermal spa

Egypt

The Arab Republic of Egypt is situated between the **Red Sea** to the east, the **Mediterranean Sea** to the north, and the **Sahara Desert** to the west and south. The vast majority of Egypt's more than 70 million inhabitants are concentrated in around 5 % of the country's territory along the banks of the Nile. Most of Egypt's territory is covered by large sand or stony deserts. Egypt has an arid climate with high temperatures during

most of the year. During winter, nighttime temperatures in the deserts often fall below 0° C and the country's Mediterranean coast gets heavy rainfall.

The **Nile**, Africa's longest river, is the lifeline of Egypt. The Nile Valley, a fertile oasis on both sides of the river, has a maximum width of 25 kilometers and is surrounded

A tranquil section of the Nile Valley near Aswan. **Mg33**

by deserts. The Nile enters Egypt as Lake Nasser, a large reservoir created after the construction of the **Aswan High Dam** in the 1960s. The Nile Valley extends north from the lake to the area around **Cairo**. The Nile Delta is a fertile plain crossed by branches of the river and the most important center of agriculture in Egypt.

The **Suez Canal** connects the Red Sea to the Mediterranean Sea. The canal was completed in 1869 and remains one of the

Marsa Matruh The westernmost major city in Egypt – Cleopatra's Bath – bay on the Mediterranean Sea – Siwa Oasis. **Md30**

White Desert Between the Baharija and Farafra oases – stunning white limestone formations created by erosion. **Me32**

Cairo Egypt's capital has an impressive collection of Islamic art and architecture. The Mosque of Amr is the oldest mosque in Africa. During the 10th century, the Fatamid dynasty founded the Al-Azhar University, the oldest university in the Muslim world. The Sultan Hasa Mosque (top photo) was founded in the 14th century. Cairo's museums contain ancient Roman, Christian, and Islamic art. **Mf30**

Mount Catherine Monastery Located in southern Sinai on Mount Catherine (2,637 m) – Greek-Orthodox monastery with an important collection of religious icons – historic basilica. **Mg31**

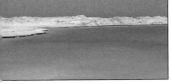

Red Sea Large coral reefs between Marsa Alam and Hurghada – good diving venues – abundant marine life. **Mh32**

St Simeon's Monastery Site of a monastic settlement between the 7th and 13th centuries – archeological site. **Mg33**

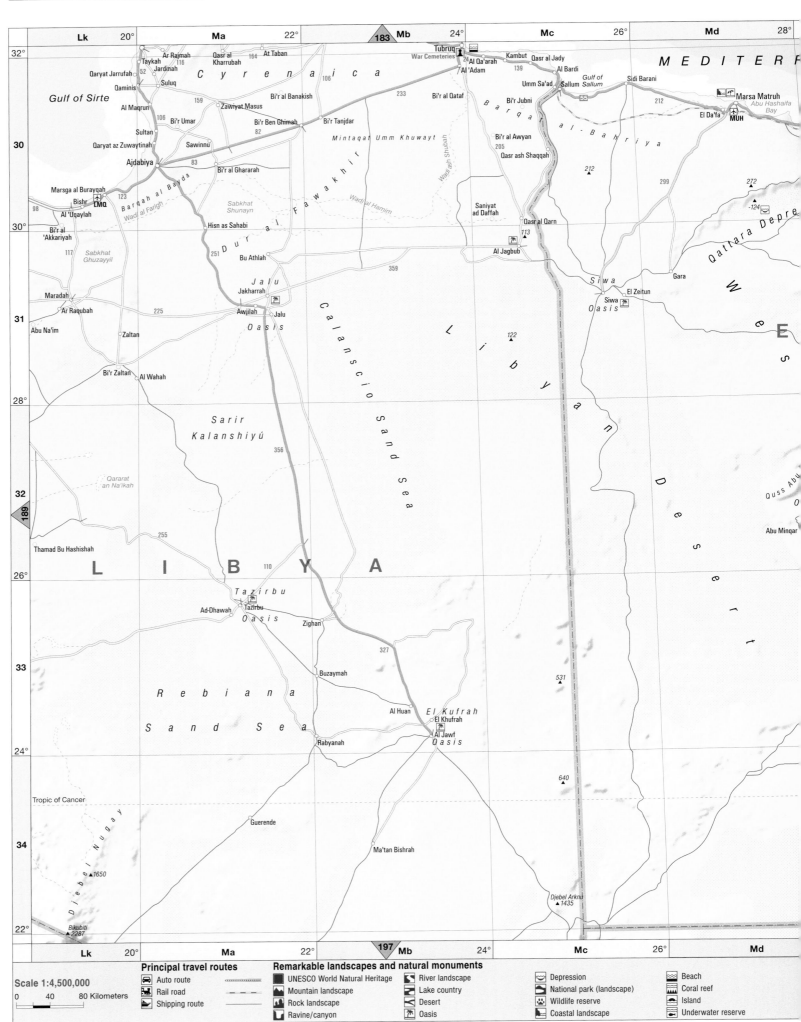

Scale 1:4,500,000
0   40   80 Kilometers

Principal travel routes
- Auto route
- Rail road
- Shipping route
- ---- (route line)

Remarkable landscapes and natural monuments
- UNESCO World Natural Heritage
- Mountain landscape
- Rock landscape
- Ravine/canyon
- River landscape
- Lake country
- Desert
- Oasis
- Depression
- National park (landscape)
- Wildlife reserve
- Coastal landscape
- Beach
- Coral reef
- Island
- Underwater reserve

Egypt

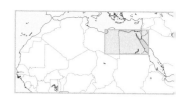

most economically important waterways in the world. East of the canal, the mountainous **Sinai Peninsula** is home to Egypt's tallest mountain, ⛰ Mount Catherine (2,637 m). The Sinai is also home to beautiful canyons and unique stone formations formed by erosion. The waters off the eastern coast of Egypt and around the Sinai Peninsula contain many colorful 🪸 **coral reefs**. The reefs with their biodiversity and natural beauty are popular

tourist attractions. Tourism is an important sector of the Egyptian economy. In addition to seaside resorts and beaches, Egypt's biggest attractions are its many historic and archeological sites. The country's cultural attractions include remnants from the civilization of the ancient Egyptians, ancient Christian monuments, and Islamic architecture.

During ancient times, important overland trade routes passed along a series of oases through the deserts of Egypt and Libya into the continent's interior. The **Qattara Depression** in Egypt's interior is situated 134 meters below sea level and is one of the lowest points in Africa. **Libya** has a total land area of approximately 1.76 million km². Most of the country consists of sandy deserts located in a large basin. In the far south of Libya the ⛰ **Tibesti Mountains** rise along the border to Chad. While the

southern and central sections of Libya have extremely arid climates, the country's coastal region has a pleasant Mediterranean climate. The coastal regions are home to more than 95 % of Libya's five million inhabitants. Of this population, a large minority are concentrated in two cities: **Benghazi** and the capital city **Tripoli**. Both cities and their surroundings are home to many well-preserved 🏛 ruins from the Roman era.

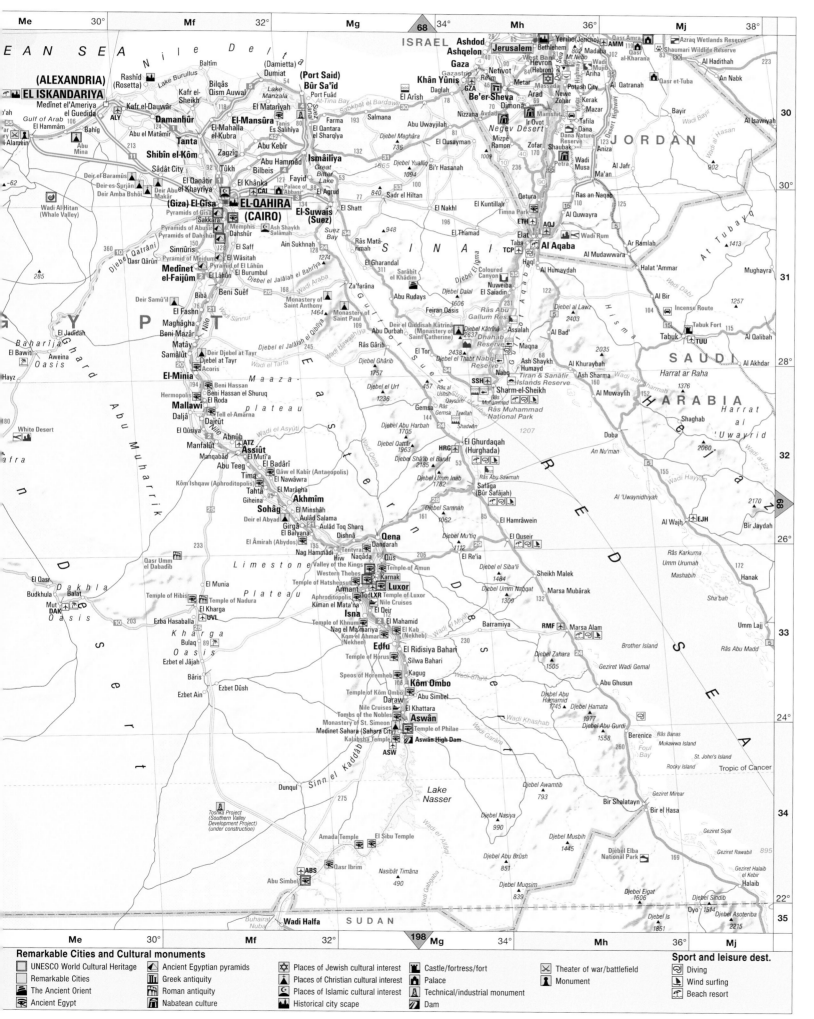

Ancient Egypt The age of the pharaohs encompasses thirty dynasties. The history of ancient Egypt is divided into three periods: the Old Kingdom (2660–2160 BC) – when most Egyptian pyramids were built, the Middle Kingdom (2040–1785 BC), and the New Kingdom (1552–1070 BC). The years between these three periods were times of conflict and instability. Egypt contains many remnants from the civilization of the pharaohs. Photos from top to bottom: Sphinx (Giza) (**Mf31**), Hatshepsut Temple, Tomb of Tutankhamen, Karnak (**Mg33**), Temple of Isis, Aswan (**Mg33**), El Seboua Temple, Lake Nasser (**Mg34**), Temple of Ramses II. (Abu Simbel) (**Mf34**).

Aswan City in southern Egypt – 🏝 Elephantine Island and the Temple of Satet (Satis) – 🌊 two large dams in the surrounding area – Aswan has the largest Nubian population of any Egyptian city – traditional 🏪 marketplaces. **Mg33**

Remarkable Cities and Cultural monuments

- ▢ UNESCO World Cultural Heritage
- ▢ Remarkable Cities
- The Ancient Orient
- Ancient Egypt
- Ancient Egyptian pyramids
- Greek antiquity
- Roman antiquity
- Nabatean culture
- Places of Jewish cultural interest
- Places of Christian cultural interest
- Places of Islamic cultural interest
- Historical city scape
- Castle/fortress/fort
- Palace
- Technical/industrial monument
- Dam
- Theater of war/battlefield
- Monument

Sport and leisure dest.

- Diving
- Wind surfing
- Beach resort

The 🏝 **Canary Islands** and the Moroccan territory of Western Sahara are separated by a narrow stretch of the Atlantic Ocean. The Canary Islands are situated off the northwestern coast of Africa. The island group belongs to Spain and consists of seven islands; **Gran Canaria**, **Tenerife**, **Lanzarote**, **La Palma**, **La Gomera**, **El Hierro**, and **Fuerteventura**. All of the islands are of volcanic origins but most of the volcanoes on the Cana-

ries are dormant. Popular tourist destinations for many decades, the Canary Islands are home to many beach resorts and fascinating diverse landscapes. The western and central islands are dominated by craggy volcanic peaks. In contrast to this, the landscapes on the geologically older eastern islands have been smooth-

Pico del Teide: the highest mountain on the Canary Islands. **Kb31**

The Canary Islands The seven Canary Islands are home to many contrasting landscapes. Ocean currents bring abundant rainfall to the smaller western islands. These islands **El Hierro**, **La Palma**, and **La Gomera** are home to lush green vegetation. Farther east, the island **Tenerife** contains stunning landscapes in its interior and beautiful beaches on its coast. **Gran Canaria** encompasses diverse landscapes including the beautiful stretch of sand dunes at Playa de Maspalomas. **Fuerteventura** and **Lanzarote** are the oldest islands in the group and contain mostly craggy volcanic landscapes. Photos from top to bottom: the observatory at Roque de Los Muchachos (La Palma) (**Kb31**), Agulo in northern La Gomera (**Kb31**), Garajonay National Park (**Kb31**), Pico del Teide (Tenerife) (**Kb31**), Playa de Maspalomas (Gran Canaria) (**Kc32**), Fuerteventura (**KcKd31**), Montañas del Fuego (Lanzarote) (**Kd31**).

Scale 1:4,500,000

0   40   80 Kilometers

Principal travel routes	Remarkable landscapes and natural monuments		
🚗 Auto route	■ UNESCO World Natural Heritage	🗻 Extinct volcano	🍃 Nature park
🚂 Rail road	▲ Mountain landscape	🗺 Cave	🏞 National park (landscape)
⚓ Shipping route	🪨 Rock landscape	⚔ Desert	🌸 National park (flora)
	🏔 Ravine/canyon	🌴 Oasis	🦌 National park (fauna)
			🔄 Biosphere reserve
			🏖 Coastal landscape
			🏖 Beach

ed by many centuries of erosion. The arrival of the Spanish colonists after the 15th century wiped out most traces of the indigenous African peoples who once inhabited the Canary Islands. The indigenous people, the Gaunches, are generally believed to have been related to the Berber ethnicities of mainland North Africa. Before the 1970s, the desert region between Morocco and Mauritania was Spanish Sahara, a territory of Spain. After

the sparsely populated region was granted its independence from Spain in 1976, the area was occupied by Morocco and Mauritania. Today the region is the Moroccan territory of **Western Sahara**. The local independence movement Polisario Front has campaigned, with the support of Algeria and often with violence, for the region's independence from Morocco. The majority of Western Sahara's around 250,000 inhabitants are

native **Sahrawis**. Western Sahara landscapes are dominated by gravel and sand deserts. There are numerous salt flats scattered throughout the region, and the **Grand Erg Oriental** – near the border to Algeria – contains large wandering sand dunes.

Many of the trade routes that once connected North Africa and Sub-Saharan Africa passed through the western sections of the Sahara. Many of the scattered

oasis towns in the region were once important trade centers. **Ouadâne** and **Chinguetti**, two oasis towns in Mauritania, are now both important pilgrimage sites for local Muslims. The two towns contain fascinating historic architecture including homes, libraries, and mosques made of adobe. Together with several other Mauritanian desert towns, Ouadane and Chinguetti, have been designated a UNESCO world heritage site.

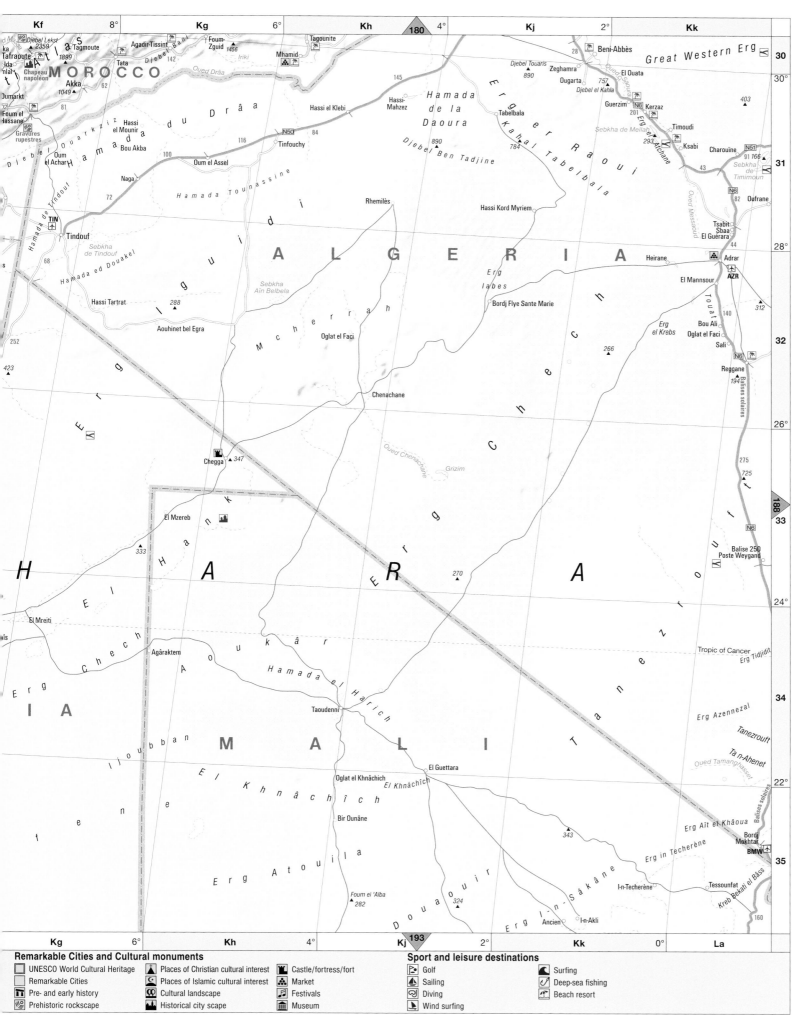

Anti-Atlas Mountain range in Morocco featuring many unusual granite formations. The region is the traditional homeland of several large Berber ethnic groups. The Chapeau Napoleon (top photo), a high stone hill, was named for its resemblance to Napoleon's hat. The red-colored villages around Tafraoute (middle photo) blend into their mountainous desert surroundings. February – when the almond trees bloom – is generally considered the best month to visit the region (bottom photo). **Kf31**

Tan-Tan The city is the administrive and economic center of Morocco's far south – camels are traded at the local livestock market (photo) once a week. **Ke31**

Adrar Principal town in the Touat oasis – dwellings made from red clay in traditional Saharan style – lively market. **Kk32**

Atâr Market in the Mauritanian desert – surrounded by gravel deserts, steep hills, and fields of sand dunes. **Kd35**

Adrar Massif Northeastern Mauritania – tall plateau shaped by erosion – a caravan route connecting Western Sahara and Morocco passes through the sparsely populated area. **Ke35**

Remarkable Cities and Cultural monuments

- ☐ UNESCO World Cultural Heritage
- ☐ Remarkable Cities
- ☐ Pre- and early history
- ☐ Prehistoric rockscape
- ☐ Places of Christian cultural interest
- ☐ Places of Islamic cultural interest
- ☐ Cultural landscape
- ☐ Historical city scape
- ☐ Castle/fortress/fort
- ☐ Market
- ☐ Festivals
- ☐ Museum

Sport and leisure destinations

- ☐ Golf
- ☐ Sailing
- ☐ Diving
- ☐ Wind surfing
- ☐ Surfing
- ☐ Deep-sea fishing
- ☐ Beach resort

Central Sahara

The ⬚ **Sahara Desert** occupies almost the entire northern half of the African continent. The center of the desert features interesting landscapes and cultural attractions. Five nations have borders in the central Sahara; Algeria, Libya, Chad, Niger, and Mali. Several ▲ mountain ranges form the highlands of the central Sahara including the **Hoggar** and **Tassili n'Ajjer** in Algeria, the **Aïr Mountains** in Niger, and the **Tibesti range** in Chad. All

of the mountain ranges in the central Sahara were formed during the Precambrian era and originally consisted of smooth granite, quartz, and crystallized stone. Erosion and volcanic activity altered the shape of the region's mountains and formed the many unique stone formations throughout the central Sahara.

Heavily eroded mountains in the Hoggar Range. **Lc-Lg34**

In Salah ⬚ Oasis in central Algeria – mosque and old town buildings made of red clay – surrounded by large sand dunes. **Lb32**

Tassili n'Ajjer National Park UNESCO world heritage site – mountainous desert region – 🖼 ancient rock paintings. **Le33**

Ancient Rock Paintings in the Desert Remnants of ancient cultures that once inhabited the Sahara are scattered through Tassili n'Ajjer National Park. Scientists believe the Sahara once experienced periods of heavy rainfall in the distant past. **Le32/33**

Hoggar Mountains Mountain range in the deserts of southern Algeria – eroded ▲ volcanoes – inhabited by Tuareg communities – main settlement, Tamanrasset. **Lc-Ld34**

Tuareg merchants once dominated trade in the Sahara. The Tuareg are now scattered throughout the Sahara and the northern Sahel. Though related to the Berbers, the Tuareg have a unique culture and social structure.

Iferouâne ⬚ Oasis in the Aïr Mountains of Niger – large Tuareg community – 🖼 Aïr-Ténéré National Park. **Le36**

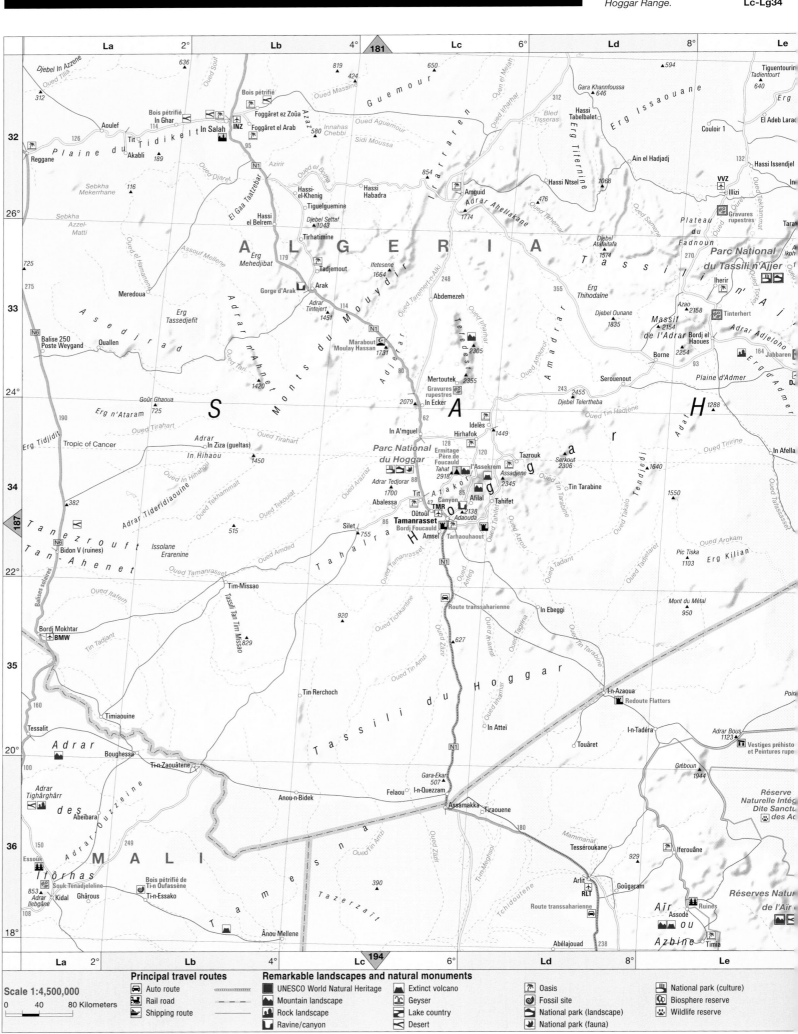

Scale 1:4,500,000
0   40   80 Kilometers

Principal travel routes
- 🚗 Auto route
- 🚆 Rail road
- 🚢 Shipping route

Remarkable landscapes and natural monuments
- ▪ UNESCO World Natural Heritage
- ▲ Mountain landscape
- 🗻 Rock landscape
- Ravine/canyon
- ▪ Extinct volcano
- Geyser
- Lake country
- Desert
- Oasis
- Fossil site
- National park (landscape)
- National park (fauna)
- National park (culture)
- Biosphere reserve
- Wildlife reserve

Central Sahara

The Hoggar Mountains are home to many dark chimney-shaped formations created by volcanic activity. The highlands of **Libya** and the Tibesti Mountains encompass many small lakes that glitter under the desert sun.

The tallest mountain ranges in the central Sahara rise more than 3,000 meters above seal level. Emi Koussi (3,415 m) in the Tibesti Mountains is the highest mountain in the region.

During prehistoric times, the highlands of the central Sahara were inhabited by hunter and gatherer populations which later turned to raising livestock for survival. Many ancient stone carvings and **rock paintings** depicting wild animals, livestock, gods, and dances have been found throughout the region. Many of the ancient paintings indicate that many sections of the Sahara were fertile and hospitable areas 10,000 years ago. The southern sections of the central Sahara contain many ergs – large fields of sand dunes. Most of the remaining salt caravans of the Tuareg people pass through the **Ténéré Desert** – a barren wilderness located east of the Aïr Mountains. During winter, powerful sand storms are common in the desert. The Tuareg caravans carry sorghum to oasis communities which they exchange for salt with local people. This trading relationship between the Tuareg and the isolated oasis villages of the Central Sahara has existed for centuries.

The **Tuareg** were once called the "knights of the Sahara" by Europeans because of their traditional weapons and the hierarchical structure of their society. Centuries ago, Tuareg merchants controlled trade throughout the Sahara and Tuareg warriors were feared by most communities in the Central Sahara.

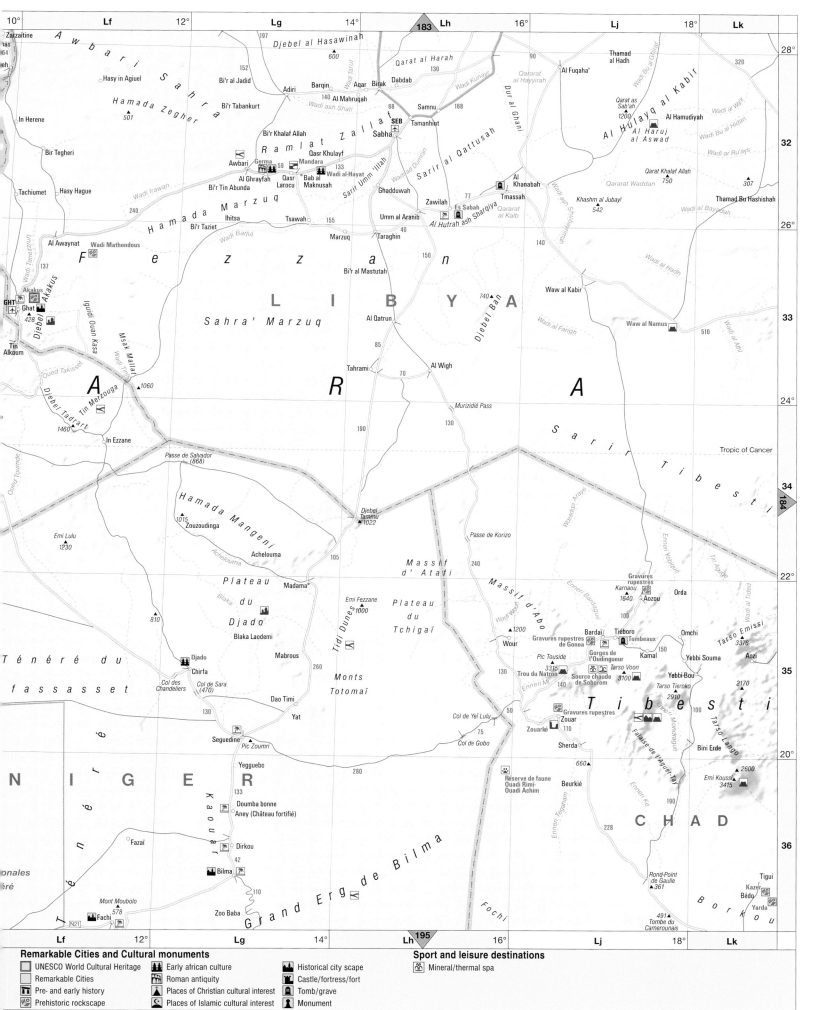

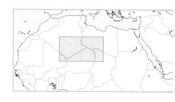

Acacus Mountains Mountain range in Libya with interesting stone formations – sand dunes and canyons – the Fozzigiaren stone arch (photo). **Lf33**

Prehistoric Art in the Acacus Mountains UNESCO world heritage site – ancient depictions of animals, dances, and peoples – between 2,000 and 20,000 years old. **Lf33**

Ghat Oasis in the Acacus Mountains – beautiful abandoned old town with narrow alleys – abandoned French fort. **Lf33**

Tin Merzouga Tassili n'Ajjer – desert landscapes – red sand dunes and tall column-shaped stone formations. **Lf33/34**

Ancient Burial Sites of Fezzan Burial site of ancient sultans in the Libya's Fezzan region – Sahel style architecture with significant Hausa influences. **Lh32**

Waw al Namus Volcano crater with a diameter of ten kilometers – a colorful saline lake is located inside the crater. **Lj33**

Stone Arches of the Djado Plateau Mountainous plateau in the Tenere Desert (Niger) – ruins of Djado – major center of overland trade until the 19th century. **Lg35**

Cape Verde Islands, Senegal, Gambia

Historians remain divided on the question of whether or not Greek sailing vessels traveled to the coast of Senegal during ancient times. In 1445, the Venetian sailor Alvise de Mosto reached the uninhabited **Cape Verde Islands** aboard a Portuguese trade ship. The Portuguese had already established their first base on mainland Africa near the Senegal River delta a decade before Mosto explored the Cape Verde Islands. Eventually the Cape

Verde Islands became a major center of the slave trade as a station between the mainland coast, where most slaves originated, and the European colonies in the Americas. This dark chapter of the region's history continued for several centuries before the slave trade was finally ended in the 19th century.

The beautiful old town of Mindelo on the island Saõ Vicentes. **Jh37**

Trarza ⊠ Desert region south of Nouakchott in Mauritania – inhabited by nomadic camel herders (photo). **Kc37**

Nouakchott Capital of Mauritania – ⊠ attractive mosques built in typical North African style – important ⊠ market – the city was a small fishing village before it became the nation's capital in 1958. **Kc36**

Cape Verde Islands The island group near the coast of mainland Africa is home to Iberian style colonial ⊠ architecture on Saõ Vicente, ⊠ sandy beaches on the islands Sal and Maio, beautiful cliffs on ⊠ Santo Antão (top photo, **Jh37**), and the volcano ⊠ Pico on Fogo (bottom photo, **Jh38**).

Saint Louis Former capital of the French colony Senegal – Mauritania – ⊠ colonial architecture – ⊠ beaches. **Kb37**

Dakar Senegal's capital city – modern business and port district, Ville Nouvelle (photo) – old town with ⊠ markets and colonial buildings. **Kb38**

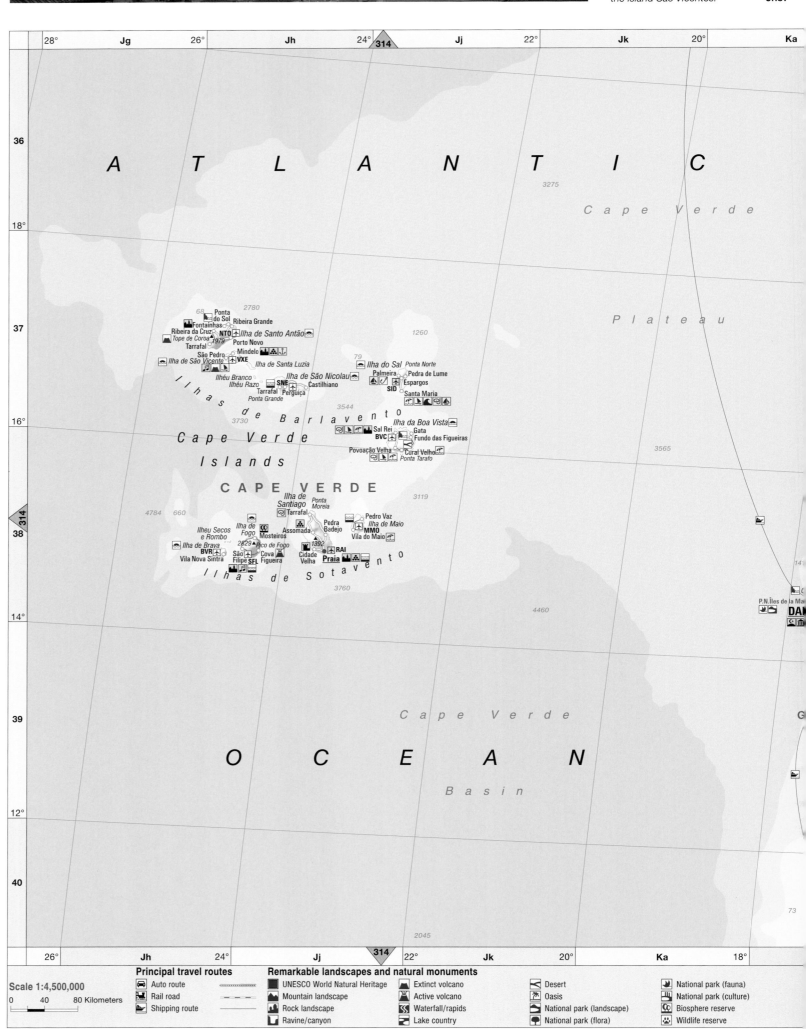

Scale 1:4,500,000

0   40   80 Kilometers

Principal travel routes
- 🚗 Auto route
- 🚂 Rail road
- ⛴ Shipping route

Remarkable landscapes and natural monuments
- ■ UNESCO World Natural Heritage
- Mountain landscape
- Rock landscape
- Ravine/canyon
- Extinct volcano
- Active volcano
- Waterfall/rapids
- Lake country
- Desert
- Oasis
- National park (landscape)
- National park (flora)
- National park (fauna)
- National park (culture)
- Biosphere reserve
- Wildlife reserve

Cape Verde is an archipelago of ten major islands and numerous smaller islands with a total land area of 4,033 km². Uninhabited until the arrival of the Portuguese, the Cape Verde Islands now have a diverse population. Around 71 % of the Cape Verde Island's population is of mixed white European and black African descent. Most of the remaining population is of black African (28 %) or Portuguese (1 %) descent. The majority of the country's population is concentrated on two islands: **Santiago** and **Saõ Vicente**.

The Cape Verde Islands are all of volcanic origin and there are several active volcanoes in the archipelago. In 1995, the volcano **Pico** (2,829 m) on the island of Fogo was the site of a major eruption. The large western islands have mountainous interiors with many gorges and coastal cliffs.

On the African mainland between the deserts of Mauritania and the tropical forests of Guinea lies a strip of savannahs that stretches through most of Senegal and sections of Mali. The northern regions of Senegal and Mali are both occupied by sections of the Sahel, an arid transition zone south of the Sahara Desert. Severe droughts are common in both countries. The basin of the **Casamance River** in Senegal is a fertile region with abundant rainfall and lush vegetation. **Niokolo-Koba National Park** in southern Senegal is home to expansive tropical rainforests.

Senegal was a French colony for centuries and French remains the dominant language of commerce, government and education in the country. The country's capital Dakar is generally considered one of the most beautiful and culturally vibrant cities in West Africa.

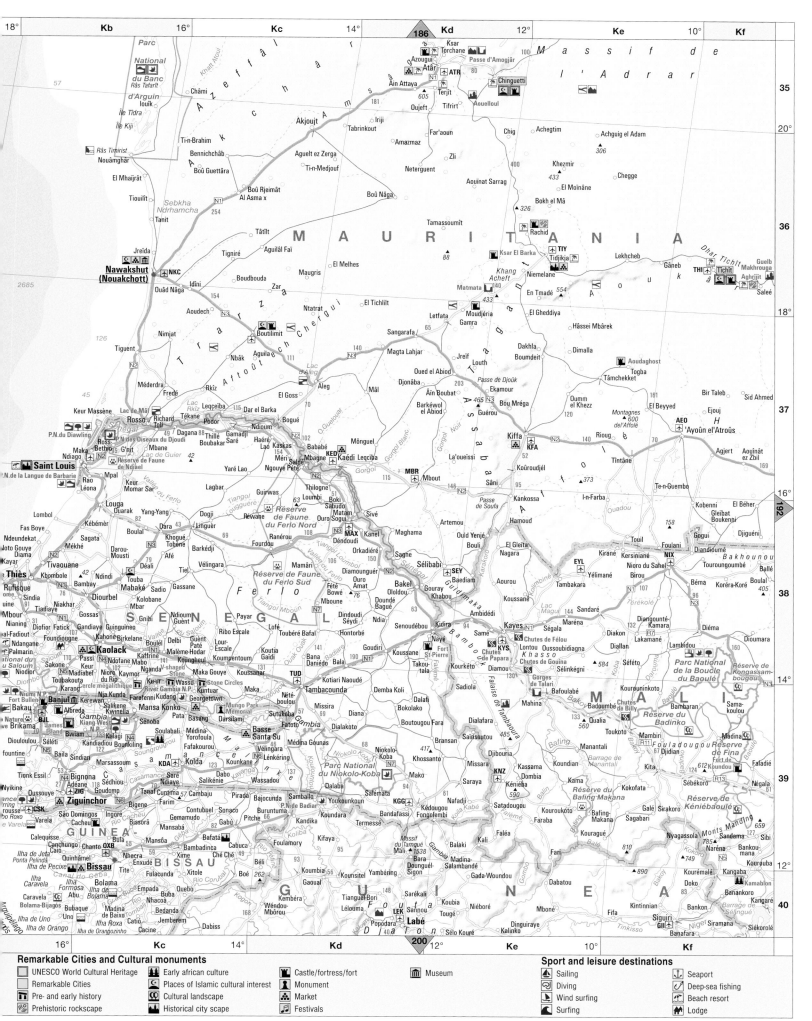

Gorée Island was a major station for European slave ships. At least two million Africans were transported from the island to slavery in the Americas. The island is now a UNESCO world heritage site with several historic sites linked to the brutal slave trade. Kb38

Mbour Coastal town located south of Dakar – traditional fishing industry – large resort hotels – beaches (photo). Kb38

Touba Important spiritual center of the Murid Muslims, Senegal's largest religious community – Great Mosque (photo). Kc38

Brikama Fishing village in Gambia – center of traditional wood carving and drum production. Kb39

Gambia River 1,120 kilometers – important transport route – fertile basin – photo: village near Banjul. Kb-Kc39

Wassu Stone Circles Prehistoric stone monument in eastern Senegal – consists of several stone pillars up to 2.5 meters tall – may have once been used as burial site or for religious ceremonies. Kc39

Remarkable Cities and Cultural monuments

- UNESCO World Cultural Heritage
- Remarkable Cities
- Pre- and early history
- Prehistoric rockscape
- Early african culture
- Places of Islamic cultural interest
- Cultural landscape
- Historical city scape
- Castle/fortress/fort
- Monument
- Market
- Festivals
- Museum

Sport and leisure destinations

- Sailing
- Diving
- Wind surfing
- Surfing
- Seaport
- Deep-sea fishing
- Beach resort
- Lodge

Mali

The ⬛ Niger, Africa's third longest river, flows from its source in the highlands of Guinea to the arid and ⬛ semi-arid regions of Mali and Niger. The crescent-shaped river has one of the most unusual forms of any major waterway in the world. The river's course was a mystery to the western world for many centuries and several explorers lost their lives while attempting to study the Niger. The Niger flows northeast from Guinea

into Mali, where it continues to flow northeast through the country's desert. In eastern Mali, the Niger suddenly changes direction and the river flows south into the neighboring country Niger. Farther south, the river enters Nigeria and flows to its delta on the Gulf of Guinea coast.

Wetlands along the banks of the Niger River in the region of Gao. **Kk37**

Chinguetti Mauritanian trade center – ⬛ historic mosque, a pilgrimage site – ⬛ old town with abandoned homes buried beneath sand dunes. **Kd35**

Tichît On the caravan route between Chinguetti and Timbuktu – ⬛ desert region with large sand dunes. **Kf36**

Falaise de Tambaoura ⬛ Stone hills near Kayes in western Mali – highest point, 485 meters. **Ke39**

Bamako Capital city of Mali – lively ⬛ Marché Rose market (photo) – ⬛ National Museum with traditional masks and relics. **Kf39**

Mopti Port city on the Niger River – ⬛ adobe mosque (photo) – large ⬛ marketplace near the harbour where local products are sold – center for the production of traditional Fulbe clothing. **Kh38**

Djenné ⬛ Ancient trade center on the Bani River – Islamic schools and ⬛ mosques – large adobe mosques – ⬛ weekly market – UNESCO world heritage site. **Kh39**

Korientzé Port city on the Niger River – beautiful traditional architecture – ⬛ historic mosque – ⬛ livestock market. **Kj38**

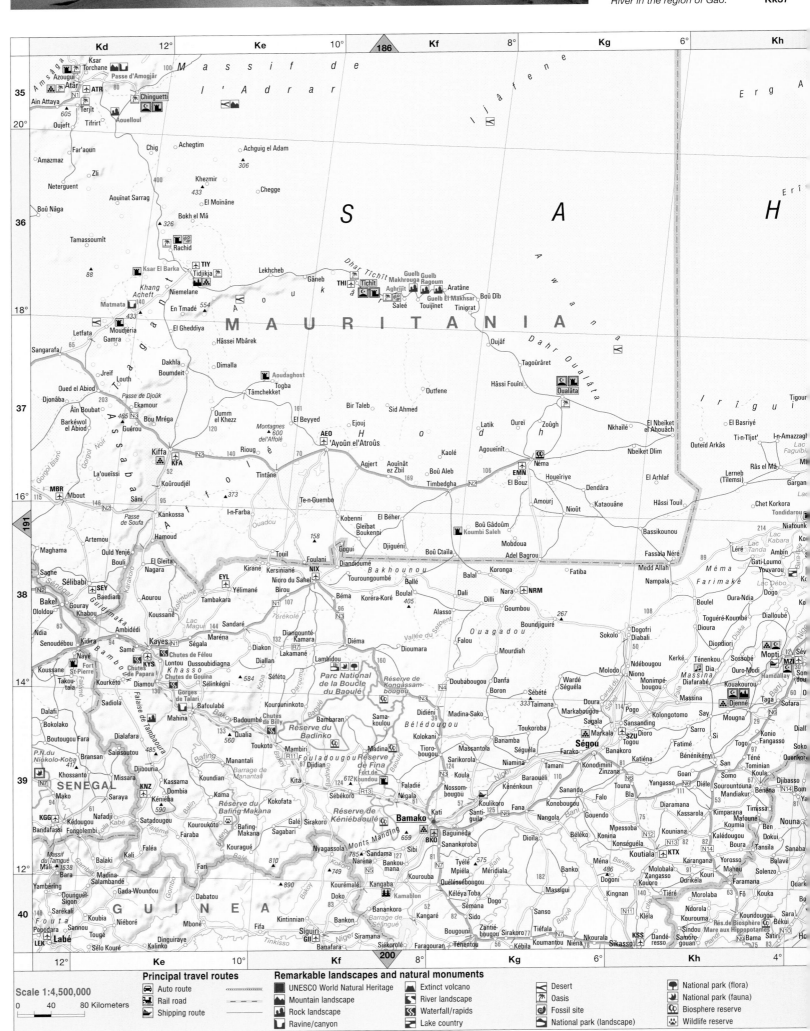

Scale 1:4,500,000

0   40   80 Kilometers

Principal travel routes
- 🚗 Auto route
- 🚂 Rail road
- 🚢 Shipping route

Remarkable landscapes and natural monuments
- ⬛ UNESCO World Natural Heritage
- ⬛ Mountain landscape
- ⬛ Rock landscape
- ⬛ Ravine/canyon
- ⬛ Extinct volcano
- ⬛ River landscape
- ⬛ Waterfall/rapids
- ⬛ Lake country
- ⬛ Desert
- ⬛ Oasis
- ⬛ Fossil site
- ⬛ National park (landscape)
- ⬛ National park (flora)
- ⬛ National park (fauna)
- ⬛ Biosphere reserve
- ⬛ Wildlife reserve

Mali

The Niger has been an important 🚢 transportation route over the centuries and many important cities and trade bases developed along the river's banks. Centuries ago, **Timbuktu** was a wealthy center of trade and education. In many cultures, the name Timbuktu has become a synonym for distant and exotic places. Timbuktu's golden age has long ended and a small settlement between the Sahara and the Niger River is all that remains of the

once glorious African city. Other ancient cities near the Niger River including Mali's capital **Bamako** have continued to grow in population and economic importance. Only ruins remain of **Kumbi (Koumbi Saleh)**, the last capital of the powerful Ghana Empire and once the largest city in West Africa. Today few caravans travel through the southern Sahara. Most modern caravans are led by Berber or Tuareg salt traders who carry their pro-

ducts from northern Mali to river ports on the Niger.

Mali and **Niger** are two of the most sparsely populated countries in Africa. Both countries have land areas of around 1.3 million km² and around ten million inhabitants. The arid northern sections of Mali and Niger are the most sparsely populated regions in both countries.

Burkina Faso, known as Upper Volta before 1984, is located south of Mali

and Niger. The country has a total area of 274,000 km² and its territory consists mostly of savannahs. The countryside is home to vast plains and numerous small villages consisting of adobe structures. More than 160 distinct ethnic groups inhabit the country. The Mossi people are the largest ethnic group in the country. Between the 11th and 19th centuries the Mossi ruled a large and powerful empire.

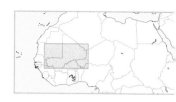

Timbuktu (Tombouctou) Historic city in Mali – 🕌 Sankore and Djinguere-Ber mosques – 🛒 Tuareg markets – UNESCO world heritage site.　　　**Kj37**

Goundam River port on a tributary of the Niger River – 🕌 mosque in traditional Sudanese style (photo).　　　**Kj37**

Niger River Important 🚢 transport route (4,160 km) – the river flows through West Africa, from Guinea to Nigeria.　　　**Kk37**

Hombori Highlands Heavily eroded 🏔 plateau in Mali – highest point, Hombori Tondo (1,155 m).　　　**Kj38**

The central plateau of Mali is home to the **Dogon**, a people who have preserved many aspects of their culture. Photos from top to bottom: Bandiagara cliffs, Dogon village, Dogon in traditional masks.　　　**Kj38**

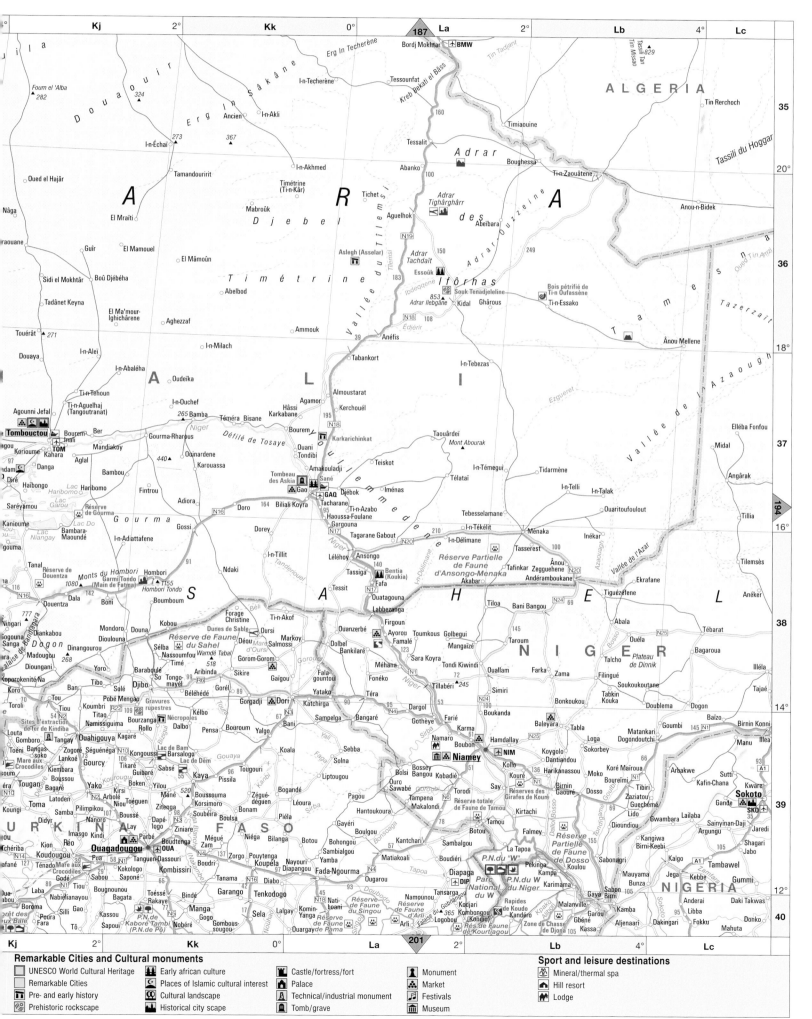

Arab traders and cartographers named the transition zone between Sahara and the savannahs of Africa the **Sahel**, an Arabic word for shore or boundary. Drought and land erosion are common problems throughout the Sahel. For centuries, the Sahel has been expanding into once fertile regions to its south. Desertification has also expanded the Sahara into areas that were once part of the Sahel. ⊡ **Lake Chad** is one of the

most interesting geographic features in the Sahel. The lake is the remnant of an ancient inland sea that once covered a large section of western Africa. After the climate in the region changed and the Sahara began to expand, the inland sea was greatly reduced in size. Although several rivers flow into Lake Chad, the

The barren Ténéré Desert in north-eastern Niger. Le36/37

Teguidda-n-Tessoumt Important center of salt production in Niger – salt is produced using ancient techniques – the salt mines are open to visitors. **Ld37**

Agadez Historic trade and political center on the edge of the Aïr Mountains – 🕌 adobe mosque built in the 15th century (photo) – important regional market – home to the Aïr-Tuareg sultans. **Ld37**

Niamey Capital city of Niger – population of 400,000 – 🏪 markets – 🏛 Anthropology Museum (photo: national day). **Lb39**

W National Park 🐘 National Park in Niger between forests and savannahs – UNESCO world heritage site – elephant, buffalo, and hippopotamus populations. **Lb39**

Zaria One of several historic 🏛 Hausa city states (pop. 360,000) in northern Nigeria – 🏛 historic palace (photo) – the city is surrounded by a well preserved defensive wall – large traditional 🏪 marketplace. **Ld40**

Kainji Lake National Park Nigeria's oldest national park – 5,340 km² of savannahs and forests – buffalo, warthog, baboon, and waterbuck populations. **Lc41**

Scale 1:4,500,000

0   40   80 Kilometers

Principal travel routes
- Auto route
- Rail road
- Shipping route

Remarkable landscapes and natural monuments
- UNESCO World Natural Heritage
- Mountain landscape
- Rock landscape
- Ravine/canyon
- Extinct volcano
- Geyser
- River landscape
- Waterfall/rapids
- Lake country
- Desert
- Oasis
- National park (landscape)
- National park (flora)
- National park (fauna)
- Biosphere reserve
- Wildlife reserve

lake continues to decrease in size every year. Lake Chad now covers a maximum area of 17,000 km² but its area varies significantly depending on the level of rainfall in the region.

Baobab trees, acacias, bushes and hard grass are the most common types of vegetation found throughout the Sahel. The semi-nomadic **Tuareg** and **Fulbe** peoples both graze livestock in the Sahel regions of southern Niger and northern Nigeria.

In contrast to the western sections of the Sahara, the desert regions of **northern Niger** offer many interesting and unique landscapes. The region contains the beautiful natural terraces in the ⛰ Aïr Mountain range and the vast sand dune fields of the Ténéré Desert – located in the ⬚ **Aïr et du Ténéré National Nature Reserve**. Unique stone formations, **Aïr-Tuareg** villages, and the historic town of ⬚ **Agadez** are just a few of the

numerous noteworthy tourists attractions in northern Niger.

Between the 16th and 19th centuries, the city states of the Hausa people flourished throughout **southern Niger** and **northern Nigeria**. ⬚ **Sokoto**, **Kano**, and **Zaria** in Nigeria as well as **Maradi** and **Zinder** in Niger were all powerful city states which often formed alliances and fought wars against one another. The power of the city states came to an

abrupt end after European colonizers gained control of the region. Some of the cities and towns in the region feature historic palaces and mosques built when the city states were at their most powerful. Despite influence from other cultures, the Hausa still value their culture and traditional social structures. Symbolic visits from members of the nobility are common during ceremonies in Hausa communities.

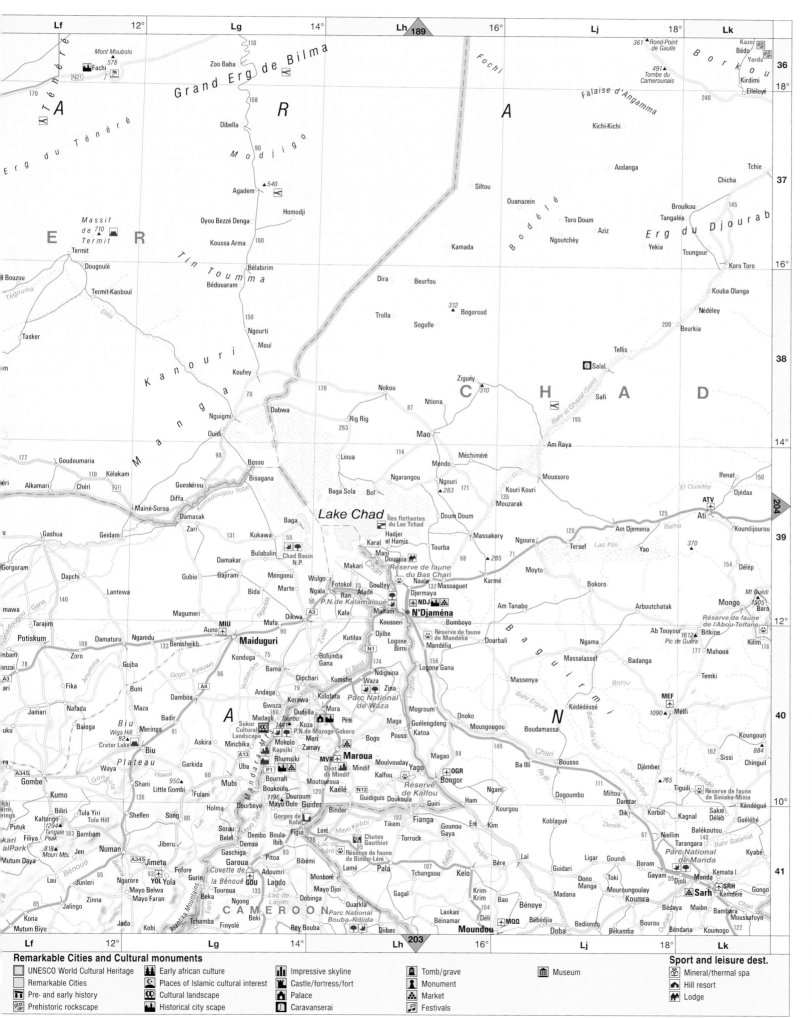

Aïr et du Ténéré National Nature Reserve ⬚ The sand dunes and the granite mountains of the Aïr range are inhabited by a variety of rare desert animals including antelopes and ostriches. The reserve is a UNESCO world heritage site. **Le36/37**

Fachi ⬚ Oasis on the caravan route between Agadez and Blima – rest stop with subterranean wells (photo) – ⬚ traditional adobe architecture. **Lf36**

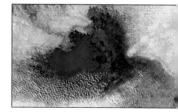

Lake Chad Shallow lake with a maximum depth of 1.5 meters – maximum area (during rainy season) of around 20,000 km² – large hippopotamus populations. **Lg-Lh38/39**

Mandara Mountains The local people live in small villages (top photo) and cultivate their land in northern Cameroon and Nigeria according to ancient methods of terrace farming and livestock (bottom photo) grazing. **Lg40**

Remarkable Cities and Cultural monuments

- ⬚ UNESCO World Cultural Heritage
- ⬚ Remarkable Cities
- ⬚ Pre- and early history
- ⬚ Prehistoric rockscape
- ⬚ Early african culture
- ⬚ Places of Islamic cultural interest
- ⬚ Cultural landscape
- ⬚ Historical city scape
- ⬚ Impressive skyline
- ⬚ Castle/fortress/fort
- ⬚ Palace
- ⬚ Caravanserai
- ⬚ Tomb/grave
- ⬚ Monument
- ⬚ Market
- ⬚ Festivals
- ⬚ Museum

Sport and leisure dest.
- ⬚ Mineral/thermal spa
- ⬚ Hill resort
- ⬚ Lodge

Northern Chad

Northern **Chad** is situated on the eastern edges of the central Sahara Desert. The sparsely populated region is relatively unexplored and remains difficult to access. The **Tibesti Mountain** range is an ancient group of volcanoes in northern Chad and southernmost Libya. Many of the ancient ▲ volcanoes' peaks collapsed after the mountains became inactive leaving behind gigantic craters, which often contain small lakes.

Many deep and narrow ⊔ gorges cut through the older sections of the Tibesti Mountain range. Water from rainfall and underground springs often accumulates inside the gorges, transforming them into fertile oases with lush vegetation. Because of the labyrinth-like shape of the gorges in the Tibesti Mountains, many are

Trou du Natron: an ancient caldera in the Tibesti Mountains. **Lj35**

Bardai Fertile ☑ oasis at the foot of the Tibesti Mountains – ancient ☑ rock paintings and pre-Islamic burial sites. **Lj35**

Rock Paintings of Gonoa ☑ Prehistoric art including depictions of people, elephants, cattle, and giraffes. **Lj35**

Tibesti Mountains The mountain range is located mostly in northern Chad but also extends into the neighboring countries of Libya and Niger. The ancient highlands extend over an area of more than 100,000 km² and feature a variety of interesting natural attractions including volcanic craters up to ten kilometers in diameter and the mountain Emi Koussi. **Lj-Lk35**

Zouar Oasis Located on the edge of the Tibesti Mountains – Zoarke Valley has water holes (gueltas) and dense vegetation – ancient rock paintings. **Lj35**

Faya ☑ Oasis city and important ⊔ trade center for Tubu and Daza merchants in central Chad – along the caravan route between Lake Chad and Sudan. **Lk37**

Salai Caravansary One of several ⊔ trade centers along the caravan route between Lake Chad and Tripoli via Largeau (Faya) – livestock market. **Lj38**

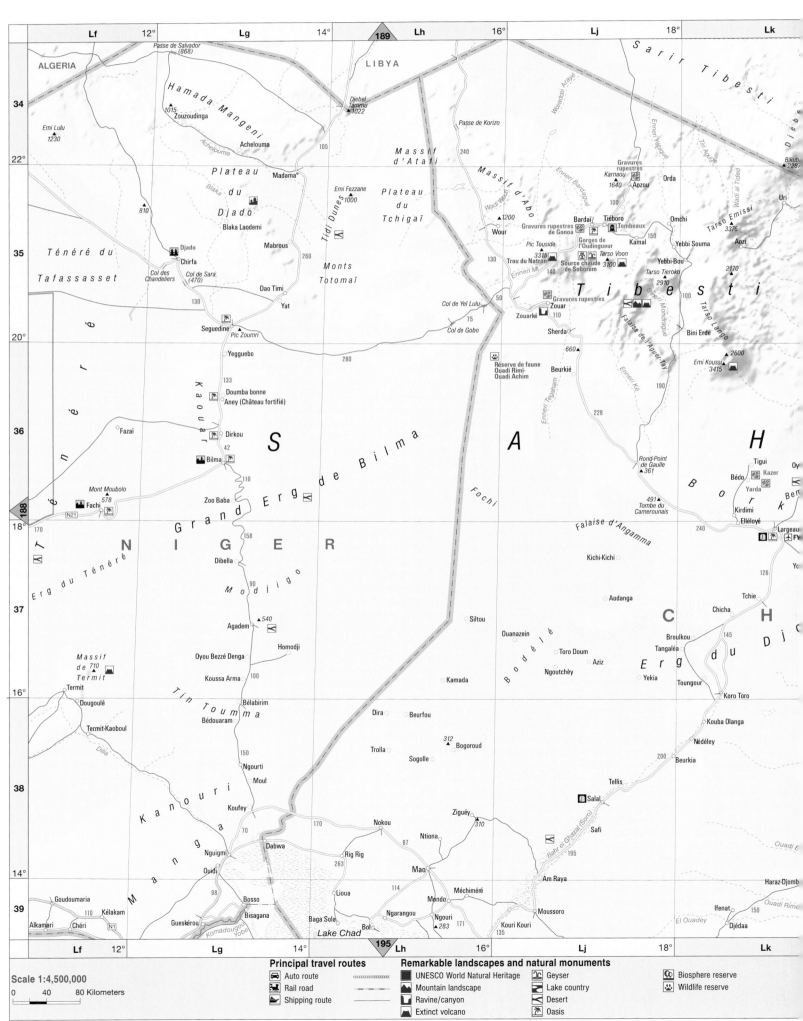

Scale 1:4,500,000

0   40   80 Kilometers

Principal travel routes
- 🚗 Auto route
- 🚆 Rail road
- 🚢 Shipping route

Remarkable landscapes and natural monuments
- ■ UNESCO World Natural Heritage
- ☑ Mountain landscape
- ☑ Ravine/canyon
- ▲ Extinct volcano
- ☑ Geyser
- ☑ Lake country
- ☑ Desert
- ☑ Oasis
- ☑ Biosphere reserve
- ☑ Wildlife reserve

difficult to access and are rarely visited by people from outside the region.

The Tubu, a semi-nomadic group of livestock breeders, are one of the larger ethnic groups in the isolated highlands. They have a reputation as an independent people that avoids contact with other communities. For centuries, the Tubu resisted the domination of Islamic sultans and continue to resist the influence of modern Chad's central government.

To the south, Chad borders the junction of Nigeria, Niger, and Cameroon around **Lake Chad**.

As in other areas of the Sahara, several caravan routes once passed through northern Chad. These routes were, however, far more dangerous and less widely traveled than most other caravan routes through the Sahara. In the 19th century, western explorers traveled to northern Chad to study the region. Some

of these explorers lost their lives there and northern Chad has remained a dangerous area for outsiders, even in modern times. The region's underdeveloped infrastructure, the xenophobia of the Tubu people, and the countless land mines planted by the Libyan army are some of the factors and dangers that complicate travel in northern Chad.

West of the Tibesti Mountains lies the **Djado Plateau**, a large elevated tableland.

The plateau features several sites with ancient rock paintings created by prehistoric cultures that once inhabited the region. The **Enneri Blaka Valley** stretches through the Djado Plateau. During prehistoric times, the valley was a fertile region with lush vegetation. The area was home to a large population of livestock breeders and hunters. These ancient peoples left behind fascinating relics that depict the area as it once was.

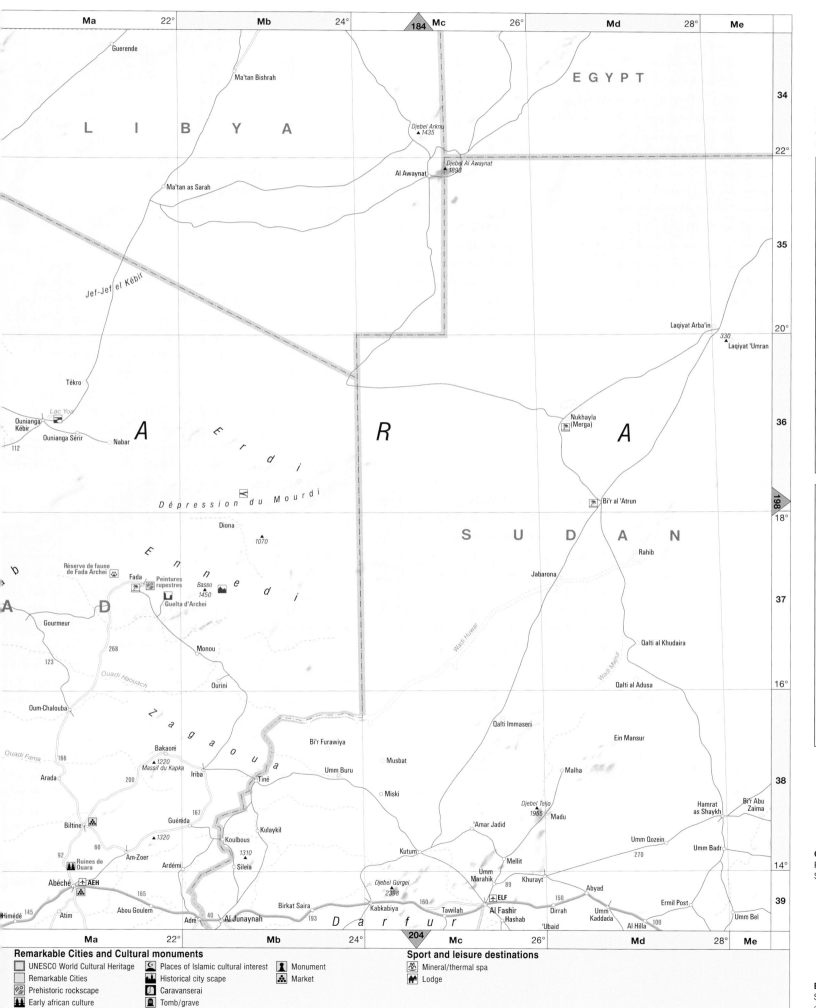

Lac Yoa Saline ⌑ lake situated below sea level between the Tibesti and Ennedi Plateau – fascinating landscapes with dunes and stone formations. **Ma36**

Historic Caravan Routes Until the 19th century caravans transported goods between Tripoli on the Mediterranean coast and the kingdoms around Lake Chad. Today the caravans are limited to local trade between communities in northern Chad. Most modern caravans in the region are led by Tuareg or Tubu merchants. Camels remain the principal means of overland travel through the regions. **Lj-Lk37/38**

Ennedi Plateau The region is a transition zone between the Tibesti Mountains and the Sahara. Ancient rock paintings depict the once fertile region before the expansion of the Sahara Desert. **Ma-Mb37**

Guelta d'Archei ⌑ Canyon in the Ennedi Plateau region – natural springs – habitat of Saharan crocodiles. **Ma37**

Biltine Important ⌂ market for the Tubu, Shoa, and Wadai peoples – ruins of the ancient city Ouara. **Ma38**

Remarkable Cities and Cultural monuments

UNESCO World Cultural Heritage	Places of Islamic cultural interest
Remarkable Cities	Historical city scape
Prehistoric rockscape	Caravanserai
Early african culture	Tomb/grave
Monument	
Market	

Sport and leisure destinations

Mineral/thermal spa	
Lodge	

Northern Sudan, Eritrea

Around 38 million people live in **Sudan**, Africa's largest country with a total area of 2.5 million km². Sudan borders Egypt to the north and Kenya, Uganda, and Congo to the south. The country also borders the Red Sea, Eritrea, and Ethiopia to the east. North of Sudan's capital **Khartoum**, the Nile River valley separates the ⊷ **Libyan** and **Nubian Deserts**. The sections of the Nile Valley near the Nubian Desert are home to many histo-

ric cultural sites built by ancient Egyptians and Nubians. Lake Nasser, a large reservoir created after Egypt dammed the Nile in the 1970s, extends across the Egyptian border into the northernmost region of Sudan around Wadi Halfa. In Khartoum, the Blue Nile and White Nile merge to form the Nile River proper. The

The oasis of Wadi Baraka (Eritrea) is surrounded by barren deserts. **Mj38/39**

Wadi Halfa Town in northern Sudan – the older sections of the town were submerged after the creation of Lake Nasser. **Mf36**

Dongola Sudanese city founded in the 19th century – date palm groves – ruins of Kawa including an ancient ⊞ temple. **Mf37**

Karima Ruins of an ancient ⊞ imperial city – ⊞ pyramids (photo) containing the graves of Kushite monarchs – UNESCO world heritage site. **Mf37**

Meroe Capital of the Kush Kingdom after the 7th century BC – ⊞ royal burial site after the 3rd century BC – tall pyramids – subterranean burial chambers. **Mg38**

Musawwarat es Sufra ⊞ Ancient temple dedicated to the lion god Apademak – built around 220 BC – reliefs depicting gods – restored between 1960 and 1970. **Mg38**

Naqa ⊞ Temple of Apademak built during the 1st century BC – Temple of Amun built in the 1st century BC – Roman ruins from the 3rd century AD. **Mg38**

Omdurman One of Sudan's major cities – large ⌂ marketplace – old Derwish monasteries – ⌂ mausoleum of the Mahdi, a 19th century Sudanese religious leader. **Mg39**

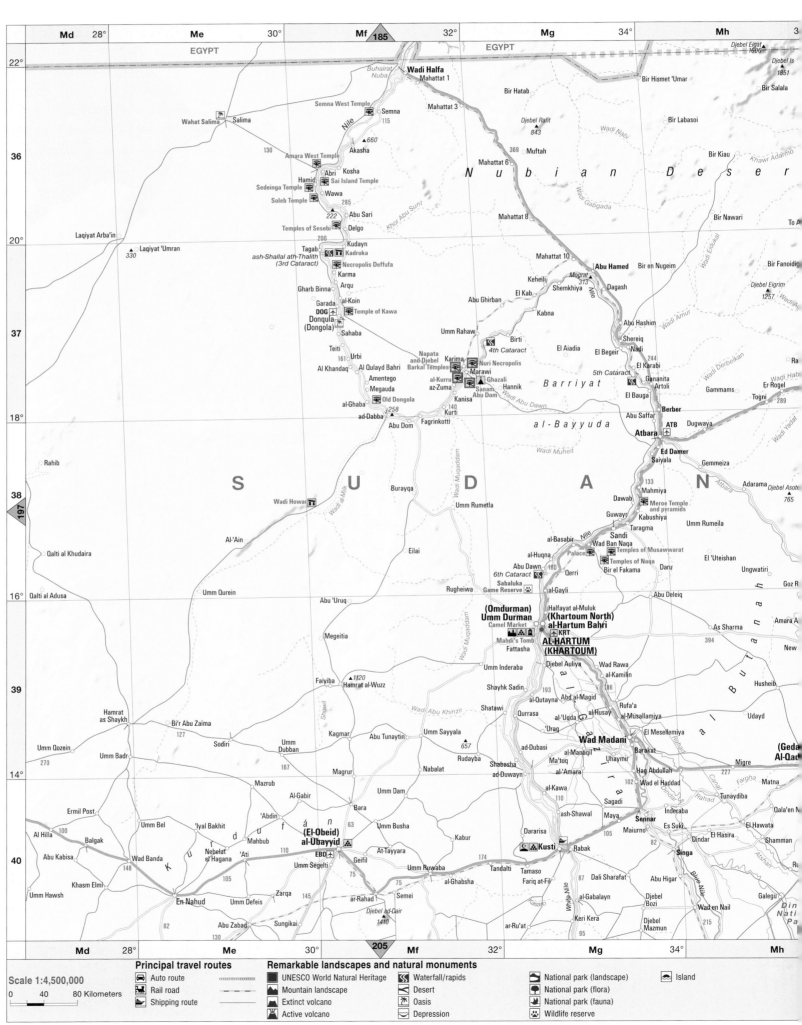

Scale 1:4,500,000
0   40   80 Kilometers

Principal travel routes	Remarkable landscapes and natural monuments		
🚗 Auto route	■ UNESCO World Natural Heritage	⧨ Waterfall/rapids	⊡ National park (landscape)	⬤ Island
🚂 Rail road	▲ Mountain landscape	⬚ Desert	⬤ National park (flora)	
Shipping route	▲ Extinct volcano	⬚ Oasis	⬤ National park (fauna)	
	▲ Active volcano	⬚ Depression	⬚ Wildlife reserve	

Atbara River, the Nile's northernmost major tributary, flows from Ethiopia to the city of Atbara in Sudan, where it enters the Nile. Al-Jazirah (Gezira), a Sudanese region between the **Blue Nile** and **White Nile** is a leading center of agriculture. A long ⛰ mountain range with a maximum height of 2,259 meters stretches along the **Red Sea** coast of Sudan. ◫ **Dindar National Park** near the Sudanese-Ethiopian border is home to interesting wild-

life including lion, leopard, elephant, and giraffe populations. Northern Sudan has an arid hot climate with sparse rainfall. **Eritrea** is a small nation located on East Africa's Red Sea coast. The country has a total area of 121,444 km² and a population of 3.5 million. An ancient ⛰ mountain range stretches from north to south over much of Eritrea's territory. A narrow and arid strip of coastal plains separates the Eritrean highlands from the Red Sea.

The ⊰ stony deserts of the northern highlands are inhabited mostly by nomadic peoples, while the population of the southwestern highlands consists largely of subsistence farmers. Southeastern Eritrea is dominated by mountains and sections of the arid Danakil Plain. The northern highlands of Ethiopia extend to the country's borders with Eritrea and Sudan. These highlands are the source of several rivers – including the Blue Nile and

Atbara Rivers. The highlands of Ethiopia have a mostly subtropical climate with heavy rainfall during summer. In Simien National Park and around Ethiopia's highest mountain, **Ras Dashen** (4,620 m), snow occasionally falls during winter. The arid ⊰ **Danakil** plain, an extension of the Great Rift Valley, is situated at an average elevation of 116 meters below sea level in northeastern Ethiopia and southern Eritrea.

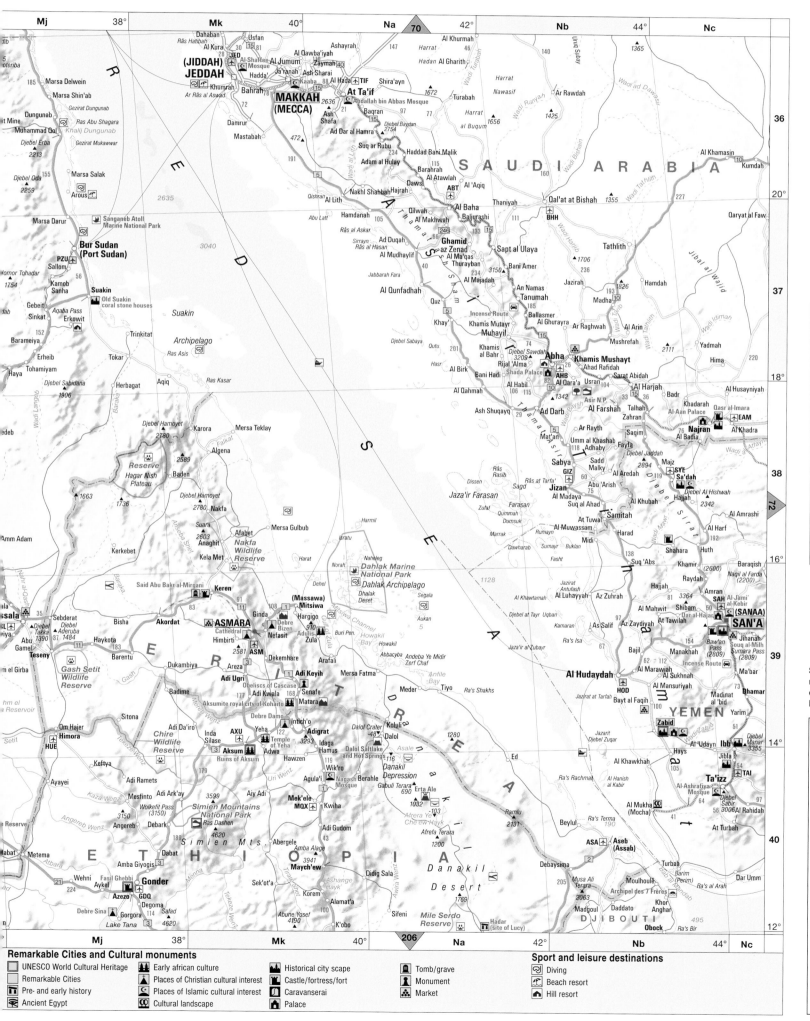

Sanganeb Atoll Large coral reefs in the Red Sea – interesting 🤿 diving sites – the atoll was designated a national park in 1990, because of its fascinating marine life. **Mj37**

Wadi Baraka ⊰ Stony desert in the northern highlands (1,000–1,500 m) of Ethiopia – inhabited by nomadic livestock breeders during the rainy season. **Mj38/39**

Axum The ancient city in northern Ethiopia was the capital of the Kingdom of Axum. The city features many historic sites (top photo). The Ethiopian Orthodox Church believes the Ark of the Covenant is housed in Axum. **Mk39**

Simien Mountains National Park Temperate 🏔 highlands (1,900–4,430 m) in northern Ethiopia – habitat of the Walia ibex, Dschelada baboon and Simien fox. **Mk40**

Gondar The city was the capital of Ethiopia between the 17th and 19th centuries AD. During the reign of Emperor Fasilidas many grand buildings, including palaces (top photo), churches (bottom photo), and monasteries, were built in the city. The local architecture features Arabian and Portuguese influences. **Mj40**

Remarkable Cities and Cultural monuments

- ▢ UNESCO World Cultural Heritage
- ▢ Remarkable Cities
- ▢ Pre- and early history
- ▢ Ancient Egypt
- Early african culture
- Places of Christian cultural interest
- Places of Islamic cultural interest
- Cultural landscape
- Historical city scape
- Castle/fortress/fort
- Caravanserai
- Palace
- Tomb/grave
- Monument
- Market

Sport and leisure destinations

- Diving
- Beach resort
- Hill resort

West Africa

The landscapes of West Africa range from semi-desert areas along the southern edges of the Sahel to dense tropical forests. Several long rivers – including the ⬛ **White Volta** (Ghana) – flow through the region to the Atlantic Ocean. The ⬛ **Niger River**, one of Africa's longest waterways, rises in the highlands of Guinea. West Africa has a largely smooth coast with only a few major lagoons and bays. The region's coastal areas consist

mostly of large mangrove forests and swamps. In contrast to the low-lying coast, West Africa's interior consists mostly of expansive flat plateaus broken by scattered mountain ranges. Most of West Africa was once covered by dense tropical rainforests. Most of the region's forests have been cleared in recent cen-

Traditional fishers on the Comoé River in Côte d'Ivoire.　　**Kj41**

Freetown Sierra Leone's capital – 🏛 King James market – heavily damaged during a recent civil war.　　**Kd41**

Yawri Bay Deep 🌊 bay on Sierra Leone's Atlantic coast – home to many marine animals including turtles, crabs, and a variety of fish species – fishing villages.　　**Kd41**

Tiwai Island Wildlife Sanctuary 🐾 Nature reserves (13 km²) on a small island in the Moa River – large primate population (colobus monkeys) – home to crocodiles and more than 120 bird species.　　**Ke42**

Man Major city in western Côte d'Ivoire – located at the foot of the heavily forested Toura Mountains – traditional 🎭 mask festivals, mostly in February.　　**Kg42**

Lac du Buyo Manmade lake on the Sassandra River in Côte d'Ivoire – important power plant – 🌊 beautiful shoreline – abundant animal life.　　**Kg42**

Parc National de Taï 🌿 Conservation area (33,000 km²) in Côte d'Ivoire – UNESCO world heritage site – tropical rainforests – abundant wildlife.　　**Kg43**

Yamoussoukro Administrative capital of Côte d'Ivoire – 🏛 presidential palace – 🏛 Notre Dame de la Paix (photo).　　**Kh42**

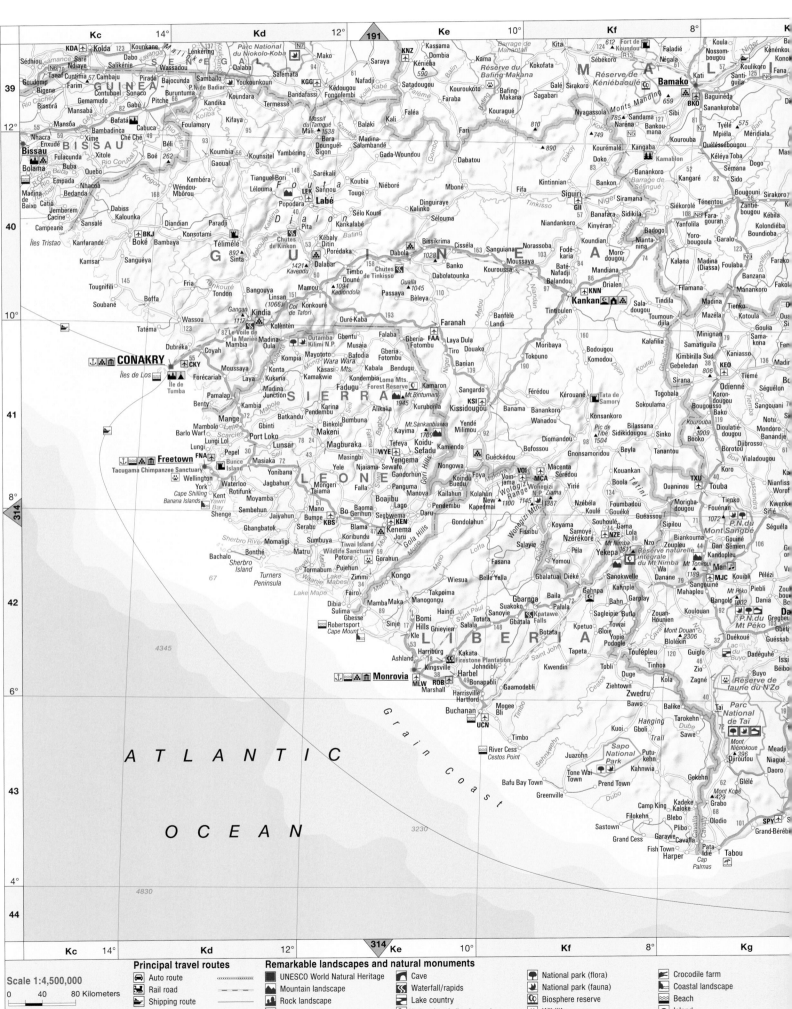

Scale 1:4,500,000
0　　40　　80 Kilometers

Principal travel routes
- 🚗 Auto route
- 🚆 Rail road
- 🚢 Shipping route

Remarkable landscapes and natural monuments
- UNESCO World Natural Heritage
- Mountain landscape
- Rock landscape
- Ravine/canyon
- Cave
- Waterfall/rapids
- Lake country
- National park (landscape)
- National park (flora)
- National park (fauna)
- Biosphere reserve
- Wildlife reserve
- Crocodile farm
- Coastal landscape
- Beach
- Island

turies for cultivation or to create space for settlements. The region is rich in **mineral resources,** including diamonds and gold. These natural resources drew European traders to the region after the 17th century. The Portuguese constructed several forts and trading bases along the West African coast before the start of colonialism. The region was a center not only for the trade of minerals but also ivory and, tragically, millions of human slaves.

Several powerful kingdoms flourished in West Africa before the start of the colonial era, including the kingdoms of Dahomey and Ashanti. Many West African kingdoms offered serious resistance to the European powers. Modern West Africa is home to an incredible variety of ethnic groups. Many ethnic groups in the region are now separated by borders created during the colonial era without regard to local demographics and history.

Despite foreign influences, most West African peoples were able to maintain many of their traditions. Indigenous animist beliefs are widely practiced throughout the region as is Christianity. Vodun, a naturist religion centered on ancestor worship, originated on the coast of West Africa and was carried to the Americas by slaves from the region. During the 1990s, West Africa was the scene of several bloody civil wars. **Liberia** and

Sierra Leone have been devastated by long armed conflicts. Several West African countries, however, have recently experienced significant economic and political developments – most notably **Ghana**, which is now a democracy after decades of dictatorship. Unlike most other African regions, West Africa has plentiful potential energy sources. The region's rivers are a convenient source of electricity for several countries.

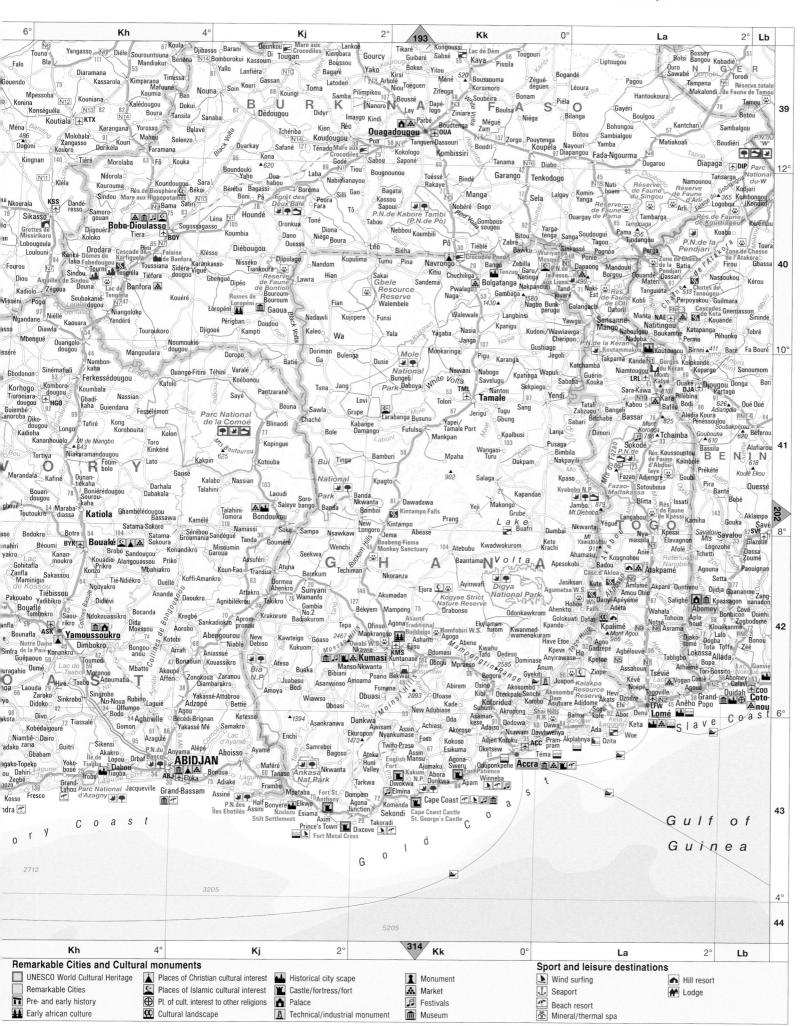

Bobo-Dioulasso The second largest city in Burkina-Faso – adobe mosques and dwellings (photo) – large marketplace – annual music festival. **Kh40**

Parc National de la Comoé Conservation area (11,500 km²) in Côte d'Ivoire – UNESCO world heritage site – sacred sites of the Lobi and Dyula peoples. **Kj41**

Abidjan Economic and cultural center of Côte d'Ivoire – population two million – large markets – St. Paul's cathedral – national museum. **Kh43**

Lake Volta Man-made lake created in 1965 on the White Volta River in Ghana – power plant in Akosombo Dam – ferry and freighter traffic – fishing boats (photo) – Digya National Park. **Kk-La41/42**

Ashanti Largest ethnic group in Ghana – the city of Kumasi, a UNESCO world heritage site, is the traditional center of Ashanti culture – traditional wooden art. **Kk42**

St. George's Castle One of several forts founded by the Portuguese on West Africa's coast – UNESCO world heritage site – once a center for slave trading. **Kk43**

Abomey Once the capital of the powerful Dahomey Kingdom – royal palace built in the 17th century, a UNESCO world heritage site – museum. **La42**

Remarkable Cities and Cultural monuments

- UNESCO World Cultural Heritage
- Remarkable Cities
- Pre- and early history
- Early african culture
- Places of Christian cultural interest
- Places of Islamic cultural interest
- Pl. of cult. interest to other religions
- Cultural landscape
- Historical city scape
- Castle/fortress/fort
- Palace
- Technical/industrial monument
- Monument
- Market
- Festivals
- Museum

Sport and leisure destinations

- Wind surfing
- Seaport
- Beach resort
- Mineral/thermal spa
- Hill resort
- Lodge

Southern Nigeria, Cameroon

The vast  delta of the Niger stretches through an area 200 kilometers wide in southern Nigeria on the country's coast along the Gulf of Guinea and Bight of Benin. North of Nigeria's swampy and low lying coastal areas is a region of rolling hills. The hills of southern Nigeria stretch east to the **Adamaoua Mountains** in Cameroon, which rise to a maximum height of 2,460 meters. The mountain range is covered mostly by tropical forests, and several national parks shelter the area's abundant flora and fauna. Western Cameroon is home to several tall active and inactive volcanoes. The summit of the highest volcano in the region, **Mount Cameroon** (4,095 m), is the highest point in West Africa. **Isla de Bioko**, a volcanic island off of Came-

Tropical rainforests in Dja Nature Reserve (Cameroon). **Lg44**

Vodun and other **animist religions** are widely practiced in West and Central Africa. Respect for ancestors and nature spirits are among the central beliefs of most indigenous religions in the regions. **Lb42**

Lac Nokoué The village **Ganvié** with its floating market and unique traditional homes is located in a small lagoon on the edge of Lake Nokoue in southern Benin. **Lb42**

Lagos Most of Nigeria's largest city is built on several islands near the country's southern coast – National Museum and Balogun Market on Lagos Island. **Lb42**

Osogbo Spiritual center of several indigenous religious groups, located in Nigeria – shrine to the deity Osun (photo). **Lc42**

Lake Nyos Lake in a volcanic crater – in 1986 the lake erupted releasing a cloud of poisonous gas that killed many people. **Lf42**

Principal travel routes

Scale 1:4,500,000
0   40   80 Kilometers

- Auto route
- Rail road
- Shipping route

Remarkable landscapes and natural monuments

- UNESCO World Natural Heritage
- Mountain landscape
- Rock landscape
- Active volcano
- Cave
- River landscape
- Waterfall/rapids
- Lake country
- Nature park
- National park (landscape)
- National park (flora)
- National park (fauna)
- National park (culture)
- Biosphere reserve
- Coastal landscape
- Beach

roon's coast, is an extension of the large volcanic mountain range on the mainland. The 918-kilometer-long Sanaga River flows into the Atlantic Ocean at its delta in southernmost Cameroon.

The Adamaoua highlands are a transition zone between the semi-arid regions of northern Cameroon and the country's humid tropical south, which encompasses some of the wettest areas on the planet. Northern Cameroon consists mostly of semi-arid savannahs, while the south and the coastal regions are home to large tropical rainforests.

To the south, Cameroon is bordered by the Republic of Congo, a country in the Congo River basin, which shares its name with the larger Democratic Republic of Congo, once known as Zaire. The Ubangi River, the largest tributary of the Congo, is fed by several smaller rivers that rise in the highlands of Cameroons. The Ubangi forms sections of the border between the Republic of Congo (capital: Brazzaville) and the Democratic Republic of Congo (capital: Kinshasa). The sections of the Congo basin west of the Ubangi are covered by large swampy wetlands. These wetlands are mostly nourished by the many tributaries of the Ubangi and the area contains expansive rainforests. In densely populated southern Nigeria, large rainforest areas have been cleared in recent decades for use as agricultural land. Southern Cameroon, Gabon, and the two Congo states, however, still contain vast and intact tropical rainforests. The rainforests in the Congo Basin constitute the second largest area of tropical rainforests on the planet. These vast forests are inhabited by many animals including several endangered ape species.

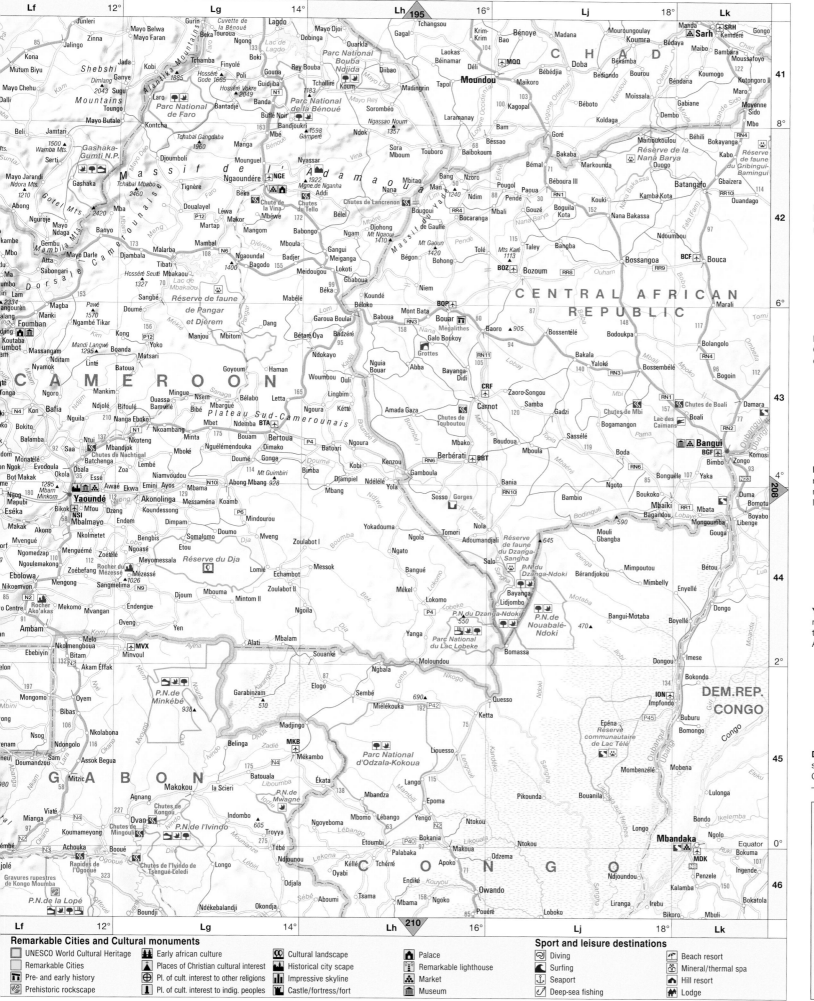

Korup National Park Large national park in western Cameroon (1,255 km²) – tropical rainforests – ape colonies. **Le43**

Rey Bouba Fulani sultanate in northern Cameroon – traditional festivals in honor of the local sultan Baba. **Lh41**

Foumban Capital of a sultanate in Cameroon – sultan's palace – anthropology museum – Tam Tam house with ten-meter-long drums (photo). **Lf43**

Yaoundé Cameroon's capital city (pop. 1.4 millions) – modern skyline – presidential palace (photo) – Museum of African Art – central marketplace. **Lf44**

Dja Faunal Reserve Nature reserve in southeastern Cameroon (5260 km²) – UNESCO world heritage site – tropical rainforests – gorilla colonies. **Lg44**

Pygmies of Central Africa Several hunter and gatherer pygmy groups live in the rainforests of Central Africa. The pygmies live in small close-knit clans.

Remarkable Cities and Cultural monuments

- UNESCO World Cultural Heritage
- Remarkable Cities
- Pre- and early history
- Prehistoric rockscape
- Early african culture
- Places of Christian cultural interest
- Pl. of cult. interest to other religions
- Pl. of cult. interest to indig. peoples
- Cultural landscape
- Historical city scape
- Impressive skyline
- Castle/fortress/fort
- Palace
- Remarkable lighthouse
- Market
- Museum

Sport and leisure destinations

- Diving
- Surfing
- Seaport
- Deep-sea fishing
- Beach resort
- Mineral/thermal spa
- Hill resort
- Lodge

Central African Republic, Southern Sudan

The region between the ⊠ **Sahel's** southern edges in Sudan and the **tropical rainforests** of Central Africa offers a variety of landscapes and climates. The northern sections of the region – in southern Sudan and the Central African Republic – consist of arid land with eroded soil and sparse vegetation. Nomadic livestock herders including the Tubu people form a large proportion of the inhospitable area's population. The ◪ **Marrah Moun-**

tain range (Jabal Marra), a chain of ◪ extinct volcanoes stretching through sections of Sudan and Chad, is one of the most fascinating geographic features in this region. In stark contrast to the barren surrounding plains, the sides of the mountains are covered by dense vegetation. Southern Chad is a transition

A small Nuba village in the highlands of southern Sudan. **Mf39/40**

Marrah Mountains The chain of extinct ◪ volcanoes is a relatively fertile ◪ mountain range with a maximum height of 3,088 meters. **Mc39**

Saint Floris National Park The large nature reserve in the Central African Republic is a ◪ habitat for cheetahs and rhinoceroses (middle photo). The park's wetlands are home to flocks of pelicans (bottom photo). **Ma41**

Ubangi ⊠ River along the border between the Central African Republic and the Republic of Congo – ⊠ rapids near Gele. **Lk43**

Chutes de Boali 50 meters high and 250 meters wide ⊠ waterfall near Bangui in the Central African Republic. **Lk43**

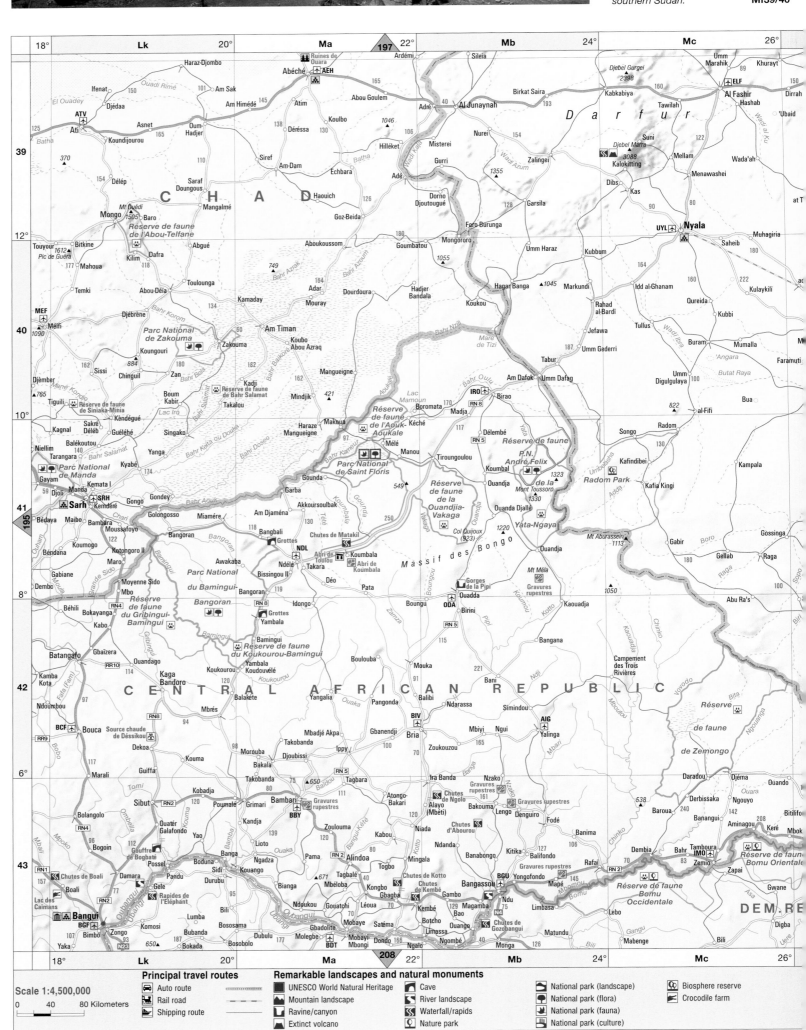

Scale 1:4,500,000

0   40   80 Kilometers

Principal travel routes
- Auto route
- Rail road
- Shipping route
- ········· (route)

Remarkable landscapes and natural monuments
- UNESCO World Natural Heritage
- Mountain landscape
- Ravine/canyon
- Extinct volcano
- Cave
- River landscape
- Waterfall/rapids
- Nature park
- National park (landscape)
- National park (flora)
- National park (fauna)
- National park (culture)
- Biosphere reserve
- Crocodile farm

zone between the arid Sahel and the vast tropical rainforests of Central Africa. The region consists of a flat basin dissected by countless streams and ⮑ rivers. The **Chari (Shari)**, one of southern Chad's principal rivers, contributes most of the water that flows into Lake Chad. Most of southern Chad's population consists of subsistence farmers and Sudanic language-speaking ethnicities. The culture of the **Sara people**, a collection

of closely related ethnicities, includes a complex and ancient mythology well studied by Western anthropologists, before and after the colonial era.
The **White Nile River (Al-bahr Al-abyad)** flows north from the city of Malakal through southern and central Sudan before it merges with the Blue Nile in Khartoum. The Sudd is a swampy plain in southern Sudan that is watered by several rivers including the White Nile.

The area's terrain is greatly affected by the water levels of these rivers. In addition to large papyrus swamps, the **Sudd** also encompasses large grasslands that frequently are flooded in summer.
In Chad and Sudan the border between the arid Sahel and the fertile forests and savannahs to its south are also borders between different religious communities. In both countries, tensions between Muslim, Christians and Animists have

led to violent conflicts. Both Chad and Sudan have experienced drawn out civil wars between the Muslims in their northern regions and the mostly Christian and Animist communities in their southern regions. In Chad, the civil war lasted for almost three decades before a ceasefire was agreed upon in the mid 1990s. Southern Sudan remains the site of violent conflicts and widespread human rights abuses.

Nuba Mountains Fertile ⛰ mountainous region in eastern Sudan – inhabited by Nuba ethnicities and Arabic-speaking nomads. **Mf39/40**

The Nuba This group of ethnicities inhabits the mountainous regions of Sudan and has preserved many of its ancient traditions. The Nuba, who are considered backward by their Arabic-speaking neighbors, have suffered from government-supported expulsions and discrimination.

Sudd ⮑ Marshland along the edges of the White Nile in central Sudan – inhabited by livestock breeders. **Mf41/42**

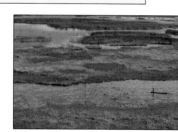

Shambe National Park 🏞 Swamp south of the Sudd region – habitat of the Nile lechwe and fascinating birds (photo). **Mf42**

Boma National Park 🏞 Savannah in southeastern Sudan – wild dogs – important habitat for antelope herds. **Mg42**

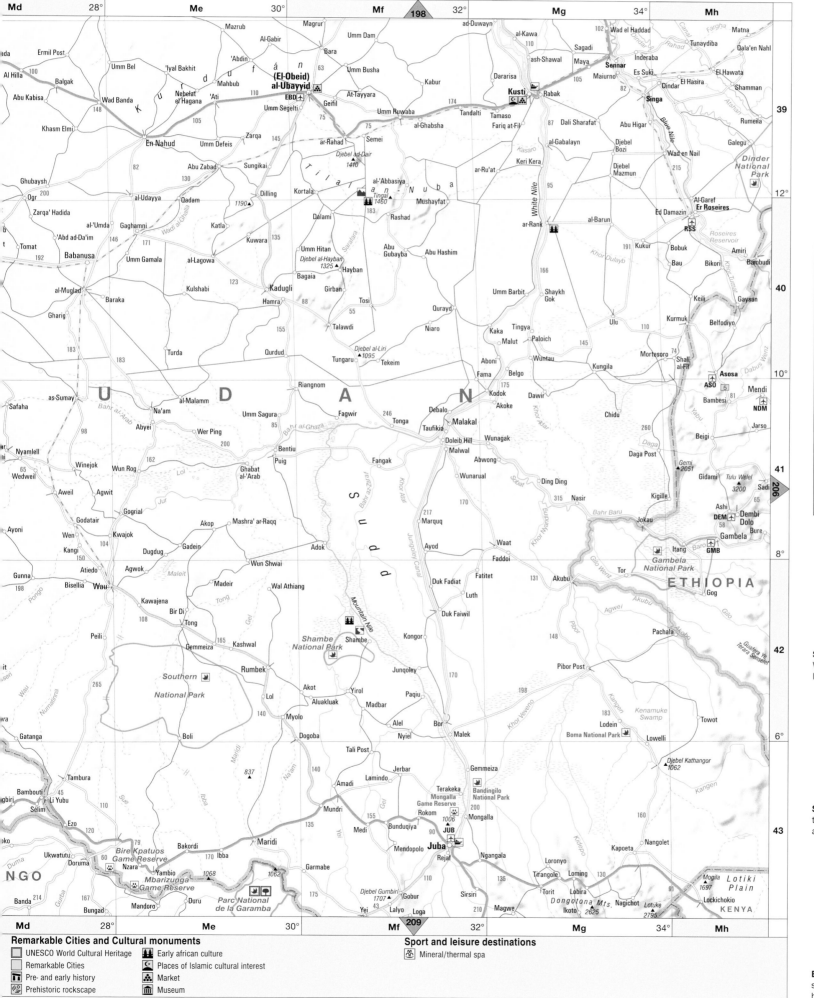

Remarkable Cities and Cultural monuments

- ◻ UNESCO World Cultural Heritage
- ◻ Remarkable Cities
- 🗿 Pre- and early history
- ◻ Prehistoric rockscape
- 🏛 Early african culture
- ◻ Places of Islamic cultural interest
- 🏪 Market
- 🏛 Museum

Sport and leisure destinations

- 🛁 Mineral/thermal spa

Highlands of Ethiopia, Horn of Africa

Ethiopia in East Africa is a mountainous country with a total area of 1.13 million km². The country's capital, **Addis Ababa**, has a population of nearly three million and is situated at a height of 2,400 meters above sea level. Ras Dashen Terara (4,260 m) in the Simien Mountains is the country's highest mountain. Ethiopia's highlands have a mostly temperate climate with temperatures below 20° C during most of the year.

The highlands decline in steps to the eastern section of the country, a region dominated by savannahs and ⊟ deserts. Eastern Ethiopia is an arid region with sparse rainfall. The Danakil Plain, in northeastern Ethiopia and southeastern Eritrea is one of the hottest and driest areas in the world.

Traditional two-story dwellings with thatched roofs in Ethiopia. **Mk39**

Daga Estifanos ▲ Ancient mausoleum containing the tombs of several Ethiopian emperors – on an island in Lake Tana – monasteries and churches in the area. **Mj40**

Abuna Josef Massif ▲ Heavily eroded mountain (4,190 m) – one of the highest peaks in the Ethiopian highlands. **Mk39**

Lalibela Important spiritual center of Ethiopian Christianity, often called the Ethiopian Jerusalem – monolithic cave churches, UNESCO world heritage sites – ▲ Beta Georgis church (photo). **Mk39**

Lower Valley of the Awash River ⊞ Excavation sites containing ancient hominid remains, the oldest are more than 3.2 million years old – world heritage site. **Na40**

Lake Assal ⊟ Body of water situated 155 meters below sea level – one of the deepest points on the Earth's surface – salt caravan routes between the lake and Bati. **Nb40**

Harer ▣ Principal city of Ethiopia's Muslim minority – founded in 1520 – walled ▣ old town – more than 90 mosques. **Nb41**

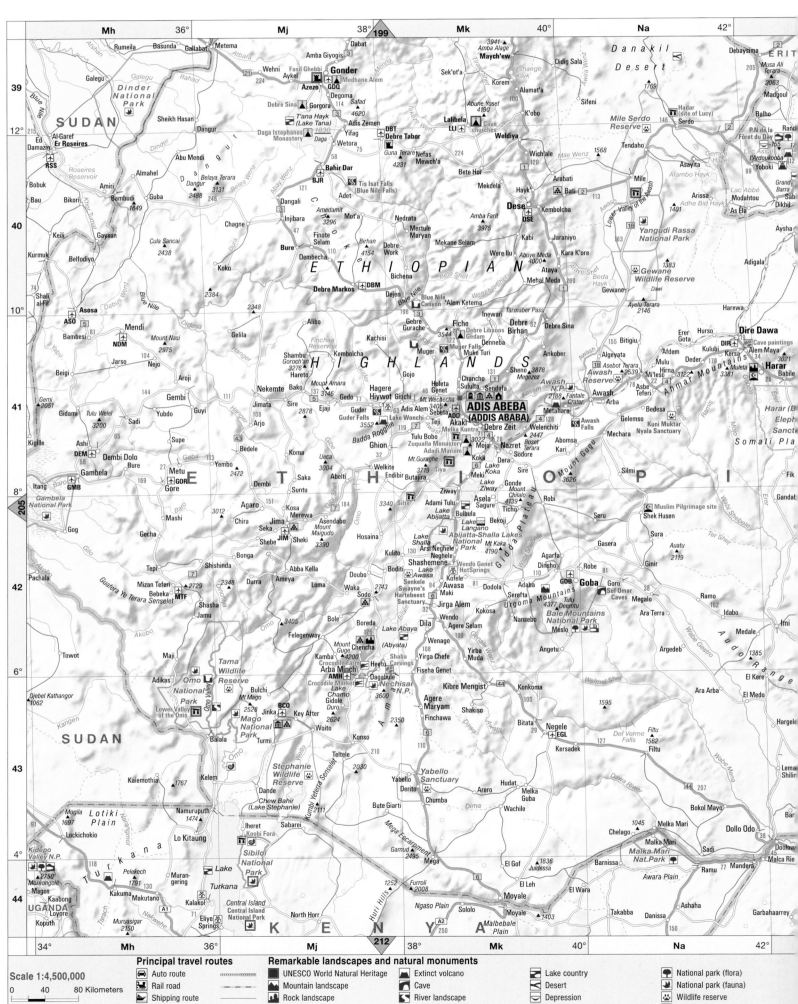

Principal travel routes

- 🚗 Auto route
- 🚂 Rail road
- ⚓ Shipping route

Scale 1:4,500,000

0   40   80 Kilometers

Remarkable landscapes and natural monuments

- ▪ UNESCO World Natural Heritage
- ▪ Mountain landscape
- ▪ Rock landscape
- ▪ Ravine/canyon
- ▲ Extinct volcano
- ⌂ Cave
- ▬ River landscape
- ▬ Waterfall/rapids
- ⊟ Lake country
- ⊟ Desert
- ⊟ Depression
- ⊟ National park (landscape)
- ▪ National park (flora)
- ▪ National park (fauna)
- ▪ Wildlife reserve
- ▪ Crocodile farm

The western edges of the Ethiopian highlands are more fertile and receive significantly more rainfall than the eastern edges. **Lake Tana**, in the northwestern highlands, is the largest body of water in Ethiopia with an area of around 3,000 km². The lake is also the source of the **Blue Nile River**. The **Omo River**, one of Ethiopia's principal rivers, rises in the southern highlands and flows to **Lake Turkana** (Rudolf) in Kenya. Gambela

National Park near the Sudanese border consists of marshy savannahs crossed by many rivers and streams. The **Great Rift Valley** runs through the middle of the Ethiopian highlands. In Ethiopia, the Great Rift Valley encompasses a chain of large lakes. **Lake Assal**, on the Danakil Plain in Djibouti, is one of the deepest points on the Earth's surface with an average elevation of 155 meters below sea level. **Djibouti**, a small nation with an area of

23,200 km², is situated on East Africa's coast next to the Gulf of Aden and the Red Sea. Like the countries it borders, Djibouti consists primarily of deserts and volcanic highlands. **Somalia** has a 3,025-kilometer-long coastline along the Gulf of Aden and the Indian Ocean. Somalia's terrain consists of hilly deserts and mountainous highlands along the country's northern coast. Humidity levels on the northern coast

regularly exceed 80 % during the rainy season. Somalia's capital **Mogadishu** is also the largest city in the country. Ethiopia and the Horn of Africa region are home to more than 70 ethnic groups who speak dozens of different languages. Most Ethiopians are Christians. The Ethiopian Orthodox Church was founded in the 4th century AD. Somalia has been a predominantly Muslim nation since the 12th century.

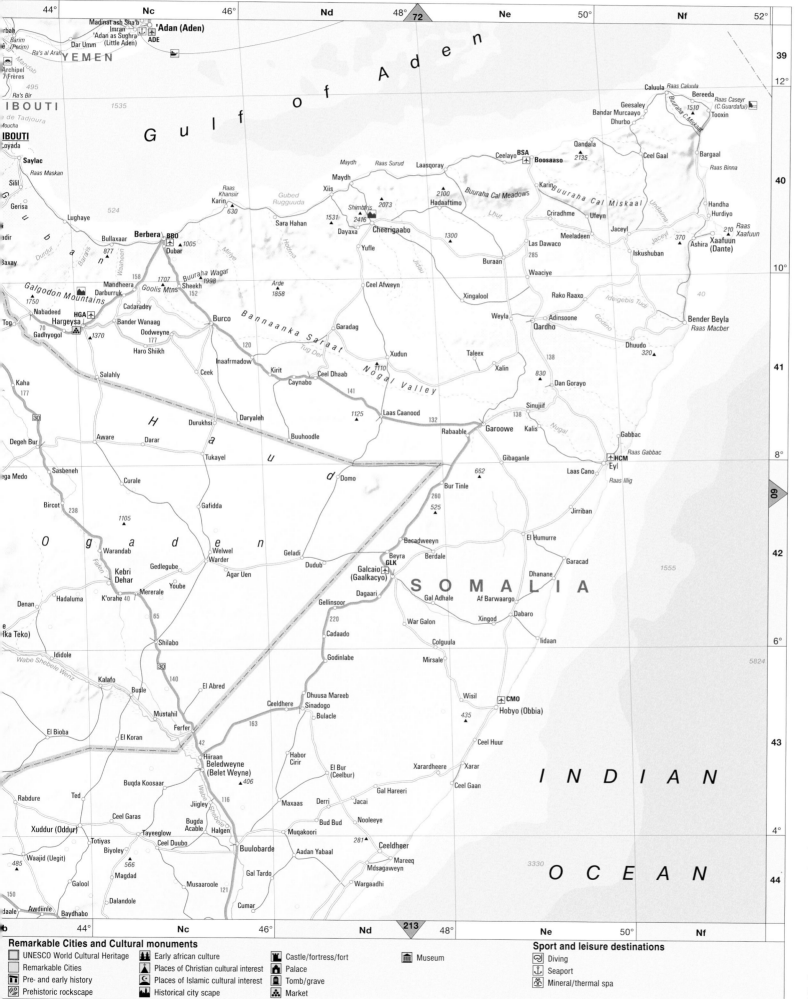

Awash National Park Fantale crater (2,007 m) – habitat for oryx antelopes, leopards, and Kudus. Mk-Na41

Addis Ababa Ethiopia's capital – St. George's cathedral (photo) – Menelik Mausoleum – Gebbi Palace – Anthropology Museum – marketplace. Mk41

Nechisar National Park Ethiopian national park in the Great Rift Valley – home to rare animal species. Mj42/43

Mursi The nomadic Mursi people have lived in the Omo River Valley in southwestern Ethiopia for hundreds of years. Adult Mursi women wear large plates (photo) in their ears and lower lips. Mj43

Hargeysa Commercial center in northwestern Somalia – located in an agricultural region – marketplace (photo). Nc41

Somali Desert The arid regions of Somalia are inhabited mostly by nomadic herders – frequent sand storms. Nc-Ne40/41

Webe Shebel River The river rises in Ethiopia's highlands – numerous agrarian villages along the river's banks. Nc43

Northern Congo, Northern Democratic Republic of Congo

The gigantic basin of the ◤ **Congo River** consists of vast tropical rainforests and swamps. It stretches through most of Central Africa. Situated near the equator, the region has a tropical climate with high temperatures and heavy rainfall throughout the year. Countless unique tropical plant and animal species inhabit the largely inaccessible rainforests in the region. The construction of roads stretching from east to west though the rain-

forests and ship traffic on the river has greatly expanded the limits of human settlement in the region. Large sections of Central Africa's rainforests have been cleared in recent decades by miners, loggers, and a growing population in need of farming land. Habitat loss, poaching, and civil wars have brought several spe-

The Ruwenzori Mountains are covered by thick tropical vegetation. **Me45**

Wagenia Fishing Grounds Fishing area on the Congo River near ◤ Boyoma Falls – the local fishermen still rely on centuries-old traditional methods (photo) – near the city of ◪ Kisangani (pop. 200,000). **Mc45**

Okapi Wildlife Reserve ◪ Conservation area and habitat for endangered Okapis in eastern Congo – UNESCO world heritage site – several waterfalls. **Me45**

Aka Pygmies The Aka, a group of Pygmy communities, live in the upper valley of the Congo River. Like most other Pygmies, the Aka are hunter-gatherers and live in small clans. They reside in heavily forested areas. Their traditional lifestyles are increasingly threatened by outside influences. Traditional knowledge and beliefs are passed down the generations though songs and storytelling.

Rutshuru Small city on the southern edge of ◪ Virunga National Park – large produce market (photo) – ◤ Rutshuru waterfalls: three kilometers outside of the city. **Me46**

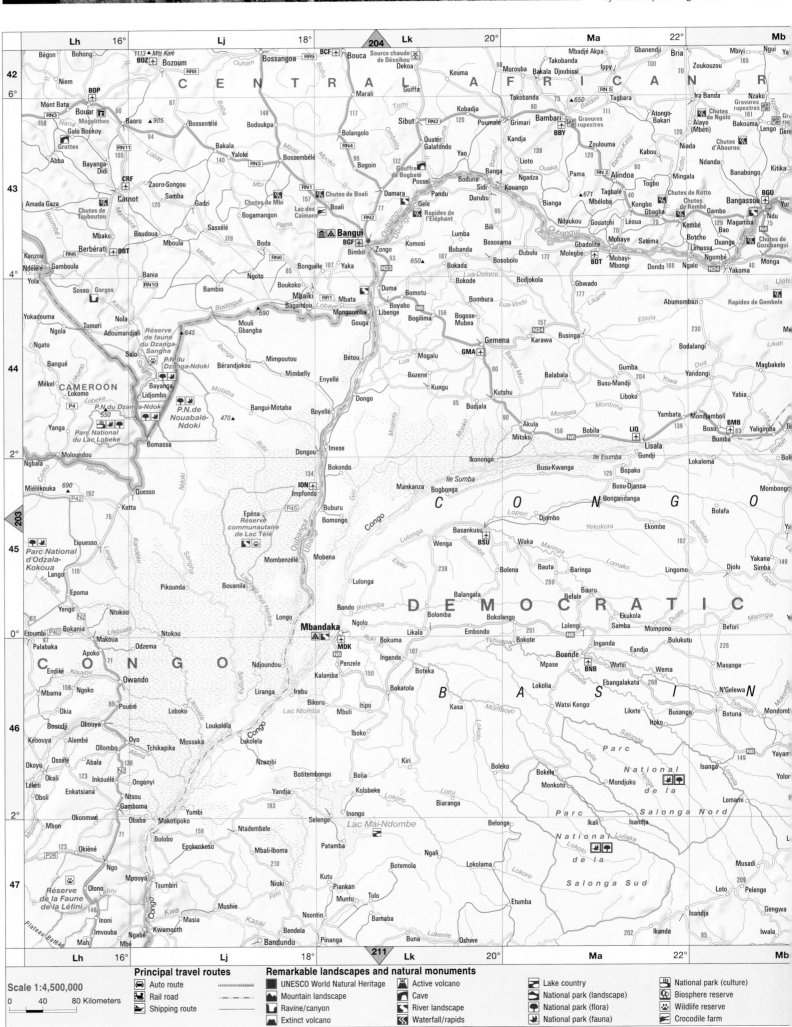

Scale 1:4,500,000

0   40   80 Kilometers

Principal travel routes
- Auto route
- Rail road
- Shipping route

Remarkable landscapes and natural monuments
- UNESCO World Natural Heritage
- Mountain landscape
- Ravine/canyon
- Extinct volcano
- Active volcano
- Cave
- River landscape
- Waterfall/rapids
- Lake country
- National park (landscape)
- National park (flora)
- National park (fauna)
- National park (culture)
- Biosphere reserve
- Wildlife reserve
- Crocodile farm

cies in the Congo basin including the region's mountain gorillas and forest elephants to the verge of extinction. The Congo basin is the traditional homeland of several hunter-gatherer ethnic groups collectively referred to as Pygmies because of their small statures. Most Pygmies live in small clans and music plays an important role in the culture of almost all of their communities. The majority of the basin's population is formed by mem-

bers of Bantu-language-speaking ethnicities. The ancestors of the Bantu-speaking ethnicities arrived in the Congo basin after they migrated from their original homelands in the borders of modern-day Nigeria at least 2,000 years ago.
Most of the Congo basin consists of flat low-lying areas. However, the eastern edge of the basin near Lake Victoria is a mountainous region encompassing countless large and small lakes. The ▲

Ruwenzori and ▲ **Vurangi** mountain ranges are situated on the eastern edge of the Albertine (Western) Rift Valley, an extension of the Great Rift Valley. The jagged Ruwenzori Mountain range rises to a maximum height of 5,109 meters and encompasses several large glaciers. These rainy and humid highlands are home to unique endemic vegetation including unusually large flowers and weeds. Among the animals in the Ruwen-

zori Mountains, the region's birds and primates are the most fascinating and studied. Many historians believe the Ruwenzori Mountains are the "Mountains of the Moon" described by the Greco-Egyptian geographer Ptolemy during the 2nd century AD. Ptolemy and many other geographers believed the mountain range contained the source of the Nile River. In the 19th century, explorers proved that the White Nile rises from Lake Victoria.

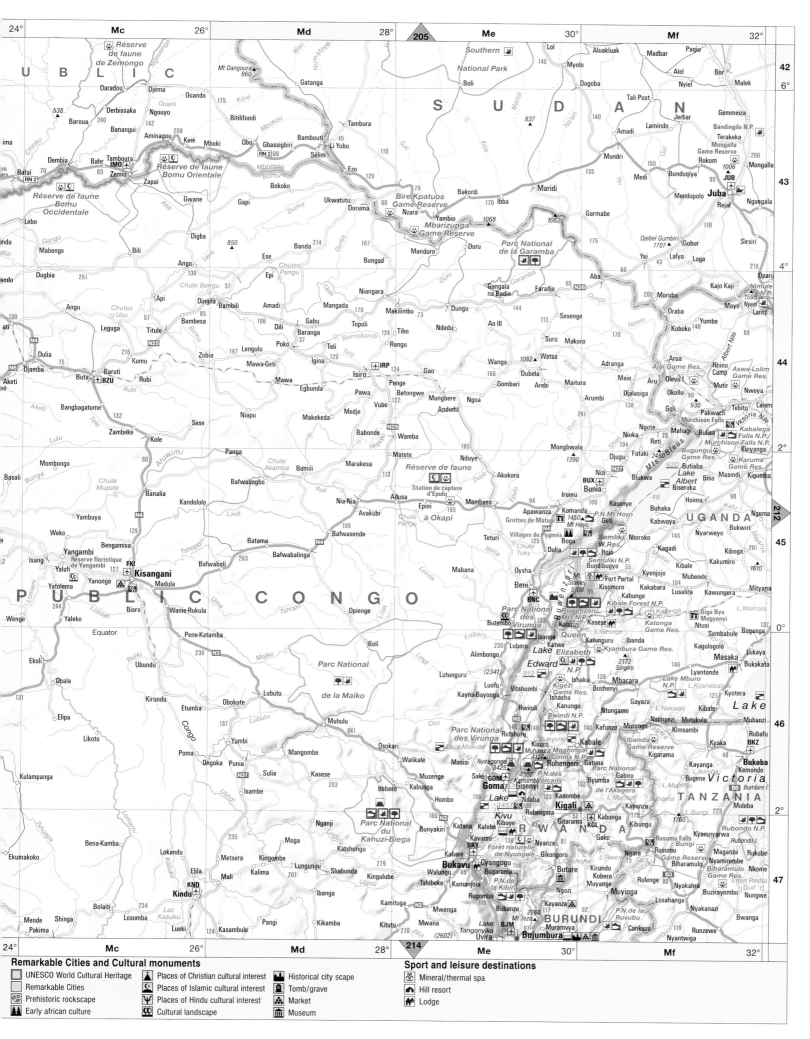

Ruwenzori National Park/Virunga National Park The two neighboring ▣ national parks are located along the border between Uganda and the Democratic Republic of Congo. Both parks encompass volcanic mountain chains and contain many unique plants species. Photos from top to bottom: mountain valley, giant lobelias, Jackson's chameleon. **Me45**

Mountain Gorillas Virunga and Ruwenzori National Parks are home to around 250 mountain gorillas. Their survival is threatened by poaching and wars. **Me46**

Volcanoes of Central Africa Virunga National Park is home to several active ▲ volcanoes. The 3,425-meter-high volcano Nyiragongo is the most active in the region. **Me46**

Remarkable Cities and Cultural monuments

- ☐ UNESCO World Cultural Heritage
- ☐ Remarkable Cities
- ☐ Prehistoric rockscape
- ☐ Early african culture
- ▲ Places of Christian cultural interest
- ▲ Places of Islamic cultural interest
- ▲ Places of Hindu cultural interest
- ☐ Cultural landscape
- ☐ Historical city scape
- ☐ Tomb/grave
- ☐ Market
- ☐ Museum

Sport and leisure destinations

- ☐ Mineral/thermal spa
- ☐ Hill resort
- ☐ Lodge

Southern Congo, Southern Democratic Republic of Congo, Northern Angola

The powerful **Congo River** gives its name to two nations in central Africa: the **Republic of Congo**, also known as Congo-Brazzaville, and the **Democratic Republic of Congo** or Congo-Kinshasa, formerly Zaire. Both Congo nations contain vast areas of dense tropical rainforests and the Congo River is the most important transportation route in the region. **Kinshasa** (population: 4.5 million) and **Brazzaville** (population:

950,000), the two capital cities of the Congo nations, are both located on the banks on the river.

Gabon (267,667 km²), a nation to the north of the Republic of Congo has a terrain and tropical climate similar to that of the two Congo Nations. Gabon's coastal areas consist of flat plains, while the inter-

The Congo River: Africa's second longest river.

ior consists mostly of low hills. Almost all of Gabon's territory is located in the basin of the **Ogooue River**. The 850-kilometer-long river rises in the Republic of Congo and flows to its delta on Gabon's Atlantic coast.

Gabon and the two Congo nations have **equatorial tropical climates** with high levels of humidity and heavy rainfall throughout the entire year. All three countries are home to vast tropical rainforests

Lambaréné 🏥 Hospital in the rainforests of Gabon – founded in 1913 by Dr. Albert Schweitzer, who was buried nearby. **Lf46**

Moukalaba-Doudou National Park Large conservation area in southwestern Gabon – Nyanga savannah, rainforests, and swamps – elephants and gorillas. **Lf47**

Conkouati-Douli National Park Sea turtle habitats – elephants, gorillas, chimpanzees (photo). **Lf47/48**

Kinshasa The capital of the Democratic Republic of Congo – cathedrals and mosques – large marketplaces. **Lh48**

The **Congo River** (4,374 km) has the largest river basin in Africa. The river is a vital transport route for Central Africa and several large cities are located on its banks.

Scale 1:4,500,000

0   40   80 Kilometers

Principal travel routes
- 🚗 Auto route
- 🚂 Rail road
- Shipping route
- Mountain landscape

Remarkable landscapes and natural monuments
- 🏛 UNESCO World Natural Heritage
- Mountain landscape
- Rock landscape
- Ravine/canyon
- Cave
- River landscape
- Waterfall/rapids
- Lake country
- National park (landscape)
- National park (flora)
- National park (fauna)
- National park (culture)
- Biosphere reserve
- Wildlife reserve
- Whale watching
- Turtle conservation area

Southern Congo, Southern Democratic Republic of Congo, Northern Angola

with amazing levels of biodiversity. Several ■ **national parks** have been created in the region's rainforests to protect indigenous flora and fauna from the effects of deforestation and habitat loss. The region's primates, including gorillas and chimpanzees, are especially endangered and several reserves have been created solely for the protection of these animals. Bantu-language-speaking ethnic groups form the vast majority of Central Africa's

population. Before the beginning of European colonization in the 19th century, the region was dominated by several powerful African kingdoms. The Luba-Lunda kingdoms were famous for their wealth of gold reserves and controlled large areas in the Congo Basin before the colonial era. By the beginning of the 20th century most of the Congo Basin had fallen under the control of European colonial powers. In recent decades, the vast

mineral wealth of the Congo Basin has been a driving force behind the region's frequent armed conflicts and civil wars. Tension between the many ethnic groups in Central Africa has also been a major factor behind the region's conflicts and political instability.

Northern **Angola**, unlike the rest of the country, has a wet tropical climate similar to other regions near the equator. The climate along Angola's long ■ **At-**

lantic coast is strongly influenced by ocean currents, such as the Benguela Current. The **central plateau** in Angola's interior rises to heights above 2,000 meters. The plateau declines gradually in the north and more abruptly in the south. Most of Angola's territory is covered by savannahs and semi-arid regions. Angola has large deposits of natural resources, including oil, copper, and diamonds.

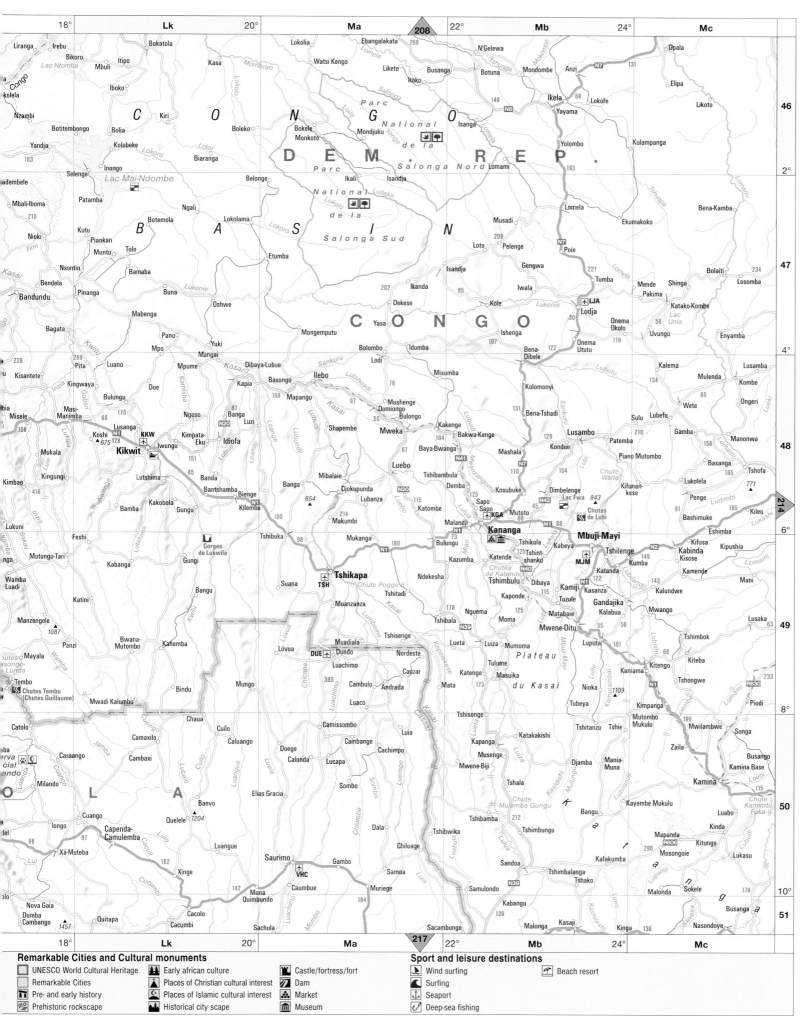

Salonga National Park ■ The world's largest tropical rainforest reserve (36,000 km²) is a UNESCO world heritage site and is home to fascinating animals including elephants and chimpanzees. The park is accessible only by river boat. Photos from top to bottom: rainforest, mandrill baboon, mustached monkey, a group of bonobos.　　　**Ma46/47**

Katanga Ethnically diverse region in the Democratic Republic of Congo (Kinshasa) – photo: medicine man.

Uganda, Kenya, Northern Tanzania

The **East African Rift System** is the most spectacular geographic feature in East Africa. The East African Rift System is part of a larger rift system called the Afro-Arabian Rift Valley. The Afro-Arabian Rift Valley was formed more than 30 million years ago after the African and Asian continental plates separated from one another. The 7,000-kilometer-long rift valley extends from the Jordan Valley in Israel through the Red Sea and down to

the southern edges of East Africa. The width of the East African Rift System ranges between 50 and 300 kilometers. In East Africa, the Rift Valley diverges into two sections: the Eastern (Great) Rift Valley and the Western Rift Valley. Both sections of the East African Rift System contain volcanic mountain ranges

Masai-Mara Reserve in Kenya features fascinating flora and fauna. **Mh46**

Lake Turkana (Rudolf) ⇄ Lake (6,000 km²) in northwestern Kenya – traditional homeland of the Turkana people. **Mh-Mj43/44**

The Afro-Arabian Rift Valley 7,000 kilometers long – extends from Israel to East Africa – volcanic mountain ranges. **Mj44/45**

Lake Bogoria ⇄ Located in the Great Rift Valley – high salt and mineral content – geysers – flamingo flocks (photo). **Mj45**

The Masai This famed group of semi-nomadic livestock herders lives in several East African countries. The Masai have maintained many of their traditions despite increasing contact with other ethnic groups.

Masai Mara National Reserve The northernmost section of the Serengeti is divided into two zones by Tanzania's government. The northern zone is inhabited by Masai herders and the southern zone is a conservation area for wildlife. The reserve is home to large herds of gnus (top photo), lions (middle photo), and water buffalo (bottom photo). **Mh46**

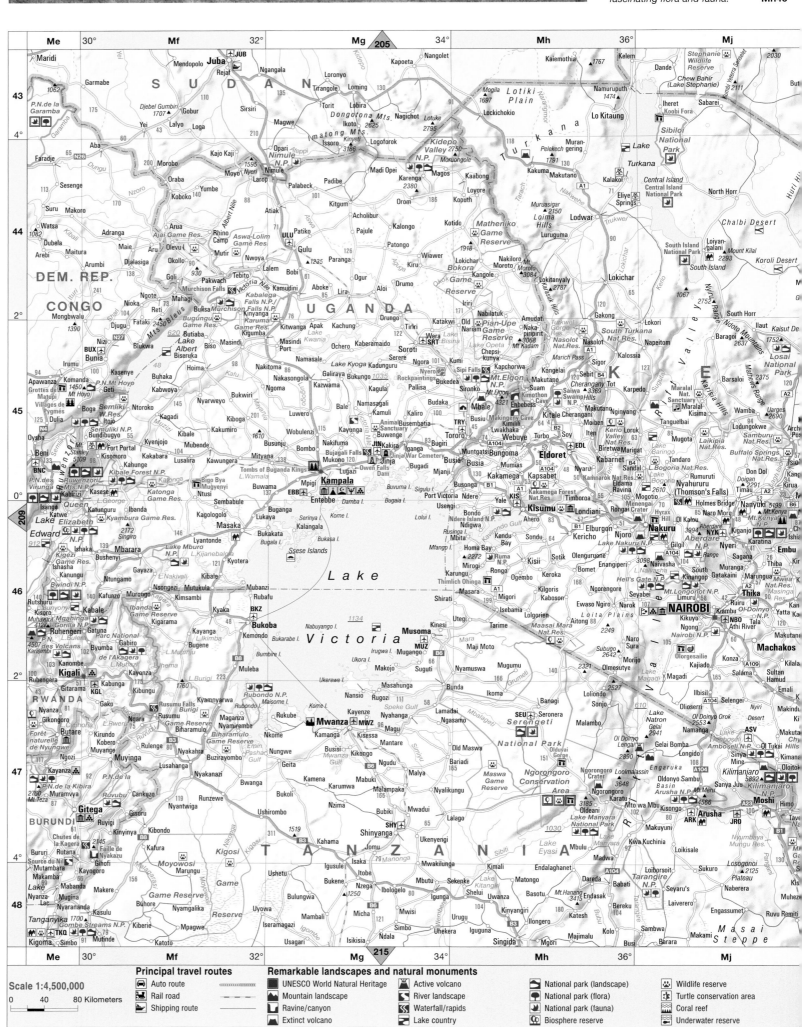

Scale 1:4,500,000

0   40   80 Kilometers

Principal travel routes
- Auto route
- Rail road
- Shipping route

Remarkable landscapes and natural monuments
- UNESCO World Natural Heritage
- Mountain landscape
- Ravine/canyon
- Extinct volcano
- Active volcano
- River landscape
- Waterfall/rapids
- Lake country
- National park (landscape)
- National park (flora)
- National park (fauna)
- Biosphere reserve
- Wildlife reserve
- Turtle conservation area
- Coral reef
- Underwater reserve

including the **Virunga Mountains** along the Ugandan-Rwandan border and the **Ruwenzori Range**. The Great Rift Valley of East Africa also contains a series of large lakes. ⚓ **Lake Victoria**, the world's second largest freshwater lake, is located in a large basin between the eastern and western sections of the rift system. Many important archeological ⚫ discoveries have been made in the Great Rift Valley during modern times. The

Great Rift Valley's climate and terrain are ideal for the preservation of organic remains and the bones of prehistoric humans, and extinct hominid species have been discovered at many sites throughout East Africa.

Both Kenya and Tanzania contain a series of highlands that stretch from the countries' coasts into their interiors. These **highlands** rise to 2,000 meters in elevation and the savannahs they

encompass are home to many large wild animals, including elephants and lions. The Serengeti, a wilderness in northern Tanzania, contains several nature reserves with abundant wildlife and beautiful landscapes. The highlands of Tanzania and Kenya feature several of Africa's highest mountains, including ▲ **Mount Kenya** (5,199 m) and ▲ **Mount Kilimanjaro** (5,892 m) – the second highest and highest mountain on the

continent. The 400-kilometer-long **Tana River**, which flows from Kenya's interior to the Indian Ocean, is the most important river in the highlands. Somalia is situated on a plateau with an average elevation of 500 meters. Most of the country's terrain consists of semi-arid savannahs and deserts. A narrow strip of humid plains stretches along the country's coast, and northern Somalia features a region of arid highlands.

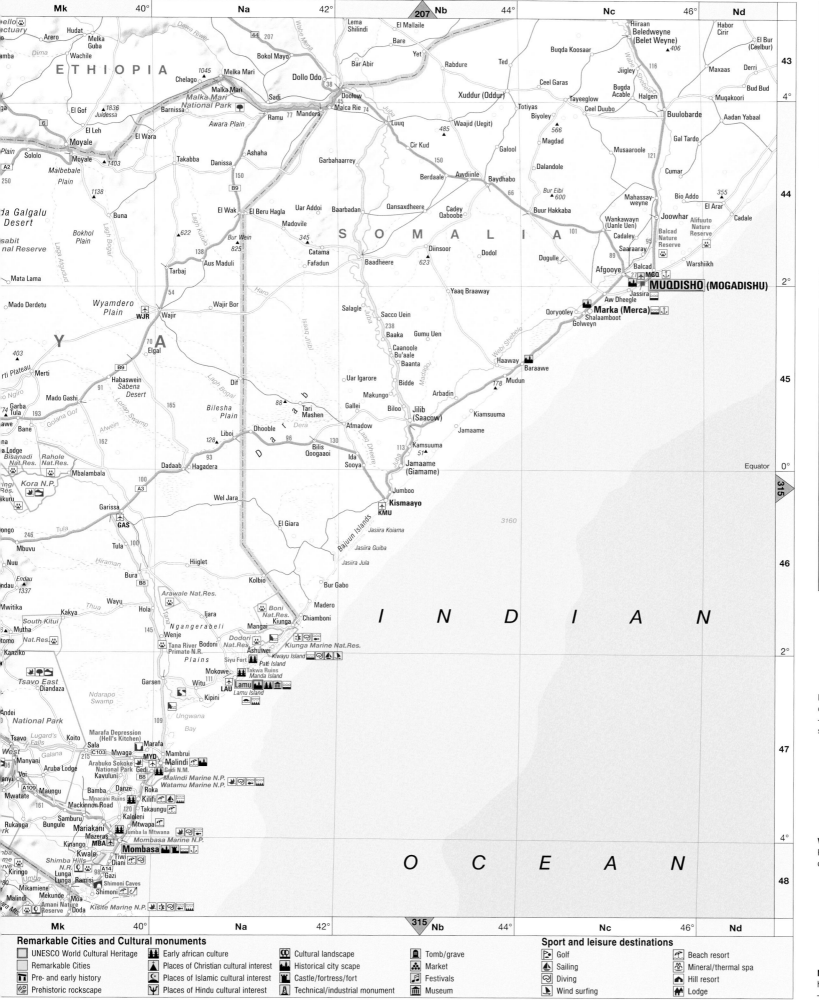

Samburu The Samburu people of central Kenya are closely related to the Masai. Like the Masia, the Samburu were traditionally semi-nomadic cattle herders.

Samburu National Reserve 🏕 Conservation area in a semi-arid region with large antelope herds (photo) and gerenuks. **Mj45**

Amboseli National Park The national 🦏 park (400 km²) at the foot of Mount Kilimanjaro has a wet tropical climate and is inhabited by diverse wildlife. Amboseli National Park's unique vegetation (top photo) and large elephant herds (bottom photo) are the park's major attractions. **Mj47**

Lamu UNESCO world heritage site – port city located on an island in the Indian Ocean – 🏛 Swahili architecture in the well-preserved old town – 🏖 beaches. **Na47**

Watamu Bay Beautiful 🏖 beaches on the Kenyan coast – 🏕 Marine National Park with coral reefs – 🤿 diving sites. **Na47**

Mombasa 🏛 Kenya's leading port city – 🏰 historic Fort Jesus, built in the 17th century – 🏛 Swahili old town. **Mk48**

Remarkable Cities and Cultural monuments

▣	UNESCO World Cultural Heritage
▫	Remarkable Cities
🛕	Pre- and early history
🪨	Prehistoric rockscape
◉	Early african culture
✝	Places of Christian cultural interest
☪	Places of Islamic cultural interest
🕉	Places of Hindu cultural interest
◫	Cultural landscape
🏙	Historical city scape
🏰	Castle/fortress/fort
⚙	Technical/industrial monument
⚰	Tomb/grave
🛒	Market
🎵	Festivals
🏛	Museum

Sport and leisure destinations

⛳	Golf
⛵	Sailing
🤿	Diving
🏄	Wind surfing
🏖	Beach resort
♨	Mineral/thermal spa
🏨	Hill resort
🏔	Lodge

Rwanda, Burundi, Tanzania

East Africa and the eastern sections of Central Africa comprise many landscapes and geographic regions. The **Mitumba Mountain range** in western East Africa stretches over a distance of 1,200 kilometers parallel to Lake Tanganyika. In the west, the range borders the basin of the Congo River. The section of the Mitumba range south of **Lake Kivu** rises to a height of 2,600 meters and descends in elevation abruptly near the Great Rift Val-

ley. The most remarkable geographic feature in this region is the East African Rift System, which is divided into two sections: the Western (Albertine) and Eastern (Great) Rift Valley. The Western Rift Valley contains numerous lakes including Lake Kivu and **Lake Tanganyika**, the longest lake in Africa.

Storm clouds above the savannahs of the Serengeti in Tanzania. **Mh47**

Lake Victoria The world's second largest freshwater lake (68,800 km²) – source of the White Nile River – the lake's endemic fauna is threatened by the Nile perch. **Mg46/47**

Akagera National Park 2,800 km² – located in the Kagera (Akagera) River basin – buffalo and antelope populations. **Mf46**

Nyungwe National Park The 970-km²-large nature reserve encompasses tropical rainforests inhabited by many rare birds and endangered primates including chacma baboons (bottom photo). **Me47**

Gombe Streams National Park The national park's main attraction is its chimpanzee population, made famous by the work of Jane Goodall. Despite the creation of the nation park, the primates remain endangered. **Me48**

Rusha National Park The third largest national park in Tanzania with an area of 12,800 km² – hotels and camp sites in the park – views of Mount Kilimanjaro. **Mh49**

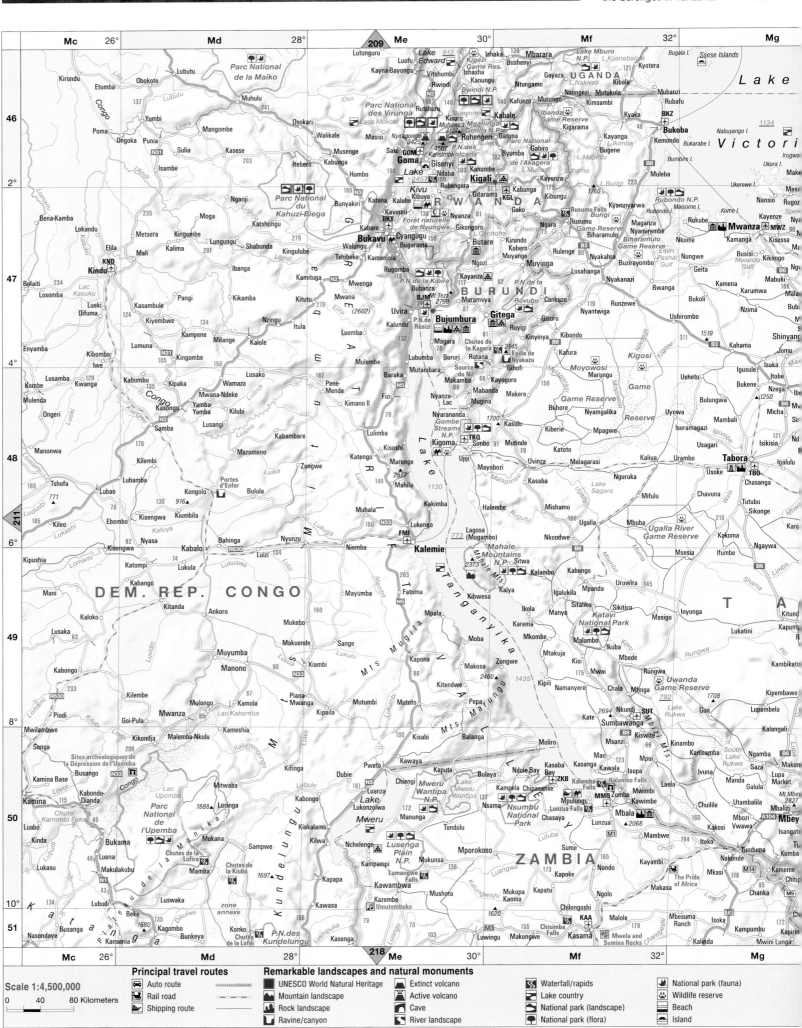

Scale 1:4,500,000

0   40   80 Kilometers

Principal travel routes
- Auto route
- Rail road
- Shipping route

Remarkable landscapes and natural monuments
- UNESCO World Natural Heritage
- Mountain landscape
- Rock landscape
- Ravine/canyon
- Extinct volcano
- Active volcano
- Cave
- River landscape
- Waterfall/rapids
- Lake country
- National park (landscape)
- National park (flora)
- National park (fauna)
- Wildlife reserve
- Beach
- Island

The mountains of the 🏔 **Ruwenzori** and **Virunga ranges** are located to the east of Lake Kinu. The mountains in both ranges are covered by dense tropical rainforests inhabited by endangered mountain gorillas. The foothills of the Ruwenzori Mountains are the source of the Kagera (Akagera) River, the most isolated source of the Nile River. The area between the western and eastern sections of the East African Rift System contains a large, flat basin. Much of this basin is occupied by 🌊 **Lake Victoria**, Africa's largest lake. The savannahs of Tanzania's 🦁 **Serengeti National Park** are located directly south of Lake Victoria. Many large animals inhabit the park including groups of lions, elephants, buffalos, zebras, and leopards. The most interesting geographic feature in the national park is the Ngorongoro crater, which has an area of 260 km².

The Great (Eastern) Rift Valley stretches through Kenya and Tanzania. Like the Western Rift, it contains a series of large lakes including Lake Natron, Lake Eyasi, and Lake Manyara. **Lake Natron**, located in northern Tanzania, contains numerous active geysers and water with high mineral content. The large volcanic mountains on the edge of the Eastern Rift have been dormant for centuries or thousands of years. One of these mountains,

🏔 **Mount Kilimanjaro**, is the highest mountain in Africa with a height of 5,892 meters. Although generally considered inactive, many geologists believe molten lava continues to accumulate within Mount Kilimanjaro and that the volcano could erupt in the future.

East Africa's coastal regions consist of a narrow strip of low-lying plains. The coast has been a meeting point for African and Asian cultures for many centuries.

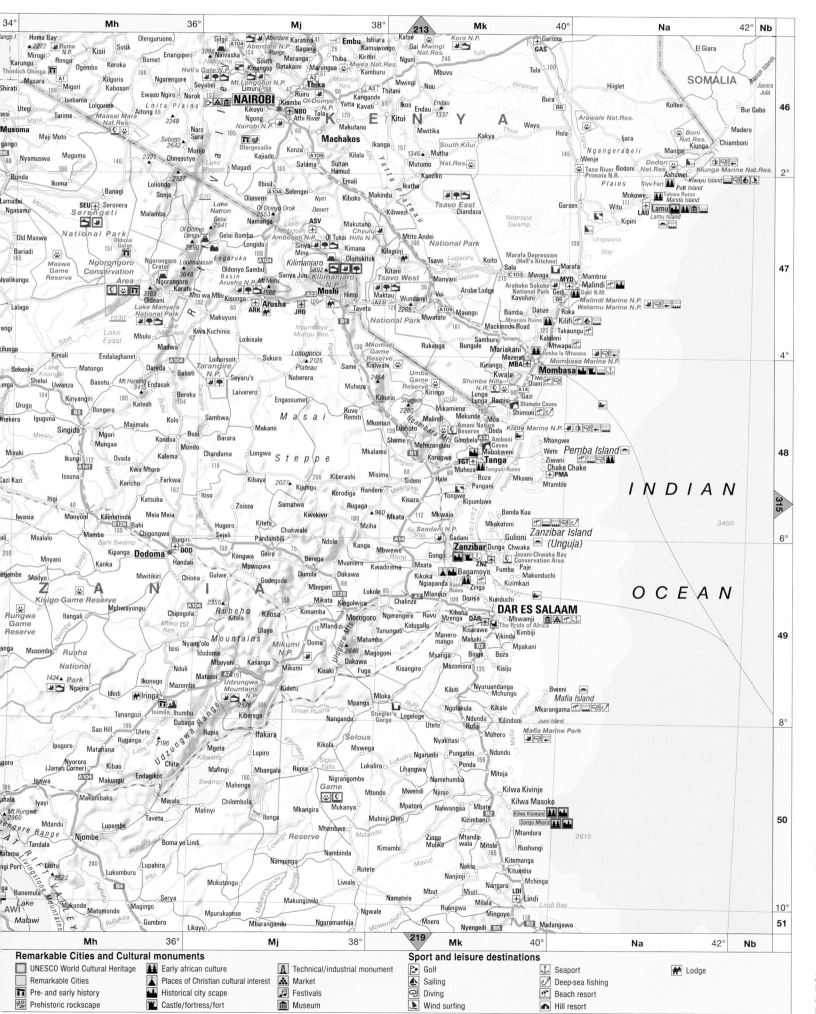

Serengeti National Park 14,500 km² – incredible abundance of 🦁 wildlife – UNESCO world heritage site. **Mh47**

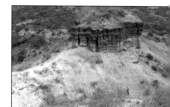

Olduvai Gorge Ngorongoro Conservation Area – 🏛 archeological site containing tools created by Homo erectus hominids, the ancestors of modern humans. **Mh47**

Ngorongoro Conservation Area 🏛 The area around the 260 km² large and up to 2,286-meter-high Ngorongoro volcanic crater is a UNESCO world heritage site and is inhabited by large herds of gnus and zebras. The Masai people graze their cattle in the area during certain times of the year. **Mh47**

Kilimanjaro Africa's tallest 🏔 mountain (5,892 m) – national park, a UNESCO world heritage site – temperate vegetation. **Mj47**

Lake Manyara Mineral rich 🌊 lake in the Great Rift Valley – 🦁 national park inhabited by lions and a large flamingo population (photo). **Mh47**

Zanzibar 🏛 UNESCO world heritage site – historic 🏛 Stone Town contains traditional Swahili architecture – vibrant ⚓ harbor – 🏖 beaches – 🤿 diving sites. **Mk49**

Remarkable Cities and Cultural monuments

- 🏛 UNESCO World Cultural Heritage
- 🏛 Remarkable Cities
- 🏛 Pre- and early history
- 🏛 Prehistoric rockscape
- 🏛 Early african culture
- 🏛 Places of Christian cultural interest
- 🏛 Historical city scape
- 🏛 Castle/fortress/fort
- 🏛 Technical/industrial monument
- 🏛 Market
- 🏛 Festivals
- 🏛 Museum

Sport and leisure destinations

- ⛳ Golf
- ⛵ Sailing
- 🤿 Diving
- 🏄 Wind surfing
- ⚓ Seaport
- 🎣 Deep-sea fishing
- 🏖 Beach resort
- 🏔 Hill resort
- 🏨 Lodge

Southern Angola, Western Zambia

The western and southern sections of Angola encompass two distinct geographic regions: the 🏖 coastal lowlands near the Atlantic Ocean and the highlands of the Bié Plateau. The climate of the coastal lowlands is heavily influenced by ocean currents and the vast ▨ **Namib Desert** stretches along Angola's coast. The width of the Namib Desert ranges between 80 and 130 kilometers in Angola. Dense fog frequently

blankets the areas directly on Angola's Atlantic coast. Rainfall is extremely sparse in the coastal lowlands farther away from the ocean.

The fertile **Bié Plateau** is a flat elevated plateau with an average elevation of 1,500 meters. The highest point on the plateau is the summit of the mountain

The Cunene River flows through Namibia and Angola. **Lg54**

Luanda Angola's capital city has historic 🏛 Portuguese colonial architecture in its old town, lively 🛒 markets, and beautiful sandy 🏖 beaches on the Ilha de Luanda. **Lg50**

Angola's National Parks While some 🐾 animals, including the African bush viper (top photo) and the Angolan colobus monkey (bottom photo), continue to flourish in the country's national park, others such as the sable antelope (middle photo) remain endangered.

Epupa Falls River rapids and a 35 meter tall 💧 waterfall on the Cunene River – inhabited by the nomadic Himba people – baobabs – large crocodile population. **Lg54**

Skeleton Coast Dangerous 🏖 coast stretching through Namibia and Angola – frequent fog and a large number of sandbars – numerous shipwrecks – 🏞 national park. **Lf54/55**

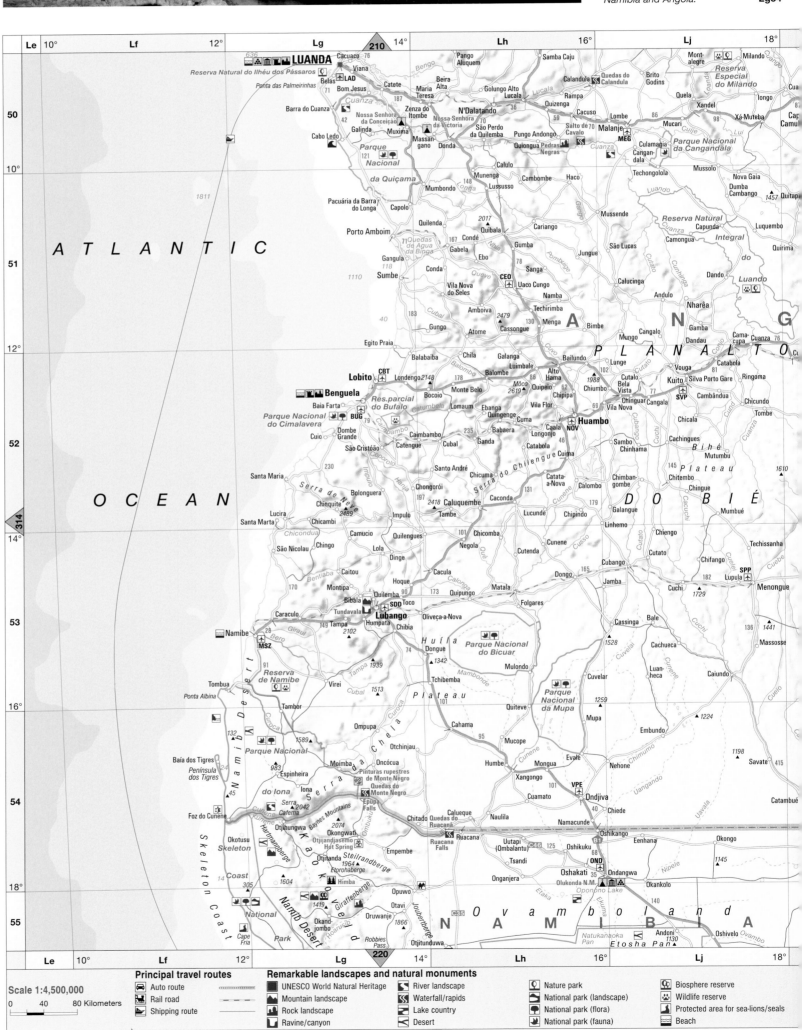

Scale 1:4,500,000

0   40   80 Kilometers

Principal travel routes
- 🚗 Auto route
- 🚃 Rail road
- ⋯⋯ Shipping route

Remarkable landscapes and natural monuments
- ■ UNESCO World Natural Heritage
- ▲ Mountain landscape
- Rock landscape
- Ravine/canyon
- River landscape
- Waterfall/rapids
- Lake country
- Desert
- Nature park
- National park (landscape)
- National park (flora)
- National park (fauna)
- Biosphere reserve
- Wildlife reserve
- Protected area for sea-lions/seals
- Beach

Moco (2,619 m). Many rivers and small streams flow through the plateau. Most of the larger rivers in the region flow south towards the Okavango River basin or north to the Cuanza (Kwanza) River and its many tributaries. The lower course of the **Cunene River** forms a long section of the border between Namibia and Angola. The Bié Plateau comprises several distinct vegetation zones including temperate savannahs in the south and tropical rainforests in the plateau's northwestern sections. Angola is rich in mineral resources – including oil, diamonds, iron ore, copper, and gold. These resources (especially oil) are the country's most valuable exports and dominate its trade with other nations. Despite the growing importance of mining, most of Angola's people work as farmers or agricultural laborers.

The **highlands of Zambia** consist primarily of dry forests and large marshlands (near the country's rivers). The country is home to abundant fauna; large herds of elephants, buffalos, and zebras inhabit Zambia's savannahs. The border region around the junction of Angola, Namibia, Zambia, and Botswana is dominated by two large rivers: the Okavango River (1,800 km) rises on the Bié Plateau in Angola and the **Zambezi** (2,736 km), which rises in northwestern Zambia. The Zambezi River forms the Victoria Falls (128 m) when it flows over a narrow gorge near the border between Zimbabwe and Zambia. The **Caprivi Strip** was created by colonial officials who wanted to control the route between Namibia (then a German colony) and the Zambezi River. Consisting of marshlands, the area is home to many hippopotamuses and crocodiles.

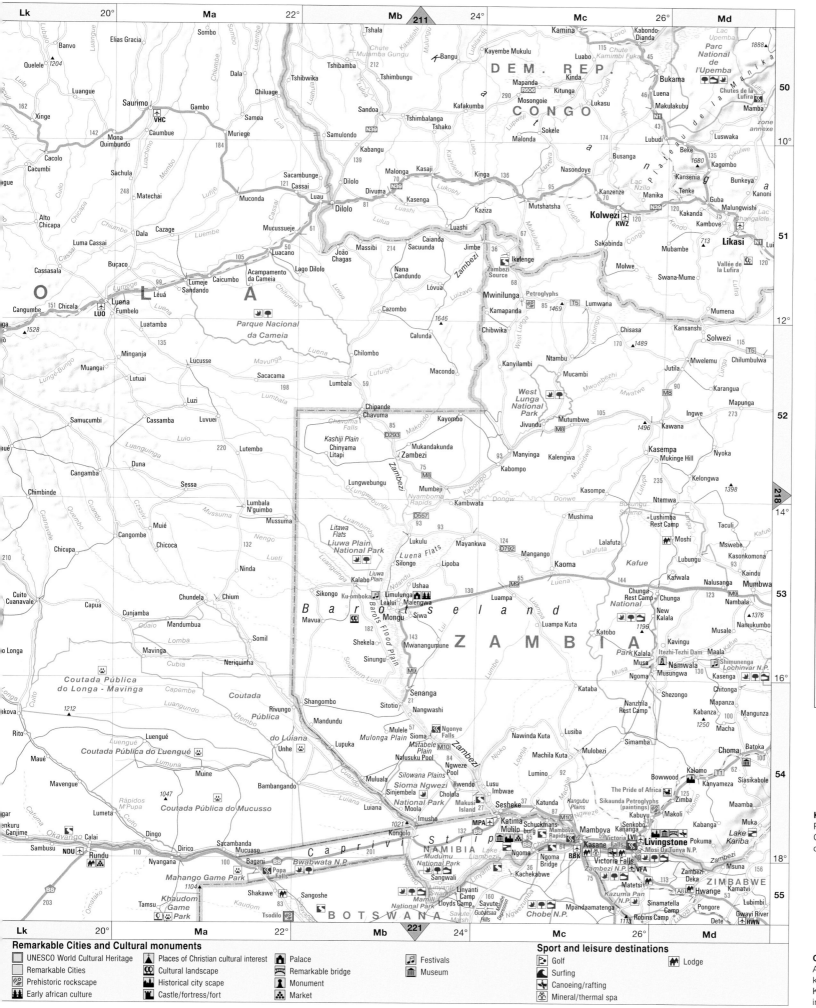

West Lunga National Park Swamps and swampy forests between the West Lunga and Kabompo Rivers – elephants, buffalos, and hippopotamuses. **Mc52**

Zambezi Major river in southern Africa (2,750 km) – rises in northern Zambia – several national parks in the river basin – river boat tours. **Mb-Mc54**

Victoria Falls The waterfalls, a UNESCO world heritage site, are situated on the border between Zimbabwe and Zambia. Victoria Falls drop more than 100 meters off the side of a long narrow gorge. **Mc54**

Kwando River The river rises on the Bié Plateau in Angola and flows through the Caprivi Strip – Mudumu National Park – crocodiles and hippopotamuses. **Mb55**

Okavango River The Okavango rises in Angola and flows over a distance of 1,800 kilometers to a large inland delta in the Kalahari Desert – ancient San rock paintings in the Tsodilo Hills. **Lk-Ma54/55**

Remarkable Cities and Cultural monuments

- UNESCO World Cultural Heritage
- Remarkable Cities
- Prehistoric rockscape
- Early african culture
- Places of Christian interest
- Cultural landscape
- Historical city scape
- Castle/fortress/fort
- Palace
- Remarkable bridge
- Monument
- Market
- Festivals
- Museum

Sport and leisure destinations

- Golf
- Surfing
- Canoeing/rafting
- Mineral/thermal spa
- Lodge

Eastern Zambia, Malawi, Northern Mozambique

The majority of Zambia's territory is covered by dense tropical forests. Two major rivers rise in the country: the ◧ **Zambezi River** rises in northern Zambia and the **Luapula River**, which rises in the **Bangweulu Swamps**. The Zambezi (2,736 km) forms a long section of the border between Zambia and Zimbabwe. Zambia contains around 45 % of southern Africa's freshwater reserves. The banks of the Zambezi and its major tributaries contain large swampy areas. Zambia's vast tropical forests are home to many endangered animals including elephants and chimpanzees. The country's government has created several national parks in the recent decades in an effort to protect local wildlife. Along Zambia's northern border with the

Lake Malawi has a wealth of unique flora and fauna. **Mg–Mh50/53**

Chimfunshi Chimpanzee Sanctuary ⬚ Africa's largest wildlife orphanage rescues injured and orphaned chimpanzees. **Md52**

South Luangwa National Park (Zambia, 9,050 km²) – ▣ lions, elephants, giraffes, and leopards. **Mf52**

Kafue National Park (Zambia, 22,400 km²) – large forests – endangered ▣ elephant population – antelopes (photo). **Mc-Md53**

Cabora Bassa Dam Major dam on the Zambezi River – ▨ 200-kilometer-long reservoir – important source of electricity for Mozambique. **Mf-Mg53**

Mana Pools National Park The park, a UNESCO world heritage site, is located in the Zambezi River basin. During the dry season, the area teems with wildlife including Nile crocodiles (bottom photo) and rare white rhinoceroses (top photo). **Me53/54**

Lake Kariba Large ▨ reservoir created by the Kariba Dam on the Zambezi River – recreation facilities. **Md-Me54**

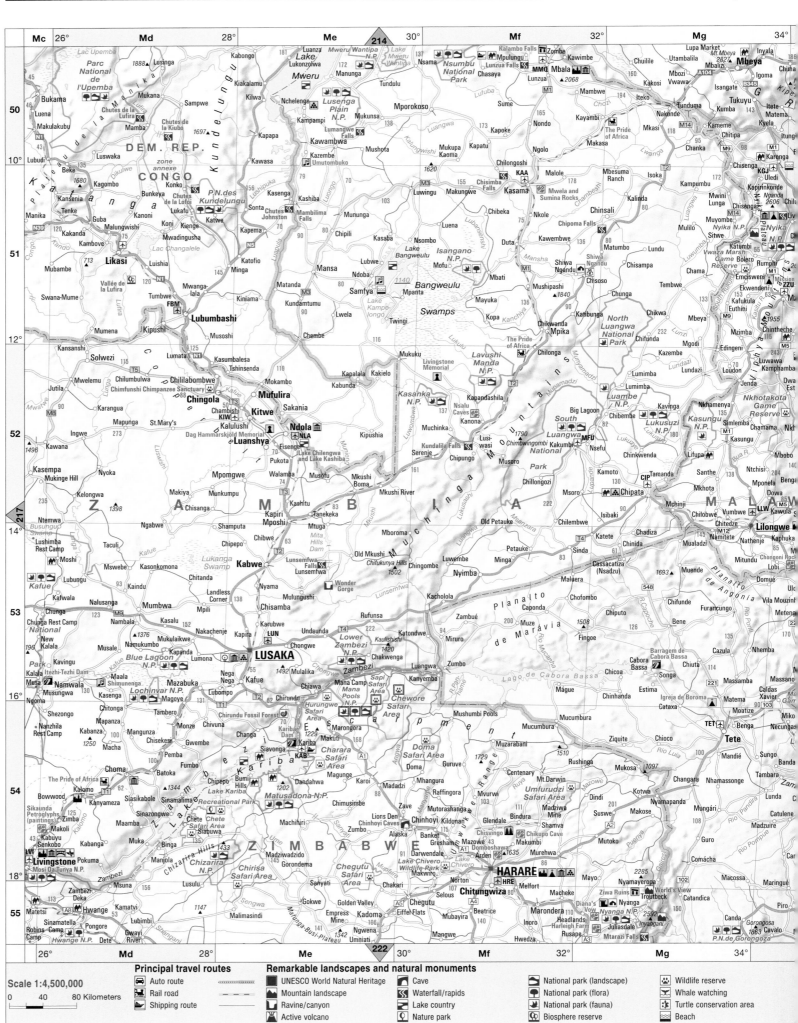

Scale 1:4,500,000

0   40   80 Kilometers

Principal travel routes
- 🚗 Auto route
- 🚂 Rail road
- ⛴ Shipping route

Remarkable landscapes and natural monuments
- ◼ UNESCO World Natural Heritage
- Mountain landscape
- Ravine/canyon
- Active volcano
- Cave
- Waterfall/rapids
- Lake country
- Nature park
- National park (landscape)
- National park (flora)
- National park (fauna)
- Biosphere reserve
- Wildlife reserve
- Whale watching
- Turtle conservation area
- Beach

Eastern Zambia, Malawi, Northern Mozambique

Democratic Republic of Congo lies the so-called **"copper belt"** – a region with abundant mineral resources. The ⛰ **Muchinga Mountains** (1,840 m), in northeastern Zambia, form the largest mountain range in the country.

⛰ **Lake Malawi**, also widely known as Lake Nyasa, is located in the southern section of the **Great Rift Valley**, which stretches from north to south through most of Malawi. Africa's third largest lake has a total length of 600 kilometers from north to south and 90 kilometers from east to west. More than 1,000 endemic fish species inhabit the lake, including around 500 species of perch. The lake is surrounded by a series of ⛰ highlands: Viphya Highlands, Livingstone Mountains, and Nyika Plateau. Mozambique borders Malawi, Zambia, Zimbabwe, and South Africa in the west; and the Indian Ocean in the east.

The northern half of Mozambique is a flat region with an average elevation of 1,000 meters above sea level and abundant rainfall. Several isolated highland areas are scattered throughout northern Mozambique. In general, the region's elevation rises gradually from east to west. Mount Namuli, the tallest mountain in Northern Mozambique, rises 2,420 meters. Vast tropical forests once covered large sections of northern Mozambique. Most of the remaining tropical rainforests in the country are located in the far north around ⛰ Lake Malawi.

Northern Mozambique has a ⛰ **rocky coastline** with many steep cliffs. Numerous ⛰ small islands and long ⛰ coral reefs are situated directly off the coast. Many of the islands near the coast are home to abundant animal life and beautiful, isolated beaches.

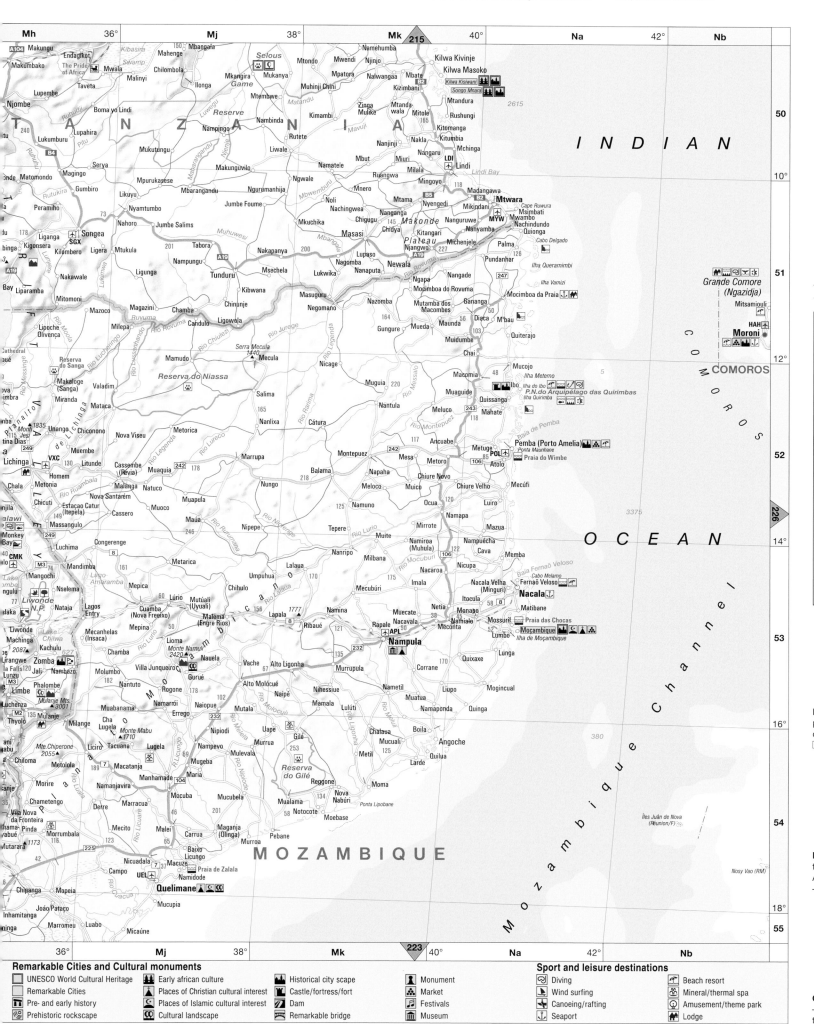

Lake Malawi National Park UNESCO world heritage site – abundant marine life – ⛰ cormorants and egrets – (photo) Monkey Bay. **Mh53**

Liwonde National Park ⛰ Located in the Shire River basin – the ⛰ local wildlife is threatened by poaching – large lion and elephant populations. **Mh53**

Mulanje Mountains The ⛰ mountain Sapitwa (3,001 m) in southeastern Malawi is the highest mountain in the range (top photo) and the country. Tropical rainforests cover large sections of the mountains and their foothills, while other sections are covered by shrubs and grass. The area features extensive hiking trails. **Mh53**

Ilha do Ibo Island in the Quirimbas Archipelago – ⛰ Portuguese fort – ⛰ sandy beaches – large ⛰ coral reefs off the coast – ⛰ sea turtles. **Na52**

Ilha de Moçambique UNESCO world heritage site – former capital of Portuguese East Africa – ⛰ Fort Sao Sebastiao – ⛰ mosques – ⛰ churches. **Na53**

Gurué ⛰ Highland region in Mozambique – Monte Namuli (2,240 m) – good hiking-trails ⛰ tea plantations (photo). **Mj53**

Remarkable Cities and Cultural monuments

- ⬜ UNESCO World Cultural Heritage
- ⬜ Remarkable Cities
- ⬜ Pre- and early history
- ⬜ Prehistoric rockscape
- ⬜ Early african culture
- ⬜ Places of Christian cultural interest
- ⬜ Places of Islamic cultural interest
- ⬜ Cultural landscape
- ⬜ Historical city scape
- ⬜ Castle/fortress/fort
- ⬜ Dam
- ⬜ Remarkable bridge
- ⬜ Monument
- ⬜ Market
- ⬜ Festivals
- ⬜ Museum

Sport and leisure destinations

- ⬜ Diving
- ⬜ Wind surfing
- ⬜ Canoeing/rafting
- ⬜ Seaport
- ⬜ Beach resort
- ⬜ Mineral/thermal spa
- ⬜ Amusement/theme park
- ⬜ Lodge

Namibia, Botswana, Western Zimbabwe

The Caprivi Strip: a sparsely populated wilderness in Namibia. **Mb54**

The two countries, **Botswana** and **Namibia**, consist mostly of semi-arid and arid regions such as the ⊠ **Kalahari Desert**. The ⊠ **Namib Desert** stretches over 1,500 kilometers along the southwestern coast of Africa. It is generally considered one of the most barren and inhospitable deserts in the world. The Namib contains no large oases or significant bodies of water. The desert does however contain several **dry watercourses** that occasionally carry water through the desert after periods of heavy rainfall in Namibia's highlands.

The ⊠ **Sossusvlei** area in the Namib Desert contains the tallest sand dunes in the world. Some of the sand dunes in the area are more than 300 meters tall. Namibia's Atlantic coast features many long

Kaokoveld ⌂ Mountainous region in northwestern Namibia – homelands of the Himba people (photo) – deep mountain valleys – desert elephants. **Lg54/55**

Etosha National Park The park (22,000 km²) encompasses the large Etosha saltpan and is home to many large wild animals. Guided tours on good trails (pads) provide visitors the chance to see lions (top photo), antelopes, zebras, gnus (bottom photos) and other animals up close. **Lh-Lj55**

Spitzkoppe The "Matterhorn" of Namibia – ⌂ granite formation in southern Damaraland – ⌂ ancient San rock paintings – popular destination for rock-climbers. **Lh56**

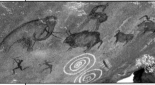

Erongo Mountains The ⌂ mountain range between the Namib Desert and Namibia's Central Highlands features many unusual eroded stone formations (top photo). Ancient rock paintings found in the area suggest the region was once considerably more fertile than it currently is. **Lh56**

Namib-Naukluft Park ⌷ Protected desert wilderness – ⌂ Naukluft Mountains – ⊠ sand dunes in Sossusvlei (photo). **Lh57/59**

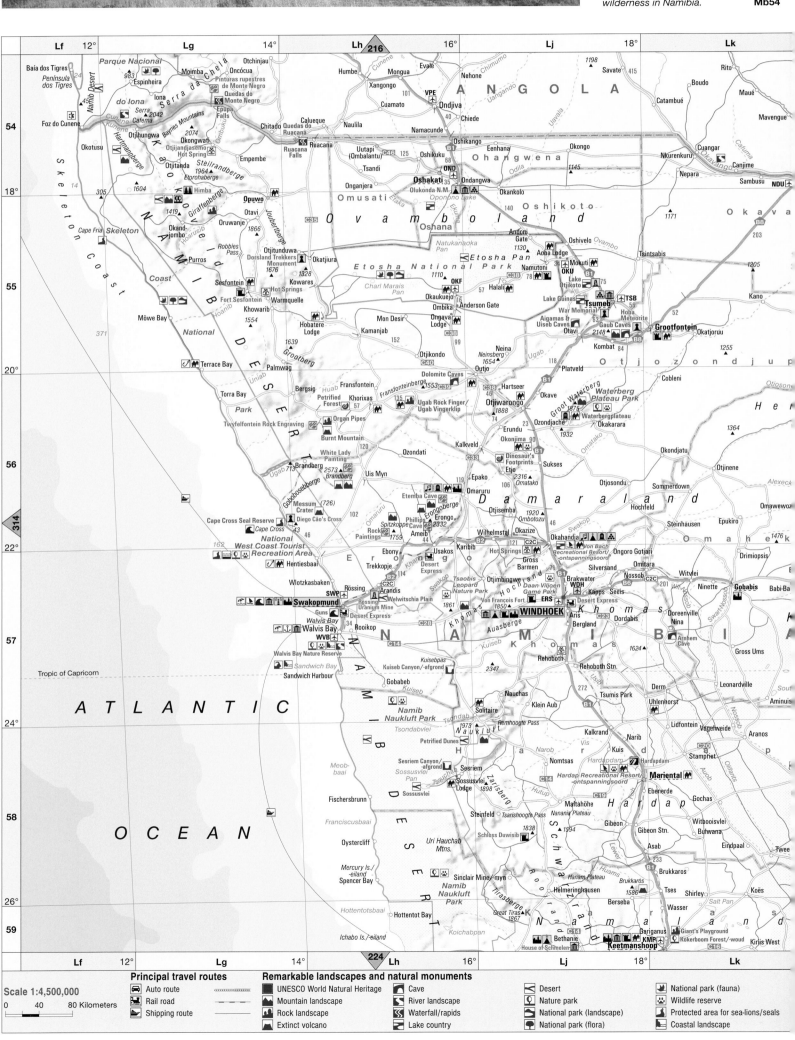

Scale 1:4,500,000

0   40   80 Kilometers

Principal travel routes
- Auto route
- Rail road
- Shipping route

Remarkable landscapes and natural monuments
- UNESCO World Natural Heritage
- Mountain landscape
- Rock landscape
- Extinct volcano
- Cave
- River landscape
- Waterfall/rapids
- Lake country
- Desert
- Nature park
- National park (landscape)
- National park (flora)
- National park (fauna)
- Wildlife reserve
- Protected area for sea-lions/seals
- Coastal landscape

sand dunes and the waters directly off the coast contain countless small sand bars. Namibia's northern coast is known as the "Skeleton Coast" because the large number of sandbars and dense fog once led to frequent shipwrecks in the area. The Kalahari Desert is significantly more fertile and hospitable than the Namib. The region's desert plants survive in the arid climate by storing water collected during the rainy season.

Located in Botswana, the 🖼 **Okavango River** delta is the largest inland river delta in the world. During much of the year, water from the Okavango turns this section of the Kalahari Desert into a fertile wetland with small islands and swamps. Both the Okavango delta and the areas surrounding it are home to abundant flora and fauna. Large sections of the Okavango delta have been declared 🖼 conservation areas by the governments of Namibia and Botswana.

Namibia's Central Highlands stretch through much of the country's interior between the Namib Desert and the arid plains of eastern Namibia. The region consists of ancient, craggy mountains. The southern section of the highlands is particularly arid and rainfall is extremely sparse in the area. The northern sections of the highlands ("the copper triangle") get moderate rainfall and the area is heavily cultivated.

Namibia is one of the most sparsely populated countries in the world with a population of less than two million. The country's economy is dominated by the export of natural resources, such as diamonds and uranium. Namibia's neighbor, **Botswana**, is also a sparsely populated nation with valuable natural resources. Botswana also has a long history of impressive economic growth and political stability.

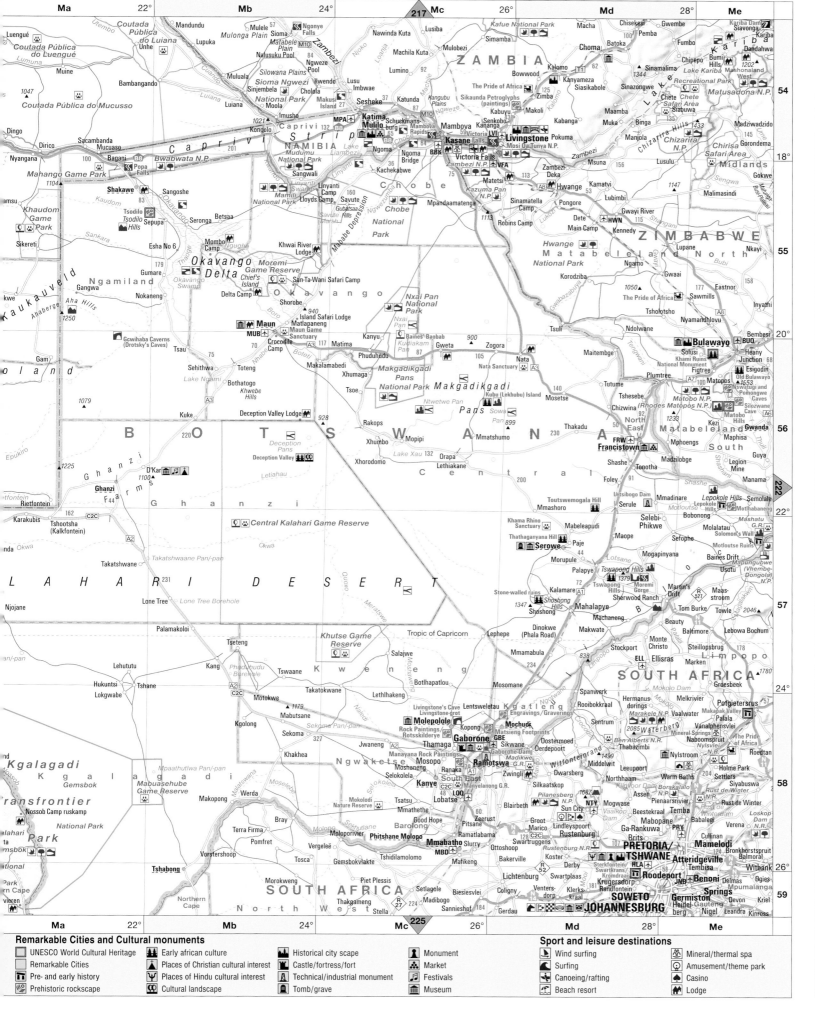

Chobe National Park 🖼 National Park along the Chobe River in Botswana – home to large elephant herds. **Mc55**

Okavango Delta The UNESCO world heritage site comprises the world's largest inland delta. During the rainy season, the 🖼 Okavango River floods large sections of the Kalahari Desert (top photo). The delicate ecosystem in the delta supports a diverse collection of plants (middle photo) and wild animals (bottom photo). **Mb55**

The San, also known as Bushmen, have inhabited southern Africa longer than any other group. Over time, the San have been pushed into the less fertile areas of the region. Most of the San in Namibia and Botswana have abandoned their traditional nomadic hunter-gatherer lifestyles.

Remarkable Cities and Cultural monuments

▢ UNESCO World Cultural Heritage	▲ Early african culture	▣ Historical city scape
▢ Remarkable Cities	▼ Places of Christian cultural interest	▣ Castle/fortress/fort
● Pre- and early history	▽ Places of Hindu cultural interest	⚙ Technical/industrial monument
● Prehistoric rockscape	◆ Cultural landscape	✝ Tomb/grave

▣ Monument	
🏛 Market	
♫ Festivals	
🏛 Museum	

Sport and leisure destinations

Wind surfing	Mineral/thermal spa
Surfing	Amusement/theme park
Canoeing/rafting	Casino
Beach resort	Lodge

Eastern Zimbabwe, Southern Mozambique

The beautiful  mountainous landscapes of eastern Zimbabwe and northern South Africa with their abundant wildlife are a major contrast to the coastal lowlands of Mozambique. The variety of **Zimbabwe's** landscapes range from the barren arid sections of the Kalahari Basin in the west to the mountainous regions covered by dense tropical vegetation in the country's east. The highlands of central and eastern Zimbabwe, like the highlands on

the other side of the **Limpopo River** in South Africa, consist of ancient mountain ranges. Zimbabwe's tallest mountain, **Inyangani**, rises 2,592 meters above sea level in the border region near Mozambique. The area of forested savannahs along the Limpopo River between South Africa and Zimbabwe is known as

A pristine forest in the Umfurudzi Safari Area (Zimbabwe).   **Mf54**

Domboshawa Area in Zimbabwe with ancient cave paintings – holy site for several local communities.   **Mf54**

Matobo National Park Nature reserve in Zimbabwe with many ancient stone formations and rock paintings – UNESCO world heritage site.   **Me56**

Great Zimbabwe (UNESCO world heritage site) Historic ruins of a powerful African kingdom that flourished between the 12th and 15th centuries. Great Zimbabwe was once home to 20,000 people. The ruins constitute one of sub-Saharan Africa's greatest archeological sites.   **Mf56**

Nyanga National Park Mountainous region in Zimbabwe with tropical forests and several waterfalls – Remains of abandoned settlements built in the 17th and 18th centuries – Rhodes Museum.   **Mg55**

Scale 1:4,500,000

0   40   80 Kilometers

Principal travel routes
- Auto route
- Rail road
- Shipping route

Remarkable landscapes and natural monuments
- UNESCO World Natural Heritage
- Mountain landscape
- Rock landscape
- Ravine/canyon
- Cave
- River landscape
- Waterfall/rapids
- Lake country
- Fossil site
- Nature park
- National park (landscape)
- National park (flora)
- National park (fauna)
- Wildlife reserve
- Whale watching
- Turtle conservation area

the **lowveld**. The region is home to many wild animals and encompasses several ⊟ nature reserves including Matusadona National Park in Zimbabwe. The **Great Dyke**, a long series of ⛰ hills and ridges, stretches through northwest Zimbabwe around 60 kilometers west of the capital Harare. The ancient geological formation consists of Precambrian-era stone containing an abundance of natural resources.

Mozambique has a total area of 812,379 km² and around 17 million inhabitants. In contrast to neighboring Zimbabwe, only the northern and western sections of Mozambique are mountainous. Most of the country consists of low-lying plains crossed by several major rivers, including the ↙ **Zambezi** and **Limpopo Rivers**. Most of Mozambique's regions have tropical or subtropical climates with abundant rainfall. The only significant excep-

tions are the country's northern highlands which have more temperate climates because of their relatively high elevations. The **Great Limpopo Transfrontier Park** (30,000 km²) is a multinational nature reserve created to protect the threatened flora and fauna in the border region between Zimbabwe, Mozambique, and South Africa. The western section of the park, created in 2002, encompasses South Africa's famous

Kruger National Park. Mozambique's Indian Ocean coast is also home to several nature reserves, created in recent decades to protect the area's biodiversity on land and in the waters off the coast. Across the **Mozambique Channel**, the coast areas of **Madagascar** are inhabited by many rare and endangered animals. The waters around Madagascar contain large coral reefs with fascinating marine life.

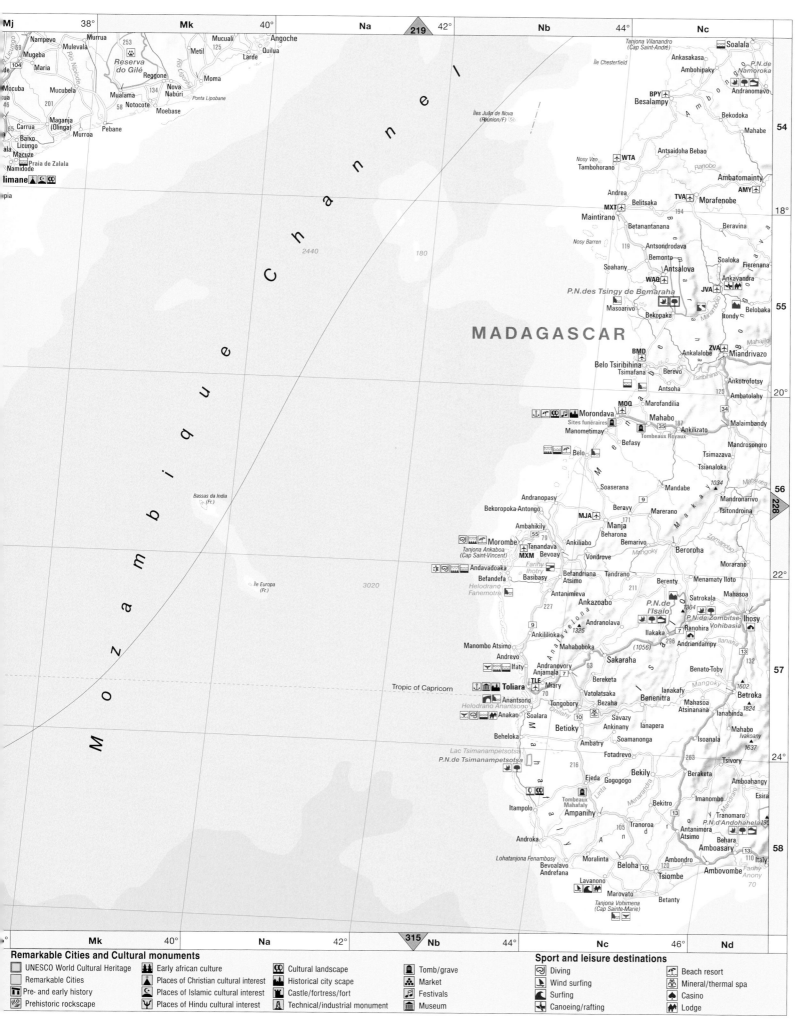

Kruger National Park ⊟ The South African park (20,000 km²) was founded in 1898. More than 150 mammals inhabit the park including leopards (top photo), giraffes (middle photo), and buffalo (bottom photo). The Great Limpopo Transfrontier Park (36,000 km²), founded in 2002, encompasses Kruger National Park and areas in Zimbabwe and Mozambique. **Mf57/58**

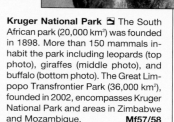

Blyde River Canyon South African canyon ⊔ – 26 kilometers long and 800 meters deep – the three ⛰ rondavels. **Mf58**

Swaziland ⛰ The kingdom of Swaziland is a mountainous country with a total area of 17,363 km². Swaziland maintained at least nominal independence through centuries of European colonization in southern Africa. Ethnic Swazis form the overwhelming majority of the population and the king holds supreme power over the country's government. **Mf58/59**

Maputo Mozambique's capital city – ▣ Portuguese colonial architecture and art nouveau train station designed by Gustave Eiffel – lively 🏛 markets – 🏛 modern art museum – vibrant cultural scene. **Mg58**

Remarkable Cities and Cultural monuments

◻ UNESCO World Cultural Heritage	⛪ Early african culture
◻ Remarkable Cities	⛪ Places of Christian cultural interest
🅣 Pre- and early history	☪ Places of Islamic cultural interest
🅟 Prehistoric rockscape	卐 Places of Hindu cultural interest
▦ Cultural landscape	▦ Tomb/grave
▦ Historical city scape	▦ Market
▦ Castle/fortress/fort	▦ Festivals
▦ Technical/industrial monument	▦ Museum

Sport and leisure destinations

▢ Diving	▣ Beach resort
▢ Wind surfing	▣ Mineral/thermal spa
▢ Surfing	▣ Casino
▢ Canoeing/rafting	▣ Lodge

South Africa, Lesotho, Swaziland

With a population exceeding 40 million and a total area of 1.2 million km², the Republic of South Africa is one of the largest and most populous countries in sub-Saharan Africa. Together with Namibia and the kingdoms Lesotho and Swaziland, South Africa comprises a region with an amazing diversity of landscapes and topographies. The region encompasses semi-arid areas in the Karoo and the Namib Desert, subtropical forests

near the Indian Ocean coast, and the craggy mountains of the Drakensberg Range, a section of southern Africa's Great Escarpment. The many national parks and nature reserves in southern Africa are refuges for many of the region's animals, some of which are threatened by extinction. Kruger National

Southern Africa's arid regions feature beautiful and unique vegetation.

Fish River Canyon National Park 161-kilometer-long and 550 meter deep canyon – largest canyon system in Africa. **Lj59**

Augrabies Falls National Park Stunning waterfalls and stone formations – Oranje River – antelope, leopard, and rhinoceros populations. **Ma60**

West-Coast-Nationalpark Beautiful conservation area around a lagoon near the village of Langebaan – a diverse collection of birds inhabit the area. **Lk62**

Cape Town South Africa's most beautiful city is located on a peninsula between the Indian and Atlantic Oceans. The city has become one of Africa's most visited destinations since the end of apartheid. Cape Town's historic district and modern busi-ness center (top photo) are situated at the foot of Table Mountain. The sur-rounding areas feature spectacular landscapes (bottom photo). **Lk62/63**

Little Karoo Semi-arid region near the Swart Mountains (1,500 m) – ostrich farms – numerous vineyards. **Ma62**

Garden Route Beautiful landscapes along South Africa's southern coast – sandy beaches (photo). **Mb63**

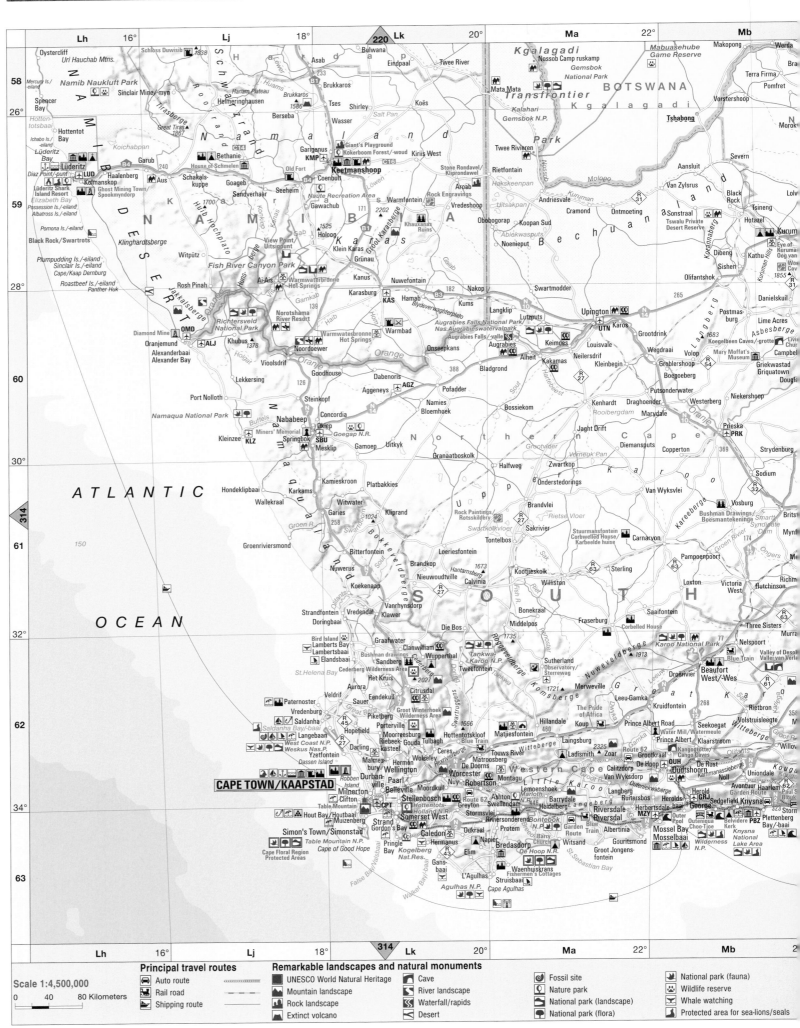

Scale 1:4,500,000

0   40   80 Kilometers

Principal travel routes
- Auto route
- Rail road
- Shipping route
- — Auto route (dashed)
- ··· Shipping route (dotted)

Remarkable landscapes and natural monuments
- UNESCO World Natural Heritage
- Mountain landscape
- Rock landscape
- Extinct volcano
- Cave
- River landscape
- Waterfall/rapids
- Desert
- Fossil site
- Nature park
- National park (landscape)
- National park (flora)
- National park (fauna)
- Wildlife reserve
- Whale watching
- Protected area for sea-lions/seals

Park in South Africa is the most famous nature reserve in the region. The park is home to many of the animals typically associated with the region, including elephants, lions, and rhinoceroses. The Indian and Atlantic Ocean coasts of South Africa are popular areas for whale, dolphin, and seal watching.

The region around the Cape of Good Hope has a Mediterranean climate. The Cape Region is also home to a unique type of vegetation called Fynbos, the smallest of the world's floral kingdoms. The Fynbos classification comprises more than 8,500 different plant species, all of which are found within a 70,000 km²-large-area in southwestern South Africa. South Africa has a wealth of natural resources. Johannesburg, the largest city in southern Africa, developed into a major city after a gold rush in nearby mines during the late 19th century. Uranium, nickel, and platinum are also important resources produced in South Africa. South Africa has the largest and most developed economy in Africa.

Although black Africans form a majority of the country's population, South Africa is also home to millions of Asians, whites, and people of mixed ethnicity. For several decades South Africa was ruled by a government that enforced strict racial segregation and denied most of the country's people the right to vote. Although apartheid was ended in the 1990s, there are still major economic differences between the ethnic groups of South Africa. Most urban black and mixed-race South Africans live in townships, areas with mostly substandard housing. The largest ethnic groups in the country are the Xhosa and Zulu peoples. The San people (Bushmen) have lived in southern Africa for thousands of years.

Johannesburg Major industrial and financial center in South Africa – 712,000 inhabitants (with Soweto 2.5 millions) – important 🏛 museums. **Md-Me59**

Lesotho The mountainous kingdom of the Sotho people (2 million inhabitants, 30,355 km², capital city Maseru) features the highest mountain in southern Africa – ⛰ Thabana Ntlenyana (3,482 m) – beautiful highland regions. Traditional means of locomotion are the Sotho ponies. **Md-Me60/61**

Drakensberg 250-kilometer-long ⛰ mountain range with a maximum height of 3,842 meters – San rock painting. **Me60**

Greater St. Lucia Wetland Park Coastal marshlands – UNESCO world heritage site – crocodiles, rhinoceros, and hippopotamuses – whale watching. **Mg59**

Zulu The more than ten million Zulus form the largest ethnic group in South Africa. Most of the region's Zulu population is concentrated in the KwaZulu-Natal region and around Johannesburg. During the 19th century, the Zulus fiercely resisted European colonization under the reign of Shaka Zulu.

Durban South African port city on the Indian Ocean coast – large Indian community – Juma Mosque – Victoria Street Market – Sea World aquarium – beaches and beachside hotels. **Mf60**

Remarkable Cities and Cultural monuments

- UNESCO World Cultural Heritage
- Remarkable Cities
- Pre- and early history
- Prehistoric rockscape
- Places of Christian cultural interest
- Places of Hindu cultural interest
- Cultural landscape
- Historical city scape
- Castle/fortress/fort
- Technical/industrial monument
- Dam
- Theater of war/battlefield
- Monument
- Market
- Museum
- Theater

Sport and leisure destinations

- Race track
- Sailing
- Diving
- Wind surfing
- Surfing
- Beach resort
- Mineral/thermal spa
- Casino

Most of the large islands scattered in the **Indian Ocean** were created millions of years ago when the landmass **Gondwanaland** drifted apart, forming the different continents of our planet. Sri Lanka and Madagascar are the largest of the many islands scattered throughout the sections of the Indian Ocean between Asia and Africa. Other large islands that once dotted the ocean were submerged after a rise in global sea level. The Sey-

chelles are the peaks of a mountain chain that once stretched across one of these landmasses that disappeared beneath the ocean.
The Comoros were created through volcanic activity, millions of years later than the Seychelles or Madagascar. ▲ **Karthala** (2,361 m) on the island Grand

Palm trees and sandy beaches on the island of La Digue (Seychelles). **Nh48**

Flora and Fauna of Madagascar
Madagascar is home to countless endemic plants and animals, many of which remain undiscovered. Madagascar's unique animals developed in isolation from other regions, and new species are still being discovered on the island. The government of Madagascar has created several nature reserves to protect the island's biodiversity. Photos from top to bottom: golden bamboo lemur, octopus trees, Parson's chameleon, baobab trees.

Nosy Be Island with beautiful long white sandy ▤ beaches – thick tropical vegetaton and ▲ volcanoes – ▥ Nosy Faly – the island's main town ▥ Hell-Ville features attractive colonial architecture. **Ne52**

Réserve Spéciale d'Ankarana Karst landscapes with numerous subterranean ⌂ caves – subterranean rivers – crocodile population – ⊕ baobab groves containing the graves of local kings. **Ne52**

Cirque Rouge Beautiful ▤ stone formation near the city of Mahajanga – popular tourist destination. **Nd53**

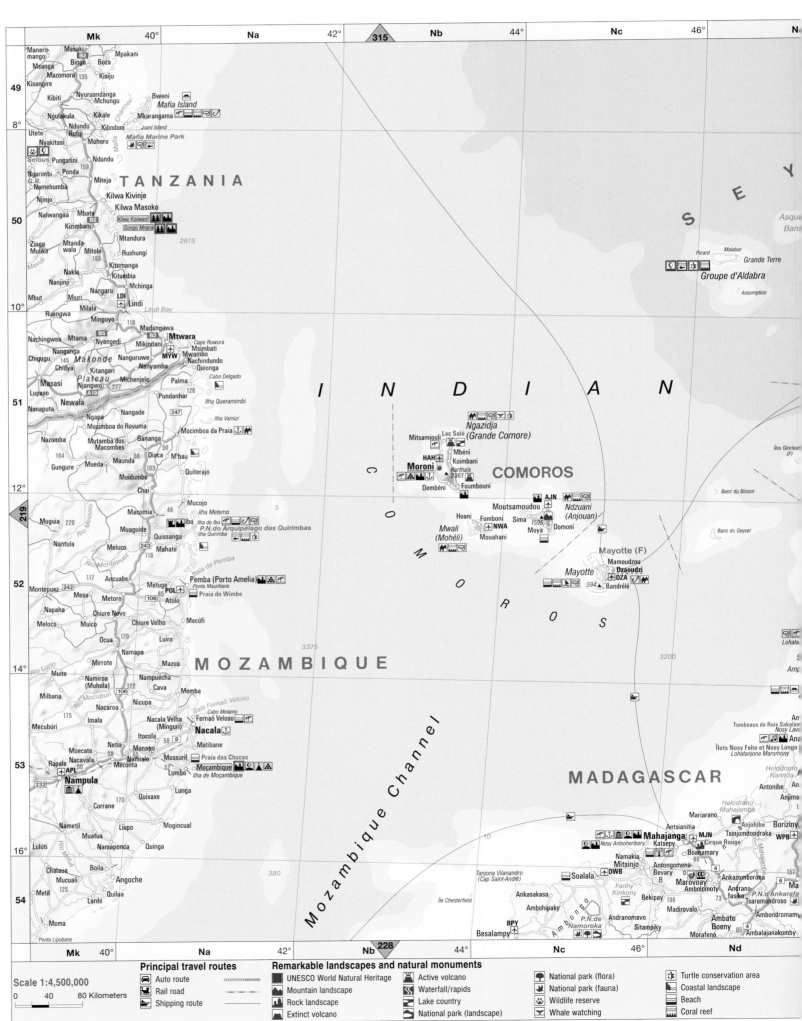

Scale 1:4,500,000
0   40   80 Kilometers

Principal travel routes
- 🚗 Auto route
- 🚆 Rail road
- Shipping route

Remarkable landscapes and natural monuments
- ■ UNESCO World Natural Heritage
- ■ Mountain landscape
- ■ Rock landscape
- ■ Extinct volcano
- ▲ Active volcano
- Waterfall/rapids
- Lake country
- National park (landscape)
- National park (flora)
- National park (fauna)
- Wildlife reserve
- Whale watching
- Turtle conservation area
- Coastal landscape
- Beach
- Coral reef

Comoros, Seychelles, Northern Madagascar

Comore (Ngazidja) is the youngest and one of the more active volcanoes in the island group. The volcanoes on Mayotte and Moheli, the oldest of the Comoro Islands, have been dormant for centuries. All of the major Comoro Islands have mountainous interiors surrounded by narrow strips of flat coastal land. The flora and fauna of the islands is similar to that of Madagascar. Many of the islands' indigenous species have become extinct in recent centuries because of human activities including logging and farming. The discovery of a live coelacanth in the waters around the Comoros in 1938 shocked the scientific world. Before this discovery, the unusual fish-like creatures were believed to have become extinct millions of years ago.

 Madagascar (590,000 km²), the world's fourth largest island, is situated 400 kilometers off the coast of mainland Africa. The island encompasses several topographies and distinct climate zones ranging from humid subtropical to semi-arid. Madagascar's isolation from other landmasses led to the development of many unique plants and animals. The island's lemur population is widely studied by scientists from around the world. Like Madagascar, the Seychelles (454 km²) are home to an abundance of unique endemic flora and fauna. Thousands of Seychelles green turtles and several rare bird species inhabit the Aldabra Atoll. The Seychelles are an archipelago of more than 100 islands, only a third of which are inhabited. The central islands, including Mahe and Praslin, have mountainous interiors. These islands have heavy levels of rainfall during most of the year and are covered by dense green vegetation. The outer islands of the Seychelles are mostly flat coral islands with arid climates.

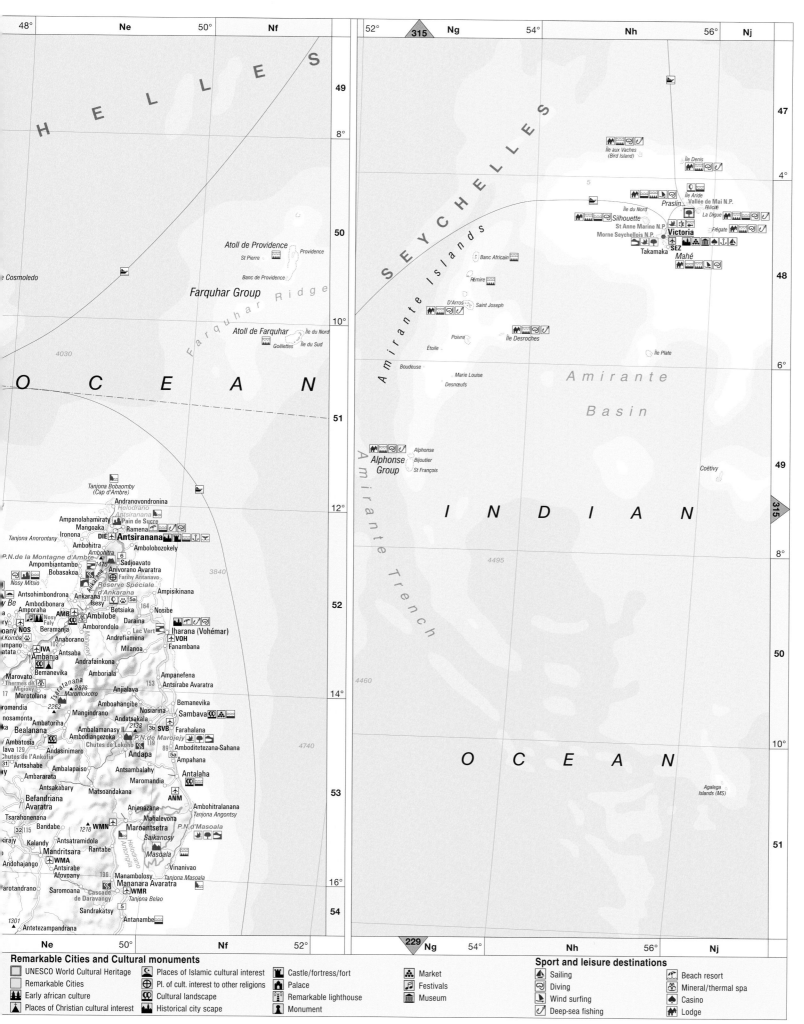

Comoros Moroni (top photo) on the island Grande Comore is the capital of the Comoros. The island of Anjouan (bottom photo) has beautiful undeveloped beaches. **Nb-Nc51/52**

Aldabra Atoll The islands (UNESCO world heritage site) are home to many animals including red-footed boobies (top photo) and large manta rays (bottom photo). **Nd50**

Praslin Vallée de Mal, a UNESCO world heritage site, contains coco-de-mer palm forests – diving sites. **Nh48**

St. Anne National Marine Park Five islands (photo) – spawning ground for turtles – diving sites. **Nh48**

Frégate Island Privately owned island in the Seychelles – beaches and diving sites – exclusive holiday resort. **Nh48**

Remarkable Cities and Cultural monuments

- ☐ UNESCO World Cultural Heritage
- ☐ Remarkable Cities
- Early african culture
- Places of Christian cultural interest
- Places of Islamic cultural interest
- Pl. of cult. interest to other religions
- Cultural landscape
- Historical city scape
- Castle/fortress/fort
- Palace
- Remarkable lighthouse
- Monument

Sport and leisure destinations

- Market
- Festivals
- Museum
- Sailing
- Diving
- Wind surfing
- Deep-sea fishing
- Beach resort
- Mineral/thermal spa
- Casino
- Lodge

Madagascar, Réunion, Mauritius

The islands of  **Madagascar**,  **Mauritius**, and  **Réunion** are situated on the western edge of the Indian Ocean. This region features a unique mixture of African and Asian cultural influences. The majority of Mauritius' population consists of people whose ancestors came from the Indian subcontinent to work as field laborers on the island. The French territory Réunion has large ethnic European (especially French), African, and Asian

communities. Madagascar is home to dozens of distinct indigenous ethnic groups and religious communities. The majority of Madagascar's people, however, are the descendants of both (Malay) Southeast Asians and black African ancestors. Eastern Madagascar's terrain is dominated by ancient mountains (up to

Lac d'Itasy (Madagascar): a lake surrounded by volcanic highlands.   **Nd55**

Antananarivo Madagascar's capital and largest city – vibrant weekly 🖼 market on Fridays: Zoma – 🏛 wooden royal palace: Rova – 🏚 colonial-era architecture.   **Nd55**

Lac d'Itasy Beautiful lake situated 2,300 meters above sea level, west of Antananarivo – 🗻 volcanic landscapes – home to large bird populations.   **Nd55**

The **Tsingy de Bemaraha Strict Nature Reserve** features fascinating heavily eroded 🗻 landscapes (bottom photo) and is a designated UNESCO world heritage site. Tall baobab trees (top photo) are common throughout the area. The dense tropical rainforests in the reserves are home to many lemurs and birds.   **Nc55**

Rocher d'Ifandana 🗻 Granite hills in Madagascar's southern highlands – located near 🌳 Andringitra National Park, which also feature numerous granite formations.   **Nd56**

Isalo National Park (81,540 ha) Mountainous conservation area featuring unique 🗻 stone formations – deep 🏞 gorges with beautiful tropical vegetation.   **Nc57**

Befandefa Town on Madagascar's southwestern coast – 🪸 coral reefs and isolated 🏖 beaches – sheltered lagoons.   **Nb57**

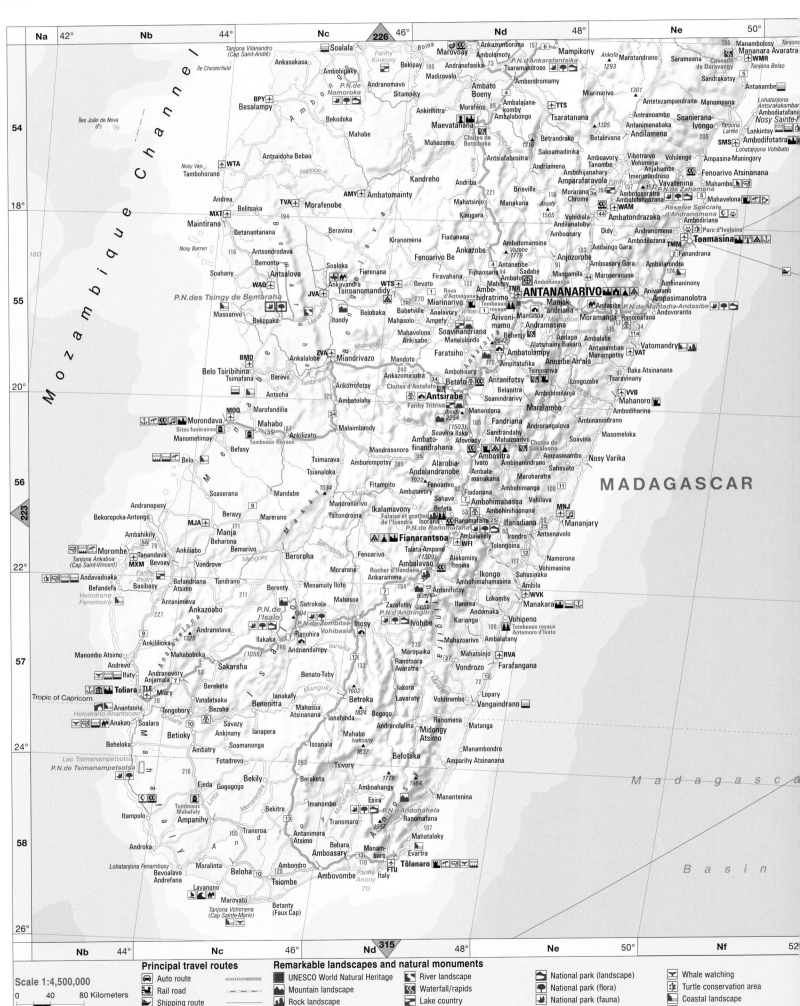

Scale 1:4,500,000

0   40   80 Kilometers

Principal travel routes
- 🚗 Auto route
- 🚂 Rail road
- ⛴ Shipping route

Remarkable landscapes and natural monuments
- ▪ UNESCO World Natural Heritage
- ▪ Mountain landscape
- ▪ Rock landscape
- ▪ Extinct volcano
- ▪ River landscape
- ▪ Waterfall/rapids
- ▪ Lake country
- ▪ Fossil site
- ▪ National park (landscape)
- ▪ National park (flora)
- ▪ National park (fauna)
- ▪ Wildlife reserve
- ▪ Whale watching
- ▪ Turtle conservation area
- ▪ Coastal landscape
- ▪ Beach

3,500 m high) including the ⛰ **Ankaratra Mountains**. The eastern edges of these mountain ranges are covered by dense tropical rainforests. Due to ocean currents and moist winds, Madagascar's eastern coast is a region of heavy rainfall and high humidity. Southwestern Madagascar is bounded to the north and east by two high mountain massifs. The region is largely arid with sparse rainfall throughout the year and scattered dry forests.

Much of Madagascar's land is cultivated including the country's large highlands. Rice, the staple food of most Madagascans, is widely cultivated for domestic consumption, while coffee is the leading export crop. Madagascar's amazing abundance of unique endemic flora and fauna is largely the result of the island's geographic isolation. The island's fifteen endemic lemur species are perhaps the most fascinating and studied native creatures found there. Of the more than 230 reptiles on Madagascar around 95 % are native to the island, including 38 types of chameleons.

The small islands of Réunion and Mauritius are both part of the Mascarene Archipelago in the Indian Ocean. The archipelago developed above a so-called hot spot, an area on the ocean's floor where magma rises from the Earth's mantle. Mauritius, the oldest island in the group, is around eight million years old, while Réunion was formed three million years ago. The volcano ⛰ **Piton de la Fournaise** (2,632 m) on Réunion is one of the world's most active in terms of lava production. The ⛰ highlands around the dormant volcano ⛰ **Piton de Neiges** are covered by dense tropical vegetation. A long ring of ⬚ **coral reefs** surround Mauritius.

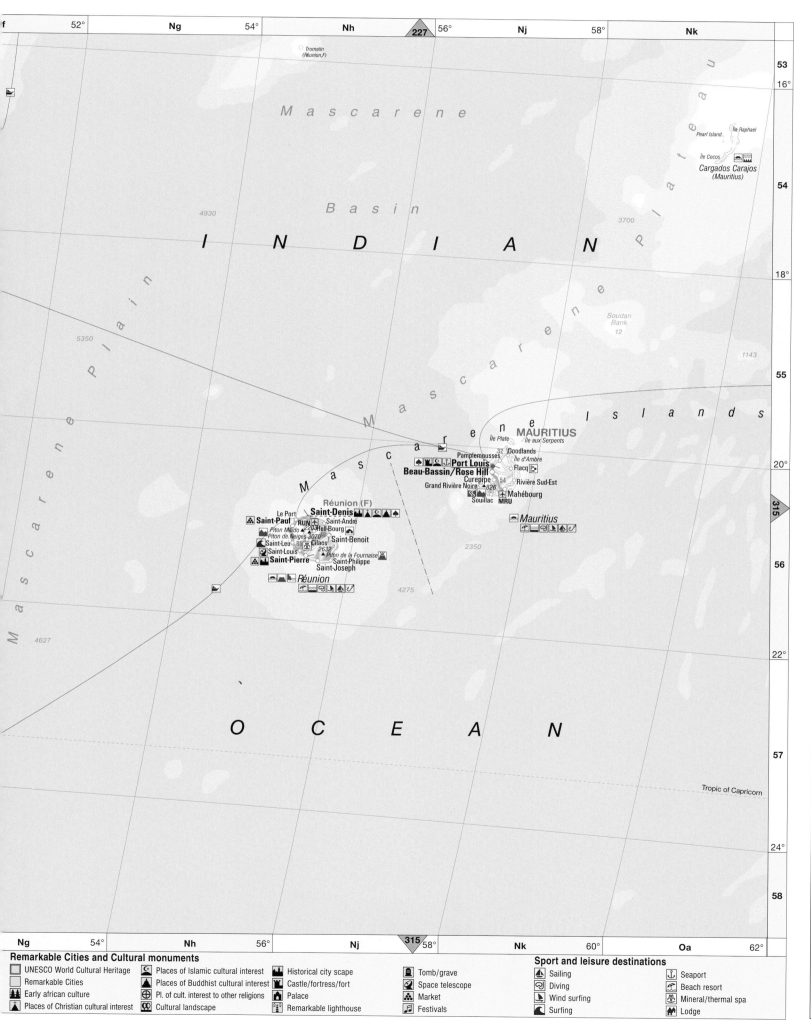

Andringitra National Park ⛰ Mountainous national park in southeastern Madagascar – fascinating endemic 🌸 flora including numerous rare orchids – also home to several lemur species and rare butterflies. **Nd57**

Mahafaly Tribal Tombs 🏛 Sacred site for the Mahafaly people – wooden statues and animal horns adorn the tombs. **Nc58**

Réunion The island (2,500 km²) features beautiful ⛰ volcanic highlands. ⛰ **Piton de la Fournaise** (top and bottom photos) frequently releases large amounts of lava from its summit (middle photo: Cirque de Salazie). **Nh56**

Mauritius has several interesting stone formations including ⛰ **Trois Mamelles** (top photo) and **Morne Brabant** (middle photo). Ethnic Indians (bottom photo) form the majority of Mauritius' population. **Nj56**

Remarkable Cities and Cultural monuments

- ☐ UNESCO World Cultural Heritage
- ☐ Remarkable Cities
- ▲ Early african culture
- ▲ Places of Christian cultural interest
- ☪ Places of Islamic cultural interest
- ☸ Places of Buddhist cultural interest
- ✚ Pl. of cult. interest to other religions
- ⬛ Palace
- ⬛ Cultural landscape
- ⬛ Historical city scape
- ⬛ Castle/fortress/fort
- ⬛ Remarkable lighthouse
- ⬛ Tomb/grave
- ⬛ Space telescope
- ⬛ Market
- ⬛ Festivals

Sport and leisure destinations

- ⛵ Sailing
- 🤿 Diving
- 🏄 Wind surfing
- 🏄 Surfing
- ⚓ Seaport
- 🏖 Beach resort
- ♨ Mineral/thermal spa
- 🏡 Lodge

Chicago (top): The modern skyline of the city glitters next to Lake Michigan.
Joshua Tree National Park (bottom): Sunset above California's Joshua Trees.

Yucátan Peninsula (left): Ancient remnants of the Maya civilization on the Caribbean coast.
Cascade Mountains (right): Snow and glaciers cover Mt. Rainier (4,392 m) in Washington State.

North and Central America

The Golden Gate and vibrant San Francisco, the red rock formations of Monument Valley, the Grand Canyon, endless prairies, the legacy of the Maya, Aztecs, and immigrants from all corners of the globe, the colonial towns of Mexico, Caribbean Islands, historic Route 66 and Highway No. 1, and New York City... Welcome to North America.

North and Central America · The continent

The northern continent of the Western Hemisphere stretches from the Arctic Ocean to the Caribbean Sea. North America can be divided into three large geographic regions running from north to south. The western portion of the continent is dominated by the **Cordilleras**, a series of mountain ranges which contains Alaska's Mount McKinley (6,194 m), the continent's tallest mountain. The Appalachian Mountains stretch through much of eastern North America. In between these two regions lie the vast Central Plains of North America. One of the continent's most interesting geographic attractions is Death Valley, the lowest point on the planet's surface.

The **Rocky Mountains**, the largest mountain chain in North America, extend through the United States and Canada. In the American Southwest, the Rocky Mountains border the Sierra Madre mountain range which extends through most of Mexico and into Central America. The Isthmus of Panama is only 50 kilometers wide. The islands of the **Caribbean** form a large chain running from Cuba to South America and are separated into two groups: the Lesser Antilles and the Greater Antilles.

The Rocky Mountains are 4,300 kilometers long.

One of the world's largest nations, the United States of America is home to many diverse landscapes, including (photos from top to bottom) the glaciers of Alaska's Glacier Bay, the peaks of the Rocky Mountains, the Great Plains, and Monument Valley in the deserts of the Southwest.

The Alaska Range (photo: Mount McKinley, 6,194 m), the Rocky Mountains (Mount Elbert, 4,396 m), and the Coast Mountains (Mount Waddington, 4,016 m) all belong to the **North American Cordilleras**, a series of mountain ranges.

The 6,020 kilometers long Mississippi-Missouri river system is the largest river system in North America. Rising in Minnesota, the Mississippi River flows south to its delta on the Gulf of Mexico. The enormous drainage basin of the Mississippi River covers an area of 3,208,000 km². The Mackenzie and Yukon Rivers in Canada are the second and third longest rivers on the continent.

The world's largest island, Greenland (2,175,600 km²), and the world's fifth largest island, Baffin Island (517,890 km²), are among the many arctic islands surrounding the North American mainland. The largest islands in the Caribbean Sea are Cuba (111,000 km²), Hispaniola (76,000 km²), and Jamaica (10,990 km²). St. Lucia (photo) is one of the smaller Caribbean nations with an area of 616 km².

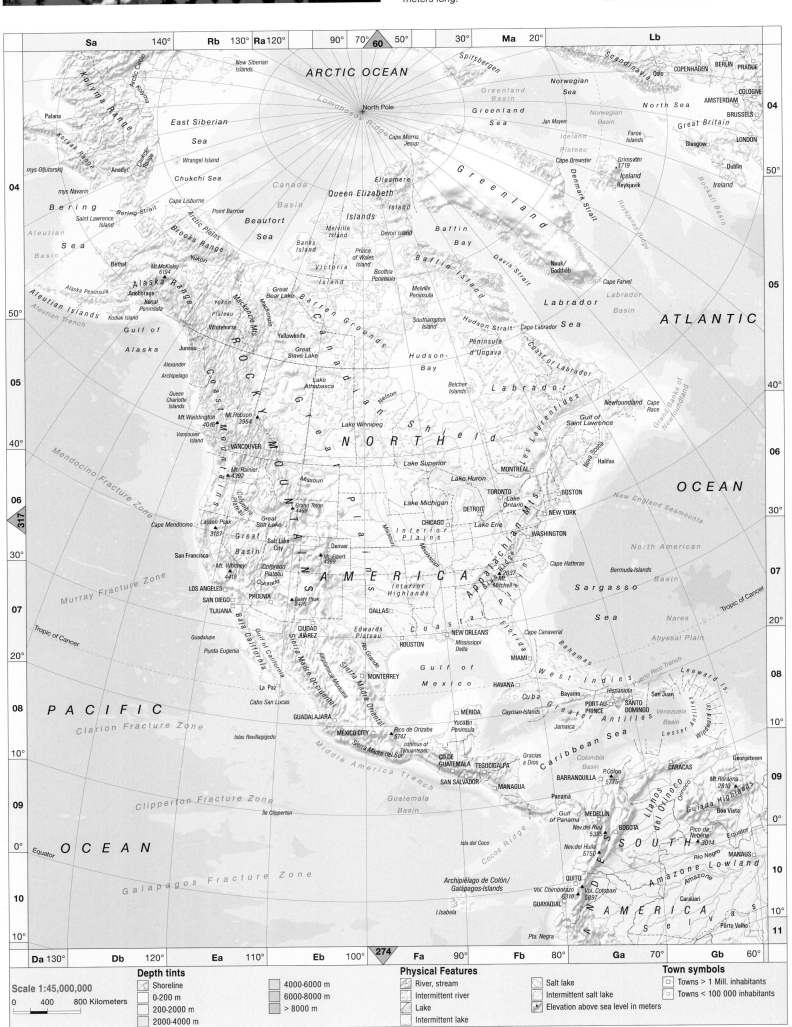

Scale 1:45,000,000

0   400   800 Kilometers

Depth tints			Physical Features			Town symbols	
Shoreline			River, stream		Salt lake		Towns > 1 Mill. inhabitants
0-200 m		4000-6000 m	Intermittent river		Intermittent salt lake		Towns < 100 000 inhabitants
200-2000 m		6000-8000 m	Lake		Elevation above sea level in meters		
2000-4000 m		> 8000 m	Intermittent lake				

In addition to the three larger nations on the continent (Canada, Mexico, and the United States) there are numerous smaller North American nations. The **indigenous people** (Native Americans and Inuit) form only a small portion of the population in Canada and the United States, while most Mexicans and Central Americans are at least of partial indigenous descent.
Over the centuries millions of European immigrants settled in North America and most of the continent's population is of European descent. Millions of North Americans, mostly in the United States and the Caribbean, are of African descent. Canada and the USA attract a large number of immigrants every year, including many migrants from neighboring Mexico.

North America is a continent with many different faces.

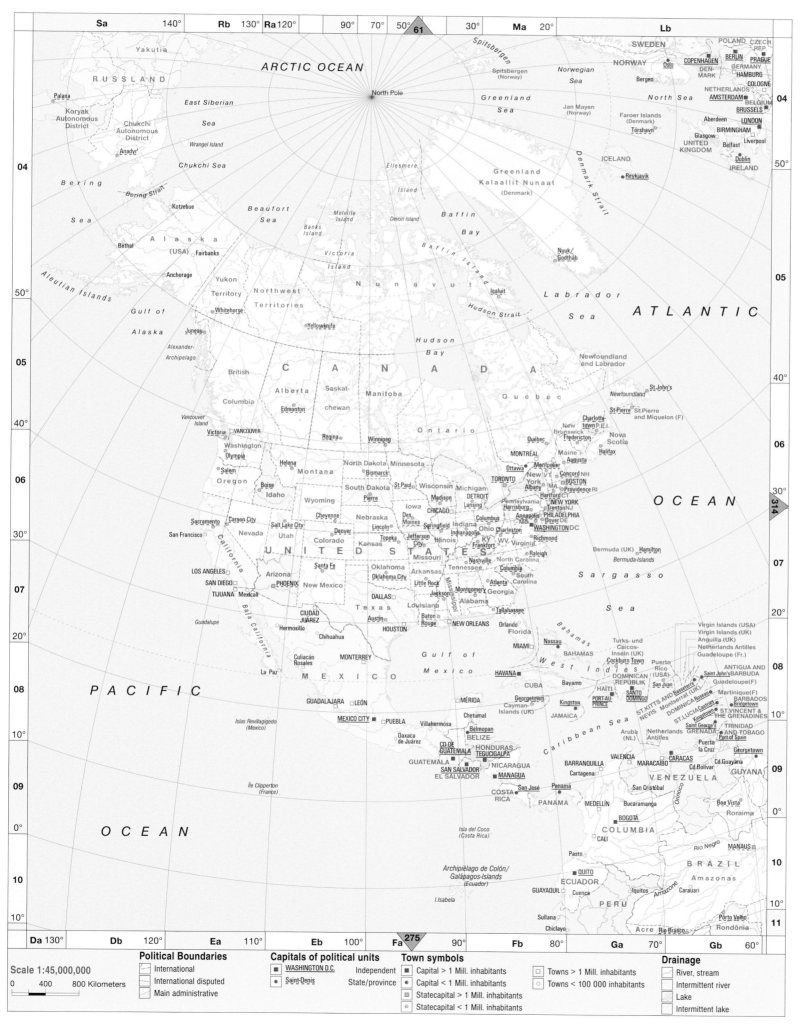

Countries and Flags

Antigua and Barbuda
Bahamas
Barbados
Belize
Canada
Costa Rica
Cuba
Dominica
Dominican Republic
El Salvador
Grenada
Guatemala
Haiti
Honduras
Jamaica
Mexico
Nicaragua
Panama
Saint Kitts and Nevis
Saint Lucia
St. Vincent and the Grenadines
Trinidad and Tobago
United States of America

The **indigenous people of North America** continue to struggle for recognition and equal rights, including ownership of land. In Canada, the Inuit (top photo: Inuit couple) have won control of their own self-governing region called Nunavut. Many of the Amerindians in the United States live in so-called reservations. Among the most well known Native American tribes in the United States are the Seminole in the Southeast, the Iroquois in the Northeast, the Cheyenne and Lakota Sioux in the Great Plains states, and the Navajo in the Southwest. Today, Native Americans (middle photo) form only a small percentage of the American population. Central America's indigenous people form a large part of the region's population but have limited political influence (bottom photo: Cuba woman in Panama).

Scale 1:45,000,000
0 400 800 Kilometers

Political Boundaries
International
International disputed
Main administrative

Capitals of political units
■ WASHINGTON D.C. Independent
● Saint-Denis State/province

Town symbols
■ Capital > 1 Mill. inhabitants
● Capital > 1 Mill. inhabitants
● Statecapital > 1 Mill. inhabitants
○ Statecapital < 1 Mill. inhabitants
□ Towns > 1 Mill. inhabitants
□ Towns < 100 000 inhabitants

Drainage
River, stream
Intermittent river
Lake
Intermittent lake

Alaska, Canada, Greenland

Canada and Alaska cover the northern half of the North American continent. 10 % of the region is covered by bodies of water. Alaska and Canada are home to one-third of the world's freshwater supply. The region borders three oceans: the Pacific, Atlantic, and Arctic Oceans. The vast majority of Canada's population lives within 300 kilometers of the American-Canadian border. Large sections of the region are sparsely popula-

ted or totally uninhabited. The Hudson Bay plain is the lowest region of Canada. The Canadian (Precambrian) Shield forms a horseshoe around the **Hudson Bay region** and is one of the world's oldest geologic features. During the ice age the entire region was covered by gigantic glaciers. To the east of the **Canadian**

An arctic sunset in Alaska's beautiful Glacier Bay. **Da07**

The Bering Strait Located between the American state Alaska and Siberia in Russia – 85 kilometers wide at its narrowest point – (photo: Saint Lawrence Island).

Alaska Range The northernmost range in the North American Cordilleras – (photo: Wonder Lake in Denali National Park).

Kluane National Park Wilderness area in the St. Elias Mountains (Yukon Territory) – glaciers and snowfields: Icefield Ranges – Taiga wildlife and vegetation.

Gulf of Alaska Glacier Bay National Park is home to 16 flowing glaciers – the Alexander Archipelago contains over 11,000 islands.

The Northern Rockies The Canadian Rockies are home to glaciers and snow-covered mountains. The region also contains diverse wildlife including a large bear population. Several major rivers incuding the Columbia and Athabasca Rivers rise in the Rockies.

Scale 1:18,000,000

0   160   320 Kilometers

Depth tints
- Shoreline
- 0-200 m
- 200-2000 m
- 2000-4000 m
- 4000-6000 m
- 6000-8000 m
- > 8000 m

Physical Features
- River, stream
- Intermittent river
- Lake
- Intermittent lake
- Salt lake
- Intermittent salt lake
- Elevation above sea level in meters

Shield lie the mountainous regions of Labrador and Baffin Island – both areas with subarctic climates. Between the Canadian Shield and the mountainous regions of eastern Canada lies the narrow valley of the St. Lawrence River. The lower river valley is one of Canada's most populated and economically important regions. To the west of the Canadian Shield lies the Great Plains region. These vast plains were formed during the ice ages as gigantic migrating glaciers flattened the land they passed over. The Canadian Rockies are a section of the Cordilleras, a long system of mountain ranges extending through South and North America. The Coast Mountains to the west of the Rockies also belong to the Cordilleras. The mountains of the Cordilleras extend into the American state of Alaska. Alaska is home to some of the continent's highest mountains including Mount McKinley (6,194 m), the highest peak in North America. The Bering Strait borders Alaska to the west. During the last ice age, the strait formed a land bridge that connected the Asian and North American continents. It was here that the ancestors of today's Native Americans crossed into the Americas. This land bridge was also crossed by migrating animals, many of which evolved into new species found only in the Americas. Between the Canadian mainland and Greenland lies the Arctic Archipelago. The mountainous islands in this group have peaks rising 2,000 meters above sea level. To the northeast of Canada lies the world's largest island, Greenland. The island has a jagged coast and most of its land is covered by a layer of ice. Greenland, a Danish territory, is sparsely populated and the majority of its inhabitants are Inuits.

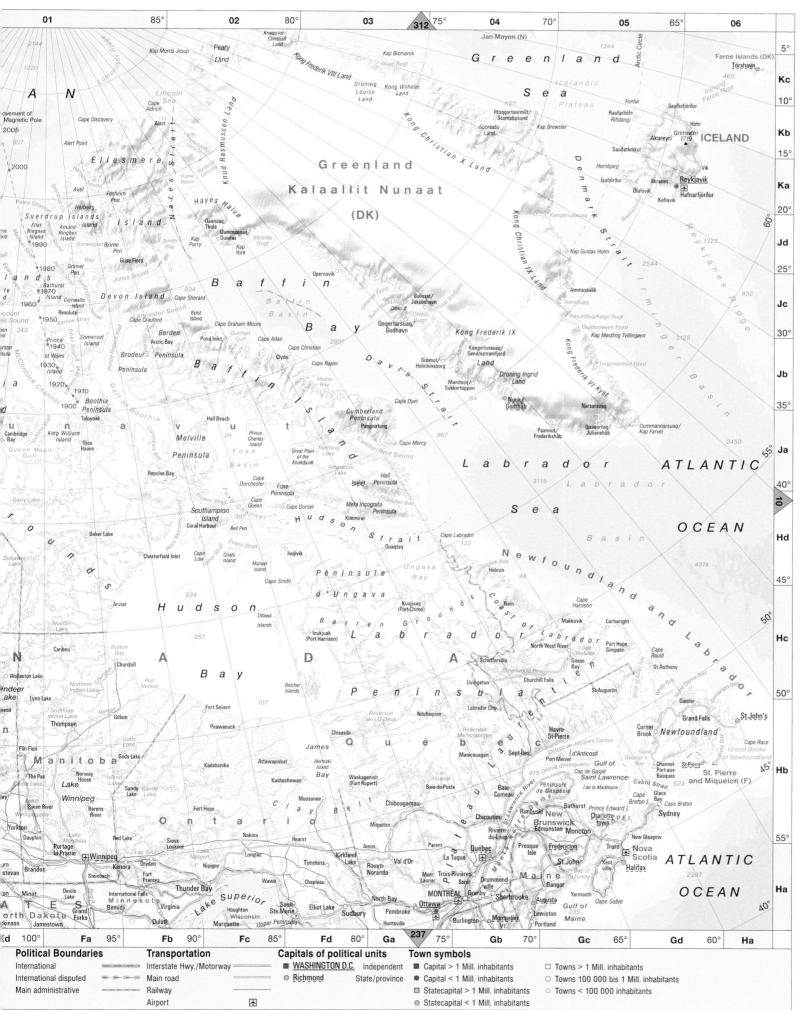

The Barren Grounds Tundra landscape covered by permafrost and sparse vegetation – subarctic flora and fauna.

Manitoba One of Canada's three Prairie Provinces. Most of Manitoba lies on the Canadian Shield – Conservation areas include Riding Mountain National Park (photo).

Nunavut Canada's youngest and largest province. The region's population is 85 % Inuit. Nunavut covers 20 % of Canada's land area. There are few paved roads in the region and most of the territory consists of treeless tundra.

Hudson Bay Inland sea in northeastern Canada – ice-free during four months of the year – rarely more than 200 meters deep – connected to the Atlantic at the Hudson Strait.

Newfoundland Easternmost province of Canada – the provincial capital is St. John's – Gros Mourne National Park (photo).

New England Historic region in the northeastern United States – wooded mountains – bays – pleasant resort islands – historic cities and picturesque villages.

Legend

Political Boundaries
International
International disputed
Main administrative

Transportation
Interstate Hwy./Motorway
Main road
Railway
Airport

Capitals of political units
■ WASHINGTON D.C. Independent
● Richmond State/province

Town symbols
■ Capital > 1 Mill. inhabitants
■ Capital < 1 Mill. inhabitants
□ Statecapital > 1 Mill. inhabitants
● Statecapital < 1 Mill. inhabitants
□ Towns > 1 Mill. inhabitants
○ Towns 100 000 bis 1 Mill. inhabitants
○ Towns < 100 000 inhabitants

USA, Central America

The Pacific coast is the most geologically active region in North America. Along this coast the Pacific and American tectonic plates meet and collide with one another. Tectonic activity is also responsible for the emergence of large mountain ranges (Sierra Nevada, Rocky Mountains) in western North America. Earthquakes and tremors are common throughout the region. The Nazca and Cocos tectonic plates, which collide with the

smaller Caribbean plate, are located beneath Central America. Most of the Caribbean islands and the deep **Cayman Trench** lie along the edges of the Caribbean plate. The Caymen Trench, one of the world's deepest trenches, lies in the waters between Central America and Cuba. This geologically active re-

Arizona's Grand Canyon is one of the world's most visited natural attractions.

Sierra Nevada Mountain range in California and Nevada – Highest Peak: Mount Whitney, 4,418 meters.

The southern Rockies They stretch over 2,500 kilometers from the Canadian to the Mexican border. Grand Teton (bottom photo) rises 4,198 meters.

Colorado Plateau The Rocky Mountains contain beautiful sandstone formations including Monument Valley (top photo) and Arches NP (bottom photo).

The Deserts of the Southwest North of Mexico's Sierra Madre Mountains lie the vast deserts of the Southwestern United States. Photos from top to bottom: Death Valley in California, Organ Pipe Cactus National Monument in Arizona, Mojave Desert.

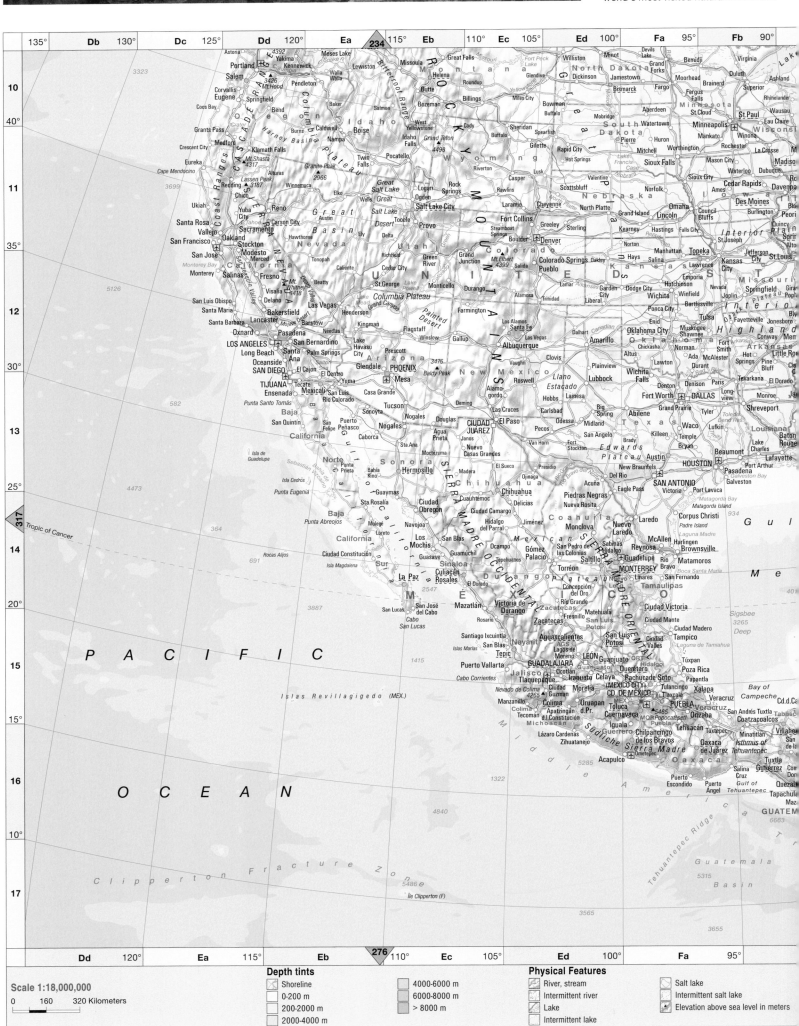

Scale 1:18,000,000

0   160   320 Kilometers

Depth tints
- Shoreline
- 0–200 m
- 200–2000 m
- 2000–4000 m
- 4000–6000 m
- 6000–8000 m
- > 8000 m

Physical Features
- River, stream
- Intermittent river
- Lake
- Intermittent lake
- Salt lake
- Intermittent salt lake
- Elevation above sea level in meters

gion is home to a high number of active volcanoes. Eastern North America's present topography was created during the ice ages. Enormous migrating glaciers shaped the **Appalachian Mountains**. The glaciers also created large basins, where large lakes, such as the Great Lakes, were eventually formed.
The contiguous United States and Central America are home to many different climate zones. The northern regions of the United States have temperate climates and four distinct seasons. These temperate regions are bordered in the south by subtropical and arid regions which extend to the tropics of Central America. In the tropical regions of the Caribbean and Central America there are two distinct seasons: a rainy season and a dry season. The Caribbean islands and the coastal areas bordering the Gulf of Mexico and Caribbean Sea are often threatened by hurricanes. **Hurricanes** are powerful tropical cyclones that can cause major destruction when they hit land. Central America also suffers from powerful winds usually called **"nortes."** These winds bring bitterly cold air and rain from the United States and Canada to the Caribbean and Central America. The Atlantic coast of the United States is the most heavily populated region on the continent. The coast is home to an almost continuous area of urban and suburban development stretching north from Washington DC to Boston in New England. The United State's incredible wealth of arable land and natural resources (coal, iron ore, gold) were vital to its emergence as the world's largest economic power. The beautiful and historic colonial towns of Mexico's highlands were built with wealth generated from the region's gold and silver mines.

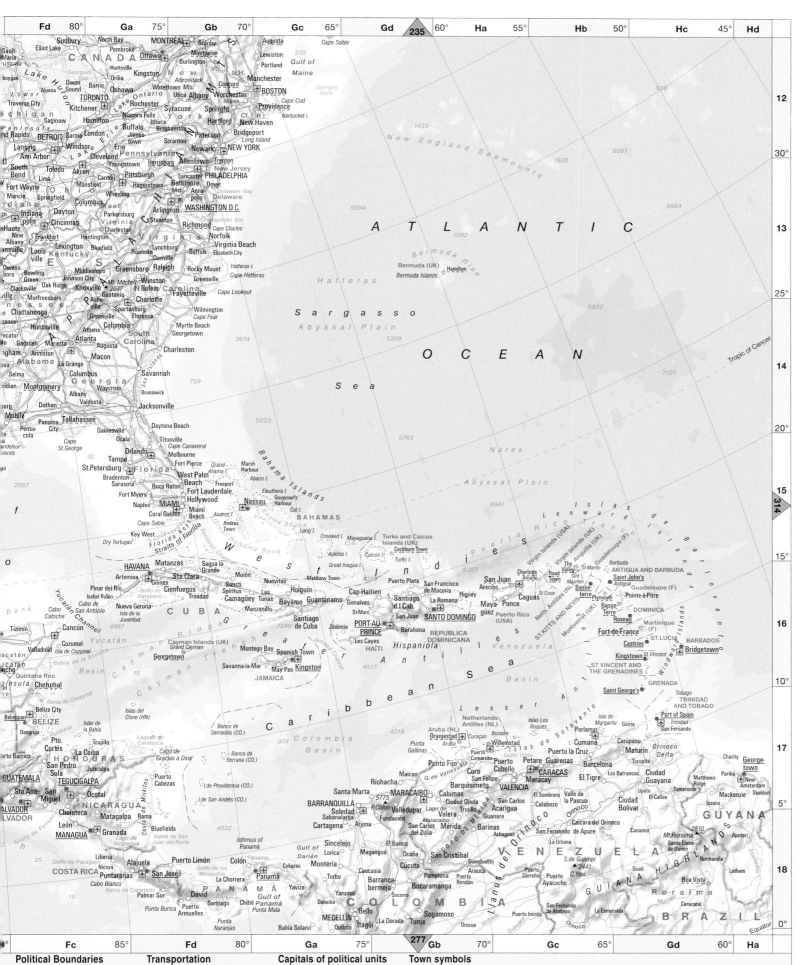

The Great Lakes The largest group of freshwater lakes in the world. Lake Michigan (top photo) is the only lake entirely in the US. Niagara Falls (bottom photo) drops into Lake Ontario.

The Appalachians The Great Smokey Mountains (top photo) are a UNESCO world heritage site. The Ridge Mountains (bottom photo) are covered by woodlands.

Sierra Madre Mountains Divided into two ranges: the Sierra Madre Oriental and Occidental – the ranges feature many volcanoes including Popocatepetl (5,452 m).

The Caribbean Islands Consisting of the Bahamas, the Greater Antilles, and the Lesser Antilles – the Caribbean Sea encompasses beautiful coral and volcanic islands (photo: St. Lucia).

Central American Cordilleras Mountain ranges between the Gulf of Tehuantepec and Columbia – more than 300 active volcanoes in the region.

Political Boundaries
International
International disputed
Main administrative

Transportation
Interstate Hwy./Motorway
Main road
Railway
Airport

Capitals of political units
■ WASHINGTON D.C. Independent
● Richmond State/province

Town symbols
■ Capital > 1 Mill. inhabitants
● Capital < 1 Mill. inhabitants
◐ Statecapital > 1 Mill. inhabitants
○ Statecapital < 1 Mill. inhabitants
□ Towns > 1 Mill. inhabitants
○ Towns 100 000 bis 1 Mill. inhabitants
○ Towns < 100 000 inhabitants

Western Alaska

Alaska with an area of 1.5 million km² is the largest of the 50 American states. Alaska is a large peninsula on the north-western edge of North America. The state shares a long border with Canada. The distance between this border and the westernmost of Alaska's ⛰ Aleutian Islands is over 3,900 kilometers. The **Aleutian Islands** are a chain of small islands stretching into the North Pacific. These stormy islands lie near the edge

A colorful mountain lake in Alaska.

of a continental tectonic plate and are home to several active ⛰ volcanoes. Earthquakes are also common in this geologically active region.
Southern Alaska is home to several mountain ranges including the Alaska and the Aleutian Ranges. ⛰ **Mount McKinley** in 🏞 Denali National Park is the tallest mountain in North America. The

mountain was named after President William McKinley in 1897, but the state of Alaska also recognizes its indigenous name, Denali. With its base at sea level and its peak at 6,194 meters, Mount McKinley has one of the steepest vertical rises in the world.
The Alaska Range shelters **Anchorage**, Alaska's largest city, and its suburbs from the bitter cold winds of northern Alaska. The average temperature in the

Kotzebue Inuit settlement – large zinc deposits in the area – 🏛 Nana Museum of the Arctic – (photo: Kotzebue Sound). **Bj12**

Unalakleet Traditional fishing harbor on the Norton Sound – wonderful locations for ⛴ fishing, Quinnat-salmon in June. **Bk14**

Inuit The name Inuit means people and since the 1970s the term has ganed in popularity over the name Eskimo (raw meat eaters). The Inuit once lived from fishing and hunting but many now work in Alaska's oil industry.

National Parks and Nature Reserves Alaska has 🏞 16 nature reserves including the 🏞 Alaska Maritime National Wildlife Refuge **(Bd16)**. The reserves provide protected living space for Alaska's flora and fauna. The Yukon Flats National Wildlife Refuge **(Cg12)** is home to moose, grizzlies, and wolves.

Shishaldin ⛰ On Unimank Island, one of the most active volcanoes in the Aleutians, 2862 meters – last eruption in 1999. **Bj18**

Aniakchak National Monument National park in the Aleutian Range – beautiful ⛰ volcanoes (photo). **Cb17**

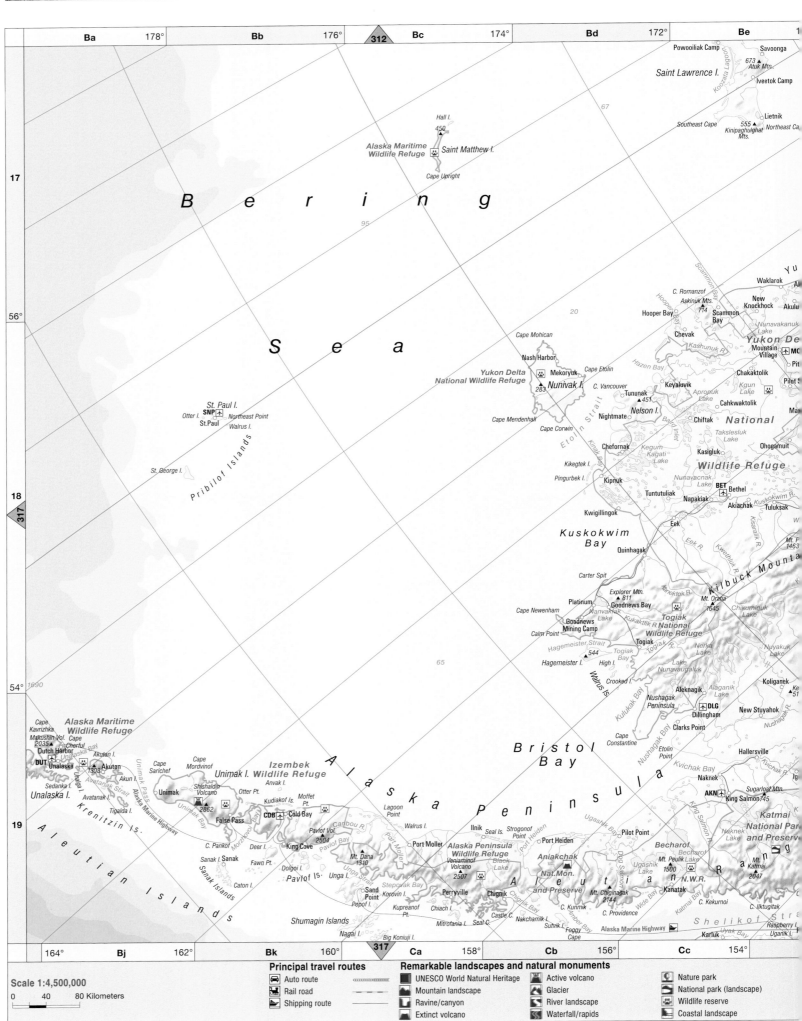

Scale 1:4,500,000

0   40   80 Kilometers

Principal travel routes
- 🚗 Auto route
- 🚃 Rail road
- 🚢 Shipping route

Remarkable landscapes and natural monuments
- ⬛ UNESCO World Natural Heritage
- Mountain landscape
- Ravine/canyon
- Extinct volcano
- Active volcano
- Glacier
- River landscape
- Waterfall/rapids
- Nature park
- National park (landscape)
- Wildlife reserve
- Coastal landscape

region is around -11°C in winter and 15°C during the mild summer months. The **Kenai Peninsula**, south of Anchorage, is one of many regions in Alaska with a large number of spectacular glaciers. The **Columbia Glacier** in Prince William Sound is the fastest moving glacier in the world and one of the most beauiful in Alaska. **Wrangell-St. Elias National Park** where the Wrangell-St. Elias, Churgach, and Alaska Ranges

meet, is a UNESCO world heritage site containing numerous glaciers, mountains and icefields.
Western Alaska's terrain is mostly hilly with jagged coastlines, numerous bays, and natural harbors. The region is also home to the **Yukon Delta** with its abundance of wildlife. Central Alaska extends from the Brooks Range to the Arctic Circle. The **Yukon River** flows through most of central Alaska. The region con-

sists primarily of marshy treeless land covered by permafrost, rock or soil that remains frozen throughout most of the year. **Fairbanks**, the largest city in the region and the second largest in Alaska, is only frost-free during the months of June and July. The region north of the **Brooks Range** consists of tundra with average temperatures far below freezing for most of the year. This is the so-called land of the midnight sun, a region where

the sun continuously shines from May to August only to disappear during winters. The discovery of natural resources in Alaska has also been the driving force behind the state's settlement and development for over 100 years. During the 19th century, a gold rush brought a flood of migrants to the state. Despite population growth and the exploitation of natural resources, most of Alaska remains a pristine, sparsely settled wilderness.

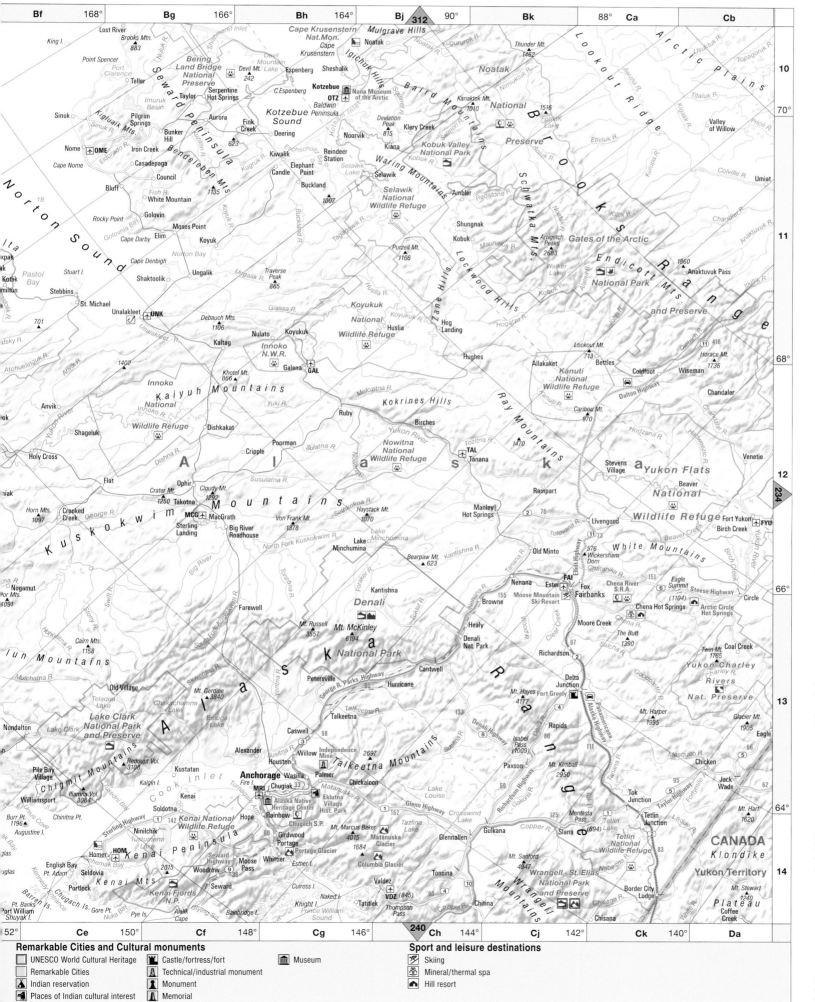

The Alaska Highway This roadway (2,432 km) stretches through the North American wilderness. The highway starts in Dawson Creek, British Columbia and ends in Delta Junction, Alaska. **Ch14**

Fairbanks Alaska's second largest city (35,000 inhabitants) – amusement park Alaskaland – University of Alaska Museum (local history and art museum). **Cg13**

Mount McKinley The highest mountain in North America (6,194 m) – beautiful white mountain face – Wonder Lake at the foot of the mountain. **Ce14**

Denali National Park Mount McKinley is the major attraction in this national park – typical tundra landscape – home to herds of caribou, moose, bears and wolves. **Ce14**

Anchorage Alaska's largest city and leading economic center – founded in 1914 – population of 250,000 and the economic center of the state – Anchorage Museum of History and Art. **CfBc**

Homer Small port city on the mountainous Kenai Peninsula – nearby Kenai Mountains – gravel bar, Homer Spit – Pratt Museum (indigenous culture). **CeBb**

Portage Glacier and Lake This area lies east of Anchorage – large icebergs fall from the glaciers into the lake. **CfBc**

Remarkable Cities and Cultural monuments
- UNESCO World Cultural Heritage
- Remarkable Cities
- Indian reservation
- Places of Indian cultural interest
- Castle/fortress/fort
- Technical/industrial monument
- Monument
- Memorial
- Museum

Sport and leisure destinations
- Skiing
- Mineral/thermal spa
- Hill resort

Southern Alaska, Northwestern Canada, Hawaiian Islands

The **Alaskan Panhandle** stretches from ⌂ Wrangell-St. Elias National Park south to the Canadian border at the Portland Inlet. It is home to numerous fjords and large sections of the Panhandle including the **Alexander Archipelago** are covered by temperate rainforest. The climate in this part of Alaska is influenced by warm ocean currents. The average temperature in the region is -6° C in January and 13° C in June. Rain or snow is very common

throughout the year. Fall and winter are the seasons with the most precipitation. The region's dense rainforests thrive in this wet climate. Many of the region's most beautiful rainforests are located in spectacular fjords – several of which, including the ⌂ **Misty Fjord National Monument**, are protected by conserva-

The Mendenhall Glacier near Alaska's capital city Juneau. **Dc16**

tion laws. Every year between July and September, Pacific salmon migrate into the rivers of Alaska to spawn. Without the salmon, the bear population in the region would not be able to survive. Tours along the Alaskan coast give cruise ship passengers the opportunity to observe Orcas, humpback whales, and other types of whales. The ⌂ **Inside Passage** in southeast Alaska is one of the best areas for whale watching in the state. While the

Kodiak Island Alaska's largest island has ⌂ green coastline and snow covered mountains – home to the world's largest bears – the brown bears in the ⌂ Kodiak National Wildlife Refuge live on a diet consisting mostly of salmon. **Cc-Cd17**

Chugach Mountains ⌂ Mountain range with a large number of glaciers – home to large grizzly and wolf populations. **Ch-Cj15**

Mount Huxley Tall mountain with a height of 3,828 meters in ⌂ Wrangell-St. Elias National Park. **Ck15**

Alexander Archipelago Islands in southeastern Alaska – fjords – the ⌂ Inside Passage – humpback whale pods. **Dc-Dd17/18**

The Hawaiian Islands The archipelago is 2,400 kilometers long and has an incredible variety of landscapes including beaches, mountains, active volcanoes, canyons, waterfalls, and tropical forests. **Bk-Cc34/36**

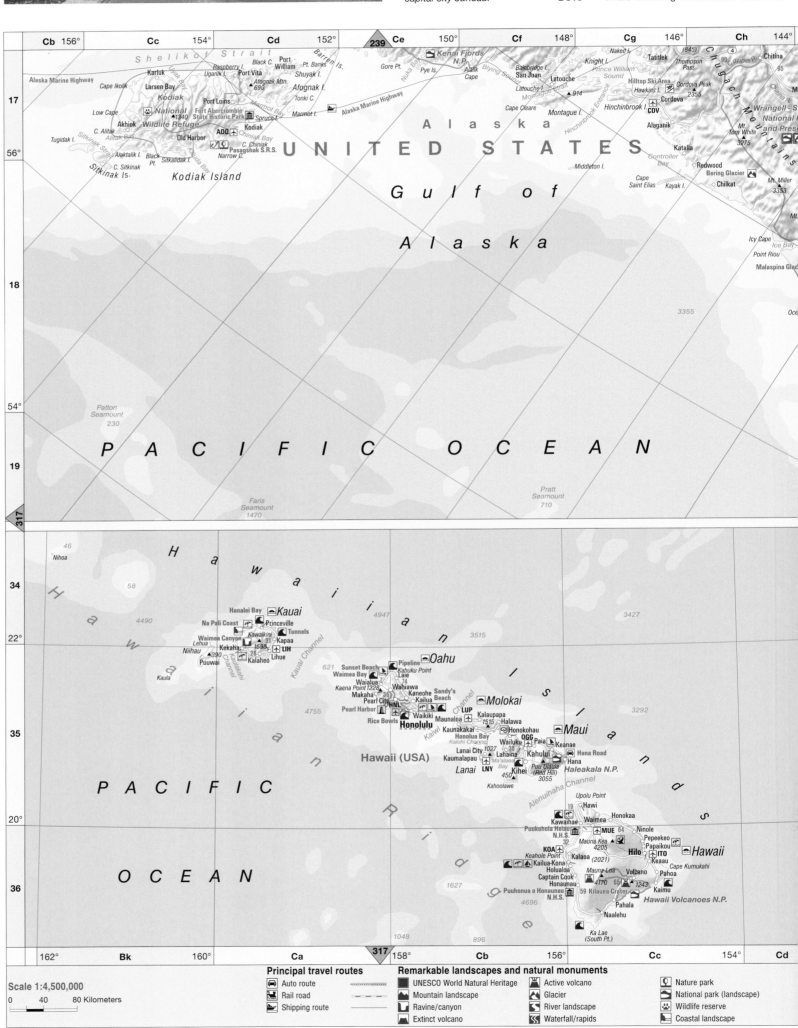

Scale 1:4,500,000

0   40   80 Kilometers

Principal travel routes

- 🚗 Auto route
- 🚂 Rail road
- 🚢 Shipping route

Remarkable landscapes and natural monuments

- ⬛ UNESCO World Natural Heritage
- Mountain landscape
- Ravine/canyon
- Extinct volcano
- Active volcano
- Glacier
- River landscape
- Waterfall/rapids
- Nature park
- National park (landscape)
- Wildlife reserve
- Coastal landscape

Southern Alaska, Northwestern Canada, Hawaiian Islands

Panhandle has a maritime climate and heavy rainfall, the regions to its north as well as those farther inland are drier and have colder winters. The region around  **Mount Logan** (5,959 m) to the north of the Panhandle and the interior regions away from the coast have continental climates with less rainfall and large variations in temperature during the year. In Canada's Yukon Territory and along the eastern edges of the Rockies temperatures near -50° C are not uncommon during winter. In the late 19th century, the **Yukon Territory** made news around the world when large gold deposits were discovered in the area around the Klondike River. Fortune seekers from many nations came to the territory in search of wealth. Today the territory is one of the most sparsely populated regions in Canada.

Hawaii, the southernmost American state, lies in the Pacific Ocean nearly 4,000 kilometers away from the west coast of the American mainland. The state consists of six main islands: Oahu, Kauai, Maui, Lanai, Molokai, and Hawaii and at least 130 smaller islands and islets. This archipelago of volcanic islands owes its existence to a hot spot in the earth's crust. Molten lava from the hot spot hardened and accumulated over time forming underwater mountains and eventually the islands. The Hawaiian Islands are home to a variety of landscapes; tropical rainforests, white sandy beaches, black volcanic sand beaches, cliffs and canyons can all be found on the islands. Travelers on the islands can also visit the lava pools and lava flows in Hawaii Volcanoes National Park near the crater of Kilauea. Daytime temperatures on the islands range between 25° C and 30° C during most of the year.

Kluane National Park This national park is a world heritage site. Located in the Yukon Territory, the park contains large inaccessible glaciers and Canada's tallest mountain, Mount Logan (top photo). The park is home to wolves and grizzly bears. There are several hiking paths along Kathleen Lake (bottom photo). **Ck-Db15**

Nahanni National Park In the Northwest Territories – world heritage site – mountain ranges, canyons, and rivers. **Dh15**

Haines Town at the northern edge of the Inside Passage – local culture in the Chilkat Center for the Performing Arts. **Dc16**

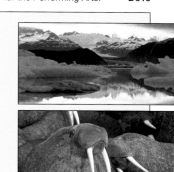

Glacier Bay National Park Glacier Bay encompasses 16 glaciers, twelve of which descend into the bay. The area is now a UNESCO world heritage site. Seals, walruses, and whales all live in the bay. The John Hopkins Glacier is the most active in the bay and regularly releases large amounts of ice into the water. **Db16**

Hazleton Historic architecture from the colonial era – K'san Indian Village Museum: recreation of a Native American village. **Dg18**

Remarkable Cities and Cultural monuments

- UNESCO World Cultural Heritage
- Remarkable Cities
- Places of Christian cultural interest
- Places of Indian cultural interest
- Technical/industrial monument
- Dam
- Monument
- Memorial
- Space telescope
- Museum

Sport and leisure destinations

- Sailing
- Diving
- Wind surfing
- Surfing
- Canoeing/rafting
- Deep-sea fishing
- Beach resort

Southwestern Canada, Northwestern USA

Southwestern Canada is a region of mountain ranges (Rocky Mountains, Coast Mountains) and vast plains that encompass parts of three Canadian provinces: British Columbia, Alberta, and Saskatchewan. Southwestern Canada is bordered by three northwestern American states: Washington, Idaho, and Montana. The tall mountains in this region, including the ◢ **Rockies**, have a major effect on the climate. Along the ◢ Pacific coast, moun-

tains block the path of air into the interior; the rising air cools, condenses and falls to the ground as snow or rain. The coast is not only wetter than the interior, it also has milder temperatures during winter. The Pacific coast is also home to **Vancouver** and **Seattle**, the two largest urban areas in the region.

Longmire Valley in Mount Rainier National Park.   **Dk22**

Vancouver The 🏙 city has a beautiful natural setting between mountains and the ocean – Gastown – large Chinatown – Stanley Park and its aquarium – 🏛 Museum of Anthropology (MOA).   **Dj21**

Olympic National Park Temperate ◢ rainforest – Hoh Rainforest – Rialto Beach – ◢ Makah Indian Reservation (museum and cultural center).   **Dh-Dj21/22**

Seattle The largest 🏙 city in the American Northwest is a vibrant cultural center – The Space Needle (158 m) was built for the 1962 World's Fair – ◢ Pike Place Market – Seattle Aquarium – 🏛 Seattle Art Museum. **Dj22**

Mount Rainier National Park Popular area for hiking – 26 ◢ glaciers – ◢ Wonderland Trail Grove of the Patriarch – ◢ volcano (last eruption in 1963).   **Dk22**

Mount St. Helens In 1980 this ◢ volcano erupted and blew away the summit as well as the north face of the mountain leaving a large crater. Coldwater Ridge Visitors Center provides information about the eruption and impressive views of the mountain. **Dj22**

Cannon Beach Attractive coastal town – long ◢ sandy beaches – Haystack Rock (72 meters tall free-standing rock). **Dj23**

Legend

Scale 1:4,500,000

0   40   80 Kilometers

Principal travel routes
- 🚗 Auto route
- 🚂 Rail road
- Shipping route

Remarkable landscapes and natural monuments
- ■ UNESCO World Natural Heritage
- Mountain landscape
- Rock landscape
- Active volcano
- Glacier
- River landscape
- Waterfall/rapids
- Nature park
- National park (landscape)
- National park (flora)
- National park (fauna)
- National park (culture)
- Wildlife reserve
- Coastal landscape
- Beach
- Underwater reserve

The region's interior has a continental climate. Summers in the interior are considerably warmer than on the coast and the winters are far colder. Latitude also determines climate in the region – the farther north a location in the interior is, the rawer its climate. In Edmonton, the capital of Alberta, temperatures can reach -25° C in winter.

Vancouver Island was once covered by virgin rainforests, but logging has reduced the forests to a few areas including Clayoquot Sound and **Pacific Rim National Park**.

The **Queen Charlotte Islands** lie 80 kilometers away from mainland British Columbia and are home to an abundance of wildlife. The eastern **Rocky Mountains** contain interesting landscapes and some of the most beautiful **national parks** in North America, including Banff and Jasper National Parks.

The Icefields Parkway, running through these two parks, is one of the world's most spectacular mountain highways. The mountains in the eastern Rockies are covered by snow and surrounded by ice and snowfields. The eastern Rockies are heavily forested and there are countless mountain lakes scattered throughout the region. To the east of the Rockies lies a region of vast prairies and grasslands. **Calgary**, the largest city in Alberta, lies at the foot of the Rockies while Edmonton, the northernmost large city in Canada, is surrounded by plains. The province Saskatchewan has an economy dominated by agriculture. The province produces around 60 % of Canada's wheat. Mining (uranium and potash) also plays an important role in the province's economy. While southern Saskatchewan is covered by fields, the north is mostly forests and marshland.

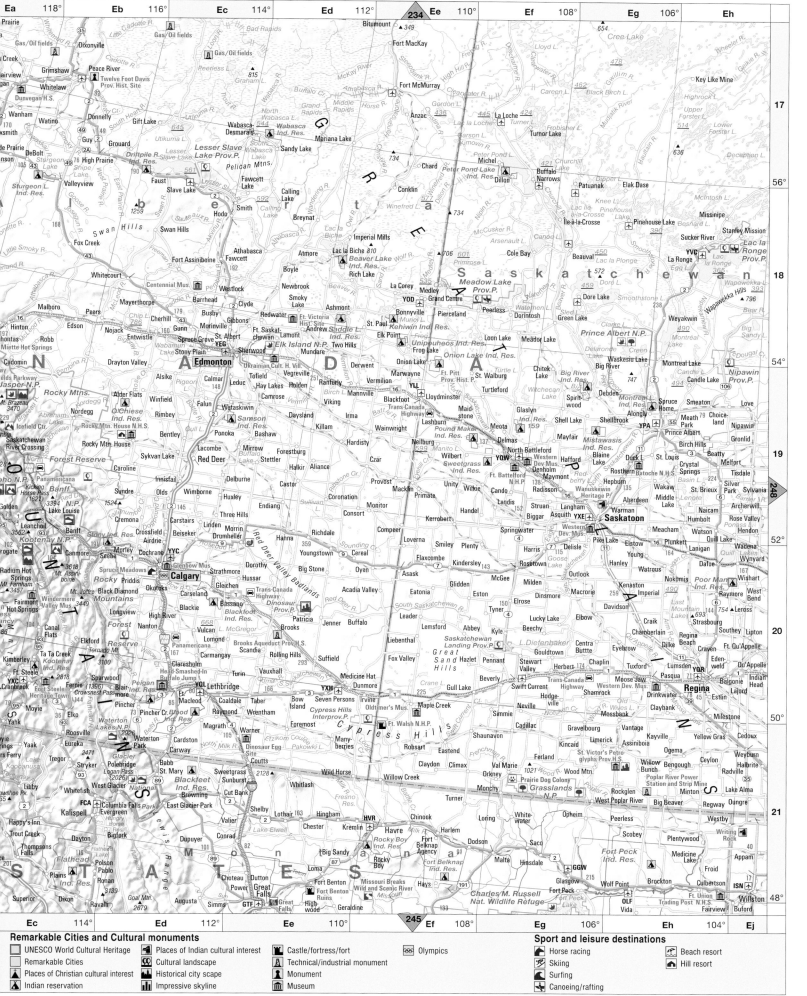

Clearwater River Romantic river in Canada's Wells Gray Provincial Park – Dawson Falls (18 m high) – Helmcken-Falls (137 m high). **Dk–Ea19**

Jasper National Park Largest national park in the Rocky Mountains (10,878 km²) – Athabasca Glacier and Athabasca Falls – Spirit Island in Maligne Lake. **Ea19**

Glacier National Park (Montana, US) 400 glaciers – more than 140 kilometers of hiking trails – extreme weather conditions – Connaught train tunnel. **Eb20**

Banff National Park Canada's oldest national park, founded in 1885 (6,641 km²) – resort town of Banff – rafting on the Bow River – glacial lakes including Lake Louise and Moraine Lake. **Ec20**

Mount Assiniboine Mountain in Kootenay National Park – mountain wilderness in the western Rockies – Marble Canyon – the town Radium Hot Springs. **Ec20**

Dinosaur Provincial Park Prehistoric dinosaur gravesite in Alberta: UNESCO world heritage site – Dinosaur Trail – bus tours to excavation sites. **Ee20**

Waterton Lakes National Park National park in southern Alberta – Upper Waterton Lake – Red Rock Canyon – the historic Prince of Wales Hotel. **Ec21**

Remarkable Cities and Cultural monuments

- UNESCO World Cultural Heritage
- Remarkable Cities
- Places of Christian cultural interest
- Indian reservation
- Places of Indian cultural interest
- Cultural landscape
- Historical city scape
- Impressive skyline
- Castle/fortress/fort
- Technical/industrial monument
- Monument
- Museum

Sport and leisure destinations

- Olympics
- Horse racing
- Skiing
- Surfing
- Canoeing/rafting
- Beach resort
- Hill resort

Western USA

This section of the American West stretches from the Pacific coast to the eastern edges of the 🏔 **Rocky Mountains**. The Pacific coast between Oregon and Southern California is heavily developed but still contains many pristine 🏖 beaches. The San Andreas Fault runs from Southern California to the northern part of the state and passes through the heavily populated metropolitan area of **San Francisco**. Mountain ranges like the Cascade and

Coast Ranges in the north and the **Sierra Nevada** mountains in the south have a major effect on the climate of the Pacific coast. These mountains form a natural barrier that traps moisture in the coastal areas, forming a rain shadow in the interior. California contains nine national parks, more than any other state in the

Yosemite National Park: fascinating landscapes and wildlife. Ea26/27

Crater Lake National Park 🏞 The intense blue-colored Crater Lake is surrounded by a high crater wall – hiking trails. **Dj24**

Redwood National Park Home to the 🌲 Redwoods trees (sequoia sempervirens) – the tallest: Tall Tree (120 m). **Dh-Dj25**

Lassen National Park This 🏞 nature reserve covers 440 km² – Bumpass Hell has geothermal springs and boiling mud pools – 💧 Burney Falls (40 m). **Dk25**

San Francisco Northern California's largest city – city population 725,000 – attractions: Fisherman's Wharf, Lombard Street, cable cars, Coit Tower, Chinatown, and Market Street shopping area. **Dj27**

Lake Tahoe Azure blue 🏞 mountain lake on the state border between Nevada and California – the area is a popular vacation destination during summer and winter. **Dk-Ea26**

Yosemite National Park 🏞 Mountainous landscapes on 3,082 km² in western California – deep 🏞 canyons, diverse wildlife, Yosemite Falls (740 m) – panoramic views from Glacier Point. **Ea26/27**

Mono Lake Remnant of an ancient 🏞 inland sea – mating area for California's seagull population – unusual chalk formations called tufus. **Ea26/27**

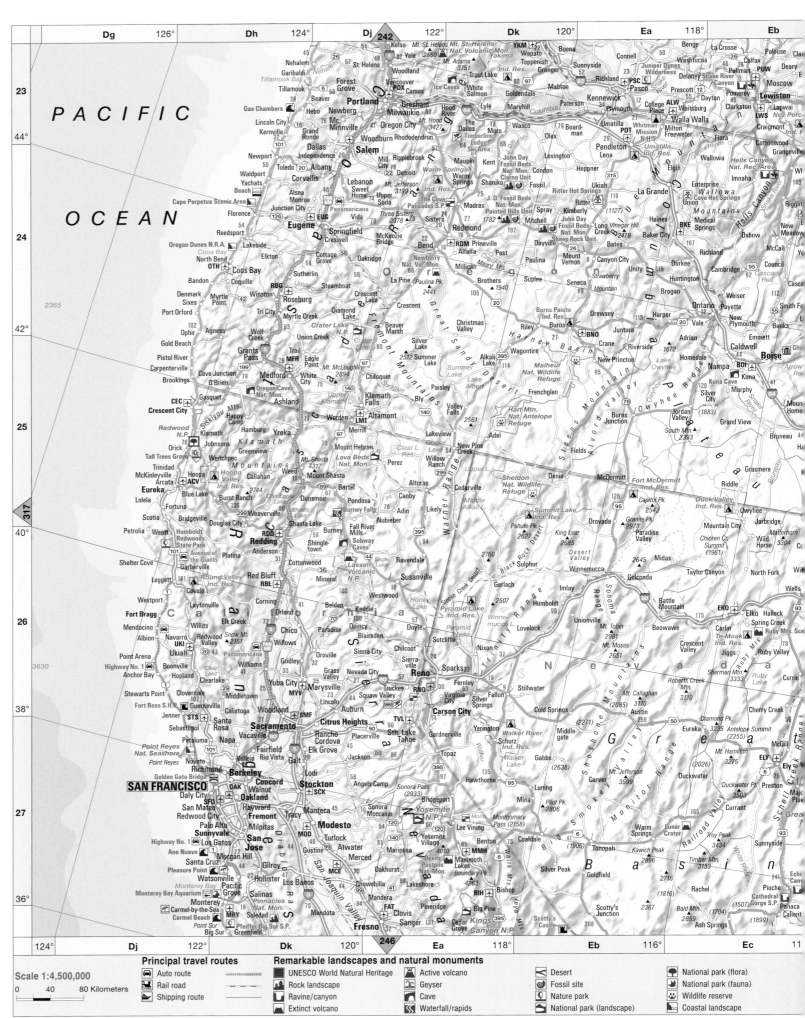

Map legend

Scale 1:4,500,000
0   40   80 Kilometers

Principal travel routes
- 🚗 Auto route
- 🚂 Rail road
- ⚓ Shipping route

Remarkable landscapes and natural monuments
- ⬛ UNESCO World Natural Heritage
- Rock landscape
- Ravine/canyon
- Extinct volcano
- 🌋 Active volcano
- Geyser
- Cave
- Waterfall/rapids
- Desert
- Fossil site
- Nature park
- National park (landscape)
- National park (flora)
- National park (fauna)
- Wildlife reserve
- Coastal landscape

country. ◨ **Yellowstone National Park** in western California is the most visited national park in the state.
The Cascade Range is part of the Pacific Ring of Fire and the range is home to numerous active volcanoes. Many volcanoes in the range, including Mount Hood (Oregon) and Mount Shasta (California), have picturesque snow-covered peaks. To the east of the Cascade lies the volcanic **Columbia Plateau**. Farther

south, the Sierra Nevada Mountains are bordered in the east by the **Great Basin**. The Great Basin is the largest arid region in North America. The Great Basin is home to Death Valley – the lowest point in the United States – and the ◨ Great Salt Lake Desert in Utah.
The Great Basin is bordered to the east and northeast by the Rocky Mountains. ◨ Yellowstone National Park became the world's first national park when it was

established in 1872. The national park is divided between three states – Idaho, Wyoming, and Montana – and lies in a volcanically active region. In addition to its geologic attractions including its famous ▨ geysers, the park also has an abundance of wildlife, including bears and buffalos. The mountains of Colorado make the state one of the most popular destinations in the western United States. The Colorado town of Vail is the

site of the largest ski area in the country. Utah boasts five national parks. ◨ **Bryce Canyon** in Utah has an impressive collection of interesting stone formations. Utah's **Zion National Park** is most famous for its beautiful cliffs and canyons, while **Arches National Park's** major attractions are its many natural sand-stone arches. East of the Rocky Mountains are the vast and fertile prairies of the Great Plains.

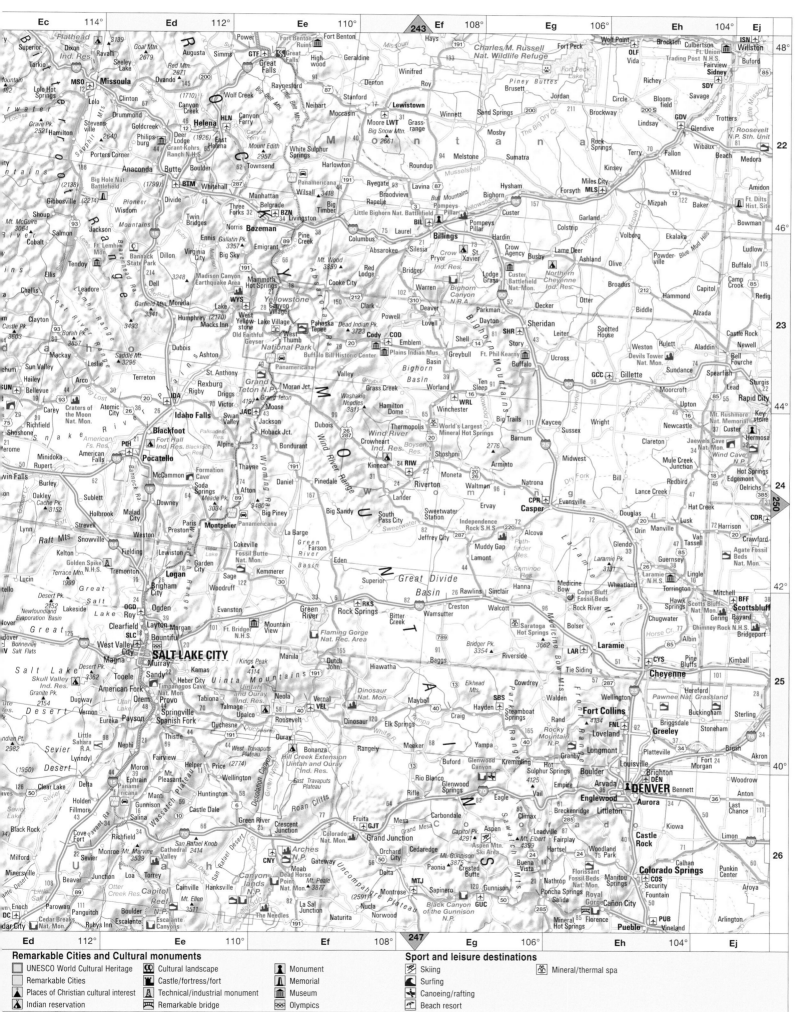

Yellowstone National Park ◨ The world's oldest national park (established in 1872, 9,000 km²) lies at an elevation of 2,400 meters in the Rocky Mountains. Yellowstone National Park is home to bears, buffalo, and elk. The geologically active park contains numerous hot springs and around 200 ▨ geysers. **Ee23**

Grand Teton National Park ◨ National Park in the Rocky Mountains – The Grand Teton (mountain) rises 4,197 meters – numerous ☷ mountain lakes. **Ee24**

Salt Lake City Capital city of Utah – city population 175,000 – founded by Mormon settlers – Host city of the 2002 ▨ Winter Olympic games. **Ee25**

Arches National Park Erosion created the more than 200 natural stone arches in the ◨ national park. **Ef26**

Canyonlands National Park ◨ National park at the meeting point of the Colorado and Green Rivers – panoramic views from the Grand View Point Overlook. **Ee-Ef26**

Kings Canyon National Park ◨ River valley surrounded by high canyon walls – home to the General Grant Tree (America's Christmas tree). **Ea27**

Remarkable Cities and Cultural monuments

▢ UNESCO World Cultural Heritage	⛰ Cultural landscape
▢ Remarkable Cities	⛫ Castle/fortress/fort
▢ Places of Christian cultural interest	⚙ Technical/industrial monument
▢ Indian reservation	⌁ Remarkable bridge
⛩ Monument	
⛿ Memorial	
⌂ Museum	
⛀ Olympics	

Sport and leisure destinations

⛷ Skiing	♨ Mineral/thermal spa
⛱ Surfing	
⛵ Canoeing/rafting	
⛱ Beach resort	

Southwestern USA

There are few regions in the world that can offer visitors the chance to visit more fascinating natural attractions than the American Southwest. The 🏞 **Grand Canyon** surveyor John Wesley Powell was enthralled by what he described as a "wilderness of rocks; deep gorges, where the rivers are lost below cliffs and towers and pinnacles; and beyond them, mountains blending with the clouds." The Southwest encompasses five states: Ne-

vada, Colorado, Utah, Arizona, and New Mexico. The region's terrain is dominated by large basins and plateaus which are broken by tall mountains ranges such as the 🏔 **Rocky Mountains** and deep river valleys. Covering 110,000 km², the Colorado Plateau encompasses some of the most beautiful national parks in the

The Mitten Buttes in Monument Valley (Arizona). **Ee27**

Big Sur Coastal area along California's Highway 1 – beautiful cliffs – 🏖 Julia Pfeiffer State Park (beaches), 🌲 Pfeiffer Big Sur State Park (redwood forests). **Dk27**

Death Valley National Park 🏜 Spectacular desert landscapes and an extreme climate – 🧂 salt lakes 🏞 – canyons 🏜 large sand dunes. **Eb27/28**

Las Vegas The city is a popular tourist destination – neon-lit Glitter Gulch has numerous 🎰 casinos – large theme hotels and casinos – 🎡 amusement parks. **Ec27**

Los Angeles Second largest city in the United States – population: city 3.6 million, county 9.4 million – with impressive 🏙 skyscrapers – 🎡 Disneyland – 🏖 beach communities including Venice Beach and Santa Monica – interesting 🏛 museums: Getty Center and Paul Getty Museum in Malibu. **Ea29**

Joshua Tree National Park Uninhabited 🏜 nature reserve in the Mojave Desert – ten meters tall Yucca trees (Joshua Trees) and unique cacti. **Eb-Ec28/29**

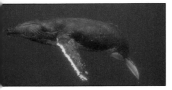

El Vizcaíno Reserve The world's first 🐋 marine reserve for the protection of whales – whale watching 🚤 – boat tours. **Ec31**

Organ Pipe Cactus National Monument 🏜 wilderness in the Sonora Desert – interesting desert plants. **Ed29/30**

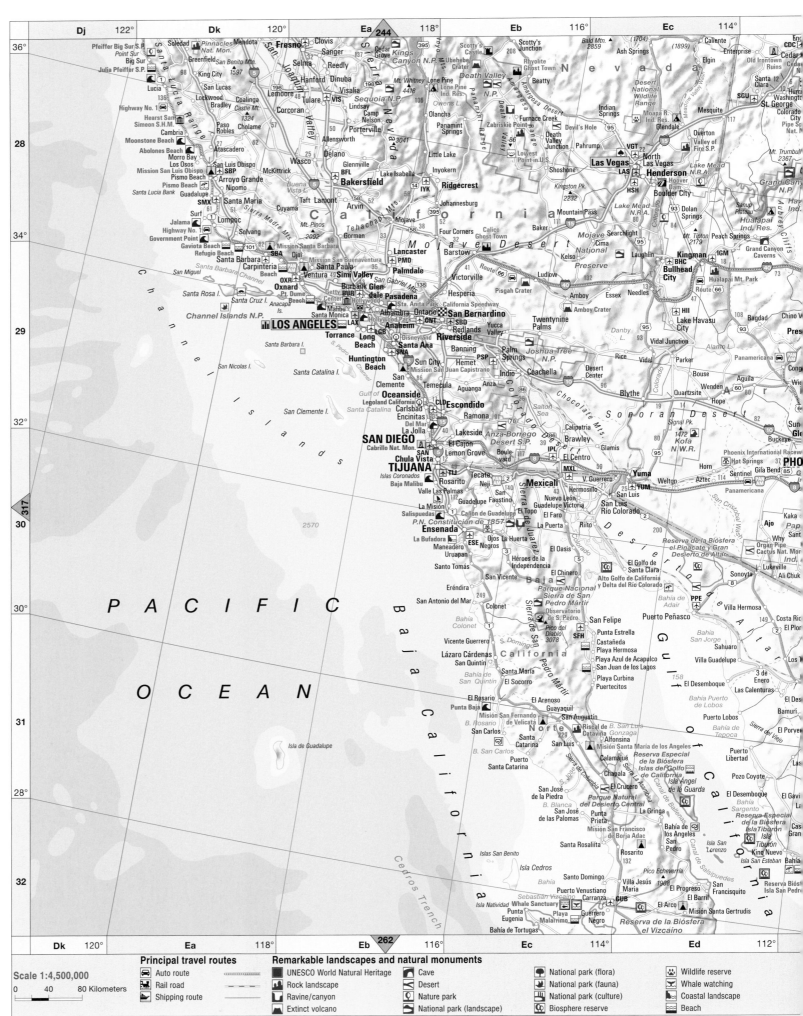

Scale 1:4,500,000

0   40   80 Kilometers

Principal travel routes
- 🚗 Auto route
- 🚆 Rail road
- Shipping route

Remarkable landscapes and natural monuments
- UNESCO World Natural Heritage
- Rock landscape
- Ravine/canyon
- Extinct volcano
- Cave
- Desert
- Nature park
- National park (landscape)
- National park (flora)
- National park (fauna)
- National park (culture)
- Biosphere reserve
- Wildlife reserve
- Whale watching
- Coastal landscape
- Beach

Southwest including Grand Canyon, Bryce, Zion, and Arches National Park. The ⬛ **Colorado River** is the longest and most important river in the region. The construction of dams in the last century has created several large 🜄 artificial lakes in the region including Lake Mead and Lake Powell. The construction of the Hoover Dam is considered one of the greatest engineering achievements of the 20th century. Without the energy supplied by dams, 🜄 **Las Vegas** would never have become a bright and vibrant metropolis in the middle of a ⬛ desert. Large sections of Nevada, Southern California and most of the border region are covered by rocky or sandy deserts.

In addition to its natural sights, the region also offers cultural attractions, many connected to the history and culture of local Native Americans. The ancient history of the local Native Americans is displayed in the region's pueblos. The most visited pueblos are 🜄 **Taos Pueblo** with its adobe buildings, 🜄 **Acoma Pueblo** the "Sky City," 🜄 **Mesa Verde National Park's** 700-year-old cliff buildings, and sites in Arizona's 🜄 reservations.

To the west of the ⬛ **Sierra Nevada** mountains lies Southern California with its beautiful 🜄 beaches and the exciting urban areas of Los Angeles and San Diego. While the coastal area of Southern California is densely populated and highly developed, the interior contains many pristine wilderness areas.

The Mexican coasts along the **Gulf of California** (Sea of Cortez) are surrounded by extremely dry ⬛ deserts. Many of the islands in the gulf are conservation areas. Along the coast of **Baja California** several 🜄 marine reserves have been created for the protection of local whales and dolphins.

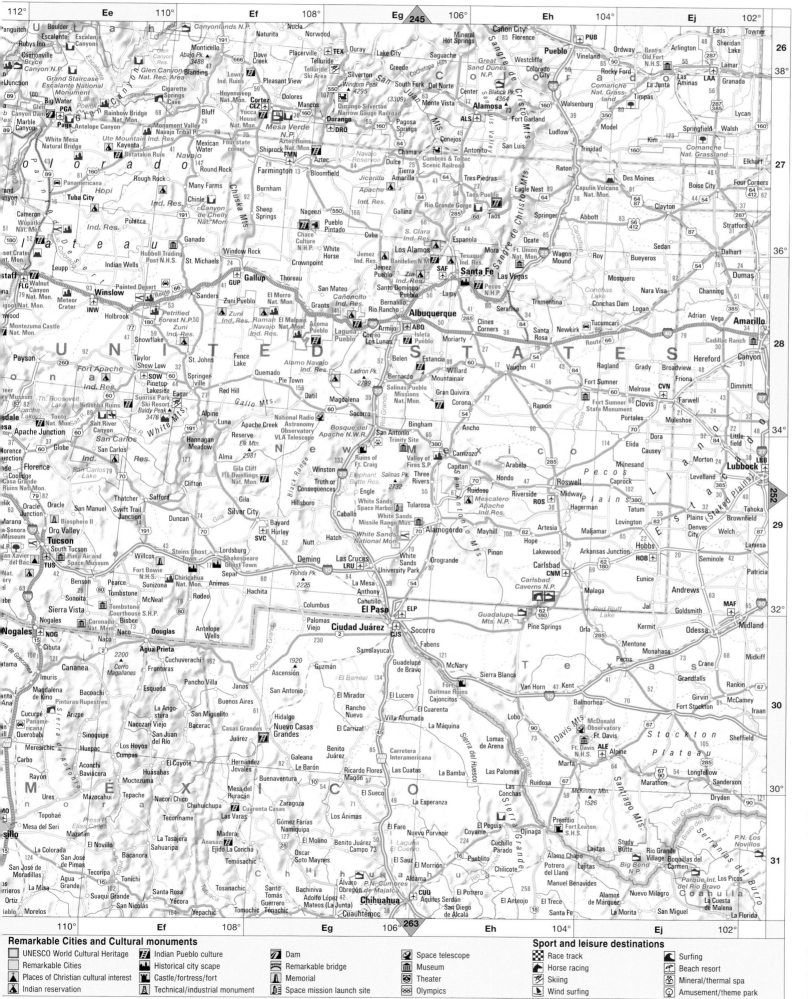

Bryce Canyon National Park Red 🜄 stone formations called Hoodoos – large horseshoe shaped natural amphitheaters. **Ed27**

Grand Canyon National Park The largest 🜄 canyon in the world. The Grand Canyon lies in northwest Arizona and stretches 350 kilometers, created by the Colorado River over millions of years – 🜄 national park – panoramic views. **Ed-Ee27/28**

Meteor Crater 🜄 Meteor impact crater in Arizona – 170 meters deep and 1,250 meters wide – 40,000 years old. **Ee28**

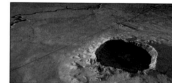

Mesa Verde National Park 🜄 Canyons in southwestern Colorado – well preserved 🜄 cliff settlements constructed by the Anasazi Native Americans. **Ef27**

Chaco Culture N.H.P. Remnants of ancient 🜄 Pueblo culture – the 🜄 remains of Pueblo Bonito, a structure that was once five stories tall and had 600 rooms. **Ef-Eg27/28**

Acoma Pueblo 🜄 Native American village – one of the oldest permanently inhabited settlements in the Americas (founded in 1075) – often called "Sky City". **Eg28**

Carlsbad Caverns National Park 🜄 Extensive network of more than 100 caves with stunning rock formations in southern New Mexico – the 🜄 Big Room, a 545-meter-long chamber. **Eh29**

Remarkable Cities and Cultural monuments

- ⬜ UNESCO World Cultural Heritage
- ⬜ Remarkable Cities
- ⬜ Places of Christian cultural interest
- ⬜ Indian reservation
- ⬜ Indian Pueblo culture
- ⬜ Historical city scape
- ⬜ Castle/fortress/fort
- ⬜ Technical/industrial monument
- ⬜ Dam
- ⬜ Remarkable bridge
- ⬜ Memorial
- ⬜ Space mission launch site
- ⬜ Space telescope
- ⬜ Museum
- ⬜ Theater
- ⬜ Olympics

Sport and leisure destinations

- ⬜ Race track
- ⬜ Horse racing
- ⬜ Skiing
- ⬜ Wind surfing
- ⬜ Surfing
- ⬜ Beach resort
- ⬜ Mineral/thermal spa
- ⬜ Amusement/theme park

Southern Canada

The northern regions of the provinces Manitoba, Saskatchewan, Quebec, and Ontario are covered by the Canadian Shield, one of the oldest geological features on the Earth's surface. The **Canadian Shield** extends out from both sides of the Hudson Bay and covers almost half of Canada's total land area. The area's topography was shaped to a great extent by glaciers during the ice age. In terms of mineral wealth, the Canadian

Shield is one of the richest regions in the world. The vast **Hudson Bay Lowlands** are a region of lakes and flat swampy land on the southern and western coasts of the bay. The province of Ontario alone encompasses several hundred thousand lakes. Central Canada has a typical continental climate with dry

Pukaskwa National Park on the shore of Lake Superior. **Fg-Fh21**

Pisew Falls Waterfall on the Grass River – located in Manitoba's Paint Lake Provincial Park. **Fa18**

Grass River Provincial Park Undeveloped wilderness with countless lakes – most of the park's land is covered by permafrost – scattered forests. **Ek18**

Lake Winnipeg The largest lake in Manitoba – dunes and beaches – surfing and recreational sailing areas. **Fa-Fb19/20**

Hollow Water First Nation Land Native reservation in Manitoba – on the southern shore of Lake Winnipeg. **Fb20**

Woodland Caribou Provincial Park Conservation area containing numerous lakes – caribou and bear populations. **Fc20**

Lake Manitoba The smallest of Manitoba's three largest lakes (4,624 km²) – name comes from the Ojibwa language and means "Straits of the Great Spirit". **Fa20**

Winnipeg Capital city of Manitoba – population 690,000 – Winnipeg Art Gallery – French district, St. Boniface – Centennial Centre with the Manitoba Museum of Man and Nature. **Fb21**

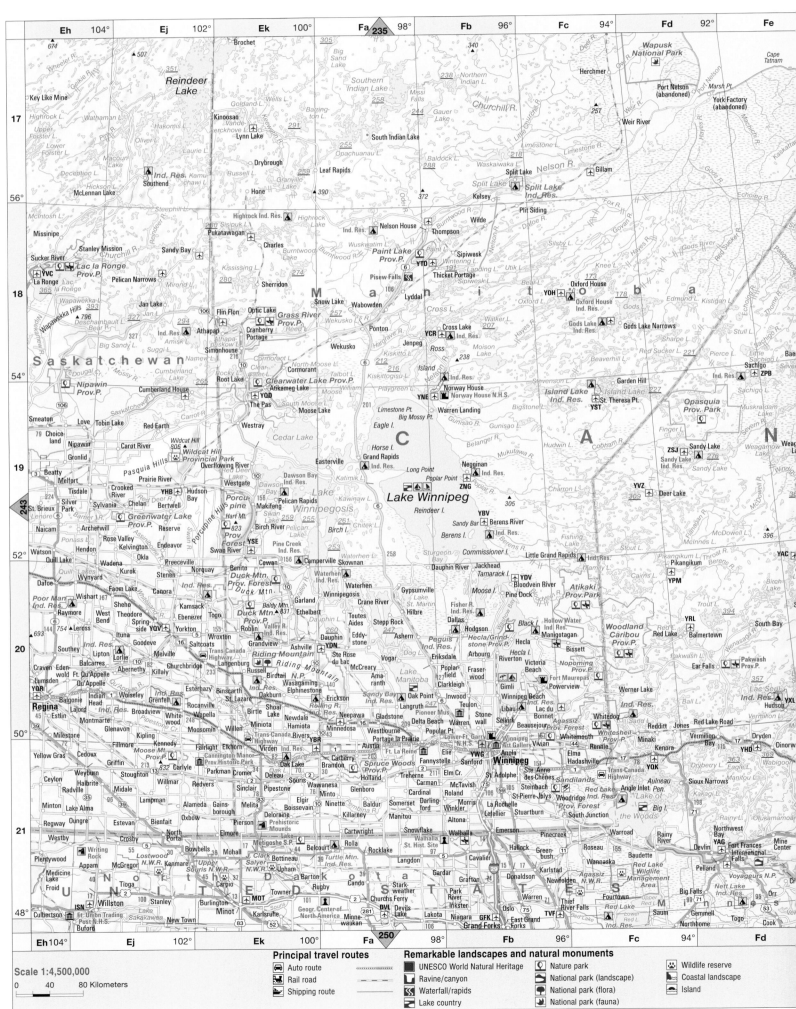

Scale 1:4,500,000

0   40   80 Kilometers

Principal travel routes
- Auto route
- Rail road
- Shipping route

Remarkable landscapes and natural monuments
- UNESCO World Natural Heritage
- Ravine/canyon
- Waterfall/rapids
- Lake country
- Nature park
- National park (landscape)
- National park (flora)
- National park (fauna)
- Wildlife reserve
- Coastal landscape
- Island

hot summers and bitter cold winters that are five months long in the south and even longer in northern areas. Winter temperatures around -25° C and summer temperatures exceeding 25° C are typical for the region. Because of the raw climate and terrain in the northern sections of southern Canada most of the region's population is concentrated in the far south near the American border. The pristine forests and lakes are best ex-

plored from the many hunting and fishing lodges scattered throughout southern Canada. Fishing and hunting in the great outdoors are favorite pastimes for much of the region's population. Southern Canada has many accessible waterways for canoeing and kayaking. The Trans Canada Highway stretches from the Atlantic coast to the Pacific coast, and driving along the highway provides travelers with a good impression of

the country's landscapes. The highway passes through forests and along lakes in Ontario, into the wheat fields and grasslands of the Prairie Provinces. The Great Plains begin west of Winnipeg in Manitoba and rise in elevation from east to west. Lake Winnipeg, one of the largest lakes in Canada, has many sandy white beaches along its edges. In addition to Lake Winnipeg, Manitoba is also home to two other large lakes, Lake Manitoba and

Lake Winnipegosis, and countless smaller lakes scattered throughout the province.The central and southern sections of Saskatchewan are covered by vast fields used for agriculture and the province is widely known as the "breadbasket of Canada." While most of Saskatchewan is covered by flat plains, the northern section of the province, like much of neighboring Manitoba, is covered by countless lakes.

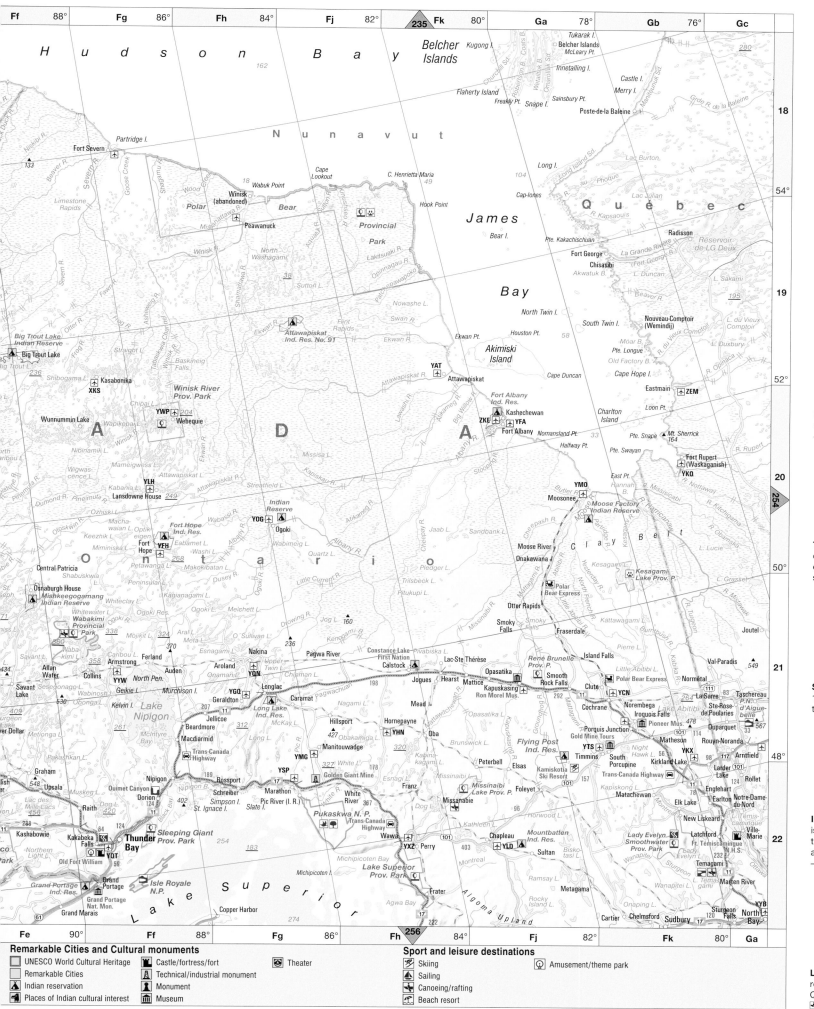

James Bay Home to Cree Indian communities – seal, whales, and walrus populations – hydroelectric projects on the Quebec coast. **Fj-Ga18-20**

Ouimet Canyon Five kilometers long and up to 150 meters deep canyon in Ontario – contains rare alpine-arctic vegetation – panoramic views from platforms. **Ff21**

Kakabeka Falls The Native American name means the "waterfall over tall rocks" – the falls are 39 meters high. **Ff21**

Thunder Bay Town on the northwestern coast of Lake Superior – major port for the export of Canadian grain – historic museum Old Fort William. **Ff21**

Sleeping Giant Land formation (330 m x 12 km) – according to legend the Giant "protects" the entrance to Thunder Bay. **Ff21**

Isle Royale National Park Unihabited island in the north of Lake Superior – part of the American state Michigan – the isolated area is only accessible by boat or seaplane – hiking areas. **Ff21/22**

Lake Temagami Beautiful lake surrounded by forests – in Ontario near the Quebec border – popular with fishers and kayakers. **Fk-Ga22**

Remarkable Cities and Cultural monuments

- UNESCO World Cultural Heritage
- Remarkable Cities
- Indian reservation
- Places of Indian cultural interest
- Castle/fortress/fort
- Technical/industrial monument
- Monument
- Museum
- Theater

Sport and leisure destinations

- Skiing
- Sailing
- Canoeing/rafting
- Beach resort
- Amusement/theme park

Northern Great Plains

Most of the American Midwest is covered by the vast flat prairies of the **Great Plains**. The western sections of the Great Plains border the  **Rocky Mountains**. The area within 200 kilometers of the Rockies is dotted by several isolated hilly areas such as Badlands National Park, the Smoky Hills, and the Sandy Hills. North of the Smoky Hills lies the geographic center of the mainland United States; a monument marks the exact

location. The Great Plains tend to decline in elevation from west to east. The **Missouri Plateau** is a large plateau in the center of the United States. It borders the **Coteau des Prairies** and the **Coteau du Missouri**, two smaller significant plateaus in the region. The Midwest is home to several large river basins including the

Ft. Pierre Grassland National Park in South Dakota. **Ek23**

Devil's Tower tall rim of an inactive volcano (264 m) – national monument in the state of Wyoming. **Eh23**

Mount Rushmore The faces of four American presidents carved in stone: Washington, Jefferson, Lincoln, and Roosevelt – all around 18 meters tall. **Ej24**

Wind Cave National Park Extensive network of caves – Custer State Park – buffalo herds. **Ej24**

Badlands National Park Large region of heavily eroded arid land – eagle, hawk and falcon populations. **Ej24**

Chimney Rock 46 meters tall rock formation near the North Platte River in Nebraska. **Ej25**

Denver Capital city of Colorado – metropolitan population: 2.4 million – Cherry Cheek shopping area – Country Club District – LoDo: downtown neighborhood with bars, art galleries, and boutiques – Colorado History Museum. **Eh26**

Aspen Ski resort: popular with the wealthy and celebrities – dozens of ski areas – tree-lined streets. **Eg26**

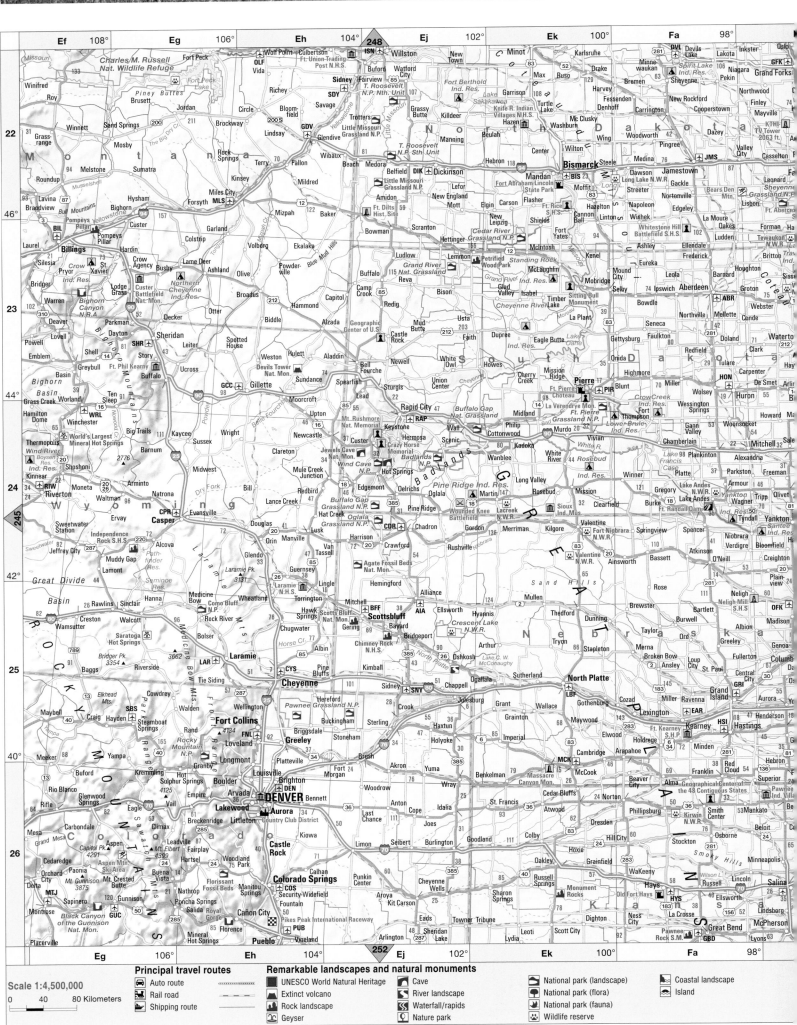

Scale 1:4,500,000
0   40   80 Kilometers

Principal travel routes
- Auto route
- Rail road
- Shipping route

Remarkable landscapes and natural monuments
- UNESCO World Natural Heritage
- Extinct volcano
- Rock landscape
- Geyser
- Cave
- River landscape
- Waterfall/rapids
- Nature park
- National park (landscape)
- National park (flora)
- National park (fauna)
- Wildlife reserve
- Coastal landscape
- Island

basin of the 3,725 meters long 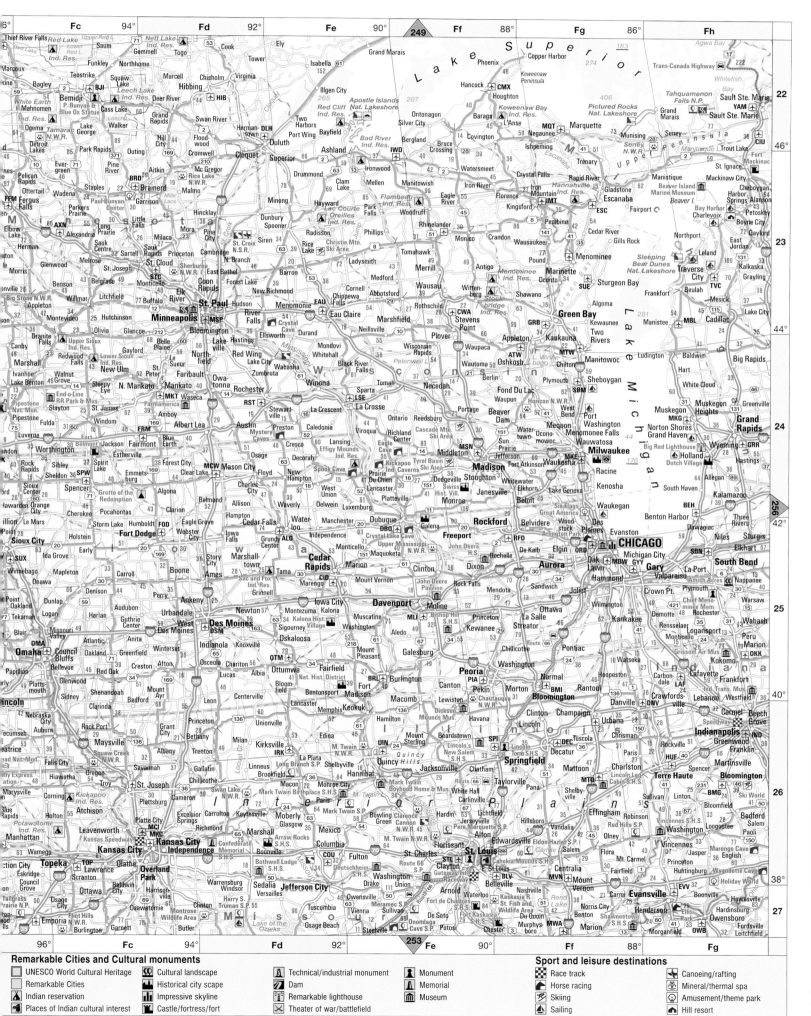**Missouri River**. The Missouri River begins in Montana and there are several large dams along the river's path.

The **Great Lakes**, divided between the United States and Canada, are the largest group of freshwater lakes in the world. The five Great Lakes cover a combined total of 245,000 square kilometers. **Chicago** on Lake Michigan is the largest city in the Midwest and one of the most

important economic centers on the continent. America's Midwest has large deposits of mineral resources including iron ore, oil, and coal. The most important river in the region is the **Mississippi**, the continent's longest river. The basin of the Mississippi River is a fertile region that is home to countless farms. Near **St. Louis**, the Mississippi River joins with the Illinois and Missouri Rivers. The Midwest has experienced several

major floods in the recent decades. Many dams and levees have been built throughout the region to protect against floods which can cause major damage to homes and agricultural areas.

Some of the most important historic sites in the United States are in the Midwest, including sites connected to the history of the region's Native Americans. **Wounded Knee** in South Dakota was the site of one of the most controversial

events in the region's history. On December 29, 1890, at least 150 Lakota (Sioux) men, women, and children lost their lives in a clash with the United States army. The Midwest has four distinct seasons characterized by hot summers and very cold winters. Rainfall is heaviest in the eastern sections of the Midwest and significantly less in the western parts of the region. Major droughts hit the region at least once every 25 years.

Minneapolis-St. Paul "Twin Cities" on the Mississipi River – Minnesota Capitol building (photo) in St. Paul – skyscrapers in Minneapolis – St. Anthony Falls. **Fd23**

Milwaukee Largest city in Wisconsin – Performing Arts Center – historic district with 19th century architecture. **Fg24**

Holland, Michigan Founded by Dutch settlers – Dutch Village theme park – Big Red Lighthouse (photo). **Fg24**

Chicago The third largest city in the United States. Chicago's metro population exceeds eight million. The city has an impressive skyline including the Sears Tower (top photo). The Art Institute of Chicago has a famous collection of art. Other attractions: beaches on the shore of Lake Michigan and an active jazz scene. **Fg25**

St. Louis Largest city in Missouri – The Jefferson National Expansion Memorial with the Gateway Arch (photo). **Fe26**

Remarkable Cities and Cultural monuments

- ☐ UNESCO World Cultural Heritage
- ■ Remarkable Cities
- ▲ Indian reservation
- ● Places of Indian cultural interest
- ♦ Cultural landscape
- ⬚ Historical city scape
- ▦ Impressive skyline
- ♜ Castle/fortress/fort
- ▲ Technical/industrial monument
- ▲ Dam
- ♦ Remarkable lighthouse
- ✕ Theater of war/battlefield
- ▲ Monument
- ▦ Memorial
- ⛪ Museum

Sport and leisure destinations

- 🏁 Race track
- 🏇 Horse racing
- ⛷ Skiing
- ⛵ Sailing
- 🛶 Canoeing/rafting
- ♨ Mineral/thermal spa
- ◉ Amusement/theme park
- ⛰ Hill resort

The basin of the 🚂 **Mississippi-Missouri River** covers a large section of the mainland United States. The basin stretches over the territory of eleven states: New Mexico and Colorado in the west; Tennessee, Alabama and Mississippi in the east; Louisiana and Texas in the south; Oklahoma and Arkansas in the basin's center; and Kansas and Missouri in the north. To the west of the basin rise the 🏔 **Rocky Mountains** with peaks over 4,000

meters high. To the east of the basin are the heavily forested 🏔 **Appalachian Mountains**. The flat plains extending from the east and west banks of the Mississippi River are called the **Interior Plains**. Farther west is a region called the Interior Highlands encompassing the Ozark Plateau and the **Ouachita Mountains**.

White Sands National Monument in New Mexico. **Eg29**

Durango Silverton Narrow Gauge Railroad 🚂 Historic steam engine train – travels daily between Durango and Silverton in southern Colorado. **Eg27**

Rio Grande Gorge Scenic deep 🏞 canyon (200 meters) – west of Taos, New Mexico – 🛶 canoe and paddle boat tours. **Eh27**

Taos Pueblo This 🏛 Native American settlement in the 🏞 Rio Grande Valley has been inhabited for almost 1,000 years – UNESCO world heritage site – ⛪ Spanish mission. **Eh27**

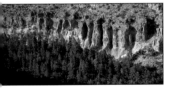

Bandelier National Museum West of Santa Fe – ruins of Anasazi Native American 🏛 cave settlements. **Eg28**

Santa Fe Capital city of New Mexico – located at 2,100 meters above sea level – artist colonies – historic adobe buildings – numerous art galleries and craft shops along Canyon Road. **Eh28**

White Sands Space Harbor The isolated area is is used by 🚀 NASA as a training area for space shuttle pilots – the 🏛 White Sands Missile Range Museum has an interesting collection of rockets. **Eg29**

San Antonio Large 🏙 city in Texas with strong Hispanic-Mexican heritage – the Alamo: originally a ⛪ Spanish mission built in 1755 and the site of a historic battle, "cradle of Texan independence". **Fa31**

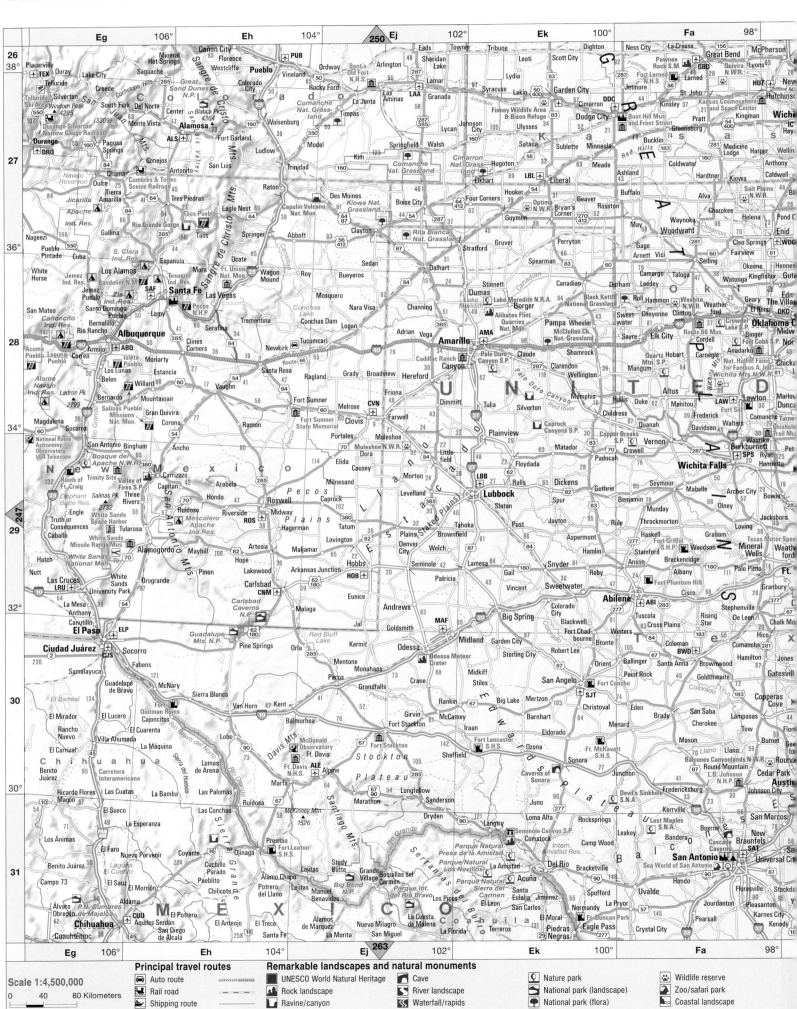

Scale 1:4,500,000

0   40   80 Kilometers

Principal travel routes
- Auto route
- Rail road
- Shipping route

Remarkable landscapes and natural monuments
- UNESCO World Natural Heritage
- Rock landscape
- Ravine/canyon
- Extinct volcano
- Cave
- River landscape
- Waterfall/rapids
- Desert
- Nature park
- National park (landscape)
- National park (flora)
- National park (fauna)
- Wildlife reserve
- Zoo/safari park
- Coastal landscape

This region is heavily forested and has deep river valleys. It is crossed by many waterways including the Arkansas, Canadian, and Pecos Rivers. The Rio Grande River flows over 2,480 kilometers from its source in Colorado to the Gulf of Mexico. East of El Paso the Rio Grande forms a natural border between Texas and Mexico.
South of the Mississippi-Missouri Basin lie the extremely flat and low-lying Gulf

Coast plains which extend to the coast. This region is very humid and covered by extensive swamplands. The numerous Pueblos of New Mexico give visitors the chance to discover the history and culture of local Native Americans. Many of the region's Native Americans also welcome visitors to their traditional ceremonies and festivals. Oklahoma was once called "Indian Territory" and it was in this territory that most of the

southeastern Native Americans who were expelled during the Trail of Tears were forcibly settled. There are several memorials in the state dedicated to this sad chapter in American history. For many people around the world Texas is still a land of cowboys and vast empty plains. Nowadays, many Texans live in large modern cities such as Dallas, San Antonio, and Houston. The state is also a major center for several high tech

industries and the home of NASA's Lyndon B. Johnson Space Center in Houston. The Gulf Coast states – Mississippi, Alabama, and Louisiana – contain many historic sites including restored antebellum plantations and relics from the Spanish and French colonial eras. New Orleans, at the mouth of the Mississippi, is a vibrant city with well-preserved Spanish colonial architecture and a distinct local culture.

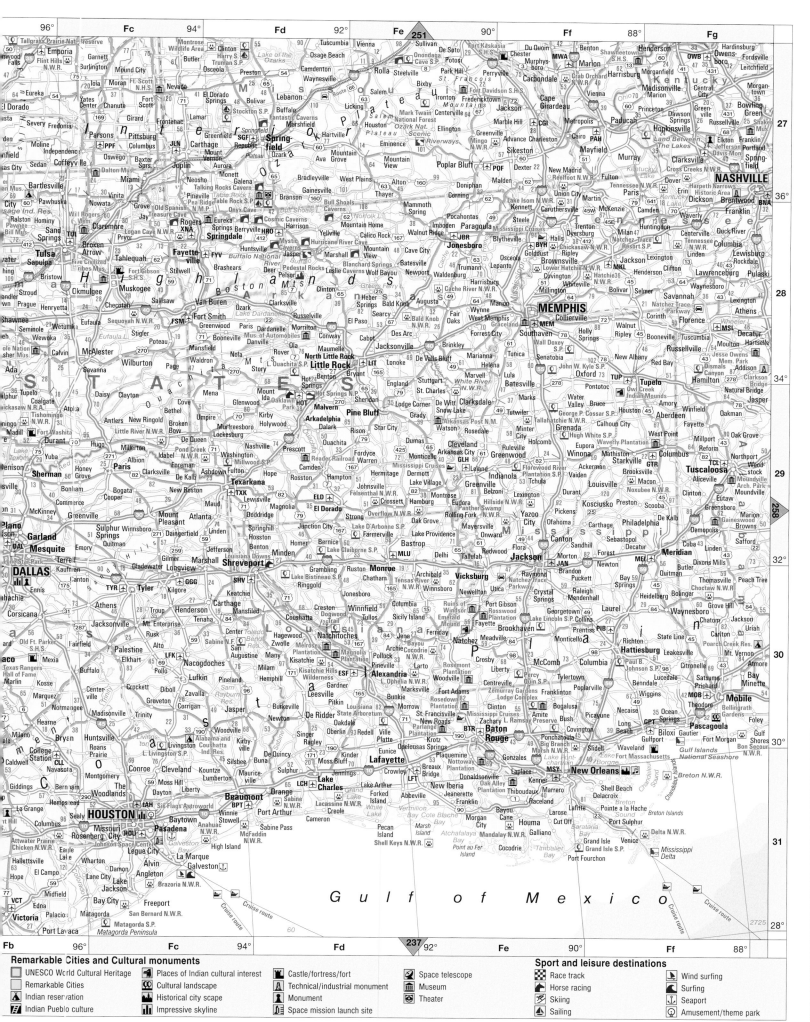

Dallas Second largest city in Texas – beautiful modern skyline – John F. Kennedy Memorial. **Fb29**

Houston Important center for the oil and petrochemical industries – modern skyscrapers – Six Flags Astroworld – Lyndon B. Johnson Space Center (NASA). **Fc31**

Natchez Port city on the Mississippi – antebellum houses – Natchez African American History Museum. **Fe30**

Oak Alley Plantation Sugar plantation on the Mississippi River – several movies were filmed in the area. **Fe31**

New Orleans Port city in the Mississippi Delta region – lively jazz scene – birthplace of Louis Armstrong – French Quarter – Mardi Gras. **Fe31**

The Mississippi River The longest river in North America. The Mississippi flows south from its source in Minnesota to its delta on the Gulf of Mexico. Tourists can take steamboat tours down the river and discover the river basin's landscapes. **Ff-Fe27/31**

Remarkable Cities and Cultural monuments

- UNESCO World Cultural Heritage
- Remarkable Cities
- Indian reservation
- Indian Pueblo culture
- Places of Indian cultural interest
- Cultural landscape
- Historical city scape
- Impressive skyline
- Castle/fortress/fort
- Technical/industrial monument
- Monument
- Space mission launch site

Sport and leisure destinations

- Space telescope
- Museum
- Theater
- Race track
- Horse racing
- Skiing
- Sailing
- Wind surfing
- Surfing
- Seaport
- Amusement/theme park

Newfoundland, Southeastern Canada

Newfoundland, Canada's easternmost province, consists of two distinct regions – the large island of Newfoundland and the mainland region of Labrador. Newfoundland is home to the majority of the province's inhabitants. Most of the island has a maritime climate, while sparsely populated Labrador has a sub-arctic climate. Both areas are home to large forests and crystal clear lakes. The province of New Brunswick encom-

passes the northernmost sections of the Appalachian Mountains. To the west of New Brunswick lies the Saint Lawrence River which flows north into the Gulf of Saint Lawrence. The Saint Lawrence is 3,000 kilometers long and is bordered by fertile plains on both sides. The river is connected to the Great

Lighthouse on Cape Enrage in New Brunswick. **Gg23**

Labrador Heavily forested, sparsely populated peninsula in eastern Canada – long cold winters – mostly tundra. **Gc19**

Les Laurentides ▣ Popular weekend destination for people from the surrounding regions – winter sports facilities – abundant wildlife – beautiful autumn foliage. **Ge22**

Québec City French is the dominant language in Québec's capital and second largest city. Québec City is divided into two sections. The lower town contains the military museum 🏛 Musee du Fort and the 🏛 Basilique cathedrale Notre Dame built in 1647. The Upper Town contains the picturesque Petit-Champlain district with its historic architecture. The two sections of the inner city are connected by stairways and a funicular. **Ge22**

Montréal Population: 3.5 million – interesting mix of architectural styles (skyscrapers and Victorian homes). **Gd23**

Acadia National Park ▣ US-State Maine – oldest national park in the eastern United States – Cadillac Mountain (466 m). **Gf23**

La Verendrye Nature Reserve ▣ Nature reserve covering 13,615 km² – numerous lakes and rivers – bears and elk herds. **Gb22**

Scale 1:4,500,000

0   40   80 Kilometers

Principal travel routes
- 🚗 Auto route
- 🚂 Rail road
- 🚢 Shipping route

Remarkable landscapes and natural monuments
- ▣ UNESCO World Natural Heritage
- ▣ Rock landscape
- ▣ Nature park
- ▣ National park (landscape)
- ▣ National park (flora)
- ▣ National park (fauna)
- ▣ Wildlife reserve
- ▣ Coastal landscape

Newfoundland, Southeastern Canada

Lakes by a series of canals. **Québec** has a land area of 1.5 million km² and is the largest of Canada's ten provinces. The province borders Ontario in the west, Newfoundland and Labrador in the east, and New Brunswick in the southeast. Québec also shares borders with the U.S states of Maine, New Hampshire, Vermont, and New York.

Canada's Atlantic provinces have long cold winters and the region gets heavy precipitation during the entire year. The region's climate is greatly influenced by ocean currents and winds from the continent's interior regions. Most of central and southern Québec has a continental climate with hot summers, cold winters, and abundant rainfall. September and October are the best months to visit the region. During these months visitors can enjoy the beautiful autumn colors of the region's forests.

Eastern Canada comprises large undeveloped regions with abundant wildlife including large caribou and bear populations. Many aquatic birds inhabit the region's coasts and whales can be seen in the Saint Lawrence River.

More than half of the Canadian population lives in the Southeast of the country. Like the rest of the population, most of Canada's 970,000 indigenous people live in the country's eastern provinces.

The state of **Maine** shares a border with the Canadian provinces of New Brunswick and Québec. There are countless small bays and islands along the jagged coast of Maine. Maine is the most sparsely populated and least developed of the New England states. The state has an abundance of wildlife including caribous and beavers. Maine's capital city, Augusta, is one of the smallest state capitals in the United States.

Signal Hill 170-meter-high cliff in the harbour of Newfoundland's provincial capital, St. John's – Cabot Tower (photo) lies atop the coastal cliff – interesting radio and Morse code museum. **Hd22**

Gros-Morne National Park Mountainous national park (1,805 km²) with fjords – fascinating wildlife. **Hb21**

Avalon Peninsula Peninsula in western Newfoundland – location of the provincial capital, St. John's – numerous fishing villages and large bays. **Hd22**

Prince Edward Island Hilly island in the Gulf of Saint Lawrence – the smallest Canadian province – lakes and attractive villages – pink sandy beaches in the south. **Gj22**

Cape Breton Island Narrow peninsula in New Brunswick – mild climate – beautiful rugged landscape – distinctive local culture – Cabot Trail. **Gk22/23**

Fortress of Louisbourg On Cape Breton Island – founded by the French during the colonial era – reconstructed fort with museum. **Gk23**

Lunenburg Picturesque port city south of Halifax in Nova Scotia – Cape Breton Island – Victorian architecture and brightly painted houses – UNESCO world heritage site – fisheries museum. **Gh23**

Legend

Remarkable Cities and Cultural monuments

- UNESCO World Cultural Heritage
- Remarkable Cities
- Places of Christian cultural interest
- Indian reservation
- Historical city scape
- Castle/fortress/fort
- Technical/industrial monument
- Dam
- Remarkable lighthouse
- Remarkable bridge
- Monument
- Museum
- World exhibition
- Olympics

Sport and leisure destinations

- Horse racing
- Skiing
- Sailing
- Canoeing/rafting

Great Lakes Region, Mid-Atlantic States

The five ⛵ **Great Lakes** were formed at the end of the last ice age when massive glaciers carved out huge basins in the Earth's surface. When the glaciers melted these basins filled with water and formed the Great Lakes. Lake Superior is the largest and deepest of the Great Lakes with a surface area of 82,350 km² and a maximum depth of 200 meters. Lake Erie, with an average depth of 62 meters, is the shallowest of the

Great Lakes and drains into Lake Ontario at the spectacular Niagara Falls (60 m high). Niagara Falls consists of three separate falls and together the falls are one of the most visited natural attractions on the continent. With a combined surface area of 245,000 km², the Great Lakes are the largest group of fresh-

A beautiful sunset above Lake Superior. Fe-Fh21/22

Bruce Peninsula National Park 100-kilometer-long ⛵ peninsula northwest of Toronto – 🏖 beaches – Bruce Trail. **Fk23**

Detroit Largest city in Michigan – center of the American automobile industry – 🏛 Henry and Edsel Ford Auditorium – downtown with the civic center and philharmonic – Renaissance Center. **Fj24**

Cleveland Ohio port city on the shore of Lake Erie – 🏛 Rock and Roll Hall of Fame (music history museum) – art deco 🏬 shopping center, Tower City – 🎭 Playhouse Square encompasses four theaters. **Fk25**

Toronto 4.9 million inhabitants, located on Lake Ontario – 🗼 CN Tower – the financial district with modern 🏛 art galleries. **Ga24**

Niagara Falls 🌊 Falls descend from the Niagara River – in Ontario and New York – three separate falls: American Falls, Horseshoe Falls, and Bridal Veil Falls. **Ga24**

Allegany State Park 🌲 Conservation area, east of Lake Erie – heavily forested area – beautiful meandering rivers. **Ga24**

Philadelphia Largest city in Pennsylvania – population 1.7 million – historic sites including the Independence Hall in 🏛 Independence Historical Park – excellent art collections in the 🏛 Philadelphia Museum of Art and Franklin Institute. **Gc26**

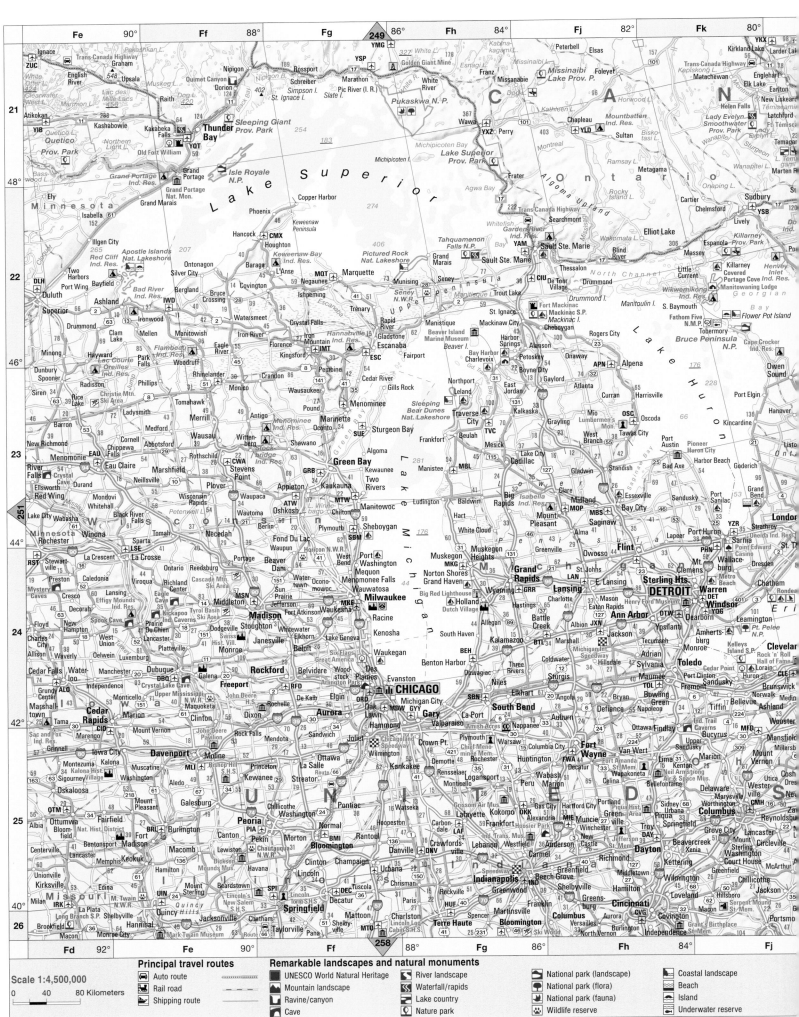

Scale 1:4,500,000

0   40   80 Kilometers

Principal travel routes	Remarkable landscapes and natural monuments		
🚗 Auto route	▪ UNESCO World Natural Heritage	〽 River landscape	🌲 National park (landscape)	⛰ Coastal landscape
🚂 Rail road	▲ Mountain landscape	💧 Waterfall/rapids	❀ National park (flora)	🏖 Beach
⚓ Shipping route	⩗ Ravine/canyon	🦆 Lake country	🐾 National park (fauna)	▣ Island
	⌂ Cave	🍃 Nature park	🐾 Wildlife reserve	▦ Underwater reserve

water lakes in the world. The Great Lakes, which lie along the American-Canadian border, also represent the world's largest supply of potable water. The ⬛ **Appalachian Mountains** stretch from the southeastern United States to the Canadian province of Québec. The mountains form a natural barrier between the Eastern Seaboard of the United States and the Midwest. During the ice ages, the Appalachians were re-

shaped by glaciers which left the mountains shorter and rounder.
The climate of New York and **New England** is greatly influenced by ocean currents and winds. This region has hot summers with temperatures regularly exceeding 30°C and cold winters with temperatures below -10°C. More than 70% of New England's land is covered by deciduous forests and during autumn, the region's foliage displays bright fiery

colors that attract visitors from around the world. The coniferous forests to the north of the Great Lakes are darker and less accessible than their New England counterparts. These forests are home to abundant wildlife including large elk herds and bear populations. The western Appalachians have rich coal deposits and the area around the Great Lakes is fertile and well suited for large-scale agriculture. The Great Lakes Region and the

surrounding Midwestern states are responsible for most of America's grain production. The ⬛ Saint Lawrence seaway is a series of canals that connect the Great Lakes to the Atlantic. The seaway was completed in 1959 and is administered by the United States and Canada. The Northeastern United States and the Great Lakes region comprise one of the world's wealthiest and most economically productive regions.

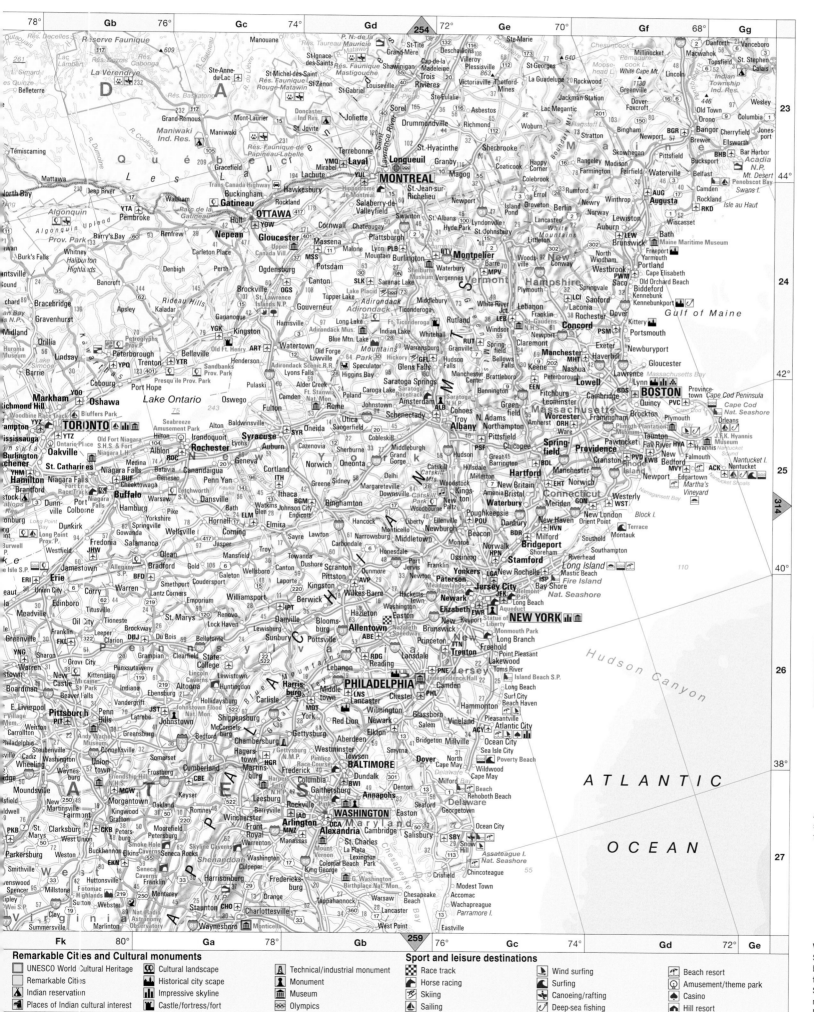

Boston New England's largest city – historic architecture – 🚶 Freedom Trail – Quincy Market – 🏙 panoramic views from the J. Hancock Tower. **Ge24**

Martha's Vineyard 🏝 Island south of Cape Cod – 🏖 beaches – Victorian architecture – popular weekend destination. **Ge25**

Nantucket Popular tourist destination – major 🚢 whaling port in the 18th century – 🏖 beaches and historic architecture. **Ge25**

New York City 🏙 Largest city in the United States with a population over eight million. Visitors can enjoy views of the city's skyline from the top of the Empire State Building. The 🏛 Metropolitan Museum, Museum of Modern Art and the Guggenheim contain world class art collections. **Gc-Gd25**

Atlantic City 🎰 Gaming center in New Jersey – large 🏨 casino-hotel resorts – the famous Boardwalk. **Gc26**

Washington D.C. Capital of the United States – home to important government buildings including the 🏛 White House and the 🏛 Capitol building (photo) – 🏛 The Smithsonian Institute is one of the world's most impressive collections of museums – National Gallery of Art. **Gb26**

Remarkable Cities and Cultural monuments

☐ UNESCO World Cultural Heritage	▣ Cultural landscape	▣ Technical/industrial monument			
● Remarkable Cities	▣ Historical city scape	▣ Monument			
▣ Indian reservation	▣ Castle/fortress/fort	▣ Museum			
▣ Places of Indian cultural interest		▣ Olympics			

Sport and leisure destinations

▣ Race track	▣ Wind surfing	▣ Beach resort	
▣ Horse racing	▣ Surfing	▣ Amusement/theme park	
▣ Skiing	▣ Canoeing/rafting	▣ Casino	
▣ Sailing	▣ Deep-sea fishing	▣ Hill resort	

Southern States

In the United States, the southeastern region of the country is commonly referred to as **"the South."** Next to New England the South is the American region with the clearest identity. Around the world people associate the South with images of old cotton plantations, southern gentry and the region's history of racial divisions. The South usually refers to the southeastern states between Texas and the District of Columbia. To the south of

the region lies the Gulf of Mexico and to the east, the Atlantic Ocean. The coastlines in the region are uneven and contain numerous bays, river deltas, barrier islands, and large natural harbors such as **Chesapeake Bay** in Virginia. The Gulf Coast is a humid area with many swamps, bayous, and river deltas. The flat watery

A colorful "Indian summer" in the mountains of North Carolina. **Fk27**

Mark Twain National Forest Protected forest in southern Missouri – hiking and bike trails, horse riding, and canoeing. **Fe27**

Table Rock State Park On the northern shore of Table Rock Lake, a reservoir on the White River – camping areas. **Fd27**

Ozark Plateau An upland region mostly in Arkansas and Missouri; partially in Kansas and Oklahoma. There are around 1,500 limestone caves in the region. **Fd-Fe27**

Memphis The Memphis Pyramid (top photo) is the most famous landmark of the city's skyline. The city has strong musical traditions. In addition to its famous connection to Blues, the city is also home to Graceland and Beagle Street (bottom photo) contains numerous live music venues. **Ff28**

Nashville Capital of Tennessee – population 500,000 – center of the country music industry – Country Music Hall of Fame and the Grand Ole Opry. **Fg27**

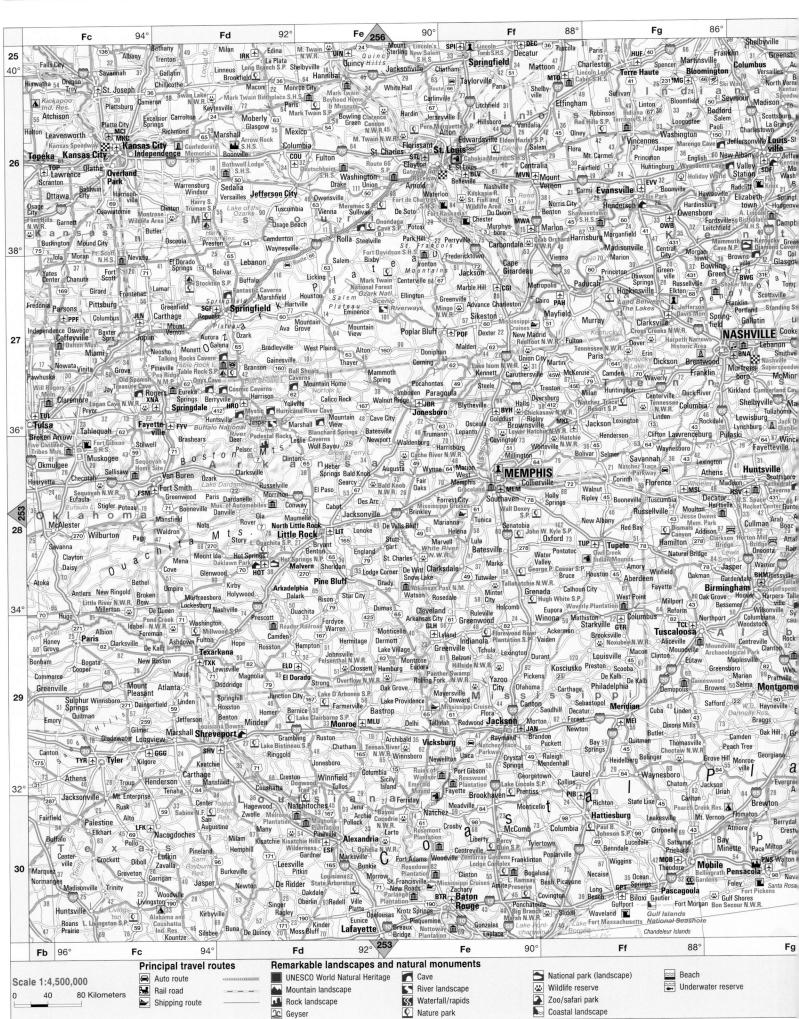

Scale 1:4,500,000

0   40   80 Kilometers

Principal travel routes
- Auto route
- Rail road
- Shipping route
- (dotted line)

Remarkable landscapes and natural monuments
- UNESCO World Natural Heritage
- Mountain landscape
- Rock landscape
- Geyser
- Cave
- River landscape
- Waterfall/rapids
- Nature park
- National park (landscape)
- Wildlife reserve
- Zoo/safari park
- Coastal landscape
- Beach
- Underwater reserve

plains along the Gulf Coast extend up to 800 kilometers into the region's interior. The **Mississippi River** is the longest river in North America. Near St. Louis, the Illinois and Missouri Rivers merge into the Mississippi and the river flows into the Gulf of Mexico at New Orleans. The **Appalachian Mountains** extend through the interior of the South. The highest peak in these relatively low mountains is Mount Mitchell in North Carolina which rises 2,037 meters. The southern Appalachians are home to two beautiful national parks: **Shenandoah National Park** and **Great Smoky Mountains National Park**. The 760 kilometer long **Blue Ridge Parkway** winds through the Appalachian Mountains and passes through or near many of the most beautiful areas in the region.

Many remnants of the antebellum South can still be found in the region, including historic plantations and small towns with historic districts. Some cities in the South – such as Savannah, Georgia and Charleston, South Carolina – have large collections of interesting historic architecture from the 18th and 19th centuries. Louisiana is home to the unique French influenced culture of the Cajuns who are famous for their distinct dialect and cuisine. The South boasts many sites connected to the history, culture, and arts of African-Americans, including the Martin Luther King Jr. National Historic Site in Atlanta.

Large southern cities, including Atlanta, New Orleans, and Memphis, give visitors an impression of the region's economic revival in recent decades and the rich musical heritage of the South. Jazz, Blues, Country Music, and Rock and Roll all have their roots in the Southern United States.

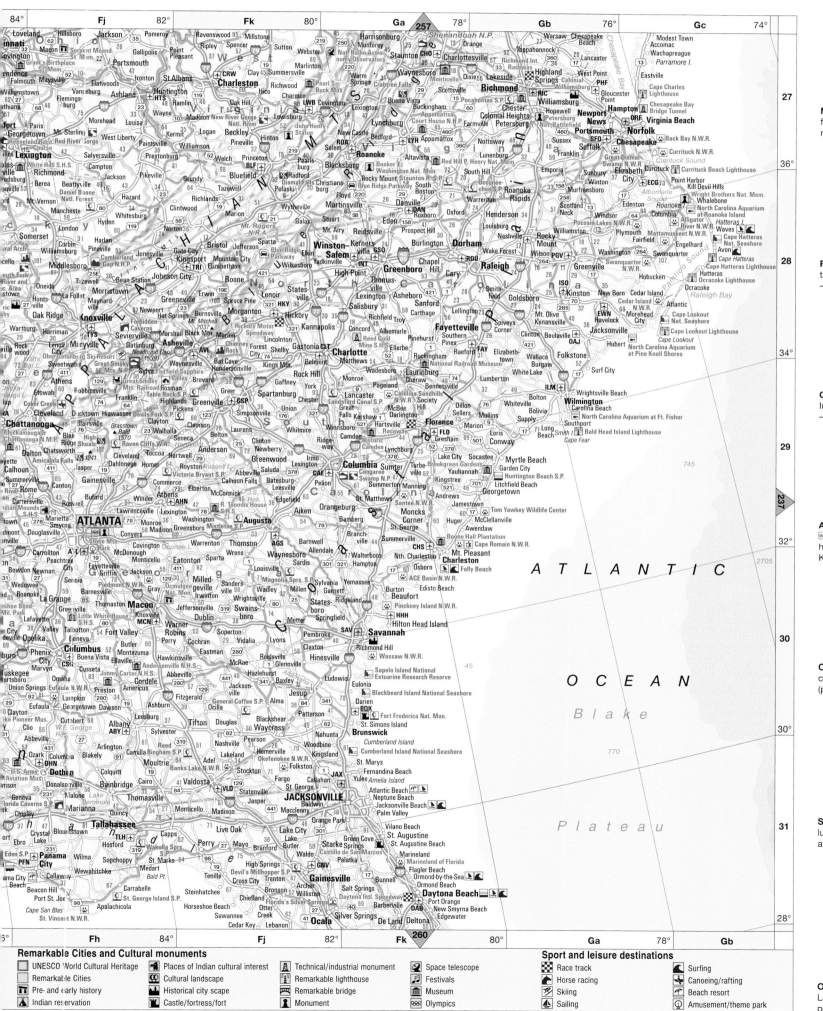

Monticello Private estate of Thomas Jefferson – designed by Jefferson in a combination of styles – world heritage site. **Ga27**

Richmond Capital of Virginia and capital of the Confederacy during most of the civil war – Museum of the Confederacy. **Gb27**

Great Smoky Mountains National Park In the Appalachians – world heritage site – Cherokee Native American land. **Fj28**

Atlanta Georgia's state capital – site of the 1996 Olympics – CNN and Coca Cola are headquartered in the city – Martin Luther King Jr. National Historic Site. **Fh29**

Charleston Historic architecture in the city center – luxury homes on East Battery (photo) – Boone Hall Plantation. **Ga29**

Savannah Historic district with antebellum and Victorian architecture – tree-lined avenues – beautiful squares. **Fk29**

Okefenokee National Wildlife Refuge Large swampland in Georgia – peat deposits up to five meters thick – alligators.**Fj30**

Remarkable Cities and Cultural monuments

UNESCO World Cultural Heritage	Places of Indian cultural interest	Technical/industrial monument
Remarkable Cities	Cultural landscape	Remarkable lighthouse
Pre- and early history	Historical city scape	Remarkable bridge
Indian reservation	Castle/fortress/fort	Monument

Space telescope	
Festivals	
Museum	
Olympics	

Sport and leisure destinations

Race track	Surfing
Horse racing	Canoeing/rafting
Skiing	Beach resort
Sailing	Amusement/theme park

Florida, Bahamas

The state of Florida consists of an 800-kilometer-long peninsula and a narrow "panhandle" in the north of the state. No part of the state is more than 100 kilometers away from the coast. To the east of Florida lies the Atlantic; to the west and south of the panhandle lies the Gulf of Mexico. The 🏖 **Florida Keys** are a chain of small islands that extend along the Straits of Florida and into the **Gulf of Mexico**. The Florida Keys are con-

nected to the mainland by the Overseas Highway, a series of bridges and streets. **Key West** is the southernmost point of the mainland United States. Florida is a flat state with no major elevations; the highest areas in the state are the **Northwest Plateau** around Tallahassee and the **Central Highlands**.

Sandy white beach in Delnor Wiggins State Park near Naples. **Fk32**

Ringling Museum of Art (Sarasota) Important 🏛 collection of Flemish art including works from Peter Paul Rubens – Circus Museum. **Fj32**

Big Cypress Seminole Indian Reservation 🔺 Nature reserve with swamps and cypress forests – home to the last Florida panthers. **Fk32**

Everglades National Park 🏞 This unique and delicate ecosystem covers 1.5 million acres. The Everglades are a vast flat tropical marshland covered by sawgrass and cypress trees. The national park covers only 20 % of the Everglades' area. The Everglades are home to alligators, Florida panthers, and at least 300 bird species. **Fk33**

Overseas Highway This famous 180-kilometer-long 🛣 highway connects the Florida Keys to the mainland. **Fk33**

Key West Westernmost island of the Florida Keys – 🏛 Hemingway House (museum) – Key West Aquarium on Mallory Square – Conch House in Old Town (photo). **Fk33**

St. Augustine Oldest city in the United States – 🏛 historic center with Spanish colonial architecture – major attraction is the 🏰 Castillo de San Marcos (photo). **Fk31**

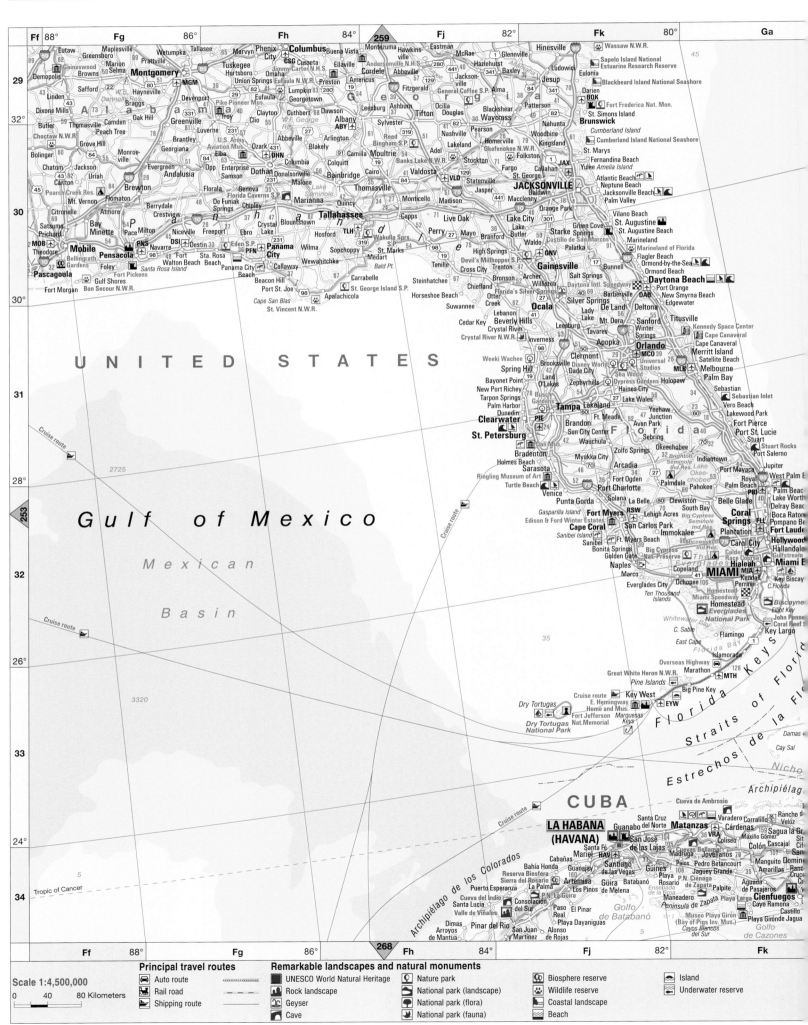

Legend

Scale 1:4,500,000
0   40   80 Kilometers

Principal travel routes
- 🚗 Auto route
- 🚆 Rail road
- Shipping route

Remarkable landscapes and natural monuments
- ■ UNESCO World Natural Heritage
- Rock landscape
- Geyser
- Cave
- Nature park
- National park (landscape)
- National park (flora)
- National park (fauna)
- Biosphere reserve
- Wildlife reserve
- Coastal landscape
- Beach
- Island
- Underwater reserve

The state of Florida has a total area of 151,714 km² of which 11,500 km² are covered by water. Florida is home to countless 🜊 lakes including Lake Okeechobee, the second largest freshwater lake entirely in the United States. 🜊 The **Everglades**, a large tropical marshland with unique flora and fauna, begins just south of Lake Okeechobee. Florida's coastlines total 13,000 kilometers including at least 1,800 kilometers of white

sandy beaches. The **Barrier Islands** along the state's Atlantic coast are a series of islets and sandbanks that protect the coast from strong ocean waves. Many of Florida's eco-systems including the lagoons around Cape Canaveral are threatened by development. The sea turtles that gave the 🜊 **Dry Tortugas** Islands their name are an endangered species like many of the state's indigenous animals.

The **Bahamas** are an island group of more than 700 🜊 islands and 2,000 islets off the southeastern coast of Florida. Because of their location, the Bahamas have a tropical climate cooled by ocean breezes. Temperatures between 28° C and 33° C are normal during the humid summer days. The islands get an abundance of sunshine during the entire year and most rainfall occurs between May and October.

The Bahamas have very few sources of drinkable water and there are no rivers on the islands. Because of this shortage of freshwater, the Bahamas have very few indigenous land animals. There is however an impressive variety of 🜊 marine life in the surrounding waters, including large coral reefs and countless species of fish. Because of the abundant marine life, the Bahamas are a popular destination for recreational 🜊 divers.

Daytona Beach Popular 🜊 beach town – major car racing center – annual Harley Davidson Bike Week. **Fk31**

Walt Disney World Located near Orlando – four 🜊 theme parks: Magic Kingdom, Epcot Center, Animal Kingdom, and Disney-MGM Studios. **Fk31**

Cape Canaveral Site of Kennedy Space Center where most American space missions start – 🜊 NASA Visitors Center – 🜊 Astronaut Hall of Fame. **Fk31**

Miami The largest urban area in Florida – population of two million in the metro area – Port of Miami – Little Havana, center of the Cuban-American cummunity – Miami Seaquarium. **Fk33**

Miami Beach Part of Greater Miami – 🜊 Art Deco architecture along Ocean Drive – numerous night clubs and restaurants. **Fk33**

The Bahamas Millions of tourists enjoy the beautiful 🜊 beaches, shopping centers, and 🜊 casinos in the Bahamas each year. The Out Islands are more peaceful, less developed, and less visited than popular Nassau and Freeport and are home to the pristine 🜊 Exuma Cays Land and Sea Park (400 km²). **Gb33**

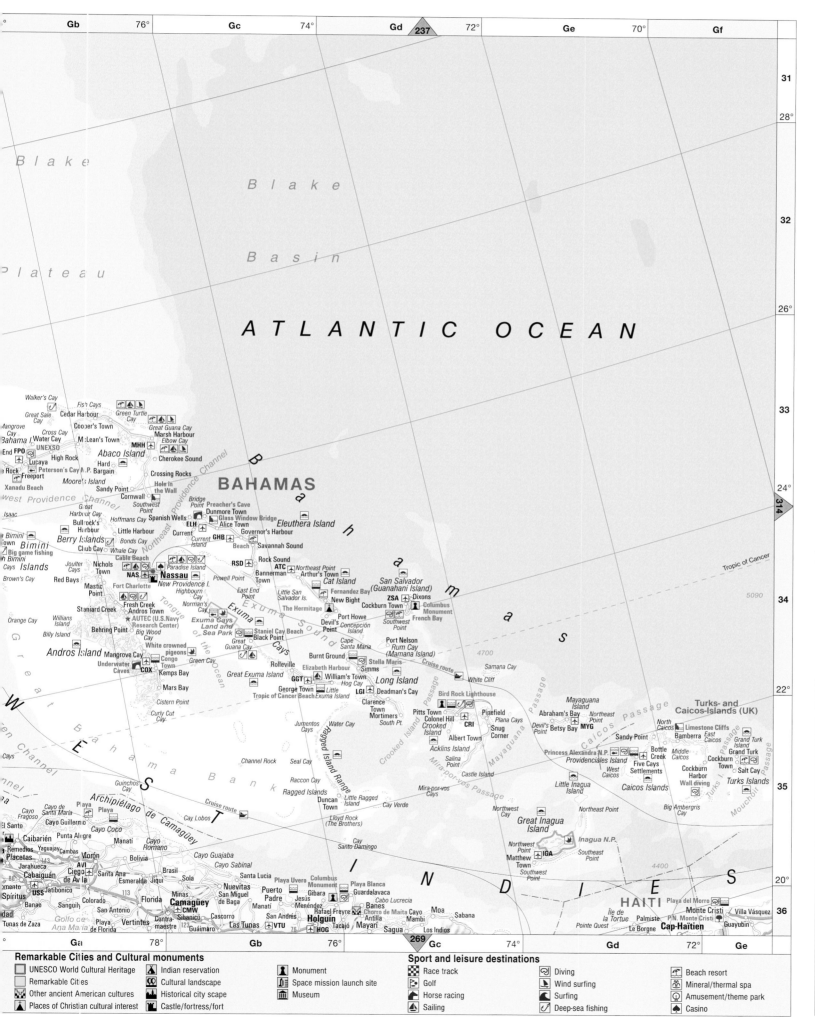

Remarkable Cities and Cultural monuments

🜊 UNESCO World Cultural Heritage	🜊 Indian reservation
🜊 Remarkable Cities	🜊 Cultural landscape
🜊 Other ancient American cultures	🜊 Historical city scape
🜊 Places of Christian cultural interest	🜊 Castle/fortress/fort

🜊 Monument	
🜊 Space mission launch site	
🜊 Museum	

Sport and leisure destinations

🜊 Race track	🜊 Diving	🜊 Beach resort
🜊 Golf	🜊 Wind surfing	🜊 Mineral/thermal spa
🜊 Horse racing	🜊 Surfing	🜊 Amusement/theme park
🜊 Sailing	🜊 Deep-sea fishing	🜊 Casino

Northern Mexico

Mexico is located in a very geologically active region. The country's territory lies in an area where three tectonic plates meet. Along the southern coast, the Cocos plate collides with and slides beneath the larger North American plate. The Cocos plate also collides with the Pacific plate along its western edges. The three plates are moving through the Earth's interior at a rate of around five centimeters per year. The tectonic activi-

ty in the region makes Mexico a country that is frequently shaken by earthquakes and tremors.

Northern Mexico is home to numerous mountain ranges including the different Sierras in **Baja California** and the large mountain ranges that extend from north to south through the country's interior.

El Arco stone formations near Cabo San Lucas in Baja California. **Ef34**

The two largest mountain ranges in the country are the parallel 🏔 **Sierra Madre Oriental** (eastern) and **Sierra Madre Occidental** (western). The Sierra Madre Occidental declines steeply to the Pacific coast on its western side and in the east the range declines gradually in stages through the **Mexican Highlands**. The highest mountains in the Sierra Madre Oriental range rise over 3,000 meters above sea level.

La Pintada 100-meter-long 🏔 cave – contains ancient cave paintings from between 1100 BC and 1480 AD. **Ed32**

San Javier 🏔 Jesuit mission in Baja California – built in 1699 – most beautiful Jesuit mission in Baja California. **Ee33**

La Paz 🏔 Port city in southern Baja California – palm-tree-lined promenade with cafes and seafood restaurants. **Ee33**

Cascadas de Basaseachic The highest 🏔 waterfall in Mexico – 246 meters high – surrounded by tropical forests. **Ef31**

Álamos Colonial city – once a center of silver mining – 🏔 Nuestra Señora de la Concepción (photo). **Ef32**

Barranca del Cobre (Copper Canyon) A series of 🏔 canyons – six rivers flow through the area – lush vegetation. **Eg32**

Sierra Madre Oriental 🏔 Mountain range, parallel to the Sierra Madre Occidental – peaks rising over 3,000 meters. **Ej-Ek31-33**

Principal travel routes
- Auto route
- Rail road
- Shipping route

Scale 1:4,500,000
0   40   80 Kilometers

Remarkable landscapes and natural monuments
- UNESCO World Natural Heritage
- Mountain landscape
- Rock landscape
- Ravine/canyon
- Extinct volcano
- Active volcano
- Cave
- Waterfall/rapids
- Nature park
- National park (landscape)
- National park (fauna)
- Biosphere reserve
- Whale watching
- Coastal landscape
- Beach
- Underwater reserve

The ▲ **Sierra Volcanica Transversal** is a chain of active volcanoes that crosses Mexico between the 19th and 21st parallels of latitude. This range is home to the beautiful volcano **Popocatépetl** as well as Mexico's highest peak, the snow covered volcano **Pico de Orizaba** (5,747 m).

The coastal regions in northern Mexico have humid tropical or subtropical climates. The Gulf of Mexico coastal region gets heavy rainfall during the entire year. Bitter cold north winds called Nortes (northers) often bring sudden cold temperatures and violent storms south into Mexico. These winds frequently cause extensive crop damage in the country's agricultural region. During summer and fall the Pacific coast is often threatened by typhoons while the eastern coasts are at risk from hurricanes.

☒ **Baja California** is an arid area and indigenous plants include several species of giant cacti. The body of water between Baja California and mainland Mexico is usually called the Sea of Cortez but is also known as the Gulf of California. The Sea of Cortez is home to at least 800 different animal species.

The indigenous people of northern Mexico traditionally lived through hunting, and the cultivation of crops (especially corn and beans), and by gathering local plants including agave and yucca plants. Wine has been produced in the areas around ☒ **Parras de Fuente** since the early colonial period. The far north is home to numerous large cattle ranches and wheat farms. Irrigation is used throughout northern Mexico to support agriculture in the region. The major source of Mexico's wealth during the colonial era was silver from the mines in the Sierra Madres.

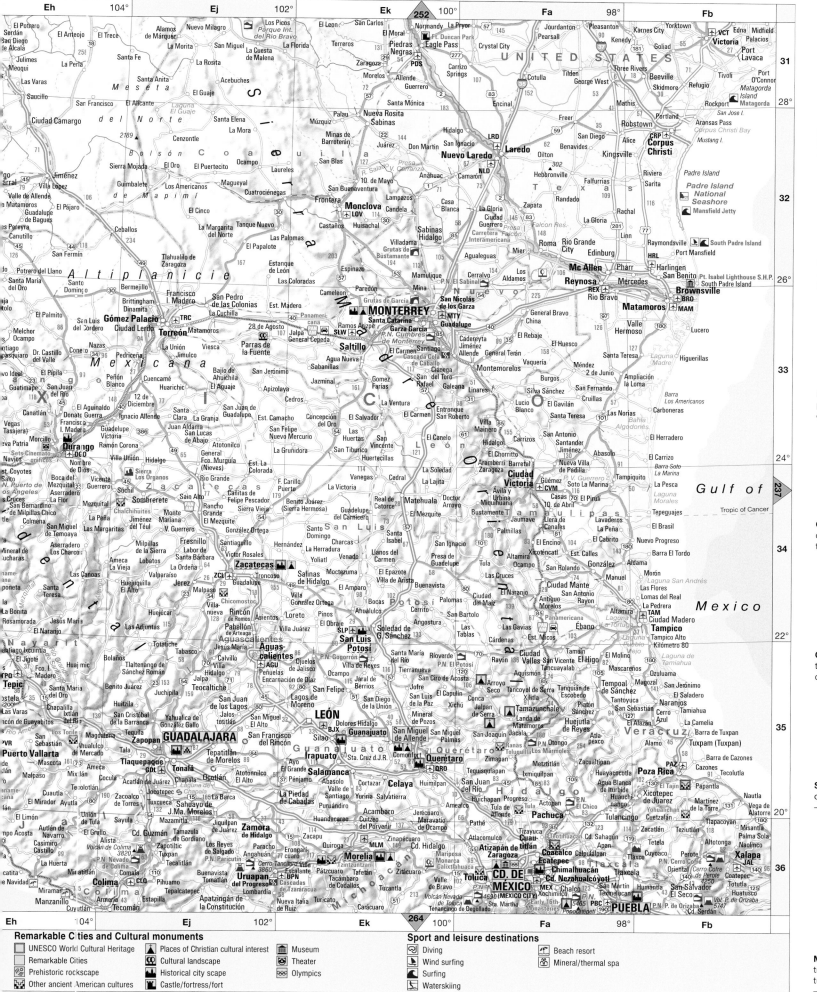

Monterrey Third largest city in Mexico – Faro del Comercio (photo) on the Gran Plaza – ▲ Cathedral. **Ek33**

Zacatecas ☒ Colonial city founded in 1546 – the old town is a UNESCO world heritage site – ▲ baroque cathedral (photo). **Ej34**

Puerto Vallarta ☒ Popular tourist resort – population: 350,000 – ☒ sandy white beaches – old town on the Rio Cuale. **Eh35**

Guadalajara ☒ Second largest city in Mexico – population six million – colonial architecture – large ☒ market place. **Ej35**

Guanajuato Once an important mining town – one of Mexico's most charming ☒ city centers – world heritage site. **Ek35**

San Miguel de Allende ☒ Small city with colonial architecture – cobblestone streets – ▲ Templo de San Francisco (photo). **Ek35**

Morelia Founded in 1541 this city in Central Mexico has restored colonial architecture in its ☒ center – beautiful ▲ cathedral – palatial colonial homes. **Ek36**

Remarkable Cities and Cultural monuments
- ☐ UNESCO World Cultural Heritage
- ☐ Remarkable Cities
- ☐ Prehistoric rockscape
- ☐ Other ancient American cultures
- ☐ Places of Christian cultural interest
- ☐ Cultural landscape
- ☐ Historical city scape
- ☐ Castle/fortress/fort
- ☐ Museum
- ☐ Theater
- ☐ Olympics

Sport and leisure destinations
- ☐ Diving
- ☐ Wind surfing
- ☐ Surfing
- ☐ Waterskiing
- ☐ Beach resort
- ☐ Mineral/thermal spa

Southern Mexico, Guatemala

In geography, the region known as Central America begins to the east of the Mexican Isthmus of Tehuantepec. Most of **Mexico** (Latin America's third largest nation) belongs to the North American continent. Mexico's capital, Mexico City, lies at an elevation of 2,242 meters in the **central highlands** which are surrounded by the  **Sierra Madre Oriental** and **Sierra Madre Occidental** mountains. The southern boundary of this region is defined by

the **Sierra Volcánica Transversal**, a volcanic mountain chain. Well-known volcanoes in this chain include ▲ Popocatépetl (5,465 m), Iztaccihuatl (5,286 m) and the highest peak, Pico de Orizaba (5,747 m). In the heart of the **Yucatán Peninsula** lies the expansive tropical rain forest ▨ Biósfera Calakmul/Biósfera Maya. This

The Mayan ruins of Tulum on Mexico's Caribbean coast.
Fg35

Mexico City ▥ Templo Mayor (top photo) on Plaza de la Constitucion is a reminder of this city's Aztec heritage. Much of the city was once covered by a lake. The ▣ Cathedral Metropolitana and the famous ▦ National Anthropology Museum are important attractions. **Fa36**

Popocatépetl Active ▲ volcano – the surrounding area has interesting churches (UNESCO world heritage sites) – ▣ Nuestra Señora de los Remedios. **Fa36**

Puebla Plaza de Armas – ▣ cathedral – views of ▲ Popocatépetl and Iztaccíhuatl – ▣ Iglesia Santo Domingo – the old town is a UNESCO world heritage site. **Fa36**

El Tajín ▨ historic ruins – 17 ancient ball sports areas – several pyramids and viewing platforms – ▦ museum. **Fb35**

Oaxaca ▣ Plaza de Armas is the city's main square – Alameda de Léon has an interesting ▣ arts and crafts market – colonial architecture in Centro Cultural de Santo Domingo (world heritage site). **Fb37**

Monte Alban Pre-Columbian ▨ ruins above Oaxaca Valley – los Danzantes, carved stone figures – the burial grounds are UNESCO world heritage sites. **Fb37**

Scale 1:4,500,000

0   40   80 Kilometers

Principal travel routes
- 🚗 Auto route
- 🚃 Rail road
- 🚢 Shipping route

Remarkable landscapes and natural monuments
- ▪ UNESCO World Natural Heritage
- ▪ Mountain landscape
- ▪ Extinct volcano
- ▪ Active volcano
- Geyser
- Cave
- Waterfall/rapids
- Nature park
- National park (landscape)
- National park (flora)
- Biosphere reserve
- Coastal landscape
- Beach
- Coral reef
- Island
- Underwater reserve

region which is home to countless species of flora and fauna is divided between Mexico and Guatemala.

Throughout Mexico there are numerous historic sites from the civilizations of pre-Columbian Mayans and Aztecs. Today the Mayans constitute 60 % of Guatemala's population; a further 800,000 ethnic Mayans live in Mexico.

The southern regions of **Guatemala** are defined by a series of ⛰ mountain chains.

The southern and eastern highlands encompass numerous 🌋 volcanoes (some active) and several lakes including ⛵ **Lago de Atitlán**. The areas north of Guatemala City, Alta, and Baja Veracruz are covered by an expansive grassland with diverse vegetation.

Belize, the smallest Central American nation, has practically no noteworthy elevations. Belize is most famous for its 🏝 Cayes, a collection of small islands in the Caribbean Sea. Belize is also home to the world's second largest coral reef, the 🌊 **Gran Recife Maya** also known as the Belize Barrier Reef.

Mayan ruins and mountain chains can be found throughout **El Salvador**. Along El Salvador's southern coast, a thin plain gives way to a mountain chain comprising more than 20 active 🌋 volcanoes. Near the border to **Honduras**, the Lempa river valley seperates the ⛰ **Matepan** and **Chalatenango** mountains. There are many remnants of Mayan civilization in the region. The ruins at ⛰ **Copán** are a designated UNESCO world heritage site.

Several river valleys extend from southwestern Honduras to the Caribbean coast in the North. In eastern regions of the country, the coast becomes increasingly wide. South of the Honduran highlands the Pacific coast is bordered by a plain.

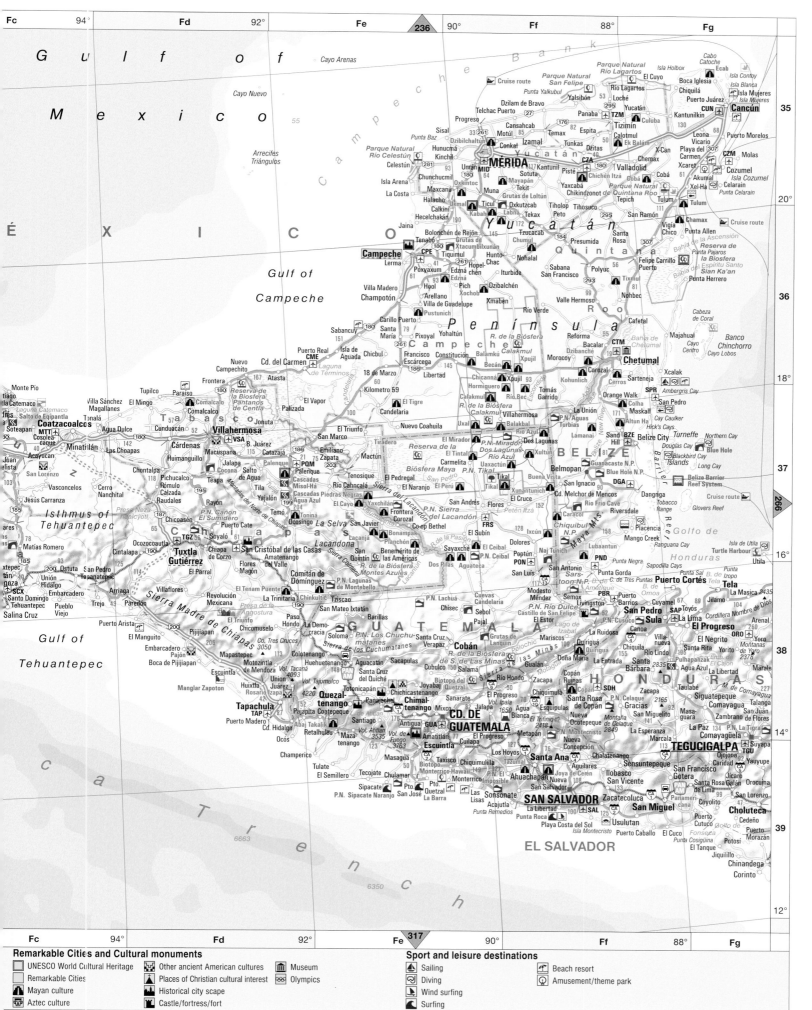

The Realm of the Maya
Even today there are mysteries surrounding the pre-Columbian Mayan culture. Several ruins of this civilization belong to UNESCO's list of World Heritage Sites including Chichén Itzá with its Pyramid of Kukulcán. The site also includes a field for ball sports and a warrior temple. Uxmal in Mexico contains an impressive pyramid; another attraction here is the so-called Governor's Palace, once an important residence for the local Maya elite. The ruins at Palenque cover an area of 16 km², but only a small portion of the site has been excavated including the Palacio with its distinctive towers. Tikal, in Guatemala, is surrounded by dense jungle but remains one of the most important Mayan archaeological sites. Photos from top to bottom: Chichén Itzá (Ff35), Uxmal (Ff35), Palenque (Fd37), Tikal (Ff37), Quiriguá (Ff38).

Belize Barrier Reef/Gran Recife Maya 🌊 300-kilometer-long coral reef – hundreds of small coral islands (Cayes) – UNESCO world heritage site. **Fg37**

Antigua Former capital city of Guatemala with colonial achitecture – ⛪ cathedral (1545) – La Merced church (1749) – Las Capuchinas monastery, 18th century. **Fe38**

Remarkable Cities and Cultural monuments
- ▫ UNESCO World Cultural Heritage
- ◾ Remarkable Cities
- ▲ Mayan culture
- ▲ Aztec culture
- ▲ Other ancient American cultures
- ✝ Places of Christian cultural interest
- 🏙 Historical city scape
- 🏰 Castle/fortress/fort
- 🏛 Museum
- Olympics

Sport and leisure destinations
- ⛵ Sailing
- Diving
- Wind surfing
- Surfing
- 🏖 Beach resort
- Amusement/theme park

Honduras, El Salvador, Nicaragua, Costa Rica, Panama

Many geographers consider Mexico's Isthmus of Tehauntepec the starting point of Central America but the region is usually defined as consisting of the six countries between Mexico and Columbia. The mountainous border region separating Guatemala from El Salvador and Honduras runs through an area where the North American tectonic plate collides with the Caribbean plate. The climate in Central America is overwhelmingly tropi-

cal with the exception of a few regions. Central America is home to a diverse collection of plants and animals. Many of the region's animals are unique hybrids created from the mixing of North and South American species. The thin strip of land forming the Isthmus of Panama connects North America and South Amer-

Arenal in Costa Rica, one of many active volcanoes in this region. **Fh40**

ica. At its narrowest, the isthmus has a width of 46 kilometers.
Expansive rainforests cover the eastern plains of Nicaragua and Honduras. This region is dissected by numerous rivers, most of which flow into the Caribbean Sea. Much of western Nicaragua is covered by a large basin containing the region's largest lake ▣ **Lago de Nicaragua** (8,150 km²). South of Lago de Nicaragua rise the volcanoes of the ▣

Islas de la Bahía Archipelago of ▣ coral islands off the northern coast of Honduras – Roatán is the largest island – ▣ conservation areas on the coasts. **Fg37**

Copán Large ▣ Mayan temple complex in Honduras – contains many statues, all dated to between 400 and 700 AD – UNESCO world heritage site. **Ff38**

Río Platano Biosphere Reserve ▣ This nature reserve is inhabited by many endangered and rare species including tapirs, jaguars (photo), red macaws, and fish species. The biosphere is also home to unique plants. Around 5,000 Paya and Miskito Amerindians live in the area. **Fh38**

Guanacaste ▣ National park in Costa Rica – savannahs and dry forests – rainforests along the slopes of ▣ inactive volcanoes – UNESCO world heritage site. **Fh40**

La Amistad International Park The core of a large ▣ biosphere reserve in Panama and Costa Rica. The park stretches from the swampy coast into the highlands of the Cordillera Talamanca. The area has been designated a UNESCO world heritage site. **Fj41**

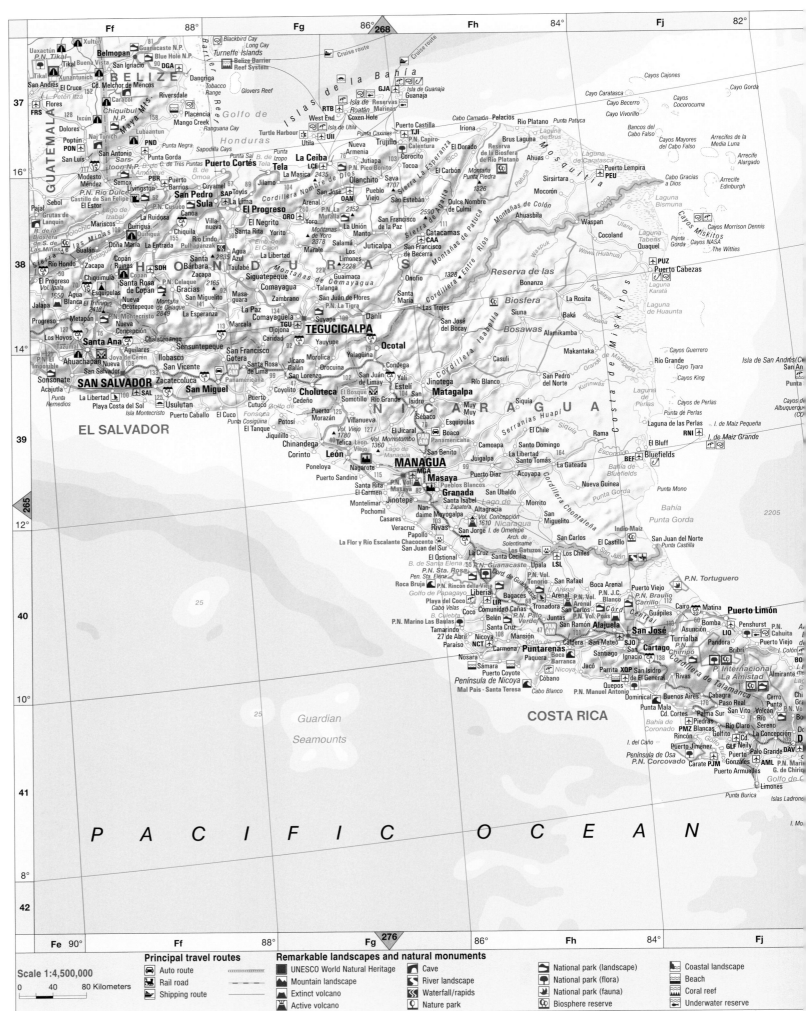

Principal travel routes

- Auto route
- Rail road
- Shipping route

Scale 1:4,500,000

0   40   80 Kilometers

Remarkable landscapes and natural monuments

- UNESCO World Natural Heritage
- Mountain landscape
- Extinct volcano
- Active volcano

- Cave
- River landscape
- Waterfall/rapids
- Nature park

- National park (landscape)
- National park (flora)
- National park (fauna)
- Biosphere reserve

- Coastal landscape
- Beach
- Coral reef
- Underwater reserve

Cordillera Central and  Cordillera de Talamanca mountain ranges. The highest summits in these ranges rise over 3,000 meters and several of the volcanoes are still active including Arenal (1,633 m). As with the active volcanoes, the frequent earthquakes and tremors in this region are the result of plate tectonics. In 1972, Nicaragua's capital city, Managua, was devastated by a powerful earthquake. Despite its small size,

Costa Rica has a diverse collection of flora and fauna and several distinct climate zones. Many of the country's rainforests have been designated national parks. Many of the western areas of the country have dry savannah-like landscapes, while the eastern coast is covered by humid swampland. Most of the country's rainforests lie in the central highlands, while the northwest contains expansive dry forests. Both coasts are

home to rare and endangered sea turtles. Tortuguero National Park was established solely for the protection of sea turtles and is only accessible by boat. The waters off the Caribbean coast of Central America contain several large coral reefs. The best diving areas in the region include Panama's **San Blas Islands**, the **Bocas del Toro Archipelago** in Costa Rica, and many small islands off the coast of Nicaragua and Hondu-

ras. The legacy of Spanish colonialism can be seen in the region's culture and historic architecture.

Costa Rica's Central Valley attracted more European settlers that any other area in the region because of its mild climate and good conditions for coffee cultivation and dairy farming. Many of the coastal areas and plains in Central America contain large fruit plantations which produce fruit primarily for foreign markets.

Costa Rica's Volcanoes The volcanoes along the edges of Costa Rica's Central Valley can be easily visited from the capital, San José. Many of the craters are filled with water, natural fountains often spring from their centers. The crater of Arenal has been crowned by a plume of smoke ever since the volcano's last eruption in 1968, after a century of being dormant. **Fh40**

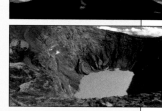

Portobelo Port city on Panama's Caribbean coast – Spanish style colonial architecture in the historic city center – UNESCO world heritage site. **Ga41**

Panama City Capital city of Panama – historic buildings in the old town (UNESCO-world heritage site) – international hotels and restaurants – the city has impressive modern skyscrapers along the bay. **Ga41**

The Panama Canal Construction of the canal began in 1881 and it was opened in 1914 – 67.5 kilometers long – under American jurisdiction until 1999 – panoramic views of the canal from the Miraflores locks. **Ga41**

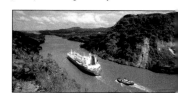

Darién National Park National park (580,000 ha) in one of most undeveloped regions of Panama – has an abundance of unique flora and fauna – UNESCO world heritage site – Tapir (photo). **Gb42**

Remarkable Cities and Cultural monuments

- UNESCO World Cultural Heritage
- Remarkable Cities
- Mayan culture
- Other ancient American cultures
- Places of Christian cultural interest
- Historical city scape
- Castle/fortress/fort
- Technical/industrial monument
- Monument

Sport and leisure destinations

- Sailing
- Diving
- Wind surfing
- Surfing
- Canoeing/rafting
- Deep-sea fishing
- Beach resort

Cuba, Jamaica

The 120-kilometer-wide **Yucatan Channel** separates the Yucatan Peninsula from Cuba, the largest and westernmost of the four Greater Antilles. In addition to Cuba, the **Greater Antilles** includes the islands of Jamaica, Puerto Rico, and Hispaniola. Cuba, together with the Cayman Islands and the Bahamas, lies along the southern edges of the North American tectonic plate. Jamaica and Hispaniola lie along the northern edges of the

Montego Bay in Jamaica lures many tourists to its fine beaches. **Gb36**

relatively small Caribbean plate. South of these two islands, the Caribbean Sea has an average depth of 5,000 meters below sea level.

The 1500-meters-deep Nicholas Channel is located off the northern coast of **Cuba**, between the island and Florida. Between the Bahamas and Cuba lies the Great

Bahama Bank, a large area of relatively shallow waters. There are countless coral reefs near the coast of Cuba and the island is surrounded by numerous groups of small islands and sandbanks including the **Archipiélago de Sabana** and the **Archipiélago de los Jardines de la Reina**. These ⛱ tropical coral islands, along with the ⛱ **Isla de la Juventud** off the southwest coast, are excellent areas for diving. The abundance of coral reefs in

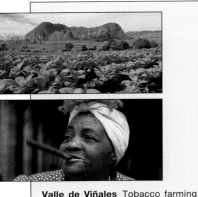

Valle de Viñales Tobacco farming has been the main industry in the rural region around ⛱ Pinar del Río for centuries. The region is also the location of many unique ⛰ round stone formations (top photo). **Fj34**

Havana Cuba's capital has impressive colonial architecture, much of which is in need of restoration. The most important landmark in the ⛱ old town (with the fortress UNESCO world heritage sites) is the Cathedral. **Fj34**

Cienfuegos Important port city for the sugar industry – ⛱ Piaza Marti has beautiful historic architecture – Palacio del Valle, built in Moorish style. **Fk34**

The Cayman Islands The islands are the peaks of underwater mountains. The ⛱ Caymans, a British territory, are one of the best ⛱ areas for diving in the Caribbean. **Fk36**

Scale 1:4,500,000

0   40   80 Kilometers

Principal travel routes	Remarkable landscapes and natural monuments		
🚗 Auto route	🏛 UNESCO World Natural Heritage	🌳 Nature park	⬡ Biosphere reserve	⬡ Island
🚂 Rail road	⛰ Rock landscape	🏕 National park (landscape)	🏖 Coastal landscape	⬡ Underwater reserve
🚢 Shipping route	🕳 Cave	🌷 National park (flora)	🏖 Beach	
	💧 Waterfall/rapids	🦌 National park (fauna)	🪸 Coral reef	

the region can be attributed to the warm temperature, moderate salinity, and clearness of the water in the region.

The island of Cuba is over 1,250 kilometers long and 190 kilometers at its widest. Huge round stone formations can be found in the 🏔 **Valle de Viñales** and **Sierra de los Órganos** regions of eastern Cuba. The tallest stone formations (Mogotes) in these areas rise 700 meters above sea level. Pico Turquino,

Cuba's tallest mountain, lies in the 🏔 **Sierra Maestra** Range and rises 1,972 meters. The small Cayman Islands are the summits of an underwater mountain chain. The 🏝 **Cayman Islands** are a British territory consisting of three main islands: Grand Cayman, Little Cayman, and Cayman Brac. The **Cayman Trench** extends underwater north and west of the Cayman Island and descends 7,240 meters at its deepest point. The center of

Jamaica is a mountainous region, while the coastal regions consist of plains with many beautiful beaches. The beaches and the warm climate are the two main reasons Jamaica has become one of the most famous Caribbean destinations. The island rises in elevation from east to west. The **Blue Mountains** are a series of tall hills and mountains in eastern Jamaica. They are heavily forested and feature many of the island's most beautiful

landscapes. The mountains also support an important coffee growing industry. Blue Mountain Peak, the tallest mountain on the island, rises 2,292 meters.

Hurricanes pose a major threat to almost all of the islands in the Caribbean region, including Jamaica and Cuba. During hurricane season (July to October) the region is at high risk of being struck by devastating hurricanes and tropical storms.

Trinidad Restored 🏛 colonial-era city at the foot of the Sierra de Escambray mountain range in southwestern Cuba – UNESCO world heritage site – traditional Cuban colonial architecture – beautiful beaches at 🏖 Playa Ancon. **Fk-Ga35**

Santiago de Cuba Second largest 🏛 city in Cuba – strong influence on Cuban music and dance – grave of Cuban national hero José Marti in the ⛪ Cathedral at Parque Céspedes – 🏛 colonial history museum in the Casa de Diego Velázquez. **Gc35**

El Cobre Important ⛪ pilgrimage site for Cuban Catholics since the 17th century – Basilica, built in the 20th century. **Gc35**

Jamaica The island's population is 2.7 million. Tourism is very important for the Jamaican economy. The major attractions in Negril are 🏖 Eight Mile Beach, the local bars and nightclubs. Montego Bay and Ocho Rios are home to numerous beautiful small bays and 🌊 Dunn's River Falls. The 🏔 Blue Mountains in eastern Jamaica encompass some of the most breathtaking landscapes on the island and the last remnants of Jamaica's virgin tropical forests. Photos from top to bottom: A bay on the north coast, Ocho Rios, Dunn's River Falls, Cockpit County. **Gb36**

Remarkable Cities and Cultural monuments
- 🏛 UNESCO World Cultural Heritage
- Remarkable Cities
- Mayan culture
- Other ancient American cultures
- Places of Christian cultural interest
- Cultural landscape
- Historical city scape
- Castle/fortress/fort
- Palace
- Tomb/grave
- Monument
- Museum

Sport and leisure destinations
- Sailing
- Diving
- Wind surfing
- Seaport
- Deep-sea fishing
- Beach resort
- Mineral/thermal spa
- Amusement/theme park
- Casino

Hispaniola and Lesser Antilles

Hispaniola, Puerto Rico, and the Lesser Antilles form a bow of islands along the eastern edges of the Caribbean tectonic plate. In this area the North American tectonic plate pushes underneath the smaller Caribbean plate. Like other regions near the collision zone of two tectonic plates, this region is home to many mountain ranges, including the ▲ highlands in the **Dominican Republic** which rise to a height of 3,200 meters above sea

level. The tectonic activity is also responsible for the ▲ volcanism on many of the smaller islands in the region. **Barbados** is the region's only large island created entirely from coral formations. The last major volcanic eruption in region occurred in 1995/96 when the volcano ▲ Soufrière devastated the small island

The Virgin Islands are surrounded by beautiful tropical coasts. **Gh36**

Citadelle La Ferrière and Sans Souci Palace historic ▲ fortress (40 m tall) in northern Haiti – 🏛 built in 1807 and modeled after Versailles; today partly in ruins. **Gd36**

Samaná Peninsula Peninsula with 🏖 beautiful beaches in the Dominican Republic – 🏠 small villages – 🐋 whale watching in Bahía de Samaná. **Gf36**

Parque Nacional Los Haïtises National park in the Dominican Republic – home to unique 🐟 fish and bird species – accessible caves – exotic vegetation. **Gf36**

Santo Domingo Capital of the Dominican Republic – founded in 1496 – 🏛 colonial old town has historic palatial homes and monasteries – 🏛 Cathedral (photo) – 🏛 Faro a Colon/Columbus Lighthouse. **Gf36**

Dominican Republic The country's economy is now heavily dependent on tourism. The country has a wealth of beautiful beaches in and windsurfing is popular. The Dominican Republic also has many diving areas and large resort hotels.

San Juan Capital of Puerto Rico – 🚢 cruise ship port – 🏛 restored colonial architecture – historic sites including UNESCO world heritage sites. **Gg36**

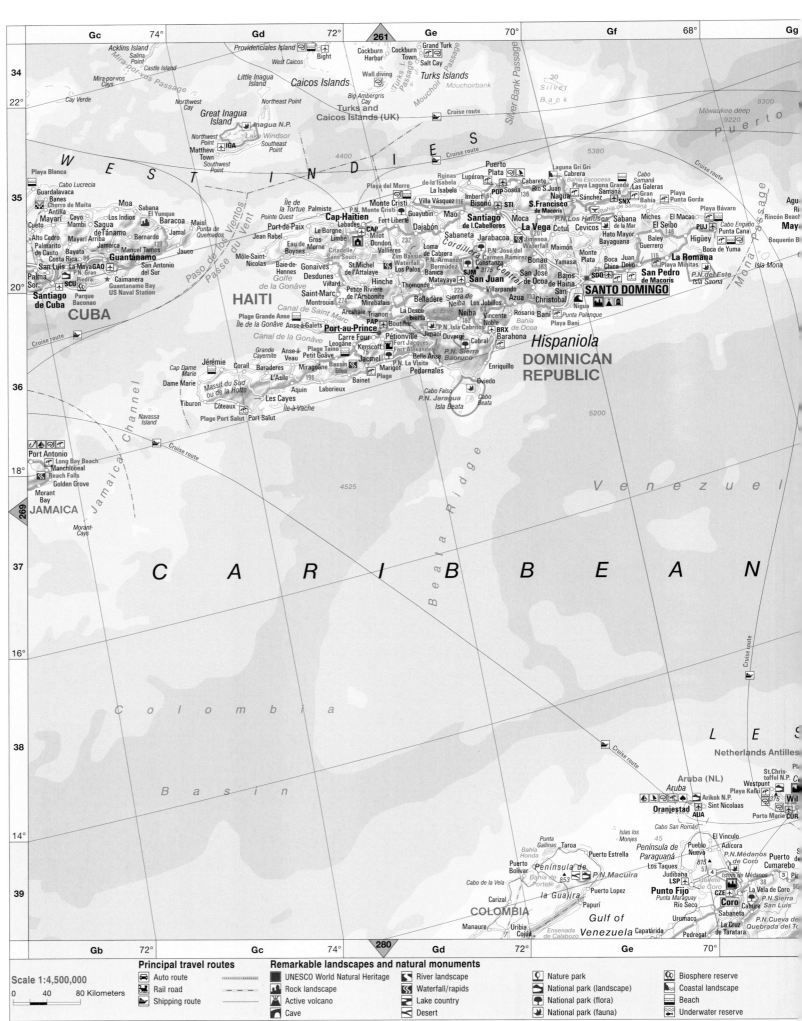

Scale 1:4,500,000

0   40   80 Kilometers

Principal travel routes
- Auto route
- Rail road
- Shipping route
- ···· (dotted route)
- ---- (dashed route)

Remarkable landscapes and natural monuments
- UNESCO World Natural Heritage
- Rock landscape
- Active volcano
- Cave
- River landscape
- Waterfall/rapids
- Lake country
- Desert
- Nature park
- National park (landscape)
- National park (flora)
- National park (fauna)
- Biosphere reserve
- Coastal landscape
- Beach
- Underwater reserve

Montserrat. Hispaniola, the second largest island in the Caribbean, is home to several mountain ranges. The tallest mountains on the island are in the Cordillera Central. Hispaniola's tallest mountain, Pico Duarte, rises 3,175 meters. The mountains in the central highlands of Puerto Rico rise to heights around 1,300 meters above sea level.

The Lesser Antilles are divided into two groups of islands: the Leeward Islands in the north and the Windward Islands in the south. In addition to their famous white beaches, many of the islands, including St. Lucia and Dominica, also have black beaches with dark volcanic sand. The tropical climate and fertile soil in the region make the islands ideal for the farming of tropical plants. Several islands still contain remnants of virgin tropical rainforests with unique flora and fauna. While most islands in the Lesser Antilles are covered by lush tropical forests, a few islands (most notably Aruba) have dry desert-like interiors with sparse vegetation. Because of their warm sunny climates, countless beaches, and beautiful landscapes, the Lesser Antilles attract many tourists from beyond the region. In recent decades, tourism has become the dominant industry in the region. Between July and October, the Lesser Antilles are threatened by hurricanes and many of the islands have been devastated by these powerful storms in the past. The southern islands of the Lesser Antilles are less threatened by hurricanes and have far drier climates than their northern counterparts.

The Netherlands Antilles – consisting of Curaçao, Bonaire, and Aruba – is the southernmost island group in the Lesser Antilles and has some of the best diving sites in the Caribbean.

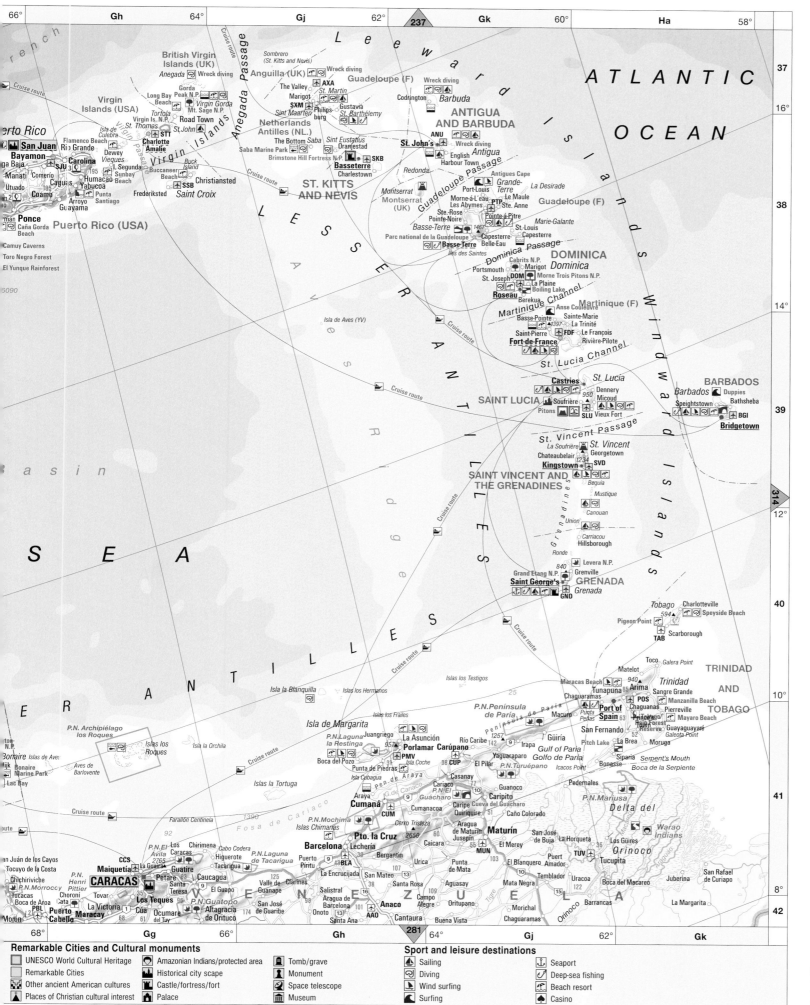

English Harbour Bay on the southern coast of Antigua – popular sailing area – site of the Antigua Sailing Week.   **Gk37**

Guadeloupe Overseas department of France – two distinct regions: mountainous west and flat east – coffee fields rise along the slopes of the island's volcanoes.   **Gk37**

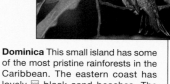

Dominica This small island has some of the most pristine rainforests in the Caribbean. The eastern coast has lovely black sand beaches. The island's northwestern section is covered by large banana fields. Trois Pitons National Park encompasses the island's virgin rainforests and is a UNESCO world heritage site.   **Gk38**

Soufrière Small town on St. Lucia – sulfur springs – Pitons: round stone mountains: the highest rising 800 meters.   **Gk39**

Barbados The easternmost of the Lesser Antilles islands – old sugar plantations and historic colonial estates – Harrison's Cave has stalactite-covered chambers – beautiful white beaches on the coasts.   **Ha39**

St. George's Grenada's capital has a beautiful harbor – the island's culture and architecture display both British and French influences – Fort George.   **Gk39**

Remarkable Cities and Cultural monuments

- ☐ UNESCO World Cultural Heritage
- ☐ Remarkable Cities
- ☐ Other ancient American cultures
- ☐ Places of Christian cultural interest
- Amazonian Indians/protected area
- Historical city scape
- Castle/fortress/fort
- Palace
- Tomb/grave
- Monument
- Space telescope
- Museum

Sport and leisure destinations

- Sailing
- Diving
- Wind surfing
- Surfing
- Seaport
- Deep-sea fishing
- Beach resort
- Casino

Atacama (top): A snow covered beauty on the edge of Chile's most fascinating desert.
Iguaçu Falls (bottom): The roaring waters of South America's widest falls.

Machu Picchu (left): The remnants of an Incan "lost city" in the Peruvian highlands.
Rio de Janeiro (right): Beaches and sunshine; South America's most hedonistic city.

South America

From the green rainforests of the Amazon basin to the icecaps of the world's tallest volcanoes and the glaciers of Patagonia, South America has a wealth of fascinating and unique landscapes. The cultural highlights of the continent include ancient sites of Incan civilization and the legacy of European colonialism.

Compared to the other continents South America is a relatively compact land-mass. The continent has smooth coast-lines and a consistently flat relief – outside of the Andes. The southern continent of the western hemisphere is 7,500 kilometers long from north to south and the greatest distance from east to west measures 4,800 kilometers. The continent borders Central (and North) America at the Isthmus of Panama.

Parinacota (6,400 m), a volcano in Chile's Lauca National Park.

The Andes Mountains, the world's second highest mountain range after the Himalayas, rise to the east of the continent's Pacific coast. Aconcagua in Argentina is the highest mountain in the Western Hemisphere. Other significant mountain ranges in South America include the Pakaraima Mountains in the north and the Serra do Mar in Brazil. Between these two mountainous regions lies the vast basin of the Amazon River. With a length of 6,400 kilometers, the Amazon is the second longest river in the world after the Nile. The marshy land of the Gran Chaco is located north of the fertile Pampas and the sparsely populated region of Patagonia. The flat basin of the Orinoco River (2,140 km) occupies a large area in northern South America.

The **Andes mountain system** extends north to south along the entire length of South America (200–400 km width). The Andes are also the longest mountain chain on the planet. Aconcagua (top photo) located in the border region between Argentina and Chile is the highest mountain in the Andes. The highest active volcano in the Andes is Cotopaxi (bottom photo), located in Ecuador. Cotopaxi rises 5,897 meters high and has a beautiful snow-capped summit.

The drainage basin of the **Amazon River** is home to the world's largest collection tropical rainforests (middle photo). The Amazon River basin stretches 3,500 kilometers from east to west, and more than 2,000 kilometers from north to south. The Rio Negro is the largest tributary of the Amazon River and has a drainage basin with an area of 600,000 km². Many sections of the river basin are covered by dense vegetation (bottom photo). Trees in the Amazon Forest can grow over 90 meters high (top photo). The area's rainforests are home to incredibly diverse animals and plants.

The **Iguaçu (Iguazu) Falls** are located on the border between Brazil and Argentina. The falls are between 65 and 70 meters high and three kilometers wide (top photo). **Lake Titicaca** (8,559 km²) is the highest lake in the Andes with an elevation of 3,182 meters. Lake Maracaibo is the largest lake in South America (13,512 km²).

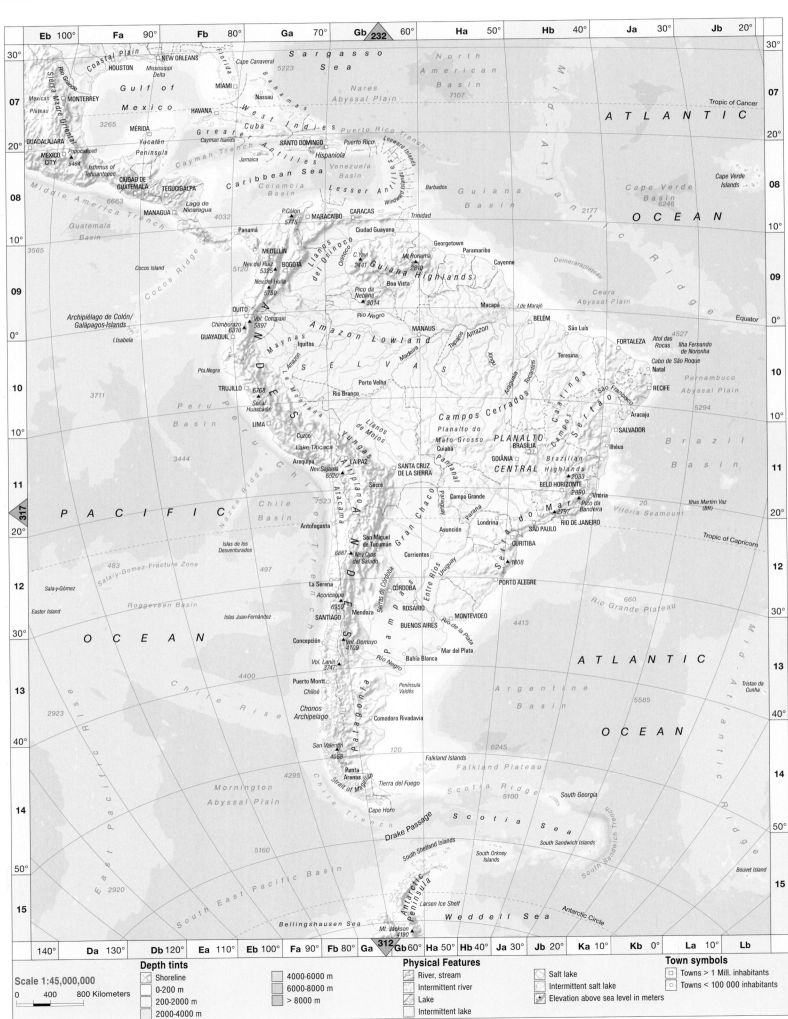

Scale 1:45,000,000

0   400   800 Kilometers

Depth tints
- Shoreline
- 0-200 m
- 200-2000 m
- 2000-4000 m
- 4000-6000 m
- 6000-8000 m
- > 8000 m

Physical Features
- River, stream
- Intermittent river
- Lake
- Intermittent lake
- Salt lake
- Intermittent salt lake
- Elevation above sea level in meters

Town symbols
- Towns > 1 Mill. inhabitants
- Towns < 100 000 inhabitants

There are twelve independent nations in South America as well as French Guiana, a territory of France. South America is home to 304 million people, more than half of this population lives in Brazil. Centuries of contact between Europeans, Amerindians and Africans has made the population of South America the most ethnically and racially mixed in the world.

No other continent is as religiously homogeneous as South America. Almost 90 % of the continent's people are Roman Catholics.

Migration from rural areas to cities continues to expand the population of cities in the region. In recent decades, the continent's cities have grown explosively. Most of South America's large cities are surrounded by large slums, home to the poorest members of society.

Left: Quetchua woman (Peru).
Right: Yanomami in the Amazon basin.

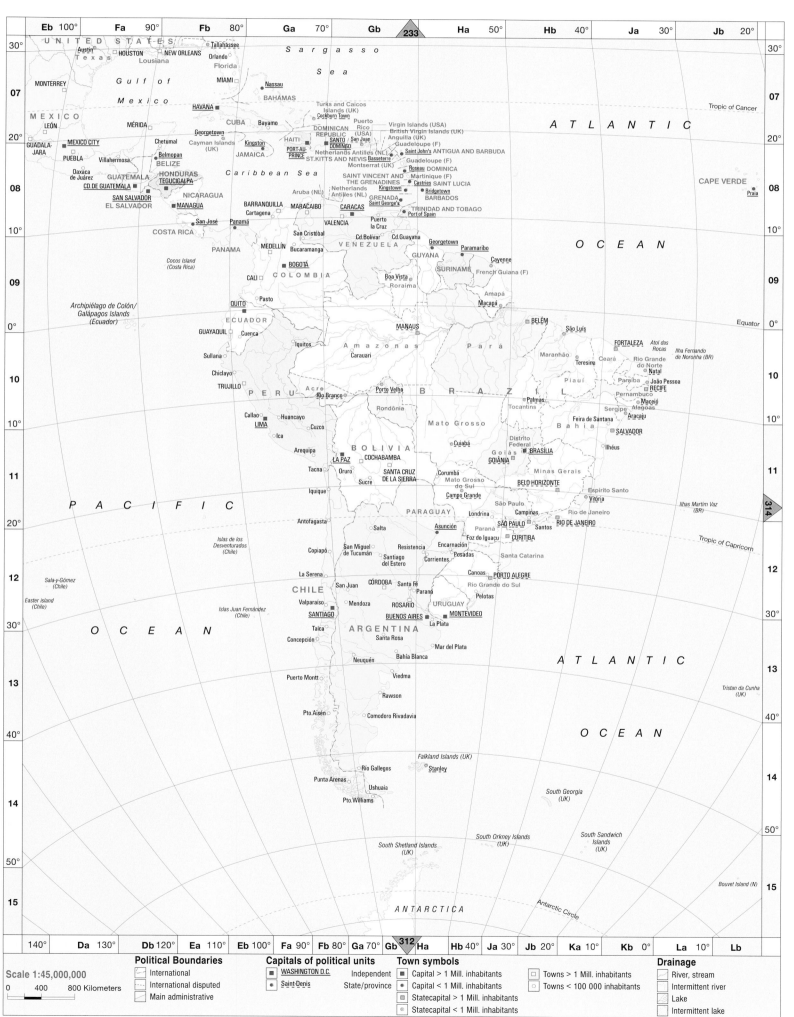

Countries and Flags

	Argentina
	Bolivia
	Brasil
	Chile
	Colombia
	Ecuador
	Guyana
	Paraguay
	Peru
	Suriname
	Uruguay
	Venezuela

The **indigenous populations** of South America face many threats to their cultures and traditional lifestyles. One significant issue is the increasing exploitation of natural resources in the Amazon region and Andean highlands. In the next few decades, only the most isolated tribes in sparsely populated inhospitable regions will be able to preserve their traditional lifestyles in the face of pressure from the outside world. The Quechua in the Andes were traditionally llama and alpaca herders. The Yanomami are one of the largest tribes in the Amazon region, numbering at least 20,000 in Brazil and Venezuela. The Suya of Brazil are a people of farmers and hunters and gatherers. The Suya are well known for the large plates they wear in their ears and lips. Photos from top to bottom: Quechua women in Peru, Quechua girl in traditional clothing, Yanomami in the Amazon region, Suya in the Brazilian state Mato Grosso.

Scale 1:45,000,000

0   400   800 Kilometers

Political Boundaries	Capitals of political units	Town symbols		Drainage
☐ International	■ WASHINGTON D.C. Independent	■ Capital > 1 Mill. inhabitants	☐ Towns > 1 Mill. inhabitants	☐ River, stream
☐ International disputed	● Saint-Denis State/province	■ Capital < 1 Mill. inhabitants	☐ Towns < 100 000 inhabitants	☐ Intermittent river
☐ Main administrative		■ Statecapital > 1 Mill. inhabitants		☐ Lake
		■ Statecapital < 1 Mill. inhabitants		☐ Intermittent lake

Northern South America

Western South America is home to the **Andes Mountains**, one of the longest mountain ranges in the world. The Andes are an ancient mountain range created through the collision of tectonic plates. The mountain range rises 6,000 meters above sea level. Active volcanoes and frequent earthquakes are evidence that the Andes remain a geologically active region. There are several long ocean trenches off the coast of South America

including the 8,000-meter-deep **Atacama Trench**. The northern Andes in Columbia are comprised of three parallel mountain ranges: the Occidental, Central, and Oriental Cordilleras.
In Ecuador, south of Colombia, the Andes are divided into two separate ranges. In Peru, long mountain valleys divide the

The Amazon rainforests are home to an incredible abundance of flora and fauna.

The Galapagos Islands This archipelago of volcanic islands is famous for its unique flora and fauna. Charles Darwin did much of his important research on these islands. The islands are a UNESCO world heritage site.

The Northern Andes Numerous active volcanoes – Chimborazo (photo) is the highest mountain in Ecuador (6,310 m).

The Peruvian Andes In Peru, the Andes are divided into several ranges. In the north, the Andes are divided by the Marañón River. In the south, the mountains border the Altiplano plateau. Photos from top to bottom: Cordillera Blanca, the Cordillera Villacabamba range near Cuzco, Lake Titicaca.

La Montaña (Peru) Region of lush rainforests in the eastern foothills of the Andes Mountains – abundance of wildlife and tropical plants.

Salt Lakes in the Bolivian Andes Fascinating lakes at heights between 3,000 and 4,500 meters above sea level – unique ecosystems.

Scale 1:18,000,000

0   160   320 Kilometers

Depth tints
- Shoreline
- 0-200 m
- 200-2000 m
- 2000-4000 m
- 4000-6000 m
- 6000-8000 m
- > 8000 m

Physical Features
- River, stream
- Intermittent river
- Lake
- Intermittent lake
- Salt lake
- Intermittent salt lake
- Elevation above sea level in meters

Andes into several distinct ranges. Altiplano, in southern Peru, is a large plateau surrounded by the tall mountains of the **Cordillera Oriental** and **Cordillera Occidental**. The **Altiplano** contains numerous salt pans and lakes including **Lake Titicaca**, the highest navigable lake in the world. The Andes reach their maximum width in Bolivia extending more than 700 kilometers east from the Pacific coast. The **Guiana and Brazilian Highlands**, the massive Amazon River basin, the **Llanos del Orinoco** marshland, and the plains of the **Gran Chaco** are all situated in the north of South America, to the east of the Andes. The **Amazon Basin**, the world's largest river basin, has a maximum width of 6500 km². The Amazon has more than 300 tributaries, many of which are interconnected by natural canals (iguarapes). Many of the rivers in the region split into two or more rivers – a process called bifurcation. The **Casiquiare** River, one of the longer branches of the Orinoco River, flows into the Amazon. Most of the Amazon basin is covered by thick tropical rainforests. In many of the region's rainforests, the ground is permanently covered by a shallow layer of water.

The climate in the Amazon rainforest is humid and hot with an average annual temperature around 26° C. Despite human impact on the rainforest, the region is still home to an incredible abundance of unique animal and plant species. In recent decades, environmental activism and international interest in the rainforests has led to increased government protection of the region. But the biodiversity of the Amazon remains threatened. The Amazon basin contains more than half of the world's remaining rainforest areas and has a significant impact on the planet's climate.

The Windward Islands The southern islands in the Lesser Antilles – Trinidad and Tobago (photo) lie near the South American coast.

Guiana Highlands One of the oldest geological formations. Angel Falls (top photo) in Venezuela's Canaima National Park descend from a height of more than 1,000 meters. The park is also home to Hacha Falls (bottom photo).

The Amazon Basin The world's largest river basin is nourished by the mighty Amazon River as well as its hundreds of tributaries.

Brazilian Highlands The region borders the Amazon River basin and is covered by savannahs and forests.

Pantanal One of the world's largest series of wetlands. The Pantanal covers more than 230,000 km² – UNESCO world heritage site.

Legend

Political Boundaries
- International
- International disputed
- Main administrative

Transportation
- Interstate Hwy./Motorway
- Main road
- Railway
- Airport

Capitals of political units
- ■ WASHINGTON D.C. — Independent
- ○ Richmond — State/province

Town symbols
- ■ Capital > 1 Mill. inhabitants
- ● Capital < 1 Mill. inhabitants
- ■ Statecapital > 1 Mill. inhabitants
- ● Statecapital < 1 Mill. inhabitants
- □ Towns > 1 Mill. inhabitants
- ○ Towns 100 000 bis 1 Mill. inhabitants
- ○ Towns < 100 000 inhabitants

Southern South America

The cone-shaped southern portion of South America extends to within a few hundred kilometers of Antarctica. Mount Aconcagua, the highest mountain in South America, lies in western Argentina and rises 6963 meters. In the far south of the continent, the **Andes Mountain Range** tends to decrease in height and width. The island **Tierra del Fuego** is the southernmost region of South America. The highest mountains on the island, the last

segment of the Andes, reach to a height of no more than 2500 meters. Massive glaciers can be found in the Patagonia region of Argentina as well as on the barren **South Georgia** and **South Sandwich Islands**. The landscapes south of **Puerto Montt** in Chile look remarkably similar to the fjords of Norway and Alaska. **Argen-**

Barren mountain landscape in the southern Andes.

The Atacama Desert The world's driest desert is surrounded by mountain ranges and is home to several salt lakes (top photo) and active geysers including El Tatio (bottom photo).

Argentinean Lake District Argentina's Lake District encompasses snow-capped mountains and many beautiful lakes. The region is a popular tourist destination.

Patagonia Patagonia is the most sparsely settled region in Argentina. The area contains many glaciers and tall stone formations created by erosion. Photos from top to bottom: Torres del Paine National Park, Los Glaciares National Park, Mount Fitz Roy.

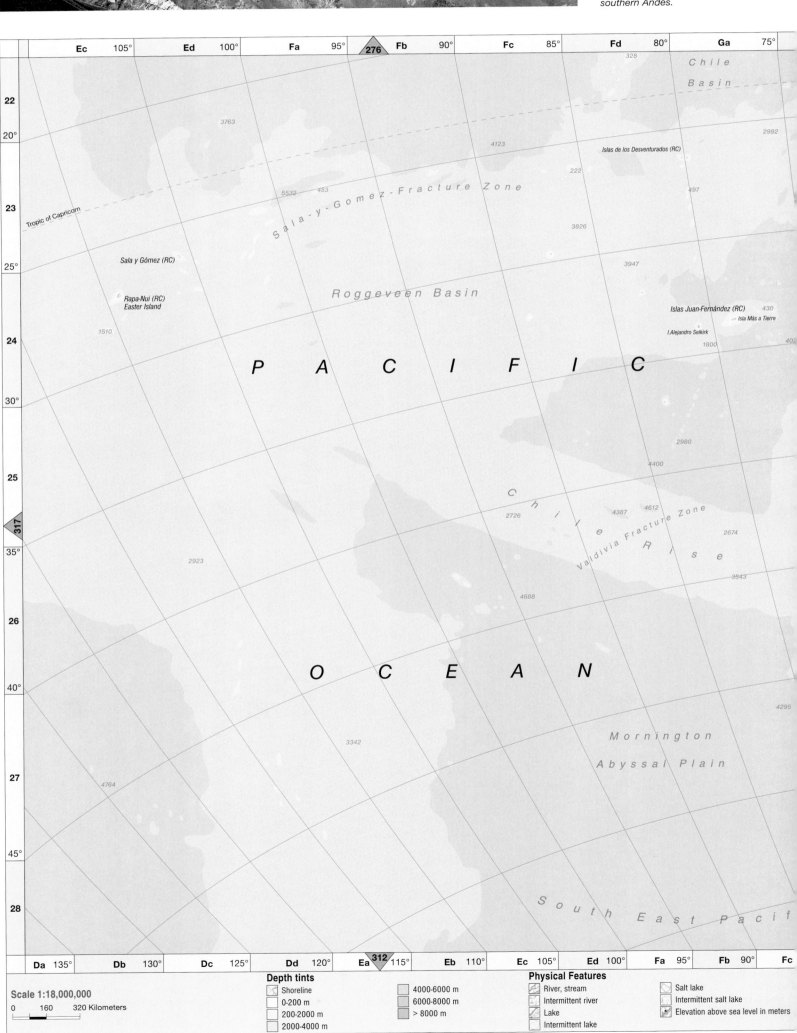

Scale 1:18,000,000

0   160   320 Kilometers

Depth tints

- Shoreline
- 0-200 m
- 200-2000 m
- 2000-4000 m
- 4000-6000 m
- 6000-8000 m
- > 8000 m

Physical Features

- River, stream
- Intermittent river
- Lake
- Intermittent lake
- Salt lake
- Intermittent salt lake
- Elevation above sea level in meters

tina's **Lake District**, around San Carlos de Bariloche, is a region of mountains, forests and crystal-clear lakes that reminds many visitors of Switzerland. The lakes were created during the ice ages by large moving glaciers. North of the Puerto Natales in Chile, lies the **Torres del Paine** National Park with breathtaking natural sights and unique wildlife.

The subtropical regions of northern Chile are home to numerous volcanoes, salt lakes, and deserts including the Atacama Desert. The **Atacama Desert** is the driest area in the world. High mountain ranges surround the desert on both sides, preventing moist air from entering the region. Northern Chile's many salt lakes support delicate ecosystems with unique flora and fauna including colonies of flamingos and llamas. Two large regions cover the vast plains between the Andes in the west and the **highlands** of southern Brazil in the east – the **Gran Chaco** and the **Pampas**. Spanish settlers were the first people to bring cattle to South America, and today the Pampas and Gran Chaco are major centers for cattle ranching. The sections of the Pampas to the south and west of Buenos Aires are used mainly for crop cultivation (especially corn and wheat); Argentina is a major exporter of foodstuffs.

Patagonia is a cool, windswept, and sparsely populated region. Sheep farming is a major industry in this Argentinean frontier. The regions at the extreme south of the continent and the **Falkland Islands (Islas Malvinas)** have cool climates with abundant precipitation. Much of southern South America's population is concentrated in a few large coastal cities such as Buenos Aires, Valparaiso, and Montevideo.

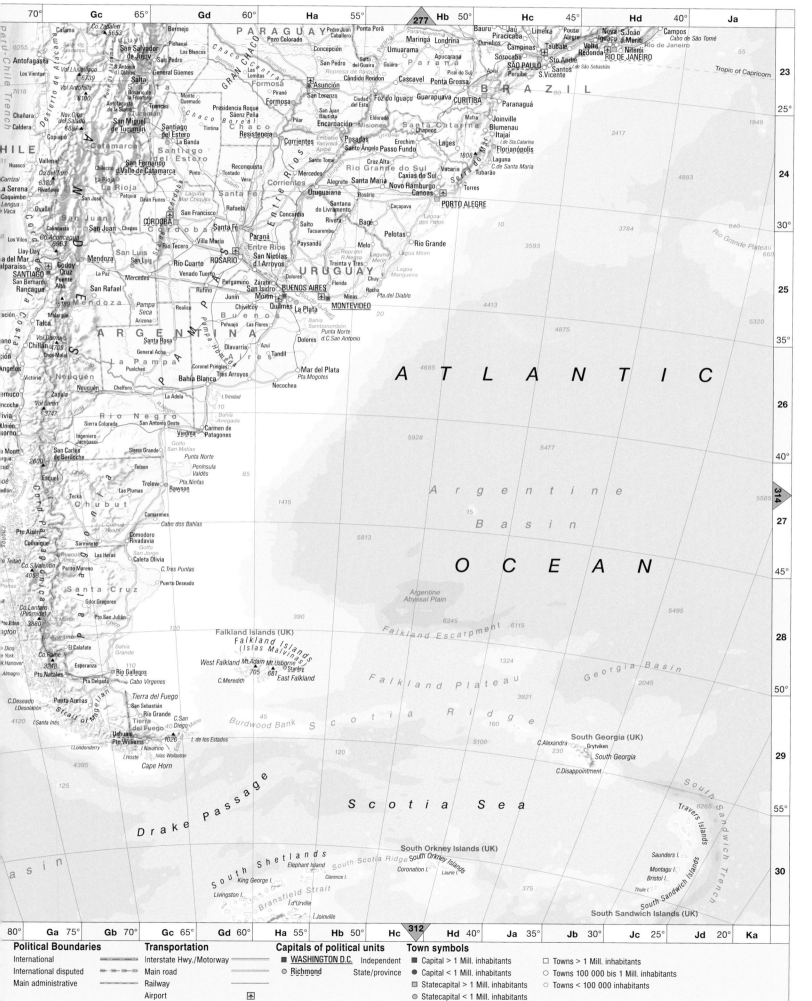

Gran Chaco Expansive grassland region in Argentina and Paraguay – subject to floods and frequent drought – pawpaw trees (photo) are common to the Gran Chaco.

La Pampa Seca This dry section of the Pampas lies in the rain shadow of the Andes – major center of the Argentinean cattle ranching industry.

The Pampas A region of vast fertile plains extending north and west of the Rio de la Plata – crop farming and sheep herding.

The Falkland Island (Islas Malvinas) Island group in the South Atlantic – British territory – site of the 1982 Falklands War.

South Georgia Discovered in 1675 – more than 160 glaciers descend from the island into the ocean – abandoned whaling station.

South Shetland Islands First explored in 1819 – four island groups with a total land area of 3,687 km² – highest peak, Mount Foster (2,105 m) – large penguin colonies.

South Sandwich Islands Group of islands west of a large ocean trench – active volcanoes – the islands are covered by glaciers.

Political Boundaries
International
International disputed
Main administrative

Transportation
Interstate Hwy./Motorway
Main road
Railway
Airport

Capitals of political units
■ WASHINGTON D.C. Independent
◉ Richmond State/province

Town symbols
■ Capital > 1 Mill. inhabitants
■ Capital < 1 Mill. inhabitants
□ Statecapital > 1 Mill. inhabitants
◉ Statecapital < 1 Mill. inhabitants
□ Towns > 1 Mill. inhabitants
○ Towns 100 000 bis 1 Mill. inhabitants
○ Towns < 100 000 inhabitants

Western Venezuela, Northern Colombia

The geological history of this South American region goes back to the early periods of the Earth's development. The mountains of the 🏔 **Guiana Highlands**, east and south of the Orinoco River, were first formed during the Precambrian period. The oldest sections of this range were created around 2.5 billion years ago on the prehistoric super-continent Gondwanaland. The western portions of the Guiana Highlands are covered by the up-

land plains of the Gran Sabana. The Pemon Amerindians who inhabit the region refer to the mountains, which they consider sacred, as tepuis.

To the east of the **Gran Sabana** lies an area of plateaus and mesas. Because of their height and steep rises many of the plateaus and mountains in the highlands

A colorful island in the Los Roques Archipelago National Park. **Gg40**

are isolated from surrounding regions. This isolation has led to the development of unique vegetation in many areas. Since the 1950s, the Orinoco basin in Venezuela has become increasingly important for the country's economy because of its vast deposits of mineral resources. An even larger segment of the Venezuelan economy relies on the oil deposits in the region around **Lake Maracaibo**. Thanks to its large reser-

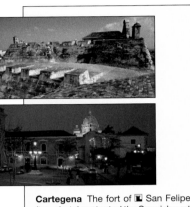

Cartegena The fort of 🏰 San Felipe (top photo) protected the Spanish port Cartagena during the colonial era. The beautiful 🏛 old town (bottom photo) is still surrounded by a city wall. **Gc40**

Santa Cruz de Mompox 🏛 Colonial city founded in 1537 – historic ⛪ Santa Barbara church was built in Moorish style. **Gc41**

Río Magdalena This river was the most important transport route in the region during pre-Colombian times – several floating markets (photo). **Gd41/44**

Los Katios National Park Columbian 🌳 national park adjoined to Panama's Darien National Park. **Gb42**

Villa de Leyva Picturesque village in the Boyaca Highlands of Colombia – cobblestoned streets and squares – historic architecture from the colonial era. **Gd43**

Bogotá Capital city of Colombia – population 6.8 million – historic old town: La Candelaria – modern high rises – historic architecture around 🏛 Plaza Bolivar – 🏛 gold museum. **Gc43**

Scale 1:4,500,000

0   40   80 Kilometers

Principal travel routes
- 🚗 Auto route
- 🚂 Rail road
- Shipping route

Remarkable landscapes and natural monuments
- ■ UNESCO World Natural Heritage
- ■ Mountain landscape
- ▲ Extinct volcano
- ▲ Active volcano
- Cave
- River landscape
- Waterfall/rapids
- Lake country
- Desert
- Nature park
- National park (landscape)
- National park (flora)
- National park (fauna)
- National park (culture)
- Coastal landscape
- Beach

ves, Venezuela is one of the world's leading oil producers and exporters. The country's oil deposits were formed billions of years ago in an undersea basin along the edge of the South American tectonic plate.

Collisions between the Nazca and South American tectonic plates led to the formation of the ■ **Andes Mountains** (divided into three separate ranges in this region). There are several moun-

tains rising more than 5,000 meters in the region including snow covered **Pico Bolivar** in the Sierra de Merida, 5,215-meter-high **Nevado de Tolima**, and the active 5,352-meter-high ■ volcano **Nevado der Ruiz**. Many of the numerous valleys in the Colombian Andes were formed by powerful rivers such as the **Rio Atrato** and **Rio Magdelena**.
The **Llanos** are a hot region of expansive prairies in the **Orinico River** basin

region of Colombia and Venezuela. Because of powerful trade winds, the coastal areas in this part of northern South America are relatively dry – especially during winter. Colombia and Venezuela get most of their rainfall during the humid summer months.

During the early 19th century, the German explorer and naturalist Alexander von Humboldt became the first person to identify the incredible diversity of flora and

fauna in the region. Ecotourism has become an important industry in Venezuela recently with an increasing number of tourists visiting the country's wilderness areas. The rainforest and savannahs in the region often border mountainous regions with cool climates and rugged vegetation. In addition to its abundant vegetation, northwestern South America is also home to many fascinating and unique animal species.

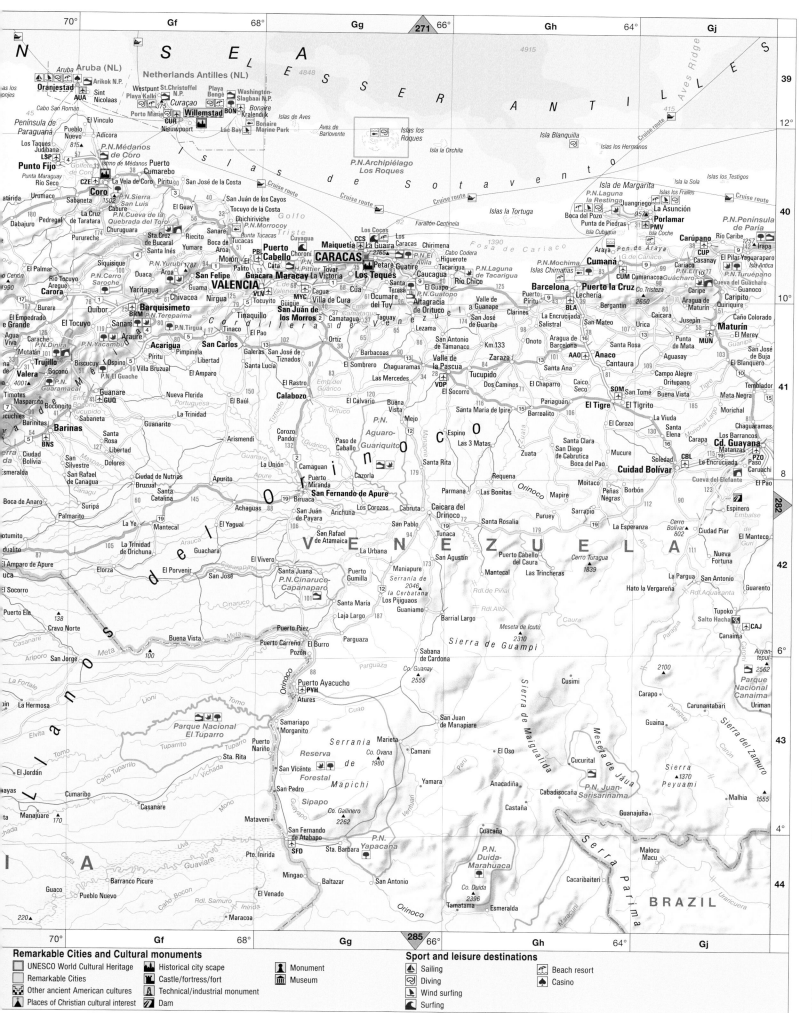

Willemstad Capital of the Netherland Antilles – on Curaçao – historic quarter with Dutch architecture – oil refinery. **Gf39**

Coro Historic city founded in 1527 (population: 175,000) – Cathedral (1583) – UNESCO world heritage site. **Gf40**

Caracas Capital of Venezuela – population of five million – historic cathedral and San Francisco Church – Casa Natal del Libertador: birthplace of Simon Bolivar. **Gg40**

The Orinoco River The longest river (2140 km) in Venezuela, passes through rainforests (top photo) including the homelands of the Yanomami (middle photo). **Gg-Gj41/44**

Salto Hacha Terraced waterfalls along the dark Río Carrao in the Laguna de Canaima (Venezuela). **Gj42**

Remarkable Cities and Cultural monuments

- ☐ UNESCO World Cultural Heritage
- ◆ Remarkable Cities
- ◆ Other ancient American cultures
- ◆ Places of Christian cultural interest
- ■ Historical city scape
- ▲ Castle/fortress/fort
- ⚒ Technical/industrial monument
- ⬚ Dam
- 👤 Monument
- 🏛 Museum

Sport and leisure destinations

- ⛵ Sailing
- 🤿 Diving
- 🏄 Wind surfing
- 🏄 Surfing
- 🏖 Beach resort
- 🎰 Casino

Eastern Venezuela, Guyana, Suriname

Northeastern South America comprises eastern Venezuela, the French territory French Guiana and two of the smallest nations in South America – Suriname and Guyana. The region is home to many diverse landscapes and natural attractions including tropical rainforests, high plateaus, the world's tallest waterfall, prairies, and sandy white beaches. The majority of the region's population is concentrated in eastern **Venezuela's** coastal

areas. This coastal region was one of the first areas to be settled during the Spanish colonization of South America. Many of the cities along the Venezuelan coast, including Puerto la Cruz, experienced a major hotel construction boom in the 1980s. There are still, however, undeveloped beaches in places such as 🏖

Auyán-tepuí is the largest mesa in the Guiana Highlands. **Gj43**

Trinidad und Tobago Pigeon Point is a beautiful series of 🏖 beaches in western Tobago (top photo). Trinidad has one of the largest carnivals in the Caribbean. This small nation has a diverse population and is the birthplace of calypso music. **Gk40**

Mochima National Park National Park in northern Venezuela – includes uninhabited islands, creeks, and beaches. **Gh40**

Warao Amerindians The Warao Amerindians live in the Orinoco Delta – stilt houses are common in Warao villages. **Gk41**

Angel Falls The tallest 🌊 waterfalls in the world – 978 meters tall – discovered in 1936 by the American pilot Jimmy Angel. **Gj42/43**

Quebrada de Jaspe 🌊 Terraced riverbed in a tropical rainforest – unusual, dark reddish-orange colored stone. **Gk43**

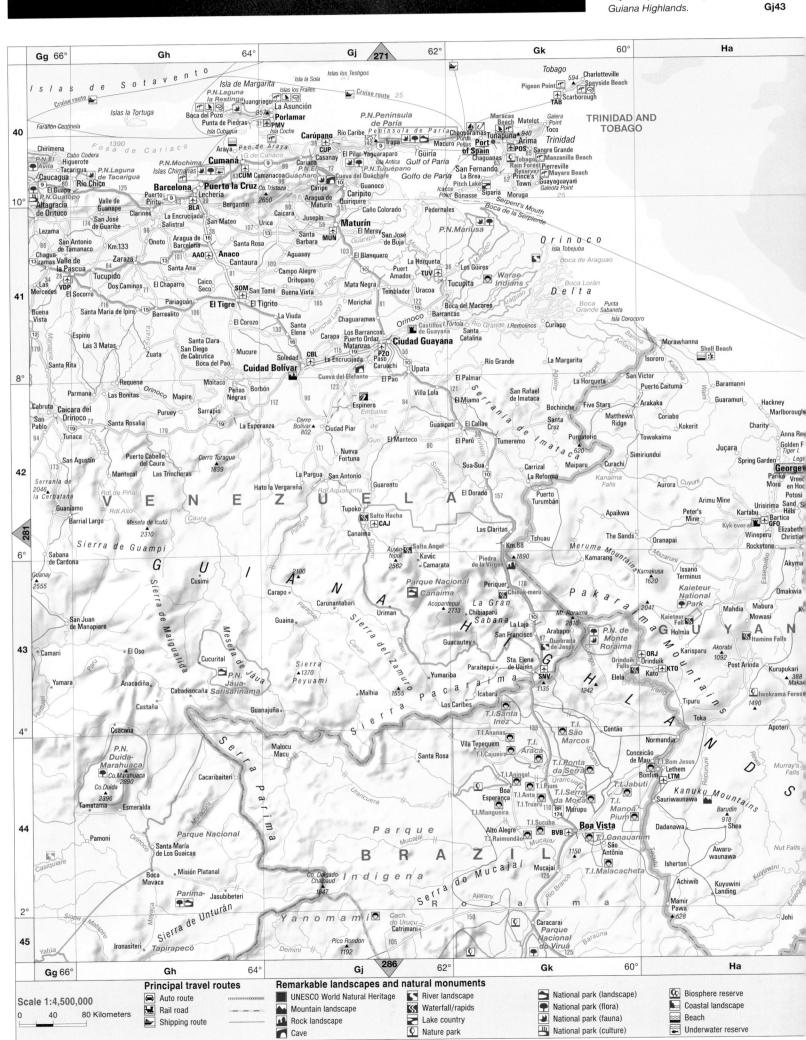

Principal travel routes

Scale 1:4,500,000

0   40   80 Kilometers

- 🚗 Auto route
- 🚂 Rail road
- 🚢 Shipping route
- ········ (dotted line)
- – – – (dashed line)

Remarkable landscapes and natural monuments

- ◻ UNESCO World Natural Heritage
- ◻ Mountain landscape
- ◻ Rock landscape
- ◻ Cave
- 🌊 River landscape
- 🌊 Waterfall/rapids
- 🌊 Lake country
- 🌊 Nature park
- National park (landscape)
- National park (flora)
- National park (fauna)
- National park (culture)
- Biosphere reserve
- Coastal landscape
- Beach
- Underwater reserve

Mochima National Park.  **Isla Margarita**, an island off the Venezuelan coast is one of the most popular tourist destinations in the region. **The Orinoco River** is the most important river in the region. Two major cities are located along the Orinoco: Ciudad Bolivar, a major port city and Ciudad Guyana, a leading industrial center. The Casiquiare River connects the Orinoco to the Rio Negro, a tributary of the Amazon River.

High water levels in the Rio Negro often cause the Casiquiare to change its direction and flow backwards into the Orinoco. The **Guiana Highlands** block the path of the Orinoco and force the river to make a 1,000 kilometer detour on its way to the ocean. These highlands are one of the oldest mountain regions in the world and were once a part of the prehistoric Guiana Shield. The **Gran Sabana** in the southeastern Guiana Highlands offers fascinating landscapes. The region is home to isolated mesas (called tepuis locally) that rise above lush rainforests. Roraima Tepui lies along the border between Venezuela, Guyana, and Brazil. To the east of the Orinoco Delta in Venezuela are the three countries sometimes collectively known as the Guianas. **Guyana** is the westernmost of these three countries and is home to the beautiful Kaieteur Falls. East of Guyana lies **Suriname**, a former Dutch colony with an attractive capital city. **French Guiana**, the easternmost of the Guianas, is an overseas territory of France. This small territory is the location of the European Space Agency's launch center and infamous Devil's Island, a former French penal colony. Because the interior of the Guianas is covered by thick hot rainforests, the populations of all three countries are concentrated along the coast.

Paramaribo Capital of Suriname – Fort Zeelandia (photo) – Suriname National Museum – colonial wooden houses – UNESCO world heritage site. **Hc43**

Kaieteur Falls Spectacular waterfall in Guyana – 226-meter-drop – the surrounding region is home to unique wildlife including tapirs, armadillos, and anteaters. **Ha43**

Central Suriname Nature Reserve Protected ecosystem – home to rare poisonous frogs – covered by thick rainforests – UNESCO world heritage site. **Hb-Hc43/44**

Kourou Site of the European Space Agency's launch center – space exploration museum – in French Guiana. **Hd43**

Îles du Salut Island group includes Ile du Diable (Devil's Island), once the site of an infamous French penal colony. **Hd43**

Remarkable Cities and Cultural monuments

- UNESCO World Cultural Heritage
- Remarkable Cities
- Amazonian Indians/protected area
- Historical city scape
- Castle/fortress/fort
- Dam
- Space mission launch site

Sport and leisure destinations

- Sailing
- Diving
- Wind surfing
- Deep-sea fishing
- Beach resort

Ecuador, Southern Colombia, Northern Peru

The equatorial region in western South America stretches into three countries: Ecuador, Peru, and Colombia. This compact region encompasses coastlines, mountainous highlands, and tropical forests. The Andes in this region are divided into three separate ranges: the **Cordillera Real** in the west, the **Cordillera Oriental** in the east, and the Cordillera Central which runs between the previous two. The three ranges, which contain

several peaks above 5,000 meters, are separated by hilly highlands. The highest mountain in the region, 🗻 Chimborazo (6,310 m), is an inactive volcano. 🗻 Cotopaxi, the world's highest active volcano, lies in central Ecuador. Many of the region's rivers have their sources in the western Cordilleras and flow through to

Cotopaxi: one of the most beautiful peaks in the Andes. **Ga46**

Galápagos Islands Swallow-tailed gulls, Galapagos land iguanas, and Galapagos giant tortoises, are a few of the many unique species on this group of islands. The 🏝 islands are a UNESCO world heritage site. The Galapagos also feature unique 🗻 volcanic landscapes and plant species. **Fe-Ff45/46**

San Agustín Archeological Park Site containing more than 🗿 500 sculptures created between the 6th and 12th centuries – UNESCO world heritage site. **Gb45**

El Angel Ecological Reserve 🌿 Nature reserve containing rugged alpine vegetation – at heights between 3400 and 4150 meters – in northern Ecuador. **Ga-Gb45**

Quito Ecuador's capital lies 2850 meters above sea level – founded in 1534 – the old town is a UNESCO world heritage site – 🏛 16th century cathedral – 🏛 La Compania and San Francisco (photo). **Ga46**

Cotopaxi 🗻 The world's highest active volcano – crater diameter of 5897 meters – hardy alpine vegetation lies below the snow-covered rim. **Ga46**

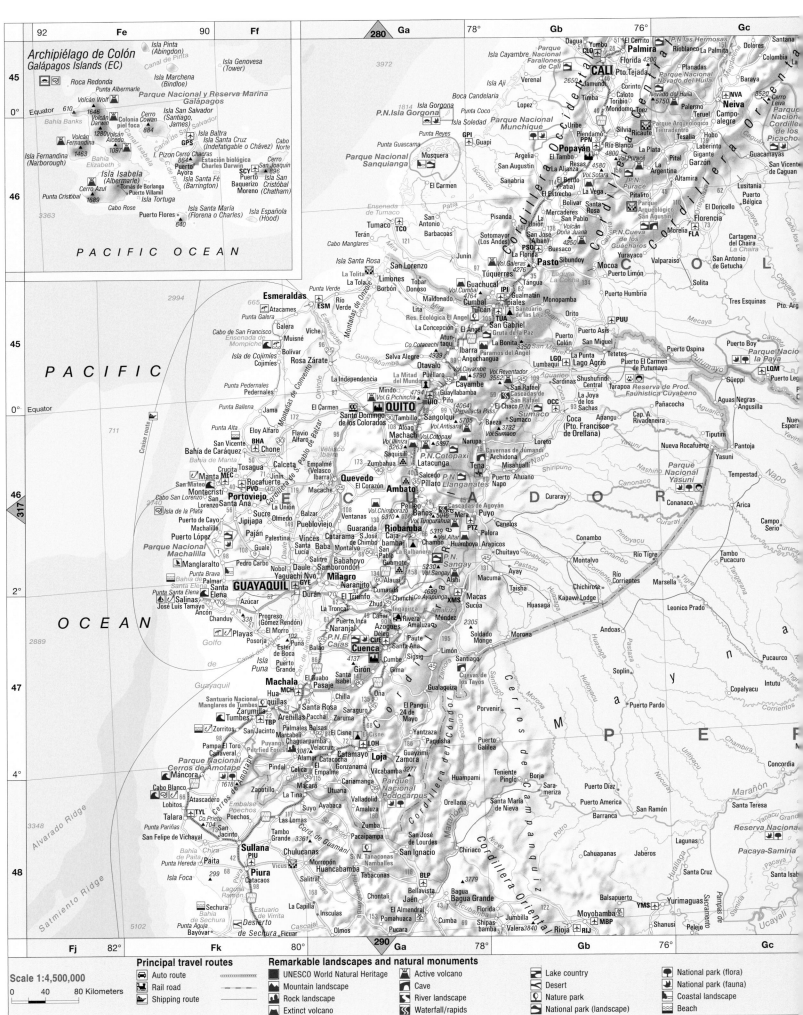

Scale 1:4,500,000

0   40   80 Kilometers

Principal travel routes
- 🚌 Auto route
- 🚂 Rail road
- Shipping route
- Mountain landscape

Remarkable landscapes and natural monuments
- ■ UNESCO World Natural Heritage
- 🗻 Active volcano
- Cave
- River landscape
- Waterfall/rapids
- Lake country
- Desert
- Nature park
- National park (landscape)
- National park (flora)
- National park (fauna)
- Coastal landscape
- Beach
- Rock landscape
- Extinct volcano

coastal areas where they deposit fertile soil important to local agriculture. Several important tributaries of the **Amazon River** such as the Rio Napo and Rio Santiago rise in the eastern Cordilleras. The heavily forested eastern Cordilleras are bordered to the east by the plains of the **Amazon River basin**. This region of dense rainforest is largely inaccessible with the exception of areas where natural resources (natural gas and oil) are

exploited. The Brazilian section of the Amazon basin contains several large land reserves created to protect the traditional lifestyles of local Amerindians. The **Galápagos Islands** are a group of volcanic islands formed on top of a so-called mantle plume. Mantle plumes are columns of molten rock that rise from deep within the earth's surface. These columns of rock force the earth's crust to rise forming volcanoes and in some

cases volcanic islands. The tallest volcano on the Galápagos Islands is **Cerro Azul** rising more than 5,000 meters from the ocean floor and 1,689 meters above sea level. **Cerro Wolf**, the second tallest peak on the islands, rises 1,646 meters. The islands are slowly drifting eastwards toward the South American mainland. The western islands are the youngest in the group. The Galápagos Islands are most famous for their

unique wildlife and the work of Charles Darwin, who conducted some of his most important research on the islands. Alcedo Crater is home to the largest colony of **Galápagos Giant Tortoises**. These famous tortoises are the largest in the world and can live as long as 150 years. The island's unique wildlife is a result of the Galápagos' geographic isolation from other land areas and the lack of large predators on the islands.

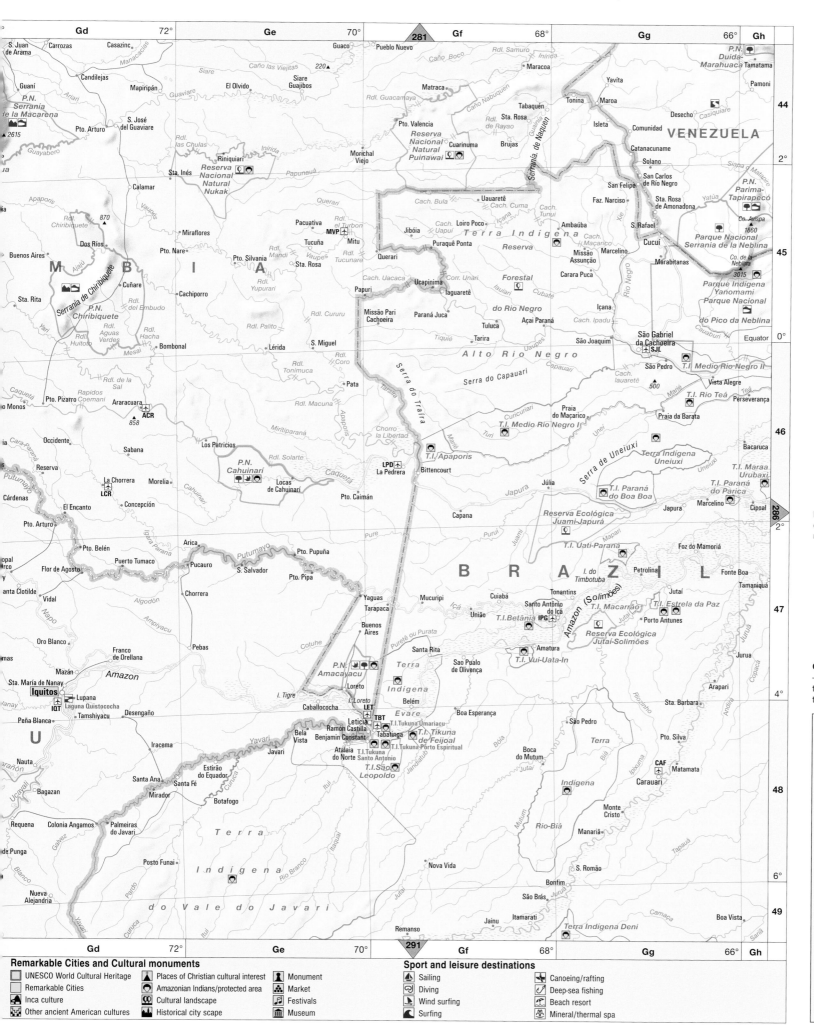

Chimborazo The highest 🏔 mountain in Ecuador (6,310 m) – inactive volcano – 16 glaciers – ice covered craters. **Ga46**

Machalilla National Park 🗺 National park on the Pacific coast – extensive forests – good areas for bird watching. **Fk46**

Sangay National Park 🗺 National park in Ecuador – 🏔 Sangay volcano (5,230 m) – home to endangered tapirs. **Ga46/47**

Ingapirca Built around 1500 – 🏛 complex of Incan inns and troop lodgings – once a major stop on the Incan road system. **Ga47**

Cuenca Founded by the Spanish in 1557 – 🏛 Catedral Nueva (photo) – historic 🏙 old town with 17th and 18th century architecture – UNESCO world heritage site. **Ga47**

The Amerindians of the western Amazon region The Amazon basin has been inhabited by humans for at least 12,000 years. The Huaorani are one of the last nomadic tribes in Ecuador. Many of the region's Amerindians live on protected land reservations.

Remarkable Cities and Cultural monuments

- ☐ UNESCO World Cultural Heritage
- ☐ Remarkable Cities
- ▣ Inca culture
- ☐ Other ancient American cultures
- ▲ Places of Christian cultural interest
- 🛕 Amazonian Indians/protected area
- ∞ Cultural landscape
- ▣ Historical city scape
- ▣ Monument
- ▣ Market
- 🎵 Festivals
- 🏛 Museum

Sport and leisure destinations

- ⛵ Sailing
- 🤿 Diving
- 🏄 Wind surfing
- 🏄 Surfing
- 🚣 Canoeing/rafting
- 🎣 Deep-sea fishing
- 🏖 Beach resort
- ♨ Mineral/thermal spa

Amazonian Lowlands

The Amazon River basin is the largest  river basin in the world. The drainage area of the Amazon River is larger in size than the continent of Australia. Technically the Amazon River only begins where it merges with the **Rio Negro**, 18 kilometers southeast of Manaus. The section of the river upstream from Manaus is known to Brazilians as the **Rio Solimões**. Further upstream in Peru, the name of the river reverts back to Amazon. In Peru, several rivers that originate in the Andes, including the Maranon and Huallaga, flow into the Amazon. The Amazon has several large tributaries such as the powerful Rio Negro which flow south into the Amazon. Other major tributaries such as the **Rio Madeira**, **Rio Tapajos**, and **Rio Xin-**

Sunrise above the steamy Amazon rainforest.

Amazon Amerindians The 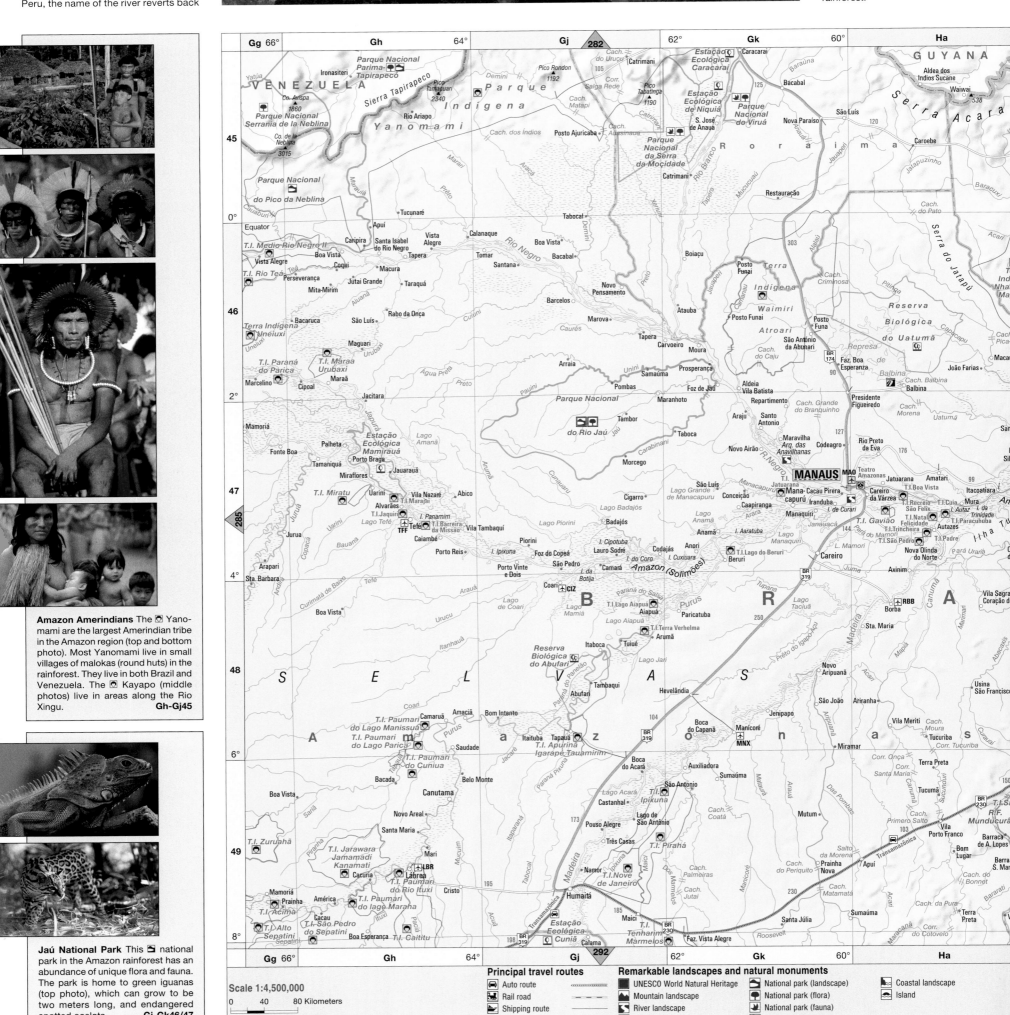 Yanomami are the largest Amerindian tribe in the Amazon region (top and bottom photo). Most Yanomami live in small villages of malokas (round huts) in the rainforest. They live in both Brazil and Venezuela. The Kayapo (middle photos) live in areas along the Rio Xingu. **Gh-Gj45**

Jaú National Park This national park in the Amazon rainforest has an abundance of unique flora and fauna. The park is home to green iguanas (top photo), which can grow to be two meters long, and endangered spotted ocelots. **Gj-Gk46/47**

Scale 1:4,500,000

0   40   80 Kilometers

Principal travel routes
- Auto route
- Rail road
- Shipping route

Remarkable landscapes and natural monuments
- UNESCO World Natural Heritage
- Mountain landscape
- River landscape
- Nature park
- National park (landscape)
- National park (flora)
- National park (fauna)
- Biosphere reserve
- Coastal landscape
- Island

gu flow north into the river. The water level fluctuation of the Amazon River can be as great as 15 meters. Downstream from Manaus the river widens and is rarely less than five kilometers wide. One exception to this pattern is the narrow area of the river around **Óbidos** where the Amazon is 100 meters deep and only two kilometers wide. Modern geologists believe that the Amazon was created in the section of Africa where the Sahara

Desert is now located. It is also known that the Amazon once flowed towards the Pacific – the opposite direction of its present course. Millions of years ago, Africa and South America formed one continent. When this continent began to break apart, and South America drifted westwards, the Andes began to form. The rising mountains forced the Amazon to finally change direction around six million years ago.

The Amazon rainforest is the largest continuous forested area in the world. Because of its dense vegetation and poor soil it remains a sparsely populated region. Logging and land clearing have done considerable damage to the rainforest. But in recent decades increased environmental awareness has led to activism and government action for the defense of the Amazon rainforest. Large sections of the rainforest are now protected in natio-

nal parks such as **Jau National Park**, **Yanomami Indigenous Park**, and **Tumucumaque Park**. In the 15th century, before the arrival of Europeans, there were at least one million Amerindians living in the rainforest – today there are less than 100,000. Many tribes were enslaved, kidnapped, or wiped out by diseases during the co-lonial period. There are now at least 100 fewer tribes in the region than at the start of the 20th century.

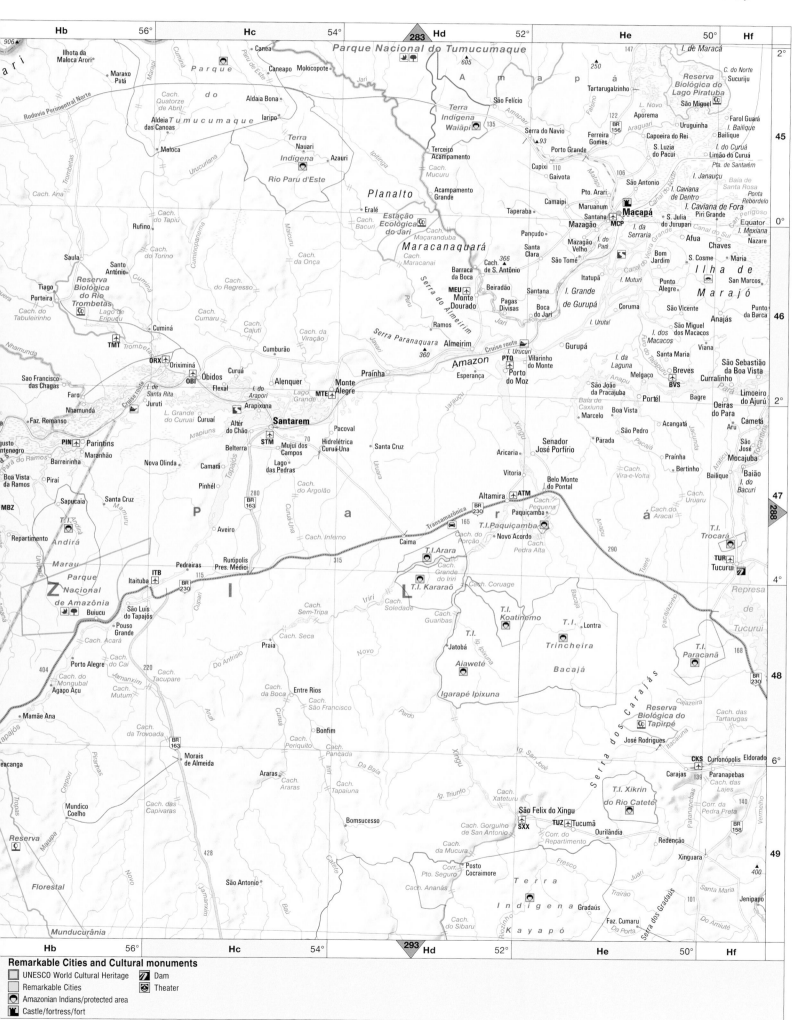

Macapá Capital of the Brazilian state Amapá – historic Fort São José was built in 1763 – Zoobotanico Park: a nature reserve inhabited by local wildlife. **He45**

Along the Amazon The Amazon River is the most important transport route into the Amazon region. Because of the thick almost inaccessible rainforests many towns in the Amazon region are only connected to the outside world by ships traveling up and down the river.

Rio Negro Famous for its dark colored water, the Rio Negro is a major tributary of the Amazon. Due to the high acidity and low mineral content of its water, the Rio Negro is inhabited by few animals and insects. The river (over 1,700 km long) lies mostly in Brazil. It begins as the Rio Guainia in Columbia and reaches its maximum width (2 km) near Manaus. The luxury hotel Ariaú Tower in Manaus has a viewing platform which offers good views over the river and surrounding rainforests.

Manaus Large city in the Amazon region – center of Brazil's 19th century rubber boom – Teatro Amazonas opera house. **Gk47**

Remarkable Cities and Cultural monuments
- ☐ UNESCO World Cultural Heritage
- ☐ Remarkable Cities
- ☐ Amazonian Indians/protected area
- ☐ Castle/fortress/fort
- ⚡ Dam
- ☐ Theater

Northeastern Brazil

Northeastern Brazil is one of the most distinct regions in the country. The Northeast, a tropical region, is located just south of the equator which passes through the ⬚ **Ilha de Marajó** in the Amazon Delta. The Ilha de Marajo has a land area roughly the size of Switzerland and is one of the largest river islands in the world. During much of the year, half of the island's land is submerged beneath the ⬚ **Amazon**, **Pará**, and **Tocantins Rivers**.

In recent decades, water buffalos from India have been introduced to the area. The water buffalos are used primarily for cargo transportation – there are now thousands of them in the region. One of the most interesting natural phenomena in the Amazon delta is a large tidal wave called **Pororoca**. The wave appears from

The area around Canoa Quebrada has numerous beautiful, colorful cliffs. **Jb48**

Ilha de Marajó One of the largest ⬚ river islands in the world – covers 48,000 km² – surrounded by rivers including the Amazon and the Tocantins. **He-Hf46**

Baía de Marajó Large channel in the Amazon river delta – rich fishing grounds – dense ⬚ mangrove rainforests line both banks of the channel. **Hf46**

Belem Largest ⬚ port in the Amazon region – ⬚ Ver-o-Peso market hall (photo) – ⬚ Museo Goeldi: natural history museum – ⬚ Forte de Castelo (1616). **Hf46**

Alcântara ⬚ Historic city with colonial architecture – Plaza Gomez de Castro – 17th century houses and churches. **Hh47**

São Luís Capital city (population: 750,000) of Maranhão – vibrant reggae music scene – ⬚ historic city center – ⬚ Catedral de Sé (UNESCO world heritage site; photo). **Hh47**

Lençóis Maranhenses National Park ⬚ Countless large sand dunes – shallow lakes are formed during the rainy season. **Hj47**

Kayapó Indigenous Land ⬚ Amerindian land reserve in the Central Brazilian Highlands – most Amerindians live traditional lifestyles – large forests. **He49**

Scale 1:4,500,000

0   40   80 Kilometers

Principal travel routes
- 🚗 Auto route
- 🚂 Rail road
- 🚢 Shipping route

Remarkable landscapes and natural monuments
- ⬛ UNESCO World Natural Heritage
- Cave
- River landscape
- Nature park
- National park (landscape)
- National park (flora)
- National park (fauna)
- National park (culture)
- Biosphere reserve
- Turtle conservation area
- Coastal landscape
- Beach
- Island

February to May when water in the **Perigoso Channel** (between the islands Caviana de Fora and Mexiana) is pushed out to sea by powerful currents from the Amazon. This frightening wave is often five meters tall and more than a kilometer in length.

The areas south and east of the Amazon Delta, including portions of the **Central Brazilian Highlands**, are significantly drier than the regions in the delta. The vegetation in these areas also differs from that in the Amazon Delta. The humid **tropical rainforests** with their heavy rainfall extend south to the area near the city of São Luís. Vast grasslands called **Campos Cerrados**, with only scattered clusters of trees, border the rainforests. Between Natal and Fortaleza in the easternmost region of Brazil, the climate is shaped by strong coastal winds.

The interior regions of northeastern Brazil are covered by dry forests known as **Caatinga** in Brazilian Portuguese. These dry regions receive less than 50 millimeters of rainfall annually and are subject to frequent droughts. This is also one of the poorest regions in Brazil with many of its inhabitants living in severe poverty. The Atlantic coast has many large sand dunes and long sandy beaches. The coastal areas south of Natal have humid rainy climates. During much of the colonial era, the Northeast's sugar crops were Brazil's greatest source of wealth.

Fernando de Noronha is a tropical archipelago comprising 21 volcanic islands, 350 kilometers off the coast of mainland Brazil. In an effort to preserve the archipelago's pristine beaches and unique marine life, most of the islands and the waters around them have been designated a national marine park.

Fernando de Noronha Archipelago of volcanic islands 350 kilometers off the Brazilian coast – underwater national park around the islands – diving areas. **Jd47**

Jericoacoara National Park Beautiful beaches along the Atlantic coast – sand dunes – abandoned fishing villages. **Hk47**

Fortaleza Capital of the state of Ceará – population of two million – José de Alencar theatre (1910) – popular beaches – vibrant nightlife in Iracema district. **Ja47**

Olinda Historic city on Brazil's east coast. Olinda's old town is a designated UNESCO world heritage site. São Francisco convent (top photo) and Nossa Senhora do Carmo church (bottom photo) are two of the most beautiful buildings in the city. **Jc49**

Recife Capital of Pernambuco – population: 1.35 million – historic city center around the São Pedro cathedral (photo) – Recife Antigo, lively portside district. **Jc50**

Southern Peru, Northwestern Bolivia

Despite its location between the ocean and mountains the Peruvian coast is a relatively infertile and dry area. The cool **Humboldt Current**, a shallow current carrying Antarctic water, runs along the coast of **Peru**. Large fog clouds extend from the coast into the interior; however, the region gets very little rainfall. Lush green vegetation grows along the bottom edges of mountains with frequent fog coverage. A few scattered river oases are

the only areas in the region capable of supporting agriculture. While the coast itself is relatively barren, the waters off the coast contain an incredible abundance of marine life. Nutrient rich water from the deep **Peru-Chile Trench** (-6,600 m) supports a complex food chain with plankton at the bottom and

Lake Titicaca in Peru and Bolivia is the largest lake in South America. Gf53/54

Moche Pyramids near Lambayeque Terraced ⬜ adobe pyramids (dried loam) – ancient burial complex. **Ga49**

Chan-Chan Ancient capital of the ⬜ Chimú kingdom – founded in the 12th century – UNESCO world heritage site. **Ga49**

Huascarán National Park Mount Huascarán rises 6,768 meters (photo) – deep ravines and glacial lakes. **Gb50**

Chavín de Huántar Large settlement built by the ⬜ Chavín culture around 800 BC – UNESCO world heritage site. **Gb50**

Lima Capital of Peru – population: approx. 8.5 million – colonial ⬜ old town – historic 17th and 18th century ⬜ churches – Plaza San Martín (photo). **Gb52**

Nazca Lines ⬜ A series of geometric lines and forms in the Peruvian desert – made by the Nazca between 200 and 600 BC. **Gc53**

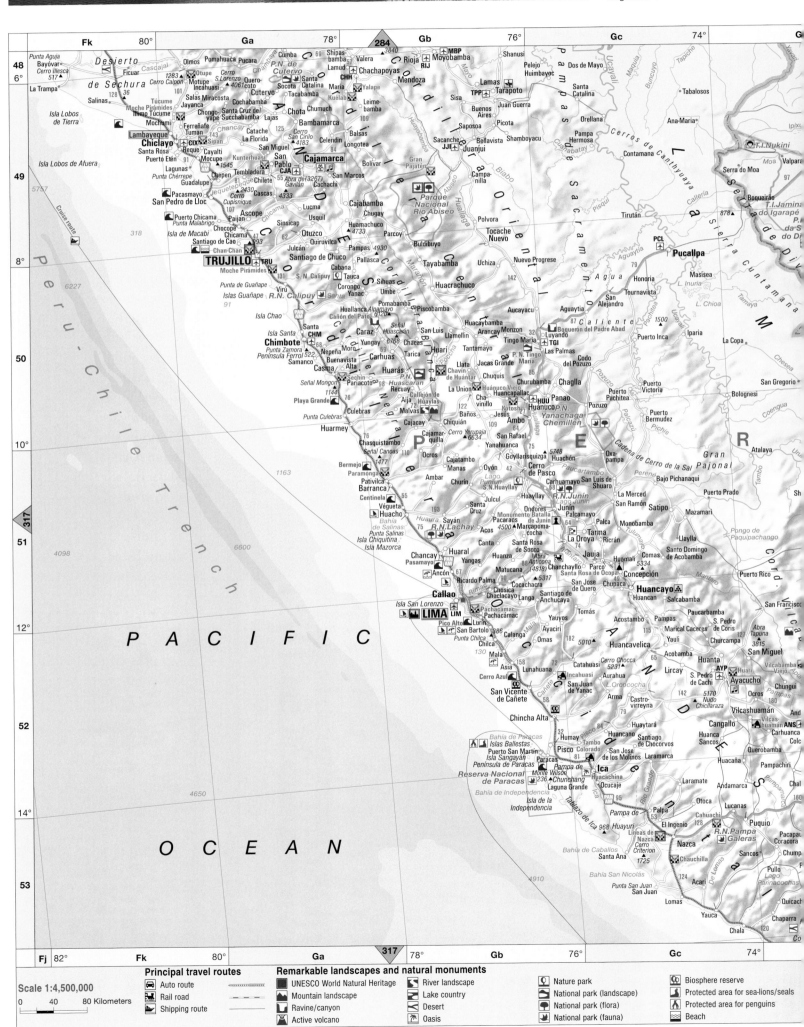

ocean predators and aquatic birds at the top. **El Niño** is an natural phenomenon that causes the waters in the eastern Pacific to warm, resulting in significant changes to the region's weather pattern. The anomaly occurs at irregular intervals every two to seven years. El Niño has a negative impact on fishing and agriculture in western South America and often results in the appearance of destructive floods along the Peruvian coast.

The heavy rainfall during El Niño is a serious threat to the ancient adobe settlements built by pre-Incan coastal Amerindian cultures. These historic buildings are amongst the oldest remaining Amerindian sites in the Americas.

East of Trujillo on Peru's southern coast, the ☒ **Callejón de Huaylas Valley** separates the ⛰ **Cordillera Negra** and ⛰ **Cordillera Blanca Mountains**. The Ucayali River flows through the Cordillera Oriental and Cordillera Central mountain ranges. The river is one of many that feed the Amazon.

The Incas were once the most powerful nation in South American. From their capital city ⛯ **Cuzco**, the Incas administered a vast empire. During the colonial era, Peru's highlands were the major center of gold mining in South America.

⛵ **Lake Titicaca**, situated 3,821 meters above sea level, is the largest lake in South America with an area of 8,300 km². In addition to the coast (La Costa) and the highlands (La Sierra), Peru has a third distinct region. The third region, **La Selva** is a region of rainforest-covered plains. The Selva covers more than two thirds of Peru and contains several ☒ land reserves created to protect Amerindians. The Selva has a stable climate throughout the year with warm temperatures, high humidity, and heavy rainfall.

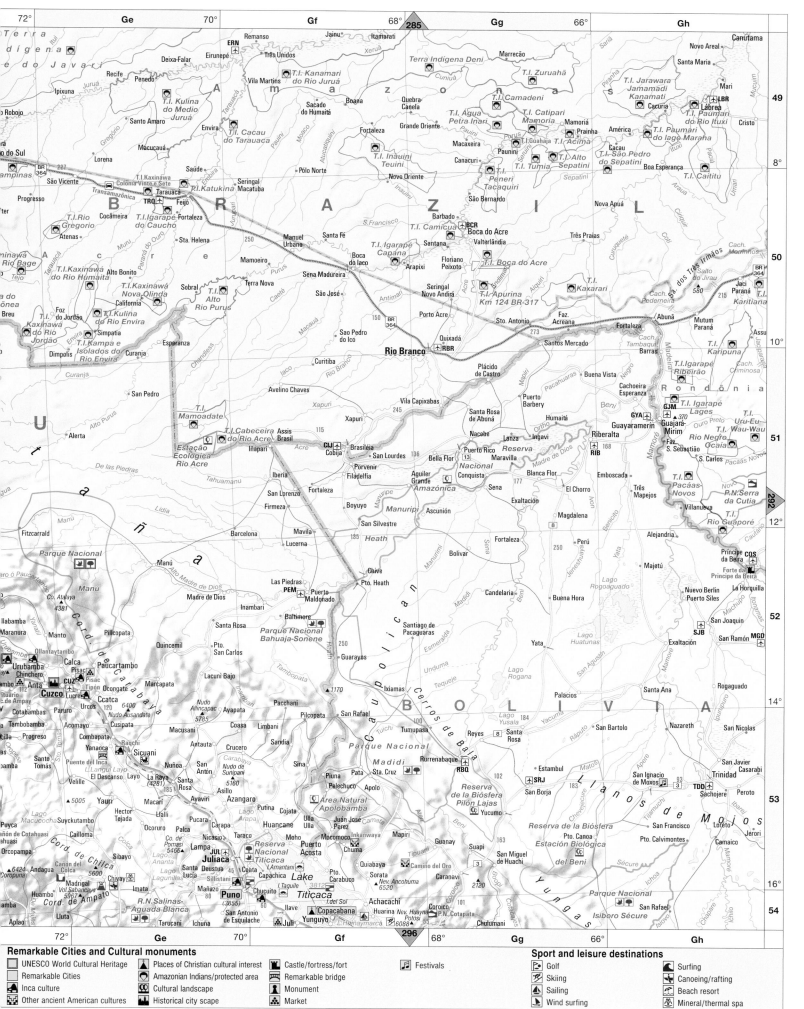

Manú National Park ☒ National Park covering 15,000 km² – over 1,000 bird species including Aras (photo).   Gd-Ge51/52

Bahuaja-Sonene National Park 10,914 km² – consisting of ☒ rainforests and grasslands – unique mixture of rainforest and savannah flora and fauna.   Gf52

Machu Picchu Ancient Incan fortress city located 2,400 meters above sea level. It was rediscovered in 1911. The city consists of a temple complex surrounded by dwellings.   Gd52

Cuzco The city was once the center of the ⛯ Incan Empire. ☒ Plaza de Armas (bottom photo) was built on top of an Incan ritual site. The remnants of the ⛯ Incan fortress Sacsayhuaman (top photo) are near the city.   Gd52

Sillistani Tall towers containing burial tombs built in the pre-Incan and Incan periods – located near a small lake.   Ge53

Puno The largest city on Lake Titicaca – 3,855 meters above sea level – founded in 1668 – ☒ historic cathedral.   Ge53

Remarkable Cities and Cultural monuments

☐ UNESCO World Cultural Heritage	▲ Places of Christian cultural interest	⛫ Castle/fortress/fort
☐ Remarkable Cities	☒ Amazonian Indians/protected area	⛉ Remarkable bridge
☐ Inca culture	☒ Cultural landscape	▲ Monument
☐ Other ancient American cultures	☒ Historical city scape	▲ Market

☒ Festivals	

Sport and leisure destinations

⛳ Golf	⛷ Surfing	
⛷ Skiing	⛵ Canoeing/rafting	
⛵ Sailing	⛱ Beach resort	
☒ Wind surfing	♨ Mineral/thermal spa	

Mato Grosso, Northeastern Bolivia

It was only after paved roads were built between the cities of Porto Velho and Cuiaba that large scale agriculture and settlement came to Mato Grosso, a Brazilian state in the country's  Planalto Central region. Across the border, northeastern Bolivia remains a sparsely populated and in some areas uninhabited region. The border between Brazil and northeastern Bolivia is marked by the Marmore and Guapore Rivers.

A flooded area of the Pantanal during the rainy season   HbHc54

In Portuguese, the name **Mato Grosso** means "thick grass." The region comprises two Brazilian states – Mato Grosso and Mato Grosso do Sol. Both of these states contain vast grasslands. The dry season in Mato Grosso begins in July and lasts until October. Many of the local tree species have adapted to the environment – hard rubbery leaves and thick bark to protect them against water loss and fire. In addition, many trees store water in complex underground root systems.

The so-called **Campos Cerrados** (300 to 800 m high) with its many rivers and forests lie in the southern Mato Grosso and is home to several Amerindian land reserves. Despite the land reserves, many of the local Amerindian peoples are finding it increasingly hard

The Amerindians of Rondonia Rondonia (243,000 km²) is home to 40 different Amerindian tribes. Many of them still lead traditional lives in the state's tropical forests. **Gh-Gk50/52**

Noel Kempff National Park National park covering 15,230 km² – tropical plains and wooded plateaus – UNESCO world natural heritage site. **Gk52/53**

The Mission Churches of Chiquitos The Bolivian region is the location of six historic mission churches. The churches were built between 1696 and 1760 by Jesuit missionaries and local Amerindians. **Gj-Gk54**

Chapada dos Guimarães National Park Brazilian national park with a total land area of 330 km². The park features many interesting stone formations including the so-called "Cidade da Pedra", the city of stone (top photo). **Hc53**

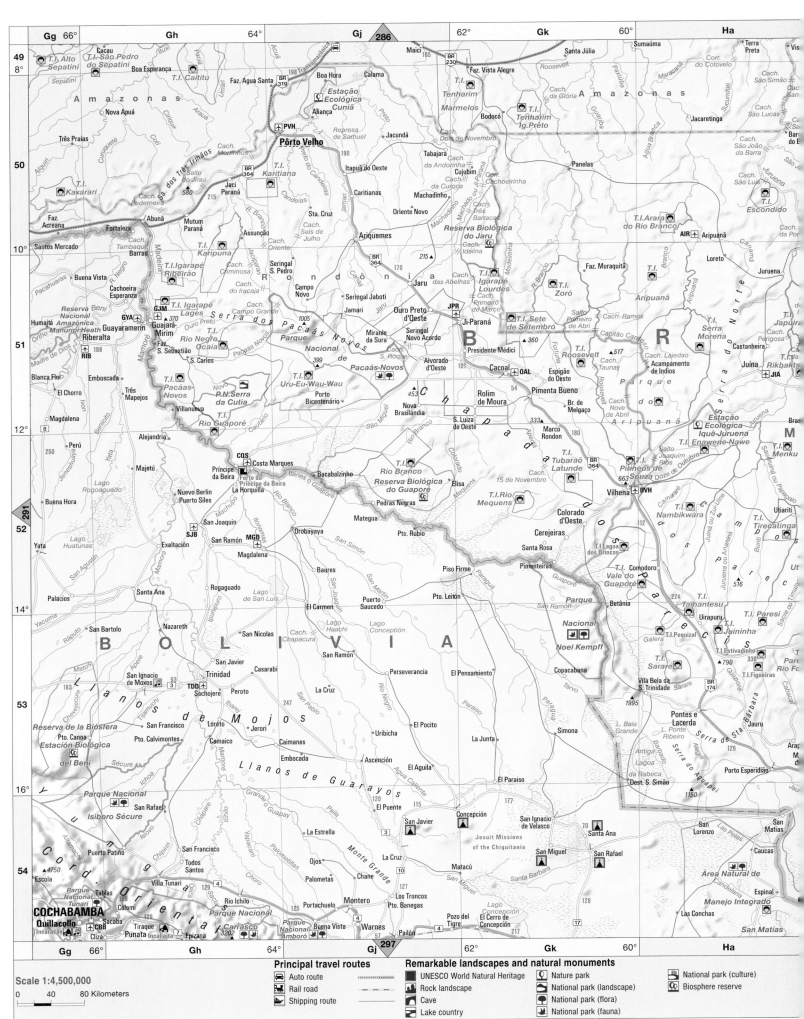

Scale 1:4,500,000

0   40   80 Kilometers

Principal travel routes
- Auto route
- Rail road
- Shipping route

Remarkable landscapes and natural monuments
- UNESCO World Natural Heritage
- Rock landscape
- Cave
- Lake country
- Nature park
- National park (landscape)
- National park (flora)
- National park (fauna)
- National park (culture)
- Biosphere reserve

to maintain traditional lifestyles. Much of the land in the Campos Cerrados is used for livestock ranching. The ranching industry has devastated local wildlife which the Amerindians have traditionally hunted. Another environmental threat to the region's ecosystems and indigenous people comes from mining. Mercury and other waste substances from mines are polluting the region's rivers and their basins.

To the east of the Campos Cerrados lies the Pantanal, one of the world's largest wetlands. Because of its incredible abundance of plant and animal species, the **Pantanal** is sometimes called the "Noah's Ark" of South America. The area has a total land area of 230,000 km² of which a mere 1,350 km² is protected in conservation areas.

Between the months of December and March, the region gets extremely heavy rainfall. During these months many of the Pantanal's rivers flood their banks covering large sections of the region with water. Many of the area's animals seek shelter from the floods in the treetops or on hills. The Pantanal is inhabited by many fascinating animals and is one of the best areas in South America to view wildlife. The region is home to rare birds, large cats, and at least 230 species of fish. Capybaras, the largest rodents in the world, are common throughout the region. Anteaters, giant otters, and jaguars are just a few of the many fascinating animals visitors can see in this area.

Cuiabá, the state capital of Mato Grosso, is known as the northern gateway to the Pantanal. The city is the best base for any expedition into the Pantanal. It lies near the geographic center of South America. With about half a million inhabitants, Cuiabá is the largest city in the region.

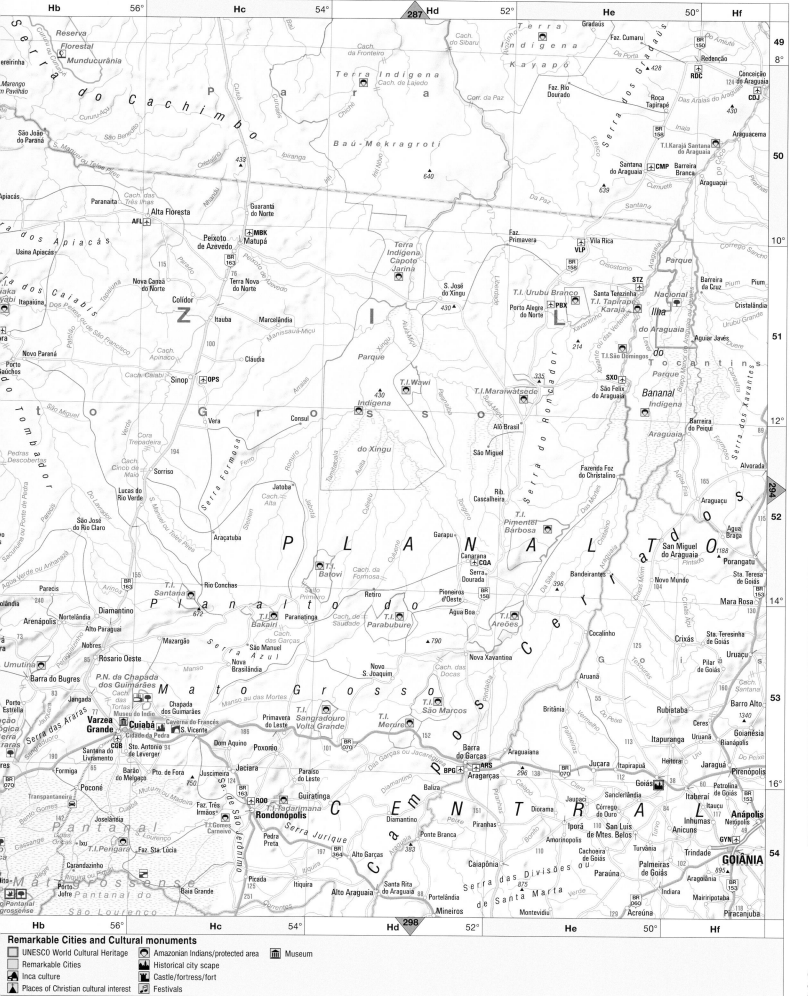

Xingu Indigenous Park Large Amerindian land reserve along the Xingu River – primarily marshland. **Hd51/52**

Cuiabá State capital of Mato Grosso – the "gateway" to the Pantanal – Museo do Indio: Amerindian culture museum. **Hb53**

Pantanal One of the world's largest wetland areas. The Pantanal covers 230,000 km² and is home to many different species of birds, fish, amphibians and land animals. The dry season between May and September is the best time to visit the area. **Hb-Hc54**

Goiás Attractive mining town with historic european architecture – the town is a UNESCO world heritage site. **He53**

Remarkable Cities and Cultural monuments

- ▢ UNESCO World Cultural Heritage
- ▢ Remarkable Cities
- Inca culture
- Places of Christian cultural interest
- Amazonian Indians/protected area
- Historical city scape
- Castle/fortress/fort
- Festivals
- Museum

Eastern Brazil

The highlands of the  **Planalto Central** lie south of the Amazon River basin. Several tributaries of the Amazon River, including the Araguaia and Tocantins Rivers drain the western highlands of eastern Brazil. These rivers nourish huge tropical marshlands including the 300 kilometer-long **Ilha do Bananal**. These large lush tropical areas are still home to numerous Amerindian tribes. The construction of the planned capital

city – **Brasília** – brought domestic and international attention to the sparsely populated Brazilian interior. The city was completed in the 1960s and features a unique collection of 20th century architecture. Soybeans are the most important crop grown on the relatively dry savannahs in the interior. The **Serra**

Chapada Diamantina National Park boasts spectacular gorges. **Hk52**

Ilha do Bananal This large "island" is a 320-kilometer-long tropical marshland surrounded by rivers including the **Rio Araguaia**. The area is home to the Javae and Karaja Amerindians (middle photo). The northern section contains a national park, home to wood storks (bottom photo) and river dolphins. **He51**

Chapada dos Veadeiros National Park National park on a large plateau – numerous lakes, waterfalls and ponds. **Hg52/53**

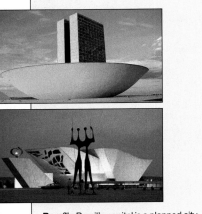

Brasília Brazil's capital is a planned city built in the 1960s. Most of the city's architecture was designed by Oscar Niemeyer, including the congress building (top photo) and Plaza of the Three Powers (bottom photo). **Hg53**

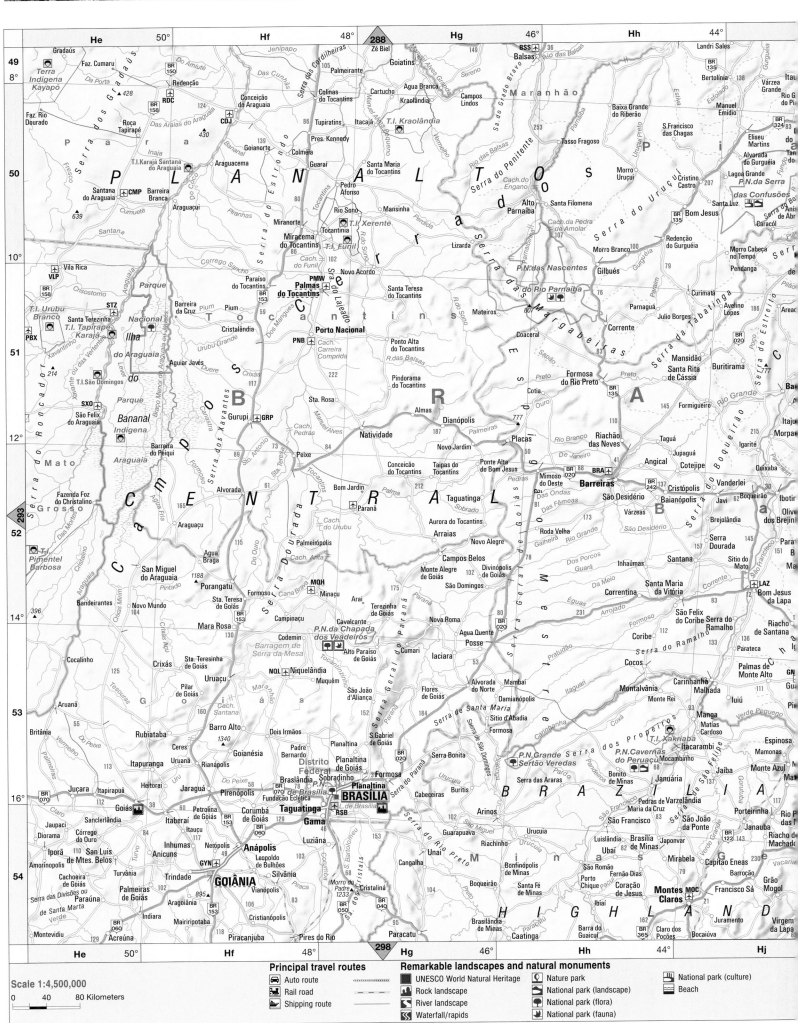

Scale 1:4,500,000

0   40   80 Kilometers

Principal travel routes
- Auto route
- Rail road
- Shipping route

Remarkable landscapes and natural monuments
- UNESCO World Natural Heritage
- Rock landscape
- River landscape
- Waterfall/rapids
- Nature park
- National park (landscape)
- National park (flora)
- National park (fauna)
- National park (culture)
- Beach

Geral do Paranã and the **Serra Geral do Goiás** mountain ranges are the sources of many rivers which flow into and feed the 3000-kilometer-long ⟨⟩ **São Francisco River**. The São Francisco River is the third largest river in Brazil and one of the most important in the northeastern region. The river was once a major transport route before ⟨⟩ dams and reservoirs made ship travel along the river impractical.

The **Barragem de Sobradinho** is a large reservoir along the São Francisco River in the Brazilian state of Bahia. The reservoir, with a total area of 4,220 km², was created after the construction of a dam built to generate electricity. **Sertão**, known as the poorhouse of Brazil, is an extremely dry region in the interior of eastern and northeastern Brazil. The Sertao gets less than 50 millimeters of rainfall annually and long droughts are common in the region. Many

of the rivers in this area dry up and disappear into the briar covered savannahs. The coastal areas of eastern Brazil get abundant rainfall and the region is one of the world's major centers of **sugarcane production**. It was sugar production that once made the northeastern coast the richest region in colonial Brazil. Millions of African slaves were brought here to work in the sugar fields and the region's culture (including the local cuisine and

religious practices) were strongly influenced by African traditions. **Cocoa farming**, concentrated near the coast, is also an important industry in the region. The Brazilian highlands contain many fascinating geological attractions – most of them formed through erosion caused by the area's many rivers. The canyons in ⟨⟩ **Chapada Diamantina** National Park feature some of the most fascinating landscapes in the region.

Serra da Capivara National Park 🏞 Nature reserve in Brazil's interior– 2,000 prehistoric 🖼 rock paintings. **Hj50**

Chapada Diamantina National Park Vast ⟨⟩ savannahs broken by tall, flat-topped mountains – 🏔 beautiful canyons – numerous 🌊 waterfalls including the 340-meterhigh Cachoeira da Fumaça. **Hk52**

Salvador da Bahia Historic ⚓ port city founded in 1549. The city has fascinating architecture. 🏛 São Francisco (bottom photo) and the other historic churches in Salvador were built during the city's golden age in the 17th and 18th centuries. The 🏛 Pelourinho district (top photo) contains many Baroque buildings and is a UNESCO world heritage site. Salvador is a major center of 🎵 Afro-Brazilian culture. **Ja52**

Ilha de Itaparica Island in the Baía de Todos os Santos (239 km²) – long 🏖 sandy beaches – picturesque village of Itaparica. **Ja52**

Ilha do Boipeba Island (293 km²) south of Salvador – undeveloped white 🏖 beaches – tropical forests. **Ja52**

Porto Seguro 🏛 Atmospheric small town on the coast with a historic town center – Passarela do Álcool promenade. **Ja54**

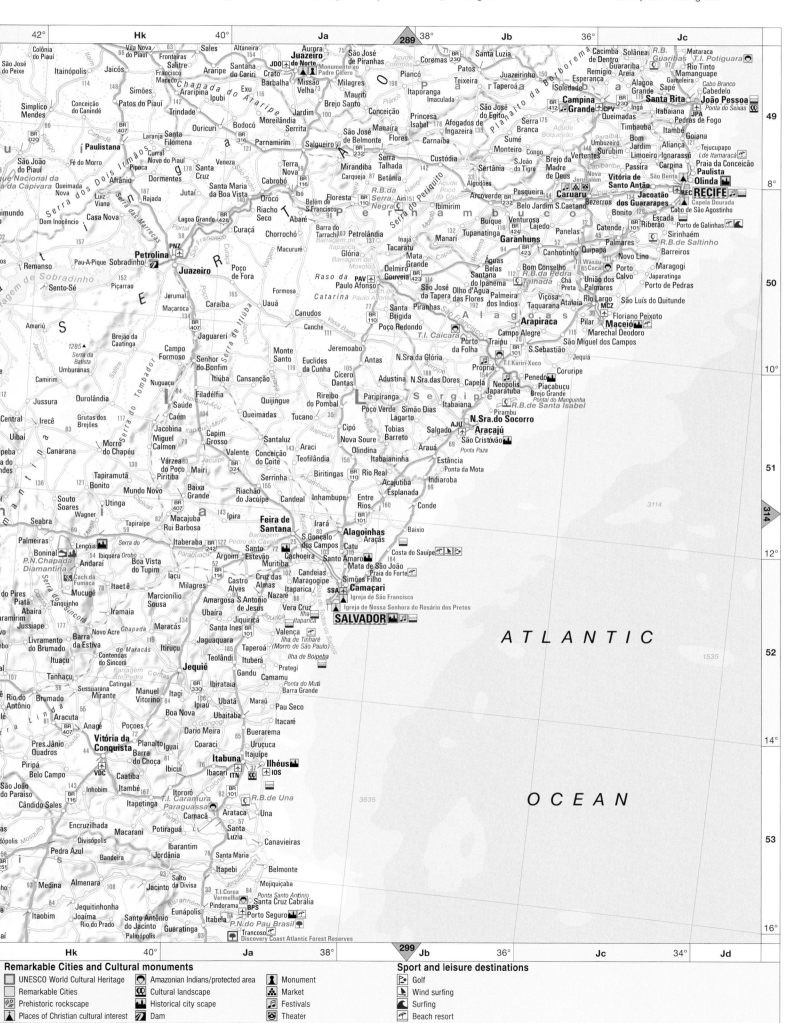

Northern Chile, Southern Bolivia, Pantanal, Gran Chaco

The ⛰ Andes Mountains, between the 17th and 24th parallels of latitude, lie in an area with a subtropical climate. The mountain range is at its widest here, stretching several hundred kilometers into the continent's interior. To the east of this section of the Andes is the ⬗ **Gran Chaco**, a vast subtropical savannah. The Gran Chaco stretches through parts of Argentina, Bolivia, Paraguay and Brazil. In this part of South America the

level of precipitation tends to decrease from east to west. The wetlands of the Pantanal and Paraguay Chaco Borreal are nourished by the waters of the large Paraguay-Parana river system. The ⬗ **Pantanal** is the largest area of wetlands in South America. During the rainy season between December and March

A row of snow-capped volcanoes near the Atacama Desert. **Gf-Gg57/58**

Iquique Port founded in 1730 – once a major export harbor for nitrates – part of Chile since 1883 – 🏛 Naval History Museum – ⬚ interesting coastline. **Ge56**

Salar de Uyuni The largest and highest ⬚ salt flat in the world – situated at a height of 5000 meters above sea level – much of the flat's surface is red due to algae – groups of flamingos. **Gf-Gg56**

Chuquicamata The world's largest ⛏ copper mine – produces five percent of global copper output – 800 meters deep. **Gf57**

The Atacama Desert The Atacama is the world's driest desert. Salar de Atacama, a large salt flat to the west of Cordillera Domeyko, covers 3000 km². Near the salt flat, the Valle de la Luna, "Valley of the moon", has strange landscapes resembling the moon's surface. Just outside of the Atacama Desert, the ⬚ El Tátio Geyser Field contains a large number of active geysers in a small area. The azure blue Lake Verde in Bolivia, located at the foot of the active volcano ⛰ Licancábur (5916 m), can be reached from the Atacama through the Jama mountain pass. Photos from top to bottom: El Tátio Geyser Field, Valle de la Luna, Salar de Atacama, Lake Verde. **Gf57/58**

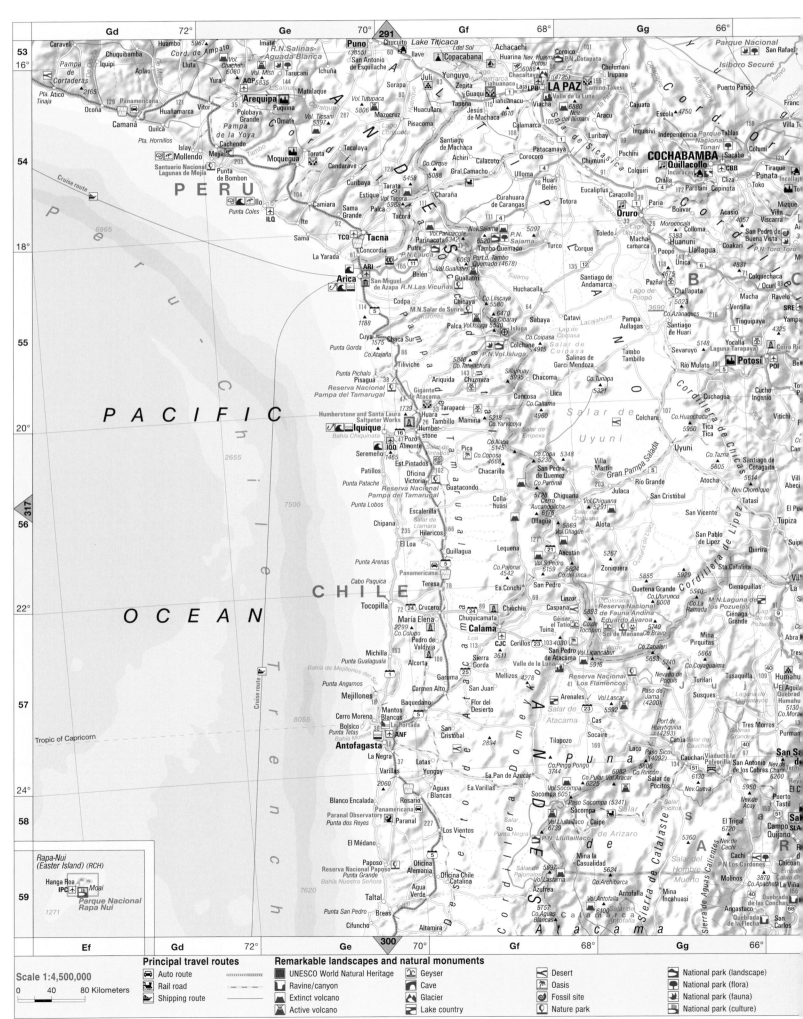

Scale 1:4,500,000

0   40   80 Kilometers

Principal travel routes
- 🚗 Auto route
- 🚂 Rail road
- ⛴ Shipping route
- ········ Ravine/canyon
- ——— Extinct volcano
- ——— Active volcano

Remarkable landscapes and natural monuments
- ⬛ UNESCO World Natural Heritage
- Geyser
- Cave
- Glacier
- Lake country
- Desert
- Oasis
- Fossil site
- Nature park
- National park (landscape)
- National park (flora)
- National park (fauna)
- National park (culture)

much of the region lies under a shallow layer of water. The unique plant and animal life in the Pantanal is threatened by increased tourism and agriculture.

The Andes Mountains increase significantly in width south of Lake Titicaca. A chain of narrow mountains covered by dense mountain rain forest rises along the eastern edges of the Gran Chaco. The 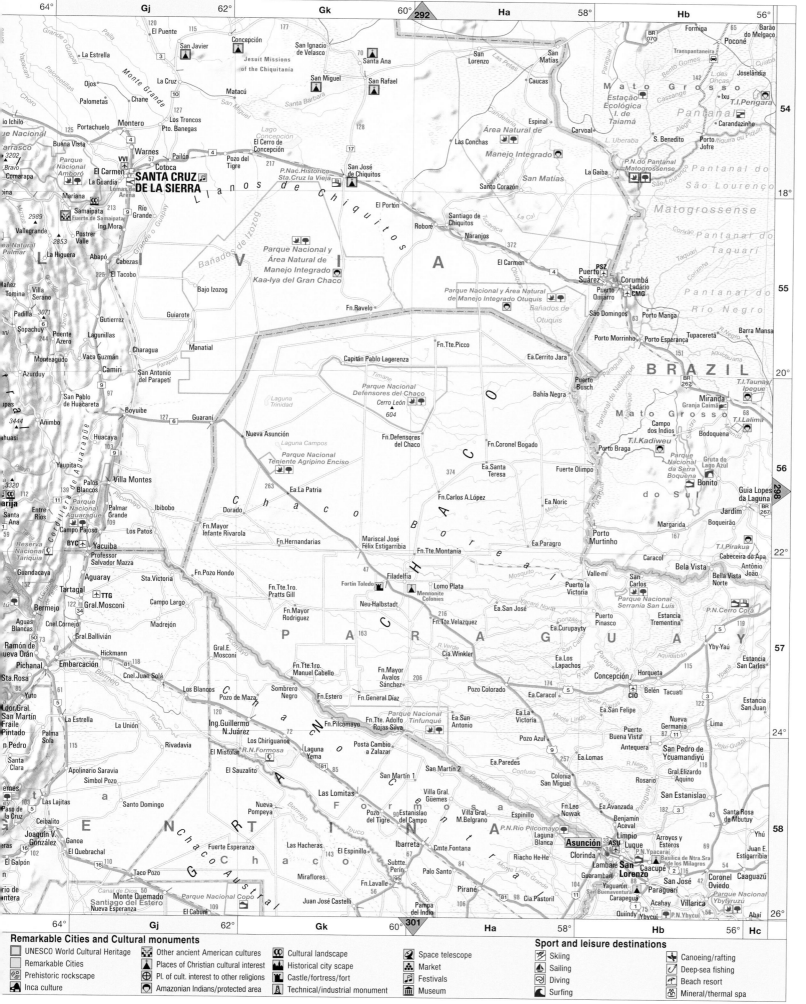 **Yungas** in southern Bolivia is a region of highland rainforests between

the Andes and the Amazon Basin. This transition zone is home to dense rainforests and mountainous vegetation. The watershed or divide between the Amazon and Paraguay river basins runs along the 18th parallel of latitude.

In the center of the Andes mountain range in southern Bolivia lies the **Altiplano**, a large plateau high above sea level. The Puna – the section of the Altiplano in Argentina and Chile – has unique flora

and fauna. This part of South America contains many large ⊠ **salt flats** (salares) scattered throughout the drier section of the Andes. Llamas, vicunas, and alpacas are among the many unique endemic animal species found in the Andes.

The largest plateau in the Andes begins near the 27th parallel of latitude in the Cordillera Domeyko range and stretches to an area of the Cordillera Oriental range just south of La Paz. Salar de Atacama

and Salar de Uyuni are the most fascinating of the many salt lakes in this region. The Salar de Uyuni is the remnant of a prehistoric lake that once covered most of southern Bolivia. Salar de Uyuni, which is dry during most of the year, is also the world's largest and highest salt flat. Numerous ⊠ active volcanoes and ⊠ geysers are among the many other natural attractions in this fascinating region of South America.

Tiwanaku (Tiahuanaco) Once the center of a large pre-Columbian ⊠ Amerindian empire – the historic site now encompasses the remnants of four ancient temples and pyramids – Puerto del Sol (photo). **Gf54**

La Paz The highest major city in the world located between 3,300 and 4,000 meters above sea level – founded in 1548 – ⊠ historic city center with ⊠ marketplace. **Gf54**

Altiplano Large plateau region in the Andes – most of the local Amerindians have retained many of their traditions – interesting villages and markets. **Gf-Gg54-56**

Sucre Capital of Bolivia – ⊠ historic old town with colonial architecture – ⊠ cathedral built in the 17th century – UNESCO world heritage site. **Gh55**

Potosí Historic mining town – ⊠ Casa Nacional de la Moneda: coin minting museum – UNESCO world heritage site. **Gh55**

Cordillera de Sama ⊠ Conservation area in Altiplano (108.5 km²) – fascinating valley – contains four large lakes. **Gh56**

Quebrada de Humahuaca 130-kilometer-long ⊔ gorge in Argentina – the Río Grande flows through the gorge – the gorge is surrounded by high stone walls. **Gh57**

Remarkable Cities and Cultural monuments

☐ UNESCO World Cultural Heritage	⊠ Other ancient American cultures	⊠ Cultural landscape	**Sport and leisure destinations**		
☐ Remarkable Cities	⊠ Places of Christian cultural interest	⊠ Historical city scape	⊠ Space telescope	⊠ Skiing	⊠ Canoeing/rafting
☐ Prehistoric rockscape	⊕ Pl. of cult. interest to other religions	⊠ Castle/fortress/fort	⊠ Market	⊠ Sailing	⊠ Deep-sea fishing
☐ Inca culture	⊠ Amazonian Indians/protected area	⊠ Technical/industrial monument	⊠ Festivals	⊠ Diving	⊠ Beach resort
			⊞ Museum	⊠ Surfing	⊠ Mineral/thermal spa

Southeastern Brazil

Southeastern Brazil is the wealthiest and most heavily populated region in the country. The Southeast is home to almost half of the country's population as well as Brazil's two largest cities – **São Paulo** and **Rio de Janeiro**. A series of coastal mountain ranges, including the ☐ **Serra da Mantiqueira**, stretch along the southeastern coast. The region also features many tall and striking stone formations such as Rio's famous **Sugar-**

loaf. These stone formations are the remnants of ancient volcanoes.

Away from the coast, the land in the Southeast declines in elevation. Only a few rivers flow through the valleys in the coastal mountains. The region's interior contains several powerful rivers many of which flow through the **Brazilian Highlands** into the

The Sugarloaf and Corcovado: the most famous of Rio's many hills. **Hj57**

Tingua Nature Reserve ☐ Nature reserve in Rio de Janeiro state – extensive virgin tropical forests. **Hj57**

Serra do Mar Coastal mountain range near Rio – popular weekend destination for city residents – tropical forests. **Hh57**

Parati ☐ City with historic architecture – ☐ Santa Rita de Cássia – ☐ Museum de Arte Sacra (religious artwork). **Hh57**

São Paulo The largest city and economic center in Brazil – metro population of at least 20 million – ☐ São Paulo Museum of Art – ☐ Teatro Municipal: historic opera house. **Hg57**

Atlantic Forest Southeast Reserves A group of 25 separate nature reserves protecting virgin tropical forests. **Hg58**

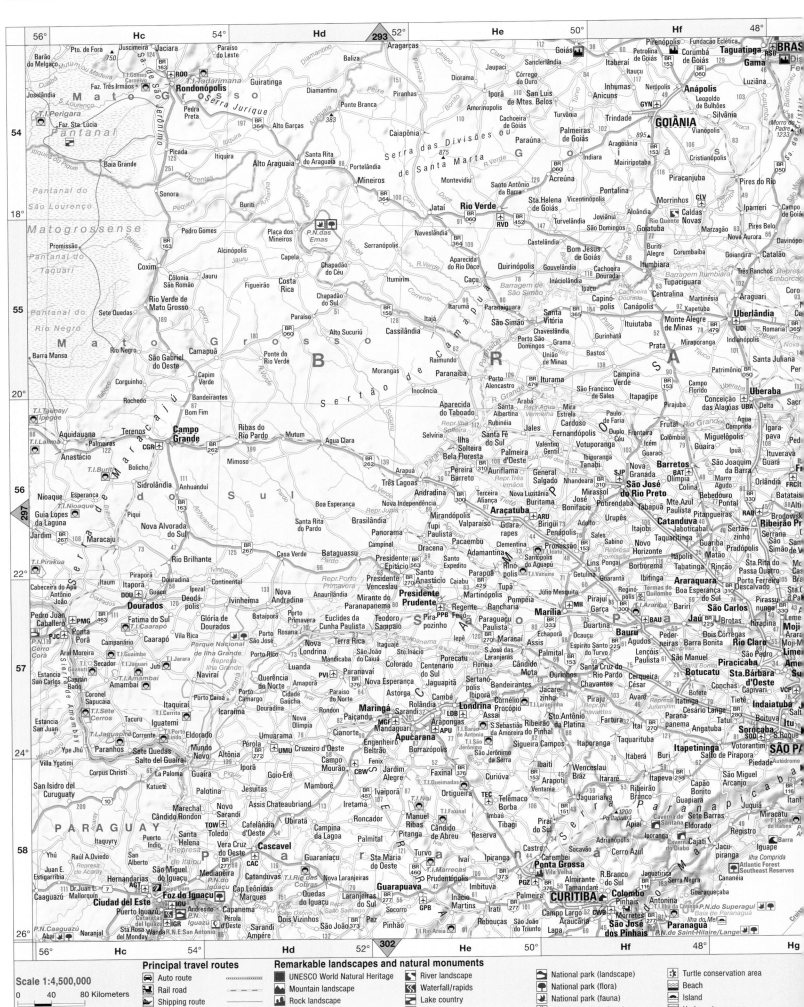

Principal travel routes

Scale 1:4,500,000

0   40   80 Kilometers

🚗 Auto route
🚂 Rail road
⚓ Shipping route

Remarkable landscapes and natural monuments

━━━ River landscape
☐ UNESCO World Natural Heritage
☐ Mountain landscape
☐ Rock landscape
☐ Cave
🔊 Waterfall/rapids
☐ Lake country
☐ Nature park

☐ National park (landscape)
☐ National park (flora)
☐ National park (fauna)
☐ National park (culture)

☑ Turtle conservation area
☐ Beach
☐ Island
☐ Underwater reserve

Paraná and Paranaíba Rivers. The Rio Iguaçú begins in the mountains of southern Brazil. Along its course the river flows over an 80-meter-high escapement creating the most beautiful waterfalls in the country. **Iguaçú Falls** – along the border between Argentina and Brazil – are a crescent shaped series of 275 separate falls over two kilometers in length.

The Pantanal, a large marshland covering 230,000 km², is located to the west of the **Mato Grosso** region with its vast grasslands. The **Pantanal**, one of the world's largest wetlands, is home to unique flora and fauna. The region's delicate ecosystems are increasingly threatened by agriculture and tourism.

The vast grasslands of the Mato Grosso are used mostly for livestock grazing. The highlands of southeastern Brazil are major centers for **coffee production**. Coffee farming is concentrated primarily in the area's moist river valleys. In recent decades, sheep farming and other agricultural activities have reduced the highlands' once-total dependence on coffee crops. The state of **Minas Gerais**, with an area the size of France, boasts many of Brazil's most impressive historic buildings. This beautiful architecture is a legacy of the region's history as an important and wealthy mining center during the colonial era. Diamonds, gold, and iron are just a few of the mineral resources that have been mined in the state. Even today, the state produces over 90 % of the precious stones mined in Brazil. The name Minas Gerais means "general mines" in Portuguese and reflects the state's historic connections to natural resources. The state's highest mountain, Pico da Bandeira, rises 2,890 meters above sea level.

Bom Jesus de Matosinhos Sanctuary
Baroque pilgrimage church – UNESCO world heritage site. Hj56

Ouro Preto City with numerous Baroque buildings including São Francisco de Assis church. Ouro Preto was once a mining center. Hj56

Serra dos Orgãos National Park The second oldest national park in Brazil – lush tropical vegetation. Hj57

Rio de Janeiro The city, with a population of twelve million, is famous for its beaches, breathtaking natural setting and Carnival. There are several mountains in the city. Hj57

Remarkable Cities and Cultural monuments

- UNESCO World Cultural Heritage
- Remarkable Cities
- Places of Christian cultural interest
- Amazonian Indians/protected area
- Historical city scape
- Dam
- Festivals
- Museum

Sport and leisure destinations

- Arena/stadium
- Race track
- Horse racing
- Diving
- Wind surfing
- Surfing
- Beach resort
- Mineral/thermal spa

North Central Chile, Central Argentina, Uruguay

The section of South America between the 26th and 35th parallels of latitude exhibits a remarkable variety of landscapes and climates. The western part of the region is dominated by the ■ **Andes Mountains**. The **South American continental shield**, which encompasses the Brazilian and Guiana highlands, is located to the north and northeast of this area. Between the Brazilian highlands and Chile lies a series of vast flat plains

comprising two distinct regions: the **Pampas** in Argentina and the **Gran Chaco** in both Paraguay and Argentina. **Uruguay** consists mostly of rolling hills and low-lying coastal plains. Uruguay's principal rivers are the ☰ **Rio Uruguay** – along the border to Argentina – and the ☰ **Río Negro**.

Fascinating sandstone formations in Talampaya National Park **Gf-Gg60/61**

La Silla One of three large ☑ observatories in the Andes south of La Serena – twelve large telescopes. **Ge60**

La Serena The second oldest city in Chile, founded in 1544 – ☐ seaside town with beaches – historic and modern architecture – the ☐ lighthouse is a city landmark. **Ge60**

Valparaíso Chile's largest coastal city – the lower city features the harbor and a historic marketplace – funiculars connect the lower and upper city – ☐ Museo a Cielo Abierto, modern art museum. **Ge62**

Aconcagua South America's tallest ☐ mountain (6963 m) – ☐ Jesus statue on the Argentinean side of the mountain. **Ge62**

Puente del Inca Natural bridge in western Argentina – 28 meters wide and 20 meters above the Rio Mendoza – created by mineral deposits from a natural spring. **Gf62**

Santiago de Chile Capital of Chile (established in 1541) – population of five million – historic buildings including ☐ San Francisco around Cerro Santa Lucia and Cerro San Cristobal – ☐ Museo de Arte Precolombino (pre-Columbian art) – artist district Bellavista. **Ge62**

Mendoza Modern city in Argentina – ☐ Wine Museum – several wine cellars open to the public – Casa Giol (photo). **Gf62**

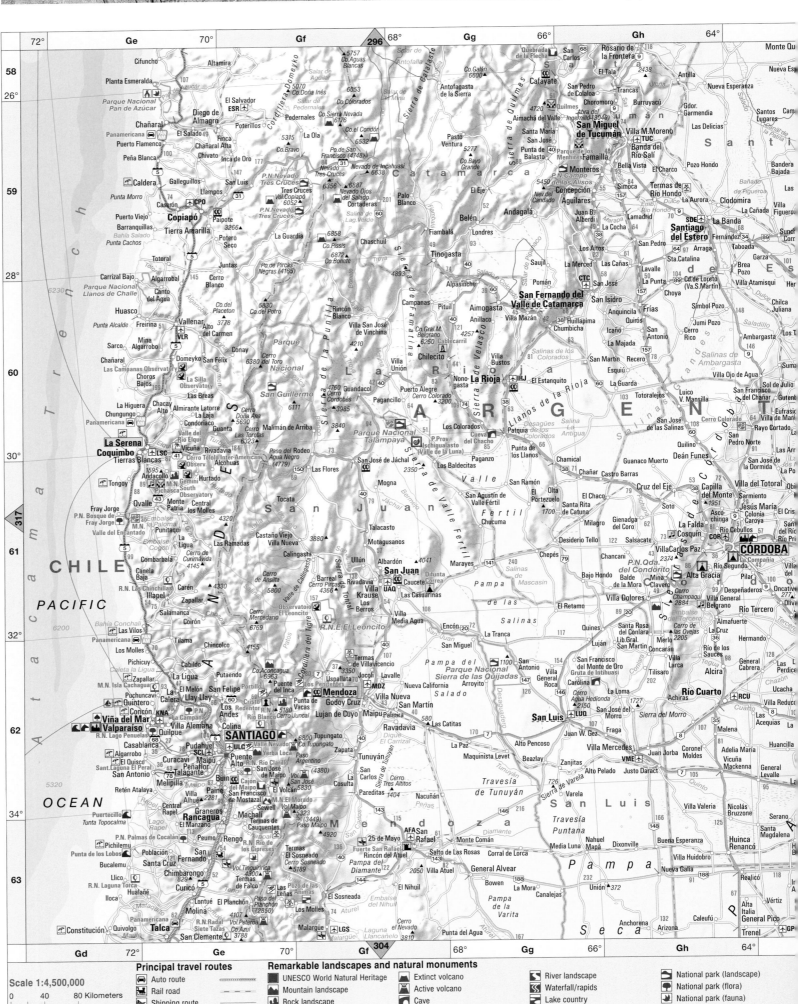

Principal travel routes

Scale 1:4,500,000

0   40   80 Kilometers

- 🚗 Auto route
- 🚂 Rail road
- ⚓ Shipping route

Remarkable landscapes and natural monuments

- ◻ UNESCO World Natural Heritage
- ◻ Mountain landscape
- ◻ Rock landscape
- ◻ Ravine/canyon
- ▲ Extinct volcano
- ▲ Active volcano
- ◻ Cave
- ◻ Glacier
- ◻ River landscape
- ◻ Waterfall/rapids
- ◻ Lake country
- ◻ Oasis
- ◻ National park (landscape)
- ◻ National park (flora)
- ◻ National park (fauna)
- ◻ National park (culture)

The 🚢 **Río de la Plata** is an estuary between southern Uruguay and northern Argentina. The estuary ranges between 48 and 200 kilometers in width before it flows into the Atlantic Ocean. West of Montevideo, the Rio de la Plata is a freshwater body – the section of the estuary east of the city contains salt-water.
The Pampas in Argentina is one of the world's most important centers for grain production. Livestock ranching is the most important industry in the semi-arid Gran Chaco region. Argentina's Mendoza Province and Chile's 🏞 **Central Valley (Valle Central)** both have subtropical climates. The two regions are also the leading centers for wine production in South America.
The ⛰ **Andes Mountains** stretch the entire length of Chile. South of Chile's capital city Santiago, the Andes are divided into a coastal and interior range separated from one another by the fertile Central Valley. The interior range in this section of the Andes features **Aconcagua**, South America's highest mountain. Aconcagua rises 6963 meters above sea level and is surrounded by a large national park containing numerous glaciers and pristine mountain lakes.
The northern edges of central Chile consist of arid and semi-arid areas. Most of central Chile however has a pleasant Mediterranean climate and fertile soil. The warmer sections of central Chile are the most densely populated areas of the country and contain its two largest cities: Valparaiso and Santaigo de Chile. Santiago de Chile, the capital city of Chile, is a modern urban area with scattered historic buildings, tall skyscrapers, and a population around five million inhabitants.

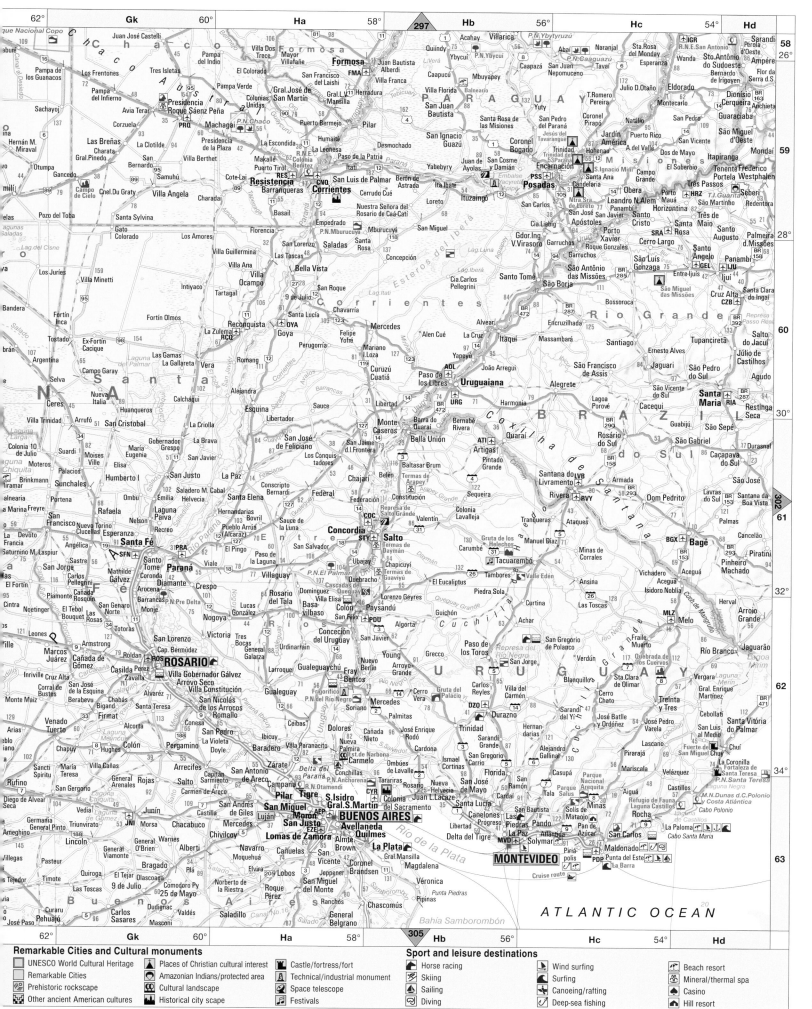

Los Menhires Park Open air museum containing 129 ancient 🗿 stone monoliths (4th to 9th centuries) – located in Argentina's Tafí del Valle. **Gh59**

Talampaya National Park 🏞 National park containing large sandstone formations – UNESCO world natural heritage site – 🖼 pre-Columbian rock paintings. **Gf-Gg60/61**

Córdoba Second largest city in Argentina – population 1.2 million – location of a major university – 🏛 historic Baroque Iglesia Compañía de Jesús church – ⛪ cathedral and city hall on the Plaza San Martín. **Gh61**

Buenos Aires The largest city and capital of Argentina was founded in 1536. Buenos Aires and its suburbs are home to 12 million people, one third of Argentina's population. The sophisticated and cosmopolitan city is famous as the birthplace of tango. 🏛 La Boca is a colorful and lively neighborhood near the city's harbor. Photos from top to bottom: La Boca district, tango dancers, Plaza de la Republica. **Ha63**

Montevideo Capital of Uruguay – important 🚢 port city – population: 1.3 million – 🏖 popular sandy beaches – Parliament building (photo). **Hb63**

Remarkable Cities and Cultural monuments

- ⬜ UNESCO World Cultural Heritage
- ◻ Remarkable Cities
- ◼ Prehistoric rockscape
- ◻ Other ancient American cultures
- 🔺 Places of Christian cultural interest
- 🔺 Amazonian Indians/protected area
- 🔺 Cultural landscape
- 🔺 Historical city scape
- 🏰 Castle/fortress/fort
- 🏭 Technical/industrial monument
- 📡 Space telescope
- 🎵 Festivals

Sport and leisure destinations

- 🐎 Horse racing
- ⛷ Skiing
- ⛵ Sailing
- 🤿 Diving
- 🏄 Wind surfing
- 🏄 Surfing
- 🛶 Canoeing/rafting
- 🎣 Deep-sea fishing
- 🏖 Beach resort
- ♨ Mineral/thermal spa
- 🎰 Casino
- ⛰ Hill resort

Southern Brazil, Southern Paraguay

From Salvador in the north to Porto Allegre, a continuous series of plateaus and uplands run parallel to the **Brazilian** coast. These elevations were created millions of years ago when South America separated from the prehistoric supercontinent Gondwanaland. This region features numerous fertile valleys, unusual stone formations, and beautiful green mountains. Large remnants of the virgin tropical forest that once covered most of coastal

Brazil can be found in the ⬛ **Atlantic Forest Southeast Reserves**. This group of 25 nature reserves covers an area around 4,700 km² large.
The few rivers in the region that flow eastward are relatively short. Most of the rivers in the region flow westward into the ⬛ Uruguay, Paraná, or São Fran-

Iguaçu Falls: a conglomerate of more than 270 separate waterfalls. Hc58

Asunción Capital city of Paraguay – population 1.2 million – Panteón Nacional de los Héroes (photo). Hb58

Itaipu Dam 7,700-meter-long ⬛ dam – part of the world's largest ⬛ hydroelectric power facility – 20 generators. Hc58

Iguaçu National Park The national park around the spectacular 🔲 Iguaçu Falls (up tp 6,500 km³ water daily) is a UNESCO world heritage site. Hc58

Jesuit-Guarani Missions More than ⬛ 30 historic missions along the Paraná River. The 18th-century buildings once housed Jesuit missionaries and converted Amerindians. Hc59

Esteros del Iberá Large marshland and savannah region – unique plants – more than 300 bird species. Hb59/60

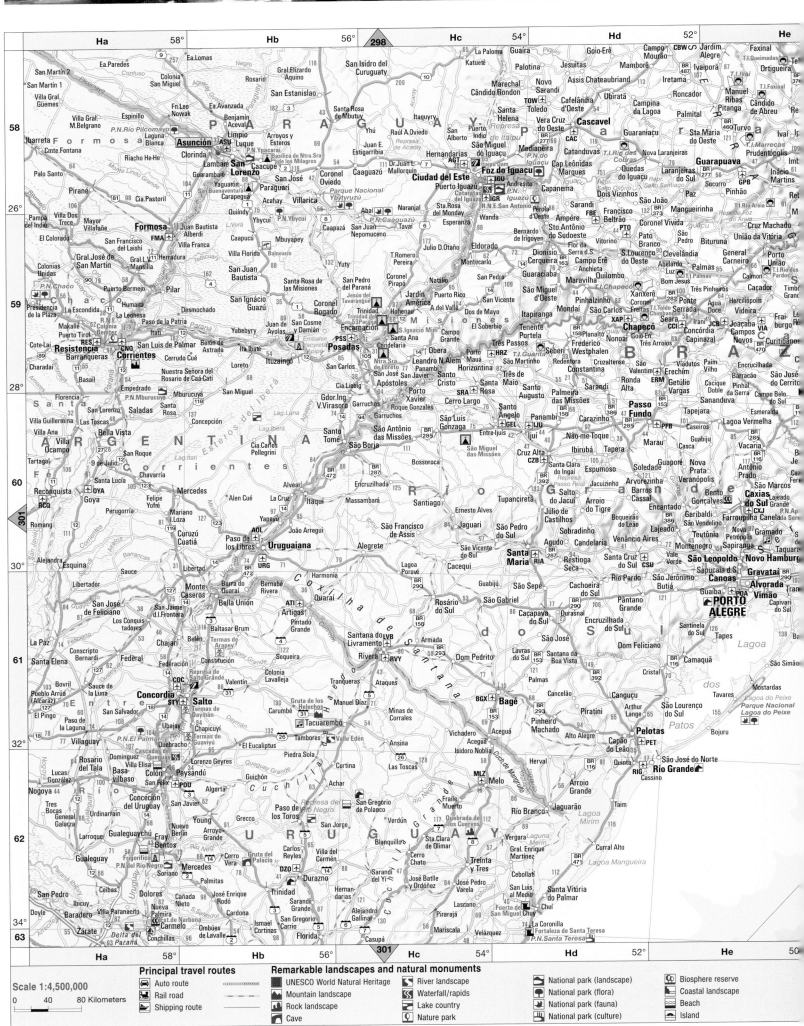

Scale 1:4,500,000
0   40   80 Kilometers

Principal travel routes
- Auto route
- Rail road
- Shipping route

Remarkable landscapes and natural monuments
- UNESCO World Natural Heritage
- Mountain landscape
- Rock landscape
- Cave
- River landscape
- Waterfall/rapids
- Lake country
- Nature park
- National park (landscape)
- National park (flora)
- National park (fauna)
- National park (culture)
- Biosphere reserve
- Coastal landscape
- Beach
- Island

Southern Brazil, Southern Paraguay

cisco River. The **Iguaçu River** flows over an 80 meter high drop on its way to merge with the Parana River. Over centuries the river's eroding forces formed one of the greatest natural attractions in South America. The ◼ **Iguaçu Falls** are a group of 275 separate waterfalls stretched out over two kilometers. The ◼ subtropical forests of southern Brazil are home to many interesting animals including tapirs and rare bird species.

The **Esteros del Iberá** is a large marshland with abundant wildlife, located between the Uruguay and Paraná Rivers. There are several large lagoons along the coast of southern Brazil including the **Lagoa dos Patos**.
The mild subtropical climate and fertile soil of southern **Brazil** and southern **Paraguay** attracted millions of European immigrants to the region. The influence of German, Italian, and other Euro-

pean settlers is still evident in the region's culture and tradtions. Every year, the residents of Blumenau in Brazil celebrate the largest German style Oktoberfest in Latin America. Due to careful urban planning, Curitiba (the state capital of Paraná), is generally considered the most livable urban area in Brazil. The **Planalto Meridional** is an area of hills and evergreen forests stretching from southern Brazil into Uruguay. Many

of the rainforests in southern Brazil, including those around the Iguaçu Falls and east of Curitiba, are protected by conservation laws.
The ◼ **Serra Geral** and **Serra Gaúcha** ranges around Porto Alegre contain temperate vegetation. The area features many vineyards and is an important center for wine production. This is also one of the few places in Brazil where snow falls during winter.

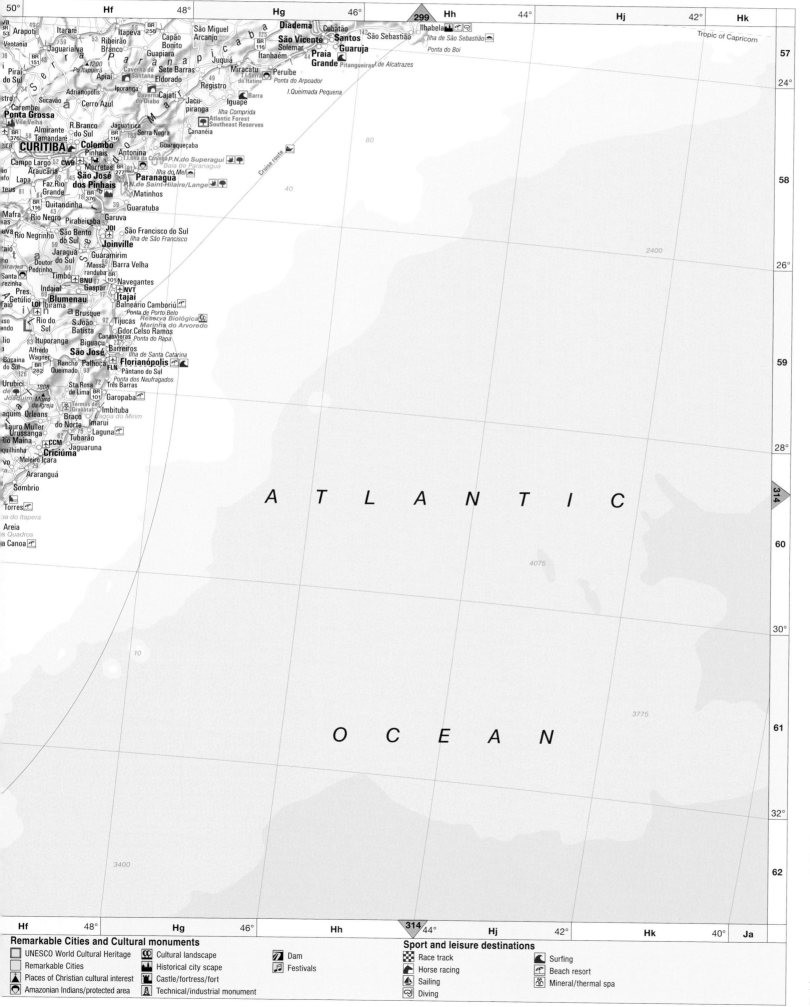

Atlantic Forest Southeast Reserves A group of 25 ◼ nature reserves containing virgin tropical forests. **Hg58**

Curitiba One of Brazil's most "livable" cities – excellent public transport system – several parks – ◼ Ópera de Arame. **Hf58**

Train Route Curitiba-Paranagua ◼ Train route passing through the Serra do Mar – built between 1880 and 1885 – 110-kilometer-long route with beautiful views. **Hf58**

Blumenau Brazilian city founded by German immigrants – numerous ◼ half-timbered buildings – ◼ Oktoberfest. **Hf59**

Florianópolis The state capital of Santa Catarina – part of the city is on an island – ◼ Ponte Hercílio Luz suspension bridge, built in the 1920s. **Hf59**

Porto Alegre Large city in Southern Brazil – German and Italian cultural influences – ◼ São Pedro Theatre – ◼ Mercado Público market – ◼ historic cathedral. **He61**

Aparados da Serra National Park Contains the seven-kilometer-long ◼ Itaimbezinho gorge – two ◼ waterfalls. **He60**

Remarkable Cities and Cultural monuments

- ◻ UNESCO World Cultural Heritage
- ◻ Remarkable Cities
- ◻ Places of Christian cultural interest
- ◻ Amazonian Indians/protected area
- ◻ Cultural landscape
- ◻ Historical city scape
- ◻ Castle/fortress/fort
- ◻ Technical/industrial monument
- ◻ Dam
- ◻ Festivals

Sport and leisure destinations

- ◻ Race track
- ◻ Horse racing
- ◻ Sailing
- ◻ Diving
- ◻ Surfing
- ◻ Beach resort
- ◻ Mineral/thermal spa

South Central Chile, Pampas

The section of South America below the 36th parallel of latitude tends to rise in elevation from east to west. The Andes Mountains in the west include numerous volcanoes and are separated from the Pacific Ocean by a narrow coastal strip of land. The border between Chile and Argentina runs through the Andes in this region. South America features many of the world's tallest active volcanoes. The volcanism in the Andes is the result of col-

lisions between three tectonic plates of the Earth's crust; the Nazca, Antarctic, and South American plates. Tectonic activity was also responsible for the creation of the 7,500 meter deep **Peru-Chile Trench** situated off the western coast of South America in the Pacific Ocean. The 38th parallel of latitude marks the geo-

Villarrica (2,847 m): one of many beautiful active volcanos in Chile. **Gd65**

Villarrica National Park Located on the southern edge of a large lake, the park ⬛ includes the volcanoes ▲ Villarrica (2,847 m), Quetrupillán and some parts of Lanín. **Ge65**

Lanín National Park The volcano ▲ Lanín (3,747 m) is situated in the center of this Argentinean ⬛ national park – popular destination for mountain climbers. **Ge65**

Chile's Lake District Scenic region in the Chilean Andes. The volcano ▲ Osomo (top photo) and ⬛ Lago Llanquihue (bottom photo) are two of the many stunning natural attractions in this area north of Puerto Montt. **Gd66**

Isla Grande de Chiloé Large ⬛ island off the coast of Patagonia – around 160 ⬛ churches (Gothic and Baroque wooden buildings) – Castro Cathedral (photo) – UNESCO world heritage site. **Gd67**

Corcovado Active volcano (2,300 m) next to the Gulf of Corcovado – several lakes in the surrounding area. **Gd67**

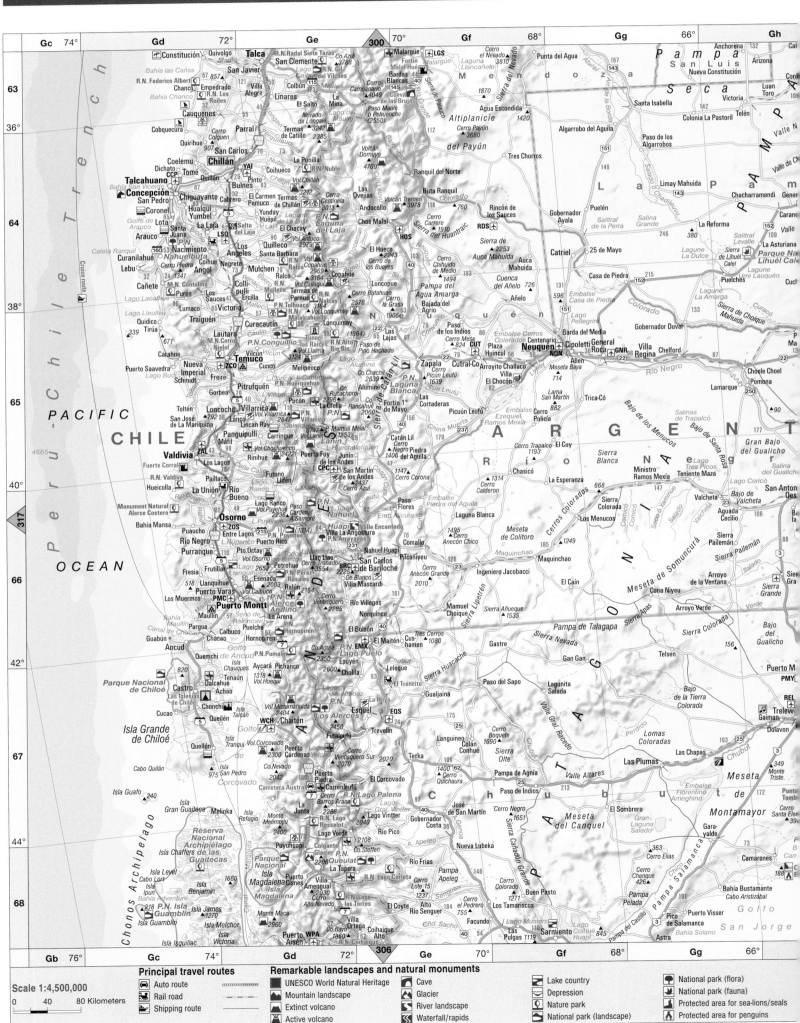

Principal travel routes

- 🚗 Auto route
- 🚂 Rail road
- ⚓ Shipping route
- ······· Cruise route

Scale 1:4,500,000

0   40   80 Kilometers

Remarkable landscapes and natural monuments

- ⬛ UNESCO World Natural Heritage
- ⬛ Mountain landscape
- ▲ Extinct volcano
- ▲ Active volcano
- ⬛ River landscape
- ⬛ Waterfall/rapids
- ⬛ Cave
- ⬛ Glacier
- ⬛ Lake country
- ⬛ Depression
- ⬛ Nature park
- ⬛ National park (landscape)
- ⬛ National park (flora)
- ⬛ National park (fauna)
- ⬛ Protected area for sea-lions/seals
- ⬛ Protected area for penguins

graphic border between two distinct sections of the Andes: the Central and **⬛ Southern Cordilleras**. The Southern Cordilleras extend through Patagonia and onto the island Tierra del Fuego. The range decreases in elevation from north to south.

A large number of mountain lakes and large ⬛ glaciers are scattered throughout the Southern Cordilleras. During the ice ages, gigantic glaciers created large val-

leys and unique stone formations throughout the Andes Mountains. At the end of the last ice age, water released from melting glaciers caused the sea level around the region to rise. The many ⬛ **fjords** along the southwestern coast of South America were created when mountainous inland areas were partially submerged by the rising ocean. Ice age glaciers also formed many new bodies of water in the Andes. Several areas in the

region, including the ⬛ **Chilean Lake District**, have an incredible concentration of beautiful lakes.

Ancient layers of stone are located beneath the surface of Patagonia and the Pampas in Argentina. The vast prairies of the Pampas are used primarily for grain cultivation and to a lesser extent for livestock ranching. Patagonia, the most sparsely populated section of Argentina, has a cool and dry climate. Sheep herd-

ing and mining are the most important sectors of Patagonia's economy. The Andes and the Chilean coast in this region are covered by thick evergreen forests. Many fascinating animals inhabit the eastern coast of Argentina. Punta Tombo is home to large penguin colonies and the ⬛ **Valdés Peninsula** has the largest sea elephant population in Argentina. Whale watching season in the region is between July and December.

Cerro Payún High inactive ⬛ volcano (3,680 m) – large elliptical main crater (8 x 10 km), several smaller craters and up to ten-kilometer-long fields of lava.　　**Gf64**

Laguna Blanca National Park This national park in the eastern Andes has several mountain ⬛ lakes – created for the protection of rare black-necked swans.　　**Ge65**

Nahuel Huapi National Park National park in ⬛ mountainous western Argentina – tallest mountain Cerro Tronador (3,554 m) – 100-kilometer-long glacial lake.　　**Ge66**

Mar del Plata Popular ⬛ holiday destination on Argentina's Atlantic coast – many visitors in summer – ⬛ large casino.　　**Hb65**

Valdés Península The peninsula on Argentina's Atlantic coast is home to an abundance of ⬛ wildlife. The cliffs at ⬛ Punta Delgada and ⬛ Punta Norte are inhabited by large sea elephant populations. ⬛ Caleta Valdés has the area's largest population of sea lions (bottom photo). Whale watching season in the area is between July and December.　　**Gj67**

Cabo dos Bahías This remote coastal area is home to a large colony of Magellan penguins (photo).　　**Gh68**

Remarkable Cities and Cultural monuments

☐ UNESCO World Cultural Heritage	⬛ Castle/fortress/fort	⬛ Dam
☐ Remarkable Cities	⬛ Technical/industrial monument	
☐ Places of Christian cultural interest	⬛ Market	
☐ Historical city scape	⬛ Festivals	

Sport and leisure destinations

⬛ Race track	⬛ Diving	⬛ Deep-sea fishing
⬛ Golf	⬛ Wind surfing	⬛ Beach resort
⬛ Horse racing	⬛ Surfing	⬛ Mineral/thermal spa
⬛ Skiing	⬛ Canoeing/rafting	⬛ Casino

Southern Chile, Patagonia, Falkland Islands

South America stretches south to just below the 55th parallel of latitude. While the areas along the 55th parallel of latitude in the northern hemisphere are covered by ice sheets and tundras, the southern tip of South America has a cool but temperate climate with abundant precipitation. The southernmost regions of the continent are frequently swept by powerful storms in the Pacific Ocean. Constant storms and strong winds make

the area off of the coast one of the world's most dangerous ship passages.
In the mountains of the 🖼 Peruvian Andes snow begins to fall at elevations between 4,900 and 5,300 meters above sea level. In central Chile, the so-called snow line begins at elevations around 2,000 meters. In Chile's far south, the snow line is

Torres del Paine: spectacular land-scapes in the southern Andes. **Gd71**

J. Ormachea Petrified Forest Argentinean 🍃 petrified forest with 70-million-year old remnants of tall trees that were once up to 100 meters high. **Gf68**

Laguna San Rafael National Park Large 🍃 nature reserve (1.74 ha) in Chile with the 45-kilometer-long 🏔 San Rafael Glacier – icebergs and fjords. **Gc-Gd69**

Río Baker Valley Partially forested 🏞 canyons between northern and southern icefields in Chile – turquoise blue 🏞 river – good fishing area. **Gd69**

Cueva de las Manos The isolated 🏞 canyons along the Rio Pinturas (top photo) featuring caves with 10,000-year-old 🖼 paintings. These caves are a UNESCO world heritage site. The cave paintings show handprints in different colors (bottom photo). **Ge69**

Los Glaciares National Park Beautiful 🍃 national park and UNESCO world heritage site between Lago Viedma and Lago Argentino. The park has many peaks including 🏔 Mount Fitz Roy (top photo). The 🏔 Perito Moreno Glacier (bottom photo) flows into Lago Argentino. **Gd70/71**

Scale 1:4,500,000
0   40   80 Kilometers

Principal travel routes
- Auto route
- Rail road
- Shipping route

Remarkable landscapes and natural monuments
- UNESCO World Natural Heritage
- Mountain landscape
- Rock landscape
- Extinct volcano
- Active volcano
- Cave
- Glacier
- Lake country
- Fossil site
- Nature park
- National park (landscape)
- National park (fauna)
- Biosphere reserve
- Whale watching
- Protected area for penguins
- Coastal landscape

located a mere 700 meters above sea level. Large evergreen trees flourish along Chile's southwestern coast, an area with abundant rainfall. The western sections of the southern Andes exhibit sparse moorland vegetation. The easternmost sections of the southern Andes – in Argentina – feature vast temperate forests and alpine vegetation. This area is often called ⛰ **Argentina's Switzerland** and also has many large mountain

lakes including ⚐ **Lago Argentino** at the foot of the Andes. The southern tip of South America comprises numerous bays, peninsulas, and lakes. The archipelago ⛰ **Tierra del Fuego** is the southernmost region of South America. The archipelago consists of countless tiny islets, five smaller islands, and one large island also called Tierra del Fuego. In 1520, Ferdinand Magellan became the first European to visit the archipelago.

During the 19th century, the discovery of gold attracted a large number of migrants to the region. Tierra del Fuego is now a sparsely populated region divided between Argentina and Chile.
Ushuaia in Argentina is the southernmost city in the world. The city lies on the **Beagle Channel**, which was named after the famous ship that Charles Darwin sailed with to South America. West of Ushuaia lies a mountain range named

after Darwin himself, the Cordillera Darwin. ⛰ Southern Patagonia is a land of fire and ice. Patatgonia features both active volcanoes, including Mount Viedma (1,305 m), as well as numerous large glaciers. The 🏝 **Falkland Islands**, known as **Islas Malvinas** in Spanish, are a British overseas territory off the southeastern coast of South America. The Falklands are home to large penguin colonies and at least 60 bird species.

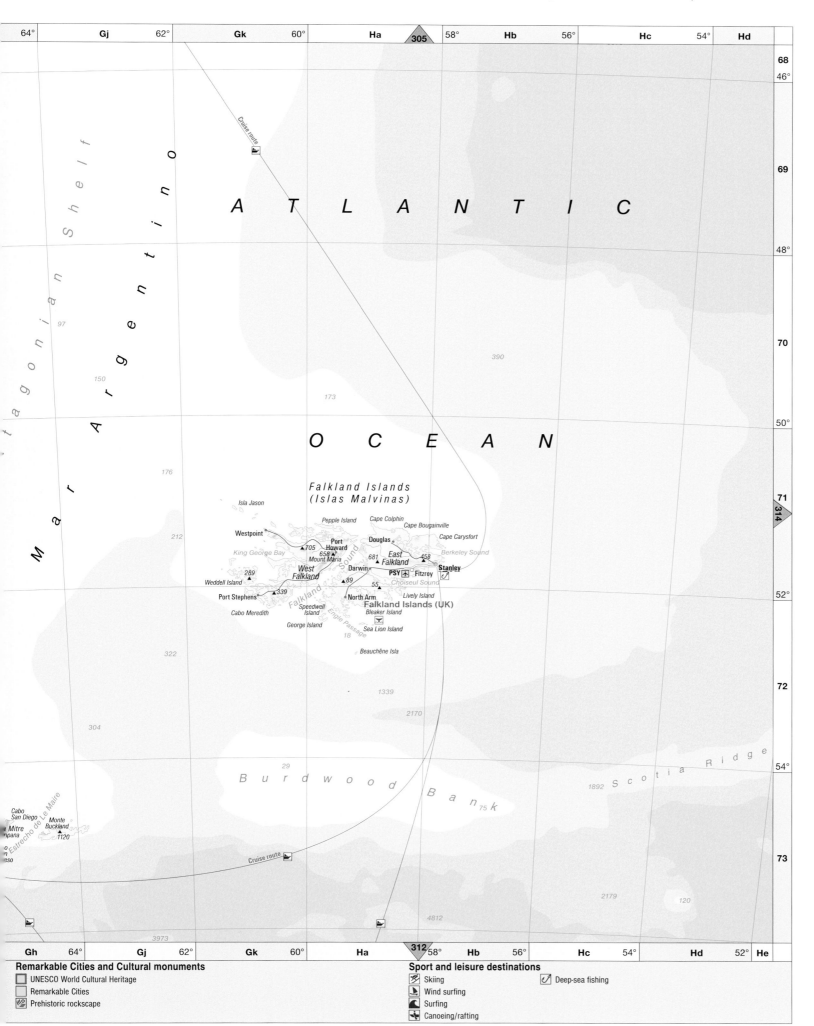

Torres del Paine National Park Chilean 🏝 national park on the edge of an ice field – the park has several hiking trails that pass through some of the more scenic areas – Rio Paine waterfalls. **Gd71**

Punta Arenas ⚓ Port city on the Straits of Magellan – beautiful cemetery – 🏛 regional history museum. **Ge72**

Tierra del Fuego National Park 🏝 Protected mountainous region in Tierre del Fuego – only the southern portions of the park are accessible. **Gf73**

Ushuaia The southernmost city in the world – 🏛 Museo del Fin del Mundo, regional and natural history museum. **Gg73**

Cape Horn 🏝 The southern tip of South America on the island Isla de Hornos – surrounded by stormy waters. **Gg73**

The Falkland Islands/Isla Malvinas
The islands are covered by grasslands. Sheep herding and fishing are the major industries. The areas outside of Port Stanley boast large bird colonies and good 🎣 fishing areas. **Gk-Hb71/72**

Remarkable Cities and Cultural monuments
- ☐ UNESCO World Cultural Heritage
- ☐ Remarkable Cities
- 🗺 Prehistoric rockscape

Sport and leisure destinations
- 🎿 Skiing
- 🏄 Wind surfing
- 🏄 Surfing
- 🛶 Canoeing/rafting
- 🎣 Deep-sea fishing

Eiderstedt (top): Historic lighthouse near Wester-hever, North Frisia in Germany.
Okayama (bottom): A stunning sunset above islands in Japan's Inland Sea.

The Atlantic (left): Colorful marine inhabitants of the deep blue sea.
The Pacific (right): Huge waves demonstrate the incredible power of the oceans.

Arctic Region, Antarctica, Oceans

The immense oceans shape the face of our "blue planet." The Pacific, Atlantic, Indian, and Arctic oceans cover more than two thirds of the planet's surface. Even today most of the oceans' landscapes remain unexplored. Around the polar regions the world's oceans give way to the barren ice masses of the Arctic and Antarctica. These inhospitable regions were a magnet to famous explorers including Admiral Richard E. Byrd and Robert F. Scott.

Arctic Region

Unlike most of the world's regions, the Arctic has no clear geographic definition. The Arctic usually refers to the cold treeless regions around the North Pole. The Arctic encompasses the Arctic Ocean and its adjacent bodies of water – including Baffin Bay, the Beaufort Sea, the Greenland Sea, the Laptev Sea, and the Bering Sea. The Arctic also consists of the countless islands in the region and some sections of mainland

North America (Canada and Alaska), Europe, and Asia.
The **Arctic** has a total area of 28 million km². Of the ten million km² of land in the Arctic, five million km² lie in **Canada**; around four million km² is equally divided between **Greenland** and **Russia**, and the remaining arctic land lies in **Alaska**

The Arctic is home to several large mammal species including Polar Bears.

Many of the ice-covered areas along **Alaska's Arctic coast** (photo) are only navigable by icebreakers.

Ellesmere Island Canadian island near northeastern Greenland – mountainous island with peaks rising to 3,000 meters – covered by glaciers.

Baffin Island Canada's largest arctic island – the north is mountainous and covered by enormous glaciers – the western section of the island is marshy and flat.

Icebergs can travel the oceans for up to ten years – most of an iceberg's mass lies underwater – photo: icebergs in the Labrador Sea.

Greenland covers 2.17 million km² and is the largest island in the world. The island is self-governing but politically associated with Denmark. Geographically is Greenland a section of the North American continent. It has around 56,000 inhabitants, mostly Inuit. In the Inuit language, Greenland is called Kalaallit Nunaat (land of people). Over 80 % of the island's surface is covered by ice of which the thickest layer measures around 3,400 meters. The Humboldt Glacier is the largest in the Northern Hemisphere (over 100 km wide).

Scale 1:18,000,000

0   160   320 Kilometers

Depth tints

Shoreline	4000-6000 m
0-200 m	6000-8000 m
200-2000 m	> 8000 m
2000-4000 m	

Physical Features

River, stream	Salt lake
Intermittent river	Intermittent salt lake
Lake	Elevation above sea level in meters
Intermittent lake	

and **Norway**. The center of the Arctic is covered by water and ice masses.

The **Arctic Ocean** is the smallest of the world's four oceans. The Arctic Ocean is separated from the Pacific Ocean by the narrow Bering Strait. It also shares a much longer border with the Atlantic Ocean. The Arctic Ocean has a total area of around 14 million km². In winter, most of the ocean's surface is covered by a layer of **ice** between three to four meters

thick. During summer the extent of this ice layer decreases and the coastal areas around the ocean become navigable for ships. The Arctic is the shallowest of the oceans with an average depth around 1,200 meters. Fram Basin is the deepest point with a maximum depth of 4,665 meters. A large percentage of the Arctic's land area, especially in Greenland and Canada, is covered by ice during the entire year. Most of the remaining land is

covered by **permafrost**, layers of frozen soil or rock that temporarily thaw in summer covering the land with water. Most of the Arctic's landscapes, including the many beautiful fjords in the region, were formed during or near the end of the last ice ages.

Life in the Arctic is strongly influenced by the extreme days and nights in the region. Long dark winter months with little sunshine are followed by short sum-

mers with almost continuous daylight. Despite the extreme climate, the Arctic is home to many fascinating animal species including polar bears, reindeer and walruses. The North Pole is warmed by ocean currents and is therefore not the coldest place in the Arctic. Ojmjakon, in northeastern Siberia, has the coldest average temperatures in the region. Temperatures around -78° C have been recorded in the area.

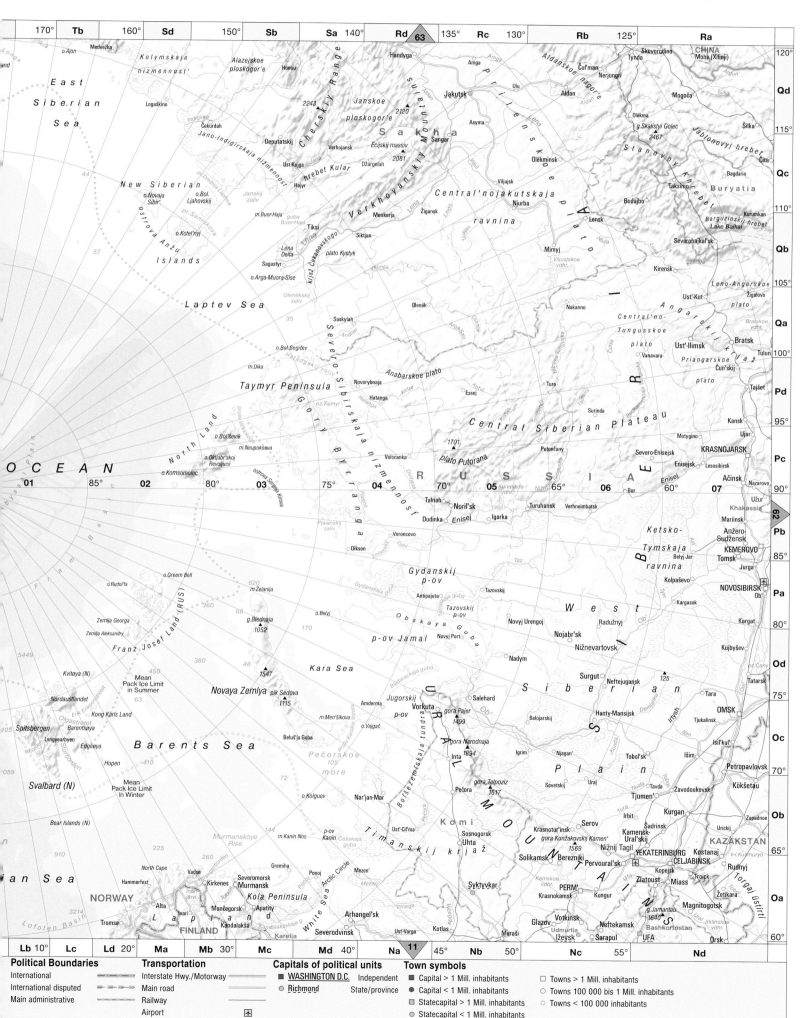

The Geographic **North Pole** is also known as True North. Unlike the Magnetic North Pole, the Geographic North Pole has a fixed position. The North Pole lies in the Arctic Ocean and is occasionally free of ice, despite the cold temperatures in the area.

The ice sheet on the Arctic Ocean often reaches the **Siberian coast**. At least ten million km² of Arctic Ocean is covered by ice.

The **Monaco Glacier** (photo) in the Liefdefjord is one of the most spectacular glaciers on the Norwegian island Spitsbergen.

Despite its raw climate the Arctic is home to many species of animal life. Some **animals**, like Arctic foxes, are active throughout the year while others including polar bears hibernate during the coldest months. Adult polar bears can weigh over 1,000 kilograms and are the largest predators in the Arctic. Whales, walruses, caribou, and reindeer continue to play an important part in the diet of indigenous people in the Arctic. Photos from top to bottom: Polar bears, walruses, Arctic foxes.

Political Boundaries

International	
International disputed	
Main administrative	

Transportation

Interstate Hwy./Motorway	
Main road	
Railway	
Airport	✈

Capitals of political units

■ WASHINGTON D.C.	Independent
◉ Richmond	State/province

Town symbols

■ Capital > 1 Mill. inhabitants	☐ Towns > 1 Mill. inhabitants
● Capital < 1 Mill. inhabitants	◯ Towns 100 000 bis 1 Mill. inhabitants
◉ Statecapital > 1 Mill. inhabitants	◯ Towns < 100 000 inhabitants
◉ Statecapital < 1 Mill. inhabitants	

Antarctica

Antarctica occupies most of the area in the Antarctic Circle. The **Antarctic Peninsula** extends over 1,900 kilometers towards South America. Most of the continent is covered by a layer of ice that is, in some places, up to 4,000 meters thick. Less than five percent of the continent is free of ice; primarily coastal areas including Victoria Land and Wilkes Land. Antarctica has an average land area of around 14 million km² but it increases or

decreases in size depending on the season. The **ice layer** is thickest at the center of the continent and declines in thickness towards Antarctica's edges. Mount Vernon is the highest mountain on the continent. The mountain is 4,897 meters high and it was first climbed in 1966. The area around the **South Pole** is situated 2,804 meters above sea level. The

The Transantarctic Mountains.

Because of its extremely cold temperatures and brutal storms Antarctica is an almost uninhabitable landmass. Penguins (photo) live in large colonies in order to survive in this harsh environment.

The **Antarctic Peninsula** lies between the Weddell Sea and the Bellingshausen Sea. The Peninsula is over 1,200 kilometers long. Mount Jackson is the highest point in the region, rising almost 4,190 meters.

Every year huge ice masses break away from Antarctica and flow into the oceans as new **icebergs**. In May 2002, a massive iceberg measuring 6,336 km² (larger than the US state of Delaware) broke away from the Ross Shelf. Photo: Icebergs in the Amundsen Sea.

The **Transantarctic Mountains** are located near the South Pole. The highest peak is Mount Kirckpatrick with a total height of 4,528 meters above sea level.

The American research base **Amundsen-Scott Base** (photo) lies near the Geographic South Pole. Other American bases lie on the Ross Sea (McMurdo) and on Anvers Island (Palmer Station). The station was built in 1956 and has been in use since then. A geodesic dome forms part of the station.

Mount Minto (4,165 m) is the highest mountain in Victoria Land. Many volcanoes rise high above the ice covered surface of Antarctica.

Scale 1:18,000,000

0   160   320 Kilometers

Depth tints

- Shoreline
- 0-200 m
- 200-2000 m
- 2000-4000 m
- 4000-6000 m
- 6000-8000 m
- > 8000 m

Physical Features

- River, stream
- Intermittent river
- Lake
- Intermittent lake
- Salt lake
- Intermittent salt lake
- Elevation above sea level in meters

Antarctica

average elevation of the continent is 2,340 meters. The large bays in the Ross Sea and Weddell Sea divide western Antarctica from the rest of the continent. Between these two regions lies the **Transantarctic Moutain Range**. Mount Kilpatrick, the highest peak in this range, rises 4,528 meters.

The ice mass covering the continent is frozen but active. Large glaciers frequently break away from the continent's edges and become icebergs. Rivers of ice in the continent's interior continously create new glaciers. There are several large ice shelves on the continent including the Ross Shelf (490,000 km²) and Filchner Ronne Shelf (450,000 km²). The continent is surrounded by the world's stormiest waters.

Antarctica is the coldest place on Earth. Temperatures reaching -89.2°C have been recorded at Vostok Climate Station in western Antarctica. Even in summer most of Antarctica has temperatures below the freezing point. The Antarctic Peninsula, which extends to South America, is Antarctica's warmest region. Geologists believe Antarctica has large reserves of natural resources including oil, gold and natural gas. **The Antarctic Treaty**, signed in 1959, declares that the continent will be used peacefully for the mutual benefit of all mankind. The Antarctic Treaty Sytem has stopped any potential mining efforts or permanent land claims on the continent. Antarctica is the only continent with no permanent human inhabitants and there are also no large land animals on the continent. In 1985 scientists discovered a hole in the **ozone layer** above Antarctica. At the beginning of the 21st century the hole – believed to be a result of industrial pollution – was four times the size of Australia.

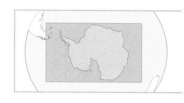

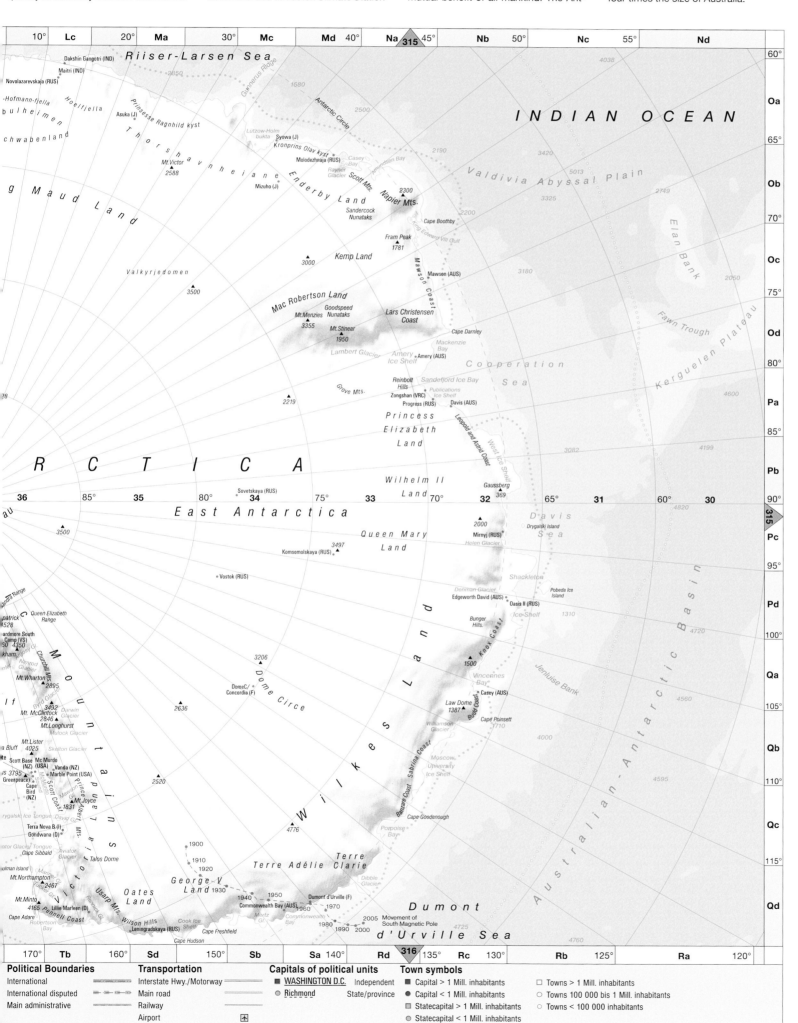

As many as 2,500 scientists work in the over **50 international research stations** in Antarctica at any one time. In addition, almost 12,000 tourists visited the continent in 2001/2002 and the number of tourist is expected to rise.

On January 17, 1912 Robert F. Scott reached the **South Pole** after Amundsen. Scott died on the way back (photo: a memorial to Scott).

Mount Erebus (3,795 m) on Ross Island is the highest still active volcano in Antarctica.

Lützow-Holm-Bay (photo) lies between Enderby Land and Queen Maud Land – impressive glaciers.

The Mawson Coast (photo) is the location of the Australian Antarctica research station (Mawson Station).

Cape Darnley (photo) borders MacKenzie Bayin the north. This area is home to a large colony of Emperor penguins.

Political Boundaries
International
International disputed
Main administrative

Transportation
Interstate Hwy./Motorway
Main road
Railway
Airport

Capitals of political units
■ WASHINGTON D.C. Independent
◉ Richmond State/province

Town symbols
■ Capital > 1 Mill. inhabitants
● Capital < 1 Mill. inhabitants
▣ Statecapital > 1 Mill. inhabitants
◉ Statecapital < 1 Mill. inhabitants
□ Towns > 1 Mill. inhabitants
○ Towns 100 000 bis 1 Mill. inhabitants
○ Towns < 100 000 inhabitants

Atlantic Ocean

With its adjacent seas, the Atlantic covers 106.6 million km² of the Earth's surface and is (after the Pacific) the second largest ocean. The Atlantic is bounded by four continents. The largest of these seas are the Mediterranean (three million km²) and the North Sea (575,000 km²) to the east of the Atlantic and the Caribbean Sea (2.6 million km²) and Gulf of Mexico (1.8 million km²) to the ocean's west. The Mid-Atlantic Ridge, an underwater mountain system, runs through the middle of the ocean. The deepest point in the Atlantic is Milwaukee Deep (-9,219 m) in the Puerto Rico Trench. Many of the islands in the Atlantic – such as the Azores and Cape Verde Islands – are the peaks of vast underwater mountain systems.

A lighthouse on the rocky Atlantic coast of Maine.

Many of the **marine animals** in the Atlantic Ocean travel great distances during the year. Some animals including dolphins (photo) and whales migrate in groups called pods or schools.

The **Mediterranean Sea** The largest sea adjacent to the Atlantic. It connects with the Atlantic at the Strait of Gibraltar. Major islands in the sea include Sicily, Cyprus, Crete, Corsica, and Malta. Photo: The Greek island Mykonos.

The largest **island** in the Atlantic is Greenland (2,175,600 km²), which lies north of mainland North America. The largest island in the Carribean is Cuba (111,000 km²). Great Britain (219,801 km²) and Iceland (103,000 km²) are the largest European islands in the Atlantic. Photos from top to bottom: Iceland, Ireland, an island in the Carribean Sea, the Falkland Islands.

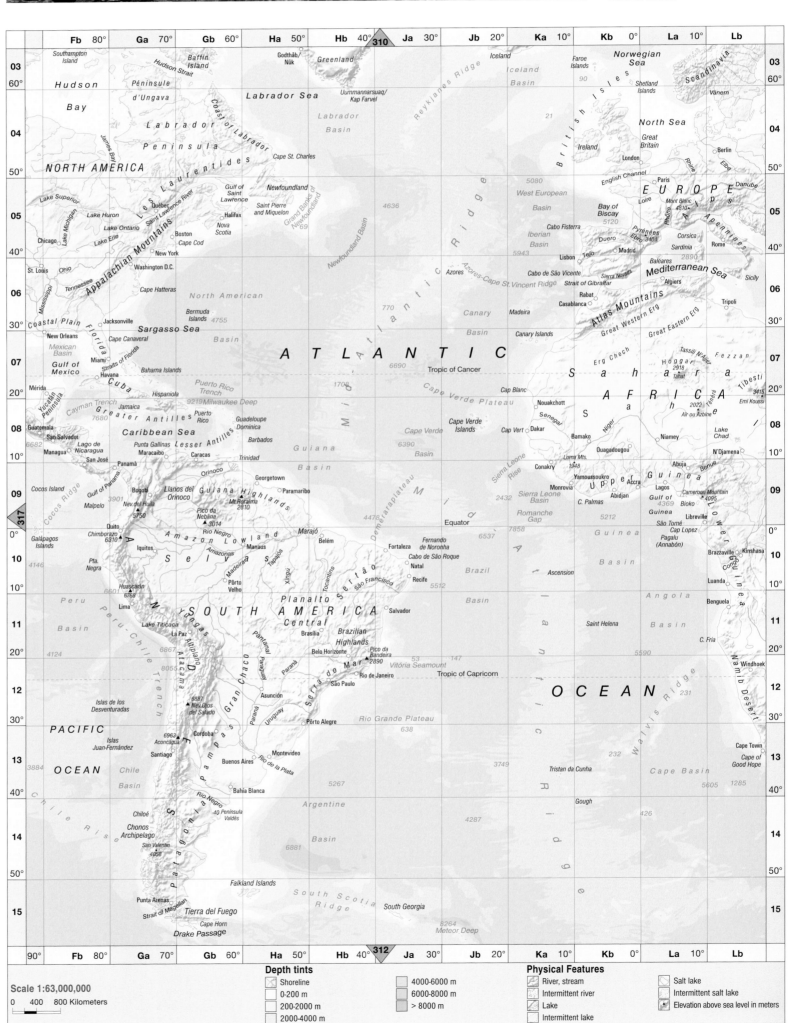

Scale 1:63,000,000

0   400   800 Kilometers

Depth tints
- Shoreline
- 0–200 m
- 200–2000 m
- 2000–4000 m
- 4000–6000 m
- 6000–8000 m
- > 8000 m

Physical Features
- River, stream
- Intermittent river
- Lake
- Intermittent lake
- Salt lake
- Intermittent salt lake
- Elevation above sea level in meters

Indian Ocean

The Indian Ocean covers arround 74.1 million km² and is the world's third largest ocean. The Indian Ocean is surrounded by four continents; Africa, Asia, Australia, and Antarctica. It borders the Atlantic Ocean on the meridian at 20 degrees east and the Pacific Ocean on the meridian at 147 degrees east. There are numerous bodies of water adjacent to the Indian Ocean, including the Red Sea, Persian Gulf, Arabian Sea, the Great Australian Bight, and the Bay of Bengal. The deepest point in the Indian Ocean is the **Java Trench** which extends 7,450 meters below the surface. The average depth of the ocean is around 3,850 meters. Java, Sumatra, Sri Lanka and Madagascar are the largest islands in the ocean.

Sunset over the Arabian Sea near the coast of southern India.

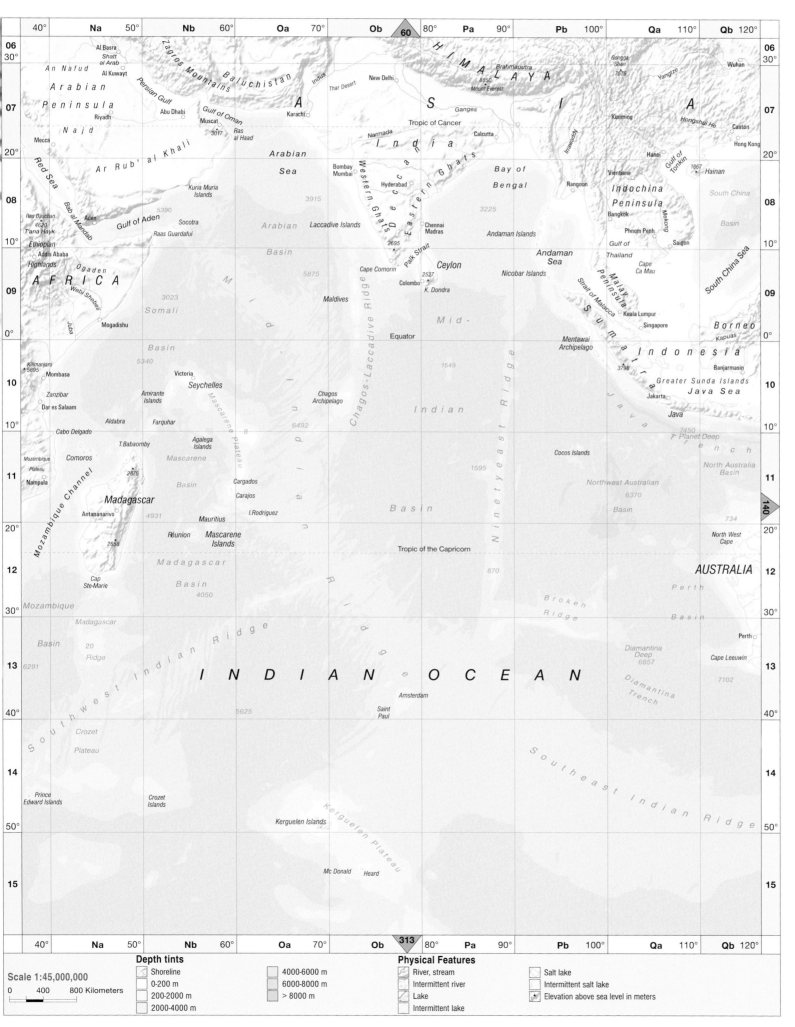

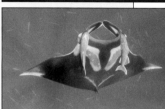

The Indian Ocean is home to diverse **marine life** and many areas are open to divers. Whale sharks (top photo) are often 15 meters long. Manta rays (bottom photo) live near the ocean floor and belong to a family of fish related to sharks.

Because of high temperatures and evaporation many of the Indian Ocean's **adjacent seas**, including the Red Sea (top photo), have a high salt content. In many of the large gulfs around the ocean, water temperatures can reach 32° C. (bottom photo: Gulf of Thailand).

Five tectonic plates are situated beneath the Indian Ocean. Many of the ocean's volcanic islands lie near the edges of these plates. Mauritius (top photo) is of volcanic origin. The Seychelles (bottom photo) are coral islands. Madagascar (587,040 km²) is the largest island in the Indian Ocean.

Scale 1:45,000,000

0   400   800 Kilometers

Depth tints
- Shoreline
- 0-200 m
- 200-2000 m
- 2000-4000 m
- 4000-6000 m
- 6000-8000 m
- > 8000 m

Physical Features
- River, stream
- Intermittent river
- Lake
- Intermittent lake
- Salt lake
- Intermittent salt lake
- Elevation above sea level in meters

Pacific Ocean

The **Pacific** is the superlative of the world's four oceans. The ocean was first named the "Pacific" (peaceful) by 16th century European explorers who mistook it for a calm body of water. It is the largest ocean in the world with an area of 181.6 million km² and it covers more than a third of the planet's surface. Even without its adjacent seas the Pacific covers 166.2 million km², a larger area than all the land on the planet combined.

Beautiful Bora Bora in French Polynesia.

The Pacific is also the deepest of the oceans with an average depth of 4,280 meters. The deepest point in the Pacific is the Challenger Deep in the **Marianas Trench** with a depth of 11,034 meters. More than half of the unfrozen water on the planet is contained in the Pacific. The **International Date Line** runs through the middle of the ocean.

Most of **the Pacific's animals** live between the ocean's surface and a depth of 200 meters and eat plankton and algae. Photos from top to bottom: Giant Pacific octopus, blue whales, giant jellyfish, tiger shark.

The **Great Barrier Reef** off the northeastern coast of Australia covers an area of 205,000 km². The reef is home to more than 400 species of coral, 2,000 species of fish, and many other forms of marine life.

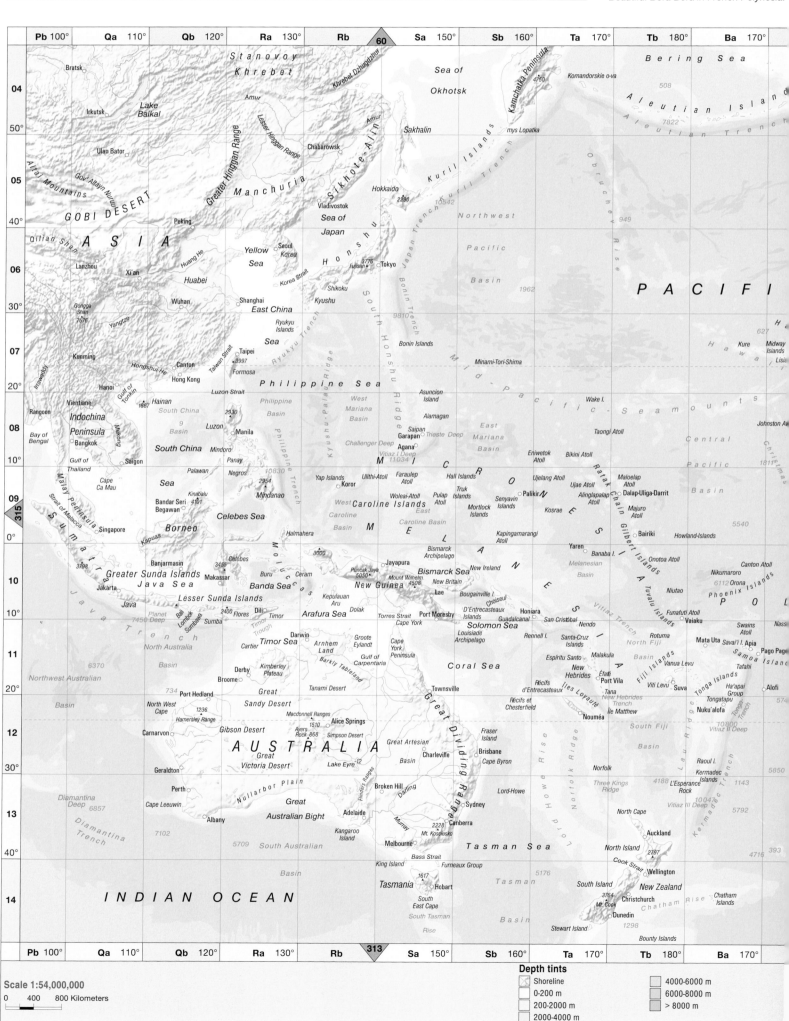

Scale 1:54,000,000

0   400   800 Kilometers

Depth tints

Shoreline	4000-6000 m
0-200 m	6000-8000 m
200-2000 m	> 8000 m
2000-4000 m	

The largest bodies of water bordering the Pacific include the East China Sea and Yellow Sea in the west, the Gulf of Alaska and Bering Sea in the north, the Sea of Cortez in the east, and the Ross Sea in the south. The farthest distance from north to south in the Pacific – from the Bering Strait to Antarctica – covers around 15,500 kilometers. The Straits of Malacca are often considered the westernmost section of the Pacific. From east to west between the Straits of Malacca and Panama the greatest distance in the Pacific Ocean measures around 17,500 kilometers.

There are an estimated 25,000 islands in the Pacific, more than in all the other oceans combined. Most of the Pacific's islands lie south of the equator.

Several large underwater mountain chains rise in the Pacific Ocean. The East Pacific Rise is an **underwater mountain chain** stretching 8,700 kilometers through the Pacific, parallel to the South American coast. It is one section of the Pacific's massive mid-oceanic ridge. Magma from the earth's core runs out of these mountains, hardens, and becomes part of the ocean's floor.

The Pacific "Ring of Fire" encircles the entire ocean and is a zone of frequent volcanic eruptions and earthquakes. The zone contains numerous mountain ranges and trenches including the Mariana Trench, the Japan Trench and Cascade Mountains. In addition to earthquakes and eruptions, the coastal areas in the Pacific are also threatened by powerful cyclones and tsunamis. Many of the islands near the Asian mainland, including New Guinea, the Philippines and Taiwan, are of volcanic origin. In the southern and central Pacific the countless islands are divided into three regions: Polynesia, Micronesia, and Melanesia.

The Pacific region features **a ring of active volcanoes**. Especially the **Kamtchaka Peninsula** (top photo) and the **Chilenean Andes Mountains** (bottom photo) encompass some of the world's most active volcanoes.

Mauna Kea (4,205 m) on **Hawaii** is a spectacular sight. The mountain stretches 5,500 meters from the ocean's floor to its surface. Its total height is around 9,700 meters.

The islands of Melanesia and Micronesia are situated in the western Pacific, northeast of Australia. Palau archipelago (photo) belongs to Micronesia.

The **island archipelagos of Polynesia** lie in the central Pacific. The Samoan Islands (top photo) lie near the western edges of Polynesia. The Marquesas Islands (bottom photo) are a part of French Polynesia.

The **Easter Islands** lie 3,500 kilometers off the coast of South America. Its famous statues (photo) are called Moai.

Physical Features
- River, stream
- Intermittent river
- Lake
- Intermittent lake
- Salt lake
- Intermittent salt lake
- Elevation above sea level in meters

The index explained

All of the places named on the maps in the atlas are listed in the atlas index. The place names are listed alphabetically. Special symbols and letters including accents and umlauts are ignored in the order of the index. For example, the letters Á, Ä, Â are all categorized under A, and Ź, Ż, Ž are all treated as the standard Latin letter Z. Written characters consisting of two letters joined together (ligatures) are treated as two separate characters in the index: for example, words beginning with the character Æ would be indexed under AE.

The most commonly used abbreviations in the atlas – including N.P. for national park or N.W.R. for national wildlife refuge – are also used in the index. These abbreviations are listed and explained on this page (below). Generic geographic terms (sea, bay, etc.) and word articles (the, le, el, etc.) were used in the order of the index: for example, the Gulf of Mexico is listed under G and Le Havre, France is listed under L.

A special aspect of the atlas is the detailed and specially developed system of pictograms it features. These pictograms highlight famous travel routes, scenic landscapes, natural attractions, man-made attractions, cultural sites, as well as sporting, vacation, and recreation facilities. These pictograms also appear in the index (up to three per place name). The pictograms provide a basic overview of the attractions featured in a particular area. The meanings of all of the pictograms featured in the atlas are explained on the following page. In addition to these pictograms, the index also features special symbols to provide information about the political status of certain places including states,

Abbreviations

Abb.	Abbey, abbaye (French), abbadia (Span.), abbazia (Ital.)
Abor.	Aboriginal (indigenous inhabitants of Australia)
Aborig.	Aboriginal (indigenous inhabitants of Australia)
Ad.	Adas (Turkish) = Island
Ág.	Ági -os, -a, -i (Greek) = Saint
A.L.	Aboriginal Land = Aboriginal land reserve in Australia
Ban.	Banjaran (Malaysian) = mountain range
Bol'.	Bol'-šoj, -šaja, -šoe (Russian) = large-
C.	Cape, cap (French), cabo (Span./Port.), capo (Ital.)
Can.	Canal
Cast.	Castle, castel (French.), castillo (Span.), castelo (Port.), castello (Ital.)
Cd.	Ciudad (Span.), cidade (Port.) = city
Co.	Cerro (Span.) = mountain, hill
Conv.	Convento (Span.) = monastery
Cord.	Cordillera (Span.) = mountain range
Corr.	Corrente (Port.), corriente (Ital./Span.) = river
Cr.	Creek
D.	Dake (Jap.) = mountain
D.	Danau (Indonesian) = lake
Dağ.	Dağlar, dağlari (Turkish) = mountain range
Ea.	Estancia (Span.) = estate
Emb.	Embalse (Span.), embassament (catalonian) = reservoir
Ens.	Ensenada (Span./Port.) = small bay
Erm.	Ermita (Span.) = hermitage
Est.	Estación (Span.) = rail station
Faz.	Fazenda (Port.) = estate
Fl.	Fleuve (French) = river
Fs.	waterfalls
g.	gawa (Jap.) = river
G.	Gora (Russian), góra (Polish), gunung (Indonesian) = mountain
Gde.	Grande (Span./French) = large
Geb.	Gebirge (German), gebergte (Dutch) = mountain range
Grd.	Grand (French) = large
Gt.	Great-
Hist.	Historic, historical
Hr.	Hrebet (Russian) = high
Ht.	Haut (French) = high-
Hte.	Haute (French) = high-
Hts.	Haut -s, -es (French) = high-
Hwy.	Highway
I.	Isla (Span.), ilha (Port.) = island
Î.	Île (French) = island
Ind.	Indian/ Native Americans
Ind.Res.	Indian Reservation = Native American land reserves in North America
Is.	Islands
Îs.	Îles (French) = islands
Jaz.	Jazovir (Bulg.) = reservoir
Jct.	Junction
Jez.	Jezioro (Pol.), jezero (Czech/Slovak./Serb./Croat./Slov.) = lake
Kan.	Kanal (Turk./Rus.), kanaal (Dutch), kanał (Pol.) = canal
Kep.	Kepulauan (Malaysian) = archipelago
Kg.	Kampong (Malaysian), kampung (Khmer) = village
Kör.	Körfezi (Turk.) = gulf, bay
L.	Lake, lac (French), lago (Ital./Span./Port.), loch, lough (Gaelic)
M.	Mys (Rus./Ukr.) = cape
Mal.	Malo, -yj, -aja, -oe (Rus.) = small
Mem.	Memorial
Mon.	Monastery, monastère (French.), monasterio (Span.), monastero (Ital.)
M.P.	Milli Parki (Turk.) = national park
Mt.	Mount, mont (French)
Mta.	Montagna (Ital.), montaña (Span.) = mountain range
Mte.	Monte (Ital./Span./Port.), montagne (French) = mountain
Mtes.	Montes (Span./Port.), montagnes (French) = mountains
Mţi.	Munţii (Romanian) = mountain range
Mti.	Monti (Ital.) = mountain range
Mtn.	Mountain
Mtns.	Mountains
Mts.	Mountains, Monts (French)
Mus.	Musée (French), museo (Span.), museu (Port.) = museum
N.	North, Northern, Norte (Ital./Span./Port.), Norra (Swedish), Nørdre (Norwegian), Nørre (Danish), Nord (German)
Nac.	Nacional (Span.), Nacional'-nyj, -aja, -oe (Russian) = national
Naz.	Nazionale (Ital.) = national
N.B.C.A.	National Biodiversity and Conservation Area = protected natural area
Nev.	Nevado (Span.) = snow-covered mountain peaks
N.H.P.	National Historic Park
N.H.S.	National Historic Site
Niž.	Niž-e, -nij, -naja, -neje (Russian) = lower-
Nižm.	Nižmennost' (Rus.) = plain
N.M.P.	National Military Park
N.P.	National Park, Nationalpark (Swedish), nasjonal park (Norwegian), Nemzeti Park (Hungarian)
N.R.	Nature Reserve, Natuurreservaat (Dutch)
N.R.A.	National Recreation Area
N.S.	National Seashore
N.Sra.	Nossa Senhora (Port.) = our lady (Mary, the mother of Jesus)
Nva.	Nueva (Span.) = new-
Nvo.	Nuevo (Span.) = new-
N.W.R.	National Wildlife Refuge
o.	Ostrov (Rus.) = island
P.	Port (English and French), puerto (Span./Port.), porto (Ital.) = harbor
Peg.	Pegunungan (Indonesian) = mountain
Pen.	Peninsula, péninsule (franz.), península (Span.), penisola (Ital.)
Pk.	Peak
P.N.	Parc National (French), parque nacional (Span./Port.), parco nazionale (Ital.) = national park
p-ov.	Poluostrov (Rus.) = peninsula
Pres.	Presidente (Span./Port.) = president
Prov.	Provincial, Province
Pse.	Passe (French) = Pass
Pso.	Paso (Span.), passo (Ital.) = Pass
Pt.	Point
Pta.	Punta (Span./Port.) = point
Pte.	Pointe (French) = point
Pto.	Punto (Ital.) = point
Q.N.P.	Quasi National Park (Jap.) = national park
R.	River, rivière (French), río (Span.), ribeiro, rio (Port.), ríu (Romanian), reka (Bulgarian)
Ra.	Range
Rep.	Republic, république (French), república (Span./Port.), republicca (Ital.)
Repr.	Represa (Port.) = dam
Res.	Reserva (Span.), réserve (French) = nature reserve
Res.	Reservoir, réservoir (French)
Resp.	Respublika (Russian) = Republik
s.	San (Jap.) = mountain
S.	San (Span./Ital.), são (Port.) = saint
Sanc./Sanct.	Sanctuary
Sd.	Sound, sund (German, Danish, Norwegian, Swedish)
Sel.	Selat (Indonesian) = strait
Sg.	Song (Vietnamese) = river
S.H.P.	State Historic Park
S.H.S.	State Historic Site
Sk.	Shuiku (Chinese) = reservoir
S.M.	State Monument
S.P.	State Park
Sr.	Sredn -e, -ij, -jaja (Russian) = central, middle
Sra.	Sierra (Span.), serra (Port./Ital.) = mountain range
St./St	Saint (English and French), sankt (German, Dutch)
Sta.	Santa (Span./Port./Ital.) = saint
Star.	Star -o, -yj, -aja, -oe (Russian) = old-
Ste	Sainte (French) = saint
Sth.	South, southern
St.Mem.	State Memorial
Sto.	Santo (Span./Port.) = Saint
Str.	Street, Strait, stretto (Italian), stræde (Danish), stret (Norwegian)
t.	tau (Kaz.) = mountain
T.	Take (Jap.) = peak, summit
T.	Temple
Tel.	Teluk (Indonesian) = bay
Tg.	Tanjung (Indonesian) = cape
T.I.	Terra Indígena (Port.), territorio indigena (Span.) = indigenous land reservation in Latin America
Vdhr.	Vodohranilišče (Russian) = reservoir
Vel.	Velik -o, -ij, -yki, -oe (Rus.) = large-
Verh.	Verhn -ee, -ie, -ij, -jaja (Rus.) = mountain
Vill.	Village
vlk.	Vulkan (Rus.) = volcano
Vol.	Volcano, volcan (French), volcán (Span.)
Vul.	Vulkan (German), Vulcano (Ital./Romanian) = volcano
W.A.	Wilderness Area
Wildl.	Wildlife
W.S.	Wildlife Sanctuary
Y.	Yama (Jap.) = mountain, mountain range
Zal.	Zaliv (Russian), zalew (Polish) = bay
Zap.	Zapovednik (Russian) = nature reserve
Z.B.	Nature reserve in the People's Republic of China
Zp.	Zapadn -e, -ji, -aja, -noe (Russian) = west, western

provinces, and capital cities. Virtually all of the places listed in the atlas have a country reference; these nations are identified by their international license (registration) plate codes. The various international license codes are identified on this page. In the case of communities and areas that are located on or between the borders of two nations, the license plate codes of both nations are listed and separated by a backslash.

The names of areas and geographic features that cannot be assigned to specific states, such as the Atlantic Ocean, are followed by the page number of a map featuring the area and the number of the map grid box in which the area is depicted on the map.

Antigua	🏝 ⛰ 🏔	**AG**	271	Gk37
Place name	Pictograms	Nation	Page	Map grid

International license (registration) plate code

A	Austria	CV	Cape Verde	GUY	Guyana	MH	Marshall Islands	RG	Guinea	THA	Thailand
AFG	Afghanistan	CY	Cyprus	H	Hungary	MK	Macedonia	RH	Haiti	TIM	East Timor
AG	Antigua and Barbuda	CZ	Czech Republic	HN	Honduras	MNG	Mongolia	RI	Indonesia	TJ	Tajikistan
AL	Albania	D	Germany	HR	Croatia	MOC	Mozambique	RIM	Mauritania	TM	Turkmenistan
AND	Andorra	DARS	Western Sahara	I	Italy	MS	Mauritius	RL	Lebanon	TN	Tunisia
ANG	Angola	DJI	Djibouti	IL	Israel	MV	Maldives	RM	Madagascar	TO	Tonga
ARM	Armenia	DK	Denmark	IND	India	MW	Malawi	RMM	Mali	TR	Turkey
AUS	Australia	DOM	Dominican Republic	IR	Iran	MYA	Burma	RN	Niger	TT	Trinidad and Tobago
AZ	Azerbaijan	DVRK	Korea, North	IRL	Ireland	N	Norway	RO	Romania	TUV	Tuvalu
B	Belgium	DY	Benin	IRQ	Iraq	NAM	Namibia	ROK	Korea, South	UA	Ukraine
BD	Bangladesh	DZ	Algeria	IS	Iceland	NAU	Nauru	ROU	Uruguay	UAE	United Arab Emirates
BDS	Barbados	E	Spain	J	Japan	NEP	Nepal	RP	Philippines	USA	United States of
BF	Burkina Faso	EAK	Kenya	JA	Jamaica	NIC	Nicaragua	RSM	San Marino		America
BG	Bulgaria	EAT	Tanzania	JOR	Jordan	NL	Netherlands	RT	Togo	UZB	Uzbekistan
BH	Bahrain	EAU	Uganda	K	Cambodia	NZ	New Zealand	RUS	Russia	V	Vatican City
BHT	Bhutan	EC	Ecuador	KIR	Kiribati	OM	Oman	RWA	Rwanda	VN	Vietnam
BIH	Bosnia and	ER	Eritrea	KN	Saint Kitts and Nevis	P	Portugal	S	Sweden	VRC	China
	Herzegovina	ES	El Salvador	KS	Kyrgyzstan	PA	Panama	SA	South Africa	VU	Vanuatu
BOL	Bolivia	EST	Estonia	KSA	Saudi Arabia	PAL	Palau	SD	Swaziland	WAG	Gambia
BR	Brazil	ET	Egypt	KWT	Kuwait	PE	Peru	SGP	Singapore	WAL	Sierra Leone
BRN	Bahrain	ETH	Ethiopia	KZ	Kazakhstan	PK	Pakistan	SCG	Serbia and	WAN	Nigeria
BRU	Brunei	F	France	L	Luxembourg	PL	Poland		Montenegro	WD	Dominica
BS	Bahamas	FIN	Finland	LAO	Laos	PNG	Papua New Guinea	SK	Slovakia	WG	Grenada
BU	Burundi	FJI	Fiji	LAR	Libya	PY	Paraguay	SLO	Slovenia	WL	Saint Lucia
BY	Belarus	FL	Liechtenstein	LB	Liberia	Q	Qatar	SME	Suriname	WS	Samoa
C	Cuba	FSM	Micronesia	LS	Lesotho	RA	Argentina	SN	Senegal	WV	Saint Vincent and
CAM	Cameroon	G	Gabon	LT	Lithuania	RB	Botswana	SOL	Solomon Islands		the Grenadines
CDN	Canada	GB	Great Britain	LV	Latvia	RC	Taiwan	SP	Somalia	YE	Yemen
CH	Switzerland	GCA	Guatemala	M	Malta	RCA	Central African	STP	São Tomé and	YV	Venezuela
CI	Cote d'Ivoire	GE	Georgia	MA	Morocco		Republic		Principe	Z	Zambia
CL	Sri Lanka	GH	Ghana	MAL	Malaysia	RCB	Republic of the Congo	SUD	Sudan	ZW	Zimbabwe
CO	Colombia	GNB	Guinea-Bissau	MC	Monaco	RCH	Chile	SY	Seychelles		
COM	Comoros	GQ	Equatorial Guinea	MD	Moldova	RDC	Democratic Republic	SYR	Syria		
CR	Costa Rica	GR	Greece	MEX	Mexico		of the Congo	TCH	Chad		

Symbols used in the index

⬭ City
▪ State
● Capital
▢ Province
◉ Provincial Capital

Principal travel routes

Auto route
Rail road
Highspeed train
Shipping route

Remarkable landscapes and natural monuments

UNESCO World Natural Heritage
Mountain landscape
Rock landscape
Ravine/canyon
Extinct volcano
Active volcano
Geyser
Cave
Glacier
River landscape
Waterfall/rapids
Lake country
Desert
Oasis
Fossil site
Depression
Nature park
National park (landscape)
National park (flora)
National park (fauna)
National park (culture)
Biosphere reserve

Wildlife reserve
Whale watching
Turtle conservation area
Protected area for sea-lions/seals
Protected area for penguins
Zoo/safari park
Crocodile farm
Coastal landscape
Beach
Coral reef
Island
Underwater reserve

Remarkable Cities and cultural monuments

UNESCO World Cultural Heritage
Pre- and early history
Prehistoric rockscape
The Ancient Orient
Ancient Egypt
Ancient Egyptian pyramids
Minoan culture
Phoenecian culture
Early African culture
Etruscan culture
Greek antiquity
Roman antiquity
Nabatean culture
Vikings
Ancient India
Ancient China
Ancient Japan
Mayan culture
Inca culture
Aztec culture
Other ancient American cultures
Places of Jewish cultural interest

Places of Christian cultural interest
Places of Islamic cultural interest
Places of Buddhist cultural interest
Places of Hindu cultural interest
Places of Jainist cultural interest
Places of Sikh cultural interest
Places of Shinto cultural interest
Places of cultural interest to other religions
Places of cultural interest to indigenous peoples (native peoples)
Aborigine reservation
Places of Aboriginal cultural interest
Indian reservation
Indian Pueblo culture
Places of Indian cultural interest
Amazonian Indians/protected area
Cultural landscape
Historical city scape
Impressive skyline
Castle/fortress/fort
Caravanserai
Palace
Technical/industrial monument
Dam
Remarkable lighthouse
Remarkable bridge
Tomb/grave
Theater of war/battlefield
Monument
Memorial
Space mission launch site
Space telescope
Market
Festivals
Museum
Theater
World exhibition
Olympics

Sport and leisure destinations

Arena/stadium
Race track
Golf
Horse racing
Skiing
Sailing
Diving
Windsurfing
Surfing
Canoeing/rafting
Seaport
Deep-sea fishing
Waterskiing
Beach resort
Mineral/thermal spa
Amusement/theme park
Casino
Hill resort
Lodge

Special index pictograms

Bodies of Water
Canal
Other physical names
Pass
Underwater topography

Al Jagbub – Anar Darreh

Al Jagbub LAR 184 Mc31
Al Jalamid KSA 69 Na30
Al-Jami'al-Kebir YE 72 Nc38
Al Jawb KSA 71 Nf34
Al Jawf KSA 69 Mk31
Al Jawf LAR 184 Mb33
Al Jaza'ir DZ 181 Lb27
Aljenaari WAN 194 Lb40
Aljezur P 30 Km47
Al Jihrah KSA 70 Nb32
Al Jubaylah KSA 71 Nd33
Al Jufra Oasis LAR 176 Ld13
Al Jumailiyah Q 78 Nf33
Al Jumum KSA 70 Mk35
Al Junaynah SUD 204 Mb39
Al Jurayd KSA 71 Ne32
Al Jussah KSA 70 Na34
Aljustrel P 30 Km47
Al Kabar SYR 69 Mk28
Al Kadhimiya IRQ 69 Nc29
Al-Kaf Palace YE 72 Ne37
Alkali Lake USA (OR) 244 Ea24
Alkamari RN 195 Lf39
Al- Kamil OM 79 Nk34
al-Kamilin SUD 198 Mg39
Al Karabilah IRQ 69 Na28
Al Karameh SYR 69 Mk28
Al Kararim LAR 183 Lh29
al-Kawa SUD 198 Mg40
Al-Khabb UAE 79 Nh33
Al-Khabbah OM 79 Nk34
Al Khabra KSA 71 Nb32
Al-Khabura OM 79 Nj34
Al Khadra KSA 72 Nc37
Al Khafah KSA 70 Nb32
Al Khalf KSA 70 Na33
Al Khalis IRQ 69 Nc29
Al Khamasin KSA 71 Nc35
Al Khanabah LAR 189 Lh32
Al Khandaq SUD 198 Mf37
Al Kharfah KSA 71 Nd34
Al Kharj KSA 71 Nd33
Al Khawkhah YE 72 Nb39
Al Khawrah UAE 78 Nh33
Al Khawtamah YE 72 Nb38
Al Khidr IRQ 69 Nc30
Al Khobar KSA 71 Nf32
Al Khor Q 78 Nf33
Al Khottah KSA 70 Na32
Al Khubah KSA 72 Nb37
Al Khums LAR 182 Lh29
Al Khuraybah KSA 68 Mh31
Al Khurmah KSA 71 Nb35
Al Khushaybi KSA 71 Nb33
Al-Kidan KSA 78 Ng34
Al Kifl IRQ 69 Nc29
Al Kisrah SYR 69 Mk28
Alkmaar NL 34 Le38
al-Koin SUD 198 Mf37
Al Kufah IRQ 69 Nc29
Al Kumayt IRQ 69 Nd29
Al Kura KSA 70 Mk35
al-Kurru SUD 198 Mf37
Al Kut IRQ 69 Nc29
Al Kuwayt KWT 78 Nd31
Al Kuwayt KWT 78 Nd31
Al Labbah KSA 69 Na31
Allada DY 202 Lb42
Al Ladhqiyah SYR 66 Mh28
Allagash USA (MA) 254 Gf22
Allagash River USA 254 Gf22
al-Lagowa SUD 205 Me40
Allagudda IND (APH) 115 Ok39
Allahabad = Tirth Raj Prayag IND (UPH) 113 Pa33
Al Lahabah KSA 71 Nd32
Allahdurg IND (APH) 112 Oj37
Allahganj IND (UPH) 111 Ok32
Allakaket USA (AK) 239 Cd12
Allanche F 27 Lc45
Allandale AUS (SA) 149 Rh59
Allanmyo MYA 118 Ph36
Allanridge SA 225 Md59
Allansford AUS (VIC) 159 Sb65
Allan Water CDN (ON) 249 Fe20
Allapalli IND (MHT) 113 Pa36
Allardville CDN (NB) 255 Gh22
Allariz E 28 Kn52
Allauch F 27 Lf47
Alldays SA 222 Me57
Alleen N 14 Lh32
Allegan USA (MI) 256 Fh24
Allegany S.P. USA 257 Ga24
Allemanskraaldam SA 225 Md60
Allen RA (RN) 304 Gg65
Allen RP 125 Rc39
Allendale USA (SC) 259 Fk29
Allende MEX (COH) 263 Ek31
Allende MEX (NL) 263 Ek33
Allen Island AUS (QLD) 154 Rk54
Allensworth USA (CA) 246 Ea28
Allentown USA (PA) 257 Gc25
Alleppey = Alappuzha IND (KER) 114 Oj41
Alleppey Beach IND 114 Oj42
Aller D 35 Ll38
Aller = Cabañaquinta E 28 Kp53
Allersberg D 37 Lm41
Allevard F 27 Lg45
Allgäu D 36 Ll43
Allgäuer Alpen D/A 36 Ll43
Alliance USA (NE) 250 Ej24
Alliance USA (OH) 257 Fk25
Allier F 27 Ld44
Alliford Bay CDN (BC) 242 De19
Alligator Pond JA 269 Gb37
Alligator River N.W.R. USA 259 Gc28
Allinge DK 17 Lp35
Al Lisafah KSA 71 Nd32
Allison USA (IA) 251 Fd24
Allison Island PNG 165 Sb46
Al Lith KSA 70 Na35
Allo E 29 Ks52
Allomo WAN 202 Ld42
Allones F 24 La43
Allora AUS (QLD) 157 Sf60
Allos F 27 Lg46
All Soul's Memorial Church (Kanpur) IND 111 Pa32
Allu RI 133 Ra48
Al Luhayyah YE 72 Nb38
Allur IND (APH) 115 Pa39
Alma AUS (NSW) 159 Sc62
Alma CDN (QC) 254 Ge21
Alma CDN (NB) 255 Gh23
Alma USA (NM) 247 Ef29
Alma USA (NE) 250 Fa25
Alma USA (MI) 256 Fh24
Alma USA (GA) 259 Fj30
Al Ma'aniyah IRQ 69 Nb30
Almacelles E 32 La49
Al Machmin IRQ 69 Nb30
Almada P 30 Ki48
Al Madaya KSA 72 Nb37
Almaden AUS (QLD) 155 Sc54
Almadén E 30 Kq48
Al Madina KSA 70 Mk33
Al Madinah KSA 70 Mk33
Almafuerte RA (CD) 300 Gh62
Al Magharim YE 72 Nd38
Almagro E 31 Kr48
Al Mahash KSA 70 Na32
Al Mahatta Ath'thania SYR 69 Na28
Al Mahbas DARS 187 Kf32
Al Mahdoom SYR 68 Mj27
Almahel ETH 206 Mh40
Al Mahfid YE 72 Nd38
Al Mahmudiyah IRQ 69 Nc29
Al Mahrah YE 73 Nf38
Al Mahruqah LAR 189 Lh32
Al Mahwit YE 72 Nb38
Al Majadah KSA 72 Na36
Al Majm'ah KSA 71 Nc33
Al Makhwah KSA 70 Na36
al-Malamm SUD 205 Me41
Al-Malkyer SYR 69 Nb27
Alma, Mount AUS 157 Sf58
Al Manajier SYR 69 Na27
Al Manama BRN 78 Nf32
al-Manaqil SUD 198 Mg39
Almandar IR 76 Nc26
Almansa E 31 Kt48
Al-Mansura SYR 69 Mk28
Al Mansuriyah YE 72 Nb38
Almanza E 28 Kp52
Alma Peak CDN 241 Dg17
Al Ma'qas KSA 70 Na36
Al Maqrun LAR 183 Ma30
Almar AFG 82 Oc28
Al Marah KSA 71 Ne33
Al Marawiah YE 72 Nb38
Almaraz E 30 Kp49
Al-Mariyyah UAE 78 Ng34
Al Marj LAR 183 Ma29
Almarza E 29 Ks51
Almas BR (TO) 294 Hg51
Almaty KZ 81 Oj24
Al Mawsil IRQ 69 Nb27
Al-Mawsil IRQ 69 Nb27
Al Mayadin SYR 69 Na28
al-Maysar OM 79 Nk34
Al Mayyah KSA 70 Nb32
Almazán E 29 Ks51
Almeida P 28 Ko50
Almeirim BR (PA) 287 Hd46
Almeirim P 30 Km49
Almel IND (KTK) 112 Oj37
Almelo NL 34 Lg38
Almenara BR (MG) 299 Hk54
Almenara E 31 Ku49
Almenar de Soria E 29 Ks51
Almendo MW 219 Mh54
Almendral E 30 Ko48
Almendralejo E 30 Ko48
Almere NL 34 Lf38
Almería E 31 Ks46
Almerimar E 31 Ks46
Al'met'evsk RUS (TAR) 55 Ng18
Älmhult S 17 Lp34
Al-Midhar Mosque YE 72 Ne38
Al Midhnab KSA 71 Nc33
Al-Mihrad KSA 78 Ng35
Al Mina RL 68 Mh28
Al-Mintirib OM 79 Nk34
Almirante PA 266 Fj41
Almirante Brown RA (BA) 301 Ha63
Almirante Latorre RCH 300 Ge60
Almirante Tamandaré BR (PR) 298 Hf58
Al-Mirfa UAE 78 Ng33
Almiropótamos GR 50 Me52
Almirós GR 50 Mc51
Al Mish'ab KSA 71 Ne31
Al Mistannah KSA 71 Ne33
Almodôvar P 30 Km47
Almodóvar del Campo E 31 Kq48
Almodóvar del Río E 30 Kp47
Almofala BR (CE) 289 Ja47
Almoharin E 30 Ko49
Almonte E 30 Ko47
Almora AUS (QLD) 154 Rk55
Almora IND (UTT) 111 Ok31
Almoustarat RMM 193 La37
Älmsta S 15 Lt31
Al Mubarraz KSA 71 Ne33
Al-Mudaiba OM 79 Nk34
Al Mudawwara JOR 68 Mh31
Almudévar E 29 Ku52
al-Muglad SUD 205 Md40
Al Muharraq BRN 78 Nf32
Al Mukalla YE 72 Ne38
Al Mukha YE 72 Nb39
Al Mulayhah al Gharbiyah KSA 71 Ne34
Almuñécar E 30 Kr46
Almunge S 15 Lt31
Al Muqdadiyah IRQ 69 Nc29
Al-Musalla OM 79 Nk34
al-Musallamiya SUD 198 Mg39
Al-Musana'a OM 79 Nj34
Al Musayjid KSA 70 Mk33
Al Musaymir YE 72 Nc39
Al Musayyib IRQ 69 Nc29
Al Muwassam KSA 72 Nb37
Al Muwayh KSA 70 Na34
Al Muwaylih KSA 70 Mh32
Al Muzahmiyah KSA 71 Nd33
Al Muzaylif KSA 70 Na36
Al Naqub YE 72 Nc38
Alnaši RUS 55 Ng17
Alness GB 21 Kq33
Alness GUY 283 Hb42
Alnif MA 180 Kh30
Alnön S 15 Ls28
Alnwick GB 21 Kt35
Alo FJ 170 Ba53
Alo FIN 18 Mc30
Aloåg EC 284 Ga46
Aloândia BR (GO) 298 Hf54
Alô Brasil BR (MT) 293 He52
Aloft Is. NZ 170 Bf55
Alogatina G 202 Lf45
Aloi EAU 212 Mg44
Aloja LV 19 Me33
Aloja LV 19 Me33
Aloma WAN 202 Le42
Along IND (ARP) 116 Ph31
Alongly CDN (SK) 243 Eh19
Alongshan VRC (NMZ) 95 Rb20
Alónissos GR 50 Md51
Alonso de Rojas C 268 Fj34
Alor E 30 Kn48
Alor RI 136 Rc50
Álora E 30 Kq46
Alorna IND 112 Og38
Alor Setar MAL 120 Qa42
Alot IND (MPH) 112 Oh34
Alota BOL 296 Gg56
Alotau PNG 166 Sf51
Alpachiri RA (LP) 305 Gj64
Alpalhão P 30 Kn49
Alpamayo PE 290 Gb50
Alpasinche RA (LR) 300 Gg60
Alpena USA (MI) 256 Fj23
Alpera E 31 Kt48
Alpercatas BR 288 Hh49
Alpes du Valais CH 36 Lh44
Alpha AUS (QLD) 155 Sd57
Alpha Cordillera 310 Ea01
Alphen a/d Rijn NL 34 Le38
Alphonse SY 227 Ng49
Alphonse Group SY 227 Ng49
Alpiarça P 30 Km49
Alpi Carniche I 43 Lo44
Alpi Lepontine I/CH 36 Lj44
Alpi Marittime I 42 Lh46
Alpine USA (WY) 245 Ee24
Alpine USA (AZ) 247 Ef29
Alpine USA (TX) 247 Ej30
Alpine Lake Wilderness USA 242 Dk22
Alpine N.P. AUS 159 Sd64
Alpi Oróbie I 42 Lk44
Alpi Veroste I 42 Ll44
Alpouro DY 194 Lb41
Alps 10 Lb09
Alpu TR 53 Ml51
Alpujarras E 31 Kr46
Al Qa'amiyat KSA 72 Ne36
Al Qa'arah LAR 184 Mc30
Al-Qabil OM 79 Nh34
Al-Qadarif SUD 198 Mh39
Al-Qaffay UAE 78 Nf33
Al Qafrah YE 72 Nc38
Al Qahmah KSA 72 Na37
Al Qa'iyah KSA 70 Nb33
Al Qa'iyah KSA 71 Nc32
Al Qala'a LAR 182 Lh30
Al Qalibah KSA 68 Mj31
Al Qara'a KSA 72 Nb36
Al Qardabah LAR 183 Mb29
Al Qarn YE 72 Nc38
Al Qaryah ash Sharqiyah LAR 182 Lg30
Al Qaryah al Gharbiyah LAR 182 Lg30
Al Qasab KSA 71 Nc33
Al Qasabat LAR 183 Lh29
Al Qath YE 72 Ne38
Al Qatif KSA 71 Nf32
Al Qatranah JOR 68 Mj30
Al Qatrun LAR 189 Lh33
Al Qawba'iyah KSA 70 Mk35
Al Qaysumah KSA 71 Nd31
Al-Q'nitra MA 180 Kg28
Al-Qua'a UAE 78 Nh34
Al Quasir SYR 68 Mj28
Alquézar E 32 La48
Al Qulayd Bahri SUD 198 Mf37
Al Qulayyib KSA 71 Ne32
Al Qunfadhah KSA 70 Na36
Al Qurayn KSA 71 Nd33
Al Qurayrah KSA 70 Nb33
Al Qurnah IRQ 69 Nd30
Al Qusayr IRQ 69 Nc30
Al Qutaifeh SYR 68 Mj29
al-Qutayna SUD 198 Mg39
Al Quwarah KSA 71 Nb32
Al Quwayiah KSA 71 Nc33
Al Quzah YE 72 Ne38
Al Rahibat LAR 182 Lf30
Al Rahidah YE 72 Nc39
Al Rassafa SYR 69 Mk28
Al Rawdah YE 72 Nd38
Al Rayyan Q 78 Nf33
Alroy Downs AUS (NT) 145 Rj55
Als DK 16 Lk35
Als DK 16 Ll34
Alsace F 25 Lh42
Alsace F 25 Lh43
Alsa Craig GB 20 Kp35
Al-Samha UAE 78 Nh33
Alsasua E 29 Ks52
Alsea USA (OR) 244 Dj23
Alsek River CDN 241 Da15
Alsfeld D 34 Lk40
Al-Shafee Mosque KSA 70 Mk35
Al Shaykh 'Uthman YE 72 Nc39
Alshi EC 284 Ga47
Al Shihr YE 72 Ne38
Al Sidarah YE 72 Ne38
Alsike CDN (AB) 243 Ec19
Alsike S 15 Ls31
Alsterbro S 17 Lq34
Alstermo S 17 Lq34
Al Sufal YE 72 Ne38
Al Sukhnah YE 72 Nb38
Al Surrah YE 72 Nd39
Alta N 13 Mb11
Alta Badia I 42 Lm44
Alta Floresta BR (MT) 293 Hc50
Altagracia NIC 266 Fh40
Altagracia YV 280 Ge40
Alta Gracia RA (CD) 300 Gh61
Altagracia de Orituco YV 281 Gg41
Alta Italia RA (LP) 300 Gh63
Altajskij zapovednik RUS 89 Pe20
Altamachi BOL 292 Gg54
Altamaha USA 259 Fk30
Altamira BR (PA) 287 Hd47
Altamira CO 284 Gc44
Altamira MEX (TM) 263 Fa34
Altamira MEX (TM) 263 Fb34
Altamira PE 296 Gf58
Altamira do Maranhão BR (MA) 288 Hh48
Altamont USA (OR) 244 Dk24
Altamura I 45 Lr50
Alta Murgia, P.N. dell' I 45 Lr50
Altanbulag MNG 94 Pj21
Altanbulag MNG 94 Qd22
Altaneira BR (CE) 289 Ja49
Altan ovoo VRC/MNG 89 Pf23
Altan Ovoo MNG 94 Qa22
Altar MEX (SO) 246 Ee30
Altar-Est DZ 182 Le31
Altar, Volcán EC 284 Ga46
Altata MEX (SL) 262 Eg33
Altavista USA (VA) 259 Ga27
Altay MNG 94 Pj21
Altay MNG 94 Pg22
Altay RUS 62 Pb08
Altay VRC (XUZ) 89 Pe22
Altay Mountains MNG 86 Pc09
Altayn Caadah Gov' MNG 96 Pj24
Altay Shan VRC 89 Pd21
Altdorf CH 36 Lj44
Altdorf D 37 Lm41
Altea E 31 Ku48
Altenberg D 35 Lo40
Altenburg D 35 Ln40
Altenkirchen D 34 Lh40
Altenmarkt A 37 Lo43
Altenmarkt A 37 Lp43
Altensteig D 36 Lj42
Altentreptow D 35 Lo37
Altér do Chão BR (PA) 287 Hc47
Alter do Chão P 30 Kn49
Alte Saline Bad Reichenhall D 37 Ln43
Al Thaura SYR 69 Mk28
Altheim A 37 Lo42
Althofen A 37 Lp44
Altîna RO 46 Me45
Altinbesik TR 53 Mm54
Altındere Vadisi Milli Parkı TR 67 Mk25
Altınekin TR 53 Mn52
Altınhisar TR 53 Mp52
Altınkaya Barajı TR 66 Mh25
Altin Köprü IRQ 69 Nc28
Altinópolis BR (SP) 298 Hg56
Altinova TR 52 Mg51
Altıntaş TR 52 Ml51
Altıntepe TR 67 Mk26
Altınyaka TR 53 Ml54
Altınyayla TR 52 Mk53
Altiplanicie del Payún RA 304 Gf64
Altiplano BOL 296 Gf54
Altiri IND (ORS) 116 Pd35
Altja EST 18 Mg31
Altkirch F 25 Lh43
Altmark D 35 Lm38
Altmühl D 37 Lm42
Altnaharra GB 21 Kq32
Alto USA (TX) 253 Fc30
Alto Alegre BR (RR) 282 Gk44
Alto Alegre BR (RS) 302 Hd61
Alto Araguaia BR (MT) 298 Hd54
Alto Bonito BR (AC) 291 Ge50
Alto Bonito BR (PA) 288 Hg46
Alto Cedro C 269 Gb35
Alto Changane MOC 222 Mg58
Alto Chicapa ANG 217 Lk51
Alto de Carmen RCH 300 Ge60
Alto de Tamar CO 280 Gc42
Alto Garças BR (MT) 298 Hd54
Alto Golfo de California y Delta del Río Colorado MEX (BC) 246 Ec30
Alto Hama ANG 216 Lh52
Alto Ligonha MOC 219 Mk53
Alto Longá BR (PI) 289 Hj48
Alto Madre de Dios PE 291 Ge52
Alto Molócué MOC 219 Mj53
Alton GB 23 Ku39
Alton USA (IL) 251 Fe26
Alton USA (MO) 253 Fe27
Alton USA (NY) 257 Gb24
Altona CDN (MB) 248 Fb21
Alto Nevado, Cerro RCH 304 Gd68
Altônia BR (PR) 298 Hd57
Altoona USA (PA) 257 Ga25
Alto Paraguai BR (MT) 293 Hb53
Alto Paraíso de Goiás BR (GO) 294 Hg53
Alto Parnaíba BR (MA) 294 Hh50
Alto Pelado RA (SL) 300 Gg62
Alto Pencoso RA (SL) 300 Gg62
Alto Purus PE 291 Ge51
Alto Rio Guamá, T.I. BR 288 Hg47
Alto Rio Mayo RA (CB) 306 Ge68
Alto Rio Negro, T.I. BR 285 Gf45
Alto Rio Purus, T.I. BR 291 Ge50
Alto Río Senguer RA (CB) 304 Ge68
Altos BR (PI) 289 Hj48
Alto Santo BR (CE) 289 Ja48
Alto Sepatini, T.I. BR 291 Gg49
Alto Sucuriú BR (MS) 298 Hd55
Altotonga MEX (VC) 264 Fb36
Altötting D 37 Ln42
Alto Turiaçu, T.I. BR 288 Hg47
Altun VRC (XUZ) 91 Pe26
Altun-alem džamija SCG 48 Ma47
Altun Ha BH 265 Ff37
Altun Shan VRC 91 Pc27
Altun Shan VRC 91 Pg26
Altura E 31 Ku49
Alturas USA (CA) 244 Dk25
Alturitas YV 280 Gd41
Altus USA (OK) 252 Fa28
Altyn Arashan KS 81 Ok24
Altyn-Mosque VRC 90 Oj26
Aluakluak SUD 205 Mf42
Al Ubaydi IRQ 69 Na28
Al Ubaylah KSA 71 Nf34
al-Ubayyid SUD 205 Mf39
Al Udailiyah KSA 71 Ne33
Al 'Udayn YE 72 Nb39
al-Udayyah SUD 205 Me39
Alu Grottos VRC 117 Pk33
Alūksne LV 19 Mh33
Al 'Ula KSA 70 Mj32
al-'Umda SUD 205 Md40
Aluminé RA (NE) 304 Ge65
Aluminé RA 304 Ge65
Alunda S 15 Lt30
Alungdaw Kathapa National Park MYA 116 Ph34
Aluoi VN 119 Qd37
Alupka UA 57 Mh23
Al 'Uqaylah LAR 183 Lk30
Al Uqayr KSA 71 Nf33
al-'Uqda SUD 198 Mg39
Alur IND (MHT) 112 Oj37
Alur IND (APH) 115 Oj39
Al 'Urayq KSA 68 Mk31
Al-Uruq al-Muraridah KSA 73 Ng36
Alušta UA 57 Mh23
Al Uwayailah KSA 69 Nb30
Al 'Uwayja KSA 71 Nf34
Al 'Uwaynid KSA 71 Nc33
Al 'Uwaynidhiyah KSA 70 Mh32
Al Uzaym KSA 70 Nb32
Al Uzayr IRQ 69 Nd30
Alva USA (OK) 252 Fa27
Alvalade P 30 Km47
Älvängen S 16 Ln33
AlvarAalto-museo FIN 18 Mf28
Alvarado CO 280 Gc43
Alvarado MEX (VC) 264 Fc36
Alvarães BR (AM) 286 Gh47
Alvaréz RA (SF) 301 Gk62
Alvaro Obregón MEX 262 Ef32
Alvaro Obregón MEX (CHH) 247 Eg31
Alvdal N 14 Ll28
Älvdalen S 15 Lo30
Älvdalen S 15 Lp29
Alvear RA (CR) 301 Hb60
Alvesta S 17 Lp34
Älvho S 15 Lp29
Älvik N 14 Lg30
Alvin USA (TX) 253 Fc31
Alvinópolis BR (MG) 299 Hj56
Alvito P 30 Kn48
Älvkarleby S 15 Ls30
Alvorada BR (RS) 302 He61
Alvorada BR (TO) 294 Hf52
Alvorada do Gurguéia BR (PI) 294 Hj50
Alvorada do Norte BR (GO) 294 Hg53
Alvorado d'Oeste BR (RO) 292 Gj51
Alvord Valley USA 244 Ea24
Alvøy N 14 Le30
Älvros S 15 Ln29
Älvros S 15 Lp28
Älvsbyn S 12 Ma13
Älvsered S 17 Ln33
Al Wahah LAR 183 Lk31
Al Wajh KSA 70 Mj32
Al Wakrah Q 78 Nf33
Alwar IND (RJT) 110 Oj32
Al Wari'ah KSA 71 Nd32
Al Widyan IRQ/KSA 69 Na29
Al Wigh LAR 189 Lh33
Al Wittyah LAR 182 Lf29
Alxa Gaoyuan VRC 96 Qa25
Alxa Youqi VRC (NMZ) 96 Qa26
Alxa Zuoqi VRC (NMZ) 96 Qc26
Alyangula AUS (NT) 145 Rj52
Al Yaroubiyeh SYR 69 Nb27
Al-Yasat UAE 78 Ng33
Alyawarra & Katitja A.L. AUS 149 Rh56
Alytus LT 19 Me36
Alz D 37 Ln42
Alzada USA (MT) 245 Eh23
Alzey D 36 Lj41
Alzira E 31 Ku49
Ama MYA 118 Ph38
Ama PNG 164 Sa48
Amacayacu, P.N. CO 285 Gf47
Amaciá BR (AM) 286 Gh48
Amaculi MEX (DGO) 262 Eg33
Amacuro YV 282 Gk41
Amada Gaza RCA 203 Lh43
Åmådalen S 15 Lp29
Amada Temple ET 185 Mg34
Amadi BD 116 Pe34
Amadi RDC 209 Md44
Amadi RDC 209 Me44
Amadi SUD 209 Mf43
Amadjuak Lake CDN 234 Gb05
Amadora P 30 Kl48
Amadrar DZ 188 Ld33
Amadror CO 280 Gc42
Amager DK 16 Ln35
Amahai RI 134 Re47
Amakouladji RMM 193 Kk37
Amakusa N.P. J 107 Re29
Amakusa-shoto J 107 Re29
Amal OM 73 Nh36
Åmål S 15 Ln31
Amalapuram IND (APH) 113 Pb37
Amalfi CO 280 Gc42
Amalfi I 44 Lp50
Amalia SA 225 Mc59
Amaliáda GR 50 Mb53
Amalner IND (MHT) 112 Oh35
Amaluza EC 284 Ga47
Amaluza EC 284 Ga48
Amamá RA (SE) 300 Gj59
Amamapare RI 135 Rj48
Amambai BR (MS) 298 Hc57
Amambai, T.I. BR 298 Hc57
Amami Islands J 107 Re32
Amanã BR 287 Hb48
Amanab PNG 164 Sa47
Aman Abad IR 77 Nk27
Amancio Rodríguez C 269 Gb35
Amandit River Rafting RI 130 Qh47
Amándola I 43 Lo48
Amaneyé, T.I. BR 288 Hf47
Amanganj IND (MPH) 113 Pa33
Amani Nature Reserve EAT 215 Mk48
Amantea I 45 Lr51
Amanzimtoti SA 225 Mf61
Amapá BR 277 Hb18
Amapá BR (AP) 283 He44
Amapari BR 287 Hd45
Amapora BR (PR) 298 Hd57
Amar ETH 206 Mj43
Amara RO 47 Mh46
Amara Abu Sin SUD 198 Mh39
Amaradia RO 46 Md46
Amara, Mount ETH 206 Mj41
Amarante BR (PI) 289 Hj49
Amarante P 28 Km51
Amarante do Maranhão BR (MA) 288 Hg48
Amaranth CDN (MB) 248 Fa20
Amărăştii de Jos RO 48 Me47
Amara West Temple SUD 198 Mf36
Amarbayasgalant Monastery MNG 94 Qc21
Amardalay MNG 94 Qd22
Amareleja P 30 Kn48
Amargosa BR (BA) 295 Ja52
Amargosa Desert USA 246 Eb27
Amargosa Range USA 246 Eb27
Amarillas C 268 Fk34
Amarillo USA (TX) 252 Ek28
Amárinthos GR 50 Md52
Amariú BR (BA) 295 Hk51
'Amar Jadid SUD 197 Mc38
Amarkantak IND (MPH) 113 Pa34
Amarnath IND (MHT) 112 Og36
Amarnath Cave PK 83 Oh28
Amarpatan IND (MPH) 113 Pa33
Amarpur IND (TRP) 116 Pf34
Amaru RO 47 Mg46
Amarwara IND (MPH) 113 Ok34
Amasya TR 66 Mh25
Amata AUS (SA) 148 Rg59
Amatari BR (AM) 286 Ha47
Amatenango del Valle MEX (CHP) 265 Fd37
Amatitlán GCA 265 Fe38
Amatrice I 44 Lo48
Amatura BR (AM) 285 Gf47
Amau PNG 165 Se51
Amaya E 29 Kq52
Amazmaz RIM 191 Kd36
Amazon 277 Hb19
Amazonas BR 276 Gc20
Amazon Cone 277 Hc17
Amazônia, P.N. de BR 287 Hb48
Amazon Shelf 277 Hc18
Amba Alage ETH 199 Mk40
Ambad IND (MHT) 112 Oh36
Ambae VU 168 Td53
Amba Farit ETH 206 Mk40
Ambagarh Chauki IND (CGH) 113 Pa35
Amba Giyogis ETH 199 Mj40
Ambah IND (MPH) 111 Ok32
Ambahikily RM 228 Nb56
Ambajogai IND (MHT) 112 Oj36
Ambala IND (HYA) 111 Oj30
Ambalabe RM 228 Ne55
Ambalabongo RM 228 Nd54
Ambalajanakomby RM 228 Nd54
Ambalakely RM 228 Nd56
Ambalakirajy RM 227 Ne53
Ambalamanakana RM 228 Nd56
Ambalamanasy II RM 227 Ne53
Ambalangoda CL 115 Pa43
Ambalantota CL 115 Pa43
Ambalapaiso RM 227 Ne53
Ambalarondra RM 228 Ne55
Ambala Sadar IND (HYA) 111 Oj30
Ambalatany RM 228 Nd57
Ambalavao RM 228 Nd56
Ambam CAM 203 Lf44
Ambanja RM 227 Ne52
Ambar PE 290 Gb51
Ambararata RM 227 Ne53
Ambargasta RA (SE) 300 Gj60
Ambasa IND (TRP) 116 Pf34
Ambasamudram IND (TNU) 115 Oj42
Ambathala AUS (QLD) 157 Sc58
Ambato EC 284 Ga46
Ambato RM 228 Nd55
Ambato Boeny RM 228 Nd54
Ambatofinandrahana RM 228 Nd56
Ambatolahy RM 228 Nd56
Ambatolampy RM 228 Nd55
Ambatomainty RM 228 Nc54
Ambatomanoina RM 228 Nd55
Ambatondrazaka RM 228 Ne54
Ambatoriha RM 227 Ne53
Ambatosia RM 227 Ne53
Ambatovory RM 228 Nd56
Ambatry RM 228 Nc57
Ambaúba BR (AM) 285 Gg45
Ambazac F 26 Lb45
Ambelákia GR 48 Mc51
Ambelau RI 134 Rd47
Ambelónas GR 50 Ma51
Ambelónas GR 48 Mc51
Amber Bay USA 238 Cb17
Ambered ARM 74 Nc25
Amber Fort IND 110 Oh32
Amberg D 37 Lm41
Ambergris Cay BH 265 Fg36
Ambérieu-en-Bugey F 27 Lf45
Ambert F 27 Ld45
Ambidédi RMM 191 Ke38
Ambikanagar IND (WBG) 116 Pd34
Ambikapur IND (CGH) 113 Pb34
Ambila RM 228 Nd56
Ambil Island RP 124 Ra39
Ambilobe RM 227 Ne52
Ambin RMM 192 Kh38
Ambinanindrano RM 228 Nd56
Ambinanindrano RM 228 Ne56
Ambinanitromby RM 228 Ne55
Ambioa, T.I. BR 288 Hf49
Ambitle Island PNG 166 Sg48
Ambjörby S 15 Lo30
Amble GB 21 Kt35
Ambler USA (AK) 239 Cb12
Ambleside GB 23 Ks36
Ambo PE 290 Gb51
Amboahangibe RM 227 Ne53
Amboahangy RM 228 Nd58
Amboasary RM 228 Nd55
Amboasary RM 228 Nd58
Amboasary Gara RM 228 Ne55
Amboavory RM 228 Ne54
Ambodiangezoka RM 227 Ne53
Ambodiatafana RM 228 Ne54
Ambodibonara RM 227 Ne52
Ambodifototra RM 228 Ne54
Ambodiharina RM 228 Ne55
Ambodilazana RM 228 Ne55
Ambodiriana RM 228 Ne54
Ambodítetezana-Sahana RM 227 Nf53
Ambohidratrimo RM 228 Nd55
Ambohijanahary RM 228 Ne54
Ambohimahamasina RM 228 Nd56
Ambohimahasoa RM 228 Nd56
Ambohimanga RM 228 Nd55
Ambohimanga RM 228 Nd56
Ambohimilanja RM 228 Nd55
Ambohimitaonana RM 228 Nd56
Ambohipaky RM 228 Nc54
Ambohisary RM 228 Nd55
Ambohitra RM 227 Ne52
Ambohitra RM 227 Ne52
Ambohitralanana RM 227 Nf53
Ambohitsilaozana RM 228 Ne54
Amboise F 24 Lb43
Amboiva ANG 216 Lh51
Amboli IND (MHT) 112 Og38
Ambolobozo RM 226 Nd53
Ambolobozokely RM 227 Ne52
Ambolomoty RM 228 Nd54
Ambon RI 134 Rd47
Ambon RI 134 Re47
Ambondro RM 228 Nc58
Ambondromamy RM 228 Nd54
Ambongo RM 226 Nc54
Amboni Caves EAT 215 Mk48
Amboriala RM 227 Ne52
Amborompotsy RM 228 Nd56
Amborondolo RM 227 Ne52
Amboró, P.N. BOL 297 Gj54
Amboseli N.P. EAK 212 Mj47
Ambositra RM 228 Nd56
Ambotosoratra RM 228 Ne54
Ambovombe RM 228 Nd58
Amboy USA (CA) 246 Ec28
Amboy USA (MN) 251 Fc24
Amboy Crater USA 246 Ec28
Amboyna Cay 126 Qg42
Ambrim VU 168 Te54
Ambriz ANG 210 Lg49
Ambrolauri GE 74 Nb24
Ambuaki RI 134 Rg46
Ambulong Island RP 125 Ra39
Ambunten RI 132 Qg49
Ambunti PNG 165 Sb48
Ambur IND (TNU) 115 Ok40
Am Dafok RCA 204 Mb40
Am-Dam TCH 204 Ma39
Amdassa RI 137 Rf49
Amderma RUS 62 Oa05
Am Djeména RCA 204 Ma41
Am Djemena TCH 195 Lj39
Amdo VRC (TIB) 93 Pf29
Amealco MEX (QRT) 264 Ek35
Ameca MEX (JLC) 263 Eh35
Ameca La Vieja MEX (ZCT) 263 Eh34
Amedamit ETH 206 Mj40
Ameghino RA (BA) 301 Gj63
Ameib NAM 220 Lh56
Ameixial P 30 Kn47
Ameland NL 34 Lf37
Amélia I 44 Ln48
Amelia Island USA 259 Fk30
Amélie-les-Bains F 26 Lc48
Amelinghausen D 35 Ll37
Améloud RN 194 Ld37
Amelup AUS (WA) 150 Qk63
Amendolara I 45 Lr51
Ameng VRC (YUN) 100 Qc34
Amenia USA (NY) 257 Gd25
Amentego SUD 198 Mf37
Ameri IR 78 Nf30
América BR (AM) 286 Gh49
Americana BR (SP) 298 Hg57
American Falls USA (ID) 245 Ed24
American Fork USA (UT) 245 Ee25
American Fs. Res. USA 245 Ed24
American Samoa USA 141 Bb11
Americus USA (GA) 259 Fh29
Amersfoort NL 34 Lf38
Amersfoort SA 225 Me59
Amery ANT (AUS) 313 Oc32
Amery Ice Shelf ANT 313 Od32
Ames USA (IA) 251 Fd24
Amesbury GB 23 Kt39
Ameya ETH 206 Mj42
Amfiklia GR 50 Mc52
Amfilohía GR 50 Mb52
Ámfissa GR 50 Mc52
Amfiteatri AL 48 Lu49
Amga RUS 63 Rc06
Amga RUS 63 Rc06
Amgala DARS 186 Ke32
Amgaon IND (MHT) 113 Pa35
Amgu RUS 103 Rj23
Amguid DZ 188 Lc32
Amgun' RUS 102 Rh20
Amguri IND (ASM) 116 Pg32
Amherst CDN (NS) 255 Gh23
Amherst = Kyaikkami MYA 118 Pj37
Amherst USA (MA) 257 Gd24
Amhertsburg CDN (ON) 256 Fj24
Am Himédé TCH 204 Ma39
Amhuinnsuidhe Castle GB 20 Ko33
Amicalola Falls USA 259 Fh28
Amidon USA (ND) 250 Ej22
Amiens F 25 Lc41
Amik Gölü TR 66 Mj27
Amile NEP 92 Pb32
Amili IND (ARP) 117 Ph31
Amilly F 25 Lc43
Aminagou RCA 209 Mc43
Amindeo GR 48 Mb50
Amindivi Islands IND 114 Og41
Amini Island IND 114 Og41
Åminne S 17 Lt33
Amino J 105 Rh28
Aminuis NAM 220 Lk57
Amir Abad IR 77 Oa27
Amirante Basin 227 Nh49
Amirante Islands SY 227 Ng48
Amirante Trench 227 Ng49
Amir Chah PK 84 Ob31
Amiri SUD 205 Mh40
Amirkala IR 76 Ng27
Amish Acres USA 256 Fg25
Amisk Lake CDN 248 Ej18
Amite USA (LA) 253 Fe30
Amity Point AUS (QLD) 157 Sg59
Amizmiz MA 180 Kf30
Amkunj IND (AAN) 115 Pg39
Amkusa-nada J 107 Re29
Amla IND (MPH) 113 Ok35
Amlakhi IND (ASM) 116 Pg33
Amlamé RT 201 La42
Amlekhganj NEP 92 Pc32
Åmli N 14 Lj32
Amlwch GB 22 Kq37
'Amm Adam SUD 199 Mj38
Amman JOR 68 Mh30
Ammarnäs S 12 Lj13
Ammaroo AUS (NT) 149 Rh56
Ammassalik DK 235 Ja05
Ammersee D 37 Lm43
Ammochostos CY 53 Mo55
Ammochostos Bay CY 53 Mp55
Ammochostos = Gazimağusa CY 53 Mo55
Ammouk RMM 193 Kk36
Amnat Charoen THA 119 Qc38
Amnok Gang DVRK/VRC 104 Rd25
Amoama GH 201 Kj42
Amol IR 76 Ng27
Amoliani GR 49 Md50
Amon MA 180 Ke31
Amontada BR (CE) 289 Ja47
Amores RA 301 Ha59
Amorgós GR 51 Mf54
Amorgós GR 51 Mf54
Amorinopolis BR (GO) 298 He54
Amory USA (MS) 253 Ff29
Amos CDN (QC) 254 Ga21
Åmot N 14 Lj31
Åmot N 14 Lk31
Åmot N 14 Ll29
Åmot S 15 Lr30
Amotape, Cerros de PE 284 Fk48
Åmotfors S 14 Ln31
Amotopo SME 283 Hb44
Amou F 26 Ku47
Amou RT 201 La42
Amouguér MA 180 Kh29
Amou Oblo RT 201 La42
Amoy = Xiamen VRC (FJN) 101 Qk33
Amoya GH 201 Kj42
Ampah RI 130 Qh46
Ampahana RM 227 Nf53
Ampalu RI 128 Qa46
Ampana RI 131 Ra46
Ampanefena RM 227 Ne52
Ampang RI 133 Qj50
Ampani IND (ORS) 113 Pb36
Ampaniby RM 228 Nc58
Ampanolahamiraty RM 227 Ne52
Ampara CL 115 Pa43
Amparafaravola RM 228 Ne54
Amparihy Atsinanana RM 228 Nd57
Amparo BR (SP) 299 Hg57
Ampasimanolotra RM 228 Ne55
Ampasimatera RM 226 Nd53
Ampasina-Maningory RM 228 Ne54
Ampasinambo RM 228 Ne56
Ampefy RM 228 Nd55
Amper D 37 Lm42
Amper WAN 194 Le41
Ampère BR (PR) 302 Hd58
Ampère Seamount 176 Kb12
Ampezzo I 43 Ln44
Amphitheâtre d'El Djem TN 182 Lf28
Amphitrite Group RP 124 Qg37
Ampisikinana RM 227 Ne52
Ampitatafika RM 228 Nd55
Ampiyacu PE 285 Gd47
Amplepuis F 27 Le45
Ampliación la Loma MEX (TM) 263 Fa33
Ampombiantambo RM 227 Ne52
Amporaha RM 227 Ne52
Amposta E 32 La50
Amqui CDN (QC) 254 Gg21
Amrabad IND (APH) 113 Ok37
Amran YE 72 Nb38
Amrapara IND (JKD) 116 Pd33
Amrati IND (CGH) 113 Pa36
Amravan IR 76 Nh28
Amravati IND (MHT) 112 Oj35
Am Raya TCH 195 Lj38
Amreli IND (GUJ) 112 Of35
Amritsar IND (PJB) 110 Oh30
Amroha IND (UPH) 111 Ok31
Amrum D 34 Lj36
Amsāga RIM 186 Kd35
Am Sak TCH 204 Lk39
Amsel DZ 188 Lc34
Amsterdam NL 34 Le38
Amsterdam SA 225 Mf59
Amsterdam USA (NY) 257 Gc24
Amsterdam 315 Ob13
Amsterdamøya N 13 Lf06
Amstetten A 37 Lp42
Amtali BD 116 Pf34
Am Tanabo TCH 195 Lj39
Am Timan TCH 204 Ma40
Amudalavalsa IND (APH) 113 Pb36
Amudarja TM 75 Ob26
Amudarjo UZB 75 Nk24
Amu-Dar'ya TM 77 Oc27
Amudat EAU 212 Mh45
Amulung RP 125 Ra37
Amund Ringnes Island CDN 235 Fa03
Amundsen Bay 313 Nc32
Amundsen Glacier 312 Ca36
Amundsen Gulf CDN 234 Dd04
Amundsen Ridge ANT 312 Eb32
Amundsen Sea ANT 312 Ec32
Amungen S 15 Lq29
Amungwiwa, Mount PNG 165 Sd49
Amuntai RI 130 Qh47
Amur RUS 63 Ra08
Amur RUS/VRC 87 Ra08
Amurang RI 131 Rc45
Amursk RUS 102 Rj20
Amursko-Zejskaja ravnina RUS 102 Rd19
Amusquillo E 28 Kq51
Amvrakikós Kólpos GR 50 Ma51
Amyl RUS 89 Ph19
Amzacea RO 47 Mj47
Am-Zoer TCH 197 Ma38
Anaa Atoll F (FPY) 171 Ch54
Anabanua RI 131 Ra47
Anabar RUS 63 Qc04
Anabarskoe plato RUS 62 Qb04
Anaborano RM 227 Ne52
Anacadiña YV 281 Gh43
Anacapa Is. USA 246 Ea29
Anaco YV 281 Gh41
Anaconda USA (MT) 245 Ed22
Anacortes USA (WA) 242 Dj21
Anadarko USA (OK) 253 Fb28
Anadyr RUS 63 Tc05
Anadyr' RUS 63 Td06
Anadyrskoye Ploskogor'ye RUS 63 Tc05
Anáfi GR 51 Mf54
Anáfi GR 51 Mf54
Anafonitria GR 50 Ma53
Anagé BR (BA) 295 Hk53
Anaghit ER 199 Mk38
Anagni I 44 Lo49
Anagodu IND (KTK) 114 Oj39
Anah IRQ 69 Na28
Anaharavi GR 50 Lu51
Anaheim USA (CA) 246 Eb29
Anahidrano RM 226 Nd53
Anahim Lake CDN (BC) 242 Dh19
Anahita IR 76 Ne28
Anáhuac MEX (NL) 263 Ek32
Anahuac N.W.R. USA 253 Fc31
Anai Mudi IND 115 Oj41
Anajás BR (PA) 288 Hf46
Anajatuba BR (MA) 288 Hh47
Anakalang RI 133 Qk50
Anakao RM 228 Nb57
Anakapalle IND (APH) 113 Pb37
Anakch DARS 186 Kd32
Anakie AUS (QLD) 155 Sd57
Anakopia Caves GE 74 Na24
Anaktuvuk Pass USA (AK) 239 Ce11
Anaktuvuk River USA 239 Ce11
Analalava RM 226 Nd53
Analavelona RM 228 Nc57
Analavory RM 228 Nd55
Anamã BR (AM) 286 Gk47
Anamaduwa CL 115 Pa43
Ana-Maria PE 290 Gc49
Anambe, T.I. BR 288 Hf47
Anambra WAN 202 Ld42
Anamorium TR 66 Mg27
Anamur TR 66 Mg27
Anamur TR 53 Mn54
Anamur Burnu TR 66 Mg27
Anan J 105 Rh29
Ananás BR (TO) 288 Hf49
Ananas, T.I. BR 282 Gk44
Anand IND (GUJ) 112 Og34
Ananda CI 201 Kh42
Anandgarh IND (RJT) 110 Og31
Anandpur IND (ORS) 116 Pd35
Anandpur Sahib IND (PJB) 111 Oj30
Anan'evo KS 81 Oj24
Añangu EC 284 Gb46
Anangu Pitjantjatjara A.L. AUS 148 Rf59
Anan'iv UA 47 Mk43
Ananthapur IND (APH) 115 Oj39
Anantnag 83 Oh29
Anantsono RM 228 Nb57
Anapa RUS 57 Mj23
Anápolis BR (GO) 298 Hf54
Anapu BR 287 He46
Anapu BR 287 He47
Anapurus BR (MA) 289 Hj47
Anar IR 76 Nh30
Anarak IR 76 Nf29
Anar Darreh AFG 82 Oa29

Catambué – Chamburi Kalat

Catambué ANG 216 Lk54
Catanacuname YV 285 Gg44
Catanauan RP 125 Rb39
Catandica MOC 222 Mg55
Catanduanes Island RP 125 Rc39
Catanduva BR (SP) 298 Hf56
Catanduvas BR (PR) 298 Hd58
Catangalo BR (RJ) 299 Hj57
Catanhede BR (MA) 288 Hh47
Catánia I 44 Lq53
Catán Lil RA (NE) 304 Ge65
Catanzaro I 45 Lr52
Catanzaro Marina I 45 Lr52
Catarama EC 284 Ga46
Cataratas del Iguazú BR/RA 298 Hc58
Catarina BR (CE) 289 Ja49
Catarman RP 125 Rc39
Catata-a-Nova ANG 216 Lh52
Catatumbo YV 280 Gd41
Catatumbo-Barí, P.N. CO 280 Gd41
Catavi BOL 296 Gf55
Catauá MOC 218 Mg53
Catazajá MEX (CHP) 265 Fd37
Catbalogan RP 127 Rc40
Cat Ba N.P. VN 100 Qd35
Cat-Bazar KS 81 Og24
Cat Cays BS 261 Ga33
Catechane MOC 222 Mg57
Catedral de Ávila E 28 Kq50
Catedral de Barbastro E 32 La48
Catedral de Burgos E 29 Kr52
Catedral de Ciudad Rodrigo E 28 Ko50
Catedral de Cuenca E 31 Ks50
Catedral de León E 28 Kp52
Catedral de Sal CO 280 Gd43
Catedral de Sigüenza E 31 Ks51
Catedral de Toledo E 31 Kq49
Catedral de Tortosa E 32 La50
Catedral de València E 31 Ku49
Catedral de Viseu P 28 Kn50
Catedral de Zamora E 28 Kp51
Catedral La Seo de Zaragoza E 29 Ku51
Cateel Bay RP 127 Rd42
Catemaco MEX (VC) 265 Fc36
Catembe MOC 225 Mg59
Catende BR (PE) 295 Jc50
Catengue ANG 216 Lg52
Cateraggio F 33 Lk48
Catete ANG 210 Lg50
Catete BR 287 Hh49
Cathcart SA 225 Md62
Cathedral Cave AUS (QLD) 157 Sd58
Cathedral Caverns USA 258 Fg28
Cathedral Cove NZ 160 Th64
Cathédrale de Clermont-Ferrand F 27 Ld45
Cathédrale de Lausanne CH 36 Lg44
Cathédrale de Narbonne F 27 Ld47
Cathédrale de Reims F 25 Le41
Cathédrale de Saint-Bertrand-de-Comminges F 26 La47
Cathédrale de Strasbourg F 25 Lh42
Cathédrale de Vienne F 27 Le45
Cathédrale d'Orléans F 25 Lb43
Cathédrale du Puy-en-Velay F 27 Ld45
Cathedral Gorge S.P. USA 244 Ec27
Cathedral Peak SA 225 Me60
Cathedral Prov. Park CDN 242 Dk21
Cathedral Rock N.P. AUS 157 Sg61
Cathedral Valley USA 245 Ee26
Catingal BR (BA) 295 Hk53
Catió GNB 191 Kc40
Catipari Mamoria, T.I. BR 291 Gg49
Cat Island BS 261 Gc33
Catkal KS 80 Of25
Catkal kyrka toosu KS 80 Of25
Cat Lake CDN (ON) 248 Fe20
Cat Lake CDN 248 Fe20
Catoco Cangola ANG 210 Lh50
Cato Island AUS 143 Sd23
Catolé do Rocha BR (PB) 289 Jb49
Catolo ANG 211 Lj50
Caton Island USA 238 Bj18
Catoute E 28 Ko52
Catriel RA (RN) 304 Gg64
Catriló RA (LP) 305 Gj64
Catrimani BR (RR) 286 Gj45
Catrimani BR 286 Gj45
Catrimani BR (RR) 286 Gk45
Catskill USA (NY) 257 Gd24
Catskill Mts. USA 257 Gc24
Catskill Park USA 257 Gc25
Cattedrale di Bari I 45 Lr49
Cattedrale d'Otranto I 45 Lt50
Cat Tien N.P. VN 119 Qd40
Cattle Creek AUS (NT) 145 Rf54
Cattólica I 43 Ln47
Cattolica di Stilo I 45 Lr52
Catu BR (BA) 295 Ja52
Catúa RA (PJ) 296 Gg57
Catuane MOC 225 Mg59
Catulene MOC 218 Mh54
Catumbela ANG 216 Lh52
Cátura MOC 219 Mk52
Caturama BR (BA) 295 Hj52
Čatyrkël KS 81 Oh25
Catyrtaš KS 81 Oj25
Cauaburi BR 285 Gg45
Cauale ANG 210 Lj49
Căuaș RO 46 Mc43
Cauayan RP 125 Ra37
Cauayan RP 127 Rb41
Cauca ANG 210 Lh50
Cauca CO 280 Gc42
Caucagua YV 281 Gg40
Caucaia BR (CE) 289 Ja47
Caucas BOL 297 Ha54
Caucasia CO 280 Gc41
Caucasus RUS/GE 64 Na10
Caucete RA (SJ) 300 Gf61
Cauchari RA (PJ) 296 Gg58
Caudry F 25 Ld40
Cauit Point RP 127 Rd41
Caumbue ANG 211 Ma50
Caumont-l'Éventé F 24 Ku41
Caunes-Minervois F 26 Lc47
Čaunskaja Guba RUS 63 Tb04
Caupolican BOL 291 Gf52
Cauquenes RCH 304 Gd63
Caura YV 281 Gh42
Caurés BR 286 Gj46
Cauro F 33 Lj49
Causapscal CDN (QC) 254 Gg21
Căușeni MD 47 Mk44
Causey USA (NM) 247 Ej29
Caussade F 26 Lb46
Cautário BR 291 Gh52
Cauterets F 26 Ku48
Cautin RCH 304 Gd65
Cauto Embarcadero C 269 Gb35
Cauvery IND 115 Ok41
Cava MOC 219 Na53
Cava de'Tirreni I 44 Lp50
Cavaillon F 27 Lf47
Cavalaire-sur-Mer F 27 Lg47
Cavalcante BR (GO) 294 Hg52
Cavalese I 42 Lm44
Cavalier USA (ND) 248 Fb21
Cavalla LB 200 Kg43
Cavalla LB 200 Kg43
Cavally CI 200 Kg43
Cavalo MOC 222 Mh55
Cavan IRL 20 Kn37
Căvăran RO 46 Mc45
Çavdarhisar TR 52 Mk51
Çavdır TR 52 Mk53
Cave NZ 161 Tf68
Cave City USA (AR) 253 Fe28
Cave Junction USA (OR) 244 Dj24
Cavendish AUS (VIC) 158 Sb64
Cave paintings (Alem Maya) ETH 206 Na41
Caverna de Santana BR 298 Hf58
Caverna do Diabo BR 298 Hf58
Caverna do Francês BR 293 Hc53
Cavernas de Júmandí EC 284 Gb46
Cavernas do Peruaçu, P.N. BR 294 Hh53
Caverns of Sonora USA 252 Ek30
Cave Rock SA 225 Mf61
Cave Temple (Dambulla) CL 115 Pa43
Cavili Island RP 127 Ra41
Cavite RP 125 Ra38
Cavnic RO 46 Md43
Cavour I 42 Lh46
Cavtat HR 45 Lt48
Cavustepe TR 67 Nb26
Čavusy BY 54 Mf19
Cawayan RP 127 Rb40
Cawdor Castle GB 21 Kr33
Caxambu BR (MG) 299 Hh56
Caxias BR (MA) 288 Hj48
Caxias do Sul BR (RS) 302 He60
Caxito ANG 210 Lg50
Caxuxa BR (MA) 288 Hh48
Çay TR 53 Mm52
Çayağzı TR 52 Mk49
Cayaltí PE 290 Ga49
Cayambe EC 284 Ga45
Cayambe, Volcán EC 284 Ga45
Cayapas EC 284 Ga45
Çaybeyi TR 66 Mj27
Cay Caulker BH 265 Fg37
Çayeli TR 67 Na25
Cayenne F 283 Hd43
Cayeux-sur-Mer F 25 Lb40
Çaygören Baraj TR 52 Mj51
Çayhan TR 53 Mp53
Çayıralan TR 53 Mq51
Çayırhan TR 53 Mm50
Çayırova = Agios Theodoros CY 53 Mp55
Çayırözü TR 53 Mq52
Çaylar TR 67 Na26
Çayli AZ 74 Nd25
Cay Lobos C 269 Gb34
Caylus F 26 Lb46
Cayman Brac GB 269 Ga36
Cayman Islands GB 268 Fk36
Cayman Ridge 268 Fj36
Cayman Trench 268 Fj37
Cay Marino 126 Qh41
Cayñabo SP 207 Nd41
Cayo Arenas MEX 265 Fe34
Cayo Becerro HN 266 Fj38
Cayo Becerro HN 266 Fj38
Cayo Caballones C 269 Ga35
Cayo Cabeza del Este C 269 Ga35
Cayo Cantiles C 268 Fj35
Cayo Caratasca HN 266 Fj37
Cayo Caratasca HN 266 Fj37
Cayo Centro MEX 265 Fg36
Cayo Coco C 269 Ga34
Cayo del Rosario C 268 Fj35
Cayo de Santa María C 269 Ga34
Cayo Fragoso C 269 Ga34
Cayo Gorda HN 266 Fj38
Cayo Gorda HN 266 Fj38
Cayo Grande C 269 Ga35
Cayo Guajaba C 269 Gb35
Cayo Guillermo C 269 Ga34
Cayo Largo C 268 Fj35
Cayo Largo C 268 Fk35
Cayo Lobos MEX 265 Fg36
Cayo Mambí C 269 Gc35
Cayo Nuevo MEX 265 Fd35
Cayo Ramona C 268 Fk34
Cayo Romano C 269 Gb34
Cayo Sabinal C 269 Gb35
Cayos Anctitas C 269 Ga35
Cayos Blancos del Sur C 268 Fk34
Cayos Cajones HN 266 Fj37
Cayos Cajones HN 266 Fj37
Cayos Cinco Balas C 269 Ga35
Cayos Cocorocuma HN 266 Fj38
Cayos Cocorocuma HN 266 Fj38
Cayos de Albuquerque CO 266 Fk39
Cayos de E.S.E. CO 267 Fk39
Cayos de Perlas NIC 266 Fj39
Cayos de Roncador CO 267 Fk39
Cayos de San Felipe C 268 Fj35
Cayos Guerrero NIC 266 Fj39
Cayos King NIC 266 Fj39
Cayos los Indios C 268 Fj35
Cayos Mayores del Cabo Falso HN 266 Fj38
Cayos Mayores del Cabo Falso HN 266 Fj38
Cayos Miskitos NIC 266 Fj38
Cayos Morrison Dennis NIC 266 Fj38
Cayos NASA NIC 266 Fj38
Cayo Tyara NIC 266 Fj39
Cayo Vivorillo HN 266 Fj38
Cayo Vivorillo HN 266 Fj38
Cay Sal BS 260 Fk34
Cay Santo Damingo BS 261 Gc35
Cayuga Lake USA 257 Gb24
Cay Verde BS 261 Gc35
Cazage ANG 217 Ma51
Cazalla de la Sierra E 30 Kp47
Čažaši GE 74 Nb24
Cazaubon F 26 Ku47
Cazenovia USA (NY) 257 Gc24
Cazin BIH 43 Lq46
Čazma HR 43 Lr45
Cazombo ANG 217 Mb51
Cazones MEX (VC) 264 Fb35
Cazorla E 31 Ks47
Cazorla YV 281 Gg41
Cazula MOC 218 Mg53
Cazuza Ferreira BR (RS) 302 He60
Ccatca PE 291 Ge52
Čėrven' BY 54 Me19
Čėrykav BY 54 Mf19
Cea E 28 Kq52
Ceadâr-Lunga MD 47 Mj44
Ceahlău, P.N. RO 47 Mf43
Ceanu Mare RO 46 Md44
Ceará BR 277 Ja19
Ceara Abyssal Plain 277 Hd18
Ceará-Mirim BR (RN) 289 Jc48
Ceará-Mirim BR 289 Jc48
Ceatalchioi RO 47 Mj45
Ceballos MEX (DGO) 263 Eh32
Čeboksary RUS (CHU) 55 Nd17
Cebollati ROU 301 Hc62
Cebollati ROU 301 Hd62
Cebreros E 28 Kq50
Čebrikove UA 47 Ml43
Cebu RP 127 Rb40
Cebu RP 127 Rc40
Čečava BIH 43 Ls46
Ceccano I 44 Lo49
Cece H 41 Lt44
Čečel'nyk UA 47 Mk42
Čechtice CZ 40 Lq41
Cecil Plains AUS (QLD) 157 Sf59
Cécina I 42 Ll47
Cécina I 42 Ll47
Cedar Bay N.P. AUS 153 Sc53
Cedar Bluffs USA (KS) 250 Ek26
Cedar Breaks Nat. Mon. USA 246 Ed27
Cedar City USA (UT) 246 Ed27
Cedaredge USA (CO) 245 Eg26
Cedar Falls USA (IA) 251 Fd24
Cedar Grove USA (CA) 246 Ea27
Cedar Harbour BS 261 Gb32
Cedar Island USA (NC) 259 Gb28
Cedar Island N.W.R. USA 259 Gb28
Cedar Key USA (FL) 260 Fj31
Cedar Lake CDN 248 Ek19
Cedar Park USA (TX) 252 Fb30
Cedar Point USA 256 Fj25
Cedar Rapids USA (IA) 251 Fe24
Cedar River USA (MI) 256 Fg23
Cedar River Grassland N.P. USA 250 Ek22
Cedartown USA (GA) 259 Fh29
Cedarvale CDN (BC) 241 Df18
Cedarville SA 225 Me61
Cedarville USA (CA) 244 Dk25
Cedeira E 28 Km53
Cedeño HN 266 Fg39
Cederberg SA 224 Lk62
Cederberg Wilderness Area SA 224 Lk62
Cedillo E 30 Kn49
Cedoux CDN (SK) 248 Ej21
Cedral BR (MA) 288 Hh46
Cedral MEX (SLP) 263 Ek34
Cedrillas E 31 Ku50
Cedro BR (CE) 289 Ja49
Cedros MEX (ZCT) 263 Ek33
Cedros Trench 246 Eb31
Ceduna AUS (SA) 158 Rg62
Cée E 28 Kl52
Ceek SP 207 Nc41
Ceel Afweyn SP 207 Nd41
Ceelayo SP 207 Ne40
Ceel Baxay ETH 207 Nb40
Ceelbur = El Bur SP 207 Nd43
Ceel Dhaab SP 207 Nd41
Ceeldheer SP 207 Nd44
Ceeldhere SP 207 Nd43
Ceel Duubo SP 213 Nc44
Ceel Gaal SP 207 Nf40
Ceel Gaan SP 207 Nd41
Ceel Garas SP 207 Nc43
Ceel Huur SP 207 Ne43
Cefalù I 44 Lp52
Cegdomyn RUS 102 Rg20
Ceglèd H 41 Lu43
Céglie Messápica I 45 Ls50
Cehegin E 31 Kt48
Ceheng VRC (GZH) 100 Qc33
Čehotina SCG 48 Lu47
Čehov RUS 54 Mj18
Čehov RUS 103 Sb22
Cehu Silvaniei RO 46 Md43
Ceibalito RA (SA) 297 Gh58
Ceibal, P.N. GCA 265 Ff37
Ceibas RA (ER) 301 Ha62
Céide Fields IRL 20 Kl36
Čejč CZ 40 Lr42
Čekerek TR 53 Mq50
Çekirge TR 53 Mn51
Čekiške LT 19 Md35
Čekmaguš RUS 55 Nh18
Čekunda RUS 102 Rg20
Čekurdah RUS 63 Sb04
Celano I 44 Lo48
Celanova E 28 Kn52
Celaque, P.N. HN 265 Ff38
Celaraín MEX (QTR) 265 Fg35
Celaya MEX (GJT) 264 Ek35
Čelbas RUS 57 Mk22
Celbridge IRL 22 Ko37
Celebes RI 122 Ra19
Celebes Basin RP 127 Ra42
Celebes Sea RI 122 Ra18
Celebi TR 53 Mo51
Čelebići BIH 48 Lt47
Celendin PE 290 Ga49
Celestún MEX (YT) 265 Fe35
Čelić BIH 46 Lt46
Celica EC 284 Ga48
Celilabad AZ 74 Ne26
Celina RUS 57 Na22
Celina USA (OH) 256 Fh25
Celina USA (TN) 258 Fh27
Čelinac Donji BIH 43 Ls46
Čeljabinsk RUS 62 Oa07
Celjachany BY 39 Mf38
Celje SLO 43 Lq44
Cella E 31 Kt50
Celldömölk H 40 Ls43
Celle D 34 Ll38
Celle Ligure I 42 Lj46
Čelny RUS 102 Rh21
Celorico da Beira P 28 Kn50
Cel'ovce SK 41 Mb42
Celtic Sea 22 Kn40
Çeltik TR 53 Mm51
Çeltikçi TR 53 Ml53
Çeltikli TR 53 Mn51
Cemaru, Gunung RI 130 Qh45
Čemerno BIH 43 Lt47
Cemilbey TR 53 Mq50
Cemilköy TR 53 Mp52
Çemişgezek TR 67 Mk26
Cenderawasih Marine Reserve RI 135 Rh47
Cenepa PE 284 Ga47
Cenovo BG 49 Mf47
Centani SA 225 Me62
Centelles E 32 Lc49
Centenario RA (NE) 304 Gf65
Centenario do Sul BR (PR) 298 He57
Centenary ZW 218 Mf54
Centennial Museum, Barrhead CDN 243 Ec18
Center USA (CO) 247 Eg27
Center USA (ND) 250 Ek22
Center USA (TX) 253 Fc30
Center Hill Lake USA 258 Fh28
Centerville USA (TX) 253 Fc30
Centerville USA (IA) 251 Fd25
Centerville USA (MO) 253 Fe27
Centerville USA (TN) 258 Fg28
Centinela PE 290 Gb51
Centinela PE 290 Gb51
Centinela, Cerro RA 304 Ge64
Cento I 42 Lm46
Centovalli Express CH/I 36 Lj44
Central Buttle CDN (SK) 243 Eg20
Central BR (BA) 295 Hj51
Central RB 221 Mc56
Central African Republic 175 Lb09
Central Australia A.L. AUS 148 Re57
Central Balkan, N.P. BG 49 Me48
Central Brahui Range PK 84 Od31
Central City USA (NE) 250 Fa25
Central City USA (KY) 258 Fg27
Central Desert A.L. AUS 145 Rf55
Central Eastern Rainforest Reserves AUS 157 Sg60
Centralia USA (WA) 242 Dj22
Centralia USA (IL) 251 Ff26
Centralina BR (MG) 298 Hf55
Central Island EAK 206 Mj44
Central Island N.P. EAK 212 Mj44
Central Kalahari Game Reserve RB 221 Mb57
Central Karakorum N.P. PK 83 Oj28
Central los Molles RCH 300 Ge61
Central Makran Range PK 84 Oc32
Central Mosque (Pattani) THA 121 Qa42
Central Mount Wedge AUS 148 Rf57
Central'nojakutskaja ravnina RUS 63 Qd06
Central'notungusskoe plato RUS 62 Pd06
Central Pacific Basin 316 Ba08
Central Patricia CDN (ON) 249 Fe20
Central Range LS 225 Me60
Central Range PNG 165 Sb48
Central Rapel RCH 300 Ge62
Central Reserve A.L. AUS 147 Re58
Central Siberian Plateau RUS 62 Pc05
Centre F 24 Lb43
Centre USA (AL) 259 Fh28
Centre Island AUS 145 Rj53
Centre minier de Lewarde F 25 Ld40
Centre Spatial Guyanais F 283 Hd43
Centreville USA (MS) 253 Fe30
Centreville USA (AL) 258 Fg29
Cenxi VRC (GZG) 100 Qf34
Cenzontle MEX (COH) 263 Ej32
Čepigova MK 48 Mb49
Čepin HR 43 Lt45
Cepu RI 132 Qf49
Cer MK 48 Mb49
Čerachavka BY 54 Mf19
Ceram RI 134 Re47
Ceram Sea RI 134 Rd47
Cerbère F 26 Ld48
Cercal P 30 Km47
Cercle mégalithique SN 191 Kc39
Čerdakly RUS 55 Ne18
Cerdeira P 28 Kn50
Cère F 26 Lb46
Cereal CDN (AB) 243 Ee20
Cerejeiras BR (RO) 292 Gk52
Ceremhovo RUS 94 Qb19
Čeremoš UA 47 Mf42
Ceremošnja Pecina SCG 46 Mb46
Cerëmuški RUS (CHK) 89 Pf19
Čerencovo RUS 54 Mg16
Čerepiški manastir BG 48 Md47
Čerepovec RUS 54 Mj16
Ceres BR (GO) 294 Hf53
Ceres RA (SF) 301 Gk60
Ceres SA 224 Lk62
Čereševo BG 49 Mg47
Ceresole Reale I 42 Lh45
Céret F 26 Lc48
Cerete CO 280 Gc41
Cerezo de Abajo E 29 Kr51
Cerfontaine B 25 Le40
Cerga RUS (ALT) 89 Pc20
Cerignola I 45 Lq49
Çerıklı TR 53 Mp51
Cerillos RA (SA) 296 Gh58
Cerillos RCH 296 Gf57
Cérilly F 27 Lc44
Cerizay F 24 Ku44
Čerkasovo RUS 18 Mj30
Čerkasy UA 56 Mg21
Çerkeş TR 53 Mo50
Čerkessk RUS (KCH) 74 Nb23
Cerkev Marijinega oznanjanja SLO 43 Lp44
Çerkezköy TR 52 Mj49
Cerknica SLO 43 Lp45
Čermasa RUS 55 Nh18
Cermei RO 46 Mb44
Çermik TR 67 Mk26
Cermoltan KZ 81 Oj24
Čern' RUS 54 Mj19
Cerna HR 43 Lt45
Cerna RO 46 Mc46
Cerna RO 47 Mj45
Cerna Domogled, P.N. RO 46 Mc46
Cernaja RUS 95 Qk19
Cerna-Sat RO 46 Mc45
Černava RUS 55 Mk19
Černava RUS 55 Mk19
Cernavodă RO 47 Mj46
Cernay F 25 Lh43
Cernégula E 29 Kr52
Černëvo RUS 18 Mj32
Cernica RO 47 Mg46
Černihiv UA 54 Mf20
Černi Lom BG 49 Mg47
Černivci UA 47 Mf42
Černjachiv UA 56 Me20
Černjaevo RUS 102 Rd19
Černjahovsk RUS 19 Mb36
Černjanka RUS 54 Mj20
Cernovice CZ 40 Lp41
Černozemel'skij kanal RUS 74 Nc23
Černyševsk RUS 95 Qj19
Černyškovskij RUS 55 Nb21
Cerovačke Špilje HR 43 Lq46
Cerovica SCG 48 Mc47
Cerqueira César BR (SP) 298 Hf57
Cerralvo MEX (NL) 263 Fa32
Cerrigydrudion GB 23 Kr37
Cërrik AL 48 Lu49
Cerrito CO 280 Gd42
Cerrito MEX (SLP) 263 Ek34
Cerrito, T.I. BR 298 Hc57
Cerro Aconcagua RA 300 Ge62
Cerro Agua Hedionda RA 300 Gg62
Cerro Aguas Blancas RA/RCH 296 Gf58
Cerro Aguja RA/RCH 304 Ge67
Cerro Aguja RCH 306 Gf73
Cerro Aiguilete RCH 306 Gd71
Cerro Alto Nevado RCH 304 Gd68
Cerro Anecón Chico RA 304 Gf66
Cerro Anecón Grande RA 304 Ge66
Cerro Apacheta RA 296 Gg58
Cerro Archibarca RA 296 Gg58
Cerro Arenales RCH 306 Gd69
Cerro Atajaña RCH 296 Ge55
Cerro Atalaya PE 291 Ge52
Cerro Aucanquilcha RCH 296 Gf56
Cerro Avispa BR/YV 285 Gh45
Cerro Ayapunga PE 284 Gc47
Cerro Azanaques BOL 296 Gg55
Cerro Azul BR (PR) 298 Hf58
Cerro Azul EC 284 Fe46
Cerro Azul MEX (VC) 264 Fb35
Cerro Azul PE 290 Gb52
Cerro Azul RA 304 Ge66
Cerro Azul RCH 300 Ge63
Cerro Balmaceda RCH 306 Gd71
Cerro Barros Arana RCH 304 Gd67
Cerro Bayo RCH 304 Gd68
Cerro Bayo Grande RA 300 Gg59
Cerro Belgrano RA 306 Ge69
Cerro Blanco RA 304 Ge66
Cerro Blanco RCH 300 Ge60
Cerro Bolívar 802 YV 281 Gj42
Cerro Bonete RA 300 Gf59
Cerro Boquete RA 304 Gf67
Cerro Bravo BOL 296 Gg57
Cerro Bravo BOL 297 Gh54
Cerro Bravo RCH 300 Gf59
Cerro Butahuao RA 304 Ge65
Cerro Calderón RA 304 Gf66
Cerro Calpon PE 290 Ga49
Cerro Caltama BOL 296 Gf56
Cerro Campanario RA/RCH 304 Ge63
Cerro Cangrejo RA 306 Gd70
Cerro Carrere RA 304 Gf64
Cerro Centinela RA 304 Ge64
Cerro Cerrón YV 281 Ge40
Cerro Chachil RA 304 Ge65
Cerro Chacras EC 284 Fe46
Cerro Champaquí RA 300 Gh61
Cerro Chato ROU 301 Hc62
Cerro Chenque RA 304 Gg68
Cerro Chihuido de Medio RA 304 Gf64
Cerro Chocca PE 290 Gc52
Cerro Chulluncani BOL 297 Gh55
Cerro Cibaray BOL 296 Gf55
Cerro Cirque BOL 296 Gf54
Cerro Cofre de Perote MEX 263 Fb36
Cerro Cofre, P.N. MEX 264 Fb36
Cerro Coipasa BOL 296 Gf55
Cerro Cojudo Blanco RA 306 Gf69
Cerro Colorado MEX (SO) 262 Ef32
Cerro Colorado RA 304 Gf68
Cerro Colorado RA 300 Gg60
Cerro Colorado RA 300 Gj61
Cerro Colorados RA/RCH 300 Gf59
Cerro Colquen RCH 304 Gd64
Cerro Colupo RCH 296 Ge57
Cerro Convento RA 306 Gf71
Cerro Copa BOL/RCH 296 Gf56
Cerro Coposa RCH 296 Gf56
Cerro Corá BR (RN) 289 Jb49
Cerro Corá RA (MI) 301 Hc59
Cerro Corá, P.N. PY 297 Hb57
Cerro Cordobés RA 300 Gf60
Cerro Corona RA 304 Ge66
Cerro Cotacachi EC 284 Ga45
Cerro Cowan EC 284 Fe46
Cerro Coyaguaima RA 296 Gg57
Cerro Criterion PE 290 Gc53
Cerro Cumbrera RCH 306 Gd69
Cerro Cupisnique PE 290 Ga49
Cerro de Ansilta RA 300 Gf61
Cerro de Curimávida RCH 300 Ge61
Cerro de la Neblina EC 284 Fk46
Cerro de las Ovejas RA 300 Gh62
Cerro Delgado-Chalbaud BR/YV 282 Gj44
Cerro del Inca BOL/RCH 296 Gf56
Cerro de los Bueyes RA 304 Ge64
Cerro del Placeton RCH 300 Ge60
Cerro del Potro RA/RCH 300 Gf60
Cerro del Toro RA/RCH 300 Gf60
Cerro de Pasco PE 290 Gb51
Cerro de Pomasi PE 291 Ge53
Cerro de Tocopuri BOL 296 Gg57
Cerro Doña Ana RCH 300 Ge60
Cerro Doña Inés RCH 300 Gf59
Cerro el Condór RA 300 Gf59
Cerro el Ford RCH 306 Ge72
Cerro Elías RA 304 Gg68
Cerro el Nevado RA 300 Gf63
Cerro el Pedrero RA 304 Gf68
Cerro Fundición RA 296 Gh57
Cerro Galán RA 300 Gg59
Cerro Gallinero YV 281 Gg43
Cerro General M. Belgrano RA 300 Gg60
Cerro Guanay YV 281 Gg43
Cerro Hatscher RA 306 Gd70
Cerro Hoya, P.N. PA 267 Fk42
Cerro Huanchaca BOL 296 Gg56
Cerro Hudson RCH 306 Gd69
Cerro Hyades RCH 306 Gd69
Cerro Igle RA 306 Gd71
Cerro Illesca PE 290 Fk49
Cerro Jeinemeni RCH 306 Gd69
Cerro Juncal RA/RCH 300 Gf62
Cerro la Campana RCH 306 Gd71
Cerro la Criolla RA 306 Ge71
Cerro la Grasa RA 304 Ge65
Cerro La Ramada BOL/RA 296 Gg57
Cerro Largo BR (RS) 302 Hc60
Cerro Las Torolas RA/RCH 300 Gf60
Cerro Lautaro RCH 306 Gd70
Cerro Leiva CO 285 Gf44
Cerro León PY 297 Gk56
Cerro Lique BOL 296 Gh56
Cerro Lliscaya BOL/RCH 296 Gf55
Cerro Lote 15 RA 304 Ge68
Cerro Magallanes MEX 247 Ef30
Cerro Mellizo Sur RCH 306 Gd70
Cerro Mercedario RA 300 Ge61
Cerro Mesa RA 304 Gf65
Cerro Mina CO 280 Gd41
Cerro Mirador RCH 306 Ge72
Cerro Monte León RA 306 Gf71
Cerro Morado RA 296 Gh57
Cerro Moreno RCH 296 Ge57
Cerro Murallón RA/RCH 306 Gd70
Cerrón, Cerro YV 281 Ge40
Cerro Nanchital MEX (VC) 265 Fc37
Cerro Napa BR/RCH 296 Gf56
Cerro Negro RA 304 Ge65
Cerro Negro RA 304 Gf68
Cerro Nevado RCH 304 Gd67
Cerro Norte RA 306 Gd70
Cerro Ovana YV 281 Gg43
Cerro Paine Grande RCH 306 Gd71
Cerro Pajonal RCH 296 Gf56
Cerro Pan de Azúcar RA 306 Gf70
Cerro Paroma BOL/RCH 296 Gf56
Cerro Payún RA 304 Gf64
Cerro Peineta RA 306 Gd71
Cerro Picudo RA 306 Gf69
Cerro Picún Leufú RA 304 Gf65
Cerro Piedra RCH 304 Gd64
Cerro Pináculo RA 306 Gd71
Cerro Pingo Pongo RCH 296 Gf58
Cerro Pintado RA 306 Gd70
Cerro Pircas RA 300 Gf61
Cerro Pissis RA 300 Gf59
Cerro Policia RA (RN) 304 Gf65
Cerro Prieto PE 284 Fk48
Cerro Pular RCH 296 Gf58
Cerro Punta PA 266 Fj41
Cerro Punta Gruesa RA 306 Ge71
Cerro Quichaura RA 304 Ge67
Cerro Rancahué RA 304 Ge65
Cerro Rico BOL 296 Gh55
Cerro Rico RA (SE) 300 Gh60
Cerro Rincón RA/RCH 296 Gg58
Cerro Rucachoroi RA 304 Ge65
Cerros BH 265 Ff36
Cerro Sanchez RA 306 Gf71
Cerro San Cirilo PE 290 Ga49
Cerro San Joaquín EC 284 Ff46
Cerro San Lorenzo PE 290 Ga49
Cerro Santa Elena RA 304 Gh68
Cerro San Valentín RCH 306 Gd69
Cerro Saroche, P.N. YV 281 Gf40
Cerros Colorados RA 304 Gf66
Cerros de Amotape PE 284 Fk48
Cerros de Amotape, P.N. PE 284 Fk48
Cerros de Bala BOL 291 Gg53
Cerros de Campanquiz PE 284 Gb48
Cerros de Canthyuaya PE 290 Gc49
Cerro Sierra Nevada RCH/RA 300 Gf59
Cerro Sin Nombre RCH 306 Gd68
Cerro Sosneado RA 300 Gf63
Cerro Steffen RA/RCH 304 Ge68
Cerro Tamaná CO 280 Gb43
Cerro Tatajachura RCH 296 Gf55
Cerro Tazna BOL 296 Gg56
Cerro Tetari CO/YV 280 Gd40
Cerro Tololo Inter-American Observatory RCH 300 Ge61
Cerro Trapalco RA 304 Gf65
Cerro Tres Altitos RA 300 Gf62
Cerro Tres Cruces MEX 265 Fd38
Cerro Tres Picos RA 305 Gj65
Cerro Tristeza YV 281 Gj40
Cerro Tronador RA/RCH 304 Ge66
Cerro Tunapa BOL 296 Gg55
Cerro Tupungato RA/RCH 300 Gf62
Cerro Turagua YV 281 Gh42
Cerro Uturuncu BOL 296 Gg57
Cerro Ventisquero RA 304 Ge66
Cerro Ventisquero Sur RCH 304 Ge67
Cerro Vera ROU 301 Hb62
Cerro Yarvicoya RCH 296 Gf56
Cerro Yerupaja PE 290 Gb51
Cerro Zapaleri BOL/RA/RCH 296 Gg57
Cerrudo Cué RA (CR) 301 Hb59
Čerskij RUS 63 Ta05
Certaldo I 42 Lm47
Čertegui CO 280 Gb43
Čertižné SK 41 Mb41
Čertkovo RUS 55 Na21
Certosa di Padula I 45 Lq50
Certosa di Pavia I 42 Lk45
Čerusti RUS 55 Na18
Cervales E 30 Kp49
Cervantes AUS (WA) 150 Qh61
Cervantes RP 125 Ra37
Cervaro I 45 Lq49
Červena Skalá SK 41 Ma42
Červená Voda CZ 40 Lr40
Červen Brjag BG 48 Me47
Cervera E 32 Lb49
Cervera del Río Alhama E 29 Kt52
Cervera de Pisuerga E 28 Kq52
Cervéteri I 44 Ln49
Cérvia I 42 Ln46
Cervignano di Friuli I 43 Lo45
Červonoarmijs'ke UA 47 Mj45
Červonohrad UA 39 Me40
Červonoznam'janka UA 47 Ml43
Cesano I 43 Ln47
César CO 280 Gd40
Cesário Lange BR (SP) 298 Hg57
Cešaulja BY 19 Mf37
Cesena I 42 Ln46
Cesenático I 42 Ln46
Cēsis LV 19 Mf33
Česká Kamenice CZ 40 Lp40
Česká Kubice CZ 40 Ln41
Česká Lípa CZ 40 Lp40
České Budějovice CZ 40 Lp42
České Švýcarsko, N.P. CZ 40 Lp42
České Velenice CZ 40 Lp42
Český Brod CZ 40 Lp40
Česky Dub CZ 40 Lp40
Český Krumlov CZ 40 Lp42
Česky ráj CZ 40 Lq40
Český Těšín CZ 40 Lt41
Çeşme TR 51 Mg52
Çeşmelisebil TR 53 Mn52
Češskaja guba RUS 62 Nb05
Cessnock AUS (NSW) 159 Sf62
Cestos LB 200 Kf42
Cestos Point LB 200 Kf43
Cesvaine LV 19 Mg34
Cétar VRC (QHI) 96 Qa27
Cetatea de Baltă RO 46 Me44
Cetatea Heracleea RO 47 Mj46
Cetățeni RO 47 Mf45
Cetingrad HR 43 Lq45
Cetinje SCG 48 Lt48
Çetinkaya TR 67 Mj26
Çetinkaya TR 67 Na27
Cetraro I 45 Lq51
Ceuta E 180 Kh28
Ceuta E 180 Kh28
Ceuta YV 280 Ge41
Ceva I 42 Lj46
Cevedale = Zufallspitze I 42 Ll44
Cévennes F 27 Ld46
Cévennes, P.N. des F 27 Ld46
Cevicos DOM 270 Gf36
Cevizli TR 53 Mm53
Cewice PL 38 Ls36
Ceyhan TR 66 Mh27
Ceyhan Nehri TR 66 Mj27
Ceylanpınar TR 67 Na27
Ceylon CDN (SK) 243 Eh21
Ceylon CL 108 Pa17
Cèze F 27 Le46
Chaacha TM 77 Oa27
Cha-am THA 118 Pk39
Cha'anpu VRC (HUN) 99 Qf31
Chababar IR 79 Oa33
Chabanais F 26 La45
Chabás RA (SF) 301 Gk62
Chabet el Akra DZ 182 Lc27
Chabeuil F 27 Lf46
Chabi IND (MPH) 113 Pa34
Chablis F 25 Ld43
Chaboksar IR 76 Nf27
Chabovičy BY 39 Me38
Chabris F 24 Lb43
Chacabuco RA (BA) 301 Gk63
Chacabuco RCH 306 Gd68
Chacaltaya BOL 296 Gf54
Chacaltongo de Hidalgo MEX (OAX) 264 Fb37
Chacane MOC 222 Mh58
Chacao RCH 304 Gd66
Chacarilla RCH 296 Gf56
Chacas PE 290 Gb50
Chaca Sur RCH 296 Gf55
Chacay Alto RCH 300 Ge60
Chachani, Volcán PE 296 Ge54
Chachapoyas PE 290 Gb49
Chacharan PK 85 Of31
Chacharramendi RA (LP) 304 Gh64
Chaché GH 201 Kj41
Chachil, Cerro RA 304 Ge65
Chachoengsao THA 118 Qa39
Chachro PK 85 Of33
Chaclacayo PE 290 Gb52
Chaco RA 279 Gd24
Chaco Austral RA 301 Gk59
Chaco Boreal PY 297 Gk56
Chaco Central RA 297 Gk58
Chaco Culture N.H.P. USA 247 Ef28
Chacoma BOL 296 Gf55
Chaco, P.N. RA 301 Ha59
Chacras, Cerro EC 284 Fe46
Chad 175 Lb08
Chadakori RN 194 Ld39
Chadaouanka RN 194 Ld38
Chad Basin N.P. WAN 195 Lg39
Chadegan IR 76 Nf29
Chadiza Z 218 Mg53
Chadron USA (NE) 250 Ej24
Chadyang VRC (GDG) 101 Qj34
Chae Hom THA 118 Pk36
Chaek KS 81 Oh25
Chaeryong DVRK 104 Rc26
Chae Son N.P. THA 118 Pk36
Chafe WAN 194 Ld40
Chafo WAN 194 Lc40
Chagai PK 84 Oc31
Chagai Hills PK 84 Ob31
Chagalamarri IND (APH) 115 Ok39
Chaghalvandi IR 76 Ne29
Chaghcharan AFG 82 Oc28
Chaglla PE 290 Gc50
Chagne ETH 206 Mj40
Chagny F 27 Le44
Chagos-Laccadive Ridge 60 Ob11
Chagres, P.N. PA 267 Ga41
Chaguanas TT 282 Gk40
Chaguaramas TT 282 Gk40
Chaguaramas YV 281 Gg41
Chaguaramas YV 282 Gj41
Chaguarpamba EC 284 Ga47
Chagyl TM 75 Nh25
Chahar Borjak AFG 82 Ob30
Chahar Rustal IR 78 Nf31
Chahbounia DZ 181 Lb28
Chahe VRC (YUN) 117 Qb32
Chah-e Ab AFG 82 Oe27
Chah-e-Mosafar IR 77 Nj28
Chahjam IR 76 Nh28
Chah Kavr IR 76 Nh30
Chah Pahn IR 78 Nf32
Chah Sagak IR 77 Oa29
Chah Sorkh IR 78 Ng31
Chah Zardar IR 79 Nk32
Chah Zebar IR 78 Nh31
Chai MOC 219 Na51
Chai Badan THA 118 Qa38
Chaibasa IND (JKD) 113 Pc34
Chail IND (UPH) 113 Pa33
Chaillé-les-Marais F 24 Kt44
Chainat THA 118 Qa38
Chaîne de l'Atakora DY 201 La40
Chaîne des Bibân DZ 181 Lc27
Chai Pra Kan THA 118 Pk36
Chaiqiao VRC (ZJG) 106 Ra31
Chaitanya Temple BD 116 Pf33
Chaitén RCH 304 Gd67
Chaiwopu VRC (XUZ) 89 Pd24
Chaiya THA 120 Pk41
Chaiyaphum THA 118 Qb38
Chajari RA (ER) 301 Ha61
Chajian VRC (AHU) 106 Qk29
Chakachamna Lake USA 239 Cd15
Chakai IND (BIH) 116 Pd33
Chakaktolik USA (AK) 238 Bj15
Chakar PK 84 Oe31
Chakari ZW 222 Me55
Chakavel IND (KTK) 115 Ok40
Chak Chak IR 76 Nh29
Chakchoka IND (WBG) 116 Pe32
Chakdaha IND (WBG) 116 Pe34
Chake Chake EAT 215 Mk48
Chakhansur AFG 82 Ob30
Chak Kompong Som K 119 Qb40
Chakkrarat THA 119 Qb38
Chakradharpur IND (JKD) 113 Pc34
Chakrata IND (UTT) 111 Oj30
Chaksu IND (RJT) 110 Oh32
Chak Swari 83 Og29
Chakur IND (MHT) 112 Oj36
Chak Véal Rénh VN/K 121 Qc40
Chakwal PK 83 Og29
Chakwale EAT 215 Mj48
Chakwenga Z 218 Me53
Chala EAT 214 Mf49
Chala MOC 219 Mh52
Chala PE 290 Gc53
Chalais F 26 La45
Chalakudi IND (KER) 114 Oj41
Chalalou PNG 165 Sc49
Chalamera E 32 La49
Chalamont F 27 Lf45
Chalatenango ES 265 Ff38
Chalaua MOC 219 Mk54
Chalawa WAN 194 Le40
Chalbi Desert EAK 212 Mj44
Chalcatzingo MEX 264 Fa36
Chalchihuites MEX 263 Ej34
Chalco MEX (MEX) 264 Fa36
Chalengkou VRC (QHI) 91 Pg26
Châlette-sur-Loing F 25 Lc42
Chaleur Bay CDN 255 Gh22
Chalhuanca PE 290 Gd53
Chalia = Shehuen RA 306 Ge70
Chaling VRC (HUN) 101 Qg32
Chalinze EAT 215 Mk49
Chalisgaon IND (MHT) 112 Oh35
Chalk Mountain USA (TX) 252 Fb29
Chalky Inlet AUS 161 Td69
Challa AUS (WA) 150 Qk60
Challa BOL 296 Gg54
Challakere IND (KTK) 115 Oj39
Challans F 24 Kt44
Challapalle IND (APH) 113 Pa37
Challapata BOL 296 Gg55
Challenger Deep 162 Sa16
Challis USA (ID) 245 Ec23
Cha Lo VN 119 Qc37
Chaloem Rattanakosin N.P. THA 118 Pk38
Châlons-en-Champagne F 25 Le42
Chalon-sur-Saône F 27 Le44
Chalt 83 Oh27
Cha Lugela MOC 219 Mj54
Châlus F 26 La45
Chalus IR 76 Nf27
Cham CH 36 Lj43
Cham D 37 Ln41
Chama USA (NM) 247 Eg27
Chama Z 218 Mg51
Chamah, Gunung MAL 121 Qa42
Chamama MW 218 Mg52
Chaman PK 82 Od30
Chaman Soltan IR 76 Ne29
Chamba EAT 219 Mj51
Chamba IND (HPH) 111 Oj29
Chamba MOC 219 Mj53
Chamba IND 111 Ok32
Chambak ARM 74 Nc25
Chambaya PE 290 Ga49
Chamberlain CDN (SK) 243 Eh20
Chamberlain USA (SD) 250 Fa24
Chamberlain Lake USA 254 Gf22
Chamberlain River AUS 144 Rd54
Chambers Bay AUS 145 Rf52
Chambersburg USA (PA) 257 Gb26
Chambers Pillar AUS 148 Rg58
Chambéry F 27 Lf45
Chambeshi Z 214 Mf51
Chambira PE 284 Gc48
Chambishi Z 218 Me52
Chambley F 25 Lf41
Chambly F 25 Lc41
Chambo EC 284 Ga46
Chambord CDN (QC) 254 Gd21
Chambord F 24 Lb43
Chambri Lake PNG 165 Sb48
Chamburi Kalat PK 84 Oc32

Chitado – Coguno

Chitado ANG 216 Lg54
Chitalwana IND (RJT) 110 Of33
Chitanda Z 218 Md53
Chi Tanh VN 119 Qe39
Chitedze MW 218 Mg52
Chitek Lake CDN (SK) 243 Eg19
Chitek Lake CDN 248 Fa19
Chitembo ANG 216 Lj52
Chitengo MOC 222 Mh55
Chitina USA (AK) 240 Ch15
Chitina River USA 240 Cj15
Chitipa MW 214 Mg50
Chitobe MOC 222 Mg56
Chitolo MOC 222 Mg57
Chitonga Z 218 Md54
Chitose J 103 Sa24
Chitradurga IND (KTK) 115 Oj39
Chitrakot IND (CGH) 113 Pa36
Chitrakut IND (UPH) 113 Pa33
Chitral PK 83 Of28
Chitré PA 267 Fk42
Chittagong BD 116 Pf34
Chittaranjan IND (JKD) 116 Pd34
Chittaurgarh IND (RJT) 110 Oh33
Chittaurgarh Fort IND (RJT) 110 Oh33
Chittoor IND (APH) 115 Ok40
Chittor = Chittaurgarh IND (RJT) 110 Oh33
Chitungwiza ZW 222 Mf55
Chituta MOC 222 Mg56
Chityal IND (APH) 113 Ok36
Chityal IND (APH) 113 Ok37
Chiuchiu RCH 296 Gf57
Chium ANG 217 Ma53
Chiumbe ANG 211 Ma50
Chiumbo ANG 216 Lj52
Chiure Novo MOC 219 Mk52
Chiure Velho MOC 219 Mk52
Chiusa = Klausen I 42 Lm44
Chiusi I 42 Lm47
Chiuta MOC 218 Mg53
Chiva E 31 Ku49
Chivacoa YV 281 Gf40
Chivasso I 42 Lh45
Chivato RCH 300 Ge59
Chivay PE 291 Ge53
Chive BOL 291 Gf52
Chivhu ZW 222 Mf55
Chivilcoy RA (BA) 301 Ha63
Chivirico C 269 Gb36
Chivuna Z 218 Md54
Chizarira Hills ZW 218 Md54
Chizarira N.P. ZW 218 Md54
Chizu J 105 Rh28
Chizwina RB 221 Md56
Chlef DZ 181 La27
Chłudowo PL 38 Lr38
Chlumec nad Cidlinou CZ 40 Lq40
Chmel'nyc'kyj UA 56 Md21
Chmielnik PL 39 Ma40
Chmil'nyk UA 56 Md21
Choam Khsant K 119 Qc38
Choam Sla K 119 Qb40
Choapa RCH 300 Ge61
Chobe RB 221 Mc55
Chobe RB/NAM 221 Mc54
Chobe N.P. RB 221 Mc55
Chocca, Cerro PE 290 Gc52
Chocianów PL 38 Lq39
Chociwel PL 38 Lq37
Chocolate Hills RP 127 Rc41
Chocolate Mts. USA 246 Ec29
Chocontá CO 280 Gd43
Chocope PE 290 Ga49
Choctaw N.W.R. USA 258 Ff30
Chodavaram IND (APH) 113 Pa37
Chodavaram IND (APH) 113 Pb37
Cho Do DVRK 104 Rc26
Chodoriv UA 41 Me41
Chodov CZ 40 Ln40
Chodová Planá CZ 40 Ln41
Chodzież PL 38 Lr38
Choele Choel RA (RN) 304 Gh65
Chofombo MOC 218 Mf53
Choharwa NEP 92 Pd32
Chohtan IND (RJT) 110 Of33
Choiceland CDN (SK) 243 Eh19
Choirokoitia CY 53 Mo56
Choiseul SOL 166 Sj49
Choiseul Sound GB 307 Ha71
Choix MEX (SL) 262 Ef32
Chojbalsan MNG 95 Qh21
Chojna PL 38 Lp38
Chojnice PL 38 Ls37
Chojniki BY 54 Me20
Chojnów PL 38 Lq39
Chokai Q.N.P. J 105 Rk26
Chokai-san J 105 Sa26
Chok Chai THA 119 Qb38
Choke ETH 206 Mj40
Chókué MOC 222 Mg58
Chokwe = Chókué MOC 222 Mg58
Cholame USA (CA) 246 Dk28
Chola Shan VRC 98 Pk30
Chola Shankou VRC 98 Pk30
Cholchol RCH 304 Gd65
Cholet F 24 Ku43
Cholila RA (CB) 304 Ge67
Cholistan Desert PK 85 Of31
Chołola Z 217 Mb54
Cholopyči UA 39 Me40
Cholpon-ata KS 81 Oj24
Cholsan DVRK 104 Rc26
Choluteca HN 266 Fg39
Ch'olwon ROK 104 Rd26
Choma Z 218 Md54
Chom Bung THA 118 Pk39
Chom Phra THA 119 Qb38
Chomsk BY 39 Mf38
Chom Thong THA 118 Pk36
Chomutov CZ 40 Lo40
Chona EAT 215 Mg48
Ch'onan ROK 104 Rd27
Chon Buri THA 118 Qa39
Chonchi RCH 304 Gd67
Chon Daen THA 118 Qa37
Chondung Temple ROK 104 Rd27
Chone EC 284 Fk46
Chongchon Gang DVRK 104 Rc26
Chongjin DVRK 104 Re25
Chongju DVRK 104 Rc26
Ch'ongju ROK 104 Rd27
Chongju ROK 104 Rd28
Chong Kal K 119 Qb39
Chonglong VRC (SCH) 98 Qc31
Chongming VRC (JGS) 106 Ra30
Chongoene MOC 222 Mg58
Chongoni Rock Art MW 218 Mh53
Chongorói ANG 216 Lg52
Chongoyape PE 290 Ga49
Chong Phan THA 120 Pk41
Chongp'yong DVRK 104 Rd26
Chongqing VRC 87 Qb13
Chongqing VRC (CGQ) 99 Qd31
Chong Qing-Temple VRC 96 Qb28
Chongren VRC (JGX) 106 Qj32
Chong Samui THA 120 Pk41
Chongsan Do ROK 107 Rd28
Chongshen Monastery VRC 117 Qa33
Chong Tao THA 120 Pk41
Chongwe Z 218 Me53
Chongwe Z 218 Me53
Chongwu VRC (FJN) 101 Qk33
Chongyang VRC (HUB) 106 Qh31
Chongyi VRC (JGX) 101 Qh33
Chongzhou VRC (SCH) 98 Qb30
Chongzuo VRC (GZG) 100 Qd34
Chonju ROK 104 Rd28
Chonkham IND (ARP) 117 Pj32
Chonogol MNG 95 Qh23
Chonos Archipelago RCH 304 Gc68
Chontali PE 284 Ga48
Chontalpa MEX (TB) 265 Fd37
Chon Thanh VN 119 Qd40
Cho Oyo NEP/VRC 92 Pd31
Chopan IND (UPH) 113 Pb33
Chopda IND (MHT) 112 Oh35
Chopim BR 302 Hd59
Choqa Zanbil IR 76 Ne29
Chorea MA 180 Kh30
Chorhat IND (MPH) 113 Pa33
Chorkerup AUS (WA) 150 Qj63
Choro BOL 292 Gh54
Choró BR (CE) 289 Ja48
Chorol UA 56 Mg21
Chorolque, Nevado BOL 296 Gh56
Choromoro RA (TU) 300 Gh59
Choroní YV 281 Gg40
Choros Bajos RCH 300 Ge60
Choroszcz PL 39 Mc37
Chorozinho BR (CE) 289 Ja48
Chorrera PE 285 Ge47
Chorrochó BR (BA) 295 Ja50
Chorro de Maíta C 269 Gc35
Chorro El Indio, P.N. YV 280 Gd41
Chorro la Libertad CO 285 Gf46
Chorzele PL 39 Ma37
Chorzów PL 39 Lt40
Ch'osan DVRK 104 Rc25
Choshi J 105 Sa28
Choshuenco, Volcán RCH 304 Gd65
Chosica PE 290 Gb51
Chos Malal RA (NE) 304 Ge64
Chosong DVRK 104 Rd25
Choszczno PL 38 Lq37
Chota PE 290 Ga49
Chota Nagpur Plateau IND 113 Pa34
Chota Udaipur IND (GUJ) 112 Oh34
Choteau USA (MT) 243 Ed22
Chotilsko CZ 40 Lp41
Chott Ech Chergui DZ 181 La28
Chott el Fedjadj TN 182 Le28
Chott el Gharbi DZ 181 Kk29
Chott el Gharsa TN 182 Ld28
Chott el Hodna DZ 181 Lc28
Chott el Jerid TN 182 Le29
Chott el Malah DZ 182 Lc29
Chott Melrhir DZ 182 Ld28
Chott Merouane DZ 182 Ld29
Chotyn UA 47 Mg42
Chouf RL 68 Mh29
Choûm RIM 186 Kd35
Chowchilla USA (CA) 244 Dk27
Choya RA (SE) 300 Gh60
Choyr MNG 94 Qe22
Chozi Z 214 Mf50
Chrám CZ 40 Lq40
Chr'aščevka RUS 55 Ne19
Chréa DZ 181 Lb27
Chréa, P.N. de DZ 181 Lb27
Chreïrik RIM 186 Kd35
Chrisí Ammoudiá GR 49 Me50
Chrisman USA (IL) 256 Fg26
Chrissiesmeer SA 225 Mf59
Christchurch GB 23 Kt40
Christchurch NZ 161 Tg67
Christiana SA 225 Mc59
Christianburg GUY 282 Ha42
Christiansburg USA (VA) 259 Fk27
Christiansfeld DK 16 Lk35
Christiansholm N 14 Lh32
Christiansø DK 17 Lq35
Christian Sound USA 241 Dc17
Christiansted USA (VI) 271 Gh37
Christie Island MYA 120 Pj41
Christie Mtn. Ski Area USA 256 Fe23
Christina Lake CDN (BC) 242 Eb21
Christina River CDN 243 Ee17
Christmas Creek AUS (WA) 144 Rc55
Christmas Creek AUS 144 Rd55
Christmas Island AUS 122 Qb21
Christmas Ridge 316 Bb08
Christmas Valley USA (OR) 244 Dk24
Christoval USA (TX) 252 Ek30
Chrudim CZ 40 Lq41
Chrystynivka UA 56 Me21
Chrzanów PL 39 Lu40
Chu KS 81 Oh24
Chu = Shu KZ 80 Oe23
Chuadanga BD 116 Pe34
Chuave PNG 165 Sc49
Chubalung VRC (SCH) 98 Pk31
Chub Cay BS 261 Gb33
Chubu-Sangaku N.P. J 105 Rj27
Chubut RA 279 Gc27
Chubut RA 304 Gg67
Chuchi Lake CDN 242 Dh18
Chuchiliga GH 201 Kk40
Chucuito PE 291 Gf53
Chucuma RA (SJ) 300 Gg61
Chucurí CO 280 Gc42
Chu Dang Sin VN 119 Qe39
Chufut-Kale UA 57 Mg23
Chugach Is. USA 239 Ce16
Chugach Mountains USA 240 Ch15
Chugach S.P. USA 239 Cf15
Chugay PE 290 Gb49
Chugiak USA (AK) 239 Cf15
Chugoku-sanchi J 105 Rg28
Chugwater USA (WY) 245 Eh25
Chuhuichupa MEX (CHH) 247 Ef31
Chuí BR (RS) 302 Hd62
Chuilile EAT 214 Mg50
Chuitayo EC 284 Gb46
Chuka EAK 212 Mj46
Chukchi Autonomous District RUS 63 Tb05
Chukchi Plateau 310 Bd03
Chukchi Sea RUS 63 Uc04
Chukmpalli IND (MHT) 113 Pa36
Chuknagar BD 116 Pe34
Chukotskiy Poluostrov RUS 63 Ua05
Chulamar GCA 265 Fe39
Chulaphon Reservoir THA 118 Qa37
Chula Vista USA (CA) 246 Eb29
Chullúncani, Cerro BOL 297 Gh55
Chulucanas PE 284 Fk48
Chulumani BOL 296 Gg54
Chuluut gol MNG 94 Qa21
Chuma BOL 291 Gf53
Chumba ETH 206 Mk43
Chumbicha RA (CA) 300 Gg60
Chumbo BR (MG) 299 Hg55
Chumda VRC (QHI) 93 Pj29
Chumphae THA 118 Qb37
Chumphon THA 120 Pk40
Chumphon Buri THA 119 Qb38
Chum Phuang THA 119 Qb38
Chumpi PE 290 Gd53
Chumsaeng THA 118 Qa38
Chumuch PE 290 Ga49
Chumul MEX 265 Ff36
Chun THA 118 Qa36
Chun'an VRC (ZJG) 106 Qk31
Chunchi EC 284 Ga47
Ch'unch'on ROK 104 Rd27
Chunchucmil MEX (YT) 265 Fe35
Chundela ANG 217 Ma53
Chunga Z 217 Mc53
Chunga Z 218 Mg51
Chungang DVRK 104 Rd25
Chunga Rest Camp Z 217 Mc53
Ch'ungju ROK 104 Rd27
Ch'ungmu ROK 104 Re28
Chungui PE 290 Gd52
Chungungo RCH 300 Ge60
Chungyang Shanmo RC 101 Ra34
Chunian PK 83 Og30
Chunshui VRC (HNN) 99 Qg29
Chunwan VRC (GDG) 100 Qf34
Chunya EAT 214 Mg50
Chuor Phnom Kravanh K 119 Qb39
Chuor Phnum Dangrek K 119 Qb38
Chupaca PE 290 Gc52
Chupanan IR 76 Nh29
ChuPha VN 119 Qd39
Chu Prong VN 119 Qd39
Chuquibamba PE 291 Gd53
Chuquibambilla PE 291 Gd53
Chuquicamata RCH 296 Gf57
Chuquis PE 290 Gb50
Chur CH 36 Lk44
Churachandpur IND (MNP) 116 Pg33
Churcampa PE 290 Gc52
Churchbridge CDN (SK) 248 Ek20
Churchill CDN 235 Fa07
Churchill CDN 235 Fb07
Churchill Falls CDN 235 Gd08
Churchill Lake CDN 243 Ef17
Churchill Mountains 313 Sc35
Churchill River CDN 243 Ef18
Churchill Sound CDN 249 Ga17
Churchs Ferry USA (ND) 248 Fa21
Church Stretton GB 23 Ks38
Churia Range NEP 92 Pa31
Churia Range NEP 92 Pb32
Churín PE 290 Gb51
Churki IND (CGH) 113 Pb34
Churu IND (RJT) 110 Oh31
Churubamba PE 290 Gb50
Churuguara YV 281 Gf40
Chu Se VN 119 Qe39
Chushaf 83 Ok29
Chuska Mts. USA 247 Ef27
Chu-sonji J 105 Sa26
Chust UA 41 Md42
Chust UZB 80 Of25
Chute Akamba RDC 209 Md45
Chute Bangu RDC 209 Mc44
Chute de la Vina CAM 203 Lg42
Chute-des-Passes CDN (QC) 254 Ge21
Chute Kamimbi Fuka RDC 211 Mc50
Chute Mulamba Gungu RDC 211 Mb50
Chute Mupele RDC 209 Mc45
Chute Penge RDC 209 Me45
Chute Pogge II RDC 211 Ma49
Chutes d'Abourou RCA 204 Mb43
Chutes d'Antafofo RM 228 Nd55
Chutes de Béla RCB/RDC 210 Lh48
Chutes de Betsiboka RM 228 Nd54
Chutes de Billy RMM 192 Kf39
Chutes de Boali RCA 204 Lk43
Chutes de Bouenza RCB 210 Lg47
Chutes de Dibouangui G 210 Lf46
Chutes de Félou RMM 191 Ke38
Chutes de Gouina RMM 191 Ke38
Chutes de Gozobangui RDC 208 Mb43
Chutes de Katende RDC 211 Mb49
Chutes de Kembé RCA 204 Ma43
Chutes de Kinkon RG 200 Kd40
Chutes d'Ekom CAM 202 Lf43
Chutes de Kongou G 203 Lg45
Chutes de Kotto RCA 204 Ma43
Chutes de la Kagera BU 214 Me47
Chutes de la Kiubo RDC 214 Md50
Chutes de la Lobé CAM 202 Le44
Chutes de la Lofoi RDC 218 Md51
Chutes de la Lufira RDC 214 Md50
Chutes de la Madelaine F 168 Td57
Chutes de Lancrenon CAM 203 Lh42
Chutes de l'Ankofia RM 227 Ne53
Chutes de l'Ivindo de Tsengué Leledi G 203 Lg46
Chutes de Livingstone RDC 210 Lg48
Chutes de Lokoho RM 227 Ne53
Chutes de Loufoulakari RCB/RDC 210 Lh48
Chutes de Lubi RDC 211 Mb49
Chutes de Matakil RCA 204 Ma41
Chutes de Mbi RCA 203 Lj43
Chutes de Mingouli G 203 Lg45
Chutes de Nachtigal CAM 203 Lf43
Chutes de Ngolo RCA 204 Mb43
Chutes de Papara RMM 191 Ke38
Chutes de Poubara G 210 Lg46
Chutes de Sakaleona RM 228 Nd56
Chutes de Tanougou DY 201 La40
Chutes de Tinkisso RG 200 Ke40
Chutes de Touboutou RCA 203 Lh43
Chutes de Zongo RCB/RDC 210 Lh48
Chutes d'Inga RDC 210 Lg48
Chutes du Tello CAM 203 Lg42
Chutes Gauthiot TCH 195 Lh41
Chutes Guillaume = Chutes Tembo RDC 211 Lj49
Chutes Johnston RDC 218 Me51
Chutes Kasongo-Lunda RDC 211 Lj49
Chutes Pangu RDC 209 Md44
Chutes Tembo RDC 211 Lj49
Chutes Usu RDC 209 Mc44
Chute Toky RDC 209 Me45
Chute Walfe RDC 211 Mb48
Chutine Landing CDN (BC) 241 De17
Chuvashia RUS 55 Nd18
Chuwangsan N.P. ROK 104 Re27
Chuxiong VRC (YUN) 117 Qa33
Chuy ROU 301 Hd62
Chuzhou VRC (AHU) 106 Qk29
Chuzmiza RCH 296 Gf55
Chvaletice CZ 40 Lq40
Chwaka EAT 215 Mk49
Chwałowice PL 39 Mb40
Chwaszczyno PL 38 Lt36
Chynów PL 39 Mb39
Chynthiana USA (KY) 259 Fh26
Chyriv UA 41 Mc41
Chyulu Hills N.P. EAK 212 Mj47
Ciamis RI 132 Qe49
Cianjur RI 132 Qd49
Cianorte BR (PR) 298 Hd57
Ciawi RI 132 Qd49
Cibadak RI 132 Qd49
Cibaray, Cerro BOL 296 Gf55
Cibinong RI 132 Qd49
Cibit RUS (ALT) 89 Pd20
Cibuta MEX (SO) 247 Ee30
Çiçekdağı TR 53 Mp51
Cícero Dantas BR (BA) 295 Ja51
Ćićevac SCG 48 Mb47
Cicheng VRC (ZJG) 106 Ra31
Cicia FJI 169 Ua54
Cidade da Pedra BR 293 Hc53
Cidade Gaúcha BR (PR) 298 Hd57
Cidade Medieval de Évora P 30 Kn48
Cidade Velha CV 190 Jj38
Cide TR 66 Mg25
Ciechanów PL 39 Ma38
Ciechanowiec PL 39 Mc38
Ciechocinek PL 38 Lt38
Ciego de Ávila C 269 Ga34
Ciego de Ávila C 269 Ga35
Ciemnik PL 38 Lq37
Ciemnoszyje PL 39 Mc37
Ciénaga de Ayapel CO 280 Gc43
Ciénaga de Oro CO 280 Gc41
Ciénaga de Pedeguita CO 280 Gb42
Ciénaga de Zapata, P.N. C 268 Fk34
Ciénaga de Zapatosa CO 280 Gd41
Ciénaga Grande CO 280 Gc41
Ciénaga Grande RA (PJ) 296 Gg57
Ciénaga Grande de Santa Marta CO 280 Gc40
Ciénaga Guájaro CO 280 Gc40
Ciénaga Iguana CO 280 Gc41
Ciénagas de Catatumbo, P.N. YV 280 Ge41
Cienaguillas RA (PJ) 296 Gh57
Ciénega CO 280 Gc40
Ciénega del Toro MEX (NL) 263 Ek33
Ciénega Prieta MEX (CHH) 262 Eg32
Cienfuegos C 268 Fk34
Čierny Balog SK 41 Lu42
Cieszanów PL 39 Md40
Cieszyn PL 40 Lt41
Cieza E 31 Kt48
Ciężkowice PL 39 Lu40
Cifrapalota H 41 Lu44
Çiftehan TR 53 Mp53
Çifteler TR 53 Mm51
Çifte Minare Medresesi TR 67 Na26
Çiftlik TR 53 Mp52
Cifuentes C 268 Fk34
Cifuentes E 31 Ks50
Cifuncho PE 296 Ge58
Cigarette Springs Cave USA 247 Ee27
Cigarro BR (AM) 286 Gj47
Cigel'ka SK 41 Mb41
Cigliano I 42 Lj45
Cihanbeyli TR 53 Mn52
Cihanbeyli Yaylası TR 53 Mn52
Cijawung RI 132 Qc49
Cijulang RI 132 Qe49
Cikajang RI 132 Qd49
Cikalong RI 132 Qe49
Cikampek RI 132 Qd49
Cikarang RI 132 Qd49
Cikatomas RI 132 Qe49
Cikobia FJI 169 Ua53
Čikoj MNG 95 Qf21
Cikoj RUS (BUR) 94 Qd20
Cikoj RUS 94 Qd20
Čikokon RUS 95 Qf20
Cilacap RI 132 Qe49
Cilaos F 229 Nh56
Çıldır TR 67 Nb25
Çıldır Gölü TR 67 Nb25
Ciledug RI 132 Qe49
Cilegon RI 132 Qd49
Cilento I 44 Lq50
Cilento e Vallo di Diano, P.N. del I 44 Lq50
Čilgar RUS (KAL) 57 Nc22
Cili VRC (HUN) 99 Qf31
Cilibia RO 47 Mh45
Çilimli TR 53 Mm50
Cillas E 31 Kt50
Cilleros E 30 Ko50
Cillium TN 182 Le28
Čil'na RUS 55 Ne18
Cima USA (CA) 246 Ec28
Cimalavera, P.N. do ANG 216 Lg52
Cimarron USA (KS) 252 Ek27
Cimarron USA 252 Ek27
Cimarron Nat. Grassland USA 252 Ek27
Cimbur RI 136 Rc50
Çimenlik TR 52 Mg50
Çimenliyeniköy TR 66 Mg26
Cimetières des Dinosaures de Gadafawa RN 194 Le37
Cimitarra CO 280 Gd42
Cimljansk RUS 57 Nb22
Cimljanskoe Vodohranilišče RUS 55 Nb21
Cimoszki PL 39 Mc37
Cimpu RI 131 Ra47
Çimşit TR 53 Mn51
Çınar TR 67 Na27
Çınarcık TR 52 Mk50
Cinaruco YV 281 Gf42
Cinaruco-Capanaparo, P.N. YV 281 Gg42
Cincinnati USA (OH) 256 Fh26
Çine TR 52 Mj53
Ciney B 25 Lf40
Cinfães P 28 Km51
Cíngoli I 43 Lo47
Cinque Island IND 115 Pg40
Cinque Terre I 42 Lk46
Cinque Terre, P.N. delle I 42 Lk46
Cintalapa MEX (CHP) 265 Fd37
Cintei RO 46 Mb44
Cintra RA (CD) 301 Gj62
Cioara MD 47 Mj44
Ciocănești RO 47 Mf43
Ciochina RO 47 Mh46
Cioclovina RO 46 Md45
Ciolacu Nou MD 47 Mh43
Ciorani RO 47 Mg46
Ciorăști RO 47 Mh45
Cipanas RI 132 Qd49
Cipatujah RI 132 Qe49
Cipó BR (BA) 295 Ja51
Cipoal BR (AM) 286 Gh46
Cipoletti RA (RN) 304 Gg65
Čiprovski manastir BG 48 Mc47
Čir RUS 55 Nb21
Çirax Qala Sassanid Castle AZ 74 Ne25
Circeo, P.N. del I 44 Ln49
Circle USA (AK) 239 Ch13
Circle USA (MT) 245 Eh22
Circleville USA (OH) 256 Fj26
Circuit de Catalunya E 32 Lc49
Circuit Nelson Piquet BR 299 Hj57
Circuito de Jerez E 30 Kp46
Circuit Ricardo Tormo E 31 Ku49
Circular Reef PNG 165 Sd47
Cirebon RI 132 Qe49
Cirema, Gunung RI 132 Qe49
Cirencester GB 23 Kt39
Cirey-sur-Vezouze F 25 Lg42
Ciriè I 42 Lh45
Ciripcău MD 47 Mj43
Ciriquiri BR 291 Gh50
Cir Kud SP 213 Nb44
Cirò I 45 Ls51
Cirò Marina I 45 Ls51
Čirpan BG 49 Mf48
Cirque, Cerro BOL 296 Gf54
Cirque de Jaffar MA 180 Kh29
Cirque de Navacelles F 27 Ld47
Cirque Rouge RM 226 Nd53
Cisco USA (TX) 252 Fa29
Cislău RO 47 Mg45
Cismișlia MD 47 Mj44
Císneros CO 280 Gc42
Cisowsko-Orłowińsk Park Krajobrazowy PL 39 Ma40
Cisséla RG 200 Ke40
Cisterna di Latina I 44 Ln49
Cistern Point BS 261 Gb34
Cistierna E 28 Kp52
Čita RUS 95 Qg19
Čita RUS 95 Qh19
Citadelle/Sans Souci RH 269 Gd36
Citadelle de Calvi F 33 Lj48
Citeureup RI 132 Qc49
Čitluk BIH 43 Ls47
Citronelle USA (AL) 253 Ff30
Citrusdal SA 224 Lk62
Citrus Heights USA (CA) 244 Dk26
Città Alta di Bergamo I 42 Lk45
Cittadella I 42 Lm45
Città della Pieve I 42 Ln48
Città del Palladio I 42 Lm45
Città di Castello I 42 Ln47
Città Sant'Ángelo I 44 Lp48
City Palace (Jaipur) IND 110 Oh32
City Palace (Udaipur) IND 112 Og33
Ciucea RO 46 Mc44
Ciucurova RO 47 Mj46
Ciudad Altamirano MEX (GUR) 264 Ek36
Ciudad Bolívia YV 281 Ge41
Ciudad Camargo MEX (CHH) 263 Eh32
Ciudad Constitución MEX (BCS) 262 Ee33
Ciudad Cortes CR 266 Fj41
Ciudad de Guatemala GCA 265 Fe38
Ciudad del Carmen MEX (CAM) 265 Fe36
Ciudad del Este PY 298 Hc58
Ciudad del Maíz MEX (SLP) 263 Fa34
Ciudad de México MEX (MEX) 264 Fa36
Ciudad de México MEX (MEX) 264 Fa36
Ciudad de Nutrias YV 281 Gf41
Ciudad Encantada E 31 Ks50
Ciudad Guayana YV 282 Gj41
Ciudad Guerrero MEX (TM) 263 Fa32
Ciudad Guzmán MEX (JLC) 264 Ej36
Ciudad Hidalgo MEX (MHC) 264 Ek36
Ciudad Hidalgo MEX (CHP) 265 Fd38
Ciudad Huitzuco MEX (GUR) 264 Fa36
Ciudad Insurgentes MEX (BCS) 262 Ee33
Ciudad Ixtepec MEX (OAX) 265 Fc37
Ciudad Juárez MEX (CHH) 247 Eg30
Ciudad Lerdo MEX (DGO) 263 Ej33
Ciudad Lerdo de Tejada MEX (VC) 265 Fc36
Ciudad Madero MEX (TM) 263 Fb34
Ciudad Mante MEX (TM) 263 Fa34
Ciudad Melchor de Mencos GCA 265 Ff37
Ciudad monumental de Cáceres E 30 Ko49
Ciudad Mutis = Bahia Solano CO 280 Gb42
Ciudad Neily CR 266 Fj41
Ciudad Nezahualcóyotl MEX (MEX) 264 Fa36
Ciudad Obregon MEX (SO) 262 Ef32
Ciudad Ojeda YV 280 Ge40
Ciudad Perdida CO 280 Gd40
Ciudad Piar YV 282 Gj42
Ciudad Real E 31 Kr48
Ciudad Rodrigo E 28 Ko50
Ciudad Sahagún MEX (HDG) 264 Fa36
Ciudad Serdán MEX (PUE) 264 Fb36
Ciudad Valles MEX (SLP) 264 Fa35
Ciudad Victoria MEX (TM) 263 Fa34
Ciuperceni RO 46 Md46
Ciutadella E 32 Ld50
Ciutești MD 47 Mj43
Cividale del Friuli I 43 Lo44
Civil'sk RUS (CHU) 55 Nd18
Cívita Castellana I 44 Ln48
Civitanova Marche I 43 Lo47
Civitavécchia I 44 Lm48
Civitella del Tronto I 44 Lo48
Civitella Roveto I 44 Lo49
Civray F 26 La44
Çivril TR 52 Mk52
Cixi VRC (ZJG) 106 Ra30
Cizre TR 67 Nb27
Cjurupyns'k UA 56 Mg22
Čkalovsk RUS 55 Nb17
Čki-Naryn KS 81 Oj25
Clacton-on-Sea GB 23 Lb39
Clain F 24 La44
Clair Engle Lake USA 244 Dj25
Clairview AUS (QLD) 155 Se57
Clamecy F 25 Ld43
Clam Lake USA (WI) 251 Fe22
Clan Donald Centre GB 20 Kp33
Clanton USA (AL) 258 Fg29
Clanville SA 225 Md61
Clanwilliam SA 224 Lk62
Claonaig GB 20 Kp35
Claquato Church USA 242 Dj22
Clara Island MYA 120 Pj40
Clara, Mount NZ 161 Tg67
Claraville AUS (NT) 149 Rh57
Claraville AUS (QLD) 154 Sa55
Clare AUS (SA) 158 Rk62
Clare AUS (QLD) 155 Sc57
Clare AUS (QLD) 155 Sd55
Clare USA (MI) 256 Fh24
Clare Island IRL 20 Kk37
Claremont USA (NH) 257 Gd24
Claremont Point AUS 153 Sb52
Claremore USA (OK) 253 Fc27
Claremorris IRL 20 Kl37
Clarence NZ 161 Tg67
Clarence Cannon N.W.R. USA 251 Fe26
Clarence Island 312 Hb31
Clarence Strait AUS 145 Rf52
Clarence Strait USA 241 Dd18
Clarence Town BS 261 Gc34
Clarendon USA (TX) 252 Ek28
Clarens SA 225 Me60
Clarenville CDN (NF) 255 Hc21
Claresholm CDN (AB) 243 Ed20
Clareton USA (WY) 245 Eh24
Clarinda USA (IA) 251 Fc25
Clarines YV 281 Gh41
Clarion USA (IA) 251 Fd24
Clarion USA (PA) 257 Ga25
Clarion Fracture Zone 317 Cb08
Clark USA (WY) 245 Ef23
Clark USA (SD) 250 Fb23
Clarke-City CDN (QC) 254 Gg20
Clarke Island AUS 158 Se66
Clarke Lake CDN 243 Eg18
Clarke River AUS (QLD) 155 Sc55
Clarkia USA (ID) 242 Eb22
Clarkleigh CDN (MB) 248 Fa20
Clark Range AUS (QLD) 155 Sd56
Clarksburg USA (WV) 257 Fk26
Clarksdale USA (MS) 253 Fe28
Clark's Harbour CDN (NS) 255 Gh24
Clarkson SA 225 Mc63
Clarkson Bridge USA 258 Fg28
Clarks Point USA (AK) 238 Ca16
Clarkston USA (WA) 244 Eb22
Clarksville USA (TX) 253 Fc29
Clarksville USA (AR) 253 Fd28
Clarksville USA (TN) 258 Fg27
Claro BR 293 He54
Claro BR 298 He54
Claro dos Poções BR (MG) 299 Hh54
Claromecó RA (BA) 305 Gk65
Classical Gardens VRC 106 Ra30
Claude USA (TX) 252 Ek28
Cláudia BR (MT) 293 Hc51
Claudio BR (MG) 299 Hh56
Clausthal-Zellerfeld D 35 Ll39
Claveria RP 125 Ra36
Claveria RP 125 Rb39
Claxton USA (GA) 259 Fk29
Clay USA (WV) 259 Fk26
Claybank CDN (SK) 243 Eh20
Clay Belt CDN 249 Fk20
Clay Center USA (KS) 250 Fb26
Claydon CDN (SK) 243 Ef21
Clayoquot Sound CDN 242 Dg21
Clayton AUS (SA) 149 Rk60
Clayton USA (ID) 245 Ec23
Clayton USA (NM) 247 Ej27
Clayton USA (OK) 253 Fc28
Clayton USA (MO) 251 Fe26
Clayton USA (AL) 259 Fh30
Clayton USA (GA) 259 Fj28
Clear Creek USA 239 Cg13
Cleardale CDN (AB) 243 Ea17
Clearfield USA (UT) 245 Ed25
Clearfield USA (SD) 250 Ek24
Clearfield USA (PA) 257 Ga25
Clearlake USA (CA) 244 Dj26
Clear Lake USA 244 Dj26
Clear Lake USA (UT) 245 Ed26
Clear Lake USA (SD) 251 Fb23
Clear Lake USA (IA) 251 Fd24
Clear Lake Reservoir USA 244 Dk25
Clear Prairie CDN (AB) 243 Ea17
Clearwater CDN (BC) 242 Dk20
Clearwater USA 244 Eb22
Clearwater USA (FL) 260 Fj32
Clearwater Creek CDN 241 Dg14
Clearwater Lake CDN 248 Ek18
Clearwater Lake Prov. Park CDN 248 Ek18
Clearwater Mountains USA 245 Ec22
Clearwater River CDN 243 Ee17
Clearwater West Lake CDN 248 Fd21
Cleburne USA (TX) 252 Fb29
Cle Elum USA (WA) 242 Dk22
Cleethorpes GB 23 Ku37
Clejani RO 47 Mf46
Clelles F 27 Lf46
Clementina BR (SP) 298 He56
Clemson USA (SC) 259 Fj28
Cleopatra Needle RP 126 Qk40
Cleo Springs USA (OK) 252 Fa27
Clermont AUS (QLD) 155 Sd57
Clermont F 25 Lc41
Clermont USA (FL) 260 Fk31
Clermont-en-Argonne F 25 Lf41
Clermont-Ferrand F 27 Ld45
Clermont-l'Hérault F 27 Ld47
Clerval F 25 Lg43
Clervaux L 25 Lg40
Cles I 42 Lm44
Cleugh Passage IND 115 Pg39
Cleve AUS (SA) 158 Rj62
Clevedon GB 23 Ks39
Cleveland USA (TX) 253 Fc30
Cleveland USA (MS) 253 Fe29
Cleveland USA (TN) 259 Fh28
Cleveland USA (GA) 259 Fj28
Cleveland USA (OH) 256 Fk25
Clevelândia BR (PR) 302 Hd59
Clevelan Pen. USA 241 Dd18
Cleveleys GB 23 Kr37
Clew Bay IRL 20 Kl37
Clewiston USA (FL) 260 Fk32
Clifden IRL 20 Kk36
Clifden NZ 161 Td69
Clifden Castle IRL 20 Kk36
Cliffdale River AUS (QLD) 154 Rk54
Cliffs of Moher IRL 22 Kl38
Cliffs of the Nullarbor AUS 151 Re61
Clifton AUS (QLD) 157 Sf59
Clifton SA 224 Lk62
Clifton USA (AZ) 247 Ef29
Clifton USA (TN) 258 Fg28
Clifton Bridge GB 23 Ks39
Clifton Hills AUS (SA) 149 Rk59
Cli Lake CDN 241 Dj15
Climax CDN (SK) 243 Ef21
Climax USA (CO) 245 Eg26
Climax USA (MN) 250 Fb22
Clinch Mts. USA 259 Fj27
Clines Corners USA (NM) 247 Eh28
Clinton CDN (BC) 242 Dk20
Clinton NZ 161 Te69
Clinton USA (WA) 242 Dj21
Clinton USA (MT) 245 Ed22
Clinton USA (OK) 252 Fa28
Clinton USA (MO) 251 Fd26
Clinton USA (AR) 253 Fd28
Clinton USA (IA) 251 Fe25
Clinton USA (LA) 253 Fe30
Clinton USA (IL) 256 Ff25
Clinton USA (AL) 258 Fg29
Clinton USA (SC) 259 Fk28
Clinton USA (NC) 259 Ga28
Clinton-Colden Lake CDN 234 Ec06
Clintwood USA (VA) 259 Fj27
Clio USA (AL) 259 Fh30
Clipperton Fracture Zone 317 Cb09
Clisson F 24 Kt43
Člista RUS (KAL) 57 Nc22
Clitheroe GB 23 Ks37
Cliza BOL 296 Gg54
Clodomira RA (SE) 300 Gh59
Cloghan IRL 22 Kn37
Clogherhead IRL 22 Ko37
Clogher Head IRL 22 Ko37
Clonagh AUS (QLD) 154 Sa56
Clonakilty IRL 22 Km39
Clonbrook GUY 283 Hb42
Cloncurry AUS (QLD) 154 Sa56
Cloncurry River AUS (QLD) 154 Sa56
Clones IRL 20 Kn36
Clonmacnoise IRL 22 Kn37
Clonmel IRL 22 Kn38
Cloppenburg D 34 Lj38
Cloquet USA (MN) 251 Fd22
Cloquet USA 251 Fd22
Cloridorme CDN (QC) 255 Gh21
Clorinda RA (FO) 297 Hb58
Cloudy Mount USA 239 Cb14
Clovelly GB 22 Kq40
Cloverdale USA (CA) 244 Dj26
Clovis USA (CA) 244 Ea27
Clovis USA (NM) 247 Ej28
Cloyes-sur-le-Loir F 24 Lb43
Čl'ton RUS 55 Nd21
Clucellas RA (SF) 301 Gk61
Cluj-Napoca RO 46 Md44
Cluny AUS (QLD) 156 Rk58
Cluny F 27 Le44
Cluses F 27 Lg44
Clusone I 42 Lk45
Clute CDN (ON) 249 Fk21
Clutha River AUS 161 Te68
Clyde CDN (AB) 243 Ed18
Clyde CDN 235 Gc04
Clyde GB 21 Kr35
Clydebank GB 21 Kq35
Clyde River CDN (NS) 255 Gh24
Cna RUS 55 Na19
Coacalco MEX (MEX) 264 Fa36
Coaceral BR (BA) 294 Hh51
Coachella USA (CA) 246 Eb29
Coahuila MEX 236 Ed13
Coakari BOL 296 Gg55
Coalcomán de Vázquez Pallares MEX (MHC) 264 Ej36
Coal Creek USA (AK) 239 Cj13
Coaldale CDN (AB) 243 Ed21
Coaldale USA (NV) 244 Eb26
Coalgate USA (OK) 253 Fb28
Coalinga USA (CA) 246 Dk27
Coal River CDN 241 Dg15
Coal River CDN (BC) 241 Dg16
Coamo USA (PR) 271 Gg36
Coaraci BR (BA) 295 Ja53
Coari BR 286 Gh48
Coari BR (AM) 286 Gj48
Coarnele Caprei RO 47 Mh43
Coasa PE 291 Ge53
Coastal Plain USA 232 Fa06
Coast Mountains CDN/USA 232 Db04
Coast of Labrador CDN 235 Gd07
Coast Ranges USA 236 Dd11
Coata PE 291 Gf53
Coatepec MEX (VC) 264 Fb36
Coatepeque GCA 265 Fe38
Coaticook CDN (QC) 257 Ge23
Coats Bay CDN 249 Ga17
Coats Island CDN 235 Fd06
Coats Land ANT 312 Jb34
Coatzacoalcos MEX (VC) 265 Fc36
Cobá MEX (QTR) 265 Fg35
Cobá MEX 265 Fg35
Cobadin RO 47 Mj46
Cobalt USA (ID) 245 Ec23
Cobán GCA 265 Fe38
Çobanlar TR 53 Ml52
Cóbano CR 266 Fh41
Cobar AUS (NSW) 157 Sc61
Cobblestones AUS 150 Qh62
Cobden AUS (VIC) 159 Sb65
Cobh IRL 22 Km39
Cobham AUS (NSW) 156 Sb61
Cobham River CDN 248 Fc19
Cobija BOL 291 Gf51
Cobleni NAM 220 Lk56
Cobleskill USA (NY) 257 Gc24
Cobos RA (SA) 297 Gh58
Cobourg CDN (ON) 257 Ga24
Cobourg Peninsula AUS 145 Rg51
Cobquecura RCH 304 Gd64
Cóbué MOC 219 Mh52
Coburg D 37 Ll40
Coburn AUS (WA) 146 Qh59
Coca E 28 Kq51
Coca EC 284 Gb46
Coca EC 284 Gb46
Cocachacra PE 290 Gb51
Cocal BR (PI) 289 Hk47
Cocalinho BR (MT) 293 He53
Cocalinho BR (MA) 288 Hh47
Cocameira BR (AC) 291 Ge50
Cochabamba BOL 296 Gg54
Cochabamba PE 290 Ga49
Cochem D 36 Lh40
Cochetopa Hills USA 247 Eg27
Cochin = Kochi IND (KER) 114 Oj42
Cochran USA (GA) 259 Fj29
Cochrane CDN (AB) 243 Ec20
Cochrane CDN (ON) 249 Fk21
Cochrane RCH 306 Gd69
Cockaköl KZ 88 Of21
Cockatoo AUS (QLD) 157 Sf58
Cockatoo Island AUS 144 Rb54
Cockburn Bank 22 Km41
Cockburn Harbor GB 261 Ge35
Cockburn Town BS 261 Gc33
Cockburn Town GB 261 Ge35
Cockermouth GB 21 Kr36
Cocklebiddy AUS (WA) 151 Rd62
Coclecito PA 267 Fk41
Coco CR 266 Fh40
Coco HN/NIC 266 Fj38
Cocobeach G 202 Le45
Cococá BR (CE) 289 Hk49
Coco Channel IND 115 Pg39
Cococi BR (CE) 289 Hk49
Cocodrie USA (LA) 253 Fe31
Cocoland NIC 266 Fj38
Cocona MEX 265 Fd37
Cocoparra N.P. AUS (NSW) 159 Sd63
Cocorna CO 280 Gc42
Cocos BR (BA) 294 Hh53
Cocos Island CR 276 Fc17
Cocos Islands AUS 122 Pd21
Cocos Ridge 276 Fc18
Cocuite MEX (VC) 264 Fb36
Cocula MEX (JLC) 264 Ej35
Codajás BR (AM) 286 Gj47
Codeagro BR (AM) 286 Gk47
Codemin BR (GO) 294 Hf53
Codfish Island NZ 161 Td69
Codigoro I 42 Ln46
Codlea RO 47 Mf45
Codó BR (MA) 288 Hj48
Codo del Pozuzo PE 290 Gc50
Codogno I 42 Lk45
Codozinho BR (MA) 288 Hh48
Codpa RCH 296 Gf55
Codrington AG 271 Gk37
Codróipo I 43 Ln45
Codru MD 47 Mj44
Cody USA (WY) 245 Ef23
Coelemu RCH 304 Gd64
Coelho Neto BR (MA) 289 Hj48
Coenbult NAM 224 Lk59
Coengua PE 290 Gd51
Coeur d'Alene Ind. Res. USA 242 Eb22
Coeur d'Alene Lake USA 242 Eb22
Coesfeld D 34 Lh39
Coëtivy SY 227 Nj49
Coeur d'Alene USA (ID) 242 Eb22
Coevorden NL 34 Lg38
Coffee Bay SA 225 Me62
Coffee Bay Beach Point SA 225 Me62
Coffee Creek CDN (YT) 241 Da14
Coffeyville USA (KS) 253 Fc27
Coffin Bay AUS (SA) 158 Rh63
Coffin Bay AUS 158 Rh63
Coffin Bay N.P. AUS 158 Rh63
Coffs Harbour AUS (NSW) 157 Sg61
Cofimvaba SA 225 Md61
Cofre de Perote, Cerro MEX 263 Fb36
Cogâlnic MD 47 Mj44
Čoghadak IR 78 Nf31
Coghinas I 33 Lk50
Coghtan SA 225 Me61
Cogla Downs AUS (WA) 146 Qj59
Cognac F 26 Ku45
Cogne I 42 Lh45
Cogolin F 27 Lg47
Čograjskoe vodohranilišče RUS 74 Nc23
Çoğun TR 53 Mp51
Coguno MOC 222 Mh58

Index **341**

Great Yarmouth – Gurgaon

Great Yarmouth GB 23 Lb38
Great Zab IRQ 69 Nb28
Great Zimbabwe National Monument ZW 222 Mf56
Grebbestad S 14 Lm32
Grebenhain D 34 Lk40
Grebinka UA 56 Mg20
Grębocin PL 38 Lt37
Gréboun RN 188 Le35
Grecco ROU 301 Hb62
Greece 9 Ma06
Greeley USA (CO) 245 Eh25
Greeley USA (NE) 250 Fa25
Green Bay USA (WI) 256 Fg23
Green Bay USA 256 Fg23
Greenboro USA (NC) 259 Ga27
Greenbush USA (MN) 248 Fb21
Green Cape AUS 159 Sf64
Green Cay BS 261 Gb33
Green Cove Springs USA (FL) 260 Fk31
Greene USA (NY) 257 Gc24
Greeneville USA (TN) 259 Fj27
Greenfield USA (CA) 246 Dk27
Greenfield USA (IA) 251 Fc25
Greenfield USA (MO) 253 Fd27
Greenfield USA (IN) 256 Fh26
Greenfield USA (OH) 256 Fj26
Greenfield USA (MA) 257 Gd24
Green Head AUS (WA) 150 Qh60
Greenhill Island AUS 145 Rg51
Green Island AUS (QLD) 155 Sd54
Green Island = Lutao RC 101 Ra34
Green Island Bay RP 126 Qk40
Green Islands PNG 166 Sh48
Green Lake CDN (SK) 243 Eg18
Greenland DK 235 Hd03
Greenland Basin 8 Kb02
Greenland Sea 8 Kb02
Greenlaw GB 21 Ks35
Greenly Island AUS 158 Rh63
Green Mts. USA 257 Gd24
Greenock GB 21 Kq35
Greenodd GB 23 Kr36
Greenough AUS (WA) 150 Qh60
Greenough River AUS 150 Qh60
Green Point SA 225 Mf61
Green River PNG 164 Sa47
Green River USA (UT) 245 Ee26
Green River USA (WY) 245 Ef25
Green River USA 245 Ef26
Green River Basin USA 245 Ef24
Greensboro USA (AL) 258 Fg29
Greensboro USA (GA) 259 Fj29
Greensburg USA (KS) 252 Fa27
Greensburg USA (IN) 256 Fh26
Greensburg USA (KY) 258 Fh27
Greensburg USA (PA) 257 Ga25
Green Turtle Cay BS 261 Gb32
Greenvale AUS (QLD) 155 Sc55
Greenview USA (CA) 244 Dj25
Greenville CDN (BC) 241 Df18
Greenville LB 200 Kf43
Greenville USA (TX) 253 Fb29
Greenville USA (MO) 253 Fe27
Greenville USA (MS) 253 Fe29
Greenville USA (KY) 258 Fg27
Greenville USA (AL) 258 Fg30
Greenville USA (MI) 256 Fh24
Greenville USA (OH) 256 Fh25
Greenville USA (GA) 259 Fh29
Greenville USA (SC) 259 Fj28
Greenville USA (PA) 257 Fk25
Greenville USA (NC) 259 Gb28
Greenville USA (ME) 254 Gf23
Greenwater USA (WA) 242 Dk22
Greenwater Lake Prov. Park CDN 248 Ej19
Greenwich GB 23 La39
Greenwood AUS (WA) 146 Qj59
Greenwood CDN (BC) 242 Ea21
Greenwood USA (AR) 253 Fc28
Greenwood USA (MS) 253 Fe29
Greenwood USA (IN) 258 Fg26
Greenwood USA (SC) 259 Fj28
Greer USA (ID) 242 Eb22
Greer USA (SC) 259 Fj28
Greers Ferry Lake USA 253 Fe28
Greetsiel D 34 Lh37
Gregbeu CI 200 Kg42
Gregório BR 291 Ge49
Gregory USA (SD) 250 Fa24
Gregory Downs AUS (QLD) 154 Rk55
Gregory N.P. AUS 145 Rf53
Gregory N.P. AUS 145 Rf54
Gregory Range AUS 146 Ra56
Gregory Range AUS (QLD) 154 Sb55
Gregory River AUS (QLD) 154 Rk55
Gregory Springs AUS (QLD) 154 Sc55
Greifenburg A 37 Lo44
Greifswald D 35 Lo36
Greifswalder Bodden D 35 Lo36
Grein A 37 Lp42
Greiz D 35 Ln40
Gremiha RUS 62 Md05
Gremjač'e RUS 55 Mk20
Grenaa DK 16 Ll34
Grenada CO 280 Gc41
Grenada USA (MS) 253 Ff29
Grenada WG 271 Gk40
Grenada 271 Gk39
Grenade F 26 Lb47
Grenade-sur-l'Adour F 26 Ku47
Grenadines WV 271 Gk39
Grenchen CH 36 Lh43
Grenen DK 16 Ll33
Grenfell AUS (NSW) 159 Se62
Grenfell CDN (SK) 248 Ej20
Grenoble F 27 Lf45
Grenville WG 271 Gk39
Gresford AUS (NSW) 159 Sf62
Gresham USA (OR) 244 Dj23
Gresham USA (SC) 259 Ga29
Gresham ZW 218 Mf54
Gresik RI 132 Qg49
Gressåmoen n.p. N 12 Lg13
Gressoney-la-Trinité I 42 Lh45
Gretna Green GB 21 Kr36
Greve in Chianti I 42 Lm47
Greven D 34 Lh38
Grevená GR 48 Mb50
Grevenbroich D 34 Lg39
Grevenmacher L 25 Lg41
Grevesmühlen D 35 Lm37
Greve Strand DK 16 Ln35
Grevie S 16 Ln34
Greybull USA (WY) 245 Ef23
Greybull USA 245 Ef23
Grey Cairns GB 21 Kr32
Grey Hunter Peak CDN 241 Dc14
Greylingstad SA 225 Me59
Grey Mare's Tail GB 21 Kr35
Greymouth NZ 161 Tf67
Grey Range AUS 156 Sb60
Grey Range AUS 156 Sc59
Grey River CDN (NF) 255 Hb22
Grey River CDN 255 Hb22
Greystone ZW 222 Me56
Greystones IRL 22 Ko37
Greyton SA 224 Lk63
Greytown SA 225 Mf60
Grgurnica MK 48 Mb49
Grianan of Aileach IRL 20 Kn35
Gribanovskij RUS 55 Na20
Gribbelt Island CDN 242 Df19
Gribingui RCA 204 Lk42
Gridley USA (CA) 244 Dk26
Griekwastad SA 224 Mb60
Grieskirchen A 37 Lo42
Griffin CDN (SK) 248 Ej21
Griffin USA (GA) 259 Fh29
Griffith AUS (NSW) 159 Sd63
Grigor'evskoe RUS 55 Nb17
Grigoriopol MD 47 Mk43
Grik MAL 121 Qa43
Grillby S 15 Ls31
Grillon, Mount USA 241 Db16
Grimari RCA 208 Ma43
Grimma D 35 Ln39
Grimmen D 35 Lo36
Grimsby GB 23 Ku37
Grimsey IS 12 Kb12
Grimshaw CDN (AB) 243 Eb17
Grímsstaðir IS 12 Kb13
Grimstad N 14 Lj32
Grimsvötn IS 12 Kb13
Grinăuți MD 47 Mh43
Grindavík IS 12 Jj14
Grindelwald CH 36 Lj44
Grindsted DK 16 Lj35
Grinell USA (IA) 251 Fd25
Grinkiškis LT 19 Md35
Grinnel Peninsula CDN 235 Fb03
Grintavec SLO 43 Lp44
Gripsholm S 15 Ls31
Griquatown SA 224 Mb60
Grise Fiord CDN 235 Fc03
Griškabūdis LT 19 Md36
Grisolles F 26 Lb47
Grisslehamn S 15 Lt30
Grissom Air Mus. USA 256 Fg25
Grivenskaja RUS 57 Mk23
Grivița RO 47 Mh46
Grizim DZ 187 Kj33
Grjady RUS 54 Mf16
Grjazi RUS 55 Mk19
Grjazovec RUS 54 Na16
Grmeč BIH 43 Lr46
Groaíras BR (CE) 289 Hk47
Grobiņa LV 19 Mb34
Groblersdal SA 222 Me58
Groblershoop SA 224 Mb60
Grobniza BG 49 Mf48
Grocka SCG 46 Ma46
Gródek PL 39 Md37
Gröditz D 35 Lo39
Gródki PL 39 Ma37
Gródki PL 39 Mc40
Grodków PL 38 Ls40
Grodziczno PL 39 Lu37
Grodzisk Mazowiecki PL 39 Ma38
Grodzisk Wielkopolski PL 38 Lr38
Groeninge-Museum B 25 Ld39
Groen Rivier SA 224 Lj61
Groen Rivier SA 224 Mb61
Groenriviersmond SA 224 Lj61
Groesbeek SA 222 Me57
Groix F 24 Kr43
Groix F 24 Kr43
Grójec PL 39 Ma39
Grombalia TN 182 Lf27
Grömitz D 35 Ll36
Gromnik PL 41 Ma41
Gröna Lund S 15 Ls31
Gronau D 34 Lh38
Grong N 12 Lg13
Grong Grong AUS (NSW) 159 Sd63
Gröningen D 35 Lm39
Groningen NL 34 Lg37
Groningen SME 283 Hc43
Groninger Museum NL 34 Lg37
Gronlid CDN (SK) 243 Eh19
Grønligrotta N 12 Lh12
Grönskåra S 17 Lq33
Grootberg NAM 220 Lh55
Grootdraaidam SA 225 Me59
Grootdrink SA 224 Ma60
Groote Eylandt AUS 145 Rj53
Groote Eylandt A.L. AUS 145 Rj53
Grootfontein NAM 220 Lk55
Groot Henar SME 283 Hb43
Groot Jongensfontein SA 224 Ma63
Groot Karasberge NAM 224 Lk59
Grootkraal SA 224 Mb62
Groot Letaba SA 222 Mf57
Groot Marico SA 221 Md58
Groot Rivier SA 224 Ma62
Groot Rivier SA 224 Mb62
Grootrivierhoogte SA 224 Mb62
Grootvloer SA 224 Ma60
Groot Waterberg NAM 220 Lj55
Grootwinterhoekberge SA 225 Mc62
Groot Winterhoek Wilderness Area SA 224 Lk62
Gropeni RO 47 Mh45
Gros Morne CDN 255 Hb21
GrosMorne RH 270 Gd36
Gros Morne N. P. CDN 255 Hb21
Gross Barmen NAM 220 Lj57
Gross Barmen Hot Springs NAM 220 Lj57
Großenhain D 35 Lo39
Großenkneten D 34 Lj38
Großer Arber D 37 Lo41
Großer Beerberg D 35 Ll40
Großer Feldberg D 36 Lj40
Großer Garten D 34 Lk38
Großer Inselsberg D 35 Ll40
Großer Peilstein A 37 Lq42
Großer Plöner See D 35 Ll36
Großer Pyhrgas A 37 Lp43
Großer Rachel D 37 Lo42
Grosses AUS (SA) 158 Rh61
Große Sandspitze A 37 Ln44
Grosseto I 42 Lm47
Grosseto Prugna F 33 Lj49
Grossevići RUS 103 Rk22
Groß-Gerau D 36 Lj41
Groß Gerungs A 37 Lp42
Großglockner A 37 Ln43
Großglockner Straße A 37 Ln43
Grossos BR (RN) 289 Jb48
Großpetersdorf A 37 Lr43
Großräschen D 35 Lo39
Gross Ums NAM 220 Lk57
Großvenediger A 37 Ln43
Grosuplje SLO 43 Lp45
Grotli N 14 Lh29
Groton USA (SD) 250 Fa23
Grotta Azzurra I 44 Lp50
Grotta del Genovese I 44 Ln52
Grotta di Nettuno I 33 Lj50
Grotta di San Michele I 33 Lk50
Grottáglie I 45 Ls50
Grottaminarda I 44 Lq49
Grottammare I 43 Lo47
Grotte de Clamouse F 27 Ld47
Grotte de Grand-Roc F 26 La46
Grotte de Lascaux F 26 Lb45
Grotte de Niaux F 26 Lb48
Grotte de Pech Merle F 26 Lb46
Grotte des Demoiselles F 27 Ld47
Grotte de Villars F 26 La45
Grotte di Castellana I 45 Ls50
Grotte di Catullo I 42 Ll45
Grotte di Frasassi I 43 Ln47
Grotte du Mas-d'Azil F 26 Lb47
Grottes (Bangbali) RCA 204 Ma41
Grottes d'Azé F 27 Le44
Grottes de Beni-Add DZ 181 Kk28
Grottes de Bétharram F 26 Ku47
Grottes de Bongolo G 210 Lf47
Grottes de Dimba et Ngovo RDC 210 Lh48
Grottes de Matupi RDC 209 Me45
Grottes de Missirikoro RMM 201 Kh40
Grottes de Remouchamps B 25 Lf40
Grottes de Yambala RCA 204 Ma42
Grottes du Galo Boukoy RCA 203 Lh43
Grotto of the Redemption USA 251 Fc24
Grouard CDN (AB) 243 Eb18
Groumania CI 201 Kj42
Groundbirch CDN (BC) 242 Dk18
Groundhog River CDN 249 Fj21
Groupe d'Aldabra SY 226 Nd50
Grov N 12 Lj11
Grove USA (OK) 253 Fc27
Grove City USA (OH) 256 Fj26
Grove City USA (PA) 257 Fk25
Grove Hill USA (AL) 258 Fg30
Grövelsjön S 14 Ln28
Grove Mountains 313 Oc32
Groveton USA (TX) 253 Fc30
Groveton USA (NH) 257 Ge23
Grožnjan HR 43 Lo45
Groznyj RUS (CHE) 74 Nc24
Grube GH 201 Kk41
Grube Messel D 36 Lj41
Grubišno Polje HR 43 Ls45
Grudusk PL 39 Ma37
Grudziądz PL 38 Lt37
Grumento Nova I 45 Lq50
Grumeti EAT 212 Mh46
Grums S 15 Lo31
Grünau NAM 224 Lk59
Grünberg D 34 Lj40
Grundkallen 15 Lt30
Grundy USA (VA) 259 Fj27
Grundy Center USA (IA) 251 Fd24
Grünstadt D 36 Lj41
Grunwald PL 39 Ma37
Grupe GH 201 Kj41
Gruppo di Sella I 42 Lm44
Gruszka PL 39 Ma39
Gruta de Intihuasi RA 300 Gh62
Gruta de la Paz EC 284 Gb45
Gruta de las Maravillas E 30 Ko47
Gruta de los Helechos ROU 301 Hb61
Gruta del Palacio ROU 301 Hb62
Gruta de Ubajara BR 289 Hk47
Gruta do Lago Azul BR 297 Hb56
Grutas de Bustamante MEX 263 Ek32
Grutas de García MEX 263 Ek33
Grutas de Lanquin GCA 265 Ff38
Grutas de Loltún MEX 265 Ff35
Grutas de Xtacumbilxunán MEX 265 Fe36
Grutas dos Brejões BR (BA) 295 Hk51
Grutas Lázaro Cárdenas MEX 265 Fc37
Gruver USA (TX) 252 Ek27
Gruža SCG 48 Ma47
Gruzdžiai LT 19 Md34
Grybów PL 41 Ma41
Grycksbro S 15 Lq30
Gryfice PL 38 Lq37
Gryfino PL 38 Lp37
Gryfów Śląski PL 38 Lq39
Grykë AL 48 Lu50
Gryllefjord N 12 Lj11
Gryt S 17 Lr32
Grythyttan S 15 Lp31
Gstaad CH 36 Lh44
Gua EAT 214 Mg49
Guabalá PA 267 Fk41
Guabijú BR (RS) 302 Hc61
Guabiju BR (RS) 302 He60
Guabún RCH 304 Gd66
Guacamayas CO 284 Gc44
Guacamayas CO 281 Ge43
Guacara YV 281 Gg40
Guacautey YV 282 Gk43
Guachara YV 281 Gf42
Gua Charah MAL 121 Qb43
Guachimetas de Arriba MEX (DGO) 262 Eg33
Guachipas RA (SA) 296 Gh58
Guachochi MEX (CHH) 262 Eg32
Guachucal CO 284 Gb45
Guaco CO 281 Ge44
Guaçu BR (MS) 298 Hc57
Guaçuí BR (ES) 299 Hk56
Guadalajara E 31 Kr50
Guadalajara MEX (JLC) 264 Ej35
Guadalcanal E 30 Kp48
Guadalcanal SOL 167 Sk50
Guadalest E 31 Ku48
Guadalupe BR (PI) 288 Hj49
Guadalupe MEX (ZCT) 263 Ej34
Guadalupe MEX (NL) 263 Ek33
Guadalupe PE 290 Ga49
Guadalupe USA (CA) 246 Dk28
Guadalupe de Bagues MEX (CHH) 263 Eh32
Guadalupe Mts. N.P. USA 247 Eh30
Guadalupe y Calvo MEX (CHH) 262 Eg32
Guadeloupe F 271 Gk37
Guadeloupe Passage 271 Gk37
Guadelupe de Bravo MEX (CHH) 247 Eg30
Guadelupe del Carnicero MEX (SLP) 263 Ek34
Guadelupe de los Reyes MEX (SL) 262 Eg33
Guadelupe Victoria MEX (BC) 246 Ec29
Guadelupe Victoria MEX (DGO) 263 Eh33
Guadix E 31 Kr47
Guaduas CO 280 Gc43
Guafera Ye Terara Senselet ETH 206 Mh42
Guahaja, T.I. BR 291 Gg49
Guaíba BR (RS) 302 He61
Guaimaca HN 266 Fg38
Guáimaro C 269 Gb35
Guaimbe, T.I. BR 298 Hc57
Guaina YV 282 Gj43
Guainía CO 285 Gf44
Guaíra BR (PR) 298 Hc58
Guaíra BR (SP) 298 Hf56
Guajará BR (AM) 291 Gd49
Guajará-Mirim BR (RO) 292 Gh51
Guajirú BR (CE) 289 Ja47
Gualán GCA 265 Ff38
Gualaquiza EC 284 Ga47
Gualdo Tadino I 42 Ln47
Guale EC 284 Fk46
Gualeguay RA (ER) 301 Ha62
Gualeguay RA 301 Ha62
Gualeguaychú RA (ER) 301 Ha62
Gualjaina RA (CB) 304 Ge67
Guallatiri RCH 296 Gf55
Guallatiri, Volcán RCH 296 Gf55
Gualmatán CO 284 Gb45
Guam USA 141 Sa08
Guamá BR 288 Hg46
Guama YV 281 Gf40
Guamal CO 280 Gc41
Guamal San Martin CO 280 Gd44
Gua Mampu RI 133 Ra48
Guamini RA (BA) 305 Gj64
Guamo CO 280 Gc43
Guamote EC 284 Ga46
Guamúchil MEX (SL) 262 Ef33
Guamués CO 284 Gb45
Gua Musang MAL 121 Qb43
Gu'an VRC (HBI) 97 Qj26
Guanabo C 268 Fj34
Guanacaste N.P. BH 265 Ff37
Guanacaste, P.N. CR 266 Fh40
Guanacevi MEX (DGO) 262 Eh33
Guanaco Muerto RA (CD) 300 Gh61
Guanahani Island = San Salvador BS 261 Gc33
Guanaja HN 266 Fh37
Guanajay C 268 Fj34
Guanajuato MEX (GJT) 264 Ek35
Guanajuato MEX 263 Ek35
Guanajuña YV 282 Gj43
Guanambi BR (BA) 294 Hj53
Guanare YV 281 Gf41
Guanare YV 281 Gf41
Guanarito YV 281 Gf41
Guanay BOL 291 Gg53
Guanay, Cerro YV 281 Gg43
Guancheng VRC (ZJG) 106 Ra30
Guandacaya BOL 297 Gh57
Guandacol RA (LR) 300 Gf60
Guandiping VRC (HUN) 99 Qf31
Guandong VRC 87 Qc14
Guang'an VRC (SCH) 99 Qd30
Guangang VRC (AHU) 106 Qj31
Guangba VRC (SCH) 99 Qd29
Guangchang VRC (JGX) 106 Qj32
Guangde VRC (AHU) 106 Qk30
Guangfenghai VRC (GZH) 100 Qc32
Guanghai VRC (GDG) 101 Qg35
Guangmao Shan VRC 117 Qa32
Guangnan VRC (YUN) 100 Qc33
Guangning VRC (GDG) 100 Qg34
Guangrao VRC (SDG) 97 Qk27
Guangshan VRC (HNN) 106 Qh30
Guangsheng Si VRC 97 Qf27
Guangshui VRC (HUB) 106 Qh30
Guangshuishi VRC (HUB) 99 Qg30
Guangshun VRC (GZH) 100 Qd32
Guangtong VRC (YUN) 117 Qa33
Guangxi Zhuangzu Zizhiqu VRC 87 Qb14
Guangyuan VRC (SCH) 99 Qc29
Guangze VRC (FJN) 106 Qj32
Guangzhou VRC (GDG) 101 Qg34
Guanhães BR (MG) 299 Hj55
Guaní CO 285 Gd44
Guaniamo YV 281 Gg42
Guanica USA (PR) 271 Gg37
Guanipa YV 281 Gj41
Guanling VRC (GZH) 100 Qc33
Guanoco YV 282 Gj40
Guanqiao VRC (NHZ) 96 Qc27
Guanta RCH 300 Ge60
Guantánamo C 269 Gc35
Guantanamo Bay US Naval Base USA 269 Gc36
Guantao VRC (HBI) 97 Qh27
Guanyun VRC (JGS) 106 Qk28
Guapé BR (MG) 299 Hh56
Guapi CO 284 Gb44
Guapiara BR (SP) 298 Hf58
Guápiles CR 266 Fj40
Guaporé BOL 292 Gk52
Guaporé BR 292 Ha53
Guaporé BR 302 Hd60
Guaporé BR (RS) 302 He60
Guaqui BOL 296 Gf54
Guará BR (SP) 298 Hg56
Guará BR 294 Hh52
Guara E 29 Ku52
Guaraci BR (SP) 298 Hf56
Guaraciaba BR (SC) 302 Hd59
Guaraciaba do Norte BR (CE) 289 Hk48
Guaraí BR (TO) 294 Hf50
Guaramacal, P.N. YV 281 Ge41
Guarambaré PY 297 Hb58
Guaramirim BR (SC) 303 Hf59
Guaramuri GUY 282 Ha42
Guaranda EC 284 Ga46
Guaraní BOL 297 Gj56
Guaraniaçu BR (PR) 298 Hd58
Guarantã BR (SP) 298 Hf56
Guarantã do Norte BR (MT) 293 Hc50
Guarapari BR (ES) 299 Hk56
Guarapuava BR (PR) 298 He58
Guarapuava BR (MG) 299 Hg54
Guaraqueçaba BR (PR) 303 Hf58
Guararapes BR (SP) 298 He56
Guarariba BR (PB) 289 Jc49
Guaratinga BR (BA) 299 Ja54
Guaratingueta BR (SP) 299 Hh57
Guaratuba BR (PR) 303 Hf58
Guarayos BOL 291 Gf52
Guarda P 28 Kn50
Guardalavaca C 269 Gc35
Guardamar del Segura E 31 Ku48
Guarda-Mor BR (MG) 299 Hg54
Guardiagrele I 44 Lp48
Guardia Mitre RA (RN) 305 Gj66
Guardo E 28 Kq52
Guareña E 30 Ko48
Guarento YV 282 Gj42
Guari PNG 165 Sd50
Guariba BR 292 Gk50
Guariba BR (SP) 298 Hf56
Guárico YV 281 Gg41
Guarita, T.I. BR 301 Hd59
Guarujá BR (SP) 299 Hg58
Guarulhos BR (SP) 299 Hg57
Guasave MEX (SL) 262 Ef33
Guasca CO 280 Gd43
Guasdualito YV 281 Ge42
Guasipati YV 282 Gk42
Guasizaco MEX (CHH) 262 Ef32
Guasopa PNG 166 Sg50
Guastalla I 42 Ll46
Guasuti, T.I. BR 298 Hc57
Guatacondo RCH 296 Gf56
Guataqui CO 280 Gc43
Guatemala 265 Fe38
Guatemala Basin 236 Fa16
Guatimape MEX (DGO) 263 Eh33
Guatire YV 281 Gg40
Guatopo, P.N. YV 281 Gg40
Guatraché RA (LP) 305 Gj64
Guaviare CO 281 Gf44
Guaxupé BR (MG) 299 Hg56
Guayabal C 269 Gb35
Guayabero CO 285 Gd44
Guayabones YV 280 Ge41
Guayaguayaré TT 282 Gk40
Guayama USA (PR) 271 Gg37
Guayapo YV 281 Gg43
Guayaquil EC 284 Ga47
Guayaquil MEX (BC) 246 Ec31
Guayaramerín BOL 291 Gh51
Guayas CO 284 Gc45
Guaycurú RA 301 Ha59
Guayliabamba EC 284 Ga45
Guayllabamba EC 284 Ga46
Guaymas MEX (SO) 262 Ee32
Guayquiaró RA 301 Ha61
Guayubin DOM 270 Ge36
Guayzimi EC 284 Ga48
Guba ETH 206 Mh40
Guba RDC 218 Md51
guba Buor-Haja RUS 63 Rc04
Guban SP 207 Nb40
Gubat RP 125 Rc39
Gubatsaa Hills RB 217 Mc55
Gúbbio I 42 Ln47
Gubed Rugguuda SP 207 Nd40
Guben D 35 Lp39
Gubi WAN 194 Le40
Gubin PL 38 Lp39
Gubio WAN 195 Lg39
Gubkin RUS 55 Mj20
Gubra IND (MPH) 113 Ok34
Guča SCG 48 Ma47
Gucheng VRC (SAX) 99 Qf28
Gucheng VRC (HUB) 99 Qf29
Guci Hot Water Spring RI 132 Qe49
Gudalur IND (TNU) 114 Oj41
Gudauta GE 74 Na24
Gudbrandsdalen N 14 Lk29
Gudenå DK 16 Lk34
Guder ETH 206 Mj41
Guder ETH 206 Mj41
Guder Falls ETH 206 Mj41
Gudermes RUS (CHE) 74 Nd24
Guderup DK 16 Lk36
Gudgaon IND (MPH) 113 Oj35
Gudha IND (RJT) 110 Oj32
Gudhjem DK 17 Lp35
Gudi WAN 194 Le41
Gudivada IND (APH) 113 Pa37
Gudiyattam IND (TNU) 115 Ok40
Gudong VRC (YUN) 117 Pk33
Güdül TR 53 Mn50
Gudur IND (APH) 115 Ok39
Gudvangen N 14 Lg30
Gudžal RUS 102 Rg20
Guéassou RG 200 Kf41
Guebwiller F 25 Lh43
Guechémé RN 193 Lb39
Guéckédou RG 200 Ke41
Guelb El Makhsar RIM 192 Kf36
Guelb El Rhein RIM 186 Kd34
Guelb er Richât RIM 186 Ke35
Guelb Makhrouga RIM 192 Kf36
Guelb Ragoum RIM 192 Kf36
Guelb Zednes RIM 186 Ke33
Guéléhé TCH 204 Lk41
Guélengdeng TCH 195 Lh40
Guellala TN 182 Lf29
Guelltat Sidi Saad DZ 181 La28
Guelma DZ 182 Ld27
Guelmim MA 180 Ke31
Guelta d'Archei TCH 197 Ma37
Guémar DZ 182 Ld29
Guémené-Penfao F 24 Kt43
Guémené-sur-Scorff F 24 Kr42
Güémez MEX (TM) 263 Fa34
Guemour DZ 181 Lc32
Guènt Paté SN 191 Kc38
Guépaouo CI 201 Kh42
Güeppí PE 284 Gc46
Guer F 24 Ks43
Güer Aike RA (SC) 306 Gf71
Guérande F 24 Ks43
Guerara DZ 181 Lc29
Guercif MA 181 Kj28
Guéréda TCH 197 Mb38
Guerende LAR 184 Ma34
Guéret F 26 Lb44
Guerguarat DARS 186 Kb35
Guérin-Kouka RT 201 La41
Guermessa TN 182 Lf29
Guerneville USA (CA) 244 Dj26
Guernsey GB 24 Ks41
Guernsey USA (WY) 245 Eh24
Guérou RIM 191 Ke37
Guerrero MEX (CHH) 247 Eg31
Guerrero MEX (COH) 263 Ek31
Guerrero MEX 264 Ek36
Guerrero, P. V. MEX 263 Fa34
Guerrero Negro MEX (BCS) 262 Ec32
Guerzim DZ 181 Kk31
Gueskérou RN 195 Lg39
Guéssabo CI 200 Kg42
Guésséyo CI 200 Kg42
Guessou South DY 194 Lb40
Gueugnon F 27 Le44
Guéyo CI 200 Kg43
Guézaoua RN 194 Le38
Guffertspitze A 37 Lm43
Guge, Mount ETH 206 Mj42
Gugești RO 47 Mh45
Guglionesi I 44 Lp49
Guguan USA 123 Sb15
Guguang, Gunung RI 130 Qj44
Gugu, Mount ETH 206 Mk41
Gugurtli UZB 80 Ob25
Guhagar IND (MHT) 112 Og37
Guia Lopes da Laguna BR (MS) 297 Hb56
Guiana Basin 277 Hb16
Guiana Highlands 276 Gd17
Guiana Plateau 277 Hb17
Guiarote BOL 297 Gj55
Guibaré BF 193 Kk39
Guibéroua CI 200 Kg42
Guicán CO 280 Gd42
Guichi VRC (AHU) 106 Qj30
Guichón ROU 301 Hb62
Guidan-Roumji RN 194 Ld39
Guidari TCH 195 Lj41
Guider CAM 195 Lg41
Guidiguir RN 194 Le39
Guidiguis CAM 195 Lh40
Guidimaka RIM/RMM 191 Ke38
Guidimouni RN 194 Le39
Guiding VRC (GZH) 100 Qd32
Guidjiba CAM 203 Lg41
Guidong VRC (HUN) 101 Qg32
Guiembé CI 201 Kh41
Guiendana CI 201 Kh41
Guiengola MEX 265 Fc37
Guiffa RCA 204 Lk42
Guigang VRC (GZG) 100 Qe34
Guiglo CI 200 Kg42
Güigüe YV 281 Gg40
Guihua Temple VRC 98 Pk31
Guihuayuan VRC (SCH) 99 Qc30
Guihulñgan RP 127 Rb40
Guijuelo E 28 Kp50
Guilderton AUS (WA) 150 Qh61
Guildford GB 23 Ku39
Guiler Gol VRC 95 Ra22
Guilin VRC (GZG) 100 Qf33
Guillaumes F 27 Lg46
Guillestre F 27 Lg46
Guilmara DY 201 La40
Guilvinec F 24 Kq43
Guimarães BR (MA) 288 Hh47
Guimarães P 28 Km51
Guimaras Island RP 127 Rb40
Guimba RP 125 Ra38
Guimbalete MEX (COH) 263 Ej32
Guimiliau F 24 Kr42
Guinagourou DY 194 Lb41
Guinchos Cay BS 261 Ga34
Guindulman RP 127 Rc41
Guinea 175 Ka08
Guinea Basin 174 Kb10
Guinea-Bissau 175 Ka08
Güines C 268 Fj34
Guînes F 25 Lb40
Guingamp F 24 Kr42
Guinguineo SN 191 Kc38
Guipavas F 24 Kq42
Guiping VRC (GZG) 100 Qf34
Guîr RMM 193 Kj36
Güira de Melena C 268 Fj34
Guiratinga BR (MT) 298 Hd54
Guiri CAM 195 Lh40
Güiría YV 282 Gj40
Guiripa CO 280 Ge43
Guirwas SN 191 Kc38
Guisa C 269 Gb35
Guisborough GB 23 Kt36
Guiscard F 25 Ld41
Guise F 25 Ld41
Guishi Shuiku VRC 100 Qf33
Guissat RN 194 Le37
Guissèr MA 180 Kg29
Guissona E 32 Lb49
Guitiriz E 28 Kn53
Guitri CI 201 Kh43
Guiuan RP 127 Rc40
Guiyang VRC (GZH) 100 Qd32
Guiyang VRC (HUN) 100 Qg33
Gui Yuan Si VRC 106 Qh30
Guizhou VRC 87 Qb13
Guizhou VRC (HUB) 99 Qf30
Gujan-Mestras F 26 Kt46
Gujarat IND 108 Oc14
Gujar Khan PK 83 Og29
Gujba WAN 195 Lf40
Gujiao VRC (SAX) 97 Qg27
Gujranwala PK 83 Oh29
Gujrat PK 83 Oh29
Gujri IND (MPH) 112 Oh34
Gukovo RUS 57 Mk21
Gulabgarh 83 Oj29
Gulagambone AUS (NSW) 157 Se61
Gulang VRC (GSU) 96 Qb27
Gulangyu RC 101 Qk33
Gulbarga IND (KTK) 112 Oj37
Gulbarga Fort IND 112 Oj37
Gulbene LV 19 Mg33
Gulbin Ka WAN 194 Lc40
Gul'ca KS 81 Og25
Gul'ca KS 81 Og26
Guldenløves Fjord DK 235 Ja06
Guledagud IND (KTK) 112 Oh38
Gulf Islands National Seashore USA 253 Ff30
Gulf of Aden 64 Nb16
Gulf of Alaska USA 234 Cc07
Gulf of Aqaba ET/KSA 68 Mh31
Gulf of Arab ET 185 Me30
Gulf of Bahrain KSA 71 Nf33
Gulf of Bone RI 131 Ra48
Gulf of Boothia CDN 235 Fc05
Gulf of Bothnia S/FIN 12 Lk15
Gulf of California MEX 236 Eb13
Gulf of Carpentaria AUS 142 Rd21
Gulf of Corinth GR 50 Mc52
Gulf of Darién PA/CO 267 Gb41
Gulf of Finland 18 Md31
Gulf of Gdansk PL 38 Lt36
Gulf of Genoa I 42 Lj46
Gulf of Guinea 176 La18
Gulf of Hikma ET 184 Me30
Gulf of Kachchh IND 112 Oe34
Gulf of Khambhat IND 112 Og35
Gulf of Liaotung VRC 104 Ra25
Gulf of Lingayan RP 124 Ra37
Gulf of Maine USA 257 Gf24
Gulf of Mannar IND/CY 115 Ok42
Gulf of Martaban T 118 Pj38
Gulf of Masirah OM 73 Nk35
Gulf of Mexico 237 Fb13
Gulf of Oman 64 Nd14
Gulf of Panama PA 267 Ga42
Gulf of Papua PNG 165 Sc50
Gulf of Paria YV 282 Gj40
Gulf of Riga EST/LV 19 Md33
Gulf of Saint Lawrence CDN 255 Gj21
Gulf of Sallum ET 184 Mc30
Gulf of Salonica GR 48 Mc50
Gulf of Santa Catalina USA 246 Ea29
Gulf of Sirte LAR 183 Lj30
Gulf of Suez ET 185 Mg31
Gulf of Taranto I 45 La50
Gulf of Tehuantepec MEX 265 Fc38
Gulf of Thailand T 122 Qa16
Gulf of Tolo RI 131 Rb47
Gulf of Tomini RI 131 Ra46
Gulf of Tonkin VN/VRC 100 Qd36
Gulf of Valencia E 32 La51
Gulf of Venezuela YV 280 Ge40
Gulf of Venice I 43 Ln45
Gulf of Zula ER 199 Mk39
Gulfport USA (MS) 253 Ff30
Gulf Saint Vincent AUS 158 Rk63
Gulfstream Park USA (FL) 260 Fk33
Gulganj IND (MPH) 113 Ok33
Gulgong AUS (NSW) 159 Se62
Gulioni EAT 215 Mk49
Gulir RI 134 Rf48
Guliston UZB 80 Oe25
Guljanci BG 49 Me47
Guljanic'ke UA 47 Ml43
Gul Kach PK 82 Oe30
Gul'keviči RUS 57 Na23
Gullbrandstorp S 16 Ln34
Gullfoss IS 12 Jk13
Gull Lake CDN 243 Ed19
Gull Lake CDN (SK) 243 Ef20
Gullspång S 15 Lp32
Güllü TR 52 Mk52
Güllü Dağları TR 67 Na25
Güllük TR 51 Mh53
Güllük Körfezi TR 51 Mh53
Gulmarg 83 Oh28
Gülpınar TR 52 Mg51
Gülşehir TR 53 Mp52
Gulshat KZ 88 Oh22
Gulsvik N 14 Lk30
Gulu EAU 212 Mg44
Gülük Dagı Milli Parkı TR 53 Ml54
Gulumba Gana WAN 195 Lh40
Gulwe EAT 215 Mj49
Guma = Pishan VRC (XUZ) 90 Ok27
Gumaca RP 125 Ra39
Gumare RB 221 Mb55
Gumba ANG 216 Lh51
Gumba RDC 208 Ma44
Gumbardo AUS (QLD) 157 Sc59
Gumbiro EAT 219 Mh51
Gumdag TM 75 Nh26
Gumel WAN 194 Le39
Gumgarhi NEP 92 Pb31
Gumi RI 134 Rd45
Gumiel de Hizán E 29 Kr51
Gumine PNG 165 Sc49
Gumla IND (JKD) 113 Pc34
Gumlu AUS (QLD) 155 Sd55
Gummersbach D 34 Lh39
Gummi WAN 194 Lc39
Gumsi WAN 195 Lf39
Gümüldür TR 51 Mh52
Gümüşçay TR 52 Mh50
Gümüşhane TR 67 Mk25
Gümüşkent TR 53 Mp52
Gümüşova TR 53 Ml50
Gümüşsu TR 52 Ml52
Gumu Uen SP 213 Nb45
Gumzai RI 135 Rh48
Guna IND (MPH) 113 Oj33
Guna Terare ETH 206 Mk40
Gunbad-e-Haruniyeh IR 77 Nk27
Gundabooka N.P. AUS (NSW) 157 Sc61
Gundardehi IND (CGH) 113 Pa35
Gundelfingen D 36 Ll42
Gundji RDC 208 Ma44
Gündoğmuş TR 53 Mn54
Gundulpet IND (KTK) 115 Oj41
Güneşli TR 53 Mq52
Güney TR 52 Mj52
Güney TR 52 Mk52
Güney Doğu Toroslar TR 66 Mj26
Gunga ANG 217 Lk53
Gungadei AUS (NSW) 159 Se63
Gungi RDC 211 Lk49
Gungo ANG 216 Lh51
Gungu RDC 211 Lk48
Gungure MOC 219 Mk51
Gunisao Lake CDN 248 Fb19
Gunisao River CDN 248 Fb19
Guniujiang Z.B. VRC 106 Qj31
Gunlom A.L. AUS 145 Rg52
Gunn CDN (AB) 243 Ec19
Gunna SUD 205 Md42
Gunnaur IND (UPH) 111 Ok31
Gunnebo S 17 Lr33
Gunnedah AUS (NSW) 157 Sf61
Gunnerus Ridge 313 Mc32
Gunning AUS (NSW) 159 Se63
Gunnison USA (UT) 245 Ee26
Gunnison USA (CO) 245 Eg26
Gunnison, Mount USA 245 Eg26
Gunpowder AUS (QLD) 154 Rk55
Guns NAM 220 Lh57
Günsang VRC (TIB) 92 Pb30
Gunt TJ 81 Og27
Gunta WAN 194 Le40
Guntakal IND (APH) 115 Oj39
Guntersville USA (AL) 258 Fg28
Guntin de Pallares E 28 Kn52
Guntur IND (APH) 113 Pa37
Gununa AUS (QLD) 154 Rk54
Gunungagung RI 129 Qc48
Gunung Ambang Reserve RI 131 Rc45
Gunung Angemuk RI 135 Rk47
Gunung Antares RI 135 Sa48
Gunungapi RI 136 Rd49
Gunungapi RI 136 Rd49
Gunung Api RI 134 Re48
Gunung Argopuro RI 132 Qg49
Gunung Bakayan RI 130 Qj44
Gunung Balease RI 131 Ra47
Gunung Basakan RI 130 Qj44
Gunung Batubrok RI 130 Qh45
Gunung Batukau RI 133 Qh50
Gunung Besar RI 132 Qg48
Gunung Bromo RI 132 Qg49
Gunung Butak RI 132 Qg49
Gunung Cemaru RI 130 Qh45
Gunung Chamah MAL 121 Qa42
Gunung Cirema RI 132 Qe49
Gunung Daku RI 131 Ra45
Gunung Dempo RI 129 Qb47
Gunung Dom RI 135 Rj47
Gunung Gading N.P. MAL 130 Qe45
Gunung Gagau MAL 121 Qb42
Gunung Gambuta RI 131 Rb45
Gunung Gandadiwata RI 131 Qk47
Gunung Guguang RI 130 Qj44
Gunung Halimun RI 132 Qd49
Gunung Harden RI 130 Qh43
Gunung Irau RI 134 Rg46
Gunung Kambuno RI 131 Ra47
Gunung Katoposo RI 131 Ra46
Gunung Kemal RI 130 Qj45
Gunungkembang RI 129 Qb47
Gunung Kerihun RI 130 Qh45
Gunung Kerinci RI 128 Qa46
Gunung Kinabalu MAL 126 Qj42
Gunung Kujat RI 130 Qj44
Gunung Kwoka RI 134 Rg46
Gunung Lawit RI 130 Qg45
Gunung Lawu RI 132 Qf49
Gunung Leuser N.P. RI 120 Pj44
Gunung Liangmangari RI 130 Qg46
Gunung Liangpran RI 130 Qh45
Gunung Liman RI 132 Qf49
Gunung Loi RI 130 Qg45
Gunung Lompobatang RI 133 Ra48
Gunung Lumaku MAL 126 Qh43
Gunung Lumut RI 130 Qh46
Gunung Malabar RI 132 Qd49
Gunung Malea RI 128 Pk45
Gunung Malino RI 131 Ra45
Gunung Masurai RI 128 Qa47
Gunung Mata Bia TIM 136 Rd50
Gunung Mebo RI 135 Rg46
Gunungmegang RI 129 Qb48
Gunung Meja Reserve RI 135 Rg46
Gunung Mekongga RI 131 Ra47
Gunung Menyapa RI 130 Qj45
Gunungmeraksa RI 129 Qc47
Gunung Merapi RI 132 Qf49
Gunung Merapi RI 133 Qh50
Gunung Mulu N.P. MAL 126 Qh43
Gunung Muria RI 132 Qf49
Gunung Mutis RI 136 Rc50
Gunung Nanti RI 129 Qb48
Gunung Niut RI 130 Qe45
Gunung Noring MAL 121 Qa42
Gunung Pancungapang RI 130 Qh45
Gunung Pangrango RI 132 Qd49
Gunung Payang RI 130 Qh45
Gunung Ranakah RI 133 Ra50
Gunung Rantemario RI 131 Ra47
Gunung Ratai RI 129 Qc48
Gunung Raung RI 133 Qh50
Gunung Raya RI 128 Qa47
Gunung Raya RI 130 Qg46
Gunung Rinjani RI 133 Qj50
Gunung Saran RI 130 Qf46
Gunung Sebayan RI 130 Qf46
Gunung Seblat RI 128 Qb47
Gunung Semeru RI 132 Qg50
Gunungsitoli RI 128 Pj45
Gunung Slamet RI 132 Qe49
Gunung Tahan MAL 121 Qb42
Gunung Takan RI 133 Qj50
Gunung Tamborra RI 133 Qj50
Gunung Tampu Inanajing RI 128 Pk45
Gunung Tata Mailau = Mount Ramelau TIM 136 Rc50
Gunung Tebak RI 129 Qc48
Gunung Tenamatua RI 131 Ra46
Gunung Tentolomatinan RI 131 Rb45
Gunung Tibau RI 130 Qh45
Gunung Trus Madi MAL 126 Qj43
Gunungtua RI 128 Pk45
Gunung Tuham RI 130 Qg45
Gunung Ubia RI 135 Rj48
Gunung Umsini RI 135 Rg46
Gunung Wanggamet RI 133 Ra51
Gunung Welirang RI 132 Qg49
Gunupur IND (ORS) 113 Pb36
Gunupur IND (ORS) 113 Pb36
Gunwara IND (MPH) 113 Pa33
Günyüzü TR 53 Mm51
Günz D 36 Ll42
Günzburg D 36 Ll42
Gunzenhausen D 37 Ll41
Guocheng VRC (GSU) 96 Qc27
Guodao VRC (SAX) 97 Qg27
Guo He VRC 106 Qj29
Guoquanyan VRC 98 Qb30
Guoyang VRC (AHU) 106 Qj29
Guozhen VRC (SAA) 99 Qd28
Gupeng VRC (GZG) 100 Qe34
Gupis 83 Og27
Guptapur IND (ORS) 113 Pc36
Gur RUS 103 Rj21
Guraghe, Mount ETH 206 Mk41
Gura Haitii RO 47 Mf43
Gurahonț RO 46 Mc44
Gura Humorului RO 47 Mf43
Gurais 83 Oh28
Gurampod IND (APH) 113 Ok37
Guran IR 79 Nh32
Gurasada RO 46 Mc45
Gurba RDC 205 Md43
Gurbantünggüt Shamo VRC 89 Pd23
Gurdaspur IND (PJB) 110 Oh29
Gurdim IR 79 Oa33
Gurdžaani GE 74 Nc25
Güre TR 52 Mk52
Gur'evsk RUS 19 Ma36
Gurgaon IND (HYA) 111 Oj31

Jaab Lake – Jiuzhan

J

Jaab Lake CDN 249 Fj20
Jaala FIN 18 Mg29
Ja'ar YE 72 Nc39
Jääsjärvi FIN 18 Mg29
Jabal os Sara AFG 82 Oe28
Jabalpur IND (MPH) 113 Ok34
Jabarona SUD 197 Md37
Jabbarah Fara KSA 70 Na36
Jabbaren DZ 188 Le33
Jaberos PE 284 Gb48
Jabiru AUS (NT) 145 Rg52
Jablah SYR 68 Mh28
Jablanac HR 43 Lp46
Jablanica BG 48 Me47
Jablanica BIH 43 Ls47
Jablanica SCG 48 Mb48
Jablonec nad Nisou CZ 40 Lq40
Jablonica SK 40 Ls42
Jablonka PL 41 Lu41
Jabłonowo Pomorskie PL 39 Lu37
Jabluniv UA 41 Me42
Jablunkov CZ 40 Lt41
Jabo WAN 194 Lc39
Jabonga RP 127 Rc41
Jabotá BR 293 Hc52
Jaboticabal BR (SP) 298 Hf56
Jaboticatubas BR (MG) 299 Hj55
Jabra IND (JKD) 113 Pc33
Jabrin OM 79 Nj34
Jabugo E 30 Ko47
Jabuka SCG 48 Lu47
Jabukovac SCG 46 Mc46
Jabukovik SCG 48 Mc48
Jabuti, T.I. BR 282 Gk44
Jaca E 29 Ku52
Jacai SP 207 Nd43
Jacala MEX (HDG) 264 Fa35
Jacaré BR 286 Gj49
Jacaré BR 295 Hk51
Jacareacanga BR (PA) 287 Hb49
Jacareí BR (SP) 299 Hh57
Jacaretinga BR (AM) 292 Ha50
Jacarezinho BR (PR) 298 Hf57
Jacas Grande PE 290 Gb50
Jaceyl SP 207 Nf40
Jaceyl SP 207 Nf40
Jáchal RA 300 Gf61
Jaciara BR (MT) 298 Hc54
Jacinto BR (MG) 299 Hk54
Jaciparaná BR 291 Gh51
Jaci Paraná BR (RO) 292 Gh50
Jacitara BR (AM) 286 Gh47
Jack Daniels Distillery USA 258 Fg28
Jackhead CDN (MB) 248 Fb20
Jackman Station USA (ME) 257 Ge23
Jackpot USA (NV) 245 Ec25
Jacksboro USA (TX) 252 Fa29
Jackson USA (CA) 244 Dk26
Jackson USA (MT) 245 Ed23
Jackson USA (WY) 245 Ee24
Jackson USA (MN) 251 Fc24
Jackson USA (MS) 253 Fe29
Jackson USA (MO) 253 Ff27
Jackson USA (TN) 253 Ff28
Jackson USA (AL) 258 Fg30
Jackson USA (MI) 256 Fh24
Jackson USA (OH) 256 Fj26
Jackson USA (KY) 259 Fj27
Jackson USA (GA) 259 Fj29
Jackson, Mount ANT 6 Gd33
Jackson's Arm CDN (NF) 255 Hb21
Jacksonville USA (TX) 253 Fc30
Jacksonville USA (AR) 253 Fd28
Jacksonville USA (IL) 251 Fe26
Jacksonville USA (AL) 259 Fh29
Jacksonville USA (GA) 259 Fj30
Jacksonville USA (FL) 259 Fk30
Jacksonville USA (NC) 259 Gb28
Jacksonville Beach USA (FL) 259 Fk30
Jacktown USA (OK) 253 Fb28
Jack Wade USA (AK) 239 Ck13
Jacmel RH 270 Gd36
Jacó CR 266 Fh41
Jacoatão dos Guararapes BR (PE) 295 Jc50
Jacobina BR (BA) 295 Hk51
Jacob Lake USA (AZ) 247 Ed27
Jacobsdal SA 225 Mc60
Jacques Cartier, Mount CDN 254 Gh21
Jacqueville CI 201 Kh43
Jacquinot Bay PNG 166 Sf48
Jacuba BR 298 Hd55
Jacuí BR 302 Hd60
Jacuipe BR 295 Ja51
Jacuizinho BR (RS) 302 Hd60
Jacundá BR (RO) 292 Gj50
Jacundá BR 287 He47
Jacup AUS (WA) 150 Qk62
Jacupiranga BR (SP) 298 Hf58
Jacurici BR 295 Ja51
Jada WAN 195 Lg41
Jadar SCG 46 Lu46
Jadcherla IND (APH) 112 Ok37
Jadebusen D 34 Lj37
Jadewari PK 84 Od33
Jadib YE 73 Ng37
Jädraås S 15 Lr30
Jadraque E 31 Ks50
Jadu LAR 182 Lg30
Jaén E 31 Kr47
Jaén PE 284 Ga48
Jafarabad IND (MHT) 112 Oh35
Jafarah LAR 182 Lf29
Jaffna CL 115 Pa42
Jägala EST 18 Mf31
Jagalur IND (KTK) 115 Oj39
Jagannath Temple IND 113 Pc36
Jagare BIH 43 Ls46
Jagbahun WAL 200 Kd41
Jagdalpur IND (CGH) 113 Pb36
Jagdaqi VRC (NMZ) 102 Rc20
Jagdish Temple IND 112 Og33
Jagdispur IND (UPH) 111 Pa32
Jagersfontein SA 225 Mc60
Jaggang VRC (TIB) 92 Ok29
Jaggayyapeta IND (APH) 113 Pa37
Jaght Drift SA 224 Ma60
Jaghuri AFG 82 Od29
Jagishiri-to J 103 Sa23
Jaglot 83 Oh28
Jagna RP 127 Rc41
Jagodina SCG 48 Mb47
Jagodnoe RUS 63 Sb06
Jagraon IND (PJB) 110 Oh30
Jagst D 36 Lk41
Jagtial IND (APH) 113 Ok36
Jaguapire, T.I. BR 298 Hc57
Jaguapitã BR (PR) 298 He57
Jaguaquara BR (BA) 295 Ja52
Jaguarão BR (RS) 302 Hd62
Jaguarão BR 301 Hd62
Jaguaré BR (ES) 299 Hk55
Jaguareri BR (BA) 295 Hk51
Jaguaretama BR (CE) 289 Ja48
Jaguari BR (RS) 302 Hc60
Jaguariaiva BR (PR) 298 Hf58
Jaguaribe BR (CE) 289 Ja48
Jaguaribe BR 289 Ja48
Jaguari, T.I. BR 298 Hc57
Jaguaruana BR (CE) 289 Jb48
Jaguaruna BR (SC) 303 Hf60
Jaguatirica BR (PR) 298 Hf58
Jagüé RA 300 Gf60
Jaguey Grande C 268 Fk34
Jahangira PK 83 Og29
Jahangirabad IND (UPH) 111 Ok31
Jahangirganj IND (UPH) 111 Pb32
Jahazpur IND (RJT) 110 Oh33
Jahotyn UA 56 Mf20
Jahrah KWT 78 Nd31
Jahrom IR 78 Ng31
Jaíba BR (MG) 294 Hj53
Jaicós BR (PI) 289 Hk49
Jaigarh Fort IND 110 Oh32
Jailolo RI 134 Rd45
Jailolo = Halmahera RI 134 Re45
Jaina MEX (CAM) 265 Fe35
Jainpur IND (UPH) 111 Pb32
Jainti IND (WBG) 116 Pe32
Jaintiapur BD 116 Pg33
Jainu BR (AM) 285 Gf49
Jaipur IND (RJT) 110 Oh32
Jaipur IND (ASM) 117 Ph32
Jaipurhat BD 116 Pe33
Jais IND (UPH) 111 Pa32
Jais Aben Resort PNG 165 Sc48
Jaisalmer IND (RJT) 110 Of32
Jaisalmer Fort IND 110 Of32
Jaisamand Lake IND 112 Og33
Jaisamand Sanctuary IND 112 Oh33
Jaisinghnagar IND (MPH) 113 Pa34
Jaiyahun WAL 200 Kd42
Jajarkot NEP 92 Pb31
Jajarm IR 77 Nj27
Jajce BIH 43 Ls46
Jakabszállás H 41 Lu44
Jakalj SCG 48 Lu46
Jakar BHT 116 Pf32
Jakarta RI 132 Qd49
Jakes Point AUS 150 Qh59
Jakharrah LAR 183 Ma31
Jakiri CAM 203 Lf42
Jakkalsberge NAM 224 Lj60
Jäkkvik S 12 Lj12
Jakobabad PK 84 Oe31
Jakobshavn = Ilulissat DK 235 Hc05
Jakobstad FIN 13 Mb14
Jakolevo RUS 55 Mj20
Jakoruda BG 48 Md48
Jakpa WAN 202 Lc43
Jakunvara RUS (KAR) 13 Mf14
Jakutsk RUS 63 Rb06
Jal USA (NM) 247 Ej29
Jalaid Qi VRC (NMZ) 102 Rb22
Jalai Nur VRC (NMZ) 95 Qj21
Jalalabad AFG 83 Of28
Jalalabad IND (UPH) 111 Ok32
Jalal-Abad KS 81 Og25
Jalalpur IND (UPH) 111 Pb32
Jalalpur PK 83 Og29
Jalama USA (CA) 246 Dk28
Jalance E 31 Kt49
Jalandhar IND (PJB) 110 Oh30
Jalang RI 133 Ra48
Jalangi IND (WBG) 116 Pe33
Jalapa = Xalapa MEX (VC) 264 Fb36
Jalapa MEX (TB) 265 Fd37
Jalapa GCA 265 Ff38
Jalasjärvi FIN 18 Mc28
Jalaun IND (UPH) 111 Ok32
Jalawla IRQ 69 Nc28
Jaldag AFG 82 Od30
Jaldiyan IR 76 Nc27
Jales BR (SP) 298 He56
Jalesar IND (UPH) 111 Ok32
Jaleshwar IND (ORS) 116 Pd35
Jalez AFG 82 Oe28
Jalgaon IND (MHT) 112 Oh35
Jalgaon IND (MHT) 112 Oh36
Jalgaon IND (MHT) 112 Oj35
Jali MW 219 Mh53
Jalibah IRQ 69 Nd30
Jalingo WAN 195 Lf41
Jalisco MEX 263 Eh36
Jallo Park PK 83 Oh30
Jalna IND (MHT) 112 Oh36
Jalnagar IND (CGH) 113 Pb34
Jalor IND (RJT) 110 Og33
Jalostotitlán MEX (JLC) 264 Ej35
Jalpa MEX (ZCT) 264 Ej35
Jalpa MEX (COH) 263 Ek33
Jalpaiguri IND (WBG) 116 Pe32
Jalpan de Serra MEX (HDG) 264 Fa35
Jalta UA 57 Mh23
Jalu LAR 183 Ma31
Jaluit Atoll MH 163 Tb17
Jalu Oasis LAR 183 Ma31
Jama EC 284 Fk46
Jamaame SP 213 Nb45
Jamaame SP 213 Nb45
Jamaica C 269 Gc35
Jamaica JA 269 Ga37
Jamaica Channel JA 269 Gc37
Jamal AFG 82 Oe28
Jamalpur BD 116 Pe33
Jamalwal PK 82 Oe30
Jama Masjid IND 113 Ok33
Jamanxim BR 287 Hb48
Jamari BR 292 Gj50
Jamari BR (RO) 292 Gj50
Jamari WAN 195 Lf40
Jamarovka RUS 95 Qf20
Jamb IND (MHT) 113 Ok35
Jamba ANG 216 Lj53
Jamba ANG 211 Lk50
Jambahal IND (ORS) 113 Pc34
Jambi RI 129 Qb46
Jambo GH 201 La41
Jamboeye RI 120 Pj43
Jambol BG 49 Mg48
Jambongan MAL 126 Qj42
Jambongan MAL 126 Qj42
Jambusar IND (GUJ) 112 Og34
Jamda IND (JKD) 113 Pc34
Jame Mosque IR 76 Ne29
Jame Mosque IR 76 Nf28
Jame Mosque IR 76 Ng28
Jame Mosque IR 76 Nh27
Jameos del Agua E 186 Kd31
Jamesabad PK 85 Oe33
James Bay CDN 235 Fd08
James Cook Museum AUS 153 Sc53
James Corner = Nyororo EAT 215 Mh50
James Craik RA (CD) 300 Gj62
James Island WAG 191 Kb39
James Range AUS 148 Rg58
Jamestown AUS (SA) 158 Rk62
Jamestown SA 225 Md61
Jamestown USA (ND) 250 Fa22
Jamestown USA (NY) 257 Ga24
Jamestown USA (TN) 259 Fh27
Jamestown USA (SC) 259 Ga29
Jämijärvi FIN 18 Mc29
Jaminawá Arara do Rio Bage, T.I. BR 291 Gd50
Jaminawá do Igarapé Preto, T.I. BR 290 Gd49
Jamindan RP 127 Rb40
Jäminkipohja FIN 18 Me29
Jämjö S 17 Lq34
Jam Jodhpur IND (GUJ) 112 Of35
Jamkhandi IND (KTK) 112 Oh37
Jamkhed IND (MHT) 112 Oh36
Jammalamadugu IND (APH) 115 Ok39
Jammerbugten DK 16 Lk33
Jammersdrif SA 225 Md60
Jam, Minaret of AFG 82 Oc28
Jammu 83 Oh29
Jammu and Kashmir IND 108 Od12
Jamnagar IND (GUJ) 112 Of34
Jamnagar Fort IND (GUJ) 112 Of34
Jamnice CZ 40 Lq41
Jampur PK 85 Of31
Jämsä FIN 18 Mf29
Jämsänkoski FIN 18 Mf29
Jamshedpur IND (JKD) 116 Pd34
Jamtara IND (JKD) 116 Pd34
Jamtari WAN 203 Lf42
Jämtland S 12 Lh14
Jamu ETH 205 Mh42
Jamui IND (BIH) 116 Pd33
Jamuna Bridge BD 116 Pe33
Jamundi CO 284 Gb44
Jamunkira IND (ORS) 113 Pc35
Jana KSA 71 Ne32
Jana RUS 63 Rd05
Janakpur NEP 92 Pc32
Janan IND (GUJ) 112 Of34
Janannah UAE 78 Ng33
Janauba BR (MG) 294 Hj53
Jand PK 83 Og29
Jandaq IR 76 Nh28
Jandiatuba BR 285 Gf48
Jandola PK 83 Of29
Jandowae AUS (QLD) 157 Sf59
Janesville USA (WI) 256 Ff24
Jang GH 201 Kj41
Jang IND (ARP) 116 Pf32
Janga GH 201 Kk40
Jangada BR (MT) 293 Hb53
Jangamo MOC 222 Mh58
Jangaon IND (APH) 113 Ok37
Jangipur IND (WBG) 116 Pe33
Jangjay AFG 82 Od29
Jangkar RI 133 Qh49
Jangra IND (ORS) 113 Pc35
Janja BIH 46 Lu46
Janjina HR 43 Ls48
Janjira IND 112 Og36
Jan Kempdorp SA 225 Mc59
Jan Lake CDN (SK) 248 Ej18
Jan Lake CDN 248 Ej18
Jan Mayen N 8 Kb02
Jan Mayen N 8 Kb02
Jan Mayen N 10 Kc04
Jano-Indigirskaja nizmennost' RUS 63 Rd04
Jano-Indigirskaja nizmennost' RUS 63 Sa04
Janos MEX (CHH) 247 Ef30
Jánoshalma H 41 Lu44
Jánosháza H 40 Ls43
Jánossomorja H 40 Ls43
Janów PL 39 Lu40
Janów PL 39 Md37
Janów Lubelski PL 39 Mc40
Janowo PL 39 Ma37
Janów Podlaski PL 39 Md38
Jansenville SA 225 Mc62
Janskij zaliv RUS 63 Rd04
Janskoe ploskogor'e RUS 63 Rc05
Jantan RI 135 Rh47
Jantarnyj RUS 39 Lu36
Jantia Hills IND 116 Pg33
Jantingue MOC 222 Mg58
Jantra BG 49 Mf47
Januária BR (MG) 294 Hh53
Janville F 25 Lb42
Janzé F 24 Kt43
Japan J 61 Sa06
Japan Basin 87 Rc10
Japanese World War II Bunker RI 134 Rg48
Japanese World War II Headquarter RI 134 Rd45
Japan Trench J 87 Sa11
Japaratinga BR (AL) 295 Jc50
Japaratuba BR (SE) 295 Jb51
Japca MD 47 Mj43
Japerica BR (PA) 288 Hg46
Japeri BR 289 Jc49
Japonvar BR (MG) 299 Hh54
Jäppilä FIN 18 Mh28
Japuíba, T.I. BR 292 Ha51
Japur IR 79 Nj30
Japura BR 285 Gf46
Japurá BR (AM) 285 Gg46
Japurá BR 286 Gh47
Japura RI 128 Qb46
Japvo IND 116 Ph33
Jaqué PA 267 Ga42
Jaquiri, T.I. BR 286 Gh47
Jarabacoa DOM 270 Ge36
Jarablos SYR 68 Mj27
Jaraguá BR (GO) 294 Hf53
Jaraguá do Sul BR (SC) 303 Hf59
Jaragua, P.N. DOM 270 Ge37
Jarahueca C 269 Ga34
Jaraicejo E 30 Kp49
Jaraíz de la Vera E 30 Kp50
Jaral de Berrios MEX (GJT) 264 Ek35
Jaramillo RA (SC) 306 Gg69
Ja'ranah KSA 70 Mk35
Jarandilla de la Vera E 30 Kp50
Jaraniyo ETH 206 Mk40
Jaransk RUS 55 Nd17
Jaranwala PK 83 Og30
Jarara, T.I. BR 298 Hc57
Jarauçu BR 287 Hd47
Jarawara Jamamadi Kanamati, T.I. BR 286 Gh49
Järbo S 15 Lr30
Jarbridge USA (NV) 244 Ec25
Jarcevo RUS 54 Mg18
Jardim BR (MS) 297 Hb56
Jardim BR (CE) 289 Ja49
Jardim Alegre BR (PR) 298 He58
Jardim do Serido BR (RN) 289 Jb49
Jardinah LAR 183 Ma30
Jardín América RA (MI) 301 Hc59
Jardine River AUS 152 Sb51
Jardine River N.P. AUS 152 Sb51
Jard-sur-Mer F 24 Kt44
Jaredi WAN 194 Lc39
Jaremča UA 41 Me42
Jaremča UA 41 Me42
Jargalant MNG 89 Pf22
Jargalant MNG 94 Pj23
Jargalant MNG 94 Qa22
Jargalant MNG 94 Qc20
Jargalant MNG 94 Qc21
Jargalant MNG 94 Qd21
Jargalant Uul MNG 94 Pj23
Jargaltkhaan MNG 95 Qe22
Jargeau F 25 Lc43
Jarha IND (MPH) 113 Pa34
Jari BR 287 Hd46
Järlåsa S 15 Ls31
Jarlshof GB 21 Kt31
Jarmen D 35 Lo37
Jarmolynci UA 56 Md21
Järna S 15 Lp30
Järna S 15 Ls31
Jarnac F 26 Ku45
Jarny F 25 Lf41
Jarn Yaphour UAE 78 Nh33
Jaro RP 127 Rc40
Jarocin PL 38 Ls39
Jaroměř CZ 40 Lq40
Jaroměřice CZ 40 Lq41
Jaroměřice nad Rokytnou CZ 40 Lq41
Jaroslavl' RUS 54 Mk17
Jarosław PL 39 Mc40
Jarosławiec PL 38 Lr36
Järpen S 12 Lg14
Jarqo'rg'on UZB 80 Od27
Jarrahdale AUS (WA) 150 Qj62
Jarrar KSA 70 Nb33
Järsnäs S 17 Lp33
Jarso ETH 205 Mh41
Jartai VRC (NMZ) 96 Qc26
Jartai Yanchi VRC 96 Qc26
Jaru BR (RO) 292 Gj51
Jaru BR 292 Gj51
Jarub YE 73 Ng37
Jarud Qi VRC (NMZ) 95 Ra23
Järva-Jaani EST 18 Mf31
Järvakandi EST 18 Me32
Järvelä FIN 18 Mf30
Järvenpää FIN 18 Mf30
Järvsö S 15 Lr29
Jaryšiv UA 47 Mh42
Jasaan RP 127 Rc41
Jasanova AL 48 Lu48
Jasa Tornič SCG 46 Ma45
Jasel'da BY 39 Mf38
Jasenice HR 43 Lq46
Jasenskaja RUS 57 Mk22
Jashpurnagar IND (CGH) 113 Pc34
Jasienica PL 38 Lp39
Jasiira Guiba SP 213 Nb46
Jasiira Jula SP 213 Nb45
Jasiira Koiama SP 213 Nb46
Jasikan GH 201 La42
Jasil'kul' TJ 81 Og27
Jasinja UA 41 Me42
Jašiūnai LT 19 Mf36
Jask IR 79 Nj33
Jaškul' RUS (KAL) 57 Nc22
Jasło PL 41 Mb41
Jasmund, N.P. D 35 Lo36
Jasná SK 41 Lu42
Jasnaja RUS 95 Qh20
Jasna Poljana BG 49 Mh48
Jasnoe RUS 19 Mb36
Jasnogorsk RUS 54 Mj18
Jasnomorskij RUS 103 Sa24
Jasov SK 41 Ma42
Jasper CDN (AB) 243 Ea19
Jasper USA (AR) 253 Fd27
Jasper USA (TX) 253 Fd30
Jasper USA (IN) 258 Fg26
Jasper USA (AL) 258 Fg29
Jasper USA (FL) 259 Fj30
Jasper USA (NY) 257 Gb24
Jasper USA (GA) 259 Fh28
Jasper Lake CDN 242 Ea19
Jasper N.P. CDN 243 Eb19
Jasper USA (TN) 258 Fh28
Jasper Tramway CDN 243 Eb19
Jasrana IND (UPH) 111 Ok32
Jassan IRQ 69 Nc29
Jassan IRQ 69 Nc28
Jastarnia PL 38 Lt36
Jastrebarsko HR 43 Lq45
Jastrowie PL 38 Lr37
Jastrząbka PL 39 Mb37
Jastrzębia Gora PL 38 Lt36
Jastrzębie Zdrój PL 40 Lt41
Jasubibeteri YV 282 Gh44
Jasynuvata UA 57 Mj21
Jászalsószentgyörgy H 41 Ma43
Jászapáti H 41 Ma43
Jászárokszállás H 41 Lu43
Jászberény H 41 Lu43
Jatai BR (GO) 298 He54
Jatapu BR 286 Ha47
Jatapuzinho BR 286 Ha45
Jath IND (MHT) 112 Oh37
Jati PK 84 Oe33
Jatibarang RI 132 Qe49
Jatibonico C 269 Ga35
Jatijajar Cave RI 132 Qe49
Jatiraga RI 132 Qf49
Jatiwangi RI 132 Qe49
Jatni IND (ORS) 113 Pc35
Jatobá BR (MT) 293 Hc52
Jatobá BR (GO) 294 Hf54
Jatobá BR (PA) 287 Hd48
Jatobá BR (MA) 288 Hj48
Jatobá do Piauí BR (PI) 289 Hk48
Jatoi PK 85 Of31
Jättendal S 15 Ls29
Jatuarana BR (AM) 286 Ha47
Jatuarana, T.I. BR 286 Gk47
Jaú BR 286 Gj47
Jaú BR (SP) 298 Hf57
Jauaperi BR 286 Gk46
Jauaruá BR (AM) 286 Gh47
Jáua-Sarisariñama, P.N. YV 281 Gh43
Jauco C 269 Gc35
Jauja PE 290 Gc51
Jaumave MEX (TM) 263 Fa34
Jaungulbene LV 19 Mg33
Jaunkalsnava LV 19 Mf34
Jaunpiebalga LV 19 Mg33
Jaunpils LV 19 Md34
Jaunpur IND (UPH) 113 Pb33
Jaupaci BR (GO) 298 He54
Jauquara BR 293 Hb53
Jaurin RUS 102 Rf21
Jauru BR (MT) 292 Ha53
Jauru BR 292 Ha54
Jauru BR (MS) 298 Hc55
Jauru BR 298 Hd55
Java RI 132 Qf50
Java SME 283 Hc43
Javalambre E 31 Kt50
Javand AFG 82 Oc28
Javanrub IR 76 Nd28
Javari BR (AM) 285 Ge48
Javari BR 287 Hd46
Java Ridge RI 132 Qe50
Javartkhoshuu MNG 95 Qg21
Java Sea RI 132 Qg48
Java Trench 122 Qa20
Jávea = Xàbia E 31 La48
Javi BR (BA) 294 Hj52
Javkhlant MNG 95 Qf21
Javkhlant MNG 95 Qg22
Javoriv UA 41 Md41
Javorivskyj N.P. UA 41 Md41
Javornik CZ 40 Ls40
Jaw BRN 78 Nf33
Jawai IND 110 Og33
Jawai Bandh IND 110 Og33
Jawan Tomb KSA 71 Ne32
Jawatha Mosque KSA 71 Ne33
Jawhar IND (MHT) 112 Og36
Jawi RI 130 Qe46
Jawor PL 38 Lr39
Jawor Solecki PL 39 Mb39
Jaworzno PL 39 Lu40
Jawoyn A.L. AUS 145 Rg53
Jay USA (OK) 253 Fc27
Jayakwadi IND 112 Oh36
Jayanca PE 290 Ga49
Jayapatna IND (ORS) 113 Pb36
Jayapura RI 135 Sa47
Jaynagar IND (BIH) 116 Pd32
Jayton USA (TX) 252 Ek29
Jaza'ir al Zubayr YE 72 Nb38
Jaza'ir Farasan KSA 72 Na37
Jazarit Djebel Zuqar YE 72 Nb38
Jazirah KSA 72 Nb36
Jazirat Al Batinah KSA 71 Ne32
Jazirat Antufash YE 72 Nb38
Jazirat at Tarfah YE 72 Nb38
Jazireh-ye Abu Musa IR 78 Nh33
Jazireh-ye Forur IR 78 Nh32
Jazireh-ye Hendorabi IR 78 Ng32
Jazireh-ye Hengam IR 79 Nj32
Jazireh-ye Hormoz IR 79 Nj32
Jazireh-ye Jabrin IR 78 Nf32
Jazireh-ye Khark IR 78 Nf31
Jazireh-ye Kish IR 78 Ng32
Jazireh-ye Larak IR 79 Nj32
Jazireh-ye Lavan IR 78 Ng32
Jazireh-ye Qeshm IR 79 Nj32
Jazireh-ye Sirri IR 78 Nh33
Jazireh-ye Tonb-e Bozorg IR 78 Nh32
Jazminal MEX (COH) 263 Ek33
Jazovir Iskăr BG 48 Md48
Jazovir Mandra BG 49 Mh48
Jazovir Tiča BG 49 Mg47
Jazovir Žrebčevo BG 49 Mf48
Jdiriya DARS 186 Ke32
Jeanerette USA (LA) 253 Fe31
Jean Rabel RH 270 Gd36
Jebba WAN 194 Lc41
Jebel RO 46 Mb45
Jebri PK 84 Oc32
Jedburgh GB 21 Ks35
Jedda RI 129 Qc46
Jeddah KSA 70 Mk35
Jedlińsk PL 39 Mb39
Jednorożec PL 39 Mb37
Jedrzejów PL 39 Ma40
Jedwabne PL 39 Mc37
Jedwabno PL 39 Ma37
Jeedamya AUS (WA) 150 Ra60
Jefawa SUD 204 Mb40
Jefferson USA (TX) 253 Fc29
Jefferson USA (WI) 256 Ff24
Jefferson USA (NC) 259 Fk27
Jefferson City USA (MO) 251 Fd26
Jefferson Davis Mon. USA 258 Fg27
Jefferson, Mount USA 244 Dk23
Jefferson, Mount USA 244 Eb26
Jeffersontown USA (KY) 258 Fh26
Jeffersonville USA (IN) 256 Fh26
Jeffersonville USA (GA) 259 Fj29
Jeffrey City USA (WY) 245 Eg24
Jeffreys Bay SA 225 Mc63
Jef-Jef el Kébir TCH 197 Ma35
Jega WAN 194 Lc39
Jege WAN 202 Lc41
Jehanabad IND (BIH) 113 Pc33
Jeinemeni, Cerro RCH 306 Gd69
Jejevo SOL 167 Sk50
Jejuí-Guazú PY 297 Hb58
Jēkabpils LV 19 Mf34
Jelai RI 130 Qf47
Jelanec' UA 56 Mf22
Jelbart Ice Shelf 312 Kd33
Jelcz-Laskowice PL 38 Ls39
Jelekangphu Gang IND 116 Pe31
Jelenia Góra PL 38 Lq40
Jelenino PL 38 Lr37
Jelgava LV 19 Md34
Jeli MAL 121 Qa43
Jellicoe CDN (ON) 249 Fg21
Jelling DK 16 Lk35
Jelmusibak RI 130 Qh46
Jelovac SCG 48 Mb46
Jeløy N 14 Ll31
Jelsa N 14 Lg31
Jelutung RI 129 Qd47
Jema GH 201 Kk42
Jemaa Ida Oussemlal MA 180 Kf31
Jemâa-Sahi MA 180 Kf29
Jemaja RI 121 Qc44
Jemaluang MAL 121 Qb44
Jember RI 132 Qg50
Jemberem GNB 191 Kc40
Jemez Ind. Res. USA 247 Eg28
Jemez Pueblo USA (NM) 247 Eg28
Jemielno PL 38 Lr39
Jeminay VRC (XUZ) 89 Pc22
Jemma WAN 194 Le40
Jemma WAN 194 Le41
Jempara RI 130 Qh47
Jen WAN 195 Lf41
Jena D 35 Lm40
Jena USA (LA) 253 Fd30
Jenakijeve UA 57 Mk21
Jenbach A 37 Lm43
Jenda MW 218 Mg52
Jendarata MAL 120 Qa44
Jendouba TN 182 Le27
Jenerhodar UA 56 Mh22
Jeneshuaya BOL 291 Gg52
Jengish Chokusu KS 81 Pa24
Jenin IL 68 Mh29
Jenipapo BR (AM) 286 Gk48
Jenipapo BR (TO) 288 Hf49
Jenipapo BR 288 Hf48
Jenluise Bank 313 Qb31
Jenner CDN (AB) 243 Ee20
Jenner USA (CA) 244 Dj26
Jennersdorf A 37 Lr44
Jennings USA (LA) 253 Fd30
Jennings River CDN 241 De16
Jenny SME 283 Hc43
Jenpeg CDN (MB) 248 Fa18
Jepara RI 132 Qf49
Jeppener RA (BA) 301 Ha63
Jequeri BR (MG) 299 Hj56
Jequetepeque PE 290 Ga49
Jequiá BR (AL) 295 Jb51
Jequié BR (BA) 295 Hk52
Jequitaí BR (MG) 299 Hh54
Jequitaí BR 299 Hh54
Jequitibá BR (MG) 299 Hj55
Jequitinhonha BR (MG) 299 Hk54
Jequitinhonha BR 295 Ja53
Jerada MA 181 Kj28
Jeramungup AUS (WA) 150 Qk62
Jerangle AUS (NSW) 159 Se63
Jerantut MAL 121 Qb44
Jerash JOR 68 Mh29
Jerbar SUD 209 Mf43
Jerdera RI 135 Rh49
Jerécuaro MEX (GJT) 264 Ek35
Jereh IR 78 Nf31
Jérémie RH 270 Gc36
Jeremoabo BR (BA) 295 Ja51
Jerer ETH 207 Nb41
Jereweh RI 133 Qj50
Jerez MEX (ZCT) 263 Ej34
Jerez de la Frontera E 30 Ko46
Jerez de los Caballeros E 30 Ko48
Jergucat AL 48 Ma51
Jericho AUS (QLD) 155 Sd57
Jericho IS 68 Mh30
Jerichow D 35 Ln38
Jericoacoara, P.N. de BR 289 Hk47
Jerigu GH 201 Kk41
Jerilderie AUS (NSW) 159 Sc63
Jerka PL 38 Lr39
Jerkoh MAL 121 Qa43
Jerko La VRC 92 Pa30
Jerome USA (ID) 245 Ec24
Jerori BOL 292 Gh53
Jersey GB 24 Ks41
Jersey City USA (NJ) 257 Gc25
Jerseyville USA (IL) 251 Fe26
Jersey Zoo GB 24 Ks41
Jeršov RUS 55 Ne20
Jertih MAL 121 Qb43
Jerudong Park BRU 126 Qh43
Jerumal BR (BA) 295 Hk50
Jerumenha BR (PI) 288 Hj49
Jerusalem IS 68 Mh30
Jeruzalem SLO 43 Lr44
Jervis Bay AUS (NSW) 159 Sf63
Jervis Inlet CDN 242 Dj20
Jervois Range AUS 149 Rh57
Jerzens A 37 Ll43
Jerzu I 33 Lk51
Jesenice CZ 40 Lp41
Jesenice SLO 43 Lp44
Jeseník CZ 40 Ls40
Jesi I 43 Lo47
Jesmond CDN (BC) 242 Dj20
Jésolo I 43 Ln45
Jessen D 35 Ln39
Jesse Owens Mem. Park USA 258 Fg28
Jesser Point SA 225 Mg59
Jessheim N 14 Lm30
Jessore BD 116 Pe34
Jesuitas BR (PR) 298 Hd58
Jesuit Missions of the Chiquitania BOL 292 Gk54
Jesup USA (GA) 259 Fk30
Jesús PE 290 Gb51
Jesús PY 301 Hc59
Jesús Carranza MEX (VC) 265 Fc37
Jesús del Tavarangué PY 301 Hc59
Jesús de Machaca BOL 296 Gf54
Jesús María MEX (NYT) 263 Eh34
Jesús María MEX (AGS) 264 Ej35
Jesús María RA (CD) 300 Gh61
Jesús Menéndez C 269 Gb35
Jetavana Dagoba CL 115 Pa42
Jeti-Ögüz KS 81 Ok24
Jetmore USA (KS) 252 Fa26
Jetpur IND (GUJ) 112 Of35
Jeumont F 25 Le40
Jeuram RI 120 Pj43
Jevargi IND (KTK) 112 Oj37
Jever D 34 Lh37
Jevnaker N 14 Ll30
Jevpatorija UA 56 Mg23
Jewar IND (UPH) 111 Oj31
Jewels Cave Nat. Mon. USA 250 Ej24
Jewish Autonomous Region RUS 63 Rc09
Jew Town IND 114 Oj42
Jeypur IND (ORS) 113 Pb36
Jeziorany PL 39 Ma37
Jezioro Bukowo PL 38 Lr36
Jezioro Jamno PL 38 Lr36
Jezioro Jeziorak PL 39 Lu37
Jezioro Jeziorsko PL 38 Lt39
Jezioro Kopan PL 38 Lr36
Jezioro Łebsko PL 38 Ls36
Jezioro Mamry PL 39 Mb36
Jezioro Śniardwy PL 39 Mb37
Jezioro Wicko PL 38 Lr36
Jezioro Zegrzyńskie PL 39 Mb38
Jeżów PL 39 Lu39
Jeżowe PL 39 Mc40
Jezzine RL 68 Mh29
Jhabua IND (MPH) 112 Oh34
Jhajha IND (BIH) 116 Pd33
Jhajjar IND (HYA) 111 Oj31
Jhal PK 84 Od31
Jhalakati BD 116 Pf34
Jhalawar IND (RJT) 112 Oj33
Jhalida IND (WBG) 116 Pd34
Jhalod IND (GUJ) 112 Oh34
Jhang PK 83 Og30
Jhanjharpur IND (BIH) 116 Pd32
Jhansi IND (UPH) 111 Ok33
Jhansi Fort IND 113 Ok33
Jhanzi IND (ASM) 116 Ph32
Jhargram IND (WBG) 116 Pd34
Jharkhand IND 108 Pa14
Jharol IND (RJT) 112 Og33
Jharsuguda IND (ORS) 113 Pc35
Jhatpat PK 84 Oe31
Jhelum PK 83 Og29
Jhelum PK 83 Og30
Jhenaidah BD 116 Pe34
Jhenida BD 116 Pe34
Jhimpir PK 84 Od33
Jhudo PK 85 Oe33
Jhunjhunun IND (RJT) 110 Oh31
Jiachuan VRC (SCH) 99 Qd29
Jiading VRC (SHG) 106 Ra30
Jiahe VRC (HUN) 100 Qg33
Jiajiang VRC (SCH) 98 Qb31
Jialing Jiang VRC 99 Qc30
Jiamusi VRC (HLG) 102 Rf22
Jian IR 78 Ng30
Ji'an VRC (JXI) 106 Qh32
Ji'an VRC (JLN) 104 Rd25
Jianchang VRC (LNG) 97 Qk25
Jianchaxi VRC (GZH) 99 Qe31
Jianchi VRC (HUB) 99 Qe30
Jianchuan VRC (YUN) 117 Pk32
Jiande VRC (ZJG) 106 Qk31
Jiang VRC 106 Qj31
Jiang'an VRC (SCH) 98 Qc31
Jiangbei VRC (CGQ) 99 Qd31
Jiangcheng VRC (YUN) 117 Qa34
Jiangchuan VRC (YUN) 117 Qb33
Jiangdi VRC (YUN) 117 Qb32
Jiangdu VRC (JGS) 106 Qk29
Jiange VRC (SCH) 99 Qc29
Jiangjin VRC (CGQ) 99 Qd31
Jianghong VRC (GZG) 100 Qe35
Jianghua VRC (HUN) 100 Qf33
Jiangjunmiao VRC (XUZ) 89 Pf23
Jiangkou VRC (CGQ) 99 Qe30
Jiangkou VRC (GZH) 100 Qe32
Jiangling VRC (HUB) 99 Qg30
Jiangluo VRC (GSU) 99 Qc29
Jiangmen VRC (GDG) 101 Qg34
Jiangshan VRC (ZJG) 106 Qk31
Jiangshan VRC (ZJG) 106 Ra31
Jiangsu VRC 87 Qd12
Jiangxi VRC 87 Qd13
Jiangyin VRC (JGS) 106 Ra30
Jiangyong VRC (HUN) 100 Qf33
Jiangyou VRC (SCH) 98 Qc30
Jianhe VRC (GZH) 100 Qe32
Jianhu VRC (JGS) 106 Qk29
Jianle VRC (FJN) 106 Qj32
Jianli VRC (HUB) 99 Qg31
Jianmen Path VRC 99 Qc29
Jianning VRC (FJN) 106 Qj32
Jian'ou VRC (FJN) 106 Qk32
Jianping VRC (LNG) 97 Qk25
Jianshui VRC (YUN) 117 Qb34
Jian Xi VRC 106 Qk32
Jianyang VRC (SCH) 98 Qc30
Jianyang VRC (FJN) 106 Qk32
Jiaode VRC (YUN) 100 Qa31
Jiaohe VRC (JLN) 104 Rd24
Jiaohe Gucheng VRC 91 Pe24
Jiaojiang VRC (ZJG) 106 Ra31
Jiaokou VRC (SAX) 97 Qf27
Jiaoling VRC (GDG) 101 Qj33
Jiaonan VRC (SDG) 97 Qk28
Jiaotelo VRC (TIB) 92 Pd31
Jiaozhou VRC (SDG) 104 Ra27
Jiaozuo VRC (HNN) 99 Qg28
Jiasa VRC (YUN) 117 Qa33
Jiashan VRC (ANH) 106 Qj29
Jiashan VRC (ZJG) 106 Ra30
Jiashi VRC (XUZ) 90 Oj26
Jia Xian VRC (SAA) 97 Qf26
Jia Xian VRC (HNN) 99 Qg29
Jiaxing VRC (ZJG) 106 Ra30
Jiayin VRC (HLG) 102 Rf21
Jiayu VRC (HUB) 99 Qg31
Jiayu G. VRC 96 Pk26
Jiayuguan VRC (GSU) 96 Pk26
Jibert RO 47 Mf45
Jibia WAN 195 Ld39
Jibjaat OM 73 Nh37
Jibla YE 72 Nc39
Jibóia BR (AM) 285 Gf45
Jibou RO 46 Md43
Jicarilla Apache Ind. Res. USA 247 Eg27
Jícaro Galán HN 266 Fg39
Jichang VRC (GZH) 100 Qc32
Jichang VRC (GZH) 100 Qd33
Jičín CZ 40 Lq40
Jidau SP 207 Nd40
Jiddah KSA 70 Mk35
Jiddat al-Harasis OM 73 Nh36
Jiele Golden Pagoda VRC 117 Pj33
Jielong VRC (CGQ) 99 Qd31
Jieshi VRC (GDG) 101 Qh34
Jieshi Wan VRC 101 Qh34
Jieshou VRC (ANH) 106 Qh29
Jiexi VRC (GDG) 101 Qh34
Jiexiu VRC (SAX) 97 Qf27
Jieyang VRC (GDG) 101 Qj34
Jieznas LT 19 Me36
Jiggalong AUS (WA) 146 Ra57
Jiggalong Aboriginal Reserve AUS 146 Ra57
Jiggs USA (NV) 244 Ec25
Jigme Dorji N.P. BHT 116 Pe32
Jigongshan VRC 106 Qh30
Jiguaní C 269 Gb35
Jihanah YE 72 Nc38
Jihlava CZ 40 Lq41
Jihua Dao VRC 104 Ra25
Jiigley SP 207 Nc43
Jijel DZ 182 Lc27
Jijie VRC (YUN) 117 Qb34
Jijiga ETH 207 Nb41
Jijona = Xixona E 31 Ku48
Jiju VRC (SCH) 98 Qa31
Jilamo HN 266 Fg38
Jilan IR 77 Nh27
Jilava RO 47 Mg46
Jilavele RO 47 Mg46
Jilbadji Nature Reserve AUS (WA) 150 Qk61
Jilia RO 47 Mg43
Jilib SP 213 Nb45
Jili Hu VRC 89 Pd22
Jilin VRC 87 Rb10
Jilin VRC (JLN) 104 Rd24
Jilin Hada Ling VRC 104 Rc24
Jima ETH 206 Mj42
Jim Abad IR 77 Nk27
Jimani DOM 270 Ge36
Jimata ETH 206 Mj41
Jimbe ANG 217 Mb51
Jimbolia RO 46 Ma45
Jimda VRC (TIB) 93 Pg31
Jimei VRC (FJN) 101 Qk33
Jimena de la Frontera E 30 Kp46
Jiménez MEX (CHH) 263 Eh32
Jiménez MEX (COH) 252 Ek31
Jimenez RP 127 Rb41
Jiménez del Téul MEX (ZCT) 263 Ej34
Jimenoa Waterfall DOM 270 Ge36
Jimeta WAN 195 Lg41
Jimi River PNG 165 Sc48
Jim Jim Falls AUS 145 Rg52
Jimmy Carter N.H.S. USA 259 Fh29
Jimo VRC (SDG) 104 Ra27
Jimsar VRC (XUZ) 89 Pe24
Jimulco MEX (COH) 263 Ej33
Jinan VRC (SDG) 97 Qj27
Jinchai VRC (GZG) 100 Qe33
Jinchang VRC (GSU) 96 Qb26
Jincheng VRC (YUN) 117 Qb33
Jincheng VRC (SAX) 99 Qg28
Jinchuan VRC (SCH) 98 Qb30
Jinci Si VRC 97 Qg27
Jind IND (HYA) 111 Oj31
Jindabyne AUS (NSW) 159 Se64
Jindare AUS (NT) 145 Rf53
Jindian VRC 117 Qb33
Jindřichov CZ 40 Ls40
Jindřichův Hradec CZ 40 Lq41
Jinfo Shan VRC 99 Qd31
Jing'an VRC (JXI) 106 Qh31
Jingbian VRC (SAA) 96 Qe27
Jingchuan VRC (GSU) 99 Qd28
Jingde VRC (AHU) 106 Qk30
Jingdezhen VRC (JGX) 106 Qj31
Jingdong VRC (YUN) 117 Qa34
Jingellic AUS (NSW) 159 Sd63
Jingemarra AUS (WA) 146 Qj59
Jinggangshan VRC (JGX) 101 Qh32
Jinggangshan VRC 101 Qh32
Jinggu Daizu VRC (YUN) 117 Qa34
Jinghe VRC (XUZ) 88 Pb23
Jing He VRC 99 Qe28
Jinghong VRC (YUN) 117 Qa34
Jingjiang VRC (JGS) 106 Ra29
Jingle VRC (SAX) 97 Qf26
Jingmen VRC (HUB) 99 Qg30
Jingning VRC (GSU) 99 Qc28
Jingpo VRC (HLG) 102 Re24
Jingpo Hu VRC 102 Re24
Jingshan VRC (HUB) 99 Qg30
Jingtai VRC (GSU) 96 Qc27
Jingtieshan VRC (GSU) 91 Pj26
Jingtie Shan VRC 91 Pj26
Jingxi VRC (GZG) 100 Qd34
Jing Xian VRC (AHU) 106 Qk30
Jingxiang VRC (SDG) 106 Qj28
Jingxing VRC (HBI) 97 Qh27
Jingxing VRC (HLG) 102 Rb22
Jingyu VRC (JLN) 104 Rd24
Jingyuan VRC (GSU) 96 Qc27
Jingyu Hu VRC 91 Pe27
Jingyu Nao VRC 99 Qe29
Jingzhou VRC (HUN) 100 Qe32
Jinhe VRC (SCH) 117 Qa32
Jinhe VRC (NMZ) 95 Ra20
Jinhua VRC (ZJG) 106 Qk31
Jinín EC 284 Fk46
Jining VRC (NMZ) 97 Qg25
Jining VRC (SDG) 106 Qj28
Jinja EAU 212 Mg45
Jinja War Cemetery EAU 212 Mg45
Jinjiang = Panzhihua VRC (SCH) 117 Qa32
Jinjiang VRC (YUN) 117 Qa32
Jinka ETH 206 Mj43
Jinkou VRC (HUB) 106 Qh30
Jinning VRC (YUN) 117 Qb33
Jinniu VRC (HUB) 106 Qh31
Jinotega NIC 266 Fh39
Jinotepe NIC 266 Fg40
Jinping VRC (YUN) 117 Qb34
Jinping VRC (GZH) 100 Qe32
Jinqian He VRC 99 Qe29
Jinsha VRC (GZH) 100 Qd32
Jinsha VRC (JGS) 106 Ra29
Jinsha Jiang VRC 86 Qa13
Jinshan VRC (SHG) 106 Ra30
Jinshanlin VRC 97 Qj25
Jinshatan VRC (SAX) 97 Qg26
Jinshi VRC (HUN) 99 Qf31
Jinshiqiao VRC (HUN) 100 Qf32
Jinta VRC (GSU) 96 Pk26
Jintan VRC (JGS) 106 Qk30
Jintololo Island RP 127 Rb40
Jintotolo Channel RP 127 Rb40
Jintur IND (MHT) 112 Oj36
Jinxi VRC (JGX) 106 Qj32
Jinxi VRC (LNG) 104 Ra25
Jin Xi VRC 106 Qj32
Jinxian VRC (JGX) 106 Qj31
Jinyang VRC (SCH) 117 Qb32
Jinyun VRC (ZJG) 106 Ra31
Jinzhou VRC (LNG) 104 Ra25
Jinzhou VRC (LNG) 104 Ra26
Ji-Paraná BR (RO) 292 Gk51
Jipijapa EC 284 Fk46
Jiquí C 269 Ga35
Jiquilillo NIC 266 Fg39
Jiquilpan de Juárez MEX (MHC) 264 Ej35
Jiquiriçá BR (BA) 295 Ja52
Jiquiriçá BR 295 Ja52
Jiqzhi VRC (QHI) 98 Qa29
Jirampal IND (CGH) 113 Pa36
Jirga Alem ETH 206 Mk42
Jiri NEP 92 Pd32
Jirkov CZ 40 Lo40
Jiroft IR 79 Nj31
Jirriban SP 207 Ne42
Jirwan KSA 71 Nf34
Jishan VRC (SAX) 99 Qf28
Jishou VRC (HUN) 99 Qe31
Jishui VRC (JXI) 106 Qh32
Jitarning AUS (WA) 150 Qj62
Jitia RO 47 Mg45
Jitian VRC (SCH) 98 Qc30
Jitra MAL 120 Qa42
Jitzamuri MEX (SL) 262 Ef32
Jiu RO 48 Md47
Jiucai Ling VRC 100 Qf33
Jiuchang VRC (GZH) 100 Qd32
Jiuhuajie VRC (AHU) 106 Qj30
Jiuhuashan VRC 106 Qj30
Jiujiang VRC (JGX) 106 Qh31
Jiuling Shan VRC 106 Qh31
Jiulong = Kowloon VRC (HKG) 101 Qh34
Jiulong Shan VRC 106 Qk31
Jiuquan VRC (GSU) 96 Pk26
Jiurongcheng VRC (SDG) 104 Rb27
Jiusuo VRC (HAN) 100 Qe36
Jiutai VRC (JLN) 102 Rc23
Jiuxu VRC (GZG) 100 Qd33
Jiuyishan VRC 100 Qg33
Jiuzhaigou VRC (GSU) 98 Qb29
Jiuzhaigou VRC 98 Qb29
Jiuzhan VRC (HLG) 102 Rc20

Lianghe ◎ VRC (CGQ) 99 Qe31
Lianghekou ◎ VRC (GSU) 98 Qc29
Liangmangari, Gunung ▲ RI 130 Qg46
Liangping ◎ VRC (CGQ) 99 Qd30
Liangpran, Gunung ▲ RI 130 Qh45
Liang Qu ≋ VRC 98 Qa31
Liangshan ◎ VRC (SDG) 97 Qj28
Liangshan ◎ VRC (SDG) 106 Qj28
Liangzi Hu ≋ VRC 106 Qh30
Lianhua ◎ VRC (JGX) 101 Qg32
Lianhua Shan ▲ VRC 101 Qh34
Lianjiang ◎ VRC (GDG) 100 Qf35
Lianjtang ◎ VRC (FJN) 106 Qk32
Lianokládi ◎ GR 50 Mc52
Lianping ◎ VRC (GDG) 101 Qh33
Lianshan ◎ VRC (GDG) 100 Qg33
Lianshui ◎ VRC (JGS) 106 Qk29
Liantang ◎ VRC (GZG) 100 Qf33
Liantang ◎ VRC (JGX) 106 Qj31
Lian Xian ◎ VRC (GDG) 100 Qg33
Lianyuan ◎ VRC (HUN) 100 Qf32
Lianyungang ◎ VRC (JGS) 106 Qk28
Lianyungang ◎ VRC (JGS) 106 Qk28
Liaocheng ◎ VRC (SDG) 97 Qh27
Liaodun ◎ VRC (XUZ) 91 Pg24
Liao He ≋ VRC 104 Rb24
Liaoning ☐ VRC 87 Ra10
Liaotung Peninsula ▲ VRC 104 Rb26
Liaoyang ◎ VRC (LNG) 104 Rb25
Liaoyuan ◎ VRC (JLN) 104 Rc24
Liaozhong ◎ VRC (LNG) 104 Rb25
Liaquatpur ◎ PK 85 Of31
Liard Highway ■ CDN 241 Dj16
Liard Plateau ▲ CDN 241 Dg15
Liard River ≋ CDN 241 Dj16
Liard River Corridor ■ ■ CDN 241 Dh16
Liari ◎ PK 84 Od33
Liat ▲ RI 129 Qd47
Liatorp ◎ S 17 Lp34
Liawang Shan ▲ VRC 117 Qb33
Libagon ◎ RP 127 Rc40
Libano ◎ CO 280 Gc43
Líbano ◎ RA (BA) 305 Gk64
Libao ◎ VRC (JGS) 106 Ra29
Libau ◎ CDN (MB) 248 Fb20
Libba ◎ WAN 194 Lc40
Libby ◎ USA (MT) 243 Ec21
Libenge ◎ RDC 208 Lk44
Liberal ◎ USA (KS) 252 Ek27
Liberator General San Martin ◎ RA (SL) 300 Gh62
Liberdade ≋ BR 293 Hd51
Liberec ◎ CZ 40 Lp40
Liberia ◎ CR 266 Fh40
Liberia ■ 175 Ka09
Libertad ◎ MEX (CAM) 265 Fe36
Libertad ◎ RA (CR) 301 Hb61
Libertad ◎ ROU 301 Hb63
Libertad ◎ YV 281 Gf41
Libertad ◎ YV 281 Gf41
Libertador ◎ RA (CR) 301 Ha61
Libertador General San Martín ◎ RA (PJ) 297 Gh57
Liberty ◎ USA (TX) 253 Fc30
Liberty ◎ USA (NY) 257 Gc25
Liberty ◎ USA (LA) 253 MS
Libiąż ◎ PL 39 Lu40
Libina ◎ CZ 40 Ls41
Libjo ◎ RP 127 Rc40
Libmanan ◎ RP 125 Rb39
Libo ◎ VRC (GZH) 100 Qd33
Libode ◎ SA 225 Me61
Libohovë ◎ AL 48 Ma50
Liboi ◎ EAK 213 Na45
Liboko ◎ RDC 208 Ma44
Libon ◎ RP 125 Rb39
Libona ◎ RP 127 Rc41
Liboumba ≋ G 203 Lg45
Libourne ◎ F 26 Ku46
Libramont-Chevigny ◎ B 25 Lf41
Libreville ● ■ ⌂ G 202 Le45
Libya ■ 175 Lb07
Libyan Desert ▲ LAR/ET 184 Mc31
Licancábur, Volcán ▲ RCH 296 Gg57
Licata ◎ I 44 Lo53
Lice ◎ TR 67 Na26
Lich ◎ D 34 Lj40
Licheng ◎ VRC (SAX) 97 Qg27
Licheng ◎ VRC (JGS) 106 Qk29
Lichinga ◎ ■ MOC 219 Mh52
Lichtenau ◎ D 34 Lj39
Lichtenburg ◎ SA 225 Md59
Lichtenfels ◎ D 37 Lm40
Lichtenvoorde ◎ NL 34 Lg39
Lichuan ◎ VRC (HUB) 99 Qe30
Lichuan ◎ VRC (JGX) 106 Qj32
Liciro ◎ MOC 219 Mj54
Licking ◎ USA (MO) 253 Fe27
Lički Osik ◎ HR 43 Lq46
Ličko Lešće ◎ HR 43 Lq46
Lida ◎ BY 19 Mf37
Liden ◎ S 15 Lr28
Lidfontein ◎ NAM 220 Lk58
Lidhult ◎ S 17 Lo34
Lidia ≋ PE 291 Ge51
Lidingö ◎ S 15 Lt31
Lidjombo ◎ RCA 203 Lj44
Lidköping ◎ S 15 Lo32
Lido ◎ RN 193 Lb39
Lido di Jésolo ◎ ■ I 43 Ln45
Lido di Metaponto ◎ ■ I 45 Lr50
Lidoríki ◎ GR 50 Mc52
Lidzbark ◎ PL 39 Lu37
Lidzbark Warmiński ◎ PL 39 Ma36
Liebenburg ◎ D 35 Ll38
Liebenthal ◎ CDN (SK) 243 Ef20
Liebenwalde ◎ D 35 Lo38
Lieberose ◎ D 35 Lp38
Liebig, Mount ▲ AUS 148 Rf57
Liechtenstein ■ FL 36 Lk43
Liechtensteinklamm ■ A 37 Lo43
Liège ◎ ■ B 25 Lf40
Lieksa ◎ ■ FIN 13 Mf14
Lielauce ◎ LV 19 Mc34
Lielstraupe ■ LV 19 Me33
Lielupe ≋ LV 19 Md34
Lielvārde ◎ LV 19 Me34
Liemianzhen ◎ VRC (SCH) 99 Qc30
Lienz ◎ ■ A 37 Ln44
Liepāja ◎ ■ ≋ LV 19 Mb34
Liepene ◎ LV 19 Mb33
Lieplievka ◎ BY 39 Md39
Liepna ◎ LV 19 Mh33
Lier ◎ ☐ ■ B 25 Le39
Lierbyen ◎ N 14 Ll31
Liesjärven kansallispuisto ■ FIN 18 Md30
Liestal ◎ CH 36 Lh43
Lietnik ◎ USA (AK) 238 Bf14
Lieto ◎ FIN 18 Mc30
Lievestuore ◎ FIN 18 Mg28
Liévin ◎ F 25 Lc40
Liezen ◎ A 37 Lp43
Lifamatola ▲ RI 134 Rd46
Liffol-le-Grand ◎ F 25 Lf42
Lifford ◎ IRL 20 Kn36
Lifou ▲ F 168 Td56
Lifuka Island ▲ TO 170 Bc55
Lifune ≋ ANG 210 Lh50
Lifupa ◎ ■ MW 218 Mg52
Liganga ◎ EAT 219 Mh51
Ligao ◎ RP 125 Rb39
Ligar ◎ TCH 195 Lj41
Ligera ◎ EAT 219 Mh51
Lighthouse Prov. H.S. ⌂ CDN 255 Hd21
Lightning Ridge ◎ AUS (NSW) 157 Sd60
Lignano Sabbiadoro ◎ ■ I 43 Lo45
Lignières ◎ F 25 Lc44
Ligny-en-Barrois ◎ F 25 Lf42
Ligny-le-Châtel ◎ F 25 Ld43
Ligowola ◎ EAT 219 Mj51
Ligueil ◎ F 24 La43
Ligui ◎ MEX (BCS) 262 Ee33
Ligunga ◎ EAT 219 Mj51
Ligúria ☐ I 42 Lj46
Ligurian Sea ≋ I/F 42 Lj47
Lihangwa ◎ EAT 215 Mk50
Lihás ◎ GR 50 Mc52
Lihir Group ▲ PNG 166 Sg47
Lihir Island ▲ PNG 166 Sg47
Lihoslavl' ◎ RUS 54 Mh17
Lihou Reefs and Cays ▲ AUS 155 Sg54
Lihovskoj ◎ RUS 57 Na21
Lihue ◎ USA (HI) 240 Ca35
Lihuél Calel, P.N. ■ RA 304 Gh64
Lihula ◎ EST 18 Md32
Lijiang ◎ ☐ ■ VRC (YUN) 117 Qa32
Lijiang ■ VRC 100 Qf33
Lijiang ≋ VRC 100 Qf33
Lijiang River cruises ■ VRC 100 Qf33
Likala ◎ RDC 208 Lk45
Likame ≋ RDC 208 Ma44
Likasi ◎ RDC 218 Md51
Likati ◎ RDC 209 Mb44
Likati ≋ RDC 208 Mb44
Likely ◎ CDN (BC) 242 Dk19
Likely ◎ USA (CA) 244 Dk25
Likenäs ◎ S 15 Lo30
Likete ◎ RDC 208 Ma46
Likhmisar ◎ IND (RJT) 110 Og32
Liki ◎ RI 128 Qa46
Likiep Atoll ▲ MH 163 Tb16
Likisia ◎ TIM 136 Rc50
Liknes ◎ N 14 Lg32
Likódimo ▲ GR 50 Mb54
Likoma Island ▲ MW 219 Mh51
Likoto ◎ RDC 209 Mc46
Likouala ≋ RCB 203 Lh45
Likouala aux Herbes ≋ RCB 203 Lj45
Likovskoe ◎ RUS 18 Mj31
Liku ◎ RI 130 Qe45
Likum ◎ PNG 165 Sc49
Likupang ◎ RI 131 Rc45
Likuyu ◎ EAT 219 Mj51
Lilarea ◎ AUS (QLD) 155 Sc57
l'Île de Zembra, P.N. ■ TN 182 Lf27
Lilienfeld ◎ A 37 Lq42
Lilienthal ◎ D 34 Lj37
Liling ◎ VRC (HUN) 101 Qg32
Liljendal ◎ FIN 18 Mg30
Lilla Creek ◎ AUS (NT) 148 Rh58
Lilla Edet ◎ S 16 Ln32
Lillärdal ◎ S 15 Lp29
Lille ⦿ ☐ ■ F 25 Ld40
Lillebonne ◎ F 24 La41
Lillehammer ◎ ■ N 14 Ll29
Lillers ◎ F 25 Lc40
Lillesand ◎ ■ N 14 Lj32
Lillestrøm ◎ N 14 Lm31
Lilli ◎ EST 18 Mf33
Lillie Marleen ◎ ANT (D) 313 Tc33
Lillo ◎ E 31 Kr49
Lillooet ◎ CDN (BC) 242 Dk20
Lillooet River ≋ CDN 242 Dj20
Lilo ≋ RDC 209 Mc46
Lilong ◎ IND (MNP) 116 Ph33
Lilongwe ● ■ ■ MW 218 Mg52
Liloy ◎ RP 127 Rb41
Lilydale ◎ AUS (SA) 158 Rk62
Lim ≋ RCA 203 Lh42
Lim ≋ SCG 48 Lu47
Lima ● ☐ ■ PE 290 Gb52
Lima ◎ PY 297 Hb57
Lima ◎ S 15 Lo30
Lima ◎ USA (OH) 256 Fh25
Limache ◎ RA (CD) 301 Gj60
Lima Duarte ◎ BR (MG) 299 Hj56
Limah ◎ OM 79 Nj33
Liman ◎ RUS 74 Nd23
Liman ◎ UA 57 Mj21
Limanáki ◎ GR 50 Mb52
Liman, Gunung ▲ RI 132 Qf49
Limanowa ◎ PL 41 Ma41
Limão do Curuá ◎ BR (AP) 287 He45
Limar ◎ RI 136 Rd49
Limas ◎ RI 129 Qc45
Limasawa Island ▲ RP 127 Rc41
Limassa ◎ RCA 208 Mb43
Limassol ◎ CY 53 Mo56
Limatambo ◎ PE 291 Gd52
Limavady ◎ GB 20 Ko35
Limay ≋ RA 304 Gf65
Limay ◎ RP 124 Ra38
Limay Mahuida ◎ RA (LP) 304 Gg64
Limba ≋ EAT 214 Mg49
Limbani ◎ PE 291 Gf53
Limbasa ◎ RDC 208 Mb43
Limbaži ◎ LV 19 Me33
Limbda ◎ IND (GUJ) 112 Of35
Limbdi ◎ IND (GUJ) 112 Of34
Limbé ◎ ■ ■ CAM 202 Le43
Limbe ◎ MW 219 Mh53
Limbé ◎ RH 270 Gd36
Limboto ◎ RI 131 Rb45
Limbuak ◎ MAL 126 Qj42
Limbung ◎ RI 131 Qk47
Limbunya ◎ AUS (NT) 145 Re54
Limburg ◎ D 34 Lj40
Lime Acres ◎ SA 224 Mb60
Limeira ◎ BR (SP) 298 Hg57
Liménas Géraka ◎ GR 50 Md54
Liménas Hersonissou ◎ GR 51 Mf55
Limerick ◎ CDN (SK) 243 Eg21
Limerick ◎ IRL 22 Km38
Limes ☐ ■ D 36 Lj40
Limestone Cliffs (Middle Caicos) ■ GB 261 Ge35
Limestone Lake ≋ CDN 248 Fc17
Limestone Plateau ▲ ET 185 Mf33
Limestone Pt. ▲ CDN 248 Fa19
Limestone Rapids ≋ CDN 249 Ff18
Limestone River ≋ CDN 248 Fc17
Limfjorden ≋ DK 16 Lk34
Liminangcong ◎ RP 126 Qk40
Limingen ≋ N 12 Lg13
Limmared ◎ S 17 Lo33
Limmen Bay ≋ AUS 145 Rh53
Limmen Bight River ≋ AUS 145 Rh53
Límnes ◎ GR 50 Mc53
Límni ◎ GR 50 Md52
Límni Aliákmona ≋ GR 48 Mc50
Límni Ilíki ≋ GR 50 Md52
Límni Kastoriás ■ GR 48 Mb50
Límni Kerkínis ■ GR 48 Md49
Límni Korónia ≋ GR 48 Md50
Límni Mikrí Préspa ■ GR 48 Mb50
Límni Trihonída ≋ GR 50 Mb52
Límni Vegoritída ≋ GR 48 Mb50
Límni Vólvi ≋ GR 48 Md50
Límni Vouliagménis ◎ GR 50 Mc52
Límnos ■ ■ GR 49 Mf51
Limoeiro ◎ BR (PE) 295 Jc49
Limoeiro do Ajurú ◎ BR (PA) 288 Hf46
Limoeiro do Norte ◎ BR (CE) 289 Ja48
Limoges ⦿ ⌂ F 26 Lb45
Limón ◎ EC 284 Ga47
Limon ◎ USA (CO) 250 Ej26
Limone Piemonte ◎ I 42 Lh46
Limones ◎ EC 284 Ga45
Limones ◎ PA 266 Fj41
Limousin ▲ F 26 Lb45
Limousin ☐ F 26 Lb45
Limoux ◎ F 26 Lc47
Limpio ◎ PY 297 Hb58
Limpopo ☐ SA 222 Me57
Limpopo ≋ SA/ZW 222 Mf57
Limski kanal ■ HR 43 Lo45
Limulunga ◎ ■ ■ Z 217 Mb53
Limuru ◎ EAK 212 Mj46
Lin ◎ AL 48 Ma49
Linah ◎ KSA 69 Nb31
Linahamari ◎ RUS 13 Mf11
Linao Bay ≋ RP 127 Rb42
Linapacan Island ▲ RP 126 Qk40
Linapacan Strait ≋ RP 126 Qk40
Linares ◎ E 31 Kr48
Linares ◎ MEX (NL) 263 Fa33
Linares ◎ RCH 304 Ge63
Linariá ◎ GR 50 Me52
Linbana ■ S 12 Lk13
Lincang ◎ VRC (YUN) 117 Qa34
Lincan Ray ◎ ■ RCH 304 Gd65
Linchang ◎ VRC (SAA) 99 Qe29
Linchuan ◎ VRC (JGX) 106 Qj32
Lincoln ◎ ■ GB 23 Ku37
Lincoln ◎ RA (BA) 301 Gk63
Lincoln ◎ USA (CA) 244 Dk26
Lincoln ◎ USA (KS) 250 Fa26
Lincoln ⦿ USA (NE) 251 Fb25
Lincoln ◎ USA (IL) 256 Ff25
Lincoln ◎ USA (ME) 254 Gf23
Lincoln Birthplace N.H.S. ⌂ USA 258 Fh27
Lincoln Caverns ■ USA 257 Ga25
Lincoln City ◎ USA (OR) 244 Dj23
Lincoln Highway ■ AUS 158 Rj62
Lincoln Island ▲ RP 124 Qg37
Lincoln Log Cabin S.H.S. ⌂ USA 251 Ff26
Lincoln N.P. ■ AUS 158 Rj63
Lincoln Sea ≋ CDN/DK 235 Ha02
Lincolnshire Wolds ▲ GB 23 Ku37
Lincoln's New Salem S.H.S. ⌂ USA 251 Ff26
Lincoln's New Salem S.H.S. ⌂ USA 256 Ff26
Lincoln Tomb S.H.S. ■ USA 251 Ff26
Lincoln Tomb S.H.S ■ USA 256 Ff26
Lincolnton ◎ USA (NC) 259 Fk28
Lind ◎ DK 16 Lj34
Lind ◎ USA (WA) 242 Ea22
Lindås ◎ N 14 Lf30
Lindau ◎ ■ D 36 Lk43
Linde ◎ LV 19 Me34
Linde ≋ RUS 63 Ra05
Lindela ◎ MOC 222 Mh58
Lindelse ◎ DK 16 Ll36
Lindeman Group ▲ AUS 155 Se56
Lindeman Islands N.P. ■ AUS 155 Se56
Linden ◎ CDN (AB) 243 Ed20
Linden ◎ D 34 Lj40
Linden ◎ GUY 282 Ha42
Linden ◎ USA (TX) 253 Fc29
Linden ◎ USA (TN) 258 Fg28
Linden ◎ USA (AL) 258 Fg29
Linderödsåsen ▲ S 17 Lo35
Lindesberg ◎ S 15 Lq31
Lindesnes ▲ N 14 Lh33
Lindesnes ◎ N 14 Lh33
Lindholm Høje ■ DK 16 Lk33
Lindi ◎ EAT 215 Mk50
Lindi ≋ RDC 209 Md45
Lindian ◎ VRC (HLG) 102 Rc22
Lindi Bay ≋ EAT 215 Mk50
Lindis Valley ◎ NZ 161 Te68
Lindley ◎ SA 225 Md59
Lindleyspoort ◎ SA 221 Md58
Lindome ◎ S 16 Ln33
Lindos ◎ ■ GR 51 Mj54
Lindoso ◎ P 28 Km51
Lindow ◎ D 35 Lo38
Lindsay ◎ CDN (ON) 257 Ga23
Lindsay ◎ USA (CA) 246 Ea27
Lindsay ◎ USA (MT) 245 Eh22
Lindsay ◎ USA (OK) 252 Fb28
Lindsborg ◎ USA (KS) 250 Fb26
Lindsdal ◎ S 17 Lr34
Linduri ◎ VU 168 Td53
Líneas de Nazca ☐ ■ PE 290 Gc53
Line Islands ▲ 317 Bb09
Linevo ◎ RUS 55 Nc20
Linfen ◎ VRC (SAX) 97 Qf27
Lingadaw ◎ MYA 116 Ph35
Lingal ◎ IND (APH) 113 Ok37
Lingala ◎ IND (APH) 115 Ok39
Linga Linga ▲ MOC 222 Mh57
Linganamakki Reservoir ≋ IND 114 Oh39
Lingaraja Temple ■ IND 113 Pc35
Lingayen ◎ RP 124 Ra38
Lingbao ◎ VRC (HNN) 99 Qf28
Lingbi ◎ VRC (AHU) 106 Qj29
Lingbim ◎ CAM 203 Lh43
Lingbo ◎ S 15 Lr29
Linge ◎ N 14 Lh28
Lingen ◎ D 34 Lh38
Lingga ▲ RI 129 Qc46
Lingga Karo Batak Village ■ RI 120 Pk44
Linggi ◎ MAL 121 Qb44
Linghai ◎ VRC (LNG) 104 Ra25
Linghem ◎ S 15 Lq32
Lingig ◎ RP 127 Rd41
Lingi Point ▲ AUS 145 Rf51
Lingle ◎ USA (WY) 245 Eh24
Lingomo ◎ RDC 208 Mb45
Lingomo ◎ RDC 208 Mb46
Lingqi Dong ■ VRC 106 Qk31
Lingqiu ◎ VRC (SAX) 97 Qh26
Lingshan ◎ VRC (GZG) 100 Qe34
Lingshan Dao ▲ VRC 104 Ra28
Lingshan Han Tombs ■ VRC 97 Qh26
Lingshi ◎ VRC (SAX) 97 Qf27
Lingshui ◎ VRC (HAN) 100 Qf36
Ling Shui ■ VRC 100 Qe34
Lingsugur ◎ IND (KTK) 112 Oj37
Lingtai ◎ VRC (GSU) 99 Qd28
Lingtou ◎ VRC (HAN) 100 Qe36
Linguaglossa ◎ I 44 Lq53
Linguèr ◎ SN 191 Kc38
Lingwu ◎ VRC (NHZ) 96 Qd26
Ling Xian ◎ VRC (HUN) 101 Qg32
Lingyan Si ▲ VRC 97 Qj27
Lingyin Si ▲ VRC 106 Qk30
Lingyuan ◎ VRC (LNG) 97 Qk25
Lingyun ◎ VRC (GZG) 100 Qd33
Linhai ◎ VRC (ZJG) 106 Ra31
Linhai ◎ VRC (HLG) 102 Rc20
Linhares ◎ BR (ES) 299 Hk55
Linhe ◎ VRC (NMZ) 96 Qd25
Linhemo ◎ ANG 216 Lj52
Linia ◎ PL 38 Ls36
Linjiang ◎ VRC (JLN) 104 Rd25
Lin Jiang ≋ VRC 106 Ra31
Linji Temple ▲ VRC 97 Qh27
Linköping ◎ S 15 Lq32
Linkou ◎ VRC (HLG) 102 Rf23
Linkuva ◎ LT 19 Md34
Linli ◎ VRC (HUN) 99 Qf31
Linlithgow ◎ GB 21 Kr35
Linn ◎ USA (TX) 263 Fa32
Linna ■ FIN 18 Mc30
Linnansaaren kansallispuisto ■ ■ FIN 18 Mj28
Linneus ◎ USA (MO) 251 Fd26
Linnoitus ■ FIN 18 Mj30
Linping ◎ VRC (ZJG) 106 Ra30
Linqing ◎ VRC (SDG) 97 Qh27
Linqu ◎ VRC (SDG) 97 Qk27
Linquan ◎ VRC (AHU) 106 Qh29
Lins ◎ BR (SP) 298 Hf56
Linsan ◎ RG 200 Kd40
Linsell ◎ S 15 Lo28
Linshu ◎ VRC (SDG) 106 Qk28
Linshui ◎ VRC (SCH) 99 Qd30
Linshuize ◎ VRC (YUN) 100 Qc33
Linstead ◎ JA 269 Gb36
Linta ≋ RM 228 Nc58
Lintan ◎ VRC (GSU) 98 Qb28
Lintao ◎ VRC (GSU) 98 Qb28
Linté ◎ CAM 203 Lf43
Linton ◎ USA (ND) 250 Ek22
Linton ◎ USA (IN) 258 Fg26
Lintong ◎ VRC (SAA) 99 Qe28
Linxi ◎ VRC (NMZ) 97 Qk24
Linxi ◎ VRC (HBI) 97 Qk26
Linxia ◎ VRC (GSU) 98 Qb28
Lin Xian ◎ VRC (SAX) 97 Qf27
Lin Xian ◎ VRC (HNN) 97 Qg27
Linxiang ◎ VRC (HUN) 99 Qg31
Linyanti ■ RB 221 Mc55
Linyanti Camp ◎ RB 221 Mb55
Linyanti Swamp ≋ NAM/RB 217 Mb55
Linyi ◎ VRC (SDG) 97 Qj27
Linyi ◎ VRC (SDG) 106 Qk28
Linying ◎ VRC (HNN) 99 Qg29
Linz ◎ ■ A 37 Lp42
Linz ◎ D 34 Lh40
Linze ◎ VRC (GSU) 96 Qa26
Linzhen ◎ VRC (SAA) 97 Qe27
Linzolo ◎ RCB 210 Lh48
Linzor ◎ RCH 296 Gf57
Lioma ◎ MOC 219 Mj53
Lioni ≋ CO 281 Gf43
Lions Den ◎ ZW 218 Mf54
Lioppa ◎ RI 136 Rd49
Lioto ◎ RCA 208 Ma43
Lioua ◎ TCH 195 Lh39
Liouesso ◎ RCB 203 Lh45
Lipa ◎ RP 125 Ra39
Lipany ◎ SK 41 Ma41
Liparamba ◎ EAT 219 Mh51
Lípari ◎ ■ I 44 Lp52
Lipari Islands ▲ I 44 Lp52
Lipcani ◎ MD 47 Mg42
Lipeck ◎ RUS 55 Mk19
Liperi ◎ FIN 13 Me14
Lipiany ◎ PL 38 Lp37
Lipica ■ SLO 43 Lo45
Lipicy-Zybino ◎ RUS 54 Mj19
Lipik ◎ HR 43 Ls45
Lipin Bor ◎ RUS 13 Mk15
Lipka ◎ PL 38 Ls37
Lipki ◎ RUS 55 Mj19
Lipljan ◎ SCG 48 Mb48
Lipniak ◎ PL 39 Md36
Lipnica ◎ PL 38 Ls36
Lipnica Murowana ◎ ☐ ■ PL 41 Ma41
Lipniďki ◎ BY 19 Mf37
Lipník nad Bečvou ◎ CZ 40 Ls41
Lipno ◎ PL 39 Lu38
Lipoba ◎ Z 217 Mb53
Lipoche Olivença ◎ MOC 219 Mh51
Lipolist ◎ SCG 46 Lu46
Lipova ◎ RO 46 Mb44
Lipovcy ◎ RUS 102 Rf23
Lipoven'ke ◎ UA 47 Ml42
Lipovljani ◎ HR 43 Lr45
Lippe ≋ D 34 Lh39
Lippstadt ◎ D 34 Lj39
Lipsí ■ GR 51 Mg53
Lipsk ◎ PL 39 Md37
Lipsko ◎ PL 39 Mb39
Lipson ◎ AUS (SA) 158 Rj63
Lipton ◎ CDN (SK) 248 Ej20
Liptougou ◎ BF 193 La39
Liptovský Hrádok ◎ SK 41 Lu41
Lipu ◎ VRC (GZG) 100 Qf33
Liqen i Butrintit ≋ AL 48 Ma51
Liqeni i Banjës ≋ AL 48 Ma50
Lique, Cerro ▲ BOL 296 Gh56
Liqueni i Fierzös ≋ AL 48 Ma48
Lira ◎ EAU 212 Mg44
Liranga ◎ RCB 208 Lj46
Lirangwe ◎ MW 219 Mh53
Lircay ◎ PE 290 Gc52
Liri ≋ I 44 Lo49
Lisa Gora ◎ UA 47 Mm42
Lisala ◎ RDC 208 Ma44
Lisboa ● ■ ■ P 30 Kl48
Lisbon ● ■ ■ P 30 Kl48
Lisbon ◎ USA (ND) 250 Fb22
Lisbon Falls ■ SA 222 Mf58
Lisburn ◎ GB 20 Ko36
Liscannor Bay ≋ IRL 22 Kl38
Liscomb Game Sanctuary ■ CDN 255 Gj23
Lisdoonvarna ◎ ■ IRL 22 Kl37
Liseberg ■ S 16 Ln33
Lishan ◎ VRC (SCH) 99 Qd30
Lishan Z.B. ■ VRC 99 Qf28
Lishi ◎ VRC (SAX) 97 Qf27
Lishizhen ◎ VRC (CGQ) 99 Qd31
Lishu ◎ VRC (JLN) 104 Rc24
Lishui ◎ VRC (JGS) 106 Qk30
Lishui ◎ VRC (ZJG) 106 Qk31
Li Shui ≋ VRC 99 Qf31
Lisieux ◎ F 24 La41
Lisitu ◎ EAT 215 Mh50
Liskeard ◎ GB 22 Kq40
Liski ◎ RUS 55 Mk20
L'Isle-Adam ◎ F 25 Lc41
L'Isle-en-Dodon ◎ F 26 La47
L'Isle-Jourdain ◎ F 26 La44
L'Isle-Jourdain ◎ F 26 Lb47
L'Isle-sur-la-Sorgue ◎ F 27 Lf47
L'Isle-sur-le-Doubs ◎ F 25 Lg43
Lismore ◎ AUS (VIC) 159 Sb64
Lismore ◎ AUS (QLD) 157 Sf59
Lismore ◎ AUS (NSW) 157 Sg60
Lismore ▲ GB 20 Kp34
Lismore ◎ IRL 22 Kn38
Lisnaskea ◎ GB 20 Kn36
Lišov ◎ CZ 40 Lp41
Lissadell ◎ AUS (WA) 144 Re54
Lissenung Island Resort ■ PNG 166 Sf47
Lissington ◎ AUS (NSW) 157 Sd60
List ◎ D 34 Lj36
Listafjorden ≋ N 14 Lg32
Lister, Mount ▲ 313 Ta34
Listowel ◎ CDN (ON) 256 Fk24
Listowel ◎ IRL 22 Kl38
Listvjanka ◎ RUS 94 Qc20
Lita ◎ EC 284 Ga45
Litang ◎ VRC (SCH) 98 Qa31
Litang ◎ VRC (GZG) 100 Qe34
Litawa Flats ▲ Z 217 Mb53
Litchfield ◎ USA (MN) 251 Fc23
Litchfield Beach ◎ USA (SC) 259 Ga29
Litchfield N.P. ■ AUS 145 Rf52
Liteni ◎ RO 47 Mg43
Lithgow ◎ AUS (NSW) 159 Sf62
Lithuania ■ LT 19 Mc35
Lití ◎ GR 48 Mc50
Litija ◎ SLO 43 Lp44
Litipara ◎ IND (JKD) 116 Pd33
Litóhoro ◎ GR 48 Mc50
Litoměrice ◎ ■ CZ 40 Lp40
Litomyšl ◎ CZ 40 Lr41
Litoral ▲ RO 47 Mj46
Litovel ◎ CZ 40 Ls41
Litovko' ◎ RUS 102 Rh21
Little Abitibi Lake ≋ CDN 249 Fk21
Little Abitibi River ≋ CDN 249 Fk20
Little Aden = 'Adan as Sughra ◎ ■ YE 72 Nc39
Little Andaman ▲ IND 115 Pg40
Little Avalon ■ AUS 159 Sf62
Little Barrier Island ▲ NZ 160 Th64
Little Bay ◎ CDN (NF) 255 Ha22
Little Belt ≋ DK 16 Lk35
Little Belt Mts. ▲ USA 245 Ee22
Little Bighorn Nat. Battlefield ■ USA 245 Ef23
Little Cadotte River ≋ CDN 243 Eb17
Little Cayman ■ GB 269 Fk36
Little Churchill River ≋ CDN 248 Fc17
Little Coco Island ▲ MYA 115 Pg39
Little Colorado ≋ USA 247 Ee28
Little Current ◎ CDN (ON) 256 Fk23
Little Current River ≋ CDN 249 Fh20
Little Desert ▲ AUS 158 Sa64
Little Desert N.P. ■ ■ AUS 158 Sa64
Little Exuma Island ▲ BS 261 Gc34
Little Falls ◎ USA (MN) 251 Fc23
Littlefield ◎ USA (TX) 247 Ej29
Little Fort ◎ CDN (BC) 242 Dk20
Little Gombi ◎ WAN 195 Lg40
Little Grand Rapids ◎ CDN (MB) 248 Fc19
Little Halibut Bank ■ 21 Kt32
Little Harbour ◎ BS 261 Gb33
Little Inagua Island ■ BS 261 Gd35
Little Lake ◎ USA (CA) 246 Eb28
Little Mecatina River ≋ CDN 255 Gk19
Little Missouri ≋ USA 250 Ej22
Little Missouri Grassland N.P. ■ USA 250 Ej22
Little Nicobar Island ▲ IND 115 Pg42
Little Ragged Island ▲ BS 261 Gc34
Little River Canyon ■ USA 259 Fh28
Little River N.W.R. ■ USA 253 Fc28
Little Rock ⦿ USA (AR) 253 Fd28
Little Ruaha ≋ EAT 215 Mh50
Little Sachigo Lake ≋ CDN 248 Fd18
Little Sahara R.A. ■ USA 245 Ed26
Little Salmon Lake ≋ CDN 241 Dc14
Little Salt Lake ≋ USA 245 Ed27
Little Sandy Desert ■ AUS 146 RA58
Little San Salvador Is. ▲ BS 261 Gc33
Little Scarcies ≋ WAL 200 Kd41
Little Smoky River ≋ CDN 243 Eb18
Littleton ◎ USA (CO) 245 Eh26
Littleton ◎ USA (NH) 257 Ge23
Little White House S.H.S. ⌂ USA 259 Fh29
Little Zab ≋ IRQ 69 Nb27
Lituhu ◎ EAT 219 Mh51
Litunde ◎ MOC 219 Mh52
Lituya Bay ≋ USA 241 Db16
Litvínov ◎ CZ 40 Lo40
Liuba ◎ VRC (SAA) 99 Qd29
Liuchiu Yü ▲ RC 101 Ra34
Liuhe ◎ VRC (JLN) 104 Rc24
Liujiachang ◎ VRC (HUB) 99 Qf30
Liujiang ◎ VRC (GZG) 100 Qe33
Liu Jiang ≋ VRC 100 Qe34
Liujing ◎ VRC (GZG) 100 Qf34
Liujixia Shiku ▲ VRC 96 Qb28
Liuku ◎ VRC (YUN) 117 Pk33
Liuli ◎ EAT 219 Mh51
Liulin ◎ VRC (SAX) 97 Qf27
Liuliu ◎ SOL 166 Sj49
Liupan Shan ▲ VRC 99 Qc28
Liupanshan Z.B. ■ VRC 99 Qd28
Liupanshui ◎ VRC (GZH) 100 Qc32
Liupo ◎ MOC 219 Mk53
Liurongsi Huata ▲ VRC 101 Qg34
Liushi ◎ VRC (ZJG) 106 Ra31
Liushilipu ◎ VRC (AHU) 106 Qh29
Liuwa Plain ▲ Z 217 Mb53
Liuwa Plain N.P. ■ ■ Z 217 Mb53
Liuxu ◎ VRC (GZG) 100 Qe34
Liuyang ◎ VRC (HUN) 99 Qg31
Liuzhai ◎ VRC (GZG) 100 Qd33
Liuzhou ◎ VRC (GZG) 100 Qe33
Liuzhuang ◎ VRC (JGS) 106 Ra29
Livada ◎ RO 46 Md43
Livaderó ◎ GR 48 Mb50
Livaderó ◎ GR 49 Me49
Livádi ◎ GR 51 Me53
Livadiá ◎ GR 50 Mc52
Livadia Palats ■ UA 57 Mh23
Livadohóri ◎ GR 49 Mf51
Livāni ◎ LV 19 Mg34
Livari ◎ SCG 48 Lu48
Livarot ◎ F 24 La42
Lively ◎ CDN (ON) 256 Fk22
Lively Island ▲ GB 307 Ha72
Livengood ◎ USA (AK) 239 Cf13
Live Oak ◎ USA (FL) 259 Fj30
Livera ◎ CY 53 Mn55
Liverpool ◎ AUS (NSW) 159 Sf62
Liverpool ◎ CDN (NS) 255 Gh23
Liverpool ◎ ☐ ■ GB 23 Ks37
Liverpool Bay ≋ GB 23 Kr37
Liverpool Range ▲ AUS 157 Sf61
Livezi ◎ RO 47 Mg44
Liv Glacier ≋ 312 Bc35
Livigno ◎ ■ I 42 Ll44
Livikó Pélagos ≋ GR 51 Md55
Livingston ◎ CDN 235 Gc08
Livingston ◎ GB 21 Kr35
Lívingston ◎ GCA 265 Ff38
Livingston ◎ USA (MT) 245 Ee23
Livingston ◎ USA (TX) 253 Fc30
Livingston ◎ USA (TN) 258 Fh27
Livingstone ◎ ■ ■ Z 217 Mc54
Livingstone Church ■ SA 224 Mb60
Livingstonegrot ■ RB 221 Mc58
Livingstonekerk ■ SA 224 Mb60
Livingstone Memorial ■ Z 218 Mf52
Livingstone Mountains ▲ EAT 215 Mh50
Livingstone's Cave ■ RB 221 Mc58
Livingstonia ◎ ■ ■ MW 218 Mh51
Livingston Island ▲ 312 Gd31
Livizile ◎ RO 46 Md44
Livno ◎ BIH 43 Lr47
Livny ◎ RUS 55 Mj19
Livonia ◎ USA (MI) 256 Fj24
Livorno ◎ ■ I 42 Ll47
Livramento do Brumado ◎ BR (BA) 295 Hk52
Livron-sur-Drôme ◎ F 27 Le46
Liw ◎ PL 39 Mb38
Liwa ◎ OM 79 Nj33
Liwa ◎ RI 129 Qc48
Liwale ◎ EAT 215 Mj50
Liwa Oasis ■ ■ UAE 78 Ng34
Imperial Tombs of the Ming and Qing Dynasties (Nanjing) ☐ ■ VRC (JGS) 106 Qk29
Li Wenzhong, Tomb of = Imperial Tombs of the Ming and Qing Dynasties ☐ ■ VRC (JGS) 106 Qk29
Liwiec ≋ PL 39 Mb38
Liwonde ◎ MW 219 Mh53
Liwonde N.P. ■ ■ MW 219 Mh53
Li Xian ◎ VRC (SCH) 98 Qb30
Li Xian ◎ VRC (GSU) 99 Qc28
Li Xian ◎ VRC (HUN) 99 Qf31
Lixin ◎ VRC (AHU) 106 Qj29
Lixoúri ◎ GR 50 Ma52
Lixus ■ MA 180 Kg28
Liyang ◎ VRC (JGS) 106 Qk30
Li Yubu ◎ SUD 209 Md43
Lizarda ◎ BR (TO) 294 Hg50
Lizard Island ■ AUS 153 Sc53
Lizard Point ▲ GB 22 Kp41
Lizespasts ◎ LV 19 Mg33
Lizotte ◎ CDN (QC) 254 Gd21
Lizums ◎ LV 19 Mg33
Ljachavičy ◎ BY 39 Mg37
Ljady ◎ RUS 54 Me16
Ljamca ◎ RUS 13 Mj13
Ljangar ◎ TJ 81 Og27
Ljig ◎ SCG 48 Ma46
Ljørndalen ◎ N 15 Ln29
Ljuban' ◎ BY 54 Me19
Ljuban' ◎ RUS 54 Mf16
Ljubar ◎ UA 56 Md21
Ljubašivka ◎ UA 47 Ml43
Ljubča ◎ BY 19 Mg37
Ljubešiv ◎ UA 39 Mf39
Ljúbija ◎ BIH 43 Lr46
Ljubim ◎ RUS 55 Na16
Ljubinje ◎ BIH 43 Lt48
Ljubiš ◎ SCG 48 Lu47
Ljubljana ● ■ SLO 43 Lp44
Ljuboml' ◎ UA 39 Me39
Ljubovija ◎ SCG 48 Lu46
Ljubuški ◎ BIH 43 Ls47
Ljubymivka ◎ UA 57 Mj22
Ljubytino ◎ RUS 54 Mg16
Ljudinovo ◎ RUS 54 Mh19
Ljugarn ◎ S 17 Lt33
Ljukkum ▲ KZ 88 Oj22
Ljung ◎ S 17 Lo33
Ljunga ◎ S 15 Lr32
Ljungan ≋ S 15 Lr28
Ljungaverk ◎ S 15 Lq28
Ljungby ◎ S 17 Lp34
Ljungbyhed ◎ S 17 Lo34
Ljungbyholm ◎ S 17 Lr34
Ljungdalen ◎ S 15 Ln28
Ljunghusen ◎ S 17 Ln35
Ljungsbro ◎ S 15 Lq32
Ljungskile ◎ S 14 Lm32
Ljusdal ◎ S 15 Lr29
Ljusfallshammar ◎ S 15 Lq32
Ljusnan ≋ S 15 Lq29
Ljusterö ▲ S 15 Lt31
Ljustorp ◎ S 15 Ls28
Ljutomer ◎ SLO 43 Lr44
Lkhachinvandad Uul Nature Reserve ■ ■ MNG 95 Qh23
Llagostera ◎ E 32 Lc49
Llaima, Volcán ▲ RCH 304 Ge65
Llallagua ◎ BOL 296 Gg55
Llalli ◎ PE 291 Ge53
Llamellin ◎ PE 290 Gb50
Llampos ◎ RCH 300 Ge59
Llanberis ◎ GB 22 Kq37
Llandeilo ◎ GB 22 Kr39
Llandovery ◎ GB 22 Kr39
Llandrindod-Wells ◎ GB 23 Kr38
Llandudno ◎ GB 23 Kr37
Llanelli ◎ GB 22 Kq39
Llanes ◎ E 28 Kq53
Llanganates, P.N. ■ EC 284 Ga46
Llangollen ◎ GB 23 Kr38
Llangurig ◎ GB 22 Kr38
Llanidloes ◎ GB 22 Kr38
Llano ◎ USA (TX) 252 Fa30
Llano ≋ USA 252 Fa30
Llanobajo ◎ CO 280 Gb44
Llano de Magdalena ▲ MEX 262 Ee33
Llano Estacado ▲ USA 247 Ej29
Llano Mariato ◎ PA 267 Fk42
Llanos de Challe, P.N. ■ RCH 300 Ge60
Llanos de Chiquitos ▲ BOL 297 Gk55
Llanos de Guarayos ▲ BOL 292 Gj53
Llanos de la Rioja ▲ RA 300 Gg60
Llanos del Carmen ◎ MEX (SLP) 263 Ek34
Llanos del Orinoco ▲ CO/YV 281 Ge42
Llanos de Mojos ▲ BOL 291 Gh53
Llanquihue ◎ RCH 304 Gd66
Llanrheidol ◎ AUS (QLD) 154 Sa57
Llanrwst ◎ GB 23 Kr37
Llanwddyn ◎ GB 23 Kr38
Llanwrtyd Wells ◎ GB 22 Kr38
Llao Llao ◎ RA (RN) 304 Ge66
Llata ◎ PE 290 Gb50
Llaylla ◎ PE 290 Gc51
Llay-Llay ◎ RCH 300 Ge62
Lleida ◎ ■ E 32 La49
Llera de Canales ◎ MEX (TM) 263 Fa34
Llerena ◎ E 30 Ko48
Lleyn ▲ GB 22 Kq38
Llica ◎ BOL 296 Gf55
Llico ◎ RCH 300 Gd63
Llifén ◎ RCH 304 Gd66
Llíria ◎ E 31 Ku49
Lliscaya, Cerro ▲ BOL/RCH 296 Gf55
Llivynci ◎ UA 47 Mg42
L'Ile-Rousse ◎ ■ F 33 Lj48
Llorente ◎ RP 127 Rc40
Lloret de Mar ◎ ■ E 32 Lc49
Lloyd Bay ≋ AUS 153 Sb52
Lloyd Lake ≋ CDN 243 Ef17
Lloydminster ◎ CDN (SK) 243 Ef19
Lloyd Rock ▲ BS 261 Gc35
Lloyds Camp ◎ RB 221 Mc55
Llucena ◎ E 31 Ku50
Llucmajor ◎ E 32 Lc51
Llullaillaco, P.N. ■ RCH 296 Gf58
Llullaillaco, Volcán ▲ RCH/RA 296 Gf58
Lluta ◎ PE 296 Gd54
Lnáře ◎ CZ 40 Lo41
Loa ≋ RCH 296 Gf56
Loa ◎ USA (UT) 245 Ee26
Loaita Bank ■ 126 Qh40
Loaita Island ▲ 126 Qh40
Loajanan ◎ RI 131 Qj46
Loakulu ◎ RI 131 Qj46
Loanda ≋ ANG 211 Lj50
Loanda ◎ G 210 Le46
Loandji ≋ RDC 211 Lk48
Loange ≋ RDC 211 Ma48
Loango ◎ RCB 210 Lf48
Loango ◎ RDC 210 Lg48
Loango, P.N. de ■ ■ G 210 Le47
Loanja ≋ Z 217 Mc54
Loano ◎ I 42 Lj46
Loay ◎ RP 127 Rc41
Lobatos ◎ MEX (ZCT) 263 Ej34
Lobatse ◎ RB 221 Mc58
Löbau ◎ D 35 Lp39
Lobay ≋ RCA 203 Lj43
Lobaye ≋ RCA 203 Lk44
Lobaye ≋ RDC 209 Mc45
Lobcovo ◎ RUS 55 Na17
Lobeke ≋ CAM 203 Lh44
Lobenstein ◎ D 35 Lm40
Lobería ◎ RA (BA) 305 Ha65
Löberöd ◎ S 17 Lo35
Łobez ◎ PL 38 Lq37
Lobi ◎ MW 218 Mh53
Lobira ◎ SUD 205 Mg43
Lobito ◎ ANG 216 Lg52
Lobitos ◎ PE 284 Fk48
Lobo ≋ CAM 203 Lg44
Lobo ◎ RI 135 Rh47
Lobo ◎ ■ RP 125 Ra39
Lobo ◎ USA (TX) 247 Eh30
Loboko ◎ RCB 208 Lj46
Lobonäs ◎ S 15 Lq29
Lobos ≋ MEX 262 Eg33
Lobos ◎ RA (BA) 301 Ha63
Lobougoula ◎ RMM 201 Kh40
Loburg ◎ D 35 Ln38
Łobżenica ◎ PL 38 Ls37
Locarno ◎ CH 36 Lj44
Locas de Cahuinarí ◎ CO 285 Ge46
Lochaline ◎ GB 20 Kp34
Loch Awe ≋ GB 21 Kp34
Lochboisdale ◎ GB 20 Kn33
Loch Broom ≋ GB 21 Kp33
Loché ◎ MEX (YT) 265 Ff35
Loch Earn ≋ GB 21 Kq34
Lochearnhead ◎ GB 21 Kq34
Lochem ◎ NL 34 Lg38
Loch Ericht ≋ GB 21 Kq34
Loches ◎ ■ F 24 Lb43
Loch Fyne ≋ GB 20 Kp35
Lochgilphead ◎ GB 20 Kp34
Lochiel ◎ SA 225 Mf59
Lochinvar N.P. ■ ■ Z 218 Md53
Lochinver ◎ GB 21 Kp32
Loch Katrine ≋ GB 21 Kq34
Loch Ken ≋ GB 21 Kq35
Loch Lilly ◎ AUS (NSW) 158 Sa62
Loch Linnhe ≋ GB 21 Kp34
Loch Lochy ≋ GB 21 Kq34
Loch Lomond ≋ GB 21 Kq34
Loch Lomond and The Trossachs N.P. ■ ■ GB 21 Kq34
Loch Loyal ≋ GB 21 Kq32
Lochmaddy ◎ GB 20 Kn33
Loch Maree ■ GB 21 Kp33
Loch Naver ≋ GB 21 Kq32
Loch Ness ■ GB 21 Kq33
Łochów ◎ PL 39 Mb38
Loch Rannoch ≋ GB 21 Kq34
Lochranza ◎ GB 20 Kp35
Loch Roag ≋ GB 20 Ko32
Lochsa ≋ USA 245 Ec22
Loch Shin ≋ GB 21 Kq32
Loch Sport ◎ AUS (VIC) 159 Sd65
Loch Tay ≋ GB 21 Kq34
Lochvycja ◎ UA 54 Mg20
Lociel ◎ AUS (SA) 158 Rk62
Lock ◎ AUS (SA) 158 Rh62
Lockeport ◎ CDN (NS) 255 Gh24
Lockerbie ◎ GB 21 Kr35
Lockesburg ◎ USA (AR) 253 Fc29
Lockhart ◎ AUS (NSW) 159 Sd63
Lockhart ◎ USA (TX) 252 Fb31
Lockhart River ◎ AUS (QLD) 152 Sb52
Lockhart River A.L. ■ AUS 152 Sb52
Lock Haven ◎ USA (PA) 257 Gb25
Lockichokio ◎ EAK 205 Mh43
Löcknitz ◎ D 35 Lp37
Lockwood ◎ USA (CA) 246 Dk28
Lockwood Hills ▲ USA 239 Cc12
Locminé ◎ F 24 Ks43
Loc Ninh ◎ VN 119 Qd40
Locri ◎ I 45 Lr52
Locri Epizefiri ■ I 45 Lr52
Locronan ◎ ■ F 24 Kq42
Loctudy ◎ F 24 Kq43
Locust CRiver ≋ USA 251 Fd26
Lod ◎ IL 68 Mh30
Lodein ◎ SUD 205 Mg42
Lodejenoe Pole ◎ RUS 13 Mg15
Löderup ◎ S 17 Lp35
Lodève ◎ F 27 Ld47
Lodge Corner ◎ USA (AR) 253 Fe28
Lodge Creek ≋ CDN 243 Ee21
Lodge Grass ◎ USA (MT) 245 Eg23
Lodhran ◎ PK 85 Of31
Lodi ◎ I 42 Lk45
Lodi ◎ RDC 211 Ma48
Lodi ◎ USA (CA) 244 Dk26
Løding ◎ N 12 Lh12
Lødingen ◎ N 12 Lj11
Lodja ◎ RDC 211 Mb47
Lodosa ◎ E 29 Ks52
Lödöse ◎ S 16 Ln32
Lodoyo ◎ RI 132 Qg50
Lodrani ◎ IND (GUJ) 112 Of34
Lodungokwe ◎ EAK 212 Mj45
Lodwar ◎ EAK 212 Mh44
Łódź ◎ PL 39 Lu39
Loei ◎ THA 118 Qa37
Loeka ≋ RDC 208 Mb44
Loémé ≋ RCB 210 Lg48
Loeng Nok Tha ◎ THA 119 Qc37
Loeriesfontein ◎ SA 224 Lk61
Løfallstrand ◎ N 14 Lg30
Lofé ◎ SN 191 Kc38
Lofer ◎ A 37 Ln43
Loffa ≋ LB 200 Ke42
Lofoten ■ N 12 Lg12
Lofoten Basin ■ 8 La03
Lofsdalen ◎ ■ S 15 Lo28
Loftahammar ◎ S 17 Lr33
Lofthus ◎ N 14 Lg30
Lofty Range ▲ AUS 146 Qk58
Lofty Ranges, Mount ▲ AUS 158 Rk63
Log ◎ RUS 55 Nb21
Loga ◎ RN 193 Lb39
Loga ◎ SUD 209 Mf43
Logan ◎ USA (UT) 245 Ee25
Logan ◎ USA (NM) 247 Ej28
Logan ◎ USA (IA) 251 Fc25
Logan ◎ USA (OH) 256 Fj26
Logan ◎ USA (WV) 259 Fk27
Logan Cave N.W.R. ■ USA 253 Fc27
Logan Glacier ■ CDN 241 Ck15
Logan, Mount ▲ CDN 241 Ck15
Logan Mountains ▲ CDN 241 Df15
Logan Pass ■ USA 243 Ec21
Logansport ◎ USA (IN) 256 Fg25
Logatec ◎ SLO 43 Lp45
Loge ≋ ANG 210 Lh49
Logeloge ◎ EAT 215 Mk49
Logobou ◎ BF 201 La40
Logoforok ◎ SUD 212 Mg44
Logone ≋ CAM/TCH 195 Lh40
Logone Birni ◎ CAM 195 Lh40
Logone Gana ◎ TCH 195 Lh40
Logone Occidental ≋ TCH 203 Lh41
Logone Oriental ≋ TCH 203 Lj41
Lógos ◎ GR 50 Mc52
Logozohe ◎ DY 202 Lb42
Logroño ⦿ ■ E 29 Ks52
Logrosán ◎ E 30 Kp49
Løgstør ◎ DK 16 Lk34
Logtak Lake ≋ IND 116 Pg33
Løgumkloster ◎ DK 16 Lj35
Lohaghat ◎ IND (UTT) 111 Pa31
Lohals ◎ DK 16 Ll35
Lohara ◎ IND (CGH) 113 Pa35
Lohardaga ◎ IND (JKD) 113 Pc34
Lohatanjona Angadoka ▲ RM 226 Nd52
Lohatanjona Antsirakakambana ▲ RM 228 Nf54
Lohatanjona Fenambosy ▲ RM 228 Nc58
Lohatanjona Maromony ▲ RM 226 Nd53
Lohatanjona Vohibato ▲ RM 228 Ne54
Lohawat ◎ IND (RJT) 110 Og32
Lohikoski ◎ FIN 18 Mj29
Lohit ≋ IND 117 Ph32
Lohja ◎ FIN 18 Me30
Lohmar ◎ D 34 Lh40
Lohne ◎ D 34 Lj38
Lohr ◎ D 36 Lk40
Loi ◎ PNG 165 Sc49
Loibltunnel ▲ A/SLO 37 Lp44
Loiborsoit ◎ EAT 215 Mj48
Loi, Gunung ▲ RI 130 Qg45
Loi-kaw ◎ MYA 118 Pj36
Loikisale ◎ EAT 215 Mj47
Loi-lawm ◎ MYA 117 Pj34
Loile ≋ RDC 208 Ma46
Loimaa ◎ FIN 18 Md30
Loima Hills ▲ EAK 212 Mh44
Loimijoki ≋ FIN 18 Mc29
Loir ≋ F 24 Ku43
Loire ☐ ■ F 24 Ku43
Loire ≋ F 24 Lb43
Loiro Poco ◎ BR (AM) 285 Gf45
Loi Sang ▲ MYA 117 Pj35
Loi Song ▲ MYA 117 Pj34
Loita Plains ▲ EAK 212 Mh46
Loi Tawngkyaw ▲ MYA 117 Pj34
Loitz ◎ D 35 Lo37
Loiyangalani ◎ ■ EAK 212 Mj44
Loja ◎ E 30 Kq47
Loja ◎ EC 284 Ga47
Lojanice ◎ SCG 46 Lu46
Lojmola ◎ RUS (KAR) 13 Mf15
Lojsthajd ▲ S 17 Lt33
Lokači ◎ UA 39 Me40
Lokalema ◎ RDC 208 Mb45
Lokandu ◎ RDC 214 Mc47
Lokan tekojärvi ≋ FIN 13 Md12
Lokapur ◎ IND (KTK) 112 Oh37
Lokata ◎ RI 134 Rf46
Lökbetan ◎ AZ 74 Ne25
Løken ◎ N 14 Lm31
Lokeren ◎ B 25 Ld39
Loket ■ CZ 40 Ln40
Lokgwabe ◎ RB 221 Ma58
Lokichar ◎ EAK 212 Mh44
Lokichar ≋ EAK 212 Mh44
Lokichar ◎ EAU 212 Mh44
Lokitanyaly ◎ EAK 212 Mh44
Lo Kitaung ◎ EAK 205 Mh43
Loknja ◎ RUS 54 Mf17
Loko ◎ WAN 202 Ld41
Lokofe ◎ RDC 209 Mb46
Lokoja ◎ WAN 202 Ld42
Lokolama ◎ RDC 211 Lk47
Lokolia ◎ RDC 208 Ma46
Lokolo ≋ RDC 208 Lk46
Lokomby ◎ RM 228 Nd57
Lokomo ◎ CAM 203 Lh44
Lokomo ≋ CAM 203 Lh44
Lokon ▲ RI 131 Rc45

M

Maji – Manuel Alves Grande

Maji ETH 205 Mh42
Majiahewan VRC (NHZ) 96 Qc27
Majie VRC (YUN) 117 Qb33
Majilovac SCG 46 Mb46
Majimalu EAT 215 Mh48
Maji Moto EAT 212 Mh46
Majkop RUS (ADY) 57 Na23
Majli-Saj KS 81 Og25
Majorskij RUS 57 Na22
Majors Place USA (NV) 244 Ec26
Majskij RUS (KBA) 74 Nc24
Majskij RUS 102 Re19
Majuba Hill SA 225 Me59
Majuro Atoll MH 163 Tc17
Majz YE 72 Nb37
Maka LB 200 Ke42
Maka SN 191 Kb37
Maka SN 191 Kc39
Makabana RCB 210 Lg47
Makado ZW 222 Me56
Maka Gouye SN 191 Kc39
Makaha USA (HI) 240 Ca35
Makah Ind. Res. USA 242 Dh21
Makak CAM 203 Lf44
Makaka RCB 210 Lg47
Makalamabedi RB 221 Mb56
Makale RI 131 Qk47
Makalehi RI 127 Rc44
Makallé RA (CH) 301 Ha59
Makaloge MOC 219 Mh52
Makalondi RN 193 La39
Makalu-Barun N.P. NEP 92 Pd32
Makalu I NEP/VRC 92 Pd31
Makamba BU 214 Me48
Makami EAT 215 Mj48
Makanda RCB 210 Lg47
Makanjila MW 219 Mh52
Makanshy KZ 88 Pb22
Makantaka NIC 266 Fh39
Makapak Valley SA 222 Me58
Makaranangang RI 133 Qk49
Makar'evskaja RUS 13 Mh15
Makarevyči UA 39 Mf39
Makarfi WAN 194 Ld40
Makari CAM 195 Lh39
Makari GUY 282 Ha43
Makaroa NZ 161 Te68
Makarov RUS 103 Sb21
Makarov Basin 310 Ed01
Makarovo RUS 55 Nb19
Makarska HR 43 Ls47
Makasa Z 214 Mf50
Makassar RI 131 Qk48
Makassar Strait RI 131 Qj47
Makat KZ 11 Nc09
Makatéa F 171 Cf53
Makaw MYA 117 Pj32
Makay RM 228 Nc56
Makedade TIM 136 Rc50
Makedonien GR 48 Mb50
Makekeda RDC 209 Md44
Makekeda RDC 209 Me44
Makemo Atoll F (FPY) 171 Cj54
Makeni WAL 200 Kd41
Makere EAT 214 Mf48
Maketu NZ 160 Tj64
Makgadikgadi Pans RB 221 Mc56
Makgadikgadi Pans N.P. RB 221 Mc56
Makhaleng LS 225 Md60
Makhdumnagar IND (UPH) 111 Pb32
Makhmur IRQ 69 Nb28
Makhtal IND (APH) 112 Oj37
Makhu IND (PJB) 110 Oh30
Maki ETH 206 Mk42
Maki RI 135 Rh47
Makifeng CDN (MB) 248 Ek19
Makijivka UA 57 Mk21
Makina SOL 167 Ta50
Makindu EAK 215 Mj47
Makingeny Cave EAK 212 Mh45
Makira SOL 167 Ta51
Makiya Z 218 Md52
Makkah KSA 70 Mk35
Makkovik CDN 235 Gd08
Makkuva IND (APH) 113 Pb36
Makli Hills PK 84 Od33
Maknassy TN 182 Le28
Makó H 41 Ma44
Mako SN 191 Kd39
Makojo EAT 212 Mg46
Makokibatan Lake CDN 249 Fg20
Makokou G 203 Lg45
Makoli Z 218 Md54
Makona LB/RG 200 Kf41
Makonde EAT 219 Mh51
Makonde Plateau EAT 219 Mk51
Makondo Z 217 Mb52
Makongo GH 201 Kk41
Makongolosi EAT 214 Mg50
Makoop Lake CDN 249 Fe19
Makopong RB 221 Mb58
Makor CAM 203 Lg42
Makosa RDC 214 Me49
Makose ZW 218 Mg54
Makotipoko RCB 208 Lj46
Makou VRC (HUB) 99 Qg30
Makoua RCB 203 Lh46
Makoua TCH 204 Ma41
Makov SK 40 Lt41
Makovo MK 48 Mb49
Makovo RUS 74 Ne22
Mąkowarsko PL 38 Ls37
Maków Mazowiecki PL 39 Mb38
Makrakómi GR 50 Mc52
Makran Coast Range PK 84 Ob33
Makrany BY 39 Me39
Makrigialós GR 51 Mf55
Makrinítsa GR 50 Md51
Makriráhi GR 50 Md51
Makronísi GR 50 Me53
Maksatiha RUS 54 Mh17
Maksi IND (MPH) 112 Oj34
Maksudangarh IND (MPH) 112 Oj33
Maktau EAK 215 Mk47
Makthar TN 182 Le28
Maku IR 76 Nc26
Makuende RDC 214 Me49
Makulakubu RDC 214 Mc50
Makum IND (ASM) 117 Ph32
Makumbako EAT 215 Mh50
Makumbi RDC 211 Ma48
Makumbi ZW 218 Mf54
Makunda RB 221 Ma57
Makunduchi EAT 215 Mk49
Makungo SP 213 Nb45
Makungu EAT 215 Mh50
Makunguvilo EAT 215 Mj50
Makungwe Z 218 Mf51
Makunudu Atoll MV 114 Og42
Makurazaki J 107 Rf30
Makurdi WAN 202 Le42
Makushin Vol. USA 238 Bg19
Makusi Island Z 221 Mc54
Makutano EAK 212 Mh44
Makutano EAK 212 Mh45
Makutano EAK 212 Mh45
Makutano EAK 212 Mj46
Makutano EAK 215 Mj47
Makuti ZW 218 Me54
Makuyeh IR 78 Ng31
Makuyuni EAT 215 Mj47
Makwate RB 221 Md57
Makwiro ZW 218 Mf54
Mâl RIM 191 Kd37
Mala PE 290 Gb52
Mala PE 290 Gb52
Mala RI 134 Rf46
Malå S 12 Lk13
Mala A.L. AUS 148 Rf56
Malabang RP 127 Rc42
Malabar SY 226 Nd50
Malabar Coast IND 114 Og40
Malabar, Gunung RI 132 Qd49
Malabo GQ 202 Le44
Malabo RI 131 Qk47
Malabuñgan RP 126 Qj41
Malacacheta BR (MG) 299 Hj54
Malacacheta, T.I. BR 282 Gk44
Malacca IND (AAN) 115 Pg41
Malacca MAL 121 Ob44
Malacky SK 40 Lr42
Malad City USA (ID) 245 Ed24
Maladzečna BY 19 Mg36
Malá Fatra, N.P. SK 41 Lu41
Málaga CO 280 Gd42
Málaga E 30 Kq46
Malaga USA (NM) 247 Eh29
Malagan Beach Resort PNG 166 Sf47
Malagarasi EAT 214 Mf48
Malagarasi EAT 214 Mf48
Malagón E 31 Kr49
Malahar RI 133 Ra50
Malahide Castle IRL 22 Ko37
Mălăiești RO 46 Mc45
Malaimbandy RM 228 Nc56
Malaita SA 222 Me58
Malaita SOL 167 Ta50
Malaja Belaja RUS 94 Qb19
Malaja Kuril'skaja grjada RUS 103 Sd24
Malaja Višera RUS 54 Mg16
Malakal SUD 205 Mf41
Malakand PK 83 Of28
Malakata PNG 165 Se46
Malakheti NEP 92 Pa31
Mala Kladuša BIH 43 Lq45
Malaknagiri IND (ORS) 113 Pa36
Malakula VU 168 Td54
Malakwa CDN (BC) 242 Ea20
Malakwal PK 83 Og29
Malala PNG 165 Sc48
Malala PNG 165 Sd48
Malalamai PNG 165 Sd48
Malalaua PNG 165 Sd50
Malam PNG 165 Sb50
Malambo EAT 214 Mf49
Malambo EAT 215 Mh47
Mala Mechet UA 47 Mj45
Malam Jabba Ski resort PK 83 Og28
Malammaduri WAN 194 Le39
Malampaka EAT 214 Mg47
Malampuzha IND (KER) 114 Oj41
Malanda AUS (QLD) 155 Sc54
Malandji RDC 211 Mb48
Malang RI 132 Qg49
Malanga MOC 219 Mj52
Malangas RP 127 Rb42
Malangbong RI 132 Qe49
Malangke RI 131 Ra47
Malanje ANG 210 Lj50
Malanów PL 38 Lt39
Malanut Bay RP 126 Qk41
Malanville DY 194 Lb40
Malapatan RP 127 Rc43
Malar PK 84 Oc32
Malarba CAM 203 Lg42
Mälaren S 15 Lr31
Malargüe RA (MD) 300 Gf63
Malargüe RA 300 Gf63
Malartic CDN (QC) 254 Ga21
Malaryta BY 39 Me39
Malasait PNG 166 Sf48
Mala Serdoba RUS 55 Nc19
Malaspina Glacier USA 240 Ck16
Malatswana RB 221 Mb58
Malatya TR 67 Mk26
Malaut IND (PJB) 110 Oh30
Malavalli IND (KTK) 115 Oj40
Malavi IR 76 Nd29
Mala Vyska UA 56 Mf21
Malawali MAL 126 Qj42
Malawan IND (UPH) 111 Ok32
Malawi 175 Mb11
Malawiya SUD 199 Mj39
Malay RP 127 Ra40
Malaybalay RP 127 Rc41
Malayer IR 76 Ne28
Malay Peninsula MAL 121 Qb43
Malaysia MAL 61 Qa09
Malazgirt TR 67 Nb26
Malbaza RN 194 Lc39
Malbebale Plain EAK 206 Mk44
Malbhanguwa NEP 92 Pa31
Malbon AUS (QLD) 154 Sa56
Malbon Vale AUS (QLD) 154 Rk56
Malbooma AUS (SA) 158 Rh61
Malbork PL 38 Lu36
Malboro CDN (AB) 243 Eb19
Malbrán RA (SE) 301 Gj60
Malbuisson F 27 Lg44
Malca Rie SP 213 Na44
Malcésine I 42 Ll45
Malchin D 35 Ln37
Malchow D 35 Ln37
Malcolm AUS (WA) 150 Ra60
Maldegem B 25 Ld39
Malden USA (MO) 253 Ff27
Maldives MV 61 Ob09
Maldives MV 108 Oc17
Maldon AUS (VIC) 159 Sc64
Maldon GB 23 La39
Maldonado EC 284 Ga45
Maldonado ROU 301 Hc63
Maldybai KZ 81 Og24
Małdyty PL 39 Lu37
Malè I 42 Ll44
Male MV 114 Og43
Male MYA 117 Pj34
Male PNG 165 Sc48
Male WAL 200 Ke42
Malea, Gunung RI 128 Pk45
Malealea LS 225 Md60
Malee Downs AUS (SA) 158 Sa64
Małe Gacno PL 38 Lt37
Malegaon IND (MHT) 112 Oh35
Malegaon Jahagir IND (MHT) 112 Oj35
Malei MOC 219 Mj54
Maleit SUD 205 Me42
Malek SUD 205 Mf42
Malekan IR 76 Nd27
Malé Karpaty CZ 40 Ls42
Malélé RCB 210 Lg48
Malema MOC 219 Mj53
Malé Malé RN 194 Le39
Malemba-Nkulu RDC 214 Md50
Máleme GR 50 Md55
Malème-Hodar SN 191 Kc38
Malena RA (CD) 300 Gh62
Malendo WAN 194 Lc40
Malendok Island PNG 166 Sg47
Malengwa Z 217 Mb53
Malente D 35 Ll36
Malesherbes F 25 Lc42
Malestan AFG 82 Od29
Malestroit F 24 Ks43
Maleta RUS 94 Qe20
Maletsunyane Falls LS 225 Me60
Malgobek RUS (ING) 74 Nc24
Malgrat de Mar E 32 Lc49
Malha SUD 197 Md38
Malhada BR (BA) 294 Hj53
Malhah IRQ 69 Nb28
Malhanskij hrebet RUS 94 Qe20
Malheur Nat. Wildlife Refuge USA 244 Ea24
Malhia YV 282 Gj43
Mali RDC 214 Md47
Mali RG 191 Kd39
Mali 175 Kb08
Mália GR 51 Mf55
Malian He VRC 96 Qd27
Malibu USA (CA) 246 Ea29
Mali Đerdap SCG 46 Mb46
Maligaya RP 125 Ra38
Malihabad IND (UPH) 111 Pa32
Mali Hka MYA 117 Pj33
Mali Island MYA 118 Pk39
Maliku RI 131 Rb46
Malili RI 131 Ra47
Målilla S 17 Lq33
Mali Lošinj HR 43 Lp46
Malimán de Arriba RA (SJ) 300 Gf60
Malimasindi ZW 222 Me55
Malimbong RI 131 Qk47
Malinalco MEX 264 Fa36
Malinau RI 130 Qj44
Malindang, Mount RP 127 Rb41
Malindi EAK 215 Na47
Malindi EAT 215 Mk48
Malindi Marine N.P. EAK 213 Na47
Malinga G 210 Lg47
Malingping RI 132 Qd49
Malin Head IRL 20 Kn35
Maliniec PL 38 Lt38
Malinke SN 191 Kc39
Malino RI 133 Qk48
Malino RI 131 Ra46
Malino, Gunung RI 131 Ra45
Malinska HR 43 Lp45
Malinyi EAT 215 Mj50
Malipari IND (WBG) 116 Pe32
Maliq AL 48 Ma50
Mal i Qarrishtë AL 48 Ma50
Mal i Shpatit AL 48 Ma49
Malita RP 127 Rc42
Maliya IND (GUJ) 112 Of34
Maljamar USA (NM) 247 Ej29
Maljiševo SCG 48 Ma48
Malka Mari EAK 206 Na43
Malka Mari N.P. EAK 213 Na43
Malkapur IND (MHT) 112 Og37
Malkapur IND (MHT) 112 Oj35
Malkapur IND (APH) 113 Ok37
Malkara TR 52 Mg50
Malko Tărnovo BG 49 Mj49
Malla IND (KTK) 112 Oj37
Mallacoota AUS (VIC) 159 Se64
Mallacoota Inlet AUS 159 Se64
Mallaig GB 20 Kp34
Mallala AUS (SA) 158 Rk63
Mallanganee AUS (NSW) 157 Sg60
Mallaoua RN 194 Le39
Mallaranny IRL 20 Kl37
Mallawî ET 185 Mf32
Malleco RCH 304 Gd65
Mallee Cliffs N.P. AUS 159 Sb63
Mallee Highway AUS 158 Sa63
Mallén E 29 Kt51
Málles Venosta = Mals im Vinschgau I 42 Ll44
Mallet BR (PR) 302 He58
Mallnitz A 37 Lo44
Mallorca E 32 Ld51
Mallow IRL 22 Km38
Mallwyd GB 22 Kr38
Malmal PNG 166 Sf48
Malmbäck S 17 Lp33
Malmbanan S/N 12 Lk11
Malmberget S 12 Ma12
Malmédy B 25 Lg40
Malmesbury GB 23 Ks39
Malmesbury SA 224 Lk62
Malmköping S 15 Lr31
Malmö S 17 Lo35
Malmo USA (MN) 251 Fd22
Malmslätt S 15 Lq32
Malmyž RUS 55 Nf17
Malngin A.L. AUS 145 Re54
Malo VU 168 Td53
Maloaini SOL 166 Sh49
Maloarhangel'sk RUS 54 Mj19
Maloarhangel'sk RUS 94 Qe20
Maloca BR (PA) 287 Hc45
Maloca do Gonçalo BR (PA) 287 Hb49
Maloca Velha BR (PA) 283 Hc44
Malocu Macu BR (RR) 282 Gj44
Maloe BY 19 Me37
Maloelap Atoll MH 163 Tc17
Malojapass CH 36 Lk44
Malojaroslavec RUS 54 Mj18
Malokuril'skoe RUS 103 Sd24
Malole Z 218 Mf51
Malolo FJI 169 Tj54
Malolo Plantation Lodge PNG 165 Sc48
Malolos RP 125 Ra38
Malolotja Nature Reserve SD 225 Mf59
Malom PNG 166 Sf47
Małomice PL 38 Lq39
Malonda RDC 211 Mc50
Malone USA (FL) 259 Fh30
Malone USA (NY) 257 Gc23
Malong VRC (YUN) 117 Qb33
Malonga RDC 217 Mb51
Ma³opolska PL 39 Ma40
Måløy N 14 Lf29
Mal Pais - Santa Teresa CR 266 Fh41
Malpartida de Plasencia E 30 Ko49
Malpas Hut AUS (QLD) 154 Sb55
Malpaso MEX (JLC) 263 Eh35
Malpaso MEX (ZCT) 263 Ej34
Malpe Beach IND 114 Oh40
Malpica de Bergantiños E 28 Km53
Mālpils LV 19 Me33
Malpura IND (RJT) 110 Oh32
Mals im Vinschgau = Málles Venosta I 42 Ll44
Malta I 44 Lp55
Malta LV 19 Mg34
Malta LV 19 Mh34
Malta M 44 Lp55
Malta USA (MT) 243 Eg21
Malta USA (OH) 257 Fk26
Maltahöhe NAM 220 Lj58
Maltam CAM 195 Lh39
Maltatal A 37 Lo44
Maltee AUS (SA) 158 Rg62
Malton GB 23 Ku36
Malu VRC (GZG) 100 Qd35
Maluera MOC 218 Mf53
Małujowice PL 38 Ls40
Malukalukuang RI 133 Qj48
Maluku RDC 210 Lh48
Malumfashi WAN 194 Ld40
Malum Islands PNG 166 Sh47
Malunda RI 131 Qk47
Malung S 15 Lo30
Malungsfors S 15 Lo30
Malungwishi RDC 218 Md51
Malur IND (KTK) 115 Oj40
Maluso RP 127 Ra42
Maluszyn PL 39 Lu40
Malut SUD 205 Mg40
Maluti LS 225 Me60
Maluu SOL 167 Ta50
Malvan IND (MHT) 112 Og37
Malvas PE 290 Gb50
Malvern USA (AR) 253 Fd28
Malwal SUD 205 Mf41
Malya EAT 214 Mg47
Malyj Abakan RUS 89 Pe20
Malyj Čuraševo RUS (CHU) 55 Nd18
Malyj Derbety RUS (KAL) 55 Nc22
Malyj Enisej RUS 94 Pj20
Malyj Naryn KS 81 Oj25
Malyn UA 56 Me20
Mały Płock PL 39 Mc37
Malyševo RUS 55 Na18
Mamad RP 127 Rb42
Mamadys RUS (TAR) 55 Nf18
Mamãe Ana BR (PA) 287 Hb48
Mamaevom kurgane RUS 55 Nc21
Mama Hatun Türbesi TR 67 Na26
Mamaia RO 47 Mj46
Mamak TR 53 Mn51
Mamala MOC 219 Mk53
Mamallapuram IND (TNU) 115 Pa40
Mamallapuram IND 115 Pa40
Mamallapuram Beach IND 115 Pa40
Mamalyha UA 47 Mg42
Mamana Island = Rum Cay BS 261 Gc34
Mamanguape BR (PB) 289 Jc49
Mamanuca Group FJI 169 Tj54
Mamâri SN 191 Kd38
Mamasa RI 131 Qk47
Mamasın Baraj TR 53 Mp52
Mamasiware RI 135 Rh47
Mamba EAT 215 Mh48
Mamba LB 200 Ke42
Mamba RDC 214 Md50
Mambai BR (GO) 294 Hg53
Mambajao RP 127 Rc41
Mambal CAM 203 Lg42
Mambali EAT 214 Mg48
Mambasa RDC 209 Me45
Mambeco MOC 222 Mg57
Mamberamo RI 135 Rk47
Mamberamo Delta RI 135 Rj46
Mamberamo-Foja Mountains-Rouffaer Reserves RI 135 Rk47
Mambéré RCA 203 Lh43
Mambi RI 131 Qk47
Mambia RG 200 Kd41
Mambila Mountains CAM/WAN 203 Lf42
Mambili RCB 203 Lh45
Mambilima Falls Z 218 Me51
Mambiri RMM 192 Kf39
Mambolo WAL 200 Kd41
Mambonde ANG 216 Lh53
Mamborê BR (PR) 298 Hd58
Mambova Z 217 Mc54
Mambova Rapids RB/NAM 221 Mc54
Mambrui EAK 215 Na47
Mamburao RP 124 Ra39
Mambusao RP 127 Rb40
Mambwe Z 214 Mf50
Mamcai RI 135 Rh46
Mamda IND (APH) 113 Ok36
Mamedkala RUS (DAG) 74 Ne24
Mameigwess Lake CDN 249 Ff19
Mamelodi SA 221 Me58
Mamers F 24 La42
Mamfe CAM 202 Le43
Mamili N.P. NAM 221 Mb55
Mamiña RCH 296 Gf56
Maminigui CI 201 Kh42
Mamir Pawa GUY 282 Ha44
Mamisi RI 135 Rh47
Mamit IND (MZR) 116 Pg34
Mammanat RN 188 Ld36
Mammoth Cave AUS 150 Qh63
Mammoth Cave N.P. USA 258 Fg27
Mammoth Hot Springs USA (WY) 245 Ee23
Mammoth Lakes USA (CA) 244 Ea27
Mammoth Springs USA (AR) 253 Fe27
Mamoadate, T.I. BR 291 Ge51
Mamoeiro BR (AC) 291 Gf50
Mamonas BR (MG) 294 Hj53
Mamonovo RUS 39 Lu36
Mamoré BOL/BR 291 Gh51
Mamoriá BR (AM) 291 Gg49
Mamou RG 200 Kd40
Mamoudzou F 226 Nc52
Mampikony RM 228 Nd54
Mampodre E 28 Kp53
Mampong GH 201 Kk42
Mampongtin Range GH 201 Kk42
Mamshit IL 68 Mh30
Mamu WAN 202 Lb42
Mamudo MOC 219 Mj52
Mamue Choique RA (RN) 304 Ge66
Mamuil Malal, P. RA/RCH 304 Ge65
Mamuju RI 131 Qk47
Mamulique MEX (NL) 263 Ek32
Mamuno RB 221 Ma57
Mamure Kalesi TR 66 Mg27
Mamuru BR 287 Hb47
Mamykovo RUS (TAR) 55 Nf18
Man CI 200 Kg42
Man RCA 203 Lh42
Mana F 283 Hd43
Mana F 283 Hd43
Manacacias CO 280 Gd44
Mana Camp ZW 218 Me53
Manacapurú BR (AM) 286 Gk47
Manacapurú BR 286 Gk47
Manacor E 32 Ld51
Manadhoo MV 114 Og43
Manado RI 131 Rc45
Manaďv UA 41 Mf41
Managua NIC 266 Fg39
Manah OM 79 Nj34
Manaíra BR (PB) 289 Ja49
Manajuare CO 281 Ge43
Manakamana NEP 92 Pc31
Manakana RM 228 Nd54
Manakara RM 228 Nd57
Manak Chowk and Havelis (Jaisalmer) IND 110 Of32
Manakha YE 72 Nb38
Manalalondo RM 228 Nd55
Manali IND (HPH) 111 Oj29
Manama UAE 79 Nh33
Manama ZW 222 Me56
Manamadurai IND (TNU) 115 Ok42
Manambaro RM 228 Nd58
Manambolo RM 228 Nc55
Manambolosy RM 228 Ne54
Manambondro RM 228 Nd57
Manamensalo FIN 13 Md13
Manami RI 135 Rh47
Manam Island PNG 165 Sc48
Manamo YV 282 Gj41
Manamoc Island RP 127 Ra40
Mananara RM 228 Nd57
Mananara Avaratra RM 228 Ne54
Manandona RM 228 Nd56
Mananga RI 136 Rb50
Manangatang AUS (VIC) 159 Sb63
Manangoora AUS (NT) 145 Rj53
Mananjary RM 228 Ne56
Manankoro RMM 200 Kg40
Manantali RMM 191 Ke39
Manantenina RM 228 Nd58
Manantoddy IND (KER) 114 Oj41
Mananur IND (APH) 113 Ok37
Manaparai IND (TNU) 115 Ok41
Mana Pass VRC/IND 92 Ok30
Mana Pools N.P. ZW 218 Me53
Manaprie YV 281 Gg41
Manaquiri BR (AM) 286 Gk47
Manari BR (PE) 295 Jb50
Manari PNG 165 Sd50
Manariã BR (AM) 285 Gg48
Manas PE 290 Gb51
Manas VRC (XUZ) 89 Pd23
Manasarowar = Mapam Yumco VRC 92 Pa30
Manas He VRC 89 Pc23
Manas Hu VRC 89 Pd23
Manaskent RUS (DAG) 74 Nd24
Manaslu I NEP 92 Pc31
Manassas USA (VA) 257 Gb26
Manas Tiger Reserve IND 116 Pf32
Manas Tiger Reserve IND 116 Pf32
Manastir Dečani SCG 48 Ma48
Manastir Đurđevi Stupovi SCG 48 Lu48
Mănăstirea RO 47 Mg46
Mănăstirea Bistrița RO 47 Mg44
Mănăstirea Cocoș RO 47 Mj45
Mănăstirea Cozia RO 46 Me45
Mănăstirea Hîncu MD 47 Mj43
Mănăstirea Humorului RO 47 Mf43
Mănăstirea Hurezi RO 46 Md45
Mănăstirea Sinaia RO 47 Mf45
Mănăstirea Snagov RO 47 Mg46
Manastir Gračanica SCG 48 Mb48
Mănăstirile Basarabi RO 47 Mj46
Manastir Kalenić SCG 48 Ma47
Manastir Ljubostinja SCG 48 Mb47
Manastir Manasija SCG 48 Mb46
Manastir Mileševa SCG 48 Lu47
Manastir Ostrog SCG 48 Lu48
Manastir Ravanica SCG 48 Mb47
Manastir Savina SCG 48 Lt48
Manastir Sopoćani SCG 48 Ma47
Manastir Studenica SCG 48 Ma47
Manastir Žiča SCG 48 Ma47
Manat KZ 89 Pb21
Manatí C 269 Ga34
Manatí C 269 Gb35
Manati USA (PR) 271 Gg36
Manatial BOL 297 Gj55
Manatuto TIM 136 Rc50
Manau PNG 165 Sd50
Man'aung MYA 118 Pg36
Manaure CO 280 Gd40
Manaus BR (AM) 286 Gk47
Manavgat TR 53 Mm54
Manavgat Baraj TR 53 Mm54
Manavgat Şelâlesi TR 53 Mm54
Manawar IND (MPH) 112 Oh34
Manawoka RI 134 Rf48
Manay RP 127 Rd42
Manayana Rock Paintings RB 221 Mc58
Mañazo PE 291 Ge53
Manba VRC (YUN) 117 Qa34
Manbazar IND (WBG) 116 Pd34
Manbej SYR 68 Mj27
Mancha Khiri THA 119 Qb37
Mancha Real E 31 Kr47
Mancheng Hanmu Tombs VRC 97 Qh26
Manchester GB 23 Ks37
Manchester USA (IA) 251 Fe24
Manchester USA (TN) 259 Fh28
Manchester USA (KY) 259 Fj27
Manchester USA (CT) 257 Gd25
Manchester USA (NH) 257 Ge24
Manchester Center USA (VT) 257 Gd24
Manchhar Lake PK 84 Od32
Manching D 37 Lm42
Manchirayal IND (APH) 113 Ok36
Manchis MAL 121 Qb44
Manchok WAN 194 Le41
Manchuria VRC 87 Ra10
Manciano I 44 Lm48
Máncora PE 284 Fk48
Mancos USA (CO) 247 Ef27
Mand PK 84 Ob32
Manda BD 116 Pe33
Manda EAT 214 Mg50
Manda EAT 219 Mh51
Manda TCH 204 Lk41
Mandabe RM 228 Nc56
Mandagadde IND (KTK) 114 Oh40
Mandaguari BR (PR) 298 He57
Mandah RI 129 Qb46
Mandai PK 84 Oe31
Manda Island EAK 213 Na47
Mandal MNG 94 Pk21
Mandal MNG 94 Qd21
Mandal N 14 Lh32
Mandalay MYA 117 Pj35
Mandalay N.W.R. USA 253 Fe31
Mandalgarh IND (RJT) 110 Oh33
Mandalgov' MNG 94 Qd23
Mandali IRQ 69 Nc29
Mandamabgwe ZW 222 Mf56
Mandan USA (ND) 250 Ek22
Mandaon RP 125 Rb39
Mandapeta IND (APH) 113 Pb37
Manda, P.N.de TCH 195 Lk41
Mandara LAR 189 Lg32
Mandara Mountains CAM/WAN 195 Lg40
Mándas I 33 Lk51
Mandasip RI 128 Pk45
Mandaue RP 127 Rb40
Mandel AFG 82 Oa29
Mandélia TCH 195 Lh40
Mandem IND (CGH) 113 Pa36
Mandera EAK 213 Na44
Mandera USA (CA) 244 Dk27
Mandeville JA 269 Gb36
Mandheera SP 207 Nc41
Mandi IND (GUJ) 112 Og35
Mandi IND (HPH) 111 Oj30
Mandiakoy RMM 193 Kj37
Mandiakur RMM 192 Kh39
Mandiana RG 200 Kf40
Mandi Bahauddin PK 83 Og29
Mandi Burewala PK 83 Og30
Mandicaba BR (PR) 298 Hd57
Mandi Dabwali IND (PJB) 110 Oh31
Mandié MOC 218 Mg54
Mandi Langwé CAM 203 Lf43
Mandimba MOC 219 Mh53
Mandioli RI 134 Rd46
Mandira IND 113 Pc34
Mandji = Sangala G 210 Lf46
Mandla IND (MPH) 113 Pa34
Mandlakazi MOC 222 Mg58
Mando WAN 194 Ld40
Mandoli IND (RJT) 110 Og33
Mandon RI 135 Rj46
Mandor RI 130 Qe45
Mandoro RDC 209 Me43
Mandoto RM 228 Nd55
Mandoul TCH 203 Lj41
Mandouri RT 201 La40
Mândra RO 46 Md45
Mandráki GR 51 Mh54
Mandrare RM 228 Nd58
Mandritsara RM 227 Ne53
Mandronarivo RM 228 Nc56
Mandrosonoro RM 228 Nd56
Mandsaur IND (MPH) 112 Oh34
Mandu IND 112 Oh34
Mandu IND (JKD) 113 Pc34
Mandul RI 131 Qj44
Mandumbua ANG 217 Ma53
Mandundu Z 217 Mb54
Mandurah AUS (WA) 150 Qh62
Mandúria I 45 Ls50
Mandvi IND (GUJ) 112 Oe34
Mandwa Beach IND 112 Og36
Mandya IND (KTK) 115 Oj40
Mané BF 193 Kk39
Måne N 14 Lj31
Maneadero C 268 Fk34
Maneadero MEX (BC) 246 Eb30
Manegaon IND (MPH) 113 Ok34
Mané Kondjo TCH 195 Lk40
Maner IND (BIH) 113 Pc33
Manèrbio I 42 Ll45
Maneromango EAT 215 Mk49
Maneron Beach RI 132 Qg49
Maneroo AUS (QLD) 154 Sb57
Manevyči UA 39 Mf39
Manfalût ET 185 Mf32
Manfeilong VRC (YUN) 117 Qa35
Manfred AUS (WA) 146 Qj59
Manfred Downs AUS (QLD) 154 Sa56
Manfredónia I 45 Lq49
Manga BF 201 Kk40
Manga BR (MG) 294 Hj53
Manga CAM 203 Lg42
Manga PNG 166 Sg48
Manga RN 195 Lg38
Mangada RDC 209 Md44
Mangada RDC 209 Me44
Manga Grande ANG 210 Lg49
Mangai EAK 213 Na46
Mangai PNG 166 Sf47
Mangai RDC 211 Lk48
Mangaïzé RN 193 La38
Mangalagiri IND (APH) 113 Pa37
Mangalia RO 47 Mj47
Mangalmé TCH 204 Lk39
Mangalore AUS (VIC) 159 Sc64
Mangalore AUS (QLD) 157 Sd59
Mangalore IND (KTK) 114 Oh40
Mangalvedha IND (MHT) 112 Oh37
Mangamaunu NZ 161 Tg67
Mangamila RM 228 Nd55
Mangango Z 217 Mc53
Manganti RI 128 Qa46
Mangaon IND (MHT) 112 Og36
Mangarwar IND (RJT) 112 Oh33
Mangawah IND (MPH) 113 Pa33
Mangaweka NZ 160 Th65
Mangaweka NZ 160 Tj65
Mangchang VRC (GZG) 100 Qd33
Mangdangshan VRC 106 Qj28
Mange PNG 165 Sd49
Mange WAL 200 Kd41
Mangen N 14 Lm31
Manger N 14 Lf30
Manggar RI 129 Qe47
Manggasi RI 135 Rj47
Manggopoh RI 128 Qa46
Mangho Pir PK 84 Od33
Manghystau KZ 74 Nf24
Manghystau shyghanaghy KZ 74 Nf23
Manghystau üstirti KZ 75 Ng24
Mangial IND (MHT) 112 Oj36
Mangindrano RM 227 Ne53
Mang'it UZB 75 Oa24
Mangkururrpa A.L. AUS 148 Re56
Manglaralto EC 284 Fk46
Manglares CO 280 Gb43
Mangla Reservoir PK 83 Og29
Manglar Zapoton MEX 265 Fd38
Mangnai VRC (QHI) 91 Pf27
Mangnai Zhen VRC (QHI) 91 Pf26
Mangoaka RM 227 Ne52
Mangochi MW 219 Mh53
Mango Creek BH 265 Ff37
Mango Creek BH 265 Ff37
Mangoky RM 228 Nc56
Mangoky RM 228 Nc57
Mangole RI 134 Rc46
Mangom CAM 203 Lg42
Mangombe RDC 209 Md46
Mangonui NZ 160 Tg63
Mangoro RM 228 Ne55
Mangoudara BF 201 Kh41
Mangral IND (GUJ) 112 Of35
Mangrove Cay BS 261 Ga32
Mangrove Cay BS 261 Gb33
Mangrul Pir IND (MHT) 112 Oj35
Mangshan VRC 99 Qg28
Mangualde P 28 Kn50
Manguchar PK 84 Od31
Mangueigne TCH 204 Ma40
Mangueira, T.I. BR 282 Gk44
Mangueirinha BR (PR) 302 Hd58
Manguel Creek AUS (WA) 144 Rb54
Mangui VRC (NMZ) 95 Rb19
Manguito C 268 Fk34
Mangum USA (OK) 252 Fa28
Mangungu RDC 210 Lj48
Mangunza Z 218 Md54
Mangut RUS 95 Qg21
Mangwe ZW 222 Mf55
Manhamade MOC 219 Mj54
Manhao VRC (YUN) 117 Qb34
Manhattan USA (MT) 245 Ee23
Manhattan USA (KS) 251 Fb26
Manhica MOC 222 Mg58
Manhuaçu BR 299 Hj55
Manhuaçu BR (MG) 299 Hj56
Manhumirim BR (MG) 299 Hk56
Manhup Kale UA 57 Mg23
Mani CO 280 Gd43
Máni GR 50 Mc54
Mani RDC 211 Mc49
Mani TCH 195 Lh39
Mani WAN 194 Ld39
Mania RM 228 Nd56
Maniago I 43 Ln44
Mania-Muna RDC 211 Mb50
Maniapure YV 281 Gg42
Manicaland ZW 222 Mf55
Manicani Island RP 127 Rc40
Manicoré BR (AM) 286 Gk48
Manicoré BR 286 Gk49
Manicouagan CDN (QC) 254 Gf20
Manifah KSA 71 Ne32
Maniganggo VRC (SCH) 98 Pk30
Manigotagan CDN (MB) 248 Fb20
Manihari IND (BIH) 116 Pd33
Manihi Atoll F (FPY) 171 Ch53
Manihiki Atoll NZ 163 Ud21
Manika IND (JKD) 113 Pc34
Manika RDC 217 Mc51
Manikganj BD 116 Pe34
Manikpur IND (UPH) 113 Pa33
Manila RP 125 Ra38
Manila USA (UT) 245 Ef25
Manila Bay RP 125 Ra38
Manilaid EST 18 Me32
Manildra AUS (NSW) 159 Se62
Manilla AUS (NSW) 157 Sf61
Maningrida AUS (NT) 145 Rh52
Maninjau RI 128 Qa46
Manipa RI 134 Rd47
Manipur IND 109 Pc13
Manisa TR 51 Mh52
Manises E 31 Ku49
Manissauá-Miçu BR 293 Hc51
Manistee USA (MI) 256 Fg23
Manistique USA (MI) 256 Fg23
Manitisque Lake USA 251 Fh22
Manitoba CDN 235 Fa08
Manito Lake CDN 243 Ef19
Manitou CDN (MB) 248 Fa21
Manitou CDN (QC) 254 Gh20
Manitou USA (OK) 252 Fa28
Manitou Lake CDN 248 Fd21
Manitoulin Island CDN 256 Fj23
Manitounuk Sound CDN 249 Gb18
Manitou Springs USA (CO) 245 Eh26
Manitouwadge CDN (ON) 249 Fh21
Manitowaning Lodge CDN 256 Fk23
Manitowish USA (WI) 251 Fe22
Manitowoc USA (WI) 256 Fg23
Manitsoq = Sukkertoppen DK 235 Hb05
Maniwaki CDN (QC) 254 Gc22
Maniwaki Ind. Res. CDN 254 Gb22
Maniwori RI 135 Rh47
Manizales CO 280 Gc43
Manja RM 228 Nc56
Manjakandriana RM 228 Nd55
Manjamba MOC 219 Mh52
Manjar Sumba IND (MHT) 112 Oh36
Manjeri IND (KER) 114 Oj41
Manjhand PK 84 Oe33
Manjira Wildlife Sanctuary IND 112 Ok36
Manjira W.S. IND 112 Ok37
Manjlegaon IND (MHT) 112 Oj36
Manjo CAM 202 Le43
Manjola ZW 218 Md54
Manjou CAM 203 Lg43
Manjra IND 112 Oj36
Mankachar IND (ASM) 116 Pe33
Mankanza RDC 208 Lk45
Månkarbo S 15 Ls30
Man Kat MYA 117 Pk35
Mankato USA (KS) 250 Fa26
Mankato USA (MN) 251 Fd23
Mankera PK 83 Of30
Mankhan MNG 94 Qa20
Mankhan Nature Reserve MNG 89 Pg22
Manki CAM 203 Lf43
Mankim CAM 203 Lg43
Mankono CI 201 Kg41
Mankpan GH 201 Kk41
Mankrangso GH 201 Kk42
Mankulam CL 115 Pa42
Manley Hot Springs USA (AK) 239 Ce13
Man Li MYA 117 Pj34
Manlleu E 32 Lc49
Manmad IND (MHT) 112 Oh35
Manna RI 129 Qb48
Manna Hill AUS (SA) 158 Rk62
Man-Namlet MYA 117 Pk34
Mannar CL 115 Ok42
Mannemkonda IND (ORS) 113 Pa36
Manners Creek AUS (NT) 149 Rj57
Mannheim D 36 Lj41
Manni VRC (TIB) 92 Pd28
Manning USA (ND) 250 Ej22
Manning USA (SC) 259 Fk29
Manning Prov. Park CDN 242 Dk21
Manning Range, Mount AUS 150 Qk60
Manning Strait SOL 167 Sj49
Manningtree GB 23 Lb39
Mann Ranges AUS 148 Re58
Mann River AUS 145 Rh52
Mannum AUS (SA) 158 Rk63
Mannville CDN (AB) 243 Ee19
Mano LB/WAL 200 Ke42
Mano WAL 200 Kd41
Manoá Pium, T.I. BR 282 Gk44
Manogongu LB 200 Ke42
Manohardi BD 116 Pf33
Manokwari RI 135 Rh46
Manokwari RI 135 Rh47
Manole BG 49 Me48
Manoleasa RO 47 Mh43
Manolo Fortich RP 127 Rc41
Manoma RUS 103 Rj21
Manombo Atsimo RM 228 Nb57
Manometimay RM 228 Nc56
Manompana RM 228 Ne54
Manonga EAT 212 Mg47
Manono RDC 214 Md49
Manonwa RDC 211 Mc48
Manor IND (MHT) 112 Og36
Manorhamilton IRL 20 Km36
Manori Beach IND 112 Og36
Manosque F 27 Lf47
Manou RCA 204 Ma41
Manouane CDN (QC) 254 Gc22
Manova WAL 200 Ke41
Manp'o DVRK 104 Rd25
Manpur IND (CGH) 113 Pa35
Manqabâd ET 185 Mf32
Manra KIR 163 Ub19
Manresa E 32 Lb49
Mansa IND (PJB) 110 Oh31
Mansa Z 218 Me51
Mansabá GNB 191 Kc39
Mansa Konko WAG 191 Kc39
Mansalay RP 125 Ra39
Man Sam MYA 117 Pj34
Mansar IND (MHT) 113 Ok35
Mansehra PK 83 Og28
Mansel Island CDN 235 Fd06
Mansfeld D 35 Lm39
Mansfield AUS (VIC) 159 Sd64
Mansfield GB 23 Kt37
Mansfield USA (AR) 253 Fc28
Mansfield USA (OH) 256 Fj25
Mansfield USA (PA) 257 Gb25
Mansfield Jetty USA (TX) 263 Fb32
Mansfiled USA (LA) 253 Fd30
Mansha Z 218 Mf51
Mansi MYA 117 Ph33
Mansiari IND (UTT) 111 Pa30
Mansidão BR (BA) 294 Hh51
Mansilla E 29 Kr52
Mansilla E 29 Ks52
Mansilla de las Mulas E 28 Kp52
Mansinha BR (TO) 294 Hg50
Mansión CR 266 Fh40
Mansle F 26 La45
Manso BR 293 Hc53
Mansôa GNB 191 Kc39
Manso au das Mortes BR 293 Hc53
Manson Creek CDN (BC) 241 Dh18
Manso-Nkwanta GH 201 Kk42
Mansoura DZ 181 Lc27
Mansourah DZ 181 Kk28
Mansur Abad IR 78 Ng31
Mansur Abad IR 77 Nk29
Mansura Ruins PK 85 Oe33
Manta DY 201 La40
Manta EC 284 Fk46
Mantadia-Andasibe, P.N.de RM 228 Ne55
Mantalinga RI 131 Ra47
Mantalingajan, Mount RP 126 Qj41
Mantamádos GR 51 Mg51
Mantanai Besar MAL 126 Qj42
Mantare EAT 214 Mg47
Mantaro PE 290 Gc51
Mantasoa RM 228 Nd55
Mantawa RI 131 Rb46
Manteca USA (CA) 244 Dk27
Mantecal YV 281 Gf42
Mantecal YV 281 Gh42
Mantehage RI 131 Rc45
Mantena BR (MG) 299 Hk55
Mantes-la-Jolie F 25 Lb42
Mantes-la-Ville F 25 Lb42
Manthani IND (APH) 113 Ok36
Manthiréa GR 50 Mc53
Manti USA (UT) 245 Ee26
Manticao RP 127 Rc41
Manto HN 266 Fg38
Manto PE 291 Gd52
Mantorp S 15 Lq32
Mantos Blancos RCH 296 Ge57
Mántova I 42 Ll45
Mantralayam IND (APH) 112 Oj38
Mäntsälä FIN 18 Mf30
Mänttä FIN 18 Me28
Mantua C 268 Fh34
Mantuan Downs AUS (QLD) 157 Sd58
Mantung AUS (SA) 158 Sa63
Mantup RI 132 Qg49
Manturovo RUS 55 Nc16
Mäntyharju FIN 18 Mg29
Mäntyluoto FIN 15 Mb29
Manu IND (TRP) 116 Pg34
Manú PE 291 Ge51
Manú PE 291 Ge52
Manu WAN 194 Lc39
Manuae Atoll F (FPY) 171 Cc54
Manua Islands USA 170 Bf53
Manubepium RI 135 Rh46
Manuc Bei MD 47 Mj44
Manuel MEX (TM) 263 Fa34
Manuel Alves BR 294 Hf51
Manuel Alves Grande BR 288 Hg49

X

Xichang – Yumbel

Xichang VRC (GZG) 100 Qe35
Xichang VRC (SCH) 117 Qb32
Xichong VRC (SCH) 99 Qc30
Xichou VRC (YUN) 100 Qc34
Xichú MEX (GJT) 264 Ek35
Xichuan VRC (HNN) 99 Qf29
Xicoténcatl MEX (TM) 263 Fa34
Xicotepec de Juarez MEX (PUE) 264 Fb35
Xidi VRC 106 Qk31
Xie BR 285 Gg45
Xieng Ngeun LAO 118 Qb36
Xien Hon LAO 118 Qa36
Xiezhou Guandimiao VRC 99 Qf28
Xifeng VRC (GSU) 99 Qd28
Xifeng VRC (GZH) 100 Qd32
Xifeng VRC (LNG) 104 Rc24
Xigangzi VRC (HLG) 102 Rd21
Xigaze VRC (TIB) 92 Pe31
Xihan Shui VRC 99 Qc29
Xi He VRC 96 Qa24
Xiheying VRC (HBI) 97 Qh26
Xi Hu VRC 106 Ra30
Xihua VRC (HNN) 106 Qh29
Xiis SP 207 Nd40
Xiji VRC (NHZ) 99 Qc28
Xi Jiang VRC 100 Qf34
Xijin Shuiku VRC 100 Qe34
Xijir Ulan Hu VRC 93 Pf28
Xijishui VRC (GSU) 96 Qc27
Xikou VRC (ZJG) 106 Ra31
Xikouzi VRC (NMZ) 95 Ra19
Xikrin do Rio Catete, T.I. BR 287 He49
Xilamuren Caoyuan VRC 97 Qf25
Xi Liao He VRC 104 Rb24
Xilin VRC (GZG) 100 Qc33
Xi Ling Xia Li VRC 99 Qf30
Xilinhot VRC (NMZ) 97 Qj24
Xilinji = Mohe VRC (HLG) 95 Rb19
Xıllı AZ 74 Ne26
Xilókastro GR 50 Mc52
Xilong-Shan Z.B. VRC 98 Qb28
Xime GNB 191 Kc40
Ximeng VRC (YUN) 117 Pk34
Ximucheng VRC (LNG) 104 Rb25
Xin VRC 106 Qj31
Xin'anjiang Sk. VRC 106 Qk31
Xin'ansuo VRC (YUN) 117 Qb34
Xinavane MOC 222 Mg58
Xin Barag Youqi VRC (NMZ) 95 Qj21
Xin Barag Zuoqi VRC (NMZ) 95 Qk21
Xinbin VRC (LNG) 104 Rc25
Xincai VRC (HNN) 106 Qh29
Xinchang VRC (GZH) 100 Qd33
Xinchang VRC (ZJG) 106 Ra31
Xincheng VRC (HBI) 97 Qh26
Xincheng Weijin Mu VRC 96 Pk26
Xinchuan Gang VRC 106 Ra29
Xindeng VRC (ZJG) 106 Qk31
Xindian VRC (HLG) 102 Rd23
Xindu VRC (SCH) 98 Qc30
Xinduqiao VRC (SCH) 98 Qa30
Xinfeng VRC (JGX) 101 Qh33
Xinfengjiang Shuiku VRC 101 Qh34
Xingalool SP 207 Ne41
Xing'an VRC (GZG) 100 Qf33
Xingan VRC (JGX) 106 Qh32
Xingcheng VRC (LNG) 104 Ra25
Xinge ANG 211 Lk50
Xingfeng VRC (GDG) 101 Qh33
Xingguo VRC (JGX) 101 Qh32
Xinghe VRC (NMZ) 97 Qg25
Xinghua VRC (JGS) 106 Qk29
Xingkai Hu VRC 102 Rg23
Xinglong VRC (HAN) 100 Qe36
Xinglong VRC (HBI) 97 Qj25
Xingning VRC (GDG) 101 Qh33
Xingod SP 207 Ne42
Xingou VRC (HUB) 99 Qg30
Xingpan VRC (GZG) 100 Qe35
Xingren VRC (GZH) 100 Qc33
Xingrenbu VRC (NHZ) 96 Qc27
Xingshan VRC (HUB) 99 Qf30
Xingtai VRC (HBI) 97 Qh27
Xingtang VRC (HBI) 97 Qh26
Xingu BR 277 Hb20
Xinguara BR (PA) 288 Hf49
Xingwen VRC (SCH) 99 Qc31
Xing Xian VRC (SAX) 97 Qf26
Xingxingxia VRC (XUZ) 91 Ph25
Xingyi VRC (GZH) 100 Qc33
Xinhe VRC (XUZ) 90 Pb25
Xinhuang VRC (HUN) 100 Qe32
Xining VRC (QHI) 96 Qa27
Xiniujiao VRC (GZG) 100 Qe35
Xinji VRC (HBI) 97 Qh27
Xinjian VRC (JGX) 106 Qh31
Xin Jiang VRC 106 Qj31
Xinjie VRC (YUN) 117 Qb33
Xinjie VRC (YUN) 100 Qc34
Xinjin VRC (SCH) 98 Qb30
Xinkai He VRC 104 Ra24
Xinlicheng VRC 104 Rc24
Xinlong VRC (SCH) 98 Qa30
Xinmin VRC (LNG) 104 Rb25
Xinning VRC (HUN) 100 Qf32
Xinqing VRC (HLG) 102 Re21
Xinshizhen VRC (SCH) 98 Qb31
Xintai VRC (SDG) 97 Qj28
Xintian VRC (HUN) 100 Qg33
Xin Xian VRC (HNN) 106 Qh30
Xinxiang VRC (HNN) 99 Qg28
Xinxing VRC (GDG) 100 Qg34
Xinxing VRC (HAN) 100 Qe36
Xinxu VRC (GZG) 100 Qd34
Xinyang VRC (HNN) 106 Qh29
Xinye VRC (HNN) 99 Qg29
Xinyi VRC (GDG) 100 Qf34
Xinyi VRC (JGS) 106 Qk28
Xinying VRC (HAN) 100 Qe36
Xinyu VRC (JGX) 106 Qh32
Xinyuan VRC (XUZ) 88 Pb24
Xinzhan VRC (GZH) 99 Qd32
Xinzhan VRC (HLG) 102 Rc23
Xinzhao Shan VRC 96 Qd26
Xinzhelin Shuiku VRC 106 Qh31
Xinzheng VRC (HNN) 99 Qg28
Xinzhou VRC (GZG) 100 Qd33
Xinzhou VRC (SAX) 97 Qg26
Xinzhu VRC (HUB) 106 Qh30
Xinzo de Limia E 28 Kn52
Xinzuotang VRC (GDG) 101 Qh34
Xiongyuecheng VRC (LNG) 104 Rb25
Xiping VRC (HNN) 99 Qf29
Xiping VRC (HNN) 106 Qh29
Xi Qiao VRC 101 Qg34
Xiqu VRC (SCH) 117 Qa32
Xique-Xique BR (BA) 295 Hj51
Xirdalan AZ 74 Ne25
Xishaqundao VRC 124 Qg37
Xishui VRC (GZH) 99 Qd31
Xishui VRC (HUB) 106 Qh30
Xi Shui VRC 106 Qh30
Xi Taijnar Hu VRC 91 Pg27
Xitole GNB 191 Kc40
Xi Ujimqin Qi VRC (NMZ) 95 Qj23
Xiushui VRC (JGX) 106 Qh31
Xiu Shui VRC 106 Qh31
Xiuwen VRC (GZH) 100 Qd32
Xiuwu VRC (HNN) 99 Qg28
Xiuyan VRC (LNG) 104 Rb25
Xiuying VRC (HAN) 100 Qf36
Xiwu VRC (QHI) 93 Pj29
Xixabangma Feng VRC 92 Pc31
Xixia VRC (HNN) 99 Qf29
Xi Xian VRC (HNN) 106 Qh29
Xi Xian VRC (SAX) 97 Qf27
Xixiang VRC (SAA) 99 Qd29
Xixia Wangling VRC 96 Qd26
Xixona E 31 Ku48
Xiyang VRC (SAX) 97 Qg27
Xizang Zizhiqu VRC 87 Pb12
Xmaben MEX (CAM) 265 Ff36
Xocavand AZ 74 Nd26
Xochiapa MEX (VC) 264 Fc37
Xochicalco MEX 264 Fa36
Xochimilco MEX (MEX) 264 Fa36
Xochob MEX 265 Ff36
Xo'jayli UZB 75 Nk24
Xom Tang VN 100 Qc35
Xovos UZB 80 Oe25
Xpujil MEX (CAM) 265 Ff36
Xpujil MEX 265 Ff36
Xuan'en VRC (HUB) 99 Qe31
Xuanhan VRC (SCH) 99 Qd30
Xuanhua VRC (HBI) 97 Qh25
Xuankong Monastery VRC 97 Qg26
Xuan Loc VN 119 Qd40
Xuan Mai VN 100 Qc35
Xuanwei VRC (YUN) 100 Qc32
Xuanzhong Si VRC 97 Qg27
Xuanzhou VRC (AHU) 106 Qk30
Xuchang VRC (HNN) 99 Qg28
Xudat AZ 74 Ne25
Xu Da, Tomb of = Imperial Tombs of the Ming and Qing Dynasties VRC (JGS) 106 Qk29
Xuddur SP 207 Nb43
Xudun SP 207 Nd41
Xuebao Ding VRC 98 Qb29
Xuefeng Shan VRC 99 Qf32
Xuejiadao VRC (SDG) 104 Ra28
Xueshan VRC 96 Qc27
Xugui VRC (QHI) 93 Pj28
Xultún GCA 265 Ff37
Xumishan Shiku VRC 96 Qc27
Xunantunich BH 265 Ff37
Xundian VRC (YUN) 117 Qb33
Xungru VRC (TIB) 92 Pc31
Xun He VRC 99 Qe29
Xun He VRC 102 Re21
Xunhua VRC (QHI) 96 Qb28
Xun Jiang VRC 100 Qf34
Xunke VRC (HLG) 102 Re21
Xunwu VRC (JGX) 101 Qh33
Xun Xian VRC (HNN) 97 Qh28
Xunyang VRC (SAA) 99 Qe29
Xunyi VRC (SAA) 99 Qe28
Xupu VRC (HUN) 100 Qf32
Xushui VRC (HBI) 97 Qh26
Xuwen VRC (GDG) 100 Qf35
Xuyi VRC (JGS) 106 Qk29
Xuyong VRC (SCH) 99 Qc31
Xuzhou VRC (JGS) 106 Qj28
Xylofagou CY 53 Mg55
Xylóskalo GR 50 Md55

Y

Yaak USA (MT) 243 Ec21
Yaamba AUS (QLD) 155 Sf57
Ya'an VRC (SCH) 98 Qb31
Yaaq Braaway SP 213 Nb45
Yaba RI 134 Rd46
Yaba-Hita-Hikosan N.P. J 107 Rf29
Yabassi CAM 202 Le43
Yabayo CI 200 Kg43
Yabebyry PY 301 Hb59
Yabello ETH 206 Mk43
Yabelo Sanctuary ETH 206 Mk43
Yabia RDC 208 Mb44
Yablonovyy Range RUS 63 Qc08
Yabroud SYR 68 Mj29
Yabucoa USA (PR) 271 Gh36
Yabuli VRC (HLG) 102 Re23
Yabus ETH 205 Mh41
Yabuyanos PE 285 Gd46
Yacambú, P.N. YV 281 Gf41
Yacaré Norte PY 297 Ha57
Yacata FJI 169 Ua54
Yachats USA (OR) 244 Dh23
Yacheng VRC (HAN) 100 Qe36
Yacimiento Rio Turbio RA (SC) 306 Gd71
Yacuiba BOL 297 Gj56
Yacuma BOL 291 Gg53
Yadagiri Gutta IND 113 Ok37
Yadavindra Gardens IND 111 Oj30
Yadgir IND (KTK) 112 Oj37
Yadibikro CI 201 Kh42
Yadkinville USA (NC) 259 Fk27
Yadmah KSA 72 Nc36
Yafase RI 135 Sa47
Yafran LAR 182 Lg29
Yagaba GH 201 Kk40
Yagaji RN 194 Le38
Yagasa Cluster FJI 169 Ua55
Yago CAM 195 Lh40
Yagradagzê Shan VRC 93 Ph28
Yaguachi Nuevo EC 284 Ga47
Yaguajay C 269 Ga34
Yaguaraparo YV 282 Gj40
Yaguarón PY 297 Hb58
Yaguarón ROU 301 Hd62
Yaguas CO 285 Ge47
Yaha THA 120 Qa42
Yahekou VRC (HNN) 99 Qg29
Yahk CDN (BC) 242 Eb21
Yaho BF 201 Kj40
Yahsihan TR 53 Mo51
Yahsiyan TR 53 Mo51
Yahualica de González Gallo MEX (JLC) 264 Ej35
Yahuma RDC 208 Mb45
Yahyalı TR 53 Mq52
Yaibrai VRC (NMZ) 96 Qb26
Yaita J 105 Rk27
Yajalón MEX (CHP) 265 Fd37
Yajiang VRC (SCH) 98 Qa30
Yaka RCA 208 Lk43
Yakana RDC 208 Mb45
Yakarra AUS (QLD) 156 Sb60
Yakassé-Attobrou CI 201 Kj42
Yakassé Mé CI 201 Kj43
Yakeshi VRC (NMZ) 95 Ra21
Yakima USA (WA) 242 Dk22
Yakima Ind. Res. USA 242 Dk22
Yakkabog UZB 80 Od26
Yakmach PK 84 Ob31
Yako BF 193 Kj39
Yakoma RDC 208 Mb43
Yakote J 105 Sa26
Yaku J 107 Rf30
Yaku-jima J 107 Rf30
Yakumo J 103 Sa24
Yakushima N.P. J 107 Rf30
Yakutat USA (AK) 241 Da16
Yakutat Bay USA 241 Da16
Yakutia RUS 63 Qc05
Yala EAK 212 Mh45
Yala GH 201 Kk40
Yala THA 121 Qa42
Yalagüina NIC 266 Fg39
Yalakdere TR 52 Mk50
Yalaki RDC 208 Mb45
Yalama AZ 74 Ne25
Yala N.P. CL 115 Pa43
Yalape PE 290 Gb49
Yalardy AUS (WA) 146 Qh59
Yalata AUS (SA) 151 Rf61
Yalata A.L. AUS 151 Rf61
Yalbalgo AUS (WA) 146 Qh58
Yale CDN (BC) 242 Dk21
Yale EAK 212 Mh45
Yale USA (WA) 242 Dj22
Yaleko RDC 209 Mc45
Yalgar River AUS 146 Qk59
Yalgo BF 193 Kk39
Yalgoo AUS (WA) 150 Qj60
Yalgorup N.P. AUS 150 Qh62
Yali BF 193 La39
Yali NIC 266 Fg39
Yaligimba RDC 208 Mb44
Yalıhüyük TR 53 Mn53
Yalıkavak TR 51 Mh53
Yalıköy TR 52 Mj49
Yalinga RCA 204 Mb42
Yallalong AUS (WA) 146 Qh59
Yalleroi AUS (QLD) 157 Sc58
Yallingup AUS (WA) 150 Qh62
Yallo BF 192 Kj39
Yalock AUS (NSW) 159 Sc62
Yaloké RCA 203 Lj43
Yalong Jiang VRC 98 Pk29
Yalong Jiang VRC 117 Qa32
Yalongwa RDC 208 Mb45
Yaloupi F 283 Hd44
Yalova TR 52 Mk50
Yalpirakinu A.L. AUS 148 Rg57
Yalsihon MEX (YT) 265 Ff35
Yalta UA 57 Mh23
Yalufi RDC 209 Mc45
Yalu Jiang VRC/DVRK 104 Rd25
Ya'lujiang Kou DVRK 104 Rc26
Yalvaç TR 53 Mm52
Yamada J 105 Sa26
Yamagata J 105 Sa26
Yamaguchi J 105 Rf28
Yamakawa J 105 Rf28
Yamal Nenets Autonomous District RUS 62 Oc05
Yamal Poluostrov RUS 62 Ob04
Yamanashi J 105 Rk28
Yamanlar TR 52 Mk52
Yamara YV 281 Gg43
Yamarna AUS (WA) 147 Rb59
Yamasa DOM 270 Ge36
Yamasaki J 105 Rh28
Yamatan VRC (QHI) 98 Pk28
Yamato Rise 87 Rc11
Yamatsun J 105 Sa27
Yamba AUS (NSW) 157 Sg60
Yamba BF 193 La39
Yambala RCA 204 Ma42
Yambala Koudouvélé RCA 204 Ma42
Yambarran Range AUS 145 Rf53
Yambata RDC 208 Ma44
Yamba-Yamba RDC 214 Md48
Yambéring RG 200 Kd40
Yambi G 210 Lf46
Yambio SUD 209 Me43
Yambuya RDC 209 Mc45
Yamdena RI 137 Rf49
Yamethin MYA 117 Pj35
Yamnotri IND (UTT) 111 Ok30
Yamoussoukro CI 201 Kh42
Yampa USA (CO) 245 Eg25
Yampa USA 245 Ef25
Yamparaez BOL 296 Gh55
Yamuna IND 111 Ok30
Yamuna IND 111 Pa33
Yamunanagar IND (HYA) 111 Oj30
Yamzho Yumco VRC 93 Pf31
Yan MAL 120 Qa43
Yanaba Island PNG 166 Sf50
Yanac AUS (VIC) 158 Sa64
Yanac PE 290 Gb50
Yanachaga Chemillén, P.N. PE 290 Gc51
Yanacu Grande PE 284 Gc48
Yanadani J 107 Rg29
Yanahuanca PE 290 Gb51
Yanai J 105 Rg29
Yanam IND (PND) 113 Pb37
Yanam Pondicherry IND 113 Pb37
Yanan VRC (GDG) 100 Qf34
Yan'an VRC (SAA) 97 Qe27
Yanaoca PE 291 Ge53
Yanatili PE 291 Gd52
Yanbian VRC (SCH) 117 Qa32
Yanbu al Bahr KSA 70 Mk33
Yancannia AUS (NSW) 156 Sb61
Yanchang VRC (SAA) 97 Qf27
Yancheng VRC (JGS) 106 Ra29
Yanchi VRC (NHZ) 96 Qd27
Yanco AUS (NSW) 159 Sd63
Yanco Glen AUS (NSW) 156 Sa61
Yancun VRC (GDG) 101 Qh34
Yandal AUS (WA) 146 Ra59
Yandang shan VRC 106 Ra32
Yandaran AUS (QLD) 157 Sg58
Yandaxkak VRC (XUZ) 91 Pe26
Yandev WAN 202 Le42
Yandil AUS (WA) 146 Qj59
Yandina SOL 167 Sk50
Yandina Plantation Resort SOL 167 Sk50
Yandja RDC 208 Lj46
Yandon MYA 118 Ph37
Yandongi RDC 208 Mb44
Yandun VRC (XUZ) 91 Ph24
Yanfolila RMM 200 Kf40
Yanga CAM 203 Lh44
Yanga TCH 204 Lk41
Yangalia RCA 204 Ma42
Yangambi RDC 209 Mc45
Yangara TCH 196 Lk35
Yangas PE 290 Gb51
Yangasso RMM 192 Kh39
Yangbajain VRC (TIB) 93 Pf30
Yangchang VRC (YUN) 100 Qc32
Yangcheng VRC (SAX) 99 Qg28
Yangchun VRC (GDG) 100 Qf34
Yangcun VRC (TJN) 97 Qj26
Yangdok DVRK 104 Rd26
Yangga RI 164 Sa50
Yang He VRC 97 Qh25
Yangi Qal'eh AFG 82 Oe27
Yangiqishloq UZB 80 Od25
Yangirabot UZB 80 Oc25
Yangiyer UZB 80 Oe25
Yangiyo'l UZB 80 Oe25
Yangizang UZB 80 Od27
Yangjiang VRC (GDG) 100 Qf35
Yanglin VRC (YUN) 117 Qb33
Yangling VRC (SAA) 99 Qe28
Yangluo VRC (HUB) 106 Qh30
Yangmingshan N.P. RC 101 Ra33
Yangon MYA 118 Pk37
Yangpingguan VRC (SAA) 99 Qd29
Yangpu Gang VRC 100 Qe36
Yangquan VRC (SAX) 97 Qg27
Yangquangu VRC (SAX) 97 Qf27
Yangqu Shan VRC 97 Qg26
Yangshan VRC (GDG) 100 Qg33
Yangshuo VRC (GZG) 100 Qf33
Yangtouyan VRC (YUN) 117 Qa33
Yangtze VRC 87 Qb12
Yangudi Rassa N.P. ETH 206 Na40
Yangxi VRC (GDG) 100 Qf35
Yangxin VRC (HUB) 106 Qh31
Yang-Yang SN 191 Kc38
Yangyuan VRC (HBI) 97 Qh25
Yangzhou VRC (JGS) 106 Qk29
Yangzi'e Z.B. VRC 106 Qk30
Yanhu VRC (TIB) 92 Pb29
Yanhuitlán MEX 264 Fb37
Yanji VRC (JLN) 104 Re24
Yanjin VRC (YUN) 98 Qc31
Yanjing VRC (CGQ) 99 Qd31
Yankari National Park WAN 195 Lf41
Yankton USA (SD) 250 Fb24
Yankton Ind. Res. USA 250 Fa24
Yanling VRC (HNN) 106 Qh28
Yanmen VRC (YUN) 98 Pk31
Yanmen G VRC 97 Qg26
Yanonge RDC 209 Mc45
Yanqi VRC (XUZ) 91 Pd24
Yanqing VRC (BJG) 97 Qh25
Yanqul OM 79 Nj34
Yanrey AUS (WA) 146 Qh57
Yanshan VRC (HBI) 97 Qj26
Yanshan VRC (YUN) 100 Qc34
Yanshou VRC (HLG) 102 Re23
Yansoribo RI 135 Rg46
Yantabulla AUS (NSW) 157 Sc60
Yantai VRC (SDG) 104 Ra27
Yantou VRC (ZJG) 106 Ra31
Yantzaza EC 284 Ga47
Yanxi VRC (HUN) 99 Qf31
Yanyuan VRC (SCH) 117 Qa32
Yanzikou VRC (GZH) 100 Qc32
Yao RCA 208 Lk43
Yao TCH 195 Lj39
Yao'an VRC (YUN) 117 Qa33
Yaodian VRC (GSU) 99 Qd28
Yaodian VRC (SAA) 97 Qe27
Yaolin Dong VRC 106 Qk31
Yaoundé CAM 203 Lf44
Yaowang Shan VRC 99 Qe28
Yao Xian VRC (SAA) 99 Qe28
Yapacana, P.N. YV 281 Gg44
Yapacani BOL 292 Gh54
Yapei GH 201 Kk41
Yapen RI 135 Rj46
Yapero RI 135 Rj48
Yapeyú RA (CR) 301 Hb60
Yapıldak TR 53 Ml51
Yap Islands FSM 162 Rh17
Yappar River AUS (QLD) 154 Sb55
Yapraklı TR 53 Mo50
Yap Trench 162 Rd17
Yapuparra A.L. AUS 147 Rd59
Yaqui MEX 247 Ef31
Yara C 269 Gb35
Yaraka AUS (QLD) 156 Sc58
Yaraligöz Dağı TR 66 Mh25
Yarawin AUS (NSW) 157 Sd61
Yarbasan TR 52 Mj52
Yarda TCH 196 Lk36
Yardea AUS (SA) 158 Rh62
Yardımcı Burnu TR 66 Mf27
Yardimli AZ 74 Ne26
Yare GB 23 Lb38
Yaré Lao SN 191 Kc37
Yaren NAU 163 Tb19
Yargatenga BF 201 Kk40
Yargatti IND (KTK) 112 Oh38
Yari CO 285 Gd45
Yarıkkaya TR 53 Mm52
Yarim YE 72 Nc38
Yaringa North AUS (WA) 146 Qh58
Yarısli Gölü TR 53 Mk53
Yaritagua YV 281 Gf40
Yarkant = Shache VRC (XUZ) 90 Oj26
Yarkant He VRC 90 Oj27
Yarlarweelor AUS (WA) 146 Qj58
Yarloop AUS (WA) 150 Qh62
Yarlung Zangbo Jiang VRC 93 Pf31
Yarma TR 53 Mn53
Yarmouth CDN (NS) 255 Gg24
Yarmouth USA (ME) 257 Ge24
Yaro Lund PK 85 Oe32
Yarpuz TR 53 Mm53
Yarra DY 194 Lb40
Yarrabubba AUS (WA) 146 Qj59
Yarraden AUS (QLD) 152 Sb53
Yarram AUS (VIC) 159 Sd65
Yarra Ranges N.P. AUS (VIC) 159 Sc64
Yarrie AUS (WA) 146 Ra56
Yarronvale AUS (QLD) 157 Sc59
Yarrowitch AUS (NSW) 157 Sg61
Yarrowmere AUS (QLD) 155 Sc56
Yarrum AUS (QLD) 154 Rk54
Yarumal CO 280 Gc42
Yarvicoya, Cerro RCH 296 Gf56
Yasa RDC 211 Ma47
Yasawa FJI 169 Tj54
Yasawa Group FJI 169 Tj54
Yashi WAN 194 Ld39
Yashikera WAN 194 Lb41
Yashiro-jima J 105 Rg29
Yasinza'i Kalay AFG 82 Oc30
Yasothon THA 119 Qc38
Yass AUS (NSW) 159 Se63
Yasuj IR 76 Nf30
Yasun Burnu TR 67 Mj25
Yasuni EC 284 Gb46
Yasuni PE 284 Gc46
Yasuni, P.N. EC 284 Gc46
Yat RN 189 Lg35
Yata BOL 291 Gg52
Yata BOL 291 Gh52
Yata RCA 204 Mb41
Yatağan TR 52 Mj53
Yatako BF 193 La38
Yatang VRC (YUN) 117 Pk32
Yate F 168 Td57
Yates Center USA (KS) 253 Fc27
Yatha MYA 117 Ph34
Yathon AUS (NSW) 159 Sc62
Yathon Nature Reserve AUS 159 Sc62
Yati CO 280 Gc42
Yatolema RDC 209 Mc45
Yatsushiro J 107 Rf29
Yatsu-take J 105 Rk28
Yatta EAK 212 Mj46
Yatta Plateau EAK 212 Mj46
Yatúa YV 285 Gg45
Yauca PE 290 Gc53
Yauco USA (PR) 271 Gg36
Yauhannah USA (SC) 259 Ga29
Yauli PE 290 Gc52
Yaupita BOL 297 Gh56
Yauri PE 291 Ge53
Yauyos PE 290 Gc52
Yauyupe HN 266 Fg39
Yaval IND (MHT) 112 Oh35
Yavari BR/PE 285 Ge48
Yavaros MEX (SO) 262 Ef32
Yavaşlar TR 66 Me26
Yavatmal IND (MHT) 113 Ok35
Yavero ó Paucartambo PE 291 Gd52
Yavineto PE 284 Gc46
Yavita YV 285 Gg44
Yaviza PA 267 Gb41
Yavsan Tuzlası TR 53 Mo52
Yavuzeli TR 66 Mj27
Yawatahama J 107 Rg29
Yawatongguzlangar VRC (XUZ) 90 Pb27
Yawatoutou, Mount GH/RT 201 La42
Yawgu GH 201 La40
Yawimu RI 164 Rk49
Yawngo MYA 117 Pk34
Yawri Bay WAL 200 Kd41
Yaxcabá MEX (YT) 265 Ff35
Yaxchilán MEX (CHP) 265 Fe37
Yayama RDC 208 Mb46
Yaygölü TR 53 Mq52
Yaylacık TR 53 Mn53
Yayvantepe TR 67 Na27
Yazd IR 76 Nh30
Yazdan IR 77 Oa29
Yazhou VRC (GZH) 100 Qd33
Yazıçayırı TR 53 Mo51
Yazıhan TR 67 Mk26
Yazılıkaya TR 53 Ml51
Yazitepe TR 53 Mr50
Yazman PK 85 Of31
Yazoo City USA (MS) 253 Fe29
Ybbs A 37 Lp42
Ybbs A 37 Lq42
Ybycuí PY 301 Hb59
Yby-Yaú PY 297 Hb57
Ydby Hede DK 16 Lj34
Ye MYA 118 Pj38
Yea AUS (VIC) 159 Sc64
Yebawmi MYA 117 Ph33
Yebbi-Bou TCH 196 Lj35
Yebbi Souma TCH 189 Lj35
Yebok MYA 118 Pg36
Yebya MYA 116 Ph35
Yecheng VRC (XUZ) 90 Oj27
Yecla E 31 Kt48
Yécora MEX (SO) 262 Ef31
Yedisu TR 67 Na26
Yedseram WAN 195 Lg40
Yeehaw Junction USA (FL) 260 Fk32
Yeelanna AUS (SA) 158 Rh63
Yeelirrie AUS (WA) 146 Ra59
Yeggebo RN 196 Lg36
Yegheghnadzor ARM 74 Nc26
Yégué RT 201 La41
Yegyi MYA 118 Ph37
Yeha ETH 199 Mk39
Yei SUD 209 Mf43
Yei SUD 205 Mf43
Yeji GH 201 Kk41
Yeji VRC (AHU) 106 Qh30
Yekaterinburg RUS 62 Oa07
Yekepa LB 200 Kf42
Yekia TCH 195 Lj37
Yekokora RDC 208 Ma45
Yek Shaba IR 76 Nd27
Yelahanga IND (KTK) 115 Oj40
Yela Island PNG 166 Sh51
Yelbarsli TM 77 Oa27
Yelcho RCH 304 Gd67
Yelcho ANT (RCH) 312 Gd31
Yele WAL 200 Ke41
Yeleğen TR 52 Mj52
Yelerbon AUS (QLD) 157 Sf60
Yélimané RMM 191 Ke38
Yelkaturti IND (APH) 113 Ok36
Yell GB 21 Kt30
Yellabinna Regional Reserve AUS 151 Rg61
Yellandu IND (APH) 113 Pa37
Yellapur IND (KTK) 114 Oh39
Yellareddi IND (APH) 112 Oj36
Yellowdine AUS (WA) 150 Qk61
Yellowdine Nature Reserve AUS (WA) 150 Qk61
Yellow Grass CDN (SK) 243 Eh21
Yellowhead Pass CDN 242 Ea19
Yellowknife CDN 234 Eb06
Yellow Pine USA (ID) 244 Ec23
Yellow River VRC 87 Qc11
Yellow Sea 87 Ra11
Yellowstone USA 245 Eg22
Yellowstone National Park USA 245 Ee23
Yell Sound GB 21 Kt30
Yellville USA (AR) 253 Fd27
Yelma AUS (WA) 147 Ra59
Yeloten TM 77 Ob27
Yelvertoft AUS (QLD) 154 Rk56
Yelwa WAN 194 Lc40
Yelwa WAN 194 Le41
Yema RDC 210 Lg48
Yema Nanshan VRC 91 Ph26
Yema Shan VRC 91 Ph26
Yemassee USA (SC) 259 Fk29
Yembo ETH 205 Mh41
Yemen YE 61 Na08
Yemnu PNG 164 Sb47
Ye-myet-ni MYA 116 Ph35
Yen CAM 203 Lg44
Yenagoa WAN 202 Ld43
Yenan-gyaung MYA 116 Ph35
Yen Bai VN 100 Qc35
Yenchang VRC (TIB) 93 Pe30
Yen Chau VN 100 Qc35
Yendé Milimou RG 200 Ke41
Yendéré BF 201 Kh40
Yendi GH 201 Kk41
Yénéganou RCB 210 Lg47
Yenge RDC 208 Ma46
Yengema WAL 200 Ke41
Yengisar VRC (XUZ) 90 Oj26
Yengi Kand IR 76 Nd27
Yengo RCB 203 Lh45
Yengo N.P. AUS 159 Sf62
Yenibaşak TR 67 Na26
Yeniçağa TR 53 Mn50
Yenice TR 52 Mj53
Yenice TR 53 Mn49
Yenice TR 53 Mn51
Yeniceoba TR 53 Mn52
Yeniçubuk TR 66 Mj26
Yenifakılı TR 53 Mq51
Yenifoça TR 51 Mg52
Yenihisar TR 51 Mh53
Yenikent TR 53 Mn51
Yenikent TR 53 Mo52
Yeniköy TR 52 Mj51
Yeniköy TR 52 Mj52
Yenimehmetli TR 53 Mn51
Yenipazar TR 52 Mj53
Yenipazar TR 52 Ml50
Yenipazar TR 53 Mq51
Yenişarbademli TR 53 Mm53
Yenişehir TR 52 Mk50
Yenişehir TR 52 Mk52
Yeniyıldız TR 53 Mp53
Yen Ly VN 119 Qc36
Yenne F 27 Lf45
Yéno G 210 Le46
Yéno G 210 Lf46
Yentna River USA 239 Ce14
Yeola IND (MHT) 112 Oh35
Yeo Lake AUS 147 Rc59
Yeo Lake Nature Reserve AUS 151 Rc60
Yeoval AUS (NSW) 159 Se62
Yeovil GB 23 Ks40
Yepachic MEX (CHH) 262 Ef31
Yepes E 31 Kr49
Yeppoon AUS (QLD) 155 Sf57
Yeraltı şehri (Derinkuyu) TR 53 Mp52
Yerba Loca RCH 300 Ge62
Yercaud IND (TNU) 115 Ok41
Yeremarou DY 194 Lb41
Yerevan ARM 67 Nc25
Yergara IND (KTK) 112 Oj37
Yeriho IS 68 Mh30
Yerilla AUS (WA) 150 Ra60
Yerington USA (NV) 244 Ea26
Yerköprü TR 66 Mg27
Yerköprü TR 53 Mn52
Yerköy TR 53 Mp51
Yermala IND (MHT) 112 Oh36
Yeröö gol MNG 94 Qd21
Yerupaja, Cerro PE 290 Gb51
Yerville F 24 La41
Yesagyo MYA 117 Ph35
Yesan ROK 104 Rd27
Yeshin MYA 116 Ph34
Yeshwant Sagar IND 112 Oh34
Yesilbağ TR 53 Mm53
Yeşil Camii (Bursa) TR 52 Mk50
Yeşil Camii (İznik) TR 52 Mk50
Yeşildağ TR 53 Mm53
Yeşil Gölük TR 53 Mp52
Yeşilhisar TR 53 Mq52
Yeşilırmak TR 66 Mh25
Yeşilova TR 52 Mk53
Yeşilova TR 53 Mo52
Yeşilöz TR 53 Mn51
Yeşilvadi TR 52 Mk49
Yeşilyurt TR 53 Mn51
Yeşilyurt TR 53 Mr51
Yeste E 31 Ks48
Yesterday River CDN 249 Fk20
Yet ETH 207 Nb43
Yetla de Juárez MEX (OAX) 264 Fb37
Yetman AUS (NSW) 157 Sf60
Ye-u MYA 117 Ph34
Yevlax AZ 74 Nd25
Ye Xian VRC (HNN) 99 Qg29
Yexiangqu VRC 117 Qa34
Yeyik VRC (XUZ) 90 Pb27
Yeyungou VRC (XUZ) 90 Pc25
Yhú PY 298 Hc58
Yi ROU 301 Hb62
Yi'an VRC (HLG) 102 Rc22
Yibin VRC (SCH) 98 Qc31
Yichang VRC (HUB) 99 Qf30
Yicheng VRC (HUB) 99 Qg30
Yicheng VRC (SAX) 99 Qf28
Yichuan VRC (HNN) 99 Qg28
Yichuan VRC (SAA) 99 Qf28
Yichun VRC (HLG) 102 Re22
Yichun VRC (JGX) 106 Qh32
Yidun VRC (SCH) 98 Pk30
Yiewi RI 134 Re45
Yifag ETH 206 Mj40
Yifeng VRC (JGX) 106 Qh31
Yığılca TR 53 Mm50
Yihuang VRC (JGX) 106 Qj32
Yijun VRC (SAA) 99 Qe28
Yilan VRC (HLG) 102 Re22
Yıldırım Camii TR 52 Mh51
Yıldız Dağları TR 52 Mh49
Yıldızeli TR 66 Mj26
Yilehuli Shan VRC 102 Rc20
Yiliang VRC (YUN) 117 Qb33
Yiliang VRC (YUN) 100 Qc32
Yilingyan VRC 100 Qe34
Yilong VRC (SCH) 99 Qd30
Yilou BF 193 Kk39
Yilui PNG 164 Sb47
Yima VRC (HNN) 99 Qf28
Yimen VRC (SAA) 99 Qd28
Yimin VRC (NMZ) 95 Qk21
Yimni River PNG 165 Sb48
Yimuhe VRC (NMZ) 95 Ra19
Yinan VRC (SDG) 97 Qk28
Yinchuan VRC (NHZ) 96 Qd26
Yindi AUS (WA) 150 Rb61
Yingcheng VRC (HUB) 99 Qg30
Yingchengzi Tomb VRC 104 Rb26
Yingde VRC (GDG) 101 Qg33
Yinggehai VRC (HAN) 100 Qe36
Yinghe VRC (AHU) 106 Qj29
Ying He VRC 106 Qj29
Yingjiang VRC (YUN) 117 Pj33
Yingjin He VRC 97 Qk24
Yingkou VRC (LNG) 104 Rb25
Yingkou VRC (LNG) 104 Rb25
Yingpanshan VRC (YUN) 100 Qc32
Yingshan VRC (AHU) 106 Qj29
Yingshan VRC (SCH) 99 Qd30
Yingtan VRC (JGX) 106 Qj31
Yingui CAM 202 Lf43
Ying Xian VRC (SAX) 97 Qg26
Yingxian Mu Ta VRC 97 Qg26
Yingxiuwan VRC (SCH) 98 Qb30
Yining VRC (XUZ) 88 Pa24
Yiningarra A.L. AUS 148 Re56
Yinjiang VRC (GZH) 99 Qe32
Yinjiang VRC (GZH) 100 Qe32
Yinma He VRC 102 Rc23
Yin Shan VRC 97 Qe25
Yinxu VRC 97 Qh27
Yipinglang VRC (YUN) 117 Qa33
Yiqikai VRC (QHI) 98 Pk28
Yirba Muda ETH 206 Mk42
Yirga Chefe ETH 206 Mk42
Yirie RG 200 Kf41
Yirol SUD 205 Mf42
Yirrkala AUS (NT) 145 Rj52
Yirshi VRC (NMZ) 95 Qk22
Yishui VRC (SDG) 97 Qk28
Yitong VRC (JLN) 104 Rc24
Yitong He VRC 102 Rc23
Yitulihe VRC (NMZ) 95 Ra20
Yiwu VRC (XUZ) 91 Ph24
Yiwu VRC (ZJG) 106 Ra31
Yi Xian VRC (HBI) 97 Qh26
Yixing VRC (JGS) 106 Qk30
Yiyang VRC (HUN) 99 Qg31
Yiyang VRC (JGX) 106 Qj31
Yiyu IND (ARP) 116 Ph31
Yiyuan VRC (SDG) 97 Qk27
Yizhang VRC (HUN) 101 Qg33
Yizheng VRC (JGS) 106 Qk29
Yizhou VRC (GZG) 100 Qe33
Yizhou VRC (LNG) 104 Ra25
Ylakiai LT 19 Mb34
Ylämaa FIN 18 Mj30
Yläne FIN 18 Mc30
Yli-Kitka FIN 13 Me12
Ylimarkku = Övermark FIN 15 Mb28
Ylitornio FIN 13 Mb12
Ylivieska FIN 13 Mc13
Ylöjärvi FIN 18 Md29
Yngaren S 15 Lr32
Yngen S 15 Lp31
Yoakum USA (TX) 253 Fb31
Yoboki DJI 207 Nb40
Yocalla BOL 296 Gh55
Yof SN 191 Kb38
Yofor RI 135 Rj48
Yogoum TCH 197 Lk37
Yogyakarta RI 132 Qf49
Yohaltún MEX (CAM) 265 Fe36
Yoho N.P. CDN 243 Eb20
Yohualichan MEX 264 Fb35
Yoichi J 103 Sa24
Yokadouma CAM 203 Lh44
Yok Don N.P. VN 119 Qd39
Yokkaichi J 105 Rj28
Yoko CAM 203 Lg43
Yokoate-jima J 107 Re31
Yokoboué CI 201 Kh43
Yokohama J 105 Rk28
Yokohama J 103 Sa25
Yokosuka J 105 Rk28
Yola CAM 203 Lh43
Yola WAN 195 Lg41
Yolande F 283 Hd43
Yolcular TR 67 Nb26
Yoliatl MEX (SLP) 263 Ek34
Yolombo RDC 208 Mb46
Yolüstü TR 67 Na26
Yomou RG 200 Kf42
Yomuka RI 164 Rk49
Yonago J 105 Rg28
Yoneshiro-gawa J 105 Sa25
Yonezawa J 105 Sa27
Yong'an VRC (FJN) 101 Qj33
Yongchang VRC (GSU) 96 Qa26
Yongcheng VRC (HNN) 106 Qj29
Yongcheng VRC (JGX) 106 Qk31
Yongchuan VRC (CGQ) 99 Qc31
Yongde VRC (YUN) 117 Pk34
Yongdeng VRC (GSU) 96 Qb27
Yongding VRC (FJN) 101 Qj33
Yongdok ROK 104 Re27
Yongfeng VRC (JGX) 106 Qh32
Yongfeng VRC (JGX) 106 Qh32
Yongfu VRC (GZG) 100 Qe33
Yonghung DVRK 104 Rd26
Yongjia VRC (ZJG) 106 Ra31
Yongjing VRC (GSU) 96 Qb28
Yongju ROK 104 Re27
Yongkang VRC (ZJG) 106 Qk31
Yongle VRC (GZH) 100 Qe32
Yonglegong VRC 99 Qf28
Yongling Tomb VRC 104 Rc25
Yongning VRC (GZG) 100 Qe34
Yongning VRC (NHZ) 96 Qd26
Yongofondo RCA 208 Mb43
Yong Peng MAL 121 Qb44
Yongping VRC (JGX) 106 Qj31
Yongping VRC (SAA) 97 Qe27
Yongping VRC (YUN) 117 Pk33
Yong Quan Si VRC 106 Qk32
Yongren VRC (YUN) 117 Qa32
Yongshan VRC (YUN) 98 Qb31
Yongsheng VRC (YUN) 117 Qa32
Yongshun VRC (HUN) 99 Qe31
Yongxing VRC (HUN) 101 Qg32
Yongxin VRC (JGX) 101 Qh32
Yongxiu VRC (JGX) 106 Qh31
Yongzhou VRC (HUN) 100 Qf32
Yonibana WAL 200 Kd41
Yonkers USA (NY) 257 Gd25
Yonne F 25 Ld43
Yontai VRC (FJN) 101 Qk33
Yopal CO 280 Gd43
Yopie Podogle LB 200 Kf42
Yopurga VRC (XUZ) 90 Oj26
Yorazlar TR 53 Mm52
Yorito HN 266 Fg38
York AUS (WA) 150 Qj61
York GB 23 Kt37
York USA (NE) 250 Fb25
York USA (PA) 257 Gb26
York USA (SC) 259 Fk28
York WAL 200 Kd41
Yorke Peninsula AUS 158 Rj63
Yorketown AUS (SA) 158 Rj63
Yorkeys Knob AUS (QLD) 155 Sc54
York Factory (abandoned) CDN 248 Fd17
Yorkshire USA (NY) 257 Ga24
Yorkshire Dales N.P. GB 23 Ks36
Yorkshire Downs AUS (QLD) 154 Sa56
Yorkshire Wolds GB 23 Ku36
Yorkton CDN (SK) 248 Ej20
Yorktown USA (TX) 252 Fb31
Yornaning AUS (WA) 150 Qj62
Yoro HN 266 Fg38
Yoro RMM 193 Kj38
Yorobougoula RMM 200 Kg40
Yoron J 107 Re32
Yoron-jima J 107 Re32
Yorosso RMM 192 Kh39
Yorubaland Plateau WAN 202 Lb41
Yosemite N.P. USA (CA) 244 Ea27
Yosemite Village USA (CA) 244 Ea27
Yoshino-gawa J 105 Rg28
Yoshino-Kumano N.P. J 105 Rh29
Yoshino sacred site J 105 Rh28
Yosu ROK 104 Rd28
Yosua PNG 164 Sb48
Yotai-santi J 103 Sa24
Youangarra AUS (WA) 150 Qk60
Youanmi Downs AUS (WA) 150 Qk60
Yoube ETH 207 Nc42
Youdunzi VRC (QHI) 91 Pf26
Youghal IRL 22 Kn39
Youghal Bay IRL 22 Kn39
Youkounkoun RG 191 Kd39
You Le Yuan VRC 98 Qc30
Youllemmedene RMM 193 La37
Young AUS (NSW) 159 Se63
Young CDN (SK) 243 Eh20
Young ROU 301 Hb62
Youngerina AUS (NSW) 157 Sc61
Younghusband Peninsula AUS 158 Rk63
Youngstown CDN (AB) 243 Ee20
Youngstown USA (OH) 257 Fk25
Youssoufia MA 180 Kf29
Youvarou RMM 192 Kh38
You Xian VRC (HUN) 101 Qg32
Youyang VRC (CGQ) 99 Qe31
Youyi Feng VRC 89 Pd21
Youzhou VRC (HNN) 99 Qg28
Yowa RDC 208 Ma44
Yowergabbie AUS (WA) 150 Qj60
Yo Yo Park AUS (QLD) 157 Sd59
Yozgat TR 53 Mp51
Yozgat Camlığı Milli Parkı TR 53 Mp51
Ypäjä FIN 18 Md30
Ypané PY 297 Hb57
Ype Jhú PY 298 Hc57
Ypsilanti USA (MI) 256 Fj24
Yreka USA (CA) 244 Dj25
Ysabel Channel PNG 165 Se46
Yset N 14 Ll28
Yssingeaux F 27 Le45
Ystad S 17 Lo35
Ystyk KS 81 Oh25
Ytre Arna N 14 Lf30
Ytre Oppedal N 14 Lf29
Ytre Sula N 14 Le29
Ytterhogdal S 15 Lp28
Yttermalung S 15 Lo30
Yu RI 134 Re46
Yuanbao Shan VRC 100 Qe33
Yuanjiang VRC (YUN) 117 Qb34
Yuan Jiang VRC 117 Qa34
Yuan Jiang VRC 99 Qf31
Yuanlin RC 101 Ra34
Yuanlin VRC (NMZ) 95 Ra21
Yuanling VRC (HUN) 99 Qf31
Yuanmou VRC (YUN) 117 Qa33
Yuanping VRC (SAX) 97 Qg26
Yuanqu VRC (SAX) 99 Qf28
Yuantan VRC (AHU) 106 Qj30
Yuantouzhu VRC 106 Ra30
Yuanyang VRC (YUN) 117 Qb34
Yuba USA (OK) 253 Fb29
Yuba City USA (CA) 244 Dk26
Yubari J 103 Sa24
Yubdo ETH 205 Mh41
Yubetsu J 103 Sb23
Yubetu-dake J 103 Sa24
Yucatán MEX (YT) 265 Fg35
Yucatán MEX 265 Ff35
Yucatán Basin 268 Fh35
Yucatán Channel 268 Fh35
Yucatán Peninsula MEX 265 Ff35
Yucca House Nat. Mon. USA 247 Ef27
Yucca Valley USA (CA) 246 Eb28
Yücebağ TR 67 Na26
Yuchán RA (SE) 300 Gj59
Yuci VRC (SAX) 97 Qg27
Yucumo BOL 291 Gg53
Yudi Shan VRC 95 Rb19
Yudu VRC (JGX) 101 Qh33
Yuechi VRC (SCH) 99 Qd30
Yueliang He VRC 102 Rb23
Yuelushan VRC 99 Qg31
Yuendumu AUS (NT) 148 Rf57
Yuendumu A.L. AUS 148 Rf57
Yueqing VRC (ZJG) 106 Ra31
Yuexi VRC (AHU) 106 Qj30
Yueyang VRC (HUN) 99 Qg31
Yueyang VRC (SCH) 99 Qc30
Yufle SP 207 Nd40
Yugan VRC (JGX) 106 Qj31
Yugia VRC (QHI) 91 Ph26
Yuğluk Dağı TR 66 Mg27
Yuhe VRC (SAA) 97 Qe27
Yuhe VRC (SDG) 106 Qj28
Yuhomae J 107 Rf29
Yuhong VRC (GZG) 100 Qd33
Yuhuan VRC (ZJG) 106 Ra31
Yuhuan Dao VRC 106 Ra31
Yuin AUS (WA) 146 Qj59
Yuinmery AUS (WA) 150 Qk60
Yu Jiang VRC 100 Qe34
Yukarıçamözü TR 67 Mj26
Yukarı Sakarya Ovaları TR 53 Mm51
Yuki RDC 211 Lk47
Yuki River USA 239 Cb13
Yukon Charley Rivers Nat. Preserve USA (AK) 239 Cj13
Yukon Delta USA 238 Bj14
Yukon Delta National Wildlife Refuge USA (AK) 238 Bh15
Yukon Flats National Wildlife Refuge USA 239 Cg12
Yukon Plateau CDN 241 Db14
Yukon River USA 239 Cd13
Yukon Territory CDN 234 Da06
Yüksekova TR 67 Nc27
Yukuhashi J 107 Rf29
Yulara AUS (NT) 148 Rf58
Yuleba AUS (QLD) 157 Se59
Yulee USA (FL) 259 Fk30
Yule River AUS 146 Qk56
Yuli RC 101 Ra34
Yuli VRC (XUZ) 91 Pd25
Yuli WAN 194 Lf41
Yulin VRC (GZG) 100 Qf34
Yulin VRC (SAA) 97 Qe26
Yulinsi Shiku VRC 91 Ph25
Yulong Xueshan VRC 117 Qa32
Yuma USA (AZ) 246 Ec29
Yuma USA (CO) 250 Ej25
Yumare YV 281 Gf40
Yumariba YV 282 Gj43
Yumbarra Conservation Park AUS 158 Rg61
Yumbe EAU 209 Mf44
Yumbel RCH 304 Gd64

Abbreviations:
C = Corbis
DFA = Das Fotoarchiv
G = Getty
H = Huber
M = Mauritius
mcs = Mediacolors
P = Premium
JAI = JonArnoldImages

Page I–II: Spacecapes, PhotoDisc Vol. 34. page II–III: ©Geospace/EDC 2002. page IV–V: World Landmarks and Travel, PhotoDisc Vol. 60. page VI–VII: P/Stimpson/Pl. page VIII–IX: 1, 2, 3 P; 3 H/Damm. page X–XI: 1 Monheim; 2, 3 P; 4 IFA/Jacobs. page XII–XIII: 1 G/Tomlinson; 2 G/Waite; 3 P/Petsch; 4 G/Layda. page XIV: 1 DFA; 2 H/Damm. page XV: P. page XVI–XVII: 1 P/S.Bunka; 2 IFA; 3 P/NGS; 4 P/Schwabel. page XVIII: P/Raymer/NGS. page 2: top P; 1 G/TCL; 2, 3, 5, 6 P; 4 M; 7 H/Damm. page 3: 1, 3, 4, 6, 7 P/Marka; 2 zefa/Putz; 5 W. + C. Kunth. page 4: top C; 1 G; 2 Mau; 3–5 dpa. page 5: 1 H/Bertsch; 2, 3, 6 P; 4 K.U.Müller; 5, 7 G/Cornish. page 6 – page 8.1, 5 P; page 8: 2 Wandmacher; 3 IFA; 6 mcs. page 9: 1 Schapowalow/Holm; 2 DFA/ Morris. page 10: top P; 1 G; 2, 6 P; 3 Bieker; 5 mcs; 7 IFA. page 11: 1 H; 2 Böttcher; 3, 7 mdc; 4, 5 IFA; 6 C. page 12: top, 1 P; 2 IcelandicImages; 3, 7 Laif; 4 P; 5 M/sipa; 6 DFA/Tack. page 13: 1 IFA; 2 Laif/Modrow; 3 M; 4–6 C; 7 H/Giovanni. page 14: top, 2 G; 1, 3, 6, 7 P; 4, 5 Klammet. page 15: 1, 2 Laif/Meier; 3 C; 4 Laif; 5, 7 P; 6 H. page 16: top C; 1, 5 Klammet; 2, 7 P; 3 Nordis; 4 Pix; 6 DFA. Page 17: 1 P; 2 Laif; 3 Klammet; 4–7 – page 18: top Laif; 1 IFA; 2 Laif; 3 Nordis; 4 P/Sekai Bunka; 5 DFA; 6 P; 7 G. page 19: 1, 6 M; 2, 4 H; 3, 5 P. page 20: top, 1, 3–7 P; 2 M/ACE. page 21: 1 DFA/ Babowic; 2–4, 6 P; 5 G; 7 M/Nägele. page 22: top, 4 P; 5 M/Kord; 6 Klammet; 7 G/Waite. page 23: 1, 3–5, 7 P; 2 G; 6 Klammet. page 24: top IFA; 1 DFA/Mayer; 2 M; 3 NN; 4 G; 5, 6 P; 7 Herzig. page 25: 1–6 P; 7 DFA. page 26: top, 2, 5, 6 P; 1 IFA; 3 Monheim; 4 G; 7 H. page 27: 1 IFA; 2, 4 P; 3, 5, 7 H; 6 M. page 28: top, 4, 5 P; 1 Laif; 2 Nägele/KM; 3 H; 6 G/Cornish; 7 Pix/Silberbauer. page 29: 1 G/Thiele; 2, 6, 7 P; 3, 4 H; 5 IFA. page 30: top, 2, 3, 6, 7 P; 1 Gonzalez; 4 Klein/Laif; 5 C/Frerck. page 31: 1 G/Everts; 2 Monheim; 3–5 P; 6 Transglobe/Winter; 7 IFA. page 32: top Gonzalez/Laif; 1, 3, 5–7 P; 2 IFA; 4 GM Schmid. page 33: 1, 3 Bednorz/Monheim; 2, 5 Laif; 4, 7 IFA; 6 M/Raga. page 34: top, 1, 4–7 P; 2 H; 3 M. page 35: 1, 6 H; 2 Dr. Zahn; 4, 5 Böttcher. page 36: top, 1 G; 2 M/Hänel; 3, 5 H; 4 Freyer; 6, 7 P. page 37: 1, 5 Romeis; 2, 3 Freyer; 4 H; 6 Radelt/KM; 7 P. page 38: top Laif; 1 Kalmar; 2 H/Schmid; 3 von Götz; 4, 6 DFA; 5, 7 P. page 39: 1, 2, 5, 6 P; 3 Laif; 4 Freyer; 7 C/Libra. page 40: top H; 1 IFA; 2, 4, 6 P; 3 Laif; 5 M; 7 Jano/Pix. page 41: 1, 5 P; 2 H; 3, 6 M; 4 Huber/Laif. page 42: top–2, 5, 7 P; 3, 6 Klammet, Nägele; 4 G. page 43: 1, 2 P; 3 G; 4 Freyer; 5 IFA; 6, 7 H. page 44: top IFA; 2–3, 5, 7 P; 4 G/Layda; 6 M. page 45: 1, 3–5 P; 2 M; 6 H; 7 NN. page 46: top H; 1, 5, 7 DFA/Zippel; 2–4, 6 IFA. page 47: 1 Klammet; 2 G/Tschanz; 3 IFA; 4 C/Wheeler; 5 G/Jecan; 6 IFA; 7 DFA/Riedmiller. page 48: top, 2 IFA; 1 G; 3 mcs; 4 M/Rossenbach; 5–7 P. page 49: 1, 4–7 Henseler/Laif; 2 Evans; 3 P. page 50 top – page 51.3: P; 4, 7 H/Mehlig; 5 M; 6 DFA. page 52: top–3, 6 P; 4 Laif; 5 C. page 53: 1, 2 P/NGS; 3 M/Hänel; 4, 6 H/ Schmid; 5 Krause/Laif; 7 mcs. page 54: top Klasen; 1–5 P; 6 G; 7 Kalmar. page 55: 1, 2, 6 H; 3, 4 P/Buss; 5, 7 C/Schmid. page 56: top C; 1, 2 DFA/Müller; 3 – page 57.2: C; 3 H; 4–7 C. page 58–59 P. page 60: top M/Krinninger; 1, 2 IFA; 3, 4 G; 5 DFA/Morrow; 6 C. page 61: 1 DFA/Riedmiller; 2 Emmler/Laif. page 62: top Arthus- Bertrand/C; 1 Essik/Arora; 2 B. & C. Alexander Photography/Alamy; 3 P/Mikhailov; 4 Klasen; 5 Hilger/Laif; 6 Pölking/TG; 7 P/IC; Page 63: 1 S.Brown/pd; 2–4 Langewin; 5–7 Arthus-Bertrand/C. page 64: top C. page 64: 1 DFA/Cristofori; 2–4 IFA; 5 Wheeler/C; 7 Westermann. page 65: 1, 2, 4, 7 C; 3, 5 IFA; 6 M. page 66: top Pictor/P; 1 Tophoven/Laif; 2, 3, 5, 6 P. page 66: 4 Antrobus/C; 7 Klammet. page 67: 1 G/Thiele; 2 P; 3–6 IFA; 7 Evans; 8 M/Pigneter. page 68: top P; 1, 2 Laif; 3 H/Schmid; 4 DFA/Künzig; 5 mcs; 6 IFA; 7 H. page 69: 1 G/Mollenhauer; 2, 3 IFA; 4–7 C. page 70: top IFA/Aberham; 1, 3 Kaehler; 2 Stier; 6 Shandiz. page 71: 1 O'Rourke; 2 Houser; 3 Thévenart/C. page 72: top IFA/Rölle; 1, 2 C; 3–5 IFA; 6 – page 73: 1, 5 B. Kreißl. page 73: 2–4, 6, 7 IFA. page 74: oben C; 1 IFA; 2 Chatelin/Focus; 3 Pix/Steenmans; 4 G/Weinberg; 5 P; 6 – page 75: 1, 3 G.M.Schmid; 2 Laif; 4 C; 5 G/Wedewarth. page 76: top–2, 5, 7 C; 3, 6 IFA; 4 P. page 77: 1, 2, 5, 7 C; 3 M; 4, 6 P/NGS. page 78: top C; 1 IFA; 2 P; 3 G/Maroon; 4, 6 IFA/Tschanz; 5 Westermann; 7 C; page 79: 1 DFA/Sasse; 2 IFA; 3, 4, 7 Westermann; 5 IFA/Aberham; 6 C. page 80: top C; 1 zefa/Anderle; 2 C; 3, 4, 6 M/O'Brien; 5 P/Maiburg. page 81: 1 C; 2–4 P; 5 zefa/Minden/Lanting; 6, 7 C. page 82: top C; 1, 2, 4 DFA/Maeder; 3 C; 5, 6 IFA; 7 C. page 83: 1 P; 2, 3 C; 4–7 K.U.Müller. page 84: top M; 1 C; 2 IFA; 3 Hub/Laif; 4–6 DFA/Bolesch; 7 – page 85.1 C; 2 Evrad/TG; 3 DFA/Bolesch; 4–7 C. page 86: top–2 P; 3 Sparks/C; 4 P; 5 K.U.Müller; 6 IFA/Fried; 7 Fiedler. page 86.8 – page 87.1 P; 2 IFA/Warter; 3 C; 4, 6 P; 5 DFA/Zippel; 7 Moore. page 88: top P/Sekai Bunka; 1 Su/C; 2 Nasa/C; 3 Zhuoming/C; 4 Wier/C; 5 Twight/Aurora; 6 IFA. page 89: 1, 2 IFA/Jung; 3 Wier/C; 4 P; 5 Arbib/C; 6, 7 K.U.Müller. page 90: top P; 1 Su/C; 2 – page 91.5 K.U. Müller; 6 IFA/Aberham. page 92: top–2 P; 3 G; 4, 6 DFA/Gordon, Bolesch; 5 K.U. Müller. page 93: 1, 2, 7 P; 3 H; 4 M; 5, 6 K.U.Müller. page 94: top Pölking/TG; 1 Su/ C; 2 Bailey/C; 3 DFA/Cristoph; 4, 7 C; 5, 6 IFA. page 95: 1, 2 DFA/Cristoph; 3–5 C; 6 IFA; 7 M/Morandi. page 96: top P; 1 IFA; 2–4, 7 K.U. Müller; 5 P; 6 IFA/Schmidt. page 97: 1 IFA/Aberham; 2 K. U.Müller; 3 P; 4 interfoto/TG; 5, 6 P. page 98: top P; 1 Slater/C; 2 Chun Li/C; 3, 4 P/Minden; 5 mcs; 6 C. page 99: 1 K.U.Müller; 2 H; 3 M; 4 DFA/ Zippel; 5 C; 6 de Bode/Laif; 7 P. page 100: top IFA/Aberham; 1, 3 P; 4 G/ Su; 5 IFA/ Nok; 6 DFA/Wheeler; 7 Raymer. page 101: 1, 3 K.U. Müller; 2 P/Mac Killop; 4 DFA/ Sasse; 5 M/Blockhuis; 6, 7 IFA/Arakaki. page 102: top, 3 IFA; 1, 5 mcs; 2, 7 DFA; 4, 6, 7 P. page 103: 1–3, 5, 6 P; 4 IFA. page 104: top G; 1 K.U.Müller; 2, 7 DFA/ Stark; 3, 5 M/Gierth; 4 G; 6 P. page 105: 1 Hiroshi Suga/Focus; 2 G/Ehlers; 3 IFA/Aberham; 4, 5 P/Orion; 6 H/Orient; 7 Shintani/MT/ P. page 106: top P; 1 K.U.Müller; 2–6 P. page 107: 1, 3, 5–7 Kumamoto/, Orion/P; 2 DFA/Sasse; 4 K.U. Müller. page 108: top IFA; 1–5 P; 6 DFA/Scheibner; 7 P. page 109: 1, 4, 6, 7 P; 2 M/Krinninger; 3 G; 5 K.U.Müller. page 110: top – 2 P; 3 DFA/Riedm.; 4–6, 8 P, 7 C. + W. Kunth. page 111: 1 Cooke/C; 2 Calder/ C; 3 Cassidy/P; 4 Wedewarth/G; 5 P; 6 K.U. Müller. page 112: top Wolinsky/Aurora; 1–5 C; 6 Huber/Laif; 7 H. page 113: 1, 4–7 C; 2 P; 3 DFA. page 114: top Sekai Bunka/ P; 1 Fiala/P; 2 Huber/Laif; 3, 4 P; 5, 6 DFA/Scheibner. page 115: 1, 2, 4, 5 H; 3, 6 P. page 116: top P; 1 G/Chesley; 2 Baldev/Sygma/C; 3, 5, 6 P; 4 K.U. Müller; 7 Horner/C. page 117: 1, 7 K.U. Müller; 2, 6 Yamashita/C; 3 Strachan/G; 4, 5 P. page 118: top, 1 P; 2 G/Kavanagh; 3 C; 4, 6 DFA; 5 P; 7 – 119.1 H; 2, 7 C; 3, 5, 6 P; 4 Pix/Rahn. page 120: top P, 1 DFA; 2 G/Merill; 3, 4 DFA/Müller; 5, 6 DFA/Sasse. page 121: 1–3 C. + W. Kunth; 4, 6 P, 5 DFA/Sasse. page 122: top, 1, 3 P; 2 IFA/ Adams; 4–6 C/Holmes, Lawler. page 123: 1–4, 6 P; 5 G/Austen. page 124: top Pacific Stock/P; 1 Transglobe; 2 H/Fantuz; 3 C; 4 DFA/Tack; 5 P; 6, 7 C. page 125: 1 P; 2, 4, 7 C; 3, 5 mcs; 6 IFA. page 126: top H; 1 Laif/Riehle, 2 P/Minden; 3, 5 C; 4 P/Lanting; 6, 7 DFA. page 127: 1, 4 P; 2, 5 DFA; 3 H; 6, 7 Laif/Riehle. page 128: top G; 1 IFA; 2 K.U.Müller; 3–5 C; 6 K.U.Müller. page 129: 1, 2, 4–6 C; 5 IFA. page 130: top, 1 C; 2 Eisele; 3 P; 4 Su/G; 5 P/NGS; 6 Fields/C. page 131: 1, 2 Frink/Fogden/C; 3 P; 4 mcs; 5 Fields/C; 6, 7 P. page 132: top IFA; 1 G/Ehlers; 2, 5, 6 C; 3 IFA; 4 P. page 133: 1 P; 2 mcs; 3 G; 4 Emmler/Laif; 5 C; 6 Bilderberg. page 134: top IFA; 1 P/Bavendamm; 2, 3 Wheeler, Lenars/C. page 135: 1 Lawler/C; 2, 3 Schaefer/C; 4 Lenars/C; 5 IFA; 6, 7 B. + C. Alexander/Alamy. page 136: top Stephen Frink Collection/Alamy; 1, 2 Stauder/IPN; 3, 4 Lawler/Fields/C; 5, 7 IFA/Bail; 6 Wheeler/C. Page 137: 1, 2, 4–6 Fields/ C; 3 IFA; 7 Lenars/C. page 138/139 top, 1, 2 P; 3 DFA/Hympendahl. page 140: top IFA; 1 Kaehler/C; 2 Hugh Brown/IPN; 3 Houser/C; 4 IFA; 5 G; 6 P; 7 M. page 141: 1, 2 M; 1 P; 2 Schapowalow/Pratt; 3 TG/Ryman; 4 DFA/Wheeler. page 142: top, 1, 6 C; 2, 5 IFA; 3, 4, 7 P/APL. page 143: 1, 7 IFA; 2, 5 Probst/C; 3, 6 P; 4 DFA. page 144: top IFA; 1, 2, 5 Arthus-Bertrand/C; 3 Garwood/C; 4 Garvey/C; 6, 7 IFA. page 145: 1 Tweedie/C; 2 IFA; 3, 4 H; 5 TG/Schmitz; 6 IFA/Gottschalk; 7 P. page 146: top Hugh Brown/IPN; 1, 2 C; 3, 7 IFA; 4 M/Nakamura; 5, 6 P. page 147: 1–4 Hugh Brown/IPN; 5 Garvey/C; 6, 7 P. page 148: top P; 1 Pix; 2 M/Drecoli; 3 Nowitz/C, 4 H; 5 Souders/C; 6 IFA. page 149: 1 P; 2 IFA; 3–5 C; 6, 7 P/APL. page 150: top P; 1 C; 2 IFA/Siebig; 3, 4 P/APL; 5, 6 IFA; 7 Gardner/Lane Agency/C. page 151: 1, 2, 7 IFA; 3, 6 P; 4 Gardner/Lane/C; 5 Garwood/C. page 152: top P; 1 Tweedie/Alamy; 2 Lenars/C; 3 Hugh Brown/IPN; 4 Holmes/C; 5, 6 P; 7 Arthus Bertrand/C. page 153: 1 Glover, Ecoscene/C; 2–4 P; 5, 7 IFA; 6 DFA/Tack. page 154: top, 1 P; 2 Orezzoli/ C; 3–6 P. page 155: 1, 2 Arthus-Bertrand, Lehman/C; 3 Matsumoto/DFA; 4, 6, 7 Chesley/G; 5 P/Minden. page 156: top, 1, 3 P/ APL; 2, 4, 5, 6 C. page 157: 1 P. page 157: 2 Emmler/Laif; 3, 4 IFA; 5, 6 C; 7 P. page 158: top P; 1, 2 Houser/C; 3 IFA; 4 Heaton/C; 5 Souder/C; 6 Rowell/C. page 159: 1–4 P; 6 IFA; 5, 7 C. page 160: top G; 1–3, 4 G; 5–7 P. page 161: 1 G; 2–7 P. page 162: top, 1 P; 2, 7 G; 3 Aurora/Ernsting/Bilderberg; 4 IFA; 5 P; 6 zefa/Bell. page 163: 1, 2 Bond/ 4, 5 Sarkis/ 6 Peebles Phot./Alamy; 7 La Roque/Laif. page 164: top, 2, 3 C, 1 Robert Harding/Alamy; 4–6 Minden/P. page 165: 1, 3–7 C; 5 mcs. page 166: top, 1, 2 C; 3, 5 Essik/Aurora; 4 Lenars/C; 6, 7, page 167: 1, 4, 5, 7 C; 2 P; 3 Frink Collection/Alamy; 6 Helms. page 168: top, 1 P; 2 Helms; 3, 4 C; 5 Essik/Aurora; 6 P. page 169: 1, 2, 5, 6 C; 3, 4 P. page 170: top, 1, 2 C; 3–5 Pacific Stock/ P. page 171: 1, 2, 4–6 P; 3 IFA/JAI. page 172–173 P, 4 H. page 174: top Cook/Alamy; 1 P; 2 Pix; 3 G/Parfitt; 4 mcs; 5 M; 6 IFA. page 175: 1 Laif; 2 Cristofori. page 176: top P; 1–3 IFA; 4–6 C. page 177: 1, 3 P; 2 DFA/Riedmiller; 4 Melters/missio/DFA; 6 Scheibner/DFA; 5, 7, 8 C. page 178: top–3 P; 4 Image State/Alamy; 5 IFA; 6, 7 Emmler/Laif. page 179: 1 P; 2 G/Parfitt; 3 P; 4, 7 DFA; 5 Laif; 6 IFA. page 180: top, 7 IFA/Diaf; 1 Laif; 2 M; 3 G/Grigoriou; 4, 5 H; 6 P. page 181: 1 DFA; 2, 3, 5 IFA; 4 G/Kanus; 6 P; 7 Laif. page 182: top, 7 P; 1 M; 2 G/WPS; 3 IFA; 4 H; 5 M; 6 Laif. page 183: 1–4 IFA; 5 P; 6 H; 7 Laif. page 184: top H; 1, 2, 6 IFA; 3, 7 P; 4 DFA; 5 G/Pigneter. page 185: 1, 3, 7 P; 2, 5 G/Hellier; 4 mcs; 6, 8 IFA. page 186: top P; 1, 4–7 IFA; 2 H; 3 Look/Richter. page 187: 1 P; 2 DFA; 3 IFA; 4, 6, 7 C; 5 Pix. page 188: top G; 1 IFA; 2, 6 Laif; 3 Pix; 2, 4, 5 C; 7 mcs. page 189: 1 Laif; 2 M; 3 IFA; 4, 7 C; 5, 6 IFA. page 190: top, 3, 4 IFA; 1 C; 2, 5 P; 6 – page 191. 1, 2, 4–7 DFA; 3 P. page 192: top P; 1 DFA; 2, 3, 5, 7 C; 4 P; 6 M. page 193: 1 Uluntuncok/Laif; 2 IFA; 3 Arthus-Bertrand/C; 4 P; 5, 7 C; 6 mcs. page 194: top, 1, 3 C; 2, 4 P; 5, 6 DFA. page 195: 1, 3 C; 2 IFAM; 4 Geospace/EDC; 5, 6 DFA/Christoph. page 196: top, 3, 7 P; 1, 2, 4, 5 IFA; 6 Laif. page 197: 1, 4, 5 IFA; 2, 6, 7 P; 3 Laif. page 198: top IFA; 1, 2, 4–6 C; 3 DFA; 7 Laif. page 199: 1, 2, 5 IFA; 3, 4 Laif; 6, 7 DFA. page 200: top C; 1, 6 P; 2 IFA; 3–5 C. page 201: 1–4 C; 5 AKG; 6, 7 DFA. page 202: top P; 1 DFA/ Christoph; 2 Buck; 3 Laif/Krause; 4 IFA; 5 Pix/Havi; 6 M; 7 C. page 203: 1, 3 DFA/ Buck; 2 DFA/Christoph; 4 C; 5 P; 6 M/de Foy. page 204: top Oswald Iten; 1, 2 Laif/ Riehle; 3, 4 P; 5 Save/Jecan; 6 Victor Englebert. page 205: 1 Davenport/Aurora; 2–4 O.Iten; 5 Caputo/IPN; 6 M/Ritschel; 7 Campbell/Aurora. page 206: top P; 1 DFA/ Scheibner; 2 IFA/Fiedler; 3 Riehle/Laif; 4 H; 5 M; 6 P. page 207: 1, 3, 4 IFA; 2 P; 5 Uluntuncok/Laif; 6 C. page 208: top M; 1 Caputo/Aurora; 2 G/Lange; 3–5 Sygma/C; 6 IFA. page 209: 1, 2 H; 3 C; 4, 6 P; 5 IFA. page 210: top, 2, 3 C; 1 Dr. Janicke; 4 Reporters/Laif; 5–7 Caputo/IPN. page 211: 1, 4 P; 2 M; 3 Gallo/C; 5 Caputo/IPN. page 212: top P; 1, 3 IFA; 2 G/Parfitt; 4 DFA/Stark; 5 G/Petersen; 6 P; 7 C. + W. Kunth. page 213: 1, 5 Riehle/Laif; 2 C. + W. Kunth; 3 P/Sixty-Six; 4 Pölking/P; 6 IFA; 7 Caputo/Aurora. page 214: top IFA/Aberham; 1–3 Ariadne van Zanbergen; 4, 5 C; 6 M/Rosing; 7 P. page 215: 1 P. page 207: 2 Okapia; 3–5 P; 6 DFA/Thomashoff; 7 DFA/Wheeler. page 208: top C; 1 ImageState/Alamy; 2 A. Vitale/Alamy; 3 C; 4, 5, 7 P; 6 DFA/Honzera. page 217: 1 Malie Rich-Griffith/Alamy; 2 M/Eichhorn; 3, 4 H; 5 Morgan/Alamy; 6 IFA/BCI. page 218: top Pix; 1, 3 C; 2, 7 P; 4 DFA; 5 M; 6 R. König. page 219: 1 C; 2 Meier/Laif; 3 zefa/Boehnke; 4 DFA/Stark; 5–7 IFA/Pickford. page 220: top, 3 C. + W. Kunth; 1, 2 P; 4–6 IFA; 7 G/Chard. page 221: 1 C. + W. Kunth; 2 IFA; 3, 4 P; 5 Schapowalow. page 222: top –3, 7 C; 4, 5 IFA/Mielke. page 223: 1, 3, 4 P; 2 G; 5, 6 Emmler/Laif. page 224: top P; 1, 2 IFA; 3–6 Laif; 7 DFA. page 225: 1, 2, 5 Emmler/Laif; 3 IFA/Aberham; 4 Riehle/Laif; 6 IFA/Welsh. page 226: top, 4, 6 P; 5 IFA; 7 C. page 227: 1, 4 P; 2, 5, 6 IFA; 3 C. page 228: top, 2 Arthus-Bertrand/C; 1 DFA; 3, 4 P/Minden; 5 – page 229.1 Hellier/C; 2 DFA; 3–6 IFA; 7, 8 P. page 230–231 P. page 232: 1, 3, 4, 7 P; 2, 6 G/TCL; 5 M. page 233: 1 P/NGS; 2 DFA/ Wheeler; 3 G/Hiser; 4 P/Brandenburg; 5 Gonzalez/Laif. page 234: top – 1 C; 2, 7, 8 P; 3–5 G; 6 H. page 235: 1 G/Walker; 2–4 P; 5, 6 C; 7 H. page 236–237.1 P; 2 M; 3 G/Till; 4 Look/Heeb; 5 C; 6 G/Everts; 7 G/Waugh. page 238: top P; 1, 2 C; 3 M; 4, 5 P; 6 – page 239.3 C; 4 P; 5, 6 C. page 230: top, 1 C; 2–4 P; 5, 6 Pix/Pacific Stock; 7 G/Schafer/Hill. page 241: 1 Panorama Images; 2 Pix/Masterfile; 3 C; 4 Minden/Clifton/P; 5, 6 P; 7 C. page 242: top – 5 P; 6 G/Marshall; 7 P/NGS. page 243: 1 IFA/Hartmann; 2 P/Westlight; 3, 4 Yanagi/P; 5 G/Kennan; 6 DFA/Schmid; 7 – page 244. top P/Sisk; 1 G/Wells; 2 P/Gilchrist; 3 DFA/Schmid; 4, 5 P/Kosuge; 6 G/ Coleman; 7 P/Weyers. page 245: 1, 3, 5–7 P/Roda; 2 Pix/Minden/Fitzharris; 4 DFA/ Schmid. page 246 – 247.1 P; 2 G/Craddock; 3 P/NGS/Blair; 4 M/AGE; 5 Huber/Laif; 6 G; 7 P. page 248: top, 5 C; 1–3, 6, 7 P; 4 Essick/Aurora. page 249: 1, 2 First Light/P; 3 Kennedy/ C; 4, 5 P; 6 Schermeister/C; 7 M/Canstock. page 250: top IFA/Arnold; 1–4, 6, 7 P; 5 IFA. page 251: 1–3, 5, 6 P; 4 G/Wells. page 252: top P/ Sekai Bunka; 1, 2 DFA/Tack; 3 G/PP; 4 DFA/Schumacher; 5 P/Frilet/Stock Image; 6 DFA/Fessel; 7 DFA/Matsumoto. page 253: 1 IFA/Panstock; 2 P; 3, 5 DFA/Tack; 4 DFA/Moore; 6 G/Bean. page 254: top – 2 C; 3 G/Marcoux; 4 Souders/C; 5 DFA/Müller; 6 Lewis/C. page 255: 1 Wheeler/C; 2 P/NGS; 3 Souders/C; 4 Probst/C; 5 Steedman/C; 6 Kaehler/C; 7 Nowitz/C. page 256: top P; 1 C; 2–4 P; 5 G; 6 M; 7 – page 257: 1 P; 2, 3 DFA/Müller; 4, 5, 7 P; 6 C. page 258: top P/Watts/First Light; 1 Zobel/C; 2 Muench/C; 3 Fleming/C; 4 Purcel/C; 5 IFA/ Aberham; 6 DFA/Tack; 7 P. page 259: 1 Huber/Laif; 2 DFA/Wheeler; 3 Olson/Aurora; 4–6 DFA; 7 P. page 260 top –3, 6, 7 P; 4 R. König; 5 DFA/Tack. page 261: 1 DFA/Schmid; 2–5 P; 6 M/visa image; 7 DFA/Tack. page 262: top – page 263.1 C; 2 P/Siepmann; 3, 6 C; 4, 7 P; 5 G. page 264: top P; 1 G/Frerck; 2 Gonzalez/Laif; 3 P/Brimberg; 4, 6, 7 Pix/Raga; 5 P. page 265: 1, 2 G; 3, 4 P; 5 Gonzalez/Laif; 6, 7 H. page 266: top Schafer/C; 2 Arthus-Bertrand/C; 3 G/Höröld; 4, 5, 7 P; 6 H. page 267: 1 mcs; 2, 3 P; 4, 5 Lehmann/C; 6 M/AGE; 7 P. page 268: top IFA; 1 Pix; 2 Look/Raach; 3 P; 4 M; 5, 7 C; 6 IFA. page 269: 1 H; 2 Gonzalez/Laif, 3–7 C. page 260: top NN; 1, 2, 6 mcs; 3 C; 4 G; 5 IFA; 7 P. page 271: 1 Eisele; 2 C; 3 H/Giovanni; 4 R. König; 5 M/Pearce; 6 H/Gräfenhain; 7 P. page 272–273. 1 Woodhouse; 2, 3 P; 4 G. page 274: top, 1 G; 2 Woodhouse; 3, 5 Holz; 4, 6 P; 7 Photopress/Köck. page 275: 1 P; 2, 3 G/Pile; 4 Schapowalow/Hiller; 5 DFA; 6 Focus/Fordrelli. page 278: top G/Prior; 1, 3 P/ Pecha; 2 Rowell/C; 4 P/Roda; 5 Woodhouse; 6 Wald/Aurora; 7 mcs. page 277: 1 IFA; 2 Gonzalez/Laif; 4 P/Siering; 5, 6 Jo Holz. page 278: top, 1, 2 P/ Hummel; 3 G; 4 DFA/ Schmid; 5 C; 6, 7 P/ Roda. Page 279: 1 P; 2, 3 G; 4 Schafer/C; 6 Leask/C; 7 Kaehler/ C; 5 P. page 280: top Arthus-Bertrand/C; 1 Horner/C; 2, 3 DFA/Zippel; 4 G/Horner; 5 H/Giovanni; 6 Via/Gross; 7 M/AGE. page 281: 1 P; 2 Gonzalez/Laif; 3, 7 C; 4–6 Caputo/Aurora. page 282: top, 1 P; 2 G/Armand; 3, 4 C; 5 G/Fisher; 6 Gonzalez/Laif. page 283: 1 C; 2 Randy Olson/Aurora; 3 P; Henseler/ Laif. page 284: top Corral/C; 1–3 P; 4 DFA/ Zippel; 5 Horner/C; 7 Rowell/C; 6 IFA. page 285: 1 P/Pecha; 2 Schaefer/C; 3 Creed/C; 4 Corral/C; 5, 6 Kaehler/C. page 286: top Rowell/C; 1 IFA; 2 M; 3 Delevingue/Focus; 4 P/Pecha; 5 R.König; 6 P. page 287: 1 Photobrazil; 2 P; 3 Kaehler/C; 4 G/Prior; 5 M/Wendler; 6 P; 7 Lehmann/C. page 288: top Fordyce/C; 1 Bosshart/C; 2 Laif; 3 Kaehler/C; 4, 5 Bosshart/C; 6 Photobrazil; 7 Azoury/C. page 289: 1 Kaehler/C; 2 Maze/C; 3 Garg/C; 4 Fordyce/C; 5 M/Raga; 6 IFA/Jon Arnold Images. page 290: top Woodhouse; 1 Benn/C; 2 Dagli Orti/C; 3 Gonzalez/Laif; 4 Orti/C; 5, 6 P. page 291: 1 Fogden/C; 2 Braasch/C; 3 C; 4 Laif; 5 Woodhouse; 6 Soumar/C; 7 Archivo iconografico/C. page 292: top P; 1, 2 Branco/Magnum/Focus; 3 Vega; 4, 5 Hodalic; 6 TG/Moody; 7 P. page 293: 1 Feanny; 2 P; 3 Save/Ziesler; 4, 5 Allofs/C; 6 P/Minden; 7 Photobrazil. page 294: top Piepenburg/Laif; 1, 3 Genevieve Vallee/Alamy; 2 Robert Harding Picture Library/Alamy; 4 Gonzalez/Laif; 5 M/Wendler; 6 World Wide Picture Library/Alamy. page 295: 1 Orezzoli/ C; 2, 3 Piepenburg/Laif; 4 DFA; 5 Yspeert/C; Red/Alamy; 7 P. page 296: top Woodhouse; 1, 2 P; 3–7 DFA/Tack. page 297: 1 M/AGE; 2 IFA/TPC; 3 DFA/Christoph; 4 mcs; 5, 6 Sparshatt/C; 7 Pitamitz/C. page 298: top, 5, 6 P/Barbudo; 1 Creed/C; 2, 3, 7 mcs; 4 Jo Holz. page 299: 1 mcs; 2 Piepenburg/Laif; 3 IFA/Jon Arnold Images; 4 P/Minden/Lanting; 5 IFA; 6, 7 P. page 300: top –2, 4, 5, 7 Gonzalez/Laif; 3 Harscher/Laif; 6 zefa/Damm. page 301: 1–5 Gonzalez/Laif; 6 P; 7 Kristensen/Laif. page 302: top P; 1 IFA; 2 Laif; 3 G/Parfitt; 4 P/Minden/Lanting; 5 Look/Richter; 6, 7 Gonzalez/Laif. page 303: 1 DFA/Meyer; 2 P; 3 IFA/Seidenberger; 4, 5, 7 P; 6 mcs. page 304: top P/Hummel; 1, 5, 7 Rowell/C; 2 mcs; 3 Stadler/C; 4 Everton/C; 6 P. page 305: 1 Arthus-Bertrand/C; 2 Shok/C; 3–5 IFA; 6 P; 7 Stadler/C. page 306: top P; 1 Modic/C; 2 Kaehler/C; 3, 4 Stadler/C; 5 Gonzalez/Laif; 6 H; 7 P. page 307: 1 IFA; 2 DFA/Tack; 3 P/Abel/NGS; 4 IFA; 5 mcs; 6 Röchner/TG, 7 C. page 308–309: P/Sekai Bunka. page 310: top P; 1 Amos/C; 2 Widstrand/C; 3 Pinneo/Aurora; 4 G/TCL; 5 G/Beatty; 6 G/Heacox; 7 McLain/Aurora. page 311: 1, 3 Rowell/C; 2 Sygma/C; 4 Schafer/C; 5–7 P. page 312: top, 1, 3 P/Hummel; 2 G/Osborne; 4 G/Rogers; 5 Rowell/C; 6 Hawthorne/C. page 313: 1 Beebe/C; 2 Rainier/C; 3, 4 Rowell/C; 5–7 P/Hummel. page 314: top Randlev/C; 1 P; 2 G/Grigoriou; 3 G/Krechichwost; 4 P; 5 IFA; 6 P. page 315: top, 1, 2, 4 P; 3 M/Bibikow; 5 IFA; 6 Pitamitz/C. page 316–317.1, 3, 7 P; 2, 4, 6 C.

Credits/Contributers

© 2006 Verlag Wolfgang Kunth GmbH & Co. KG, Munich
© GeoGraphic Publishers GmbH & Co. KG, Munich
Innere Wiener Straße 13
81667 Munich
Tel.: (49) 89 45 80 20-0
Fax: (49) 89 45 80 20-21
info@geographicmedia.de
www.kunth-verlag.de

© Cartography: GeoGraphic Publishers GmbH & Co. KG, Munich

Map relief 1 : 2,25 Mio./1 : 4,5 Mio./1 : 18 Mio./1 : 27 Mio./1 : 45 Mio./
1 : 54 Mio./1 : 63 Mio./1 : 85 Mio. MHM ® Copyright © Digital Wisdom, Inc.

© English translation: Verlag Wolfgang Kunth GmbH & Co. KG, Munich

English language distribution:

GeoCenter International Ltd
The Viables Centre, Harrow Way
Basingstoke, Hants RG22 4BJ
England
Tel.: (44) 1256 817 987
Fax: (44) 1256 817 988
sales@geocenter.co.uk
www.insightguides.com

ISBN 981-258-070-0

Concept: Wolfgang Kunth
Cartography: GeoKarta – Ralf van den Berg, Jens Ewers, Bernd Hilberer, Doris Kordisch, Peter Krause, Gabriele Luber, Karen Morlok, Heiner Newe, Beate Reußner, Bernhard Spachmüller, Karin Stemmer

Texts: Manuela Blisse & Uwe Lehmann, Peter Daners, Christian Gehl, Christine Hamel, Bernd Helms, Dr. Siegmar Hohl, Dr. Bernhard Jendricke, Marlis Kappelhoff, Barbara Kreißl, Angelika Kunth-Jakobs, Frank Meinshausen, Michael Schaeffer, Daniela Schetar, Trudie Trox

Editing: Eckard Schuster; CLP • Carlo Lauer & Partner
Proofreading: Michael Kaiser
Coordination: Heiner Newe, Claus-Peter Waider, Michael Kaiser
Picture Research: Max Oberdorfer

Coordination and editing English version: Katja Baldewein
Text Translation: Demetri Lowe
Proofreading English version: Alison Moffat-McLynn

Design, Layout: Umḃruch, Munich
Cover design: Umḃruch, Munich
Final artwork: Dorothea Happ
Reproduction: Fotolito Varesco, Auer (Italy)
Print: Appl Aprinta, Wemding

Printed in Germany